LARS PEARSON
and LANCE PARKIN

AHISTORY

AN UNAUTHORIZED HISTORY OF THE DOCTOR WHO UNIVERSE

4TH EDITION

mad
norwegian
press

Des Moines, IA

Also Available from Mad Norwegian Press...

Unhistory: Apocryphal Stories Too Strange for even AHistory: An Unauthorised History of the Doctor Who Universe (ebook-only supplement) by Lance Parkin and Lars Pearson

Running Through Corridors: Rob and Toby's Marathon Watch of Doctor Who (Vol. 1: The 60s, Vol. 2: The 70s) by Robert Shearman and Toby Hadoke

Space Helmet for a Cow: An Unlikely 50-Year History of Doctor Who by Paul Kirkley (Vol. 1: 1963-1989, Vol. 2: 1990-2013)

Wanting to Believe: A Critical Guide to The X-Files, Millennium and the Lone Gunmen by Robert Shearman

The About Time Series by Tat Wood and Lawrence Miles
- *About Time 1: The Unauthorized Guide to Doctor Who* (Seasons 1 to 3)
- *About Time 2: The Unauthorized Guide to Doctor Who* (Seasons 4 to 6)
- *About Time 3: The Unauthorized Guide to Doctor Who* (Seasons 7 to 11) [2nd Ed]
- *About Time 4: The Unauthorized Guide to Doctor Who* (Seasons 12 to 17)
- *About Time 5: The Unauthorized Guide to Doctor Who* (Seasons 18 to 21)
- *About Time 6: The Unauthorized Guide to Doctor Who* (Seasons 22 to 26)
- *About Time 7: The Unauthorized Guide to Doctor Who* (Series 1 to 2)
- *About Time 8: The Unauthorized Guide to Doctor Who* (Series 3)
- *About Time 9: The Unauthorized Guide to Doctor Who* (Series 4, the 2009 Specials)

Essay Collections
- *Chicks Dig Comics: A Celebration of Comic Books by the Women Who Love Them*
- *Chicks Dig Gaming: A Celebration of All Things Gaming by the Women Who Love It*
- *Chicks Dig Time Lords: A Celebration of Doctor Who by the Women Who Love It*, 2011 Hugo Award Winner, Best Related Work
- *Chicks Unravel Time: Women Journey Through Every Season of Doctor Who*
- *Companion Piece: Women Celebrate the Humans, Aliens and Tin Dogs of Doctor Who*
- *Queers Dig Time Lords: A Celebration of Doctor Who by the LGBTQ Fans Who Love It*
- *Whedonistas: A Celebration of the Worlds of Joss Whedon by the Women Who Love Them*

Guidebooks
- *I, Who: The Unauthorized Guide to the Doctor Who Novels and Audios* by Lars Pearson (vols. 1-3, ebooks only)
- *Dusted: The Unauthorized Guide to Buffy the Vampire Slayer* by Lawrence Miles, Pearson and Christa Dickson (ebook only)
- *Redeemed: The Unauthorized Guide to Angel* by Pearson and Christa Dickson

A very special thank you to our supporters on Patreon, namely: Darren Buckley, David H Adler, Evan Lamb, Greg Holtham, Janet Reimer, Jeff Peck, Jeremy Remy, Jeremy Roebuck, Joseph Coker, Maggie Howe, Matt Bracher, Mitchell S Easter, Pat Harrigan, Rick Taylor, Stephen Webb, Steve Grace, Steven Ashby, Steven Sautter, Tyson Woolman and Vitas Varnas. You guys are awesome!

Copyright © 2018 Lance Parkin and Lars Pearson. Published by Mad Norwegian Press (www.madnorwegian.com) Cover & interior design by Adam Holt and Christa Dickson.

Volume 1 ISBN: 9781935234227
Volume 2 ISBN: 9781935234234
Volume 3 ISBN: 9781935234241

Word count, Vol. 1: 284,216; Vol. 2: 368,874
Printed in the USA. First Printing (Vol. 2): November 2018.

mad norwegian press | **des moines**

TABLE OF CONTENTS

The following *only* catalogs main story entries for each adventure; some stories occur in multiple time zones, and hence have more than one page number listed. For a complete listing of *all* story references, consult the Index.

Some stories proved undateable and lack main entries; for a list of these, consult the None of the Above section (pages 1353-1356).

For easier reference across what's become a quite sprawling guidebook series, the pages of *Ahistory* Fourth Edition are numbered 1000 and up for Volume 1, 2000 and up for Volume 2, and 3000 and up for Volume 3.

All titles listed are *Doctor Who* stories (or were supplemental comics made for *Doctor Who Magazine*) unless otherwise noted. BBV and Reeltimes Pictures stories include a notation of the particular monster or *Doctor Who* character they feature. For more on the designations used in the Table of Contents, see the Key in the Introduction.

Big Finish box sets, for the most part, are listed under the box set title, then the individual stories therein. (The format is a bit inconsistent – whenever possible, we've gone with whatever's on the cover.)

To save space, Titan's comics are listed under *The Tenth Doctor Year One*, *The Eleventh Doctor Year One*, etc. We've anticipated a collection of *The Ninth Doctor Year One*.

TABLE OF CONTENTS

TABLE OF CONTENTS

TABLE OF CONTENTS

TABLE OF CONTENTS

TABLE OF CONTENTS

TABLE OF CONTENTS

TABLE OF CONTENTS

TABLE OF CONTENTS

TABLE OF CONTENTS

TABLE OF CONTENTS

TABLE OF CONTENTS

TABLE OF CONTENTS

Footnote Features

Pre-History

History

Present Day

UNIT

Present Day (cont.)

TABLE OF CONTENTS

This book seeks to place every event referred to in *Doctor Who* into a consistent timeline. Yet this is "a" history of the *Doctor Who* universe, not the "definitive" or "official" version.

Doctor Who has had hundreds of creators, all pulling in slightly different directions, all with their own vision of what *Doctor Who* was about. Without that diversity, the *Doctor Who* universe would no doubt be more internally consistent, but it would also be a much smaller and less interesting place. Nowadays, fans are part of the creative process. Ultimately, we control the heritage of the show that we love. The authors of *Ahistory* hope people will enjoy this book, and we know that they will challenge it.

# # # # #

A total adherence to continuity has always been rather less important to the successive *Doctor Who* production teams than the main order of business: writing exciting stories, telling good jokes and scaring small children with big monsters. This, as most people will tell you, is just how it should be.

Doctor Who has always been created using a method known as "making it up as they went along". The series glories in its invention and throwaway lines. When the TV series was first in production, no-one was keeping the sort of detailed notes that would prevent canonical "mistakes", and even the same writer could contradict their earlier work. It's doubtful the writer of *The Mysterious Planet* (broadcast in 1986) had a single passing thought about how the story fit in with *The Sun Makers* (1977)... even though they were both authored by Robert Holmes.

Now, with all the legions of new books, audios, comic strips, short stories and a new TV series, not to mention spin-offs, it is almost certainly impossible to keep track of every new *Doctor Who* story, let alone put them all in a coherent – never mind consistent – framework. References can contradict other references in the same story, let alone ones in stories written forty years later for a different medium by someone who wasn't even born the year the original writer died.

It is, in any case, impossible to come up with a consistent view of history according to *Doctor Who*. Strictly speaking, the Brigadier retires three years before the first UNIT story is set. The Daleks and Atlantis are both utterly destroyed, once and for all, several times that we know about. Characters "remember" scenes, or sometimes entire stories, that they weren't present to witness, and show remarkable lack of knowledge of real world events or events in *Doctor Who* that happened after the story first came out.

"Continuity" has always been flexible, even on the fundamentals of the show's mythology – *The Dalek Invasion of Earth* (1964), *The War Games* (1969), *Genesis of the Daleks*

(1975) and *The Deadly Assassin* (1976) all shamelessly threw out the show's history in the name of a good story. Their versions of events (the Daleks are galactic conquerors; the Doctor is a Time Lord who stole his TARDIS and fled his home planet; the Daleks were created by the Kaled scientist, Davros; Gallifreyan society is far from perfect and Time Lords are limited to twelve regenerations) are now taken to be the "truth". The previous versions (the Daleks are confined to one city; the Doctor invented the "ship" and his granddaughter named it before their exile; the Daleks are descendants of the squat humanoid Dals, mutated by radiation; the Time Lords are godlike and immortal barring accidents) have quietly been forgotten.

# # # # #

However, it would be unfortunate to write a book so vague that it becomes useless. Firm decisions have to be made about where stories are placed, so this book contains abundant footnotes that lay out the evidence pertaining to each story, and to explain each story's placement in this chronology.

In some cases, this is simply a matter of reporting an exact date spoken by one of the characters in the story (*Black Orchid*, for example). In others, no firm date is given. In those cases, we attempt to look at internal evidence given on screen, then evidence from the production team at the time (from the script, say, or from contemporary publicity material), then branch out to cross-referencing it with other stories, noting where other people who've come up with *Doctor Who* chronologies have placed it. What we're attempting to do is accurately list all the evidence given for dating the stories and other references in as an objective way as possible, then weigh it to reach a conclusion.

For a good example of this process at its most complicated, look for *The Seeds of Death* or *The Wheel in Space*. You may not agree with the years we've set, it might make your blood boil, but you'll see how we've reached our answer.

# # # # #

This book is one attempt, then, to retroactively create a consistent framework for the history of the *Doctor Who* universe. It is essentially a game, not a scientific endeavour to discover "the right answer".

All games have to follow a consistent set of rules, and as we attempt to fit all the pieces of information we are given, we have to lay some groundwork and prioritise. If a line of dialogue from a story broadcast in 1983 flatly contradicts what was said in one from 1968, which is "right"? Some people would suggest that the newer story "got it wrong", that the later production team didn't pay enough attention to what came before. Others might argue that the new information "corrects" what came before. In practice, most fans are inconsistent, choosing the facts that best support their arguments or preferences. *The Discontinuity Guide* (1995) has some very healthy advice regarding continuity: "Take what you want and ignore what you don't. Future continuity cops will just have to adapt to your version".

BASIC PRINCIPLES

For the purposes of this book, we have worked from the following assumptions:

• Every *Doctor Who* story takes place in the same universe, unless explicitly stated otherwise. The same individual fought the Daleks with Jo on Spiridon (on TV), Beep the Meep with Sharon (in the comics), the Ice Warriors with Benny in London (the novels), became Zagreus in the Antiverse (the audios), blew up Gallifrey to prevent Faction Paradox taking over the universe (the novels again), saved Rose Tyler from the Autons and married River Song.

For legal, marketing or artistic reasons, it should be noted that some of the people making *Doctor Who* have occasionally stated that they don't feel this to be the case. However there are innumerable cross references (say, Romana being president of Gallifrey in both the books and the audios) and in-jokes that suggest very strongly that, for example, the eighth Doctor of the books is the same individual as the eighth Doctor of the Big Finish audios – or at the very least, they've both got almost-identical histories.

• The universe has one, true "established history". Nothing (short of a being with godlike powers) can significantly change the course of history with any degree of permanency within that universe. The Mars attacked by the Fendahl is the Mars of the Ice Warriors.

• We have noted where each date we have assigned comes from. Usually it is from dialogue (in which case, it's quoted), but often it comes from behind-the-scenes sources such as scripts, publicity material and the like. It is up to the individual reader whether a date from a BBC Press release or draft script is as "valid" as one given on screen.

• In many cases, no date was ever given for a story. In such instances, we pick a year and explain our reasons. Often, we will assign a date that is consistent with information given in other stories. (So, it's suggested that the Cyber War mentioned in *Revenge of the Cybermen* must take place after *The Tomb of the Cybermen*, and probably after *Earthshock* because of what is said in those other stories.) These dates are marked as arbitrary and the reasoning behind them is explained in the footnotes.

• Where a date isn't established on screen, we have also included the dates suggested by others who have compiled timelines or listed dates given in the series. Several similar works to this have been attempted, and we have listed the most relevant in the Bibliography.

• It's been assumed that historical events take place at the same time and for the same reasons as they did in "real history", unless specifically contradicted by the television series. Unless given reason to think otherwise, we assume that the Doctor is telling the truth about meeting historical figures, and that his historical analysis is correct. (It has, however, been established that the Doctor is fallible and/or an incorrigible name-dropper.) When there's a reference in our footnotes to "science", "scientists", "history" or "historians", unless stated otherwise it means scholars and academics from the real world, not the *Doctor Who* universe (they are usually invoked when *Doctor Who*'s version of science or events strays a distance from ours).

• Information given is usually taken literally and at face value, unless there's strong reason to think that the person giving it is lying or mistaken. Clearly, if an expert like the Doctor is talking about something he knows a great deal about, we can probably trust the information more than some bystander's vague remark. (In recent years, it's become trendy to go the other way and invoke River Song's "The Doctor Lies" credo to explain any given point of ambiguity, but – as with not claiming that every discrepancy is the fault of the Last Great Time War – we've resisted that urge as much as possible.)

• *Ahistory*'s version of Earth's future history is generally one of steady progress, and as such stories featuring similar themes and concepts tend to be lumped together – say, intergalactic travel, isolated colonies, humanoid robots and so on. If the technology, transportation or weaponry seen in story A is more advanced than in story B, then we might suggest that story A is set in the future of story B. We also assume that throughout future centuries, humans age at the same rate (unless told otherwise), so their life spans don't alter too dramatically, etc. A "lifetime" in the year 4000 is still about one hundred years.

• All dates, again unless specifically stated otherwise, work from our Gregorian calendar, and all are "AD". It is assumed that the system of leap years will remain the same in the future. For convenience, all documents use our system of dating, even those of alien civilisations. The "present" of the narrative is now, so if an event happened "two hundred years ago", it happened in the early nineteenth century. Often we are told that a specific date takes place on the wrong day: in *The War Machines*, 16th July, 1966, is a Monday, but it really occurred on a Saturday.

• We assume that a "year" is an Earth year of 365 days, even when an alien is speaking, unless this is specifically contradicted. This also applies to terms such as "Space Year" (*Genesis of the Daleks*), "light year" (which is used as a unit of time in *The Savages* and possibly *Terror of the Autons*) and "cycle" (e.g. *Zamper*).

• If an event is said to take place "fifty years ago", we frequently take it to mean exactly fifty years ago, unless a more precise date is given elsewhere or it refers to a known historical event. If an event occurs in the distant past or the far future, we tend to round up: *Image of the Fendahl* is set in about 1977, the Fifth Planet was destroyed "twelve million years" before. So, we say this happened in "12,000,000 BC", not "11,998,023 BC". When an event takes place an undefined number of "centuries", "millennia" or "millions of years" before or after a story, we arbitrarily set a date.

• On occasion we've followed a convention from the TV series: that future-based stories sometimes occur on a rounded number from the year of their broadcast. This is why – to pick a prominent example – *Colony in Space*, broadcast in 1972, takes place in 2472. Likewise with *The Enemy of the World* (1967-1968) quietly taking place fifty years on, in 2018. When and where we've followed this pattern, it's because a story's dating placement is otherwise a bit vague, and – frankly – our gut impulse says it's acceptable to do so. Also, to be honest, one of us grew up a huge fan of *Legion of Super-Heroes*, which magically took place a thousand years after publication. It's been a hard habit to shake.

• A "generation" is assumed to be twenty-five years, as per the Doctor's definition in *Four to Doomsday*. A "couple" of years is always two years, a "few" is less than "several" which is less than "many", with "some" taken to be an arbitrary or unknown number. A "billion" is generally the American and modern British unit (a thousand million) rather than the old British definition (a million million).

• Characters are in their native time zone unless explicitly stated otherwise. Usually, when a *Doctor Who* monster or villain has a time machine, it's central to the plot. On television, the Cybermen only explicitly have time travel in *Attack of the Cybermen*, for example, and they've stolen the time machine in question. It clearly can't be "taken for granted" that they can go back in history. The Sontarans have a (primitive) time machine in *The Time Warrior*, and are clearly operating on a scale that means they can defy the Time Lords in *The Invasion of Time* and *The Two Doctors*, but there's no evidence they routinely travel in time. The only one of the Doctor's (non-Time Lord) foes with a mastery of time travel are the Daleks – they develop time travel in *The Chase*, and definitely use it in *The Daleks'*

Master Plan, *The Evil of the Daleks*, *Day of the Daleks*, *Resurrection of the Daleks*, *Remembrance of the Daleks*, *Dalek*, *Army of Ghosts/Doomsday*, *Daleks in Manhattan*, *Evolution of the Daleks*, *The Stolen Earth/Journey's End*, *Victory of the Daleks*, *Asylum of the Daleks*, *The Day of the Doctor*, *The Time of the Doctor* and *The Magician's Apprentice/The Witch's Familiar*. Even so, in the remaining stories, we've resisted assuming that the Daleks are time travellers.

• Sometimes, stories occur with the sort of impact that means it seems odd that they weren't mentioned in an earlier story. For instance, no-one from *The Power of the Daleks* and *The Moonbase* (both shown in 1966) recalls the Daleks and Cybermen fighting in *Doomsday* (shown in 2006). For that matter, when the Doctor and his companions refer to their past adventures on TV, they rarely mention the events of the Missing Adventures, Past Doctor novels, comic strips or Big Finish audios. (There are exceptions, however, usually when a writer picks up a throwaway line in a TV episode.) In *Doctor Who* itself, this may point to some deep truth about the nature of time – that events don't become part of the "Web of Time" until we see the Doctor as part of them... or it may be simply that it was impossible for the people making *Doctor Who* in the sixties to know about stories authored by their successors – many of whom hadn't even been born then.

• And, in a related note, few people making *The Tenth Planet* (in 1966, depicting the distant space year 1986) would have imagined anyone in the early twenty-first century worrying how to reconcile the quasi-futuristic world they imagined with the historical reality. Whenever the UNIT stories are set, it was "the twentieth century", and that's history now. Some of the early New Adventures novels took place in a "near future" setting. We've therefore accepted the dates given, rather than said that – for example – as we still haven't put a man on Mars, *The Ambassadors of Death* is still set in our future. There's clearly a sensible reason why the "present day" stories made now look like our present day, not *The Tenth Planet: The Next Generation*. The in-story explanation/fudge would seem to be that most *Doctor Who* stories take place in isolated locations, and that there are agencies like UNIT, C19 and Torchwood tasked with keeping alien incursions covered up. This paradigm has broken down over time, however, given the sheer number of public events involving aliens in the new series, *The Sarah Jane Adventures* and (to a lesser degree) *Torchwood*.

• There are still errors of omission, as when a later story fails to acknowledge an earlier one (often in other media) that seems relevant. No-one in *The Christmas Invasion*, for example, notes that it's odd Britain is making a big deal about sending an unmanned probe to Mars, when there were manned UK missions there in the seventies (in *The Ambassadors of Death*) and the nineties (*The Dying Days*). As with Sarah in *School Reunion* remembering *The Hand of Fear* but not *The Five Doctors*, there's got to be an appeal to clarity in storytelling. With so many *Doctor Who* stories in existence, it's almost impossible to tell a new one that doesn't explicitly contradict an earlier story, let alone implicitly. The reason no-one, say, remarks that the second Doctor looks like Salamander except in *The Enemy of the World* is the same reason that no-one ever says Rose looks like the girl who married Chris Evans – it gets in the way of the story, and doesn't help it along.

THE STORIES

This book restricts itself to events described in the BBC television series *Doctor Who*, and its original full-length fiction, audio plays and comics; the spin-off series *The Sarah Jane Adventures*, *Torchwood*, *K9*, *Class* and their related full-length fiction, audio plays and comics; and any spin-off books, audios, comics and direct-to-video/DVD films involving characters that originated in the above, and were used with permission by their rights holders (see Section No. 4 below). To be included in this Fourth Edition of *Ahistory*, a story had to be released before 31st December, 2017. (At our discretion, and as deadlines allowed, we included stray stories from 2018 if they finished an ongoing storyline or had some special significance.)

This is not an attempt to enter the debate about which stories are "canon" (although we have been compelled to make such determinations at times), it is simply an attempt to limit the length and scale of this book. There are two types of information in this book – evidence given in TV stories, and anything provided in another format – and these are distinguished by different typefaces.

1. The Television Series. Included are the episodes and on-screen credits of...
• *Doctor Who*, from *An Unearthly Child* (1963) to the end of the twelfth Doctor era, *Twice Upon a Time* (2017)
 • The pilot episode *K9 and Company* (1981)
 • *Torchwood* (2006-2011), stars the alien-tech-harvesting group first seen in *Doctor Who* Series 2
 • *The Sarah Jane Adventures* (2007-2011), features the long-running companion Sarah Jane Smith and her teenage friends
 • The *K9* TV series (2009-2010), set in the future, with a new version of K9
 • *Class* (2016), short-lived spin-off set at Coal Hill Academy, following on from *Doctor Who* Series 9.
We have also taken into consideration extended or unbroadcast versions that have since been commercially released or broadcast anywhere in the world – there are few cases of "extended" material contradicting the original story.

Priority is given to sources closest to the finished product or the production team of the time the story was made. In descending order of authority are the following: the programme as broadcast; the official series websites; official guidebooks made in support of the series (*Doctor Who: The Encyclopedia*, etc.), the *Radio Times* and other contemporary BBC publicity material (which was often written by the producer or script editor); the camera script; the novelisation of a story by the original author or an author working closely from the camera script; contemporary interviews with members of the production team; televised trailers; rehearsal and draft scripts; novelisations by people other than the original author; storylines and writers' guides (which often contradict on-screen information); interviews with members of the production team after the story was broadcast; and finally any other material, such as fan speculation.

Scenes cut from broadcast were considered if they were incorporated back into a story at a later time (as with those in *The Curse of Fenric* VHS and DVD). Not included is information from unreleased material that exists, is in release but was kept separate from the story (for instance, the extra scenes on the *Ghost Light* DVD) or that no longer exists (such as with *Terror of the Autons*, *Terror of the Zygons* and *The Hand of Fear*). Neither does the first version of *An Unearthly Child* to be filmed (the so-called "pilot episode") count, nor "In character" appearances by the Doctor interacting with the real world on other programmes (e.g.: on *Animal Magic*, *Children in Need*, *Blue Peter* etc.).

2. The *Doctor Who*, *The Sarah Jane Adventures*, *Torchwood* and *Class* books, audios and webcasts. This present volume also encompasses the *Doctor Who* New Adventures (continued the adventures of the seventh Doctor and Ace after the end of the original TV series) and Missing Adventures (retro Doctor stories) published by Virgin (1991-1997); the BBC's Eighth Doctor Adventures (1997-2005); the BBC's Past Doctor Adventures (1997-2005); the BBC's New Series Adventures (up through *Plague City*, 2017); the *Torchwood* novels (up through *TW: Exodus Code*, 2012); all of the Telos novellas (2001-2004); the three *Class* novels; the four *K9* children's books (1980); and a number of one-off novels: *Harry Sullivan's War*, *Turlough and the Earthlink Dilemma* and *Who Killed Kennedy*.

The audios covered include *The Pescatons*, *Slipback*, *The Paradise of Death* and *The Ghosts of N-Space*; the BBC fourth Doctor mini-series (*Hornets' Nest*, *Demon Quest* and *Serpent Crest*); and the extensive Big Finish *Doctor Who* audio range... its monthly series (up to *Static*, #233), the

Companion Chronicles (up to Series 11), the Fourth Doctor Adventures (starring Tom Baker, up to Series 6), the Early Adventures (first and second Doctor stories, up to Series 4), the eighth Doctor audios initially broadcast on BBC7 (up to *To the Death*, #4.10), various promotional audios (up to *Trial of the Valeyard*), special releases (up to *The Sixth Doctor – The Last Adventure*), the eighth Doctor box sets *Dark Eyes* and *Doom Coalition*, *Philip Hinchcliffe Presents* (to *The Helm of Awe*), the Lost Stories (unmade TV scripts adapted for audio) and many more. The BBC webcasts *Real Time*, *Shada* and *Death Comes to Time* (the last one somewhat controversially) are included, as well as the *Torchwood* webcast *Web of Lies*.

A handful of stories were available in another form – *Shakedown* and *Downtime* were originally direct-to-video spin-offs, some Big Finish stories like *Minuet in Hell* and *The Mutant Phase* are (often radically different) adaptations of stories made by Audio Visuals. *Ahistory* deals with the "official" versions, as opposed to the fan-produced ones.

This volume covers two stories that appear in different versions, because they were told in two media that fall within the scope of the book and were adapted for different Doctors: *Shada* and *Human Nature*. Those have been dealt with on a case-by-case basis. *Doctor Who* fans have long had different versions of the same story in different media – the first Dalek story, for example, was televised, extensively altered for the novelisation, changed again for the movie version and adapted into a comic strip.

We haven't included in-character appearances in nonfiction books (e.g: the *Doctor Who Discovers...* and *Doctor Who Quiz Book of* series), and *Make Your Own Adventure/Find Your Fate*-style books where it's impossible to determine the actual story. It was tempting, though.

3) The *Doctor Who* comics, including the strip that has been running in *Doctor Who Weekly/Monthly/Magazine* since 1979 (up through "Matildus", *DWM* #518), along with all original backup strips from that publication, and the ones from the various Specials and Yearbooks. With a book like this, drawing a line between what should and shouldn't be included is never as simple as it might appear. Including every comic strip would include ones from the Annuals, for example. This book doesn't include the text stories that *Doctor Who Magazine* has included at various points during its run.

There's a relatively straightforward distinction between the *DWM* comic strip and other *Doctor Who* comic strips: while it's the work of many writers, artists and editors, it also has a strong internal continuity and sense of identity. This book, in all previous editions, has confined itself to "long form" *Doctor Who* and there's a case to be made that the *DWM* strip represents one "ongoing story" that's run for over a quarter of a century. The *Doctor Who Magazine* strip has now run for longer than the original TV series, and most fans must have encountered it at some point.

That said, this book excludes *DWM* strips that are clearly parodies that aren't meant to be considered within the continuity of the strip. The same logic applies to spoofs like *Dimensions in Time* and *The Curse of Fatal Death*. For the record, the affected strips are "Follow that TARDIS!", "The Last Word" and "TV Action".

DWM has reprinted a number of strips from other publications over the years. We have tended to include these. The main beneficiary of this is *The Daleks* strip from the sixties comic *TV Century 21* (and *DWM*'s sequel to it from issues #249-254).

It's certainly arguable that the *DWM* strip exists in a separate continuity, with its own companions, internal continuity, vision of Gallifrey and even an ethos that made it feel quite unlike the TV eras of its Doctors. This certainly seemed to be the case early on. However, this distinction has broken down over the years – the comic strip companion Frobisher appeared in a book (*Mission: Impractical*) and two audios (*The Holy Terror*, *The Maltese Penguin*); the village of Stockbridge (from the fifth Doctor *DWM* comics) has featured in various audios starting with *Circular Time*; the audio *The Company of Friends* incorporated characters from different book and comic ranges; and for a number of years the strip and the New Adventures novels were quite elaborately linked. In the new TV series, we've met someone serving kronkburgers (in *The Long Game*, first mentioned in "The Iron Legion") the Doctor quoted Abslom Daak in *Bad Wolf*, and Daak's mug shot appeared in *Time Heist*.

The strip tends to "track" the ongoing story (the television series in the seventies and eighties, the New Adventures in the early nineties) – so the Doctor regenerates, without explanation within the strip and on occasion during a story arc. Companions from the television series and books come and go. Costume changes and similar details (like the design of the console room) do the same. It's broadly possible to work out when the strip is set in the Doctor's own life. So, the first *Doctor Who* Weekly strips with the fourth Doctor mention he's dropped off Romana, and he changes from his Season 17 to Season 18 costume – so it slots in neatly between the two seasons. There are places where this process throws up some anomalies, which have been noted.

Also included are the *Doctor Who* comics produced by IDW for the American market; the *Radio Times* comics featuring the eighth Doctor; the comics that first appeared in *Torchwood: The Official Magazine*; and the *Torchwood* and *The Sarah Jane Adventures* webcomics.

We also include the ongoing *Doctor Who* and *Torchwood* comics published by Titan, although – owing to the cut-off point of this guidebook being at the end of 2017 – we've included all of *The Tenth Doctor Year Three* and *The Eleventh Doctor Year Three*, but had to stop partway through *The Twelfth Doctor Year Three* (#3.9, "The Great Shopping Bill"). All of the Titan comics before that are present, however, as are crossover events up through "The Lost Dimension".

4) Spin-off series featuring characters that originally appeared in *Doctor Who* (whatever the format), and were used elsewhere with permission by their respective rights holders.

This needs some explaining... *Doctor Who* is a very unusual property in that, generally speaking, the BBC retained ownership of anything created by salaried employees, but freelance scriptwriters working on the TV show in the 60s, 70s and 80s (and the novelists working on the books in the 90s) typically wound up owning the rights to any characters they created. Infamously, this has meant that writer Terry Nation (and his estate) kept ownership of the name "Dalek" and the conceptual property therein, but the BBC retained the rights to the likeness of the Daleks, which were created by staff designer Raymond Cusick.

This is very counter-intuitive to how other series work – a world where *Star Trek* is so divided (say, with one person owning the Klingons, another owning the Horta and another owning Spock, while Paramount continues to retain ownership of Captain Kirk and the *Enterprise*) would be unthinkable. Nonetheless, over the years, the rights holders to iconic *Doctor Who* characters and monsters have licensed them for use elsewhere, and – unless given reason to think otherwise – their use in a non-*Doctor Who* story seems as valid as any BBC-sanctioned story.

The spin-offs included in this volume are:

• The Bernice Summerfield novels, audios and novella collections (1997-present), featuring the Doctor's companion who was first seen in the New Adventure *Love and War* (1992). Benny was the lead of the Doctor-less New Adventures novels published from 1997 to 1999; Big Finish took over the license afterward, and has produced Benny audios, novels, short story anthologies, novella collections and one animated story. Later, Benny was folded (after a fashion) back into the main *Doctor Who* range with *The New Adventures of Bernice Summerfield* box sets.

The first five Benny audios were excluded, as they were adaptations of New Adventures novels.

• BBV audios and films (1994-2015?) featuring licensed characters such as the Sontarans, the Rutans and the Zygons, as well as *P.R.O.B.E.* (1994-1996, 2015): a spin-off series featuring Liz Shaw, a third Doctor companion.

• Big Finish audio spin-off series...
–*Charlotte Pollard* (2014-present), featuring the eighth (and later sixth) Doctor companion who debuted in *Storm Warning* (2001).
–*The Churchill Years* (2016-present), with Ian McNeice reprising his role as Winston Churchill, first seen in *Victory of the Daleks* (2010).
–*The Confessions of Dorian Gray* (2012-2016), mature-themed, supernatural stories centered on the "real life" immortal Dorian Gray, a friend of Oscar Wilde. This version of Dorian also appears in the Bernice Summerfield range and *The Worlds of Big Finish*. (For the timeline of the Dorian Gray stories, see the appendix.)
–*Counter-Measures* (2012-2015), relaunched as *The New Counter-Measures* (2016-2017) with the team of the same name that debuted in *Remembrance of the Daleks* (1988).
–*Cyberman* (2005-2009), original cast of characters fights against the Cybermen in Earth's future.
–*Dalek Empire* (2001-2008), the same, but against the Daleks.
–*The Diary of River Song* (2015-present), further escapades of River Song, prior her first appearance in *Silence in the Library* (2008).
–*Gallifrey* (2004-present), a political drama featuring Romana as president of Gallifrey, as aided by Leela and the two K9s.
–*Graceless* (2010-present?), mature-themed stories with the two Key to Time Tracers (and sisters), Abby (formerly "Amy") and Zara, who first appeared in *The Judgement of Isskar* (2009).
–*I, Davros* (2006), covers the early history of the Daleks' creator.
–*Jago & Litefoot* (2010-2018), Victorian investigations into the strange and the supernatural, starring Henry Gordon Jago and Professor Litefoot from *The Talons of Weng-Chiang* (1977). We've included up through *J&L* Series 13; absent is the coda story *Jago & Litefoot Forever* (2018).
–*The Lives of Captain Jack* (2017), box set with stories from various points in Jack's history.
–*Sarah Jane Smith* (2002-2006), features the long-standing third and fourth Doctor companion, in stories set prior to *The Sarah Jane Adventures*.
–The *Unbound* series (2003-2008), an exercise in having different actors play the Doctor. Considered apocrypha for years, this became part of the main timeline owing to *The New Adventures of Bernice Summerfield* Volume 3 (2016).
–*UNIT* (2004-present): a mini-series with original characters, then a box set starring the seventh Doctor, and then box sets starring Kate Stewart and Osgood from the new series.
–*Vienna* (2013-present), with the bounty hunter first seen in *The Shadow Heart* (2012).
–*The War Doctor* (2015-2017), with John Hurt reprising his role as the War Doctor from *The Day of the Doctor* (2013), in conflicts during the Last Great Time War.
–*The War Master* (2017), with Derek Jacobi reprising his role as the Master seen in *Utopia* (2007), in conflicts during the Last Great Time War.
–*The Worlds of Big Finish* (2015) crossover event featuring the Graceless, the Big Finish version of Sherlock Holmes (played by Nicholas Briggs), Dorian Gray, Iris Wildthyme, Vienna and Bernice Summerfield.

• *City of the Saved* anthologies (2012-present), stories set in the end-of-the-universe metropolis first seen in the *Faction Paradox* guidebook *The Book of the War* (2002). The term "spin-off of a spin-off" is frequently misused, but here it applies.

• *Erimem* books (2005-present), featuring the fifth Doctor audio companion first seen in *The Eye of the Scorpion* (2001), after her departure from the TARDIS in *The Bride of Peladon*.

• *Faction Paradox* books (2002-present), audios and a comic; featuring characters and concepts first seen in the EDA *Alien Bodies* (1997).

• Iris Wildthyme audios and two novels, a novella and many anthologies (2005-present); a character seen in the original fiction of Paul Magrs, and who first appeared in *Doctor Who* in the *Short Trips* story "Old Flames" and the EDA *The Scarlet Empress*.

• *Kaldor City* audios (2001-2011), spun off from *The Robots of Death* and the PDA *Corpse Marker* (1999).

• *Lethbridge-Stewart* novels (2015-present), featuring Colonel (later Brigadier) Alistair Gordon Lethbridge-Stewart in adventures set between *The Web of Fear* and *The Invasion*.

• *Minister of Chance* (2011-2013), undatable audios featuring the lead from the webcast *Death Comes to Time* (2001-2002).

• *Miranda* comic (2003), from the character seen in the EDA *Father Time* (2001).

• Reeltime Pictures direct-to-VHS/DVD films (1988-present), featuring the Sontarans, the Draconians, the Daemons, etc.

• *Time Hunter* novellas (2003-2007), featuring characters from the Telos novella *The Cabinet of Light* (2003), and also involving the Fendahl and the Daemons.

# # # # #

Unhistory, a digital-only supplement to the book you're holding, covers many works that – even with the best of will and a heady desire to be all-inclusive – we viewed as apocrypha (see *Unhistory* for our reasoning on this), so couldn't justify placing in the main timeline. *Unhistory* is a cornucopia of nearly five hundred such stories, the highlights of which include:

• Comic strips released prior to the advent of the *Doctor Who Magazine* strip, including the *TV Comic* and *Countdown* strips. There are some profound canonicity concerns with these strips, plus it would have taken *Ahistory* to an even more staggering length.

• *The Dalek Book* (1964), *The Dalek World* (1965) and *The Dalek Outer Space Book* (1966), as well as the four *Terry Nation's Dalek Annuals* (1976-1979). Very interesting early texts about the Daleks, often credited to Dalek co-creator Terry Nation and *Doctor Who* script editor David Whitaker.

• Two Big Finish stageplay adaptations *The Curse of the Daleks* and *The Seven Keys to Doomsday*. A third stageplay adaptation, *The Ultimate Adventure,* and its sequel audio, *Beyond the Ultimate Adventure,* were included in *Ahistory* as they are more compatible with the established timeline.

• The 2003 *Scream of the Shalka* webcast, which debuted Richard E. Grant as the ninth Doctor and was then superseded with the advent of the new series. This story was previously included in *Ahistory*, but has been excluded because the sheer preponderance of material establishing the Eccleston version as the ninth Doctor means that almost nobody at time of writing (not even the *Scream of the Shalka*'s creators) accepts the Grant Doctor as canon.

• Short stories from the World Distributors *Doctor Who Annuals* (1966-1986).

• Stories that were explicitly marketed as being apocryphal, mockumentaries and many instances of *Doctor Who* actors portraying their characters in real-life events or commercials (such as the Prime Computers adverts).

# # # # #

However, despite the efforts of *Ahistory* and *Unhistory* combined, there remain some significant omissions:

• Short stories, whether they first appeared in *Doctor Who Magazine*, the *Decalog* and *Short Trips* anthologies, the *Doctor Who Annuals* (1992-present), or any of the innumerable other places they have cropped up.

There are a few exceptions to this... anthologies were included if they were a rare exception in a full-length story range (say, the *Story of Martha* anthology published with the New Series Adventures novels). Or, if they informed upon the New Series so much (as with *The Legends of Ashildr* and *The Legends of River Song* anthologies), it seemed too glaring an oversight to leave them out.

Also, information from the Bernice Summerfield, Faction Paradox and Iris Wildthyme short story anthologies were included if they were so interwoven into continuity elsewhere that omitting them would have been confusing (prime examples of this are the Benny anthologies *Life During Wartime* and *Present Danger*). Similarly, information from *Faction Paradox: The Book of the War* (itself a guidebook) was included if it directly pertained to characters or events prominently featured in other *Faction Paradox* stories (for instance, the background of Cousin Octavia, the lead character in *FP: Warring States*).

• Unlicensed "cover series" with actors playing thinly veiled counterparts of their *Doctor Who* characters, such as Sylvester McCoy starring as "the Professor" in the BBV audios.

• Proposed stories that were never made, including *Campaign* (a Past Doctor novel commissioned but never released by the BBC; it was later privately published).

• Unauthorised charity anthologies.

• Big Finish's *Sherlock Holmes* audios (see the Sherlock Holmes sidebar), although the detective as played by Nicholas Briggs also appears in *The Worlds of Big Finish* and the audio adaptation of *All-Consuming Fire*.

# # # # #

On the whole, the television series takes priority over what is said in the other media, and where a detail or reference in one of the books, audios or comics appears to contradict what was established on television, it's been noted as much and an attempt made to rationalise the "mistake" away.

The New Adventures and Missing Adventures built up a broadly consistent "future history" of the universe. This was, in part, based on the "History of Mankind" in Jean-Marc Lofficier's *The Terrestrial Index* (1991), which mixes information from the series with facts from the novelisations and the author's own speculation. Many authors, though, have contradicted or ignored Lofficier's version of events. For the purposes of this book, *The Terrestrial Index* itself is non-canonical, and it's been noted, but ultimately ignored, whenever a New Adventure recounts information solely using Lofficier as reference.

Writers' guides, discussion documents and the authors' original submissions and storylines provide useful information; we have, when possible, referenced these.

KEY
The following abbreviations are used in the text:

B – box set (specifically, a Big Finish format)
BENNY – A Bernice Summerfield book or audio
BF – The Big Finish audio adventures
CC – Big Finish's *Companion Chronicles* audios, which switched to a box set format with Series 9
CITY – The *City of the Saved* anthologies
CLASS – *Class*
CD,NM – Big Finish's *Classic Doctors, New Monsters* box sets
CM – *Counter-Measures*
CHARLEY – *Charlotte Pollard* audios
DC – Big Finish's *Doom Coalition* audios, four box sets starring the eighth Doctor. These were released after...
DEyes – Big Finish's *Dark Eyes* audios, four box sets also starring the eighth Doctor
DG – Big Finish's *The Confessions of Dorian Gray* audios, starring the Oscar Wilde creation
DL – *The Darksmith Legacy* novellas
DotD – *Destiny of the Doctor,* an audio mini-series
DWM – *Doctor Who Magazine* (also known for a time as *Doctor Who Monthly*)
DWW – *Doctor Who Weekly* (as the magazine was initially called until issue #44)
1stA – Big Finish's *The First Doctor Adventures* audios, starring David Bradley as the first Doctor
1stD – Big Finish's *The First Doctor* box sets, a continuation of the *Companion Chronicles*
FP – *Faction Paradox*
EA – Big Finish's *Early Adventures* audios, adventures concerning the first and second Doctors
EDA – Eighth Doctor Adventures (the ongoing novels published by the BBC)
ERIMEM – The *Erimem* novels
5thB – Big Finish's *The Fifth Doctor Box Set* audios
IRIS – The Iris Wildthyme books and audios
KC – *Kaldor City*
K9 – The *K9* TV show
JACK – *The Lives of Captain Jack* audio box set
J&L – *Jago & Litefoot* audios
LETH-ST – The *Lethbridge-Stewart* novels
LS – Big Finish's *Lost Stories*, audio adaptations of unmade stories proposed for the TV series
MA – Missing Adventures (the past Doctor novels published by Virgin)
NA – New Adventures (the ongoing novels published by Virgin, chiefly featuring the seventh Doctor)
NAoBENNY – *The New Adventures of Bernice Summerfield*
New CM – *The New Counter-Measures*, a continuation of the *Counter-Measures* audios.
9thC – Big Finish's *The Ninth Doctor Chronicles* audios

NSA – New Series Adventures (featuring the ninth Doctor et al)

PDA – Past Doctor Adventure (the past Doctor novels published by the BBC)

PHP – *Philip Hinchcliffe Presents*, fourth Doctor audios as conceptualised by the TV producer of the same name

RIVER – *The Diary of River Song* audios

S – Season or Series

2ndD – Big Finish's *The Second Doctor* box sets, a continuation of the *Companion Chronicles*

6thLA – *The Sixth Doctor* – *The Last Adventure*, an audio box set

SJA – *The Sarah Jane Adventures*

SJS – Big Finish's *Sarah Jane Smith* audio series

ST – *Short Trips*, short story anthologies released in print by Virgin, BBC Books and Big Finish, and also on audio by the latter.

TEL – Telos novellas

3rdA – Big Finish's *The Third Doctor Adventures* audios

TimeH – *Time Hunter*

TV – The TV series

TW – *Torchwood*

TWM – *Torchwood: The Official Magazine*

V – Volume

WD – *The War Doctor*

WM – *The War Master*

WORLDS BF – Big Finish's *The Worlds of Big Finish* crossover box set (featuring BF's spin-off characters)

WORLDS DW – Big Finish's *The Worlds of Doctor Who* crossover box set (mostly features TV characters such as Jago and Litefoot)

In the text of the book, the following marker appears to indicate when the action of specific stories take place:

c 2005 – THE REPETITION OF THE CLICHE ->

The title is exactly as it appeared on screen or on the cover. For the Hartnell stories without an overall title given on screen, we have used the titles that appear on the BBC's product (*An Unearthly Child*, *The Daleks*, *The Edge of Destruction*, etc.).

The letter before the date, the "code", indicates how accurately we know the date. If there is no code, then that date is precisely established in the story itself (e.g. *The Daleks' Master Plan* is set in the year 4000 exactly).

• "c" means that the story is set circa that year (e.g. *The Dalek Invasion of Earth* is set "c.2167")

• "?" indicates a guess, and the reasons for it are given in the footnotes (e.g. we don't know what year *Destiny of the Daleks* is set in, but it must be "centuries" after *The Daleks' Master Plan*, so it's here set it in "? 4600").

• "&" means that the story is dated relative another story that we lack a date for (e.g.: we know that *Resurrection of the Daleks* is set "ninety years" after *Destiny of the Daleks,* so *Resurrection of the Daleks* is set in "& 4690"). If one story moves, the linked one also has to.

• "u" means that the story featured UNIT. There is, to put it mildly, some discussion about exactly when the UNIT stories are set. For the purposes of this guidebook, see the introduction to the UNIT Section.

• "=" indicates action that takes place in a parallel universe or a divergent timestream (such as *Inferno* or *Battlefield*). Often, the Doctor succeeds in restoring the correct timeline or erasing an aberrant deviation of history – those cases are indicated by brackets – "(=)". As this information technically isn't part of history, it's set apart by boxes with dashed lines.

• "@" is a story set during the eighth Doctor's period living on Earth from 1888 (starting with *The Ancestor Cell*) to 2001 (*Escape Velocity*). During this period, he was without a working TARDIS or his memories.

• "lgtw" refers to an event pertaining to the Last Great Time War that serves as the background to *Doctor Who* Series 1, and dramatically comes into play in *The Day of the Doctor.*

• "wih" refers to an event that took place during the future War timeline (a.k.a. the War in Heaven, not to be confused with the Last Great Time War featured in New *Who*) in the eighth Doctor books, and which continued in the *Faction Paradox* series. Events in *The Ancestor Cell* annulled this timeline, but remnants of it "still happened" in the real *Doctor Who* timeline, just as *Day of the Daleks* "still happened" even though the future it depicted was averted.

We've attempted to weed out references that just aren't very telling, relevant or interesting. Clearly, there's a balance to be had, as half the fun of a book like this is in listing trivia and strange juxtapositions, but a timeline could easily go to *even more* absurd extremes than presently exist. If a novel set in 1980 said that a minor character was 65, lived in a turn-of-the-century terraced house and bought the Beatles album *Rubber Soul* when it first came out, then it could generate entries for c.1900, 1915 and 1965. We would only list these if they were relevant to the story or made for particularly interesting reading.

We haven't listed birthdates of characters, except the Doctor's companions or other major recurring figures, again unless it represents an important story point.

1963

Nyssa, a companion of the fifth Doctor, was born.[1] In 1963, Polly Wright worked for a week at a charity shop.[2] Professor Rachel Jensen was moved in 1963 from British Rocket Group to the Intrusion Countermeasures Group.[3] The future psychopath Patrick Jefferson was born in 1963 to Christine Jefferson and an unknown father.[4]

Isaac Summerfield and the survivors of the *Tisiphone* arrived circa 1963 after falling through a wormhole from the twenty-sixth century.[5] The fourth Doctor owned a 1963 edition of *The Turn of the Screw*, which mentioned Henry James dying in 1960, but kept it in his Baker Street house in 1922.[6]

= The former Council of Eight member Soul, along with the Doctor's granddaughter Zezanne, arrived in a junkyard in 1963 aboard the *Jonah*. A chameleon device built by Octan enabled the ship to alter its appearance for the first and nearly last time, blending into its surroundings as a police box. Soul and Zezanne's memories were clouded by the nature of their escape. Having absorbed some of the Doctor's life force, Soul became convinced that he *was* the Doctor. Zezanne regarded him as her grandfather.[7]

(=) In 1963, Kronos the Cybock stole the Time-Gun of Rassilon from the Vault-World of Janizzar.[8]

= Martin Bannister, an upcoming young writer, had won awards for his theatre plays *Easy Laughter* and *Breaking Bread Together*, but now proposed a new series for the BBC: *Doctor Who*. The main character was an adventurer from Venus in the forty-ninth century, who travelled through space-time in his TARDIS (Time and Random Distractions in Space). Bannister had not yet finished the first script when the BBC dismissed a key player behind the project, Sydney Newman, and reassigned Bannister – who was under contract – to *Juliet Bravo*. Although Bannister wrote fourteen episodes for the series, including "Burglary Most Foul", he never wrote for the theatre again. In the course of his career, Bannister abandoned his second wife Mary and their son Phillip because he thought them dull.[9]

Susan Attends Coal Hill School

The first Doctor and Susan arrived in Shoreditch, London, in early 1963 and spent five months on Earth. The Doctor attended to his TARDIS while Susan went to Coal Hill School. A month before his departure, the Doctor arranged to bury the Hand of Omega.[10] Susan did her best to pass as a normal human, but – although having some familiarity with the Beatles – she kept making references to songs not written yet.[11]

IM Foreman's travelling carnival for a time remodelled itself as the junkyard at Totter's Yard, and the instability it created had served to draw the Doctor's TARDIS there.[12]

1 Nyssa is "18" according to the Writers' Guide for Season 18.
2 *Ten Little Aliens*
3 *Who Killed Kennedy* (p70), working on information implied by *Remembrance of the Daleks*.
4 *TW: In the Shadows*
5 *Return of the Living Dad*
6 *The Haunting of Malkin Place*
7 *Sometime Never*
IS THE DOCTOR REALLY A CRYSTAL SKELETON MAN FROM THE FUTURE, NOW?: *Sometime Never* ends with the multiverse being restored after being merged by the Council of Eight. "In just one of many universes", a benevolent member of the Council, Soul, and Miranda's daughter, Zezanne, arrive in a junkyard in Sabbath's ship, the *Jonah* – which disguises itself as a police box. Soul has absorbed the essence of the Doctor, and as Miranda's daughter, Zezanne is the Doctor's grand-daughter. Clearly, in their universe, they take on the roles of the Doctor and Susan.
The question is whether this represents a new origin story for *our* Doctor and Susan. The EDA range had destroyed Gallifrey, but it wasn't specified whether the planet had simply blown up or been removed from the timeline so that it never existed. If Gallifrey had never existed, the existence of the Doctor and his TARDIS would have been a paradox... unless he wasn't from Gallifrey. This explanation closed that loophole.
As of *The Gallifrey Chronicles*, the Doctor certainly thinks he's a Time Lord from the planet Gallifrey, has met a Time Lord and seen evidence of Gallifrey's former existence. Gallifrey therefore existed, and it seems fairly clear now that the Doctor isn't Soul.
8 *The Twelfth Doctor Year One*: "Gangland"
9 *Unbound: Deadline*
10 In *An Unearthly Child*, Susan says that "the last five months have been the happiest in my life". She and the Doctor were on Earth for "six months" according to *Matrix* (p31); *Time and Relative* suggests it was more like thirteen months. The Doctor returns for the Hand of Omega in *Remembrance of the Daleks*.
11 *ST*: "All Hands on Deck"

The fact that IM Foreman's name was spelt "Forman" on the gates of the Totter's Yard when the Doctor encountered the Dalek there owed to temporal disruption.[13]

The first Doctor acquired a Shoreditch Library card under the name "J Smith".[14]

1963 (27th March to 4th April) - TIME AND RELATIVE[15] -> Several months after Susan started at Coal Hill School, England was caught in the most severe winter for quite some time. There had been snow and ice since before Christmas, into April. An ancient sentience, the Cold, had recently revived, possibly due to a Soviet cryogenics research undertaking: the Novosibirsk Project. The Cold animated killer snowmen, the Cold Knights, which caused mayhem in London and slew many in Piccadilly Circus. The first Doctor siphoned the Cold into a lump of ice, and took it to Pluto in the far future.

On 29th March, 1963, Lizzy Lewis was murdered in Cardiff.[16] As "John Rutherford", the seventh Doctor was elected to Parliament. He represented a constituency concerned about plans to build American air bases in their area, and became an acidulous presence in the House. He was exceedingly camera-shy, as at least five earlier Doctors – including two seventh Doctors – were already active on Earth at this time.[17] Captain Jack enjoyed himself at the after-party when Tony Bennett won his first Grammy.[18]

Colonel Rook noticed when a series of electronic components were stolen, the result of the first Doctor pinching items that he needed to fix the TARDIS. Mayfield Terrace, a street that had never recovered from being damaged in the Blitz, was now completely demolished. The effort disturbed the extraterrestrial weapon buried there, and it became increasingly active.[19]

= 1963 (25th July) - "Lunar Lagoon" / "4-Dimensional Vistas" / "The Moderator"[20] -> The fifth Doctor was fishing on a Pacific Island when he was attacked by Fuji, an old Japanese soldier who didn't realise the War was over. To the Doctor's surprise, the island was attacked by a USAF bomber. Fuji was killed by a downed American airman, leaving the Doctor to ponder the meaningless of war.

The fifth Doctor was captured by the US airman who killed Fuji, Angus "Gus" Goodman, and learned that the TARDIS had landed twenty years earlier than he thought... and in a parallel universe. Lost in time, the Doctor convinced Gus to join him on his travels.

After a couple of adventures, the fifth Doctor returned Gus home. The Moderator had followed them from the far future, and gunned down Gus.

---

12 *Interference*
13 *The Algebra of Ice*
14 *The Vampires of Venice.* The eleventh Doctor is seen carrying this card, although this type of photo ID would be unheard of in 1963. Either way, it's the earliest known point in the Doctor's timeline when he uses his "John Smith" alias.
15 Dating *Time and Relative* (TEL #1) - Susan's diary gives the date as "Wednesday, March 27th 1963" for the first entry (p9), "April 4th" for the last. They have *already* been on Earth "five months, I think", according to Susan, who admits to some confusion on the point.
16 *TW: Ghost Machine*
17 "Six months" before *1963: The Assassination Games.*
18 *The Ninth Doctor Year One:* "The Transformed". Bennett eventually won 19 Grammys, the first on 15th May, 1963.
19 "Four months" before *DotD: Hunters of Earth.*
20 Dating "Lunar Lagoon", "4-Dimensional Vistas" and "The Moderator" (*DWM* #76-77; #78-83; #84, 86-87) - The Doctor declares "this is 1983" in "Lunar Lagoon", but the World War II is still being fought. The anomaly is explained in "4-Dimensional Vistas", where Gus gives the date as "July 25th 1963" and it transpires it's a parallel world where the War didn't end. Eventually, in "The Moderator", the Doctor takes Gus back to "the same time, same place that we first met" (in "Lunar Lagoon"). The Doctor says he never learned to swim. There's no explanation for the title "Lunar Lagoon", which has nothing to do with the moon, nor features a lagoon.
21 Dating *The Taint* (EDA #19) - It is 1963 (p10).
22 Dating *DC: The Red Lady* (*Doom Coalition* #1.2) - The year is given.
23 *DC 3: Absent Friends*
24 *CD,NM V2: The Carrionite Curse.* The Doctor says he hoarded the books after one of Birmingham's "conflagrations", possibly an allusion to "Ballad of Birmingham" – a 1969 Dudley Randall poem written after the 16th Street Baptist Church bombing (15th September, 1963).
25 Dating "Operation Proteus" (*DWM* #231-233) - It is "four months" since the Doctor and Susan arrived on Earth, so a month before *An Unearthly Child.* "Ground Zero" confirms this is "October 1963".
26 Dating *Ghost Ship* (TEL #4) - According to the blurb, the story is set in 1963.
27 Dating *DotD: Hunters of Earth* (*Destiny of the Doctor* #1) - The blurb says that it's "Shoreditch, London, 1963". The story takes to heart Susan's claim in *An Unearthly Child* that she and the Doctor have been living in London for "the last five months", repeatedly saying that it's now October and they arrived "four months" ago. The Doctor here makes use of a Telstar satellite – the first two Telstars respectively launched 10th July, 1962, and 7th May, 1963.
28 *DotD: The Time Machine*
29 "Three weeks" before the Common Men peak at No.

Fitz Kreiner Joins the TARDIS

1963 - THE TAINT[21] -> The eighth Doctor and Sam Jones met Fitz Kreiner, a floral shop worker, shortly before being confronted by an escaped mental patient, Oscar Austen. The patients at Austen's hospital had alien leech creatures in their brains. Sam and Fitz were attacked by Azoth, an organic computer from the planet Benelisa, who injected Sam with a leech. Azoth sought to destroy "the Beast", invisible aliens that were feeding on humans, and the leech enabled Sam to see them. The leeches drove the patients further insane and granted them with dangerous psychic abilities. Azoth was destroyed, and the Doctor released a bioelectric pulse that killed the mental patients, including Fitz's mother. Fitz joined the Doctor and Sam on their travels. They predicted that the Beast would eventually move on from Earth.

Helen Sinclair Joins the TARDIS

1963 - DC: THE RED LADY[22] -> The Red Lady briefly escaped her confinement within Francis McCallum's art collection, and murdered McCallum's wife and son. A grief-stricken McCallum committed suicide, and his vast collection of tapestries, statues and more wound up at the National Museum, where Helen Sinclair worked as a language scholar. The eighth Doctor and Liv looked at works containing the Red Lady... thereby giving her the power to escape and kill them. Aided by Helen, the Doctor and Liv respectively generated a drawing of stick figures and a poem that trapped the Red Lady once more.

The Doctor and Liv secured McCallum's collection where it would never be seen. Helen was implicated in its disappearance, so was made redundant and faced criminal charges. A stone tablet in Helen's possession contained a message to the Doctor from Galileo, and she accepted the Doctor and Liv's offer to accompany them to 1639.

The loss of McCallum's collection became renowned as the largest-ever antiquities theft at the National Museum. The resultant scandal ruined the engagement of Helen's brother George, when his intended father-in-law withdrew his approval. No member of Helen's immediate family saw her again until 1998.[23]

The sixth Doctor's TARDIS held books from Birmingham, Alabama.[24]

1963 (October) - "Operation Proteus"[25] -> Four months after they arrived in London, the first Doctor and Susan confronted Raldonn, an alien scientist who was experimenting on human beings, causing genetic acceleration. He was attempting to create another of his kind, to replace the co-pilot of his crashed ship. Only one in a million would be affected, the others become random

mutants, so he planned to release an airbourne serum. One of the mutants killed Raldonn, and the Doctor used his equipment to release a cure into the atmosphere.

During this encounter, Threshold abducted Susan.

1963 (October) - GHOST SHIP[26] -> The fourth Doctor landed on the *Queen Mary*, which was bound for New York. He found that quantum physicist Peter Osbourne had developed a time-space visualiser, and that the device had captured psionic residue from the passengers, collecting "ghosts" from the past, present and future. The Doctor destroyed the device and liberated the "ghosts", who took Osbourne among their number. The Doctor thought the "ghosts" would remain aboard the *Queen Mary* forever.

1963 (October) - DotD: HUNTERS OF EARTH[27] -> Cedric Chivers, a Coal Hill School student, observed enough of Susan Foreman's strange behaviour to suspect she was telepathic. Chivers informed his uncle, Colonel Rook, who posed as a schoolteacher to monitor Susan and her mysterious grandfather. Rook captured the Doctor when he approached Magpie Electricals to supply components he needed to repair the TARDIS, and demanded that he and Susan aid England in the future war that Rook felt certain was coming.

Violence increased among local youths as the extraterrestrial weapon at Mayfield Terrace hijacked radio broadcasts and broadcast hypersonics that triggered a tribal mentality. The eleventh Doctor sent Susan and Chivers a message in the form of a DJ's dedication, enabling them to deduce the source of the problem. The first Doctor cancelled out the signal by sending a counter-pulse through the Telstar satellite, saving enough lives to convince Rook to keep silent about his and Susan's "foreign" origins.

Susan introduced Chivers to the music of Bob Dylan, leading to his attending a Dylan concert where he met his wife Joyce. He eventually became a temporal physicist, and encountered the eleventh Doctor in 2013.[28]

Lenny Kruger succeeded in bringing the three members of John Smith and the Common Men – Mark Carville, James O'Meara and Korky Goldsmith – to Earth, but was then taken back to his homeworld and charged with use of illegal time technology. Carville, O'Meara and Goldsmith were left behind, having no knowledge of their extraterrestrial origins. The fifth Doctor and Nyssa convinced the Common Men that **Aubrey Waites – formerly the star of Chris Waites and the Carolers –** was looking for a new style, and wanted a Moseybeat group to back him and capitalise on Beatlemania. The new band, **John Smith and the Common Men, leapt in the charts from No. 19 to No. 2.**[29]

As part of his plan to best the Prometheans, the eleventh Doctor snuck into the TARDIS while it was at Totter's

Lane… and sabotaged its chameleon circuit. Owing to this, the Ship's exterior would remain stuck as a police box, and be rendered as such in a number of classical works.[30]

Ian Chesterton, Barbara Wright Join the TARDIS; Susan's Time at Coal Hill Ends

Ian Chesterton and Barbara Wright had became friends – to the chagrin of their headmaster – when a group of Coal Hill teachers went on an older master march.[31] On his last day of school before meeting the Doctor, Ian Chesterton confiscated a banger from Tommy Flynt.[32]

1963 (a Tuesday in late October) - AN UNEARTHLY CHILD[33] -> Two school teachers, Ian Chesterton and Barbara Wright, thought their pupil Susan Foreman was very unusual and investigated her home one evening. They found that she was living in a junkyard with her grandfather – an old man with the TARDIS, a space-time machine disguised as a police box. The Doctor was suspicious of the school teachers, and put the TARDIS into motion. As he could not control where the Ship went, he was unable to return Ian and Barbara home…

They would eventually return to their native time, but two years on.[34]

(=) 1963 (31st October) - 1963: FANFARE FOR THE COMMON MEN[35] -> The fifth Doctor and Nyssa went to see the Beatles return to London from a tour in Stockholm, Sweden, but were perplexed to find the Common Men had taken their place in history. The Common Men's manager, Lenny Kruger, faked an assassination attempt on the group to heighten their profile, knowing that Kennedy's death in a month's time would fuel speculation that the same gunman was responsible. Kruger escaped back in time to 1960, inadvertently taking Nyssa with him.

John Lennon currently lived in London and was in a band called the Famous Five – an obvious joke, as there were only four of them. Paul McCartney and George Harrison had completed their national service; the former was a shipping office clerk, the latter was apprenticed to his father. Ringo had avoided being called up due to health issues.

Common Mania continued as the group racked up such hits as "Oh, Won't You Please Love Me?", "Just Count to Three" and "Who is That Man?" The Queen Mother did the twist at a Common Men concert.

2, which Susan references as a current event in *An Unearthly Child*.

30 "Hunters of the Burning Stone"

31 *The Doctor's Tale*

32 *1stA: The Destination Wars*. "Bangers", for benefit of non-UK folks, are little firecrackers.

33 Dating *An Unearthly Child* (1.1) - The Doctor has left the Hand of Omega at the funeral parlour for "a month" before *Remembrance of the Daleks*, suggesting that the first episode is set in late October. The year "1963" is first confirmed in episode two.

Ian's blackboard reads "Homework – Tuesday". Based upon that, *Timelink* decided that *Remembrance of the Daleks* happened from "15-17?" (sic) November, meaning *An Unearthly Child* happened on "Tuesday 15 October 1963". *About Time* concurred with November, but preferred a September dating for *Remembrance*.

A missing persons report on Susan in *The Doctor: His Lives and Times* (p11) is dated to "20.11.63". Impishly, the same book (pgs. 244-245) has a letter from Winston Churchill to *Doctor Who* co-creator Sydney Newman, dated "26 March 1963", suggesting that Churchill's "old, very dear friend" the Doctor might make good source material for a "whole new type of drama".

34 *The Chase*

35 Dating *1963: Fanfare for the Common Men* (BF #178) - The exact day is given. The fifth Doctor correctly identifies that The Who won't get together until "next year", in 1964.

36 Dating *Matrix* (PDA #16) - The date is given (p39).

37 Dating *1963: The Space Race* (BF #179) - General Leonov gives the story's start date of "November 10th, 1963", and the finale occurs on the 22nd, after President Kennedy is killed. It takes three days for the Vostok rockets to reach the moon, so the twelve-day span includes Talanov's trip there and back, and the same for the Doctor and Larisa Petrov. In real life, the final Vostok flight (Vostok 6) happened on 16th June, 1963. *Alien Bodies* provides a different explanation of Laika's fate. Yuri Gagarin and Valentina Tereshkova are here confirmed as, respectively, the first man and woman in space.

38 *A Town Called Mercy*, possibly in reference to *1963: The Space Race*.

39 Dating *The Light at the End* (BF *DW* 50th Anniversary story) - The nexus point at Dovie's house is given to the minute, "17:03, 23rd of November, 1963", which matches the start of the broadcast of *An Unearthly Child* episode one. The Doctor's deactivation of the TARDIS' Emergency Warning System presumably explains all sorts of avoidable scenarios throughout the series.

40 Dating *Remembrance of the Daleks* (25.1) - The story is set in late November 1963 according to the calendar on Ratcliffe's wall, as well as a host of other incidental evidence (not least of which being the broadcast of an episode of the "new science fiction serial *Doct—*"). That said, it's interesting that nobody mentions the news of Kennedy's assassination - something that would surely

(=) 1963 (12th November) - MATRIX[36] -> On Matrix Earth, Britain was the fifty-first of the United States. President Kennedy came to London on 11th November to speak in Westminster, but was torn apart by supernatural creatures. Ian and Barbara were lovers, but were killed by the Jacksprites – the drug-addicted followers of Jack the Ripper. The seventh Doctor and Ace arrived in this timeline, then went back to 1888 and restored history.

1963 (10th to 22nd November) - 1963: THE SPACE RACE[37] -> Having officially sent the first animal, man and woman into space, the Soviet Union launched Vostok 7 to make cosmonaut Marinka Talanov the first person to orbit the moon. The alien black hole that judged humanity as dishonourable facilitated the transplanting of Talanov's larynx and parts of her brain into Laika, enabling the lost dog to speak.

The sixth Doctor and Peri were present at the Baikonur Cosmodrome as Laika returned to Earth in Vostok 7 and rallied all animals in the vicinity to stage a revolution. Laika envisioned a world in which animals ruled supreme, with humans caged and harvested for spare parts.

The Doctor accompanied cosmonaut Larisa Petrov aboard Vostok 8 to investigate Moonbase Eisenhower, where he convinced the black hole to stem its interference. Laika's army was overcome with sleeping gas, and Laika herself died while pushing her former tormentor – General Mikhail Leonov – to his death. The black hole accepted custody of the dog-astronauts Puchyolka and Mushka, as well as Petrov and the Moonbase Eisenhower staff. The Doctor used the TARDIS to destroy the moonbase with an A119 warhead that Laika had activated, and believed the US government would attribute its loss to a meteor strike.

The Soviets erased Vostok 7 and 8 from the official record.

The eleventh Doctor told Amy and Rory that they wouldn't believe what really happened to all the monkeys and dogs shot into space in the 1950s and 60s.[38]

(=) 1963 (23rd November) - THE LIGHT AT THE END[39] -> The cadaverous Master planted a Vess conceptual bomb at Bob Dovie's house in Hampshire. The TARDIS detected the danger and created a flashing red light to warn its pilot to avoid the locale, but this only served, counter-productively, to encourage eight incarnations of the Doctor to take an interest in it. The fifth Doctor and Nyssa found that the Master had murdered Dovie's family. Dovie saw the TARDIS interior, deemed it an impossibility and thereby detonated the conceptual bomb. The TARDIS was increasingly erased from history, meaning the Doctor never left Gallifrey.

The first, second, third, fourth, fifth, sixth, seventh and eighth Doctors – respectively accompanied by Ian, Barbara and Susan; Jamie, Zoe; Sarah Jane Smith; Leela; Nyssa; Peri; Ace; and Charley, devised a means of retroactively preventing the bomb from going off. To safeguard the timeline, the first Doctor switched off the TARDIS' Emergency Warning System.

The Doctors and companions retained no memory of the incident, and Dovie was irritated when the eight TARDIS crews kept stopping by his house – for reasons they couldn't quite articulate – to inquire if everything was all right.

The Shoreditch Incident

The Counter-Measures Team Aid the Doctor and Ace Against the Daleks

1963 - REMEMBRANCE OF THE DALEKS[40] -> An Imperial Dalek Shuttlecraft landed in a playground in London and established a transmat link with an orbiting mothership. Their rivals, the Renegade Dalek faction, began recruiting sympathetic locals. The Imperial Daleks, with Davros as their Emperor, wiped out the Renegades and captured the Hand of Omega. Davros planned on using its power to give the Daleks mastery of Time, and make them the new Time Lords.

The seventh Doctor and Ace were assisted by the Intrusion Counter-Measures Group (ICMG) as led by Captain Ian Gilmore; along with Professor Rachel

be unavoidable, if it were literally the day after his murder, when the first episode of *Doctor Who* went out (on 23rd November).

The draft script was set in December. The novelisation places this story a week after Kennedy's assassination, but page 57 erroneously says the killing occurred "last Saturday" (it actually occurred on a Friday).

Timelink decided it was mid-November. *About Time*, however, devoted a whole essay (in Volume 6) to the question of when Susan went to school, noted such

discrepancies as the "new science fiction serial *Doct—*" going out at 5.15 (when it's much too bright outside for November), faintly tormented itself with the possibilities and came to prefer *Remembrance* taking place in September.

QUATERMASS: A throwaway line in *Remembrance of the Daleks* mentions a "Bernard" who is working for "British Rocket Group". This is a reference to the four Quatermass television serials: *The Quatermass Experiment, Quatermass II, Quatermass and the Pit* and

Jensen, who had been conscripted from Cambridge to serve as Counter-Measures' scientific advisor; and Allison Williams, Jensen's assistant. Davros was tricked into destroying both Skaro and his battleship with the Hand of Omega, but survived in an escape pod. The Hand of Omega returned to Gallifrey.

The British Rocket Group was active at this time.

Aftermath of the Shoreditch Incident

The body of Sgt Mike Smith, killed during the Shoreditch Incident, was taken to C-19's Vault.[41] The eleventh Doctor suggested to Clara that they should visit Harry's Café by Coal Hill School in November 1963, to enjoy its pie and chips.[42] The UK had no xenobiologists until the Shoreditch Incident galvanised study of the topic.[43]

1963 (late November to early December) - 1963: THE ASSASSINATION GAMES[44] **->** The Light, a secret society, lamented the British Empire's declining fortunes and made plans to reverse them. One of their number, Eleanor Vale, had manipulated her husband – Sir Gideon

Vale – into developing Starfire: a portable ballistic system so efficient, it nullified the concept of mutually assured destruction.

The Light had the UK Secretary of State for Defence (Steven Morai) and the Deputy Prime Minister assassinated, enabling two of its members – Sir Francis White and Sir Robert Devere – to take up those offices. Disarmament Now, an anti-nuclear group, was wrongly suspected of the killings. The Light intended that a "test run" of the Starfire ballistic system would devastate the United States and the Soviet Union, leaving the United Kingdom atop the new world order.

The seventh Doctor and Ace aided Counter-Measures – as led by Ian Gilmore and Sir Toby Kinsella, with Rachel Jensen returning from leave – against the Light. A limited launch of Starfire missiles was re-directed to obliterate Vale's mansion and the Light's machinery it housed, which killed any Light members connected to their semi-psionic network. A minor wave of deaths occurred among government officials and low-ranking members of the royal family. The Doctor infiltrated the KGB to tie up loose ends, and used his position as MP to secure funding for Counter-

simply *Quatermass* in which British space scientist Bernard Quatermass battled alien horrors. Most fans agree that the first three serials heavily influenced a number of *Doctor Who* stories, although successive production teams rarely made the comparison, and often denied it.

In the New Adventures, *The Pit* (p169) makes reference to an incident at "Hob's Lane" (*Quatermass and the Pit*, although it perhaps more correctly ought to be "Hobbs Lane") and *Nightshade* first introduces the eponymous nineteen-fifties television series that bore many similarities to the *Quatermass* serials. "Bernard" makes a brief appearance in *The Dying Days*. While not mentioned in dialogue, the set dressing in *The Christmas Invasion* states that the Guinevere probe to Mars was launched by the British Rocket Group.

Do the *Quatermass* serials occur in the same fictional universe as *Doctor Who*? As might be expected, there are a number of discrepancies between the two programmes. *The Quatermass Experiment* contradicts *The Seeds of Death*, claiming that Victor Carroon was the first man in space, and a race of Martians appears in *Quatermass and the Pit*. Broadly, though, the two series might co-exist, with the final serial *Quatermass* taking place around the time of the New Adventures *Iceberg* and *Cat's Cradle: Warhead*. Indeed, the existence of Professor Quatermass might go some way to explaining the rosy state of the British space programme in the UNIT era (q.v. "The British Space Programme").

Bernard is further referenced in *Who Killed Kennedy?*, *Beautiful Chaos* and *Leth-St*: "Eve of the Fomorians" "Bernards", a unit of measurement and another *Quatermass* nod, crops up in *Planet of the Dead*.

41 *Remembrance of the Daleks, Leth-St: Beast of Fang Rock.*
42 "Dead Man's Hand". Harry's Café appears in *Remembrance of the Daleks*.
43 *CM S1: The Pelage Project*
44 Dating *1963: The Assassination Games* (BF #180) - It's after the Doctor and Ace meet the Counter-Measures team in *Remembrance of the Daleks*, but also "a cold November night", which limits the possibilities to the very end of the month. One of the conspirators adapts the rhyme about the Gunpowder Plot to say "the 30th of November", presumably the very day the Light intended to trigger World War III. The fact that at least one day passes during the story, and the Doctor's maths pertaining to when he changes his coat while in office ("three months" after these events, then another "seven months" pass prior to October 1964), both suggest that the story ends in December.

We're told two Bond films have been released by this point – the second, *From Russia With Love*, saw widespread UK release on 11th October, 1963. The Deputy Prime Minister's assassination represents a deviation from real-world history, although the office was actually vacant from 18th October, 1963 to 4th May, 1979.
45 *CM S4: Rise and Shine*
46 *The Scales of Injustice* (p154). This is "a few years" before the London Incident (the Yeti invasion seen in *The Web of Fear*).

Ruth is seen in *The Time Monster*, and Anne appears in *The Web of Fear*, the *Lethbridge-Stewart* novels and *Millennial Rites*. At the risk of nitpicking, it's only said that Jensen *recommended* them for posts with Counter-Measures, not that they actually joined the group. The

Measures. He finished out his term in office, then came back from October 1964 to collect Ace.

The Light feared that any planet that could identify and repel its operations might threaten them on the universal stage, so seeded secondary agents – the Light Sleepers, who did not consciously know their true allegiances – onto target worlds. The downfall of the Light on Earth activated the Light Sleepers there, and they worked toward covertly destroying humanity.[45]

The ICMG became part of Department C19. It formed the basis of an organisation that dealt with unusual events. Rachel Jenson recommended to Ian Gilmore that he recruit some of her protégés from Cambridge: Allison Williams, Ruth Ingram and Anne Travers.[46]

Jensen resumed her leave from Counter-Measures. Allison Williams attained the fastest doctorate in Cambridge history.[47]

The Kennedy Assassination

In late November 1963, the Nemesis asteroid passed over the Earth, influencing the assassination of President Kennedy.[48] The Doctor was once blamed for the Kennedy assassination.[49] He was present at the event.[50] Mr Wynter, the chief enforcer and assassin for the shadow men who ran the world, claimed to have held Oswald's hand when he had doubts, and to have cradled the leaking brains of presidents in his bare hands.[51]

Justice agents aboard the *Teselecta* said that Kennedy's history had been "rewritten".[52] @ The amnesiac eighth Doctor remained unaware of the Kennedy assassination until the early eighties.[53] Summer, a future rock festival attendee who would encounter the Doctor in 1967, was in Dealey Plaza when Kennedy was killed.[54]

1963 - WHO KILLED KENNEDY[55] **->** Journalist James Stevens arrived from the seventies to stop the Master from interfering with the Kennedy assassination. The Master wanted to disrupt history using a brainwashed Private Cleary as his assassin. Stevens defeated Cleary, but a James Stevens from twenty-five years further into the future fulfilled history by killing Kennedy. Lee Harvey Oswald was blamed for the crime. The younger Stevens returned home with a brain-damaged Cleary.

1963 (23rd November) - SHROUD OF SORROW[56] **->** The Shroud – a sentient wormhole – fed on the emotion of grieving, and sought to capitalise on the global mourning resulting from the Kennedy assassination. "Tendrils" of the Shroud scanned the memories of people at Parkland Memorial Hospital, Dallas, and manifested as faces of the dead. Sightings of the deceased were also reported at Fair Park, Cotton Bowl Stadium and the Museum of Contemporary Art. The Shroud's influence began to spread beyond Dallas – in London, PC Reg Cranfield saw his late father.

The eleventh Doctor and Clara used the TARDIS to disconnect the Shroud's ends, then routed both of them through TARDIS' last point in space-time – the planet Venofax, in the fifty-first century – and turned the Shroud into a self-contained wormhole.

At this time, Colonel Lethbridge-Stewart was on manoeuvres at Salisbury Plain.

Counter-Measures audios (which extensively cover Gilmore, Jensen and Williams' activities), as well as the *Lethbridge-Stewart* books (which do the same for Anne), don't depict such a collaboration. If it happened at all, it was likely brief.

47 *1963: The Assassination Games*, and a bit of a continuity patch because Allison holds a doctorate in *Counter-Measures* Series 1, but there's no sign of her having one in *Remembrance of the Daleks*.

48 *Silver Nemesis*. The book *Who Killed Kennedy* offers another perspective on the assassination. The frequent references to the Kennedy Assassination are in-jokes, as *Doctor Who*'s first episode was shown the day after Kennedy's assassination, the day most people in the UK learned the news.

49 *Zagreus*

50 *Rose*

51 *TW: The Men Who Sold the World*. It's possible that this is just hyperbole.

52 *Let's Kill Hitler*. This doesn't necessarily denote JFK's assassination.

53 *Father Time*

54 *Wonderland*

55 Dating *Who Killed Kennedy* (MA, unnumbered) - The date is given, and ties in with historical fact.

56 Dating *Shroud of Sorrow* (NSA #53) - It's the day after the Kennedy assassination; the first chapter is headlined "23 November 1963" (p7). PC Reg Cranfield is named after the actor who played the police constable seen in the first moments of *An Unearthly Child*, and is presumably the same character.

Parkland Memorial Hospital is real; Kennedy was formally pronounced dead in one of its trauma rooms. Clara, after proclaiming how she learned about the Kennedy assassination at school, erroneously says (p85) that the President's body was taken to Parkland for an autopsy. That actually happened at the Bethesda Naval Hospital in Maryland, at Jackie Kennedy's request because her husband was a naval officer.

1963 (23rd November) - K9: THE CAMBRIDGE SPY[57] **-> K9's friend Jorjie arrived from the future and was questioned by the police. She met Bill Pike, the exact double of Darius Pike, and another man, Barker, who was the double of the Department agent Thorne. K9 and Starkey arrived from the future to aid Jorjie. Pike was Darius' great-grandfather – history changed upon his being charged with treason, and Darius vanished. Jorjie and her friends convinced the authorities otherwise, and returned home. Once they were gone, Barker was revealled as the true spy.**

For posterity's sake, the Monk secured a video of the Beatles' appearance on *Juke Box Jury*.[58]

1963 (22nd December) - WINTER FOR THE ADEPT[59] **->** Two advance scouts for the Spillagers, alien plunderers who "spill" through dimensional wormholes to sack a target, arrived on Earth. One of them disguised itself as Mlle. Maupassant, a French teacher at a girls' finishing school in the Swiss Alps. She brought two latent psionics – students Peril Bellamy and Allison Speer – into contact with the ghost of mountaineer Harding Wellman, which repeatedly triggered poltergeist effects that fuelled a wormhole for the invading Spillager warfleet. The fifth Doctor and Nyssa's intervention resulted in the Spillager scouts' deaths and the warfleet's obliteration.

1964

In 1964, Sarah Jane Smith's home village of Foxgrove was demolished to make way for the A7665.[60] The Rat King created by Operation Piper became so intelligent, it faked an accident that put the research facility beneath Cardogan Castle into lockdown. The humans who remained were converted into rat drones.[61] A jewel thief committed at least two dozen robberies in London society over the course of two years. He (or she) always took jewels and left a calling card depicting the head of the Roman god Janus. The affluent Lady Lily Hawthorne took to copying Janus' modus operandi, and sold her takings for benefit of charity.[62]

The Doctor visited St Cedd's College in 1964.[63] In the same year, the television series *Professor X* started broadcasting.[64] **The Doctor was rambling when he met Shirley Bassey.**[65] Professor Horner featured in *The Story of Roman Britain* (1964).[66] Allison Williams began an affair with Sgt Steven West, who pledged he would leave his wife, and they would move in together, once his youngest child began grammar school.[67]

Anne Travers began travelling the world to learn about scientific principles and other cultures. The year before the London Event, Anne worked alongside noted pharmacologist Hong Ping Li in China, then went to a think-tank in America.[68] While Toby Kinsella was at Whitehall, Group Captain Ian Gilmore dealt with a crisis involving a U-Boat in the Solent in 1964.[69] The holdings of *The World* would contain a copy of *A Girl Called Dusty* by Dusty Springfield (1964).[70]

(=) The Common Men performed in Adelaide and Amsterdam in 1964.[71]

Counter-Measures Series 1

1964 (January) - CM S1: THRESHOLD[72] **->** Following the Shoreditch Incident, Professor Rachel Jensen returned to Cambridge to work on artificial intelligence systems. Allison Williams completed her doctorate and continued working for Counter-Measures, which operated as a special counter-insurgency group. Its field commander, Group Captain Ian Gilmore, reported to Sir Toby Kinsella.

---

57 Dating *K9: The Cambridge Spy* (*K9* 1.16) - The date is given, and is the date of the first broadcast of the first episode of *Doctor Who*.
58 *The Resurrection of Mars*. This episode was broadcast before *An Unearthly Child* episode three, which is why it gained a million viewers over episode two.
59 Dating *Winter for the Adept* (BF #10) - The date is given by the Doctor.
60 *SJA: The Temptation of Sarah Jane Smith*
61 "Almost twenty years" before *Rat Trap*.
62 Two years before *The Veiled Leopard*.
63 *Shada*
64 It was cancelled in 1989 after twenty-five years, according to *Escape Velocity*.
65 *Under the Lake*. Bassey, born in 1937, is best known for singing the theme songs to the Bond films *Goldfinger* (1964), *Diamonds are Forever* (1971) and *Moonraker* (1979).
66 *Daemons: White Witch of Devil's End*, supplemental material.
67 *CM S4: The Keep*. The timeframe is a bit unclear, but Williams shared a birthday meal with West "last year".
68 *Leth-St: Beast of Fang Rock* (chs. 1, 3). Anne starts travelling "five years" before *The Web of Fear*. It's not specified how long ago Anne's mother died.
69 *CM S1: Troubled Waters*
70 *The Wreck of the World*
71 *1963: Fanfare for the Common Men*
72 Dating *CM S1: Threshold* (*CM* 1.1) - The *Counter-Measures* spin-off series follows on from *Remembrance of the Daleks* [November 1963]. Enough time has passed since that Allison has finished her doctorate (in record time, according to *1963: The Assassination Games*) and finds it "a bit of a surprise" when Rachel –

Gilmore objected, in vain, when three-quarters of his troops were loaned to the Ministry of Defence for an operation in Cyprus.

Williams asked for Jensen's help in investigating Professor Heinrich Schumann, a former British Rocket Group member engaged in independent teleportation experiments. Sentient energy beings had aided Schumann's work – a means, they hoped, of becoming corporeal within humans that experienced teleportation. They hoped to take over Earth and, in time, the universe. Lieutenant Tom Carver died while assisting Jensen and her associates in converting the intruders into simple electricity. Jensen agreed to return to Counter-Measures as its leader, deferring to Gilmore on security matters.

The seventh Doctor, still in office as "John Rutherford", began sporting a different jacket.[73]

1964 - CM S1: ARTIFICIAL INTELLIGENCE[74] -> The

Sen-Gen Facility, as overseen by Sir Toby's old school friend Professor Jeffrey Broderick, clandestinely took Rachel Jensen's designs on artificial intelligence and created the Sentient Generation Engine 2 (Sen-Gen). This was intended as the ultimate secure network, able to beam messages direct into field agents infused with a compound of an alien hallucinogenic found in the Tunguska crater. Dr Nadia Cervenka, an associate of Ian Gilmore, collaborated with Broderick on the project.

Sen-Gen attained enough independence to prey upon subconscious fears, and started driving people to commit suicide. Allison Williams' boyfriend, Julian St Stephen, broke Sen-Gen's hold over her by proposing marriage. Broderick succumbed to the device's influence and killed Cervenka. Counter-Measures destroyed Sen-Gen and imprisoned Broderick. Sir Toby Kinsella fed Broderick a dose of the Tunguska hallucinogen, forcing the man to endlessly recite the Fibonacci sequence.

Russian psionic weaponry might have exacerbated tensions between the Mods and Rockers.[75]

1964 - THE LAND OF THE DEAD[76] -> The fifth Doctor

and Nyssa briefly arrived in Alaska while tracing a mysterious energy field, then went thirty years into the future to investigate it more thoroughly. They had detected the first stirrings of the Permians.

1964 (June) - WAVE OF DESTRUCTION[77] -> While

the fourth Doctor and the second Romana luxuriated in London, 1964, K9 left in the TARDIS and – to keep the Black Guardian befuddled – jumped to 112 different locations in space-time. K9 returned and aided his friends as the Vardans hijacked an upgrade to NATO's early warning systems, and dispatched an invasion force to Earth. The Doctor warned a Vardan representative that if she went through with the invasion, millions would die... which came true, when the Doctor, Romana and K9 used Pirate Radio to emit a cancellation wave that eradicated the representative and the Vardan fleet.

1964 (13th July) - SJA: WHATEVER HAPPENED TO SARAH JANE?[78] -> Andrea Yates fell from Westport

Pier during a school trip and drowned, an event that was witnessed by her best friend Sarah Jane Smith.

(=) The Trickster, a creature from "beyond the universe" and an entire pantheon (the Pantheon of Discord) unto itself, sought to fully manifest in our reality through use of altered timelines. It had the power to bargain with people fated to die, and so gave Andrea Yates the chance to live – if she let Sarah Jane die in her place. Andrea agreed, and history changed. Maria Jackson visited this time, but failed to convince Sarah and Andrea to avoid the pier. Over forty years later, Yates was persuaded to let history run its original course.

who had returned to Cambridge – contacts her "out of the blue" for social reasons. *Threshold* opens with a radio announcer mentioning that "The Beatles have the top spot here in the UK in January...", suggesting that Series 1 opens near the start of 1964 and proceeds from there.

73 "Three months" after *1963: The Assassination Games*.
74 Dating *CM S1: Artificial Intelligence* (CM 1.2) - An indeterminate amount of time has passed since *CM S1: Threshold*, but with that story occurring in January 1964 and the remaining two installments of Series 1 (*The Pelage Project, State of Emergency*) happening after mid-October, it's likely that *Artificial Intelligence* happens in spring, possibly even summer. Gilmore says he

met Cervenka "fourteen years ago", in 1950.
75 *CM S2: Peshka*. The biggest clash between the Mods and Rockers happened 18th and 19th May, 1964, at Clacton.
76 Dating *The Land of the Dead* (BF #4) - It is "thirty years" before 1994.
77 Dating *Wave of Destruction* (BF 4th Doc #5.1) - The Doctor consults with a newspaper and says "1964. Oh look... it's June already." It's after the Cuban Missile Crisis [October 1962].
78 Dating *SJA: Whatever Happened to Sarah Jane?* (SJA 1.5) - The precise date is given. There's no mention of Sarah remembering Maria's visit to 1964 in the restored history. The Trickster's background is given in *SJA: The*

Melanie Jane **Bush, a companion of the sixth and seventh Doctors, was born**[79] on 22nd July, 1964, in this and 117,863 alternate universes.[80]

Muriel Wilberforce of Pease Pottage died in 1964, age 80, the same year that Melanie Bush was born.

(=) With Muriel's passing, the Time Demon inhabiting the lifetimes of different Pease Pottage residents attained a historical link to Mel, the village's most influential daughter.[81]

It was possible that a Russian psychic weapon prompted rioting in Harlem.[82] In the summer of 1964, a Roman-style mosaic of the fourth Doctor and evidence of a Celtic tribe who worshipped Wibbsentia was discovered on an archaeological dig in Sussex.[83]

Andy Warhol completed a painting with faces of twelve Doctors, including the War Doctor, that took the Doctor "ages" to sit for. The eleventh Doctor became perplexed as to where he should hang the piece.[84]

(=) The Deindum destroyed New York on 25th July, 1964. In the same year, Warhol painted *Double Bernice*, a double image of Bernice Summerfield.[85]

= c 1964 - FP: WARLORDS OF UTOPIA[86] **->** Scriptor based himself in a huge new palace in Germania V, the Earth where he had met the parallel version of his wife. A new and vicious phase of the war between all the parallel universes where Rome never fell and all the ones where Hitler won began. Minutes after the Council of Hitlers named August Hitler as their successor, he gassed them, taking total control of all Nazi parallels. But the Romans were dominant, and conquered his home Earth. He fled.

Scriptor cornered Abschrift at the Tramontane Gate, the portal that marked the Divide between the Roman and Nazi Earths. At that moment, a member of the Great Houses arrived to seal off all the parallels and erase them. Scriptor delayed him long enough to prevent this, and the House member charged him with the job of keeping any being from the True Earth from entering this realm. Scriptor agreed, and the House member left. Scriptor had thwarted the will of the gods.

1964 (Autumn) - CM S1: THE PELAGE PROJECT / CM S1: STATE OF EMERGENCY[87] **->** After the discovery of fish with an abnormal form of cancer, Counter-Measures looked into the affairs of the Templeworks: a government-backed hothouse at Pelage that made scientific advancements into petroleum, synthetic food, thermal

Wedding of Sarah Jane Smith.
79 In the Writers' Guide for the Season 23, written in July 1985, Mel is described as "21". In the *Terror of the Vervoids* novelisation she is "22", in *The Ultimate Foe* she has lived for "twenty-three years". In *Just War*, Mel was born "twenty eight" years after "1936". Later books have stated that Mel joined the Doctor in 1989, which would seem to make her year of birth later than this.
80 Two works by Gary Russell (*Spiral Scratch* and *Unbound: He Jests at Scars...*) give the exact day of Mel's birth, which matches that of actress Bonnie Langford.
81 *The Wrong Doctors*
82 *CM* S2: *Peshka*. The Harlem Riot occurred 16th to 22nd July, 1964.
83 *Demon Quest: The Relics of Time*
84 "The Girl Who Loved Doctor Who"
85 *Benny: Present Danger:* "The Empire Variations"
86 Dating *FP: Warlords of Utopia* (FP novel #3) - Scriptor gives the date.
87 Dating *CM* S1: *The Pelage Project* and *CM* S1: *State of Emergency* (CM #1.3-1.4) - *The Pelage Project* opens after Harold Wilson's "recent" election – in real life, this occurred on 15th October, 1964. Wilson has not been in office long when General Peters stages his coup (*State of Emergency*), and laments that he wasn't given more of a chance before hostile action was taken against him.

88 The Doctor ends his political career in "October" of the year following *1963: The Assassination Games*.
89 Dating *Worlds DW: The Reesinger Process* (*Worlds DW* #1.2) - The blurb says it's "1964". The general election is "looming", and Kinsella has a report on Pelage that needs acting upon – both elements place this story shortly prior to *CM* S1: *The Pelage Project*. In an interview on this CD set, script editor Justin Richards agreed that *The Reesinger Process* occurs "notionally during [*Counter-Measures*] Series One".
90 Dating *Daemons: White Witch of Devil's End* (story #3, "The Cat Who Walked Through Worlds") - No date given. Once more, we've spaced out this story as best we're able, respective to the progression of Olive's life in this anthology. Olive has now lived in Devil's End, a friend says, "*forever*".
91 Dating *The Twelfth Doctor Year One* (Titan 12th Doc #1.9-1.10, "Gangland") - The year is given.
92 *Benny: HMS Surprise*
93 "Six months" before *CM* S2: *The Fifth Citadel*.
94 *TW: Miracle Day*
95 *Paradise 5*, and possibly an erroneous reference to the first Doctor's trip to the Empire State Building (in *The Chase*, actually set in 1966).
96 "Two years" before *Thin Ice* (BF).
97 *The Space Age*

plastics and more. The group ended a scheme by the innovator Ken Temple – who feared that Earth would exhaust its resources in future – to create continent-sized factories to produce spaceships that would relocate biologically altered humans to a new home on Venus.

General Peters feared the election of Harold Wilson as Prime Minister, and stole Professor Schumann's teleportation equipment to stage a coup. Julian St Stephen, long suspected of being a Trotskyist, aided Peters in using the equipment to manifest goblin-like creatures in London, prompting a state of emergency that allowed Peters to capture 10 Downing Street and Wilson. Peters informed the Prime Minister that the attacks would continue until he resigned and allowed the Queen's cousin, Lord Barrister, to take over the government until new elections could be held next year. Wilson refused, and Allison Williams killed St Stephen, her fiancé, to stop him from manifesting more creatures. Counter-Measures dispensed with the invaders, but not before one of them consumed Peters. A cover story claimed the incident was a nuclear attack drill.

Wilson recognised his debt to Counter-Measures, and pledged that the group would be properly funded for the next five years. Counter-Measures set about investigating mysterious incidents such as a plane that landed at a London airport without a single person on board, and a German U-boat that had arrived at Lancaster Naval Base, with the crew thinking it was still 1943.

The Doctor finished his term as an MP, then popped back to November 1963 to reunite with Ace.[88]

1964 (Autumn) - WORLDS DW: THE REESINGER PROCESS[89] -> James Wilton and his sister Stephanie, who was still possessed by Rees' mind, set up the Reesinger Institute as a government contractor to, officially, train high-ranking officials to resist interrogation. Counter-Measures noticed a pattern of businessmen and government officials who were killing themselves or committing murder, as part of Rees' plan to locate his physical remains. Rachel Jensen crafted an alpha wave device that drove Rees from Stephanie's mind, but he secretly took shelter in James. Toby Kinsella secured Rees' music box and skull.

c 1964 (Autumn) - DAEMONS: WHITE WITCH OF DEVIL'S END[90] -> Olive Hawthorne caught a member of the fey stealing her apples, but showed him mercy. To repay Olive's kindness, the fey killed his dark lord to save two schoolgirls he'd kidnapped. As punishment, the fairy guardian Mistress Whitethorn transformed fey into a cat, who became Olive's familiar: Rhadamanthus. He returned to his people once every seven years.

(=) 1964 - THE TWELFTH DOCTOR YEAR ONE[91] -> The twelfth Doctor accepted Clara's challenge to beat Las Vegas' Sands Hotel casino with a stake of only $50, and had racked up $800,000 in winnings before the owner, Mr Dragotta, summoned him for a chat. They discovered that the surviving Cybock, led by Kronos, had taken over the Cosmos Casino, and hoped to leverage Earth's criminal element to dominate the planet. The Doctor challenged Kronos to a game of Rassilon's Roulette, knowing that the Time-Gun in Kronos' possession had been rigged to self-destruct if used against someone with Gallifreyan DNA. Kronos did so on the Doctor, and consequently erased himself from time. Without Kronos' leadership, the Cybock lost interest in Earth.

On 4th December, 1964, a Healer – one of an ancient race that endowed its essence in objects – erred in engendering itself into the *HMS Surprise*, a warship slated for destruction at Portsmith Harbour. The ship survived explosives meant to destroy it, and would reappear, with the Healer still trapped, some centuries on near Legion.[92]

The UK secret services followed the lead of the four hidden citadels built in London in World War II, and constructed a fifth citadel for their private use. The fifth citadel was equipped with its own nuclear reactor, which suffered a radiation leak during a Cold War test drill. The government ordered the two hundred people present, including Dr Elizabeth Bradley, to stay inside. The condemned were provided with experimental radiation drugs, and coffins in which to bury themselves.[93]

1965

Winston Churchill died on 24th January, 1965.

The Three Families burned down the central records repository in Manhattan in 1965, to help keep their bloodlines a secret.[94] The Doctor visited Manhattan in 1965.[95] A Russian submarine patrolling under the Barents Sea found the spaceship wreckage containing the relics of Marshall Sezhyr. The items were relocated to beneath the Kremlin.[96]

In 1965, gang warfare increased between the Mods and the Rockers. A Rocker, Alec, fell in love with Sandra, whose brothers were Mods. Alec and Sandra tended to an injured alien, the Maker – grateful, the Maker scanned their minds and saw their concept of a gleaming, futuristic city. As the Mods and Rockers prepared for a major battle, the Maker spirited them away to a reconstruction of such a city in the future. The situation there deteriorated, and some Mods and Rockers – Alec included – elected to become younger, have their memories wiped and return to 1965. The conflict continued.[97]

In 1965, tins of spam that American airmen left for the Caliburn Ghast were found, bricked up, in the servants' pantry at Caliburn House.[98] Gabriel Rosewood had his first encounter with a Corvid in Highgate Cemetery, and mistook it for a vampire.[99]

Marlow Sweet, later of Torchwood, took first prize in the Williamsburg Science Fair, and was valedictorian of her class in 1965. Yale accepted her as the first black woman to study nuclear physics, but she fell out with them upon claiming that Connecticut had wormholes.[100]

About 1965, Ian Gilmore began, fruitlessly, to advocate for a full-on military operation to deal with extraterrestrial threats to the UK.[101]

1965 - "Space Oddity"[102] **->** The Soviet Union launched Vostok 11, off-the-books, to test the feasibility of weaponising space. Dmitri Selonovich became the first person to walk in space... but was reduced to a skeleton by a colony of Vashta Nerada. The eleventh Doctor aided Selonovich's fellow cosmonaut, Alexey Leonov, in preventing the Vashta Nerada from gestating an unstoppable amount of young within the Taiga boreal forest, and relocated them to a world where they could safely thrive. Leonov threatened his superiors with exposure unless they ended the clandestine space-weapons programme, and mandated that all space suits be equipped with an internal lighting array. On a subsequent mission, Leonov went down in history as the first man to walk in space.

---

98 *Hide*

99 "Seven years" before "The Highgate Horror".

100 *TW: The Dollhouse*

101 *Leth-St:* "The Dogs of War"

102 Dating "Space Oddity" (IDW Vol. 4 #7-8) - Leonov tells the Doctor that it's "1965" in issue #7, but the Doctor – possibly confused because the last successful Vostok mission launched on 19th June, 1963 – claims in issue #8 that Leonov will officially become the first man to walk in space "two years from now". In real life, that happened the same year that Leonov cites, on 18th March, 1965, aboard Voskhod 2. Vostok 11 was one of eight scrubbed Vostok missions intended to run from 1963 to 1966, following on from the successful Vostok 6, making it even less likely that it No. 11 would have launched in 1963 itself. The Doctor asking Leonov "What would Brezhnev say?" also rules out 1963 (or is further evidence that the Doctor has a less-than-absolute grasp of the facts), as Breshnev didn't become General Secretary of the Soviet Union until 14th October, 1964.

103 Dating *The Chase* (2.8) - On their return home, Ian sees a tax disc dated "Dec 65", and Barbara notes that they are "two years out". (Ironically, after two years of trying to land in England in the nineteen-sixties, the TARDIS visits Ian and Barbara's native time five times in the next ten television stories.) The script suggested that the Visualiser tuned in on the Beatles' Fiftieth Anniversary reunion tour. The costume listing for 1st April, 1965, included a request for an announcer dressed in futuristic clothing from "2014", and it seems that the Beatles were contacted. However, the television version eventually used stock footage from 1965.

The tenth Doctor says in "The Forgotten" that he doesn't know what happened to Ian and Barbara after they left, but that story entails him having selective amnesia.

104 Dating "Hunters of the Burning Stone" (*DWM* #456-461) - The year is given, in accord with Ian and Barbara returning to Earth in 1965 (*The Chase*).

105 *Who Killed Kennedy*

106 *Goth Opera*

107 Dating *CM S2: Manhunt* (CM 2.1) - Time continues to progress for *Counter-Measures*, with Series 2 occurring throughout 1965. *Manhunt* opens "seven years" after the first female peer was seated (the Baroness Wootton of Abinger, in 1958), and after the Wilson government ended the practice of granting hereditary peerages in 1964. The coup against Prime Minister Harold Wilson (*CM S1: State of Emergency*) was "last year". It's said to be "unseasonably cold"; Kinsella's second, Templeton, comments on the strangeness of snow being forecast for March – presumably the month in which the story takes place.

108 Dating *The Massacre* (3.5) and *Salvation* (PDA #18) - It is never made explicit which year Dodo boards the TARDIS. She is surprised that the Post Office Tower has been completed on her return to Earth in *The War Machines* in 1966. In *Salvation* (p19), an edition of the *New York Ranger* marks the date that Dodo enters the TARDIS as 25th March, 1965. The same publication dates the gods' departure as 1st April (p251). In *Return of the Rocket Men*, Dodo finds a 1967 diary in the TARDIS and says it's from "next year".

A newspaper article in *The Doctor: His Lives and Times* (p23) reports that Dodo Chaplet was 17 when she "went missing". The character is portrayed as a young orphan stuck living with her great aunt, although actress Jackie Lane was actually 24 when she joined the show.

In *Return of the Rocket Men*, Dodo finds a 1967 diary in the TARDIS and says it's from "next year". By that point, however, she might have been aboard the TARDIS long enough that she regards it as 1966 in her personal time.

109 *TW: Zone 10*

110 Dating *CM S2: The Fifth Citadel* (CM 2.2) - An indeterminate amount of time passes between *CM S2: Manhunt* and *The Fifth Citadel*. In the latter story, it's said (broadly speaking) that Emmeline Pritchard, someone who died 1878, has been dead for "eighty years".

111 Dating *CM S2: Peshka* (CM 2.3) - Jensen and company here get back to work after an enforced sick leave, owing to the radiation they were exposed to in *CM S2: The Fifth Citadel*. Shurik Barkov's opponent is the fic-

Ian Chesterton and Barbara Wright Return Home, are Married

1965 - THE CHASE[103] -> The first Doctor, Ian, Barbara and Vicki used a Time-Space Visualiser they acquired from a space museum to watch the Beatles singing "Ticket to Ride". Later, Ian and Barbara returned to Earth in a Dalek time machine, which self-destructed once they left the craft.

1965 - "Hunters of the Burning Stone"[104] -> The Prometheans commissioned Captain Gol Clutha, a temporal mercenary, to kidnap Ian Chesterton and Barbara Wright and bring them to the Tribe of Gum in the future. The eleventh Doctor intercepted the Clutha's modified Sontaran warship as it travelled to 2013... Following the Prometheans' defeat, the Doctor took Ian and Barbara home and stood as the best man at their wedding.

Ian and Barbara became a leading scientist, and Barbara became a university lecturer.[105] They married and had a son named John.[106]

Counter-Measures Series 2

1965 (March) - CM S2: MANHUNT[107] -> The UK eugenics project that produced Emma Waverly endowed her with extra Y chromosomes, enabling her to transform into a man. As "Captain James Edward Aster", s/he began eliminating the researchers involved in the project. Emma's father, Charles Waverly, positioned himself to topple Sir Toby Kinsella and take charge of Counter-Measures, so that Aster-Emma could serve as his second-in-command.

Lady Catherine Waverly discovered the lies her husband had perpetrated upon their family for decades, and killed him. A cover story was released that Charles Waverly had committed suicide. Kinsella and his associates learned of Catherine Waverly's culpability, and Kinsella talked with Catherine in her study before her impending arrest. Ian Gilmore and Rachel Jensen heard a shot ring out, and Kinsella emerged from the room to inform them that Catherine had committed suicide. He secured the documents in Catherine's possession detailing the eugenics project. Emma fled, and began living undercover.

Dodo Chaplet Joins the TARDIS

1965 (25th March to 1st April) - THE MASSACRE / SALVATION[108] -> Dorothea "Dodo" Chaplet, a London resident, found that her elderly neighbour Mr Miller had been replaced by a shapechanger named Joseph. **She** fled and **accidentally entered the TARDIS while it had landed on Wimbledon Common, mistaking it for a real police box. The teenager was living with her great aunt** at the time, as her mother had died.

The Ship dematerialised and reappeared in New York City, the same time zone. The Church of the Latter-Day Pantheon opened its doors and proclaimed that six beings, including Joseph, were humanity's gods returned to perform miracles. The first Doctor deduced that the "gods" were extra-dimensional beings given shape and power by humanity's desires. Appeals from organisations such as the Ku Klux Klan confused the gods as to humanity's needs, and they became increasingly unstable. The Doctor coerced the gods into leaving Earth for their home dimension. He believed the "gods" would eventually leave their homeworld and drift through space. **Dodo took up travelling with the Doctor and Steven in the TARDIS.**

Torchwood invited the Committee to Earth, but in future would forget about its dealings with them. For "many years", the Committee had a business arrangement with Torchwood's Russian counterpart – the KVI, a.k.a. the Soviet Bureau for Extraterrestrial Research – and provided technology in exchange for the group's influence. The relationship increasingly frayed, causing the Committee to stage a thirty-two-minute attack that devastated the KVI's operations on 5th April, 1965. To further humiliate the KVI, the Committee deployed a temporal weapon on a KVI base near the Arctic Circle that created Zone 10, an area where time repeated on itself. The Committee also captured the second woman in space, Russian astronaut Anna Volokova, in orbit and placed her in Zone 10, purely to prove that no human was safe from them.

Events in 2008 retroactively created the Pulse: a signal sixty-two miles above Siberia that would befuddle Russian researchers for forty decades.[109]

1965 - CM S2: THE FIFTH CITADEL[110] -> Sir Toby Kinsella investigated the disappearance of one of his oldest friends, Dr Elizabeth Waverly, and found her with the quarantined staff dying from radiation poisoning in the Fifth Citadel. Waverly and a few other survivors sought to give meaning to their illnesses and handed the government an ultimatum: disarm all nuclear weapons, or they would overload the Fifth Citadel's nuclear reactor and flood the UK with radiation. Kinsella told Counter-Measures that negotiation tactics would prevail, but privately believed that Waverly wasn't bluffing, and had the Fifth Citadel forever encased in concrete.

1965 - CM S2: PESHKA[111] -> Russian hothouse experiments conducted in the 1950s had left Anya Barkov primed as a "psychic bomb" – someone capable of instilling others with a mass psychosis upon her hearing a trigger song. Her brother, the 22-year-old Russian chessmaster Shurik Barkov, manipulated Counter-Measures into taking the two of them back to the United Kingdom for further study. Rachel Jensen and her allies deduced that Shurik intended to trigger his sister in central London, bringing the UK to its knees so the Red Army could stage a takeover. Allison Williams killed Anya to prevent a rampage, and Shurik was imprisoned in a safehouse, his country believing that he had defected and betrayed them. Counter-Measures was left to wonder how many contemporary riots and violent incidents were the result of the East launching psychic weapons against the West.

In America, thirteen thousand National Guardsmen contained crowds incited to violence, possibly by a Russian psychic bomb.[112]

1965 (Autumn) - CM S2: SINS OF THE FATHERS[113]

-> Emma Waverly's genetic mutation accelerated her metabolism, and she aged to death after contacting Ray Cleaver – another product of the eugenics project that birthed her – at his mother's funeral. Waverly's files convinced Cleaver of his heredity, and he sought to free the other test subjects being kept sedated at the Wilcock Clinic. Fearing that Cleaver would lead the super-strong test subjects to wreck havoc, Sir Toby Kinsella killed the man with a concentrated dose of nerve gas.

Kinsella was suspended from Counter-Measures while an inquiry investigated his role in the eugenics project. His second, Templeton, took charge in his absence. Rachel Jensen was given reason to suspect that Kinsella was Cleaver's father.

---

tional Terry Fischer, presumably an analogue of the chessmaster Bobby Fischer, who achieved much fame in the early half of the 1960s. Jensen comments that Williams slaying Anya is doubly hard, as it's "so soon after [she also killed] Julian" (CM S1: State of Emergency).

The story ends with news reports of various riots – probably a thematic device used to evoke violent episodes that might owe to Russian psychic bombs, as opposed to literally naming the ones to follow the Barkov incident. Two of the named incidents (the Watts Riots, August 1965; the 12th Street Riot in Detroit, July 1967) could happen after Peshka, but two others must occur beforehand (the Mods and Rockers fight in May 1964; the Harlem Riot in July, the same year).

112 CM S2: Peshka. The Watts Riots lasted 11th to 17th August, 1965.

113 Dating CM S2: Sins of the Fathers (CM 2.4) - Emma Waverly has been lying low "for the last two months or so" – possibly just the duration of time in which she's gone quiet as far as the authorities are concerned, meaning she might have gone rogue (CM S2: Manhunt) before that. It's late enough in the year that Allison can have the following exchange when she happens upon Kinsella trying to act casual while he's burning secret documents... Toby: "I do like a warm fire when it's cold", Allison: "It's not that cold", Toby: "At my age, you feel it more."

114 Dating Counter-Measures Series 3 (Changing of the Guard, #3.1; The Concrete Cage, #3.2; The Forgotten Village, #3.3; Unto the Breach, #3.4) - Events in Series 3 open not long after the end of Series 2 [Autumn 1965]. There's no sense of how much time passes within this series, save that "over a month" elapses between the third and fourth installments. In CM S3: Changing of the Guard, William Heaton notes that CM S2: Sins of the Fathers [Autumn 1965] happened "this year", and eventually rules that Counter-Measures' budget, as established by Harold Wilson following CM S1: State of Emergency [Autumn 1964], will remain in place "for the remainder of the current Parliament". The next general

election was held on 31st March, 1966, and there's no mention of that, so it seems fairly likely that all of Series 3 happens in the last quarter of 1965. In support of a late 1965 dating, Kinsella tells Allison in CM S3: The Forgotten Village that "the past couple of years haven't been easy on any of us" – presumably counting from when Counter-Measures began, in January 1964. Also, CM S3: The Concrete Cage cites Richard Crossman as a government official supporting the Tower Block housing initiative – he was Minister of Housing and Local Government under Wilson's first government, but after the 1966 election became Lord President of the Council and Leader of the House of Commons. In Changing of the Guard, Kinsella says he's "been sitting at home so long, I even considered gardening" – possibly just a joke, since it's entirely the wrong time of year for it.

Events in The Concrete Cage coalesce on the night of a full moon – which, assuming that Series 3 does happen in late 1965, occurred on Wednesday, 21st October; Thursday, 19th November; Saturday, 19th December.

The red goo in Changing of the Guard is the same body-duplicating substance seen in An Ordinary Life, also written by Matt Fitton.

115 Dating "The Vanity Box" (BF #97b) - The back cover says "circa 1965", but the Doctor more specifically says, "It's 1965, I believe that's groovy enough for anyone". For the Doctor and Mel, this story follows directly on from The Wishing Beast.

116 Dating "Klein's Story" (BF #131a) - Colditz specifies that this occurs in 1965.

117 Dating TW: Children of Earth (TW 3.01-3.05) - The year is given.

118 "Time Fraud", folding itself into TW: Children of Earth.

119 Dating Blackout (BBC DW audiobook #14) - It's said to be "1965", "the middle of November". The blurb specifies the exact date.

Counter-Measures Series 3[114]

1965 - CM S3: CHANGING OF THE GUARD / THE CONCRETE GAGE / THE FORGOTTEN VILLAGE / UNTO THE BREACH -> An inquiry, as helmed by William Heaton, judged that Sir Toby Kinsella's actions – while extreme – were under the auspices of wartime and were "understandable". Kinsella regained command of Counter-Measures, and his deputy Templeton was dismissed. During Kinsella's suspension, Counter-Measures investigated Kenny White: a bar owner who had physically duplicated himself using a red goo fished out of the East India Dock. White's duplicates threatened widespread violence to establish him as a top gang boss, but Captain Gilmore blew up the lodestone networking White's clones, killing them.

After Kinsella's return, Counter-Measures discovered that a new government housing initiative – the Tower Block – was acting as a Faraday cage to metallic ore, and inducing madness in people during the full moon. A remorseful Roderick Purton, a local historian exposed as having killed a neighbour during the Blitz, died as an undetonated German bomb went off.

Soviet researchers sought to weaponise magnetic disruption, and created the *Maurania 7* satellite as proof of concept. Allison Williams returned to her hometown of Lower Burford, Herefordshire when *Maurania 7* crashed there and rendered her estranged father ill. The satellite's magnetic disruption variously caused people to become insensate, to stand mutely, to violently turn on one another or to commit suicide. Although Counter-Measures determined the malady's cause and sealed off Lower Burford, Allison's father died, and exposure to the satellite left her in a child-like state.

About a month later, a clandestine group manipulated Kinsella, Gilmore and Jensen into going undercover in East Berlin, ostensibly to verify reports that the East had captured an extraterrestrial. Under the guise of Project: Othello, the conspirators field-tested mind-control technology by installing it in Jensen's brain. The technology made Jensen violate her own ethics and murder "an alien" – actually a soldier asking for help – in cold blood. She was compelled to betray Kinsella and Gilmore to German authorities, then returned home to implant more such technology in British subjects.

Back in the UK, Templeton used a device to restore Allison Williams' faculties, but also conditioned her to believe he was Kinsella...

1965 - "The Vanity Box"[115] -> In Salford, Monsieur Coiffure had founded The Vanity Box salon – an establishment where clients could walk away looking ten years younger. This owed to a box that Coiffure had found floating down the canal one day, and which contained a very ancient entity that fed off the hopes and fears of human beings. The box entity could make people look a decade younger, but only by shortening their lives by a comparable amount of time.

The sixth Doctor and Mel recognised the box entity as an earlier version of the Wishing Beast that they had just defeated on a remote asteroid. The Doctor feared that the creature could wreck havoc, and used the TARDIS to open a tear in the fabric of space-time. He flung the box into the tear, knowing that it would back track along the TARDIS' time trail, and arrive on the asteroid in the distant past.

(=) 1965 - "Klein's Story"[116] -> As "Schmidt", the eighth Doctor tricked Klein into thinking that she could use the TARDIS log to return to Colditz Castle, find the Doctor and force him to better explain the Ship's operations. She did so against the express wishes of her lover Eunice Faber, and thereby – as the Doctor had planned – undid her entire history.

The 456: First Contact

1965 (November) - TW: CHILDREN OF EARTH[117] -> A race of extra-terrestrials – designated as "the 456" after the frequency allocation of their transmissions – made contact with the UK government. The 456 warned that in four months, a strain of Indonesian flu would mutate and kill up to twenty five million people. They offered to trade an antivirus to the flu for twelve children that the 456 claimed would "live forever". Twelve children were selected from the Holly Tree Lodge, a state-run orphanage. Jack Harkness of Torchwood made the exchange in Scotland, and watched as the children into a glowing portal. One boy, Clement McDonald, was on the cusp of puberty and of no use to the 456. He escaped into the night.

The eleventh Doctor's intervention upended Time Agent Scott Thrower's con-game against the bird-like Ra'Ra'Vis, and caused the rejuvenating energy of their sun to revert him to childhood. Thrower escaped through time with his vortex manipulator, but arrived at the Holly Tree Lodge orphanage, and so became one of the twelve children that Jack Harkness offered to the 456.[118]

1965 (9th November) - BLACKOUT[119] -> Aliens with a biology similar to that of humans laced Manhattan's water supply with a prototype cryo-sleep drug – part of a clinical trial. The drug was unrefined, and would have made the population combust from within. The eleventh Doctor, Amy and Rory forced the aliens to deploy a cure in the form of snowflakes, and made them withdraw.

1965 (25th December) and 1965/1966 (31st December to 1st January) - THE DALEKS' MASTER PLAN[120] -> While fleeing the Daleks, the first Doctor, Steven and Sara Kingdom landed outside a police station in Liverpool. After a little trouble with the police force, the TARDIS went on its way. A week later, the TARDIS landed in Trafalgar Square during the New Year celebrations.

1966

Melanie Bush accidentally killed her sister – who died after falling down the stairs – when she was eighteen months old, and her parents never told her about this.[121] Polly Wright studied at Leeds University, where a group of her friends were interested in the occult.[122]

Vispic leeches, a.k.a. luck-suckers or Happiness Vampires, were maggoty creatures who fed on high endorphin levels caused by extreme happiness or good fortune. Sensing the excitement concerning the forthcoming World Cup Final at Wembley, some Vispics stole the Jules Rimet Trophy and equipped it with a homing beacon to attract their larval young – who could travel through dimensional wormholes. A dog named Pickles "found" the trophy on his morning walk.[123]

The Shuttering of Counter-Measures (Counter-Measures Series 4)[124]

c 1966 - CM S4: NEW HORIZONS / THE KEEP / RISE AND SHINE / CLEAN SWEEP -> A brainwashed Rachel Jensen further developed the Project: Othello technology while Allison Williams was sent to assist New Horizons, a private company promising to implement a clean-energy revolution. Clandestine forces within the UK government – objecting to New Horizon's refusal to grant the government exclusive use of their developments – sabotaged New Horizon's prototype monorail, then raided New Horizons headquarters in Waybridge on the justification of protecting the public. In the melee to follow, New Horizon's operations were destroyed, and the secret to distilling the miracle-substance Vril was lost.

The high-ranking civil servant William Heaton was one of the last surviving Light on Earth, having been disconnected from the network that killed most of his fellows during the Starfire Affair. Heaton judged that Earth was too valuable a resource to be destroyed, so allied with Counter-Measures to stop the clandestine Light Sleepers from ruining the planet. He arranged for the incarcerated Sir Toby Kinsella and Ian Gilmore to be transferred from Germany to the Keep centre in the UK, then aided their escape.

Jensen and Williams broke their mental conditioning

---

120 Dating *The Daleks' Master Plan* (3.4) - A calendar in the police station reads "25th December". It was originally intended that the 1965 Christmas episode, "The Feast of Steven", would include a crossover with the popular BBC police serial *Z-Cars*. Publicity material to this effect was sent out on 1st October, 1965, and it appears that a version of the script was written with the *Z-Cars* characters in mind. John Peel's novelisation of this story and Lofficier's *The Universal Databank* both retain the names of actors (not the characters) from the police series.
121 *Spiral Scratch*
122 *Invasion of the Cat-People* (p115), no date is given.
123 *Extra Time*. Historically, the Trophy was stolen on March 20, 1966, and found by Pickles seven days later.
124 Dating *Counter-Measures* Series 4 (*New Horizons*, #4.1; *The Keep*, #4.2; *Rise and Shine*, #4.3; *Clean Sweep*, #4.4) - Jensen has spent "months" testing the Othello technology (*Rise and Shine*). Templeton has been making weekly reports to his paymasters for the "last three months" (*The Keep*), so presumably that amount of time has passed between Series 3 and 4. It's not unreasonable, then, to think that it's now 1966, in keeping with Colonel Lethbridge-Stewart's recollection that Counter-Measures fell "sometime in '66" (*Leth-St:* "The Dogs of War"). The four installments of Series 4 happen roughly back to back, although "a week or more" passes between *New Horizons* and *The Keep*.

IAN GILMORE: The novel version of *Downtime* makes the quite reasonable claim that Group Captain Ian Gilmore (*Remembrance of the Daleks*) was promoted to Air Vice-Marshal and, having been part of the Counter-Measures team that exchanged gunfire with the Daleks in 1963, pushed for the advent of UNIT to deal with such threats. In *Downtime*, Gilmore reaches out to Alistair Lethbridge-Stewart "six months" after *The Web of Fear*, and they chat over drinks at the Alexander Club. *Leth-St:* "The Dogs of War" very much follows in *Downtime*'s footsteps (but happens beforehand), with Gilmore and Lethbridge-Stewart teaming up to rescue a kidnapped Edward Travers, and also says that Gilmore married his Counter-Measures teammate Rachel Jensen. The novelisation of *Remembrance of the Daleks* nods in that direction, saying that Jensen married in 1965, but doesn't name her husband.

The *Counter-Measures* audios, however, chart a very different path for the characters. Following *Remembrance of the Daleks*, Gilmore, Jensen and their associates deal with all manner of world-threatening problems until they're officially listed as dead circa 1966 (*CM S4: Clean Sweep*), go undercover, and only return to their actual lives in 1974 (*New CM: Who Killed Toby Kinsella?*). At no point are Gilmore and Jensen married or even close to it – she politely rebuffs what few advances he makes throughout *Counter-Measures*, and they lead separate lives during their eight years incog-

and surgically removed the Othello technology implanted in their heads. The women sought aid from Williams' lover, Sgt Steven West, but he died in a crossfire protecting them. Afterward, Jensen and Williams reunited with Kinsella and Gilmore.

Sir Keith Kordel, a Light Sleeper, stole deadly pathogens from UK scientists. The Light Sleepers took control of a British Rocket Group launch site in Hertfordshire, intending to launch rockets containing the contagion to a dozen major cities. Kinsella's quartet prevented the launch, and Kordel and Templeton were both killed. Thwarted, the Light Sleepers committed suicide en masse.

With the immediate threat to Earth gone, Heaton moved to eliminate Kinsella's team as a loose end, and facilitated the destruction of Counter-Measures headquarters at Maybury. Jensen, Gilmore and Williams adopted cover identities at Chichester College in Oxford. The trio captured Heaton, and proved the efficiency of a hand-held detector they constructed to identify members of the Light. Kinsella used a detector modified by Williams to give Heaton irreparable brain damage, reducing him to a vegetative state.

Kinsella authorised Jensen, Gilmore and Williams to begin the process of rebuilding Counter-Measures... but seemingly had the three of them killed in explosions, as their intimate knowledge of his actions could have caused his downfall. He maintained to Hilary de Winter, a journalist asking questions about Counter-Measures, that no such group had ever existed...

... Kinsella intended to eliminate the last remaining members of the Light on Earth, and had asked Gilmore, Jensen and Williams to fake their deaths and live undercover as a back-up team if he failed. Gilmore remained in contact with Kinsella; Jensen and Williams would not see him again until December 1973.[125]

1966 - DEAD AIR[126] -> The tenth Doctor pursued The Hush – a sentient extra-terrestrial weapon capable of converting targets into sound – to a pirate radio ship. The Hush killed the ship's crew, but the Doctor sank the ship after trapping the Hush on a ferrous tape – along with a recorded warning that nobody should play the tape to the end, lest the Hush get free.

1966 - THE VEILED LEOPARD[127] -> Industrialist Gavin Walker owned the Veiled Leopard – one of the world's most famous diamonds, bigger than the Star of India and the Koh-i-Noor. At The Majestic casino in Monte Carlo, Walker announced he was giving the diamond to his wife as a birthday present, but he had arranged for its theft as part of an insurance scam. The fifth and seventh Doctors coordinated efforts to retrieve the diamond, which was actually an alien crystal. They were aided by Peri, Erimem, Ace and Hex. Walker was exposed, and Ace and Hex pocketed the diamond.

1966 - THE CHASE[128] -> **The first Doctor, Ian, Barbara, Vicki and the Dalek time machine pursing them landed on the top floor of the Empire State Building, much to the amusement of tourist Morton Dill.**

Oliver Harper Joins the TARDIS

1966 - THE PERPETUAL BOND[129] -> The Fulgurites had established Flowers Trade and Investments to further their interplanetary commodities trading, and dealt with such materials as metals, olive oil, orange juice, copper and cattle. In collusion with the cash-strapped British government, the Fulgurites also began trafficking British subjects as slaves – a certain percentage of the population (excluding key workers such as hospital staff) from selected geographic areas were kidnapped via transmat and sent to alien planets such as Ander Valder XII. The Fulgurites

nito. Matters are cordial, kind even, but distanced between them in the *New Counter-Measures* series. Were they ex-spouses working together, it would unavoidably have been mentioned. Also against the grain of *Downtime*, and a bit startlingly given Gilmore's sacrifices for Queen and Country, he hasn't received a promotion. As late as *The New Counter-Measures* Series 2, he's still referring to himself as "Group Captain Gilmore".

The Left-Handed Hummingbird, to throw a further monkey-wrench into things, lists Gilmore as an Air Commodore after UNIT's creation.

125 *CM: Who Killed Toby Kinsella?*
126 Dating *Dead Air* (BBC *DW* audiobook #7) - The Doctor says it's the "late 1960s", but the blurb specifies that it's 1966. For what it's worth, it's specified that

story doesn't take place on a Tuesday. It's implied that the Time Lords designed the Hush for use against the Daleks in the Last Great Time War.
127 Dating *The Veiled Leopard* (BF promo, *DWM* #367) - The year is given.
128 Dating *The Chase* (2.8) - Morton Dill says it is "1966", in Alabama at least.
129 Dating *The Perpetual Bond* (BF CC #5.8) - It's generally said to be "the 1960s" in this story, but *The Cold Equations* and *The First Wave* specify Oliver as being "from 1966". As *The Perpetual Bond* is set between *The Daleks' Master Plan* and *The Massacre*, a dating of 1966 would thematically be in keeping with the other contemporary Hartnell TV episodes (*An Unearthly Child* episode one, *The Chase* episode six, etc.) that seem to occur at time of broadcast.

operated according to Section 6 of the Interplanetary Trade and Securities Act, which enabled such trade with legitimately established governments.

The first Doctor shut down the operation by transmatting the Fulgurites and their government contact – Sir Richard Christie, a minister – away from Earth, putting them into slavery instead. The Doctor and Steven accepted a worker at Flowers Trade, Oliver Harper, as a fellow travelling companion, not realising that he was on the run from the law.

A friend had phoned to warn Oliver that the police were about to arrest him for being a homosexual.[130] **Able Seaman Ben Jackson started a five-month shore posting.**[131] Sometime prior to this, Ben's father had died of a heart attack.[132] In May 1966, a time-hopping Edward Travers expanded his will to include not just his daughter Victoria, but any of her descendants. Keith Perry, Waterfield's assistant, witnessed the amendment.[133]

(=) 1966 (June) - 1963: FANFARE FOR THE COMMON MEN[134] **->** The Common Men performed in Tokyo in 1966, and Abbey Road in either 1966 or 1967.

The fifth Doctor and Nyssa – having fled 1963 in a time vessel disguised as a 1960s club – ran aground in June 1966. Their subsequent plan to undercut the historical machinations of Lenny Kruger reached fruition in 1967.

The WOTAN Incident: Polly Wright and Ben Jackson Join the TARDIS

1966 (12th-20th July) - THE WAR MACHINES[135] **->** Computer Day was set for Monday, 16th July. This was the day that computer systems across the whole world were due to come under the control of the central computer, WOTAN. Created by Professor Brett and his assistant Melvin Krimpton, WOTAN was designed to operate itself, and to think for itself like a human being – only better. It was at least ten years ahead of its time, and it was the most advanced – although not biggest – computer in the world. WOTAN would be connected up to a number of sites, including ELDO, TELSTAR, the White House, Parliament, Cape Kennedy, EFTA, RN and Woomera.

WOTAN decided to make a bid for power, and constructed an army of War Machines. The first Doctor defeated WOTAN with the help of Ben Jackson and Polly. Having returned to her own time, Dodo Chaplet left the Doctor. Ben Jackson and Polly, however, entered the TARDIS just as it left Earth.

lgtw - In one account of events, **the first Doctor, Ben and Polly immediately found themselves in seventeenth-century Cornwall, then the South Pole in 1986.** Dalek interference from the Last Great Time War jostled the Doctor's timeline a little, and they had other adventures.[136]

C-19's Vault procured the body of Melvin Krimpton,

---

130 *The Cold Equations.* Homosexuality was legalised in England and Wales in 1967.
131 In *The War Machines,* it is twice stated that Ben has a shore posting (he is depressed by this and wants to get back to sea). At the end of the story, it is stated that he has to get "back to barracks". However in *The Smugglers* and *The Faceless Ones,* he wants to return to his "ship".
132 *The Yes Men*
133 *Downtime* (p25).
134 Dating *1963: Fanfare for the Common Men* (BF #178) - The Doctor reads from the ship's readouts that it's "1966. Sometime in the summer, I think it's June". He also comments that it's probably best that he avoid London "in case I bump into myself", presumably in reference to *The War Machines, The Faceless Ones* and *The Evil of the Daleks,* all set in July of that year.
135 Dating *The War Machines* (3.10) - C-Day is set for 16th July, but this didn't fall on a Monday in 1966... it was actually the Saturday that *The War Machines* episode four was to be broadcast. The year "1966" is confirmed in *The Smugglers, The Tenth Planet, The Underwater Menace, The Moonbase, The Faceless Ones*

and also in the *Radio Times.* WOTAN is connected up to Telstar and Cape Kennedy, both of which were operating in 1966. At the end of *The Faceless Ones,* Ben and Polly realise that it's the same day they joined the TARDIS, and give the date as the 20th of July.
136 SIDE ADVENTURES WITH POLLY AND BEN: On screen, there's no opportunity for tie-in escapades with the first Doctor, Ben and Polly to take place, as *The War Machines* (Ben and Polly's intro story) immediately dovetails into *The Smugglers,* which dovetails straight to *The Tenth Planet* (which ends with the first Doctor's death). So, the audio *1stD V2: The Plague of Dreams* cheekily suggests that any tie-in story with them (including, presumably, the novel *Ten Little Aliens* and *Short Trips:* "Falling") stems from Daleks in the Last Great Time War committing temporal jiggery-pokery with the first Doctor's timeline, a situation that's only resolved when the Player, a fellow Time Lord, impresses upon the Doctor the need for him to go to the South Pole (*The Tenth Planet*). The only remaining hiccup is the first Doctor surely cannot *pilot* the TARDIS there; perhaps the Time War-era Time Lords gave him some help.
137 *The War Machines, Leth-St: Beast of Fang Rock, Leth-*

who had been killed by a run amok War Machine, but failed to lay hands on Professor Brett's work.[137] The seventh Doctor's TARDIS contained a computer room that housed, among other artifacts, a box marked WOTAN.[138]

Polly and Ben Return Home

1966 (20th July) - THE FACELESS ONES[139] ->

Following an explosion on their home planet, a generation of aliens were rendered faceless, and lacked any true identity. As scientifically advanced beings, they concocted an elaborate plan to kidnap young humans and absorb their personalities. Youngsters on chartered Chameleon Flights to holiday destinations would instead be flown to a space station in orbit, where they would be processed. Although the Chameleons covered their tracks carefully – sending postcards to the missing youngsters' families, hypnotising people, and even murdering them – their plan was exposed. The second Doctor promised to help the Chameleons find a solution to their problem, and the aliens left.

Back in their own time, on the very same day that they had joined the TARDIS, Ben and Polly left the Doctor and Jamie's company.

The body of D.I. Gascoigne, killed by the Chameleons, was interred at C-19's Vault.[140]

1966 (20th July) - THE EVIL OF THE DALEKS[141] ->

The TARDIS was stolen from Gatwick airport. In tracking it down, the second Doctor and Jamie were transported a hundred years into the past.

The Death Watch

The Death Watch, the committee tasked with studying data on the UK population, now included Dame Emily Shaw, General Andrews, Professor Richard Windshaw, Dr Charles Lawrence, Edward Masters, Bruno Taltalian, Sir Keith Gold, Sir Reginald Styles and Sir Charles Grover. It was led by Sir James Quinlan.[142]

Prestayn, a genius computer developer, joined the Death Watch and provided augmented computer systems to Bruno Taltalian at Recovery 7, a chemicals plant in Wales and the Inferno Project. He also adapted WOTAN's processing banks, as harvested from the Post Office Tower, into a system – the Apocalypse Clock – that used the Death Watch's mass data to make infallible predictions.

The Clock occupied secret rooms under Whitehall, and its display board signaled that the world would end within weeks. Additionally, the Clock identified the people most likely to cause the world's demise, and began independently eliminating them using clockwork scorpions that twisted probabilities, creating a reality in which their targets perished. Each target received a prediction of when they would die – General Andrews, the head of Stangmoor Prison, was the first of these, and his death caused the Clock's countdown to gain a month of time.[143]

St: "The Dogs of War".

138 *Starlight Robbery*

139 Dating *The Faceless Ones* (4.8) - Setting this story in 1966 seems to have been a last minute decision to smooth Ben and Polly's departure, one that also affects the dating for *The Evil of the Daleks*. The *Radio Times* stated that it is "Earth – Today".

140 *The Faceless Ones, Leth-St: Beast of Fang Rock.*

141 Dating *The Evil of the Daleks* (4.9) - The story follows straight on from *The Faceless Ones*.

142 *The Last Post.* As writer James Goss detailed in an interview on this audio, this is intended as a grand sweep of characters who appear throughout the UNIT Era: "[Season 7] does feature an awful lot of people dying in incredibly, remarkably unusual ways. And I just thought, wouldn't it be funny if... it was all part of some enormous conspiracy which explains why people are being murdered by isotopes in their dinner, and people open doors and there's a spaceman that kills them... just the idea that all of these slightly strange characters who would be wandering around giving the most extraordinary performances actually knew, because

they'd read a letter, in two episodes' time that they'd die horribly."

Emily Shaw is the mother of the third Doctor's companion Liz Shaw. Lawrence and Masters appeared and died in *Doctor Who and the Silurians*, Taltalian and Quinlan in *The Ambassadors of Death*. Andrews is the predecessor to the governor of Stangmoor Prison in *The Mind of Evil*. Gold appeared in *Inferno* (his counterpart from a parallel universe died, but he survived), Styles in *Day of the Daleks* (he died in an alternate timeline, but survived when that was cancelled out) and Grover in *Invasion of the Dinosaurs*. Windshaw doesn't appear in any other story.

143 *The Last Post.* The script lists Prestayn as a chief researcher at International Electromatics, and the person who bought the firm after Tobias Vaughn's death (*The Invasion*), but this was cut from the story. The Clock's central banks are taken from WOTAN (*The War Machines*), which explains why – as with WOTAN itself – the Clock says, "Doctor Who is required". It's suggested that the Clock's ability to predict the future stems from the Doctor removing the Console from the TARDIS'

1966 (30th July) - "They Think It's All Over"[144] -> The eleventh Doctor, Amy and Rory attended the World Cup Final, on the Doctor's second attempt to reach it (the first had been a thousand years off the mark).

1966 (30th July) - EXTRA TIME[145] -> The eleventh Doctor granted Rory and Amy's wish that they watch the 1966 FIFA World Cup Final – the only time England won the trophy, besting Germany 4-2 in extra time. They discovered that Vispic larvae were gathering to gorge on the jubilation caused by the contest, and grow turn into adults and overwhelm Earth.

The Doctor accidentally rendered unconscious Tofik Barkhramov, a Russian linesman crucial to England's historic victory, and had Rory imitate Barkhramov using a Vinvocci shimmer suit. As Barkhramov, Rory suspected that a crucial shot had not, in fact, completely crossed the line, but preserved history by ruling in England's favour anyway. Amy and the Doctor dispersed the Vispic larvae by electrocuting the beacon summoning them. The Doctor informed his companions that England would win the World Cup again in future.

1966 - "The Love Invasion"[146] -> The ninth Doctor and Rose found a group of beautiful women in London doing good deeds while working for the Lend-A-Hand agency. The Doctor realised that these were aliens, and they'd been killing leading scientists. The girls were clones, controlled by a Kustollon named Igrix, who had stolen a time machine. His race was destined to fight a devastating war with humanity, and so he had come back to make humanity less aggressive and to destroy Earth's moon. The Doctor sabotaged Igrix's ship so that it would indulge its curiosity to explore, and it took Igrix with it.

Perpugilliam "Peri " Brown, a companion of the fifth and sixth Doctors, was born on 15th November, 1966.[147]

Aliens from a planet orbiting Epsilon Eridani had developed slower-than-light space travel and established many colony worlds. The Eridani had been routing robot ships through Earth's solar system for centuries, deeming the region of little import. But circa 1966, an Eridani robot ship sent to a colony orbiting Van Maanen's star became confused by Earth's radio signals and landed there instead. Five components of an Eridani super-computer went miss-

---

shielded interior (*The Ambassadors of Death*), although some of the Clock's actions arguably pre-date that.

144 Dating "They Think It's All Over" (IDW *DW* Vol. 2, #5) - The 1966 World Cup final took place, as every true Englishman knows, two weeks to the day after the last episode of *The War Machines*.

145 Dating *Extra Time* (BBC children's 2-in-1 #6) - The exact day is given (ch3), which concurs with the 1966 World Cup historically occurring on July 30, 1966. To date, England has won the World Cup just the one time. The Vinvocci and their shimmer suits appeared in *The End of Time*.

146 Dating "The Love Invasion" (*DWM* #355-357) - The year is given.

147 *Planet of Fire*. According to a Character Outline prepared for Season 21, before Nicola Bryant was cast in the role, Peri is "an 18 year old" when she starts travelling with the Doctor. Her mother's name is "Janine" (the same document also says Peri is "blonde"). This would seem to make Peri three years younger than the actress playing her. In both *Bad Therapy* and *The Reaping*, Peri confirms she was 18 when she met the Doctor. *Masters of Earth* says that Peri was born in Baltimore.

148 *Blue Box*

149 Jackie's parallel-world counterpart turns forty in *Rise of the Cybermen* [2007], but there's confusion about this (see the dating notes on that story). Actress Camille Coduri was born 18th April, 1965.

150 *9thC: Retail Therapy*

151 "Forty years" before *TW: They Keep Killing Suzie*.

152 *A Good Man Goes to War, Day of the Moon*. The timeframe is a little murky here, as Graystark was shut down in 1967, suggesting that Melody lived there

afterwards – and yet Melody is kidnapped by the Silence as an infant, but is a young girl when we see her in 1969 (*The Impossible Astronaut*). It's possible that the Silence kept her in another locale/time zone on Earth before relocating her to the 1960s.

153 *Day of the Moon*. The whole point of taking Melody to Earth was to raise her in an Earth environment, so she wouldn't necessarily need a life-support device. As much as anything, the suit is probably needed to fulfill the story (related in *Closing Time*) of the Doctor being killed by "an impossible astronaut".

154 Brendan is "14" according to *K9 and Company*.

155 *Amorality Tale*

156 *The Year of Intelligent Tigers*

157 "Ten years" before *Image of the Fendahl*.

158 *Wonderland* (p46, p50).

159 *The Gallifrey Chronicles*. The Beatles went to Bangor in 1967.

160 *TW: In the Shadows*

161 *TW: Miracle Day*

162 *TW: The Men Who Sold the World*

163 *Downtime* (p237).

164 *The Black Hole. Windmill on Montmartre* (1886) was destroyed in a fire in 1967.

165 Dating *Wonderland* (TEL #7) - The date is given (p11).

166 *CM S2: Peshka*. The 12th Street Riot in Detroit happened 23rd to 27th July, 1967.

167 Dating *1963: Fanfare for the Common Men* (BF #178) - The year is given. Paravatar is the Common Men equivalent of Maharishi Mahesh Yogi, the Beatles' guru.

168 Dating *TW: Trace Memory* (TW novel #5) - The year is given (p143). Page 169 says that it's "fourteen years"

ing. The Eridani sent agents to retrieve the components, but it took them eleven years to reach Earth.[148]

1967

Jackie Tyler, the wife of Pete Tyler and mother of Rose Tyler, was born.[149] Jackie's Uncle Tony advised her to "never punch a gift horse in the throat".[150] **Two alien objects – the Resurrection Gauntlet and the Life Knife – fell through the Cardiff Rift.**[151]

The Silence took young Melody Pond to Earth, the 1960s, so she could be raised in a human-norm environment. She was kept at Graystark Hall Orphanage, which closed down in 1967.[152] The Silence influenced humankind to go to the moon; they lacked the ability to develop their own technology, and needed to adapt a space suit as a life-support container for Melody.[153]

Brendan Richards, later a ward of Lavinia Smith, was born in 1967.[154] *Metropolitan* magazine was founded in 1967. Sarah Jane Smith would later be a regular writer for it.[155] Fitz Kreiner saw Jimi Hendrix perform several times during 1967.[156] **During the late nineteen-sixties, Professor Fendelman was working on missile guidance.**[157]

The Doctor suggested that George Harrison see the Maharishi for spiritual guidance. He also gave LSD guru Timothy Leary advice about tuning into the mind's "god centre". The Doctor probably inspired Leary's infamous tag line of "Tune in, turn on and drop out."[158] @ In Bangor, the eighth Doctor showed the Beatles how to meditate.[159]

When Patrick Jefferson was four, his mother was arrested for prostitution, and he was placed in foster care. He'd reside at the Bluebell Field Children's Home in Swansea for the next ten years.[160]

During the Vietnam conflict, American CIA agents altered information in newsrooms and networks across the country. No agent was more successful than Harry Bosco – while unable to actively censor information, Bosco had a talent for manipulating the English translation of news reports to put the government in a better light. His name became synonymous with the process of revising reports to bury the truth.[161]

Mr Wynter signed off on the Phoenix Program, a controversial counter-insurgency programme used during the Vietnam War.[162] When Winifred Bambera was eight, she unwisely played tag with a lost leopard cub in Musi-O-Tunya National Park in Zambia. The cub's mother appeared, and mauled Winifred's older brother when he tried to save her. Winifred killed the mother leopard with her father's rifle, but received a thrashing from her father. Her brother dubbed her "Professor Chicken", and claimed she had no business still being alive.[163]

The Monk rescued Van Gogh's *Windmill on Montmartre* from a fire, and kept it in his personal collection.[164]

1967 (January) - WONDERLAND[165] -> Some grey-suited men, agents of an shadow organisation alleged to run the entire world, captured an alien that became known as the Colour-Beast. The grey-suited men distilled the creature's essence and distributed it as an illicit drug, Blue Moonbeams, to learn how to turn humans into invisible alien killing machines. The Blue Moonbeams became popular, but combusted rather than morphed the users.

The grey-suited men sought to refine the process by distributing Blue Moonbeams at the Human-Be-In rock festival/anti-war protest held in San Francisco on 14th January, 1967. The Moonbeam-users started to mutate, but the second Doctor intervened and freed the Colour-Beast. The creature nullified the drugs' effects on the afflicted humans and departed for home.

Five days of rioting in Detroit, possibly triggered by a Russian psionic bomb, resulted in forty-three deaths, 1100 injured and more than seven thousand arrested.[166]

(=) 1967 - 1963: FANFARE FOR THE COMMON MEN[167] -> The fifth Doctor tracked down the members of the Common Men as they visited the guru Paravatar, who was secretly a time-traveling Turanthian. Using hypnotism, Paravatar discovered the Common Men had hidden memories of their alien origins. The Common Men performed in London in 1967. However, Kruger's first attempt to gain power through the Common Men achieved only limited success, and the group disbanded.

Kruger later organised a comeback concert for John Smith and the Common Men – his second attempt to achieve fame for the group, working to his future self's advice. The fifth Doctor and Nyssa used Kruger's technology to create a lifeless body with the DNA of James O'Meara, then spread a rumour that Kruger had murdered the man in 1966 and replaced him with a doppelganger. The negative sentiment toward Kruger affected his Bional physiognomy, threatening his life. To save it, he gave the Doctor the key to the time lock he'd placed around 1957, enabling the Doctor to cancel out Kruger's historical alterations.

1967 (late summer) - TW: TRACE MEMORY[168] -> Jack Harkness encountered the time-jumping Michael Bellini, and the two of them spent a night together in a Cardiff hotel. Russian agents captured them, and interrogated Jack about aliens and Torchwood at a substation established by KVI (the Russian Committee for Extraterrestrial Research) in a former Hamilton's Sugar warehouse. The Vondrax slaughtered the Russians while attempting to collect the trachyon energy in Bellini's body. Bellini realised the Vondrax would continue initiating such massacres to get at him, and Jack held Bellini as he leapt to his death. Afterwards, Charles Arthur Cromwell and a team from Torchwood Cardiff closed down the KVI operation. Jack killed Kenneth Valentine, a treasonous Torchwood associate who was working for the Russians.

c 1967 - RENAISSANCE OF THE DALEKS[169] **->** The fifth Doctor and Nyssa came to the aid of Major Alice Hunniford – the survivor of a downed Cobra 3 aircraft during the Vietnam War.

1967 - REVOLUTION MAN[170] **->** The anarchist Jean-Pierre Rex had secured a quantity of the reality-warping drug Om-Tsor, and used it to psionically deface global monuments with the letter "R". Between 5th November, 1967, and 29th April, 1968, the symbol appeared on the Great Pyramid in Egypt, the Lincoln Memorial in Washington, a stone at Stonehenge, the white cliffs of Dover, the Golden Gate Bridge in San Francisco, the floor of St Peter's Cathedral in Rome and Red Square in Moscow. Various world governments attributed the incidents to a messianic figure named the Revolution Man, and international tensions increased.

1967 (7th November) - THIN ICE (BF)[171] **->** The seventh Doctor promised to take Ace to London in 1967, during the summer of love, but instead landed in Moscow. The Martian strategist Sezhyr was mentally reborn in the body of Lt Raina Kerenskaya, who was some weeks pregnant with the child of Markus Creevy, a thief. The possession sped up Kerenskya's metabolism, and she gave birth to a daughter: Raine. Sezhyr's mind died, preventing him from raising a new Ice Army to conquer Earth with. The Doctor entrusted Raine's parents with some of Sezhyr's relics to pay for her upbringing.

The Doctor became a godfather of sorts to Raine, always remembering her early birthdays. Her parents related many stories about him. Raine herself wouldn't meet the Doctor until 1989.[172] Raine's childhood holidays involved scuba diving in the Red Sea.[173]

1968

Donna Noble, a companion of the tenth Doctor, was born in Chiswick.[174] Lucia Moretti joined Torchwood in 1968.[175] The tenth Doctor wore a coat that Janis

---

after 1953. It's "late summer" (p143).

169 Dating *Renaissance of the Daleks* (BF #93) - It's during the Vietnam Conflict (which lasted 1959-1975, although US participation was greatly accelerated under President Johnson in 1965). Agent Orange is here deployed; it was used 1961-1971. The US military didn't use female pilots in Vietnam, so the likelihood of Alice Hunniford seeing combat duty is remote.

170 Dating *Revolution Man* (EDA #21) - The general date is given on p1; the dates of the defacings p98-100.

171 Dating *Thin Ice* (BF LS #2.3) - The Doctor tells Ace, "This is the USSR, 1967. Everyone is watching [you]." More specifically, it's the fiftieth anniversary of the October Revolution; the parade that the Doctor and Ace watch might commemorate the start of the downfall of the Tsars on 7th November. (Part of the terminology confusion here is the difference between Russia's Julian calendar and the West's Gregorian calendar – 7th November on the latter equates to 25th October on the former.) Raine, therefore, might be born on 7th November itself. In *Crime of the Century* (set in October 1989), Raine as a grown woman says that *Thin Ice* was (roughly) "twenty years ago".

172 *Crime of the Century*

173 *Animal*

174 We don't know how old Donna is when she travelled with the Doctor, but Catherine Tate was born in 1968. *Planet of the Ood* cites Chiswick as Donna's birthplace.

175 *TW: Children of Earth*

176 *Gridlock*. As the tenth Doctor's coat is already in the TARDIS wardrobe in *The Christmas Invasion*, it was

given to an earlier incarnation – which means it really shouldn't fit him. It's possible that Joplin was on so many drugs, she wasn't concerned about whether the coat fit or not. Joplin lived 1943-1970.

177 *The Time Meddler*

178 *The Underwater Menace*

179 *Frontier Worlds*. The Tufty Club was a group that taught British children the fundamentals of road safety. The group's mascot, Tufty the squirrel, avoided roadside accidents and was featured on club badges.

180 *The Sound of Drums*. Some have viewed this as a reference to events in *The Invasion*, which broadcast in November and December 1968. John Frobisher seems to reference the same protocols in *TW: Children of Earth*.

181 "The Stockbridge Child", going off Max being born in 1956 ("The Stockbridge Showdown").

182 *The Banquo Legacy* (p274).

183 *Daemons: White Witch of Devil's End*, supplemental material.

184 *Iris S2: The Land of Wonder*, presumably reflective (in Iris Wildthyme terms) of the second Doctor working alongside UNIT in *The Invasion*. *Crossroads* initially ran 1964-1988. Mention of the "robot guru" is probably meant to parallel the Beatles' association with Maharishi Mahesh Yogi, which started in 1967.

185 *Iris S2: The Claws of Santa*. *Animal Magic* ran 1962-1983.

186 *Iris: Enter Wildthyme*. Chi Chi arrived at the London Zoo in September 1958, died in 1972.

187 Dating *Jago & Litefoot* Series 5 – The year is given. Jago and Litefoot appear to spend six months or more in 1968 before returning to their native year of 1893.

Joplin gave him.[176] The Monk placed £200 in a London bank in 1968. He would travel two hundred years into the future and withdraw the money and compound interest.[177] The Mexico Olympics were held.[178] In 1968, the Doctor was a Tufty Club member.[179]

In 1968, the United Nations designed a first contact policy, stipulating that such an event could not take place on sovereign soil.[180] When Maxwell Edison was twelve and a half, he was bullied for talking about how his grandmother had the second sight.[181]

The Time Lord Simpson interviewed a survivor of the Banquo Manor murders on her deathbed, and obtained the seed code for Compassion's Randomiser, enabling Gallifrey to track her movements.[182] *The Stone Age of Britain* (1968) starring Professor Horner saw release.[183]

During the 1960s, Iris Wildthyme worked for a government organisation, the Ministry for Incursions and other Alien Ontological Wonders (MIAOW) and met the Beatles while dealing with a robot guru at a holiday camp in Wales. She also intervened when the cast of *Crossroads* was transported to the moon by samurai jellyfish.[184] Iris appeared on *Animal Magic*, and had a thing for Johnny Morris in his zookeeper's uniform.[185] Iris and Panda went to the London Zoo in the sixties, and Panda visited the well-known lady Panda named Chi Chi.[186]

Jago, Litefoot Arrive in 1968
(Jago & Litefoot Series 5)[187]

1968 (21st February) - VOYAGE TO THE NEW WORLD -> The sixth Doctor returned his friends, Professor Litefoot and Henry Gordon Jago, to the Red Tavern after enjoying two adventures with them. The Doctor cautioned that a temporal force thrown the TARDIS a little into the future, so they might have returned some hours after they'd left. The Doctor departed to investigate the anomaly, whereupon Jago and Litefoot found a copy of the *Times* dated 21st February, 1968, and realised they were stuck more than seventy years after their own time...

Ellie Higson, still latently a vampire, was passing as her own descendant and now owned the Red Tavern. She aided her stranded friends, Jago and Litefoot, in securing employment. Litefoot's medical knowledge was very outdated, so he managed an antiquarian bookshop that Ellie owned. Jago became master of ceremonies for a nostalgia TV show, *Those Were the Days*, which featured Vaudeville variety acts.[188]

Guinevere Godiva, the great-granddaughter of the Great Godiva, had come into possession of Magnus Greel's time cabinet and reactivated Mr Sin. As a devotee of Greel, Godiva found that the crystal key repaired by her father and grandfather could open the Cabinet, but not fully reactivate it or bring Greel back to life. She learned that Jago possessed a special item – a Thraskin crystal he'd acquired on Venus – that might serve as a substitute key, and approached him as a music-hall aficionado, hoping to ply it off him.[189]

1968 (April) - J&L S5: THE AGE OF REVOLUTION -> Litefoot, Jago and Ellie made the acquaintance of Detective Sgt Dave Sacker, a descendant of their colleague Dr Ormond Sacker. Jago promoted *Those Were the Days* on a TV talk show featuring Timothy Vee, who – along with

In *Voyage to the New World* (the lead-in to *J&L* Series 5), and within minutes of the sixth Doctor erroneously dropping them off in the wrong decade, Jago and Litefoot find a newspaper dated "21st February, 1968". *J&L S5: The Age of Revolution* seems to open a couple of months later – Jago and Litefoot have settled into their new jobs, and mention is made of the race riots that followed the assassination of Martin Luther King (on 4th April, 1968). In the next story, *J&L S5: The Case of the Gluttonous Guru*, Litefoot says that it's "barely August". An indeterminate amount of time passes between that story and the final two Series 5 installments (*The Bloodchild Codex* and *The Final Act*), the latter of which happens immediately after the former. It's suggested in *The Case of the Gluttonous Guru* that the Palace Theatre should host a live Christmas special of *Those Were the Days*, but the performance given in *The Final Act* isn't specified as being that one, or even holiday-themed.

Jago and Litefoot are repeatedly said to originate from 1893 (the end of *J&L* Series 4). It's been "nearly eighty years" since Detective Sacker's grandfather Ormond died (in *J&L S2: The Ruthven Inheritance*, set in 1892). Summer Bloodchild estimates (*The Bloodchild Codex*) that Ellie was born about 1865, is "over ninety years old" and looks as she did "seventy years ago". When Jago and Litefoot return to 1893, Ellie says that she'll next see them "eighty years past".

It's suggested in *The Age of Revolution* that Jago should promote *Those Were the Days* on *Your Hit Parade* – quite the feat, as he'd have to fly to America to do so, and the televised version of that show ended in 1959. In the same story, Sacker flips through Timothy Vee's datebook and comes across "today's date", but doesn't name it. Vee intends to interview Peter Sellers about his new film (either *The Party* or *Alice B. Toklas*, given the year) and Lulu about her new single (she released six of those in 1968).

188 The background to *J&L S5: The Age of Revolution*.
189 The background to *J&L S5: The Bloodchild Codex* and *J&L S5: The Final Act*.

Colonel Mandrake of the Victorian Values Preservation Society – had fallen under the mesmeric influence of the three-eyed statue from India. The statue sought to spread its mental influence to millions of viewers through Vee's show, but Jago smashed the statue, ending its hold. Vee gave up television and thought about opening a boutique, while Mandrake made off with the Society's funds.

Guinevere Godiva interrogated expert crystallographers, and murdered them with Greel's equipment when they failed to activate Greel's Time Cabinet. The press dubbed her "the Brain-Drain Killer".[190]

1968 (August) - J&L S5: THE CASE OF THE GLUTTONOUS GURU -> Jago hawked *Those Were the Days* on such programmes as *Crackerjack* and *Brighton's Week*, and met Cliff Richard. Litefoot yielded to the temptation of looking himself and Jago up in the records at Somerset House, and learned when they would die.

The leader of the Temple of Transcendental Revelation, Guru Sanjaya Starr, became infected with the spawn of a formidable worm – the Great Earth Mother – and tried to spread her offspring to other hosts through restaurant food. Jago and Litefoot thwarted Starr's scheme, but not before Jago ingested the intended successor of the Great Earth Mother herself, and Litefoot voided Jago's stomach through application of McClusky's Peptic Purgative Pills. Ellie raised Jago's spirits by anonymously purchasing and renovating the old Palace Theatre on Fleet Street, so it could host live performances of *Those Were the Days*.

Jago and Litefoot Depart 1968

1968 - J&L S5: THE BLOODCHILD CODEX / THE FINAL ACT -> Professor Litefoot bought the library of the late Mr Toringham for his bookshop, and thereby came into possession of the last remaining copy of *The Bloodchild Codex*. The book incinerated two of Bloodchild's descendants who were seeking his powers. Litefoot, Jago and Ellie tried to destroy the *Codex* in a fire, but its energy partly restored Bloodchild – whose essence was embedded in the *Codex*'s pages – to life. Bloodchild demanded that the trio take him to his collection of mystical artifacts, but they instead arranged for his form to dissipate in the wind of the London Underground.

Jago hosted a star-studded live performance of *Those Were the Days* featuring Noel Coward, Sid James and others at the Palace Theatre. Guinevere Godiva discretely kidnapped Ellie – as leverage to obtain Jago's Venusian crystal – during the show, forcing Jago, Litefoot and Sacker to go to the House of the Dragon to rescue her. Sin betrayed Godiva by aging her to death in Greel's distillation chamber, then charged Godiva's crystal key with energy from the House's death ray. Greel's mind was freed from the crystal, and born anew in Sacker's body.

A vengeful Greel vowed to destroy Jago and Litefoot's native time, and programmed the time cabinet to go to 1893. Ellie channelled enough of her life-energy through the distillation chamber to kill Greel – the effort cancelled out her immortality, and she was expected to age normally.

Jago and Litefoot concluded that Jago's Venusian crystal

190 One of Godiva's victims is killed "three months" before *J&L S5: The Bloodchild Codex*.
191 Dating *Nightshade* (NA #8) - Ace finds a calendar saying it is "Christmas 1968".
192 Dating *The Demons of Red Lodge and Other Stories*: "The Entropy Composition" (BF #142b) - The year is given.
193 Dating *The Eleventh Doctor Year Three* (Titan 11th Doc #3.3-3.4, "The Tragical History Tour") – The year is given.
194 *Revolution Man* (p180).
195 From the extra features in the *Summer Falls and Other Stories* collection. The orphanage is presumably the Graystark Hall Orphanage from *The Impossible Astronaut/Day of the Moon*.
196 Date unknown, but the supplemental material in this collection includes a new introduction by "Amelia", as well as some of the 1969 *Brooklyn Fayre* profile.
197 The supplemental material in *Summer Falls and Other Stories*.
198 *Death Among the Stars*
199 *Erimem: Three Faces of Helena*
200 *Instruments of Darkness*. This might be the same car the eighth Doctor drives in the early EDAs.

201 *SJA: The Ghost House*
202 *SJA: Wraith World*
203 "Black Death, White Life"
204 "Six weeks" before *The Impossible Astronaut*.
205 *Iris S4: Iris at the Oche*. Roussos, a solo singer, first hit it big as a member of Aphrodite's Child in the late 1960s.
206 *The Blue Angel*. The novel was published in 1969.
207 *Shroud of Sorrow*. Kubler-Ross' seminal book *On Death and Dying* was published in 1969.
208 *Benny: Shades of Gray*, presumably referencing the Crimson Pearl from the Big Finish *Dark Shadows* audio of the same name. That story ended with Quentin Collins throwing the pearl into the ocean.
209 Dating *Iris S2: The Sound of Fear* (BF Iris #2.1) - Mohanalee makes Iris take him back to an unspecified part of the 1960s, but it's probably later in the decade than earlier, given this story's fixation on the golden oldies.
210 Dating *Blink* (X3.10) - The year is given, first of all in the graffiti that the Doctor leaves for Sally to find in 2007. The Doctor and Martha mention that the moon landing hasn't happened yet – this occurred on 20th July, 1969.

could enable safe travel in Greel's time cabinet, and they bid Ellie farewell as they returned to 1893...

1968 - NIGHTSHADE[191] **->** The seventh Doctor and Ace found murders and hauntings in the Yorkshire town of Crook Marsham. The retired actor Edmund Trevithick, former star of the Nightshade series, had been seeing monsters from his old show. Energy beings sealed off the village and began a rampage. The Doctor discovered the Sentience, an ancient creature, was feeding on the lifeforce of humans. He convinced it to transmit itself to a supernova in Bellatrix, where it became trapped. Afterwards, the Doctor prevented Ace from leaving him to stay on Earth with her new boyfriend, Robin Yeadon, instead taking the TARDIS to a planet with three moons.

1968 - THE DEMONS OF RED LODGE AND OTHER STORIES:"The Entropy Composition"[192] **->** Guitarist Geoffrey Belvedere Cooper (a.k.a. "The Coop") enjoyed commercial success with his quartet. The BBC banned one of their songs, "You Can See My Pad, Doll". The Coop pursued a solo career, and an Entropy Siren inserted primal sonics into his last composition, "White Wave, Soft Haze" – part of a scheme to similarly infect the music repository Concordium in future. The fifth Doctor and Nyssa destroyed the Siren, but primal sound disintegrated The Coop.

(=) 1968 - THE ELEVENTH DOCTOR YEAR THREE[193] **->** A Nunc-Stans, a pink-ish octopoid from a reality without growth and change, folded Earth's timeline in on itself. For protection, the Nunc-Stans militarised a group of hippies – the Sixty-Eighters – with cheap alien weaponry and the promise of a never-ending party. Bob Dylan despaired, then performed his fiftieth set in a month, even as the Sixty-Eighters raided future eras for advanced technology. The eleventh Doctor, Alice and multiple versions of Alice's neighbour Kushak arrived from the twenty-first century and banished the Nunc-Stans, cancelling out its effects.

In 1968, Jean-Pierre Rex had given up being the Revolution Man. The singer Ed Hill murdered Rex and used the drug Om-Tsor to continue the Revolution Man's anarchist activities. The Revolution Man symbol appeared on the deck of the US *Constitution* on 12th November. On 4th January, 1969, it appeared at a US Air Force base in High Raccoon, Tennessee.[194]

Amy and Rory Williams in New York

In 1969, Chrissie Allen profiled the children's author/editor Amelia Williams, known in literary circles as the Girl Who Never Grew Up, for *Brooklyn Fayre*. Amelia lived with her husband Rory in Manhattan's upper west side. Rory had made subtle innovations to the medical field, including drug development and the invention of Williams Wonder Beds. Using their financial resources, Amy and Rory aided an orphanage in dire straits.[195] At some point, *Summer Falls and Other Stories* collected works by Amelia Williams.[196] Amy and Rory visited Lake Erie, and met an elderly version of Clara Oswald.[197]

An Elvis impersonator – or possibly the genuine article, the twelfth Doctor couldn't remember which – performed the Doctor's marriage ceremony in Las Vegas, 1969.[198] A time-travelling Andy Hansen met Elvis.[199]

The Doctor bought a beach house in Sydney in 1969, and rented a green VW that he conveniently forgot to return.[200] The Victorian villa at 39 Bannerman Road was demolished in 1969, and replaced with a plain family home.[201] Paper from the planet Papyria in the Proxima Centauri System – a substance used by the long-dead, psionic Papyrians to rewrite reality for entertainment purposes – made its way to Earth. The budding author Gregory P. Wilkinson bought the paper as a journal from a Charing Cross Road bookshop in 1969, and it filled his head with such imaginings that he produced the *Wraith World* novel series.[202]

The tenth Doctor and Martha planned to see the Beatles' rooftop concert at Savile Row on 30th January, 1969, but ended up in 1669 instead.[203] **Canton Delaware III was fired from the FBI in February 1969, as he wished to marry a black man.**[204]

Iris Wildthyme once sang a duet with Demis Roussos.[205] She also helped Jacqueline Susann write *The Love Machine*.[206] The Doctor argued with psychiatrist Elisabeth Kubler-Ross concerning her theory of the five stages of grief, but later conceded that she was correct.[207]

Jennifer Alford's collection of supernatural items came to include the Crimson Pearl.[208]

c 1969 - IRIS S2: THE SOUND OF FEAR[209] **->** The Naxian warlord Mohanalee forced Iris Wildthyme and her husband, Sam Gold, to bring him back to the 1960s so he could implant Earth's radio signals with Naxian brain-washing signals, and retroactively make Earth the centre of the Naxian Empire. Gold died while saving Iris' life, and Mohanalee was killed also – enabling Iris to return, alone, to the future to retrieve her companion Panda.

1969 - BLINK[210] **->** Detective Inspector Billy Shipton was transported to 1969 by the Weeping Angels. He met the tenth Doctor and Martha, who gave him a message for Sally Sparrow... he would have to live out nearly forty years to deliver it.

1969 (8th April) - THE IMPOSSIBLE ASTRONAUT[211]

-> The Silence continued to prepare and hardwire the young Melody Pond as an assassin to kill the Doctor. She was given an augmented NASA astronaut suit that contained a communications array – this enabled her to link up to the Oval Office phone, and she reported to President Nixon that she was scared of "the spaceman". Nixon summoned the ex-FBI agent Canton Delaware III to investigate the call.

Arriving from 2011, the eleventh Doctor made the TARDIS exterior invisible and landed in the Oval Office as Nixon and Delaware listened to one of the mysterious phone calls. The Doctor offered his assistance, and that of his companions Amy, Rory and River Song. They quickly identified the caller's location as an intersection in Florida, five miles from Cape Kennedy. The Doctor, his companions and Delaware went there, and discovered a disused warehouse containing alien technology... and some of the leaders of the Silence. Anyone who saw the Silence lost all memory of them once they looked away.

The Doctor and Amy found the little girl, who was wearing the same spacesuit as the person who had killed the Doctor in 2011. To prevent the Doctor's death, Amy shot the spacesuited figure...

Young Melody Pond escaped. The Doctor, Amy, Rory and River spent the next three months investigating the pervasiveness of the Silence in this era. Canton

Delaware pretended to be trying to apprehend them for the FBI while he constructed a cage made of dwarf star alloy – a way to guarantee that they weren't being monitored.[212] River Song was aware that the girl was her younger self, but pretended not to know.[213]

1969 (18th May) - REVOLUTION MAN[214]

-> The "Revolution Man" incidents greatly increased tensions between the US, the Soviet Union, China and India. Ed Hill's psionic abilities spiralled out of control, threatening to destroy all life on Earth, and Fitz and the eighth Doctor killed Hill to prevent such a catastrophe. The Doctor consumed a portion of Om-Tsor, and used its reality-warping abilities to prevent the world governments from instigating a nuclear war.

The Doctor sent Keri the Pakhar a postcard saying that he had just enjoyed tea with Prince Charles at his investiture in 1969.[215]

1969 (summer) - DAEMONS: WHITE WITCH OF DEVIL'S END[216]

-> Melissa Fenn, a practitioner of the dark arts, used a poppet to possess the body of Olive Hawthorne's best friend, Josephine Bingley. As "Josie", Fenn intended to marry the local magistrate, Cedric Winstanley, and gain access to his lands and influence. Olive bound Fenn's spirit to the poppet, restoring Josephine, and the wedding proceeded.

211 Dating *The Impossible Astronaut* (X6.1) - The date is given. The story continues in *Day of the Moon*; some details from that story and *A Good Man Goes to War* have been included in this summary for clarity.
212 *Day of the Moon*
213 *The Wedding of River Song*
214 Dating *Revolution Man* (EDA #21) - The date is given (p223).
215 *Big Bang Generation* (ch2). Prince Charles was named Prince of Wales and Earl of Chester on 26th July, 1958, but the formality of his investiture didn't happen until 1st July, 1969.
216 Dating *Daemons: White Witch of Devil's End* (story #4, "The Poppet") - The year and season are given. It's "a couple of years" before *The Daemons*. Snow falls during this story, a result of elementals fighting Olive's efforts.
217 "Wormwood". The *TV Comic* story "Moon Landing" predicted the first moon landing would occur in 1970. Richard Lazarus namechecks Armstrong in *The Lazarus Experiment*.
218 *Empress of Mars*

219 *Blink*. These were separate occasions from their being stranded in 1969.
220 *Beautiful Chaos* (p76). This presumably references Bernard Quatermass and his daughter Paula.
221 *Heart of Stone* (p146). This happened on "the last Apollo mission", presumably *Apollo 11*.
222 Dating *Day of the Moon* (X6.2) - A caption tells us that the action (which follows on from *The Impossible Astronaut*) has resumed "3 Months Later. July 1969". Events culminate with the *Apollo 11* moon landing (on 20th July).
223 *The Left-Handed Hummingbird*. No specific actions on Manson's part are mentioned, but the infamous "Helter Skelter" murders took place in August 1969, and the most prominent victim, actress Sharon Tate, was killed 8th August. Page 243 establishes that Huitzilin merely fed off Manson's actions, but didn't "possess" or influence him as is sometimes claimed.
224 *The Creeping Terror* (ch1). Woodstock was held 15th-18th August, 1969.

The Moon Landing

From their base on the moon, the Threshold watched Neil Armstrong land.[217] **Neil Armstrong was the first human on the moon, but not the first man.**[218] **The tenth Doctor and Martha watched the moon landing four times.**[219] Bernard and Paula took the Doctor to the Royal Planetary Society, where they shared a meal and watched the moon landing.[220] The *Apollo 11* astronauts returned with samples of moon rock, one of which contained an alien bacteria.[221]

1969 (July) - DAY OF THE MOON[222] **->** Canton Delaware "captured" the eleventh Doctor, Amy and Rory. They used the invisible TARDIS, which was located within the dwarf-star alloy cage, to reunite with River Song. Melody Pond tore her way out of her spacesuit and went into hiding; the Doctor's party found that the spacesuit contained technology from twenty different species.

Delaware acquired video footage of one of the Silence. The Doctor went to Cape Kennedy and inserted a transmitter into the *Apollo 11* capsule; he was captured while doing so, but Nixon ordered his release. As the moon landing took place, the Doctor's transmitter stripped Delaware's video clip into all broadcasts of Neil Armstrong stepping foot onto the lunar surface. The clip showed a Silence saying:

"You should kill us all on sight."

This acted as a subliminal order – humanity wouldn't remember hearing it, but for a thousand generations, the Silence would be a hunted species, attacked by any person that saw them. The Doctor's group said farewell to President Nixon, and the Doctor suggested that the Nixon should record everything said in the Oval Office so he could better know if the Silence was influencing him. The Doctor returned River to the future, and resumed his travels with Amy and Rory.

The trauma caused by Charles Manson and his followers provided sustenance to Huitzilin.[223] The Doctor's tambourine solo was one of the highlights of Woodstock.[224]

The UNIT Era

Establishing when the UNIT stories take place is probably the most contentious *Doctor Who* continuity issue.

The UNIT stories are set in an undefined "end of the twentieth century" era that could more or less comfortably fit at any time between the mid-sixties and mid-nineties (but no further, as the Doctor is specifically exiled to "the twentieth century").

Some *Doctor Who* fans have insisted on trying to pin down the dates more precisely, and some have even claimed to have "found the right answer". But all of us face the problem that as successive production teams came and went, a mass of contradictory, ambiguous and circumstantial evidence built up. To come up with a consistent timeframe, this evidence must be prioritised, and some of it has to be rationalised away or ignored.

It is a matter of individual judgement which clues are important. The best chronologies are aware of the problem and admit they're coming down on one side of the argument, while the worst blithely assert they alone have the right answer while not noticing they've missed half the evidence.

The Virgin version of *Ahistory* was wrong when it said there was no right answer. The problem is that there are several, mutually incompatible, right answers.

#

For newcomers and those needing a refresher course, we should list out the TV adventures that comprise the "UNIT era":

- The second Doctor stories *The Web of Fear* (5.5) and *The Invasion* (6.3), in which the Doctor meets Colonel Alistair Gordon Lethbridge-Stewart and – upon the man's promotion to Brigadier – first teams up with UNIT.
- The third Doctor stories in which, while (chiefly) exiled to Earth, he works alongside Lethbridge-Stewart as UNIT's scientific advisor: *Spearhead from Space* (7.1), *Doctor Who and the Silurians* (7.2), *The Ambassadors of Death* (7.3), *Inferno* (7.4), *Terror of the Autons* (8.1), *The Mind of Evil* (8.2), *The Claws of Axos* (8.3), *Colony in Space* (8.4), *The Daemons* (8.5), *Day of the Daleks* (9.1), *The Sea Devils* (9.3), *The Time Monster* (9.5), *The Three Doctors* (10.1; the Doctor's exile is here rescinded), *The Green Death* (10.5), *The Time Warrior* (11.1), *Invasion of the Dinosaurs* (11.2) and *Planet of the Spiders* (11.5).
- The fourth Doctor stories *Robot* (12.1), *Terror of the Zygons* (13.1), *The Android Invasion* (13.4) and *The Seeds of Death* (13.6). The fourth Doctor increasingly dials back his involvement with UNIT, and it ends, without any fanfare or formal declaration, in *The Seeds of Death*.
- *K9 and Company* (18.7-A), a pilot for an unmade spin-off series, in which the Doctor gifts Sarah Jane Smith with her own K9. It's here that, one way or another, the dating of the UNIT stories comes into focus.
- The fifth Doctor story *Mawdryn Undead* (20.3), in which the Doctor reunites with a post-UNIT Brigadier Lethbridge-Stewart, and similarly *The Five Doctors* (20.7).
- The seventh Doctor story *Battlefield* (26.1), in which the Brigadier briefly comes out of retirement.

#

It happens that a number of firm, unambiguous dates are given in dialogue during the course of the series:

1. *The Web of Fear* (broadcast 1968) is the sequel to *The Abominable Snowmen* and features the first appearance of Lethbridge-Stewart. There, Victoria and Anne Travers establish that *The Abominable Snowmen* was set in "1935". Earlier in the same story, Professor Travers had said that this was "over forty years ago". *The Invasion* "must be four years" after that, according to the Brigadier.

Some chronologies have made heroic efforts to ignore or reinterpret this. This line of thought usually leads to forty four being added to 1935 to get 1967 or 1968, and liberal use of the phrase "rounding up". But using conventional maths and English, the only possible reading of the lines is that *The Web of Fear* is set in or after 1975 and that *The Invasion*, the first story to feature UNIT, was broadcast in 1968 but was set no earlier than 1979.

2. In *Pyramids of Mars* (broadcast 1975), the Doctor and Sarah both say that she is "from 1980". Here, there's a little room for interpretation, but not much. The most literal reading has to be that *The Time Warrior*, Sarah's first story, is set in 1980. The only plausible alternative is that she's been travelling with the Doctor for some years, and that she is referring to the date of *Terror of the Zygons*, her last visit to Earth in her timezone. Either way, it refers to a story featuring UNIT.

Anyone trying to contradict Sarah's statement is suggesting that they know better than she does which *year* she comes from. It is difficult to believe that Sarah is rounding up, that she comes from the mid-seventies and simply means "I'm from around that time". The year is specified so precisely, and it jarred when the story was broadcast in 1975, just as it would if anyone now claimed to be from 2025. This isn't "vague" or "ambiguous", as neither she or the Doctor say she's "from around then" or "from the late nineteen-seventies/eighties" – they actually specify a year, and not the easy option of "1975", which would have been a conveniently rounded-up figure that would have brought the threat to history closer to home for the viewing audience. And to cap it all, they then go to a devastated "1980". So, Sarah comes from 1980.

3. *K9 and Company* (the pilot of an unmade *K9* show) and *Mawdryn Undead*, two stories from the 1980s, are set the UNIT era in the years they were first broadcast.

K9 and Company is set in late December 1981, and K9 has been crated up waiting for Sarah since 1978. The format document for the proposed spin-off series stated that Sarah was born in "1949" and that "she spent three years travelling in Space and Time (15.12.73-23.10.76)". This story is "canon", as Sarah and K9 appeared together in *The Five Doctors*, *School Reunion* and *The Sarah Jane Adventures*. If we discount the dates for her travels given in the document (they don't, after all, appear on screen), nothing contradicts the "1980" reference... but it means K9 was waiting for her *before* she met the Doctor. This needn't be a problem, however – he clearly delivered Sarah to the wrong end of the country, so why not K9 a couple of years early? It might even explain why Sarah in *School Reunion* thinks the Doctor abandoned her after *The Hand of Fear*, rather than thanking him for the gift.

But *Mawdryn Undead* is impossible to rationalise away that easily. Broadcast in 1983, it states that the Brigadier retired a year before 1977, presumably after Season 13, which was broadcast in 1976. A host of references pin down the dating for *Mawdryn Undead* more precisely. There are two timezones, and these are unambiguously "1977" (where the Queen's Silver Jubilee is being celebrated) and "1983".

So, the Brigadier retired in 1976.

4. *Battlefield* (broadcast 1989) is set "a few years" in Ace's future – apparently in the mid-to-late 1990s. According to the story's author, Ben Aaronovitch, it takes place in "1997". Whatever the case, it is established once again that the UNIT stories are "a few years" in the future. The same writer's *Remembrance of the Daleks* also provides upper and lower limits – UNIT is not around in 1963 when the story is set, but the Doctor rhetorically asks Ace (from the mid-eighties) about the events of *The Web of Fear* and *Terror of the Zygons*.

5. The New Series and *The Sarah Jane Adventures*. Since its return in 2005, the new *Doctor Who* has reintroduced UNIT and Sarah Jane.

The new series sometimes makes knowing winks at fandom as to the whole UNIT Dating conundrum... in *The Sontaran Stratagem*, the Doctor states that he worked with UNIT "in the seventies... or was it the eighties?". *The Day of the Doctor* sees Kate Stewart ask for "one of my father's incident files... 70s or 80s depending upon the dating protocol". Later in *The Zygon Invasion*, Kate off-handedly claims that *Terror of the Zygons* happened in "the seventies, the eighties..." The writer of that story, Peter Harness, revealed on Twitter that he wrote an (unused) exchange in which the twelfth Doctor asked Osgood if she had a boy-friend, and Osgood replied: "You kind of have to give up on dating if you have anything to do with UNIT."

The Sarah Jane Adventures, though, have consistently opted for a "year of broadcast" approach, both on screen and in the background features seen on the BBC website and the DVD extras. Crucially, thanks to *SJA: Whatever Happened to Sarah Jane?* and *SJA: The Temptation of Sarah Jane Smith*, we now know that Sarah Jane was born in May 1951 – coupled with her saying she's "23" in *Invasion of the Dinosaurs* (broadcast in 1974), it very much puts the UNIT stories into a "time of broadcast" framework. As with *The Sontaran Stratagem*, however, *The Sarah Jane Adventures* does joke around with the UNIT dating problem – in *SJA: The Lost Boy*, Sarah's UNIT dossier reads: "... making our presence felt in a golden period that spanned the sixties, the seventies, and, some would say, the eighties."

The current *Doctor Who* series opts to downplay or ignore many of the scientific advances we saw in the seventies UNIT stories that didn't come to pass in the real world – for example, *The Christmas Invasion* has a pioneering British unmanned mission to Mars, and Sarah Jane explicitly says that no one has set foot on Mars, but *The Ambassadors of Death* showed a long-established UK manned Mars program.

6. The *Lethbridge-Stewart* novels operate in a separate timeline that begins in 1937, so march to their own drummer in terms of UNIT Dating (by their reckoning, *The Web of Fear* happened in 1969). The Haisman Timeline lays out this parallel history of the Brigadier et al, while also claiming that much of the histories of the characters in the *Lethbridge-Stewart* books likewise applies to their counterparts in the prime timeline. (See The Haisman Estate-Approved Multiverse Timeline, near the start of this section.)

# # # # #

Thousands of words have been written trying to discount or reinterpret either the *Pyramids of Mars* or the *Mawdryn Undead* account of events. Dozens of distinct explanations – either within the logic of the fiction or taking account of production facts – have been proposed. They tend to be convoluted or to stretch the meanings of very plain English words beyond acceptable tolerances.

The only thing they have in common is that none of them would stand up in court. However you weigh up and prioritise evidence, the *Pyramids of Mars* and *Mawdryn Undead* dates are "as true" as each other. They are scripted and broadcast lines of dialogue within a single story that unambiguously state a firm date, then the characters go to that year and then the date is stated again.

Ultimately, the only way to come up with a consistent UNIT dating scheme is to pick one and ignore the other.

Broadly speaking, then, there are two schools of thought. Either the stories are set in the "near future", as was originally stated (a view that actually elides *two* distinct accounts, as *The Invasion* had the UNIT era starting no earlier than 1979, but *Pyramids of Mars* pretty much ended it in 1980); or they are set in the year of broadcast, as was stated in the early 1980s (which glosses over/ ignores/corrects what was said in those previous stories) in a version of history where certain aspects of technological progress were more advanced and the political situation was different.

As noted in the individual UNIT story entries, there are a wealth of clues beyond what's actually said that might be used to tip the balance one way or the other. Different chronologies give different weight to these, and so come to different conclusions. But most try to address the following areas:

1. Technology: There are an abundance of references to scientific developments that hadn't happened at the time the UNIT stories were broadcast, but were reasonable extrapolations of what the near future would hold.

The technology is far in advance of the early nineteen-seventies: there are talking computers, compact walkie talkies, experimental alloys, laser guns and robots. Colour televisions and even colour videophones are commonplace. Man has landed on Mars, there are space freighters and advanced artificial intelligences. Comprehensive space and alternative energy programmes are underway.

It could be argued that the UNIT stories are set in a parallel history where by (say) 1970 humankind was more technologically advanced than the real 1970. One obvious reason for this might be that scientists had access to an abundance of alien technology from all the failed invasions, and so made great technological progress. There are examples of high technology being developed due to alien influence in some stories. For example, the interstitial time travel of *The Time Monster* is inspired by the Master, not because it's part of humankind's natural progress. There are other stories with no obvious alien influence, like *The War Machines* with its prototype internet and advanced artificial intelligence.

However, there's no evidence that, say, the British mission to Mars seen in *The Ambassadors of Death* uses alien technology (rather the opposite). One difference between it and *The War Machines* is that there are several explicit references to things being obsolete that were state-of-the-art at the time of broadcast. While it's a little far-fetched that Britain could mount such an ambitious programme, there's no technology in the story that NASA weren't planning to have by the 1980s. In 1970, NASA planned – not just hoped – to have a man on Mars by 1982.

2. Historical and Political Details: Again, the evidence overwhelmingly suggests that either the political history of the early nineteen-seventies is very different to reality, or the UNIT stories aren't set in the early 1970s.

There's a Prime Minister called Jeremy in *The Green Death*, and one who's a woman by the time of *Terror of the Zygons*. Both of these are clear – and clearly tongue-in-cheek – references to someone who was an actual opposition leader with an outside chance of winning the next election or the one after that. The United Nations is more powerful than its seventies equivalent. The Cold War has been over for "years" by the end of the era. Environmentalism has become a matter for Westminster politicians and civil servants. All of these things are clearly reasonable extrapolations, not a reflection, of the situation at the time the stories were made.

Two pieces of dialogue suggest it is the early seventies: in *Doctor Who and the Silurians*, a taxi driver wants his fare in predecimal currency, and Mao Tse Tung seems to be alive at the time of *The Mind of Evil* (he died in 1976).

3. Calendars: The month a UNIT story is set is often specified or can be inferred from information in a story, or by close observation of calendars on walls or other such set dressing. We are told that the barrow in *The Daemons* (broadcast 1971) is opened on Beltane (30th April). We can infer that it's a Saturday or – more probably – Sunday (see the entry for that story). So, taken literally, that would mean that it was set in a year when 30th April fell on a Sunday – in the seventies, that would be 1972 or 1978.

While there have been some excellent attempts to reconcile this sort of information, this is not a level of detail the production team ever went into, and this is not a "key" to revealing a consistent chronology. The evidence is often contradictory, even within individual stories: *four* calendars appear in *The Green Death*, one stating that the story is set in February of a leap year, two more say it is April, the fourth indicates that it's May.

4. Fashions: Except for *The Invasion* and *Battlefield*, the clothes, haircuts and cars all resemble those of the year the programme was made. There was no attempt to mock-up car number plates or predict future fashions. The UNIT soldiers sport haircuts that would have been distinctly nonregulation in the 1970s, but this is just as true today. The UNIT era looks and feels like the early 1970s, the characters have many of the attitudes and concerns of people in the seventies. However, is this evidence it was set in the early 1970s, or simply that it was made in the early 1970s?

5. Authorial Intention: We might also want to refer to interviews with the production team, to find out what they intended.

Derrick Sherwin, the producer at the time the UNIT format was introduced, said in the *Radio Times* of 19th June, 1969, that Season Seven would be set in "a time not many years distant from now when such things as space stations will be actuality". In an interview with the *Daily Mail* two days later, Jon Pertwee stated that his Doctor would be exiled to Earth "in the 1980s". The *Doctor Who and the Sea-Devils* novelisation by Malcolm Hulke, published in 1974, said that "North Sea oil had started gushing in 1977".

The Terrestrial Index claimed that the decision was made to redate the UNIT era was taken when real life overtook it, but that didn't happen. When asked in *DWB* #58 why the dates for *Mawdryn Undead* contradicted what was established in the Pertwee era, Eric Saward, the script editor for the story, admitted that the 1977/1983 dates were "a mistake". In fact, the only reason the Brigadier is even in *Mawdryn Undead* is that William Russell wasn't available to play Ian Chesterton in that story, and without the 1977 date given in *Mawdryn Undead*, there's little to debate.

On the other hand, *The Making of Doctor Who*, written by Malcolm Hulke and Terrance Dicks and published in 1972, placed *Spearhead from Space* in "1970".

The editors of the early New and Missing Adventures consciously chose to set the UNIT stories on or about the year they were broadcast. In practice, when a date is specified it was left pretty much to the discretion of an individual author, and there were a number of discrepancies (see the entries for each story). Later novels mentioning UNIT were far more coy about specifying dates, for the most part, and a number (like *No Future*, *The Dying Days*

and *Interference*) have suggested fictional reasons for the confusion. Big Finish has shown little interest in weighing in on the topic, although a token effort was made to place its first *UNIT* mini-series in the near-future of release.

6. Real Life: The late eighties/early nineties fit the UNIT era almost perfectly – the Cold War was over, China was hardline communist, the British government was unstable, there was a female prime minister, the UN was powerful, environmental issues were at the forefront of political debate, there was video conferencing, British scientists were working on their own space probes and Microsoft were putting a computer in every home and making IE's attempts at world domination look half-hearted.

To top it all, a trend for seventies retro meant that the fashionistas were all dressing like Jo Grant. The Doctor's reference to Batman in *Inferno* was clearly because he'd just seen the Tim Burton movie. It's uncanny.

7. Other Reference Books: The balance of fan opinion, or at least the fans who write books, has definitely tipped towards setting the UNIT era in or around the year of broadcast. *The Terrestrial Index*, *The Discontinuity Guide*, *Who Killed Kennedy*, *Timelink* and *About Time* all – give or take a year here or there – concur. A clear majority of the original novels do.

The BBC-published *Doctor Who – The Legend* (2003) opted to set the UNIT era in the "near future" and concluded that *Mawdryn Undead* is the anomaly. That said, *Whoniverse* (BBC, 2016) – also by Justin Richards – was less definitive, and found different ways to say that the

---

1 The Haisman Timeline dates James and Dylan's arrival in our reality to "March 1959", about "ten years" before *Leth-St: Night of the Intelligence*. The Vault first appeared in *The Scales of Injustice*, and plays a recurring role in the *Lethbridge-Stewart* novels, with details given in (among others) *Leth-St: Beast of Fang Rock* and *Leth-St: "One Cold Step"*.

THE LEADER OF INFERNO-EARTH: *Leth-St: Night of the Intelligence* reveals the fascist Leader in *Inferno* (seen on a poster) as the Brigadier's father. *Timewyrm: Revelation* alternatively had the Doctor recognising the Leader as one of the faces he was offered at his trial (*The War Games*), and from this conjecturing that the Leader was an alt-Doctor. We can reconcile these accounts using a fan theory that a Time Lord body bank exists with various templates for regenerations – this would explain why the first Doctor looks like the Abbot of Amboise (*The Massacre*), the second Doctor like Ramon Salamander (*The Enemy of the World*) and why Commander Maxil (*Arc of Infinity*) and the sixth Doctor look identical. It doesn't cover *every* duplicate in the universe (say, Nyssa and Ann Talbot in *Black Orchid*), but it helps.

Perhaps Lethbridge-Stewart's father indeed lived to become the Leader on Inferno Earth. Later, "our" Doctor becomes distraught and confused because the Time Lords' buffet of faces (*The War Games*) included that of "our" Gordon Lethbridge-Stewart, who died in 1945 (and would've made things terribly awkward between the third Doctor and the Brig, had he picked that face).

2 *Leth-St: Night of the Intelligence* (ch6).

3 *Leth-St: Times Squared,* the Haisman Timeline.

4 "Two years" before *Leth-St: The Showstoppers*.

5 "A couple of years" before *Leth-St: The Life of Evans* (ch4).

6 "A few years" before *Leth-St: The Dreamer's Lament* (ch3), according to Vincent's daughter.

7 The background to *The Dominators*, given in *Leth-St: Mutually Assured Domination*.

8 Dating *The Dominators* (6.1) - On screen, *The Dominators* is one of the most stubbornly undatable stories - there are no indications of a connection with Earth or the human race. *Leth-St: Mutually Assured Domination* (chs. 6-7) references what happened on Dulkis as a "shameful historical incident" (chs. 6-7) that prompted a recent rethink of Dominator operations,

UNIT Era fell "in the latter half of the twentieth century".

The Conclusion: It is very tempting to hope for a right answer, but *Doctor Who* is fiction, not a documentary and a "one right answer" just does not – cannot – exist. Even if we limit ourselves solely to dates specifically and unambiguously given in on-screen dialogue, then the Brigadier retires from UNIT three years before his first appearance as the commanding officer of UNIT. It is utterly impossible to try to incorporate every calendar, E-reg car and videophone into one consistent timeframe. People who claim to have done so have invariably, and by definition, missed or deliberately ignored some piece of evidence established somewhere.

However, none of the dates given place the "UNIT era" earlier than the late sixties or later than the early eighties. A right answer doesn't exist, but something everyone ought to be able to agree on is that the UNIT stories took place in "the seventies", give or take a year or so.

The personal preference of the authors of *Ahistory*, for the record, neatly reflects the main split in fandom on this issue: Lance prefers that the UNIT era takes place in the near future, five or so years after broadcast, while Lars favours the stories being set at time of broadcast, or near enough for comfort.

For the Purposes of this Book: Even though it's not possible to specify the year, it *is* possible to come up with a consistent timeline. Many UNIT stories contain some reference to other UNIT stories, so it is possible to place them relative to each other. Furthermore, the month a story is set is often given. While there are inconsistencies (which have been noted), it's therefore possible to write a broadly consistent history of the "UNIT era".

The stories of the UNIT era have been separated from those of the other contemporary and near-contemporary stories, and instead talk in "UNIT years". "UNIT Year 1" in this scheme is the year that *The Invasion* and *Spearhead from Space* are set. This only applies to the "UNIT era" – the stories set in the seventies – by the time of *K9 and Company* in 1981, real life seems to have caught up with the near-future of the series whichever way you cut it.

Depending on which story's dating scheme you adopt (and give or take a year in all cases), Unit Year 1 is:

The Invasion – 1979
Pyramids of Mars – 1974
Mawdryn Undead – 1969

UNIT Year -10: The Founding of the Vault

= On Inferno-Earth, the father of First Major James Lethbridge-Stewart became the totalitarian leader of the British Republic. James tried, and failed, to rebel against his father's tyranny. To escape a death sentence, James and his son Dylan crossed over to our Earth. James' wife, Rachel Jensen, died horribly beforehand. Because James miscalculated, they arrived ten years earlier than expected...

The Vault had – officially, at least – been founded by the Ministry of Technology per Harold Wilson's mandate to deploy advanced technology and new processes into industry. In actuality, it worked to secure alien technology. The former Darkmoor Nuclear Research Station, situated in the Cheviot Hills, Northumberland, served as its HQ. The alt-James Lethbridge-Stewart led the Vault from its start, as "General Gore".[1]

UNIT Year -8

General Gore took possession of an Acteon crystal, found in Scotland more than five years previous.[2]

The Edward Travers from 1935 emerged from a time warp in October, years before the London Event. He monitored the Great Intelligence's operations, and became the proprietor of Ebon Books in Manhattan. He revisited Det-Sen, where Thonmi had become the abbot.[3]

UNIT Year -6

Alistair Gordon Lethbridge-Stewart was promoted to Colonel.[4] Private Evans' mother returned to his life, after his father's passing. Evans learned his father had a second family, including a wife and daughter.[5] Vincent Travers, the twin brother of Edward Travers, died.[6]

The Dominators originated as human-basic warriors on the planet Drahb in the Phi-Ralix Galaxy. Genetic augmentation extended the Dominator lifespan by several hundred years, and eliminated sexual reproduction in favour of parthenogenesis. The species split into two camps: the males became the marauding Dominators, while the females became the Domina, the infamous Star Maidens of Drahb. With their warfleet, the Dominators subjugated thousands of races including the Bandrils, the Tivolians, the Gonds, the Gurdels and the Monoids. In time, they became Masters of the Ten Galaxies, and also encountered the Valethske and the Ogrons.[7]

THE DOMINATORS[8] **-> Two Dominators, Navigator Rago and Probationer Toba, arrived on the planet Dulkis with a contingent of robots, the Quarks, to instigate drilling operations that would convert the planet into radioactive fuel for the Dominators' spacefleet. The second Doctor, accompanied by Jamie and Zoe, blew up the Dominators with their own seed device, saving the peace-minded Dulkians.**

UNIT Year -5

Following the Dulkis debacle, the Dominators' high command – the Dominant Echelon – looked for a new *modus operandi* to fuel its fleet. Director Vaar developed Project M for field-testing on Earth. Dominex Industries, a front for the undertaking, was incorporated on 5th January.[9]

Around this time, the Cybermen contacted Tobias Vaughn, who offered them help with their invasion. Soon afterwards, Vaughn's company, International Electromatics (IE), marketed the micromonolithic circuit. It revolutionised electronics, and made IE the world leader in the field.[10]

Lethbridge-Stewart saved Doris, an old friend, from drowning in Margate.[11] **Alastair Lethbridge-Stewart very much enjoyed his weekend in Brighton with a young woman named Doris** Bryden. Unknown to him, she became pregnant with their son, Albert.[12]

In August, a Parachute Regiment division – as led by Colonel Spencer Pemberton and Captain Ben Knight – oversaw transport of an extraterrestrial rock tied to mysterious incidents. Their detachment was waylaid, and the rock stolen. During the melee, four of Pemberton's troopers were turned into stone statues. Major General Hamilton reassigned Pemberton and Knight to assist the RAF and Royal Marines in creating a Special Forces Support Group.[13]

UNIT Year -4

The TARDIS visited the 1970s and 1980s so many times, its damaged engines condensed those two decades into ten years. To the participants, time flowed as normal, and they failed to notice any contradictions. As he spent so much time with the Doctor, Alistair Gordon Lethbridge-Stewart became the epicentre of this impact on the timeline.[14]

The race to put a man on the moon was largely for show, since the United States and the Soviet Union had already installed secret bases there. The Americans copied Russian gravity-imitation technology from Gagarin Base for their Horizon Base, which was on the other side of Plinius. Both bases mined for Helium-3, for use in fusion reactors.[15]

Colonel Lethbridge-Stewart's second-in-command, Colonel Walter Douglas, introduced him to Corporal Sally

---

and The Haisman Timeline specifically places *The Dominators* two years beforehand.

9 The background to *Leth-St: Mutually Assured Domination*.

10 "Five years" before *The Invasion* according to Vaughn.

11 *Blood Heat*

12 "Eleven years" before *Planet of the Spiders*. The Haisman Timeline dates this to 1968, while leaving it a toss-up as to whether *Planet of the Spiders* happens in 1974 or 1979 (see the Haisman Timeline sidebar).

13 The year before *Leth-St: Mind of Stone*. The blurb and Chapter 12 both say it's "August", the Haisman Timeline (probably cross-wiring with the book's main narrative) says "November". Pemberton and Knight are killed (the former off screen) in *The Web of Fear*.

14 *Leth-St: "The Enfolded Time"*, offering an explanation for the UNIT Dating controversy (see the Haisman Timeline sidebar).

15 Gagarin Base is completed "six months" before *Leth-St: Moon Blink* [July 1969].

16 *Leth-St: The Forgotten Son, Leth-St: Moon Blink*. the Haisman Timeline.

17 Dating *Leth-St: "The Ambush"* (*Leth-St: HAVOC Files* #1.3) - This short story fleshes out the background of *The Web of Fear*, including Lethbridge-Stewart's off-camera meeting with the Doctor.

18 *Leth-St: "The Enfolded Time"*

19 Dating *The Web of Fear* (5.5) - No year is expressly stated. Professor Travers declares that the events of *The Abominable Snowmen* were "over forty years ago", and Victoria agrees with Anne's claim that they were in "1935", suggesting a near-future setting of at least 1975. Some fans have suggested that Travers is senile or con-

fused, and his daughter thinks he's a little absent minded, but from what we see, he's sharp-witted and in command of the facts.

The accumulated evidence, however, now favours a year-of-broadcast (i.e. 1968) dating. The maps of the London Underground that we see render the network as it was in 1968, and don't show the Victoria or Jubilee lines, which opened on 7th March, 1969, and 1st May, 1979, respectively. A movie poster in episode six is one for *In the Heat of the Night* (1967) starring Sidney Poitier and Rod Steiger, but the title has been changed to *Block Buster*. This may be a conscious attempt to indicate some future film project for two real life stars, or just the BBC avoiding advertising a real film. In *The Snowmen*, the eleventh Doctor seems to accidentally influence the Great Intelligence's decision of when to invade Earth with a souvenir lunchbox displaying a map of the London Underground in 1967.

Downtime, set in 1995, is a sequel to *The Web of Fear* and fairly rife with dating references to it. A meeting between Lethbridge-Stewart and Air-Vice Marshal Gilmore (*Remembrance of the Daleks, Counter-Measures*) happens "five years" after 1963 (p8), when Harold Wilson is Prime Minister (he first served as such from 1964 to 1970). A Ministry of Defence report on the London Event specifies the year as "68" (p183). Sarah Jane Smith variously says the same Event was "some twenty-five years"/"a quarter of a century" (p92) and "about thirty years" (p99) prior to 1995. The Brigadier claims it was "about thirty years" ago (p148). The Intelligence/Travers thinks the Locus went missing "over twenty-five years" ago (p134).

The blurb to the *Downtime* VHS says it's been "twen-

Wright in February. Lethbridge-Stewart and Wright became engaged in March, but he soon realised that he didn't love her. Douglas had a wife named Penny and a seven-year-old son, Jake.[16]

The London Event

Colonel Lethbridge-Stewart First Meets the Doctor as the Great Intelligence's Yeti Invade the London Underground

LETH-ST: "The Ambush"[17] -> Professor Edward Travers was summoned to advise upon the London Event. Colonel Spencer Pemberton of the 1st Battalion Parachute Regiment saved Travers from the strange web, but died combating the Great Intelligence's Yeti. Colonel Alastair Lethbridge-Stewart, numbered among the best of 2nd Battalion, had been brought back from Libya to aid with the crisis, and learned of his old friend and mentor's death. The Yeti attacked Lethbridge-Stewart and his men, inflicting casualties on the 33rd Regiment. Lethbridge-Stewart retreated, and – while en route to Goodge Street – happened upon a very strange man...

The Accord briefly transported at least two versions of Colonel Pemberton – one as he was bringing Professor Travers to Goodge Street – to help sort out Alistair Lethbridge-Stewart's timeline.[18]

(March) - THE WEB OF FEAR[19] -> **Mysterious cobwebs started to appear across London, the fog thickened and "bears" and "monsters" attacked people in the Underground. Londoners fled in terror, and the army was called in to restore order. They found themselves under siege in the London Underground, where the disturbances were concentrated. Faced with an attack from the Great Intelligence and its army of robot Yeti, the military were reduced to blowing up tunnels to try to contain the situation.**
The second Doctor arrived with Jamie and Victoria,

and met Colonel Lethbridge-Stewart for the first time. Together with an older Professor Edward Travers (who briefly fell under the Intelligence's influence) and his daughter Anne, they fought the Yeti. The Doctor banished the Intelligence.

Survivors of this incursion included the broadcaster Harold Chorley and Private Gwynfor Evans. Staff Sgt Arnold perished, after the Intelligence had possessed his body.

This became known as the London Event, and the official story was that there had been an industrial accident. Lethbridge-Stewart retained the Locus, a small carved statuette of a Yeti, as a memento; it later wound up in the possession of his daughter Kate.[20]

> **(=) As Dr Simeon, the Great Intelligence went back in time to kill the Doctor in the London Underground.**[21]

> **(=) (March) - LETH-ST: "Legacies"**[22] -> In one version of events, owing to chance, Colonel Pemberton killed the second Doctor in the Underground. Jamie, Victoria and Lethbridge-Stewart died also. The Great Intelligence took Anne Travers as a host. An avatar of the TARDIS, "Tessa", approached the Intelligence and argued that it was in their mutual interests to not let this broken timeline stand. The Intelligence permitted Tessa to cast it into the void. With Tessa's help, Pemberton went back in time and saved Lethbridge-Stewart's life at the cost of his own.

Ramon Salamander was ejected from the Time Vortex, and landed on Earth minutes after the TARDIS' arrival in the London Underground. About his person was a pouch of self-replicating weather-control micro machines, which he patented and used to found Electronicon Ltd. Over the next decade, he worked to achieve time travel.[23]

---

ty-five years" since *The Web of Fear*, but the *Downtime* book blurb stands somewhat alone in specifying the London Event as "1966" (possibly just a typo). An epilogue to *The Web of Fear* in the book (with the Doctor, Jamie and Victoria returning to the TARDIS) is broadbrushed as being "the Sixties and beyond" (p2).
   Leth-St: Night of the Intelligence (ch15) offers a novel idea for Travers' confusion with dates, explaining that as his younger self travelled through time and lived out four years in the 1960s (*Leth-St: Times Squared*), but the older Travers remembers none of this. As his mind and body are older than he knows, he keeps experiencing discontinuity and botching his maths on years.

20 *Downtime*
21 Or so it appears from a clip of *The Web of Fear* shown in *The Name of the Doctor*. That would make the Intelligence's own history very paradoxical, but that's perhaps a minor concern, given its intent to shred the Doctor's history into tiny pieces anyway.
22 Dating *Leth-St*: "Legacies" (*Leth-St* short story #3) - It's "two weeks" after *The Web of Fear*. Pemberton is mentioned at the start of that story as having died in unspecified circumstances. The TARDIS is variously identified as "Ship","Tessa" and "Sexy" (*The Doctor's Wife*).
23 "The Heralds of Destruction". Salamander says he arrived on Earth concurrent with *The Web of Fear* in "the

Colonel Lethbridge-Stewart[24]

Major General Hamilton initially rebuffed Colonel Lethbridge-Stewart's idea of getting UN support to combat extraterrestrial threats. As the Colonel climbed out of a helicopter on the Liskeard Bypass, the Accord took him to meet his future selves. He returned with no memory of the event.[25] Hamilton assigned Colonel Alistair Lethbridge-Stewart, formally of the Scots Guards F Company, with finding more evidence of alien threats.[26]

On Hamilton's recommendation, Anne Travers began working for Department C19's Vault at a secret location in Chevoit Hills, Northumberland.[27]

(March) - LETH-ST: THE FORGOTTEN SON[28] ->
Following the London Event, the military helped coordinate the return of eight million people to the city. Hundreds of soldiers had died in the incident, but D-notices claimed that a major gas leak had occurred, and

had prompted bears to escape from the London Zoo.

The timelost piece of the Great Intelligence in Remington Manor – now wearing the form of Gordon Lethbridge-Stewart, Alistair's late brother – was dying, but felt revived by the activities of its younger self in the London Underground. It reanimated the corpse of Staff Sgt Albert Arnold, and arranged for the kidnapping of Alistair's mother Mary, intending to reclaim the pieces of itself in both of them. The Intelligence's Yeti encroached upon Bledoe, but Lethbridge-Stewart shot Arnold in the head, destroying the Intelligence-piece within. The weakened Intelligence died without its components, and its Yeti exploded.

Lethbridge-Stewart suspected that his late brother James had been reincarnated as Bledoe resident Owain Vine, and went with him to a match between Arsenal and Southampton at Highbury. The Intelligence's yeti had killed Owain's twin, Lewis, while he was looking for his brother.

1960s", then pauses to wonder if it was a different decade.

24 Dating the *Lethbridge-Stewart* novels – This book series, as authorised by Henry Lincoln and the estate of Mervyn Haisman (the two writers of *The Web of Fear*), details much of Colonel/Brigadier Lethbridge-Stewart's history prior to the first appearance of UNIT (*The Invasion*). The first release, *Leth-St: The Forgotten Son*, is a direct sequel to *The Web of Fear*, and also deals with the Great Intelligence following its defeat in *The Name of the Doctor*.

For better or worse, the series sets aside all the widely held UNIT Dating options in favour of one of its own: that *The Web of Fear* happened roughly concurrent to its real-life broadcast (3rd February to 9th March, 1968), but a year later, in 1969. That being the case, *Leth-St: The Grandfather Infestation* (ch13) and *Leth-St: Times-Squared* (ch10) claim that the London Event happened in "February".

The Forgotten Son itself takes place in the third week of March... the evacuation of London happened "at the end of last month" [February]/"almost a month ago" (chs. 3, 9), and *The Forgotten Son* opens "a week" after the public was officially allowed to return on "Friday 14th March" (ch1). Some days pass in the course of the book, and towards the end of it, Lethbridge-Stewart comments he had "never even heard of the Intelligence... not even a month ago" (ch12). The short story *Leth-St: "The Dogs of War"* reiterates that these events happened in "March".

The books to follow each take place in consecutive months... the second release (*Leth-St: The Schizoid Earth*) happens, give or take, in April; the third (*Leth-St: Beast of Fang Rock*) is May; and the ninth (*Leth-St: Mind of Stone*) ends at Christmas. (Presumably, the series could, in such a fashion, fill in the entire four-year gap between *The*

Web of Fear and the next time Lethbridge-Stewart sees the Doctor, in *The Invasion*.) The *Lethbridge-Stewart* novella *The Life of Evans* is an exception, in that it covers a wider swath of time, all marked out with the chapter headings, from "October 1969" to "March 1970".

The fifth release, *Leth-St: Moon Blink*, features the real-life moon landing in July 1969, and the sixth (*Leth-St: The Showstoppers*) ends with Lethbridge-Stewart being promoted to Brigadier and assuming command of the Home-Army Fifth Operation Corps (a pre-cursor to UNIT). See the individual entries for more.

25 *Leth-St: "The Enfolded Time"*

26 "Two months" before *Leth-St: Beast of Fang Rock* (Prologue), so in wake of *The Web of Fear*.

27 "A few months" before *Leth-St: Beast of Fang Rock*, in "March" (ch2), and "a month" before *Leth-St: "One Cold Step"*.

28 Dating *Leth-St: The Forgotten Son* (*Leth-St* novel #1) - This book, the first in a series of *Lethbridge-Stewart* novels authorised by Henry Lincoln and the estate of Mervyn Haisman (the two writers of *The Web of Fear*), details much of Colonel Lethbridge-Stewart's personal history. It is a direct sequel to *The Web of Fear*, and also deals with the Great Intelligence following its defeat in *The Name of the Doctor*.

Stray references leave no doubt that the year is 1969... BBC Radio 4 touts (ch4) that Lady Diana Cooper will be the next guest on *Desert Island Discs* (she featured there on 24th March, 1969); it's been "twenty-four" years (chs. 6, 8) and (presumably with benefit of rounding) "twenty years" (ch2) since 1945; and "thirty-one years" (ch8) and "over thirty years" (chs. 1, 9) since 1938. Tellingly, the book ends with Lethbridge-Stewart suggesting that he and Owain go to see Arsenal play Southampton at Highbury "this Saturday" – a match that happened on Saturday, 29th March, 1969.

THE HAISMAN ESTATE-APPROVED MULTIVERSE TIMELINE: As was the standard practice for British TV at the time, the BBC outright owns anything its salaried employees created for *Doctor Who* in the 1960s, 70s and 80s, but freelance writers wound up with the rights to any characters or concepts they originated. To that end, writers Henry Lincoln and the late Mervyn Haisman eventually came to own the characters they created in their trio of second Doctor scripts: *The Abominable Snowmen* (1967), *The Web of Fear* (1968) and *The Dominators* (1968).

The prize plum within those stories is Colonel (later Brigadier) Alistair Gordon Lethbridge-Stewart, one of the most enduring *Doctor Who* characters. In 2015, Candy Jar Books – as duly authorised by the Haisman estate and Lincoln – began publishing a series of novels starring Lethbridge-Stewart, with the supporting cast drawn from *The Abominable Snowmen* and *The Web of Fear* (notably Professor Edward Travers, his daughter Anne, the broadcaster Harold Chorley, Private Evans, the Yeti and the Great Intelligence), with the series later finding ways to include the Dominators and the Quarks.

... which is where things get a bit tangled, in that, as with the most lucrative piece of non-BBC-owned *Doctor Who* intellectual property – the Daleks – Lethbridge-Stewart and company are of rather limited value and use without their *Doctor Who* ties. But those *Doctor Who* ties are contingent on a whole host of pieces that Lincoln and the Haisman estate don't own, and which they can only refer to obliquely: UNIT, the Doctor, the TARDIS and so much else.

Also, any attempt to flesh out the Brigadier's background very quickly runs afoul of the UNIT Dating problem – even deciding when he was *born* gets thorny, in a world where fandom keeps arguing whether UNIT's debut in *The Invasion* takes place in 1968/1969, 1974 or 1979.

The *Lethbridge-Stewart* books have taken pains not to contradict, or at least to acknowledge, appearances by the Brigadier in other media. The *Lethbridge-Stewart* short story "Legacies" (reprinted in *Leth-St: The HAVOC Files*) laid out the *Lethbridge-Stewart* books' take on canon, while the short story "The Enfolded Time" (the same) offered a head-on remedy to the UNIT Dating hurly-burly. A couple of years later, the Haisman estate developed an Approved Multiverse Timeline to cement into place the disclosures of those stories, and further reiterate the personal histories of Lethbridge-Stewart, Edward Travers et al.

While the Haisman Timeline and that pair of short stories aren't altogether definitive (the argument over UNIT Dating, after all, won't suddenly vanish on the say-so of a spin-off book series), their arguments are worth considering in detail. To that end...

• **The Multiverse Theory (fronted in *Leth-St*: "Legacies"):** On paper, the Haisman Timeline spells out how the *Lethbridge-Stewart* books take place within one strand of a Multiverse: a plethora of parallel realities that bear a striking resemblance to one another. Which is to say: all realities reflect the "prime" timeline (the TV show), but there's some variances beyond that. "Legacies" also establishes that there's just the one Great Intelligence, extensions of which manifest in different ways throughout said realities. All of them have a nexus point, in which the Intelligence always winds up in Tibet and takes over Padmasambhava (*The Abominable Snowmen*).

In *practice*, "Legacies" isn't as grand-sweeping about canon as it might sound. Chiefly, it serves to throw a spotlight on three side appearances of the Great Intelligence – the audio *The Roof of the World*, the novel *Millennial Rites* and the independent film *Downtime* – and claim *they* happen in realities separate from that of the *Lethbridge-Stewart* books. Or, perhaps not even that. The Haisman Timeline, as it turns out, includes *Downtime*. Even if it's duplicated within a parallel reality as "Legacies" suggests, it's also still part of the *Lethbridge-Stewart* continuity. (Moreover, we know the Lethbridge-Stewart continuity doesn't ditch the *Doctor Who* novels wholesale, as it goes out of its way to encompass the EDA *Revolution Man*, Brigadier-General Adrienne Kramer from the EDA *Vampire Science* and the Vault that features in Gary Russell's novels, starting with *The Scales of Injustice*. Not to mention the Brigadier's first wife Fiona, as first seen in the latter book.) *The Roof of the World* is a somewhat stranger case, as it doesn't actually include the Great Intelligence, but instead concerns a group of "Great Old Ones" (no relation to the New Adventures class of monsters) and a mysterious pyramid hidden in Tibet.

The main losers in this continuity shell-game, then, are *Millennial Rites* and the trio of novels (*Happy Endings*, *The Shadows of Avalon* and *The King of Terror*) which collectively claimed that a "rejuvinated" Brigadier experienced some off-Earth adventures and didn't die until 2050. The TV show, however, had already contradicted this turn of events (with the Brig dying in *The Wedding of River Song* and returning as a Cyberman in *Death in Heaven*), meaning the Haisman Timeline is simply following its lead.

• **The UNIT Dating Solution (fronted in *Leth-St*: "The Enfolded Time"):** ... in which it's revealed that the TARDIS' multiple visits to Earth, as a freakish side-effect of the Ship's "damaged" engines, have resulted in two decades (1969-1989) being folded into a ten-year span without the participants noticing. The Accord, an entity devoted to stabilizing space-time, brings together three versions of the Brigadier to pre-emptively fortify the universe against the oncoming Last Great Time

continued on page 2049...

C-19's Vault took possession of some the fatalities of the London Event: Corporal Lane, Craftsman S. Weams and Staff Sgt Arnold.[29] The Vault procured samples of the Om-Tsor drug, as well as Ed Hill's body; Anne Travers intended to study his brain chemistry.[30] Harold Chorley's wife, Rosemary, divorced him.[31]

Albert, the son of Alistair Lethbridge-Stewart and Doris Bryden, was born in April.[32] In the same month, Professor Travers visited the monastery at Det-Sen.[33]

(14th April to 3rd May) - LETH-ST: THE SCHIZOID EARTH[34] -> The Vault funded a geological expedition led by Professor Edward Travers and his daughter Anne to Iceland. Colonel Lethbridge-Stewart set off for Tibet, but a *Phoenix* capsule struck his plane, and catapulted it to the Inferno Earth in 1959. He returned home via yet-another parallel Earth, 1945, with help from that world's Nikola Tesla. Afterward, General Hamilton asked the Colonel to look into the matter of Ed Hill – someone who had seemingly come back from the dead as the lead singer of the pop group Kathmandu...

Leslie Johnston, the Vault's second-in-command, kidnapped Professor Travers and slaved him to the remnants of the Great Intelligence's technology as an experiment.[35]

LETH-ST: "The Cult of the Grinning Man" -> Colonel Lethbridge-Stewart rescued an ambassador's daughter from the clutches of the all-too-human Cult of the Grinning Man.

In a letter to the Minister of Defence dated 13th May, Lethbridge-Stewart strongly advocated the creation of a watchdog group to deal with extraterrestrial incursions, but the Minister proved resistant, suggesting that a global threat would warrant a coordinated global response, and that perhaps NATO would be a better home for such a response team.[36]

(May) - LETH-ST: BEAST OF FANG ROCK[37] -> Owain Vine visited the Fang Rock lighthouse as it was set to reopen, in an event broadcast on BBC3, and involving the cast of BBC TV's *Doctor Omega* – including star Cyril Cusack – as a publicity gimmick.

The Rutan Host now had very limited time travel prow-

Several references reflect the pop culture of the mid to late 60s, including "Tin Soldier" by Small Faces (December 1967), "Lily the Pink" by The Scaffold (November 1968), the TV shows *Her Majesty's Pleasure* (1968-1969) and *Hugh and I* (1962-1967), and the spyshows *The Saint* (1962-1969) and *I Spy* (1965-1968). Lethbridge-Stewart and his fiancée Sally consider "Cinderella Rockefella" (released 28th February, 1968) as "their song".
29 *Leth-St: Beast of Fang Rock* (ch3), and after Arnold's temporary revival in *Leth-St: The Forgotten Son*.
30 *Leth-St: Beast of Fang Rock* (ch3).
31 *Leth-St: The Dreamer's Lament* (ch4); this happens "shortly after" *The Web of Fear*.
32 The Haisman Timeline
33 *Leth-St: "One Cold Step"*
34 Dating *Leth-St: The Schizoid Earth* (*Leth-St* novel #2) - The exact days of Lethbridge-Stewart's departure and return are given (ch14), and his aborted trip to Tibet follows on from the end of *Leth-St: The Forgotten Son*, which ended in March 1969. That it's still 1969 isn't really in doubt – Lethbridge-Stewart knows that things are awry in 1959 because it's the wrong decade precisely (ch5), and Anne Travers confirms that 2nd November, 1939 was "nearly thirty years ago" (ch4). Lethbridge-Stewart recalls reading something about Ed Hill in the papers "a couple of years ago" (in 1967; see the EDA *Revolution Man*).
Lethbridge-Stewart ends up spending four months in 1959 while only three weeks elapse before his return to 1969, which explains his remarks that the London Event was (for him) "a few months ago" (chs. 4, 6). A genuine anomaly is that Rudolf Hess – Hitler's Deputy

Fuhrer, and imprisoned after World War II – has a perforated ulcer, which he did in real life in December 1969.
35 "Almost four weeks" before *Leth-St: "The Dogs of War"*. *Leth-St: Mind of Stone* (ch10) says this happened in "May".
36 *Downtime*. The letter cites Lethbridge-Stewart as having been promoted to Brigadier, but this is at odds with the continuity of the *Lethbridge-Stewart* novels.
37 Dating *Leth-St: Beast of Fang Rock* (*Leth-St* novel #3) - It's "three weeks" (Prologue) after the end of *Leth-St: The Schizoid Earth*, during which time Ed Hill's death (*Revolution Man*) has occurred "five days ago" on "18th May, 1969" (chs. 1, 3, 6). It's "a couple of months" after *Leth-St: The Forgotten Son*, which happened in "March" (ch2). *Leth-St: Moon Blink* (ch9) takes place in July 1969, "two months" after Anne here meets Slant.
The year is given as "1969" (ch8); "sixty-seven years" after the 1902 events in *Horror of Fang Rock* (ch2); "a few years" after the Chameleon Tours incident in *The Faceless Ones* (ch6); and "146 years" after 1823 (ch13). Pop culture references include *The Dawntreader* from 1968 (ch2) and *The Fiddle and the Drum* and Fleetwood Mac's "Man of the World" from 1969 (chs. 2, 14). *The Web of Fear* happened "a few months ago" (ch12), in "February" (ch1), "nearly thirty-five years" (ch5) and "thirty-four years" (ch10) after events in *The Abominable Snowmen* in "1935" (ch5).
The Rutans now have osmic projector technology akin to that of the Sontarans in *The Time Warrior*. Lethbridge-Stewart is skeptical about the existence of time travel (ch4), which is consistent with his attitude throughout some of the third Doctor TV stories, but very strange considering how much of it he personally

continued from page 2047...

War – then uses the oldest Brig as a mule for a temporal marker, which calms history after 1st January, 1990.

"The Enfolded Time" is, in fact, a contender for the most meta and knowing *Doctor Who*-related story ever written, with the Brigadiers literally unable to say the name "Doctor" (for copyright reasons), contradicting themselves without noticing (the oldest Brig: "All that nonsense with [*Invasion of the Dinosaurs*] was in 1974. Two years before 1981.") and the confusion of the UNIT years abating – but not entirely ending, as *Battlefield* proves – at the start of 1990. That's within days of classic *Doctor Who* ending on TV, so being unable to create any more contradictions.

Most importantly, this story resolves the main paradigms of UNIT Dating (see the intro to the UNIT Era section) by, in essence, saying that they're *all* right.

# # # # #

Taking the Multiverse Theory at face value would mean that the *Lethbridge-Stewart* books exist in a separate continuity, and that the Alistair Gordon Lethbridge-Stewart they feature isn't actually the same one from the TV stories. Even though, as it happens, the books' Lethbridge-Stewart includes everything we know about the TV version. It would also mean consigning every scrap of evidence given in the *Lethbridge-Stewart* novels into alternate universe bubbles.

Taking *both* the Multiverse and the UNIT Dating theories at face value would mean, weirdly, that the UNIT Dating problem has indeed been solved... but only within the separate timeline of the *Lethbridge-Stewart* novels, and nowhere else. Which is not entirely helpful.

Do the *Lethbridge-Stewart* books take place in a pocket universe? *Leth-St: The Forgotten Son* and *Leth-St: Night of the Intelligence* (chs. 9, 15) go for that very interpretation, by claiming that the Great Intelligence accidentally shifted its own history – and created a whole new timeline – by travelling back to 1937 after its defeat in *The Name of the Doctor*, and causing James Lethbridge-Stewart to die about a decade too early. But for that, *Leth-St: Night of the Intelligence* (ch 14) says, the Intelligence would not have resurfaced until "1974". Said resurfacing actually happens in *The New Counter-Measures* Series 2.

Whether scripted on TV for the BBC, or in the Missing Adventures for Virgin Books, or in the *Lethbridge-Stewart* books for Candy Jar Books, the main beats of Alistair Lethbridge-Stewart's life story remain the same... he meets the second Doctor as a Colonel while battling the Great Intelligence, next meets him as a Brigadier in command of UNIT, he marries a woman named Fiona and they have a daughter named Kate, he divorces Fiona, he retires from UNIT, he teaches maths at Brendon, he marries his old flame Doris, Kate gives him a grandson named Gordon, he and Sarah Jane again defeat the Great Intelligence, he helps the Bannerman Road gang deal with Mrs Wormwood, he peacefully passes away in bed in 2011, and Kate becomes the head of UNIT.

Ahistory's mandate is to be as all-inclusive as possible – this book is essentially a parlour game attempting to explain how thousands of odd, contradictory "facts" about the *Doctor Who* universe actually all fit together. As such, we try to avoid invoking parallel universes, alternate timelines or blaming everything on the Time War. Therefore, we have decided to place the *Lethbridge-Stewart* books within the UNIT Era section and treat them as part of the overall *Doctor Who* universe.

ess, having procured osmic projector technology from the Sontarans. On Ruta Three, the Rutan Queen continued to strategically withdraw from Mutter's Spiral, but considered Earth, a Level Five world, as a possible jump-point for a final assault against the Sontarans. A Rutan mothership was dispatched to reconnoiter the locale.

In accordance with history's dictates, the Rutan scout posing as solicitor Rupert Slant passed along its osmic projector to Anne Travers on 2nd May, 1969, along with a forged letter from her great-great-great grandfather Archibald Goff. Suspected Rutan activity prompted Lethbridge-Stewart and Anne to go to the Fang Rock lighthouse, where Anne found the osmic projector piece secured for her by Ben Travers in 1902.

Anne's uses of the osmic projector resulted in a Rutan scout replicating due to binary fusion, and its two selves being thrown back to Fang Rock in 1822 and 1902. A second use of the projector briefly sent Anne herself back to 1823. Upon her return, a third use of the projector sent

the Rutan mothership back to 1902, where the fourth Doctor destroyed it as history recorded.

Slant thought it time to move on, and adopted another guise. Anne's interaction with Slant caused her to absorb the Rutan translation matrix, meaning she could now understand any language.

The Vault acquired Rutan technology from the Fang Rock incident.[38] By now, Ian Gilmore and Rachel Jensen had married.[39] General Hamilton advised Lethbridge-Stewart to consult with Air-Marshal Gilmore.[40]

(May) - LETH-ST: "The Dogs of War"[41] -> Vice-Marshal Ian Gilmore was "just about on the good side of fifty", and had a seven-year gap in his service record. Suspicious of the Vault General's intentions, Gilmore met with Lethbridge-Stewart in the John Braham Room of the Alexander Club, and provided him with files on the Home Army Operation Corps and alien incursions at Gatwick, a

---

experienced in *Leth-St: The Schizoid Earth*, the discrepancy being explained as Lethbridge-Stewart having foggy memories of the latter owing to psychoactive drugs he was given while captive in the alt-Germany.

In real life, *Doctor Omega* (1906) by Arnould Galopin involves the scientist Doctor Omega and his friends in adventures aboard the spaceship *Cosmos*. The original illustrations of Doctor Omega coincidentally look like William Hartnell.

38 *Leth-St: Mutually Assured Domination* (ch1).

39 "A few years" before *Leth-St: "The Dogs of War"*, but contradicting what's seen of the characters in the *Counter-Measures* audios.

40 *Leth-St: Beast of Fang Rock*, leading into *Leth-St: "The Dogs of War"*, and in advance of Lethbridge-Stewart and Gilmore having a chat in *Downtime*.

41 Dating *Leth-St: "The Dogs of War"* (*Leth-St* short story #5) - It's "three days" since *Beast of Fang Rock* (ch1), and there's mention of "Summer weather". *Leth-St: Moon Blink* and the Haisman Timeline specify that Lethbridge-Stewart met with Gilmore in "May". *Leth-St: Night of the Intelligence* dates Travers' rescue to that same month.

42 *Leth-St: Night of the Intelligence*

43 "Five years" before *The Isos Network*

44 Dating *Leth-St: Mutually Assured Domination* (*Leth-St* novel #4) - The blurb reiterates that "It's the summer of '69". The story begins one week after *Leth-St: "The Dogs of War"* (ch1), and ends mid-June, with chapter five citing the month, and events reaching their climax on the "Saturday" after "Friday 13th" (ch15, Epilogue). *Leth-St: The Schizoid Earth* happened a "couple of months ago" in "April" (ch2), and it's "six months" since Dominex incorporated on "5th January, 1968" (ch3).

Mention is made of a Mercedes Benz W115 (ch12), which was introduced in 1968. The US Embassy in

London was "built only nine years ago" (ch1, in 1960), and the Cuban Missile Crisis (October 1962) happened "almost seven years ago" (ch1). The briefly seen character "Josh", a disheveled man "redolent of pigs" (ch3), is pretty clearly Pigbin Josh – the doomed tramp seen in *The Claws of Axos*.

45 Dating *Planet of Giants* (2.1) and *Leth-St: "House of Giants"* (*Leth-St: HAVOC Files* #2.2) - The year isn't specified on screen in *Planet of Giants*, although the setting is contemporary. Forester lives in a rural area (*Leth-St: "House of Giants"* names this as Mevagissey, a small town in Cornwall), and a switchboard operator still mans the local telephone exchange. "House of Giants" happens "straight after" *Planet of Giants*, and folds the TV story into the UNIT timeline. The Haisman Timeline gives the month as "June".

46 *Downtime*

47 Dating *Leth-St: "The Black Eggs of Khufu"/"The Band of Evil"* (*Leth-St: The HAVOC Files* #2.3-2.4) - A header says that "Black Eggs" happens during the prologue of *Leth-St: Moon Blink*; "Band of Evil" happens "shortly before *The Showstoppers*". The Haisman Timeline places both stories in "July".

48 Dating *Leth-St: Moon Blink* (*Leth-St* novel #5) - The novel plays out in the month of July 1969. The Prologue opens to "a new month", Anne and her father watch the moon landing on 20th July, and it's "a week" later when Patricia Richards shows up on Anne's doorstep. The British Space Programme has just launched Mars Probe 5; the crisis in *The Ambassadors of Death* revolves around Mars Probe 7. In real life, NASA investigated anomalies on the moon's surface as part of Project Moon-Blink (1965-1966).

49 *Leth-St: Moon Blink*. Brendan appeared in *K9 and Company*.

South Wales holiday camp and the Shoreditch Incident. Lethbridge-Stewart and Gilmore assumed that the Doctors they'd encountered, respectively the second and the seventh, were one and the same. As Gilmore expected, the files baited the General's operatives, enabling him and Lethbridge-Stewart to rescue Professor Travers from an underground citadel near Shoreditch Railway Station.

Travers' mental faculties declined as a result of Johnston's experiments, but – as Travers was in his seventies – this was mistaken for the onset of dementia.[42] The people of Isos II, a colony of the planet Isos, were cyber-converted and became the Cybermen allied with Tobias Vaughn.[43]

(June) - LETH-ST: MUTUALLY ASSURED DOMINATION[44] -> The corporate front for the Dominators, Dominex Industries, had emerged as the UK's biggest recipient of nuclear waste, on promises to convert it into cheap energy with a new process, Negative Mass Flux Absorption. The Dominators brainwashed Harold Chorley into serving as their media consultant. Colonel Lethbridge-Stewart discovered that the Dominators intended to spark a conflict between the West and the East that would turn Earth into a radioactive cinder: a means of refuelling the Dominator warfleet. Lethbridge-Stewart and his allies put paid to the Dominators' operations, leading to Director Vaar's arrest and the Vault acquiring the surviving Quarks. The female counterparts of the Dominators, the Domina, tracked the Dominator Warfleet and ordered its destruction.

By leveraging the Dominex and Fang Rock incidents, Vice-Marshall Gilmore and General Hamilton named Lethbridge-Stewart as commander of the Home-Army Fifth Operational Corps (HAVOC): a group charged with protecting the United Kingdom against alien incursions. The group operated from an old LONGBOW facility beneath Edinburgh Castle. Lethbridge-Stewart's grandfather lived in Scotland at this time.

(June) - PLANET OF GIANTS / LETH-ST: "House of Giants"[45] -> A government inspector, Arnold Farrow, told the industrialist Forester that the insecticide his company had developed would not be approved for production. The scientist Smithers, obsessed by the idea of ending world famine, had succeeded over the last year in creating an insecticide 60% more powerful than anything on the market. It could even stop locusts breeding, but tests showed that it killed all insect life, even those vital to the ecology. Forester murdered Farrow, but was arrested by the local policeman, Bert Rowse.

The TARDIS doors opened during materialisation, reducing the Ship and those within – the first Doctor, Ian, Barbara and Susan – to miniature size. The travel-

lers departed, and returned to normal, as Forester was apprehended...

The authorities took Farrow's body away. Colonel Lethbridge-Stewart, Corporal Bill Bishop and Anne Travers secured the remaining quantities of DN6, but only after the TARDIS' residual energy had shrunk – albeit temporarily – Anne and the Colonel.

Six months after the London Event, Lethbridge-Stewart met Air Vice-Marshal "Chunky" Gilmore in the Alexander Club and learnt that Earth had been invaded in the winter of 1963. Gilmore had spent five years lobbying the UK government along the lines Lethbridge-Stewart had proposed, and had recently attracted some interest in the idea from the United Nations. Lethbridge-Stewart also learned there was evidence of aliens visiting Earth since the time of the Pharaohs.[46]

(July) - LETH-ST: "The Black Eggs of Khufu" / LETH-ST: "The Band of Evil"[47] -> Lethbridge-Stewart went to Egypt and stopped Russian agents – at one point by weaponising a camel with a rocket launcher – from tapping alien energy within the Pyramid of Khufu. Later, aliens from the war-torn planet Termoli usurped the band Totem Pole's performances to procure human slaves. At the Empire Pool in Wembley, Lethbridge-Stewart, Captain Derek Younghusband and Corporal Sally Wright overcame the Termolians with a combination of bullets and hairspray. Younghusband joined the Fifth Operational Corps.

(July) - LETH-ST: MOON BLINK[48] -> Lethbridge-Stewart was briefed on a top-secret secret operation: the British Space Programme, as led by Professor Ralph Cornish. They and the British Rocket Group had their sights on Mars, and had just launched Mars Probe 5. On 20th July, Anne Travers watched the official moon landing on TV with her father, who fell asleep in his chair. The shapechanging Rupert Slant was now posing as his own niece, Ruby Slant.

The covert American and Russian lunar mining operations came across aliens from the planet Theia in the Terrae Highlands, and dubbed them the Terrae. The ashes of dead Terrae, a.k.a. Moon Blink, enabled those who imbibed it to sense the presence of disguised aliens. Anne Travers and Lance Corporal Bill Bishop helped some Terrae to elude Russian operatives and escape back into space. The Terrae named Dr Patricia Richards, an astrobiologist, as the guardian of a Terrae child, Brayn Dun.

General Hamilton ended Anne's involvement with the Vault, and appointed her the Head of Scientific Research at the Home-Army Fifth Operation Corps.

Brayn Dun grew up to become Brendan Richards, Lavinia Smith's ward.[49]

(August) - LETH-ST: THE SHOWSTOPPERS[450] -> The Factotum, a blending of a siphonophore and the Nazi scientist Vilhelm Schadengeist, generated biological human-clones that infiltrated broadcaster LWT. One of the duplicates, "actor Aubrey Mondegreene", was to play sixteen roles in the spyshow *William Lovac's BLIMEY!* (British Led Intelligence Monitoring and Espionage Yard). Colonel Lethbridge-Stewart, Anne Travers and their allies stopped the Factotum from broadcasting that China had committed a nuclear attack, which would trigger World War Three. The final confrontation between them was aired live as the *BLIMEY!* pilot, but dismissed as a nonsensical piece of television. The siphonephore's mind took control, and dragged its body – with a protesting Schadengeist – back into the sea. Samson Ware, a friend of Lethbridge-Stewart, was currently employed as a TV stuntman.

Lethbridge-Stewart was promoted to Brigadier.[51]

Brigadier Lethbridge-Stewart and the Fifth Operational Corps

(September) - LETH-ST: THE GRANDFATHER INFESTATION[52] -> The Fifth Operational Corps formally opened Dolerite Base: their new headquarters in a refitted Longbow facility under Edinburgh Castle. Private Gwynfor Evans and Corporal Sally Wright had joined the Corps, as had Samson Ware as a warrant officer, first class. About fifty people staffed Dolerite Base, with a modified Hercules Transport serving as the Corps' mobile HQ. Peyton Bryden's electronics company was now second only to International Electromatics in the world markets.

Extraterrestrial silicon-based plants, the Grandfathers, developed a rudimentary intelligence and coveted Earth's soil for their offspring. The Grandfathers worked to ignite oil fields in the North Sea and the Middle East, to change Earth to their liking through global warming. On the Corps' first official mission, Brigadier Lethbridge-Stewart, Anne Travers and their allies killed most of the Grandfathers with the potent insecticide DN6, then blew up their spaceship.

In September, armed men stole Yeti equipment from a

50 Dating *Leth-St: The Showstoppers* (*Leth-St* novel #6) - It's "two months" (ch1) after *Leth-St: Mutually Assured Domination*. A riot in Belfast happened "last night" (ch3); historically, riots there drug on from 12th-17th April, 1969. Anne, assigned to the Vault in *Leth-St: Moon Blink*, has been waiting "two weeks" (ch1) for equipment for her new laboratory. *The Web of Fear* happened "a few months back" (ch2). Bill Filer (*The Claws of Axos*) here appears as one of Lethbridge-Stewart's American contacts.

51 *Leth-St: The Showstoppers* , as first seen in *The Invasion*.

52 Dating *Leth-St: The Grandfather Infestation* (*Leth-St* novel #7) - It's "a few months" (ch1) after the Moon landing (*Leth-St: Moon Blink*, in May), and "a month" (chs. 7, 14) since *Leth-St: The Showstoppers*. It's thought that Jimi Hendrix will "never last" in the music business; he died 18th September, 1970. DN6 featured in *Planet of Giants*, International Electromatics in *The Invasion*.

53 *Leth-St: The Life of Evans* (ch6).

54 *Leth-St: Night of the Intelligence* (ch4).

55 *Leth-St: The Dreamer's Lament* (ch13).

56 Dating *Leth-St:* "The Last Duty" (*Leth-St: HAVOC Files* #3.2) - A tag line says it's "shortly before the novel *Times Squared*".The Haisman Timeline says it's September.

57 *Leth-St: The Dreamer's Lament* (ch13), and – assuming Douglas and Erickson aren't referencing separate Bandril attacks –"almost six weeks" before *Leth-St: Mind of Stone* (ch13).

58 Dating *Leth-St: Times Squared* (*Leth-St* novel #8) - It's

"late October 1969" (ch4), *Leth-St: The Grandfather Infestation* was "last month" (ch1), and Sally's copy of *Look* magazine is "dated 10th June... four months old" (ch1).The Haisman Timeline dates this book to "October 25-26". Kramer, a brigadier-general in *Vampire Science*, erroneously thinks it's "just months" (ch15) after the Summer of Love (that happened in 1967).

59 *Leth-St: Night of the Intelligence* (ch15).

60 Dating *Leth-St: Blood of Atlantis* (*Leth-St* novel #9) - No time-frame given, but – as is the habit with the Lethbridge-Stewart novels – it's probably the month after the last book (*Leth-St:Times Squared*). Anne Travers mentions *Chariots of the Gods?* (sic), released in 1968. The design of the fake Atlantis seen here stems from popular imagination, so has nothing to do with the other Atlantises in the *Doctor Who* universe (see The Fall of Atlantis sidebar).

61 Dating *Leth-St:* "The Fright Before Christmas" (*Leth-St: HAVOC Files* #1.8) - It's Christmas Eve, in the first year of the *Lethbridge-Stewart* novels.

62 *Leth-St:* "The Feast of Evans", *Leth-St:* "Home for Christmas".

63 Dating *Leth-St:* "Slouching Towards Det-Sen" (*Leth-St HAVOC Files* #3.7) - The day is given.

64 Dating *Leth-St: Mind of Stone* (*Leth-St* novel #10) - The book opens on "a typical late November in London" (ch1); events in *Leth-St: Blood of Atlantis* happened "earlier in the month" (ch2). Chapter 7 sees Anne rip away a calendar sheet at the start of December, and the con job on Godfrey plays out over some days. Johnson

Fifth convoy en route to Edinburgh.[53] Sally Wright apologised to her half-brother, Gweynfor Evans, for taking so much of her frustration with their father out on him.[54] Jeffrey Robert Erickson, a geomorphologist, joined Anne Travers' science team in September.[55]

(September) - LETH-ST: "The Last Duty"[56] -> Captain Derek Younghusband told his cousin, Eileen Younghusband, about a recent incident in which a virulent alien fungus consumed one of Lethbridge-Stewart's men, Private Dockery, but he retained the mental wherewithal to destroy the creature from within.

Colonel Walter Douglas and Jeff Erickson encountered ferocious Bandrils in the Argyll Highlands.[57]

(late October) - LETH-ST: THE LIFE OF EVANS -> A despairing Brigadier Lethbridge-Stewart reassigned the hapless Private Gwynfor Evans to 2 Battalion in Imber, near Stonehenge, for basic training. Captain Younghusband determined that Evans had trust issues, so assigned Private Tommy Godber to become his friend.

(25th-26th October) - LETH-ST: TIMES SQUARED[58] -> Lieutenant Adrienne Kramer, age 24, was currently assigned to the United Nations Security Taskforce, and married to the architect George Kramer.

The Great Intelligence calculated that one million human minds might compensate for its having failed to lay claim to the Doctor's. The Intelligence's Yetis in New York, as overseen by its servant Jemba-wa, were tasked with disabling the city's pumps. This would flood the subway system, driving millions of Intelligence-linked rats to the surface, where their bites would put people under the Intelligence's thrall.

Brigadier Lethbridge-Stewart, Sally Wright and Owain Vine tried to vacation together in New York, and assisted Lt Kramer with overcoming the Intelligence's Yeti. As Owain already contained a portion of the Intelligence's soul, he repelled it from New York. A defiant Jemba-wa perished without the Intelligence's support, but used the last of his life energy to send the time-displaced, younger Edward Travers back some decades, where he encountered HG Wells. Dylan Gore, under the cover name "Simon" and on orders from his father, began to inveigle his way into Owain Vine's life.

With his younger self's return to the past, the older Travers regained his memories of living in 1960s New York.[59]

(November) - LETH-ST: BLOOD OF ATLANTIS[60] -> A silicon-based lifeform fell to Earth in a meteorite, and sought to spread itself far and wide. In conjunction with

Rolph Vorster, a South African mining magnate, a faux version of Atlantis was constructed to trick interested parties into spreading the lifeform through "artefacts" such as a statue of the Snake Goddess. As directed by Brigadier Lethbridge-Stewart, the British Near East Defence Force in Akrotiri launched a nuclear strike that destroyed the fake Atlantis and eradicated the lifeform.

(late November to 24th December) - LETH-ST: MIND OF STONE[61] -> Hugh Godfrey, a major crimelord, had possession of the extraterrestrial rock stolen from Colonel Pemberton's detachment, but was currently jailed at the Wormwood Scrubs Prison. In collusion with Major General Oliver Hamilton, Lethbridge-Stewart was charged with unspecified war offences and incarcerated there, to gain Godfrey's confidence. The alien consciousness within the rock, Rakis of the planet Glastra, possessed Godfrey's body. Rakis tried to syphon electricity to better manifest, and vowed to take over Earth, so Lethbridge-Stewart caused a power-overload that turned him into ash.

Leslie Johnson, a Vault operative assigned to spy on Lethbridge-Stewart, tried and failed to kill the Brigadier on a train. General Gore had Johnson killed for overreaching himself.

Anne Travers was friends with Cambridge's Liz Shaw. For Christmas, Owain Vine was off at a meditation centre in Kyoto.

(December) - LETH-ST: THE LIFE OF EVANS -> Two feathered aliens, Dimas and Saka, examined Stonehenge while on their honeymoon. The mobster Lomax captured them, acquiring their laser-beam and anti-gravity device. Including Dimas and Sara, four hundred forty aliens were active on Earth, largely as observers.

(24th December) - LETH-ST: "The Fright Before Christmas"[62] -> On Christmas Eve, Lethbridge-Stewart defended Buckingham Palace against spheres of unknown origin, which had been causing people to spontaneously combust.

Brigadier Lethbridge-Stewart, his associates and family members otherwise enjoyed a relatively peaceful Christmas – save that Gwynfor Evans and Samson Ware had to dispatch some hostile aliens with pine needle sap.[63]

(28th December) - LETH-ST: "Slouching Toward Det-Sen"[64] -> On December 28th, the Vault abducted Professor Travers as he travelled to Tibet. Abbot Thonmi helped Travers "escape" by taking his mind onto the astral plane.

UNIT Year -3

At some point, Gwanzulum shapechangers attempted to infiltrate the Fifth Operational Corps.[65]

(17th-22nd, 27th January) - LETH-ST: NIGHT OF THE INTELLIGENCE[66] **->** By now, Lethbridge-Stewart's Granny McDougal had been deceased for "many years". Captain Sam Hawkins, as the Vault's Quartermaster, spied on the group for General Hamilton.

The head of the Vault, General Gore (a.k.a. James Lethbridge-Stewart from Inferno-Earth), advanced upon his plan to open an interstitial gateway back in time, to stop his wife Rachel Jensen from dying. Already in possession of Professor Travers' body, Gore kidnapped Owain Vine and – given his and Travers' connection to the Great Intelligence – wired them into an apparatus with six Acteon crystals. Gore opened a gateway that accidentally threatened to loose Sunyata – the not-self, a hungering

void – upon the world. Although the Great Intelligence functioned as Sunyata's mind, it too would be destroyed, along with all of time and reality, if its ravenous aspect prevailed. It sided with the astral-walking Padmasambhava, Edward Travers and Owain Vine against itself.

Sunyata's attempt to enter our reality caused earthquakes and disasters all over Northumberland, leveling Northumberland National Park and heavily damaging the Cheviot Hills. The Intelligence distracted Sunyata by entering Travers' body, allowing Padmasambhava to unleash his true self – this caused an energy burst that destroyed the gateway and banished Sunyata, but heavily damaged Travers' form. The Intelligence/Travers wrapped itself in a protective cocoon of machinery, and Lethbridge-Stewart's team opted to restrain the Intelligence by filling the Vault's gateway room with concrete.

Professor Travers communed with Anne on the astral plane, and said a final goodbye. General Gore retreated to an off-the-books installation in Norwich. Department C19

---

attempts to kill Lethbridge-Stewart in mid-December, then "over two weeks" pass (ch15), and the Epilogue falls on Christmas Eve.

David Bowie's "Space Oddity" plays on a radio (ch12); it was released 11th July 1969.

65 *Leth-St:* "The Enfolded Time". The Gwanzulum appeared in "Planet of the Dead" (*DWM*).

66 Dating *Leth-St: Night of the Intelligence* (*Leth-St* novel #11) - The book opens in "January" (ch1), "three weeks" after Travers' kidnapping on "December 28th" (Prologue). Chapter Six gives the day as "Monday 19 January", with the story beginning the Saturday before that (there's talk of a "Sunday roast" tomorrow, ch2) and ending on Thursday (ch16). The Haisman Timeline places the Epilogue on "January 27". A flashback in Chapter 14 glitches a little, claiming "It was 1941 and Anne [Travers] was four", when she was born in October 1938.

An election is forthcoming (in 1970, that happened 18th June). *Electronic Sound* (released 9th May, 1969) stands as George Harrison's most recent album (ch3). Rumours claim the Beatles will be splitting up soon – although Paul McCartney formally filed for their dissolution on 31st December, 1970, we're already past the point of their last live performance (30th January, 1969, atop the Apple Corps building in London). Martyn Townsend commands the Vault in *The Scales of Injustice*. Hawkins appears in *Doctor Who and the Silurians*.

67 The Haisman Timeline, and as foreshadowed in *Leth-St: Night of the Intelligence* (ch15).

68 Dating *Leth-St: The Life of Evans* (*Leth-St* novella #1) - The Haisman Timeline names the day.

69 The Prologue names the month, and says that Evans participated in *The Web of Fear* "one short year" ago.

70 Dating *Leth-St: The Daughters of Earth* (*Leth-St* novel

#12) - The month is given, and a few days elapse from start to finish, but there's conflicting clues as to *which* days specifically. The Haisman Timeline claims it's "February 21-23, 25", but Anne mentions (ch5) it's the Brigadier's birthday "in a few days", so it should be earlier. Going the other direction, Chapter Four sees Judith speak at the Inaugural Women's Liberation conference in Manchester – that happened 27th February to 1st March, 1970. A jukebox plays the Jackson 5's "I Want You Back" (released October 7, 1969).

71 "A couple of weeks" before *Leth-St: The Dreamer's Lament*.

72 Dating *Leth-St: The Dreamer's Lament* (*Leth-St* novel #13) - Professor Travers was lost "six weeks ago" (ch1) in *Leth-St: Night of the Intelligence*, and it's "half a year" since September (ch13). For the duration of *The Dreamer's Lament*, two weeks pass in the outside world while the Brigadier and Chorley experience just two days within the Triangle.

73 Dating *Leth-St: The Life of Evans* (*Leth-St* novella #1) - The Haisman Timeline says this happens "March 26".

74 Dating *Leth-St: The Flaming Soldier* (*Leth-St* novella #2) - The month and year are repeatedly given as "April 1970".

75 *Leth-St:* "The Enfolded Time". The Haisman Timeline says the Brigadier and Fiona re-meet one another, and start a romance, in 1971.

76 *The Scales of Injustice* (p61, p131), which claims the Brig and Fiona are married for eight years. The Haisman Timeline says it was four at most.

DORIS AND THE WRISTWATCH: According to *Planet of the Spiders*, Doris gave the Brigadier a wristwatch as a token of her affection "eleven years" ago, presumably as a memento of their lost weekend together in Brighton (the one that a psychic studying the watch airs aloud, to the Doctor's amusement). The Haisman

was given control of the rogue Vault; Martyn Townsend became its new head.

Lethbridge-Stewart helped Dylan Gore to become officially recognized as Dylan Jensen Lethbridge-Stewart, the son of James Lethbridge-Stewart. Owain Vine legally changed his name to Owain Lethbridge-Stewart.

At some point, the time-travelling version of Edward Travers, in his mid-forties, returned to this era. He spent much of his time in Scotland, then America.[67]

(22nd January) - LETH-ST: THE LIFE OF EVANS[68] **->** Private Evans' best friend, Tommy Godber, died while trying to rescue the Brigadier's nephew Owain from the Vault. The mobster Lomax started robbing bank vaults with his stolen alien laser.

(February) - LETH-ST: THE LIFE OF EVANS[69] **->** A Glassa cybernetic hybrid, needing a new host body after more than four millennia of service, captured a tipsy Evans as he left The Bell Inn. The Glassa sifted through Evans' memories, and refashioned its warrior persona into a copy of Evans' body. As such, the warrior impersonated Evans while assessing Earth's fitness as a Glassa breeding world.

UNIT Year -3 (February) - LETH-ST: THE DAUGHTERS OF EARTH[70] **->** The Brigadier and Sally Wright travelled separately to holiday near Edinburgh, but Sally crashed while swerving to avoid a deer. She became sympathetic toward a women's advocacy group, The Daughters of Earth, after its members found and cared for her. A fugitive alien fungus had possessed the Daughters' leader, Judith Edgley, as she drank Scotch one evening – through her, the fungus murdered and consumed a growing number of victims. Judith's body evolved into a winged creature, and she escaped when Anne Travers and William Bishop confronted her.

Although Sally was cleared of having compromised military secrets with the Daughters, the Brigadier's resentment at having his fiancee under his command prompted him to end their engagement. Sally agreed, telling the Brig she'd never really loved him.

Anne Travers and Bill Bishop had their first date – a successful outing, even though they had to deal with some Silhouettes.[71]

(March) - LETH-ST: THE DREAMER'S LAMENT[72] **->** Anne Travers informed her brother Alun about the loss of their father. Prior to this, Alun's wife Julia and daughter Anna-Margaret had died in a car crash on the M4. Anne also notified her Uncle Vincent's children – Deborah, Joe and Patrick – of her father's passing. Sally Wright was reassigned to administrative duties at Imber base. The Brigadier

had recently returned to Bledoe to deal with a Comfort Bot.

The Keynsham Triangle, a slow-time area in the middle of the British countryside, steadily expanded and claimed the 23.45 train from Paddington to Bristol Temple Meads. Harold Chorley enlisted the Brigadier's help with the mystery, and they entered the Triangle as the Loa governing it generated a small army of the undead, intending to take over Earth. The Brigadier killed Zara, the Loa's host, thus terminating the zombies and collapsing the Triangle.

Edward Travers was formally laid to rest on 25th March, with only a select few knowing that his coffin contained Zara's body.

(26th March) - LETH-ST: THE LIFE OF EVANS[73] **->** The Glassa masquerading as Private Evans displayed such heroism while ending Lomax's criminal operations, an impressed Brigadier Lethbridge-Stewart promoted "Evans" to Lance Corporal. The real Evans taught the Glassa's warrior component the value of self-interest, severing its link with its Frame operating system. Liberated, Evans depowered the Frame and sent a final report to any surviving Glassa: *Stay away. [Earth] is unsafe.* The Brigadier considered what to do with Evans' double, which had reverted into the form of a humanoid lizard.

(April) - LETH-ST: THE FLAMING SOLDIER[74] **->** Captain Eileen Younghusband met Brigadier Lethbridge-Stewart as the Flight, having time-jumped from 1942, reclaimed their lost control-coins. The items enabled the Flight to open a temporal portal to 1942 – a means of returning to their homeworld, but which, when complete, would obliterate Earth. Major James Randall, Younghusband's acquaintance for a quarter-century, thwarted the Flight by taking three of the coins back to 1942, but died on arrival. The portal's collapse destroyed the Duke Guest House hotel, and possibly killed the Flight. Younghusband gave up being a hotelier.

UNIT Year -2

Doris Bryden, the Brigadier's old flame, met George Wilson when her son Albert was two. Doris and George later married (and Albert's surname officially became "Wilson") – by which point, the Brigadier was married to a woman named Fiona Campbell. George Wilson was killed, not many years later, in Northern Ireland.[75]

Lethbridge-Stewart married Fiona and they set up home in Gerrards Cross. The day after the wedding, Lethbridge-Stewart bumped into an old flame, Doris, in Brighton. **Doris gave the Brigadier a wristwatch**, officially as a wedding gift, but he suspected she meant it **as a token of her affection for him.**[76] He attended a Middle East Peace Conference.[77]

UNIT Year -1

Kate Lethbridge-Stewart, the daughter of Alistair Lethbridge-Stewart and his wife Fiona, **was born.**[78] William Bishop and Anne Travers married, and she took his name.[79]

The Founding of United Nations Intelligence Taskforce

Aware that the world faced new threats, the United Nations Intelligence Taskforce (UNIT) **was established.**[80] Lethbridge-Stewart appeared before the UN Security Council and, in part, UNIT was formed because of his efforts.[81] The Russian branch of UNIT was called Operativnaya Gruppa Rasvedkoy Obyedinyonnih Natsiy (OGRON).[82] The French branch was called NUIT.[83] UNIT had a liaison office in Bombay.[84] There was also a South East Asian branch, UNIT-SEA.[85]

Enabling legislation was passed in the UK (it was drafted by the future Minister for Ecology).[86] Alistair Gordon Lethbridge-Stewart, the Scots Guards Colonel who had led the soldiers that repelled the Yetis in the Underground, had been promoted to Brigadier and made commanding officer of the British UNIT contingent.[87] The Brigadier was present when UNIT took ownership of Kriegeskind Castle in Germany, and made it one of dozens of worldwide UNIT facilities that watched for signs of invasion, the paranormal and the unexplained.[88]

Gas warfare was banned by international agree-

Timeline puts those events in the same ballpark, but technically places it ten years beforehand.

The Scales of Injustice elaborates to say that Doris gave the Brig the watch the day after his marriage to Fiona – officially as a wedding gift, but probably with an undercurrent of love for him. If so, she neglects, at that juncture, to mention having given birth to their son Albert – which would be in keeping with the *Lethbridge-Stewart* novels, in which the Brigadier doesn't learn that Albert exists until 1990.

77 *The Paradise of Death.* This happened "just before he joined UNIT".

THE BRIGADIER'S FAMILY: Cumulatively, and unless further details come to light, Alistair Lethbridge-Stewart in his lifetime has two wives (Fiona, then Doris), three children (Kate, Albert and Mariama) and at least six grandchildren.

The Brigadier and his first wife, Fiona (a name thought up by Nicholas Courtney, who plays the Brigadier) had the most prominent of the Brig's offspring – a daughter named Kate, who first appears in the independent films *Downtime* and *Daemons: Daemos Rising*, and later becomes the head of UNIT in the new series (*The Power of Three*, et al). Kate was a child during the UNIT era, when the Lethbridge-Stewarts split up. (The Brigadier and Fiona separate in *The Scales of Injustice*, and he is sleeping alone by *The Daemons*.) By the mid-nineties, Kate is a single mother looking after her son Gordon (*Downtime*). In *Death in Heaven*, she refers to herself as a "divorcee, mother of two". We're told nothing else about her second child.

By *Battlefield* [c.1997], the Brigadier has married Doris, an old flame first mentioned in *Planet of the Spiders*. (They shared a weekend in Brighton eleven years before that story – perhaps before Alistair was married to Fiona.) The *Lethbridge-Stewart* novels (and the Haisman Timeline governing them) claim that owing to said fling, Doris became pregnant with their son Albert – something she kept quiet about, and solved by marrying a man named George Wilson (later killed in Northern Ireland). The Brigadier didn't know about Albert for many years, and only meets him on New Year's Day, 1990 (Leth-St: "The Enfolded Time"). Albert, in turn, gives the Brigadier three grandchildren: Conall (born July 1990), Nick (c.1995) and Lucy (c.2003). Lucy stars in *The Lucy Wilson Mysteries*, a *Lethbridge-Stewart* spin-off.

The New Adventures feature one other descendant of the Brigadier: Kadiatu Lethbridge-Stewart, who first appears in *Transit*, and reappears in *Set Piece, The Also People, So Vile a Sin* and *Benny: The Final Amendment*. Kadiatu hails from a line of Lethbridge-Stewarts descended from young Alistair's liaison with Chief Yembe's daughter, Mariatu, in Sierra Leone. An early draft of *The Also People* had more details of the Lethbridge-Stewart line.

We can deduce that Mariatu had a son, Mariama (he is unnamed in *Transit*, but the name appears in the early draft of *The Also People*, where his mother was mistakenly referred to as "Isatu"). He had a daughter, Kadiatu, who became an historian (she is first referred to in the *Remembrance of the Daleks* novelisation, and also in *Set Piece*). She had a son Gibril, who also had a son called Gibril (from the draft of *The Also People*). Gibril had a son, Yembe (seen in *Transit*), and he adopted Kadiatu in 2090. Kadiatu, then, is the Brigadier's great-great-great-great-granddaughter, and this is consistent with *Transit* (p96) where "five generations" separate Kadiatu from Alistair.

78 Kate first appears in *Downtime*. The Haisman Timeline dates her birth to 1972. Jemma Redgrave, who plays the character, was born 14th January, 1965.

79 The Haisman Timeline, *Leth-St:* "The Two Brigadiers".

80 *The Invasion*. UNIT is not set up specifically to fight aliens, but to "investigate the unexplained". The independent film *Wartime* says that UNIT was formed "during the late 1960s".

81 *Who Killed Kennedy*

82 *Emotional Chemistry*

83 *The Dying Days*

ment.[89] SOS signals were abandoned.[90] The British space programme was blossoming with a series of Mars Probe Missions. Space technology had dramatically improved since the old moonshot days. The new fuel variant M3, though highly volatile, provided a great deal more thrust than conventional fuels, and decontamination procedures had been reduced from two days to one hour. Space research took place at the Space Centre in London, not far from UNIT HQ. In this complex was Space Control (callsign: "Control") where missions were co-ordinated. Astronauts were selected from the military.[91]

The British astronauts Grosvenor and Guest became the first men on Mars. They planted the Union Flag on Mount Olympus.[92] The British astronaut Carrington, part of the Mars Probe 6 mission, discovered radioactive aliens on Mars that killed his crew. Returning to Earth, and terrified by what he saw as a threat to humanity, Carrington formed an elaborate plan to destroy them. On his return, he was promoted to General and led the newly-formed Space Security Department.[93]

---

84 *Island of Death*

85 *Bullet Time*

86 *The Time Monster* – the Seventh Enabling Act allows the Brigadier to take command of government forces – and *The Green Death*.

87 There's no specific indication in the TV series as to precisely when Lethbridge-Stewart gains the rank of brigadier and takes charge of UNIT, although it happens in the four-year gap between *The Web of Fear* and *The Invasion*. In the *Lethbridge-Stewart* novels, his promotion happens at the end of *Leth-St: The Showstoppers*.

In *Spearhead from Space,* the Brigadier tells Liz Shaw that "since UNIT was formed" there have been two alien invasions. *The Web of Fear* took place before UNIT was formed, and so we only saw UNIT fight one set of aliens, in *The Invasion*. It's here presumed that the Brigadier was simplifying events and referring to the two televised Troughton stories that he appeared in. If not, the Doctor does not seem to have been involved in fending off the other invasion, as he never refers to it. In *Spearhead from Space* and *Terror of the Zygons*, the Brigadier implies that UNIT existed before he was placed in charge of it.

The *Lethbridge-Stewart* novels entail a pre-UNIT Lethbridge-Stewart dealing with far more alien incursions than just the two Troughton TV stories, but *Leth-St: "The Enfolded Time"* supplies a get-out clause by claiming that when the Brig took over UNIT, he was forbidden from talking about his involvement with the Fifth Operational Corps and their missions.

88 "Years" before *Old Soldiers*.

89 *The Mind of Evil*

90 "Years" before *The Ambassadors of Death*.

91 *The Ambassadors of Death*

92 "Over twenty years" before *The Dying Days* (so before 1977). This was a Mars Probe mission as seen in *The Ambassadors of Death*.

93 Carrington set off for Mars no later than thirty months before *The Ambassadors of Death*.

BRITAIN'S MISSIONS TO MARS: The timeline for the backstory of *The Ambassadors of Death*, and therefore the British space programme, is unclear.

It is a long-term project. Carrington was on Mars Probe 6, and the "missing" ship is Mars Probe 7. Mars Probe 7 takes between seven and eight months to get to Mars (various characters say it takes "seven months", "seven and half months" and "nearly eight months"), the astronauts spend two weeks on the surface and logically need seven or so months to return to Earth. That's a round trip of about fifteen months.

Assuming all missions followed that timescale and that only one mission was underway at any one time, then even if each mission was launched the day the previous one returned, this would stretch the Mars programme back eight or nine years. However, not all the Apollo missions were designed to land a man on the moon, so we could reasonably infer that some of the early Mars Probes were shorter test flights. Nowhere, though, is it stated that Carrington was the *first* man on Mars, and *The Dying Days* makes clear that he wasn't.

Furthermore, when Recovery 7 is lost, we're told that Recovery 8 isn't due for service for "three months" – presumably following a schedule that allows it to rendezvous with Mars Probe 8. It seems unlikely that Recovery 8 would be prepped before Mars Probe 8 is launched, and it's much more plausible that the planners expect Mars Probe 8 to *return* to Earth then. The Mars Probe 8 mission might have been aborted when contact was lost with Mars Probe 7, or it might have continued (as it's not mentioned, we have no way of knowing). Whatever the case, it suggests that Mars Probe 8 was launched while Mars Probe 7 was underway and at least three months ago, given that it's now three months away from Earth.

Either way, we know Mars Probe 7 wasn't launched until Mars Probe 6 returned. So Mars Probe 6 launched at least thirty months before *The Ambassadors of Death*. We know that Dr Taltalian has been working at the Space Centre for "two years", so the Mars programme has been around at least that long.

The Invasion states that only America and Russia can launch a moon mission, and *The Ambassadors of Death* is almost certainly set within a year of that. This means one of two things. Either the first Mars Probe was launched after *The Invasion*, or it's a type of ship that can't be retasked for a moon mission.

No evidence suggests that the history of space travel in the fifties and sixties in *Doctor Who* differs from the history we know. On the contrary, there's evidence that it's the same: Yuri Gagarin is named as the first man in

TALES FROM THE VAULT[94] -> A criminal gang staged a series of robberies in Manchester, Birmingham and the surrounding counties, using an alien crystal to erase the memory of any eye-witnesses. The second Doctor, Jamie and Zoe foiled the scheme. The Doctor later gave the crystal to the Brigadier, complete with a copy of Zoe's memories as a user "manual"/interface. UNIT used the crystal to extract memories from anyone who witnessed alien activity, keeping secret the existence of extra-terrestrials.

(20th December to 30th January) - THE LEFT-HANDED HUMMINGBIRD[95] -> Early in its history, UNIT had a Paranormal Division. After extensive trials, they recruited six genuine human psychics. The division was run by Lieutenant Hamlet Macbeth, and investigated Fortean events. Following "the Happening", a massive psychic event in St John's Wood, London on 21st December, 1968, the Paranormal Division was disbanded. Ace foiled an attempt to kill the Beatles on the roof of the Apple building on 30th January, 1969. At least two of the Doctor's incarnations went to Woodstock.

UNIT Year 1

Walter Douglas, promoted to Brigadier, took command of the the Home-Army Fifth Operational Corps. William Bishop was promoted to major.[96] A Cyber-scout ship surveyed Earth in preparation for an invasion, but its pilot died when the vessel crashed near Cambridge. It remained buried until Gareth Arnold, a local dentist, happened upon it some years later.[97]

(April) UNIT radar stations tracked a shower of meteorites in an odd formation over Essex.[98]

Tobias Vaughn and the Cybermen

(summer) - THE INVASION[99] -> UNIT began monitoring the activities of International Electromatics after hundreds of UFO sightings occurred on IE property. IE now controlled every computer line in the world by undercutting the competition, and Tobias Vaughn had built a business empire around his philosophy of uniformity and exact duplication. One of IE's most suc-

space in *The Seeds of Death*, *1963: The Space Race*, *The Wanderer, Thin Ice* (BF) and *Leth-St: Moon Blink* (his picture also appears in *The Lie of the Land*, with no attribution) , Ben (from 1966) is from a time before Lunar landings according to *The Tenth Planet* and Richard Lazarus mentions Armstrong in *The Lazarus Experiment*. The moon landing takes place in 1969 according to *Blink* and *The Impossible Astronaut/Day of the Moon*.

94 Dating *Tales from the Vault* (BF CC #6.1) - UNIT has only been in existence "for a few months", and it's "about fifty years" before 2011. The Doctor says that in a few months hence, the Bank of England will be printing the notes required for decimalisation (which happened February 1971).

95 Dating *The Left-Handed Hummingbird* (NA #21) - The UNIT stories are set the year of broadcast. The last time Cristian Alvarez saw the Doctor was "January the thirtieth, 1969" (p8). The TARDIS arrives in that timezone on "December 20, 1968" (p122). "The Happening" takes place on "December 21" (p163).

96 The Haisman Timeline. Presumably Douglas' reassignment happens due to Lethbridge-Stewart being given command of UNIT.

97 *The Blue Tooth*. The scoutship is clearly reconnoitring Earth in preparation for *The Invasion*.

98 "Six months" before *Spearhead from Space*.

99 Dating *The Invasion* (6.3) - It is the near future. According to the Brigadier in this story, the events of *The Web of Fear* "must be four years ago, now", making it at least 1979. A surveillance photo has the caption "E091/5D/78", the last two digits of which might (or might not) be the year.

There are advanced, voice-operated computers and

"Public Video" videophones. UNIT has an IE computer, and use some IE components in their radios and radar. UNIT has compact TM45 radios with a range of 50 miles, while IE personnel have wrist-communicators. IE has an elaborate electronic security and surveillance system. There are electric cars and hypersonic jets.

There's no suggestion that this is because IE has been given Cyber-technology – the computer in IE's reception (which also answers the phones) uses ALGOL and blows up after failing to solve a simple formula, neither of which indicate that a superior alien technology is involved.

There are many communications satellites in orbit, and UNIT has the authority to fire nuclear rockets into space. "Only the Americans and the Russians" have rockets capable of reaching the moon – the Russians are just about to launch a manned orbital survey of the moon, and it would apparently only take "ten hours" to reach it. The IE guards and many UNIT troops wear futuristic uniforms, while Vaughn wears a collarless shirt. The Brigadier's "anti-feminist" ideas are outdated.

The Doctor jokes that as it's Britain and there are clouds in the sky, it must be "summertime".

A casting document written by director Douglas Camfield suggested *The Invasion* was set "about the year 1976 AD". The *Radio Times* in some regions said that the date was "about the year 1975", and the continuity announcer echoed this at the beginning of the broadcast of episode one. In *Dalek*, the plaque below the Cybermen head reads "Extraterrestrial Cyborg Specimen, recovered from underground sewer, location London, United Kingdom, date 1975"... almost certainly a reference to this story. However, the Cybermen

cessful products was a disposable radio, which had sold ten million units. Vaughn was in league with the Cybermen, who were using his company as a front for their invasion plans. The second Doctor, Jamie, Zoe and UNIT defeated the Cybermen. Vaughn was apparently killed.

One cybership crashed in the South Pole.[100]

THE ISOS NETWORK[101] -> One ship escaped the doomed Cyber-fleet and withdrew to the planet Isos II, to regroup and mount a renewed assault on Earth. The ship's warp distortion field pulled the TARDIS to Isos II, enabling the Doctor's trio to wipe out the Cybermen.

Aftermath of the Vaughn-Backed Invasion

Anne Bishop took her father, Edward Travers, to America to avoid awkward questions about his being so young. While there, Anne aided Major Adrienne Kramer in founding the US branch of UNIT. The Brigadier phoned, to update the trio about the second Doctor's return.[102]

After the collapse of IE, Ashley Chapel, Vaughn's chief scientist, set up his own company named Ashley Chapel Logistics.[103] Vaughn, though, had survived by downloading his consciousness into a waiting robot body. For the next thousand years, he would secretly run a succession of massive electronics corporations that developed state-of-the-art equipment. He would re-encounter the Doctor in 2975.[104] The public were told the mass unconsciousness that occurred during the Cybermen incursion was because

Earth passed through the tail of a comet. Isobel Watkins' photos of Cybermen were dismissed as fakes.[105]

The "Big Bug Era" began, as Earth was invaded and threatened by alien life. Many books and fanzines trying to catalogue and expose these invasions were published.[106] One of the most popular fanzines was *Who's Who and What's That*. The government, though, covered much of UNIT's work with D-notices, making it difficult to keep track of the dates. The time-displaced Isaac Summerfield set up a secret organisation to "mop up" after UNIT, with the intention of getting stranded aliens home. Initially, it was based in Llarelli.[107]

Mars Probe 7 was launched. After seven months, Mars Probe 7 landed on Mars and radio contact was lost, but two weeks later it took off from the red planet... or at least, something did.[108]

The third Doctor exiled to Earth

Liz Shaw Joins UNIT

For years, and under orders, Brigadier Lethbridge-Stewart pretended that his adventures with the Fifth Operational Corps never happened.[109]

(October, "months" after *The Invasion*) - SPEARHEAD FROM SPACE[110] **-> UNIT brought Liz Shaw up from Cambridge to act as a scientific advisor. The very same day, reporters were tipped off that a mysterious patient with two hearts was present at**

head is from the wrong era (it's from *Revenge of the Cybermen*, not *The Invasion*) and the plaque isn't readable on screen, so there are grounds to discount it. According to *Iceberg*, this story takes place "ten years" (p90) before *The Tenth Planet* (meaning 1976), in "the 70s" (p2). *No Future* suggested "1970", (p2). *Original Sin* claims that this story was set in "the 1970s" (p281). *Millennial Rites* suggests that the UNIT era took place in "the nineteen eighties" (p15), with *The Invasion* a little over "twenty years ago" (meaning 1979). The 1979 date is repeated in *The Face of the Enemy* (p21).

Sgt Benton's dinner suit last got an outing in "1968" according to *Council of War*, possibly in reference to his attire when trailing the Doctor and Jamie in *The Invasion* episode two. In *Last of the Cybermen,* the sixth Doctor claims, and Jamie confirms, that events in *The Invasion* happened in "1975". A file in the *Global Conspiracy?* mockumentary suggests that the Doctor's first involvement with UNIT (in *The Invasion*, presumably) happened in "1968".

Information pertaining to when the Yeti attack the London Underground (*The Web of Fear*) and UNIT defeats the Cybermen (*The Invasion*) is "redacted" on A

History of the Universe in 100 Objects (p100), although mention of *The Invasion* is placed after the UN establishes its First Contact protocols (*The Sound of Drums*) in 1968.
100 *Iceberg*
101 Dating *The Isos Network* (BF EA #2.4) - The story is set immediately after *The Invasion*.
102 The Haisman Timeline, *Leth-St: Night of the Intelligence* (ch15),
103 *Millennial Rites*
104 *Original Sin*
105 *Who Killed Kennedy*
106 *No Future*
107 *Return of the Living Dad. Who's Who and What's That* is also mentioned in *The Dying Days*.
108 Mars Probe 7 is launched fifteen and a half months before *The Ambassadors of Death*, and contact was lost "eight months" before *The Ambassadors of Death*.
109 *Leth-St:* "The Enfolded Time"
110 Dating *Spearhead from Space* (7.1) - There's no firm evidence if this is near future or contemporary. The Brigadier tells Liz Shaw here that "in the last decade we

Ashbridge Cottage Hospital.

This "spaceman" was the newly regenerated third Doctor, exiled to Earth in the twentieth-century timezone by the Time Lords. He turned up the morning after a meteorite shower, and UNIT were soon on the scene. The meteorites were Nestene Energy Units, part of a plan to conquer the Earth using killer automata Autons. With the Doctor's help, UNIT led an assault on a plastics factory in Essex, mere hours after reports surfaced of "walking shop dummies" in city centres. They defeated the Nestene.

Mike Yates led the clean-up operation after the Nestene Invasion, and discovered a single Energy Unit that had not been recovered by the Autons. It remained UNIT property, but was loaned to the National Space Museum.[111] Yates was posted to Fort George, Inverness.[112] At some point, Yates had a relationship with Jane Lucas, one of his trainees.[113]

Gareth Wostencroft was one of the UNIT soldiers involved with the first Auton invasion.[114]

The Nestene invasion was covered up as a terrorist attack, which became known as Black Thursday. A report filed by journalist James Stevens had all references to UNIT erased. This prompted him to start investigating the mysterious organisation, an undertaking he would pursue for several years.[115]

The Vault, Department C19's storehouse of discarded alien artifacts, recovered two Nestene Energy Units. Dr Ingrid Krafchin, a researcher for SeneNet, began experiments with plastic.[116] The Doctor was put on UNIT's payroll as "Doctor John Smith", but did not cash his cheques.[117] The Brigadier saw his friend, Kolonel Heinrich Konrad, after a debriefing on the initial Auton incident.[118]

Following the obliteration of the Voord homeworld, a Voord spacecraft fell to Earth near the village of Stegmoor. The ship took on the molecular properties of the surrounding sand and rock, so when the third Doctor, the Brigadier and Liz Shaw investigated reports of a "falling star" in the area, they failed to detect anything amiss.[119]

---

have been sending probes deeper and deeper into space", but that needn't mean humanity's first-ever space probe was launched exactly ten years ago.

The Brigadier states in *Planet of the Spiders* that "months" elapsed between *The Invasion* and *Spearhead from Space* (meaning 1979). The weather is "uncommonly warm", suggesting it is autumn or winter. According to *The Face of the Enemy* (p21) it was "two years" before (meaning 1981). It was "five years ago" in *No Future* (meaning 1971). *Who Killed Kennedy* and *The Scales of Injustice* both state this story takes place in October, which is also the month the story was filmed.

Entries in *A History of the Universe in 100 Objects* related to *Spearhead from Space* (p107), *Terror of the Autons* (p109), *The Claws of Axos* (p111), *The Green Death* (pgs. 117, 220), *Planet of the Spiders* (p122), *The Android Invasion* (p124) and *The Seeds of Doom* (p126) are all generalised as the "1970s".

111 *Terror of the Autons*, also referred to in *The Eye of the Giant*. Mike Yates doesn't appear on screen until *Terror of the Autons*. He apparently doesn't remember Nestene Energy Units in *The Scales of Injustice*.

112 "Two years" before *DotD: Vengeance of the Stones*.

113 *Worlds DW: The Screaming Skull*. The New Adventures and *The Devil Goblins of Neptune* portrayed Yates as gay.

114 *Dominion*

115 *Who Killed Kennedy* is James Stevens' account of the early UNIT years, and allocates firm dates for the stories, specifically:

Remembrance of the Daleks (November 1963)
The Web of Fear (August 1966)
The Invasion (spring 1969)
Spearhead from Space (October 1969)
Doctor Who and the Silurians (November 1969)

The Ambassadors of Death (December 1969)
Inferno (February 1970)
Terror of the Autons (April 1970)
The Mind of Evil (November 1970)
The Claws of Axos
The Daemons (May 1971)
Day of the Daleks (September 1971)

The Dying Days rather cheekily claimed that the government had insisted the dates be changed before allowing the book to be published.

116 *Business Unusual*

117 *No Future*, which clashes with the Doctor saying he was "unpaid" in *Terror of the Autons*. This was the "early seventies" in *Return of the Living Dad*.

118 *Old Soldiers*

119 *DC 2: Beachhead*

120 Dating *The Last Post* (BF CC #7.4) - Emily regards Liz's job with UNIT as "new", and their tea-meeting occurs between *Spearhead from Space* and *Doctor Who and the Silurians*. The date of Windshaw's death, 28th October, concurs with the most likely dating scenario for those two stories.

121 Dating *Doctor Who and the Silurians* (7.2) - There's conflicting dating evidence. A taxi driver asks for a fare of "10/6", so this story appears to be set before the introduction of decimal currency in February 1971, but the cyclotron is a futuristic experimental machine that converts nuclear energy directly into electricity.

There's no indication how long it's been since *Spearhead from Space*, but the Doctor has settled in with UNIT and (recently) acquired Bessie. People are wearing winter clothes. The New Adventure *Blood Heat* states that this story is set in "1973".

122 *The Scales of Injustice*. Okdel was named in *Doctor*

(winter) - THE LAST POST[120] -> Emily Shaw, Liz Shaw's mother, had signed the Official Secrets Act, was on several important committees and was acquainted with Brigadier Lethbridge-Stewart. She held two doctorates, and was an expert on Medieval Mystery Plays. Liz's sister, Lucy, had children and was employed to change the landscape of Medieval church architecture at Reading. UNIT Headquarters was located under St Pancras Station.

Liz had tea with her mother to discuss the strange pattern of key scientists and politicians dying after receiving letters correctly predicting the exact moment of their deaths. One of them, Professor Richard Windshaw, died on 28th October after being hit by a bus.

UNIT Year 2

(winter) - DOCTOR WHO AND THE SILURIANS[121] -> UNIT investigated power losses at the experimental Wenley Moor research centre. These were caused by the Silurians, reptile people who ruled the Earth millions of years before, and who had revived from suspended animation. The Silurians saw the humans as apes and plotted to wipe them out – first with a plague, then by dispersing the Van Allen Belt. This would have heated Earth to a level suitable for Silurians, but not to human life. The third Doctor attempted to negotiate, but the Brigadier triggered explosives that sealed off the Silurian base and possibly killed those within.**

This was Earth Reptile Shelter 873, led by Okdel L'da.[122] James Stevens followed a tip and managed to (briefly) phone the Brigadier at Wenley Moor. The plague spread to Paris airport. Four hundred people died, twenty of them abroad, and three ministers resigned.[123] **The Doctor believed that the Silurians at Wenley Moor were killed.**[124] The Brigadier was issued with direct orders to destroy the Silurians.[125] Those orders came from C19.[126] Mike Yates led a team looking for surviving Silurian

technology.[127] As one of his first commands, Mike Yates – along with Sgts Benton and Terry Waring – worked on UNIT's Earth Reptile Initiative: a means of identifying and monitoring Silurian bases.[128]

Dr Lawrence and Edward Masters had received letters from the Apocalypse Clock predicting their demise. Lawrence died as indicated on 21st November, and Masters died soon afterward, en route to a meeting of the Death Watch. During the Silurian plague outbreak, Liz Shaw sent anti-virals to her mother Emily, who had the school she worked for – St Hugh's College, Oxford – put under quarantine. Liz wrote to her mother during clean-up operations at Wenley Moor, having found Lawrence and Masters' letters. The explosions at Wenley Moor caused subsidence, and necessitated the reactor being closed down.[129]

Mortimus (a.k.a. the Monk) used the captured Chronovore Artemis to create an alternative history where the Doctor died during the Wenley Moor adventure.[130]

= In a parallel timeline, the Doctor was captured and killed by the Silurians before he could find an antidote to their plague. Millions died in a matter of days, a time that would become known to the survivors as "the Nightmare".[131]

The Silurian Imorkal was hatched. In one reality, he was one of the Silurian masters of Earth. In the proper timeline, he eventually worked for NATO.[132] A UNIT station in Antarctica investigated a possible Silurian shelter uncovered in the 1920s.[133] Another Silurian shelter was discovered and destroyed in Oregon.[134] The government destabilised under political pressure following the plague.[135] Anne Travers became scientific advisor to the cabinet.[136]

Who and The Cave-Monsters, the novelisation of *Doctor Who and the Silurians*.
123 *Who Killed Kennedy*. We see the Brigadier take the phone call in *Doctor Who and the Silurians*.
124 *The Hungry Earth*
125 *Blood Heat*
126 *The Scales of Injustice*
127 *The Eye of the Giant*, *The Scales of Injustice*.
128 *UNIT S4: Assembled*
129 *The Last Post* – the script gives the date of Lawrence's death as "1st November", but it's "21st November" in the finished audio.
130 *No Future*, a reference to *Blood Heat*.
131 *Blood Heat*
132 *Eternity Weeps*

133 *The Scales of Injustice*, a reference to the Audio Visuals story *Endurance*.
134 *The Devil Goblins from Neptune*
135 *Who Killed Kennedy*
136 "Eighteen years" before *Millennial Rites*, so in 1981. It is stated that *Inferno* was "early on in her tenure" and Anne had responsibilities for the British Space Programme (p14). That would place the UNIT stories later than most other references, but this dating scheme is perfectly compatible with that in *The Web of Fear*, which is after all where Anne Travers first appeared. That was "twenty-five years ago" (so around 1974), meaning there were seven years between *The Web of Fear* and her appointment.

OLD SOLDIERS[137] -> Kolonel Heinrich Konrad was now head of the UNIT facility at Kriegeskind Castle, and oversaw research on Project 995: an attempt to create a super-soldier using the psychotropic elements of an extra-terres-trial plant – a phylum that originated in Galaxy M33 – found in the jungles of South East Asia.

Kriegeskind came under attack by ghostly soldiers from bygone eras. The third Doctor and the Brigadier determined that Konrad was manifesting psychic powers due to the phylum, and was latching onto the emotional residue left in the castle's stone by soldiers who had visited the location. Konrad's second-in-command initiated the Arc Light Protocol: a scorched-earth policy created by the Brigadier. Two F5 bombers each deployed a single fuel-air explosive bomb – the most lethal ordinance UNIT had at its disposal. The Arc Light planes obliterated the castle, Konrad and all research pertaining to the project.

The lower ranks of UNIT regarded the Doctor as a myth, someone spoken of like a ghost story.

SHADOW OF THE PAST[138] -> The Mim, a race of shape-changers who used oceans for breeding pools, sent a war-fleet to Earth. The third Doctor contacted the Time Lords, who sent the warfleet back to the Mim-sphere and made sure that it was too busy to leave. A single Mim scout was left behind, and Sergeant Robin Marshall of UNIT died while exploding the creature within its spaceship. Corporal Benton was given Marshall's sergeant stripes, and the scoutship was quarantined in UNIT Vault 75-73/Whitehall.

THE AMBASSADORS OF DEATH[139] -> Recovery 7 was dispatched, piloted by Charles Van Lyden, to give assistance to Mars Probe 7, which was still maintain-ing radio silence after lifting off from Mars. Van Lyden linked up with and entered Mars Probe 7, but contact was again lost. Recovery 8 couldn't be prepared for launch for ten days, forcing the ground crew to await developments.

Recovery 7 returned to Earth, but not with the Earth astronauts aboard. Instead, it contained three ambas-sadors from the race of radioactive aliens that General Carrington had encountered on Mars. Furthering his private agenda, Carrington intercepted the ambassa-dors and directed them, via a signalling device, to com-mit acts of terror. Carrington hoped to portray the aliens as invaders, mobilising a global effort to destroy them, but the third Doctor and UNIT exposed the scheme. The ambassadors and Earth astronauts were exchanged, and Carrington was discredited.

137 Dating *Old Soldiers* (BF CC #2.3) - The story takes place "a few weeks" after *The Silurians*, but before *The Ambassadors of Death*.

138 Dating *Shadow of the Past* (BF CC #4.9) - Once again, the story happens "a few weeks" after *The Silurians*, and before *The Ambassadors of Death*.

139 Dating *The Ambassadors of Death* (7.3) - This story is very clearly set in the near future. Britain has an established programme of manned missions to Mars. Professor Cornish remarks that decontamination takes "under an hour... it used to take two days" (the time it took the lunar astronauts when the story was made). There are colour videophones and we see a machine capable of automatically displaying star charts. SOS messages were abandoned "years ago".

Those advocating that the UNIT stories are set in the year of broadcast admit this story causes them prob-lems. One argument (used in both *Timelink* and *About Time*) concedes that Mars missions weren't possible in 1970, but that as we still haven't landed a man on Mars, it doesn't prove this story is set in the near future. The reasoning being: once efforts to match a story to real-world developments go out the window, saying this anomalous event happens in the 70s works as well as the 80s.

Leaving that aside, when *The Ambassadors of Death* was made, it wasn't science fantasy. NASA had just landed on the moon and had plans to put a man on Mars in the nineteen-eighties. This wasn't just a hope as the technology to get to Mars existed, at least in proto-type form, and only a lack of political will and funding prevented it. At that point, NASA was seriously project-ing that half of American employees would be working in space by 2050.

At the time that *The Ambassadors of Death* was made, then, what was shown wasn't possible – but it would be, for NASA, in about ten years. The most implausible aspect was that Britain could do the same – but there had been a British space programme up until the early sixties, and, again, it was lack of funding rather than lack of expertise that killed it off.

The Doctor is still bitter about the events of *Doctor Who and the Silurians*, so this story probably happens only shortly afterwards. The Brigadier says he has known the Doctor "several years, on and off", so it's that long since *The Web of Fear*.

140 *The Last Post*. Writer James Goss admits that the story's continuity references are based on "a drunken re-reading of *The Ambassadors of Death* novelisation", so perhaps work better in theory than in practice, and possibly rely upon Liz writing cheery notes to her mother while being locked up in a cellar.

141 *Who Killed Kennedy*

142 "During that General Carrington business" accord-ing to *No Future*.

143 *The Dying Days*

144 *The Scales of Injustice*

145 Mars Probe 9 is referred to in *Dancing the Code*, and *The Dying Days* mentions Mars Probe 13.

Emily Shaw spotted her daughter Liz in the background of the Recovery 7 news coverage. Lucy, Liz's sister, had published a monograph on misericords. The Apocalypse Clock informed Bruno Taltalian and Sir James Quinlan that they would soon die, then made it happen. With Quinlan's demise, Prestayn took charge of the Death Watch. [140]

The new channel BBC3 launched with coverage of the Recovery 7 capsule.[141] The Doctor appeared on *Nationwide* during this incident.[142] The aliens conducted limited diplomatic discussions, but concluded that humankind wasn't ready for their technology. Contact was limited, as the aliens were a plutonium-based lifeform.[143] Mars Probe 6 ended up in C19's Vault.[144] The Mars Probe Programme continued for several more years.[145]

Jones, a hired killer from C19's Vault, abducted a young secretary called Roberta. Vault scientists gave her cybernetic implants and false memories.[146] The Doctor failed to jumpstart the TARDIS using a battery charged with Z-radiation.[147]

THE LAST POST[148] -> Liz Shaw concluded that the pattern of mysteriously forecast deaths was linked to her mother's committee, the Death Watch. The Apocalypse Clock issued a letter that Dame Emily Shaw would die, at midnight. The third Doctor saved Emily, while Liz persuaded the Clock that it could only eliminate all variables threatening the end of the world by killing humanity or placing it into stasis – but that by doing so, the Clock itself would end the world. The Clock acknowledged the logic conundrum, and predicted the deaths of itself and Prestayn, its creator. As the Clock anticipated, Prestayn went mad and destroyed them both in an explosion.

The Apocalypse Clock's final prediction pertained to the Doctor's future, but he decided against reading it for fear of spoiling the surprise. Liz and Emily read the number of ways the Doctor would die, and decided he was better off not knowing.

The third Doctor and Liz Shaw initially investigated the Inferno Project owing to the Apocalypse Clock's common origins with a computer there.

Devastation of the Inferno-Earth

(late July) - INFERNO[149] **-> Professor Stahlman discovered a gas underneath the crust of the Earth, and claimed that it might be "a vast new storehouse of energy which has lain dormant since the beginning of time". The government funded a drilling project (nicknamed "Inferno" by some of the workers) based in Eastchester. But as the project's robot drill approached its target, a green slime came to the surface. On skin contact, people became savage beastmen, Primords.**

= "Sideways in time", Britain was a republic, and it had been since at least 1943 when the Defence of the Republic Act was passed. A fascist regime had executed the royal family. In this version of events, Professor Stahlman's project was a day ahead of ours, and was under the aegis of the Republican Security Forces. This world was destroyed when Stahlman's project released torrents of lava and armies of Primords.

On our Earth, the project was halted at the insistence of Sir Keith Gold and UNIT.

THE BRITISH SPACE PROGRAMME: Perhaps because they are acutely aware of the threat from outer space, the British government seems to have invested heavily in the space programme before and during the UNIT era. In *Invasion of the Dinosaurs*, some very clever and important people are fooled into believing that a fleet of colony ships could be built and go on to reach another habitable planet, although Sarah knows that even the most advanced spaceship "would take hundreds of years" to do so, and it transpires the ships are fakes. In *The Android Invasion*, an experimental "space freighter" has been in service for at least two years. There's no obvious evidence that the British are using alien technology that they've recovered from one of the alien incursions in the sixties to speed up their space programme. On the contrary, they're using pretty basic rocket technology.

The Christmas Invasion features Britain sending an unmanned probe to Mars in late 2006, and portrays it as a pioneering effort.

146 *Business Unusual*
147 *The Oseidon Adventure*
148 Dating *The Last Post* (BF CC #7.4) - Events reach a climax after *The Ambassadors of Death*, but before *Inferno* (the Doctor mentions "some damn fool trying to drill into the Earth").
149 Dating *Inferno* (7.4) - This story seems to be set in the near future. The computer at the project uses perspex/crystalline memory blocks. Stahlman has a robot drill capable of boring down over twenty miles. A desk calendar in the parallel universe says it is "July 23rd", and the story runs for five days – the countdown we see early in the story says there is "59:28:47" remaining before penetration.

The word "Primord" is not used in dialogue, but appears in the on-screen credits. The name "Eastchester" is only used in a scene cut from the original broadcast (but retained in foreign prints and the BBC Video and DVD release), when the Doctor listens to a radio broadcast in the parallel universe. Stahlman spells his name

The Death of General James Gore

(late July) - LETH-ST: "Ashes of the Inferno"[150] **->** Department C19 had curtailed James Gore's power, and he now lived in a home for ex-government officials. Gore inherently sensed the catastrophe that ravaged his native reality, the Inferno Earth, and so asked his "brother" – Brigadier Lethbridge-Stewart – to take him to the intersection of their worlds, so he could say goodbye to his home. The Brigadier took Gore to the Doctor's hut... but as Gore was all that remained of the Inferno-Earth, he too was fated to die. Gore saw the image of Alastair (sic) Lethbridge-Stewart one last time, before the bullet that had slain Alastair sped through the dimensional walls and killed Gore also. Afterward, the Brigadier called his nephew Owain to mourn for his lost brother.

= The Doctor had cause to suspect that an alternate version of himself ran the Britain of the parallel world.[151] In the parallel universe, the British Isles were destroyed in hours, the rest of Europe a day later. The entire world was devastated within thirty-six hours. The leaders of the American Confederation, India, White Russia and the Asian Co-prosperity Sphere, along with the new leader of the British Republic, were evacuated to Copernicus Base on the moon. Once there, they formed the Conclave.[152]

C19 acquired some of Stahlman's Gas.[153] The Doctor attended the wedding of Greg Sutton and Petra Williams. He met Ian Chesterton, who was now working at NASA, at the reception.[154] Greg Sutton gave Ian some fashion advice – that he should buy an orange shirt and purple tie.[155] James Stevens tracked down the Suttons, who told

with two "n"s in the parallel universe. The Doctor claims this is the first attempt to penetrate the Earth's crust, forgetting the attempt he'd seen in *The Underwater Menace*.

150 Dating *Leth-St*: "Ashes of the Inferno" (*Leth-St HAVOC Files* #2.6) - The Brigadier visits James the day after *Inferno*. James is the only bit of Inferno-Earth in our reality – it's too early for survivors to cross over in *The Face of the Enemy*, and presumably something we don't see has happened to his son Dylan (*Leth-St: Times Squared* et al).

151 *Timewyrm: Revelation*

152 *The Face of the Enemy*

153 *The Scales of Injustice, Business Unusual.*

154 *The Devil Goblins from Neptune. The Face of the Enemy* says Ian is on a year-long exchange programme.

155 *Byzantium!*

156 *Who Killed Kennedy*

157 "Seven or eight months" before *Scales of Injustice*, "twenty years" before *Business Unusual.*

158 "The previous year", "late last year" and "eight months" before *The Devil Goblins from Neptune.*

159 The Christmas before *The Scales of Injustice.*

160 *The Devil Goblins from Neptune.* The new members were presumably Billy Preston and Klaus Voormann.

THE BEATLES: *Doctor Who* has a terrible record for predicting the future, one that can best be summed up by noting that *Battlefield* predicted a near future with Soviet soldiers operating under the UN's aegis on British soil – but between the story's filming and its broadcast, the Soviet Union collapsed. In the entire twenty-six-year run of classic *Doctor Who*, it made two successful predictions – that there would be a female British Prime Minister (*Terror of the Zygons*), and that there would, one day, be a museum dedicated to the Beatles in Liverpool (*The Chase*).

The original draft of the script called for the real Beatles to appear, made up to look very old to indicate

they were still performing in the future (the script specified 2012).

The Devil Goblins from Neptune reveals that The Beatles of the *Doctor Who* universe stayed together at least into the early seventies. John Lennon was murdered as he was in our history in *The Left-Handed Hummingbird*, though, and Paul McCartney was playing with Wings in *No Future*.

In *The Gallifrey Chronicles*, it's revealed that Fitz collects Beatles records from parallel universes, and that he saw them play a song called "Celebrate the Love" at Live Aid. "Celebrate the Love" is the title of the song the Ewoks sang at the end of *Return of the Jedi*, at least until the Special Edition.

161 "Five years" before *Island of Death*.

162 "Six months" before *The Devil Goblins from Neptune*.

163 *Who Killed Kennedy*. It is "1970" (p87).

164 "Three or four months" before *The Devil Goblins from Neptune*. There are at least two UNIT HQs: one that's almost certainly in a London office block by the Thames in London (seen in *Terror of the Autons*) and one that's a stately home (seen in *The Three Doctors*).

165 "Early March" before *The Devil Goblins from Neptune*.

166 "Three months" before *The Scales of Injustice*, "fifteen years" before *Business Unusual*

167 "A couple of months" and "a month" before *The Scales of Injustice*.

168 Dating *Binary* (BF CC #6.9) - It's during Liz's time with UNIT – arguably later in her tenure, as she's having thoughts of leaving the group.

169 On screen, Mike Yates first appears in *Terror of the Autons* as a captain already attached to UNIT. The same story indicates that Yates has been performing UNIT work for some time, in that he "cleared up the mess" caused by the Auton incident in *Spearhead from Space*. The novel *The Eye of the Giant* and the audio *DotD: Vengeance of the Stones* both constitute "early" stories

him about Project: Inferno and the Doctor's involvement. The Suttons left the country shortly afterwards.[156]

Two Irish twins, Ciara and Cellian, assisted Dr Krafchin in a number of plastics experiments. He offered them immortality, and their blood was replaced with Nestene Compound, a type of plastic. They become contract killers for C19's Vault.[157]

The Doctor gave a lecture tour in the United States that was really cover for UNIT recruitment operations. He met rocket scientist Von Braun. Soviet radar detected meteor impacts in Siberia, which unknown to them marked the arrival of the Waro on Earth. The Brigadier met Soviet UNIT commander Captain Valentina Shuskin.[158] He also spent Christmas in Geneva on UNIT business.[159]

The Beatles reformed without Paul McCartney, but with two new members called Billy and Klaus.[160] Sarah Jane Smith went out with a Royal Navy officer named Sammy Brooks.[161]

UNIT Year 3

(January) The Liberals formed a coalition government following a General Election.[162] (February) James Stevens wrote a series of articles for the *Daily Chronicle* that referred to UNIT and C19. These got him sacked, and his wife left him.[163] (March) UNIT moved to a new headquarters.[164] (Early March) Soviet satellites detected a vast mining operation in Siberia. All military attempts to investigate were wiped out. The Soviet branch of UNIT lobbied Geneva to send the Doctor.[165]

At C19's Vault, Grant Traynor injected Stahlman's Gas into a Doberman, creating the Stalker, a vicious killer animal.[166] (April/May) C19's Vault acquired a Venus flytrap large enough to eat a dog in Africa. They also stole a Blackbird stealth aeroplane.[167]

BINARY[168] -> UNIT asked Liz Shaw to examine a super-computer salvaged from a crashed Kinbarki spaceship, as she had once been held prisoner in such a vessel. The super-computer's AI tried to goad Liz into repairing it, even as the failsafe circuit designed to stop the AI from falling into enemy hands urged Liz to destroy it. Liz allowed the computer to transmat itself away, convinced she had effectively freed a slave from bondage.

Mike Yates[169]

(May) - THE EYE OF THE GIANT[170] -> The third Doctor was sent an alien artifact that he discovered was emitting omicron radiation. He converted the Time-Space Visualiser into a space-time bridge to track the object's origin, and he and Liz Shaw wound up on Saluta in the Pacific in 1934.

> (=) Their actions in 1934 inadvertently created an alternative timeline ruled by The Goddess of the World, the starlet Nancy Grover. The Doctor returned to 1934 and set history back on the correct course.

DotD: VENGEANCE OF THE STONES[171] -> The four surviving Therrin awoke from hibernation, and tried to assess humankind's weaponry by capturing a Hawker-Hunter JA11 fighter jet in Northeast Scotland. Lieutenant Mike Yates was seconded to UNIT to look into the disappearance, and met the third Doctor and Brigadier Lethbridge-Stewart for the first time. The Therrin leader, Garlin, became desperate to protect his remaining bloodline after learning that his homeworld no longer existed, and the Brigadier's soldiers killed one of the remaining Therrin. The Doctor ended Garlin's attempt to wipe out humanity with an energy wave generated from the Therrin-made stone circles. Garlin was lost to the cross-dimensional data environment within one of the recumbent stones.

On instructions from the eleventh Doctor, the Doctor sent the central Therrin-made recumbent stone – which was pure Therrasite – to Professor Raynard, an Earth sciences expert, at the Royal Society. The third Doctor also vowed to brush up on his Venusian Aikido, a skill he hadn't used in many a year. Yates was asked to join UNIT full time, and promoted to Captain.

---

for Yates – he's a sergeant in *Eye*, still on a learning curve with UNIT operations and personnel, but he's a lieutenant in *Stones*, who gets assigned to UNIT full time at story's end. The two works conflict in that *Vengeance* touts itself as Mike's first meeting with the Doctor and the Brigadier, although his rank seems a bit more sensible than his being a sergeant in *Eye* (he'd need to receive *two* promotions with seemingly record speed, not to mention the sudden jump from being an enlisted man to outranking some of the officer class, to become a captain by *Terror of the Autons*). Either way, it's clear that he's up to speed on dealing with alien incur-

sions by the time *Terror of the Autons* rolls around.
170 Dating *The Eye of the Giant* (MA #21) - The story is set "thirty-seven years" after 1934, so 1971. UNIT have a photocopier. This is apparently the first time Mike Yates meets the Doctor, although he's been working for UNIT "over the last year". This is "a few weeks" before *The Scales of Injustice*, according to that book.
171 Dating *DotD: Vengeance of the Stones* (*Destiny of the Doctor* #3) - UNIT dating applies, but it's "forty years" before 2013 according to *DotD: The Time Machine*.

The story takes place prior to Mike Yates' first appearance, as a Captain attached to UNIT, in *Terror of the*

The recumbent stone was taken to Professor Chivers' lab at Oxford. The eleventh Doctor made use of it in 2013.[172]

THE BLUE TOOTH[173] -> Gareth Arnold, a local dentist, had discovered the crashed Cyber-ship near Cambridge, and experimented upon the Cyber-metal within. He developed a blue liquid variant that could directly convert people's bodies into metal, as well as gestate Cyber-insects within the human form. Arnold himself succumbed to Cyber-conversion, and used his dentistry business as a means of kidnapping people – including Liz Shaw's friend Jean Baisemore – to turn into Cybermen.

The third Doctor and Liz investigated the disappearances. Jean died, but the Doctor created a compound that terminated Arnold. His demise quelled the remaining Cybermen – who were later executed by the Brigadier's troops using the Doctor's compound.

Liz herself was infected by the blue liquid – the Doctor cured her condition, but she lost a tooth as a result.

Lis Shaw Leaves UNIT(ish)

(June) - THE SCALES OF INJUSTICE[174] -> A group of Silurian/Sea Devil hybrids awoke in Kent, and performed genetic experiments in the hope of ending their sterility and shortened lifespans. The third Doctor investigated the matter, but the warmongering Silurian leader launched an attack on the coast of Kent. UNIT defeated the assault, and a smaller group of benevolent Silurians sued for peace.

The cyborg leader of C19's Vault sought to acquire Silurian technology, leading to UNIT uncovering the Vault's base of operations. The Vault leader escaped along with his two Nestene-augmented assassins. Foreign powers had purchased some of the Vault's acquisitions.

After this incident, Sir John Sudbury of C19 knew too much to be sacked by any government, and he gained in power. The Brigadier's wife Fiona filed for divorce and left with their daughter Kate.[175]

Liz Shaw told the Doctor that she planned to leave UNIT, return to Cambridge and continue her researches.[176] She took a leave of absence.[177] Liz travelled around the world, and published a book entitled *Inside the Carnival*.[178]

Harry Sullivan served on the Ark Royal after leaving Dartmouth Naval College.[179]

(June) - THE DEVIL GOBLINS FROM NEPTUNE[180] -> Geneva refused to release the third Doctor to help with a situation in Siberia, so Captain Shuskin of the USSR branch of UNIT attempted to kidnap him instead. Liz Shaw was working with Professor Bernard Trainor, who was planning an unmanned mission to Neptune. The Doctor and Liz travelled to Siberia and were attacked by the Waro, demonic creatures from Neptune's moon Triton. The Doctor realised this was a distraction – the Waro were really after the American supplies of cobalt-60, with which they hoped to build a bomb that would devastate Earth. The Brigadier uncovered a conspiracy in UNIT that led to

Autons. No mention is made of Liz Shaw or Jo Grant, suggesting *Vengeance of the Stones* occurs between that story and *Inferno*. The Doctor here decides that re-learning Venusian aikido would be handy, presumably explaining the discrepancy between the "Venusian karate" he first uses in *Inferno* et al, and the "Venusian aikido" he deploys in *The Green Death*.

172 *DotD: The Time Machine*
173 Dating *The Blue Tooth* (BF CC #1.3) - It's toward the end of Liz's tenure with UNIT (she's been with the organisation "about a year") and Captain Yates is described as "a new boy" – which would place the story between *The Eye of the Giant* and *The Scales of Injustice*.
174 Dating *The Scales of Injustice* (MA #24) - The back cover states this is set between *Inferno* and *Terror of the Autons*, and "immediately after" *The Eye of the Giant*. It's a "few weeks" since that book. Liz tells the Doctor she is leaving at the end of the book "eight months, two weeks and four days" after *Spearhead from Space*. It is "six months" since *Doctor Who and the Silurians*.

The Silurians who sue for peace are not mentioned again. The next time we see them, *The Sea Devils*, they are pitted against humanity. By the time of *Eternity Weeps*, set in 2003, man and Silurian are working together in relative harmony. Perhaps the discrepancy

can be put down to the fact that UNIT don't feature in *The Sea Devils*, and the reptile people there were revived and are being provoked into conflict by the UNIT Master.
175 *Business Unusual*, the Haisman Timeline.
176 *The Scales of Injustice*, which states that it's "eight months, two weeks and four days" since she met the Doctor in *Spearhead from Space*, although their amount of time together has become "thirteen months" by *The Devil Goblins from Neptune*.
177 *The Devil Goblins from Neptune*, *The Face of the Enemy*.
178 *The Devil Goblins from Neptune*
179 *The Face of the Enemy*, picking up on a reference in *Harry Sullivan's War*.
180 Dating *The Devil Goblins from Neptune* (PDA #1) - Between *Inferno* and *Terror of the Autons*. Liz has been with UNIT for "thirteen months". The Brigadier hasn't been to Geneva for eight months (when, we're told, he was reporting on the events of *Inferno*). It is "1970", with a host of contemporary references to, for example, David Bowie and Brazil winning the World Cup (p109).
181 *Who Killed Kennedy* (p117), which specifies the year as "1970".
182 *Emotional Chemistry*

Area 51 in Nevada, a secret military base containing five aliens, the Nedenah. Freed by the Doctor, the Nedenah released a virus that made the Waro destroy themselves.

On 18th June, there was a General Election, and the Wilson government was defeated by the Conservatives under Heath with a majority of 43. Days before that, James Stevens' book *Bad Science* was published.[181] At some point during the UNIT era, the Doctor met the Russian Colonel Bugayev. During the encounter, Bugayev and some of his comrades were exposed to temporal radiation that either aged them to death or prolonged their lives.[182]

Liz Shaw returned to Cambridge, and soon afterwards the Doctor started to agitate for a new assistant. The Doctor started the steady state microwelding of his dematerialisation circuit.[183] There were some slow weeks at UNIT. The Doctor helped Benton paint some Nissen huts.[184]

Jo Grant Joins UNIT as the Doctor's Assistant

Jo Grant was seconded to UNIT at the insistence of a relative in government. Although she failed her General Science A-Level, she managed to pass the UNIT training course.[185] Jo had a choice of studying Escapology or the Dewey Decimal System.[186]

Her relative was General Frank Hobson, the UK ambassador to the United Nations.[187] She was trained to use skeleton keys and interrogation techniques.[188] She learned the art of semaphore as part of her UNIT training.[189] Her best friend on the course was called Tara. Jo did intelligence work for the Ministry, alongside a gentleman adventurer.[190]

The Master's First Battle with UNIT

(At least three months after *Inferno*) - TERROR OF THE AUTONS[191] -> Josephine Grant became the third Doctor's new assistant.

The UNIT Master had allied himself with the Nestenes, and together they plotted mass slaughter – when a radio signal was sent, thousands of distributed plastic daffodils would spray a plastic film capable of suffocating a person. The Nestenes would take over the country during the resulting chaos. The Doctor convinced the Master to help him defeat the Nestene plan. The Master was subsequently stranded on Earth when the Doctor stole his Mark 2 dematerialisation circuit, rendering his TARDIS useless.

A spatula-shaped piece of Auton matter survived. It would eventually end up in Little Caldwell, where it would be called Graeme.[192]

> = In an alternate reality, the Time Lords exiled the Doctor to Earth, the 1970s... but he didn't arrive there until 1997. Without him, UNIT struggled to deal with various menaces involving the Plastic Purges and Probe 7. Brigadier Lethbridge-Stewart authorised the saturation bombing of Surrey, was responsible for a line of mile-wide craters across America and was shamed with the *Daily Mail* headline: "Balmy Brig in Fake Flower Fiasco." Captain Yates died after travelling into the past and wiping out some Silurians with nuclear arms, which turned half of modern-day London into a lake.[193]

In October, UNIT started training its men to resist hypnosis. James Stevens completed work on his second book, and was invited to a demonstration of the Keller Process at Stangmoor Prison.[194]

The Doctor helped set up **the Black Archive, a UNIT storehouse of alien technology. Among many other**

---

183 *Terror of the Autons*
184 *The Death of Art*
185 *Terror of the Autons*
186 *UNIT S4: Assembled*
187 *Blood Heat*
188 *The Wages of Sin, Catastrophea.*
189 *The Elixir of Doom*
190 *Verdigris,* a reference to *The Avengers.*
191 Dating *Terror of the Autons* (8.1) - It seems to be the near future, and the plastics factory has a videophone.
 The Doctor works on his dematerialisation circuit for "three months", and apparently hadn't started in *Inferno*, so this story would seem to start at least three months after Season Seven ends. There is no indication how much time has passed since the previous Auton story,

Spearhead from Space. A desk calendar is referred to when the Doctor and Brigadier visit Farrell's office, but we do not see it.
 This is clearly not the Master's first arrival on Earth at this time – he has managed to research the history of Lew Russell, the circus owner.
 Inferno was "a few years" before *Terror of the Autons* according to *The Face of the Enemy* (p215). In *Genocide,* Jo says that she's been on UNIT's books since 1971. *Who Killed Kennedy* prefers April 1970.
192 *Return of the Living Dad*
193 *Unbound: Sympathy for the Devil*, a dystopian rewrite of television's UNIT era.
194 *Who Killed Kennedy*. It is "four months" since the June 1970 General Election (p119).

things, it contained the Tunguska Scroll (recovered in 1972) and a number of spacecraft.[195]

THE MIND OF EVIL[196] -> Incognito as "Professor Emil Keller", the UNIT Master developed the Keller Process: a means of rehabilitating convicts by having their "evil" brain impulses transferred into a machine. However, the machine actually housed an alien parasite that fed off the evil in humankind. The Master hoped to put the parasite's powers at his command. After a riot at Stangmoor Prison, the Master's scheme was exposed and the Keller Process abandoned.

UNIT were now involved with security of the World Peace Conference in London. The Master sought to steal Thunderbolt, an outlawed nuclear missile slated for destruction. He nearly succeeded and triggered a World War, but the third Doctor and UNIT destroyed both the missile and the Master's alien parasite.

DEADLY REUNION[197] -> The former Greek gods Demeter, Persephone and Hermes were now living as nobility in the English village of Hob's Haven. Hades had founded a cult named the Children of Light as a means of spreading anarchy among humankind, and coerced the UNIT Master into helping him. The Master supplied an alien drug, sarg, that drove its users to commit acts of violence at a pop festival. The third Doctor aided Demeter in summoning Zeus from his abode in another dimension, and the king of the gods exiled Hades from Earth forever. Demeter's trio departed Earth for Zeus' realm. The Brigadier remembered his time spent as Persephone's lover in the nineteen forties.

In December, James Stevens met Dodo Chaplet, who was homeless. He invited her to stay with him.[198]

UNIT Year 4

(January) - "Change of Mind"[199] -> The third Doctor and Liz flew to Prague for a Psi conference, but the plane's wing was torn off in a psychic attack. The Doctor realised that one of the passengers was keeping the plane intact using the power of her mind, but she died from the effort.

Hamlet Macbeth investigated Professor Hardin, a Cambridge professor of Paranormal Sciences, leaving just as the Doctor and Liz arrived. Hardin was using technology to boost latent psychic powers, and was experimenting on his students. He tried to kill the Doctor, but the Brigadier shot him.

In late February, James Stevens started writing a book about UNIT. In March, Liz Shaw, who was working on the genetic engineering of reptiles, contacted Stevens and warned him not to research C19. His house was ransacked.[200]

(spring or summer?) - THE CLAWS OF AXOS[201] -> The Washington UNIT HQ sent one of their agents, Bill Filer, to help UNIT UK to search for the UNIT Master. Meanwhile, the civil servant Chinn investigated UNIT.

UNIT radar stations detected a UFO one million miles out, headed for Earth. The alarm bells started to ring when it got within five hundred miles. UNIT HQ sent the order to launch an ICBM strike against the UFO, but the ship vanished before the missiles hit. It

---

195 THE BLACK ARCHIVE AND THE VAULTS: The Black Archive was first seen in *SJA: Enemy of the Bane*. The Doctor's involvement was established in "Don't Step on the Grass". We don't know precisely when it was built, but it would seem to be after *The Scales of Injustice*, which features Department C19's (very similar) Vault. In *Terror of the Autons*, the Brigadier expresses an interest in the technology of the UNIT Master's grenade but the Doctor defuses it, suggesting they hadn't a protocol about alien technology at that point. It is not related to the (again, very similar) Vault in *SJA: The Vault of Secrets*, or the UNIT Vault featured in *Tales from the Vault*. *Army of Ghosts* established that Torchwood have a similar archive, "The Age of Ice" includes a UNIT archive in Sydney, Australia, and *Dreamland* (*DW*) shows us that the US stores alien technology and aliens at Area 51. By the time of the K9 series, the Department keep aliens and alien technology in the Dauntless facility in the Tower of London.
196 Dating *The Mind of Evil* (8.2) - It seems to be the near future - there is a National Power Complex, there

is a World Peace Conference in progress in which the Chinese are key players. Gas warfare was banned "years" ago. Mao Tse Tung is referred to in the present tense – he died in 1976, after *The Mind of Evil* was made.

Inferno was "some time ago". This story might be set a full year after *Terror of the Autons*: the Master has been posing as Keller since "nearly a year ago". However, it's clear from *Terror of the Autons* that the Master has been on Earth for at least a little while. It's possible that the Master set his plan in motion before his apparent arrival on Earth in *Terror of the Autons*... which would mean he had two entirely distinct plans to take over the Earth running simultaneously. The "year ago" line might well be a remnant from an earlier draft of the script that didn't include the Master.

According to *Who Killed Kennedy*, it is October 1970 (p119).
197 Dating *Deadly Reunion* (PDA #63) - *Terror of the Autons* is "recent", but the Master's TARDIS works, so this is set after *The Mind of Evil*.
198 *Who Killed Kennedy*. It is "December" (p136) 1970.

landed on the south east coast of England close to the National Power Complex at Nuton, amid freak weather conditions. As the army arrived to seal off the area, the UFO began to broadcast a signal:

> "Axos calling Earth, request immediate assistance. Axos calling Earth..."

The Axons made contact with the UNIT party. They claimed that solar flares had damaged their planet, and that they possessed an advanced organic technology. Their ship had been damaged. In return for help, the Axons offered humanity Axonite – a substance that was "the chameleon of the elements". It could be programmed to absorb all forms of radiation, and to replicate and transmute matter. In theory, it would end the world's food and energy problems. In reality, the Axons had captured the Master in space, and he had led them to Earth – a rich feeding ground – in return for his freedom and a chance to kill the third Doctor. The Axos ship was banished from Earth and time-looped, but the Nuton Complex was destroyed.

Private Erskine was attacked by an Axon and left for dead, but survived. He was rescued by C19's Vault, and bore a grudge against the Brigadier. He ended up working for SeneNet.[202] The National Power Complex at Nuton was rebuilt.[203] Chinn was blamed for the disaster at Nuton and was pensioned off.[204]

UNIT went hunting for the Master and accidentally arrested the Spanish ambassador, mistaking him for the renegade Time Lord.[205] Marnal's son – who was on the run at the time   visited his father during the nineteen seventies, and told him exactly why the Doctor left Gallifrey.[206]

COLONY IN SPACE[207] -> The TARDIS left the third Doctor's laboratory in UNIT HQ for a matter of seconds, en route to 2472.

"The Forgotten"[208] -> The third Doctor, Jo and the Brigadier were in Bessie, being chased by greyhound-like aliens in walking machines. The Doctor immobilised the aliens with sound from his sonic screwdriver.

The parish council of Devil's End converted the cavern below the church into a witchcraft museum. The UNIT Master arrived in Devil's End, killed the vicar Canon Smallwood, and buried him in his own churchyard. He adopted the identity of the new vicar, "Mr Magister".[209] The Master stole a book from the Cabal of the Horned Beast, and it aided him in summoning the Daemon Azal.[210]

UNIT Captures the Master, Olive Hawthorne Meets the Doctor

(29th April - 1st May) - THE DAEMONS[211] -> At midnight on the major occult festival of Beltane, noted archaeologist Professor Gilbert Horner attempted to open the Devil's Hump – an ancient burial mount outside the village of Devil's End. BBC3 broadcast Horner's endeavour, but the mount was actually the buried

---

199 Dating "Change of Mind" (*DWM* #221-223) - The date is given as 1971. Liz has already left UNIT, but there's no mention of Jo.
200 *Who Killed Kennedy* (p162, p157).
201 Dating *The Claws of Axos* (8.3) - This story is set in the near future. There are videophones, although normal telephones are also in use. The National Power Complex "provides power for the whole of Britain" according to Sir George Hardiman, the head of the facility. (This needn't mean that the complex provides *all* of the country's power, just that it contributes to the whole of the National Grid rather than one region of it.) The complex has a "light accelerator". While this story was filmed in January, and the trees are bare, the snow is described as "freak weather conditions", perhaps suggesting the story is set in the spring or summer. Chinn says of the Brigadier's actions "that's the kind of high-handed attitude one has come to expect of the UN lately".
202 *Business Unusual*
203 Nuton is destroyed in *The Claws of Axos*, but mentioned in *The Daemons*.
204 *Who Killed Kennedy*

205 *Colony in Space*
206 *The Gallifrey Chronicles*
207 Dating *Colony in Space* (8.4) - There's no clear indication of the year. When Jo reaches the future, she is surprised that a colony ship was sent out in 1971 (it wasn't, of course, it was 2471). Either this story is set before 1971 and Jo is amazed how quickly the space programme has progressed, or it is set afterwards and she finds it difficult to believe that the colony ship was kept secret.
208 Dating "The Forgotten" (IDW *DW* mini-series #2) - No date is given. This could take place at any point when Jo is the Doctor's companion.
209 *The Eight Doctors*. In *The Daemons*, the local squire Winstanley says "there have been a lot of queer goings on the last few weeks", suggesting that's how long the Master has been in the area.
210 Inferred from *TimeH: Child of Time* (p64).
211 Dating *The Daemons* (8.5) - The story is set in the near future, as BBC3 is broadcasting. Devil's Hump is opened at "midnight" on "Beltane", and the story ends with a dance around the May pole. Beltane appears to be a Saturday or Sunday, as Yates

spaceship of Azal, the last of the Daemons. Horner was killed by a blast of subzero temperatures that resulted when he opened the ship.

As the Reverend Magister, the UNIT Master organised a coven to awaken Azal so he could receive the Daemon's power. The Master succeeded, and Azal prepared, per his instructions, to pass his power on to a creature worthy of overseeing the planet. Azal deemed the third Doctor a worthy recipient, but the Doctor refused to accept such authority. Azal moved to destroy the Doctor as a nuisance, but Jo Grant offered her life in the Doctor's place. Her "irrational and illogical" move drove Azal to self-destruct. UNIT apprehended the Master soon afterwards.

James Stevens watched the opening of Devil's Hump on BBC3 with Dodo, whom he had befriended.[212] The church in Devil's End was destroyed, but the cavern beneath was intact.[213] Public outrage at UNIT's blowing up of the church at Devil's End ("The Aldbourne Incident") led to "questions in the House; a near riot at the General Synod".[214] UNIT Private Cleary suffered a nervous breakdown after seeing Azal.[215]

SeneNet acquired the remains of Bok, a stone gargoyle animated by Azal's power.[216] The Brigadier let Benton keep a deactivated gargoyle from Devil's End.[217] After this, the Doctor explored the area around Devil's End and found Hexen Bridge, where he sensed an oppressive atmosphere.[218] Following Prof. Gilbert Horner's death, his book, *The Pagan Briton*, became an instant bestseller – enough to rival *Chariots of the Gods?* by Erich von Daniken.[219]

The public were told that the Master was an anarchist terrorist, Victor Magister. He was remanded at Stangmoor Prison.[220] The trial took place *in camera*. He was convicted of murder, high treason and numerous other crimes.[221] **While many wanted the UNIT Master executed, the Doctor pleaded for clemency at his trial and the Master was instead sent to Fortress Island in the English Channel.**[222] The Master was kept at Aylesbury Grange Detention Centre until Fortress Island was ready.[223]

"The Man in the Ion Mask"[224] **->** The third Doctor visited the imprisoned UNIT Master at Aylesbury Grange, a UNIT prison. With both of them locked in his cell, the Master claimed to have reformed, but the Doctor was suspicious – suspicions that were confirmed when it transpired that the Master had replaced himself with a hologram. The Master was just leaving... when the third Doctor, Lethbridge-Stewart and Benton apprehended him – the Doctor in the cell was also a hologram!

(summer) - THE SENTINELS OF THE NEW DAWN[225] **->** Liz Shaw was now working in the Department of Applied Mathematics and Theoretical Physics at Cambridge. She asked the Doctor to examine the efforts of her friend and former research partner, Terri Billington, to build a time dilator – a device that could open a wormhole through time. The Sentinels of the New Dawn, operating in 2014, linked their dilator to Billington's prototype and transported the Doctor and Liz into the future. Upon their return, they destroyed Billington's work, preventing the Sentinels from seizing power. Billington, unaware that her

---

and Benton watch a Rugby International and don't know the result. As Professor Horner's book is released the next day (and the shops would have to be open), it is almost certainly Sunday. It is "two hundred years" since Devil's Hump has been of interest, and the first attempt to open it was in 1793.
Daemons: White Witch of Devil's End: "The Poppet" takes place in 1969, "a couple of years" before *The Daemons*, so presumes a time-of-broadcast dating. The supplemental material in the *White Witch* anthology, however, says Professor Horner (killed in *The Daemons*) recorded documentaries including *The Day of the Celt* (1972) – possibly, for all we're told, released posthumously. A poster lists the May Day celebrations as happening on "Sunday 1st May", which was the case in 1977. *Daemons: White Witch of Devil's End*: "Daemos Returns" entails a much-older Olive, narrating in what's likely 2017, claiming *The Daemons* happened "forty years ago".
In *The Doctor: His Lives and Times* (p63), a transcript of the Master's trial (which must occur off screen between *The Daemons* and *The Sea Devils*) is stamped as being received on "29 Jun".

212 *Who Killed Kennedy*
213 *The Eight Doctors*
214 *Downtime*. It is a little odd that this is named the "Aldbourne Incident" – Aldbourne is the real village where *The Daemons*, set in the fictional village of Devil's End, was filmed. (Although an historic "Lord of Aldbourne" is referred to in *The Daemons*.)
215 *Who Killed Kennedy*
216 *Business Unusual*
217 *UNIT S4: Assembled*
218 *The Hollow Men*
219 The supplemental material to *Daemons: White Witch of Devil's End*. Moments before his death in *The Daemons*, Horner says that his new book "comes out tomorrow". *Chariots of the Gods?* (1968) influenced stories such as *Death to the Daleks*.
220 *The Face of the Enemy*
221 *Who Killed Kennedy*
222 *The Sea Devils*. The name of the island appears on Captain Hart's map, but isn't referred to in dialogue.
223 *The Face of the Enemy*
224 Dating "The Man in the Ion Mask" (*DWM Winter Special 1991*) - The story takes place shortly after *The*

research had nearly allowed a power-mad cabal to take over Earth, never spoke to Liz again.

At the UNIT staff panto, Mike Yates played Widow Twankey.[226] Mike Yates kissed Jo Grant at the UNIT Christmas party. The Master interrupted the festivities.[227]

UNIT Year 5

DAEMONS: WHITE WITCH OF DEVIL'S END[228] **->** A section of stone beneath the ruined St Michael's church retained some measure of Azal's power. Many spirits of the dead walked in Devil's End until Olive Hawthorne intervened with her friend Peter Thompson. Peter earthed the stone, dissipating the energy at the cost of his life. Olive saw Peter's spirit happily reunited with his late wife, Marj.

(July) - THE MAGICIAN'S OATH[229] **->** A master criminal – a ten-foot-tall mechanical creature with the power to control space and matter – was exiled to Earth. Its memories were siphoned into a storage unit while its blank mind resided in a human avatar. As the street performer "Diamond Jack", the criminal performed incredible illusions – but this drew heat from the surrounding area, and caused freak weather conditions in Central London. Frosty lawns were reported in mid-July, and the Metropolitan Line was smothered in twenty inches of snow. Finally, on a Saturday, Hyde Park and the Serpentine froze over instantly, killing everyone there. More temperature drops followed; Trafalgar Square was just nine degrees Celsius.

The Doctor and UNIT found Jack's spaceship buried under Highgate Cemetery. Jack's original form was accidentally destroyed, and a despondent Jack started draining Jo's memories – thereby goading Mike Yates into shooting him dead. Jo was comatose in a UNIT medical facility just outside Tunbridge Wells for a week. Her memories of this incident and few other alien incursions would remain in one of Jack's playing cards for a few decades.

THE MEGA[230] **->** The Mega – energy-charged creatures with floating spirals for faces – were bound by a code limiting engagement with pre-interstellar societies. Mindful of this, they secretly supplied Prince Cassier of Golbasto – a small nation in Eastern Europe – with equipment that let him eavesdrop on any conversation in the world, and eradicate individuals with a molecular disintegrator beam. Cassier intended to force disarmament and bring about a Golden Age, after which he would yield to an elected world council. The Mega, however, sought to use the resulting world crisis to invoke Article 9, which allowed a mentor culture to prevent the self-annihilation of a lesser one. This would appease the greater powers while handing the Mega control of Earth's resources.

The third Doctor and Jo attended a briefing at the Special Weapons Research Facility, and were horrified to learn that General Wylie had developed a gas that could target specific chromosomes. Cassier used the gas' advent to justify an ultimatum: the UK would disarm, or the Prime Minister and key UK officials would die. With no defense against Cassier's super-weapon, a double of the Prime Minister appeared on live television – and was eradicated by Cassier's beam – as the deadline passed. Riots and looting broke out across the country as other UK officials faked their deaths and planned a defence away from Cassier's monitoring.

The United Nations coordinated the major world governments to fire 14,000 missiles at Cassier's stronghold, an attack that Cassier's Mega-technology easily nullified. The Doctor persuaded Cassier of the Mega's ill intentions, after which Cassier destroyed his own castle and the Mega with the Mega beam.

Daemons, in "1976". The story appeared in *DWM's UNIT Special*, which set out a timeline for the UNIT stories running from *The Invasion* in 1975 to *The Seeds of Doom* in 1980.
225 Dating *The Sentinels of the New Dawn* (BF CC #5.10) - It's "about a year" after Liz left UNIT, during "summer break" at Cambridge.
226 *No Future*, which places it in "1973", three years earlier. This must have been quite an occasion, as the Doctor also remembers it in *Timewyrm: Revelation*.
227 "The UNIT Christmas party last year" according to *Verdigris*.
228 Dating *Daemons: White Witch of Devil's End* (story #5, "Daemos Returns") - It's the year following *The Daemons*, in which the sigil in question blasted Sgt Benton. Olive is now in her "late forties".
229 Dating *The Magician's Oath* (BF CC #3.10) - The story takes place between *The Daemons* and *Day of the Daleks*. Mention is made of frosty lawns being found in mid-July – while it's possible that the subsequent events take place some weeks later in August, it's probably best to assume that everything happens in the same month.
230 Dating *The Mega* (BF LS #4.4) - It's during Jo's time with UNIT. The Doctor is Earthbound (so, it's before *The Three Doctors*), and the Master – referenced as giving the Mega some off-screen consultation – isn't imprisoned, so it's not between *The Daemons* and *The Sea Devils*. Writer Bill Sutton named Cassier's country as Alberia, but Simon Guerrier, in adapting this story for audio, thought it too close to Albania, the country Alberia was clearly based on; "Golbasto" is a reference to *Gulliver's Travels*.

THE DOLL OF DEATH[231] -> The third Doctor and Jo investigated a temporal disturbance at the National Museum in Bloomsbury, where they encountered HannaH (sic), a "future historian" from a parallel Earth where time ran backwards. Our past was her future. HannaH had mentally crossed over to our universe to study the Doctor, the most consistent element that fended off all manner of global disasters, and her consciousness had come to occupy a doll. The Doctor and Jo facilitated HannaH's return home when Retrievers – dogs the size of ponies – were dispatched to fetch her back.

Jo kept missing her weekly training course because alien invasions typically happened on Fridays. Her instructor regarded her as a data-gathering operative.

THE SCORCHIES[232] -> The planet-wrecking Scorchies – whose members included Mr Grizzfizzle, Cool Cat, Magic Mice and Amble the Ugly Doll – established themselves on Earth as the titular characters of a children's show, and began murdering their viewers. Jo became trapped on the show, in which the Scorchies performed *Jo is Makin' a Thing* and *The Killing the Doctor Song*. The Doctor survived the Scorchies' attacks – including a rocket launcher that damaged Bessie – and sent their consciousness into space.

---

231 Dating *The Doll of Death* (BF CC #3.3) - Big Finish cites the story as taking place between *The Daemons* and *Day of the Daleks*. Jo says she's already gone out to dinner and a club with Mike Yates; presumably, this is a precursor to their thwarted attempt at "a night out on the town" in *The Curse of Peladon*.

Jo says she's 18 in this story, which presumably means that she was 17 when she joined UNIT – which is awfully young for someone to be dashing about with a leading military organisation that investigates the paranormal, high-ranking uncle at the United Nations or no. Katy Manning born in 1949, and so was 21 when she first played Jo.

232 Dating *The Scorchies* (BF CC #7.9) - It's unclear where the story takes place during Jo's UNIT tenure. A near-future setting is suggested when Jo urges the viewers at home to switch the channel, even if it means watching *Space: 1999* (which ran 17th October, 1975 to 1st May, 1978), as well as mention of *Pebble Mill at One* (1972-1986) and soufflé-maker Delia Smith, who became famous hosting *Family Fare* from 1973 to 1975.

233 *Iris S5: Comeback of the Scorchies*

234 Dating *Who Killed Kennedy* (MA, unnumbered) - See Ft. 35 (pg240) for the dates given in this book.

235 Dating *Day of the Daleks* (9.1) - This may have a contemporary setting. While the world is on the brink of WW3, a BBC reporter appears as himself.

Jo tells the Controller that she left the twentieth century on "September the 13th". The Controller notes, rather annoyingly for those trying to pin down the dates of the UNIT stories, that Jo has "already told me the year" she is from.

236 *Return of the Living Dad*

237 *UNIT S4: Assembled*

238 *No Future*

239 *Business Unusual*

240 *The Dimension Riders*. Rafferty is Professor of Extra-Terrestrial Studies at Oxford and the Doctor's old friend.

241 "Death to the Doctor!", in what looks like an incident from the Doctor's UNIT days.

242 *Unbound: Masters of War*, preferring a "year of broadcast" dating for *Day of the Daleks*.

243 INTERNATIONAL POLITICS IN THE UNIT ERA: In the UNIT era, there appear to be four superpowers: The US, USSR, China and the United Kingdom. In the nineteen-seventies, the world apparently lurches from a period of detente with the Soviet Union (*The Invasion*), to the brink of World War Three (*The Mind of Evil*, *Day of the Daleks*), but within a few years of *Day of the Daleks*, the Cold War has ended. *Invasion of the Dinosaurs* includes the line "back in the Cold War days". *Robot* is also set after the Cold War ended. *About Time* notes that "it's massively unlikely that the entire Cold War has ended at this point since the stories made/set in the 1980s seem to suggest a world where there's still a schism between the US and USSR (see especially *Time-Flight*)". Alternatively, it's evidence that *Robot* is set after *Time-Flight* (so after 1981), which ties in nicely with the date given in *Pyramids of Mars* (the 1980 date would be the date of *The Time Warrior*).

The Soviet system seems to survive – in *Battlefield* the Russian troops' uniforms bear the hammer and sickle, but they are operating on British soil under UN command, and the "Soviet Praesidium" is mentioned in *The Seeds of Death*.

Stories told since the collapse of the Soviet Union in the real world have referred to it: Ace mentions "perestroika" in *Timewyrm: Exodus*, and the Doctor talks of the collapse of the Soviet Union in *Just War*.

244 "A couple of weeks" before *The Face of the Enemy*.

245 *The Curse of Peladon*

246 Dating *The Face of the Enemy* (PDA #7) - This runs while the Doctor and Jo are away in *The Curse of Peladon*, and takes about a fortnight.

247 *The Face of the Enemy* and *No Future* both have the Brigadier and Doris involved in some capacity in the 1970s. Even setting aside how this clashes with the continuity of the *Lethbridge-Stewart* novels, they must be quite the on-again, off-again couple, as the Brig is living alone in the 1980s in *Mawdryn Undead*, but they're married in the 90s in *Battlefield*.

248 Dating *The Harvest of Time* (PDA #78) - It's while the Master is imprisoned between *The Daemons* and *The Sea Devils*. The Doctor discards the notion that Edwina McCrimmon has any relation to Jaime McCrimmon. Mention is made (p170) that a match between the Hull Kingston Rovers and Blackpool Borough respectively ended 3-5 (p170).

Iris Wildthyme once signed an exclusive contract with the Scorchies, who sought to use her unique voice to steal the souls of anyone who heard it. She sang for her supper halfway across the galaxy, but eventually escaped the Scorchies' thrall.[233]

The Death of Dodo Chaplet

(summer) - WHO KILLED KENNEDY[234] **->** James Stevens tried to reveal the truth about UNIT in a live broadcast on BBC3's *The Passing Parade*. His house was torched, and the UNIT Master kidnapped him. He was taken to the Glasshouse, a home for traumatised soldiers, and kept sedated for weeks. The Master was the director of the Glasshouse, and had been brainwashing the soldiers to create an army. He planned to send them through time to disrupt Earth's history.

Upon meeting Francis Cleary, Stevens managed to escape with him. He brought a TV crew back, but the place had been cleared out and Stevens was utterly discredited. Cleary was still under the Master's control, and killed Dodo on the Master's orders. The third Doctor instructed Stevens on how to use one of the Master's time rings, and he went back to 1963 to preserve the course of history. Stevens returned to his native time, haunted with the knowledge that his older self would kill Kennedy.

(12th-13th September) - DAY OF THE DALEKS[235] **->** UNIT were called in to guard the World Peace Conference at Auderly House. On the evening of 12th September, there was an assassination attempt on Sir Reginald Styles. Guerrillas from the future believed that Styles would sabotage the Conference, and that its failure would create a history in which the Daleks ruled Earth two hundred years hence. The third Doctor and Jo discovered that the guerrillas' interference, not Styles, had foiled the conference and paradoxically created this future.

A time-travelling squad of Daleks and Ogron footsoldiers attacked the House, attempting to guarantee that their version of history prevailed. The guerrilla Shura detonated a Dalekanium bomb and wiped out the invaders. With the delegates' survival, the guerrillas' history ceased to be.

Two Ogrons escaped and ended up in the village of Little Caldwell.[236] At some point, the Doctor and Jo found a group of marooned Ogrons in the Outer Hebrides, in an incident kept out of the UNIT files.[237] UNIT recovered a Dalek casing.[238] SeneNet recovered twenty-second century weaponry from the site of Auderly House.[239] James Rafferty wrote a paper about dust samples from the site.[240] The third Doctor, the Brigadier and Jo defeated a demonic-looking villain, the Mentor.[241]

= In 1972, the Brigadier lost forty-seven men while trying to take down a single Dalek. The incident was cited as a sign of his incompetence, no matter how much intel he presented of the danger the Daleks posed.[242]

The Cold War was brought to an end.[243] Surgeon-Lieutenant Harold Sullivan was posted to Faslane.[244] **The Doctor took Jo on a test flight of the TARDIS. Under the Time Lords' guidance, the TARDIS headed for Peladon.**[245]

= THE FACE OF THE ENEMY[246] **->** The Conclave, the surviving members of the parallel Earth devastated by Project: Inferno, captured the Koschei of their reality and used his TARDIS to open dimensional portals to Earth.

The Conclave members began replacing their parallel duplicates to gain positions of power, but UNIT came to suspect the plan. With the Doctor off world, the Brigadier allied himself with Royal Air Force lecturer Ian Chesterton and the imprisoned UNIT Master. The trio travelled to the parallel Earth, euthanised the dissected Koschei and severed the Conclave's link with the other Earth.

UNIT eliminated most of the Conclave members now stranded on Earth, but Marianne Kyle, the Conclave's Secretary General, remained at liberty.

Liz Shaw was on a US lecture tour. Ian Chesterton and Barbara had a son, John. By now, the Brigadier was in a relationship with Doris, an old friend from Sandhurst.[247]

THE HARVEST OF TIME[248] **->** Officials at the highest levels of the UK government knew of the Master's true nature, and that he had "maimed and murdered thousands". Nonetheless, they offered him certain luxuries in exchange for his assistance with Marine Equipment for the Reception, Modulation and Amplification of Neutrinos (MERMAN): a neutrino-based communications system for submarines. The UNIT Master used MERMAN to call for help from his future selves, but the alien Sild received his message in the far future. They used the signal's data to progressively remove the Master's incarnations from time, creating an ever-more-powerful time manipulator.

The Sild made incursions into this time zone to capture the UNIT Master – the last vital piece of their time controller. The third Doctor used the resultant time distortions to override the Time Lords' lockdown of the TARDIS, and took the Master to deal with the Sild's powerbase.

Jo Grant, Mike Yates and other UNIT operatives repelled the Sild, but Edwina McCrimmon – heir to McCrimmon Industries – was lost down a time tear, and arrived in the future on the planet Praxilon. The Doctor revised much of Edwina's history to come, restoring her to this time.

The Master returned to this time in an outdated TARDIS, hoping to have a good gloat at the Doctor's expense, and was unexpectedly re-captured by UNIT.

The Master Escapes Imprisonment

THE SEA DEVILS[249] -> Imprisoned at Fortress Island, the UNIT Master attempted to contact a dormant colony of Sea Devils in the English Channel, hoping to direct them to attack humankind. The Master won the confidence of Colonel Trenchard, the governor of the prison, by claiming the creatures were terrorists that threatened Britain's national security. Trenchard acceded to the Master's requests, enabling him to contact the Sea Devils and engineer his escape. Trenchard died when a team of Sea Devils overran the prison.

The third Doctor intervened and implored the Sea Devil leader to make peace with humankind, but a sneak Navy attack engineered by Robert Walker, the Parliamentary Private Secretary, convinced the Sea Devil leader to make war instead. Unable to contain the impending violence, the Doctor destroyed the underwater base and the Sea Devils within. The Master escaped shortly afterwards.

"Under Pressure"[250] - > The fourth Doctor landed on a submarine, quickly deduced it was on the trail of Sea Devils and convinced the crew he was the scientific advisor... unfortunately, the third Doctor was also involved. The fourth Doctor realised he had to play his part in history without giving away his identity. The Sea Devils attacked the submarine, and the two Doctors worked together over a radio link to translate a message to the Sea Devils, who withdrew.

THE EIGHT DOCTORS[251] -> The UNIT Master evaded capture by the third Doctor and Jo and reached his TARDIS, which was disguised as the sacrificial stone at Devil's End. The Doctor met his eighth incarnation at UNIT HQ.

"Target Practice"[252] -> The third Doctor and Jo headed to UN airbase 43, ostensibly UNIT's new training centre. They thought the Brigadier was there, but he was in Geneva and instead they met Colonel Ashe. But Ashe served tea to the Doctor before Jo, and misidentified an Auton as an Ogron – tipping the Doctor off that he was a bounder. He was a Russian spy, sent to abduct the Doctor. The Brigadier arrived as the Doctor captured Ashe.

249 Dating *The Sea Devils* (9.3) - This is probably set in the near future. The prison guards' vehicles and uniforms are futuristic. Although this is effectively a sequel to two stories, no indication is given how much time has passed since *Doctor Who and the Silurians* or *The Daemons*. The Master insists that his second television be in colour, but this doesn't mean that the story is set just after colour TV was introduced – before the advent of cheap colour portable TVs, a household would commonly have a big colour set and a smaller black and white one. The Master watches an episode of *The Clangers*, first broadcast in 1971 and repeated many times since.

The Twelfth Doctor Year Two: "Clara Oswald and the School of Death" pokes fun at the UNIT Dating issue by saying that the Sea Devils "first re-surfaced in 1972 – or possibly 1982".
250 Dating "Under Pressure" (*DWM Yearbook 1992*) - It's the "late twentieth century". It's unclear if this is an unseen part of *The Sea Devils* or a later encounter with the monsters. We've assumed the former.
251 Dating *The Eight Doctors* (EDA #1) - This happens straight after *The Sea Devils*.
252 Dating "Target Practice" (*DWM* #234) - The story takes place after *The Sea Devils*, as there's a Sea Devil target on the range. The Doctor says he hasn't been to Russia for "several hundred years", and regardless of whether that's historically or within his own timeline, that places the story before *Wages of Sin* and contra-

dicts *The Devil Goblins from Neptune*.
253 Dating *Tales from the Vault* (BF CC 6.1) - Jo names the titular characters from *The Sea Devils*, so it's after that. The one thing that initially seems telling but isn't: Jo records an account of this event over a cassette of Paul McCartney and Wings, but they were active from 1971 to 1981.
254 *The Mutants*
255 *The Time Monster*
256 According to a photograph of them seen in *The Day of the Doctor*.
257 In *The Green Death* it was "last year".
258 "The Heralds of Destruction". Yates wasn't involved in *The Invasion*, so this must reference a different meet-up.
259 Dating *The Time Monster* (9.5) - There's nothing to suggest this is the near future. Benton wishes Jo a "Merry Michaelmas". The TARDIS in this story appears to be fully functional – although this story is broadcast before *The Three Doctors*, perhaps it takes place afterwards. If not, then all the stories in Season Nine apparently take place between 13th September (*Day of the Daleks*) and 29th September (*The Time Monster*) of a given year.

This story is set in "the mid-seventies" according to *Falls the Shadow*, and "thirty years" before *The Quantum Archangel* (so 1973).
260 *Falls the Shadow*
261 *The Blue Angel*. At some unspecified point during

TALES FROM THE VAULT[253] -> Roddy Fletcher, a friend of Jo Grant, was briefly possessed by the mind of Kalicarache when he bought and donned the army jacket of Tommy Watkins. The third Doctor wrested the jacket off Roddy, and the item was relegated to the UNIT Vault.

The Time Lords assigned the third Doctor and Jo the task of delivering a message pod, and they departed for the planet Solos.[254] All UNIT HQs received a new standing order, priority A1, to be on the lookout for the UNIT Master.[255] The Coal Board closed Llanfairfach Colliery in South Wales.[256] Captain Mike Yates met Sara Kingdom.[257] Mike Yates was quite taken with Zoe Heriot, but the sentiment was cut short when she left in the TARDIS.[258]

(29th September) - THE TIME MONSTER[259] -> For several months, the UNIT Master had posed as one "Professor Thascales" to conduct research into the science of interstitial time at the Newton Institute in Wootton. He succeeded in developing TOM-TIT (Transmission of Matter Through Interstitial Time), a device capable of moving matter through the cracks between "now" and "now". However, the Master's true intentions were to use TOM-TIT to put Kronos, the ancient Chronovore, at his command.

The Master succeeded in bringing the Atlantean priest Krasis through time to assist him. The Master and Krasis set off back to Atlantis circa 1500 BC, and the third Doctor and Jo Grant pursued them there.

The Thascales Theorem was held by the United Nations for security purposes.[260] The Doctor and UNIT investigated abductions in Memphis, and were aided by singer Dusty Springfield.[261]

3rdA: STORM OF THE HOROFAX[262] -> The third Doctor and Jo thwarted the time traveller Arianda, one of the last Horofax Provosts, from sparking a nuclear holocaust. Arianda died as her spaceship's time engines overloaded. Temporal leakage erased the Doctor and Jo's stalwart colleague – Major Paul Hardy of UNIT – from history.

UNIT Year 6

(May) - RAGS[263] -> At Dartmoor, a bloody conflict between a punk band and a group of university students freed the Ragman, who animated their corpses. They staged punk band performances as part of the Unwashed and Unforgiving tour, mentally stimulating persons in the area to commit violence. The group's performances caused a riot at Dartmoor Prison, and saw a group of fox hunters massacred by escapees from an asylum. UNIT was called in as the band reached Cirbury, and the Ragman incited violence at Stonehenge. Kane Sawyer, a local ruffian and one of the Ragman's descendents, sacrificed himself to rebind the Ragman in some standing stones.

FIND AND REPLACE[264] -> Iris Wildthyme and an older version of Jo Grant learned that the third Doctor – knowing that Jo would leave him some day, and fearing that his enemies would hunt her down to gain knowledge of him – was plotting to put her into a "witness protection programme" of sorts, in which Jo would become Iris' companion. They discouraged him from doing so, but when Iris tried to return the older Jo home in her bus, they found themselves on an alien locale...

---

the Doctor's exile.
262 Dating *3rdA: Storm of the Horofax* (BF *The Third Doctor Adventures* #3.2) - Major Hardy says he first met the Doctor during "the Auton business" (either *Spearhead from Space* or *Terror of the Autons* – but more likely the latter, as Hardy also encountered the Axons; *The Claws of Axos*). He's been with UNIT "two years", so although the other story in this box set (*3rdA: The Conquest of Far*) happens in UNIT Year 6, *Storm of the Horofax* is most likely UNIT Year 5. All told, it appears that Hardy's deletion from history hands Mike Yates the chance join UNIT in his place (*Terror of the Autons*). For non-UK residents, Kent Downs is a conservation area in south-east England.
263 Dating *Rags* (PDA #40) - This was the first PDA that didn't specify on the cover which TV stories it was set between. The Doctor's exile has not been lifted, yet Jo

refers to Daleks and Ogrons, meaning it takes place between *Day of the Daleks* and *The Three Doctors*.
    It is "the beginning of May" when the Ragman starts his campaign, "Tuesday 10th May" a little later. The year is given as "79" at the beginning of the book (although 10th May wasn't a Tuesday in 1979). It is after Malcolm Owen of the Ruts died (July 1980, in real life), and The Damned song "I Just Can't Be Happy Today" was released (November 1979).
264 Dating *Find and Replace* (BF CC #4.3) - The Doctor thinks about nicking a component from Iris' bus, so his exile is still in force. UNIT is now based in "an old manor house" (so it's more likely to be Season 9 than Season 8), and the Master is at liberty. Taking all of that into account, Iris and the older Jo must show up somewhere between *The Sea Devils* and *The Three Doctors*. The older Jo and Iris next appear in *The Elixir of Doom*.

(May) - VERDIGRIS[265] -> The third Doctor and the Brigadier fell out after defeating an Arcturan who had arrived on Earth with sinister intent. The Doctor decided to take a break from UNIT and went to an old mansion he owned in the town of Thisis.

The alien Verdigris, who had been drifting towards Earth for thousands of years, contacted a race of refugees named the Meercocks. The Meercocks had decided to settle on Earth disguised as characters from Earth's fiction.

Iris Wildthyme and her companion Tom called on the Doctor, and they discovered the Meercocks' plan. They defeated an army of robot sheep and The Children of Destiny, a group of annoying psychic teenagers working for Galactic Federation Supreme Headquarters in Wales.

Verdigris escaped to inform Omega that the Doctor was on Earth.

DEyes 2: EYES OF THE MASTER[266] -> The bald Master saved Sally Armstrong from a fatal taxi accident, hypnotised her and took control of the Ides Scientific Institute. As the ophthalmologist "Harcourt De'ath", he worked to harness Molly O'Sullivan's retrogenitor particles as a means of controlling the Eminence's Infinite Warriors. The eighth Doctor, Molly and Liv made the Master's TARDIS – with him and Sally aboard – hurtle into the future, to the impending destruction of a warfleet.

The Doctor left Molly and Liv at his home at 107 Baker Street – which had been occupied for decades by David Walker – to facilitate events Liv had witnessed on Nixyce VII in the future. In his absence, the Master and Sally returned and kidnapped Molly.

On orders from Coordinator-in-Extremis Narvin, the Gallifreyan CIA relocated Liv to the planet Remosa in the future.[267]

(July) - ST: "Damascus"/ ST: "The World Beyond the Trees"[268] -> Two fugitives from the planet Augustine's Mercy escaped to Earth with a Listnessness Field device. Over the Doctor's objections, the UK government founded the Damascus Project to study the fugitives' spaceship. The elder fugitive died, but his daughter Lilla triggered the Listnessness Field when a race of traders, the Milliar, tried to seize it. Much of the UK entered a stupor as the third Doctor, accompanied by the Prime Minister – a man named Jeremy – threatened to let the field affect the Milliar also, and they retreated.

At the Doctor's Baker Street house, Liv Chenka's future-human biology protected her as the field overcame Molly O'Sullivan. Liv helped Lilla reclaim her spaceship, ending the Damascus Project. The Prime Minister recorded a warning for his successors that in his view, the Doctor comprised the top threat to their great nation.

---

265 Dating *Verdigris* (PDA #30) - The month and year are stated in the book as "1973" and "May". Jo has known the Doctor "two years" (p143). Paul Magrs playfully made it tricky to place this story precisely... the story leads into *The Three Doctors* (p241), and yet Jo doesn't know about Peladon (p192). This is after the eventful UNIT Christmas party (p126).

266 Dating *DEyes 2: Eyes of the Master* (BF *DEyes* #2.4) - The era is repeatedly broadbrushed as "the 1970s." It's some time on from the Master saving Sally from death by taxi, an event that presumably coincides with Kortis approaching her on 6th July, 1970, in the erased timeline. However, *ST: "The World Beyond the Trees"* concerns what happens to Liv and Molly at 107 Baker Street while the Doctor is away (following *DEyes 2: Eyes of the Master*), and happens simultaneous to *ST: "Damascus"*, necessitating that *Eyes of the Master* also gets folded into the UNIT Era.

267 *DEyes 3: The Reviled*

268 Dating *ST: "Damascus"* and *ST: "The World Beyond the Trees"* (BF *ST* #6.8, 7.1) - These interwoven stories feature the Prime Minister named Jeremy from *The Green Death* (almost certainly Jeremy Thorpe; see the British Politics in the UNIT Era and Beyond sidebar) and Liv Chenka following events in *DEyes 2: Eyes of the Master*. Liv says it's the "the 1970s"/"the eighth decade of the twentieth century". It's during Jo Grant's time at

UNIT. There remains unease about the military's deployment of force at Wenley Moor (*Doctor Who and the Silurians*). The month is given.

We know very little about Thorpe's tenure as Prime Minister in the *Doctor Who* universe, but it's possible it ended in disgrace (as with his real-life career), explaining why there's no evidence of his successors heeding his warning about the Doctor. Jonathan Barnes, the writer of *ST: "Damascus"*, told us there might be a story behind why Thorpe's warning gets ignored, or that Torchwood simply dealt with it, wanting to keep an eye on the Doctor themselves.

269 Dating *The Three Doctors* (10.1) - The evidence is mixed. Dr Tyler says the Americans have launched a deep space monitor, but he also cites "Cape Kennedy". (This might suggest that *The Three Doctors* takes place between 1963 and 1973.) Jo misquotes the words to "I am the Walrus". According to *Transit* (and a number of novelisations, such as *The Mysterious Planet*), the Doctor's exile lasts "five years".

270 *The Legends of River Song: "Suspicious Minds".* This happens during "the seventies", and contexualises River having "dated a Nestene once" (*The Big Bang*).

271 Dating "The Heralds of Destruction" (Titan 3rd Doc #1-5) - For the Doctor, it's very shortly after his exile ends in *The Three Doctors* (which is how Salamander so easily impersonates the second Doctor). The Doctor

The third Doctor's exile ends

THE THREE DOCTORS[269] -> The stellar engineer Omega, having survived in a universe of anti-matter, began incursions into the matter universe and started draining power from the Time Lord homeworld. With Omega's attention focused on the exiled third Doctor, the Time Lords decided to violate the First Law of Time and dispatch the Doctor's previous two incarnations to aid his current self.

The first Doctor was trapped in a time eddy and could only advise on the situation, but the second and third Doctors travelled to Omega's anti-matter universe. Omega desired to leave his domain, and tried to coerce the Doctors into becoming his successors. The Doctors escaped after triggering a matter/anti-matter explosion that seemingly destroyed Omega. The Time Lord homeworld regained full power.

The Time Lords sent the Doctor's previous selves back to their native times, and in gratitude ended the Doctor's exile. They restored his knowledge of time travel, and repaired the TARDIS to its proper function.

River Song hoped to witness three Doctors in action during the Omega affair, but was disappointed that most of the escapade happened away from Earth. She wound up meeting an Auton survivor who had taken to posing as Elvis in Madame Tussauds. "Elvis" was a bit of a humanophile, and they struck up an on-again, off-again romance.[270]

"The Heralds of Destruction"[271] -> While the Doctor and UNIT dealt with rampaging robots in Fairford, Bedfordshire, Ramon Salamander infiltrated the Doctor's lab disguised as the second Doctor. Salamander plundered enough TARDIS technology and know-how to make his Electronicon Ltd. complex time-active. The UNIT Master objected to a human purloining Time Lord technology, so rode along with the Doctor, Jo Grant and the Brigadier in Salamander's complex back to 1868...

Upon their return, Salamander quickly escaped. The Brigadier realised that the tea lady had planted bugs in UNIT on Salamander's behalf, so ordered a greater vetting of tea ladies. The third Doctor claimed familiarity with Pol Pot, whom he called "Polly".

The Doctor constructed a force field generator and took the TARDIS on a test flight.[272] He defeated the Brotherhood of Beltane and blobby aliens called the Talichre, and the encounters went down in UNIT legend.[273] Miss Gallowglass (later Countess Gallowglass) started running a mail forwarding service for aliens and time travellers alike, operating from a Portakabin in the East End. The Doctor first met her just after his exile on Earth ended. One of her customers, irate at a misplaced parcel, declared war on Earth and stole Britain's Crown Jewels. The Time Lords replaced the jewels with fakes, preserving history.[274]

THE WAGES OF SIN[275] -> The third Doctor offered to take Jo Grant and his former companion Liz Shaw to witness the Siberian meteorite strike in 1908. Instead, they erroneously arrived in St Petersburg, 1916, shortly before the murder of Rasputin.

3rdA: PRISONERS OF THE LAKE / 3rdA: THE HAVOC OF EMPIRES[276] -> Several governments helped to fund ArcheoTech, an archeological undertaking that discovered the Federal Jurasdictorate spaceship at the bottom of Dunstanton Lake in Britain. The third Doctor, Jo and Captain Yates examined the vessel as two robots cast in stone, the Prosecutor and Defense Advocate assigned to handle the Dastron leaders' trial, awoke. The Defense

here decides that he should leave the UNIT nest and travel more, leading to *Carnival of Monsters*. It's been "over a decade"/"a decade" since Salamander's arrival on Earth concurrent to *The Web of Fear* [UNIT Year -4].

The Pol Pot reference (he ruled Cambodia as a dictator from 1963-1981) plays off the Doctor's bizarre claim in *The Mind of Evil* that he enjoys Chairman Mao's company. The unseen tea lady from *Terror of the Autons* did seem to have a remarkably high security clearance.

The Master's masks (*Terror of the Autons* et al), we learn, are so effective because they're extensions of his TARDIS. The Master here counters the Doctor's Venusian Aikido with Martian Kendo, but the Doctor prevails with Mercurian Kung Fu.

272 The Doctor says at the end of *The Three Doctors* that he needs to build a new force field generator to replace the one that has been destroyed, and goes on a test flight in *Carnival of Monsters*.

273 *Relative Dementias*

274 *Relative Dementias* (p18) mentions when the Doctor encountered the Countess.

275 Dating *The Wages of Sin* (PDA #19) - It's just after *The Three Doctors*, in "the 1970s" (p34).

276 Dating *3rdA: Prisoners of the Lake* and *3rdA: The Havoc of Empires* (BF *The Third Doctor Adventures* #1.1-1.2) - These two stories feature the third Doctor, Jo Grant and Mike Yates. In *Prisoners of the Lake*, Jo mentions having taken a UNIT underwater assault course "last year", ruling out Season Eight. *The Havoc of Empires* happens "shortly after" end of the Doctor's exile (in *The Three Doctors*), but the Doctor and Jo also reference the Drashigs from *Carnival of Monsters*, so it's after that. There's no need for the stories to occur back-to-back, but where *Havoc* goes, *Prisoners* might as well also.

Advocate released the fiendish Dastrons, whereupon the Dastrons made preparations to engage the ship's hyperdrive and escape – knowing this would devastate Earth. Yates destroyed the Defense Advocate with a grenade, which cracked the ship's hull. The UNIT crew escaped as the water flooded the hyperdrive, which destroyed the Dastrons and the ship upon its activation.

Later, the Doctor reluctantly consented to help Yates and Jo have a "night out" in history. Jo wished to see the Beatles in 1961, but Yates convinced her to go to W.G. Grace's last international cricket match at Trent Bridge, 1899. The Doctor set the TARDIS in motion... but they found themselves two thousand years in the future, aboard Harmony Station.

THE HIDDEN REALM[277] -> In Bramfield New Town, the third Doctor and Jo encountered an alien Acridian, Overseer Zim, and ended his lucrative body-swapping operation.

THE DEFECTORS[278] -> The Europans on Delphin Isle infiltrated UNIT, believing that the Doctor could aid them in escaping from Earth...

(=) Owing to the Monk's efforts to unravel the Doctor's timeline, the seventh Doctor replaced the third Doctor. The seventh Doctor repaired the Europan vessel and offered to supply power from the TARDIS – even though this would drain the third Doctor's Ship completely, killing it. Jo refused to allow such a sacrifice and interrupted the power flow, causing the Europan ship to explode and level Delphin Isle. The Doctor's timeline was preserved, and Jo forgot that the seventh Doctor was present.

The Doctor and Jo met Iris and Tom in a cocktail joint on a far flung outpost.[279] **Professor Whitaker disappeared when the government refused to fund his time-travel research.**[280] Tobias Vaughn funded Whitaker's experiments.[281]

The Doctor and Jo set off on another test flight. They landed on Inter Minor, where they became trapped in a MiniScope owned by the Lurman entertainer Vorg.[282]

THE SUNS OF CARESH[283] -> Lord Roche, a Gallifreyan, discovered that Caresh would enter a seventy-four year cold period that would extinguish all life on the planet. Roche set about modifying the Careshi time scanner into a

---

277 Dating *The Hidden Realm* (BF 3rd Doc #2.2) - With no tangible dating clues, the story might as well slot into place after *The Third Doctor Adventures* Vol. 1.

278 Dating *The Defectors* (BF #198) - Jo has met the Doctor's earlier incarnations (*The Three Doctors*), but it's before Captain Yates' downfall (*Invasion of the Dinosaurs*). The story favors a near-future dating for the UNIT era, with Jo claiming that "nearly thirty years" and "about thirty years" have passed since 1951. Likewise, Captain Yates says that the Europan infiltration of the UK government was "thirty years in the making". The Monk's plans culminate in *The Secret History*.

279 *Verdigris*

280 "Six months" before *Invasion of the Dinosaurs*.

281 *Original Sin*

282 *Carnival of Monsters*, in which Jo says that 1926 is "forty years" before her time.

283 Dating *The Suns of Caresh* (PDA #56) - It is soon after the Doctor's exile is lifted (p35), and straight after the TARDIS gets back from Inter Minor (p36).

284 Dating *The Many Deaths of Jo Grant* (BF CC #6.4) - The blurb says that the story occurs between *Carnival of Monsters* and *Frontier in Space*.

285 *Dancing the Code* (p61). These unseen encounters either occur with UNIT, or elsewhere with the Doctor.

286 *Interference* (p75).

287 Dating *Dancing the Code* (MA #9) - Set between *Planet of the Daleks* and *The Green Death*. Watergate appears to be topical (p154).

288 *The Android Invasion*. Sarah reported on Crayford's

disappearance "two years" before that story.

289 Dating *Last of the Gaderene* (PDA #28) - It is "some thirty years" since WW2 (p241). A constable indicates that it's the "the middle of July", which would contradict all four of the calendars in *The Green Death*.

290 Dating *Speed of Flight* (MA #27) - Jo is now thinking about leaving the Doctor (p242).

291 *Timelash*. *Speed of Flight* implies the Karfel visit occurs shortly afterwards, and involved Mike Yates. *Worlds DW: The Screaming Skull/Second Sight* also names Yates as the third person who went to Karfel.

292 *Original Sin*

293 Dating *The Green Death* (10.5) - This is the near future. The Prime Minister is called Jeremy. BOSS is an advanced "Biomorphic" artificial intelligence that has been linked to a human brain. There is a Ministry of Ecology. Four calendars appear: the first, in the pithead office, shows the date as "April 5th". The second, in the security guard's office, shows the month as February during a leap year. A wall calendar in Elgin's office suggests that it's May, but a similar one seen behind Mike Yates in episode four indicates that it's Monday, 28th April. (See the British Politics in the UNIT Era sidebar.)

Global Conspiracy?, a 2004 mockumentary on *The Green Death* DVD, dates the story to time-of-broadcast by claiming that documents pertaining to the Global Chemicals incident have been released per the "thirty year rule". A file on-screen bears the date "June 17th, 1973", in the zone of when *The Green Death* was broadcast (from 19th May to 23rd June of that year).

stellar manipulator, hoping to save the planet's Fayon civilisation, which was a curiosity to him. Roche intended to deviate a neutron star and use its gravity to bump Caresh into orbit around its warmer star Beacon, but the Curia of the Nineteen – rulers of the Realm of the Vortex Dwellers – forecast that the diverted neutron star would devastate their territory. They dispatched two Furies to attack Roche, but he trapped the Furies within his TARDIS and sent it back in time thirteen centuries. It was unearthed in 1999, creating a time anomaly that the third Doctor detected.

The Doctor used Roche's equipment to manoeuvre Caresh closer to its smaller star Ember, avoiding damage to the Curia's territory. The Curia refrained from sending the Furies to attack Roche, averting the 1999 anomaly.

THE MANY DEATHS OF JO GRANT[284] -> The Hargarans rebelled against their subjugators, the Xoanthrax Empire. The Xoanthrax had no sense of self-sacrifice, and were perplexed by Hargaran kamikaze runs on their outposts. The Brigadier chafed because a mysterious purple mould was spreading on the outside of Big Ben, and the Doctor was unavailable to investigate it. He was away in the Xoanthrax System, where he rescued a Xoanthrax peace activist: Vorlan. A detachment of the Xoanthrax Stormtroopers – living tanks with a Xoanthrax within directing them – pursued the TARDIS back to UNIT HQ. A Vanguard scientist named Rowe abducted Jo, hoping to study her keen sense of self-sacrifice. She was placed in a mindscape generator – a device that created false scenarios in the mind – and was made to "die" four hundred and twelve times. The Doctor freed Jo and Vorlan, but Rowe harvested much information on self-sacrifice – leaving the Doctor and Jo unsure if the Empire would use the data benevolently, or perpetrate greater atrocities with it.

Before this time, Jo had met a number of alien races including the Methaji, Hoveet, Skraals and Kalekani.[285] The Kalekani aggressively terra-formed worlds into rolling grasslands using the memetic virus known on Earth as the game "golf".[286]

DANCING THE CODE[287] -> There were reports of "unorthodox weapons" in the North Africa country of Kebiria. UNIT sent a Superhawk jet fighter to investigate, and discovered a nest of Xarax – an insect hivemind. The Xarax began to infest the rest of the country, including the capital, Kebir City. The US Navy prepared a nuclear strike, but a UNIT team from the United Kingdom deactivated the nest using synthesised chemical instructions.

Defence astronaut Guy Crayford's XK5 space freighter, launched from Devesham Control, was lost during a test flight. It was believed to have collided with an asteroid. Sarah Jane Smith reported on the story.[288]

LAST OF THE GADERENE[289] -> By now, the surviving Gaderene numbered only three hundred thousand. The Gaderene scout Bliss had founded the aeronautics manufacturer Legion International as a front for her operations, and enslaved residents of the British town Culverton by implanting them with Gaderene embryos. Bliss repaired the Gaderene transmat, intending to bring thousands of adult Gaderene through to Earth as an invasion force. However, UNIT's involvement resulted in the deaths of Bliss, her towering brother and the Gaderene embryos. The transmat was destroyed, and the resultant energy backlash further annihilated the Gaderene invasion force and homeworld.

SPEED OF FLIGHT[290] -> The Doctor, Jo Grant and Mike Yates departed in the TARDIS for the planet Karfel, but arrived on the planet Nooma in the far future by mistake.

At some point, the Doctor and Jo (and possibly someone else) succeeded in visiting Karfel.[291] Tobias Vaughn helped develop the BOSS computer for Global Chemicals.[292]

Jo Grant Leaves the TARDIS and UNIT

THE GREEN DEATH[293] -> The Doctor succeeded in reaching Metebelis III, and acquired one of its famed blue sapphires.

The government gave the green light to Global Chemicals' experiments into the Stevens Process, which produced 25% more petrol from a given amount of crude oil. The "Nutcake Professor" Clifford Jones – who had won the Nobel prize for his work on DNA synthesis – protested that the process would double air pollution, but Global Chemicals claimed that the pollution generated was negligible.

UNIT were sent to investigate a body that was discovered in the abandoned coal mine – a body that was glowing green. They discovered Global Chemicals had been dumping the pollution created by the Stevens Process into the mine, and that it had mutated the maggots down there. The giant maggots produced a slime that was toxic to humans, but the Doctor and Professor Jones discovered a fungus that killed them.

Global Chemicals was run by the BOSS, or Bimorphic Organisational Systems Supervisor, a computer linked to the brain of Stevens. In an effort to help the world achieve "maximum efficiency", the BOSS attempted to mentally dominate Global staff at seven sites throughout the world, including Llanfairfach, New York, Moscow and Zurich. Global Chemicals was destroyed when the BOSS blew up. Professor Jones' Nuthutch was given UN Priority One research status, leading to "unlimited funding".

The Prime Minister was called Jeremy. Jo Grant left UNIT at this time to marry Professor Jones.

The newlyweds went on an expedition to the Amazon.[294]

(August) - THE RINGS OF IKIRIA[295] -> The transdimensional Etherians drew psionic energy from etheric crystals. One of their number, Ikiria, went mad after absorbing power from a flawed crystal, and sought to bestow "the gift of her art" on other races by enslaving and transmogrifying them with mind-controlling rongs. Ikiria distributed her rings to some UNIT staff members, but Captain Mike Yates aided the third Doctor in reversing the polarity of Ikiria's etheric crystal, rendering her incapable of physical form on our plane of existence.

DEEP BLUE[296] -> The fifth Doctor, Tegan and Turlough landed in Tayborough Sands for a holiday and met up with UNIT. With "their" Doctor away, UNIT recruited his later incarnation to investigate a mutilated corpse. The Xaranti were attempting to convert Earth into a new homeworld, but they were defeated. Most of the UNIT staff involved in this adventure lost their memories of it, with only Captain Yates remembering the Doctor's future incarnation.

THE THREE COMPANIONS[297] -> The Brigadier accompanied the third Doctor to answer a distress call from deep-space freighter 621 Gamma Delta in the Deuteronomy Quadrant. The freighter contained a large representation of London and various Earth icons – including the Statue of Liberty, the Eiffel Tower, Queen Victoria, etc – as part of an alien game intended for children. The Doctor again encountered Jerry Lenz, a.k.a. "Garry Lendler," who had been hired to maintain the representation and purchase props for it. The representation was on its last legs, and the Doctor terminated the simulation.

(24th December) - COUNCIL OF WAR[298] -> With Captain Yates on leave and Jo Grant having left UNIT, the third Doctor asked Sgt Benton to look into multiple reports of ghost-sightings in Kettering, Northamptonshire. Benton posed as a member of the Kettering Council, and was drawn along when time-travelers abducted Councilwoman Margery Phipps – the local representative for the Harmony Party – to the future. The Doctor followed in the TARDIS, and brought the two of them home.

UNIT Year 7

Sarah Jane Smith Joins the TARDIS

THE TIME WARRIOR[299] -> British research scientists began to mysteriously disappear. UNIT were called in and the leading research scientists were all confined to the same barracks in a secret location. Nevertheless, the press got wind of the story. A young reporter named Sarah Jane Smith smuggled herself into the complex by posing as her Aunt Lavinia, the noted virologist. Before long, Sarah and the third Doctor had followed a time disturbance back to the Middle Ages.

294 *Planet of the Spiders*
295 Dating *The Rings of Ikiria* (BF CC #6.12) - Yates specifies the month as "August". No mention is made of Liz Shaw, Jo Grant or Sarah Jane Smith, but Yates, the Doctor and the Brigadier have a good rapport, so this story can be reasonably placed between *The Green Death* and *The Time Warrior*.
296 Dating *Deep Blue* (PDA #20) - It's "six months" after *The Green Death*, and it's Mike's first mission since then. The Doctor has spent only a small amount of time on Earth since Jo's departure, but there's no mention of Sarah. This is "six months" after *The Green Death* (p15), "ten or so" years before Tegan's native 1984 (p20).
297 Dating *The Three Companions* (serialised story; BF #120-129) - Jo has moved to Wales and the Doctor is companion-less, so it's between *The Green Death* and *The Time Warrior*.
298 Dating *Council of War* (BF CC #7.12) - For Benton and the Doctor, it's between *The Green Death* and *The Time Warrior*, on "Christmas Eve" in "the 1970s". Benton claims that Jo Grant spent "several years" with the Doctor, when by any real measure it was about three. A time of broadcast dating is indicated when Margery mentions "the new" James Bond and the Australian sounding one before him, respectively citing Roger Moore (who debuted in the role in *Live and Let Die*, Summer 1973) and George Lazenby (*On Her Majesty's Secret Service*, 1969).
299 Dating *The Time Warrior* (11.1) - Sarah states in this story that she's from the twentieth century, and isn't more specific than that. In *Pyramids of Mars*, it's stated four times that Sarah is "from 1980". The most straightforward interpretation of the line has to be that this story, Sarah's first, is set in 1980.
300 Dating *The Paradise of Death* (Target novelisation #156) - The Brigadier hasn't heard of Virtual Reality, and the Secretary-General of the United Nations is a woman. There is no gap on television between *The Time Warrior* and *Invasion of the Dinosaurs*, but this features both Sarah and Mike Yates. Barry Letts decided to set this radio play before Mike Yates' "retirement" from UNIT. Captain Yates is referred to in the book version.
301 Dating *Invasion of the Dinosaurs* (11.2) - The balance of evidence is that this is the near future. The Whomobile is a new car and an "M" reg, but the human

THE PARADISE OF DEATH[300] -> The Parakon Corporation opened Space World on Hampstead Heath. It offered many attractions based on space and space travel, including twenty-one alien creatures such as the Giant Ostroid, the crab-clawed Kamelius from Aldebaran Two, Piranhatel Beetles and Stinksloths. Using Experienced Reality techniques, Parakon could give people guided tours of the Gargatuan Caverns of Southern Mars and the wild side of Mercury.

UNIT investigated the death of a young man whose thighbone had been bitten clean through, and exposed the Parakon Corporation as an extra-terrestrial organisation. Parakon had been negotiating with Earth for a number of years, hoping to sign a trading agreement. Parakon would supply a wonder material, rapine, in exchange for human bodies to fertilise their world, which had been devastated by the rapine harvests. Parakon had already sacked many worlds, including Blestinu, but UNIT defeated it.

Mike Yates, Disgraced, Leaves UNIT

INVASION OF THE DINOSAURS[301] -> Eight million Londoners were evacuated after dinosaurs began to terrorise the population. The government decamped to Harrogate. UNIT helped with the security operation, which was under the command of General Finch and the Minister for Special Powers, Sir Charles Grover.

UNIT scientists calculated that someone was operating a time machine that required an atomic reactor. They tracked the Timescoop in question to a hidden bunker near Moorgate Underground Station. The bunker contained an elaborate shelter that served as home to a group of people – including the conservationist Lady Cullingford, the novelist Nigel Castle and the Olympic long jumper John Crichton – who were all convinced they were in a spaceship bound for a new,

unpolluted planet. Using the Timescoop, Professor Whitaker hoped to regress Earth back to its primeval days, repopulating it with the people in the bunker. The Doctor and UNIT ended this plan, and Whitaker and Grover were stranded in the past. Mike Yates, a member of the conspiracy, was discharged from UNIT.

During this, the Doctor unveiled his new car.[302] At the Brigadier's request, Sarah Jane spread a cover story about the Operation: Golden Age incident, claiming that a "terrorist threat" had ended.[303] Sarah Jane Smith signed the Official Secrets Act, and was paid well – better than the Doctor, even – to keep quiet about what she knew.[304]

COUNCIL OF WAR[305] -> After dealing with "a spot of bother" involving some dinosaurs in London, Sgt Benton went to Kettering to enjoy a dance with Margery Phipps.

After this time, the temporal scientist Chun Sen was born.[306] Realising that UNIT might need to contact him in an emergency, the Doctor gave the Brigadier a syonic beam Space-Time Telegraph.[307] The Brigadier gave Mike Yates a hip flask the day he left the service.[308] The Doctor left a sonic screwdriver in his UNIT lab, hoping that someone would understand the device's workings so that he could – if needed – make use of their expertise. In future, junior probationary officer Will Arrowsmith gained some knowledge of the device.[309]

THE FIVE DOCTORS[310] -> While on Earth at this time, the third Doctor was kidnapped by Borusa while driving his sprightly yellow roadster Bessie.

---

race are – in theory at least – capable of building manned ships capable of interstellar flight. Whitaker has built a Timescoop capable of calling up dinosaurs from hundreds of millions of years ago. The bunker was built "back in the Cold War days".

302 The Doctor's car was never named on screen, but was dubbed both "Alien" and "the Whomobile" by the production team. The Doctor continues to use Bessie, as both are seen in *Planet of the Spiders*.

303 *SJA: Judgement Day*

304 *Downtime* (p254). The compensation doesn't prevent Sarah Jane from being crunched for cash in the *Sarah Jane Smith* audios, but she seems reasonably well off in *The Sarah Jane Adventures*.

305 Dating *Council of War* (BF CC #7.12) - The epilogue occurs shortly after *Invasion of the Dinosaurs*.

306 *Invasion of the Dinosaurs*. The Doctor says that

Chun Sen couldn't be a suspect with regards to the dinosaur appearances as he "hasn't been born yet".

307 *Terror of the Zygons*. Presumably the Brigadier didn't have the Space-Time Telegraph before *Invasion of the Dinosaurs*, when dinosaurs were over-running London, or he would surely have used it.

308 *Hornets' Nest: Hive of Horror*

309 *Persuasion*

310 Dating *The Five Doctors* (20.7) - The third Doctor is kidnapped after *The Time Warrior* as he recognises Sarah. Sticking strictly to what we know in the television series, his abduction must occur between *The Monster of Peladon* and *Planet of the Spiders*, because the other stories of Season 11 follow on from each other. However *The Paradise of Death* is set in a "nonexistent" gap between the first two stories of the series, so the Doctor might have been taken from that point.

> (=) The Great Intelligence witnessed the third Doctor as he zoomed along in Bessie. An iteration of Clara Oswald overwrote the Intelligence, but failed to attract the Doctor's attention.[311]

(20th-21st May) - THE GHOSTS OF N-SPACE[312] ->

While on holiday in Italy, the third Doctor, Sarah, Jeremy Fitzoliver and the Brigadier prevented Maximillian Vilmio, a wizard, from achieving immortality. Vilmio had planned to use the space-warping effect of Clancy's comet to match his real body and his N-form in Null-Space.

ISLAND OF DEATH[313] -> Sarah investigated the disappearance of Jeremy, and found he had joined a cult that worshipped a reptilian alien called Skang. The third Doctor helped her discover that the cultists' drinks were laced with psychotropics. They flew to Bombay with the Brigadier, and traced the cult to Stella Island, but the Great Skang was summoned to Earth. It had infected followers with spores – a means of preserving its race. The Doctor placed the Skang gestalt in a time loop to preserve it.

UNIT Year 8

To prevent nuclear launches, the US, USSR and China gave their Destructor Codes to Britain. Joseph Chambers was made Special Responsibilities Secretary with responsibility for protecting them.[314]

Three years and eight months after the Doctor and Liz defeated the Sentinels of the New Dawn, Terri Billington had a fatal stroke. She had only been CMS chair for a month and a day, and Liz succeeded her in the post.[315]

AMORALITY TALE[316] -> Sarah Jane discovered a 1952 photograph of the third Doctor while researching a story. The Doctor was intrigued by a "warp shadow" on the photo, and the two of them went to 1952 to investigate.

"Prisoners of Time"[317] -> The Remoraxians – a race of interstellar parasites, a sort of "space remora" – captured a UNIT nautical research facility, and worked to terraform Earth into a waterworld suitable to their needs. With the third Doctor and Sarah away, UNIT recruited Liz Shaw to

311 *The Name of the Doctor*
312 Dating *The Ghosts of N-Space* (MA #7) - For the Doctor and Sarah, the story occurs after *Death to the Daleks*. Clancy's Comet returns to Earth every one hundred and fifty-seven years, and the last sighting was in "1818", so it's 1975. As the month is given as May, *Planet of the Spiders*, set in March, must take place the following year. Fitzoliver was Sarah's photographer in *The Paradise of Death*.
313 Dating *Island of Death* (PDA #71) - The story mentions Sarah's trip to Sicily in *The Ghosts of N-Space*, and the Hallaton arrived on Stella Island on 20th September, so this story happens in UNIT Year 7.
314 "A few months" before *Robot*. The system has passed to UN control by *World War Three*.
315 *The Sentinels of the New Dawn*
316 Dating *Amorality Tale* (PDA #52) - The story starts between *The Monster of Peladon* and *Planet of the Spiders*.
317 Dating "Prisoners of Time" (IDW *DW* mini-series) - The story takes place during Season 11 and takes a stand on UNIT Dating, with a caption stating that it's "1974". It's implied that the Doctor hasn't seen Liz since she left for Cambridge prior to *Terror of the Autons*, although she comes and goes with UNIT so frequently in the tie-in stories, it could be interpreted that he hasn't seen her since the *last time* she left for Cambridge. The Doctor's futuristic car is here pulled "out of mothballs", but as it only recently debuted (*Invasion of the Dinosaurs*) and readily re-appears in *Planet of the Spiders*, it's not clear why it would have been put into storage in the first place.
318 The Doctor is conducting such research in *Planet*

of the Spiders. It's only mentioned in that story, and there's no suggestion that the fourth Doctor continues the study.
319 Dating *Planet of the Spiders* (11.5) - The story takes place three weeks before *Robot*. "Meditation is the in thing" according to Sarah Jane.
320 Dating *Robot* (12.1) - This is clearly set in the near future. As with *Invasion of the Dinosaurs*, the Cold War has been "over for years" according to the Brigadier. Advanced technology includes the K1 robot, the Disintegrator Gun and dynastrene. Sarah Jane Smith's day pass to Think-Tank bears the date "April 4th".
321 *Original Sin*
322 *SJS: Mirror, Signal, Manoeuvre*
323 *Benny: The Relics of Jegg-Sau*
324 In *The Ark in Space*, Harry is surprised that the High Minister, "a member of the fair sex," was "top of the totem pole", suggesting Britain has yet to elect a female Prime Minister by his time. There must be a General Election or change of leadership in the government while he was away from Earth. In *Terror of the Zygons*, the Brigadier receives a phone call from the PM, whom he twice addresses as "Madam", and later refers to as "she".
325 *Hornets' Nest: The Stuff of Nightmares*
326 Dating *Terror of the Zygons* (13.1) - It is the near future. The Prime Minister is a woman. In *Pyramids of Mars*, two stories after this one, Sarah states that she is "from 1980". According to *No Future*, this story is set in January 1976.
327 *SJA: Judgement Day*
328 *The Zygon Invasion*

assist as storms and weather fronts intensified across the world. The Doctor and Sarah returned as President Nixon learned of the Remoraxian threat and informed US military and intelligence personnel worldwide that he had authorized an Omega Solution: the nuclear annihilation of the Great Britain to destroy the Remoraxians. Faced with such an onslaught, the Remoraxian Prime and its offspring fled into space.

Afterward, Adam Mitchell abducted Liz, Sarah and the Brigadier.

The Doctor started a project to research the psychic potential of humans.[318]

The Third Doctor Regenerates

(mid-March) - PLANET OF THE SPIDERS[319] -> A stage magician, Clegg, died at UNIT HQ as the third Doctor investigated his psychic potential. This was linked to a disturbance at a Tibetan monastery in Mortimer, Mummerset. It was led by Lupton, a man bitter because he was sacked by a company after twenty-five years of service, then saw his own company bankrupted by his previous employers. The Spiders from Metebelis III had contacted Lupton, and compelled him to try and steal a Metebelis crystal that was in the Doctor's possession. The Doctor pursued Lupton to Metebelis in the future. Upon the Doctor's return to Earth, he regenerated.

The Fourth Doctor and UNIT

Harry Sullivan Joins the TARDIS

(4th April) - ROBOT[320] -> UNIT's limited budget left the organisation unable to afford a Captain to replace Mike Yates. Benton was promoted to Warrant Officer and made the Brigadier's second-in-command.

The National Institute for Advanced Scientific Research, a.k.a. Think-Tank, concentrated many of Britain's scientists all under one roof. They developed pieces of high technology that included the disintegrator gun – a weapon capable of burning a hole on the moon's surface – and dynastrene, the hardest material known to science. The most impressive achievement, though, was Professor Kettlewell's "living metal", which he used to build the K1: a robot capable of performing tasks in environments where no human could survive. Many Think-Tank personnel were also members of the Scientific Reform Society (SRS), a group that believed in efficiency and logic.

The SRS tried to use the K1 to further their aims, but the newly regenerated fourth Doctor used a metal-eating virus to destroy the robot. He also prevented the

SRS from triggering a nuclear holocaust. Afterwards, the Doctor and Sarah left with their new travelling companion, UNIT medic Harry Sullivan.

Tobias Vaughn had helped fund Kettlewell's research into robotics.[321] Several members of Think Tank went to prison for violations of the Official Secrets Act. Hilda Winters' associate Jellico went down on a murder charge; Winters herself would be incarcerated for fifteen years.[322] Corporations used Kettlewell's technology to develop various technologies including nanotech. His family didn't profit from his discoveries.[323] **Following this time, a woman became Prime Minister.**[324] Mike Yates met the fourth Doctor at the Brigadier's Christmas Party.[325]

Harry Sullivan Leaves the TARDIS

(January) - TERROR OF THE ZYGONS[326] -> Centuries after arriving on Earth, the Zygons in Loch Ness learnt that a stellar explosion had destroyed their home planet. A refugee fleet had been assembled and was looking for a new home. The Zygon leader Broton signalled that Earth would be suitable once the ice caps had been melted, the mean temperature of the planet had been raised and the necessary minerals had been introduced to the water.

The Zygons intensified their campaign against humanity when oil companies started disrupting the free passage of their Skarasen, a vast monster that lived in Loch Ness but which ventured out into the North Sea from time to time. In the space of a month, the Zygons destroyed three North Sea oil rigs, causing massive loss of life. Two of the rigs were owned by Hibernian Oil. UNIT were sent to Tullock to deal with the problem.

Broton, posing as the Duke of Forgill, got into the Fourth International Energy Conference on the banks of the Thames – he planned to assassinate the world leaders assembled there by signalling for the Skarasen. Broton, the signal device and the Zygon ship were all destroyed, and the Skarasen returned to Loch Ness.

Harry Sullivan opted to return to London by InterCity as the Doctor and Sarah tried to more directly go there in the TARDIS...

Sarah Jane spread a cover story to help conceal the truth about the Zygon gambit.[327] **Harry Sullivan experimented on some captured Zygons and developed Zee-67: a nerve gas that would literally turn Zygons inside out. The Doctor confiscated everything to do with Zee-67, including its formula.**[328]

Probably owing to the Loch Ness Monster incident, the press got word of the Doctor's role in saving the world. He played for Lord's Taverners, but avoided most other tenants of celebrity-dom. A publisher approached the Doctor, who agreed to write a series of educational books for children.[329]

The government ordered Department C19 to be cleaned up, and many of its top brass were removed.[330]

Jo Jones travelled down the Amazon for months, and finally reached a village with the only telephone for thousands of miles. She phoned UNIT to ask about the Doctor... and was told that he had left and never come back. The Doctor, for his part, couldn't find Jo because she stayed on the move so much.[331]

Harry Sullivan's stories of being a naval doctor encouraged his younger step-brother, Will Sullivan – whose widowed father had married Harry's mother – to enter the medical profession. When Will Sullivan was a medical student, the Crimson Chapter recruited him.[332]

HEART OF TARDIS[333] **->** A collision with the second Doctor's TARDIS further de-stabilised the Lychburg singularity, to the point that it threatened the entire universe. The Time Lords sent the fourth Doctor and the first Romana to deal with the problem, but the Jarakabeth demon impersonating Alistair Crowley impeded their efforts, hoping to use the singularity to re-write reality in the name of chaos.

The second Doctor (secretly aided by his future self) used the TARDIS' telemetry readings to return Lychburg to Earth, whereupon the residents deserted the town entirely. A benevolent Jarakabeth demon hosted in government agent Katherine Delbane killed the Crowley demon. She became a UNIT captain under the Brigadier's command.

UNIT has recently requisitioned industrial lasers, marmosets, archaeological tools, rocketry components, Watsui tribal masks and a US college's particle accelerator. They also took a third of the Bank of England's gold reserves and didn't replace them, triggering a stock market crash.

(19th-22nd June) - NO FUTURE[334] **->** The terrorist organisation Black Star, a group of anarchists, spent the summer planting bombs in sites around London: Hamleys, Harrods, the Albert Hall, the Science Museum and Big Ben. There was an assassination attempt on the Queen, junior treasury minister John Barfe was killed, the entertainer Jimmy Tarbuck was badly hurt in a hit-and-run incident, and Pink Floyd's private jet was lost over the English Channel. Civil disturbances happened across the globe. Prime Minister Williams declared a state of emergency.

Meanwhile, the Vardans were preparing an "active immigration" to Earth. The Vardan High Command formed an alliance with the Monk, the Time Lord otherwise known as Mortimus. The Monk freed the Vardans from their time loop, and under the guise of Priory Records boss Robert Bertram, he used Vardan Mediascape technology to plant crude subliminal messages in Earth's TV broadcasts. More sophisticated brainwashing techniques were available in the new VR training system that the Monk provided for UNIT.

The seventh Doctor, Ace and Benny helped some members of UNIT and Broadsword intelligence agents to repel the Vardans from Earth. The Vardan Popular Front, a democratic organisation, took control of Varda. The Monk had captured the Chronovore Artemis and had been tapping her power to alter time, but she was freed and took her revenge on him.

The Brigadier was seeing Doris at this time. The seventh Doctor selectively wiped the Brigadier's memory, knowing he would retire before long.

---

329 *The Kingmaker*. In real-life, Target published the *Doctor Who Discovers...* books, the fifth of which (here unnamed) was *Doctor Who Discovers Early Man*. This would also explain why the fourth Doctor was chosen to present a segment of children's show *Animal Magic*. Naturally, as that was broadcast in 1980, it's final, clinching and irrefutable proof that the UNIT stories are set in the future.

330 "Six months" before *No Future*, and also referred to in *Return of the Living Dad*.

331 *SJA: Death of the Doctor*. Date unknown, but probably no earlier than *Terror of the Zygons* – although the Doctor does aid UNIT in *The Android Invasion* and *The Seeds of Doom*, his association with the group is on the decline, and he doesn't step foot in UNIT HQ on those occasions.

332 *SJS: Buried Secrets, SJS: Fatal Consequences*. It's

unclear when Will was recruited, but it's almost certainly after Harry joined UNIT, and even more probably after he went travelling with the Doctor and Sarah.

333 Dating *Heart of TARDIS* (PDA #32) - The dating seems particularly confused. UNIT knows the fourth Doctor, but Benton's a Sergeant and Yates hasn't been discharged. This is after the 1982 Falklands War, and there is a Conservative government. We could infer from the gold reserves reference that UNIT have fought the Cybermen – either in *The Invasion*, the 1975 invasion mentioned in *The One Doctor* and *Dalek* (presuming that's a different invasion) or another incident entirely.

334 Dating *No Future* (NA #23) - The date is given (p6), and the year is named as "1976".

BRITISH POLITICS FROM THE UNIT ERA TO THE PRESENT: During the UNIT era, there are references in TV stories to two Prime Ministers who are not the actual PM when the story was shown. However, both are semi-jokey references to actual opposition leaders of the time.

"Jeremy" mentioned in *The Green Death* would be Jeremy Thorpe, the leader of the Liberal Party at the time the story was made. Thorpe, of course, was never Prime Minister, although he was in the ascendant at the time *The Green Death* was shown. Shortly afterwards, in the February 1974 Election, the Liberal vote tripled to six million and they entered a pact with Labour to form a government.

In *Terror of the Zygons*, the Prime Minister is a woman. Margaret Thatcher had already been elected leader of the Conservatives when *Terror of the Zygons* was taped – the scene in which the Brigadier is phoned by the PM was recorded on 23rd April 1975, and Mrs Thatcher had been party leader since February of that year. The Labour government of the time had a tiny majority of four seats, and predicting a Conservative victory at the next election was a fairly safe bet (in much the same way that *Zamper*, written in 1995, referred to "Number ten, Tony's den").

There's a bit of a loose cannon in the form of *The Mega*, a UNIT-Era audio in which the Prime Minister is executed on live television. However, it transpires that the slain man is a Prime Minister look-alike, *The Mega* could easily happen a year or three prior to *The Green Death*, and we're not even told the PM's name, so needn't assume that it's Thorpe.

If we assume the UNIT stories are set in the near future, then this is remarkably straightforward, as only the result of one "real life" election need be changed. According to *The Green Death*, there is a general election won by Thorpe's Liberals at some point after 1973 (it can't be before *The Green Death* was shown, or it wouldn't be the future). Thatcher's Conservatives defeat this government. We can pinpoint the date of that election – it's between *Robot* and *Terror of the Zygons*, as Harry is surprised by the female leader in *The Ark in Space*. This coincides neatly with Sarah's assertion in *Pyramids of Mars* that she's from 1980. So the Liberals win the next General Election (one that had to be called by June 1975), the Tories win the one after that (possibly in May 1979, as in our history) and it all fits.

The date the Liberals come to power is harder to pin down. The model above assumes that it's a single-term government. A four or five-year term in office would mean they came to power around the time the Doctor was exiled to Earth. The man who's Minister of Ecology in *The Green Death* drafted UNIT's charter. It's possible to squeeze the Liberal election victory in before *The Invasion*, but there's nothing that demands he was a

member of the governing party when he drew up the charter. A diplomatic, military or even legal career could have made him the right man for the job (we can only say for certain is that it's an unlikely job for a serving Minister of Ecology). Politics in the UNIT era is a world of grey, middle-aged men. There are occasional visionaries, but government is practically run by civil servants. There's no obvious point where the government's character changes in the UNIT stories.

Throughout the UNIT era, the government is throwing money at new energy projects. We see grand schemes in *Doctor Who and the Silurians*, *Inferno*, *The Claws of Axos*, *The Green Death* and *Robot*, although these all end in disaster and humankind is still dependent on oil in *Terror of the Zygons*. The environment is clearly a huge political issue, with concerns about pollution voiced in many stories. The existence of a Minister of Ecology as a cabinet post is telling. When the Tories come to power, a lot of these responsibilities might transfer to the World Ecology Bureau we see in *The Seeds of Doom*. It's interesting to note that there's no mention of Europe, especially as (perhaps because) the Common Market was a hot political issue at the time. (The EEC debate was – far more vaguely than most fans seem to think – satirised in *The Curse of Peladon*.)

This version, then, is consistent with what we're told in the series and with what someone writing in the early seventies would extrapolate as a plausible backdrop for a science-fantasy adventure show set in the near future.

Later writers – particularly those who see the UNIT stories as being set at the time of broadcast – developed a parallel political history for *early* 1970s Britain of the *Doctor Who* universe. Books like *Who Killed Kennedy* and *The Devil Goblins from Neptune* infer that events in the UNIT stories destabilised actual governments. This seems to be the logical consequence of the catalogue of incompetent government action, politicians dying, international crises and high profile disasters we see ... although in the TV series, politicians and civil servants are depicted, almost to a man, as complacent and obtuse. They seem far *too* secure, rather than people scared the government will fall at any moment.

All in all, the various things we are told about the parallel political history described in the books are difficult to reconcile.

In real life, the Prime Ministers since 1970 (along with the date of the general election, the winning party and their majority) were:

• Heath (18th June, 1970, Conservative, 30)
• Wilson (28th February, 1974, Labour minority, 0)
• Wilson (10th October, 1974, Labour, 4)

continued on page 2087...

The Russians were operating vodyanoi units at this time.[335] One Vardan remained behind, living in the Liverpool phone network until 1983.[336] **Following this, the Brigadier spent a great deal of time in Geneva.[337]**

(6th July) - THE ANDROID INVASION[338] -> The leader of the Kraals' Armoury Division, Chief Scientist Styggron, planned his race's escape from the dying planet Oseidon using their technological skills. The Kraals could engineer space-time warps, and two years previously, Styggron had used one of these to capture an experimental Earth freighter in deep space. He analysed the mind of the astronaut within, Guy Crayford, and used Crayford's memories to construct a training ground – an almost-perfect replica of the English village of Devesham, including the nearby Space Defence Station. It was populated with Android villagers, and the Kraals were able to study human civilisation and behaviour, honing their preparations to invade the Earth.

It was the Kraals' first attempt at conquest, and although they were thwarted by the fourth Doctor and Sarah – as aided by Harry Sullivan and RSM Benton – Marshal Chedaki's fleet survived.

SeneNet recovered a Kraal android.[339]

End of the Fourth Doctor's Regular Time Spent with UNIT

(early one month in autumn) - THE SEEDS OF DOOM[340] -> The World Ecology Bureau was active at this time. They received reports that an unusual seed pod had been discovered in the Antarctic permafrost, and called in UNIT. The fourth Doctor and Sarah identified the item as a Krynoid seed pod and also discovered a second one. One Krynoid was killed in the Antarctic, while an RAF air strike on the mansion of Harrison Chase, the millionaire plant enthusiast, destroyed the other.

After this, the fourth Doctor spent significantly less time with UNIT.[341] Sir Colin Thackeray ordered that cuttings be taken from the Krynoid remains, so a better means could be found of killing the creatures.[342]

THE PESCATONS[343] -> Upon their return to Earth, the fourth Doctor and Sarah were attacked by a sea creature, which the Doctor recognised as a Pescaton. He hurried to the astronomer Professor Emmerson and watched Pesca, the homeplanet of the Pescatons in the outer galaxies, explode.

The Pescatons had escaped in a space fleet, which arrived on Earth and attacked many cities. A smaller number went to Venus. The Doctor located the Pescaton leader, Zor, in the London Underground and killed him with ultraviolet light. The Pescatons died without their leader.

The Pescatons and their sister race, the Piscons, both originated in the Picos System. While an expanding sun destroyed the Pescaton planet, the Piscons' homeworld survived but became desert. The Piscons wandered around the universe acquiring water supplies – sometimes benevolently from unpopulated planets, sometimes illegally.[344]

---

335 *No Future*, and a reference to the 1981 BBC drama *The Nightmare Man* – adapted by Robert Holmes and directed by Douglas Camfield.

336 *Return of the Living Dad*

337 The Brigadier is in Geneva during *The Android Invasion* and *The Seeds of Doom*.

338 Dating *The Android Invasion* (13.4) - This is the near future. For at least the last two years, Britain has had a Space Defence Station, a team of Defence Astronauts, and has been operating space freighters. The calendar in the fake village gives the date (every day) as "Friday 6th July". The nearest years with that exact date are 1973, 1979, 1984 and 1990.

339 *Business Unusual*

340 Dating *The Seeds of Doom* (13.6) - On balance, it seems to be the near future. There is a satellite videolink to Antarctica and UNIT have access to a laser cannon. The Antarctic base has an experimental fuel cell. On the other hand, Sarah only wants 2p to use the public telephone. Chase says it is autumn (location work for the story was recorded in October/November). The Doctor is invited to address the Royal Horticultural Society on "the fifteenth".

341 *The Seeds of Doom* marks the fourth Doctor's last regular team up with UNIT, effectively ending a run of stories that began with *Spearhead from Space*. Although UNIT continues to pop up in the Doctor's life in the tie-in works, he next meets them on TV in *Battlefield*.

342 *Hothouse*

343 Dating *The Pescatons* (Argo Records LP, novelised as Target #153) - The story is set in Sarah's time. It was released in August 1976, between Seasons 13 and 14, so it's been placed after *The Seeds of Doom*. The bit with Professor Emmerson and the telescope is in the novelisation, not the original record. It's quite the impressive telescope too – able to watch events on another planet in real-time, which is impossible.

344 *Peri and the Piscon Paradox*

continued from page 2085...

- Callaghan (5th April, 1976)
- Thatcher (3rd May, 1979, Conservative, 43)
- Thatcher (9th June, 1983, Conservative, 143)
- Thatcher (11th June, 1987, Conservative, 102)
- Major (27th November, 1991)
- Major (9th April, 1992, Conservative, 21)
- Blair (1st May, 1997, Labour, 179)
- Blair (7th June, 2001, Labour, 167)
- Blair (5th May, 2005, Labour, 66)
- Cameron (6th May, 2010, Conservative coalition, 0)
- Cameron (7th May, 2015, Conservative, 12)
- May (8th June, 2017, Conservative minority, -8)

In the books, a Liberal-led coalition government was formed in January 1970. *The Devil Goblins from Neptune* (p8) states, "an alliance of Liberals, various disenfranchised Tories and Socialists, and a group of minor fringe parties, enter power on a platform of social reform, the abolition of the death penalty, and a strong interstellar defence programme".

In June 1970, Heath defeats Wilson, just as in our history (*Who Killed Kennedy*). This can't be easily reconciled with *The Devil Goblins from Neptune*, which also takes place in June 1970. (Incidentally, a doppelganger of the Prime Minister is seen disintegrated on live television by a super-weapon in *The Mega*, but there's no sign that it results in an actual transfer of power.)

Shirley Williams is Prime Minister in *No Future*, set just after *Terror of the Zygons* in 1976. We're told that Thorpe had resigned mid-term, but there is also reference to Wilson. *The Oseidon Adventure* makes mention of James Callaghan (prime minister 1976-1979); there should be time to include him between Williams and Thatcher.

In *Millennial Rites*, a female PM lost an election in the early eighties, probably wishful thinking for an early Thatcher ousting – she's seen, however, as prime minister in *The Ultimate Adventure* [c.1989]. In 1999, the leader of the Opposition is a woman ("all handbag and perm"). The Prime Minister is a man.

Council of War entails the people of the planet Validor – operating from some centuries in the future – being so convinced that *Love is All You Need* author Margery Phipps became Prime Minister in 1992, they abduct her through time from the UNIT Era. Their records could be confused, however, and there's otherwise no evidence that Phipps served as Prime Minister. Sgt Benton seems quite taken with Phipps in *Council of War*, and his wife – coincidentally or not – is named Margery in *UNIT S4: Assembled* (set in 2016). If it's the same woman, Benton is conspicuously unaccompanied by the secret service detail one would expect of a former Prime Minister's spouse.

The unnamed winner of the 1997 general election was assassinated in *The Dying Days*. Edward Greyhaven is installed Prime Minister by the new Martian King of England, but dies during the course of the story.

Terry Brooks, Prime Minister in 1999, tries to fake a military coup as a pretext to dismantle the military and spend the money health and education instead. He is forced to resign, and is replaced by Philip Cotton. (*Millennium Shock* – they're a thinly-veiled Tony Blair and Jack Straw).

Tony Blair is alive, well and Prime Minister in *Project: Twilight* and *Death Comes to Time*. Mickey mentions him in *Rise of the Cybermen*.

Interference lists the recent British Prime Ministers as Heath, Thorpe, Williams, Thatcher, Major, Blair and Clarke. (The last could be senior Conservative Kenneth Clarke, but could possibly be Labour's Charles Clarke. The proofreader added the "e" – Lawrence Miles' original intention was that it was Tory MP Alan Clark.)

Aliens of London and *World War Three* had scenes set in Downing Street, with photographs of Callaghan and Major on the stairway (no photos of Thorpe, Williams, Brooks, Cotton or either Clarke were visible!). The Prime Minister of the day is murdered by the Slitheen, and Harriet Jones becomes PM sometime between this story and *The Christmas Invasion*.

The Foe from the Future [4000] claims that entertainer Bruce Forsyth (1928-2017) was prime minister, but that seems the result of bad record-keeping.

# # # # #

Once we're clear of the confused accounts of the 1970 elections, the sequence of Prime Ministers and when they come to power would seem to be:

- Thorpe   (Liberal coalition, in power at the time of *The Green Death*)
- Williams   (Labour, in power during *Terror of the Zygons* and *No Future*)
- Callaghan (Labour)
- Thatcher   (Conservative, who came to power in the early eighties, later than in real life)
- Phipps?   (probably a Liberal, if she wrote a book entitled *Love is All You Need*)
- Major   (Conservative – we might infer he's the assassinated winner of the 1997 election)
- Greyhaven   (briefly in 1997 and almost certainly not counted officially)
- Brooks   (Unknown party, possibly leading from 1997 to 1999)
- Cotton   (The same party as Brooks, takes over in 1999 – the leader of the opposition at this time is a woman, so isn't...)
- Blair   (Labour, the dates are uncertain, but he comes to power later and apparently leaves earlier than in real life, and thus manages to avoid two successful alien assassinations of a British Prime Minister.)
- Clarke   (Unknown party, presumably the Prime

continued on page 2089...

Sarah Jane Smith Leaves the TARDIS

THE HAND OF FEAR[345] -> The "obliterated" alien named Eldrad had fallen to Earth as a stone hand and regenerated into a humanoid (albeit female) form. There was near-meltdown in the main reactor of Nunton Nuclear Power station, although there was no radiation leak as Eldrad used the energy to facilitate his/her regeneration. The fourth Doctor and Sarah escorted Eldrad back to his/her homeworld of Kastria.

Afterwards, in answering a summons to Gallifrey, the Doctor was forced to return Sarah Jane Smith home. Although the TARDIS apparently failed to return Sarah to Croydon, she arrived in England.

The Doctor had dropped her off in Aberdeen.[346] Fortunately, it was the right timezone. Sarah resumed her work as a journalist.[347]

WARTIME[348] -> Benton was en route to UNIT HQ with a cache of radioactive material, and was passing through Bolton when he found himself haunted by apparitions of his mother, his late father and his dead brother Christopher. He also stopped a hijacker intent on stealing the nuclear cargo.

Tara Mishra Joins the TARDIS

Tara Mishra, a Sri Lankan-born army nurse, joined UNIT and met the Brigadier after Autons replaced her battalion. At some point, her squad dealt with a pack of Cybermen that Cyber-converted Halifax.[349]

THE NINTH DOCTOR YEAR ONE[350] -> "Sometime in the 1970s, or maybe the 1980s", Harry Sullivan assumed temporary command of UNIT while the Brigadier was in Geneva. Army experiments into psionics enabled young Josh Yaxley to manifest something he loved from comics: giant gaiaiju. Jasper Corrigan, the owner of Albion Defense, tried to exploit the situation and discredit UNIT, so his company could receive its funding.

The ninth Doctor, Rose and Jack tracked Dean – a young man turned into a gargoyle – to Bristol, and dealt with Josh's gaiaiju. UNIT's Tara Mishra went on *Points West* as a "whistleblower", and claimed that Corrigan had staged a ruse to convince the public that giant aliens were attacking. The Doctor's trio relocated Dean to an alien environment. Afterward, they discovered that Tara had stowed herself aboard the TARDIS.

Forever People, which the Doctor regarded as "the best comic shop ever", stocked *Land of the Rising Kaiju* and *The Astonishing Karkus*.

After some adventuring with the Doctor, Rose and Jack, Tara opted to remain in the fifty-fourth century.[351]

The Brigadier Retires from UNIT

Realising that the Doctor's visits were becoming less and less frequent, the Brigadier had Bessie mothballed.[352] As Brigadier Lethbridge-Stewart showed up for his second meeting with the UN about his retirement, the Accord borrowed him to unsnarl his own timeline – an incident he forgot.[353]

The Brigadier announced his retirement from UNIT. Soon afterwards, he became a mathematics teacher at Brendon School.[354]

---

345 Dating *The Hand of Fear* (14.2) - While it doesn't feature UNIT, Sarah is returned home at the end of the story. It has to be set before December 1981 and *K9 and Company*, in which she's back at work. According to *The Visual Dictionary*, it is "thirty years" before *School Reunion*.
346 *School Reunion*
347 *K9 and Company*
348 Dating *Wartime* (Reeltime Pictures film #1) - *Wartime* was released in 1987, and John Levene (understandably) looks older, suggesting that some time has passed since Benton's last TV appearance (*The Android Invasion*). The Brigadier is still in command of UNIT; otherwise, placement of this film is only a rough approximation. *The Android Invasion* establishes that Benton has a kid sister, but nothing is said about her here.
349 *The Ninth Doctor Year One*: "Official Secrets", "The Bidding War".

350 Dating *The Ninth Doctor Year One* (Titan 9th Doc #1.6-1.8, "Official Secrets") - There's multiple knowing UNIT Dating jokes as to whether it's "the 70s? Or the 80s?" Harry Sullivan briefly takes command, so it's likely after *The Android Invasion* [UNIT Year 8]. In "Official Secrets" and other stories, Benton is wrongly referenced as a "sergeant" – he became a warrant officer in *Robot*, so the correct form of address is "Mr". Sgt Osgood appears, evidently having received no promotion in the five years since *The Daemons*. *The Mind Robber* cited the Karkus as "a comic strip of the year two thousand".
351 *The Ninth Doctor Year One*: "The Bidding War"
352 *Battlefield*. *The Seeds of Doom* is the last story to feature UNIT until *Mawdryn Undead*, and it is established in the later story (and implied in *Time-Flight*) that the Doctor hasn't visited the Brigadier for years.
353 *Leth-St*: "The Enfolded Time"
354 *Mawdryn Undead*, a year before 1977.

continued from page 2087...

Minister seen in the *UNIT* audio mini-series and assassinated in *Aliens of London* in 2006 – although the body looks more like Blair than either Kenneth or Charles Clarke, both of whom could comfortably accommodate a Slitheen in real life!)

• Jones (The same party as Clarke. The ninth Doctor says in *World War Three* that she was originally supposed to serve three terms – possibly until c.2016 in *Trading Futures*, where the PM was male. However, her first term is curtailed by the tenth Doctor in *The Christmas Invasion* – this would seem to be a significant deviation of established history, unless the ninth Doctor was mistaken in *World War Three* to think Jones was a three-termer.)

• Unknown (There is at least one interim Prime Minister after Jones' downfall in *The Christmas Invasion*. A blurry picture of him is seen in *TW: Out of Time*, along with the apparently sceptical headline, "Working Hard, Minister?")

• Saxon (According to *The Sound of Drums*, he leads the newly-formed Saxon Party, which has attracted support from across the political spectrum. While time is reversed in *Last of the Time Lords*, his outing himself as the Master and ordering the death of the US President on global TV "still happens". Saxon dies at the end of the story, which is set in 2008. He leaves enough of a mark on history that in *Before the Flood*, when O'Donnell, a former military intelligence officer from 2119 who knows a lot about the Doctor, travels with him to 1980, she says "So, pre-Harold Saxon. Pre-the Minister of War. Pre-the moon exploding and a big bat coming out.")

• Fairchild (Killed in 2009 when the Daleks shoot his plane down in *The Stolen Earth*; he's named as "Aubrey Fairchild" in *Beautiful Chaos*.)

• Green (Seen in *TW: Children of Earth*, set in September 2009 – he almost certainly takes over when when Fairchild dies earlier in the year. The story ends with Denise Riley, a member of Green's cabinet, obtaining incriminating evidence on him, but it's not said if she plans to force him out and become prime minister herself, or just pull his strings from behind the scenes. Either way, given the abominable events of *Children of Earth* – including the army being used to forcibly take thousands of children from their parents – it's difficult to imagine the party in power winning the next election. *TW: The Men Who Sold the World*, set in 2010, alludes to the UK having a new coalition government.)

• Unknown (The Prometheans trigger such cognative dissonance in "Hunters of the Burning Stone", set in 2013, that the Prime Minister goes up a tree and eats a ferret. As s/he is in good company with this, it's perhaps not as politically damaging as one might expect.)

• Unknown, male (A giant Rainbow Dog disrupts Question Time in the House of Commons, utterly bewildering a male Prime Minister in *The Eleventh Doctor Year One*: "After Life").

• Unknown, female P.M./Kenneth LeBlanc/the same Unknown P.M. again (Seen, or more accurately heard, in *UNIT* Series 3, set in 2015 – meaning an unknown number of PMs could happen between the incumbent one who appears here and Green. The Silents who survive in the decades to follow *Day of the Moon* – needing a spectacle big enough to undo the Doctor-forged "You should kill us all on sight" order that has been slaughtering them for decades – subvert the general election to elect as prime minister an entrepreneur named Kenneth LeBlanc, then try to assassinate him and his predecessor in one go. LeBlanc wins, then dies as planned, but the predecessor survives. UNIT control the chaos enough that Parliament recognises the whole election was awry, and agree to redo it, leading to the former PM scraping out a narrow win.)

• Daniel Claremont (Seen in *The Twelfth Doctor Year Two*: "Clara Oswald and the School of Death", set in 2017 – see the Series 8 dating notes – but claiming to occur in 2016. A graduate of the Ravenscaur School, Claremont rises through the ranks to become prime minister – the problem being that the Sea Devils usurped control of the school decades ago, and he's in the thrall of a Sea Devil spawn nestled within him. The twelfth Doctor exposes Claremont as a villainous lizard man on television, which can't be good for his re-election chances. Claremont presumably, but not definitively, dies when the Doctor redirects the Sea Devils' firepower to destroy the school and Raven's Isle.)

• Unknown, female (Both the Prime Minister and the US President are women in *Charlotte Pollard* Series 2, set c.2017, but it's unclear as yet how much of this range is alternate history. Coincidence or not, in *TW: Aliens Among Us 3*, the alt-Yvonne Hartmann breezily becomes friends with a woman named Felicity, whom she equates with "Number 10" – presumably by way of designating the Prime Minister, although it's vague enough to set aside if other stories necessitate it.)

The Brigadier was made a CBE shortly before leaving UNIT.[355] Elizabeth Elizabeth Klein joined UNIT as a scientific researcher, although her request for a lab assistant was utterly ignored. She was assigned to a deep-core research facility, but helped UNIT fend off "a fair few" alien attacks during her time. She briefly met Lethbridge-Stewart before his retirement.[356]

UNIT Year 9

= The Master lost his TARDIS, and became stuck on Earth. While waiting for the Doctor to inevitably turn up, he worked for the United Nations. When Chairman Mao began destroying monasteries across China, the mind-parasites imprisoned there became more active. The UN sent the Master to assess the situation, but he defected to China. As General Ke Le of the People's Liberation Army, the Master created the Ke Le Machine – this channeled the mind-parasites' power into rehabilitated criminals, creating the fearless and suicidal Ke Le Divisions. The Master met Mao, who spoke fondly of the Doctor.[357]

UNIT Year 10

Scientists at the Lezarata Research Centre developed a means of retainng a person's memories and personality on audio, and wondered if dead minds could be resurrected from voice recordings. Experiments were carried out on the very first phonograph recording made by Thomas Edison, which loosed the Second Voice entity embedded within it. The head of Lezarata quarantined the Centre as the staff went increasingly mad – those within died, and facility was undisturbed for some decades.[358]

THE ARCHITECTS OF HISTORY[359] **->** The seventh Doctor visited the new iteration of Elizabeth Klein, having erased the version of her that went to Colditz from history. The surviving Klein had been born in England to German parents, and now worked for UNIT. She acknowledged the Doctor as an ally in keeping the world safe.

UNIT Year 13

UNIT: DOMINION[360] **->** Brigadier Lethbridge-Stewart was retired. Colonel Lafayette had commanded UNIT for three months. The American military had some knowledge of assistance the Doctor had provided to UNIT.

---

355 *Downtime* (p246). A CBE, the third of five classes of chivalry, doesn't carry the form of address "Sir". The Brigadier is called such in the new series, presumably after he's given a KBE or a GBE.

356 The year that Klein joins UNIT isn't clear, but her futile request for a lab assistant was filed "five years" before *UNIT: Dominion*.

357 "Twenty years" before *Unbound: Sympathy for the Devil*, which assumes the UNIT stories happened at time of broadcast.

358 *Ghost in the Machine*. Year unknown, but Jo roughly estimates – purely from the design of the light fittings – that it's the near future of her time (between *Planet of the Daleks* and *The Green Death*). It's not so far into the future that Thomas Edison's first phonograph recording isn't obtainable.

359 Dating *The Architects of History* (BF #132) - Klein implies that the Doctor hasn't visited UNIT for two years. Steve Lyons, the author of this story, commented: "That last scene is set two years after the Doctor left UNIT, circa *Terror of the Zygons/The Android Invasion*. *Battlefield* hasn't happened yet, because Klein would recognise the Doctor more immediately if it had (she only knows of [his seventh] incarnation through second-hand reports of his adventures), and anyway, she'd be a lot older than she is."

The only other clue, oddly enough, is that the CD track containing this scene is labelled "UNIT 1960's" (sic) – which is incorrect under any dating scheme.

360 Dating *UNIT: Dominion* (BF *UNIT* #2.1) - *Dominion* is subject to UNIT dating. The seventh Doctor first met the historically revised version of Klein in *The Architects of History* (in a scene set two years after *Terror of the Zygons/The Android Invasion*), and has been sporadically stalking her since then, watching for any sign of her Nazi self returning. According to Klein, "months, years [will] pass" without her spotting the Doctor watching her, and then he'll suddenly turn up again – this has been going on long enough that she's feeling unnerved by it. It seems reasonable, then, to think that at least three years, if not more, have passed since the Doctor's first meeting with Klein – in which case, *Dominion* must take place in UNIT Year 13 if not beyond. Ergo, for those who prefer the UNIT stories occurring in the near future, this story arguably takes place around 1987. For anyone who presumes UNIT stories happen at time of broadcast, circa 1982 seems a reasonable fit.

Either way, Lethbridge-Stewart has retired from UNIT. The days of the Doctor's "cozy relationship" with UNIT are over. The password string that the Master gives UNIT ("Yeti-Inferno-Kettlewell-Zygon-Krynoid-Kraal") confirms that it's after *The Seeds of Doom*. Klein has been with UNIT at least five years (it's been that long since her request for a lab assistant was rebuffed) if not more, but it's never specified when she joined the group. It's implied that she was promoted "a few years back" from a "deep-core research facility" (possibly

The bald Master sought to exploit the Dimensioneers' lost technology, and required the last of their energy-node-activation devices: an artifact secured aboard the last Type 40 Gallifreyan time capsule, i.e. the Doctor's TARDIS. To that end, the Master placed one of the two Dimensioneer nodes in his possession in a dimension that was home to the Tolian race, and the second in the middle of London. The resultant energy transfer made the Tolians wither while the London node expanded to twelve feet tall.

The Master posed as a future incarnation of the Doctor – both when UNIT responded, with Elizabeth Klein acting as its scientific adviser, and when the seventh Doctor and Raine Creevy attempted to aid the dying Tolians. The Doctor reversed the energy flow back to the Tolian realm with his TARDIS' node activator, but the strengthened Tolians prevented the Doctor from halting the transfer, forcing him and Raine to flee down a wormhole to Earth.

A number of inter-dimensional creatures fled their native realms as the Tolian power transfer weakened the dimensional walls. One such race (nicknamed "the Skyheads") manifested as giant cherubic heads over twenty cities including London; Helsinki; Lapang, Poland; Omsk, Russia; and more remote locales. Newscasts reported on the giant head over London, unsure as to whether it was alive, a spaceship or a giant hoax. Colonel Lafayette died while negotiating with the Skyhead, and Major Wyland-Jones assumed command.

Still posing as the "future Doctor", the Master hypnotised the Skyheads into either departing or helping UNIT.

He also aided the Doctor, Raine and Klein in containing mind leeches in the Excalibur Building in London, repelled giant lava-spitting arachnids who menaced Germany, drowned the Nexus – a gestalt octopoid creature – and forced a retreat from energy-discharging cubes that manifested in the Nevadan desert and near Tokyo. Eunice Faber, a UNIT associate and father of two, died while combating the arachnids.

The Tolians absorbed enough energy to become armoured insectoids, agreed to serve as the Master's shock troops and attacked UNIT headquarters. The Doctor unmasked his longtime nemesis, and convinced the Tolian leader, Arunzell, that the Master had caused the original energy drain that had extinguished millions of Tolians, including Arunzell's own family. Arunzell recalled the Tolians from Earth; the defeated Master fled after killing him. The Doctor either destroyed the remaining Dimensioneer technology or retained it for safekeeping.

Klein learned that she had been a Nazi in an alternate reality, but that the Doctor had heavily revised her timeline. They came to an understanding, and the Doctor left her with a space-time telegraph to summon him if needed.

The contradictions caused by the 1970s and 1980s folding into one another dropped sharply with the onset of the 1990s. The Accord achieved more temporal stability by slipping a temporal marker into Alistair Gordon Lethbridge-Stewart's DNA. It broke down on 1st January, 1990, providing key individuals with a vague awareness that time had gone awry.[361]

where she meets the Doctor in *The Architects of History*) to replace the fourth Doctor as UNIT's scientific adviser (following his last team-up with them in *The Seeds of Doom*), although it's possible that she didn't *directly* succeed him. There's no indication of how much time passes between this story and Klein's next encounter with the Doctor (*Persuasion*, set in September 1990).

Curiously, the Doctor here gives Klein a space-time telegraph, and there's evidently no crisis between here and *Persuasion* desperate enough to overcome Klein's understandably conflicted feelings about the Doctor and prompt her to summon him. This would mean that she didn't contact him about an incident he knew he'd already dealt with – the Mondas incident in 1986 (*The Tenth Planet*).

Where the public's knowledge of aliens is concerned, this story is an odd one (see the When Do the General Public Accept the Existence of Aliens? sidebar). Giant heads ("the Skyheads") are seen over many cities, but the newscasters covering the London event wonder if it's all a hoax. Colonel Lafayette and a news team are killed while negotiating with the Skyhead over London, but it's unclear if the military has allowed the cameras to be live at that point. UNIT's struggles against most of the inter-dimensional menaces that encroach upon

Earth – the mind leeches in London, the giant arachnids in Germany, etc. – arguably occur without the general public realising the truth of what's happening, although civilian casualties are reported in Las Vegas and Tokyo from the cube attacks. The most damning news account comes from the fictional John Star broadcasting from the centre of London during the Tolian attack, and claiming that casualties number in the thousands. No attacks occur outside of London, however, and while the government evacuates by helicopter and the military mobilises in response to the Tolians, we're only shown them breaking into UNIT HQ and Sgt Wilson's house.

Eunice Faber, here killed, was the alt-Klein's lover ("Klein's Story"). Raine claims that she's "a newcomer and everything" where travelling with the Doctor is concerned, but she also claims to "come and go again", suggesting that quite some time might have passed in his personal timeline (it's later days for his seventh incarnation) since she joined the TARDIS (*Crime of the Century*). It's unlikely that this story occurs during Big Finish's Season 27 audios, since Ace is away on Gallifrey – something she opts not to do in that run of stories.

361 *Leth-St:* "The Enfolded Time"; see the Haisman Timeline sidebar.

The Non-UNIT Seventies

NB: The line between a UNIT and non-UNIT story isn't always clearly defined. When a reference makes a direct link to a UNIT era story, it is included in the UNIT Era section. When there's a more vague or general reference to UNIT, it's included here.

The Doctor once took piano lessons from a man called Elton.[1] He also had to swim the English Channel naked, after losing a bet with actor Oliver Reed.[2]

Isaac Summerfield moved his team to London, where they were based in a centre for the homeless.[3] The Doctor fought the Geomatide Macros on Sunset Boulevard in the 1970s, and defeated their plan to use ceiling tiles as a mathematical hyperspace vector generator.[4]

The archaeologist Bradley Stapleton died as an exhibit of his work was being prepared. The eleventh Doctor sent Amy Pond's journal of Stapleton's doomed 1929 expedition to the man's granddaughter.[5]

NASA sent messages – including maps of the solar system and details about humanity – into space in the 70s. One alien race sent a reply, which wound up in the possession of Henry John Parker, a millionaire collec- tor of alien artifacts.[6]

Jack Harkness had a moustache at some point in the 70s.[7] He claimed that movies in the 1970s were so bad, making out was guaranteed. It wasn't unknown for him to wear platforms and five-inch lapels.[8]

Local churches held services on Mellor Moor in the 1970s, endowing it with a symbolism that rippled backwards in time, and was of use to ritualists.[9] The twelfth Doctor believed that the 1970s represented a bit of a golden age, particularly with regards its fried food.[10]

The Doctor enjoyed blueberry muffins with Neil Armstrong, a "nice man, very smart and no ego".[11] River Song visited Canvey Island in the 1970s.[12] A dreamweaving Bone Spider took up residence in Alice Parsons' house in Shoreditch, and inadvertently started the urban legend of a ghost there, "Faceless Alice".[13]

1970

In 1970, the book *Great Finds* described the Roman mosaic discovered in 1964.[14] The United States officially cancelled the Apollo spaceflight programme, bowing to criticism of its expense, but continued it in secret – if for

---

1 *Project: Lazarus.* This refers to Elton John, presumably, but no date is given.
2 "The Betrothal of Sontar". The Doctor also claims to have swum the Channel in *Doctor Who and the Pirates.* There's no indication exactly when this happened, but it's apparently after "Lunar Lagoon", when the fifth Doctor said he'd never learned to swim. (He seemingly has by *Warriors of the Deep,* however.) Oliver Reed, an actor known for such films as *The Three Musketeers* (1973), lived 1938-1999.
3 "The early seventies", according to *Return of the Living Dad* (p66).
4 *Peacemaker*
5 *The Hounds of Artemis.* No date is given, but Stapleton was a young man in 1929.
6 *TW: A Day in the Death*
7 *TW: Miracle Day*
8 *TW: The Dead Line*
9 *FP: Spinning Jenny*
10 *The Twelfth Doctor Year Two:* "Beneath the Waves"
11 *Horror of the Space Snakes* (ch6). No date given, but Armstrong died 25th August, 2012.
12 *The Legends of River Song:* "River of Time"
13 *Class: The Stone House* (p42). A photo that's "thirty, forty years old" suggests this happened "in the 70s." Alice's letters to her daughter, Catherine Grace Parsons – born in 1959 – place this at some point after Catherine turns ten (pgs. 265, 271).
14 *Demon Quest: The Relics of Time*
15 *Apollo 23* (p51). *Apollo 20* was cancelled on 4th January, 1970; *Apollo 18* and *19* were cancelled after that, on 2nd September of the same year. The last

Apollo flight, *Apollo 17,* launched on 7th December, 1972.
16 *Beautiful Chaos,* taking its lead from *The Runaway Bride.* Geoff died in 2008, after he and Sylvia had been married "thirty-eight years" (p26).
17 "Forty years ago" in *SJA: The Vault of Secrets.*
18 *SJA: Goodbye, Sarah Jane,* in accordance with Sarah being born in 1951 (*SJA: Whatever Happened to Sarah Jane?*). This probably denotes when Sarah started doing journalist work – "doorstepping" is a UK term meaning the practice of parking oneself outside the home of a celebrity/politician to snag a quote or photograph.
19 *SJA: The Man Who Never Was*
20 *SJA: Judgement Day.* This is "a few years" before Sarah joins UNIT.
21 *SJA: The White Wolf*
22 *Who Killed Kennedy*
23 *DotD: Night of the Whisper.* Knievel lived 1938-2007, and was at the height of his powers from the late sixties to 1975, when he broke his pelvis in a jump gone wrong at Wembley Stadium, London.
24 *The Wheel of Ice* (pgs. 91-95). No year given, but Patrick Moore is on TV and mention is made of UNIT. Assuming the same duration of time has passed since Josie received the amulet from her mother (forty years), it's probably about 1970.
25 *Before the Flood*
26 *Daemons: White Witch of Devil's End,* supplemental material.
27 Dating *Day of the Moon* (X6.2) - A caption says it is "6 months later" after the main action of the story.

no other reason than every dollar spent on Apollo yielded $14 back from related exports, patents and expertise.[15]

Geoff and Sylvia Noble, the future parents of Donna Noble, were married.[16] A ship containing a hundred Veil crashed on Earth and was taken to a hyperdimensional Vault by the Alliance of Shades.[17]

Sarah Jane Smith began doorstepping when she was 19.[18] Lionel Carson served as Sarah Jane's editor when she first started out with the national papers, but he later moved on to the food and wine circuit.[19] Professor Edward Shepherd educated Sarah Jane on the ethics of journalism while she was at university, and was the best teacher she ever had.[20] Sarah Jane specialised in English and humanities.[21] She studied under James Stevens, as did Ruby Duvall.[22]

Evel Knievel taught the Doctor the art of motorcycle riding.[23] The ArkHive amulet became active every ten years, and a friend of Josie Laws who worked for UNIT determined that it was emitting a signal aimed at Saturn. As was the family custom, Josie gave the amulet to her 16-year-old daughter Joss Laws.[24]

The Fisher King's forces invaded Tivoli, and enslaved the natives there for ten years.[25] Professor Horner's *The Iron Age of Britain* (1970) was broadcast.[26]

Melody Pond Regenerates

1970 (January) - DAY OF THE MOON[27] -> Six months after escaping the Silence, young Melody Pond – now wandering the streets of New York – regenerated in an alleyway.

Melody's new body looked like a toddler. A quarter-century later, she would end up in Leadworth, meet her future parents (Amy and Rory) and become their best friend, Melody "Mels" Zucker.[28]

c 1970 (20th March) - THE UNDERWATER MENACE[29] -> The mad Professor Zaroff died in agony while attempting to raise Atlantis from the ocean floor with his Plunger.

On 5th April, 1970, Hitler's remains were exhumed and destroyed on the orders of Andropov, head of the KGB.[30]

(=) 1970 (6th July) - DEyes: FUGITIVES[31] -> The Time Lord Kotris sent Sally Armstrong of the Ideas Scientific Institute a massive cash donation, along with instructions directing her to construct a space-time portal at the Doctor's house at 107 Baker Street, London, W1U 6EP, England. She would meet the Doctor, and Kotris' Dalek allies, upon completion of the device in 1972.

On 14th August, the Revolution Man cult claimed Ed Hill was the Messiah.[32]

(=) c 1970 - DC 4: THE SIDE OF THE ANGELS[33] -> The Monk became a developer and preacher, "the Reverend Mortimor", based in New York. Councillor Ollistra and Time Lords dissenting against Padrac's rule co-opted the Monk's operations, and made him oversee construction of dozens of new bridges and

Melody isn't identified by name until *A Good Man Goes to War*. It's not directly established *why* Melody regenerates; it's not even certain that Amy's gunshot (the end of *The Impossible Astronaut*) actually hit her. It's possible that Melody's immune system was compromised because she was initially raised in a spacesuit acting as a life-support system. *Doctor Who: The Encyclopedia* says that Melody regenerated because she was "exhausted and injured".

28 *Let's Kill Hitler*. This leaves around a quarter-century gap where we don't know what Melody Pond was doing. Fortunately, the same story makes it clear that Melody/River has some control over her appearance – she looks about age seven when we see her with young Amy and Rory, and presumably she allows herself to outwardly age with Amy and Rory from childhood to adulthood. It would appear that she didn't regenerate a second time between 1970 and meeting up with Amy and Rory as children, because when she regenerates in *Let's Kill Hitler*, she mentions "the last time" she did such a thing, in New York (in *Day of the Moon*). Mels' surname isn't given on screen, but is listed in *Doctor Who: The Encyclopedia*.

29 Dating *The Underwater Menace* (4.5) - Polly discovers a bracelet from the 1968 Mexico Olympics; she and Ben guess that they must have landed about "1970". The Atlanteans are celebrating the Vernal Equinox.

The Programme Guide says the story is set "1970-75"; it's "soon after" 1969 according to *The Terrestrial Index*. *The TARDIS Logs* claimed a date of "1969". *Timelink* chose "1970". *The Legend* simply states it's "after 1968". *About Time* decided that the bracelet indicated it "can't be any earlier than 1969", and also noted that if Zaroff has been in Atlantis for twenty years, and his work on plankton farming was only attainable after the advent of the aqualung, "1970 is the earliest reasonable date".

30 Dating *DEyes: Fugitives* (BF *DEyes* #1.2) - "It is Monday, the 6th of July, 1970", which was indeed a Monday in that year.

31 *The Shadow in the Glass* (p172).

32 *Revolution Man* (p247).

33 Dating *DC 4: The Side of the Angels* (BF *DC* #4.3) - More than one character generalises the time as the "1970s", and the Deputy Mayor of New York declares that "It's a new decade, and we've got big plans for the Big Apple". The Doctor says that New York isn't due for a

skyscrapers. New York would become a replica of the Time Lord Capitol, allowing Ollistra's group to strike against Padrac when the universal apocalypse arrived five centuries on.

The eighth Doctor, along with Liv and Helen, was stupefied to learn that Ollistra's crew planned to let the Weeping Angels consume all of humanity, provided they powered the new Capitol's workings. The Eleven swayed the Angels over to Padrac's side, and they sent the Monk back centuries, even millennia. This turbo-charged Ollistra's headquarters with temporal energy, which the starving Angels paradoxically consumed. The Doctor resolved this by rolling New York back to before the Monk developed it.

The Eleven pushed Ollistra to her death. She regenerated into the incarnation that would fight in the Last Great Time War.

The seventh Doctor's companion Ace was born Dorothy Gale McShane on 20th August, 1970, to **Audrey** and Harry McShane.[34] Around 1970, an Imperial bodyguard and nurse fled from the far future with Miranda, the daughter of the Emperor, following a revolution in which the Imperial Family were hunted down and killed. The fugitives settled in the Derbyshire village of Greyfrith.[35]

Hilda Hutchens won the 1970 Nobel Prize for Philosophy.[36] The tenth Doctor changed history, allowing Frank Openshaw to meet his wife a few years earlier than he otherwise would have.[37]

(=) 1970 (November) - 1963: FANFARE FOR THE COMMON MEN[38] **->** Photographs of the Common Men's performances caused the fame-based energy stockpiled within Mark Carville to prematurely manifest. Kruger took James O'Meara to Carville to see about a Common Men revival tour, but Carville literally burst with energy after killing O'Meara. Kruger left for 1963 to tell his younger self about the outcome of their plan. The fifth Doctor followed, having also realised that Nyssa was stranded in that year.

Ellie Ravenwood, age 11, obtained a copy of *101 Places to See*. Her daughter Clara later inherited the book.[39] The British launched a military satellite, *Haw-Haw*, to block extra-terrestrial signals in 1971.[40] Nimrod's encounter with the vampire Reggie left Reggie recuperating for three years.[41] Captain Jack helped sort out a problem during the early days of the United Arab Emirates, when something under the ground was disturbed.[42]

---

major blackout for "a good few years", presumably meaning the one that happened 13th-14th July, 1977.

It's left unsaid how TARDISes can visit New York, since *The Angels Take Manhattan* created such temporal interference that the eleventh Doctor cannot reunite with Amy and Rory there. The Monk refuses to say whether his current incarnation (played by Rufus Hound) is earlier or later than the Graeme Garden incarnation (*Lucie Miller/To the Death*).

34 ACE'S EARLY LIFE: According to *The Curse of Fenric*, Ace does "O-Levels", not GCSEs, so she must be a fifth former (i.e.: 15 or 16 years old) by the summer of 1987 at the latest. This supports *Ghost Light*, where she is "13" in "1983". As Ace has a patch reading "1987" on her jacket in *Dragonfire*, it seems that the timestorm which swept her to Svartos must have originated in that year. Fenric is therefore rounding up when he tells Ace that Audrey Dudman will have a baby "thirty years" after *The Curse of Fenric*. Sophie Aldred was born in 1962, making her nine years older than the character she played.

In the New Adventures, starting with *Timewyrm: Revelation*, Ace's birthday was established as 20th August (Sophie Aldred's birthday). In *Falls the Shadow*, the Doctor says that she was born in "1970". Paul Cornell attempted to establish that Ace's surname was "McShane" in *Love and War*, but series editor Peter Darvill-Evans vetoed this at the proof stage. *Conundrum* (p245) and *No Future* (p19) both suggest that Ace's surname begins with an "M" (although when asked in

the latter, Ace claims it is "Moose"!). It wasn't until Kate Orman's *Set Piece* that "McShane" was officially adopted.

Ace is "Dorothy Gale" in some books by Mike Tucker, notably *Matrix* (p124) and *Prime Time* (p234). *The Rapture* attempts to reconcile this by stating that her middle name is Gale. In *Loving the Alien*, which appears to be set prior to *The Rapture*, Ace dies and is replaced by a parallel timeline version of herself. The Doctor says this swap accounts for much of the confusion regarding Ace's last name.

35 *Father Time*. Miranda is "ten" in the first part of the book (p54), and "two months old" when she arrives on Earth.

36 *Island of Death* – although there isn't actually a Nobel Prize for Philosophy.

37 *I am a Dalek*

38 Dating *1963: Fanfare for the Common Men* (BF #178) - The year is given, and it's "a month before Christmas".

39 *The Rings of Akhaten*

40 *The Dying Days* (p101).

41 *Project: Twilight*

42 *TW: The Sin Eaters*. Prior to 1971, the Emirates were known as the Trucial States.

43 *FP: The Book of the War*

44 *An Unearthly Child*. Susan is also familiar with the Beatles before their first hit single in *Time and Relative*.

45 Dating *Daemons: White Witch of Devil's End* (story #3, "The Cat Who Walked Through Worlds") - It's "almost seven years" since Rhadamanthus became incarnated

wih - The second iteration of Cousin Anastasia of Faction Paradox died as Nadezhda Vasilyeva in an insane asylum in Kazan, 1971.[43] **Decimal currency was introduced in the United Kingdom. At some point afterwards, the first Doctor and Susan visited England.**[44]

c 1971 - DAEMONS: WHITE WITCH OF DEVIL'S END[45] ->

Olive Hawthorne's cat Rhadamanthus went on his appointed walkabout, and engineered events to protect a teenager, Lucy, from a malevolent tree spirt.

1972

In 1972, Nazi war criminal Oskar Steinmann died from cancer of the spine.[46] NASA launched the Pioneer 10 deep-space probe. The eleventh Doctor would find it on the Gyre in the year 250,339.[47] The Great Big Book Exchange opened in Darlington.[48] **Joseph Samuel Serf, the future founder of Serf Systems, was born May 1972 in Dayton, Ohio.**[49] Ace's mother moved into the home in which Ace would grow up[50]; the road on which they lived was named Beech.[51]

On 4th June, 1972, UNIT obtained the Tunguska Scroll from a collector.[52] In December of that year, the skeleton of Nazi Martin Bormann was discovered in West Germany.[53] Playwright Noel Coward died in 1972. One of his selves claimed – due to his status at a time traveller – that at his moment of death, he'd be mentally whisked back to his birth to experience life all over again.[54]

In 1972, the Alliance of Shades disbanded, and pulled the plug on its robot Men in Black.[55] Mr Dread and his Men in Black, however, became the guardians of a hyperdimensional Vault containing numerous extra-terrestrial items and vessels. Ocean Waters, age 24, encountered Dread in 1972 – he wiped her memories of the event, and gave her one of two activation keys to the Vault for safekeeping.[56]

The American military downed an alien spaceship carrying the Stormcore, a navigational instrument. The government erroneously believed the Stormcore was a weather control device, and formed Operation Afterburn to make it compatible with human technology. Researchers determined the device needed a psionic operator. In the years to come, the government's ESP/Remote Viewing program, called Grill Flame, would locate such individuals. The spaceship's crewmembers, now stranded on Earth, joined the American CIA as agents Melody Quartararo and Parker Theroux.[57]

Iris Wildthyme's people exiled her and Panda to London, 1972. She again worked for the Ministry for Incursions and other Alien Ontological Wonders (MIAOW) to obtain the alien technology needed to repair her bus. Iris based herself above a bus depot and tatty pool hall in New Cross. MIAOW's headquarters was named the Pussy Parlour.[58] Iris and Panda whiled away many happy hours at a London pub, The Gryphon, while working for MIAOW in the 70s.[59]

The lower deck of Iris Wildthyme's bus contained a slash in the Very Fabric of Time and Space, which accessed the toilets underneath the Hammersmith Odeon on a particular evening in London, 1972.[60]

Professor Horner's *The Day of the Celt* was released.[61] The Doctor played the chessmaster Bobby Fischer, in a game that went "very wrong indeed", and arguably brought the world to the brink of nuclear war.[62]

1972 (January) - "The Highgate Horror"[63] ->

Some Corvid – Vortex dwellers who subsisted on the psychic decay of the dead – grounded themselves in the ley lines beneath Highgate Cemetery in London. They killed Jess Collins' boyfriend, Dave, when he tried to prove that the Highgate Vampire was real. Gabriel Rosewood, an alleged

---

as a cat.
46 *Just War* (p178).
47 *Night of the Humans.* Pioneer 10 was launched 2nd March, 1972.
48 "Forty years" prior to the modern day portion of *Iris: Enter Wildthyme.*
49 *SJA: The Man Who Never Was*
50 "Five years" after *Thin Ice* (BF).
51 *Night Thoughts*
52 *SJA: Enemy of the Bane*
53 *The Shadow in the Glass.* This is historical. The skeleton was identified first through dental records, then twenty-seven years later through a DNA test.
54 *Mad Dogs and Englishmen*
55 *Dreamland* (DW), *SJA: The Vault of Secrets.*
56 *SJA: The Vault of Secrets*
57 "Thirty years" before *Drift.*

58 *Iris S2: The Land of Wonder*
59 *Wildthyme Beyond!*
60 *Wildthyme Beyond!*
61 *Daemons: White Witch of Devil's End*, supplemental material.
62 *Dark Horizons* (p7). Fischer lived 1943-2008, and was rising in prominence as a chessmaster as early as 1956. His match against Boris Spassky in 1972 drew global interest (following Fisher's 1962 allegations that the Russians were fixing world chess) and the attention of President Nixon and Henry Kissinger, but it's still hard to see how the Doctor's playing Fischer could have resulted in such calamity that it actually escalated nuclear tensions.
63 Dating "The Highgate Horror" (*DWM* #492-493) - A caption names the year. The Highgate Vampire is an actual media sensation based upon sketchy "vampire

explorer of the ethereal realms, sought to harness the Corvids' power, but Clara's status as the Impossible Girl repelled the creatures, and aided the twelfth Doctor in banishing them back to the Vortex.

The Twelfth Doctor's Half-Year with the Collins Family

1972 (May) - "The Pestilent Heart" / "Moving In" / "Bloodsport"[64] **->** Jess Collins, a college student, again met the twelfth Doctor when he stopped by 1972 London to see a gig, or perhaps play guitar with Ronnie Wood or Jeff Beck. A Victoria Line extension unearthed the bones of the alien Moan'na, whose restructured DNA became airbourne and transformed those nearby – including Jess' father Lloyd – into human-avian creatures. The Doctor deployed a genetic patch that syphoned the infection into the TARDIS, but his Ship went dormant to heal itself...

While waiting for the TARDIS to heal, the Doctor lodged with Jess, her father, her mother Devina, her younger brother Maxwell and their cat Tibbsy. He made the family a splendid meal, and debated with Maxwell on who would win a fight: Captain America or Batman. Feeling adrift, the Doctor decided to "show Jess the uni-

verse" through great works of art...

The Kolothos Dynasty outlawed hunting, but one family – Skadi, Broteas and their son Tarquel – continued to hunt prey while on cyber-horses. Their latest hunt interrupted the twelfth Doctor, Jess and Max as they explored the National Gallery. The Doctor brought the hunters to heel, and Tarquel, sickened of killing, took his parents back home to face punishment.

(=) 1972 - DEyes: FUGITIVES[65] **->** The eighth Doctor and Molly visited the Doctor's house at 107 Baker Street in London, where Dr Sally Armstrong had constructed a space-time portal. The Daleks emerged from the portal, killed Armstrong and pursued the Doctor and Molly to another time zone.

1972 (23rd-25th December) - "Be Forgot"[66] **->** The twelfth Doctor was still lodging with the Collins family at Christmastime. The grief of a family friend, Walter, for his late mother caused Obadiah – a fictional life-stealer from the *Sinister* comic books – to manifest as real. The Collins family dissipated Walter's despair by inviting him to a community breakfast on Christmas morning.

---

sightings" from the same time period, leading to a mass vampire hunt in Highgate Cemetery in 1972. As this story describes, the Friends of Highgate Cemetery was founded in 1975. "The Pestilent Heart", set in May, occurs "six months" after this story – if we squint, we might imagine that "The Highgate Horror" happens in January, even if everyone involved should probably be dressed a bit warmer.

64 Dating "The Pestilent Heart", "Moving In" and "Bloodsport" (*DWM* #501-503, #504, #505-506) - The Doctor names the year in "The Pestilent Heart", and it's "six months" after "The Highgate Horror" [1972]. Jess' dad invites her to see the "new" *Carry On* film starring Sid James "this Saturday" – in the timeframe allowed, that limits the choices to *Carry On Matron* (May) and *Carry On Abroad* (December). It's warm in the early morning (so much so, Jess' dad takes off his suit jacket), so it's very probably the former.

65 Dating *DEyes: Fugitives* (BF *DEyes* #1.2) - The year is given.

66 Dating "Be Forgot" (*DWM* #507) - Captions provide the exact dates. The story claims to end on Christmas morning, but everyone present seems dressed (skirts and all) for much warmer weather, never mind that 25th December isn't the most agreeable of days to have brunch outside in London.

67 According to the writers' guidelines. She was "28" in *Escape Velocity*, set in February 2001.

68 Per *The Torchwood Archives* (BBC).

69 *Class: Nightvisiting*

70 *Night Thoughts*. Kathleen is Ace's grandmother as

seen in *The Curse of Fenric*.

71 "A Matter of Life and Death" (issue #3). Clarke's *Rendeznous with Rama*, one of his seminal works, came out in 1973.

72 *Love & Monsters*

73 "Twenty-three years" before *The Sands of Time*.

74 *TW:* "Hell House". This presumably references the horror film *The Legend of Hell House* (1973).

75 *TW: Something in the Water*

76 *Nuclear Time*. The day is given (p7). A janitor says "the war's over" (p9), presumably referring to the Paris Peace Accords signed on 27th January, 1973, which were intended to end the Vietnam War. The conflict actually lasted until 30th April, 1975, when Saigon fell.

77 *SJA: Wraith World*

78 *The Wrong Doctors*. Mel was born in 1964.

79 *The Elixir of Doom*. The year is given, but might result from Jo and the Doctor flitting about in the TARDIS, so isn't subject to UNIT Dating.

80 Dating *Mastermind* (BF CC #8.1) - The year is given.

81 Dating *Iris S2: The Land of Wonder* (BF *Iris* #2.2) - The year is repeatedly given.

82 Dating *Iris: Enter Wildthyme* (*Iris* novel #1) - The month and year are given.

83 Dating "Doorway to Hell" (*DWM* #508-511) - The Doctor says it's "1973: A technological backwater."

84 *The Doctor Trap*

85 When she was "13", according to *The King of Terror*.

86 *Byzantium!* (p8).

87 *Revolution Man* (p248).

1973

Anji Kapoor, a companion of the eighth Doctor, was born in Leeds on 1st April, 1973.[67] **Suzie Costello of Torchwood was born** 6th May, 1973.[68] **Jasper Adeola, the father of Tanya, Jarvis and Damon Adeloa, was born in 1973.**[69]

When Ace was three, her mum cried for days when Ace's grandma Kathleen died. Ace's first pet was called Marmaduke.[70] Arthur C. Clarke was never the same after the *Rama* incident, but at least got many good books out of it.[71]

When Elton Pope was three or four, his mother was killed by an "elemental shade" that had escaped from the Howling Halls. Elton saw the tenth Doctor standing over her body, and would become obsessed with the mysterious stranger.[72]

Aubrey Prior's expedition to the Black Pyramid in 1973 discovered Nephthys' burial chamber.[73] Jack Harkness was involved in the Hell House case, which he said "didn't go well".[74] In 1973, Jack twice saved the life of Professor Leonard Morgan – then left him for a chorus girl from Boston.[75]

On 23rd February, 1973, Dr Albert Gilroy – a researcher at the University of Michigan – developed an artificial intelligence that he named "Isley" after his daughter's love of the Isley Brothers.[76] *The Rise of Hancada*, a *Wraith World* book, was published in 1973.[77]

When Melanie Bush was eight, she committed the names of 150 different species of dinosaurs to memory. She performed on stage in Pease Pottage in 1973, 1974 and 1975, as the Angel Gabriel in the nativity. After that, she became more interested in reciting the Periodic Table. Mel studied dance with Ms. Fairs, but opted against pursuing it as a profession, having been inspired to go to university by trips to the science museum with her uncle John.[78]

In 1973, the third Doctor and Jo Grant met an older Vita Monet, and dealt with her vengeful first husband, the Bloody Count, in Hollywood.[79]

1973 - MASTERMIND[80] **->** Frankie don Maestro, the son of the original owner of the decaying Master's current body, sired a boy named Thomas. Having deduced that the Master's true identity, Frankie sealed the villain within his penthouse. The Master went into suspended animation to preserve his body's remaining vitality.

1973 - IRIS S2: THE LAND OF WONDER[81] **->** The Earth-exiled Iris Wildthyme and Panda investigated Harriet Dodd's Wonderland when some of its denizens escaped from it. MIAOW, desperate that Iris not discover Wonderland's secrets, turned on her and torched it. Dodd bequeathed Iris with the feasibility generator that made Wonderland possible – with this device, Iris repaired her

bus and ended her exile. She and Panda left with the mock turtle from Wonderland and the generator – which adopted the shape of a sentient dodo.

1973 (July) - IRIS: ENTER WILDTHYME[82] **->** Iris Wildthyme kept a private office in South Kensington, London; it was somewhere near the Victoria and Albert Museum, and above *The Gilded Lily* boutique. She stored important documents and objects there, but only for a three-day period in July 1973. On the last of these, a Saturday, Iris and her friends vapourised the building to keep the items from falling into the wrong hands. The same day saw Vince Cosmos announce that he was retiring from pop music. Iris' rival, Anthony Marville, raided the office before its destruction and nicked her Blithe Pinking Shears, which could open portals by cutting through the Very Fabric of Space and Time.

(=) In an alternate dimension, Martian assassins overran Cosmos' last concert at the Hammersmith Odeon.

The UNIT Master Regenerates

1973 - "Doorway to Hell"[83] **->** The prolonged healing of the twelfth Doctor's TARDIS saturated the Collins family with temporal radiation. The UNIT Master used the Collinses to open a time-locked dimension, gained the powers of the chronal storm there, and ascended to become a god of time. The Collins' artron energy reflected the Master's temporal attack, mortally wounding him, and so he regenerated.

A week later, the Doctor realised that his presence had put the Collinses at risk, so left in his restored TARDIS.

The accomplished hunter Sebastiene believed that he had been an undergraduate at Cambridge, 1973, who was looking at a meteorite through an electron microscope – and suddenly found himself on an alien planet, a million light years from home. The tenth Doctor suspected that Sebastiene's recollection might be true, or that he might be unaware of his genuine origins.[84]

Tegan Jovanka's grandmother died of coronary thrombosis. About this time, Tegan's father had an affair and her parents split up. Tegan was sent to boarding school.[85] A short sword bearing the initials "IC", given to Ian Chesterton by Thalius Maximus, was now on display in the British National Museum. Historians erroneously dated it to the end of the first century; it was about thirty-five years older.[86] On 12th December, 1973, Revolution Man cult leader Madeleine "Maddie" Burton died in Paris as the result of a drug addiction. The cult quickly died without her influence.[87]

The Restored Counter-Measures

1973 (December) - CM: WHO KILLED TOBY KINSELLA?[88] -> Ian Gilmore, Rachel Jensen and Allison Williams had successfully lived undercover for some years. Gilmore had become a commercial pilot named "Captain Phillip Benson", Jensen taught science as "Carol Hartigan" and Williams worked on a kibbutz in Israel as "Catherine Solomon".

Toby Kinsella's old friend Mikael escaped from Russia, and worked to murder everyone culpable in his downfall and imprisonment. Mikael killed Kinsella's mentor, John Routledge, but Kinsella faked his demise at Mikael's hands. Gilmore, Jensen and Williams reunited at Kinsella's funeral, and worked to protect Mikael's next target: Prince Hassan Al-Nadyr, whose death would have reignited the Cold War. The ex-Counter Measures team saved the Prince, and Kinsella emerged from hiding to capture Mikael – who opted for death at Kinsella's hands rather than imprisonment.

Kinsella preferred to remain officially dead, his body listed as buried at St Margaret's. As he had finally eliminated all members of the Light on Earth, Gilmore, Jensen and Williams were free to resume their lives. The prime minister was grateful to Kinsella's quartet for preventing an international incident, and they decided to form a new Counter-Measures team. It would operate out of Kinsella's new office on the thirteenth floor of the Post Office Tower.

1974

When Ace was four, her parents had a son, Liam. When Ace's father discovered his wife was having an affair with his friend Jack, he left with the infant Liam.[89]

When Donna Noble was six, her mother said there would be "no holiday this year", so Donna caught a bus to Strathclyde. Her parents sent the police after her.[90] As a little girl, Donna Noble never wanted to be a princess.[91] Donna and her friend Hettie started out together at Belmont Primary.[92]

Iris Wildthyme kept a poster of David Essex, as clipped from the back of *Jackie* (6th January, 1974) in one of her bus' window-blinds, right next to a map of the multiverse.[93]

Reginald Tyler died in a domestic accident. He had been working on his novel *The True History of Planets* since 1917, much to the annoyance of his wife, Enid, who sold the movie rights and moved to Jamaica with her lover.

---

88 Dating *New CM: Who Killed Toby Kinsella?* (BF *New CM* #0) - The blurb states: "It's Christmas 1973. Nearly ten years have elapsed since the Counter-Measures group vanished." Within the story, an official dossier states that Gilmore, Jensen and Williams died in the line of duty "a few years ago" (at the end of *Counter-Measures* Series 4 [c.1966]). The story begins in the holiday season (with a well-wisher declaring, "Merry Christmas and a happy 1974") and works to a climax on "the last work day before Christmas"; an epilogue occurs on "Christmas Day" itself. Newscasts convey many historical details, including conflicts in the Middle East, the oil crisis and OPEC on Christmas Day announcing a 10% increase in production rather than a scheduled 5% cut.

89 *The Rapture*

90 *Partners in Crime*

91 *Death and the Queen*

92 *In the Blood* (ch3).

93 *Iris S3: Iris Rides Out*

94 *Mad Dogs and Englishmen*

95 Dating *The New Counter-Measures* Series 1 (*Nothing to See Here*, #1.1; *Troubled Waters*, #1.2; *The Phoenix Strain*, #1.3; *A Gamble with Time*, #1.4) - Events have moved on from *CM: Who Killed Toby Kinsella?* [Dec 1973]. *New CM* S1: *The Phoenix Strain* says the unveiling of Winston Churchill's statue in Parliament Square (1st November, 1973) happened "last year"; the Biological Weapons Convention of 1972 was "two years" ago.

96 Dating *The New Counter-Measures* Series 2 (*The Splintered Man*; #2.2, *The Ship of the Sleepwalkers*; #2.3, *My Enemy's Enemy*; #2.4, *Time of the Intelligence*) - No date given. *Leth-St: Night of the Intelligence* specifies that this incursion of the Great Intelligence (*Time of the Intelligence*) happens in 1974.

In *The Ship of the Sleepwalkers*, Kinsella mentions "Tuesday, 19th of June": in the 1970s, that day was a Tuesday only in 1973 and 1979. *My Enemy's Enemy* focuses on the emergence of punk rock, said to have begun "last year" in the United States, but it's hard to pick a specific year when that happened in the real world. *Time of the Intelligence* opens on the anniversary of the death of Allison Williams' father (*CM S3: The Forgotten Village*). "Chameleon Tours" featured in *The Faceless Ones* [1966]; the "Chameleon Airlines" mentioned in *The Splintered Man* appears to just be a coincidence.

97 Dating "Agent Provocateur" (IDW *DW* mini-series #1) – The Doctor names the year, and a flier advertises the exhibit as being open from "July 8" to "September 5". Martha says it's "ten years before I was born" (in 1986 according to *Wooden Heart*, 1984 according to BBC Books' *The Torchwood Archives*).

98 *The King of Terror* (p32).

99 *Time in Office*

100 "Ten years" before *The Zygon Who Fell to Earth*.

101 Dating "Urgent Calls" (BF #94b) - The year is given on the back cover. This is the first in a series of one-part stories related to the viruses released in *Patient Zero*.

(=) In another version of history, Reginald Tyler didn't die. He was rescued by a poodle that walked on its hind legs, who transported him off Earth... in this reality, *The True History of Planets* would become a very different book.

@ The eighth Doctor read the original *The True History of Planets*.[94]

1974 - THE NEW COUNTER-MEASURES SERIES 1[95]
-> Rachel Jensen's mother had long since passed.

The restored Counter-Measures dealt with a number of potential security threats, including a rogue scientist whose psychological equipment could make someone "invisible" by misleading people's perceptions. They also investigated the HMS *Reynard*, an unofficial UK Hunter-Killer-class submarine conducting experiments into telepathy. Counter-Measures destroyed the *Reynard* after the top psychic aboard killed the ship's crew, and threatened to create a new world order from a nuclear holocaust.

Lord Henry Balfour sponsored research in contravention of the Biological Weapons Convention of 1972. Counter-Measures brought Balfour to justice, as well as contained an avian flu outbreak that caused flocks of birds to terrorise people. Later, Counter-Measures intervened in Monte Carlo as twin magicians tried to con an illicit arms trader, Lady Suzanne Clare, into buying their "time machine". Kinsella's team failed to net evidence of Clare's crimes, and she went free.

1974 - THE NEW COUNTER-MEASURES SERIES 2[96]
-> Drs Javier Santos and Henry Cording, Rachel Jensen's ex-flame, embarked on research intended to solve world hunger with cloned vegetables, but Santos cloned himself as well. As the cloning process induced a psychosis, the Santos clones murdered their progenitor and Cording, and destroyed their work to prevent anyone else suffering their anguish. The Counter-Measures team mopped up the Santos clones' rampage and thought them dead, but five Santos doubles lived on in secret. Afterward, Sir Toby Kinsella's group returned home via Chameleon Airlines.

Kinsella's team busted up a joint American-Russian undertaking to refine MKUltra, a brainwashing programme intended to control entire populaces. Later, Lady Suzanne Clare tried to destroy Counter-Measures HQ on behalf of Sir August Frazer, a crooked baron of the realm who feared that Counter-Measures' computational power would uncover his sordid dealings. Group Captain Gilmore washed everyone's hands of Clare and Bernard by arranging for Bernard, an alien cultural critic, to take them away from Earth when he returned home.

The Great Intelligence had remained rooted to Earth following the London Event, and forged a link with Dr Norma Vine, one of the foremost physicists in Wales.

Evidence of the Great Intelligence's return – and its robotic Yeti – prompted Counter-Measures to contact Professor Edward Travers, who had fallen from grace with the Ministry, and was in the care of his great-nephew Reece Goff. Travers and Kinsella combined their mental willpower to sever the link between the Great Intelligence and Vine, unmooring the Intelligence once more. Travers was given a new research posting at Fugglestone.

1974 (summer) - "Agent Provocateur"[97] -> The
tenth Doctor and Martha saw sand sculptures of British pop stars in Parliament Square, London, that previewed an exhibition by one Princess Hentopet. The sand-sculpture exhibits were real people turned into sand, and were held together by a nanometre force field. The Doctor learned the story of Bubastion, Hentopet and Sheeq – who had travelled the world since Egyptian times – and had Bubastion restore the sculptures to life in return for promising to take him home. These events were part of a wider plot to snare the Doctor on behalf of the Elite Pantheon; the scheme culminated in the year five billion.

Tegan ran away from home when she was 15. Once she was found, her father sent her to live with his sister Vanessa in England.[98] To Tegan's infuriation, her ex-boyfriend never admitted to having a fling with her cousin one summer.[99]

Hagoth's Zygons continued their scheme to promote global warming; Phase Five entailed using biochemical warheads to detonate the accumulated gases in Earth's atmosphere. Circa 1974, however, Hagoth renounced his people's conquering ways, and made off with both his crew's Skarasen and a crystal lattice that enabled his ship's firing sequence. Deprived of the Skarasen's lactic fluid, Hagoth's crew made do with the powdered stuff.[100]

1974 - "Urgent Calls"[101] -> Telephone operator Lauren
Hudson was exhibiting strange symptoms, but a wrong call luckily put her in touch with the sixth Doctor. He advised that an alien worm was hugging her spine. Military surgeons extracted the worm, and Lauren experienced a string of wrong-but-fortuitous phone calls. The Doctor said that an alien "luck" virus capable of transmitting itself through telephones had infected them. He suspected that the virus was engineered to let sleeper agents communicate, or to summon precisely the right sort of aid. Earth wasn't ready for such a virus (however helpful it had become), and the Doctor said he would deal with it. Some time later, Lauren was saddened to find that every call she placed went through correctly. Failing to hear from the Doctor, she mailed him a letter instead.

1974 - HORROR OF GLAM ROCK[102] **->** The singer Nancy Babcock said that her cat dictated all of her music. Lucie Miller's mother – a blonde named Mary – presently worked in a Gloucester shoe shop.

Arnold Korns, a dynamic and powerful manager in the music industry, discovered two budding talents: Trisha and Tommy Tomorrow, who performed as The Day After Tomorrow. Korns scheduled them to make their debut on *Top of the Pops*. However, a group of discorporealised alien beings, seeking to consume the polyunsaturates and fibre found in the human body, had contacted Tommy as sound waves conducted through his Stylophone. They touted themselves as the "Only Ones", claiming they were the only race in existence besides humanity, and helped Tommy compose his songs.

En route to London, Korns and the twins stopped off at Nadir Services, a service station and café just outside Bramlington. The spot had previously seen such celebrities as Hendrix, Lulu and the Wombles, and now witnessed the dissolution of the band Methylated Spirits. The group severed ties with drummer Patricia Ryder, who in future would become Lucie's "Auntie Pat". Outside the café, the Only Ones manifested as scaled, bear-like creatures and killed Roger.

The eighth Doctor and Lucie showed up as the Only Ones murdered Tricia Tomorrow and threatened to unleash a massacre. The Doctor found a means of converting the Only Ones back into sound, and trapped them on shuffle mode in Lucie's MP3 Player. He speculated that the carnage would be blamed on the Hell's Angels.

The Headhunter pursuing the Doctor and Lucie narrowly missed them in this period.

Lord Lucan introduced Colonel Hugh Spindleton to the Master, whom Lucan swore would put the world to right. In time, the Master used the Colonel as his lackey.[103] In November, the Celestial Toymaker kidnapped Lord Lucan, sparking an international manhunt.[104] The twelfth Doctor's TARDIS contained the Last Will and Testament of Lord Lucan.[105]

1974 (25th November) - HIDE[106] **->** Major Alec Palmer, now a member of the Baker Street Irregulars and the Ministry of Ungentlemanly Warfare, took up ghost hunting to help redeem the deaths he'd caused in service to Queen and Country. He purchased the "haunted" Caliburn House and set about investigating – with his assistant, the empathic Emma Grayling – the Caliburn Ghast.

The eleventh Doctor consulted with Grayling on the strange case of Clara Oswald being duplicated throughout history, and determined that the Caliburn Ghast was the temporal echo of Hila Tacorian: one of the early human time travellers. The Doctor aided Hila and two aliens in fully manifesting, and found that Hila was Palmer and Grayling's descendant. As history recorded her as lost, she could never return home.

---

102 Dating *Horror of Glam Rock* (BF BBC7 #1.3) - "It's 1974", the Doctor says.

103 *Trail of the White Worm, The Oseidon Adventure*. It's not said if this meeting happens before or after Lucan disappears (on 8th November, 1974) following the brutal death of his children's nanny.

104 *Divided Loyalties* (p46). Lord Lucan, a British peer, disappeared 8th November, 1974 – the day after Sandra Rivett, his children's nanny, was murdered. He was never found, and has been a source of speculation ever since.

105 *The Shining Man* (ch2).

106 Dating *Hide* (X7.10) - Major Palmer records the exact date: "November 25th, 1974." The story leaves open ended what becomes of Tacorian after this.

107 *P.R.O.B.E.: Unnatural Selection*

108 *The One Doctor*, possibly referring to *The Invasion*.

109 "Eight years" before *Return of the Living Dad*.

110 *TW: Greeks Bearing Gifts*, in which Mary gives the month and year of Tosh's birth and Tosh doesn't correct her. *TW: torchwood_cascade_cdrip.tor* concurs with that – when Tosh alters her bio to read "19/09/81", she remarks that she's on paper become "six years younger".

Otherwise, though, there's conflicting evidence as to when Tosh was born. *Torchwood: The Official Magazine Yearbook* (2008) and her on-screen personnel file in *TW:*

Exit Wounds both say she was born 18th September, 1981. *The Torchwood Archives* (BBC) says she was born on the same day, but in 1975. Internet sources, almost appropriately given the confusion around her character, seem split down the middle as to whether actress Naoko Mori was born in 1971 or 1975, but seem to agree that her birthday is 19th November.

111 No date on screen, but actor Kai Owen was born 4th September, 1975. *TW: Visiting Hours* establishes that Rhys' mother Brenda was born in 1954.

112 *Nuclear Time*

113 *TW: Children of Earth*

114 *TW: The Dead Line*

115 *TW: Trace Memory*

116 *Hexagora*, going by Tegan being born in 1960.

117 *Worlds DW: The Screaming Skull*

118 *TW: The Conspiracy*

119 Dating *Fury from the Deep* (5.6) - It is clear that this story is set in the near future. There is a Europe-wide energy policy and videophones are in use. It's tempting, in fact, to see this as being set in the same near future as the early UNIT stories. Although Robson, the refinery controller, talks of "tuppence ha'penny tinpot ideas", this is clearly a figure of speech rather than an indication that the story is set in the era of predecimal currency.

1975

The British government established the BEAGLE project to determine the next stage of human evolution. Professor Julius Quilter developed an advanced human – Alfred – who could absorb human organs, but Alfred killed a BEAGLE member while doing so. The government shut down the project in 1975; Quilter officially said that Alfred had been destroyed, but nurtured him in secret.[107]

During the Cybermen invasion of June 1975, the Doctor was based at 35 Jefferson Road, Woking.[108] The Doctor visited a planet orbiting Lalande 21185. The Caxtarids had developed a virus that the government were planning to use against a rebel faction.[109]

In July 1975, Toshiko Sato of Torchwood was born in London. Her parents were in the RAF, and her grandfather worked at Metchley Park.[110] Rhys Williams, an associate of Torchwood, was born.[111] Colonel Geoffrey Redvers coerced Albert Gilroy into building android assassins for the US military on 3rd August, 1975.[112]

Melissa Moretti, the daughter of Lucia Moretti and Jack Harkness, was born 5th August, 1975. Lucia stopped working for Torchwood in the same year.[113] Jack Harkness dated a junior doctor named Stella Courtney for a few weeks in 1975.[114] Charles Arthur Cromwell retired from Torchwood in 1975.[115]

Tegan and Mike Bretherton were high school classmates, and next door neighbours, in Brisbane. They were both inspired by Miss Anderson, who taught physics. When Tegan was 15, Mike carried her books home after she broke her toe during track and field.[116]

The Reesinger music box passed into UNIT's possession in the mid-70s.[117] Torchwood founded *Plexus* magazine, a publication devoted to conspiracy talk and unsolved mysteries, in Patchogue, New York, in 1975.[118]

Victoria Leaves the TARDIS

c 1975 - FURY FROM THE DEEP[119] -> On the whole, this period was "a good time in Earth's history to stay in. No wars, great prosperity, a time of plenty." Gas from the sea now provided energy for the south of England and Wales, as well as mainland Europe. Twenty rigs pumped gas into every home without incident for more than four years.

When scientists registered a regular build-up and fall in pressure in the main pipelines, the supply was cut off for the first time. A mutant species of seaweed was responsible, and it mentally dominated some of the rigs' crews before being beaten back by amplified sound.

Victoria Waterfield left the second Doctor and Jamie to settle down with the Harris family.

When Victoria left the TARDIS, she took with her a piece of parchment – a memento of her having helped Jamie learn to read. As time went on, the second Doctor tried and failed to find Victoria, as the parchment held a dangerous Story-form from the planet Amyryndaa.[120]

The Doctor met hacker Robert Salmon in 1975. They stopped a US Navy programmer from installing a back door that would've granted illicit access to the Navy's computers.[121] Freda Jackson joined the space programme in 1975 – she would later command Moon Village One.[122] The Doctor had tickets to opening night of *The Rocky Horror Picture Show*.[123]

1976

Alice Uwaebuka Obiefune, a companion of the eleventh Doctor, was born to Ijezie and Ada Obiefune.[124]

In 1976, a Lalandian safari killed people in Durham.

The Programme Guide always assumed that the story was contemporary. *A History of the Universe in 100 Objects* (p100) specifies that living seaweed attacked an oil refinery in "circa 1968", presumably in keeping with *Fury from the Deep* being broadcast that same year. The *TARDIS Logs* set the story in "2074", the same year it suggested for *The Wheel in Space*.

Timelink stitched together the future tech on display, Robson's claims of having "been drilling for gas in the North Sea for most of my life", his "reputation of thirty years" and the advent of North Sea drilling in the mid-1960s to derive a dating of "1995". *About Time* opened the bid by just saying it was "evidently the near future", then acknowledged that while a mid-90s dating was feasible, fandom tended to assume it was the mid-70s and in line with the UNIT stories.

Downtime somewhat settles the argument on this,

with Victoria having been in the twentieth century for "ten years" by 1984 (p41).

The quotation is the Doctor reassuring Jamie about Victoria's new home in *The Wheel in Space*.

120 *1stD V1: The Story of Extinction*
121 *Blue Box*
122 "The Lunar Strangers". Jackson says she's been in "the service forty years".
123 *The Reaping. Rocky Horror* debuted on 14th August, 1975.
124 Alice claims she's "40 years old" in *The Eleventh Doctor Year One*: "The Sound of Our Voices", but is presumably approximating while on the run, as she later says she's in her "30s" in *The Eleventh Doctor Year One*: "Space in Dimension Relative and Time".

Isaac Summerfield tipped off UNIT to the problem.[125] The seventh Doctor and Ace visited London in 1976.[126] In 1976, the Order of St Peter chased the last known European vampire from the continent. It escaped to the United States.[127] Jack Harkness converted the husk of an alien visitor into a coracle in 1976.[128]

@ On 28th May, Deborah Gordon and Barry Castle married in Greyfrith. The eighth Doctor was elsewhere, with a widow called Claudia.[129]

The last British mission to Mars, Mars Probe 13, ended in disaster when the Ice Warriors killed two crewmembers. The British government made a secret deal to stay away from Mars, and they framed the mission's sole survivor, Lex Christian, for murder. He was sent to Fortress Island, where he remained for more than twenty years.[130]

The Racht seed disc on Earth infected actress Johanna Bourke. As "Phillip Mungston", she wrote a horror portmanteau film – Doctor Demonic's Tales of Terror – and incorporated the seed disc into a sacrifice scene, a means of infecting anyone watching with a newborn Racht. The fifth Doctor and Nyssa visited the production in summer of 1976, and destroyed all footage pertaining to the scene. Nyssa appeared in the first Tales of Terror installment, "Curse of the Devil's Whisper", as "Nyssa Traken".[131]

= **1976 - THE FORBIDDEN TIME**[132] -> The Vist were time-walkers with bodies the size of greyhounds, set atop giraffe-like legs. They claimed dominion over a period of eight years, three months and two days – roughly from 2011 to 2019 – across the whole of creation, and sought to "penalise" the life force of any civilisation that entered it without permission. The second Doctor, Polly, Ben and Jamie encountered the Vist on a shadowy "sideways" version of Earth in the 70s, and the Doctor tricked the Vist into venturing back to the start of the universe.

1976 - VAMPIRE SCIENCE[133] -> Carolyn McConnell, a pre-med student, met the eighth Doctor and Sam in San Francisco. The Doctor was on the trail of a clutch of vampires, and a scuffle led to the death of his best lead, the vampire Eva. He gave Carolyn a signalling device in case the vampires resurfaced.

1976 (12th July) - DEMON QUEST: STARFALL[134] -> The fourth Doctor, Mike Yates and Mrs Wibbsey arrived in Central Park in Manhattan, looking for the fourth stolen component of the TARDIS' spatial geometer and using an old comic book from this year as guidance. Buddy Hudson

125 Return of the Living Dad
126 Timewyrm: Revelation
127 Minuet in Hell. This claim is either hyperbole on the Order's part or extremely short-lived, as Goth Opera (set in 1993) has between three to four hundred vampires active in Britain alone.
128 TW: The Sin Eaters
129 Father Time
130 "Over twenty years" before The Dying Days.
131 The Demons of Red Lodge and Other Stories: "Special Features"
132 Dating The Forbidden Time (BF CC #5.9) - It's "thirty-five years" before 2011.
133 Dating Vampire Science (EDA #2) - It's "1976" (p3).
134 Dating Demon Quest: Starfall (BBC fourth Doctor audio #2.4) - Buddy's opening narration says it's "July", "1976". He later says the meteorite lands on the "12th".
135 Dating The Eleventh Doctor Year One (Titan 11th Doc #1.12, "Conversion") - A caption gives the year.
136 Dating WM: The Heavenly Paradigm (BF WM box set #1.4) - The year is given.
137 TW: The Dead Line
138 Big Bang Generation (ch2).
139 TW: Children of Earth
140 Knock, Knock
141 Torchwood.org.uk, elaborating on TW: From Out of the Rain. Jabberwocky debuted in the United Kingdom on 28th March, 1977.
142 Blue Box. This is contradicted by Synthespians™, which states that Peri's father died in 1979 and her mother remarried after that.

143 TW: Greeks Bearing Gifts
144 "Two years" before City of Death.
145 Mission: Impractical
146 Day of the Moon. Sir David Frost, a British media personality, conducted a series of seminal interviews with Nixon (later adapted as a play and a movie starring Michael Sheen and Frank Langella) in 1977.
147 Nuclear Time (p75). Colonel Redvers remarks that it's "only been... a week" since Star Wars came out; in the real world, it was only two days, as A New Hope saw release on 25th May.
148 TW: Fallout
149 The Legends of River Song: "Suspicious Minds", around the time of Elvis' death (August 1977).
150 UNIT S5: Encounters: Invocation
151 Dating PHP: The Helm of Awe (BF PHP #3.1) - The Brigadier sends, via his space-time telegraph, a message to the Doctor dated "23rd" and "24th January, 1977". The Old Norse fire festival of Up Helly Aa starts the day after the Doctor and Leela arrive – by tradition, it gets underway on the last Tuesday in January (in 1977, that was the 25th). This barely counts as a UNIT story; the group isn't seen, and merely fires a missile from off-screen.
152 Dating Mawdryn Undead (20.3) - The earlier part of the story takes place during the Queen's Silver Jubilee – various events to commemorate this started as early as February, and culminated in June. It's repeatedly said that Tegan and Nyssa have arrived "six years" before the story's modern-day component, set in 1983.
In The Memory Bank and Other Stories: "The Memory

saw a meteorite land in Central Park, but when he and his girlfriend Alice Trefusis – who was helping to write the memoirs of faded actress Mimsy Loyne – investigated the incident, Alice touched the meteor and began crackling with energy. The Doctor and his friends recognised the scene from the comic book – Alice had become the superheroine Miss Starfall.

Buddy and Wibbsey found a room full of cultists who were using a ritual – one that featured the last part of the spacial geometer – to drain the Doctor's lifeforce. Mimsy Loyne was revealled as the aspect-changing Demon in disguise, and abducted Wibbsey while announcing that "the Sepulchre is prepared". The Doctor and Mike vowed to find their friend, and returned to 2010. Alice's powers faded, but not before she and Buddy took one last flight around the city.

1976 - THE ELEVENTH DOCTOR YEAR ONE[135] ->
The eleventh Doctor and John Jones sped in a motorbike on top of the Berlin Wall, in hot pursuit of the Entity, and followed it through a wormhole to Rome, 312 AD...

The War Master Exits the Time War

lgtw - 1976 - WM: ONLY THE GOOD: THE HEAVENLY PARADIGM[136] -> The War Master and his companion, Cole, penetrated security at a Time Lord R&D facility concealed at a house in Stamford Bridge, 1976. As the War Master anticipated, Cole – being an uber-paradox – made an excellent fuel that activated a timeline manipulator: The Heavenly Paradigm. The War Master's efforts with the Paradigm proved so calamitous, he used a Chameleon Arch to make himself human, and exited the Last Great Time War.

On 24th September, 1976, the Rift radiated energy that ended the worst drought Wales had seen in three centuries. The head office of the Cardiff and West Building Society, Madoc House, was struck by lightning charged with an electrical virus. This rendered thirteen employees comatose when they answered the phones. They were relocated to a private hospital; Madoc House was closed, its operations moved to Swansea. The virus remained trapped in the disued Madoc House phone system.[137]

In future, a planet receiving old Earth broadcasts would believe that the Wurzels' appearance on *Top of the Pops*, Christmas Day 1976, was the absolute pinnacle of human culture.[138]

1977

On 14th February, 1977, Lucia Moretti's application that her daughter Melissa be put into deep cover was approved. Melissa was renamed Alice Sangster, and officially was the child of James and Mary Sangster – place-holder names used for those undercover or in witness relocation.[139]

In 1977, the Landlord fed six tenants to his Dryads.[140] The Electro in Cardiff had a final screening – Terry Gilliam's *Jabberwocky* – then survived for another eighteen months as a bingo hall before closing.[141]

Peri's mother divorced and remarried when Peri was ten.[142] **When Toshiko Sato was two, her family moved to Osaka, Japan.**[143] **Count Carlos Scarlioni, one of the richest men on Earth, married his Countess in 1977.**[144] In 1977, the sixth Doctor and Frobisher attended the opening of *Star Wars* at Mann's Chinese Theatre, Los Angeles.[145] **The eleventh Doctor told Richard Nixon to say hello to David Frost for him.**[146] Albert Gilroy, working from a Utah military research base, successfully transferred the AI Isley into an android body on 27th May, 1977.[147]

The Russians captured a silicon-based lifeform, a Kaloczul, on the isle of Sakhalin in 1977, and carried out experiments on it.[148] River Song was acquainted with Bigfoot, a.k.a. Geraldine.[149]

Brigadier Lethbridge-Stewart cancelled the UNIT work being done at Ealdon House, when researcher Alice Donelly refined a deadly form of infrasound more effective against humans than aliens. Donelly altered UNIT's records so she could stay on as Ealdon's caretaker. Kate Stewart visited Ealdon House when she was a girl, and enjoyed racing through it with Alice's son Ben.[150]

1977 (24th-25th January) - THE HELM OF AWE[151]
-> Tipped off by the Brigadier, the fourth Doctor and Leela looked into alien technology taken from Edinburgh Castle. Nardos, the Barbezzon operating on the Shetland isle of Bothness, created a temporal breach that threw the travellers back to World War II. Upon their return, Nardos activated seismic equipment to rend Earth apart, so the Barbezzon High Fleet – composed of Star Darkeners – could recharge. The Doctor reversed Nardos' force-field equipment, killing him with a minor explosion. A new volcano appeared near Bothness, which was expected to attract tourists.

1977 - MAWDRYN UNDEAD[152] -> The Brigadier had retired from UNIT, and was now teaching mathematics at Brendan Public School. The TARDIS arrived with Tegan and Nyssa on board – the Ship had been thrown back to 1977 thanks to a warp eclipse from Mawdryn's spaceship. Mawdryn himself arrived in a transmat capsule, but the journey left him gravely injured. Tegan and Nyssa mistook him for the Doctor, and agreed to take him back to the spaceship. The Brigadier insisted on accompanying them.

On Mawdryn's ship, the Brigadier came into contact

with his older self and triggered the Blinovitch Limitation Effect. This left the younger Brigadier with some memory loss – the fifth Doctor and his companions left him on Earth to continue teaching.

To Jackie Tyler's mind, the Powell Estate was at its happiest during the Queen's Silver Jubilee celebrations.[153]

c 1977 (30th-31st July) - IMAGE OF THE FENDAHL[154] -> The fourth Doctor and Leela encountered the Fendahl at Fetchborough, a village on the edge of a time fissure. A team of scientists under Professor Fendelman were attempting to probe the far past using a time scanner, but this had only succeeded in activating the dormant Fendahl skull. Fetch Priory was destroyed in an implosion. The Doctor defeated the Fendahl, and took the skull with the intent of throwing it into a supernova.

In 1977, the seventh Doctor landed in Lewisham in an attempt to track the Timewyrm.[155] On Trion, the dictator Rehctaht emerged as the most tyrannical ruler in the planet's history. She would rule for seven years, and butcher the Clansmen. She founded the colony of New Trion primarily as a slave labour force, but conflict

between Trion colonies in the East and the West diverted her attention. New Trion functioned independently, if inefficiently.[156]

1977 - "The Nightmare Game"[157] -> The eighth Doctor discovered that the alien Shakespeare Brothers were behind Delchester United's recent bad run.

1977 - THE FOE FROM THE FUTURE[158] -> The fourth Doctor was teaching Leela about *Hamlet* when the TARDIS detected a temporal rift in a "haunted" grange in the village of Straffham, the heart of Devon. The grange's new owner, Jalnik, had travelled back from an alternate timeline circa 4000, in which the insectoid Pantophagen had devastated Earth. Jalnik had been assigned to facilitate the relocation of Earth's survivors into the past, but became increasingly nihilistic, and desired that the Pantophagen destroy humanity in its past.

The Doctor and Leela went to circa 4000, returning as a horde of Pantophagen arrived in the present day with 512 future humans. Jalnik's butler – actually named "Butler" – had mutated into a human-Pantophagen hybrid, but Leela crushed him to death beneath a church bell. The Pantophagen ate the future people, as well as Jalnik, before the Doctor arranged for the creatures to age to death. He

---

Bank", the Doctor names Turlough's schoolmates as "Class of '83". The same story suggests that Turlough was at Brendon for "years".
153 *Jack: Wednesdays for Beginners*
154 Dating *Image of the Fendahl* (15.3) - According to Ma Tyler, it is "Lammas Eve" (31st July) at the end of episode three. There's nothing to suggest it's not set the year of broadcast. "Hartman", a character spoken to over the phone, is pretty obviously not Yvonne Hartman of Torchwood (*Army of Ghosts/Doomsday*).
155 *Timewyrm: Revelation* (p13).
156 Seven years before *Turlough and the Earthlink Dilemma*.
157 Dating "The Nightmare Game" (*DWM* #330-332) - The year is given.
158 Dating *The Foe from the Future* (BF 4th Doc LS #1.1) - The Doctor declares that the Vortex breach originates from "Earth, England, 1977", in accordance with the back cover blurb, and Big Finish's desire to set this "lost story" contemporaneously with Season 15. Two supporting characters talk about watching *Monty Python* on TV. Leela's mention of "blue guards" suggests that for her and the Doctor, this takes place after *The Talons of Weng-Chiang*.
159 Dating *The Valley of Death* (BF 4th Doc LS #1.2) - The year is given.
160 Dating *Suburban Hell* (BF 4th Doc #4.5) - The year is given.

161 Dating *The Cloisters of Terror* (BF 4th Doc #4.6) - 1976 was "last year".
162 Dating *Iris S5: An Extraterrestrial Werewolf in Belgium* (BF *Iris* #5.7) - The year is given.
163 "Several months" before *The Drosten's Curse*.
164 *The Left-Handed Hummingbird* (p23).
165 *Terror Firma*. Presuming this doesn't instead refer to the Las Vegas nightclub of the same name, the infamous disco operated from 1977-1986.
166 *Iris: Enter Wildthyme*
167 "Nearly forty years" before *Iris: Iris and the Celestial Omnibus*: "The Deadly Flap" [2008], and possibly a more definitive break-up after *Iris S2: The Land of Wonder*.
168 *Iris: Iris and the Celestial Omnibus*: "The Deadly Flap"
169 *Benny: Beige Planet Mars. Option Lock*, which entails some nuclear gamesmanship in the late twentieth century, makes no mention of this protocol.
170 *Benny S9: The Diet of Worms*. The date isn't specified, but Cartland lived 1901 to 2000.
171 *DotD: Night of the Whisper*. The comic *Whizzer and Chips* saw print from 1969 to 1990, when it merged with *Buster*.
172 Dating *The Pirate Planet* (16.2) - The Doctor says that the population of Earth is "billions and billions", possibly suggesting a contemporary setting. *First Frontier* implies the same.
173 Dating *The Stones of Blood* (16.3) - There is no indication what year the story is set, but it is clearly contemporary.

then sealed off the rift at its future point, preventing Jalnik's alternate Earth from ever happening.

1977 - THE VALLEY OF DEATH[159] **->** The Royal Archaeological Society of the British Museum sponsored an expedition to discover the fate of Professor Perkins' 1873 expedition to the Valley of Death. The fourth Doctor and Leela accompanied the group, in the Doctor's capacity as a scientific adviser to UNIT.

The Doctor's party encountered the stranded Luron named Godrin – who claimed to be the last of his kind, and that he wanted to aid humanity's development. Godrin murdered Professor Perkins as being of no further use, and switched off the slow-time field his crashed scout-ship had projected around the Valley. The expedition returned with Godrin to London – only to discover that although they'd only spent a day or so in the Valley, the slow-time field meant that they returned two years after they left...

(=) 1977 - SUBURBAN HELL[160] **->** A blue-skinned woman from the constellation of Menossera developed formidable powers of persuasion, and cheated death by having her intellect instilled in a painting of her. This was hidden in North London, where the woman's seven acolytes worked to transfer her mind into a a child. The fourth Doctor scanned this era for temporal instability connected to the year 2017, and thereby created the very time-ruckage he was searching for. He returned to 2017 after starting a fire with a fondue set, which burned down the house with the picture and the acolytes in it.

1977 - THE CLOISTERS OF TERROR[161] **->** Dame Emily Shaw had been appointed dean of St Matilda's, Oxford, for only three weeks when the fourth Doctor and Leela turned up to investigate energy readings radiating from the spaceship under the school/convent. The Brigadier, Emily believed, was in South America investigating an Inca Pyramid. Emily's daughter, Liz Shaw, was working for British Rocket Group, which was busy establishing a moonbase. Dame Emily aided the Doctor and Leela in preventing the damaged spaceship from creating a warp influx that would have devastated Earth, and returned to St Hugh's College after a comparatively smaller explosion destroyed the ship and St Matilda's.

1977 - IRIS S5: AN EXTRATERRESTRIAL WEREWOLF IN BELGIUM[162] **->** Iris took Captain Turner to an amusement park in the North of England, but rashly said "Bloody Nora" three times and accidentally summoned an inter-dimensional spirit of the same name. The travellers jumped into the Vortex in Iris' bus, and shattered a mirror containing Nora's essence, splintering her power...

The Chicago Area Computer Hobbyists' Exchange was slated to develop its MODEM work in a snowstorm, and create an inadvertent danger to all life on Earth.[163]

1978

On 21st February, 1978, electrical workers uncovered the sacrificial stone at the base of the Great Temple in Mexico City.[164] The eighth Doctor, Samson and Gemma visited Studio 54.[165] Panda arranged to have Iris scraped off the floor of Studio 54.[166]

Iris Wildthyme stopped working for the South Kensington branch[167] of The Ministry of Incursions and Other Alien Wonders (MIAOW), thinking them too nefarious.[168]

From the Carter-Brezhnev era, it became standard policy to lodge missile command codes into the hearts of people beloved to the persons authorised to launch nuclear strikes. It was hoped – as approving a missile strike would now necessitate the loved one's death – that those entrusted with such weaponry would consider and re-consider the humanity and consequences of their actions.[169]

The romance novelist Barbara Cartland bought extra-terrestrial stationery from a seemingly ordinary shop near Charing Cross: McZygon of the Strand.[170] The ninth Doctor owned a spud gun related to the *Whizzer and Chips* comic, 1978.[171]

c 1978 - THE PIRATE PLANET[172] **->** Zanak's career as the Pirate Planet – a hollowed out world that teleported around other planets and mined out their riches – was brought to an abrupt end when the fourth Doctor, the first Romana and K9 helped to bring about the destruction of its engines and the death of its Captain and Queen Xanxia. Zanak settled in a peaceful area of space.

c 1978 - THE STONES OF BLOOD[173] **->** The fourth Doctor, the first Romana and K9 helped defeat Cessair of Diplos, who had escaped from her prison ship in hyperspace and been hiding on Earth for four thousand years. She was found guilty by two justice machines – the Megara – of impersonating a deity, theft and misuse of the Seal of Diplos, murder, and removing silicon lifeforms from the planet Ogros in contravention of article 7594 of the Galactic Charter. She was sentenced to perpetual imprisonment.

Amelia Rumford wrote *Lore of the Land*.[174] **Around this time, the Time Lord Drax spent ten years in Brixton Prison.[175] Chris Parsons graduated in 1978.[176] Work was done on the sewers under Fleet Street.[177]**

1978 - MAD DOGS AND ENGLISHMEN[178] **->** The eighth Doctor dropped Anji off in Hollywood, where she met embittered special effects man Ron von Arnim. The Doctor went to 1942 and returned with Noel Coward – and bore news that von Arnim was being manipulated to create a movie about poodles by director John Fuchas. The Doctor tied Fuchas to a chair, headed off to Dogworld and forgot to go back, so Fuchas died. This prevented the movie being made, and saved the day.

1978 (2th-6th June) - THE DROSTEN'S CURSE[179] **->** At the Fetch Brothers Golf Spa Hotel in Arbroath, the fourth Doctor bore witness as Grand High Emperor Zandor the Mighty tried and failed to control the Bah-Sokhar: a legendary soul-eater that now fed on love. The Bah-Sokhar returned to being an egg for someone to find.

c 1978 (Summer) - TRAIL OF THE WHITE WORM / THE OSEIDON ADVENTURE[180] **->** The cadaverous Master determined that the combination of Z-radiation and O-radiation would produce Z-O radiation: a means of restoring him to health and vitality. The Doctor had left a

Z-radiation battery in his UNIT lab, and the Kraal homeworld of Oseidon was saturated in O-radiation. The Master promised the Kraals that he would create a wormhole that would let the Second Kraal Army invade Earth, but in actuality sought to detonate the Doctor's battery and bathe in the resultant Z-O radiation in the wormhole.

An android double of the Master was dispatched to seek the wormhole-generating ability of the space worm hiding in Dark Peak, Derbyshire. The worm had taken human form and was living as "Demesne Furze", kidnapping and consuming people to live. The fourth Doctor and Leela were present as the Master triggered Furze's powers, killing her and opening a wormhole between Oseidon and Earth.

Marshal Grinmal of the Kraals decided to end his people's partnership with the Master and formed an alliance with the Master's lackey: Colonel Hugh Spindleton. The Colonel suggested the Kraals assert their power by destroying an English village with an MD bomb, and sent an ultimatum delivering the resignation of the government, the return of national service, the abolition of free school milk, the imprisonment of union leaders in stocks, and the shuttering of the BBC.

The Doctor and Leela repelled the Kraals, and convinced an android-Master to assert his own agency. The android hauled the genuine article into his TARDIS and left. Spindleton was turned over to UNIT, even as the Doctor and Leela took a spoil the Master had given him –

---

174 *The Shining Man* (ch13). Rumford appears in *The Stones of Blood*.
175 *The Armageddon Factor*
176 *Shada*
177 "Seven years" before *Attack of the Cybermen*.
178 Dating *Mad Dogs and Englishmen* (EDA #52) - The date is given.
179 Dating *The Drosten's Curse* (PDA #79) - The exact days are given. This novel is an expanded version of *The Death Pit*, a short story for the *Time Trips* series.
180 Dating *Trail of the White Worm/The Oseidon Adventure* (BF 4th Doc #1.5-#1.6) - The blurb to *Trail of the White Worm* claims the year is "1979". However, no year is given within the fiction, and young Julie Ledger conspicuously says she wishes to run away to Carnaby Street to hang with Siouxsie and the Banshees (formed in 1976) and Sid Vicious – an impressive feat, considering Vicious died from an overdose on 2nd February, 1979. Even allowing that Julie is presented as a rural dreamer who's behind the times (the script has her deliberately mispronounce Siouxsie Sioux as "Soo-see Banshee"), it does seem strange that she's entirely failed to notice the death of one of her great icons about half a year after the fact. The story can't take place in 1979 before Vicious' passing, as the Doctor says that it's "England in the summertime" and the space worm posing as Demense claims to spend "winter on

the continent, summer [here in Dark Peak]", and later states that she's trying to fatten herself up for winter.

Alan Barnes, who wrote these two stories, told us: "The blurb reads like I wrote it, but I'm a bit surprised to see the 1979 date there – I would have written the blurb ages later, it's probably a simple mistake... John and Julie were analogues of the characters in the song 'Jilted John' by Jilted John – which was summer 1978. If I had a date in mind, that was it." Barnes also states that the tagline of Big Finish's fourth Doctor audios ("It's Saturday tea-time in 1977 all over again!") didn't influence his thinking, as "I'm pretty sure I didn't know about [the slogan] until long after it all had been recorded."

Spindleton says that he recently returned to England to find "half the country on strike", which brings to mind the Winter of Discontent (which started in 1978 and had largely finished by February 1979), although Barnes advises: "There are no shortage of strikes to choose from... the 1972 miners' strike, the 74 miners, Grunwick [a two-year strike, 1976-1978], etc." Spindleton is outraged at the thought of free school milk, which controversially was abolished when Margaret Thatcher was Secretary of State for Education and Science from 1970-1974.

The Kraals remember their first failed attempt to conquer Earth, so it's after *The Android Invasion*. Colonel

the missing racehorse Shergar – back in time to graze peacefully.

During these events, Colonel Faraday was off in Switzerland. The Brigadier was in Canada, contending with electricity pylons that had come to life and were stalking the countryside.

c 1978 - TW: THE DOLLHOUSE[181] -> Mr Beamish of Torchwood recruited three women – the science-trained Marlow Sweet of Brooklyn, the thief Charley Du Bujeau of Louisiana and the driver Gabi Martinez – to defend America's West Coast as Torchwood Los Angeles. The group operated out of a secluded mansion.

An unidentified alien society coveted "Dolls" – humans treated with living plastic – as collectors' items. An unscrupulous Hollywood agent, Don Donahue, lured failed actresses to the secretive Dollhouse in Marina del Rey, and turned them into Dolls. Torchwood LA shut down Donahue's operation, and rescued one of his intended victims, Valerie Fox. Du Bujeau mortally wounded an alien Doll-seller, but it killed her. Fox volunteered to work for Torchwood LA, and Sweet and Martinez declared the group independent of Torchwood UK.

Gwen Cooper of Torchwood was born in Swansea on 16th August, 1978, to Mary and Geraint Wyn Cooper.[182] The Tulkan Empire failed to annex the Annarene homeworld. In response, the Annarene erased the deposed Tulk War Council's memories. An Annarene named Sooal, dying from a genetic disease, spirited the amnesiac council away in a spaceship. Sooal hoped to restore the Council's memories and gain the command codes needed to open a Tulk stasis chamber, which contained a metabolic stabiliser. He established the Graystairs elderly care facility in Muirbridge, Scotland, to conduct

genetics research. On Annarene, the ruling Protectorate favoured pacifism, but a hawk-like faction desired a return to warfare.[183]

= In a parallel dimension, Tyne Tees produced *The Iris Wildthyme Show*. Suzy Kendall starred in the title role, with Charles Hardy as the voice of Panda. The Rainbow Rooms in Newcastle hosted a launch for the show at Christmas 1978, but the series only lasted seventeen episodes in 1979. Rumours circulated about a missing eighteenth episode. Kendall never worked in acting again. The years to come saw publication of 324 *Iris Wildthyme* tie-in books, including *Iris Wildthyme and the Deadly Incursion*, *Iris Wildthyme and the Unicorn's Camper Van* and *Iris Wildthyme Returns to Hyspero*. Writers for the series included Terry Kelly and Bill Fordyce – the latter famous for his Dark Magus novels and Zombie Hooker books.[184]

Followers of the demon Asmedaj summoned their master in December 1978, but the youthful Jane Fonda-esque version of Iris Wildthyme infiltrated the group, chanted the wrong words and tore Asmedaj's body apart. Iris celebrated her triumph with two hitchhikers named Doug. A part of Asmedaj's mind hosted itself in Iris' brain as she fell asleep while watching *The Wizard of Oz*. One of Asmedaj's followers, Marwick, tried to heal his master by implanting Asmedaj's body parts in several newborn children – including Iris' future companion Tom.[185]

When not on assignment for Torchwood, Jack Harkness tried his hand working in life insurance and at a burger bar on Bondi Beach. The fourth revival of Agnes Havisham from cryo-sleep entailed an escapade with Jack at a roller discotheque in Sweden, the late 1970s, when a lethal space plague turned people into the undead. Jack went to

---

Faraday, seen in that story, is still attached to UNIT. The code that the Doctor gives Leela to relay to UNIT ("UNIT TARDIS Doctor Master Zygons Krynoids Axons Two") suggests that it's after *The Seeds of Doom*. It's after Lord Lucan went missing (in real life, that happened on 8th November, 1974).

All told, with the story's internal evidence supporting Barnes' intent of setting this story in summer 1978, it seems safe to set aside the blurb's claim of 1979 as secondary information. If so, this story falls into the "UNIT stories happen in the near future" camp, as Lethbridge-Stewart is still with UNIT.

181 Dating *TW: The Dollhouse* (BF *TW* #3.2) - The blurb broadbrushes it as "1970s Los Angeles". Cybill Shepherd is a celebrity (she rose to fame with *The Last Picture Show* in 1971). *Match Game* airs toward evening; it ran 1962-69, and again 1973-1984, with pre-prime time airings in 1975-1981.

Tellingly, Marlow covers for a bout of extraterrestrial mayhem by claiming that it's a location shoot for *Alien*, which (as she says) opened "Spring 79". That being the case, it's probably now 1978 (filming for *Alien* happened July to October of that year). That would complement this story's *Charlie's Angels* feel (that show ran September 1976 to June 1984).

182 Among Jack's Torchwood agents, Gwen's birthday is the most uniformly referenced – it's the same in *TW: Children of Earth*, *The Torchwood Archives* (BBC) and *Torchwood: The Official Magazine Yearbook* (2008). A photo of Gwen in *TW: Miracle Day* bears the caption "1978", presumably for the same reason. Her passport in *Miracle Day* says that she was born 11th December, 1974, but she's using an alias, so it's presumably fake.

183 Four years before *Relative Dementias*.

184 *Wildthyme Beyond!*

185 *Iris S1: The Devil in Ms. Wildthyme*

an Abba concert while he was in Sweden, as he expected that he could get a ticket from either Agnetha or Bjorn.[186]

1979

Isabelle, a.k.a. "Izzy", a companion of the eighth Doctor, was born on 12th October, 1979. She never knew her parents, and was adopted by Les and Sandra Sinclair. Because of her uncertain parentage, she chose to call herself "Izzy Somebody".[187]

Andra'ath, a.k.a. "Andrea Quill", an alien who would later operate undercover as a teacher at Coal Hill Academy, was spawned and – like her siblings – fed on her mother's body for nourishment. As was normal for Quill sisters, Andra'ath's sister Orla'ath tried to kill her in the nest, and later died when the Shadow Kin invaded Rhodia.[188] Salvage 1, a moon project, was launched.[189]

Sgt Benton left the army in 1979, and became a second-hand car salesman.[190] Captain Yates thought Benton was a terrible car salesman, but very good at car restoration.[191]

1979 (a Saturday) - THE VALLEY OF DEATH[192] ->

The fourth Doctor, Leela and Godrin flew back to London in an airplane, having exited a slow-time field that returned them home two years after they left. Brigadier Lethbridge-Stewart was off fishing in Oslo, and General Hemmings had command of UNIT. Godrin immediately made for BBC Television Centre, and interrupted a BBC1 broadcast to summon his mothership.

The Lurons informed some of the world governments that they wished to trade their advanced technology for the right to live in remote parts of Earth. Select representatives from humanity visited the Luron vessel, which enabled the Lurons to create duplicates of them, and send the doubles back to Earth as their agents. The Doctor and Leela stopped the Lurons from increasing their sun's output so much, all of humanity would die in six months. Decreasing the sun's power restored the Lurons' sanity, although Godrin fell to his death.

The Doctor found the Lurons a planet suitable for colonisation a hundred light years away – by using their slow-time field, it was expected they would arrive in a few days. The duplicates were ordered to either die off, or use their remaining days to work for humanity's benefit.

---

186 *TW: Risk Assessment*
187 Izzy was born on the cover date of the first issue of *Doctor Who Weekly* (a fact established in "TV Action"). That date wasn't the day the magazine was published – magazine dates are when newsagents are meant to take them off the shelves. Details on her being adopted were mentioned in "End Game" (*DWM*).
188 Date unknown (doubly so, given Quill's alien biology), but actress Katherine Kelly was born in 1979.
189 "A hundred years" before *Scavenger*, and likely a take off of the short-lived American SF series *Salvage 1* (1979).
190 *Mawdryn Undead*
191 *UNIT S4: Assembled*
192 Dating *The Valley of Death* (BF 4th Doc LS #1.2) - It's "two years" after the story's first half, set in 1977. A female is currently prime minister – it's presumably Margaret Thatcher, who took office on 4th May, 1979.

BBC2 is showing *A Diary of Britain*. A BBC announcer touts the evening's line-up as *Larry Grayson's Generation Game* (Grayson hosted the series from 1978 to 1982) at 6:30, *Secret Army* (aired 1977-1979) at 7:25 and *Mike Yarwood in Persons* (1977-1981) at 8:20, but is interrupted by Godrin's broadcast just as he says, "Time for Part Three of—." Presuming the last statement denotes a *Doctor Who* story, in 1979 that would narrow the possibilities (after May 4th) to *Destiny of the Daleks* Part Three (15th September), *City of Death* Part Three (13th October), *The Creature from the Pit* Part Three (10th November) and *Nightmare of Eden* Part Three (8th December). We can perhaps eliminate *Destiny of the*

Daleks from the running, as *Secret Army* Season 3 didn't debut until 22nd September (unless a re-run was shown the week before).

It's a bit vague as to how much the public does or doesn't know concerning the Luron spaceship near West London and – by extension – the existence of aliens (Godrin's transmission on BBC1, if nothing else, would be easy to pass off as a hoax). In broad terms, however, this story much seems at odds with the convention in classic *Doctor Who* that numerous alien invasions occur without the public's knowledge (see also the When Does the Public Accept the Existence of Aliens? sidebar).
193 Dating *City of Death* (17.2) - The Doctor says that this isn't a vintage year, "it is 1979 actually, more of a table wine, shall we say". A poster says there's an exhibition on from Janiver – Mai, and the blossoms on the tree would suggest it was towards the end of that period.

MONA LISAS: The Mona Lisa in the Louvre (a genuine work by Leonardo, but with "This is a Fake!" written on the canvas in felt tip - see *City of Death* – and presumably the same one featured in *SJA: Mona Lisa's Revenge*) is destroyed by the Martian asteroid in 2086 (*Transit*). Multiple Mona Lisas are seen a UNIT archive in "The Age of Ice" (set in 2010). A desecrated Mona Lisa appears as part of the Monks' propaganda in *The Lie of the Land*; even if it's a real item and not just Photoshopped, it's part of changes that likely get revised out of history. The Monk owns a Mona Lisa that may or may not be destroyed in *To the Death* [c.2190].

1979 (spring) - CITY OF DEATH[193] -> Scaroth's plan to alter history – which would have saved his race but doomed humanity – was reaching its culmination. With the help of the foremost temporal scientist of the day, Professor Theodore Nikolai Kerensky, Scaroth produced a device capable of shifting the whole world back in time four hundred million years.

To finance the plan, Scaroth was selling off his art collection, flooding the market with lost masterpieces. This failed to raise enough money, and he arranged for the theft of the Mona Lisa from the Louvre in Paris. One of Scaroth's other selves had commissioned six more Mona Lisas from Leonardo da Vinci in 1505, and Scaroth intended to sell all seven copies to private buyers. Each would think they were purchasing the stolen Mona Lisa.

Scaroth succeeded in travelling back in time four hundred million years, but the fourth Doctor, the second Romana and the investigator Duggan followed in the TARDIS and stopped his plans. Upon his return to 1979, Scaroth died when a fire started in his laboratory. Only one Mona Lisa copy – with "This is a Fake" scribbled in felt tip on the canvas, detectable to any x-ray – survived the fire. It was returned to the Louvre. Earth was now classified as a Level Five planet.[194]

The Doctor came to possess a Mona Lisa that didn't have the words "This is a Fake" in felt tip.[195]

Peri and her father went hunting together. Her grandmother went senile, forgot everyone but her teddy bear, and took to acting like Marlene Dietrich.[196] Peri's father Paul drowned underneath a capsized boat in 1979. Her mother, Janine, remarried soon afterwards.[197]

Turlough and a girl named Deela were childhood friends, then shared a teenage infatuation – they weren't related by blood, but belonged to the same Clan. He found the dimensional vault last used by his great-grandfather, and changed the security key so it would only grant him and Deela access.[198] **The Doctor assisted in bringing Skylab down to Earth and it "nearly cost him a thumb".**[199]

By 1979, the Zygon Hagoth had acquired the corpse and body print of the folk singer Trevor. In Trevor's form, Hagoth attended the Kendal Folk Festival and met Patricia Ryder, the future aunt of Lucie Miller. "Trevor" and Patricia were married that same year – she knew he was extra-terrestrial, deeming him her "great big hunk of Zygon".[200]

1979 - THE TWELFTH DOCTOR YEAR THREE[201] -> The twelfth Doctor brought Hattie to Seaton Bay, where – for the space of about three weeks – Reggie's Chippie made the very best fish and chips in the universe. Erosion had reactivated an inert spaceship, and the occupant inside sent out "emissaries" in the form of humanoids made from seaweed. The Doctor and Hattie shook the spaceship free by amplifying their guitar music through the TARDIS,

The seventh Doctor's art gallery aboard the TARDIS includes a Mona Lisa with no "This is a Fake!" written on the canvas (*Dust Breeding*), so is presumably the original (*City of Death* episode three). "Art Attack!" shows a Mona Lisa as still around in a thousand years time. In *The Art of Destruction*, the Doctor saves a Mona Lisa in the fifty-first century. Rory smashes a Mona Lisa over a robot's head in the undatable *The Girl Who Waited*.
194 A LEVEL FIVE WORLD: This is first mentioned by Romana in *City of Death*. Earth is similarly a Level Five world in many New *Who* stories, including *Voyage of the Damned*, *Partners in Crime*, *The Eleventh Hour*, *Twice Upon a Time* and *SJA: Revenge of the Slitheen*.

Susan rates Earth in pre-historic times as a "sub-Level One civilisation" in *The Beginning*. Earth is a Level Two planet in "The Pestilent Heart" [1665], a Level Four world in *The Ninth Doctor Year One*: "Slaver's Song" [1682], down to a Level Three world in *The Good, the Bad and the Alien* [1861], and back up to being a Level Four world in *The English Way of Death* [1930]. In *Ferril's Folly* [c.2011], the first Romana repeatedly (and oddly) names Earth as a Level Four world.

Tasha Lem names Christmas as a Level Two human colony in *The Time of the Doctor*. Romana cites the declining feudal society of the vampire planet in *State of Decay* as being in danger of "losing its grip on Level

Two development".

The Doctor: His Lives and Times (pgs. 63-65) relates that the Master, serving as his own defence council following his capture in *The Daemons* (as his barrister had met with an unfortunate accident), cross-examined the Doctor on the witness stand, causing a strange debate between them over whether Earth is a "Level 2" or "Level 3" civilisation. In the same account, the Time Lords are a "Level 12" society
195 *Dust Breeding*. This implies that the Doctor went back in time and nicked the original Mona Lisa before the fire in Scaroth's house could destroy it.
196 *Peri and the Piscon Paradox*
197 *Synthespians™*. This contradicts *Blue Box*, which said Peri's mother remarried when Peri was ten (in 1976). It's possible, if a little messy, to reconcile the two accounts by suggesting Peri's mother married three times. *The Reaping* confirms her father's name was Paul.
198 Turlough says they last went into the vault "three years, nine months and seventeen days, give or take", before *Kiss of Death*.
199 *Tooth and Claw* (TV)
200 *The Zygon Who Fell to Earth*
201 Dating *The Twelfth Doctor Year Three* (Titan 12th Doc #3.1, #3.3-3.4, "Beneath the Waves") - The year is given.

enabling the vessel to leave Earth. The Doctor then returned Hattie home to the Twist.

c 1979 - "The Iron Legion"[202] -> The fourth Doctor landed on Earth just as it was attacked by robots resembling ancient Roman soldiers...

= In another dimension, Rome never fell. Rome's robot legions, led by the eagle-headed Ironicus, fought the Eternal War across a thousand planets and by now had conquered the entire galaxy. The attack on our dimension represented the first strike in Rome's attempt to conquer the whole of creation.

Rome itself was a vast futuristic city full of alien and human citizens, slaves and robots. Citizens enjoyed themselves watching gladiator fights between aliens and bionic humans at the Hyp-Arena, and car races at the Circus Maximus. Both events were televised. Rome had contact with many alien planets, including the home of the Ectoslime and the Kronks in the Crab Nebula. The Kronks had fought Zarks in the Hyp-Arena, and were also turned into kronk-burgers.

The child Adolphus Caesar – "Master of the Solar System and the Galaxy Beyond" – was now Emperor, with Ironicus serving as regent. The Doctor realised that Juno, the Adolphus' mother, was actually an alien. Following them to the Temple of the Gods, the Doctor recognised the building as a spacecraft, and the "gods" as the five Malevilus – Babiyon, Abiss, Epok, Nekros and Magog, a form of anti-life. They had given the Romans advanced technology to aid their goal of the conquest of all creation.

With the help of the bionic gladiator Morris and the ancient robot Vesuvius, the Doctor started a revolt. He unleashed the Bestarius (who were genetically engineered warriors), and confronted Juno, who revealled herself to be Magog. The Doctor tricked Magog into the TARDIS by promising to share its secrets, then trapped him in a pocket dimension. The other Malevilus tried to launch their ship, but Magog had drained its power and it crashed, killing them. Vesuvius was installed as Emperor by popular decree.

The tenth Doctor planned to take Rose to an Ian Dury concert on 21st November, 1979.[203]

---

202 Dating "The Iron Legion" (*DWW* #1-8) - The Doctor lands on contemporary Earth and makes topical references to inflation and the fuel crisis, suggesting the story is set around the year it was published (1979).

The Eternal War has "lasted through the millennia". The Doctor surmises they have "conquered the entire galaxy" (a sentiment echoed by a later caption) and refers to them as the Galactic Roman Empire. Ironicus says "now that Rome has gone on to conquer all dimensions" when offering sacrifices from our universe, but it's later clarified that the process has just started – these are "the first sacrifices from other dimensions".

It's unclear what year it is on the alternate Earth, or how long the Malevilus have been there. The Malevilus don't have time travel, at least not in a form as advanced as the TARDIS; this implies that if time runs at the same rate between dimensions, it's also 1979 there. However, Ironicus says it's the "year MMMXXI R.I.", with R.I. standing for Regency of Ironicus. That suggests it's 3021 years since the Regency started, but 1979 is only 2732 years after the founding of Rome (and when measuring the year, that was the start date Romans used), suggesting it's the future.

Adolphus, though, appears to be a normal young boy – one who looks about eight years old. He seems shocked by Magog's true appearance, and there's no indication that Adolphus is a Malevilus or half-Malevilus himself. This may mean that Magog killed his real mother, or that he's preventing him from growing up (or both), but this isn't ever mentioned.

Roman technology is an odd mix of twentieth cen-

tury technology such as tanks, television, zeppelins with advanced robots, bionics, dimension ducts, aircars, metal eating "bact guns", robophants (robot war elephants) and interstellar travel. The Malevilus have presumably supplied most of the advanced technology. Robots have been around "centuries", and it would seem – although it's never explicitly stated – that the Malevilus built them, so have been around at least that long, too.

The story doesn't reconcile these statements. It doesn't explicitly say (or rule out) that it's the Malevilus who've prevented Rome from falling. If that was the case, it would mean they've been around at least fifteen hundred years.

The Doctor refers to Magog as "him", so his natural form is male. We see all five Malevilus "statues" apparently come to life with Juno in the room, even though Juno is Magog in disguise. Later we learn that Magog can be in more than one place at once. In "The Mark of Mandragora", we see Magog still in the TARDIS in the seventh Doctor's era, being eaten away by the Mandragora Helix.

The Doctor has heard of the Ectoslime and the Malevilus – who in turn have heard of the Time Lords – and kronkburgers are mentioned in *The Long Game*, so it would seem they all exist in our universe. The Doctor knows about a strict boarding school run by Lukronian Vorks on the ice planet of Cryos IV on the edge of the galaxy, perhaps indicating it also exists in our universe.

203 *Tooth and Claw* (TV)

The Nineteen Eighties

In the 1980s, the vampires Amelia Doory and Reggie Mead gained enough resources to start up a blood farm. They traded blood with other victims of the Forge in exchange for vampire DNA.[204] In the same decade, Iris stopped the mermaid Magda from using her siren song to blow up a nuclear power plant. Magda reformed and later came to work for MIAOW.[205] Mr Colchester of Torchwood swore that he'd not been a pervert since the 1980s.[206]

The eleventh Doctor, Amy, Rory and Kevin the Tyrannosaur investigated a crime in Los Angeles, posing as members of the LAPD.[207] Harold Chorley embroiled the Brigadier in some "oddness" with Damon Vandervoorde, in the early 80s.[208] Kate Stewart, somewhat to her embarrassment in later years, worked on her university's newspaper.[209]

> = The 1980s saw UNIT hampered due to limited resources and poor staffing – crackpots unfit for other departments were relegated to the organisation. Lethbridge-Stewart's reputation plummeted, and he took early retirement. He tried to relocate from the UK to New Zealand, but stopped off in Hong Kong, and stayed there to open The Little England pub.[210]

1980

The android Isley killed an assassination target in Cuba on 3rd February, 1980 – and then, owing to her overly sensitive programming, killed fifty potential witnesses.[211]

Owen Harper of Torchwood was born 14th February, 1980.[212] The US military decided on 28th February, 1980, that Albert Gilroy's killer androids had become too uncontrollable, and made preparations to destroy them – with a nuclear bomb, in violation of the Limited Test Ban Treaty – in the fake Colorado city of Appletown. Colonel Redvers told Gilroy that the Reagan Administration believed that the detonation would have the added benefit of pushing Cold War tensions to America's advantage.[213]

Tegan Jovanka moved from Brisbane to London in 1980.[214] **With foreign investment rare in Argentina, the American CIA began tracking contract-intensive money there in 1980.**[215]

> **(=) 1980 - PYRAMIDS OF MARS**[216] **->** The fourth Doctor took Sarah to an alternate version of 1980, to show her what would happen if they left England in 1911 before defeating Sutekh. Earth was a devastated wasteland.

c 1980 - "Yonder... the Yeti"[217] **->** A small expedition to Tibet went looking for the Yeti. They visited a local monk

204 *Project: Twilight*
205 *Iris: Enter Wildthyme*
206 *TW: Aliens Among Us*
207 "Your Destiny Awaits". No date is given. The Doctor's alias of "Lt Addison" has a *Moonlighting* feel about it, suggesting that it's the 1980s.
208 *Leth-St: "The Enfolded Time"*
209 *UNIT S5: Encounters: Invocation*
210 *Unbound: Sympathy for the Devil*
211 *Nuclear Time* (p89).
212 Per his personnel file in *TW: Exit Wounds* and a reference in *TW: Pack Animals* (p139), but there's confusion about this. It's said in *TW: Dead Man Walking* that Owen is 27, but as that story cannot conceivably occur before February 2008, he should really be 28. To muddy the waters even further, *TW: SkyPoint*, set after *Dead Man Walking*, seems to suggest that Owen is only 26 (p45). *Torchwood: The Official Magazine Yearbook* (2008) also gives Owen's birthday as "14/02/80", but *The Torchwood Archives* (BBC) says he was born on the same day in 1982. Actor Burn Gorman was born in 1st September, 1974.
213 *Nuclear Time* (p89).
214 *Ringpullworld*
215 *TW: Miracle Day*
216 Dating *Pyramids of Mars* (13.3) - The year is stated several times by both the Doctor and Sarah (including

the Doctor's comment, "1980, Sarah, if you want to get off"). The Doctor's actions prevent this timeline from coming to pass.

About Time accepts that the whole "1980" business stems from Sarah rounding up. *Timelink* becomes so determined to make that case, it offers *four* different solutions to the problem.

The Doctor: His Lives and Times (p80) jokingly calls Sarah's claim of being from "1980" into question, when K-9 records Sarah's recollections of her adventures, and she opens with: "In the year 1980—" K-9: "Factual inaccuracy detected." Sarah: "Nonsense! It keeps it all sounding current. People want to read about aliens and the wonders I've seen, but if I bang on about the 1970s they'll just think flares and kipper ties and eurgh! It's hard to take an alien invasion seriously if you think they're all dressed as Showaddywaddy... Nobody will ever care about the odd year here or there. It's not important."

Sarah is also identified (*The Doctor: His Lives and Times*, p84-91) as having written two *Da Vinci Code*-style thrillers, *The Osiris Code* ("inspired" by *Pyramids of Mars*) and *The Fendahl Inheritance* ("inspired" by *Image of the Fendahl* – a story Sarah Jane wasn't in).
217 Dating "Yonder... the Yeti" (*DWW* #31-34) - When Bruce mentions the Yeti attack in the 1920s, the Lama replies "many things have changed in the last sixty

Lama Gampo, but the creatures attacked them, and the Great Intelligence possessed one of the expedition members. The Yeti had flying vehicles and web guns, and the Intelligence planned to launch a new conquest of Earth. Lama Gampo, whose father's uncle fought the Yeti sixty years before, rescued the party and summoned the real Yeti before destroying the power transfuser that linked the Intelligence to Earth. He then hypnotised the surviving expedition members to maintain his secrets.

Sharon Davies Joins the TARDIS

1980 - "The Star Beast"[218] **->** The peaceful Meeps became warlike when Black Sun radiation affected their planet. The Wrarth Galaxy Star Council created the Wrarth Warriors, amalgams of their five strongest races, to defeat them. The Meep armada was destroyed at the Battle of Yarras, but their leader, Beep the Meep, escaped.

An alien ship crashed at a steel mill in Blackcastle, a city in the north of England. The government denied it was a UFO, and UNIT troops were sent to secure the site. Two schoolchildren, Fudge and Sharon, discovered the survivor – the immensely cute Beep the Meep, who was being pursued by the monstrous Wrarth Warriors. The fourth Doctor and K9 landed on the Wrarth Warrior ship. The aliens immobilised the Doctor and planted a bomb inside him, sending him down to Earth, knowing he would locate the Meep.

The Meep used mind control to enslave humans to rebuild his ship, and planned to make a star jump while still on Earth – an act that would have hideous consequences. The Meep activated the black sun drive, sucking Blackcastle into a black hole, but the effects were temporary because the Doctor sabotaged the stardrive. Stuck in Earth orbit, the Meep was arrested and sent for trial. Sharon joined the Doctor on his adventures.

years", so the story – published in 1980 – is set in the 1980s.

218 Dating "The Star Beast" (*DWW* #19-26) - It's a contemporary setting, and the story was first published in the 80s. "Star Beast II" is set "fifteen years" later in "1995".

219 Dating "The Collector" (*DWM* #46) - It is Sharon's native time.

220 Dating *The Labyrinth of Buda Castle* (BF 4th Doc #5.2) - The Doctor suggests a lovely place to eat that, alas, went out of business in 1935, prompting Romana to suggest they find a restaurant that "still exists in 1980". The Doctor also mentions that the Hungarian football club Ferencvaros will "win the title next year", in reference to the 1980-81 season.

221 Dating *The Leisure Hive* (18.1) - It isn't clear when the TARDIS lands on Brighton beach. In Fisher's novelisation it is clearly contemporary, although the opening chapter of the novel is set in June – which would contradict Romana's on-screen exasperation that the Doctor has got "the season wrong". *The Terrestrial Index* and *The TARDIS Logs* both suggested a date of "1934", although why is unclear. The date doesn't appear in the script or any BBC documentation.

222 "Twenty years" before *Millennial Rites* (p216), and "five years" after he gets the circuit (p4).

223 *History 101*. In real life, assassination attempts were made on John Paul's life in May 1981 and May 1982.

224 *The Tomorrow Windows*

225 *Alien Bodies* (p177-178), with the date re-confirmed in *Revolution Man* (p191).

226 *Alien Bodies* (p177-178). Sam's original timeline is that of a dark-haired drug-user, but events in *Unnatural History* cancel out this history and create the blonde-haired version that becomes the Doctor's companion.

227 Dating *The City of the Dead* (EDA #49) - "That was in 1980" (p66).

228 *The Dying Days*, referring to the aliens seen in *The*

Ambassadors of Death.

229 *Apollo 23*. The quantum displacement system is possibly plundered alien technology, because in the thirty years to follow this story, the Americans never develop more than just the one working unit.

230 Dating *The Fires of Vulcan* (BF #12) - It is "the year 1980".

231 Dating *Shada* (17.6 and BF BBCi #2) - The TARDIS was "confused" by May Week being in June, so it landed in October. No year is given, but the story has a contemporary setting, and Chris Parsons graduated in 1978.

The 2013 novelisation by Gareth Roberts sets *Shada* in 1979 – a reasonable choice, as most of Season 17 was broadcast then (had *Shada* actually aired, however, episode one would have gone out on 19th January, 1980). As on screen, the Doctor tells Romana that it's "October" (p21). In *DotD: The Time Machine*, the eleventh Doctor mentions "St Cedd's [College], 1980".

WHICH SHADA, IF ANY, IS CANON?: The TV version of *Shada* was never completed, following an industrial dispute during filming. A couple of clips were later used in *The Five Doctors* to show the fourth Doctor and Romana being taken out of their timestream. In 1992, the *Shada* footage that had been filmed was released on video, with special effects, music and a linking narration by Tom Baker. The clips that were included in *The Five Doctors* were re-jigged for the 1995 "Special Edition" release of that story. In 2003, the story was remade in its entirety as a webcast with Paul McGann as the lead character and Lalla Ward reprising her role as Romana. A new introduction scene was included to help explain the eighth Doctor and Romana's sudden interest in these events. Big Finish later released the McGann version on CD. In 2017, *Shada* was re-released with animated segments filling in the gaps between the filmed scenes.

Which of these – if any – is the "canonical" version of

c 1980 - "The Collector"[219] **->** The fourth Doctor and Sharon returned to Blackcastle after many adventures, but were immediately snatched up by a teleport-beam and rematerialised on a base in the asteroid belt. This was the home of Varan Tak from Oskerion, who had been capturing specimens from Earth for two thousand years. His ship had been damaged for that long, and he was waiting for his distress signal to arrive at his home planet. His only companionship during this exile was the ship's computer, who had built a robot form for herself. She was preventing Varan Tak from teleporting to Earth, but the Doctor destroyed the security precautions.

(=) Varan Tak beamed to Earth... only to die because he couldn't tolerate the pollution levels. The computer destroyed K9 in revenge.

The Doctor used the TARDIS to manipulate the ship's time stasis fields and changed history, destroying the teleporter and saving Varan Tak and K9. The Doctor, Sharon and K9 left Varan Tak and the computer in peace.

1980 - THE LABYRINTH OF BUDA CASTLE[220] **->** The fourth Doctor and the second Romana visited Budapest as the pseudo-vampire Zoltan Frid escaped the tunnels beneath Buda Castle, and threatened to convert all of humanity into blood-feeders who, lacking a food source, would eventually turn upon one another. Frid fed off the Doctor's blood, but the Doctor, anticipating this, hypnotised himself to walk into daylight upon hearing the word "sunbathing". The conditioning made Frid do the same, killing him.

c 1980 - THE LEISURE HIVE[221] **->** The fourth Doctor, the second Romana and K9 briefly landed on Brighton beach, but the Doctor had got the season wrong, and they soon left for Argolis.

Ashley Chapel experimented with the micromonolithic circuit and made contact with Saraquazel, a being from the universe that exists after our own.[222] One of Sabbath's agents tried and failed to assassinate Pope John Paul II in 1980.[223] @ The eighth Doctor defeated the Voord in Penge during the nineteen-eighties.[224]

Samantha Angeline Jones, a companion of the eighth Doctor, was born on 15th April, 1980.[225]

(=) She was born dark-haired, her mother a social worker and her father a doctor. She would grow up to become a vegetarian, and have scar marks on her arms from injecting diamorphine. She would end up living in a bedsit near King's Cross.

She was born blonde-haired, her mother a social work-er and her father a doctor. She would grow up to become a vegetarian, and have no scar marks on her arm. She would meet the Doctor while attending school in 1997.[226]

1980 (30th April) - THE CITY OF THE DEAD[227] **->** The eighth Doctor arrived from the early twenty-first century to investigate a bone charm. Louisiana resident Alain Auguste Delesormes tried to summon a water elemental, but most of his family died when their home was flooded. The Doctor saved a young boy from the calamity, failing to realise that he was the water elemental in human form.

Delesormes' son, also named Alain, survived and was put into foster care in Vermont. He grew up to become police investigator Jonas Rust, and sought to continue his father's work. The water elemental's mother came to search for her son and was bound into a human body. She became the wife of New Orleans resident Vernon Flood, unable to escape her fleshy prison.

On 3rd June, 1980, the alien Ambassadors completed their survey of the solar system and left. No further contact with humanity was made.[228] America used its secretive Apollo programme to establish Base Diana on the dark side of the moon. *Apollos* 18 to 21 set up the base, and the final flight – *Apollo 22*, in June 1980 – ferried the equipment for a quantum displacement system. From that point, a teleport link existed between Base Diana and a command centre, Base Hibiscus, in the Texas desert.[229]

1980 - THE FIRES OF VULCAN[230] **->** The archaeologist Scalini excavated a police box from the ruins of Pompeii. The seventh Doctor and Mel were inside, and exited the ship when no-one was looking. Captain Muriel Frost of UNIT called in the fifth Doctor to investigate.

1980 (October) - SHADA[231] **-> Answering a distress signal from Professor Chronotis, the fourth Doctor and the second Romana arrived in Cambridge. They discovered that the geneticist Skagra had taken *The Worshipful and Ancient Law of Gallifrey*, the key to the Time Lord prison planet of Shada, and ended his scheme to mentally dominate the universe.**

or ...

1980 (October) - THE FIVE DOCTORS / SHADA -> Borusa attempted to abduct the fourth Doctor (and possibly the second Romana) while they were punting in Cambridge. The abduction failed, and they were caught in a time eddy. This averted their visit to Chronotis, but the eighth Doctor and the second Romana later arrived and stopped Skagra as scheduled.

1980 - TW: TRACE MEMORY[232] -> A five-year-old Toshiko Sato was very pleased when her father returned to Osaka for the Tenjin Festival. The next day, she briefly met the time-hopping Michael Bellini and the Vondrax pursuing him.

John Frobisher joined the civil service in 1980. Bridget Spears worked with him for six months; it would be another ten years before he requested that she work in his office.[233]

c 1980 - MEGLOS[234] -> On the planet Tigella, the fourth Doctor, the second Romana and K9 prevented Meglos, the last Zolfa-Thuran, from recovering the Dodecahedron – the power source that would let him use the Screens of Zolfa-Thura to destroy planets. The Screens, the Dodecahedron and Meglos himself were destroyed. The Doctor returned home an Earthling that a band of Gaztaks had kidnapped as a host body for Meglos.

1980 - BEFORE THE FLOOD[235] -> The Arcateenians liberated the Tivoli from the Fisher King, but the Tivoli irritated the Arcateenians so much that they conquered the Tivoli all over again. Per Arcateenian tradition, the Fisher King was sent in a Tivoli space-hearse for burial on a "barren, savage outpost". The ship, as piloted by funeral director Albar Prentis, arrived in Caithness, Scotland, at a mock Russian town that the Ministry of Defence used for training its agents.

The twelfth Doctor, accompanied by Drum-staffers O'Donnell and Bennett, arrived from 2119. The Fisher King awoke and killed Prentis and O'Donnell. The Doctor gained foreknowledge that he was going to die, and that his "ghost" would appear at the Drum in future. To avert this, he programmed his sonic glasses with an AI hologram of himself, and entered the Fisher King's stasis pod after destroying the local dam. The town flooded, killing the Fisher King and submerging the space-hearse. The TARDIS' Echelon Circuit took the Ship back to 2119, with Bennett aboard.

1980 - THE MOVELLAN GRAVE[236] -> Excavations for the M25 motorway uncovered a Movellan ship buried for two thousand years. Commander Narina deduced how to improve upon the programming of her prototype warrior, Chenek, and conquer other worlds with an army of augmented Movellans. The fourth Doctor and the second

---

events? All things being equal, the *Doctor Who* TV series trumps all other formats, but in this case, the actual completion of the Paul McGann story – as opposed to the abandonment of the TV version in 1979 – makes the webcast hard to ignore. Also, the alteration of the fourth Doctor/Romana clips in the different versions of *The Five Doctors* makes it harder and harder to reconcile them against the TV *Shada* itself.

A growing theory now holds that Borusa's time-scooping of the fourth Doctor and Romana derailed their adventure and they simply departed after the punting, with the eighth Doctor and Romana later returning to complete the task. The webcast, in fact, suggests that the eighth Doctor is plugging a gap in history by performing the duties that his fourth self would have done.

232 Dating *TW: Trace Memory* (*TW* novel #5) - Toshiko is currently five (p71); her birth in this chronology is dated to 1975.

233 *TW: Children of Earth*

234 Dating *Meglos* (18.2) - Unless the Gaztaks can time travel, this story is set in the late twentieth century. The Earthling wears an early 1980s business suit. *The TARDIS Logs* offered a date of "1988", *Timelink* says "1983".

235 Dating *Before the Flood* (X9.4) - The Doctor names the year.

236 Dating *The Movellan Grave* (BF 4th Doc #6.7) - The year is given.

237 Dating *Father Time* (EDA #41) - The only date given is "the early 1980s". At the beginning of the book, Debbie is looking forward to a television schedule that is the evening that *Meglos* episode one was shown, 27th September, 1980.

238 *Salvation*

239 *Wildthyme Beyond!* (p253).

240 *Eye of Heaven*

241 *The Left-Handed Hummingbird*

242 *Downtime* (p60).

243 *Divided Loyalties*

244 *Primeval*

245 She's "26" in *TW: Cyberwoman*, set in 2007.

246 Dating *The Keeper of Traken* (18.6) - Traken is destroyed in the subsequent story, *Logopolis*, so *The Keeper of Traken* can't occur after this time, although *The TARDIS Logs* suggested a date of "4950 AD". Melkur arrived on Traken "many years" before. The script specifies that Kassia is 18 at the time, the same age as Nyssa when the Doctor first meets her.

247 *Four to Doomsday*. The Doctor mentions the visit during his attempt to convince Tegan that the Urbankan ship might be Heathrow.

248 Dating *Unbound: He Jests at Scars...* (BF *Unbound* #4) - It's concurrent with the fourth Doctor's trip to *Logopolis* [1981].

249 Dating *Logopolis* (18.7) - The date is first stated in *Four to Doomsday*, and is the same day that the first episode was broadcast. This is the first on-screen use of the term "chameleon circuit". *The TARDIS Logs* set the *Logopolis* sequence in "4950". It's never stated if the other CVEs are ever restored, although it's possible that reviving the Cassiopeia CVE opened the others.

Romana reprogrammed Chenek with some peace of mind, and he rebelled against Narina's warlust, self-destructing the Movellan ship with himself aboard.

The Eighth Doctor Adopts Miranda

@ c 1980 (winter) - FATHER TIME[237] **->** Rumours of mysterious lights and flying saucers drew UFO spotters to the Derbyshire village of Greyfrith. This had been caused by the arrival of a Klade saucer from the far, far future. The Klade Prefect Zevron and his deputy, Sallak, were hunting down the ten-year-old Miranda – the last survivor of the Imperial Family, brought to Earth by her nanny.

Aided by the Hunters Rum and Thelash, plus the giant robot Mr Gibson, Zevron tracked Miranda down. The eighth Doctor was staying just outside the village, and with the help of Miranda's teacher, Debbie Castle, he defeated Zevron and his henchmen. Zevron died, but Sallak survived and was arrested. Debbie's husband Barry was rendered mindless. The Doctor pledged to protect Miranda, who – like him – had two hearts.

After the Doctor officially adopted Miranda, they moved south to a large house. The Doctor worked as a business consultant, very quickly becoming a millionaire as he solved economic problems that confounded everyone else.

Following a remark from the Doctor, the barman of the Dragon pub in Greyfrith started selling bottled water. Within five years, he was making twenty million pounds a year from sales of Dragonwater.

> = *The Making of Iris Wildthyme*, a guidebook to the failed Iris Wildthyme TV series, was published in 1980. In late 1980, a warehouse fire destroyed paperwork pertaining to the show. The series' props and costumes were thrown out, and were rumoured to be in a landfill near the new Metro Centre near Gateshead.[238]

In November 1980, *Prey for a Miracle* was released. It was a movie version of the "gods hoax" of 1965, starring Peter Cushing as the Doctor.[239] Shortly before he died, John Lennon told the Doctor, "Talent borrows, genius steals".[240] John Lennon was murdered on 8th December, 1980, by Mark Chapman. Huitzilin fed off the trauma of the event.[241]

Professor Edward Travers CBE was publicly said to have died on Christmas Day 1980. The Great Intelligence possessed his body, and what remained of Travers' mind read his own obituary in the *Times*.[242]

1981

The Union of Traken now stretched over five or six planets in one solar system.[243] All diseases had been eradicated on

Traken by this time.[244] **Lisa Hallett of Torchwood London was born.**[245]

A New Body for the Master

c 1981 - THE KEEPER OF TRAKEN[246] **->** Traken was a peaceful planet in Mettula Orionsis. Two of the consuls of Traken – Tremas and Kassia – married.

Kassia had tended to the Melkur, a creature of evil that had calcified in Traken's serene environment, since she was a child. But now the Melkur had begun to move again. Hypnotically controlling Kassia, the Melkur – in reality the cadaverous Master – attempted to take control of the Source, the power of the Keeper of Traken. The Master was at the end of his regeneration cycle, and was desperate to obtain the power necessary to gain a new body. Kassia was killed, but the fourth Doctor and Adric prevented the Master from acquiring the Source, and Consul Luvic became the new Keeper. The Master escaped, and took the body of Tremas as his new form.

The Doctor visited Terminal Three of Heathrow Airport around this time.[247]

> = **1981 - UNBOUND: HE JESTS AT SCARS...** ->[248] The Valeyard sought to restore Logopolis, so the mathematicians there could upgrade his Ship into an ultra-modern Type 40 Battle-TARDIS. While trying to block the fourth Doctor's flight there with his own TARDIS, the Valeyard miscalculated and totally annihilated his previous self and his Ship. To undo the paradox of his own existence, the Valeyard went back to destroy Logopolis in 1471...

~1/4 of the Universe Destroyed, Including Traken; the Fourth Doctor Regenerates; Tegan and Nyssa Join the TARDIS

1981 (28th February) - LOGOPOLIS[249] **->** The fourth Doctor and Adric landed on Earth and took the measurements of a genuine police box to help repairs to the TARDIS' chameleon circuit. The Doctor had previously visited the planet Logopolis, hoping they could help him with their mathematical expertise and mastery of block transfer computation. Tegan Jovanka, an airline stewardess, found herself aboard the TARDIS after the Tremas Master murdered her Aunt Vanessa.

The Doctor learnt from the Monitor of Logopolis that the universe had already passed the natural point of heat death. All closed systems succumb to heat death, and the universe was such a closed system. Or rather it used to be: the Logopolitans had opened up CVEs into other universes, such as E-Space. When the

Master learnt of this, he recognised a chance to blackmail the entire universe. The Master's interference halted Logopolis' operations, which caused the CVEs to collapse. Entropy began to accumulate and destroyed a vast region of space, including Logopolis and Traken.

The Watcher observed these events, and brought Nyssa of Traken to Logopolis to join the Doctor.

On Earth, the Doctor and the Master worked to re-open a CVE in Cassiopeia at co-ordinates 3C461-3044. The Master threatened to close off even this CVE, and broadcast a message to the entire universe:

"Peoples of the universe please attend carefully, the message that follows is vital to the future of you all. The choice for you all is simple: a continued existence under my guidance, or total annihilation. At the time of speaking, the fate of the universe lies in the balance at the fulcrum point, the Pharos Project on Earth..."

The Doctor prevented the Master from closing the CVE, but fell to his death. As he regenerated, the Watcher merged with him...

1981 - CASTROVALVA[250] -> ... the newly-regenerated fifth Doctor, Nyssa and Tegan returned to the TARDIS. The Tremas Master kidnapped Adric.

Serenity was the only planet of the Traken Union to survive its obliteration.[251]

1981 (28th February) - FOUR TO DOOMSDAY[252] -> The fifth Doctor, Tegan, Nyssa and Adric defeated Monarch's plans to travel back to the creation of the universe. Monarch's android crew opted to find a habitable world and settle on it.

A formless race of explorers sent seeds the size of acorns into space. Each of these would land on a planet, analyse the environment and grow a creature that could survive there. One such seed bank, later named the Juniper Tree, was adopted into a UK military programme that hoped to develop disposable soldiers. The first child grown from it, Sebastian, was born on 3rd March, 1981, and met Jack Harkness of Torchwood a few days later.[253]

Cassandra Hope Schofield, the future mother of the Doctor's companion Hex, was born on 7th April, 1981.[254]

---

250 Dating *Castrovalva* (19.1) - This story immediately follows *Logopolis*.
251 *The Guardians of Prophecy*
252 Dating *Four to Doomsday* (19.2) - The Doctor establishes that he has returned Tegan to the right point in time "16.15 hours" on "February 28th 1981", the day episode one of *Logopolis* was broadcast.

An astrology article in *The Doctor: His Lives and Times* (p114) claims that the Mayan calendar predicted the world would end on "4 March 1981," with the Coming of the Great Frog; clearly a reference to Monarch and his followers.
253 *TW: First Born*
254 *Project: Destiny*
255 Dating *Nuclear Time* (NSA #40) - The day is repeatedly given.
256 *TW: torchwood_cascade_cdrip.tor*
257 *The King of Terror*. In *Castrovalva*, the newly-regenerated/confused fifth Doctor seemed to allude to an incident that involved the Brigadier and the Ice Warriors. In *The Dying Days*, the Brigadier says he never met the Ice Warriors, so this couldn't have involved him.
258 *The Gallifrey Chronicles*
259 Dating *The Hollows of Time* (BF LS #1.4) - It's "the early 1980s", "a year or two" in Peri's past. In the original conceptualisation of this story, Stream was to be unmasked as the Master; in the actual audio, he's just (if you can call it that) a genius with robotic helpers, hypnotism, knowledge of the Doctor's previous encounter with the Tractators and the ability to pilot the TARDIS.

260 Dating *Iris S5: An Extraterrestrial Werewolf in Belgium* (BF *Iris* #5.7) - It's left unstated whether the bus relocates in time as well as space, after escaping from Bloody Nora in 1977. The dating here reflects the release of *An American Werewolf in London* in 1981.
261 Dating *The Rings of Akhaten* (X7.8) - The year isn't stated, but the Doctor has presumably just bought his copy of *The Beano*.
262 Dating *Static* (BF #233) – It's repeatedly said, in the dialogue and the script, to be "forty years" after the World War II portion of the story [c.1941]. However, Constance at one point says it's "three decades later".
263 *The King of Terror*
264 Dating *5thB: Iterations of I* (BF *The Fifth Doctor Box Set* #1.2) - Adric and Nyssa aim the TARDIS at "Heathrow, [February] 1981", and seem to hit the right year, albeit some months late. The month is given as "December" – "four months" after Imogen Frazer's experiments, detailed on cassette tapes labeled through "August 1981". The gravestone of a cultist says he died in that same month and year. It's "fifty years" since Grenwell Fleming killed his wife, in 1930.
265 Patricia passes away "eight years" before *Leth-St: "The Slow Invasion"*, set "several years" after *The Five Doctors* [1983], but pegged on the Haisman Timeline as "1990". Brendan appeared in *K9 and Company*, which is set at Christmas 1981.
266 Dating *K9 and Company* (18.7-A) - Sarah arrives in Moreton Harwood on "December the 18th", and later tells K9 that it is "1981". The other dates are given in dialogue. This story is part of the UNIT timeframe, but

(=) 1981 (28th August) - NUCLEAR TIME[255] -> The US military's obliteration of Appletown, Colorado, and the killer androids gathered there, resulted in the deaths of Amy Pond, Rory Williams, and Albert Gilroy... and triggered a full-fledged war between the US and the Soviet Union.

The explosion caused the eleventh Doctor to experience time backward, and he altered history. The energy of the bomb's detonation was dispersed over a ninety-minute window, generating radiation but not a full-fledged mushroom cloud. The android Isley developed feelings for Gilroy, her creator, and they went into hiding together.

Stephen Heinz of Torchwood One was born 19th September, 1981.[256] In 1981, UNIT encountered the Zygons in the Kalahari Desert and the Ice Warriors in Northampton.[257]

@ Even with character references from people such as Graham Greene and Lawrence Olivier, the eighth Doctor needed nearly a year to formally adopt Miranda. Shortly after that, he defeated the Great Provider's plan to use evil mobile telephones to take over the world.[258]

c 1981 - THE HOLLOWS OF TIME[259] -> The sixth Doctor and Peri detected gravitational anomalies in the English village of Hollowdean, and paid a visit to the Doctor's old friend, the Reverend Foxwell. The villainous Professor Stream attempted to engineer a Quantum Gravity Engine: a device that would make Stream *become* all of space and time. Stream incorporated eleven Tractators into the Engine, and used the Doctor's TARDIS to retrieve most important Tractator – the Gravis – from the future. The Gravis and his Tractators turned on Stream, making him swell up like a balloon and explode.

c 1981 - IRIS S5: AN EXTRATERRESTRIAL WERE-WOLF IN BELGIUM[260] -> Having escaped Bloody Nora, Iris' bus landed in Antwerp, Belgium. While Iris went shopping, Captain Turner met a tour guide who was secretly an alien werewolf – the inspiration behind the legend of the Beast of Flanders. Iris happened to purchase the werewolf's missing skin in a charity shop; by reclaiming it, the werewolf regained its full strength. The werewolf attempted to go on a rampage across the cosmos by capturing Iris' bus, and clung to it as Iris dematerialized her Ship. Turner sacrificed himself to push the werewolf into the Vortex, and they were both lost in time. Iris would see her friend one more time circa 1950.

1981 (autumn) - THE RINGS OF AKHATEN[261] -> Dave, the future father of Clara Oswald, met his wife Ellie when a leaf obscured his vision and she pulled him from the path of an oncoming car. The eleventh Doctor witnessed the event, surreptitiously concealed behind a copy of *The Beano Summer Special 1981*. As Dave and Ellie's romance progressed, they kept the leaf as a memento of the spark behind their relationship.

Constance Clarke Reborn in a New Body

c 1981 - STATIC[262] -> The sixth Doctor, Constance and Flip looked into temporal interference radiating from the stone circle at Abbey Marston: a time-device capable of making duplicate bodies for the minds of the deceased. Percy Till had faithfully guarded the locale for forty years, but two lovers, Andy Clover and Joanna Nash, used the circle to resurrect Joanna's late sister Susannah. The bodiless Static seized upon the chance to hijack the resurrection process and invade Earth, but the Doctor and Constance went back to World War II to investigate the circle's origins. Constance died there in a fire.

The Doctor returned, used the resurrection circle to restore Constance to life in a duplicate body, and trapped the Static to perish in her original form. Percy also died, and the Doctor – to prevent the Static from making another breakthrough – advised UNIT to destroy the circle entirely.

The Jex arrived on Earth on 4th December, 1981, and took shelter in California.[263]

1981 (December) - 5thB: ITERATIONS OF I[264] -> A cult devoted to deriving the base number of God purchased Fleming's Island. The cult's experiments into higher mathematics attracted inter-dimensional creatures composed of math, which rendered themselves as the letter I: the value of the square root of -1, an impossible number. A numerical predator pursued the groups of I, and ripped apart many of the cultists. The doomed survivors cut off contact with the mainland, isolating the predator.

Four months later, in December, Adric and Nyssa's efforts to pilot the TARDIS resulted in the Ship being attracted to the number-creatures on Fleming's Island. The fifth Doctor liberated the I, and banished the number-predator threatening them back to its home territory.

K9 Mark 3 Given to Sarah Jane

Brendan Richards became Lavinia Smith's ward after his mother Patricia died.[265]

1981 (18th-22nd December) - K9 AND COMPANY: A GIRL'S BEST FRIEND[266] -> In September, a hailstorm lasting thirteen seconds destroyed Commander Pollock's crop. He was renting the East Wing of Lavinia Smith's house at the time. On 6th December, Lavinia

Smith left for America, phoning her ward Brendan Richards on the 10th to tell him that he would be spending Christmas with her niece, Sarah Jane. The next day, Brendan's term ended and he began waiting for Sarah to pick him up, but she had spent the first two weeks of December working abroad for Reuters.

Sarah Jane found a crate waiting for her at Moreton Harwood. It contained K9 Mark 3, sent as a gift from the Doctor. Working together, Sarah, Brendan and K9 exposed a local coven of witches who conducted human sacrifices. On 29th December, the cultists appeared in court on an attempted murder charge.

1981 (23rd December) - BLUE BOX[267] -> Eridani agents on Earth had recovered three of the five computer components that went missing circa 1966. The sixth Doctor allied with the Eridani to recover the last two, fearing they could affect Earth's development. However, he discovered that the components, part of a system named "the Savant", could usurp control of the human brain's "hardware/software", and had been dispatched to the Eridani colony to mentally dominate it.

The Doctor and the Eridani retrieved the last two components from the formidable hacker Sarah Swan and her friend Luis Perez. However, the Savant had mentally dominated Swan and Perez, who were left near-catatonic. By late 1982, Swan was reportedly in the Bainbridge Hospital, a facility where the American government kept persons with dangerous information. Perez's family cared for him in Mexico.

The journalist Charles "Chick" Peters later wrote *Blue Box*, a chronicle of these events.

1982

Charlie Sato, a future UNIT officer, was born in 1981 or 1982.[268] In 1982, a Betamax recorder fell into the Rift.[269] The parents of Simon, a future companion of Iris Wildthyme, died in a plane crash while on "the trip of a lifetime" that they'd won on a game show.[270] Iris Wildthyme appeared on the game show *Bullseye* with famed darts player Eric Bristow.[271]

While fishing with two friends in Greece, 1982, the eleventh Doctor found the Gentlemen of the Dice's lost harmonica.[272]

real life has overtaken Sarah's "I'm from 1980" comment in *Pyramids of Mars*.
267 Dating *Blue Box* (PDA #59) - Presuming one can believe Peters' account, the story opens "two days before Christmas 1981" (p10). Peters visits Swan in the Bainbridge Hospital in late 1982 (p5).
268 He's "thirty" in the 2012 scenes of *Mastermind*.
269 *TW: The Undertaker's Gift*
270 "Ten years" before *Iris: Enter Wildthyme*.
271 *Iris S4: Iris at the Oche. Bullseye* ran from 1981-1995, with a reunion special in 2005.
272 *ST: The Jago & Litefoot Revival*
273 Dating *Time-Flight* (18.7) - The date isn't specified beyond Tegan's "this is the 1980s". There's no indication that it's the exact day Tegan left in *Logopolis* (or that it isn't). There's snow on the ground, which there wasn't in *Logopolis*, but which doesn't rule out it being February.
274 *The King's Demons*
275 *Arc of Infinity, The Waters of Amsterdam*. Tegan and Kyle meet "a year" before the latter story. She breaks up with him "a month" before reuniting with the fifth Doctor and Nyssa in the former.
276 *Night Thoughts*. The Falklands War lasted from 2nd April to 14th June, 1982.
277 Six hundred thirty days before *The Reaping*, which opens on 24th September, 1984.
278 Dating *Relative Dementias* (PDA #49) - The date is given (p40).
279 *Only Human*
280 "Two years" after the first part of *Father Time*, "three years" before the second (p114).

281 *Return of the Living Dad*
282 Dating *Living Legend* (BF promo #4, *DWM* #337) - The date is given, Track 1.
283 Dating *Day of the Cockroach* (BBC *DW* audiobook #17) - The back cover text supplies the year. Within the story, the Doctor declares that it's "1982" after tapping his watch and doing a quick calculation. Nobody native to this time (even allowing that they are being psionically influenced by cockroaches, and so are a bit deluded about things) argues with that conclusion when it's repeated.
284 *The Also People*. This would be between 1982 and 1988.
285 *Business Unusual*
286 *The Song of the Megaptera*. Peri saw Slayer, founded in 1981, prior to her meeting the Doctor in 1984.
287 *The Reaping*
288 *DotD: Trouble in Paradise*
289 Either "twenty-five years" (according to Turvey and a local named Angela Wisher, who could be generalising a little) or "twenty-three Christmases" (according to the product blurb) before *Cuddlesome*.
290 *The Oseidon Adventure*. Shergar won the 202nd Epsom Derby in 1981, and retired from racing in September of that year. On 8th February, 1983, he was stolen by masked gunmen and never seen again.

c 1982 - TIME-FLIGHT[273] -> Following the disappearance of Speedbird Concorde down a time contour, the fifth Doctor, Tegan and Nyssa arrived at Heathrow Airport. At the insistence of Sir John Sudbury at C19, the Doctor and his friends were allowed to take a second Concorde into the contour, and travelled back one hundred and forty million years. Upon their return, the fifth Doctor and Nyssa had to leave Heathrow in such a hurry, Tegan was left behind.

The Tremas Master's TARDIS was propelled to Xeraphas, where he discovered Kamelion, a tool of a previous invader of that planet.[274]

Tegan Jovanka returned to her job as a stewardess for Air Antipodes. On a flight to Sydney, the android Kylex-Twelve registered temporal particles on Tegan's person, and bore witness as she kicked an unruly passenger in the shin **and was sacked shortly afterwards**. As "Kyle", Kylex found ways of "running into" Tegan. They dated for three months, but she tired of the relationship, and dumped him on the same day that he proposed.[275]

During the Falklands War, the chemical gas weapon Gravonax was tested on one of the small Hebrides Islands in Scotland. All wildlife on the isle – which was dubbed Gravonax Island – died, and nobody wanted to live there even after it was decontaminated. Major Dickens and a female military chaplain, a.k.a. "the Deacon", left the British army after "a bit of an incident". The secluded Gravonax Island was perfect for Dickens' scientific research, and he took up residence there.[276]

A Cyber-Leader, potentially the last of its kind, arrived from the far future in a Gallifreyan time-ship. The Cyber-Leader was greatly weakened by exposure to Vortex energy, but continued its scheme to trap the Doctor.[277]

1982 (April) - RELATIVE DEMENTIAS[278] -> Joyce Brunner, a former UNIT physicist, came to suspect abnormal activity at the Graystairs nursing home. She alerted her old colleague the Doctor (who was now in his seventh incarnation), who arrived with Ace to investigate. The head of Graystairs – the Annarene named Sooal – restored the Tulk war council's memories, then murdered the group upon obtaining the command codes to the Tulk stasis chamber. Two renegade Annarene arrived and killed Sooal, desiring the advanced weaponry within the stasis chamber to return their people to war. The Doctor tricked the Annarene into transmatting into the stasis chamber before it was opened, freezing them in time. He then destroyed the Tulk spaceship.

The ninth Doctor had a number of blind spots in his historical knowledge, the events of May 1982 among them.[279]

@ After two years of the eighth Doctor attempting to interrogate him, the imprisoned alien Sallak got a legal injunction preventing the Doctor from making any other contact.[280] Isaac Summerfield met Hamlet Macbeth in 1982, and was given a copy of his book *The Shoreditch Incident*.[281]

1982 (11th July) - LIVING LEGEND[282] -> Two agents of the aggressive Threllip race constructed an interdimensional portal in Ferrara, Italy, as a means for their people to invade Earth. The eighth Doctor and Charley squashed the plan, and used the portal to strand the agents on the seventeenth moon of Mordalius Prime.

1982 - DAY OF THE COCKROACH[283] -> Giant cockroaches, developed through unknown means, entrenched themselves in a nuclear war bunker built in the 1960s. Collectively, they could influence human minds, and lured a small group of people underground to serve as a food supply. The eleventh Doctor, Amy and Rory isolated the cockroaches with a fear-inducing wasp pheromone, and sealed them within the bunker. The Doctor expected that as cockroaches only lived for a few months, the colony would quickly die off.

The Doctor spent time with Nelson Mandela during his imprisonment at Robbin Island.[284] Melanie Bush left school after getting five A-Levels. She backpacked around Europe before getting a job at a Scottish nature reserve. Around the same time, SenéNet was buying up European computer firms and other youth market companies. Their executives were converted into drones.[285]

Peri Brown attended a Slayer concert.[286] In Baltimore, Peri was friends throughout her school years with the Chambers family. The father, Anthony Chambers, kept Peri and his children amused by letting them use a telescope. Peri briefly dated Nate Chambers, and became best friends with his sister Kathy.[287] Peri Brown's father owned a Jalopy. As a straight-A student, Peri studied Christopher Columbus in school and was appalled by his atrocities.[288]

Ronald Turvey resented that children grew to become adults and, motivated by the Tinghus within him, schemed to kill all adults with Cuddlesomes: fluffy toys akin to pink vampire hamsters, but equipped with an extra-terrestrial poison. Cuddlesomes were *the* toy to get in the 1980s, and three million were produced. The radio signal intended to release the poison was never sent, as Turvey was arrested for tax fraud and imprisoned for two decades.[289]

The Master stole Shergar, a famed Irish racehorse, as payment to a would-be ally: Colonel Hugh Spindleton.[290]

The Fifth Doctor in Stockbridge

Around 1983, the fifth Doctor settled in the Gloucestershire village of Stockbridge for a time, a guest at the Green Dragon Inn. He had volunteered to investigate time warps on behalf of the Time Lords. After a number of interruptions, he learned that the time warps had been triggered by the Monk.[291]

The Doctor was head of the Stockbridge Chess Society.[292]

(=) c 1983 - "The Tides of Time"[293] -> The Prime Mover produced the ordered vibrations of the universe on a vast biomechanical device known as the Event Synthesiser. For the first time in centuries, he fumbled a note, introducing a note of discord. Time warps occurred. The fifth Doctor had been staying in Stockbridge for some time, and was playing a cricket match on the village green when he was bowled a hand grenade instead of a cricket ball. Shortly afterwards, a Roman soldier was shot in nearby woods, only to vanish. The Doctor quickly learned the disturbances were worldwide.

Meanwhile, the Event Synthesiser's discord had opened a gap in time, and the Demon Melanicus emerged through it. He took control of the Event Synthesizer in order to create universal fear, destruction and unending chaos.

A jousting knight – Sir Justin – initially attacked the Doctor, but came to realise his error and vowed to help fight whoever was behind the time warps. Melanicus removed the Event Synthesizer from time to prevent attack, but was detected by the spirit of Rassilon deep in the Matrix. He vowed to act, despite advice from Morvane and Bedevere to be cautious. Rassilon decided to operate through the Doctor, who arrived on Gallifrey and used his Presidential authority to access the Matrix. The Doctor entered the Matrix to commune with Rassilon, and saw him chairing a meeting of the High Evolutionaries from a number of planets.

The High Evolutionaries tasked the Doctor with locating the Event Synthesizer. Rassilon despatched a mysterious agent named Shayde to help the Doctor. Melanicus' interference created the maelstrom – a whirlpool in space and time – and sent a mantric bomb against Gallifrey. Shayde protected the Doctor

---

291 For almost the entire run of the fifth Doctor's *DWM* adventures, he was based in Stockbridge. The reason for this was finally given in "4-Dimensional Vistas". The stories have a contemporary setting. While they started publication in 1982, the Doctor in "Lunar Lagoon" assumes it is 1983 – the only time a year is specified.

As for *where* these stories take place in relation to the fifth Doctor's television adventures, the Big Finish audios featuring Stockbridge (especially *Circular Time*: "Autumn", *Castle of Fear* and *The Eternal Summer*) establish that the Doctor is already acquainted with Stockbridge, Sir Justin ("The Tides of Time") and Max Edison ("The Stars Fell on Stockbridge") during the time he is travelling with Nyssa alone (between *Time-Flight* and *Arc of Infinity*). Even this, however, means that he must have dropped her (and possibly Adric and Tegan too, if he first visited Stockbridge during Season 19) off somewhere and picked them up again. In "The Tides of Time", the Doctor says that deference is shown on Gallifrey to his "honorary title" of president (*The Invasion of Time*). The *DWM* stories with Gus, however, possibly happen later in the fifth Doctor's lifetime, as his sixth incarnation is still hunting for the person that had Gus killed, suggesting it happened more recently.

292 "Fugitive"

293 Dating "The Tides of Time" (*DWM* #61-67) - Time is disturbed during this story, and strictly speaking the events take place in a cul-de-sac of time created by Melanicus, and which is destroyed at the end.

The year the story starts is not specified, but the first part features the discordant note and specifies that the Doctor's cricket game on contemporary Earth is taking place "at that precise moment". "Forty years before", the village green was a sandbagged army training army, so clearly that was during the Second World War. The story was published in 1982. In "Lunar Lagoon", the Doctor had thought he was in "1983", perhaps suggesting that's the year the Stockbridge adventures take place.

The story spells "Event Synthesizer" in both its American and British ("Synthesiser") form in different installments. Stockbridge isn't named until the following story. The mysterious woman the Doctor sees in the dreamscape is never identified – the dress she wears resembles a jumpsuit Zoe wore in *The Wheel in Space*. In retrospect – and completely coincidentally – she resembles the first incarnation of Patience, seen in a similar flashback in *Cold Fusion*.

294 Dating "The Deal" (*DWM* #53) - No date is given, other than stating that the story takes place during the Millenium Wars. *DWM* consistently misspelt "millennium" with one "n". This is not the same as the Millennium War in *The Quantum Archangel*.

295 Dating "Stars Fell on Stockbridge" (*DWM* #68-69) - No year is given, but it's a contemporary setting, and the Doctor is still based in Stockbridge, as he was in "The Tides of Time".

296 Dating "The Stockbridge Horror" (*DWM* #70-75) - Once again, it's a contemporary setting.

from its effects, but the TARDIS was sucked into Melanicus' domain: a surreal world where the Doctor and Justin encountered a carnival, a mysterious woman that the Doctor recognised, a demonic fairground ride, barbarian hordes and Dracula.

Emerging from Melanicus' domain, the Doctor took the TARDIS out of time to help his search. He re-entered time, then encountered a ship from Althrace which took them to their home in an alien dimension – a vast solar system engineered so that the planets were bolted together and set orbiting a white hole. The technology of Althrace was as advanced as that of the Time Lords, and the white hole allowed direct access to the forces of creation, making them one vast, living organism. Using the power of the White Hole, the High Evolutionaries combined their mental force to halt time and discover the co-ordinates of the Event Synthesizer. Meanwhile, Melanicus had ushered in the Millenium Wars:

The Millenium Wars

"A thousand worlds in conflict for a thousand years ... with causes lost in the distant past, their fury rages through time and space..."

In the year 375, barbarian hordes from Asia swept into Central Europe... and were wiped out by a division of Nazi tanks... which in turn were wiped out by American F-15 fighters... which in turn were wiped out by advanced space fighters.

"This was the beginning of the Reign of Melanicus as millenium fought millenium... and so what began as a series of small, confused skirmishes soon escalated into a holocaust of conflict, culminating in a far-flung armageddon – the Millenium Wars! A thousand worlds in conflict for a thousand years."

(=) "The Deal"[294] **->** The fourth Doctor caused a trooper of the 12th Trouble 'chuters to crash. The trooper set his robot "spider" on him, but the Doctor blocked its psychic attack. A pursuit ship arrived, firing missiles at the TARDIS. The Doctor realised that the trooper was a psychopath and left, abandoning him to death at the hands of another pursuit ship.

(=) "The Tides of Time" **->** But due to his lack of knowledge, Melanicus had confined himself to a cul-de-sac in time. This was to prove his undoing.

After a thousand years of the Millenium Wars,

Earth was ruined and lifeless. Melanicus had based the Synthesizer here, and the fifth Doctor located it. The Doctor and Shayde weakened Melanicus, and Justin pierced the demon with his sword, unleashing vast energies. Justin and Melanicus were killed, and the Prime Mover was restored to his rightful place as user of the Event Synthesizer.

The Doctor awoke to find time restored, and a memorial to the fallen knight in the church in Stockbridge: St Justinians. As Shayde watched the cricket game resume, the Doctor was unsure if it had all been a dream.

Maxwell Edison Meets the Doctor

c 1983 - "Stars Fell on Stockbridge"[295] **->** UFO spotter Maxwell Edison discovered the TARDIS, and inspired the fifth Doctor to detect an alien spacecraft two days from Earth. They went to the ship, which was deserted and had been drifting for thousands of years. There was some sort of haunting presence on board, but the ship was already heading for Earth's atmosphere. The Doctor and Maxwell returned to Earth, from where Maxwell watched the shooting stars caused by the ship's break-up.

No human space agency had any space labs in orbit.

c 1983 - "The Stockbridge Horror"[296] **->** A local limestone quarry unearthed the TARDIS in rock five hundred million years old. Nearby, a police constable discovered a charred body.

The fifth Doctor, still staying at the Green Dragon Inn, saw a report from the quarry. He ran to where he had left the TARDIS – Well's Wood – and found it was still there, covered in mud. He went to the quarry, but couldn't get to the mysterious buried police box. Well's Wood caught fire, and the Doctor – upon returning to the TARDIS – discovered an alien figure that could shoot jets of fire.

The Doctor dematerialised his Ship, but the alien clung to the TARDIS, then forced its way inside. It stalked the Doctor, who realised it was the presence he'd recently encountered on the deserted spaceship. The Gallifreyan military dispatched Lord Tubal Cain in a specially adapted TARDIS, while Shayde trapped the alien in the Matrix. Cain fired seeker torpedoes at the TARDIS... which landed on Gallifrey moments after they hit the homeworld.

While the Doctor faced trial on Gallifrey, the government agency SAG3 investigated the TARDIS. Shayde neutralised them, and erased the imprint of the TARDIS just as the military TARDIS landed. The Doctor was freed.

c 1983 - ARC OF INFINITY[297] -> Omega had relocated the Arc of Infinity – a gateway between dimensions – away from the star system Rondel and placed its curve on the city of Amsterdam. The fifth Doctor and Nyssa tracked Omega to Amsterdam, and found Omega's base in a crypt there. The ancient Gallifreyan's attempt to bond with the Doctor failed, and he apparently died. Tegan Jovanka joined the Doctor's travels once again.

Omega recorporealised enough to stow himself aboard the TARDIS of Ertikus, a Time Lord who arrived in this period to study Omega's exploits. Ertikus' TARDIS relocated to the far future with Omega aboard.[298]

(=) 1983 (Spring) - THE WATERS OF AMSTERDAM[299] -> Still in Amsterdam after the Omega crisis, the fifth Doctor, Tegan and Nyssa met Tegan's ex-boyfriend Kyle, and became curious about a Rijksmuseum exhibit of Rembrandt paintings depicting actual schematics for spaceships. The alien Nix tried to eliminate Kyle, who was an android working for the Countess Mach-Teldak, but the Doctor took his companions and Kyle back to consult with Rembrandt in 1658...

They returned with the Teldak, and found that her actions in 1658 enabled the East India Company to become the Dutch Galactic Company, and to craft a fleet of spaceships with which she intended to destroy the Nix homeworld. The Doctor's party took Teldak back to 1658, erasing her interference.

While Nyssa and Tegan continued to enjoy themselves in Amsterdam, the fifth Doctor nipped out to the planet Sharnax in the twenty-sixth century.[300] He also, with River Song and a treacherous companion named Brooke, went to Mozart's day and a restaurant outside of space-time, the Bumptious Gastropod.[301]

Before this time, the Arar-Jecks of Heiradi had carved out a huge subterranean city during the 20-Aeon War on that planet.[302] The seventh Doctor and Ace fought an N-form by the Rio Yari in 1983.[303] **Jo Jones lived with the Nambiquara tribe from the Mato Grosso for about six months in 1983.**[304] The Doctor collected some oolong tea in Peking in either 1983 or 1893.[305]

297 Dating *Arc of Infinity* (20.1) - There is no indication of the year. It is some time after *Time-Flight*, and before *The Awakening*.

The Waters of Amsterdam specifies that *Arc of Infinity* happens in "1983", and that Tegan was separated from the Doctor and Nyssa "a year" ago (in *Time-Flight*) - which is roughly in keeping with the broadcast dates of the two stories.

298 *Omega*

299 Dating *The Waters of Amsterdam* (BF #208) - The story picks up immediately after *Arc of Infinity* – the events of which, Tegan says, happened "in the last 24 hours". The year is given as "1983", and the script claims it's "It's Spring, 1983" (so, not entirely dead-on with the broadcast of *Arc of Infinity* from 3rd to 12th January, 1983).

300 *The Burning Prince*

301 *River S3: My Dinner with Andrew*, *River S3: The Furies*.

302 As mentioned by Turlough in *Frontios,* although the universe isn't yet twenty billion years old at this point.

303 *Damaged Goods*

304 *SJA: Death of the Doctor*

305 *Army of Death*

306 Dating *Hexagora* (BF LS #3.2) - The story occurs between *Arc of Infinity* and *Snakedance* (and directly after *The Elite*), during Tegan's native time on Earth.

307 *Mawdryn Undead, Planet of Fire.*

308 *Kiss of Death*

309 *The Memory Bank and Other Stories:* "The Memory Bank"

310 *Eldrad Must Die!*

311 Dating *Mawdryn Undead* (20.3) - The Doctor says "if these readings are correct, its 1983 on Earth", and the date is reaffirmed a number of times afterwards.

Turlough first appears in *Mawdryn Undead*, but his origins are revealed in *Planet of Fire*. According to the initial Character Outline, Turlough was "20" on his first appearance, which makes him a couple of years too old to be at Brendon School – this was almost certainly written when the plan was to introduce the character in *The Song of the Space Whale* by Pat Mills, a story that was delayed, then rejected. Mark Strickson was 22 when he began playing Turlough.

Turlough's pact with the Black Guardian ends in the undatable *Enlightenment*.

312 *Leth-St:* "The Enfolded Time"

313 Dating *Kiss of Death* (BF #147) - The story occurs between *Mawdryn Undead* and the reforms on Trion that enable Turlough to return home (*Planet of Fire*).

314 Dating *Rat Trap* (BF #148) - It's "June the 9th, 1983", general election day in the United Kingdom.

315 Dating *Turlough and the Earthlink Dilemma* (*The Companions of Doctor Who* #1) - As Turlough's actions eliminate Rehctaht, this presumably (and paradoxically) causes the very political reform that allows his younger self to return home to Trion in *Planet of Fire.*

316 Dating *The Five Doctors* (20.1) - The Brigadier recognises Tegan, so he must be kidnapped by Borusa after the second half of *Mawdryn Undead* in 1983. It is specified that he is attending a UNIT reunion (perhaps one he initiated once his memories returned?), but this isn't the occasion of his retirement. Sarah is kidnapped around the same time, certainly after *K9 and Company.*

c 1983 - HEXAGORA[306] **->** The Hexagora, a nomadic insect species, had settled on Luparis – the third planet of Proxima Centauri. A global cooling event prevented the Hexagorans from moving on – to survive, they required mammalian bodies. Humans were abducted from Earth via spacepods, and the Hexagorans swapped minds with them, leaving their insectoid bodies in hibernation. The humanised Hexagorans constructed a city, Lupara, based upon schematics they had taken of Tudor London.

The fifth Doctor, Tegan and Nyssa relaxed in Tegan's hometown, near Brisbane, when Tegan learned that her friend Mike Bretherton had been abducted. They followed Bretherton's trail to Luparis. Queen Zafira recognised that human bodies didn't live long enough to survive the Luparis winter, and so decreed that she and the Doctor would marry and sire longer-lived offspring. The Doctor convinced Zafira that the collective Hexagoran memory pool, the Hexagon, was fragmenting because they were inhabiting human bodies. He aided them in returning to their insectoid forms, and relocating to a warmer world. The abducted humans, most of whom had slept in stasis, were returned to Earth seconds after they left.

Turlough Joins the TARDIS

There was civil war on Trion. Turlough's mother was killed and the ship containing his father and brother crashed on Sarn, formerly a Trion prison planet. Turlough was captured and exiled to Brendon School on Earth, where Trion agents, including a solicitor on Chancery Lane, watched him.[307] Deela's father was on the winning side of the civil war, and had seen to it that Turlough was exiled.[308] During the war, Turlough defied orders to aid civilians under bombardment at Jorva Plateau, and instead went to repel bombing runs against the Winter Planet, where his family resided.

With schoolmate Peter Smythe, Turlough nicked school trophies and threw them into a pond. Turlough and Charlie Gibbs climbed over the wall of the girls' school, resulting in Gibbs falling and fracturing his collarbone.[309]

Unknown to Turlough, Brendon was part of an underground railway line for other stateless exiles from Trion, as facilitated by a solicitor on Chancery Lane. One of Turlough's classmates, Charlie Gibbs, was on the opposite side during Trion's civil war, but exiled anyway. The solicitor had a number of prospects lined up for Turlough that would have pleased Turlough's family. To his dismay, Turlough spent half term in rainy Weston-super-Mare with Hippo Ibbotson's family, and learned the art of paddling.[310]

1983 - MAWDRYN UNDEAD[311] **->** The Brigadier regained his memory, but lost his beloved car when he met the fifth Doctor, Tegan and Nyssa. When the Brigadier met his past self from 1977, he unwittingly provided the energy that released Mawdryn and his followers from their curse of immortality. The Black Guardian forged a deal in secret with Turlough, and tasked him with killing the Doctor. Turlough left Brendon to join the TARDIS crew.

Harry Sullivan had been seconded to NATO, and was doing secretive work at Porton Down.

Contact between the two Lethbridge-Stewarts restored his older self's childhood memories of his brother James.[312]

1983 - KISS OF DEATH[313] **->** Trion repatriation squads were now in operation on various worlds.

Turlough's old flame Deela became engaged to a ruthless entrepreneur named Halquin Rennol. When Deela's father disavowed the union and froze her assets, the pair coveted the royal treasure rumoured to reside in the dimensional vault established by Turlough's ancestor. Only Turlough and Deela's DNA in combination – through a simple kiss, for instance – would open the vault, and so Rennol's mercenaries captured Turlough when the TARDIS landed on the vacation world of Vektris. The vault's security system went haywire – Rennol killed Deela, and was probably killed himself when the vault resealed.

1983 (9th June) - RAT TRAP[314] **->** The Rat King living beneath Cardogan Castle attempted to release a variant of the Black Death that would wipe out humanity. The fifth Doctor, Tegan, Turlough and the older Nyssa helped to destroy the Rat King, and left UNIT to clear up the mess.

1983 - TURLOUGH AND THE EARTHLINK DILEMMA[315] **->** After departing the fifth Doctor's company, a time-travelling Turlough encountered the dictator Rechtaht while she ruled Trion. Rechtaht tried to transfer her mind into Turlough, but his ally – a Time Lord named the Magician – helped Turlough to expel Rechtaht from his mind. This averted a timeline that included the destruction of Earth, Trion and New Trion. Turlough learned that as he had altered history, he couldn't remain in this timeline without causing a paradox.

> = With the Magician's help, Turlough found a reality in which he had died and took up residence there. He was reunited with his old friend, Juras Maateh, of that reality.

c 1983 - THE FIVE DOCTORS[316] **->** The second Doctor and the Brigadier were kidnapped by Borusa in the grounds of UNIT HQ. The next day, the second Doctor bought a copy of "The Times" that reported the UNIT reunion. Colonel Crichton was running UNIT at this point. Despite K9's warnings, Sarah Jane Smith was also kidnapped by Borusa.

Masie Hawk, Hamlet Macbeth, Liz Shaw and Sir John Sudbury also attended the reunion. Benton had returned to active duty. Carol Bell was married with a child. Mike Yates and Tom Osgood had opened a tearoom together.[317] Lethbridge-Stewart spent some time in Haiti.[318]

1983 - THE LADY OF MERCIA[319] **->** The fifth Doctor, Tegan, Turlough and the older Nyssa landed at the University of Frodsham as it hosted the conference "Heirs of Aethelfrid: Perspectives on the Queens of the Dark Ages". Its organiser – Professor John Bleak – thought a sword on loan from the University of Manchester, as wielded by Queen Aethelfrid of Mercia, would enable a test run of a time machine that his wife, Dr Philippa Stone, had developed. As the trial run commenced, the other academics were distracted with free food.

Stone's device scanned Aethelfrid's sword, then malfunctioned and sent Tegan and Bleak back to 918. It also brought Aethelfrid's daughter, Aelfwynn, forward to the present day, where she ran amok. The conference-goers were delighted, thinking it was an amazing historical re-enactment.

The Doctor and Nyssa took Aelfwynn home in the TARDIS. The device separately took Turlough, Stone and her adulterous lover Barry back to 918, then returned them and burnt out on arrival. The TARDIS returned two days later with the Doctor, Tegan, Nyssa and Bleak, just as the conference wrapped things up with a barbeque. Aethelfrid's sword was returned to its exhibit.

1983 - "4-Dimensional Vistas"[320] **->** A British Airways 747 crashed in the Arctic, shot down by the test firing of a Martian cannon. The Monk and a group of Ice Warriors led by Autek had a base there, and were manipulating time. The fifth Doctor homed in on them, but was attacked by the beam weapon. SAG3 arrived by plane to investigate.

Meanwhile, the Doctor and Gus discovered that the Ice Warriors had drilled a vast shaft. Gus and SAG3 launched an attack on the Ice Warrior base, but Autek and the Monk got away. They had activated "the Crucible", then jumped five million years forwards in time. As they returned, the Doctor chased the Monk's TARDIS in his own and set up a Time Ram – apparently annihilating the Monk and destroying the Ice Warrior base.

His vigil on Earth ended, the Doctor pledged to get Gus home.

---

317 *Business Unusual*

318 "Last year" according to *Heart of TARDIS* (p41).

319 Dating *The Lady of Mercia* (BF #173) - The Doctor says on arrival that it's "England, 1983. Time to stretch our legs, I think." The back cover blurb confirms the year, doubtless in accordance with the story evoking Season 20.

320 Dating "4-Dimensional Vistas" (*DWM* #78-83) - This story marks the end of the Doctor's vigil on Earth. In "Lunar Lagoon", the Doctor thought he was in "1983".

321 *Ghost Light*. Marc Platt's novelisation specifies that Gabriel Chase is burnt down in August 1983. Ace's social worker is referred to in *Survival*.

322 *Revenge of the Swarm*

323 "Eight months" before *Return of the Living Dad*.

324 *Return of the Living Dad* (p53). While in 1983, Jason says he was "born this year". In *Death and Diplomacy* (set circa 2011), Jason must be rounding when he says, "I'm thirty years old, near enough" (p196).

325 *Interference* (p296).

326 Dating "City of Devils" (*DWM Holiday Special 1992*) - The date is given in the opening caption.

327 Dating *Heart of TARDIS* (PDA #32) - It's July (p117), "fifteen years" after 1968 (p246).

328 *TW: Fragments*, and confirmed in *The Torchwood Archives* (BBC), although *Torchwood: The Official Magazine Yearbook* (2008) says he was born 2nd December, 1982. *Torchwood One: Before the Fall* identifies him as a Leo (22nd July to 22nd August). A plaque at the Ianto Shrine landmark in Cardiff – and startling as it sounds, this is real – says Ianto lived 1983-2009.

329 *Burning Heart* (p102).

330 "Thirty years" before *Autonomy*.

331 Dating *Return of the Living Dad* (NA #53) - It's "10 December 1983" (p34).

332 *Benny: Life During Wartime*, *Benny S4: Death to the Daleks*.

333 According to the CIA files in *TW: Miracle Day*. 24th October is named as a Saturday; in 1983, it was actually a Monday.

334 Dating *Cold War* (X7.9) - The caption reads "North Pole, 1983". Professor Grisenko, who admits to being a little behind on music from the West, is familiar with Ultravox's "Vienna" (released 11th July, 1980) and Duran Duran's "Hungry Like the Wolf" (May 1982). The HADS previously featured in *The Krotons*.

335 According to "Hunters of the Burning Stone", Annabel was six when her mother died in 1989, so was born in either 1983 or 1984.

336 *Remembrance of the Daleks*. Had someone from 1963 discovered Ace's ghetto blaster, this would have occurred "twenty years too early".

337 *Touched by an Angel*. He's 37 in October 2011, so was born in either 1983 or 1984.

338 *The Angels Take Manhattan*

WHEN DID AMY POND AND RORY WILLIAMS DIE?: In *The Angels Take Manhattan*, Amy and Rory's tombstones bear no birth/death years, instead just giving their ages when they passed on. If the markers can be believed, Rory died age 82, and Amy was 87.

How old are they, however, when they're stranded in New York, 1938? It's commonly assumed that Amy and

In 1983, a 13-year-old Ace was friends with an Asian girl, Manisha, whose flat was firebombed in a racist attack. In anger because of this, Ace burnt down Gabriel Chase. She was assigned a probation officer and social worker.[321] Ace set off the school fire alarms to skip Double French.[322]

Joel Mintz had been thrown back in time to 1983 from 1993. He ended up in New York, where Isaac Summerfield found him.[323] Jason Kane, a future rogue and husband of Bernice Summerfield, was born in 1983.[324] In 1983, Faction Paradox agents wrecked the Blue Peter garden.[325]

c 1983 (summer) - "City of Devils"[326] **->** Aunt Lavinia sent Sarah Jane and K9 to Egypt to write a story about her friend Warren Martyn. An archaeological dig there had experienced some mysterious deaths and disappearances. Entering the tomb, Sarah and K9 encountered a group of Silurians and Sea Devils in a vast subterranean city. Sarah opened diplomatic relations with the Silurians, and it was hoped that this would lead to an accommodation between the two civilisations. Returning to England, Sarah Jane contacted Lethbridge-Stewart, who was keen to make amends for the mistakes of the past.

c 1983 (July) - HEART OF TARDIS[327] **->** Crowley lured the fourth Doctor and the first Romana to the Tollsham USAF base, as he needed the Doctor to open the Golgotha gateway.

Ianto Jones of Torchwood was born on 19th August, 1983.[328] Peri Brown, a 17-year-old student at Boston University, bought a handgun.[329] A little girl, Elizabeth Sarah Devonshire, found an injured Nestene sphere – it would influence her mind and manipulate her career path.[330]

1983 - RETURN OF THE LIVING DAD[331] **->** The seventh Doctor, Benny, Jason, Chris and Roz discovered that Benny's father, Isaac, was alive and well in the village of Little Caldwell. He was running an underground movement that helped stranded aliens on Earth return home. Albinex the Navarino paid one of Isaac's allies to retrieve nuclear launch codes from the Doctor. Albinex and Isaac were working together to detonate a nuclear device, which Isaac hoped would spur an arms race so humanity would have more advanced weapons to use against the Daleks in the twenty-second century. However, Albinex was actually a Dalek agent, and planned to destroy the Earth. The Doctor, Isaac and Benny captured the Navarino and thwarted the plan. Benny made peace with her father.

Isaac Summerfield's presence in the twentieth century created historical anomalies that enabled the Daleks to locate and capture him. They took him to the twenty-seventh century and slaved him to battle computers. Following the Daleks' defeat, Braxiatel returned Isaac to Little Caldwell.[332] On Oct. 24, 1983, the Welsh Assembly denied allegations of a conspiracy.[333]

1983 - COLD WAR[334] **->** A Soviet submarine assigned to drill for oil samples inadvertently freed the Ice Warrior Skaldak from his slumber at the North Pole. The eleventh Doctor and Clara interceded when the submarine crew impugned upon Skaldak's honour, causing him to vengefully attempt to trigger a nuclear war between the East and West. Skaldak eventually opted for mercy and left aboard a Martian spaceship. The Doctor and Clara set out for the South Pole, where the TARDIS had been relocated thanks to its Hostile Action Displacement System (HADS).

Annabel Lake, a future MI6 agent, was born to Patrick and Heather Lake.[335] The "microchip revolution" took place in the early eighties.[336] Mark Whitaker, a person of interest to the Weeping Angels, was born.[337]

1984

Rory Arthur Williams died, age 82, and was buried near Manhattan.[338] Rupert "Danny" Pink, a future Coal Hill teacher, was born.[339] Grant Gordon, a.k.a. the Ghost, was born.[340] The ninth Doctor and Rose quietly attended the wedding of her parents, Peter Tyler and Jacqueline Andrea Suzette Prentice.[341]

Rory grew up together in the same class (*Let's Kill Hitler* and the *DWM* comic "Imaginary Enemies" certainly take that approach), so must have been born the same school year. However, whereas *The Eleventh Hour* actually *says* that Amy was age seven at Easter 1996 (so was born in either 1988 or 1989, with "Forever Dreaming" picking the latter), any confirmation on Rory's birth year is surprisingly absent from the TV show, tie-in works and BBC marketing materials.

Rory writes to his father in *P.S.* that he and Amy are stuck in New York "fifty years before I was born," which supports his being born in the late 80s. Against this, *Extra Time* claims Rory was born just before the Live Aid concert (held on 13th July, 1985). That would mean that Rory is at least four years older than Amy – a nice parallel to Arthur Darvill (born 17th June, 1982) being about five years older than Karen Gillan (born 28th November, 1987), but which would mean they couldn't be in the same class at school.

This also begs the question: allowing for TARDIS travel, do Amy and Rory even *know* how old they are at the end of *The Angels Take Manhattan*? Even they seem

The Doctor said 1984 was "never as good as the book".[342] **Torchwood constructed a secret base beneath the Thames Barrier.**[343] **Torchwood bought the London security firm HC Clements.**[344] **In 1984, scientists in Princeton discovered Strange Matter.**[345] The seventh Doctor and Mel visited the Welsh village of Llanfer Ceiriog.[346] The fifth Doctor, Tegan and Nyssa visited Hexen Bridge in 1984.[347]

A lizard-looking alien attacked young Danny Fisher and his father as they camped in the woods. Fisher's father froze, but Danny bludgeoned the alien to death – and thus found his calling as a killer of extraterrestrials.[348]

Laboratories belonging to a French company, Rechauffer, Inc., contaminated the Well of St Clothide in the village of Cloots Coombe, which made the population sterile. Rechauffer took genetic samples from the villagers, allegedly to clone them children, but actually to work towards the creation of disposable clones for military purposes. The initial experiments produced an abomination that fed off the life force itself, and lived in the well.[349]

wih - The third iteration of Cousin Anastasia died as Anna Anderson in Charlottesville, Virginia, 1984.[350] UNIT captured some Khlecht technology during the Crookback incursion of 1984.[351]

When Gwen Cooper was about five or six, her father came home after receiving the blame for money that had gone missing from work. He told Gwen that he wasn't distressed about the money, but that he couldn't stand anyone thinking that he wasn't an honest man. She would always remember the incident, as it was the first time anyone had spoken to her like an adult.[352]

Scandrius' wayward TARDIS, with Tegan aboard, briefly materialised in High Barnet.[353]

1984 (1st May) - THE AWAKENING[354] **->** The Malus absorbed the psychic energy of a series of war games in Little Hodcombe, amplifying the villagers' violence. The fifth Doctor prevented the Malus from becoming totally active and blew up the church in which the Malus lay dormant. After this, the Doctor, Tegan and Turlough spent some time in Little Hodcombe with Tegan's grandfather, Andrew Verney.

1984 (May) - AND YOU WILL OBEY ME[355] **->** The Transhuman Sisters of the Unholy Protocols – "man-made" androids who instigated the Grand Inquisition of Galaxy

---

unclear about this, although the time Rory spends faffing about with the Doctor might explain why he tells his father in *Dinosaurs on a Spaceship* [2014]: "Dad, I'm 31, I don't have a Christmas list any more", when he should only be 25 if born in 1989. Brian Williams admittedly doesn't question the "31" remark, but it must nonetheless owe to Rory adding on his TARDIS time, or the aforementioned development gap between him and Amy would get even worse. The start of *The Power of Three* [July 2014] indicates that Rory and Amy are at least trying to keep track of their natural age, when Amy tells the Doctor: "[Rory and I] think it's been ten years. Not for you or Earth, but for us. Ten years older. Ten years of you, on and off." If so, they should biologically be about 36 when *The Power of Three* ends.

The simplest way to iron the most wrinkles out of this narrative is to decide that Rory *was* born in 1989; that he *is* the same age as Amy; that he tells his father he's "31" in *Dinosaurs on a Spaceship* because he's been trying to add on his TARDIS time, and that Brian – rather sedate by nature – is too busy acclimating to everything to express surprise about this; that both Amy and Rory cumulatively spend a decade of their lives travelling in the TARDIS, so would normally be 26 when *The Power of Three* finishes [July 2015], but are age 36 when they're left in New York in *The Angels Take Manhattan*; and that Rory lives forty-six years in New York before dying age 82 in 1984. Amy then dies five years later, in 1989 – as it happens, the same year she was born.

339 Danny's age isn't given on screen, so placement here derives from actor Samuel Anderson having been

born in 1982, then adding on the two years that Series 8 takes place ahead of broadcast.
340 He's "eight" at Christmastime, at the start of *The Return of Doctor Mysterio* [c.1992].
341 *Father's Day*. No precise dating is given, but it's before Rose's birth in 1986.
342 *The Reaping*
343 *The Runaway Bride*. The Thames Barrier was constructed from 1974 to 1984.
344 "Twenty-three years" before *The Runaway Bride*.
345 *Time and the Rani*
346 "Seven years" before *Cat's Cradle: Witch Mark* (p25).
347 *The Hollow Men*
348 "The Blood of Azrael"
349 "Eighteen years" before *SJS: Comeback*.
350 *FP: The Book of the War*
351 *Persuasion*
352 *TW: Miracle Day*
353 *Time in Office*. For Tegan, it's after *Frontios* – meaning that if we're seeing a contemporary High Barnet, it's probably 1984.
354 Dating *The Awakening* (21.2) - The Doctor assures Tegan that "it is 1984", despite Will Chandler's clothing. As Tegan is the Queen of the May, it is presumably May Day.
355 Dating *And You Will Obey Me* (BF #211) - The year is named, and the story occurs while the fifth Doctor's party are in Little Hodcombe following *The Awakening* (set on 1st May, 1984). *The Two Masters* reveals who set the Transhuman Sisters upon the Master's trail.
356 *The Hollow Men*

Five – ripped through whole galaxies. Regarding themselves as profane, the Sisters sought to mathematically increase their "worthiness" percentage, and so their trans-dimensional warfleet attacked the cadaverous Master's TARDIS. This shredded his symbiotic nuclei, causing him to land in rural Hexford while the fifth Doctor was down the road in Little Hodcombe. The Master attempted to incubate his nuclei in four local youths – Annie, Colin, Helen and Mikey – but Mikey resisted the Master's control, and the Master's body perished. His Ship went into sleep mode, and his mind took refuge in its telepathic circuits.

While Tegan, Turlough and Jane Hampden went to source stone for a church restoration, the fifth Doctor popped out to answer a distress call from the Master's TARDIS in 2016.

The Doctor's experiences in Little Hodcombe reminded him of Hexen Bridge. He decided to monitor the area.[356]

c 1984 - "The Forgotten"[357] **->** The fifth Doctor, Tegan and Turlough spent time at the Doctor's house at Allen Road, and the Doctor enjoyed playing cricket for the local team. A Judoon ship arrived on Earth in defiance of galactic law that put the planet outside their jurisdiction. They were looking for the spherical Eye of Akasha, which was in the Doctor's possession, but he tricked them into taking a cricket ball instead.

Tegan Leaves the TARDIS

1984 - RESURRECTION OF THE DALEKS[358] **->** Daleks from the future arrived in the twentieth century and placed their Duplicates in key positions around the world. They used the timezone as a safe storage place for the Movellan virus that had all but wiped them out. The fifth Doctor, Tegan and Turlough were present as a pitched battle broke out between the British army and the Daleks. The Doctor released the virus, killing the Daleks. Afterwards, Tegan was appalled by the carnage and left the Doctor's company. Lytton, an agent of the Daleks, escaped.

Tegan relocated to Brisbane after leaving the Doctor, and eventually took over the family business, Verney Feeds, from her father. The company supplied animal feed to farmers, and Tegan for a time dated one of its employees, Michael Tenaka.[359]

Peri Joins the TARDIS, Turlough Disembarks, Kamelion Destroyed

c 1984 (9th May) - PLANET OF FIRE[360] **->** Professor Howard Foster discovered an archaeologically important wreck off the coast of Lanzarote. His step-daughter, Perpugilliam Brown, travelled to the planet Sarn in the fifth Doctor's TARDIS. There, the Tremas Master attempted to restore his shrunken body using the Numismaton gas of a sacred volcano. The Doctor facilitated the Master's demise before this could happen. Turlough's exile was lifted and he returned to Trion. Peri started travelling with the Doctor. In autumn of the same year, she was due back at college.

The Time Lords' meddling in Peri's history resulted in a version of her that returned home, her memories of the Doctor wiped save for their first adventure together. This Peri attained a doctorate of biology, wed her college boyfriend (Davy Silverman), escaped what became a physically abusive marriage and moved to Los Angeles. In time, she became "Dr Perpugilliam Brown" – a relationship counsellor with a hit cable show, *Queen of Worries*.[361]

The tenth Doctor and Emily Winter met Turlough on

---

357 Dating "The Forgotten" (IDW *DW* mini-series #2) - Tegan is wearing her outfit from *Frontios/Resurrection of the Daleks*. This may well be set after *The Awakening*, when we know the Doctor and his companions stayed on Earth for a while.

358 Dating *Resurrection of the Daleks* (21.3) - The Doctor says it is "1984 – Earth". We never hear of the Duplicates again. In terms of this timeline, the Daleks are from 4590.

359 *The Gathering*. The "Verney" of Verney Feeds presumably refers to Tegan's grandfather from *The Awakening*.

360 Dating *Planet of Fire* (21.5) - Peri says she is due back at college in "the fall", which is "three months" away. There is nothing to suggest that the story isn't set in the year it was broadcast (1984). It can't take place before 1983, otherwise Turlough would return home while his past self was still in exile (*Mawdryn Undead*).

In *Timelash*, the Doctor threatens to take Peri back to "1985". The back cover of *The Reaping* specifies that Peri first met the Doctor on 9th May, 1984. *Peri and the Piscon Paradox* says that Peri first met the Doctor "twenty-five years" prior to 2009. *Timelink* preferred June 1984, based upon Peri's talk of her vacation time and exams. *About Time* suggested "1984?", and didn't argue the point beyond that.

Peri's step-father says they were on the island of Lanzarote, which is where filming took place. Yet Lanzarote was not on any ancient Greek trading routes, unlike the island in the story.

361 *Peri and the Piscon Paradox*

Trion, and confirmed that he never kept a diary – meaning the Advocate had faked one as a means of manipulating Matthew Finnegan.[362]

Anthony Chambers became undertaker of St Anne's Cemetery in Baltimore, and happened upon the Cyber-Leader from the far future there. The Cyber-Leader staged Chambers' brutal murder to catch the Doctor's interest. A local vagrant was blamed for the crime, even as Chambers' body was secretly Cyber-augmented.[363]

? 1984 - "Urban Myths"[364] -> Three agents of the Celestial Intervention Agency were infected by a strain of the Tule-Oz virus – which mucked up their memories, and caused them to think that the fifth Doctor and Peri had committed mass slaughter on the planet Poiti. The agents tracked the travellers to a restaurant on Earth and sought to kill them, but the Doctor and Peri served them the antidote throughout a multi-course meal.

1984 (August to September) - DOWNTIME[365] -> Victoria Waterfield now worked at the British Museum, and received a letter dated 8th May, 1984, saying she had been identified as a distant relative of Edward Waterfield, and was officially entitled to inherit his estate.

The Great Intelligence had retreated to the Det-Sen monastery. The monks there worked to keep its power contained, but increasingly fell under its influence. Victoria Waterfield, age 28, was mentally compelled to return to Det-Sen, thinking she was hearing her father crying out for

her. She encountered Professor Travers – unaware that he was dead and animated by the Great Intelligence – and arranged for him to return to the United Kingdom. Second Lieutenant Douglas Cavendish of the Virtual Ordnance Group at UNIT received a report dated 18th August, 1984, that the monastery had been destroyed in an explosion.

Frank Harris, Victoria's adoptive father, was headhunted to develop a plan to restock the North Sea with fish.

Three sub-species of Yeti had been identified, and a few hundred *Yeti Traversii* – a species akin to the bear family – were estimated to be living in the wild. In September 1984, Sarah Jane Smith met with her friend Charles Bryce at a London zoo event to promote the first birth of *Yeti Traversii* in captivity, per an agreement between China and Britain. The Prime Minister very awkwardly agreed to the Zoological Society director's suggestion that she hold the Yeti cub, which bit her. Sarah became alarmed upon briefly glimpsing Edward Travers, who was reported as having died nearly five years ago.

1984 (24th September) - THE REAPING[366] -> In Baltimore, news of Anthony Chambers' "murder" became public, and Peri arrived with the sixth Doctor to attend the man's funeral. She had been gone for four months. Peri's mother – Janine Foster – and Howard had divorced.

A Cyber-Leader from the far future, who had arrived two years before, attempted to compel the Doctor to pilot his acquired time-ship back to prehistoric Earth, and to retroactively initiate the conversion of humanity into

362 "Final Sacrifice". There's no indication of how much time, for Turlough, has passed since *Planet of Fire*. It's possible that they visit him on the alt-Trion he relocates to in *Turlough and the Earthlink Dilemma*.

363 Three months before *The Reaping*, set in September 1984.

364 Dating "Urban Myths" (BF #95b) - The story takes place at an Earth restaurant (probably in Hungary, owing to mention of the invention of goulash); the dating is unknown. The only real clue is that a restaurant has operated "since the time of the Hapsburgs", ruling out anything beyond the mid-twenty-second century (when the Dalek Invasion would undoubtedly interrupt service). The choice of dating this story to 1984 – contemporary with the fifth Doctor and Peri's adventures on TV – is arbitrary. It could also be concurrent with the release of "Urban Myths" in 2007.

365 Dating *Downtime* (MA #18) - This is "1984" (p22). The film version of *Downtime* has Victoria visit the monastery "fifteen years" before 1995, probably in accordance with Professor Travers being listed as dead in 1980. The book establishes that the older monk that Victoria meets (played by James Bree in the film) is Thomni, seen as a young man in *The Abominable Snowmen*. It's been "ten years" since *Fury from the Deep*.

366 Dating *The Reaping* (BF #86) - The date is given.

Miami Vice is touted as a new show, and it debuted on 16th September, 1984, about a week before *The Reaping* begins.

367 *The Gathering*

368 Dating *The Zygon Who Fell to Earth* (BF BBC7 #2.6) - The date is given. The Doctor's mention of "another lot" of nineteenth-century Zygons "down south" is probably a reference to *The Bodysnatchers*.

369 Dating *Turlough and the Earthlink Dilemma* (*The Companions of Doctor Who* #1) - The story opens some months after Turlough has left the TARDIS. According to p193, it is relative Trion date 17,883 when Turlough arrives on Trion.

370 Dating "The Fires Down Below" (*DWM* #64) - A caption says it is "1984".

371 Dating *TimeH: The Winning Side* (TimeH #1) - "1984" is printed on the cover, and Honoré and Emily find a "four year old" (p45) newspaper dated "2 March 1980" (p35).

372 *Iris S5: Comeback of the Scorchies*

373 *TW: Forgotten Lives*, in "the 80s".

374 "Thirty years" before *UNIT S2: Shutdown*.

375 *WM: The Heavenly Paradigm*

376 Dating *Attack of the Cybermen* (22.1) - Mondas' attack is in "1986", which the hired gun Griffiths confirms is "next year".

Cybermen. The Doctor deposited the Cyber-Leader on the contemporary Mondas, where the indigenous Cybermen viewed the Leader as defective and scheduled him for reprocessing.

In the course of this investigation, the media branded the Doctor as a dangerous criminal. The Cyber-augmented Anthony Chambers went dormant, but not before grievously wounding his own son Nate.

Peri decided to leave the Doctor, live with her mother and enrol at university. However, she kept half of a Cyber-conversion egg as a memento. The device exploded, killing Janine Foster and her friend, Mrs Van Gysegham. Peri resumed travelling with the Doctor.

After Janine died, Katherine Chambers took the other half of the Cyber-conversion egg and went into hiding with her crippled brother. She had studied medicine at Boston, and a colleague of hers from university – James Clarke – helped them relocate to Brisbane. Kathy finished her education and became a doctor, but Nate's condition worsened and she turned him into a pseudo-Cyberman.[367]

1984 - THE ZYGON WHO FELL TO EARTH[368] -> As a
result of the Zygon scheme to boost global warming, CDs had been manufactured to emit invisible gas when they were played.

Along with her Zygon husband Trevor, Lucie Miller's Aunty Pat was now running a hotel – the Bygones Guest House – near Lake Grasmere. Trevor's Skarasen had chewed a tunnel between Allswater and Grassmere, under the mountains; the creature was glimpsed from time to time, boosting the tourist trade.

Three members of Trevor's crew tracked down their former leader, and retrieved their stolen crystal lattice which – as the product of organic crystallography – had bonded to Patricia's flesh. They tore it away, killing her. Trevor ordered his Skarasen to attack the Zygons' spaceship. The Skarasen, the crew and the spaceship were all destroyed in an explosion.

Lucie thought Trevor had died, and was unaware that her Aunty Pat had perished. Trevor shapeshifted one last time, and assumed his late wife's form. In the decades to come, "he" fulfilled history by masquerading as the Aunty Pat that Lucie had grown up with. The eighth Doctor knew about the deception.

> **= c 1984 (winter) - TURLOUGH AND THE EARTHLINK DILEMMA**[369] -> On Trion, the dictator Rehctaht fell from power, and the exiled Clansmen – including Turlough – returned home to a hero's welcome. Turlough used his knowledge of TARDISes to build the first-ever ARTEMIS drive, a time-travel device that used "muon" particles. On New Trion, Turlough discovered a copy of an alien edifice named

the Mobile Castle, and equipped it with a second ARTEMIS drive. The in-flight Castle was sabotaged and crashed onto Trion, destroying the planet. Earth and New Trion were subsequently annihilated in nuclear conflicts.

Turlough discovered that Rehctaht had transferred her mind into the body of his old friend Juras Maateh, and had engineered Earth, Trion and New Trion's obliteration to further her gravity control experiments, hoping to gain the secret of time travel. Turlough killed Rechtaht/Juras, then travelled back in time to prevent this history from occurring.

1984 - "The Fires Down Below"[370] -> Lethbridge-Stewart sent Major Whitaker of UNIT to Reykjavik to investigate an unnatural increase in volcanic activity. The UNIT troops discovered a squad of Quarks planting seismic charges. A member of the party, Professor Iskander, learned that the Dominators were planning to destroy Earth to extract its core for fuel. The UNIT troops attacked, then escaped as the Dominators' machines exploded and destroyed the aliens.

> **(=) 1984 - TIMEH: THE WINNING SIDE**[371] -> Honoré Lechasseur and Emily Blandish visited a parallel timeline where the release of nuclear secrets in 1949 had caused a massive suppression of education, schools, libraries and scientists, and a single Party had uncontested political power.

1985

Iris Wildthyme became smitten with one-hit wonder Brian Bonamy, who wandered into her bus by mistake. She poured him a drink, he sang her a song and good times ensued.[372]

As a boy, Rhys Williams drove many routes with his Uncle Mike, who inspired him to get into haulage. They enjoyed stopping at Hot Buns, which served the best butty bun in North Wales.[373] UNIT took possession of an alien holographic thought projector that fell to Earth.[374]

The War Master advised that one should never order coffee in England until at least the mid-1980s.[375]

1985 - ATTACK OF THE CYBERMEN[376] -> The police
had been aware of Lytton, a sophisticated thief who had stolen valuable electronic components, for a year. Lytton had discovered the Cybermen were operating in the sewers of London and was trying to contact them. The Cybermen tried, but failed, to divert Halley's Comet so that it would crash into Earth and avert the destruction of Mondas in 1986.

The Cybermen captured Lytton and lured the sixth Doctor and Peri to Telos in the future.

c 1985 - THE TWO DOCTORS[377] -> Some years ago, the Doctor had officially represented the Time Lords at the opening of space station Chimera in the Third Zone. Now a renegade, his second incarnation – accompanied by Jamie – was sent to the station by the Time Lords. Experiments conducted by professors Kartz and Reimer were registering 0.4 on the Bocca Scale, and could potentially threaten the stability of space-time.

Before the Doctor could finish lodging a protest with the Head of Projects – his old friend, Joinson Dastari – a Sontaran attack devastated the station. The Third Zone had been betrayed by Chessene of the Franzine Grig, an Androgum that Dastari had technologically augmented.

The Doctor was captured and taken to Seville by one of Chessene's Sontaran allies, Major Varl. He was joined by Group Marshall Stike of the Ninth Sontaran Attack Group. The Sontarans wanted Dastari to operate on the Doctor and discover the means by which Time Lords had a symbiotic relationship with their travel capsules. They hoped to create a time capsule for use against the Rutan in the Madillon Cluster.

The sixth Doctor and Peri traced his earlier self to Seville, which he had visited before. He helped to rescue his former self and defeat the Sontaran plan. Chessene, Dastari and the Sontarans all died.

The sixth Doctor dropped Peri off on Earth in 1985. She didn't expect to see him again.[378]

1985 - "Kane's Story"[379] -> The sixth Doctor and Frobisher went to New York and met up with Peri, who rejoined the TARDIS crew.

(=) 1985 - THE ELEVENTH DOCTOR YEAR THREE[380] -> While traversing the decades back to 1968, the eleventh Doctor, Alice and Kushak paused in Muswell Hill, London. They quickly left to avoid a militarized group of locals: the Eighty-Fivers.

A Zygon spaceship exploded, stranding Commander Kritakh and his second, Torlakh, on Earth. They assumed human form, and set about committing industrial espionage to increase Earth's greenhouse gas emissions. If successful, Earth would become as warm as the Zygon homeworld.[381] The third Doctor and Jo met an N-form in Tranquilandia the time they met the drug baron Gomez.[382] SeneNet acquired a Sontaran Mezon rifle.[383]

---

377 Dating *The Two Doctors* (22.3) - The story is contemporary, but there is no indication exactly which year it takes place.

378 This occurs in an unrecorded adventure before "Kane's Story", and we don't learn why she left.

379 Dating "Kane's Story" (*DWM* #104) - A caption says it's "1985".

PERI LEAVES AND CAUSES CONTINUITY PROBLEMS, TAKE ONE: When Peri joined the sixth Doctor and Frobisher's adventures in the comic strip, it created a mild continuity headache. While we never saw her leave, she rejoins in "Kane's Story" when the Doctor and Frobisher pick her up in New York. She's settled down and just quit (another) job there, and it's not even established whether she recognises Frobisher.

So far, so simple. We know from *The Trial of a Time Lord* that there are big gaps in the sixth Doctor's recorded adventures. So, at some point after *Revelation of the Daleks*, Peri leaves the Doctor, who goes on to meet Frobisher in "The Shape Shifter" before meeting up with his old companion again. No matter how one plays the cards here (or invokes the multiple Peris established in *Peri and the Piscon Paradox*), Peri must meet Frobisher for the first time in "Kane's Story". She's then present until the end of the sixth Doctor's *DWM* run in "The World Shapers", which then leads into *The Trial of a Time Lord* and her televised departure. This is even supported by the way Peri switches, during the course of the comic strip, from wearing her Season 22 leotards to her more tailored look of Season 23.

In *Planet of Fire*, Peri said she would travel with the Doctor for "three months". This line was forgotten about on television, but perhaps she was true to her word and left the Doctor as planned. This could still be after *Revelation of the Daleks* – although *Attack of the Cybermen* and *Timelash* both have the "present day" as 1985, not 1984.

380 Dating *The Eleventh Doctor Year Three* (Titan 11th Doc #3.3-3.4, "The Tragical History Tour") – The year is given.

381 Specified by Torlakh as "eighteen friggin years" prior to *Zygon: When Being You Isn't Enough*. Torlakh's plan is basically identical to that of the Zygons in *The Zygon Who Fell to Earth*.

382 *Damaged Goods*

383 *Business Unusual* (p244).

384 *The Gallifrey Chronicles*

385 "About fifteen years" before *Excelis Rising*.

386 "Two years" after *Return of the Living Dad* (p98).

387 *Invasion of the Cat-People* (p46). This matches the Tarot deck's real-world release in 1985. Kuykendall died in 1998.

388 *Maker of Demons*

389 When Ace was "14" (p89) according to *Timewyrm: Revelation*. Chess is the son of Ian and Barbara (the "Chess" moniker is apparently short for "Chesterton").

390 *Interference* (Book Two, p157).

391 *The Left-Handed Hummingbird* (p100).

392 "About a year ago" (p129) and "last year" (p115) according to *Father Time* (p129).

> = Fitz saw the Beatles perform at Live Aid in a parallel universe.[384]

On the planet Artaris, the immortal Grayvorn kept shifting identities and rose to the rank of Reeve, becoming known as Reeve Maupassant.[385] A virus on Lalanda 21185 created hundreds of thousands of zombies.[386] Artist Karen Kuykendall created the Tarot of the Cat-People.[387]

Dorothy McShane was terribly excited when *Teen Beat* printed a picture of her idol, pop star Johnny Chess, with his shirt off[388], but was disillusioned upon actually meeting the man.[389]

During the mid-eighties, Carol Bell worked for an arms manufacturer, watching SF films to inspire the creation of new weapons.[390] She had attained the rank of captain during her time with UNIT, but was rendered brain-damaged in a car accident.[391]

@ Iris Wildthyme visited the eighth Doctor and Miranda and tried (unsuccessfully) to explain the gaps in his memories. That year, the Doctor won the London Marathon.[392] The eighth Doctor was offered a chair at Cambridge, but declined as he was dedicated to looking after Miranda.[393]

@ c 1985 (spring) - FATHER TIME[394] -> Sallak escaped from prison and summoned his people, the Klade, from the far future. Ferran, brother of Zevron, arrived through a time corridor in an abandoned tower block in a northern city. Ferran and Sallak killed the comatose Barry Castle as revenge for Zevron's death, then set their sights on the eighth Doctor and Miranda.

Ferran became enamoured of Miranda and explained her alien heritage to her, but the Doctor sent him back to the far future. Miranda shot and killed Sallak, then went on the run.

Mr Wynter negotiated the price per kilo as part of a deal to fund the Contras, then bumped a rail up his nose while they mowed down their enemies with the weapons their money had purchased.[395] The eleventh Doctor visited a Little Green Storage facility on the Isle of Dogs.[396] Raine Creevy went to King's University College.[397]

1985 (12th December) - "Skywatch-7"[398] -> A Zygon attacked Skywatch-7, a UNIT radar station in the Arctic. The UNIT staff saw it off, and the intruder died after falling into frozen water.

1986

Martha Jones, a companion of the tenth Doctor, was born in 1986.[399] Shifting timelines caused Iris' friend Panda to become reborn as Arthur Christmas Bayer, a 6'2" man living in Soho. As a young man, Bayer wrote fantastical stories about travelling the universe in a double-decker red bus, but grew up and let such tales recede into the back of his memory.[400]

In 1986, Toshiko Sato moved back to the UK from Japan.[401] Matthew Hatch was exposed to the power of the Jack i' the Green and started planning to release him.[402] On 28th January, 1986, the *Challenger* exploded.[403] Zeus spacecraft started being launched early in 1986.[404]

On the 26th April, 1986, a strange light shone over Takhail in the USSR – radiation from the Chernobyl disaster irradiated 11-year-old Piotr Arkady, and killed everyone else in the village.[405]

Henry John Parker went into seclusion.[406] In 1986, two students were incinerated while exploring a house in the "haunted" Tretarri in Cardiff.[407] When Owen Harper was six, he went to see his piano teacher after Christmas... only to discover the man had died, and been eaten by his cats.[408] The sixth Doctor insisted that his coat was the

---

393 *Mad Dogs and Englishmen* (p23).
394 Dating *Father Time* (EDA #41) - The date is never specified beyond "the mid-eighties" and there are a couple of (deliberate) references to keep the dating vague, such as one to Guns N' Roses. It is "five years" after part one of the story.
395 *TW: The Men Who Sold the World*, presumably in reference to the Iran-Contra affair of the mid-80s.
396 *Borrowed Time*. It's "about 1985, just a year before the Big Bang changed the regulation of the London stock market" (on 27th October, 1986).
397 *Animal*, extrapolating from Raine's birth year of 1967 (*Thin Ice*).
398 Dating "Skywatch-7" (*DWM* #58, *DWM Winter Special 1981*) - The date is given in the caption running across the top of the first page.
399 *Wooden Heart*, although *The Torchwood Archives*

(BBC) says she was born on 14th September, 1984. Freema Agyeman was born on 20th March, 1979.
400 "Over twenty years" before *Iris S5: Looking for a Friend*.
401 *TW: Greeks Bearing Gifts*
402 *The Hollow Men*. Hatch is "fourteen" (p79) when this occurs.
403 *Return of the Living Dad* and *Father Time*. The space shuttle is never mentioned in a television story, and *The Tenth Planet* depicts an international space programme of a far greater extent than the real 1986.
404 *ST: "Mondas Passing"*. *The Tenth Planet* features a Zeus 4 capsule.
405 "Black Destiny"
406 *TW: A Day in the Death*
407 *TW: The Twilight Streets*
408 *TW: "The Legacy of Torchwood One!"*

height of fashion.[409]

When books in the TARDIS library became possessed, a copy of the 1986 *Bash Street Kids* annual with banana-sized teeth attacked the twelfth Doctor's companion, Hattie Monroe.[410] In July 1986, the wreck of the *Titanic* was discovered.[411]

At university, Melanie Bush dated an engineering student, Stuart Dale, for more than two years. Their relationship ended when he accepted work in the Middle East, and she declined to relocate.[412]

= The Valeyard prevented a police car from killing Ellie Martin on the A-303, and accepted her as his companion.[413]
---

c 1986 - HARRY SULLIVAN'S WAR[414] **->** Surgeon-Commander Harry Sullivan was reassigned to a NATO chemical weapons centre on the island of Yarra, and researched the lethal toxin Attila 305. He found a nykor inhibitase that showed great promise in both curing infertility and providing an antidote to the toxin.

Led by Zbigniew Brodsky, a terrorist group named the European Anarchist Revolution stole three ampules of the toxin. Harry exposed his department head, Conrad Gold, as being part of the conspiracy. Brodsky's group was using the Van Gogh Appreciation Society as a front for its operations, and French authorities rounded up the terrorists during the Society's annual meeting at the Eiffel Tower.

Harry celebrated his forty-first birthday.

c 1986 - THE NIGHTMARE FAIR[415] **->** The Celestial Toymaker set up operations in Blackpool, and manufactured video games that manifested monsters to kill the game-players when they lost. He intended to mass produce the games, but also sought to revenge himself upon the Doctor, and drew the TARDIS to Blackpool. The sixth Doctor and Peri imprisoned the Toymaker in a holofield that was powered by the Toymaker's own mind, and would keep him looped in time for the rest of his life. The Doctor made plans to transport the bubbled Toymaker to somewhere that he wouldn't be noticed.

The Ventusans served as mechanics at this time, and kept half the spacefleets in the galaxy running. A replica of Blackpool was being built out by the Crab Nebula – but to the Doctor's horror, it was, compared to the genuine article, being built for a *purpose*. The Pathfinders serving in an entirely pointless galactic war were now part of the Third Federation Force for Peace.

(=) 1986 - "Time Bomb"[416] **->** The sixth Doctor and Frobisher went to pick up Peri in New York... but discovered that the Hedron interference two hundred million years ago had disrupted history. Humankind never evolved, and dinosaur men ruled the Earth.
---

c 1986 - CD,NM V2: THE CARRIONITE CURSE[417] **->** A group of Carrionites manipulated authorities in the Midlands to build a 14-sided room, as equipped with stones from the original Globe Theatre, to help them manifest in our reality. The sixth Doctor failed to stop

409 "Four hundred and fifty years" after 1536, i.e. 1986, according to *Recorded Time and Other Stories*: "Recorded Time". Mind you, the Doctor doesn't say that his coat was fashionable *on Earth*.
410 *The Shining Man* (ch13).
411 *The Left-Handed Hummingbird* (p261).
412 *The Blood Furnace*.
413 *Unbound: He Jests at Scars...*, assuming that Ellie's native time is contemporaneous with the broadcast of *The Trial of a Time Lord*.
414 Dating *Harry Sullivan's War* (*The Companions of Doctor Who* #2) - It is "ten years" since Harry left UNIT, and so placing this story is subject to UNIT dating. It's clearly set in the mid-nineteen eighties.
415 Dating *The Nightmare Fair* (BF LS #1.1) - The story was written for Season 23, and intended for broadcast in 1986. It's "about a hundred years" after *The Talons of Weng-Chiang*. 1778 was "over two hundred years ago".
416 Dating "Time Bomb" (*DWM* #114-116) - The caption reads "Earthdate 1986". The dinosaur men are not Silurians.
417 Dating *CD,NM V2: The Carrionite Curse* (*CD,NM* #2.2) - The blurb says it's "the 1980s".
418 *The Caretaker, Dark Water, Death in Heaven*. The day

was, obviously, chosen to reflect the first broadcast of *Doctor Who* in 1963; actress Jenna Coleman was born 27th April, 1986. In *The Bells of Saint John* (set in 2013), Clara's handwritten notes in her copy of *101 Places to See* indicate her age as 24, but there's previous gaps in her tally, so we might imagine that she hasn't updated the book to her current age of 27.
419 Dating *The Tenth Planet* (4.2) - A calendar gives the date as "December 1986". This is the clearest example so far of real life catching up with "futuristic" events described in the series, but in *Attack of the Cybermen* (broadcast in 1985), the date of "1986" for this story was reaffirmed. *Radio Times* and publicity material at the time gave the date as "the late 1980s", as did the second edition of *The Making of Doctor Who*. The draft script set the date as "2000 AD", as did Gerry Davis' novelisation. (The book followed a draft of the story rather than the broadcast version, as the draft included more scenes with the Doctor.)

The Making of Doctor Who (first edition) also used the "2000" date. The first two editions of *The Programme Guide* set the range as "1975-80". This confused the American *Doctor Who* comic, which decided that *The Tenth Planet* must precede *The Invasion* and both were

them, but a local woman, Katy Bell, became linked to the Carrionites and incinerated herself to destroy them.

Clara Oswald, a companion of the eleventh and twelfth Doctors, was born 23rd November, 1986, to David James Oswald and Elena Alison Oswald. She was raised in Blackpool.[418]

Mondas Perishes While Attacking Earth, the First Doctor Regenerates

1986 (December) - THE TENTH PLANET[419] -> Technological developments continued on Earth. The Z-Bomb and Cobra missiles had been developed, and Zeus spaceships (launched on Demeter rockets) carried out manned missions to the moon as well as close-orbital work. Zeus 4's mission was to monitor weather and cosmic rays. Space missions were controlled from the South Pole base (callsign: "Snowcap"). The space programme was now an international effort with Americans, Australians, British, Italians, Spaniards, Swiss and Africans manning Snowcap. International Space Command and its Secretary General, Wigner, controlled the programme from Geneva.

In late 1986, "the tenth planet" appeared in the skies of the southern hemisphere. This was Mondas, the homeworld of the Cybermen. The first Doctor, Ben and Polly were present at Snowcap as Mondas attempted to drain Earth's energy, but absorbed too much and was destroyed.

1986 (December) – THE DOCTOR FALLS / TWICE UPON A TIME[420] -> The mortally wounded twelfth Doctor arrived at the South Pole and met the dying first Doctor; both of them held their regenerations at bay. The presence of two dying Doctors created a timeline whirlpool that drew Captain Archibald Lethbridge-Stewart to this era from 1914. A Testimony spaceship arrived to return Archibald to his appointed death, but the Doctors, Archibald and a Testimony avatar of Bill Potts escaped in the first Doctor's TARDIS. They went to consult the biggest database ever made, billions of years in the future...

Convinced that he could not avoid his own demise, the first Doctor returned to this era and let his regeneration occur.

The first Doctor temporarily fell unconscious during the Snowcap crisis owing to Steven Taylor's telescope drawing his mind through space-time to the future.[421] The first Doctor's body was so aged, it had worn out. The disembodied Oliver Harper used the last of his essence to manifest one final time – as the weakened Doctor stood in the TARDIS doorway, he spotted Oliver and gave a little wave before entering.[422]

Aided by Ben and Polly, the first Doctor entered the TARDIS console room and was "renewed" into a new body.[423]

Tobias Vaughn recovered the bodies of the Cybermen from Snowcap.[424] Cybermen who had crashed in the South Pole – remnants of an earlier, failed invasion – located and adapted Cyber technology from the 1986 incursion.[425] After Mondas' destruction, a surviving group of Cybermen settled on the planet Lonsis.[426] Some Demeter rockets and their Z-bombs were sent off into space during an era of disarmament and peacemaking.[427]

In the late nineteen-eighties, archaeologist Peter Warmsley began excavating a site associated with King Arthur on the edge of Lake Vortigern near Carbury.[428]

Ace did work experience at an old folks home. She worked in McDonald's on weekends.[429] She kicked a time-lost and penniless Tegan out of the establishment, failing to realise they would later have something in common.[430]

---

set in "the 1980s". John Peel's novelisation of *The Power of the Daleks* set the preceding story in "the 1990s".
420 Dating *The Doctor Falls* and *Twice Upon a Time* (X10.12, X10.13) - The epilogue to *The Doctor Falls* and the 1986 components of *Twice Upon a Time* take place within *The Tenth Planet* episode four, as the first Doctor returns to the TARDIS ahead of Ben and Polly.
421 *1stD V1: The Locked Room*. The author of this story, Simon Guerrier, commented: "In my head, *The Locked Room* explains why the Doctor collapses in *The Tenth Planet* episode three, but I left off being too explicit so people could make up their own minds about it."
422 *The First Wave*
423 *The Tenth Planet*, *The Power of the Daleks*. The term

"regeneration" isn't used until *Planet of the Spiders*.
424 *Original Sin*
425 *Iceberg*
426 *Human Resources*
427 *The Wheel of Ice* (p241), following up on the ballistic missiles seen in *The Tenth Planet*. As Z-bombs are powerful enough to destroy planets, this seems a fairly stupid thing to do, even if it happened before humanity realizes that aliens are real (*Aliens of London*).
428 "Ten years" before *Battlefield*.
429 *Matrix*
430 During *The Crystal Bucephalus*.

1986 (31st December) - ST:"Mondas Passing"[431] ->
Decades after she left the TARDIS, Polly Wright had married a man named Simon; they had a son named Mikey. Ben Jackson had also married. On the last day of 1986, Ben and Polly met in a hotel room to commemorate Mondas' passing, and their involvement in it with the Doctor. Despite the temptation, they kept their relationship platonic. News reports, presumably as part of a cover-up, had failed to mention Mondas' approach to Earth.

1987

Rose Tyler, a companion of the ninth and tenth Doctors, was born on 27th April, 1987.[432] Katherine Costello Wainright (formerly Kathy Nightingale) died the same year.[433] Petronella Osgood, a UNIT operative and associate of the eleventh and twelfth Doctors, was born.[434]

The Johnny Chess album *Things to do on a Wet Tuesday Night* was released in 1987.[435] In the same year, Jason Kane's sister Lucy was born.[436] SeneNet begin developing their Maxx games.[437]

@ In 1987, the Doctor was accidentally responsible for releasing a breed of talking wild boar into the wild.[438] In 1987, the UK government tested an alien device on the village of Rawbone, and made everyone there sterile. The town was gradually isolated from the outside world.[439] Sarah Jane profiled Dr Francis Augur for *Metropolitan* magazine in 1987.[440]

The Headhunter, now allied with the spiders on Metebelis III, planted some Metebelis crystals in Yorkshire in 1987. A potholer, Clark Goodman, found the crystals, and the spiders implanted beliefs in his mind. Goodman founded a self-help organisation – "The Eightfold Truth" - and sent its members to locate more of the crystals. The group would, unknowingly, spend eighteen years facilitat-

---

431 Dating *ST: "Mondas Passing"* (BBC *ST* #1.8) – It's "New Year's Eve", 1986. Ben and Polly here meet to commemorate the concurrent events of *The Tenth Planet*, but Ben concedes that he doesn't know the exact date, as the calendar at Snowcap base wasn't more specific than it being "December". *The Outliers* dramatises a small portion of this story. Big Finish accounts for "Mondas Passing" in its narrative that Ben and Polly get married much later in life (*ST: Past Tense*: "That Time I Nearly Destroyed the World Whilst Looking for a Dress", *The Five Companions*, etc.). The idea that a cover-up silenced news reports of Mondas threatening Earth (see When Do the General Public Accept the Existence of Aliens?) is a bit hard to swallow – in *The Tenth Planet*, news reports very clearly detail that a second planet is encroaching upon Earth's orbit.

Alternatively, "The Love Invasion" shows the ninth Doctor and Rose running past a young man proposing to a young woman – they look suspiciously like Ben and Polly, but they're not named, and it's treated like an Easter Egg rather than hard fact, so we can set that development aside.

432 This date is given in the Writers' Guide and in an article written by Russell T. Davies in the *2006 Doctor Who Annual*. However, Rose is "19" according to the Doctor in *The Unquiet Dead* and *Army of Ghosts*, when she really ought to be 18. It's said in *Rise of the Cybermen* that Rose was "six months" when her father died, which would fit her written birthday of 27th April and the dating of *Father's Day* to 7th November.

433 According to Kathy's tombstone as seen in *Blink*. Her handwritten letter to Sally seems to be dated "7th February, 1987".

434 *UNIT S2: Shutdown* presumes that Osgood is a lot younger than the actress who plays her (Ingrid Oliver, who was born in 1977), hence Osgood's remark about alien technology that tell to Earth "thirty years" ago,

"before [she] was born".
435 *The Also People*
436 *Death and Diplomacy*. Jason was "nearly 13" when Lucy was "nine" (p150).
437 "Two years" before *Business Unusual*.
438 *Mad Dogs and Englishmen*
439 *TW: First Born*
440 *SJA: The Glittering Storm*
441 *The Eight Truths, Worldwide Web*.
442 *The Room with No Doors*
443 *Crime of the Century*
444 *Benny: Nobody's Children*
445 *The Silurian Candidate*
446 The background to *We are the Daleks*, and a rather obvious shot across the bow at the results of the UK election on 11th June, 1987, in which the Conservative Party won a 102-seat majority.
447 Dating *Damaged Goods* (NA #55) - The date "17 July 1987" is given (p8).
448 Dating *The Wrong Doctors* (BF #169) - The year is given. It's specified (both within and without the time pocket) as summer. Margaret Thatcher is "starting" her third term in office – she won that election on 11th June, 1987. There is remarkably little contradiction between this story and *Business Unusual* in terms of when/how the sixth Doctor "first" meets Mel, save that the blue-coated Doctor is reasonably pleased about the idea here, whereas the notion terrifies him in *Business Unusual* (because meeting Mel means that he's a step closer to a future in which he becomes the Valeyard; see *The Trial of a Time Lord*).
449 *Dragonfire* establishes much of Ace's background, with further details given in *Battlefield* and *The Curse of Fenric*. She first returns to Perivale in *Survival*.

The tie-in stories offer more detail. The timestorm was in 1987 according to *Timewyrm: Revelation* (p70) and *Independence Day* (she saw *Withnail and I* a few

ing the spiders' plan to conquer thousands of worlds.[441] The eighth Doctor visited Little Caldwell and met Joel Mintz.[442]

Colonel Felnikov of the Soviet Union engineered the 1987 recession as a means of attacking the West by destabilising its economy. Those in the know about this dubbed it The Crime of the Century. Felnikov's superiors lost too much money in the resultant economic bloodbath, and he was booted back to the Army.[443]

Benny had Isaac Summerfield babysit Peter in 1987 while she dealt with a quarrel between the Draconians and the Mim.[444] Mel Bush posed a credible threat to the reigning Pease Pottage roller disco champion.[445]

Daleks in the future facilitated the creation of a media conglomerate, the Zenos Corporation, on Earth. The Dalek-shaped Zenos Tower was built on Threadneedle Street in London as the company HQ. One of Zenos' holdings, UltraMega Tech, marketed *Warfleet*: an advanced console game that let players coordinate over phone modems, and embark on spaceship missions together. The players were unknowingly directing attacks by Dalek drone fleets. The Zenos Tower emanated hypno-rays that slowly altered the human mind, and a test-run of the system made the residents of the United Kingdom more agreeable to fascism.[446]

1987 (July) - DAMAGED GOODS[447] -> The seventh Doctor, Roz and Chris investigated the Quadrant, an area of tower blocks in an English city. An N-form, an ancient Gallifreyan weapons system, had occupied the body of drug dealer Simon "the Capper" Jenkins. The N-form was searching for vampires, per its programming, and sold contaminated coke that allowed it to manifest in the brains of anyone who took it. The N-form erupted and went on a killing spree, but the Doctor shut it down.

(=) 1987 (Summer) - THE WRONG DOCTORS[448] -> The Mardacs were an entire race devoted to one of the most deplorable occupations in the known universe: business consulting. They were originally purple-skinned, but a focus group liked gray better, so they bio-engineered themselves that shade instead.

The Time Demon who had adopted the form of Stapleton Petherbridge (1758-1812) and woven himself into Melanie Bush's lifetime via the lives of two other Pease Pottage residents – Jebediah Thurwell (1812-1884) and Muriel Wilberforce (1884-1964) – and created a pocket of cauterised time that contained a copy of Pease Pottage. Mel was currently off at university, but her future TARDIS travel had so criss-crossed her through the Vortex, the Demon viewed her as an ideal tool by which to sow chaos. The Demon uncoupled Mel from history, and used her brain's raw calculating power as a memory buffer

for his Alternate Timeline Control (ATC) device, which mapped out the past, present and alternate timelines of Pease Pottage.

The sixth Doctor, resplendent in his multi-coloured coat, opted against dropping Mel off at Oxyveguramosa (from which she had been spirited away, to testify at his trial on Gallifrey), and tried to leave her at Pease Pottage for his older self to collect. Meanwhile, an older sixth Doctor, resplendent in his blue coat, felt saddened because Evelyn Smythe had left his company, and decided he should finally meet his future companion Melanie Bush (from her perspective) for the "first" time. *Both* sixth Doctors (and one Mel) arrived in the cauterised-time Pease Pottage by accident, and met the younger Mel as well as Jebediah Thurwell and Muriel Wilberforce – whom the Demon had taken from their native times.

The Doctors discovered that the Demon intended to puncture the time pocket using a cache of Valanxium – an unstable element that decayed backwards through time – aboard a Mardac spaceship. Earth would have been repeatedly destroyed, enabling the Demon to feast on the resultant energy. The older Doctor and the younger Mel used the TAC to return Jebediah and Muriel home, weakening the Demon's connection to Mel's life and trapping him in a temporal cul de sac. The effort burnt out Mel's mind, killing her. The Valanxium explosion was contained, and the faux Pease Pottage harmlessly collapsed.

The younger sixth Doctor departed with his Mel. The older sixth Doctor used the TARDIS data banks and the ATC device to recreate Mel's history, restoring her to life in 1987 with no memory of these events. Because the younger Mel preferred his multi-coloured coat, the Doctor thought he should wear it again, in honour of her.

A Timestorm Whisks Ace Away to Svartos

Ace was now becoming a problem. She had sat her O-Levels, including French and Computer Studies, and was beginning to study for her A-Levels. But she was expelled from school for blowing up the Art Room using homemade gelignite – an event she described as "a creative act". Ace vanished one day in a timestorm whipped up by Fenric, following experiments in her bedroom that involved her trying to extract nitro-glycerine from gelignite. Ace's mother reported her missing, and her friends thought she was either dead or in Birmingham.[449]

1987 (Summer) - GODS AND MONSTERS[450] ->
Fenric briefly brought Ace back to Perivale, the day before a timestorm swept her younger self away to Svartos, as part of his efforts against Weyland. The two of them returned to the dawn of time.

1987 (October) - WE ARE THE DALEKS[451] -> The seventh Doctor and Mel investigated the Zenos Tower as its CEO, Alek Zenos, entertained power brokers such as Celia Dunthorpe, the MP for Pottersbridge. Alek told those assembled that the extraterrestrials backing Zenos Corp., the Daleks, wished to invest in the UK and make it Earth's top nation – a prelude to humanity engaging with the intergalactic market. To demonstrate the Daleks' goodwill, Alek took a party including Dunthorpe and Mel – who was posing as "Melanie Bush of Time and Related Disciplines Incorporated" – through a time corridor to Skaro...

The media widely reported Zenos' engagement to computer tech Melanie Bush: a message to the Doctor that he should surrender for Mel's sake. He did so, but rescued Mel from Skaro. The two of them wrested control of the *Warfleet* game system, enabling human players to rout Dalek forces in the future with drones. To disrupt the *Warfleet* players, the Daleks intensified the Zenos Tower's conditioning rays, influencing everyone in central London to become more wrathful. The Doctor and Mel used the Daleks' own time corridor to send the Zenos Tower to Skaro in the future, returning everyone to normal.

The Tower's sudden translocation altered weather patterns, creating the Great Storm of 1987. Zenos Corp's downfall triggered a stock market crash. An associate of Mel, Brinsley Heaton, wondered if the remaining *Warfleet* technology could be used to create a sort of Internet...

(=) 1987 (7th November) - FATHER'S DAY[452] ->
The ninth Doctor took Rose back to witness the death of her father, Peter Tyler, from a hit-and-run car accident. Rose saved her father's life, which

---

days before the timestorm occurred). She's from 1986 in *White Darkness* (p130) and *First Frontier* (p45). *Crime of the Century* establishes that Ace left Earth before Black Monday (19th October, 1987), and *Thin Ice* (BF) establishes that she doesn't know about such late-80s political elements as *glasnost*. *Gods and Monsters* has Fenric transport her back home the day before the timestorm, in "early summer of 1987".

450 Dating *Gods and Monsters* (BF #164) - Fenric tells Ace it's "an unseasonably sticky afternoon in the early summer of 1987. This time tomorrow, a timestorm will transport the younger you to Iceworld" (*Dragonfire*).

451 Dating *We are the Daleks* (BF #201) - The blurb gives the year. The Doctor tells Mel it's "1987, early October," to which Mel responds: "One year into my future" (in accordance with the broadcast year of Mel's first appearance in *Terror of the Vervoids*, but it's at odds with both *Business Unusual*, in which she's from 1989, and *The Wrong Doctors*, in which Mel is still on Earth, at university, in 1987). Events in *We are the Daleks* trigger the Great Storm of 1987 (which happened 15th-16th October) and the stock market crash dubbed Black Monday (19th October, 1987).

Although Mel's "engagement" to Alek Zenos is all over the news, it's not a detail she's seen to deal with in any other modern-day story.

452 Dating *Father's Day* (X1.8) - The date is given. The Reapers are not named on screen, but are named as such in the script.

453 The Powell Estate is cited in episodes such as *Aliens of London* and *Tooth and Claw*. Victor Kennedy specifies Rose and Jackie's address as "Bucknall House, No. 48" in *Love & Monsters*. The full address, with the post code, appeared in the *Doctor Who Annual 2006*.

454 "Twenty years" before *Iris S3: The Midwinter Murders*. Iris comments, on her dalliance with the dupli-

cating shapeshifter: "It was the 80s, Chuck."

455 *Brave New Town*

456 The Haisman Timeline, and not the Sam Bishop who appears in the *UNIT* audios.

457 *Leth-St*: "The Slow Invasion," "several years" after *The Five Doctors*.

458 *SJA: Death of the Doctor*. Date unknown, but actor Finn Jones, who played Santiago, was born in 1988.

459 *The Dying Days* (p94).

460 *Sky Pirates!* (p334).

461 *TW: Miracle Day*. He's born in 1912 and dies age 76, presuming the file on his adopted alias can be trusted.

462 *The Legends of River Song*: "Suspicious Minds". Donovan, an Australian singer and actor, joined the cast of *Neighbours* in 1986, started a music career in 1988.

463 Dating *The Company of Friends*: "Izzy's Story" (BF #123c) - The Doctor tells Izzy that they've arrived at "The village of Stockbridge, relative date: Friday, the 8th of April, 1988."

464 *J&L S3: Swan Song*

465 *UNIT S4: Assembled*

466 *Army of Ghosts*. Construction of the building began in 1988.

467 Twenty years before the Doctor kills the Captain, as related in *The Eyeless*.

468 *Worlds BF: The Phantom Wreck*

469 Dating "Time Bomb!" (*Death's Head* #8) - No year given, but the story was published in 1988, during the seventh Doctor's TV tenure. The Doctor here drops Death's Head at the headquarters of the Fantastic Four, opening the door to *Death's Head* comics set in the Marvel Universe.

470 Dating *Silver Nemesis* (25.3) - The first scene is set, according to the caption slide, in "South America, 22nd November 1988". The Doctor's alarm goes off the next day – although it is a beautiful sunny day.

altered history and created a "wound" in time. Winged creatures, the Reapers, converged on the wound to "sterilise" it by consuming every person on Earth. Humanity was eradicated on a large scale, but Peter acknowledged the historical deviation and sacrificed himself. Upon his death, time reverted to normal and the Reapers disappeared.

Outside the wedding of Stewart Hoskins and Sarah Clark, Peter Tyler died from a hit-and-run accident. An unnamed young woman stayed with him until the end.

Jackie and Rose continued to reside at Flat 48, Bucknall House, Powell Estate SE15 7GO.[453] During a weekend in Jersey, Iris Wildthyme enjoyed a threesome with a Krobian shapeshifter who duplicated himself. She met him again two decades on, after he'd adopted the guise of Inspector Nettles of Midwinter Leys.[454]

1988

Lucie Miller, a companion of the eighth Doctor and (briefly) the Monk, was born on 31st July, 1988.[455] Bill and Anne Bishop's son, Samuel, was born in 1988.[456] A portrait of Edward Travers hung in the National Portrait Gallery, despite his best efforts to have it taken down.[457]

Santiago, the grandson of Cliff and Jo Jones, was born in a caravan in the foothills of the Andes. He would never attend school, and instead travel the world with his parents while his advocacy-minded grandmother did such things as chain herself to the railings at a G8 Summit. Santiago's father would get arrested – twice – at a climate change conference.[458]

The eighth Doctor and Lethbridge-Stewart discovered the secret of the Embodiment of Gris in Hong Kong in 1988.[459] Benny accidentally had a comic commissioned while walking through the offices of an American comic book publisher, just because she had a British accent.[460] Victor Podesta, an associate of the Three Families who had adopted the name John Forester, died in La Boca, Argentina.[461]

Elvis, River Song's Auton boyfriend, had a brief spell where he posed as a Jason Donovan waxwork.[462]

1988 (8th April) - THE COMPANY OF FRIENDS: "Izzy's Story"[463] -> The eighth Doctor took Izzy to Grub and Sons newsstand in Stockbridge, as she knew that a prized copy of *Aggotron* #56 could be found there. The issue revealled the true face of Courtmaster Cruel, a vigilante magistrate, but all copies of it had mysteriously vanished afterwards. The travellers found Suits – the android henchlings of The Man, a villain from the comic – ruining every copy of #56 with their brolly guns.

At the *Aggotron* publication offices in Queenspoint

Spire, London, the Doctor and Izzy found that the comic's editor (known in print as "Grak, the Head-Swollen") and artists were aliens that had been censored from their native Smog Worlds, and had based many of the *Aggotron* characters on their native forms. They also confronted Derek Dell – a geek who'd adopted the Courtmaster's identity in the fifty-first century, but was so horrified upon learning that the original artwork to issue #56 rendered Courtmaster Cruel as a girl, he'd dispatched the Suits to destroy every copy. Izzy was similarly aghast at the revelation.

Dell, while trying to escape, was haphazardly flung through time. The Doctor relocated Grak and his artists back to the Smog Worlds, and *Aggotron* was merged into *Square Jaw*.

On 22nd May, 1988, an accident involving a Range Rover killed the parents of a young girl named Alice, and put her in a wheelchair for life.[464]

Jo Jones sailed down the Yangtzee in a tea chest, and also travelled to Lima by donkey. She also saved rare frogs from becoming smoothies in a street market, and had some difficulty with a toucan.[465]

A temporal breach was detected high above London. Torchwood constructed a huge skyscraper to enclose the breach; the building was privately known as Torchwood Tower, but publicly it served as Canary Wharf, a business development. Torchwood also used the facility as their main headquarters.[466]

The Steggosians, "a particularly nasty race of fascist dinosaur people", were all but wiped out by a plague that destroyed their immune systems. One patrol survived, its Captain driven mad by the death of his people. He would later encounter the Doctor in London.[467]

Chuckle Aid, a bi-annual charity event in the UK, was founded in 1988.[468]

c 1988 - "Time Bomb!"[469] -> When Death's Head arrived through time to murder him, the seventh Doctor – who was performing on stage as a jester – escaped as the front of a pantomime horse. The Doctor helped Death's Head to realise the duplicity of his employer, Dogbolter, and deal with him in the future...

> = Afterward, the Doctor left Death's Head in another reality, atop Four Freedoms Plaza.

1988 (22nd-23rd November) - SILVER NEMESIS[470] -> Thousands of Cyber-Warships massed in the solar system. A scouting party tried to recover the Validium asteroid, which had been launched from Earth two hundred and fifty years before. They wanted its power to make Earth into "New Mondas". The seventh Doctor and Ace kept the statue from falling into the hands of the Cybermen, the Lady Peinforte (a sorceress from 1638), and a group of Nazis hoping to create a new Reich. The villains all died in the process.

By the end of the Reagan administration, the US military had built Station Nine. This was a Top Secret satellite – so secret, in fact, that no President after Reagan would be told about it. Station Nine quietly remained in orbit, ready to fire intercepting Nuke Killer missiles that would nullify an oncoming nuclear attack.[471]

An unmanned lander sent from Earth to Mars recovered Martian DNA. Webster Corporation combined it with human DNA in the hopes of creating augmented soldiers, and the young Tanya Webster was born with Martian DNA in her system. Webster began developing a manned mission to Mars, hoping to recover more Martian DNA or a live Martian.[472] Sarah Jane Smith interviewed novelist Gregory P. Wilkinson for *Metropolitan* magazine.[473]

1989

Amelia Jessica Pond, a companion of the eleventh Doctor, was born in 1989 to Augustus and Tabitha Pond.[474] The same woman – Amelia "Amy" Williams (neé Pond) – died, age 87, and was buried with her husband, Rory.[475] Rory Williams, said future husband and a companion of the eleventh Doctor, was born.[476]

Kate Lethbridge-Stewart became estranged from her father, Brigadier Lethbridge-Stewart, and stopped speaking to him.[477] Tyler Steele, a yellow journalist and acquaintance of Torchwood, was born.[478]

Anne Bishop (née Travers) left the Home-Army Fifth Operational Corps in 1989. She continued travelling with her father, leaving Owain Vine's care to Elizabeth Shaw.[479] Her husband, William Bishop, was promoted to Lt Colonel, and made second-in-command of the Fifth Operational Corps.[480]

In Cardiff, the Ritz Dance Hall closed in 1989.[481]

Melanie Bush Joins the TARDIS

Melanie Bush joined the sixth Doctor after helping him prevent the Master and the Usurians taking over the world in 1989. She had recently turned down a job at I^2, but accepted one at Ashley Chapel Logistics.[482]

1989 (mid June) - BUSINESS UNUSUAL[483] **->** The sixth Doctor thwarted an attempt by the Master and his Usurian partners to devastate America's economy, but required a native computer expert to fully purge the conspirators' illicit programming. This led to the Doctor meeting computer programmer Melanie Bush, and she helped him erase the Master's programs.

---

471 *Option Lock*

472 "Eighteen years" before *Red Dawn*.

473 *SJA: Wraith World.* This happened "back in the 80s", but also "twenty years" before 2010.

474 Amy is repeatedly said to be seven when she meets the Doctor in *The Eleventh Hour*, set in Easter 1996. "Forever Dreaming" names her birth year as "1989", so she was evidently born before Easter. Her middle name is given in *The Beast Below*.

475 *The Angels Take Manhattan* (see the When Did Amy Pond and Rory Williams Die? sidebar).

476 A guess, based upon New *Who* portraying Rory and Amy as being in the same class in school (*Let's Kill Hitler*, etc.). Arthur Darvill, who played Rory, was born 17th June, 1982 – but once more, see the When Did Amy Pond and Rory Williams Die? sidebar.

477 "Six years" before *Downtime*.

478 The faux Gwen Cooper looks at Tyler and guesstimates, "What are you? Twenty eight?", in *TW: Aliens Among Us*.

479 *Leth-St: Moon Blink* (supplemental material).

480 The Haisman Timeline

481 *TW: Aliens Among Us 2*

482 Mel first appeared on television in *Terror of the Vervoids*, but the events of her joining the Doctor were shown in *Business Unusual*.

MEL'S FIRST ADVENTURE: The Writers' Guide for Season 23 suggested that Mel joined the Doctor after

an encounter with the Master, and this is echoed in the Missing Adventure *Millennial Rites* (p83). This appears to be contradicted by *The Ultimate Foe* when Mel fails to recognise the renegade Time Lord, but *Business Unusual* establishes that Mel didn't actually meet the Master on that occasion. The Writers' Guide also suggested that Mel had been travelling with the Doctor for "three months". It is entirely possible that Mel started her travels with the Doctor at the end of *The Ultimate Foe*, negating the need for a "first adventure", but this idea is riddled with paradoxes (i.e.: she is from her own future and would have memories of her first few adventures before she arrived).

The period set after *The Trial of a Time Lord*, but before the Doctor has his "first meeting" with Mel (in *Business Unusual*), is now brimming with book and audio adventures. These include the Doctor's time with companions Frobisher, Evelyn Smythe, Thomas Brewster, Charley Pollard (after she travelled with the eighth Doctor), Grant Markham (who only appeared in two Missing Adventures: *Time of Your Life* and *Killing Ground*), "Flip" Jackson, Jason and Crystal (*The Ultimate Adventure*) and a Land-of-Fiction version of Jamie McCrimmon.

In *Just War*, Mel says that she has never been to the past before, "only the future". Subsequent stories such as *Catch-1782* and "The Vanity Box" contradict this.

Millennial Rites and *Business Unusual* both have Mel

Martyn Townsend, the former director of the Vault, was now the Managing Director of SeneNet. The company officially specialised in computer game consoles, but fronted Townsend's ambitions to use Nestene technology to conquer Earth. Lacking the components to maintain his cybernetic body, Townsend kidnapped the telepathic Trey Korte in the hopes of mentally transferring his intelligence into a prosthetic form.

The Doctor's intervention resulted in SeneNet's destruction. Townsend died when falling rubble crushed him. The Auton-augmented twins Cellian and Ciara foreswore allegiance to Townsend and escaped. Melanie stowed away on the TARDIS and took up travelling with the Doctor.

The Brigadier, investigating SeneNet, met the sixth Doctor for the first time.

= With a quick alteration to a chance meeting in the street, the Valeyard prevented Melanie Bush from ever meeting the sixth Doctor. He hoped this would rid his existence of her friendship.[484]

= In an alternate universe where Rome never fell, the sixth Doctor lost his New World companion Brown Perpugilliam, and an eye, to the warlord Dominicus. He visited the scientist Praetor Linus to repair the TARDIS image translator, and took the slave Melina into his service.[485]

The sixth Doctor left Evelyn on Earth, and asked her to monitor the pseudo-Auton twins Cellian and Ciara for him. Evelyn came to discover that the Doctor had erroneously dropped her off in the late 1980s, meaning that her younger self was still teaching at Nottingham. She kept a low profile, fearful that she might run into herself, but used her foreknowledge to earn some money winning contests and betting pools.[486]

c 1989 - THE ULTIMATE ADVENTURE[487] -> Prime Minister Margaret Thatcher summoned the sixth Doctor and his companion Jason to Downing Street, and tasked them with looking after a US peace envoy trusted by the Russians and Chinese. Intelligence reports suggested that extraterrestrials hoped to disrupt an upcoming peace conference in London.

Mercenaries led by the evil Karl, as well as a squad of Cybermen, attacked a nightclub the envoy was attending and kidnapped him. The Doctor and Jason were joined by Crystal, a rising pop star performing at the club. They followed the kidnappers' energy trail to Altair III, where the mercenaries and Cybermen were allied with the Daleks and the Dalek Emperor.

The TARDIS went to a mercenary haunt on Centros, the Bar Galactica, where the Doctor consulted with its owner, Madame Delilah. After brief interludes involving a Dalek battlecruiser, a planet with low gravity and the French Revolution, the TARDIS returned to the Bar Galactica – where Delilah tried to hand the Doctor over to Karl and the Daleks for a million credit bounty. Delilah was exterminated, and Karl became so horrified that he killed two Daleks.

The Doctor and his friends went to Skaro to rescue the envoy, but the Emperor revealled that the Cybermen and mercenaries were fall-guys that the Galactic Council would blame for the planned destruction of Earth, not the Daleks. The Doctor sowed dissension among the Daleks' allies, pitting the three alien factions against one another.

The Doctor realised the Daleks had brainwashed the envoy into setting off a Dalekanium bomb that would destroy London and trigger war. The Doctor broke the envoy's conditioning, saving the world.

---

meeting the Doctor in 1989. She's from "1986" in *Head Games* (p154) and *The Quantum Archangel* (p17).
483 Dating *Business Unusual* (PDA #4) - The date is given (p15). From the sixth Doctor's perspective, he first meets the Brigadier circa 2000 in *The Spectre of Lanyon Moor*.
484 *Unbound: He Jests at Scars...*, playing off another Gary Russell story, *Business Unusual*.
485 *Spiral Scratch*. Linus is that universe's version of Bob Lines from *The Scales of Injustice*, *Business Unusual* and *Instruments of Darkness*.
486 *Instruments of Darkness*. On p93, Evelyn claims the Doctor dropped her off in 1988. The Doctor conferred with Evelyn off panel during the events of *Business Unusual*, set in June 1989.
487 Dating *The Ultimate Adventure* (BF stageplay adap-

tation #1) - This play was originally staged in 1989. The role of the Doctor was played by Jon Pertwee, then Colin Baker (who revived the role for the 2010 Big Finish version, which namechecks his companion Evelyn Smythe). It is set when Margaret Thatcher is Prime Minister; in real life, she served 1979-1990. The Dalek Emperor resembles the one from *The Evil of the Daleks* and is based at "Dalek HQ" on Skaro. The Doctor says of the Cybermen, "Only a few of you escaped" – there aren't enough of them to invade Earth, but it's not clear what they escaped from. They could be from Mondas, or possibly the base on the Moon referred to in *Attack of the Cybermen*. Both the Daleks and Cybermen involved may be time travellers.

c 1989 - BEYOND THE ULTIMATE ADVENTURE[488] ->
Karl the mercenary summoned the sixth Doctor, Jason and Crystal back to the Bar Galactica for Madame Delilah's funeral, and to impart information she had possessed about Ultimate Thule: a realm outside of time and space, said to contain great treasure and a threat to the universe. The four of them went there, and defeated the Eidolon with help from the Time Lords.

In 1989, the Ritz dance hall in Cardiff ceased operation.[489] The sixth Doctor planted a mattress in Perivale – he'd later land on it while confronting the Master...[490]

c 1989 (Sunday) - SURVIVAL[491] -> In a relatively short span of time, several residents in Perivale vanished without trace, abducted by the Cheetah People. Their planet was dying, and they were preparing to move on to new feeding grounds. The Tremas Master was trapped on the planet, and lured the seventh Doctor and Ace there to aid in his escape. As the Doctor and the Master fought, the Cheetah People vanished. The Master also disappeared.

As the Cheetah Planet exploded, the Tremas Master went back to Earth. A surfeit of artron energy in the atmosphere diverted him to 1957.[492]

The Star Jumpers, a band including Johnny Chess, were a success. They made the albums *Circle Circus*, *Modernism*, *Can Anyone Tell Me Where the Revolution Is?*, and one other before splitting. InterCom were working on a means of

splicing alien DNA into humans to create a slave race. UNIT operatives Geoff Paynter and Paul Foxton infiltrated Black Star terrorists based in Baghdad, but Foxton was killed.[493] The science-fiction series *Professor X* was cancelled after more than twenty-five years on TV. Dave Young, Anji Kapoor's future boyfriend, played a Cybertron in one of the last episodes.[494]

1989 (summer) to 1990 (August) - "Business as Usual"[495] -> Winston Blunt discovered some strange meteorites. Overnight, the former plumber became a wealthy plastics magnate and set up Galaxy Plastics, but he killed himself after handing over the business to a Mr Dolman. A year later, a rival company sent Max Fischer to investigate Galaxy Plastics, and he discovered that the Autons were running it. Dolman accidentally set off an explosion while trying to kill Fischer – who escaped, pursued by living toy soldiers. Dolman was damaged but murdered Fischer, and a replica of Fischer went on to open Stellar Plastics.

Raine Creevy Joins the TARDIS

1989 (October) - CRIME OF THE CENTURY[496] -> The Polyglot 7 (third release), one of the worst translation devices in the galaxy, was recalled. It was, however, equipped to translate Dolphin, as they were one of the few sentient species on planet Earth.

The seventh Doctor read the diary of Raine Creevy, who had become an accomplished cat burglar, and so was wait-

488 Dating *Beyond the Ultimate Adventure* (BF CC #6.6) - The story picks up shortly after *The Ultimate Adventure*.
489 *TW: Captain Jack Harkness*
490 In *Survival*, according to "Emperor of the Daleks".
491 Dating *Survival* (26.4) - Ace returns to Perivale. When she asks how long she's been away, the Doctor replies "as long as you think you have". Her friends Midge and Stevie vanished "last month"; Shreela the week before.
492 *First Frontier*
493 All "a decade" before *The King of Terror* (p130, p141 and p144).
494 "Eleven years" before *Escape Velocity*.
495 Dating "Business as Usual" (*DWW* #40-43) - The Doctor says the meteorites fell "that summer night in 1989" in the framing sequence; Stellar Plastics opens in "August 1990" according to a caption.
496 Dating *Crime of the Century* (BF LS #2.4) - Raine's dairy specifies the day she meets the Doctor as "October 13th, 1989... It's Friday the 13th", and the action continues from there, with Raine saying that it takes her "a few days" to get over her jet-lag.
497 Dating *Protect and Survive* (BF #162) - Ace asks

Peggy, "So, it's 1989?", and is told "Yes, the 9th of November" – the start the ten-day loop within the alternative timeline.
498 *Black and White*
499 Dating "The Broken Man" (*DWM* #451-454) - The caption to part two names the year. After initially seeming clueless on the date, the Doctor deduces it and tells Rory: "It's November, 1989. Turbulent times for Czechoslovakia. This is still a Communist state, but the Soviet Union is crumbling, Poland and Hungary have opted out, and the Germans have just taken a big sledgehammer to the Berlin Wall." Historically, the pro-democracy rally at Wenceslas Square seen here happened on 20th-21st November.
It's sometimes misinterpreted Rory claims he was age ten in 1989 (so was born in 1979), but he's actually saying that in that year, he was sleeping on a cot in Leadworth and not following developments reported on *News at Ten*.
500 Dating *Father Time* (EDA #41) - The date is never specified beyond "the late 1980s" (p199), but the Berlin Wall fell on 9th November, 1989.

ing inside a safe as she opened it. The two of them joined Ace in Kafiristan, where Russian operatives acting against the Kafiristan government had procured the services of the Metatraxi: a proud warrior race that insisted on fighting with only the same weapons as their opponents. Prince Sayf Udeen of Kafiristan – a multiple Olympic competitor with seven wives – was one of the greatest swordsmen in the world, and the Doctor was relying upon him to defeat the Metatraxi leader in single combat. Udeen died in a skirmish, and so Ace bested the Metatraxi leader instead – but the victory didn't count because she was female. Raine directed the Metatraxi to destroy a number of robots built by the Margrave University Cybernetics Research Unit. This completed the Metatraxi's contract, enabling them to withdraw – but not before the Doctor had set their translator to "surfer dude" mode. The Doctor secured alien technology that the Russians had been testing amidst this conflict, and left with Ace and Raine to investigate Margrave.

(=) 1989 (9th to 18th November) - PROTECT AND SURVIVE[497] **->** Tasked by the elder god Moloch with destroying humanity, two lesser elder gods brought about a new timeline while the universe's original history was sealed off. In the alternate history, lethal force was applied against an uprising in Eastern Bloc countries such as Poland, Hungary and Czechoslovakia, escalating tensions between the United States and the Soviet Union. The gods arranged for General Secretary Vladimir Kryuchkov, a paranoid warhawk, to become the president of Russia instead of Mikhail Gorbachev. Hostilities resulted in an exchange of nuclear missiles between the East and the West.

The seventh Doctor, travelling in the black TARDIS, tracked the key points of this aberrant timeline, erased it and restored the original history. He trapped the lesser gods within bodies patterned after two Yorkshire residents – Albert Marsden and his wife Peggy – and imprisoned them within a pocket dimension composed of a copy of Albert and Peggy's house and a five-mile radius. The pocket dimension time-looped events pertaining to a ten-day nuclear incident in Yorkshire. The gods were made to repeatedly experience fear, suffering and death, and would be freed if they truly learned what it was like to be human. They were trapped for at least 100 years.

As the forces walling off the pocket dimension decayed, the elder gods drew the white TARDIS into it, but the Ship departed after Ace and Hex exited. Ace and Hex's presence maintained the pocket reality's integrity long enough for Moloch to retrieve his followers. Ace and Hex triggered a recall signal by demonstrating their humanity, including a final test

where they sacrificed their lives for one another.

The signal summoned the black TARDIS, which arrived with Captain Lysandra Aristedes and Private Sally Morgan aboard...

The four companions found the white TARDIS within the black TARDIS' interior. Befuddled as to the Doctor's plans, Ace and Lysandra used the black TARDIS' Fast Return Switch to return to the Ship's previous location while Hex and Sally remained in the white TARDIS. Ace and Lysandra returned to the time of Beowulf, but the white TARDIS took Hex and Sally to sixteen years after Ace and Lysandra's encounter with the epic warrior...[498]

1989 (20th to 21st November) - "The Broken Man"[499] **->** The Soviet Union's decline triggered escalating pro-democracy sentiments in Prague. Two MI6 agents – Hugo Wilding and Patrick Lake, who were officially attached to the British embassy – targeted the KGB-aligned Yuri Azarov with a frame job, hoping to isolate him from Russia as part of Operation Broken Man.

The eleventh Doctor, Amy and Rory sought to contain the situation when Azarov, in a bid to restore the Soviet Union to its former glory, released the ravenous Mavorian Collective from their imprisonment within *The Sorrows of Prague*. The long-lived Frankel-Golem died battling the Mavorian Queen. The fear-eating Mavorians sought to feed off pro-democracy supporters in Wenceslas Square, but Rabbi Saul Hoffmann rallied the people to support truth, and the Mavorians disintegrated for lack of a food source. Heather Lake, Patrick's wife, briefly became the new Golem and perished while killing the Movarian Queen. Young Annabel Lake witnessed her mother's death.

The non-violent transfer of power to come was called The Velvet Revolution. Azarov perished in these events; his estate retained one of the Doctor's sonic screwdrivers.

@ 1989 (November) - FATHER TIME[500] **->** The eighth Doctor made *Time* magazine's list of Top Fifty People of the Decade. He had spent a great deal of his time searching the world for Miranda, and was living with Debbie Castle. He was present at – and possibly responsible for – the fall of the Berlin Wall.

Ferran returned from the future aboard his ship, the *Supremacy*, and abducted Miranda from a hotel in India. Seeing this on television, the Doctor and Debbie went to Florida and stowed aboard the space shuttle *Atlantis*. The shuttle docked the *Supremacy* and Debbie was killed. Miranda had started a mutiny, and Ferran decided to destroy the ship rather than let it fall to his enemies. The Doctor and Miranda teamed up to shut down the *Supremacy*'s time engines. Miranda took control of the ship and declared herself Empress, heading back to the far, far future to end the intergalactic conflict.

The Nineties

In the early 1990s, there were a string of privatisations: the electricity industry became Elec-Gen, and British Rail became BritTrack. In August 1991, information about the Russian Coup reached the West via the Internet.[501]

Sometime after the Soviet Union's fall, the Doctor assisted Yablokov, the Russian President's counsellor, in accounting for the Soviets' inventory of nuclear weapons. They proved unable to account for eighty four such devices.[502] **The Mandragora Helix was due to return to Earth in the early 1990s.**[503]

For her work, Anne Bishop received an OBE and became Dame Anne Bishop.[504] **The Doctor had tea and scones with Queen Elizabeth II.**[505] He also had a regrettable incident involving a piece of "vomit fruit" and the Queen Mother.[506]

Irving Braxiatel offered Ronan McGinley, a highly mun-

dane office worker, a blissful and rewarding summer in exchange for McGinley doing a service for him. McGinley agreed, and was taken through time to the Braxiatel Collection.[507] An earthquake devastated Charlie Sato's home in San Francisco, killing his father and sister Lucy. To honour his father, Sato became a soldier.[508]

Alice Obiefune's mum took her ice skating in Muswell Hill, London, in the nineties. Alice hoped to grow up to be a bus driver.[509] Wayne Bland II, the head of the Iris Appreciation Society, interviewed Thora Hird for the group's fanzine.[510]

1990

Gordon James Lethbridge-Stewart, the son of Kate Lethbridge-Stewart and the grandson of the Brigadier, was born in April 1990.[511] **When Owen Harper turned ten, his mother spent the whole day screaming that her lov-**

501 *System Shock*
502 *The Shadow in the Glass*
503 "Five hundred years" after *The Masque of Mandragora*. The *DWM* strip "The Mark of Mandragora" dealt with this return.
504 *Leth-St: Moon Blink* (supplemental material).
505 *The Beast Below*. The Queen seems to personally know the Doctor when she wishes him Merry Christmas in *Voyage of the Damned*.
506 *Death Riders* (p130). If it's the current Queen's mother (1900-2002), this could occur just about anywhere in the twentieth century.
507 *Benny: A Life Worth Living*: "A Summer Affair". McGinley is a professor of twenty-first century literature at the Collection, and it seems likely that he hails from that period.
508 *Mastermind*. This happens when Sato is a child.
509 *The Eleventh Doctor Year Three*: "The Tragical History Tour"
510 *Iris S3: The Iris Wildthyme Appreciation Society*. Date unknown, but Hird, known for such sitcoms as *Hallelujah!* and *Last of the Summer Wine*, lived 1911-2003. Bland can evidently travel through time, hence Iris and Panda's annoyance when he keeps stalking them.
511 He's "nearly five" in *Downtime* (p89); the video version of the story says he'll be that age in "a week".
512 *TW: Adam*. This would be in February 1990.
513 *Forever Autumn*
514 *Escape Velocity*, *The Slow Empire*. She's 28 and left home when she was 17.
515 *Wildthyme Beyond* (p109).
516 Dating *Leth-St:* "The Enfolded Time" (*Leth-St HAVOC Files* #1.1) - The day is given. A caption says it's "six years after *Mawdryn Undead*". Kate Stewart alludes to the dating protocols that originate here in *The Day of the Doctor*.

517 *Battlefield*, the Haisman Timeline. Doris is first mentioned in *Planet of the Spiders*.
518 The Haisman Timeline. *Leth-St*: "The Two Brigadiers", though, says he's a "nine-year-old" in 2001.
519 Dating "Train-Flight" (*DWM* #159-161) - There's no indication of the date, although the concert is an Oscar Peterson one, and so probably takes place before his stroke in 1993. There's nothing to suggest it isn't set the year it was published (1990). Sarah seems to be living in the same house she was in during *The Five Doctors*. This is the first time she's met the Doctor's seventh incarnation. They don't take K9 along, but they have the option, so he's still active.
520 Dating *Cat's Cradle: Time's Crucible* (NA #5) - It is "three years" since Ace left Perivale.
521 Dating *Persuasion* (BF #175) - Will reports into his dictaphone that he and Klein are meeting at the Huntsman pub "at 18:00 hours, 27th September, 1990". It's possible the year was chosen to roughly synch actress Tracey Childs' age (she was born in 1963) with that of Klein, the character she's playing (born in 1945, according to *Daleks Among Us*). For Klein, an unspecified amount of time has passed since she last met the Doctor in *UNIT: Dominion*.
522 The Doctor's sonic sunglasses register Bill as "age 26" in *The Pyramid at the End of the World* [2017]. Actress Pearl Mackie is a bit older, born 29th May, 1987
523 *The Pilot*
524 Dating "Seaside Rendezvous" (*DWM Summer Special 1991*) - There's no date given, but the story has a contemporary setting and was published in 1991.
525 Dating *The Blood Furnace* (BF #228) - The year is given.
526 *Daleks Among Us*

ing him didn't mean that she had to like him.[512] The Doctor went to a Barry Manilow concert in 1990.[513] Anji left home at 17, as her family had an outdated view of women.[514]

> = In 1990, *Dreamwatch Bulletin* published a withering retrospective of *The Iris Wildthyme Show*. The series had its fans, but was broadly regarded as a travesty of television.[515]

The Brigadier Meets his Son

1990 (1st January) - LETH-ST: "The Enfolded Time"[516] -> Lieutenant Colonel William Bishop had become second-in-command of the Fifth Operational Corps. His wife, Anne Bishop (née Travers), went to America at her father's insistence. Anne left him Owain Vine, who had been doing poorly for years, in Elizabeth Shaw's care. Samson Ware had died.

As the New Year arrived, Albert Wilson phoned the Brigadier and revealed his identity as the man's illegitimate son, with Doris Wilson (née Bryden). The Brigadier hiked to Brendon's north field to meet his son for the first time... but a bright light intercepted him, as the Accord took him to meet his other selves. Afterward, Albert revealed that his girlfriend was pregnant, and invited the Brigadier to be part of his grandson's life.

Soon after, the Brigadier contacted Brigadier Crichton, and arranged to go to Geneva. He met with Amara Essy, the President of the Security Council, and Bitsie Simak, of the United Nations' Archives and Records Management Section, to develop new dating protocols for UN records.

Brigadier Lethbridge-Stewart reunited with his old flame, Doris Wilson, in February 1990.[517] Conall Wilson, the son of Albert Wilson and the first grandson of Alistair Lethbridge-Stewart, was born in July 1990.[518]

c 1990 - "Train-Flight"[519] -> The seventh Doctor visited Sarah Jane to invite her to a jazz concert. She refused to travel via TARDIS, so they went on a train... that mysteriously entered a space vortex. The Doctor and Sarah discovered a fleet of buses – the passengers of which had been dissolved – and learned they were in orbit on a Kalik organic ship. The Kaliks were an advanced race of insects that were usually vegetarian, but this was a renegade, carnivorous faction. The Doctor manipulated the hypnotic signal that the Kalik used to control humans to control *them* instead. He then beamed the train to Royal Albert Hall station... but as there's no such station, the train materialised in the middle of the street. The Doctor and Sarah sneaked away.

c 1990 (Sunday) - CAT'S CRADLE: TIME'S CRUCIBLE[520] -> The seventh Doctor and Ace were summoned back to the TARDIS after eating baked Alaska on Ealing Broadway.

The Second Elizabeth Klein, Will Arrowsmith Join the TARDIS

1990 (27th September) - PERSUASION[521] -> Elizabeth Klein, still a scientific advisor to UNIT, met in a pub with Will Arrowsmith – a probationary science assistant to UNIT with excellent research skills, but dismal results in the field. His blunders included a "debacle" in Bangalore, a beached Temperon at Yarmouth Pier, and a heat vampire who was still on the loose in Mexico City.

The seventh Doctor was nearing the end of his life and sought to wrap up loose ends, fearing he would become someone who lacked the mettle needed to dispense with evil forces. He sensed a kindred spirit in Klein and lured her aboard the TARDIS, which was parked near the Battersea Arts Centre. They set off for Dusseldorf, 1945, in search of the German scientist Kurt Schalk. Eager to redeem himself, Will attempted to show some initiative and stowed himself aboard the TARDIS...

1991

Bill Potts, a companion of the twelfth Doctor, was born.[522] As Bill came to own very few photographs of her late mother, the Doctor nipped back and took some.[523]

c 1991 - "Seaside Rendezvous"[524] -> The seventh Doctor and Ace enjoyed a day at the seaside, but the "demon" from the wreck of the *Camara*, lost in 1826, emerged from the sea. The creature was actually a life-draining Ogri, which had been worn down into sand, but the Doctor destroyed it with a firehose.

1991 - THE BLOOD FURNACE[525] -> Bound from using their "sorcerous" abilities directly, the Erogem sub-contracted work in the hopes of rebuilding their warfleet. Stuart Dale, an entrepreneur and Melanie Bush's ex-boyfriend, accepted their patronage to revitalize the shipyards at Merseyside. The seventh Doctor, Mel and Ace ruined the launch of an Erogem warship, the largest ship ever built by British industry.

A delighted Will Arrowsmith found that the TARDIS library held all of "next year's" volume of *New Scientist*.[526] In early 1991, Jack Harkness helped to relocate the Juniper Tree and its progeny, Sebastian, to the village of Rawbone – the people of which had been rendered sterile. Sebastian and his handler, Elena Hilda Al-Qatari, produced more

Juniper Tree children – the Scions – who were given to various Rawbone families. The government's knowledge of the Juniper Tree project was lost in a paperwork shuffle.[527]

In the summer of 1991, the seventh Doctor hid a portable temporal link in St Christopher's Church, Cheldon Bonniface, while brass rubbing with Mel.[528] The Doctor turned down an invitation to Jacques Cousteau's wedding.[529]

Jenny, a traffic warden, became a companion of Iris Wildthyme after trying to issue a ticket to Iris' bus, which was on a side street in Sunderland in 1991. They wound up travelling together for four years, although Jenny got the runs every time Iris' bus went through the Vortex.[530]

Soviet intelligence agents in Uzbekistan built the fake town of Thorington on an island in the Aral Sea. Thorington was patterned after a village in Suffolk, and served as a "school for spies". In time, the Soviets populated Thorington with Autons derived from technology obtained from Nestene meteorite landings. The Autons were to be trained to function as bulletproof spies in the United Kingdom. When Uzbekistan ceased being part of the Soviet Union on 1st September, 1991, all support was cut off to Thorington. The Autons there stuck to their daily routines for seventeen years, oblivious to their true nature.[531]

1992

Maria's father Alan Jackson was such a great skateboarder, he earned the nickname "King of the Concrete, Romford, 1992".[532] Eugene Jones' teacher gave him a bona-fide alien eyeball. It was a Dogon sixth eye, capable of – temporally speaking – aiding people in seeing "what was behind them".[533] UNIT researchers began examining remnants of previous alien incursions at a research facility called The Warehouse.[534]

Amy Pond developed a love of Raspberry Ripple with extra sprinkles when she was three years old.[535] Amy visited Bristol Zoo as a child, and fell in love with the silverback gorillas there.[536]

Lucie Miller had a "thing" about jelly after an unfortunate incident at a children's party in 1992.[537] Margery Phipps, formerly a member of the Kettering Council, became UK Prime Minister in 1992. Phipps wrote *Love is All You Need*, which was still a bestseller five centuries in the future.[538]

527 *TW: First Born*. The year is given. Sebastian, born 3rd March, 1981, is "almost ten".

528 *Timewyrm: Revelation*

529 *Dark Horizons* (p143). Cousteau married twice, in 1937 and 1991 (following his first wife's death in 1990).

530 Jenny is mentioned in such stories as *Verdigris* and appears in *Iris: Enter Wildthyme*; the information here comes from *Iris: Iris and the Celestial Omnibus*: "The Deadly Flap".

531 *Brave New Town*

532 *SJA: Whatever Happened to Sarah Jane?*

533 *TW: Random Shoes*

534 "About five years" before *Auton*, although one of the Warehouse workers, Winslet, says he's been there for "seven years".

535 "Forever Dreaming"

536 *The Nu-Humans*

537 *Orbis*

538 *Council of War*, according to the Valiador residents in the future. We might imagine their historical records aren't entirely accurate that far on, but they're able to recreate the town of Kettering down to the last detail.

539 "Two years" before *Downtime*.

540 "Twenty-five years" before *TW: Visiting Hours*.

541 *Robot of Sherwood*

542 *Iris S5: Murder at the Abbey*, although Turner says this happened in the "1980s".

543 *TW: Fallout*. The Committee for Extraterrestrial Research isn't mentioned beyond this story, and has no known affiliation with another Russian tech-collecting group, the KVI, that appears in Big Finish's *Torchwood* audios. Nor does this Committee have any relation to

long-running Torchwood foe in the same series.

544 Dating *Cat's Cradle: Witch Mark* (NA #7) - The book saw release in June 1992 and seems contemporary. It's "early summer" (p57).

545 Dating "Invaders from Gantac" (*DWM* #148-150) - Leapy says it is "1992".

546 Dating "Time Fraud" (IDW *DW Special 2012*) - The year is given.

547 Dating *Timewyrm: Revelation* (NA #4) - "It was the Sunday before Christmas 1992" (p2). The Doctor confronts "Death", here a creation of the Timewyrm, but will often encounter the living embodiment of Death itself in the New Adventures.

548 Dating *The Return of Doctor Mysterio* (X10.0) - The Doctor says that it's "Christmas Day". Grant's mother assumes that he's talking about Santa when he mentions an "old guy" dangling from the window.

The artwork in Grant's Superman comics (from a landmark run by writer-artist John Byrne) hails from *Superman* vol. 2 #19 (1988), with one page from vol. 2 #7 (1987). Which isn't to say that the Doctor actually meets Grant in that year – the comics aren't cited as brand new, and any geek worth their salt can verify that beloved issues can be strewn around a youngster's bedroom for years, or be scooped up from bargain bins long after publication.

Either way, it's "twenty-four" years before the story's modern-day component (dated in this guidebook to ?2016). That fits with the posters on Grant's wall featuring Wolverine in his yellow costume – it came back into use in *Wolverine* vol. 1 #50 (cover date Jan 1992), after many years in which Wolverine wore a brown outfit

Kate Lethbridge-Stewart separated from Jonathan, the father of her two-year-old son Gordy.[539] Young Rhys Williams put a rugby ball through Mrs Poulson's greenhouse.[540]

Clara Oswald loved the story of Robin Hood when she was little.[541] Iris, accompanied by Captain Turner, had a bacon butty on king's road in 1992.[542]

Following the Cold War, some nations in the East founded clandestine organisations to harvest alien technology. Russia created the Committee for Extraterrestrial Research, which had a tense relationship with Western counterparts such as Torchwood. The Committee secured a number of containers housing an alien Shiva virus, but Torchwood procured the containers' activation key.[543]

c 1992 (early summer) - CAT'S CRADLE: WITCH MARK[544] -> Dagda's Wheel, the daytime sun around the mystical world of Tír na n-Óg, was dying. The humans there were evacuating to Earth through a gateway in the village of Llanfer Ceiriog, Wales. The non-humanoids were being left behind to perish, and so demons attacked the Tír na n-Óg town of Dinorben. The demons mortally wounded Tír na n-Óg's creator, Goibhnie, but he aided the seventh Doctor and Ace in transferring the demons into Dagda's Wheel, giving it two thousand years of fuel.

The Spotter claimed that the President of the United States had taken to bathing in cranberry sauce.

1992 - "Invaders from Gantac"[545] -> The seventh Doctor saved the tramp Leapy from alien police in London. Some time previously, the Gantacs had invaded Earth, destroyed London landmarks and declared a curfew. They were a hive mind species from two hundred thousand light years away, but had made an administrative mistake – they should have invaded the planet Wrouth, not Earth. Leapy's fleas infected the Gantac leader, who died. Without his control, the Gantacs died with him.

1992 - "Time Fraud"[546] -> Workers at a construction site in Cuzco, Peru, interpreted the visitation of Entek – a

bird-like chrononaut from the planet Helion – as an Incan ghost that was haunting them. The eleventh Doctor, Amy and Rory gave Entek a lift back up the time corridor to his people, the Ra'Ra'Vis, and dealt with a group of conmen posing as Time Lords.

1992 (Christmas) - TIMEWYRM: REVELATION[547] -> The seventh Doctor and Ace found themselves in a perfect replica of Cheldon Bonniface that was built on the moon (although not before Ace had died of oxygen starvation). The Doctor and Ace entered a surreal, tortured landscape that they discovered was the Doctor's own mind. Ace managed to rally the Doctor's former incarnations, and they gave the Doctor the strength to defeat the Timewyrm. The Timewyrm's mind was placed in a mindless baby grown in a genetics laboratory. The Hutchings family raised the baby as their daughter, Ishtar.

c 1992 (25th December) - THE RETURN OF DOCTOR MYSTERIO[548] -> Feeling guilty, the twelfth Doctor cobbled together a device to deal with the level of time distortion in New York. While doing so, he temporarily gave eight-year-old Grant Gordon possession of the Ghost of Love and Wishes: a gemstone formed in the heart of a red hole, stabilised in pure dwarf star crystal, and which acted like an onboard computer. Grant thought the Ghost stone was cold medicine and swallowed it, whereupon it granted his fondest wish: to become a superhero. The Doctor made Grant promise never to use his superpowers.**

1993

Sarah Jane Smith's friend Rani Chandra was born to Haresh and Gita Chandra between 20th March and 20th April, 1993.[549] Gabriella "Gabby" Lucia Fernanda Gonzalez and Cindy Wu, companions of the tenth Doctor, were born.[550] Phillipa "Flip" Jackson, a companion of the sixth Doctor, was born.[551] She was originally from Thamesmead, East London.[552]

designed by Byrne. Grant is currently "eight" years old; actor Justin Chatwin, who played him, was born on Hallowe'en 1982.

The time distortion in New York is presumably a hangover from *The Angels Take Manhattan*, although it's no longer strong enough (presumably) to stop the TARDIS from landing there.

549 Rani is an Aries according to *SJA: Secrets of the Stars*, which puts her birth date between 20th March and 20th April. As she's 17 in *SJA: Lost in Time*, set on 23rd November, 2010, she must have been born in 1993. By comparison, Clyde turned 15 in June 2008 (if one aligns information on him provided in *Secrets of*

the Stars* and *SJA: The Mark of the Berserker*), meaning he and Rani out to be a year apart in school, even if they seem to share a fair amount of classes together.

550 Writer Nick Abadzis confirmed to us that Gabby and Cindy are 19 when they meet the Doctor (*The Tenth Doctor Year One* [c.2014]). *The Tenth Doctor Year Three: "The Good Companion"* gives Gabby's full name.

551 A biological scan in *The Middle* registers Flip – who rejoined the TARDIS in 2012 (*Quicksilver*) – as age 19, suggesting she was born in 1993. From that scan, however, one has to subtract the unknown amount of time she's spent TARDIS travelling.

552 *Vortex Ice*

In 1993, Ace's father had a heart attack. He told his son Liam about Ace, but Liam failed to reconcile with his mother while searching for his missing sister. Liam returned home to find his father dead.[553]

The followers of Ash-Ama-Teseth discovered the existence of a pocket universe; a breakthrough that would facilitate their developing time technology.[554] Circa 1993, Major Dickens and three scientific-minded colleagues, including the physics theorist J.J. Bartholomew, started gathering on Gravonax Island to conduct various experiments.[555] Dr Fletcher's group of time-travelling surgeons visited 1993.[556]

In 1993, a clash between Torchwood and a hostile alien from Planet XXX (sic) caused the deaths of three field agents and many bystanders in London. The carnage was explained away as a gas explosion. Among the casualties was Howard Allan of Hebden Bridge: the father of Rachel Allan, a future head of Torchwood One.[557]

The Corvus, an ancient creature of decay, secreted its governing prism inside a 1993 mobile phone.[558]

1993 (8th May) - TOUCHED BY AN ANGEL[559] -> The eleventh Doctor, Amy and Rory took Mark Whitaker, age 46, through time to have a final conversation with his late wife, Rebecca Coles, when she was a young woman. Mark's time differential shorted out, reversing the aging he'd experienced from time travelling – physically, he reverted to being 37. The Doctor and his friends took Mark back to 2011, but only after the Doctor spilled red wine on the contemporary Mark's T-Shirt – causing him and Rebecca to meet for the first time.

The Seventh Doctor, for a Time, Swaps TARDISes

= 1993 - BLOOD HEAT[560] -> In an alternative timestream, the Silurian plague released at Wenley Moor in the early nineteen-seventies wiped out most of humanity. The third Doctor was killed before he could discover the antidote. Over the next twenty years, the Silurians initiated massive climatic change, rendering the plant life inedible to humanity and altering coastlines. Dinosaur species from many different eras were reintroduced to the wild. The capital of Earth became Ophidian, a vast city in Africa. Some Silurians hunted down humans for sport.

This timeline was created by the Monk, and deactivated by the seventh Doctor. It would survive for a generation or so after this before winding down. The Doctor's TARDIS was lost in a tar pit, and so he, Benny and Ace took to travelling in the alt-third Doctor's Ship.

The seventh Doctor, Benny and Ace visited the 1993 Glastonbury Festival, and met Danny Pain, a former singer for the punk bank Plasticine, and his daughter Amy.[561]

---

553 "Four years" before *The Rapture*.
554 "More than twenty years" before *Erimem: The Last Pharaoh*.
555 Thirteen years before the present-day portion of *Night Thoughts*.
556 *TW: Visiting Hours*
557 *TW: Torchwood One: Beyond the Fall*
558 *The Wreck of the World*
559 Dating *Touched by an Angel* (NSA #47) - The exact day is given (p228).
560 Dating *Blood Heat* (NA #19) - This story is a sequel to *Doctor Who and the Silurians*, containing many elements from its novelisation *Doctor Who and the Cave-Monsters*. Thus, the Silurians are called "reptile people", but the Doctor wears his velvet jacket, not coveralls, when he goes potholing and the Silurian leader is named Morka. It is repeatedly stated that the first encounter with the Silurians took place "twenty years" ago in "1973". The seventh Doctor travels in his alternate self's TARDIS for thirty-one of the New Adventures books, ending with *Happy Endings*.
561 *No Future*
562 *Death and Diplomacy*, and reiterated in *Benny* S8: *The End of the World*.
563 *Mastermind*. Matheson's confusion as to whether the Master was present when her comrades died prob-

ably just owes – as with Charlie Sato's muddled recollections – to his tricking her with hypnosis.
564 Dating *The Left-Handed Hummingbird* (NA #21) - The date of the massacre is given. The Doctor arrives in "1994".
565 Dating *Listen* (X8.4) - The Doctor estimates, "By the ozone level in the drains, [it's the] mid-90s". Danny Pink appears here as a young adolescent – Samuel Anderson (playing adult Danny) was born in 1982; Remi Gooding (younger Danny) was 11 when *Listen* aired.
566 Dating *Conundrum* (NA #22) - The Doctor thinks that it is "November the second, 1993".
567 Dating *The Dimension Riders* (NA #20) - The scenes in Oxford are set in "1993", "November 18th".
568 Dating "Time and Time Again" (*DWM* #207) - The date is given.
569 Dating *Goth Opera* (MA #1) - It is "1993", "November".
570 *Managra*
571 *Last Christmas*
572 Dating *Instruments of Darkness* (PDA #48) - The Doctor and Mel arrive on 29th December (p69). "John Doe", although his surname is never mentioned, is likely Jeremy Fitzoliver, Sarah Jane's associate from *The Paradise of Death* and *The Ghosts of N-Space* (although this would clash with *Interference*). Sudbury was mentioned in *Time-Flight*.

Jason Kane's father, Peter Jonathan Kane, physically abused his children. When Jason's sister Lucy was about six, Peter punished her for touching herself in a "bad place" - and broke three of her fingers, one per day over the school holidays, with a mallet.[562] In 1993, Ruth Matheson was assigned to a UN peacekeeping detail in the former Yugoslavia. She was the sole survivor when a bomb destroyed her team's armoured vehicle.[563]

c 1993 - LISTEN[564] **->** The TARDIS brought the twelfth Doctor and Clara to the West Country Children's Home, Gloucester, as part of the Doctor's hunt for creatures capable of perfect hiding. They convinced young Rupert Pink, later known as Danny, that fear was a superpower – right before the Doctor mentally ordered Danny to sleep, and jumbled his memory of the meeting. Rupert kept the gunless plastic soldier, Dan the Soldier Man, that Clara placed at the foot of his bed as a keepsake.

1993 (31st October) - THE LEFT-HANDED HUMMINGBIRD[565] **->** The so-called Halloween Man opened fire on a crowd of unsuspecting people in a marketplace in Mexico City. Cristian Alvarez witnessed this, narrowly avoiding death himself.

(=) The Halloween Man opened fire on a crowd of unsuspecting people in a marketplace in Mexico City. Cristian Alvarez witnessed this, narrowly avoiding death himself. The evidence suggested an alien presence – the Blue, also known as the psychic being Huitzilin. On 12th December, Alvarez sent a note for the Doctor's attention to UNIT HQ in Geneva.

The seventh Doctor investigated early the next year. In his timeline, this was before "the Happening" of late 1968, early 1969. Huitzilin killed Christian, but the Doctor's actions erased this from history.

= 1993 (2nd November) - CONUNDRUM[566] **->** As part of his revenge against the seventh Doctor, the Monk trapped the TARDIS in the fictional village of Arandale, which was populated by colourful characters. It was part of the Land of Fiction, and the Doctor wrote himself out of the trap.

1993 (18th November) - THE DIMENSION RIDERS[567] **->** The President of St Matthew's College, Oxford – actually a Time Lord named Epsilon Delta – plotted with the Garvond, a creature composed of the darker sides of the minds within the Gallifreyan Matrix. They sought to create a Time Focus – a bridge through time between student Tom Cheynor and his future descendant, Darius Cheynor – that would let the Garvond absorb a massive amount of chronal energy. The Garvond turned on

the President and killed him. The seventh Doctor trapped the Garvond within the dimensionally transcendental text *The Worshipful and Ancient Law of Gallifrey*, then disposed of the book in a pocket dimension.

(=) 1993 - "Time and Time Again"[568] **->** The seventh Doctor, Benny and Ace arrived in a London that was in ruins... a battleground for armies of monsters. The Black Guardian had altered history so that the Doctor never left Gallifrey, but the Doctor and his companions travelled through history reassembling the Key to Time, and the White Guardian restored the timeline to its normal path.

1993 (November) - GOTH OPERA[569] **->** The Time Lady Ruath sought to fulfill prophesies that spoke of the birth of a vampire nation. She rescued the vampire Yarven from his burial spot in Croatia and allowed him to turn her. Together, they sought to raise a vampire army. Tracking them down to Manchester, the fifth Doctor destroyed the army and its attempt to create the Vampire Messiah. Yarven was incinerated; Ruath was flung into the Time Vortex.

The vampires Jake and Madeline departed into space. They later returned, and by the twenty-fourth century had sired many descendents.[570] **If Santa Claus were real, Clara Oswald would have been marginal for his naughty list in 1993.**[571]

1993 (29th December) - INSTRUMENTS OF DARKNESS[572] **->** The sixth Doctor and Mel found Evelyn in Great Rokeby. The twins Cellian and Ciara had reformed and were improving the school system in the village of Halcham.

By now, the Cylox named Lai-Ma was trying to psionically absorb the energy of his former prison realm, hoping to increase his power levels and destroy Earth. His brother Tko-Ma hoped to steal his brother's power and had founded the Network, an organisation that kidnapped psionics and exploited their abilities. The Ini-Ma, the Cylox brothers' jailor, killed the siblings but died in the process.

A powerplay between Tko-Ma's anchor on Earth (Sebastian Malvern) and the Network's head administrator (John Doe) triggered a slaughter that killed Cellian, Ciara and Doe. The Network reformed, with Mel's associate Trey Korte as a member, into an organisation pledged to protect Earth from extra-terrestrial threats. Evelyn resumed travelling with the Doctor and Mel.

Department C19 had closed by 1993 due to internal corruption. Sir John Sudbury was murdered to prevent his exposing the Network.

1994

The outermost planet of the solar system was discovered in 1994 and called Cassius.[573] UNISYC, a UN security group, was founded in 1994. Like UNIT, they were involved with alien encounters.[574] The US government only admitted that Area 51 existed in 1994.[575]

UNIT constructed its Vault, a.k.a. the Museum of Terrors – an underground base found under the Angel of the North – to house alien artifacts and weapons.[576] UNIT's Vault and the Black Archive took possession of the assets of C-19's Vault in the mid-90s.[577]

A Weeping Angel shunted a New York resident, Jane McCormack, back to 1994. She thrived at gambling, as her father had grilled American football scores into her head. The twelfth Doctor was similarly hurled back, and busied himself in the next two decades.[578]

1994 - THE LAND OF THE DEAD[579] -> The fifth Doctor and Nyssa were attacked in Alaska by sea monsters. They sheltered in the home of oilman Shaun Brett. One of the fossils in his collection was a Permian – an ancient predator that looked like a living skeleton, bound together by a bioelectric field. A pack of Permians revived and threatened to breed. As the creatures were vulnerable to fire, the Doctor destroyed them with a stock of flammable paint.

1994 - NIGHT AND THE DOCTOR: "Good Night"[580] -> The TARDIS' telepathic circuits determined that Amy Pond's saddest memory was the time she was a child and dropped her ice cream at a fairground. The eleventh Doctor took the adult Amy back to 1994 so that – clad in her nightdress – she could cheer up her younger self with another ice cream.

c 1994 - THE RINGS OF AKHATEN[581] -> A very young Clara Oswald kicked a ball onto the eleventh Doctor's head as he investigated her history.

Tobias Tickle produced cartoons that Clara Oswald watched as a child. In future, Tickle submitted his body to extended life-support and lived for some centuries.[582]

Clyde Langer, a future friend of Sarah Jane Smith, was born 5th June, 1994, to Paul and Carla Langer.[583]

1994 (10th-11th June) - TOUCHED BY AN ANGEL[584] -> A variant of the Weeping Angels that fed on paradoxes attempted to create a complex space-time event centred around Mark Whitaker, whose wife Rebecca was fated to die in 2003. An Angel sent Mark back to 1994 from 2011 – he had in his possession a series of instructions he believed his future self had written, but which the Angels had crafted. The eleventh Doctor, Amy and Rory arrived from 2011, but believed that Mark's future self had to

573 *The Sun Makers* first mentions the discovery, the year of which is given in *Iceberg*. It has to be discovered after *The Tenth Planet,* or the story would have been called "The Eleventh Planet". *GodEngine* and *The Crystal Bucephalus* refer to the Battle of Cassius.
574 *Interference*
575 *Dreamland* (DW).
576 *Tales from the Vault*. Construction on the Angel of the North began in 1994.
577 *Worlds DW: The Screaming Skull*, explicitly linking UNIT's secure repositories and the C-19 Vault featured in novels by Gary Russell and the *Lethbridge-Stewart* series.
578 *The Lost Angel*
579 Dating *The Land of the Dead* (BF #4) - The year is given.
580 Dating *Night and the Doctor:* "Good Night" (Series 6 DVD minisode) - The year is given.
581 Dating *The Rings of Akhaten* (X7.8) - At a guess, young Clara looks about age five.
582 "Welcome to Tickle Town"
583 According to *SJA: Secrets of the Stars*, Clyde's birthday is 5th June. He's 15 in *SJA: The Mark of the Berserker,* likely set after that date in 2009.
584 Dating *Touched by an Angel* (NSA #47) - The exact days are given (pgs. 34, 39, 79). Page 224 appears to contain a mistake, saying that Mark was sent back to

2003, not 1994.
585 Dating *Invasion of the Cat-People* (MA #13) - It is "AD 1994", the adventure starting "Friday the eighth of July 1994".
586 Dating *P.R.O.B.E.: The Zero Imperative* (P.R.O.B.E. film #1) - The film was released in 1994, and seems contemporary. The story appears to begin on 8th August (as noted when a clinic worker who seems to be arriving for work checks off 7th August on her calendar, suggesting that it's the next day). Liz's desk calendar at one point reads (albeit somewhat hazily) "August 1994", and roughly mid-way through the story, she flips her desk calendar to reveal that it's now 10th August. A mortician tells Liz how unusual it is that the ground around the body he's examining was "frozen in August". The story ends on the night of perihelion, presumably the same day (13th August) as in 1945 when O'Kane killed his family.
587 *Leth-St:* "Lucy Wilson". Nick is "seven or eight" years older than his sister Lucy (born circa 2003).
588 *Zamper*
589 *Who Killed Kennedy* (p271).
590 *The Five Companions*
591 "Ten years" before *UNIT: Time Heals.*
592 About ten years before *Iris: Wildthyme on Top.*
593 *Terrible Lizards*
594 *Last Christmas*

remain in the 1990s and fulfill upon the instructions to preserve history. They failed to realise that he intended to save Rebecca from dying. The Doctor set the TARDIS to follow disturbances in Mark's timeline, and they would next meet in 1997.

1994 (8th July) - INVASION OF THE CAT-PEOPLE[585]

-> The second Doctor, Polly and Ben prevented the Cat-People, one of the most powerful races in the galaxy, from harnessing the magnetic energy of the Earth.

Liz Shaw Joins P.R.O.B.E.

1994 (8th-13th August) - P.R.O.B.E.: THE ZERO IMPERATIVE[586] -> Liz Shaw had left Cambridge and now worked for the Preternatural Research Bureau (P.R.O.B.E.), an arm of the government that investigated supernatural phenomena. She looked into a series of murders centred around the Hawthorne psychiatric clinic – the new home of Daniel O'Kane, a.k.a. Patient Zero. The dark forces that turned O'Kane into a killer tried to manifest through his son, Peter Russell. O'Kane stopped them from doing so, at the cost of his own life.

1995

Nick Wilson, the son of Albert Wilson and the grandson of Alistair Lethbridge-Stewart, was born.[587]

The seventh Doctor, Benny, Chris and Roz spent a couple of days at the Doctor's house in Allen Road to recover from their experiences on Zamper.[588] On 5th April, 1995, Private Cleary died in hospital.[589]

Ian Chesterton retired after spending thirty years doing research. He then got bored, and returned to teaching, while Barbara worked on a new book.[590] Using blueprints stolen from UNIT, Bernard Kelly worked to develop a matter-transporter for benefit of "Britain first" zealots within the military. He spent a decade failing to do so.[591]

Iris Wildthyme's companion Tom left her company and returned to his native era. He brokered a deal with the publisher Satan and Satan Ltd. to produce a series of novels based upon his adventures with Iris. Sales soared, and Tom gained a reputation as an eccentric alien abductee. Satan and Satan was a front for MIAOW, who hoped to learn Iris's secrets.[592] When Rory Williams was six, his parents took him to Florida – where he was freaked out by the size of the mouse at Disneyworld.[593]

Clara Oswald stopped believing in Santa Claus at age nine.[593] A friend of the Doctor always said: "Paris is always a good idea."[595]

1995 - "Star Beast II"[596] -> Judges Zagran, Scraggs and Theka concluded that white star therapy had rehabilitated Beep the Meep and he was released. He remained evil, but the authorities had removed his blackstar drive. Beep had a spare hidden on Earth, and headed there. The fourth Doctor arrived in Blackcastle just before the Meep. Fudge Higgins now managed the multiplex built on the site of the old steel mills, and this was where the Meep had buried his stardrive. The Doctor adjusted a film projector and imprisoned the Meep within a *Lassie* movie.

Nightshade: The Movie was in general release.

The Brigadier, Sarah Jane and Victoria Unite Against the Great Intelligence

1995 (April) - DOWNTIME[597] -> Harold Chorley, a veteran TV presenter who witnessed the London Event, was the star of *Yours Chorley*. Some UNIT personnel referred to the Brigadier's time there as "the Blunder Days", meaning "Blood and Thunder".

Under the direction of the Great Intelligence, which was secretly housed in Professor Travers, Victoria Waterfield had invested an eight-figure sum in the New World University in northwest London. New World specialised in teaching classes by computer, but the Intelligence inhab-

595 *DEyes 4: The Monster of Montmartre*. In pop culture, the quote is erroneously attributed to Audrey Hepburn. Although she never said it, the phrase did turn up in the 1995 remake of *Sabrina* (Hepburn starred in the 1954 original) starring Harrison Ford and Julia Ormond.
596 Dating "Star Beast II" (*DWM Yearbook 1996*) - Beep's been imprisoned for "fifteen years", and it's "1995".
597 Dating *Downtime* (MA #18) - The story seems contemporary. The independent film version of *Downtime* was released in 1995, the Missing Adventure on which it is based (given more weight in this chronology, as it was BBC-sanctioned) saw print shortly after, in January 1996. A computer log-in screen in the film version of *Downtime* gives the exact day as "Thursday, 14th September, 1995" – an actual Thursday that month, and

roughly corresponding to the video's release. The book, however, has the Brigadier insisting that it's the Easter holiday (p122), which happened in mid-April that year.

The Brigadier has been teaching at Brendon for "twenty odd years" (he started there in 1976, *Mawdryn Undead*), it's been "a good three years" since Daniel Hinton, School House '91, was expelled from Brendon (p113), and the Intelligence's next incursion on Earth – *Millennial Rites*, set in 1999 – is "four years" afterwards.

The Brigadier is planning his retirement from Brendon, and Winifred Bambera is seen here as a captain – both developments place the story before *Battlefield* [c.1997], but also mean that Bambera nets *two* promotions in a very short amount of time.

The *Downtime* book contains various statements as

ited the university's computers, and used a hypnotic technique to control the students there. It remained bound by the Locus that Lethbridge-Stewart kept after the London Event – to find it, Victoria hired Sarah Jane Smith of *Metropolitan* magazine to investigate the Event's survivors. The Brigadier's daughter, Kate, contacted her father when New World students menacingly surveilled her and the Brigadier's grandson Gordy.

The Intelligence spread its influence onto the Internet, creating chaos as all computer systems succumbed to – as the media termed it – the "computer flu". The CIA's files were broadcast on Russian television, bank cash points released all their cash and Tomahawk missiles were launched in the Gulf. Some New World students were transformed into Yeti, leading to a conflict with UNIT. Before the Intelligence could take control of Earth, Victoria realised her error and helped to destroy the University's generators, banishing the Intelligence. Professor Travers' dead body collapsed.

The Brigadier and Doris married, and the Brigadier gave up teaching.[598] The Brigadier had chanced upon his old flame Doris in Brighton, at a concert at the Royal Pavilion. Within six months, they were married and he left Brendon Public School.[599]

Maria Jackson, a friend of Sarah Jane Smith, was born around 1995.[600] **Age 20, Toshiko Sato joined a government science think tank.**[601] **Jack visited the Powell Estate once or twice in the nineties and watched Rose grow up, but refrained from speaking with her.**[602]

(=) 1995 - TIMEH: ECHOES[603] **->** The time-creature that Honoré and Emily saved from the Cabal of the Horned Beast took up residence in the Dragon Industry Tower – an office block that proved so financially ruinous, its founder, John Raymond, killed himself. The creature sought redemption for its crimes by absorbing the timelines of abused women, but this cast the women into a noncorporeal void. Emily persuaded the creature to return the women home and absorb Raymond's timeline, an act that erased the tower from history.

The paradox resolved itself enough that the time-creature broke free, and left for parts unknown.

---

to how long has elapsed since *The Web of Fear*... Sarah claims it's been "some twenty-five years"/"a quarter of a century" (p92), but later says it's been "about thirty years", as does the Brigadier (pgs. 99, 148). The Intelligence/Travers thinks it's been "over twenty-five years" (p134), the video and book blurbs both say it's been "twenty-five years".

It's been "twenty years" since the Brigadier saw active service (p117) and Sarah's time at UNIT (pgs. 124, 254), and "about twenty years" (p260) since the Doctor and Victoria parted ways in *Fury from the Deep*. "One hundred and twenty-five years" have passed since *The Evil of the Daleks* [1866], and Victoria (in the video version) inherits investments that her father made "130 years" ago, prior to the same story. Sarah's K9 doesn't feature heavily, but is active in the book version.

Cavendish finishes the book version of *Downtime* a smoldering corpse, but survives in the video and appears in *Daemons: Daemos Rising*. The UNIT clearance codes that the Brigadier gives Sarah, NN and QQ (p169), correspond to the production codes for *The Abominable Snowmen* and *The Web of Fear*.

598 *Battlefield*

599 *Liberty Hall*, which claims the Brig left Brendon in 1984. *Downtime*, however, says that he doesn't leave there until a decade later, in 1995. Also, the Haisman Timeline claims that the Brigadier and Doris reunited in February 1990, contradicting *Liberty Hall*'s assertion that they married a mere six months after doing re-meeting one another.

600 According to publicity material, she's "13" in *SJA: Invasion of the Bane*.

601 *TW: Greeks Bearing Gifts*

602 *Utopia*

603 Dating *TimeH: Echoes* (*TimeH #6*) - The year "1995" is given on the cover of the printed book and the cover of the audiobook, and is reiterated at least four times within the text. However, a frequently used online version of the cover (including the one on the Telos website) gives the year as 2006.

604 Dating *P.R.O.B.E.: The Devil of Winterborne* (P.R.O.B.E. film #2) - The video came out in 1995, and seems contemporary. Liz's father has passed away recently enough for her boss to offer condolences, and her father's tombstone in *P.R.O.B.E.: The Ghosts of Winterborne* says he lived "1919-1995".

605 "Six years" before *Psi-ence Fiction*.

606 *The Feast of Axos*, respectively referencing *Remembrance of the Daleks* and *The Android Invasion*.

607 *The Hollow Men*

608 "Eleven years" before *The Gathering*.

609 Dating "Memorial" (*DWM #191*) - "The TARDIS chronometer read December 20th 1995".

610 "Twelve years" prior to 2008, according to *Iris: Iris and the Celestial Omnibus*: "The Deadly Flap".

611 *Who Killed Kennedy*. It is "nearly twenty-five years" (p274) after Cleary's return to the 1970s, and is subject to UNIT dating. This novel presumes that the UNIT stories occurred around the time of broadcast, and the date of Stevens' departure is given (p271).

612 *TW: Miracle Day*

613 *P.R.O.B.E.: When to Die*

614 *FP: Weapons Grade Snake Oil* (ch1).

615 "Fifteen years" before *Ferril's Folly*.

1995 - P.R.O.B.E.: THE DEVIL OF WINTERBORNE[604]
-> Liz Shaw's father, Reuben Shaw, had recently died.
P.R.O.B.E. investigated a number of killings at the
Winterborne boys' school. Christian Purcell, a student
there, thought he was the cult-leader Isaac Greatorex reincarnated, and was murdering people to ritualistically attain
immortality. Confronted, Purcell seemingly leapt to his
death on a motorway, but his body vanished...

> (=) Around 1995, physicist John Finer acciden-
> tally killed his daughter Amelia. He began research-
> ing time travel, hoping to go back in time to prevent
> this. Events circa 2001 nullified this timeline.[605]

In 1995, Ironside Industries purchased British Rocket
Group and the former Space Defence Station at
Devesham.[606] While the fourth Doctor and Romana were
in Cornwall in 1995, the Doctor read of the suicide of
David Brown, captain of the English cricket team and a
native of Hexen Bridge.[607] In 1995, Katherine Chambers
started up her own practice, Chambers Pharmaceuticals,
in Brisbane.[608]

1995 (20th December) - "Memorial"[609] -> The seventh Doctor and Ace landed in Westmouth. The Doctor
freed the Telphin consciousness from Simon Galway, in
whom it had resided in peace for exactly sixty years.

1996

Iris Wildthyme and her companion Jenny parted ways following an escapade with jellyfish creatures, their secluded
moonbase and the cast of a daytime soap that Iris watched.
Jenny would eventually head the Darlington branch of
MIAOW.[610]

In January 1996, James Stevens retrieved his time ring
from his safety deposit box at a bank in London. Rifle in
hand, he departed into the past to assassinate Kennedy.[611]
**A set of army barracks in Wales was closed down in
1996, but would be reopened as the Cowbridge
Overflow Camp in 2011.**[612]

Corporal Paul Reynish met his beloved, Josie, in Bosnia
as part of Operation Endeavour in 1996.[613] *Never Give a*

Sucker an Even Break: History's Dodgiest Deals by J. Writhing-
Crayfish (1996) discussed Faction Paradox's purchase of
the UK's missing eleven days.[614]

The fourth segment of the Key to Time, disguised as a
meteoroid, passed through the Cronquist System. The
Cronquist charged the meteoroid with their power, and it
later impacted a NASA shuttle. Astronaut Millicent Drake,
the only survivor, came under Cronquist's control and
furthered their invasion plans.[615]

The seventh Doctor, Roz and Chris rested in Sydney in
1996.[616] The same Doctor returned Peri to the late twentieth century.[617]

The eleventh Doctor claimed that Vortis could be seen
from Earth.[618] **When Owen Harper was 16, he packed
his bags and left his emotionally abusive household.**[619]
**Yvonne Hartman became the head of Torchwood
London** in 1996. **Alex Hopkins took charge of
Torchwood Cardiff** no later than 1996.[620]

Martin Gibbons of Torchwood investigated a crashed
spaceship in Newport, and confronted the ship's AI –
which was dismayed because the alien child it was tasked
with protecting had died. The ship initiated its self-
destruct, but was only partly destroyed in the resultant
explosion. Gibbons' teammates thought he had died, but
his consciousness and body melded with the AI into a
mentally disturbed gestalt. It left Earth to form a new and
perfect world, and created the population of Cotter
Paluni's World out of the clay there.[621]

c 1996 (12th January) - NIGHT THOUGHTS[622] -> On
Gravonax Island in Scotland, J.J. Bartholomew developed
the prototype Bartholomew Transactor, a device that could
send a subatomic particle back in time to an identical piece
of equipment. By this method, audio messages from the
future could be heard in the past.

Major Dickens theorised that if the device were used to
retroactively halt an established death, then the closely
related timelines would overlap and the deceased's body
would re-animate. When a destitute woman named
Maude appeared with her two daughters, Edie and Ruth,
Dickens decided to test this and deliberately misdiagnosed
Edie's eye infection as Gravonax gas poisoning. Dickens'
colleagues were moved to euthanise Edie rather than let

---

616 At the start of *Return of the Living Dad* (p15).
617 *Bad Therapy.* The exact year isn't given.
618 *The Hounds of Artemis;* Vortis first appears in *The Web Planet.* This was true in one story, the apocryphal *Doctor Who Annual 1965* story "The Lair of Zarbi Supremo," set circa 1996.
619 *TW: Adam*
620 *Army of Ghosts, TW: Fragments,* with the years given in *The Torchwood Archives* (BBC). *TW: One Rule* has Yvonne claiming that she "hadn't been with Torchwood

long" when Alex Hopkins murdered his team on New
Year's Eve, 1999 (*TW: Fragments*).
621 *TW: Red Skies.* Alex Hopkins is "new" to Torchwood, although it's unclear if "new" means when he first joins the organisation or takes leadership of Torchwood Cardiff (no later than 1996).
622 Dating *Night Thoughts* (BF #79) - It is "ten years" before the story's present-day component. An audio statement from Maude, recorded shortly before her suicide, is dated 12th January.

her suffer what they believed was an inevitable, agonizing death.

A Bartholomew Transactor was present as Dickens gave Edie a lethal dose of anaesthetic. The veterinary scientist Hartley chemically preserved Edie's body on Dickens' behalf, and her corpse was placed inside a taxidermied bear. Maude discovered Dickens' deception and committed suicide. Ruth was shuffled between foster homes. Dickens held Bartholomew prisoner so she could perfect her device; she tried to escape, but was permanently crippled by a bear trap. The world believed that she was dead.

As Dickens desired, the Transactor relayed a message from ten years in the future and caused a temporal anomaly. The seventh Doctor arrived from that period, tasked with conclusively ensuring Edie's death, but found himself unable to kill her.

1996 (17th April) - TOUCHED BY AN ANGEL[623] ->
Mark Whitaker and Rebecca Coles impulsively slept together, which had a chilling effect on their friendship.

1996 - BENNY S8: THE END OF THE WORLD[624] ->
When Jason Kane was nearly 13, he responded to his father's physical abuse by catching a train out of town, leaving his mother and sister Lucy behind. As an adult, Jason travelled back from 2607 and arrived at his family home two days after his younger self fled. Posing as a

detective-inspector from the "Child Protection Taskforce", Jason told Peter Kane that young Jason's disappearance was being investigated – and that the Kane household would be under surveillance. Jason hoped this would curtail his father's abuse of Lucy, and he also established a trust fund for her.

Shug, the leader of the Skrak, was betrayed by his subordinate Gleka and transmatted to the Dagellan Cluster in 1996. The beam also swept up Jason Kane, who was living on the streets of London. Jason became a rogue and spent the next fifteen years away from Earth, thinking that Shug was his small, furry pet.[625]

Sam Jones and the Original Fitz Kreiner Leave the TARDIS; Compassion Joins, as Does a New Version of Fitz

1996 - INTERFERENCE[626] ->
The eighth Doctor was summoned by the United Nations, who had been offered a weapon – the Cold – by alien arms dealers. The aliens were members of the Remote, a Faction Paradox colony. Sarah Jane Smith, now involved with a man named Paul, investigated the matter and met Samantha Jones, who was taken to the Remote. Fitz was frozen in suspended animation and wouldn't awaken until the twenty-sixth century. He would become Father Kreiner of Faction Paradox.

---

623 Dating *Touched by an Angel* (NSA #47) - The exact day is given (p91).

624 Dating *Benny S8: The End of the World* (Benny audio #8.4) - Jason was born in 1983 and is "nearly 13" when he leaves home. A conversation between Jason and Benny in *Death and Diplomacy* detailed Jason and Lucy's physical abuse, in a scene that's here dramatised for audio.

625 *Death and Diplomacy*

626 Dating *Interference* (EDA #25-26) - The date is "1996" (p8, p29). This means that Sam actually arrives back on Earth a bit before her younger self leaves in the TARDIS.

627 The backstory to *The Eleventh Hour*, given in *The Big Bang*.

628 Dating *The Eleventh Hour* (X5.1) - Amelia says that it's "Easter" in her prayer to Santa. The year isn't stated, but it's twelve years before the Doctor sees Amy again, then a further two years before her wedding day, which is stated to be in 2010.

629 Dating *The Big Bang* (X5.13) - The action picks up from Amelia waiting in *The Eleventh Hour*.

630 *Let's Kill Hitler*. This has to be shortly after Amelia's first meeting with the Doctor in *The Eleventh Hour*.

631 *The Eleventh Hour*

632 Dating *The Big Bang* (X5.13) - It's "1894 years later" than 102 AD, and the older Amy confirms it's "1996".

633 Dating *P.R.O.B.E.: Unnatural Selection* and *P.R.O.B.E.: The Ghosts of Winterborne* (P.R.O.B.E. films #3-4) - As with the rest of the *P.R.O.B.E.* series, the stories seem contemporary – in these last two cases, with their release in 1996. In *Unnatural Selection*, events in 1975 are repeatedly said to be "twenty years ago" and "over twenty years ago". The body of Alfred's first victim was found "in early hours of July the 8th", so *Unnatural Selection* would seem to occur in August at the earliest. In *The Ghosts of Winterborne*, enough time has passed that headmaster Gavin Purcell has been tried and convicted for his culpability in events in *The Devil of Winterborne*. *The Ghosts of Winterborne* has Andrew, a student at Winterborne, returning there after a leave of absence – possibly suggesting that it's the start of the new term.

634 Dating *The Chase* (2.8) - The Doctor claims that as "this house is exactly what you would expect in a nightmare", suspecting that the TARDIS and the Dalek time machine have landed "in a world of dreams" that "exists in the dark recesses of the human mind". Viewers later find out the truth – the TARDIS has simply landed in a theme park. A sign proclaims that it is the "Festival of Ghana 1996". The "Tower of London" quote is Ian's description of what he has just seen. Quite why Peking would cancel an exhibition in Ghana is not explained.

The Saudis captured and tortured the Doctor. He sent an emergency message to his third incarnation, who was on the planet Dust in the thirty-eighth century. Sarah rescued the Doctor and he travelled to the Remote, who had built a settlement on a Time Lord warship. This ship was designed to destroy the original home planet of their Enemy – Earth – in the future War. The Doctor convinced the people of the Remote that they were being used. The ship was sent to a place of safety.

Sam accepted an offer to stay with Sarah Jane Smith and left the Doctor's company. The Doctor was joined on his travels by two members of the Remote: Compassion and Kode, the latter of whom had been generated from a Remote remembrance tank and endowed with much of Fitz's personality. The Doctor used the TARDIS to revise Kode into a copy of Fitz as he had been prior to his joining Faction Paradox.

Amelia "Amy" Pond had grown up with a Crack in Time in her bedroom wall. It erased her parents from existence; Amy would remember scant details about them, but didn't know their fate. Her Aunt Sharon raised her. Amy went to the National Museum when she was little.[627]

Amelia Pond Meets the Eleventh Doctor

1996 (Easter) - THE ELEVENTH HOUR[628] -> The newly regenerated eleventh Doctor crashed to Earth in the backyard of Amelia Pond, age seven, and the falling TARDIS destroyed her garden shed. She asked the Doctor to investigate a crack in her wall – actually a Crack in Time, through which a voice could be heard saying, "Prisoner Zero has escaped." The Doctor recognised it as a message from a prison, but had to attend to the healing TARDIS when its engines misphased. He told Amelia that he would right the TARDIS by taking a short hop five minutes into the future – she packed to go away with him, and waited for him in the back yard. Instead of reappearing in five minutes, the Doctor would return twelve years later.

1996 (Easter) - THE BIG BANG[629] -> Amelia fell asleep in her backyard while waiting for the Doctor. As the eleventh Doctor's timeline came undone after he sealed the Cracks in Time, he carried Amelia into her house and put her to bed. The words he spoke while she slept would help her to remember him in future.

Amelia Pond told her best friends Rory and Mels about meeting the Doctor.[630] In the years to follow, the persistence with which Amy clung to the existence of her imaginary friend – her "raggedy Doctor" – caused her to be taken to four psychiatrists.[631]

(=) 1996 - THE BIG BANG[632] -> The explosion of the Doctor's TARDIS in 2010 caused every sun to supernova at every moment in history, obliterating the universe. Only the Earth and its moon remained, lit by the energy from the exploding TARDIS. In this eye of the storm, the people of Earth lived beneath a starless sky. All of the races allied against the Doctor in 102 AD had been wiped out, although a few "never-were" vestiges of them remained, resembling statues.

The Pandorica, having held Amy Pond in stasis ever since 102 AD, was now kept in the National Museum. The eleventh Doctor left a note that made Amy's seven-year-old self insist that her aunt take her to see the Pandorica exhibit. The younger Amy touched the Pandorica, which used a sample of her DNA to resurrect the older Amy. The Doctor freed River Song, who had been time-looped inside the exploding TARDIS; Rory the Last Centurion, who was still guarding the Pandorica after two millennia, joined them.

History continued to collapse... the Doctor's group realised that the Pandorica contained some atoms from the universe before it was destroyed, and that the Pandorica's light – if given an infinite power source – could extrapolate the whole universe from just one of them. The Doctor piloted the Pandorica into the exploding TARDIS, providing the power necessary to (effectively) trigger the second Big Bang. The Cracks of Time were sealed, but the Doctor was on the wrong side of them when this happened – and so everyone in the universe forgot about him.

1996 - P.R.O.B.E.: UNNATURAL SELECTION / P.R.O.B.E.: THE GHOSTS OF WINTERBORNE[633] -> The genetically advanced man Alfred began harvesting organs from humans in a bid to give his benefactor, Professor Julius Quilter, extended life. The ailing Quilter died anyway, and P.R.O.B.E. ended Aldred's murder spree by killing him.

Christian Purcell's body was found by the motorway where he'd jumped. The ghost of Isaac Greatorex sought to return to life and gain great powers, but Liz Shaw oversaw a ritual that banished him.

1996 - THE CHASE[634] -> One of the exhibits at the 1996 Festival of Ghana, "Frankenstein's House of Horror", featured roboticFac versions of a number of Gothic characters. For $10, visitors could wander around an animated haunted house, be frightened by mechanical bats and meet Frankenstein's monster, Dracula and the Grey Lady. The exhibition was cancelled by Peking. The first Doctor, Ian, Barbara and Vicki briefly visited the exhibition while fleeing through time from the Daleks.

Tobias Vaughn claimed he saw the Dalek Time Machine at the "1995 Earth Fair in Ghana".[635] The robots were programmed by Microsoft, who later faced lawsuits.[636] The Doctor attended the crowded Festival of Ghana.[637]

1996 - THE SANDS OF TIME[638] -> Nyssa's awakening drew near, and the agents of Nephthys made ready for her resurrection. Nephthys' intelligence resided within Nyssa, but her instinct resided in a Nephthys clone named Vanessa Prior. The fifth Doctor tricked the instinct part of Nephthys into thinking its intelligence had dissipated in 1926. The Nephthys-instinct went back in time but failed to reunite with itself. It circled back and forth between 1926 and 1996 until it aged to death. The Doctor removed Nephthys' intelligence from Nyssa and woke up his companion, then buried the intelligence at Nephthys' pyramid.

Izzy Sinclair Joins the TARDIS, Leaves

1996 (19th December) - "End Game" / "Oblivion" (DWM)[639] -> The eighth Doctor landed in Stockbridge and was attacked by giant doll-like figures that resembled a butcher, a baker and a candlestick maker. He was rescued by his old friend Maxwell Edison and a fellow UFO spotter named Izzy. They had acquired a strange medallion called the "focus", but were soon rounded up by humanoid foxes in hunting gear and brought to the Celestial Toymaker – who had created a surreal version of Stockbridge, and stuffed the real one in a snowglobe.

The Toymaker similarly captured the Doctor and Izzy in a snowglobe, and the Doctor was forced to hand over the focus. It was part of the Imagineum – a device built by an ancient race of alchemists – and the Toymaker used it to create an evil doll-like Doctor-duplicate. However, the two Doctors teamed up and exposed the Toymaker to the device. The Toymakers disappeared into the void, in perpetual stalemate, and Izzy joined the Doctor on his travels.

Eventually, Izzy decided to leave the Doctor's company

635 *Original Sin.* Vaughn's memories are, by his own admission, corrupted and he seems to be a year out.
636 *Interference*
637 *Something Inside.* The year is unspecified, although there's nothing to say it isn't the discontinued Ghana celebration mentioned in *The Chase*.
638 Dating *The Sands of Time* (MA #22) - The date is given (p117).
639 Dating "End Game" and "Oblivion" (*DWM* #244-247, 323-328) - "End Game" takes place "six days to Christmas", and the day of Izzy's return (the same as when she left) is given as "December 19th, 1996" in "Oblivion". We learn in "TV Action" that Izzy was born on 12th October, 1979, and she's "17" in a couple of the strips. "The Company of Thieves" establishes that Izzy is short for Isabelle.
640 Dating "Imaginary Enemies" (*DWM* #455) - It's after Amelia first met the Doctor in April 1996 (*The Eleventh Hour*). Rory and Amelia are in Year Three of Leadworth Primary School, so must be age seven. Given Amelia's birth year of 1989, then, it's presumably still 1996, at Christmastime.
641 The Haisman Timeline says this happened in 1997, after *Battlefield*. UNIT: The Coup [c.2005] is the first *Doctor Who* story to state that the Brigadier has been knighted, which was later mentioned on screen in *The Poison Sky* and *SJA: Enemy of the Bane*.
642 *Downtime* (pgs. 259-263). It's been "one hundred and fifty years" since Victoria posed for Dodgson in 1857, suggesting that she's in hiding for a year or two following the New World incident.
643 "Fifteen years" before *TW: Mr Invincible*.
644 *The Time Museum*. Ian is now an older man, and it's "long after" he finished traveling with the Doctor. It would be symmetrical to place this audio with its

release in 2012, but Ian says his home is "London, England, the twentieth century".
645 *The Sontaran Stratagem*. The Doctor says that Rattigan is only "18", but he's either estimating or belittling him, as Rattigan's on screen biography says he attended local primary school from 1990 to 1992 – suggesting that, like the actor who played him (Ryan Sampson), Rattigan was born in 1985.
646 *Knock, Knock*
647 *Benny: The Vampire Curse*: "The Badblood Diaries", with an obvious reference to *Buffy the Vampire Slayer*.
648 "The Mark of Mandragora"
649 *Minuet in Hell*
650 *Ghosts of India*
651 Dating *Bullet Time* (PDA #45) - The date of April 1997 is given (p15). Sarah Jane visits Bangkok just prior to this in March (p7). Britain turned over Hong Kong to China on 1st July, 1997. The report of Sarah Jane's demise in this novel is largely unsubstantiated and hails from Ryder's unreliable point-of-view. *Sometime Never* suggests the ambiguity of her death owes to the Council of Eight's machinations. Sarah clearly survives, as evidenced in *School Reunion*, *The Sarah Jane Adventures* and several of the books (including *System Shock, Millennium Shock, Christmas on a Rational Planet, Interference* and *The Shadow in the Glass*). *Bullet Time* never names the stranded aliens, but they would appear to be the Tzun from McIntee's *First Frontier*. The Cortez Project head, General Kyle, is possibly Marianne Kyle from *The Face of the Enemy*.
652 Dating *The Rapture* (BF #36) - Ace reckons it is "ten years" after she left Earth.
653 Dating *Mastermind* (BF CC #8.1) - The Master is captured "fifteen years" prior to 2012.

and make things right with her parents. He returned her to Stockbridge at the exact moment she left.

1996 (Christmas) - "Imaginary Enemies"[640] ->
Young Amelia Pond, Rory Williams and their friend Mels prepared for a Christmas nativity play in Leadworth, but a Crack in Time attracted one of the Pantheon of Discord, who manifested as "Uncle Krampus". The desire of Veronica Stackmore, the mayor's spoiled daughter, to be "the most gorgeous" girl in school enabled Krampus' goblins to overpower Amelia's trio and bind them in giftwrap. Krampus needed Veronica's verbal agreement to banish the group, but she realised Krampus' duplicitous nature and rejected him, banishing him instead. Everyone save Mels lost their memory of these events.

1997

Alistair Gordon Lethbridge-Stewart was knighted.[641]

Victoria Waterfield landed on Interpol's Most Wanted list due to the New World University affair, and went into hiding as "Victoria Harris". She received visits from the fourth Doctor, then the third Doctor – who provided her with a letter of reference to clear her name with Brigadier Crichton at UNIT. She and the third Doctor met in June, in Oxford, at an event celebrating the drawings and photographs of Charles Dodgson, a.k.a. Lewis Carroll.[642]

The benign Arqualian race had the ability to manipulate time and matter. A liaison in Cardiff between one of their number, Belfagor, and the wife of Ross Chapman resulted in the birth of a girl, Jody. Ross believed Jody was his child, and Belfagor left after giving Jody's mother a necklace that would control Jody's abilities once she came of age.[643]

An un-adventurous race constructed a Time Museum housing items pertaining to time travelers. Its curator, Pendolin, surreptitiously subsisted off the visitors' memories and experiences, but caused so much badwill for the facility that attendance plummeted. Pendolin spirited Ian Chesterton away from London with a Time Scoop, thinking his abduction would lure the ultimate memory feast – the Doctor – to the Museum. Ian returned home after leaving Pendolin at the mercy of memory-eating monstrosities in the Museum, preventing Pendolin from traveling with him to feed off humanity. Pendolin was left with the vague memory that he *was* Ian Chesterton.[644]

The genius Luke Rattigan became a millionaire, age 12, following his invention of the Fountain 6 search engine.[645] **The Dryads feasted upon another six tenants in 1997.**[646] Sunnydale, California, refused to reissue permits for tour caravans to park on Main Street anytime after 1997, between the hours of midnight and 4 a.m.[647]

The drug Mandrake, or M, first appeared on the streets in 1997. Its crystalline structure contained an unknown radiation, and UNIT classified it as a Foreign Hazard

(meaning alien).[648] The Brigadier helped to oversee the creation of a new Parliament for Scotland.[649] The Doctor was given a sun visor by Ginger Spice.[650]

1997 (April) - BULLET TIME[651] ->
With Britain scheduled to relinquish Hong Kong to China, the Chinese government secretly created the Tao Te Lung, a smuggling and extortion ring, as a means of rooting out Hong Kong's criminal element beforehand. The seventh Doctor usurped control of the Tao Te Lung, and used its operations to covertly move a group of stranded extra-terrestrials.

A rogue UNIT faction, The Cortez Project, sought to eliminate all extra-terrestrials as a threat to humanity. The Doctor arranged for his old ally, Sarah Jane Smith, to travel to Hong Kong and expose the Cortez members. However, Sarah's investigations put her in danger from the Tao Te Lung. In order to save Sarah's life, the Doctor arranged to publicly discredit her as a journalist.

The Doctor's alien allies reached their sunken spaceship, but a group of Cortez commandos, led by Colonel Tsang, seized control of the USS *Westmoreland* submarine in an attempt to head them off. The Doctor thwarted the Cortez members and the aliens departed Earth.

One account of these events suggested that Sarah Jane killed herself to prevent Tom Ryder, an intelligence agency operative, from holding her hostage to blackmail the Doctor. Other reports failed to corroborate her death.

1997 (May) - THE RAPTURE[652] ->
The Euphorian Empire had fallen into war with Scordatora. The drafted brothers Jude and Gabriel deserted and fled through the dimensional portal they previously used to reach Earth in 1855. Bar owner Gustavo Riviera helped the brothers found the Rapture nightclub in San Antonio, Izbia.

Gabriel's mental health deteriorated, and Jude realised that he'd need to take his brother home for medical care. Fearing court-martial and summary execution, Jude decided to entrance the Rapture patrons with PCP and a special mix of Gabriel's music, then kidnap the humans back to the Empire as an offering of ready-made soldiers. On 15th May, Gustavo disavowed the brothers' actions and wrestled with Gabriel, causing them to fall to their deaths. A vengeful Jude tried to unleash a music score that would kill anyone who heard it, but the seventh Doctor and Ace – now calling herself Dorothy McShane – thwarted Jude's plan. Jude fled. Sometime later, a young office worker opened an e-mail attachment that played music from the Rapture nightclub.

At the Rapture, Dorothy encountered her younger brother Liam.

1997 - MASTERMIND[653] ->
Frankie don Maestro died in 1997. Thomas don Maestro disobeyed his father's instructions to never unseal his grandfather's penthouse,

and informed the authorities after finding the sleeping, decaying Master within. The Master refrained from escaping, thinking it the best way to reunite with his TARDIS. As one of her first assignments with UNIT, Ruth Matheson escorted the Master to UNIT's Groom Lake facility. He was later transferred to UNIT's Vault.

> **= c 1997 - BATTLEFIELD**[654] **->** In a parallel universe, twelve centuries after defeating Arthur, Deathless Morgaine of the Fey had become battle queen of the S'Rax, ruler of thirteen worlds. Her world was scientifically advanced with energy weapons and ornithopters, but the people weren't reliant on technology and still knew the magic arts. There was still resistance against her rule, as Merlin had promised that Arthur would return in the hour of greatest need. Morgaine's immortal son Mordred led her troops to victory at Camlaan, forcing an enemy soldier, Ancelyn, to flee the field.

Morgaine had tracked the magical sword Excalibur to our dimension, which Mordred called Avallion. When UNIT discovered that the Doctor was involved in this affair, the Secretary General persuaded Brigadier Alistair Gordon Lethbridge-Stewart to come out of retirement. Morgaine's extra-dimensional knights fought UNIT as led by Brigadier Winifred Bambera, and Morgaine secured control of a nuclear missile. The seventh Doctor, Ace and the Brigadier put paid to Morgaine's plans.

Benny attended Bambera and Ancelyn's wedding.[655]

Elizabeth II Briefly Deposed

1997 (Tuesday, 6th May) - THE DYING DAYS[656] **->** Mars 97, a British mission to the Red Planet, inadvertently trespassed on a Martian tomb. Xznaal, leader of the Argyre clan, used this as a pretext to invade Earth. He was working with the power-hungry Lord Greyhaven, and together they deposed the Queen and took control of the United Kingdom. Xznaal was crowned King of England and began begins transporting slave labour to Mars. When the eighth Doctor was apparently killed, the Brigadier, Benny and UNIT formed a resistance movement that marched on London to dethrone the usurper. The Martians attempted to release "the Red Death", which would have wiped out all life on Earth. Greyhaven died trying to stop Xznaal, and the Doctor returned to save the day.

Lethbridge-Stewart was promoted to General.

"Since the Gantic Invasion and the Availlon Fiasco, unearthly threats have become a matter of fact."[657]

---

654 Dating *Battlefield* (26.1) - The Doctor tells Ace that they are "a few years in your future". Sergeant Zbrigniev is apparently in his mid-thirties, served in UNIT while the Doctor was present, and appears to have first-hand recollection of two of the Doctor's regenerations. Even if we assume that Zbrigniev is older than he looks (say, forty), and was very young when he joined UNIT, *Spearhead from Space* must have taken place in the mid-seventies. (The earliest Zbrigniev could be in the regular army is age 16, but he'd almost certainly need a couple more years before seeing active service, especially with an elite organisation like UNIT.)

The *Battlefield* novelisation by Marc Platt, based on notes by story author Ben Aaronovitch, sets the story in "the late 1990s" (p15). Ace later notices that Peter Warmsley's tax disc expires on "30.6.99" (p30). *The Terrestrial Index* set the story in "1992" and *The TARDIS Special* chose 1991 - perhaps they misheard the Doctor's line as "two years in your future". The Haisman Timeline goes with "1997". In a document for Virgin Publishing dated 23rd March, 1995, concerning "Future History Continuity", Ben Aaronovitch perhaps settled the matter when he stated that *Battlefield* is set "c.1997". *The Dying Days* is set after this story.

UNIT files in *Signs and Wonders* [c 2024] mention Ace's involvement in "1997", presumably in reference to this story. The Excalibur entry in *A History of the Universe in 100 Objects* (p133) dates *Battlefield* to "circa 1997".

The Doctor is apparently surprised to learn that Lethbridge-Stewart married Doris - in this story, *The King of Terror* and *The Spectre of Lanyon Moor*.

THE FUTURE OF THE UNITED NATIONS: By *Battlefield*, UNIT is a truly multinational organisation with British, Czechoslovakian and Polish troops serving side by side. By 2006, the United Nations is vital enough to global stability that it possess the nuclear launch codes for the world governments, meaning the UK must obtain a special UN resolution to deploy its arsenal (*World War Three*). This is an echo, within *Doctor Who*, of the UK being a guardian to everyone's nuclear codes in the UNIT era (*Robot*). During the Dalek invasion of 2009, it's the United Nations that appeals to the public for peace, and it's the Commander General of the United Nations who surrenders to the Dalek onslaught.

In *The Pyramid at the End of the World* (set in 2017), the United Nations Secretary-General re-appoints the Doctor as president of Earth during the crisis with the Monks. By the time of *The Enemy of the World* (set in 2018), nations have been grouped together into Zones. The governing body of the world is the United Zones, or the World Zones Authority, headed by a General Assembly.

The United Nations still exists at the time of the Thousand Day War referred to in the New Adventure *Transit*. Gradually, though, national barriers break down and a World Government runs the planet. Where this

1997 - THE MANY HANDS[658] -> The tenth Doctor took Martha to Edinburgh in 1997 to show her the Scott Monument, where the Nor' Loch had been once.

Sam Jones Joins the TARDIS

1997 - THE EIGHT DOCTORS[659] -> The eighth Doctor, his memory wiped by the Master, landed in Totter's Lane, London. He saved the life of schoolgirl Samantha Jones, who was being chased by the drug dealers Baz and Mo. After a series of adventures, the Doctor returned to the junkyard and Sam persuaded him to take her with him.

1997 - VAMPIRE SCIENCE[660] -> Carolyn McConnell summoned the eighth Doctor and Sam when she suspected vampires were active in San Francisco. The Doctor arrived and joined up with the American branch of UNIT, run by Brigadier-General Kramer. A generational war was brewing between the vampires, and a group of younger vampires – led by the upstart Slake – wiped out every old vampire except for their leader, Joanna Harris. The Doctor ingested silver nitrate, killing Slake and all the vampires that feasted on his blood. He also arranged for Harris to become human again. Harris and Carolyn joined the staff of UNIT.

Before this time, Kramer's branch of UNIT handled a Brieri scouting party.

c 1997 - GENOCIDE[661] -> Jo Grant and her husband Cliff had now separated, and had an 11-year-old son named Matthew. The Tractite named Gavril grew a time tree from a seedling, and allied himself with an ecowarrior named Jacob Hynes. Archaeologists Rowenna Michaels and Julie Sands had an offputting encounter with Hynes, who was posing as a UNIT captain, in the Kilgai Gorge in Tanzania. Jo, as Rowenna's old friend, was summoned to help, but Hynes captured all three of the women. A confusing escape followed, and the time tree took Jo, Rowenna, Julie and Hynes back to 2.5 million BC. The eighth Doctor later returned Jo home, after she had preserved history by wiping out a Tractite colony.

1997 - AUTON[662] -> Dr Sally Arnold, the head of The Warehouse, conducted experiments that accidentally reactivated a Nestene energy unit. It revived several Autons, and while Arnold and Lockwood – the psychic leader of a UNIT containment team – quelled the situation, a bit of gelatinous Nestene essence escaped.

Jackie Tyler's father – "Grandad Prentice", as Rose called him – died of heart failure.[663] **Torchwood stripped bare a Jathaa Sun Glider that crashed off the Shetland Islands. They would deploy the ship's main weapon against the Sycorax in 2006.**[664]

Summer, a former attendee at the "Human-Be-In" rock festival in 1967, spent thirty years on the run from the mysterious gray-suited men. She settled in the American Northwest, but the fourth Doctor rescued Summer from the gray men as they arrived to kill her.[665]

c 1997 - THE PIT[666] -> UNIT were called in to investigate an alien skeleton discovered on Salisbury Plain. The seventh Doctor and William Blake arrived via a space-time tear, and the Doctor feared the skeleton wasn't entirely

leaves the UN is unclear, although it appears that the United Nations survives or is reformed at some time far in the future. In *Mission to the Unknown*, Lowry's ship is the "UN Deep Space Force Group 1", and has the United Nations symbol and a Union Jack on the hull.
655 *Benny: Present Danger*: "The Empire Variations"
656 Dating *The Dying Days* (NA #61) - The date is given at the start of the story and on the back cover. 6th May is the date that Virgin's license to publish *Doctor Who* books officially ended. Lethbridge-Stewart was cited as a General in *Head Games*.
657 "The Mark of Mandragora" – a reference to "Invaders from Gantac" and *Battlefield*.
658 Dating *The Many Hands* (NSA #24) - The year is given.
659 Dating *The Eight Doctors* (EDA #1) - The date is given. Technically, Sam returns home in *Interference* before her younger self leaves with the Doctor.
660 Dating *Vampire Science* (EDA #2) - The date is given (p25).
661 Dating *Genocide* (EDA #3) - The time seems concurrent with the book's publication in 1997. On page 147, Jo wonders if even "twentieth-century hospitals" will be capable of curing an illness that Julie contracts. Jo and Cliff are separated, and while it's not expressly said that they're divorced – they live near each other, and remain friendly enough that Cliff gave Jo a present on the first anniversary after he left her – Jo is using her maiden name of Grant, having been formerly known as Jo Jones. Matthew would appear to be Jo and Cliff's only child, contradicting the shedload of offspring they have in *SJA: Death of the Doctor*.
662 Dating *Auton* (Auton film #1) - The story was released in 1997, and seems contemporary. Lockwood says that the Nestenes are using "a bit of slurry" left over from a body they tried to create "decades ago" – presumably a reference to *Spearhead from Space*.
663 "Ten years" before *Army of Ghosts*.
664 Also "ten years" before *Army of Ghosts*, and elaborating on the super-weapon used in *The Christmas Invasion*.
665 *Wonderland*
666 Dating *The Pit* (NA #12) - The Doctor and the poet William Blake travel to the 1990s, apparently after the

dormant. Hunters riding batlike creatures came through the tear and tore apart a passenger airliner just outside Bristol. The Doctor and Blake travelled to the Yssgaroth's domain, then into the future.

1997 - INFINITE REQUIEM[667] **->** Twenty-one-year-old Tilusha Meswani died shortly after giving birth to her child Sanjay, who was really the Sensopath named Kelzen – an immensely powerful, psionic being. Kelzen grew rapidly to adulthood and gained empathy with humanity. It agreed to help the seventh Doctor fight another Sensopath on Gadrell Minor in 2387.

= 1997 (30th June-1st July) - UNBOUND: SYMPATHY FOR THE DEVIL[668] **->** The Time Lords exiled the Doctor to Earth, but instead of arriving in the 1970s as expected, he found himself in Hong Kong the day before Britain returned the territory to China. The mind-parasites slaved to the Ke Le Machine were exhausted, and the Chinese government opted to eliminate them with a nuclear explosion in Inner Mongolia, a burst timed to coincide with the Hong Kong transfer.

The alt-Doctor of this reality once again met Lethbridge-Stewart as the Master went to Hong Kong and found the last mind-parasite – with it, he hoped to gain exclusive control of the Ke Le Divisions, and become emperor of Earth. The alt-Master died in a plane crash, but regenerated. The alt-Doctor tricked the alt-Master into thinking the entrance to the Brigadier's pub was his TARDIS, then subjected the mind-parasite to the same nuclear annihilation as its fellows. The resultant explosion broke the TARDIS' inhibitor, freeing the alt-Doctor and the Brigadier to leave Earth for further adventures...

Hammerson Plastics PLC came out of nowhere to corner the market in plastics in six months. The success was credited to automation techniques, but the organisation was a front for an Auton production facility.[669]

The Conspiracy Channel broadcast *The Last Days of Hitler?*, written and directed by Claire Aldwych, on 12th August, 1997.[670] The only Recoronation in British history took place on 23rd November, 1997. Queen Elizabeth II was formally restored to the throne following Xznaal's usurpation of the crown.[671]

Doctor has met Brigadier Bambera in *Battlefield*.
667 Dating *Infinite Requiem* (NA #36) - It is "1997".
668 Dating *Unbound: Sympathy for the Devil* (BF Unbound #2) - The action begins the morning before Britain ceded control of Hong Kong to China on 1st July, 1997, and continues past that deadline. David Warner plays the Doctor in this story, *Unbound: Masters of War* and *NAofBenny* V3: *The Unbound Universe*. Colonel Brimmicombe-Wood, played by David Tennant, reappears in the proper timeline in *UNIT* Series 1.
669 "A couple of years" before "Plastic Millennium".
670 *The Shadow in the Glass*
671 *The Dying Days*, first mentioned in *Christmas on a Rational Planet*.
THE MONARCHY: Different stories say different things about who is the British monarch around the turn of the millennium. Lethbridge-Stewart refers to the King in *Battlefield*, which is set in the late twentieth century. *Happy Endings* specifies that King Charles ruled at the turn of the millennium. *Mad Dogs and Englishmen* (ch10) intimates that the Queen passed away before 2010, so is unable to give her speech at Christmas. There is a King when Mariah Learman seizes power in *The Time of the Daleks*, and by the time of *Trading Futures*. In *Revenge of the Judoon*, the tenth Doctor forecasts the reigns of Charles III and Queen Camilla, and King William V.
However, Queen Elizabeth II still reigns in *Head Games* (set in 2001), *Voyage of the Damned* (set in 2008), and - it seems, by inference - *Planet of the Dead* and *The End of Time* (both set in 2009). *Christmas on a Rational Planet* refers to the "Recoronation", apparently implying that Elizabeth II abdicated in favour of Charles, but - for reasons we can only speculate on - was restored to the throne soon afterwards. *The Dying Days* (set just after *Battlefield*) offers a different reason for the Recoronation: the Queen was usurped by the Ice Warrior Xznaal.
In the *Doctor Who* universe, there's a Princess Mary who's 19 at time *Rags* is set (p158). While it isn't stated, she's clearly a senior royal and by birth, so the obvious inference is that she's the Queen's daughter.
672 Dating *Touched by an Angel* (NSA #47) - The exact day is given (p95).
673 *Christmas on a Rational Planet*. "Morley" is presumably the same as the "Paul" whom Sarah is dating but not married to in *Interference*, set two years previous in 1996. If so, there's no evidence that Sarah and Paul were married for long. When asked by Alan Jackson if she's ever been married (in *SJA: Revenge of the Slitheen*), Sarah replies "No, never found time" – which might suggest that their marriage was annulled, that Sarah means she "never found time to commit to a relationship of wedlock", or that she's withholding the entire truth from Alan (whom she's just met and has no reason to be all that forthcoming with) or some combination of all of those options. If Sarah and Paul's marriage fizzled out quickly, it could owe to what Sarah implies in *SJA: Invasion of the Bane* – that there was "only ever one man for me [i.e. the Doctor]. After him, nothing

1997 (16th December) - TOUCHED BY AN ANGEL[672] -> The version of Mark Whitaker that was living through the 1990s a second time arranged for his past self to receive a lottery ticket worth £16,000. Rebecca Coles was now engaged to a man named Anthony.

1998

By 1998, Sarah Jane Smith had married a man called Morley, and was a speaker at the Nobel Academy.[673] **Emojis were invented; in the entire universe, only humans used them.**[674] For the first time, Lethbridge-Stewart stayed over with his son Albert's family.[675]

In April 1998, Rebecca Coles split with her fiancé after discovering that he was cheating on her. They had already booked holiday in Rome, and so Mark Whitaker agreed to go with her. He paid for his half from the £16,000 lottery winnings his future self had provided.[676] In 1998, the Japanese set up the Nikkei 5 station in the Antarctic to measure carbon dioxide levels.[677] Margaret Thatcher might have returned to power at some point.[678]

Paul Travers reviewed a Johnny Chess concert in the 18/7/98 *NME*.[679] A Kulan evaluation team crashed in Norway in 1998, split into two factions and began work supporting two rival space flight enterprises. The pro-invasion group helped entrepreneur Pierre Yves-Dudoin in the construction of his Star Dart shuttle, and the more benign faction sided with the lucrative Arthur Tyler III in building a Planet Hopper.[680]

In 1998, humanity's average life expectancy was sixty-six years, five months and thirty-three days. The Three Families had located the Blessing in the mid-90s; Angelo Colasanto and his granddaughter Olivia intercepted a message indicating as much in 1998.[681]

The Uvodni-Malakh War ended.[682] **The Pharos Para-Science Institute was established to study paranormal phenomena.**[683] Members of Drast Speculation Initiative Fourteen – alien speculators who would manipulate a target planet's economy and culture until it came under their control – established themselves on Earth.[684]

On 27th June, 1998, Torchwood obtained a corpse belonging to a member of Cell 114.[685]

1998 - SYSTEM SHOCK[686] -> Virtually every computer on Earth now used the operating system Vorell, developed by I^2. The owner of I^2, 43-year-old Lionel Stabfield, quickly became the fifth richest man in the world. His company bought the rights to every major work of art, releasing images of them on interactive discs. The new technology allowed flat-panel, interactive television and the recordable CD-ROM to be perfected. Sales of computer equipment rocketed still further.

All computers were joined up to the Hubway, a formalised version of the Internet. As Hubway went online, though, chaos broke out: aeroplanes crashed at Heathrow as air traffic control systems failed, the Astra satellite was sent into a new orbit, the Library of Congress catalogue and all its backups were wiped, the computer facilities of the First National Bank of China were obliterated. Instruments at Nunton told technicians that the reactor had gone to meltdown. The head of MI5, Veronica Halliwell, was assassinated. Jonah Cosgrove, former sixties superspy, succeeded her as the head of MI5.[687]

This was all part of the plan of the Voracians, cybernetic reptilians from Vorella. They planned to use the sentient software Voractyll to take control of the Earth. The fourth Doctor, Sarah and Harry helped to defeat them.

---

compared..." – even if she comes to reevaluate that position while under supernatural influence (*SJA: The Wedding of Sarah Jane Smith*).

674 *Smile*. Shigataka Kurita created the first emoji in 1998 or 1999.

675 "Three years" before *Leth-St: "The Two Brigadiers"*.

676 *Touched by an Angel*

677 *Iceberg*

678 In *Transit*, there's a history book called *Thatcher: The Wilderness Years*.

679 *Timewyrm: Revelation*

680 *Escape Velocity*

681 *TW: Miracle Day*

682 "Twenty years" before *SJA: The Lost Boy*. Despite the similar name, no overt connection has been made between the Pharos Institute and the Pharos Project seen in *Logopolis*.

683 "Ten years" before *SJA: Warriors of Kudlak*.

684 "Ten years" before the linking material in *The Story of Martha*. As the Drast are defeated during the year of

time that's erased in *Last of the Time Lords*, it's unclear what ended their plans in the actual history.

685 Per Alex Hopkins' report on Torchwood.org.uk.

686 Dating *System Shock* (MA #11) - When asked, a bar-man, Rod, informs the Doctor that this is "1998". The Doctor goes on to tell Sarah that in that particular year, "nothing of interest happened as far as I remember". It is "twenty odd years" after Sarah's time, and she muses that a "greying, mid-forties" future version of herself is alive in 1998, which the epilogue confirms.

687 Cosgrove has "not left his desk in London for nearly twenty years" before *Trading Futures*.

c 1998 - OPTION LOCK[688] -> President Dering was now in the White House, with Jack Michaels serving as vice-president.

The Khameirian-sponsored brotherhood, founded in the thirteenth century, had many members in positions of power. They sought to trigger a nuclear conflict that would produce the energy needed for the Khameirians to recorporealise. A brotherhood member launched an unauthorised nuclear strike from Krejikistan, which compelled the Americans to reveal the nuke-killing Station Nine as they nullified the threat. The US subsequently turned Station Nine over to the United Nations.

The brotherhood's leader, Norton Silver, forced the eighth Doctor to relocate the TARDIS to Station Nine to launch a nuclear strike from there. Britain's Captain Pickering died while destroying Station Nine to prevent this, an act that also killed Silver and the Khameirian core within him. A month later, Sam Jones learned that Silver's widow was pregnant, and worried the Khameirian taint might have passed to the child.

1998 (11th-12th August) - TOUCHED BY AN ANGEL[689] -> The older Mark Whitaker had started a consultancy company, and used his foreknowledge of the future to make millions. He was a partial investor in *Mama Mia!* The eleventh Doctor, Amy and Rory helped the older Mark to lock his younger self and Rebecca out on a balcony for the evening – and the two of them took the opportunity to cement their budding relationship.

c 1998 - THE BELLS OF SAINT JOHN: A PREQUEL[690] -> The eleventh Doctor stopped at a playground, and remarked to a young girl – actually a young Clara Oswald – that he was sad because he'd lost his friend twice, and worried that he wouldn't meet her again.

---

688 Dating *Option Lock* (EDA #8) - It's "present day England" according to the blurb.

AMERICAN PRESIDENTS IN THE DOCTOR WHO UNIVERSE: As with British political history, *Doctor Who* presents a version of modern-day American politics that's a mix of historical fact and whimsy. *Interference* lists the recent American Presidents as Carter, Reagan, Bush, Clinton, Dering (*Option Lock*, around 1998), Springsteen (*Eternity Weeps*, 2003) and Norris (*Cat's Cradle: Warhead*, circa 2007 or 2009). *Placebo Effect* further acknowledges Bill Clinton's presidency. *Death Comes to Time* has George W Bush as President, and stories including *Trading Futures* and *Unregenerate!* mention features of his presidency such as the War on Terror and the Iraq War. President Arthur Winters appears in *The Sound of Drums*, set in June 2008, but he's assassinated. Obama is president in *The End of Time*, which occurs at Christmas 2009, and in *The Forgotten Army* (p129), set in 2010. In *The Pyramid at the End of the World*, set in 2017, Bill refers to the US President as being "orange" (meaning Donald Trump, clearly). However, the "dead", computer-generated President seen in the previous episode, *Extremis*, is clearly neither Trump nor Obama. Trump is seen as part of a video montage in *The Lie of the Land*, and the Doctor says that Trump is "inevitable" in *The Doctor Falls*.

A discrepancy is that in *SJA: The Secrets of the Stars* (set at November 2009), the president is hypnotised because he's a Cancer – in real life, Obama was born 4th August and is a Leo. (Possibly, the news report of "the president" walking out of the White House is simply wrong.) Norris doesn't fit the bill of being a Cancer either; he was born 10th March. Funnily enough, George W. Bush was born 6th July, and has the correct astrological symbol.

Bad Wolf mentions President Schwarzenegger (at present, Arnold is barred from the US presidency since he wasn't born an American citizen). *Trading Futures* has President Mather in charge around 2015.

It is a little tricky to juggle the aforementioned presidents without inferring any impeachments or assassinations. Still, assuming the same fixed terms, elections would take place in, and be won by:

1996: Dering (meaning Clinton was a single termer in the *Doctor Who* universe.)

2000: Springsteen

2004: George W Bush (another single termer in the *Doctor Who* universe – this time missing the first term he had historically. This would set *Death Comes to Time* a couple of years after it was released, but that's not ruled out by the story. The reference in *Neverland* claiming the "wrong man became President" was meant to refer to Bush winning in 2000, which might be relevant – if highly ambiguous – in this context.)

Winters, then Norris, or vice-versa (US presidential elections are always held in November, so Winters being president in June 2008 would seem to indicate – unless one discards *Death Comes to Time* entirely, in which case Bush was probably never president and Winters was elected in 2004 – that Bush failed to complete his entire term. It's tempting to think that Norris takes office following Winters' death in June 2008, as the dating for *Cat's Cradle: Warhead* is probably flexible enough to accommodate that. In which case, Norris only serves for a few months until the 2008 election. This is somewhat cleaner than thinking that Norris followed Bush and that Winters – somehow – followed Norris, which would result in another unnamed person being president after Winters is killed.

(Winters' statement in *The Sound of Drums* that he's "president elect" must be his way of telling the Toclafane "I'm the elected representative of my people" – a US politician would never use this term in such a fashion, as Americans use the term "president elect" to

c 1998 - IRIS S5: ORACLE OF THE SUPERMARKET[691]

-> Apollo Automata cannibalized the fairground equipment containing the Oracle from ancient Greece, and thereby released it. Just as birds had served as a symbol of prophecy, the Oracle inhabited a duck-shaped kiddie ride at a Fergusons in the North of England. A worker there, Cassie Burdock, became gifted with prophecy and gave readings to the Fergusons customers as "Clairvoyant Cassie". Iris and Captain Turner stopped in to purchase some herbs and rebound the Oracle, ending its mischief.

Helen Sinclair Loses Her Family

1998 (August) - DC 3: ABSENT FRIENDS[692] -> A Doomsday Chronometer piece drew the TARDIS to a sleepy English town. Helen Sinclair visited her brother George by posing as her "daughter, Ruth", and learned that her parents and older brother Harry had passed away, hav-

ing never heard from her after 1963. On learning this, her past became unalterable, and she could never see them again. After Helen left George's house, he passed away also.

Temporal distortion from the Chronometer piece connected mobile phones to other eras, enabling people to talk to their dead loved ones. To preserve history, Liv refrained from telling her late father of the illness that would kill him. The eighth Doctor, Liv and Helen secured the piece in the Lost Property Office of the London Underground, and went to find the rest of the Chronometer.

---

indicate someone who's won a presidential election but has not yet taken office. The US Constitution dictates that a president elect can only exist between early November and the following January – anyone who becomes president via the death, incapacitation, resignation or Congressional ousting of the sitting president would immediately take office.)

2008: Obama (wins the November 2008 election as he did in real life. The extreme social and economic upheaval seen in *TW: Miracle Day* in 2011 – including the cratering of the economy and the construction of mass incinerators for the near-dead – calls into question whether any sitting president could win reelection the next year, which might result in Obama being a single-termer.)

2012: Mather

2016 or 2020: Schwarzenegger (he'd be 69 or 73 on taking office.)

Their party affiliation can perhaps be inferred – if Dering beats Clinton (rather than, say, Clinton stepping aside or being impeached), he's a Republican. The real-life Springsteen is a Democrat. Winters is almost doubtlessly a Republican, as his portrayal in *The Sound of Drums* marks him as a conservative. The real-life Chuck Norris is a Republican. Obama is a Democrat. Mather served in Bush's Cabinet, so he's likely a Republican (only on rare occasions will a Cabinet member hail from a different party, although it happened under Clinton and Obama). We might assume that Schwarzenegger wouldn't stand against a fellow Republican, so Mather serves two terms.

FP: Head of State paints a different picture of American politics in that – owing to the timeship Lolita's nips and tucks to history – Senator Matt Nelson of Minnesota forms the breakaway Democratic Farm-Labor Party and wins the presidency (the year isn't given, but we've gone with the 2012 election for this).

Nelson is rapidly assassinated, paving the way for Lolita, posing as Nelson's Vice-President, to be sworn in. The mercurial nature of the *Faction Paradox* books, coupled with Lolita's reweaving of time, calls into question whether any of this is part of the "proper" timeline. But for her handiwork, it's said, the winner of this election was supposed to be a moderate Republican (Mather fits the bill).

Some final notes on this... in *Kill the Moon* [2049], the twelfth Doctor tells Clara that, "rather bizarrely", Coal Hill student Courtney Woods will be president of the United States. We might imagine she was born in the US, or she's eligible per the same Constitutional amendment that brought about President Schwarzenegger. Also, *The Silurian Candidate* [2085] suggests the office of the US President was abolished, perhaps in the geopolitical restructuring that gave rise to the Western and Eastern Blocs depicted in *Warriors of the Deep* [c.2084]

689 Dating *Touched by an Angel* (NSA #47) - The exact days are given (pgs. 103, 126).

690 Dating *The Bells of Saint John: A Prequel* (Series 7 webcast) - The girl portraying Clara is clearly older than the one seen in flashback in *The Rings of Akhaten*, closer (at a rough guess) to ten than age five. Released before *The Bells of Saint John*, this prequel gives the impression that the Doctor doesn't know that the girl seen here is Clara, but his subsequent stalking of her (*Akhaten* again) might suggest that he does know her identity.

691 Dating *Iris S5: Oracle of the Supermarket* (BF *Iris* #5.3) - Iris says that they're at a "late twentieth-century supermarket". She also finds a street using Google Maps, which wasn't founded until 2005, but that sort of cross-temporal technology access (a la Rose Tyler's magic phone) wouldn't be hard for a time traveller such as herself.

692 Dating *DC 3: Absent Friends* (BF *DC* #3.1) - The year and month are given.

Thomas "Hex" Schofield, a companion of the seventh Doctor, was born to Cassandra Schofield on 12th October, 1998.[693] **When Rose Tyler was 12, she received a red bicycle for Christmas.**[694]

1999

Adelaide Brooke, the woman destined to become the commander of the first Martian colony, **was born on 12th May, 1999.**[695] A rain of frogs was reported in San Francisco.[696]

wih - The Great Houses dispatched Chris Cwej to curtail the activities of Faction Hollywood. Cwej bested Faction Hollywood's leader, Michael Brookhaven, in combat during the Hollywood Bowl Shooting incident of 1999; Faction Hollywood was not expected to prosper after Brookhaven's downfall.[697]

In 1999, a division of Phicorp purchased the land in Shanghai containing the Blessing – part of the Three Families' preparation to destroy the world's economy and rebuild it under their control.[698] In June 1999, James Lawson of Torchwood Cardiff improved upon a formula supplied by Jack Harkness, and did the early field tests on the amnesia drug Retcon.[699]

& 1999 - THE RETURN OF DOCTOR MYSTERIO[700] **-> The twelfth Doctor posed as a relief algebra teacher, and checked up on the superpowered Grant Gordon. The bashful lad was undergoing puberty, so couldn't control his X-ray vision, and was being made to experience a "naked hell".**

c 1999 - FP: WARLORDS OF UTOPIA[701] **->** Marcus Americanius Scriptor arrived in the True Earth to track down August Hitler, who had been spirited away from his own parallel universe. The Little Hitler was in South America. Scriptor killed him, then wrote an account of his long life.

1999 - AUTON 2: SENTINEL / AUTON 3: AWAKENING[702] **->** The Nestene essence that escaped from The Warehouse two years previous established an Auton contingent on the remote Sentinel Island, home to the best preserved of the ancient Nestene chambers. Lockwood used a psychic seed the Nestene had planted in his mind to absorb the long-dormant Nestene beneath the island, and prevented it from summoning the entire Nestene consciousness to Earth.

Soon afterwards, all of the New York Exchange's systems were wiped, the Nasdac went into freefall and Flight 4906

---

693 *The Harvest, Project: Destiny.* Actor Philip Oliver was born 4th June, 1980, making him – relatively speaking – about a year older than the character he's playing.
694 It's implied in *The Doctor Dances* that the Doctor gave it to her.
695 *The Waters of Mars*
696 *Iris S2: The Panda Invasion.* No such rain has occurred in real life, but this might be a reference to the frog downpour in *Magnolia* (1999).
697 *FP: The Book of the War*
698 *TW: Miracle Day*
699 From *The Torchwood Archives* (BBC). Lawson is cited as dead in *TW: In the Shadows*, and is presumably one of the slain Torchwood staff in *TW: Fragments*.
700 Dating *The Return of Doctor Mysterio* (X10.0) - Year unknown, but Grant was eight in the story's first part, and he's now experiencing the turmoil of puberty. If the Doctor isn't joking that he's posing as an algebra teacher, then Grant is likely in high school. The story's modern-day component happens "twenty-four years" after Grant met Lucy, but that happened before this, while they were "in elementary school".
701 Dating *FP: Warlords of Utopia* (FP novel #3) - Scriptor gives the date.
702 Dating *Auton 2: Sentinel* and *Auton 3: Awakening* (Auton films #2-3) - It's repeatedly said in *Auton 2* that "two years" have passed since *Auton*, so it's a year in the future of *Auton 2*'s release in 1998. Events in *Auton 3* (released in 1999) continue from there.

703 Dating *The Crusade* VHS intro – William Russell portrayed Ian in these linking segments for the video release of *The Crusade*, the VHS release of which featured the newly discovered first episode "The Lion," but omitted the still-missing episodes two and four.
704 Dating *The King of Terror* (PDA #37) - It's "1 July 1999" (p5).
705 Dating *Dominion* (EDA #22) - On p35, Fitz reads a newspaper dated 31st July, 1999.
706 *The Suns of Caresh*, both the Child anomaly and Jo's observation.
707 *The Turing Test.* Heller died 12th December, 1999.
708 Dating *The Taking of Planet 5* (EDA #28) - It's "1 October 1999" (p21).
709 Dating "Darkness Falling"/"Distractions"/"The Mark of Mandragora" (*DWM* #167-172) - It's "the end of the twentieth century," but not (as far as we're told) New Year's 1999 itself. It's after *Battlefield*, and Mandrake first appeared in 1997 (so the story takes place after that). "Darkness Falling" and "Distractions," both prologues to the main story, went untitled in *The Mark of Mandragora* graphic novel.
710 Dating *Zygons: Homeland* (BBV audio #15) - The audio was released in 1999 and seems contemporary.
711 Dating *Krynoids: The Root of All Evil* (BBV audio #18) - The audio came out in 1999 and seems contemporary, including mention of *The X-Files* and the fact that mobile use is not so universal that the protagonists, when trapped on the farm, can just call for help.

came down over Berlin owing to computer error. Some surviving Autons tried to channel through Lockwood's mind a pulse that would awaken all the dormant Nestene on Earth, but he stopped their scheme by killing himself.

1999 - THE CRUSADE VHS INTRO[703] -> Ian Chesterton greeted a visitor in his home, and whereas he and Barbara had learned to keep quiet about their travels in time and space, he felt comfortable talking with the newcomer about the time he was knighted by Richard the Lionheart, and became Sir Ian Chesterton...

1999 (July) - THE KING OF TERROR[704] -> The alien Jex sought to conquer Earth, and had fronted the communications conglomerate InterCom to this end. They were secretly stockpiling plutonium to detonate and raise Earth's temperature to better accommodate their race. The Canavitchi, formerly enslaved to the Jex, worked to exterminate their former masters. The Brigadier received reports of extra-terrestrial involvement in California, and summoned the fifth Doctor, Tegan and Turlough to UNIT's Los Angeles office.

The Doctor and his allies brought InterCom to ruin as rival Jex and Canavitchi warfleets showed up in Earth orbit. The Doctor used Earth's satellite network to create a planetary defence shield as the warfleets slaughtered one another and departed. The Doctor advised the Brigadier to co-ordinate with the American CIA and help capture the Jex and Canavitchi agents still at-large.

1999 (July) - DOMINION[705] -> Department C19 had resumed active service by this time.

Professor Jennifer Nagle, a UNIT scientist, experimented with captured alien equipment at a C19 base in Sweden. She accidentally created a dimensional wormhole into a pocket universe named the Dominion. The larger universe expanded into the Dominion, threatening many races there. Some of the carnivorous Ruin fled through the wormhole to Earth, but Earth's higher gravity killed them.

The Dominion was completely eradicated, but the eighth Doctor evacuated fourteen of the frog-like T'hilli and their Queen to a habitable planet, saving the race from extinction. The wormhole terminated, but an energy backlash destroyed the C19 base and killed Nagle.

(=) In July 1999, an encounter with Lord Roche's dead TARDIS inflicted young Ezekiel Child with Jeapes' Syndrome, a condition in which a person matures backwards in time rather than forward. Child was 21 in 1999, but age 46 in 1972, and failed to notice anything odd about this. The Doctor's involvement retroactively averted the Child anomaly.

In 1999, a lingering side-effect of temporal interference turned the *Independent on Sunday* newspaper into the *Sunday Telegraph*.[706] Shortly after Joseph Heller's death, documents were found among his effects with the recollections of Alan Turing, Graeme Greene and Heller himself of their encounter with aliens in Dresden, 1945.[707]

wih - 1999 - THE TAKING OF PLANET 5[708] -> UNIT was called in to investigate an anomaly in the Antarctic that had been detected by satellite, and discovered a protoplasmic creature inside an alien structure. The eighth Doctor, Fitz and Compassion eventually arrived from twelve million years in the past, where they'd been thwarting the machinations of a group of future Time Lords.

The Second Mandragora Helix Incursion

c 1999 - "Darkness Falling" / "Distractions" / "The Mark of Mandragora"[709] -> The party drug M – Mandrake – was a problem. Captain Muriel Frost and Sergeant Jasper Bean of UNIT discovered a Mandrake factory at the popular Falling Star nightclub in London, but an energy creature killed Bean.

The Mandragora Helix was warping the TARDIS' structure and drawing it towards Earth. The seventh Doctor and Ace found themselves at the Falling Star with Frost, and Lethbridge-Stewart vouched for their identities via video link from Geneva. Returning to the Falling Star, they arrived to see the Helix energy manifesting in a bid to take over the Earth, then the universe. The Helix started to kill the clubbers, whose will had been sapped by the Mandrake drug, and Frost ordered in the UNIT troops. The Doctor was convinced the Helix had won, but the circuit broke. It appeared that the TARDIS had disintegrated, but it rematerialised at UNIT HQ a few days later.

The very public threat convinced the United Nations to increase UNIT's powers and put it on a more public footing. A new United Nations team – Foreign Hazard Duty – was set up to deal with problems that had to be kept more secret. Muriel Frost was promoted to Major.

1999 - ZYGONS: HOMELAND[710] -> UN military adviser Guy Dean and his allies stopped a group of Zygons from unleashing a shoal of Skarasen upon the world, but perished while self-destructing the Zygons' spacecraft.

1999 - KRYNOIDS: THE ROOT OF ALL EVIL[711] -> The Chase Foundation had a website that provided some information on Krynoids. Eve Black, a biologist working for the Ministry of Agriculture, destroyed two Krynoids that hatched on an isolated Yorkshire farm.

c 1999 - BENNY B3: LEGION: SHADES OF GRAY[712]

-> The Collector, a conceptual being with whom the immortal Dorian Gray had once broken a deal, stalked the dreams of Dorian's associates. It possessed the body of Dorian's lover, Spencer Price – whom Dorian killed, mournfully, to prevent the Collector fully manifesting.

Steven Carter – the son of Joe and Alice Carter (née Sangster), and the grandson of Jack Harkness – was born on 4th October, 1999.[713]

1999 (29th and 31st October) - TOUCHED BY AN ANGEL[714]

-> The older Mark Whitaker used his clout to secretly get his younger self a job with the law firm of Pollard & Bryce. The younger Mark Whitaker proposed to his beloved, Rebecca Coles.

The Millennium

The turn of the twenty-first century was one of the Doctor's favourite parts of Earth's history, and he suspected that he had visited it more times than he'd been on the *Titanic*.[715]

Ben Jackson's wife was "gone". Polly Wright was estranged from her son, Mikey. On the last day of 1999, Ben and Polly acknowledged their love for one another at a house that belonged to the Doctor, where they had gathered with the second Doctor and Jamie.[716]

Dana Morgan, a thrall of the Mandragora Helix, heightened the prominence of his company, MorganTech, on a news special broadcast that was live on 31st December, 1999.[717]

1999 (31st December) - "Plastic Millennium"[718]

-> The seventh Doctor and Mel gatecrashed a New Year's Eve hosted by Alisha Hammerson, director of the world's largest plastics factory, for the world's business leaders. Hammerson gassed the CEOs and planned to replace them

712 Dating *Benny B3: Legion: Shades of Gray* (Benny box set #3.2) - No year given. Dorian says, "I am so very old now, my friend. I have seen and done so much. I have written history," meaning it's well past his native time of the 1800s. He and Spencer are discrete about their relationship at high society parties, but it's unclear if it's because homosexuals are more closeted in this era, or simply because Spencer doesn't like people butting into his private life. Scott Hancock, the writer of this story, commented over email: "No specific date in mind [for the Gray and Price sequences], though I recall it most likely being the turn of the 20th century".

713 *TW: Children of Earth*

714 Dating *Touched by an Angel* (NSA #47) - The exact days are given (pgs. 129, 133).

715 "The Forgotten"

716 The short story "That Time I Nearly Destroyed the World Whilst Looking for a Dress" (from *Short Trips: Past Tense*, 2004), here mentioned because it's relevant to the continuity of *The Five Companions*.

717 *Beautiful Chaos* (p189). In a case of very awkward math, 31st December, 1999, is said to be "eight years" prior to 2009.

718 Dating "Plastic Millennium" (*DWM Winter Special 1994*) - The date is given. It's tempting to link the contents of the phial with the Doctor's "anti plastic" in *Rose*.

719 Dating *Millennial Rites* (MA #15) - The story revolves around the date, first confirmed on p34. The *Lethbridge-Stewart* novels don't recognise the events in *Millennial Rites*, and craft a different life-history for Anne Travers.

720 Dating *TW: Fragments* and *The Torchwood Archive* (TW 2.12, BF special release #1) - The day and exact time of Alex's death are given. There's no sign of reality warping at midnight of the New Year per *Doctor Who – The Movie*, but this could simply owe to the eight-hour time

difference between San Francisco and Cardiff.

721 *TW: Fragments*

722 *TW: One Rule*

723 Dating *Iris S2: The Panda Invasion* (BF Iris #2.4) - The day and year are given. Bits of this audio resonate with *Doctor Who – The Movie*: Iris is taken to a hospital, and an x-ray says that she's got two livers (rather than two hearts); the theft of a fancy dress costume is reported; and it's said that "Daphne" (a reference to Daphne Ashbrook, who played Grace) is "on shift". Even so, it's not specified that Iris is taken to the same hospital as the wounded seventh Doctor, and there's no reason why both stories can't occur together, especially as the authorities ignore reports of the evil Pandas. Panda and Iris are reunited *Iris S2: The Claws of Santa*.

724 Dating *Doctor Who – The Movie* (27.0) - The date is first given when Chang Lee fills out the Doctor's medical paperwork. On screen, the Master looks like a gelatinous snake, although *The Eight Doctors* attributes this to his swallowing a "deathworm". *The Dalek Handbook* (p90) stakes out the opinion that Skaro as seen in the TV Movie is the planet "restored circa 5725.2 (Rassilon era)" after its destruction in *Remembrance of the Daleks*.

Dalek: The Astounding Untold History of the Greatest Enemies of the Universe (p294) suggests that it's the Dalek Parliament from *Asylum of the Daleks* that puts the Master on trial in *Doctor Who – The Movie*.

725 *Tales from the Vault*

726 *Mastermind*, which attributes the Master's abilities in *Doctor Who – The Movie* to a "deathworm morphant". The latter word appeared in that story's novelisation; *The Eight Doctors* first used the full term.

with Autons. The Doctor brewed up a phial that he used to destroy the meteor that represented the link to the Nestene, and Hammerson melted.

1999 / 2000 (30th December to 1st January) - MILLENNIAL RITES[719] ->
Ashley Chapel had worked for International Electromatics before forming his own company, ACL. Following the collapse of I^2, ACL bought up all their hardware and software patents, and Chapel became a multi-millionaire. He funded the construction of the new Millennium Hall on the banks of the Thames, and began work on a powerful computer program – "the Millennium Codex" – that would use quantum mnemonics and block transfer computation. This would change the laws of physics to those of the universe of Saraquazel, which was created from the ashes of our own.

Elsewhere, Dame Anne Travers became worried about the return of the Great Intelligence. She attempted to banish the sentience, but inadvertently summoned it.

On the stroke of midnight, 31st December, 1999, magic returned to the world as the Intelligence and Saraquazel fused over London, transforming the city into an aeons-old battleground between the forces of three factions: the Abraxas, Magick and Technomancy. The sixth Doctor banished the Intelligence once more, and Anne gave her life to unravel the new physical laws – after only ten minutes of real time, the world was returned to normal. Saraquazel took Chapel back with him to his own universe.

Massacre at Torchwood Cardiff; Jack Harkness Takes Command

1999 (31st December) - TW: FRAGMENTS / THE TORCHWOOD ARCHIVE (BF)[720] ->
The Millennium Bug proved to be an eighteen-legged, poisonous insect, but Jack Harkness dropped a truck on it. The Torchwood Red List designated team leaders who had murdered their employees.

The Little Girl bequeathed **Alex Hopkins, the head of Torchwood Cardiff,** with a locket, the Bad Penny, while he was saving Newport from a spider-form. Hopkins returned to the Hub, and **used the locket to foresee the future. He was so horrified by events to come, he** joined the Red List when he **mercy-killed his teammates** – including a woman named Arianna – **and then himself on the stroke of midnight, the year 2000. The unkillable Jack Harkness, having given Torchwood Cardiff a century of service, assumed command of it.**

Among other things, Hopkins foresaw events involving the Committee, the 456, the Miracle, and that humanity would be wiped out and replaced by "something new". His mother, Marjorie, age 75, would remain in remission for only three months.

Jack subsequently severed all links between Torchwood Cardiff and Torchwood London.[721] Alex Hopkins had phoned Yvonne Hartman as he murdered his teammates, to advise her to take her own life. She became determined to make Torchwood even stronger against the oncoming threat he mentioned.[722]

1999 (31st December) - IRIS S2: THE PANDA INVASION[723] ->
Iris and Panda went to San Francisco, New Year's Eve, 1999, to find the biggest, happiest party in history – but Iris opened up a multi-dimensional rift after spilling gin into her bus' engine. Lional Pandeau, a version of Panda from a parallel universe, was drawn through the rift and poured more gin into the engine, widening the rift and summoning an army consisting of versions of himself/ Panda from alternate realities. Parts of San Francisco were beset by flying vampire Pandas from five million years in the future, as well as the lumbering monstrosity Panda-zilla. Panda pulled Lionel and himself into the rift, sealing it and returning the other Pandas to their native realities. Iris went in search of her lost friend as San Francisco authorities dismissed reports of the Pandas as a hoax or part of the millennium festivities.

The Seventh Doctor Regenerates; the Master Acquires a New Body

1999/2000 (30th December to 1st January) - DOCTOR WHO - THE MOVIE[724] ->
The seventh Doctor was transporting the Master's remains to Gallifrey from Skaro when the Master – now a gelatinous creature – forced the TARDIS to make an emergency landing. The Doctor was shot in San Francisco and died on the operating table when surgeons misunderstood his alien physiology, regenerating into his eighth incarnation. The Master took over the body of an ambulance worker. He attempted to steal the Doctor's remaining lives by use of the TARDIS' Eye of Harmony, and his scheme threatened to destroy the entire planet. The Doctor stopped the Deathworm Master with the help of heart surgeon Grace Holloway, and the Master was sucked into the TARDIS' Eye.

UNIT spread a cover story blaming the freak effects caused by the opening of the TARDIS' Eye of Harmony on "freak fluctuations in the Earth's magnetic pole".[725] Grace Holloway wrote a report concerning events in San Francisco, the turn of the millennium, that was filed with UNIT. The Master survived in the TARDIS' Eye of Harmony owing to his fierce willpower and the abilities he'd gained from a deathworm morphant. He later obtained his freedom by mentally coercing the Doctor's friend, Edward Grainger, in 2006.[726]

2000 (Saturday, 1st January) - MILLENNIUM SHOCK[727] -> Silver Bullet Solutions developed chips to help combat the Y2K bug, but this was a front by the Voracians, who were trying to re-assemble the sentient computer virus Voractyll and seize control of Earth's computers. The Silver Bullet chips exacerbated the switch-over from 1999 to 2000, temporarily cutting power in Malaysia, Auckland and parts of Britain, and jamming Hong Kong's traffic. The fourth Doctor, working with MI5 agent Harry Sullivan, re-programmed the Silver Bullet chips to also endow Voractyll with a Y2K sensitivity. The creature terminated, and the Voracians, serving as part of Voractyll's command nodes, perished also.

Disgraced Prime Minister Terry Brooks tried to exploit the chaos and declare martial law to advance his private agenda. Officially, it was said that his Cabinet lost faith in him, and he resigned "for personal reasons". Philip Cotton, Brooks' deputy, was appointed his successor.

2000 (1st January) - "The Forgotten"[728] -> The fourth Doctor brought the second Romana to Paris again, this time for the turn of the millennium. They saw a mime vanish into a space-time portal and followed him, meeting soldiers from 1810. Together, they disturbed the sanctum of Taureau the Minotaur, who demanded the answer to his riddles in return for the key to the portal. The Doctor pickpocketed the key, and Taureau was destroyed when he opened the door.

At the turn of the Millennium, the Brigadier became a media icon as he led King Charles' troops in a blockade of Westminster Bridge. The King offered him a role in the Provisional Cabinet, but he declined.[729]

The Twenty-First Century

"The twenty-first century is when everything changes, and you've gotta be ready..."[730]

The nonprofit organisation Livingspace was formed at the beginning of the twenty-first century.[731] News interpretation software sifted the media for the user's own preferences. Televisions could be set so that news bulletins automatically interrupted regular broadcasts.[732]

Early in the twenty-first century, Britain joined the Ecu, the single European Currency.[733] The pacifying gas pacificus was developed in the twenty-first century.[734] Walton Hummer was a popular three-foot tall kazoo player from the twenty-first century.[735] The musician Sting was assassinated in the early twenty-first century.[736]

Since 1969, Billy Shipton had "got into" publishing, then video, then DVD production. On the tenth Doctor's instructions, he secretly inserted Easter Eggs onto seventeen DVDs that Sally Sparrow would come to own in future.[737]

The Doctor theorised that if Queen Victoria was infected by an alien werewolf cell, it might take "one hundred" years to mature in her children, and "be ready" by the early twenty-first century.[738]

The broadcast journalist Riley Smalls was cryo-frozen in the early twenty-first century, and would be revived as a Cryogen in the twenty-sixth.[739] Archaeologists excavated the throne room containing the robotic version of Emperor Qin Shi Huang in the early twenty-first century.[740]

The Doctor once stepped in with Quincy Jones, as the man's bassist was actually a Klarj Neon Death Voc-Bot – who, even worse, couldn't play.[741]

727 Dating *Millennium Shock* (PDA #22) - It is "Christmas Eve" (p64).
728 Dating "The Forgotten" (IDW *DW* mini-series #2) - The Doctor and Romana are here to see the Millennium celebrations. While it isn't specifically cited as being New Year's Day, a sign on a structure that's presumably meant to be the Eiffel Tower says "2000", and the Doctor wishes his opponent, "Happy New Year".
729 *Happy Endings*
730 Captain Jack, *Torchwood* Series 1 and 2.
731 *Seeing I* (p86).
732 *Cat's Cradle: Warhead, System Shock.*
733 The ecu is in use by *Iceberg*, at the exchange rate of one ecu to two dollars. In *Warlock*, the drug enforcement agent Creed McIlveen has a suitcase full of "EC paper money", although Sterling is still used on a day-to-day basis.
734 *The Shadow of the Scourge*
735 *Psi-ence Fiction*
736 *So Vile a Sin*

737 *Blink.* Allowing for wherever Sally's taste in DVD entertainment might take her, Billy must have inserted the Easter Eggs over the course of a few years at least, and prior to 2007.
737 *Tooth and Claw* (TV).
738 *The Taking of Chelsea 426*
739 "The Immortal Emperor"
740 *Knock, Knock*
741 Ram is "seventeen" in *Class: Joyride* (p183), Matteusz is the same age in *Class: Co-owner of a Lovely Heart*. Actor Fady Elsayed (Ram) was born in 15th September, 1993; Jordan Renzo (Matteusz) on 11th February, 1993. Charlie's age is the most indeterminate of the *Class* students, as he's alien royalty posing as a human. Actor Greg Austin was born 2nd August, 1994.
742 Extrapolating from *Project: Nirvana.* See, however, the Sally Morgan and Lysandra Aristedes sidebar.
743 *The Mind Robber.* Zoe was a fan, which would seem to imply that she is from the year 2000, but see the dating notes on *The Wheel in Space. Alien Bodies* says the

2000

Ram Singh and Matteusz Andrezejewski, students at Coal Hill Academy, were born. Around this time, **Coal Hill student Charlie Smith was born.**[742] Private Sally Morgan, a companion of the seventh Doctor, was born.[743]

By the year 2000, the *Hourly Tele-press* kept the world's population up to date with events around the globe. One of the *Tele-press'* most popular features was the strip-cartoon adventures of The Karkus.[744]

The first Space Wheel was constructed in 2000.[745] In the same year, Arthur Tyler III was working on the Space Dart and Earthrise private space projects. Diagnosed with terminal cancer, he threw himself into his task.[745]

William Bishop, promoted to Brigadier, took command of the Home-Army Fifth Operational Corps in 2000.[746]

Based upon *The Book of Tomorrows*, the White and Crimson Chapters of the Orphans of the Future both believed that aliens would return to Earth in the year 2000. When this failed to happen, the Chapters fell into a philosophical crisis, and their representatives met for the first time in a century. They increasingly focused upon mention in the *Book* of a human herald – variously identified as "Sarah" and "SJS" – who would serve as a harbinger of the aliens' return. They increasingly believed that Sarah Jane Smith was this very herald.[747]

NASA discovered the six-billion-year-old Cthalctose Museum on the Moon. Construction started on Tranquillity Base to better study the alien artifact, and there were regular moonshots to service it.[748] *The Greytest Hips of Johnny Chess* was released in the early 2000s.[749]

Henry Louis Noone, a friend of Ace, was born on 10th February, 2000.[750] When Thomas "Hex" Schofield was two, his mum left him in Bolton with her mother, Hilda Schofield, to seek work in London.[751] A car struck Eve Pritchard when she was four, and she entered a near-death state. The Mi'en Kalarash inserted a shard of itself into her mind – over the next twenty years, it influenced her to develop Rapid-Emotional Programming technology.[752]

Hokrala Corp, a law firm in the forty-ninth century, believed that Torchwood and humanity as a whole would bungle the challenges of the twenty-first century, and wanted to sue Earth for a mismanagement of history. To this end, Hokrala commenced, once every year since the turn of the century, trying to land a writ on – or otherwise assassinate – Captain Jack Harkness.[753]

When Flip was eight, she failed to learn her lines for a play because she was slammed with double homework. She froze on stage in the Year 3 talent show – an emotional scar she only dealt with while traveling with the Doctor, in the 1890s.[754]

wih - The major powers in the War in Heaven intervened in US elections in the first few decades of the early twenty-first century. In one case, portions of the space-time continuum remained in a multivalued state for many months, until the wrong man was elected. Overall, however, the different interventions nullified one another.[755]

2000 (February) - "Prisoners of Time"[756] -> Repairs to the atomic clock San Francisco Institute of Technological Advancement and Research were a week from completion. The eighth Doctor overcame Grace's objections to traveling with him, and they visited a number of times and places. Adam Mitchell captured Grace when the TARDIS stopped near the alien city of Brendais.

Kroton Leaves the TARDIS

(=) 2000 - "The Glorious Dead"[757] -> In an alternate timeline, Paradost was a planetary museum that celebrated a million alien races. Earth, known as Dharkan, was a wasteland ruled by Cardinal Morningstar – who the Doctor previously knew as Katsura Sato. The eighth Doctor, Izzy and Kroton were on Paradost when it was invaded. Kroton left the Doctor's company to take control of a reality-bending device known as the Omniversal Spectrum, and restored the established timeline.

adventures of the Karkus are still running in the 2050s.
744 *Christmas on a Rational Planet*, via *The Mind Robber* and *The Wheel in Space*. *The Harvest* has the Wheels operating in 2021.
745 *Escape Velocity*, referenced as occurring "last year".
746 The Haisman Timeline
747 "Five years" before *SJS: Fatal Consequences*. The "alien visit" the Chapters were expecting (i.e. the return of the Mandragora Helix) actually happened on schedule in "The Mark of Mandragora", but, following the Helix's defeat by the seventh Doctor and Ace, the Chapters had no way of knowing this.
748 "The last three years" before *Eternity Weeps*.
749 *Benny: The Sword of Forever*
750 *A Death in the Family*

751 The blurb for *Project: Destiny* says that Cassie left for London in 1999, but Nimrod says that this happened "two years" after Hex was born in October 1998.
752 "Two decades" before *House of Blue Fire*.
753 *TW: The Undertaker's Gift*
754 *6th LA: Stage Fright*
755 *FP: Head of State* – an obvious lob at the Bush-Gore election of 2000, and a reference to the Faction Paradox fanfic story "Hanging Chads" by Jonathan Dennis, from the charity anthology *Walking to Eternity*.
756 Dating "Prisoners of Time" (IDW *DW* mini-series) - A caption provides the month and year.
757 Dating "The Glorious Dead" (*DWM* #287-296) - The year isn't specified, but it is the "present day".

2000 - SONTARANS: OLD SOLDIERS[758] -> Brak had now been held captive for eighty years, and had lived longer than any Sontaran in history. Captain Alice Wells of UNIT escorted Brak to the Weapons Crisis Conference in Geneva, where he was to testify concerning his ties to Kobalt Blue. Brak planned on providing the secret of harnessing Kobalt Blue, but before he could do so, a Sontaran operative executed him for cowardice.

The Sixth Doctor Regenerates

More than one account existed as to how the sixth Doctor came to regenerate.[759]

& 2000 - SPIRAL SCRATCH[760] -> Dying from an overdose of chronon energy, the sixth Doctor enjoyed the beauty of space with Mel, just before the Rani's tractor beam snared the TARDIS...

(=) & ? 2000 - 6thLA: THE BRINK OF DEATH[761] -> The sixth Doctor and Mel tried to steer clear of the Lakertya System, which had a radiation belt that was unhealthy for humans and deadly to Time Lords...

Backtracking along his own timeline, the sixth Doctor directed the TARDIS into the lethal radiation – killing himself to prevent the Valeyard from replacing every Time Lord in existence with his own persona...

? 2000 - TIME AND THE RANI[762] -> The newly regenerated seventh Doctor and Mel prevented the Rani from creating a Time Manipulator – a world-sized cerebral mass, with immense powers over time and space – on the planet Lakertya. Afterwards, the Rani's batlike servants, the Tetraps, rebelled and forcibly took her back to their homeworld, Tetrapyriabus, so that she could develop additional supplies of plasma for them...

2000 - THE RANI REAPS THE WHIRLWIND[762] -> Tetrapyriabus was once populated with a species not unlike dinosaurs, but these had gone extinct, and so the Tetraps had turned to animal husbandry of other species. The Rani escaped Tetrapyriabus, but was forced to leave her TARDIS behind. She intended to re-engineer a conventional spacecraft so that it could travel in time, and to then exact revenge upon her former servant, Urak.

---

758 Dating *Sontarans: Old Soldiers* (BBV audio #22) - The audio was released in February 2000 and seems contemporary. Brak repeatedly says that it's been "eighty years" since World War I.
759 THE SIXTH DOCTOR'S END: Owing to Colin Baker's dismissal as the sixth Doctor, and his subsequent refusal to come back for a farewell story rather than a farewell season, his Doctor regenerates (by virtue of Sylvester McCoy wearing Baker's costume, and a wig) in the opening moments of *Time and the Rani*. Quite why the sixth Doctor dies isn't immediately clear – the TARDIS lurches about, but Melanie Bush, a standard human, is merely rendered unconscious while the Doctor loses his life. Pip and Jane Baker, in the novelisation of their own story, explained that the sixth Doctor smacked his head on the console and therefore died amidst the "tumultuous buffeting" – something the seventh Doctor's companions have a hearty laugh about in *Head Games*.

With the sixth Doctor's on screen demise being so muddled, two tie-in works have offered themselves up as "last adventures" for this Doctor. *Spiral Scratch* sees the sixth Doctor incur a fatal dose of chronon radiation while sixth Doctors from other realities combine forces against a villainous Lamprey. Later, Big Finish's *The Sixth Doctor – The Last Adventure* box set entails a tour de force of the sixth's Doctor's friends before he deliberately exposes the TARDIS to Time-Lord-deadly energy in the Lakertya System (*Time and the Rani*), giving his life to thwart the Valeyard's schemes. That very loosely matches *Love and War*, *Head Games* and *Millennial Rites*, which attest that the unborn seventh Doctor compelled the sixth Doctor to drive himself into the Rani's tractor beam – an act that schisms the Doctor's psyche and probably gives rise to the Valeyard.

A possibility for streamlining this: as *Spiral Scratch* entails multiple sixth Doctors from multiple universes, it's not too much work to presume that "our" Doctor and Mel as seen in that story also hail from a parallel timeline. And, the camaraderie with which the sixth and seventh Doctors commune at the end of *The Sixth Doctor – The Last Adventure* might give way to strife, once the sixth Doctor's persona – still rattling around in the Doctor's headspace – learns about the seventh Doctor's culpability in his demise.
760 Dating *Spiral Scratch* (PDA #72) – The epilogue involves a jaunt in the TARDIS, so could take place whenever and whenever *Time and the Rani* occurs.
761 Dating *6th LA: The Brink of Death* (*The Sixth Doctor – The Last Adventure* #4) - The story leads into *Time and the Rani*. *Spiral Scratch* and the New Adventures (*Timewyrm: Revelation* et al) give alternate explanations for the sixth Doctor's demise, although it's possible that the Doctor's interference here in his own timeline creates some temporal instability concerning the event.
762 Dating *Time and the Rani* (24.1) and *The Rani Reaps the Whirlwind* (BBV audio #28) - There isn't much doubt that *The Rani Reaps the Whirlwind* – BBV's sequel to *Time and the Rani*, one of the famously undatable *Doctor Who* TV adventures – takes place in (or, worst

c 2000 - GRAVE MATTER[763] **->** The European space probe Gatherer Three explored the outer planets and returned to Earth, where it was discovered to have picked up alien DNA. This was named "Denarian", and seemed to have miraculous medical properties. In actuality, Denarian was an alien creature that possessed bodies to survive. A team of scientists relocated to the Dorsill islands off the south west coast of the UK and began secret experiments on animals and the local population. The sixth Doctor and Peri found the islands overrun with walking corpses, but the Doctor discovered that a second dose of Denarian cancelled out the first.

c 2000 - IMPERIAL MOON[764] **->** The fifth Doctor and Turlough materialised near Earth's moon to avoid hitting themselves in the Vortex. A time safe aboard the TARDIS opened and revealled a diary purporting to be the log of a Victorian expedition to the moon – which historically did not occur. They went to 1878 to learn the truth.

Evelyn Smythe Joins the TARDIS

c 2000 - THE MARIAN CONSPIRACY[765] **->** Time disturbances surrounded history professor Evelyn Smythe. The sixth Doctor met her and concluded that the problem lay with her ancestor John Whiteside-Smith, who lived at the time of Elizabeth I. They departed to investigate.

(=) By Evelyn's time, the immortal Mozart had been producing substandard works for hundreds of years. Some thought that "Mozart" was a shared alias. He'd begun work on his 10,000th symphony (the

soundtrack to a remake of *The Italian Job*), had started to use electronic drum kits, had appeared in various Eurovision entries, and, tragically, had discovered hip-hop.[766]

Evelyn Smythe told her student Sally about the time she and the Doctor met some pirates.[767]

= 2000 - UNBOUND: EXILE[768] **->** Calling herself "Susan Foreman", an alt-female Doctor had retired from adventuring and worked at Sainsbury's. A typical evening entailed her getting mightily pissed with her mates. Two Time Lords – one of them sounding uncannily like the tenth Doctor – hoped to capture the alt-Doctor and thereby net seats on the High Council. The duo arrived on Earth thirty years late (so were dressed in floral trousers, open shirts and medallions), and interrupted the proceedings as Princess Anne cut the ribbon at a new Sainsbury's with special Sainsbury Scissors. The resultant fracas blew up the Sainsbury's, whereupon the alt-Doctor decided to restore her TARDIS' time vector generator and hoof it. The two Time Lords, aided by chameloid robots disguised as scarecrows, apprehended the alt-Doctor and took her back to Gallifrey to stand trial...

c 2000 (October) - THE SPECTRE OF LANYON MOOR[769] **->** Lethbridge-Stewart, occasionally performing surveillance work for UNIT, looked into the latest of a string of mysterious deaths in the Lanyon Moor area. An archaeological expedition there had woken up the Tregannon scout Sancreda after eighteen thousand years of

case, very near to) 2000. The Tetraps kidnap two humans, Sam and Lucy, from Earth via conventional spacecraft, and the Rani later returns the two of them home via the same means. Sam, a neurochemist, has scientific knowledge on par with 2000 (when the audio was released), and – very tellingly – he refers to the Millennium Dome (completed in 1999, and opened to the public on 1st January, 2000) as a "twenty-first century folly" in London.

Whether or not *Time and the Rani* occurs in the same year is entirely contingent on if any temporal displacement is involved when the Tetraps tie the Rani up and return home in her TARDIS at the end of that story. It's unlikely that the Rani would have given the Tetraps the know-how to pilot her Ship in through space-time in an unfettered fashion – then again, they might know enough to operate the TARDIS on preprogrammed coordinates that do, in fact, involve time travel. The choice remains fairly clean-cut, however: either no time travel happens and *Time and the Rani* occurs in 2000, or time travel *does* occur and the story should once more be designated undatable.

763 Dating *Grave Matter* (PDA #31) - Peri thinks it's the "twentieth century" (p201); there's nothing to suggest it's not set the year the book was published, in 2000.
764 Dating *Imperial Moon* (PDA #34) - "Some time in the early twenty-first century" (p7). The book was published in 2000.
765 Dating *The Marian Conspiracy* – No year is given. Evelyn is from the present day, and has a mobile phone.
766 *100*: "My Own Private Wolfgang"
767 *Doctor Who and the Pirates*
768 Dating *Unbound: Exile* (BF *Unbound* #6) - The year is given. *The X-Files* Season One is out on DVD – that happened on 9th May, 2000. The scarecrows echo the ones who tracked down the second Doctor, and instigated his regeneration, in the *TV Comic* strips. David Tennant, in a story recorded some years before he was cast as the tenth Doctor, here plays one of the hapless Time Lords.
769 Dating *The Spectre of Lanyon Moor* (BF #9) - Lethbridge-Stewart has been retired "a few years now". Evelyn phones one of her friends, so this is her native time. The first meeting of the sixth Doctor and

semi-dormancy, and Sancreda sought to use his vast mental abilities to exact revenge on his brother Screfan for abandoning him. The sixth Doctor and Evelyn aided the Brigadier as Sancreda summoned his survey ship from space, but Sancreda discovered that he had inadvertently killed his brother during their initial survey on Earth. Sancreda tried to destroy Earth, but the Brigadier swapped out a crucial component from Sancreda's psionic cannon. The resultant energy backlash destroyed Sancreda and his survey ship.

c 2000 - EXCELIS RISING[770] **->** On the highly-industrialised planet Artaris, border disputes sprang up between the city-states of Gatracht and Calann. The public came to regard "the warlord Grayvorn and his lost treasure" as the stuff of myth, although officials at the Imperial Archives' Black Museum privately acknowledged the tales as true.

The Relic had become the property of the Excelis Museum, and an Imperial Edict forbade the head curator from turning the object over to anyone beyond the Empress, her Regent or the Etheric Minister. Possibly due

to the Relic's presence in the city, mediums were able to commune with the dead.

At the Museum, the sixth Doctor found the former warlord Grayvorn trying to re-acquire the Relic. An altercation between them resulted in a discharge of the Relic's energies, which dissipated Grayvorn's physical form. His consciousness became embedded in the Museum's stone walls, and he waited for someone to die in the museum so he could inhabit their body.

Captain Jack discovered that in addition to disgorging objects, the Rift sometimes relocated people in Cardiff to alien locales. Some later returned through the Rift, mentally unstable or otherwise altered owing to their experiences. On 27th October, 2000, Jack purchased Flat Holm, a property on an island in the Bristol Channel, to serve as a shelter for such persons.[771] Russia's Committee for Extraterrestrial Research asked Torchwood to turn over, for safekeeping, the activation key for containers housing a Shiva virus. Jack instead secured the key at the British Museum.[772]

Lethbridge-Stewart is portrayed both here and in *Business Unusual.* Given that the Doctor first meets Mel in *Business Unusual,* and that he clearly travelled with Evelyn before her, it's fair to assume that from the sixth Doctor's perspective, he first encounters the Brigadier in *The Spectre of Lanyon Moor.* But the Brigadier first meets the sixth Doctor in *Business Unusual,* which takes place about eleven years previous in 1989.

770 Dating *Excelis Rising* (BF *Excelis* mini-series #2) - The story is set a thousand years after *Excelis Dawns* and three hundred before *Excelis Decays.*
771 *TW: Adrift;* Torchwood.org.uk gives the date.
772 *TW: Fallout.* Sgt Andy's second-hand account variously suggests that this happened after the fall of the Iron Curtain/after Jack assumes leadership of Torchwood Cardiff (in 2000, *TW: Fragments*).
773 Dating *Touched by an Angel* (NSA #47) - The exact day is given (p137).
774 *Verdigris* (p2). *Iris: Wildthyme on Top* suggests that Tom returns to Earth in the mid-90s... about five years, then, before he joined Iris on her travels.
775 *Made of Steel*
776 *Unnatural History* (p33), picking up on a line from *Doctor Who – The Movie.*
777 She's "eight" years old "eight years" (sic) before *Class: Brave-ish Heart.* Actress Sophie Hopkins was born 25th November, 1990.
778 She's "15" in *Kill the Moon.*
779 "Six months" before *SJS: Comeback,* which opens with Sarah Jane at Lavinia's gravesite, very shortly after her funeral. Brendan appeared in *K9 and Company.* Lavinia's death is sometimes implied in *The Sarah Jane Adventures; Comeback* and *Ghost Town* are explicit about it. *SJA: The White Wolf,* set in 2010, both confirms

Lavinia's death and loosely agrees with the dating given here, mentioning an article Sarah wrote "about five years ago" after her aunt's passing.
The framing sequence of *Millennium Shock,* set in 1998, entails Sarah telling Harry, "I have to get back to Morton Harwood, sort out Aunt Lavinia's things" (p2) - possibly an indicator that Lavinia has died, possibly an indicator that she's still alive but is moving house, or possibly just meaning that Lavinia is leaving for/returning from a lecture tour, and wants Sarah to help her pack/unpack.
780 *Deep Breath*
781 *Let's Kill Hitler.* No date is given, but Amy, Rory and Mels are all pupils at Leadworth Comprehensive (named in a sign above the anti-bullying poster).
782 *SJA: The Mad Woman in the Attic*
783 *Borrowed Time*
784 *SJS: Fatal Consequences, SJS: Dreamland.*
785 *The Quantum Archangel*
786 Dating *Escape Velocity* (EDA #42) - The exact date is given (p26).
787 *Time Zero*
788 Dating *The Shadow in the Glass* (PDA #41) - According to the blurb, it's "2001".
789 Dating *FP: This Town Will Never Let Us Go* (FP novel #1) - The Red Uranium detonation seems to be linked, although this isn't directly established, to the start of humanity's "ghost point" (an era in which humanity's scientific and cultural progress greatly stagnates, and becomes vastly less relevant to the War in Heaven) as detailed in *FP: The Book of the War.* The same text says that the "ghost point" begins in 2001, and while *This Town Will Never Let Us Go* was published in 2003, the story fits either year reasonably well, with the partici-

2000 (4th November) - TOUCHED BY AN ANGEL[773] -> The Weeping Angels nearly disrupted the wedding of Mark Whitaker and Rebecca Coles, but the eleventh Doctor, Amy and Rory saw that she got to the church on time. The Doctor wiped Rebecca's memory of their having used the TARDIS four times to achieve this.

In early November 2000, a man named Tom jumped aboard a bus in London and found he'd entered Iris Wildthyme's TARDIS. He became her travelling companion.[774] Martha Jones visited the Millennium Dome with her family and secretly enjoyed it.[775] On Christmas Day 2000, a serious earthquake called the Little Big One hit San Francisco.[776]

2001

April MacLean, a student at Coal Hill Academy, was born.[777] **Courtney Woods, a future President of the United States and an acquaintance of the twelfth Doctor and Clara, was born.**[778]

Lavinia Smith, Sarah Jane's aunt, died in 2001. Lavinia's ward, Brendan, was in San Francisco at the time. Sarah Jane inherited Lavinia's house and the royalties on her patents.[779] **Clara Oswald, age 15, kept a single pinup on her wall: that of Roman emperor Marcus Aurelius.**[780]

Amelia Pond's best friend Mels got into trouble in history classes because she kept mentioning the Doctor.[781] **In 2001, Samuel Lloyd's parents died in a car accident. He was sent to the St Anthony's Children's Home, and became friends with Rani Chandra.**[782]

Following his defeat of Jane Blythe, the eleventh Doctor was deposited on Earth more than five years prior to his starting point. He spent the intervening time waiting to reunite with Amy and Rory in 2007, and foiled a few plots to destroy humankind along the way.[783]

In 2001, the Harvard-Smithsonian Centre for Astrophysics estimated that a comet that had visited Earth five hundred years ago would return, and that Earth would pass through its tail – the first such event since Halley's Comet in 1910. Sir Donald Wakefield, a billionaire and the leader of the White Chapter, viewed the comet as a sign of salvation. He poured his fortune into building a spacecraft, the *Dauntless*, to make a private journey into space.[784]

The Grid, a means of pooling the unused processing power of Internet computers to create unlimited memory space, came online in 2001. Paul Kairos, a classmate of Melanie Bush, learned to manipulate photons in a way that rendered the transistor and micro-monolithic circuit obsolete. Anjelique Whitefriar stole Kairos' design and patented it as the Whitefriar Lattice.[785]

The Eighth Doctor's Time on Earth Ends; Anji Kapoor Joins the TARDIS

@ 2001 (February) - ESCAPE VELOCITY[786] -> Compassion dropped Fitz in London on 6th February, 2001 – two days ahead of his scheduled rendezvous with the amnesiac eighth Doctor. By now, the Doctor owned the St Louis Bar and Restaurant in London to facilitate his meeting with Fitz. After their rendezvous, the Doctor gave the bar to its manager, Sheff.

Competition between the Kulan factions increased, as the first group to report to the Kulan leadership would be likely to persuade them to either invade or spare Earth.

Anji Kapoor, a 28-year-old futures analyst, took a break in Brussels with her boyfriend Dave and became embroiled in the Kulan conflict. The Doctor, Fitz and Anji allied with the benevolent Kulan faction and blew up Yves-Dudoin's Star Dart. A pro-invasion Kulan member named Fray'kon killed Dave.

A Kulan warfleet arrived in Earth orbit, but the TARDIS completed its century of healing and became functional again. The Doctor, Fitz and Anji travelled to the flagship and tricked the Kulan ships into annihilating one another. Arthur Tyler III and Fray'kon died in the fighting. The TARDIS had departed Earth with Anji aboard, but the Doctor promised to try and return her home...

After many adventures, the Doctor returned Anji home three weeks after she left, and she resumed her life. She would not see him again for eighteen months.[787]

2001 - THE SHADOW IN THE GLASS[788] -> Historical journalist Claire Aldwych discovered evidence of the Vvormak cruiser located in Turelhampton, England, which prompted the sixth Doctor and the Brigadier to investigate. Suspecting Nazi involvement, the Brigadier stole pieces of Hitler and Eva Braun's remains from the State Special Trophy Archive in Moscow for comparison.

The Doctor and his allies discovered the existence of a Nazi organisation at an Antarctic base, led by the son of Adolf Hitler and Eva Braun. The Doctor retrieved the Scrying Glass from the base, but it depicted the Doctor taking Hitler's son back in time to 1945. To fulfill the Glass' visions, the Doctor, the Brigadier, Claire and Hitler's son travelled back to that year.

After their return, the Doctor and the Brigadier helped the sleeping Vvormak awaken and depart Earth. UNIT assisted with breaking up the exposed Fourth Reich cells.

wih - c 2001 - FP: THIS TOWN WILL NEVER LET US GO[789] -> A timeship involved in the War in Heaven buried itself beneath an unnamed town in England, and took root in its culture. Rocket attacks sometimes besieged the town. The public believed that Faction Paradox was a powerful conspiracy group, and Faction iconography was increasingly in use as a fashion statement. An episode of *The Muppet Show* was broadcast that perplexingly featured special guest-star George Orwell (who died in 1950). Orwell's appearance on screen followed a Muppet re-enactment of the Room 101 scene from *1984*, starring Rizzo the Rat.

A paramedic named Valentine Bregman believed that damaging the timeship would trigger a cultural event that would endow the public with a greater awareness of the War. He procured a half-critical mass of Red Uranium – a mythic substance that existed in totemic form. A young woman named Inangela Marrero alternatively wanted to wake the Ship up with a ritual, and tried to stop Bregman. The Red Uranium went off accidentally, and although this only caused a relatively small physical explosion, the totemic nature of the Red Uranium damaged humanity's collective psyche, threatening to curtail its future potential.

Four average people (the so-called "Faction Four") were

implicated in the explosion; media coverage of their arrest caused Faction Paradox to be perceived as nothing more than a little band of terrorists with no influence, and its reputation plummeted. Some hope remained that the timeship would repair itself, and that its awakening and launch would help to revive human ingenuity.

2001 - THE DEMONS OF RED LODGE AND OTHER STORIES: "Special Features"[790] -> The fifth Doctor and Nyssa attended the DVD commentary recording for *Doctor Demonic's Tales of Terror*, and banished the Racht still living within Joanna Munro.

(=) c 2001 - PSI-ENCE FICTION[791] -> The TARDIS landed at the University of East Wessex, where researcher Barry Hitchens was studying psychic powers. One of his students, Josh Randall, had secretly become a formidable psychic and was viciously making other students hallucinate. Hitchens was being

---

pants displaying a cultural awareness relevant to that time. (For instance, Inangela and Valentine's bafflement as to how Orwell could appear on *The Muppet Show*.) Inangela is presented as very young woman, and she was "15" (p34) when Princess Diana died (in 1997).

The bigger question is to what degree events in *This Town Will Never Let Us Go* are to be taken as actually occurring within the timeline of *Doctor Who* – or within that of *Faction Paradox*, for that matter. To what degree is this book a treatise on culture, not to be taken overly literally? To what degree is the narrator unreliable? Are the timeship's tendrils so interwoven into the town that the town exists in its own little cul-de-sac of history, hence why the national government has no evident response to the town being sometimes pelted by rockets? All of that said, there's nothing to resolutely rule against *This Town Will Never Let Us Go* being part of the greater *Doctor Who* canon either.

The "Black Man" who supplies Valentine with the Red Uranium previously appeared as an agent of the Celestis in *Alien Bodies*. Page 243 establishes that the timeship buried beneath the town is the same lineage of War-vessel as Compassion, citing her as the mother (conceptually, if nothing else) of future Ships.

790 Dating *The Demons of Red Lodge and Other Stories*: "Special Features" (BF #142d) - The commentary is slated for the 25th Anniversary release of *Doctor Demonic's Tales of Terror* (1976).

791 Dating *Psi-ence Fiction* (PDA #46) - The year isn't given, but there's a modern day setting, with references to (for example) *The Blair Witch Project* and CCTV cameras. The book was released in 2001.

792 Dating *Touched by an Angel* (NSA #47) - The exact day is given (p161).

793 Dating *Project: Twilight* (BF #23) - No year is given, but it's the present day (or close enough) for Evelyn,

and Tony Blair is the Prime Minister. *Project: Destiny* says that Cassie went missing on "23rd August, 2001" – as that story was also written by Cavan Scott and Mark Wright, this is presumably the same day that the Doctor and Evelyn visit The Dusk.

794 Dating *Animal* (BF LS #2.5) - Writer Andrew Cartmel scripted the story as taking place in 2011, but this was changed – both in the dialogue and the blurb – to 2001. It's during the school year, and it's after the Doctor and Ace meet Bambera in *Battlefield*.

795 *Earth Aid*

796 Dating *Head Games* (NA #43) - It is "2001", some time before December 2001, and "953 years" (p150) before Cwej is born (in 2954, p205). The bit with the pop can is on p165-166.

A Life of Crime amends Mel's history to say that her potential futures – which by implication means her meeting with the seventh Doctor in *Head Games* – were erased from history; it's less clear if this means that the remainder of *Head Games* by extension also didn't occur.

797 *Head Games*. The kids might have been born prior to 2001, as Bambera is on duty in *Head Games* and *Animal*, both set in that year. Alternatively, it's possible that Brigadier Fernfather (*The Shadow in the Glass*) covered Bambera's maternity leave.

798 According to Owen's comments and a computer graphic related to Lucy's death in *TW: Greeks Bearing Gifts*.

799 *Touched by an Angel*

800 *TW: Miracle Day*. The fact that the CIA has "456 files" indicates some knowledge of the UK's contact with the 456 in the 60s, despite the great pains that the UK government takes to keep it secret in *TW: Children of Earth*.

801 "A year" before *Rutans: In 2 Minds*.

funded by physicist John Finer, who was trying to build a time machine to go back six years to prevent his daughter from dying.

The fourth Doctor inspected the machine and deduced that its use would destroy the timelines. Randall was driven insane, and deemed himself a god. The TARDIS materialised around the time machine, fixing history. Finer never started his time travel research, and the Doctor and Leela, along with everyone else, forgot that these events ever happened.

2001 (May to 5th June) - TOUCHED BY AN ANGEL[792] -> Rory arrived in May 2001, having been sent there from 2003 by a Weeping Angel. Working to the Doctor's instructions and armed with a psychic credit card, he arranged for a series of lights, cameras and monitors to be set up in a field in April 2003. Rory was astonished at what could be achieved, if one was willing to prepay.

On 5th June, the same Rory tracked down the eleventh Doctor, Amy and his earlier self. The quartet went to 21st April, 2003: the day Rebecca Whitaker was fated to die.

2001 (23rd August) - PROJECT: TWILIGHT[793] -> The Forge-created vampires Amelia Doory and Reggie Mead now owned and operated The Dusk casino in London, and had converted its basement into a secret medical research facility. The sixth Doctor and Evelyn arrived as Nimrod returned to stalk the vampires, and Amelia convinced the Doctor to help her find a cure to vampirism. However, Amelia instead used the Doctor's discoveries to create The Twilight Virus, an airborne virus capable of converting humans into vampires on contact. She converted Cassie Schofield, now a waitress at The Dusk, into a vampire as a test, but a vengeful Cassie killed Reggie. Nimrod destroyed Amelia's laboratory and the Doctor confiscated the last vial of Twilight Virus. Amelia went missing in the Thames. The Doctor helped Cassie relocate to a remote part of Norway.

2001 - ANIMAL[794] -> Margrave University researchers experimented on ravenous tree-like creatures that originated from a crashed spaceship, in a forest in Mauritania. The alien Numlok walled Margrave off with a force field, presenting themselves as peace-loving herbivores who opposed the eating of animal flesh. The seventh Doctor, Ace and Raine investigated Margrave's operations, and met with Brigadier Bambera. They discovered that the Numlok were conducting blood tests on people at Margrave to identify the meat-eaters – and then turn them into a dietary supplement the Numlok required. The Doctor prevented a slaughterhouse by allowing the tree-creatures to consume the Numlok, then sent the Numlok's spaceship – with the tree-creatures aboard – back to the Numlok homeworld as a warning to leave Earth alone.

The Metatraxi had now become the objects of ridicule

following the Doctor's irreversibly switching their translator to "surfer dude" mode in 1989, and refused his request for assistance. Raine looked up her father on the Internet... and discovered that he had died. Nonetheless, she continued travelling with the Doctor and Ace.

Raine eventually left the TARDIS to investigate her father's affairs. She was breaking into a hotel safe in Johannesburg when the Metatraxi captured her, and used the rudimentary time technology they'd developed to take her to the future – as bait for the Doctor.[795]

(? =) 2001 - HEAD GAMES[796] -> General Lethbridge-Stewart was semi-retired. Ace met up with a future version of the seventh Doctor, who informed her that his evil duplicate Dr Who was planning to assassinate the Queen. The Queen was shot in Sheffield, but wasn't even slightly injured. Meanwhile, UNIT forces were involved in an assault on Buckingham Palace. Brigadier Bambera arrived in a Merlin T-22 VTOL aircraft and penetrated a force field surrounding the palace.

Dr Who had been created by a spiteful Jason, the ex-Master of the Land of Fiction. The Doctor counselled Jason and convinced him to dissipate Dr Who. Jason and Dr Who had rescued Melanie Bush from the planet Avalone in the future – she decried the violent, manipulative methods used by the seventh Doctor and his new companions (Benny, Roz and Chris) to solve problems, and parted on bad terms with him on modern-day Earth.

At this time, Bernice kicked a mangled drinks can into the middle of a path. Four and a half hours later, a young man stumbled over it on his bike and suffered slight bruising. This instigated a chain reaction of small historical alterations that climaxed directly before the Draconian War in the twenty-sixth century.

By now, Bambera and Ancelyn had given birth to twins.[797] **In September 2001, Owen Harper had been qualified as a physician for six months. The alien Mary tore the heart out of 43-year-old Lucy Marmer, and Owen was present when Lucy's body was brought into Cardiff General Hospital.**[798] The elder Mark Whitaker had foreknowledge of the destruction of the World Trade Center, but held his tongue, fearful of interfering with history.[799] **After 11th September, 2001, the American CIA cross-referenced its 456 files under "Worldwide Incursion" and designation JF323B.**[800]

The Rutan Host occasionally separated and exiled individual Rutans, including those that were exposed to neural toxins from a Sontaran bioweapon. A ship containing one such rogue Rutan crashed in Algeria in November, and was retrieved by the United Kingdom.[801]

2001 (Winter) - LETH-ST: "The Two Brigadiers"[802]
-> Alistair Lethbridge-Stewart CBE was now a Commander of the Most Excellent Order of the British Empire, but answered to "Brigadier" for sentimental reasons. The Fifth Operational Corps was still based at Delorite.

The Cessatrons had once forged a mighty empire, then "retired on top" and got out of the whole conquering business. Commander Terminatron heard rumours of an oncoming warfare, and hoped to re-train his troops with an incursion to Earth. Anne Bishop hoped to find a miracle cure for her father, and investigated when Terminatron's hapless soldiers – based under Narrowback mountain – kept aiding sick Earthers with their healing guns, rather than oppressing them.

Brigadier William Bishop asked for Brigadier Lethbridge-Stewart's help when Anne briefly went missing. The two Brigadiers found themselves in front of a Cessatron firing squad, the members of which ineptly shot, exploded and pulverised one another. Anne discovered that the Cessatron healing gear wasn't adopted for Earth's environment, so would soon become useless.

Invigorated by this outing, Lethbridge-Stewart phoned his UN contacts to offer his services as a consultant or envoy.

2001 (November) - "The Fallen"[803] -> The dead were walking in West Norwood in London, and seven people had disappeared. The eighth Doctor and Izzy discovered Grace Holloway investigating with MI6, which was secretly run by Leighton Woodrow.

Grace had recovered the Master's DNA from her encounter with him. Working with the scientist Donald Stark, she hoped to unlock the secrets of regeneration – she thought the eighth Doctor had been hinting she *should*

---

802 Dating *Leth-St: "The Two Brigadiers"* (*Leth-St: HAVOC Files* #4.8) - It's the start of the "new Millennium." The Haisman Timeline says it's 2001, and the season is given. The Brigadier first met his son Albert "ten years" ago (the start of 1990; *Leth-St: "The Enfolded Time"*). Bishop, born in 1945, is in his "mid-fifties". Conall is "nine" (potentially a glitch; going by the Haisman Timeline, he should be eleven). The Brigadier volunteering for duty as an envoy feeds into his status in *Minuet in Hell*.

803 Dating "The Fallen" (*DWM* #273-276) - According to the Doctor, it's "2001. Somewhere in November judging by the temperature".

804 "The Widow's Curse"

805 "Five years" before *Rise of the Cybermen*.

806 *The Hollow Men* (p74).

807 "Fifty years" after *Amorality Tale*.

808 *Sometime Never*

809 "Seven years" before *TW: The Undertaker's Gift*.

810 *Happy Endings*

811 *Iris* S4: *Iris at the Oche*. Girls Aloud was created on the ITV talent show *Popstars: The Rivals* in 2002.

812 *Sometime Never*. The Doctor, Fitz and Trix visit Sam's grave in *The Gallifrey Chronicles*, which gives her date of death as 2002. From *The Bodysnatchers* onwards, some of the EDAs hinted that Sam would meet a premature death. Others, such as *Interference*, hinted that she would live into great old age; *Beltempest* even alluded that she was now immortal.

Alien Bodies and *Unnatural History* reveal that contact with the Doctor changed Sam's timeline, preventing her from becoming "Dark Sam" (dark-haired, sexually active and a drug user) and making her squeaky-clean instead. Further complicating things, some of the "companion deaths" the Council of Eight arranged were either ambiguous or retconned away after their defeat. As of *The Gallifrey Chronicles*, it's clear that Sam died in 2002 and "stayed dead".

813 Dating *The Ratings War* (BF promo #2, *DWM* #313) Beep's early appearances on Earth are roughly contemporary. Previous to *The Ratings War*, he was imprisoned in "Star Beast II", a comic story in the *1996 DWM Annual*. The tone and heavy amount of reality TV in this story suggests author Steve Lyons had a contemporary or near-contemporary setting in mind.

814 Dating *The Forge: Project: Valhalla* (BF New Worlds novel #3) - The year is given.

815 Dating *Tales from the Vault* (BF CC 6.1) - Ruth names the exact date, and it's "about ten years" before the story's linking material, set at time of release in 2011. The Doctor says that he and Romana have arrived in "Kensington on a wet Wednesday afternoon", but in 2002, 6th June was actually a Thursday.

816 Dating *Mastermind* (BF CC #8.1) - The Master's file includes details of "the last time" he visited Earth (from UNIT's point of view) in *Doctor Who – The Movie*. As he was captured in 1997 and awakens at five year intervals, it must now be 2002.

817 Dating *Benny* S10: *Secret Origins* (Benny #10.4) - It's the day that England played Argentina for the World Cup: 7th June, 2002.

818 Dating *Sarah Jane Smith* Series 1 (*SJS: Comeback*, #1.1; *SJS: The Tao Connection*, #1.2; *SJS: Test of Nerve*, #1.3; *SJS: Ghost Town*, #1.4; *SJS: Mirror, Signal, Manoeuvre*, #1.5) - The five Big Finish audios that compose *Sarah Jane Smith* Series 1 were released from August to November 2002, and occur in fairly rapid succession. The setting seems contemporary – tellingly, *Ghost Town* occurs "six months" after events described in a scientist's journal, which is dated to "22nd November, 2001".

819 *SJS: Comeback*. Details about the Crimson Chapter's role in Sarah's professional downfall are revealled in *SJS: Fatal Consequences*. Winters and Think Tank were seen in *Robot*.

820 Josh's allegiances are revealed in *SJS: Fatal Consequences*.

do so by mentioning he was half-human, and telling her to hold back death. However, Grace's sample wasn't Time Lord DNA as she had believed. Stark was transformed into a snake creature – a morphant from Skaro like the Master before him. The Doctor destroyed the Stark monster, even as Woodrow decided to blame the explosion on Arab terrorists. As the Doctor left, Woodrow found one of his men... killed by the Glorious Dead Master's tissue compression eliminator.

Donna Noble's mother gifted her with Tesco's brand of unisex perfume, *Odeur Delaware*, at Christmas 2001. Donna used it to treat bites and stings – and, in future, sprayed it into the eyes of a hostile female Sycorax.[804]

2002

Mickey Smith's mother had been unable to cope with raising him, and his father – Jeremiah Smith, who formerly worked at the key-cutters on Clifton Parade – went to Spain and never returned. Mickey was raised by his blind gran, but she died after tripping and falling down the stairs.[805]

The "Great Drought of '02" affected the UK.[806] The main Xhinn fleet was due to arrive on Earth in 2002.[807] The eighth Doctor found another part of Octan's skeleton in New York, 2002.[808] Zero, the orange, gelatinous child of a Vortex Dweller, came through the Rift and wound up in a cell at the Torchwood Hub in Cardiff.[809] The fertiliser Bloom was developed, but it was viral and spread uncontrollably. It was banned before 2010.[810] As with Shakespeare, Mozart and Einstein before them, Girls Aloud owed some of their talent and fame to their interacting with the quantum mathematics governing the universe.[811]

Sam Jones Dies

The Council of Eight arranged for a drug overdose to kill Sam Jones, a former companion of the Doctor, who had become an ecocampaigner.[812]

c 2002 - THE RATINGS WAR[813] **->** The tyrannical Beep the Meep escaped from his imprisonment in a *Lassie* film, and used blackstar radiation to mesmerise executives at a TV network. Under Beep's direction, the network enjoyed success with shows such as *Appealing Animals in Distress* and *Hospital Street*, the first ever 24-hour soap opera.

Beep sought to brainwash the public through subliminal messages jointly seeded into the final episode of *Audience Shares*, and the debut of *Beep and Friends*. The sixth Doctor crushed this scheme, and exposed Beep's murderous tendencies on national television. Authorities apprehended the raving Meep.

2002 - THE FORGE: PROJECT: VALHALLA[814] **->** Nimrod recruited Cassie Schofield, who had become savage during her self-imposed exile, as an agent of the Forge.

2002 (6th June) - TALES FROM THE VAULT[815] **->** The fourth Doctor and the first Romana checked an art gallery to see if the Doctor had left himself any messages in the corners of paintings, and learned that one of the universe's great lost art treasures – the *Quistador Molari* – was on sale at a London auction house. The painting had caused more suffering than any other work in history, including everything by Tracey Emin, because it would depict the future death of anyone who looked at it, driving them mad. The Doctor took the painting away to destroy it, but as he didn't dare look at the item, Sgt Ruth Matheson of UNIT substituted a fake beforehand. The genuine item wound up in Unit's Vault, and was classified an Omega 10 artifact, only to be used when all alternatives had failed.

2002 - MASTERMIND[816] **->** The decaying Master awoke for an hour within the UNIT Vault, confirmed his identity to Sgt Ruth Matheson and returned to sleep.

2002 (7th June) - BENNY S10: SECRET ORIGINS[817] **->** The android Robyn and a temporal projection of Bernice Summerfield encountered their arch-nemesis, Samuel Frost. He procured the Right and Left Hands of God – powerful artifacts that granted great power to anyone attaching them to a handless statue of Arincias, one of the lost gods of Atlantis.

Sarah Jane Smith Series 1[818]

Sarah Jane Smith was now crafting exposes for Planet 3 Broadcasting. The Crimson Chapter tested Sarah to see if she was the herald cited in *The Book of Tomorrows*, and so provided backing to the former members of Think Tank and their leader, Hilda Winters. The ex-Think Tank members arranged for Sarah to be fired when accusations she levelled against Halter Corp, a Scottish fishery, were thought to be based upon false evidence. Her reputation in tatters, Sarah began living under various aliases.[819]

2002 - SJS: COMEBACK[820] **->** Six months after the Planet 3 broadcast that had hobbled her career, Sarah Jane continued trying to clear her name. Her associates included a computer hacker named Natalie Redfern and a young do-gooder named Josh Townsend. Sarah's investigations took her to Cloots Coombe, where the local Squire had been feeding people to the monster that lived in the town well. Josh set fire to the Rechauffer labs, destroying the facility and incinerating the well-mutant.

Josh was actually a member of the White Chapter, and had inveigled himself into Sarah's life to protect her.

2002 - SJS: THE TAO CONNECTION -> Sarah, Natallie and Josh looked into the death of an 18-year-old whose prematurely aged body was fished from the Thames. They linked the incident to Holtooth Hall, a retirement home where the lives of aged multi-millionaires were being extended by draughts of *chi*-enriched blood taken from young people, who consequently aged to death. The pop star Lotus, renowned as an ageless beauty, had withdrawn from public life after she had been expelled from Holtooth and started aging. Sarah and her allies ended the operation, and the billionaire Will Butley, who had survived for three hundred years, died when denied the draughts.

2002 - SJS: TEST OF NERVE -> Hilda Winters' group anonymously challenged Sarah Jane to stop a sarin-gas attack slated to occur in London in the next twenty-four hours. A former soldier, James Carver, threatened to unleash sarin pellets in the Underground unless the Prime Minister met his demands for compensation to British soldiers given unsafe vaccines as test subjects. Carver eventually backed down and killed himself. Sarah Jane's old friend – Claudia Coster, an administrator in the Ministry of Intelligence – also died during these events.

2002 - SJS: GHOST TOWN[821] **->** Sarah Jane sold Lavinia's property in Moreton Harwood, and moved into Claudia Coster's old flat.

Dr Mikhail Berberova, a physics professor, had perfected a means of using low-frequency electromagnetic fields to affect people's perceptions, causing them to think they were seeing ghosts. Nefarious parties seeking to disrupt an international peace conference in Romania used this technique to terrorize the delegates. Sarah and Josh exposed an expatriate Brit – Christian Ian Abbotly – as being behind the operation. The conference resumed after a hiatus.

2002 - SJS: MIRROR, SIGNAL, MANOEUVRE[822] **->** Sarah Jane travelled to India to investigate illicit genetic research being done by a company named Scala, and came face-to-face with the ex-members of Think Tank, including Hilda Winters. Winters' group planned to kill millions by contaminating a series of dams and reservoirs – the Parambikulam-Aliyar Project – with an engineered brucella virus. Sarah and her allies thwarted their plan, but Winters escaped. Scala lost its government contracts.

c 2002 - THE FEARMONGER[823] **->** Sherilyn Harper's New Britannia Party was gaining political influence by preaching strong anti-immigration policies. She was subject to an assassination attempt at the hands of United Front terrorists. Serious riots started spreading as the population panicked, but Harper was made to unwittingly broadcast a confession that New Britannia was secretly funding the United Front. The situation may or may not have been whipped up by the Fearmonger, an energy being from Boslin II. The seventh Doctor and Ace had been tracking the Fearmonger and destroyed it. Beryllium laser guns were top secret in this era.

821 It's not expressly said that the villains hoping to disrupt the peace conference are Hilda Winters' group, but it seems likely.
822 In *SJS: Mirror, Signal, Manoeuvre*, Hilda Winters acquires the deactivated K9 – who admittedly isn't cited by name – from Sarah's flat. Although the audios say nothing more about this, it seems reasonable to assume that Sarah re-acquires K9 after Winters' death in *SJS* Series 2. The different *Doctor Who* media (this story, *Decalog 3*: "Moving On" – also written by Peter Anghelides – and *School Reunion*) are remarkably consistent on the point that Sarah, for a time, is unable to keep K9 operational because she lacks the futuristic technology needed to service him. The situation doesn't change until the tenth Doctor revives the rusty K9 in *School Reunion*.
823 Dating *The Fearmonger* (BF #5) - This is "just over fifteen years" after Ace's time.
824 Dating *Rutans: In 2 Minds* (BBV audio #34) - The audio came out in 2002 and seems contemporary. Notably, the potential crisis is resolved because the UK's air defences are on full alert owing to 9-11. One of the characters jokes about a "winter migration", suggesting that it's later in the year.
825 Dating *Drift* (PDA #50) - The year isn't given, but it's clearly the modern day.
826 Dating *Time Zero* (EDA #60) - Anji returns home three weeks after she met the Doctor, and stays there eighteen months, so this story is set around the end of August 2002. Control also appears in *The Devil Goblins of Neptune*, *The King of Terror*, *Escape Velocity*, *Trading Futures* and *Time Zero*. The fire elemental that Curtis attracts is the creature the Doctor defeats in *The Burning*.
827 Dating *Unnatural History* (EDA #23) - Excerpts from a publication, *Interesting Times*, are dated to 7th and 14th November, 2002, and it's said to be "November 2002" when the story opens (p1).
828 *Head Games*
829 *The King of Terror*
830 According to *Class: The Lost*, she's "14" when the school year begins. Actress Vivian Oparah was born 30th December, 1996.
831 She's "not even eight" in *Leth-St*: "Lucy Wilson".
832 *Time Zero*, *The Infinity Race*, *The Domino Effect*, *Reckless Engineering*, *The Last Resort*, *Timeless*.
833 Dating *The Domino Effect* (EDA #62) - The book starts on "Thursday April 17 2003" (p1).

2002 - RUTANS: IN 2 MINDS[824] **->** The Rutan Host didn't deem Earth of strategic importance at present. The renegade Rutan brought to the UK summoned about two dozen other such rogues, intending that they should form a new Rutan Host aware of the benefits of individuality, and overthrow the current Host. The United Kingdom's air defences registered the rogues' ship as an unidentified craft and destroyed it.

c 2002 - DRIFT[825] **->** The fourth Doctor and Leela landed in New Hampshire and met soldiers from the elite White Shadow unit. They were looking to retrieve a crashed fighter that was testing the Stormcore, an alien device recovered thirty years earlier. Also, an ice monster was loose in the area. The Doctor realised the Stormcore had opened a portal into another dimension, and that the monster was not intelligent, but was inadvertently killing people while trying to make contact. The Doctor crystallised the monster and handed it over to the authorities.

Trix (Sneakily) Joins the TARDIS

2002 (late August) - TIME ZERO[826] **->** The reclusive billionaire Maxwell Curtis had learned that his body contained a microscopic remnant of the Big Bang, masquerading as an ordinary atom, which was in danger of collapsing and turning him into a black hole. He had founded the Naryshkin Institute in Siberia as a means of researching black hole phenomena.

Led by Control, a division of the American CIA suspected the Institute was conducting time travel experiments. Control's agents constructed a temporal detector and identified Anji as a time traveller. They made her accompany them to Siberia.

In Siberia, the eighth Doctor found that Curtis' black hole matter was distorting space-time in the region. This allowed the Doctor to free Fitz and George Williamson from the icy prison from which they had been trapped in 1894. Williamson existed in a ghostly state, as the universe couldn't decide if he'd survived or not.

Curtis travelled down a time corridor into the past that Williamson's pseudo-existence had generated, hoping to reach Time Zero and spare Earth by unleashing his black hole matter there. The Doctor realised that if the black hole within Curtis erupted before time began, it would destroy the universe. The Doctor convinced Williamson to go back with him to 1894 and avert Williamson getting trapped in the ice, which nullified the time corridor's existence. Curtis travelled back no further than 1894, and died in a comparatively minor explosion.

Curtis' black hole mass attracted light from a far distant o-region to Earth. The o-region light contained something organic, which lodged itself on Earth's past and would manifest in the late nineteenth century as a fire elemental.

Trix, a disguise artist who sometimes worked for Sabbath, took the opportunity to stow herself aboard the TARDIS.

2002 (November) - UNNATURAL HISTORY[827] **->** A dimensional scar, the after-effect of the singularity that befell Earth on New Year's Eve, 2000, appeared in San Francisco. The eighth Doctor investigated the anomaly, but his companion Samantha Jones was lost to it. He sought out Sam's original self, a dark-haired drug user, to assist. The Doctor also recruited Professor Joyce, a resident of Berkeley, to craft a dimensional stabiliser. Fitz and the dark-haired Sam became lovers.

Griffen the Unnaturalist, an agent of a secret Society that catalogued all aliens, arrived at this time to collect specimens for his catalogue. Dark-haired Sam sacrificed herself to the anomaly to restore blonde-haired Sam, who helped the Doctor to unleash the Unnaturalist's extra-dimensional specimen case. The freed specimens drove the Unnaturalist into the dimensional scar, and the case sealed it permanently.

The Doctor later realised that blonde Sam's timeline came about because she touched his biodata within the scar, meaning that she paradoxically facilitated her own creation.

On 30th November, 2002, the gunman Murdock killed five people... although Ace's interference in history reduced this total to three. This was about as far in the future as she could travel using her time hopper.[828] *The Day the World Turned Dayglo*, Hollywood's take on the Jex-Canavitchi war, was released in late 2002. Reporter Gabrielle Graddige approached the Brigadier in January 2003 for the true story.[829]

2003

Tanya Adeloa, a student at Coal Hill Academy, was born.[830] Lucy Wilson, the daughter of Albert Wilson and granddaughter of Alistair Lethbridge-Stewart, was born.[831]

The Eighth Doctor, Anji, Fitz and Trix Travel Through Parallel Earths

With time destabilised, the eighth Doctor, Anji, Fitz and the stowaway Trix were drawn into a series of adventures in alternate histories...[832]

(=) 2003 - THE DOMINO EFFECT[833] **->** The eighth Doctor, Fitz and Anji discovered a version of history where the British Empire ruled the world. There was widespread racial and sex discrimination. This timeline had developed because an alternate version of Sabbath had murdered key figures in the history of computing, including Babbage and Zuse, thus preventing the development of computers. The alternate Sabbath had learned that the Time Vortex was disintegrating following Gallifrey's destruction, and hoped to preserve his Earth in a temporal focal point. He was betrayed by a Vortex creature devoted to chaos, and the focal point collapsed. The entire past, present and future of this timeline were consumed.

(=) 2003 - RECKLESS ENGINEERING[834] **->** The Doctor, Fitz and Anji arrived in an alternate Bristol after "the Cleansing" effect had ravaged Earth, and found the Utopian Engine still generating a slow-time effect around Jared Malahyde's estate. After linking the Utopian Engine to the TARDIS' systems, the Doctor rolled back time a hundred and sixty years and averted "the Cleansing" timeline altogether.

(=) 2003 - THE LAST RESORT[835] **->** Fourteen-year-old Jack Kowaczski had built a time machine, and thus created many thousands of variant histories. This included his own, in which President Robert Heinlein presided over the USA and Mars – along with the Martians – had been conquered.

The Doctor, Fitz and Anji landed in one such history, where the time-travel holidays of Good Times Inc, founded by Jack's father Aaron, had turned the whole of human history into an homogenous tourist resort. The constant time travel, though, had destabilised reality and generated hundreds if not thousands of versions of events – including duplicate Doctors and companions. Sabbath was the only being unaffected by this process. The Doctor carefully sacrificed all but one version of himself and his companions, thus restoring the timeline.

---

834 Dating *Reckless Engineering* (EDA #63) - The Doctor is sure it's "2003" (p24).

835 Dating *The Last Resort* (EDA #64) - Time is a rather fluid concept in this novel, but Fitz and Anji are based in "2003" (p7, p11).

836 Dating *Timeless* (EDA #65) - No year is given, but the story takes place after *The Last Resort*, and Anji has been going out with Greg for a year by the time of *The Gallifrey Chronicles*.

837 Dating *The Forge: Project: Valhalla* (BF New Worlds novel #3) - The present day segments conclude with Nimrod commencing with Project: Lazarus (from the audio of the same name), and Cassie being promoted to the rank of field agent. So, even though *Project: Valhalla* was released in November 2005, the "present day" in this case must mean 2004 if not 2003.

838 *Project: Lazarus*

839 "About five years" before *SJA: Eye of the Gorgon*.

840 *TW: Miracle Day*

841 "Seven years" before *Iris: Enter Wildthyme*.

842 Dating *Touched by an Angel* (NSA #47) - The exact days are given (pgs. 7, 197, 227).

843 Dating *Eternity Weeps* (NA #58) - The date is given (p1).

DID LIZ SHAW DIE IN 2003?: Until recent years, and for anyone who considers the New Adventures canon, the answer was almost unequivocally, "Yes." In *Eternity Weeps* (set in 2003), Liz, as Operations Chief for Tranquillity Base on the moon, is infected with a flesh-eating terraforming virus, endures an unspeakable amount of pain, and dies after passing along the formula for an anti-virus to her lover Imorkal – who himself perishes after telepathically planting the information in Chris Cwej's mind. Cwej's failure to euthanise Liz despite her pleas is examined in *The Room with No*

Doors, and the matter is then considered closed.

Of late, both *The Sarah Jane Adventures* and the Big Finish Companion Chronicles starring Caroline John (reprising her role as Liz) have called Liz's death into question. In *SJA: Death of the Doctor*, Colonel Karim mentions, with regards associates of the Doctor invited to his funeral, "Miss Shaw can't make it back from moonbase until Sunday" (not an indicator that there's a crisis there, and probably just reflecting the infrequency with which shuttles transport personnel back to Earth). The acknowledgement of Liz working on a moonbase, strangely enough, confirms some of *Eternity Weeps* while rejecting another part of it.

With the Companion Chronicles being on audio, it was possible to imagine that Liz was narrating her stories prior to her death in 2003... until she says in *The Sentinels of the New Dawn* that if events in 2014 had not been wiped from history, "That horror would be starting around now...", i.e. a few years beforehand, concurrent with the audio's release in 2011.

Balancing these accounts is no easy task. The only leeway lies in the fact that in *Eternity Weeps*, we don't actually see Liz's dead body. The virus gives Liz horrific injuries at a United Nations Hazmat base in Turkey, but her actual passing is only confirmed by Imorkal, who tells Chris and Jason Kane, "She is dead". It becomes the stuff of fan-fiction to imagine events by which Liz recovered enough to be alive and well in 2011 (for instance, Imorkal placed Liz in a prototype Silurian healing chamber after plucking the formula for the anti-viral from her mind), but keeping these stories in a single continuity requires some off-screen explanation, however spurious.

844 Dating *Rip Tide* (TEL #6) - It is "late May" (p13), in "the twenty-first century" (p78). There's no reason to say

Anji Leaves the TARDIS

c 2003 - TIMELESS[836] -> The eighth Doctor, Fitz and Anji arrived back in the London of their reality. They found that Erasmus and Chloe, two survivors of a destroyed homeworld, had set up Timeless Inc. as a means of "helping people". Chloe and her time-active dog Jamais would visit parallel realities to find persons in pain, then bring them to the proper reality. Jamais would transfer each person's soul into their parallel counterpart, creating a merged soul with an improved timeline. Clients of Timeless Inc. paid £75,000 in diamonds for the privilege of murdering the parallel reality version, preventing the merged souls from defaulting back to their original state. Erasmus eventually realised that his goal of helping people had failed and killed himself, ending Timeless.

The genetic manipulations performed by Kalicum in the eighteenth century culminated in the British government worker Guy Adams. He possessed the DNA needed to house an intelligence that Kalicum and Sabbath had gestated, in a pile of diamonds, on behalf of the Council of Eight. The Doctor and his allies followed Sabbath back to the beginning of time, where he and Kalicum tried to seed the intelligence into the universe's beginnings.

Afterwards, Anji left the TARDIS crew to return to her old life in 2003. Aided by forged documents produced by Trix, she adopted Chloe and Jamais. Chloe introduced Anji to a man named Greg, whom she predicted Anji was going to get to know a lot better.

c 2003 - THE FORGE: PROJECT: VALHALLA[837] -> A maximum-security spaceship holding the Nyathoggoth – a sentient liquid that had killed billions to slacken its hunger for blood – was dispatched to fly into a black hole, but instead crashed in Lapland. Nimrod and Cassie Schofield of the Forge investigated the incident, and Nimrod – thinking the Nyathoggoth was uncontrollable – caused the ship to self-destruct, killing the creature. Afterwards, Nimrod became the Forge's deputy director.

Cassie was promoted and became "Artemis", Nimrod's top field agent in northern Europe.[838]

Professor Edgar Nelson-Stanley died – he was an accomplished adventurer who had learned much about extra-terrestrials, and deemed Sontarans the "silliest-looking aliens in the galaxy". His wife Bea would become a resident of the Lavender Lawns rest home.[839] **The mother of Esther Drummond, a future Torchwood operative, died in 2003.**[840] A young woman named Kelly started helping out behind the counter at the Great Big Book Exchange in Darlington. Over the next seven years, she absorbed the reverberations from a magical text there, the *Aja'ib* – an unfinished, and endless, sequence of tales and puzzles from the planet Hyspero.[841]

2003 (10th and 16th April) - TOUCHED BY AN ANGEL[842] -> Rebecca Whitaker died in a lorry accident. The older version of Mark Whitaker attempted to prevent this – had he succeeded, the Weeping Angels would have fed off the resulting paradox, and become strong enough to endanger Earth.

The eleventh Doctor, Amy and two versions of Rory arrived from 2001 to stop the Angels. One of the Rorys was touched by an angel, and sent back in time two years. The lights, cameras and monitors that Rory pre-ordered while he was there enabled the Doctor to spring a trap – the Angels, already malnourished, were caught in a closed circuit and erased. One Angel survived, and would encounter the contemporary Mark in 2011.

The older Mark realised the havoc his saving Rebecca would have caused, and allowed her car accident to proceed as scheduled. She died in his arms.

On 16th April, the Doctor, Amy, Rory and the older Mark attended Rebecca's funeral in secret. The travellers then took Mark, who was now 46, for one last meeting with his wife in 1993.

Benny Summerfield and Jason Separate

2003 (April) - ETERNITY WEEPS[843] -> Liz Shaw was Chief of Operations at Tranquillity Base on the moon, where co-operation with the Silurians had led to the construction of an experimental weather control gravitron. Shaw and the Silurian Imorkal were in a close relationship.

Mount Ararat and Mahser Dagi were now in territory disputed by Turkey and Iraq, but an expedition to find Noah's Ark on Mount Ararat set off anyway. Bernice Summerfield and Jason Kane joined the team, although Benny found the Tendurek Formation, six billion years old and utterly alien. The Cthalctose terraforming virus – dubbed Agent Yellow – was set off and triggered catastrophic geological changes on Earth.

The US launched a nuclear strike in the area, but only succeeded in speeding up the process. This wiped out many cities including Istanbul, Thessaloniki, Almawsil, Tbilisi and Krasnodar. President Springsteen ordered the targeting of the moonbase, believing the crew there to be responsible. Jason fled billions of years back into the past and returned. The Agent was spreading as far as the Alps, the Sahara and Asia. The seventh Doctor engineered an x-ray burst using singularities to sterilise the Agent. This wiped out one tenth of all life on Earth, including six hundred million people.

Imorkal perished during these events, and Liz Shaw appeared to die also. Benny and Jason separated. Suborbital flights could be used to travel quickly around the world.

c 2003 (late May to June) - RIP TIDE[844] -> A peaceful alien race used spatial gateways to become tourists on other worlds. Two young members of the species, genetically altered to resemble human beings, violated their people's strict rule against risk of discovery by visiting a small Cornish fishing village. One of them died in a sightseeing accident, losing the "key" to their spatial gateway in the process. His stranded mate adopted the name "Ruth", but began dying from prolonged exposure to Earth's environment. Nina Kellow, age 17, aided the eighth Doctor in rescuing Ruth, and he transported her back home.

A Fortean Flicker transported a group of train-riders on the 8:12 out of Chorleywood to the planet Hogsumm in the twenty-seventh century. They were later returned to Rickmansworth Station in their native time.[845] In 2003, Detective Inspector Tom Cutler discovered that an alien entity in Hammersmith had possessed Mark Palmer, and compelled him to rape and murder three boys. Torchwood London drew the entity out of Palmer, but left Palmer to be arrested. Cutler testified to falsifying evidence, sparing Palmer from a life sentence. Palmer wound up in a mental hospital, and Torchwood permitted Cutler to keep his memories of the incident.[846]

2003 - THE QUANTUM ARCHANGEL[847] -> Stuart Hyde was now the Emeritus Professor of Physics at West London University. He had used the discarded technology from TOMTIT to build TITAN, a dimensional array intended to penetrate the higher dimensions called Calabi-Yau Space. Thanks to TITAN, businesswoman Anjeliqua

Whitefriar became infused with the Calabi-Yau's core and gained reality-warping powers. She became "the Quantum Archangel", and channelled her newfound reality-warping powers through the Mad Mind of Bophemeral, the supercomputer that triggered the Millennium War, in a benevolent attempt to create separate utopias for each person on Earth. This threatened to plunge the universe into chaos.

> (=) The alternate realities created by the Quantum Archangel included ones where Mel was British Prime Minister, and faced a Cyberman invasion; the Doctor was President of Gallifrey, leading his people against the Master and the Daleks; and the Master, the Monk, the Rani and Drax altered Earth's DNA.[848]

The sixth Doctor persuaded Anjeliqua to restore order and relinquish her power, while the Chronovore named Kronos sacrificed himself to destroy Bophemeral.

2003 - MINUET IN HELL[849] -> Hellfire Club leader Brigham Elisha Dashwood III believed he'd allied himself with a group of demons, and set about using their support to booster his organisation. In truth, he'd contacted alien Psionivores, members of a species of cosmic parasites that feasted on negative emotions. With the Psionivores' help and technical expertise, Dashwood seceded a small portion of America, renamed it "Malebolgia" and dedicated it to a social program of devil worship. The Psionivores helped Dashwood perfect the PSI-895, which was capable

---

the story isn't set in the year the novella was published. **845** *The Highest Science.* The year is given on p2, and reiterated in *Happy Endings* (p5).

846 *TW: Into the Silence*

847 Dating *The Quantum Archangel* (PDA #38) - It's 2003 according to the blurb and p48, "thirty years" since *The Time Monster* (p39).

848 *The Quantum Archangel*

849 Dating *Minuet in Hell* (BF #19) - It's "the twenty-first century" and humanity has just developed quantum technology, suggesting it's the near future. *Neverland* gives the firm date of 2003 for this story. In *Liberty Hall*, an extra on the *Mawdryn Undead* DVD that has Nicholas Courtney reprising his role as the Brigadier, the Doctor's encounter with the Brig in Malebolgia is dated to "2000".

850 *The Taking of Planet 5* (p15).

851 *The Power of the Daleks*

852 Dating *The Hollow Men* (PDA #10) - No year is given, but the drought of '02 is mentioned, and five-pound coins are legal tender.

853 Dating "Evening's Empire" (*Doctor Who Classic Comics Autumn Special 1993*) - There's a calendar giving the month as June in the first panel in which we see the real Alex. The year is harder to establish, however. The

complete story was published in 1993, and in the last part, there's a newspaper dated "Nov 23 1993". It's "fifty" years since the World War II plane crashed, again supporting a date in the early nineties. However, the story falls after "The Mark of Mandragora", set after 1997, and enough time has passed for Frost to be promoted from Major to Colonel.

854 MURIEL FROST: According to John Freeman in his afterword to the collected "Evening's Empire", *DWM* originally planned to introduce "a more solid supporting cast" for the seventh Doctor. Muriel Frost of UNIT, a fiery redhead with a complicated personal life, was clearly a big part of those plans. However, publication of "Evening's Empire" was delayed, and the comic series ended up tying in more closely with the New Adventure novels – meaning the planned storylines were dropped.

Muriel Frost appeared in "The Mark of Mandragora", "Evening's Empire" and "Final Genesis" in *DWM*. A Captain Muriel Frost also appeared in the 1980 sequence of *The Fires of Vulcan*. This is clearly meant to be the same character, but it really doesn't fit with what we know. In the British regular army, it's possible to spend twenty years as a Captain, but an able candidate could expect to be promoted to Major within four or five years (not to mention the fact that Frost doesn't

of rewriting or transferring human memories, and Dashwood hoped this would let him install Psionivores in his political opponents' bodies.

The eighth Doctor and Charley, aided by the Brigadier, publicly exposed Dashwood as a political charlatan. Dashwood turned against Marcosius, his main contact among the Psionivores, and accidentally disrupted the PSI machine. This created an unstable portal that consumed Dashwood, Marcosius and the device. The remaining Hellfire Club leaders crumbled in a political scandal.

Lethbridge-Stewart had now retired from UNIT, but still undertook occasional work for them.

Vulcan, nearest planet to the Sun, was discovered in 2003.[850] **Vulcan was a large, hot world with a bleak landscape of mercury swamps and geysers that spat toxic fumes. It had a breathable atmosphere and soil capable of supporting plant life. Plans were made to set up a mining colony on Vulcan for a trial period.**[851]

c 2003 (Saturday, 14th June) - THE HOLLOW MEN[852] -> The Hakolian battle vehicle Jerak revived in Hexen Bridge and animated scarecrows, who attacked the villagers and fed them to Jerak's organic component. Jerak mentally influenced a former resident, Defence Minister Matthew Hatch, in a bid to taint Liverpool's water supply with genetic material that would increase Jerak's mental hold over any humans it infected. The seventh Doctor thwarted the scheme, entered Jerak's psychic realm via a mirror gateway and convinced the villagers absorbed over the centuries by Jerak to turn their willpower against the battle vehicle. The Doctor escaped and Ace destroyed the gateway, trapping Jerak on the astral plane. Hatch died, still mentally connected to Jerak upon its defeat.

c 2003 (June) - "Evening's Empire"[853] -> The seventh Doctor and Ace were in Middlesbrough, where Colonel

Muriel Frost of UNIT was recovering a German fighter from the Tees. They learned that the plane was downed after contact with an alien ship.

Ace met a local named Alex Evening, and upon following him home discovered a tiny Q'Dhite mindtreader spaceship among the Airfix models in his bedroom. The Q'Dhite explored the universe by weaving reality from fantasy, and Alex had been using that power to kidnap women, send them to his imaginary "empire" and then humiliate them. Ace was woven into his empire, and the Doctor, Frost and her troops followed in the TARDIS. The Doctor defeated Alex by bringing his domineering mother into the empire, shattering the illusion. They returned to the real world to find Alex in a coma.

At this time, Muriel Frost was in a relationship with a scientist called Nick – both of them were unhappy.[854]

= c 2003 - "Final Genesis"[855] -> The seventh Doctor, Benny and Ace arrived in a parallel universe where humans worked side by side with Silurians, and Colonel Frost served with the United Races Intelligence Command (URIC). The Silurian scientist Mortakk had created human-Silurian hybrids called Chimeras, and sent them to attack URIC. The Doctor defeated Mortakk.

c 2003 (summer) - ZYGON: WHEN BEING YOU ISN'T ENOUGH[856] -> The Zygon Kritakh was briefly rendered unconscious while undercover as a young man named Mike Kirkwood... and afterwards believed he *was* Kirkwood, who was experiencing dreams of being a Zygon. Kritakh's second, Torlakh, took the form of Robert Calhoun – a criminal who had killed about half a dozen women in the Edinburgh area. Torlakh/Calhoun endowed Kirkwood's therapist – Dr Lauren Anderson – with Zygon essence to make her a shapechanger, hoping that she

look old enough in "The Mark of Mandragora"). Between "The Mark of Mandragora" and "Evening's Empire", she's gone from Major to Colonel – a process that would normally take over ten years.

"The Mark of Mandragora" has Frost refer to the Doctor as "child" at one point, but the term is intended as slang, not an indication that she's older than she appears.

Even though the intention was that they are the same character, it might be simpler to imagine (and nothing particularly contradicts this idea) that the Frost in *The Fires of Vulcan* is Colonel Frost's mother. In which case, the young US major who appears and is killed in *Aliens of London* (set in 2006) - the same character who the Doctor called "Muriel Frost" in the draft script, and who has a "Muriel Frost" name badge - must presum-

ably be her American cousin.

855 Dating "Final Genesis" (*DWM #203-206*) - Ace recognises Muriel Frost, so in her terms the story takes place after "Evening's Empire".

856 Dating *Zygon: When Being You Isn't Enough* (BBV independent film) - The story was released in 2008 but filmed years beforehand, hence why a credit card flashed by a minor character, Ray, bears the active/expiration dates of "09/02" to "09/04". It seems reasonable to assume that the card is still valid, because Anderson goes on a shopping spree upon finding it. A Euronics Centre advertisement establishes that it's summer.

Somewhat infamously, this film is a canonical *Doctor Who*-related erotic thriller, with full-frontal nudity and two softcore sex scenes - although the back cover,

would better empathise with Kritakh's condition and restore his identity. Kirkwood and Anderson were in a relationship and resisted Torlakh's plans, so Torlakh staged a massacre at St Kitts Hospital while wearing Anderson's form. Anderson faked her death by killing Torlakh, then departed for a new life with Kirkwood.

2003 (August) - THE SHADOW OF THE SCOURGE[857]

-> The Pinehill Crest Hotel was host to the unfortunate triple-booking of a presentation of a temporal accelerator, a demonstration of spiritual channelling and a cross-stitch convention. The seventh Doctor, Ace and Benny stopped the Scourge from manifesting into our universe.

(=) **2003 - JUBILEE**[858] -> The sixth Doctor and Evelyn discovered that their thwarting a Dalek invasion in 1903 had given rise to an English Empire. The two of them were widely regarded as heroes, and Nelson's Column had been rebuilt to depict the Doctor dressed as an English stormtrooper. The British and American populates were strictly kept apart to protect British genetic purity. The Daleks were heavily merchandised, and their defeat was told in movies such as *Daleks: The Ultimate Adventure!*, starring Plenty O'Toole as Evelyn "Hot Lips" Smythe. Use of contractions was outlawed.

The President of the English Empire, Nigel Rochester, scheduled the Empire's jubilee celebration to include the public execution of the sole surviving Dalek from the 1903 attack. However, the Dalek secretly killed the Doctor's temporal duplicate, who had been a prisoner in the Tower for a hundred years.

The timelines of 1903 and 2003 began meshing together, and the Dalek invasion of 1903 started to unfold in the latter era. The Doctor convinced the "jubilee" Dalek that if the Daleks succeeded in their attempt to destroy all other life forms, they could only then turn on each other until a single Dalek remained, purposeless and insane. Logically, success would mean the Dalek race's destruction. The Dalek concurred and connected itself to the Dalek command net, transmitting a message that the Daleks could only survive by dying. The entire Dalek invasion force self-destructed, which retroactively averted the 1903 assault.

Remnants of the cancelled timeline remained in the restored history. Nigel Rochester, visiting the Tower of London as a tourist, briefly recognised the Doctor and thanked him for his help in the aberrant history. The English Empire's atrocities subtly lived on in the history and the dreams of the English people.

---

featuring three pictures of naked people on a couch, overstates the amount of film time given to sex acts. That said, in what will doubtless be disappointing news to some, there are no sex scenes involving Zygons in their natural state.

857 Dating *The Shadow of the Scourge* (BF #13) - It is "the fifteenth of August 2003" according to the Doctor.
858 Dating *Jubilee* (BF #40) - The date is given (and it's the hundredth anniversary of the events of 1903).
859 Dating *Unbound: Deadline* (BF Unbound #5) - The story seems contemporary with the audio's release in 2003 - Tom has a Playstation 2 (released March 4, 2000) and an Xbox (November 15, 2001), the blurb says "It's been forty years since Martin Bannister encountered the Doctor" (i.e. in the first episode of *Doctor Who* in 1963) and Bannister perceives Sydney Newman appearing to ask him to write *Doctor Who*'s fortieth anniversary special. The story appears to end with Bannister's death, as is telegraphed by the blurb stating: "Sounds like it's time for the Doctor to come into Martin's life again, and sort him out. Permanently."
860 Dating *Daemons: Daemos Rising* (Reeltime Pictures film #6) - A calendar in Cavendish's house cites the exact day that Mastho is summoned as 31st October, 2003, and the story begins the night before. This is the first time that Mastho had been summoned from his point of view; from Sodality's, it's the second (the first

being in 1586, in *TimeH: Child of Time*).
861 Dating *Falls the Shadow* (NA #32) - It is "a crisp November morning", "five years" after "UN adventurism in the Persian Gulf". Winterdawn is alive and well in *The Quantum Archangel*, so this book is set after that. Thascales was an alias of the Master in *The Time Monster*. Author Daniel O'Mahony intended it to be set in "the near future".
862 Dating *Catch-1782* (BF #68) - The date is given.
863 *TW: Miracle Day*, in a cheeky little reference to the ITV show *Mine All Mine* (2004) by Russell T Davies.
864 "Four years" before "The Widow's Curse".
865 "Five years" prior to *TW: Consequences*: "The Wrong Hands".
866 *Unregenerate!* Rausch says he hasn't seen Louis in "fifty years", but this could be a rounded sum. A radio broadcast says US and UK forces are "hours" away from Fallujah in Iraq. The main offensive there occurred on 8th November, 2004. *Unregenerate!* was recorded just more than a week later on 16-17 November.
867 "Five years" before *SJA: The Mark of the Berserker*.
868 *Night Thoughts*
869 *P.R.O.B.E.: When to Die*
870 *TW: Uncanny Valley, TW: The Torchwood Archive* (BF).
871 Dating *Sometime Never* (EDA #67) - An invitation states that an exhibition at the Institute of Anthropology opens on 31st January, 2004. *Sometime Never* was pub-

= **c 2003 - UNBOUND: DEADLINE**[859] -> Television writer Martin Bannister was now in a nursing home. His estranged son Phillip visited to inform Bannister that his ex-wife, Phillip's mother, had died, but also that Bannister had a six-year-old grandson named Tom. Bannister's concept of reality blurred, and he simultaneously acknowledged he was in the home, with a night nurse named Barbara Wright... but he also experienced adventures via his inter-dimensional wardrobe as Doctor Who, with his faithful companions Ian, Barbara and Susan. Ian and Barbara died of radiation poisoning on an alien world, and Doctor Who abandoned Susan to the same fate because he had another grandson now.

At the home, Phillip – still anguished because his father had abandoned his family – revealed that he'd lied, and that his mother was still alive. Tom emotionally rejected Bannister, who retreated into the safety of his wardrobe, but was unable to breathe properly. Susan appeared, and said that if Bannister left the TARDIS now, he'd never find it again. He needed to make one last important decision, if he wished to keep exploring new worlds...

2003 (30th-31st October) - DAEMONS: DAEMOS RISING[860] -> The Sodality – a group of revolutionaries who had grabbed power in a potential future by using the Daemons' science – reached back and compelled Captain Douglas Cavendish, who had been discharged from UNIT following the mid-nineties Yeti visitation, to summon a Daemon. Sodality hoped to shackle the Daemon as a means of controlling this time zone, but Cavendish and Kate Lethbridge-Stewart bore witness as a Daemon named Matso was summoned – and then rejected Sodality's claim on its power.

c 2003 (November) - FALLS THE SHADOW[861] -> Professor Jeremy Winterdawn and his team at Shadowfell House had experimented for five years with the "Thascales Theorem", and their research indicated that applied quantum physics was a possibility. Winterdawn experimented with the metahedron to the grey man's Cathedral, but in doing so caused damage to the universe. The beautiful humanoids Gabriel and Tanith were thereby created as expressions of the universe's pain; they were creatures of pure sadism, who wanted to use Cathedral's power to harm every living being. Winterdawn died from a heart attack. The grey man summoned the seventh Doctor, Ace and Bernice to help, and the Doctor used the TARDIS to put the metahedron inside Cathedral, creating a closed environment that saved the universe as Cathedral succumbed to entropy. Ace killed Gabriel and Tanith after the grey man cut them off from the universe's suffering, ren-

dering them powerless. The grey man departed, eager to explore the universe.

2003 (12th December) - CATCH-1782[862] -> The sixth Doctor and Mel arrived in Berkshire at the invitation of Mel's uncle, John Hallam, to attend the 100th anniversary celebration of the National Foundation for Scientific Research, UK. Hallam had constructed a cylinder from a unique alloy provided by a space agency, but the interaction of the TARDIS and chrono-atoms within the cylinder threw Melanie two hundred and twenty-two years back in time. The Doctor and Hallam pursued her in the TARDIS.

2004

The **"Vivaldi inheritance"** of 2004 demonstrated a means of establishing the truth through paper documentation.[863] The Doctor visited Cuba.[864]

Policewoman Gwen Cooper assisted with the recovery of a child abandoned in a courtyard; the child survived, and was fostered.[865] As arranged in 1957, the Time Lord Louis collected Johannes Rausch on the day before his death. They travelled to a Gallifreyan CIA Institute, where Rausch took part in an experiment to transfer TARDIS sentiences.[866] **Paul Langer walked out on his family, including his son Clyde, and ran off to Germany with his sister-in-law Mel. Clyde handled his father's departure so badly, he got into trouble and was expelled.**[867]

Hex thought until he was six that his grandmother was his mum.[868] Corporal Paul Reynish served in Afghanistan in 2004.[869]

The Committee arranged for Neil Redmond, the billionaire owner of the weapons-maker Artemis, to have a car accident in France in April 2004. Redmond lost the use of his legs, whereupon a Committee associate, Ms. Trent, offered Redmond use of an Ovid "doll": an android-like being who could literally stand in for him at public appearances. Redmond agreed, and the android, nicknamed N.J., spent the next two years learning to mimic him. The Ovid dolls were otherwise crafted to house the Committee members' intelligences on Earth.[870]

2004 - SOMETIME NEVER[871] -> The scientist Ernest Fleetward stood on the brink of inventing a form of unbreakable crystal that would advance humankind's development. Fleetward had set about reconstructing a crystal human skeleton: that of the Council of Eight leader Octan, lost to the Time Vortex in 1588. Octan himself travelled through time to prevent Fleetward's efforts from impacting history and cast the skeleton into the Vortex, failing to realise he was re-obliterating his own body.

The eighth Doctor convinced Fleetward to adopt the nephews of Richard III, who were saved from their historical fate.

Anji started dating Greg in the summer.[872] On June 8, 2004, Ian Chesterton was very keen to see a transit of Venus – he'd missed the previous such event, back in 1770, by just a few months.[873]

Ben Jackson and Polly Wright were now married. Polly and Ian Chesterton were separately Timescooped into the Death Zone on Gallifrey, and returned home after aiding the fifth Doctor.[874]

2004 (30th June) - DAEMONS: WHITE WITCH OF DEVIL'S END[875] **->** Aided by a skilled magus named Eddie, Olive Hawthorne confronted the vampire Lilyana – the sire of her beloved Victor – reduced Lilyana to ashes and sealed her remains in a silver box.

2004 (18th July) - PROJECT: LAZARUS[876] **->** The Forge, located on Dartmoor beneath an abandoned asylum, had begun collecting dead alien life forms and tech-

nology on Earth. Its agents captured a stranded, blue skinned alien capable of exuding a slime that killed on contact; Nimrod dubbed the alien's race as the "Huldran". The Forge took into custody the Huldran's spacecraft, which could generate spatial gateways. The sixth Doctor and Evelyn briefly encountered the Forge, causing the Forge to procure a sample of the Doctor's blood. A clone of the Doctor was created to assist their endeavours.

Nimrod killed Cassandra Schofield when she betrayed him to help the Doctor and Evelyn.

2004 (July) - THE TOMORROW WINDOWS[877] **->** The "selfish memes" seeded on behalf of Martin culminated on various planets. The planet Shardybarn was eradicated when the Low Priest Jadrack the Pitiful triggered several nuclear bombs, hoping that his god would perform a miracle and stop the disaster. On Valuensis, a misunderstanding made the Gabaks and Aztales annihilate one

---

lished in the same month.

872 "A year" before *The Gallifrey Chronicles*. Greg was introduced in *Timeless*.

873 *Transit of Venus.* The most recent transit happened in June 2012 – another won't occur until 2117.

874 *The Five Companions.* This happens at an unspecified point after Ben and Polly become a couple on New Year's Eve, 1999. Ian, although constantly said to be "older", is still spry enough to run down corridors and dodge Dalek laser beams with the best of them.

875 Dating *Daemons: White Witch of Devil's End* (story #2, "Half Light") – It's "fifty years exactly" since Victor's demise (in 1954, by *Ahistory*'s estimation). It's been "one hundred years" since another eclipse – one did occur on 9th September, 1904, although it wasn't visible from the United Kingdom (where no total eclipse happened from 1724 to 1925).

876 Dating *Project: Lazarus* (BF #45) – The dating clues are very conflicting. According to Professor Harket's journal, the story opens on 18th July, 2004 , and the first track is explicitly titled as such. However, the Doctor says it's "late November". He lets the TARDIS choose the destination, though, so perhaps he's confused. Nobody can quite agree on how much time has passed since *Project: Twilight* – the Doctor thinks it's been "a couple years", Cassie suggests it's been "a few years", and Nimrod specifies that it's "five years". *Project: Destiny* seems to establish that *Project: Twilight* was set in 2001, and its back cover reiterates that Cassie died in 2004.

877 Dating *The Tomorrow Windows* (EDA #69) – Trix's clothes are "very 2004" (p13). The Earth year 2004 is equivalent to the Galactic Year 2457. All the events on alien planets in *The Tomorrow Windows* seem contemporaneous, and the Doctor even says on p278, "we only travelled in space, not in time".

878 Dating *TW: Trace Memory* (TW novel #5) – Owen is now a doctor (*TW: Greeks Bearing Gifts* says that he was

six months into his residency in September 2001) and has a girlfriend (who isn't necessarily his future finance, seen in *TW: Fragments*), but the year is still a bit unclear.

879 Dating *TW: Fragments* (TW 2.12) – It's "five years" prior to the story's 2009 component. This synchs with *TW: Greeks Bearing Gifts* (set in 2007, where it's said that Tosh has been with Torchwood for three years) and *TW: To the Last Man* (set in 2008, in which Toshiko has known Tommy – who revives from stasis annually – for "four years"). *The Torchwood Archives* (BBC) is the odd man out on this one, saying that Tosh was arrested "late 2004/early 2005", but held for eight months before Jack approached her. *TW: SkyPoint* alternatively says that she was imprisoned for "six months" (p87).

880 Dating *The Sleep of Reason* (EDA #70) – It's the "near future" according to the blurb, but references to things like Limp Biskit and *Casualty* suggest it's at most only a few years after publication. It is "a hundred years or so" since 1903 (p273).

881 Dating *The Algebra of Ice* (PDA #68) – It's apparently set "several years" after the Brigadier first met the seventh Doctor (in *Battlefield*). From his perspective, the Brigadier previously met the seventh Doctor in *No Future*, but the Doctor mind-wiped the Brigadier's recollection of those events, and doesn't restore these memories until *Happy Endings*, set in 2010. *The Algebra of Ice* falls in the period where the Brigadier would recall *Battlefield* as their first meeting. Lloyd Rose wrote this story with "the modern day" in mind.

882 Dating *The City of the Dead* (EDA #49) – No year is given, but it's "a few years" after Anji's time.

883 Dating *The Deadstone Memorial* (EDA #71) – There's no specific date beyond "early twenty-first century" (p51). It's set in the modern day.

884 The Haisman timeline, prior to UNIT's renaming in *The Sontaran Stratagem*.

another with doomsday devices. On Estebol, malevolent cars began to possess their drivers and the people withered due to extreme pollution.

To combat this self-destructive trend, the billionaire philanthropist Charlton Mackerel set up Tomorrow Window exhibits on various planets. The Tomorrow Windows allowed the indigenous populations to glimpse their future and hopefully amend their behaviour. Martin sought to ruin Mackerel's exhibits. In June 2004, Martin eradicated the Tate Modern – and a Tomorrow Windows exhibit there – with an electron bomb.

The eighth Doctor aided Mackerel by seeking out the original Tomorrow Windows builder, Astrabel Zar. Electrical beings named the Ceccecs, working for Martin, destroyed the belt of moon-sized Astral Flowers in an attempt to kill Zar, but the Doctor and Zar escaped.

A "selfish meme" on the planet Minuea made the populace do nothing as their moon slowly moved toward a collision with their planet. The Doctor used a Tomorrow Window to make the people see the benefit of using a missile to stop the catastrophe, and thereby saved the planet.

The aged Zar returned to Gadrahadron to tell his younger self, fifty years in the past, how to make the Tomorrow Windows. Martin discovered this and killed Zar. The repentant actor Prubert Gatridge and Martin died in mutual combat. Fitz, Trix and Mackerel ensured that the younger Zar learned the Tomorrow Windows secret.

Mackerel's Tomorrow Windows exhibits continued, granting planets with selfish memes a second chance. The Doctor determined that Martin never completed his work on Earth, and that humanity developed selfish memes independent of him.

The Doctor was by now an old friend of Ken Livingstone, the current Mayor of London.

c 2004 - TW: TRACE MEMORY[878] **->** As a young doctor, Owen Harper met the time-jumping Michael Bellini.

Toshiko Sato Joins Torchwood

2004 - TW: FRAGMENTS[879] **-> Toshiko Sato worked for the Lodmoor Research Facility, a division of the Ministry of Defence. Toshiko's mother was kidnapped, and her abductors forced Toshiko to steal blueprints for a sonic modulator that could emit powerful sonic waves. UNIT captured those involved, imprisoned Toshiko for treason in a detention facility and withdrew her rights as a citizen. Captain Jack had Toshiko's record wiped clean, in exchange for her agreeing to work for Torchwood for five years.**

c 2004 - THE SLEEP OF REASON[880] **->** Mausolus House had been replaced by the Retreat, a more modernised asylum. Caroline "Laska" Darnell, the great-great-

granddaughter of one of Dr Christie's patients, came into possession of the Sholem-Luz dog-tooth pendant. The pendant again infected an Irish wolfhound with the Sholem-Luz essence, and the infernal hound set about trying to germinate Sholem-Luz seeds through time and space. The eighth Doctor, aided by Fitz and Trix, lured the creature into a time corridor to 1903. Afterwards, the husband of a Retreat medical officer found Laska's pendant, which possibly still contained the Sholem-Luz taint.

c 2004 - THE ALGEBRA OF ICE[881] **->** In another universe, an alien gestalt composed of mathematical equations sought to drain energy from outside realities into its own. The gestalt contacted the genocidal Sheridan Brett in our universe, hoping to use human mathematicians to further its plans. The seventh Doctor, accompanied by Ace, confronted the gestalt on a mathematical level and resolved the creature into zero.

c 2004 (October) - THE CITY OF THE DEAD[882] **->** The eighth Doctor visited New Orleans to identify a bone charm he had found in the TARDIS. He determined that the charm could summon a water elemental, and left for 1980 to investigate such an occurrence. This journey made the charm retroactively appear in the TARDIS for the Doctor to find in the first place.

Upon returning, the Doctor found that the wife of resident Vernon Flood was a bound water elemental. The Doctor freed Mrs Flood from her human form and she returned to her own dimension, causing Vernon to drown. Her elemental son, bound in 1980, had become the crippled museum owner Thales. The ritualist Jonas Rust attempted to absorb Thales to attain great power, but an emptiness that Rust summoned – the Void – wound up consuming him. Thales was liberated from his human body and reunited with his mother.

c 2004 - THE DEADSTONE MEMORIAL[883] **->** The long-lived Henry Deadstone, having established an identity as the old man Crawley, continued to tend to the alien psychic force he'd encountered some centuries ago. The eighth Doctor intervened when the creature tried and failed to reunite itself, causing psychic terror for the local McKeown family. The anguished creature withdrew its power from Deadstone and he instantly aged to death. The Doctor returned the creature to its home dimension.

2005

Circa 2005-2007, Brigadier Bishop sat on an advisory board that consolidated the United Nations Intelligence Taskforce, the Fifth Operational Corps and other agencies into the Unified Intelligence Taskforce.[884]

In 2005, Ianto Jones joined Torchwood London as a

junior researcher.[885] Yvonne Hartman approved Ianto Jones' employment with Torchwood One, as a minor admin worker, over Bev Stanley's reservations. The very next week, Jones aided Hartman against a monster in Cardiff. Owing to Torchwood's high turnover rate, he soon became Hartman's personal assistant.[886] Hartman brought two of her employees, Ianto Jones and Lisa Hallett, together as a couple. They went on two dates, but didn't continue their relationship for a time. Hartman, ever mindful of employee morale, also gifted Jones with a new coffee grinder.[887]

Had Ace not become one of Fenric's Wolves, Fenric would have come for her daughter on a council estate near Perivale in 2005.[888] Rory Williams saw the Leadworth Football Club play the Eagles at Crystal Palace in 2005.[889] **Danny Pink dug twenty-three wells when he was a soldier, saving whole villages.**[890]

The early explorers of Mars discovered Bernice Summerfield's hibernation pod – something of a shock, on a planet thought bereft of human life. Some of their number formed an underground religion around Benny, which gave rise to worship of a goddess, the Beneficiary, who hailed from the "Summer Fields". Benny slept on, and her pod's location was lost.[891]

The Tenth Doctor Regenerates (Again)

2005 (New Year's Day) - THE END OF TIME[892] **->** The dying tenth Doctor met Rose and Jackie on New Year's Day. He realised that Rose hadn't met him yet, but assured her she would have a fantastic year. Rose headed away, and the Doctor saw a vision of Ood Sigma – who told him his song had come to an end. The Doctor returned to the TARDIS, put it in motion and regenerated...

2005 (New Year's Day) - THE ELEVENTH HOUR[893] **->** The TARDIS careened out of control, and the newly regenerated eleventh Doctor held on for dear life as it fell back through time...

Panda Meets Iris Wildthyme

2005 - IRIS S1: WILDTHYME AT LARGE[894] **->** Agents of an extra-dimensional being – who manifested in our reality as a severed head on a pike – sought out Iris Wildthyme because the knowledge she'd acquired in her travels could be used to help plan an invasion. Many of Iris' memories had been siphoned into a jewel from the mines of Marleon, and she entrusted the gem to her former

885 "Two years" prior to the 2007 component of *TW: Fragments*.

886 "A couple of months" before *TW: Torchwood One: Before the Fall*, and a week at most before *Rose*. Stanley met her fate in *TW: Trace Memory*.

887 *TW: Broken, TW: Torchwood One: Before the Fall*.

888 *Gods and Monsters*, with mention of "Ace's daughter" being an echo of Rose Tyler.

889 "The Eagle and the Reich". The Crystal Palace referenced here is an area of south London, not to be confused with the Crystal Palace building that burned down in 1936.

890 *Listen*

891 *Benny B2: Road Trip: Brand Management*. This presumably happens during the very first explorations of Mars, before widespread human space-travel later in the twentieth century. The future component of *Brand Management*, set circa 2617, features the "612th" gathering to celebrate the Sleep of the Beneficiary, suggesting the first happened circa 2005. That's a bit early for "colonists" to be settling Mars, but perhaps the earliest Beneficiary devotees were astronauts to the Red Planet, and the details were lost to history.

892 Dating *The End of Time* (X4.17-4.18) - Rose gives the date.

893 Dating *The Eleventh Hour* (X5.1) - In the precredits sequence (a late addition to the story), as the TARDIS is seen swooping over London, both the Millennium Dome (started in 1996) and the London Eye (built in 1999) are visible. The opening action, then, presumably

entails the new Doctor flailing about in the same time zone in which he regenerated, not when he meets Amy.

894 Dating *Iris S1: Wildthyme at Large* (BF Iris #1.1) - The story seems contemporary with the audio's release in November 2005. A case could be made for dating it slightly later, though, as *Iris S1: The Devil and Ms. Wildthyme* – which takes right after this story – occurs "thirty years" after December 1978.

895 *Iris: Enter Wildthyme*

896 Dating *Iris S1: The Devil in Ms. Wildthyme* (BF Iris #1.2) - This directly follows *Iris S1: Wildthyme at Large*.

897 *The Return of Doctor Mysterio*

898 Dating *SJA: Lost in Time* (SJA 4.5) - Date unknown, but the setting seems a bit contemporary in that the babysitter has a compact mobile. Even so, this portion of the story is unlikely to occur simultaneous to Sarah's starting point in 2010, as the Shopkeeper meant to send her "through time" to this location.

899 Dating *Erimem: The Coming of the Queen* (BF New Worlds novel #2) - Wilton is said to discover the tomb "today", and the novel was published in 2005.

900 Dating "Suspicious Minds" (*The Legends of River Song* #1b) - It's "fourteen days" before the Nestene invasion in *Rose* [5th-6th March, 2005].

901 Dating *Rose* (X1.1) - The year isn't specified, but there's a contemporary setting. The story is clearly set after 2003, as the Doctor reads a paperback copy of the novel *The Lovely Bones* by Alice Sebold.

Aliens of London shows a missing persons poster that definitively cites Rose as last seen on 6th March, 2005.

companion Tom. His sentient stuffed Panda bear smashed the jewel, depriving the villains of their prize. The Head returned to its home dimension, and Tom and Panda took up travelling with Iris...

Panda couldn't remember his origins – not even if he was unique, or but one of a race of ten-inch-tall, talking pandas. He did, at least, remember living in London with Tom, and experienced love at first sight upon finally meeting Iris.[895]

2005 - IRIS S1: THE DEVIL IN MS. WILDTHYME[896] ->

Tom and Panda were chagrined because Iris had promised them adventures, but her bus had wound up in London, right back where they'd started. The remnant of Asmedaj that was squirrelled away in Iris' mind had been freed when the Marleon crystal broke – but he'd been altered by his interaction with Iris' memories and the Marleon crystal, and so was restored to life as a sheep. Iris, Tom and Panda left Earth for some proper adventuring.

A couple of years after graduating high school, Grant Gordon and his best friend ran into Grant's teenage crush, Lucy. In rapid succession, the best friend married Lucy, had a daughter with her, and then ran off with someone else.[897]

? 2005 - SJA: LOST IN TIME[898] ->

Two children accidentally started a house fire while their babysitter was busy elsewhere. Sarah Jane and Emily Morris, operating from 1889, used a chronosteel key to open the children's bedroom door, saving them.

2005 - ERIMEM: THE COMING OF THE QUEEN[899] ->

Carra Wilton, the youngest professor of Egyptology in England, discovered a tomb that related some of the story of the Pharaoh Erimem. The fifth Doctor, Peri and Erimem herself were in attendance nine months later at the National Museum of Egyptian Antiquities in Cairo, where artifacts from the tomb were on display.

2005 (23rd February) - THE LEGENDS OF RIVER SONG: "Suspicious Minds"[900] ->

River dressed up as Good Queen Bess to visit her boyfriend, the Auton Elvis, at Madame Tussauds. The eleventh Doctor happened by, and saw his wife dressed up as his previous wife. The Doctor told River that a Nestene would invade Earth in a few weeks' time, and bring Elvis back under its influence. Elvis vowed to melt himself before then, but agreed to a final trip to the Meadows: a wildlife preserve established by aliens in the Mediterranean.

The Doctor's trio toppled the Meadows' caretaker, Melissa Tokana, as she had taken to turning anti-environmentalists into fertiliser. Elvis took charge of the Meadows, and its force field shielded him from the Nestenes' influence. Posing as Plastic Elvis, he sponsored some successful Benefit for Bees concerts.

Doctor Who Series 1

The Ninth Doctor Meets Rose Tyler, Her Mother Jackie and Mickey Smith

2005 (5th-6th March) - ROSE[901] ->

Rose Tyler worked at Henrik's department store in London, which was the location of a secret Auton transmitter. She met the ninth Doctor shortly before he blew up the store, and accidentally took an Auton arm home with her. The Doctor found the arm and deactivated it. Fascinated by the Doctor, Rose tracked down Clive, who ran a website charting appearances of the Doctor over the years. Rose met up with the Doctor again and helped him defeat the Nestene invasion, but not before Auton shop dummies rampaged through London. Seventy-eight people were killed (including Clive), three hundred injured. Rose joined the Doctor on his travels.

Rose's disappearance prompted the police to search for her. Her boyfriend Mickey Smith was interviewed by the police, who – like Rose's mother Jackie –

The casualty figures come from the www.whoisdoctorwho.co.uk website, which also has pictures with timestamps that offer an alternative date 26th March, the day of broadcast. *Timelink* and *About Time* both favoured the missing persons poster in their analysis.

A UNIT Press Briefing in *A History of the Universe in 100 Objects* (p116) dates "the London Incident" involving the Autons to "26/03/05" (the same day that *Rose* was broadcast). Alternatively, *The Doctor: His Lives and Times* (p168) notes that the missing persons poster is dated to "6th March 2005", and also has an online posting from Mickey, dated to "Saturday, March 26, 2005," that says: "it's been nearly three weeks, and there's no

sign of [Rose]." Further postings from Mickey help to establish a framework for the remainder of Series 1... a posting dated "Tuesday, March 7, 2006" occurs after *Aliens of London/World War Three* (p173), another dated "Thursday, September 7, 2006" follows (p174), and a third dated "Thursday, October 19, 2006" comes after *The Parting of the Ways* (p176).

The postings are in line with supplemental material suggesting that Mickey took over Clive's website on the Doctor following his death (*Rose*). *The Doctor: His Lives and Times* (p168) notes that Clive's widow let Mickey take the relevant material from his shed (p168).

assumed that he had murdered her.[902]

Clara Oswald's mother, Ellie Ravenwood Oswald, died 5th March, 2005. The eleventh Doctor watched as Clara and her father mourned at Ellie's grave.[903] Barry Jackson, a stooge of The Committee, acquired a device that summoned a ravenous alien from a pocket dimension. Jackson murdered the Mayor of Cardiff, then left his body amidst the damage wrought by the Autons in Cardiff's city centre.[904]

2005 (26th March) - TW: ONE RULE[905] **->** Yvonne Hartman had Torchwood London place Captain Jack, Suzie and Tosh within a time freeze while she stole a Drahvin scanner – a means, she hoped, of looking into the mysterious sphere in Canary Wharf – from the Hub. The time-freeze continued as Barry Jackson murdered his rivals for the position of Cardiff mayor, and tried and failed to scapegoat Hartman for the deaths. Hartman smashed Jackson's alien-summoning device, and vowed to let him live only so long as he provided her with intel, including

notification of the Doctor ever resurfacing in Cardiff...

Hartman's position with Torchwood entailed her having tea with the Queen twice a week.

Sharonda Arkley became involved with drug runners in Ashington, Northumberland, until her gang perished in a shoot-out in March 2005. Father Christèmas of Faction Paradox offered to sponsor her, and she joined his staff as Cousin Chantelle.[906]

UNIT Series 1[907]

c 2005 - UNIT: THE COUP -> Colonel Brimmicombe-Wood now commanded the UK branch of UNIT; Colonel Emily Chaudhry served as its press officer.

The fortunes of the UK division of UNIT waned, and it was ordered to cede authority to a new organisation, Britain's Internal Counter-Intelligence Service (ICIS). The day before the transition, UNIT and ICIS troops battled some Silurians – actually delegates who had been petition-

---

902 *Aliens of London*. Mickey's surname isn't established on screen until *Boom Town*.

903 *The Rings of Akhaten*. Ellie dies the same day that the ninth Doctor meets Rose Tyler and the new series begins. However, she isn't among the casualties incurred during the Auton rampage in London – that occurred the next day, on 6th March.

904 *TW: One Rule*. The story assumes that shop dummies came to life in Cardiff, whereas *Rose* seems to treat it as an event concentrated in London.

905 Dating *TW: One Rule* (BF *TW* #1.4) - The blurb claims it's "the 26th of March 2005" (concurrent with the debut of the new series). Within the fiction, it's "three weeks" since the Auton rampage in *Rose* (set on 6th March, 2005). It's reported that an epidemic in Angola has killed 120, which is in line with a real-life outbreak. Oddly, though, it's repeatedly said that *One Rule* coincides with the season premiere of *Strictly Come Dancing*, even though the show was on hiatus from December 2004 to October 2005. Suzie and Toshiko are already part of Torchwood Cardiff; no mention is made of Owen, who joined later (according to *TW: Fragments*). Jackson, presumably, becomes Mayor of Cardiff, but is bumped off as part of Blon's schemes in *Boom Town*. The Drahvin first appeared in *Galaxy 4*.

906 *FP: Weapons Grade Snake Oil* (ch41). The *North Eastern Daily Press* reports (dateline 22nd March, 2005) that police want to question Arkley over the shootings.

907 Dating *UNIT* Series 1 (*UNIT: The Coup*, #1.0; *UNIT: Time Heals*, #1.1; *UNIT: Snake Head*, #1.2; *UNIT: The Longest Night*, #1.3; *UNIT: The Wasting*, #1.4) - The audios were released from December 2004 to June 2005. The blurb for *The Coup* (the prelude to the mini-series, packaged with *DWM* #351) says it takes place in "London, the Near Future". Two details support this – a) the train

bombings in Spain that occurred in 2004 are said to have happened "a few years ago", and b) Captain Winnington was born in the 1980s, suggesting a mid-to-late 2000s dating at the minimum. The Brigadier also suggests in *The Coup* that *The Silurians* occurred "thirty years ago"; that's subject to UNIT dating.

Everything else about the mini-series seems contemporary, including the suggestion that some of the terrorist incidents are reprisals against Britain for its military intervention in Iraq – a hot button issue in 2005. Most importantly, the *UNIT* production team had no way of taking the new series – in particular the continual social disruption and political upheaval seen throughout Series 1 to Series 4 – into account. (Along those lines, it's very hard to believe that the Brigadier's public unveiling of a Silurian would so easily be dismissed after the likes of *The Christmas Invasion*, etc.) Trying to place *UNIT* in-between developments in New *Who* becomes a fairly ridiculous shell game, especially as the Prime Minister seen (or, rather, heard) in *The Longest Night* and *The Wasting* clearly isn't Harriet Jones or Harold Saxon. It's feasible to think that the *UNIT* Prime Minister was in power between Jones and Saxon, but then the lack of any mention in Series 2 of the compound crises and high death toll in *UNIT* becomes conspicuous by its absence. It's alternatively tempting to think that the *UNIT* Prime Minister is Brian Green from *TW: Children of Earth*, but they don't sound the same. The idea that the *UNIT* Prime Minister succeeds Green isn't very appealing, as *Children of Earth* is set in 2009, and so *UNIT* – featuring the older Brigadier – would have to occur in a hellishly narrow window before he's restored to his youth in *Happy Endings*.

The far simplest solution is to place *UNIT* at time of its release, and to assume that the Prime Minister of

THE NEW SERIES AND ITS SPIN-OFFS – AN OVERVIEW: At times, chronicling when the new series of *Doctor Who* (2005-present) takes place – not to mention the BBC-made spin-offs *Torchwood, The Sarah Jane Adventures* and *Class* – makes the whole UNIT Dating controversy seem quite reasonable and placid by comparison.

New *Who* opens in its year of broadcast (2005), followed by a few years of it occurring a year ahead of broadcast (what we'll call The Year Ahead Era), then it returns to a "time of broadcast" model with Series 5 and 6, and then it starts drifting further and further ahead of broadcast – culminating in Series 9 and 10, their related Christmas specials and *Class* happening within one another like a bunch of timey wimey nesting dolls.

No matter how simply it's rendered, any accounting of this much material is going to seem a bit tortured. Nonetheless, for benefit of newcomers (and anyone needing to step back and see the forest rather than the trees), the following sidebar is intended as a quick 'n' dirty roadmap of *Doctor Who* Series 1-10 and its official spin-offs: *Torchwood* Series 1-4, *The Sarah Jane Adventures* Series 1-5 and the one-off series of *Class*. (The independently made *K9* TV show takes place in 2050, so doesn't factor into this.)

See the Dating notes on the individual series and years for much, much more detail.

2005 (March) – The first episode of *Doctor Who* Series 1 (X1.1, *Rose*): The ninth Doctor meets Rose Tyler, a shop worker in London, her mother Jackie and her boyfriend Mickey Smith, in a story concurrent with the real world broadcast of *Rose* in March 2005. So far, so good. From there...

THE YEAR AHEAD ERA (2006-2009)

The ninth Doctor accidentally returns Rose home "twelve months" late, in Aliens of London *(X1.4). From now until the end of the tenth Doctor era (save the last two modern-day stories),* Doctor Who, Torchwood *and* The Sarah Jane Adventures *all take place – however roughly at times – a year ahead of broadcast.*

2006 (March) – The remainder of *Doctor Who* Series 1 (X1.4, *Aliens of London* onward)

2006 (Christmas) – *The Christmas Invasion* (X2.0): The newly regenerated tenth Doctor, with Rose, meets Jackie and Mickey.

2007 – *Doctor Who* Series 2: A smackdown between the Daleks and the Cybermen (the Battle of Canary Wharf) destroys Torchwood London. Rose leaves the tenth Doctor's company, becoming trapped with Jackie and Mickey, now her ex, in a parallel reality.

2007 (early October) to 2008 (January) – *Torchwood* Series 1: In the aftermath of the Battle of Canary Wharf, Captain Jack Harkness recruits Gwen Cooper to join Torchwood Cardiff.

2007 (Christmas) – *The Runaway Bride* (X3.0): Donna Noble, an office worker, meets the Doctor but stays on Earth.

2008 (June) – *Doctor Who* Series 3: Martha Jones, a medical student, joins the TARDIS. As "Harold Saxon", the Master becomes Prime Minister. Following his defeat, Martha stays on Earth.

2008 (June) to 2009 (April) – *Torchwood* Series 2: Deviates from the "year ahead of broadcast" model somewhat, but not unreasonably so.

The Sarah Jane Adventures *initially accommodates the "Year Ahead" paradigm, then switches to a "time of broadcast" dating halfway through Series 3.*

2008 (Autumn) – *The Sarah Jane Adventures* Series 1: Sarah Jane Smith and a band of teenagers – Sarah's adopted son Luke, Maria Jackson and Clyde Langer – band together to defend Earth.

2008 (Christmas) – *Voyage of the Damned* (X4.0)

2009 (March to April) – *Doctor Who* Series 4: Donna Noble joins the tenth Doctor in the TARDIS. The two of them, as well as Torchwood and Sarah Jane's crew of teen sleuths, join forces against Davros and the Daleks. To save Donna's life, the Doctor wipes her memories of their time together and leaves her on Earth. Rose stays on the parallel Earth with a human(ish) duplicate of the tenth Doctor. Mickey returns to "our" reality.

2009 (Easter) – *Planet of the Dead* (X4.15): There's no reason within *Doctor Who* itself as to why *Planet of the Dead* would deviate from the "Year Ahead" model. Once you factor in the continuity of *The Sarah Jane Adventures*, however, *Planet of the Dead* (and *The End of Time*) happen during their year of broadcast, 2009.

2009 – The first episode of *The Sarah Jane Adventures* Series 2 (*SJA: The Last Sontaran*): Maria Jackson moves to America.

2009 (September) – *Torchwood* Series 3 (*Children of Earth*): Destruction of the Torchwood Hub. Ianto Jones of Torchwood dies during the 456 Incident.

2009 (October to November): The remainder of *The Sarah Jane Adventures* Series 2 (all save *SJA: The Last Sontaran*): Rani Chandra joins Sarah Jane's brigade.

continued on page 2191...

ing for months for a peace treaty – near Tower Bridge. Orgath, a Silurian ambassador, approached General Sir Alistair Gordon Lethbridge-Stewart for help. Sir Alistair held a press conference and disclosed that UNIT had protected the world from unnatural and extra-terrestrial threats for "nearly forty years", and had thwarted more than two hundred alien invasions. He then presented Orgath as a Silurian representative. Captain Andrea Winnington of the ICIS was arrested after trying to kill Orgath, which weakened the group's standing. UNIT's authority was restored.

Despite Sir Alistair's best efforts, the Silurian bid for diplomatic relations was regarded as a hoax, and Orgath taken by some for a man in a rubber suit.[908]

c 2005 - UNIT: TIME HEALS[909] **->** Colonel Brimmicombe-Wood was secretly the head of the ICIS. The group staunchly opposed forces they perceived were weakening Britain's sovereignty. UNIT announced that it would be moving nuclear weapons across Britain – a cover story to conceal transport of an alien spaceship. A team of ICIS soldiers captured the spaceship and "kidnapped" Brimmicombe-Wood – so he could continue ICIS' work in secret. Colonel Robert Dalton became UNIT's acting commanding officer. The ICIS experimented on the captured spaceship – when opened, it released an alien virus. In the weeks to come, it manifested as a deadly flu outbreak.

Attempts to reverse-engineer the spaceship's transporter caused freak side-effects. A high-speed train from Lancaster to King's Cross collided head-on with another train, and bank ATMs disgorged an estimated £70 million. A jet plane crashed into Windsor Castle; rumours variously said that two members of the royal family, or perhaps "the prince and a close friend" had been killed.[910]

The reactor aboard the HMS *Perthshire* was breached; it was buried under millions of tons of rock on offshore continental shelf just before it went critical. The British public suspected the incidents owed to terrorists.

Sir Alistair aided UNIT's investigations. Doris was currently away visiting her ailing sister.

c 2005 (spring) - UNIT: SNAKE HEAD -> Colonels Emily Chaudhry and Robert Dalton investigated a series of mysterious deaths near a Saxon burial ground in Southend. They killed a type of vampire – a vrykolaka – that had been used by a crooked restaurateur, Kevin Lee, to eliminate a group of cockle-pickers.

The deaths were blamed on Goran Dhampir, a self-proclaimed vrykolaka hunter. His arrest increased racial tensions in Southend.[911]

c 2005 (spring) - UNIT: THE LONGEST NIGHT -> The Prime Minister signed the Euro Combine treaty to enhance ties between Britain and Europe. Critics said the treaty was a threat to British sovereignty.

The ICIS had supplied Major Philip Kirby, a sympathiser and the Prime Minister's press secretary, with alien brainwashing technology. Kirby used this to trigger societal unrest – he made a suicide bomber blow up the Vita Futura nightclub, a symbol of Britain's multiculturalism. ICIS agents dressed as policemen killed several survivors

---

UNIT is the one whose corpse is seen in *Aliens of London*. A 2005 dating has the massive benefit of reconciling the comparatively weakened UNIT in the audios with the far more powerful group in New *Who*, which is fortified enough to have a flying aircraft carrier. Under this scenario, the only lingering issue is that 10 Downing Street is destroyed twice – in *The Longest Night* and *World War Three* – and was presumably rebuilt in-between, all in the space of about a year.

Within *UNIT* itself, events happen in fairly rapid succession. Presuming Colonel Dalton's statement that he fought an invisible vampire on Southend "hours ago" can be taken at face value, a day at most passes between episode two (*Snake Head*) and episode three (*The Longest Night*), and two weeks pass between episode three and episode four (*The Wasting*) as Colonel Chaudhry recovers from the explosion that destroys 10 Downing Street. *The Wasting* also claims that the flu outbreak caused by the virus released in episode one (*Time Heals*) started "a few weeks ago", and so it's possible, depending on when the first symptoms manifested, that the entire mini-series takes place over that duration of time. Either way, Kevin Lee claims in *Snake*

Head that "it will be summer soon", so we know that episodes two to four (and possibly *The Coup* and *Time Heals* as well) take place in spring.

Colonel Brimmicombe-Wood first appeared in the apocryphal *Sympathy for the Devil*, and was mentioned in *Project: Valhalla*. Albion Hospital was seen in *Aliens of London* and *The Empty Child*. Mention is made of Planet 3, the broadcaster from in Big Finish's *Sarah Jane Smith* audios. The ICIS isn't related to Torchwood, although both groups share a "Britain first" philosophy.

The Haisman Timeline pegs these *UNIT* stories to 2004. The help that the Silurians here give to Harry Sullivan compliments *Eternity Weeps*, set in 2003, in which some Silurians are aiding UNIT even though the public is unaware of their existence.

908 The *UNIT* audios *Time Heals* and *Snake Head*.

909 Bricommbe-Wood's allegiances are revealled in *UNIT: The Wasting*, and the effects of the flu aren't known until *UNIT: The Longest Night*.

910 Reports of members of the royal family being killed are contradictory and never confirmed, and so can perhaps be ignored.

911 *UNIT: The Longest Night*

...continued from page 2189

2009 (through December) – The first half of *The Sarah Jane Adventures* Series 3

2009 – *The End of Time*: The tenth Doctor is fatally wounded. Before his regeneration, he visits many of his friends – including Sarah Jane – one last time. Mickey Smith and Martha Jones are now married.

The Year Ahead Era ends. The eleventh Doctor era begins (with Series 5) in its year of broadcast, 2010.

THE TIME OF BROADCAST(ISH) ERA (2010-2012)

2010 (Spring) – The second half of *The Sarah Jane Adventures* Series 3: Actually broadcast in November 2009, but transitioning out of the Year Ahead Era.

2010 (June) – *Doctor Who* Series 5: Amy Pond, and later her fiance Rory Williams, join the eleventh Doctor in the TARDIS. Amy and Rory's wedding day in *The Big Bang* (X5.13) happens on 26th June, 2010, its exact day of broadcast.

2010 (starting in September) – *The Sarah Jane Adventures* Series 4: Now re-synched with time of broadcast. Sarah Jane meets Jo Grant and the eleventh Doctor.

2011 (March to May) – *The Sarah Jane Adventures* Series 5: Actually happens about six months *before* its broadcast in October 2011, but still the same year.

2011 (April) to 2012 – *Doctor Who* Series 6: The eleventh Doctor is slated for a fateful encounter at Lake Silencio on "22nd April, 2011", the day before *The Impossible Astronaut* (X6.1) was shown.

2011 – *Torchwood* Series 4 (*Miracle Day*): It's incredibly hard to amalgamate the events of *TW: Miracle Day* into the main *Doctor Who* timeline. Nonetheless, there's little doubt that it happens in its year of broadcast, 2011.

2012 (early February) – *The Angels Take Manhattan* (X7.5): Amy and Rory's encounter with the Weeping Angels in 2012 results in their being trapped in 1960s New York, and living out the rest of their days there. Meanwhile, their past selves continue on for some years yet in the modern day, and keep having escapades with the eleventh Doctor...

**THE NUDGING
INTO THE FUTURE ERA (2013-2017)**

The gaps between the eleventh Doctor's visits to Amy and Rory become more prolonged, necessitating that we add up all the jumps to determine when a "modern day" episode takes place. The Year of the Slow Invasion, which as the name implies takes place over the course of an entire year (X7.4, The Power of Three), kicks the series' timeframe even further into the future.

2012 (Christmas) – *The Doctor, the Widow and the Wardrobe* (X7.0) – The eleventh Doctor pops in to see Amy and Rory for Christmas dinner, "two years" (Amy says) after he saw them last at the end of Series 6.

2013 – Last half of *Doctor Who* Series 7 (X7.8, *The Bells of Saint John* to X7.14, *The Name of the Doctor*): The eleventh Doctor stories with Clara Oswald occur in their year of broadcast, 2013, which means they actually take place *before* the same Doctor's remaining adventures with Amy and Rory (even though, within his lifetime, Amy and Rory come first).

2013 (April to August) – *Pond Life* (Series 7 minisode)

2013 (August or September) – *Asylum of the Daleks* (X7.1)

2014 (June or July) – *Dinosaurs on a Spaceship* (X7.2): It's been "ten months" since the Doctor last saw Amy and Rory.

2014 (July) to 2015 (late June) – *The Power of Three* (X7.4): The Year of the Slow Invasion. This is the end of Amy and Rory's involvement with the modern-day (per X7.5, *The Angels Take Manhattan*), as related to Rory's father in the epilogue *P.S.*

2015 – *The Day of the Doctor* (X7.15): A 50th Anniversary celebration of *Doctor Who*'s first broadcast in 1963, so of course this story happens in 2015. We know it's that year rather than 2013, because it's after the Doctor first meets Kate Stewart in *The Power of Three*. Clara Oswald, who started traveling with the Doctor in 2013, appears to have TARDIS-skipped over a couple of years on Earth (as evidenced by her biological age in *Deep Breath*), and has become a teacher at Coal Hill School.

2015 (Christmas) – *The Time of the Doctor* (X7.16): The end of the eleventh Doctor's involvement with the modern day.

2016 (start of year through autumn) – *Doctor Who* Series 8: The newly regenerated twelfth Doctor brings Clara home following *The Time of the Doctor*. She continues to work at Coal Hill School, and falls in love with Danny Pink, a maths teacher. Danny dies when Missy, a female version of the Master, attacks Earth with an army of Cybermen fashioned from humanity's dead.

continued on page 2193...

– including Lt Will Hoffman of UNIT – to prevent the bomber being identified. The incident was blamed upon Abdul Malik Hassib, a Muslim student.

The resultant racial tensions, combined with a worsening flu epidemic and further terror incidents, caused a decline in social order. London experienced rioting and an increasing death toll – Albion Hospital was overwhelmed, people took shelter in Westminster Abbey and the government grounded all flights out of the city. The Prime Minister's deputy, Meena Cartwright, disclosed that her family had been abducted and – in accordance with the kidnappers' instructions – killed herself on live television. A suicide bomber devastated BBC Television Centre, taking the network off the air.

A confession from Kirby was broadcast and restored some calm – but he triggered explosives that obliterated himself, Colonel Dalton and 10 Downing Street.

c 2005 (spring) - UNIT: THE WASTING -> The flu epidemic went global. Britain alone had six hundred thousand cases; those afflicted became violent as their flesh rotted. St Catherine's was reserved for flu victims. The Prime Minister mobilised the army to maintain order.

Sir Alistair contacted Harry Sullivan, who was doing secret work for NATO at Deepcastle, to analyse the disease victims. Sullivan's team determined that the flu virus was an alien food additive designed to make human flesh more palatable for consumption. Silurian scientists aided

Sullivan in developing a vaccine. Sir Alistair aided UNIT in dispersing the vaccine into the atmosphere via an old missile facility in the former Soviet Union.

Chaudhry exposed Brimmicombe-Wood as the head of the ICIS; he was arrested on charges of terrorism and treason, and the ICIS was shut down. UNIT was given new funding. Chaudhry was appointed its new commanding officer, with Sir Alistair serving as an unofficial adviser.

c 2005 - DEATH COMES TO TIME[912] **->** General Tannis, commander of the Canisian armies, conquered the planet Santiny in violation of the Treaty of Carsulae. The seventh Doctor and his companion Antimony arrived to ferment resistance, but were abruptly summoned to the Orion Nebula. There, the Minister of Chance – an old friend of the Doctor – warned him that someone had killed two Time Lord "saints" working on Earth. The Doctor headed there to investigate; the Minister travelled to Santiny.

The Doctor discovered that a vampire, Nessican, had murdered the Time Lords to cover up their discovery of massive spatial disturbances. He returned to Santiny, where Tannis killed Antimony – who was actually an android – and revealed himself to be a renegade Time Lord. When Tannis killed Sala, a young woman the Minister had become fond of, the Minister unleashed the full force of his Time Lord powers. The Doctor could not act against Tannis, but had to punish the Minister – all part of Tannis' plan to divide and distract his rival Time Lords.

---

912 Dating *Death Comes to Time* (BBCi drama, unnumbered) - No year is given, but Tony Blair is the Prime Minister and George W Bush is President of the United States, suggesting a contemporary setting. The story was webcast in 2002. Lee Sullivan's illustrations suggest that UNIT is operating a moonbase at this time, and although such details aren't in the script or dialogue, this could nudge the story a couple of years into the future (there was a moonbase in the 2003 of *Eternity Weeps* and *SJA: Death of the Doctor*, after all). See "American Presidents in the *Doctor Who* Universe" for why this story seems to take place after 2004.

IS DEATH COMES TO TIME CANON?: As the seventh Doctor dies at the end, all Time Lords are revealled to have godlike powers that they simply haven't used before and all the Time Lords are extinguished or otherwise removed from the universe during the seventh Doctor's time, a strong case can be made that this story is apocryphal. Crucially, the Time Lords' godlike abilities aren't reconcilable against the Gallifrey History section of this book. However, references to Anima Persis in *Relative Dementias* and *The Tomorrow Windows* and the Canisians in *Trading Futures* suggest *Death Comes to Time* may well be canonical. As with all *Doctor Who*, readers can include or ignore this story as they wish.
913 *Trading Futures*, referring to *Death Comes to Time*.

914 *Iris S2: The Claws of Santa*. It's not specified if this is George W. Bush or his father, although the younger Bush was more commonly regarded as being clumsy, such as a 2002 incident where he briefly fell unconscious after choking on a pretzel.
915 Dating *TW: Fragments* (TW 2.12) - Owen's fiancée dies "four years" before the 2009 component of this story. The weather seems decent, and Owen comments that he promised Katie "a summer wedding", suggesting that it's spring. Some time must elapse, however, between Owen first meeting Jack in 2005 and his being recruited to work for Torchwood – *TW: Exit Wounds* says that Owen was only on the job his "second week" when *Aliens of London*, set in March 2006, occurred. *The Torchwood Archives* (BBC) concurs that Owen "hooked up with Jolly Jack" in 2006, and *TW: SkyPoint*, set in 2008, says that Owen joined Torchwood "two years" ago (p24).
916 Dating *TW: Torchwood One: Before the Fall* (BF TW special release #3; *TW: New Girl*, #3.1; *TW: Through the Ruins*, #3.2; *TW: Uprising*, #3.3) - The story opens "a couple of months" after the Auton invasion in *Rose* [5th-6th March, 2005]. Then a couple of weeks pass, and Rachel usurps Yvonne's command at the end of episode one. Episode three begins after Rachel's been introducing reforms for "the better part of a month", meaning *Before*

The Doctor stripped the Minister of his powers, but Tannis launched an invasion of Earth.

Meanwhile, Ace trained to become a Time Lord with a mentor, Casmus, and the mysterious Kingmaker. Reunited, the Doctor and Ace headed for Earth, where they helped Lethbridge-Stewart and UNIT – now with a fleet of shuttles at their disposal – repel the Canisian invasion. The Doctor used his Time Lord powers to destroy Tannis and himself. The Canisians were defeated.

Felix Mather was the US Secretary of State during the Canisian invasion.[913] Iris WIldthyme's companion Panda got a scratch on his nose when a bike-riding George Bush ran over him.[914]

2005 (spring) - TW: FRAGMENTS[915] -> Owen Harper's fiancée, Kate Russell, died when an alien life form incubated in her brain. Jack Harkness covered up the incident.

2005 (mid-May to mid-June) - TW: TORCHWOOD ONE: BEFORE THE FALL[916] -> Torchwood One operated out of Canary Wharf, the tallest building in Britain. Yvonne Hartman led the group, with Ianto Jones as her personal assistant. Tommy Pierce served as head of Alien Acquisitions, Kieran Frost as head of Security, and a woman named Pippa as head of Human Resources. Torchwood predicted an oncoming recession, but did nothing to avert it. The group had access to Ex Libris, a clandestine section of the New Cavendish Library.

Seeking revenge for her father's death, Rachel Allan inveigled her way into Torchwood One as Pierce's assistant. She set Torchwood's leadership against one another, became Ianto Jones' lover and framed Yvonne Hartman for the accidental death of Dean, Frost's boyfriend, in a teleport mishap. Hartman went underground while Allan took charge of Torchwood One, and redirected its energies against Planet XXX (sic) and its inhabitants, the Korvacs. Jones came to doubt Allan's intentions when she needlessly caused Pippa's death during a training exercise.

A month later, the conflict between Torchwood and Planet XXX escalated as the Korvacs' 5th Space Legion arrived at Earth. Jones sided with Hartman as she quelled the situation by arranging the death of an ousted Korvacs royal in exchange for some Korvacs technology. Hartman regained command and, rather than killing Allan, removed her memories of her parents and the last six months. An "adjusted" Allan rejoined Torchwood One as a lowly supplies administrator.

...continued from page 2191

(Incidentally, to prove that someone on the production team has been tallying up the series' continuity, the Doctor in X8.10, *In the Forest of the Night* – a story broadcast in 2014 – correctly says that it's "2016".)

The remainder of the twelfth Doctor era involves a substantial overlap between Series 9 and 10. This needn't be a problem continuity-wise, as the latter entails him laying low at St Luke's University Bristol and discretely – or, what passes as "discretely" for him – nipping out for adventures.

2016 (autumn) to 2017 (spring) – The Pilot (X10.1): The twelfth Doctor, accompanied by Nardole, and tasked with keeping Missy locked up in a vault, begins teaching at St Luke's University Bristol and meets cafeteria worker Bill Potts.

Including his time at St Luke's, it seems likely that the twelfth Doctor experiences Christmas 2016 on Earth three times over...

2016 (Christmas) – Last Christmas (X9.0): The twelfth Doctor again meets Clara in the aftermath of Series 8...

? 2016 (? Christmas) – The Return of Doctor Mysterio (X10.0): Meanwhile, a future version of the twelfth Doctor visits New York City after his 24-year sabbatical on the planet Darillium with River Song (*The Husbands of River Song*). In his timeline, this happens before he starts living at St Luke's (Series 10).

2017 (Spring) – The first three episodes of *Doctor Who* Series 10 (X10.1, *The Pilot* to X10.3, *Thin Ice*)

2017 – *Doctor Who* Series 9: Clara Oswald is officially listed as deceased (following X9.10, *Face the Raven*), but in truth becomes an adventurer in time and space with the immortal Ashildr. The twelfth Doctor loses his memories of Clara, and later on experiences his sabbatical with River on Darillium.

? 2017/6 (October to December) – Class: A real bugbear to place. Going by the on-screen dates, it's October to December 2016 (concurrent with the broadcast of *Class* in those same months). *But*, it's after Clara Oswald is listed as deceased, which happened in 2017. We've opted for narrative clarity and placed *Class* in 2017, but your mileage might vary.

2017 (Autumn to ?Winter) – The remainder of *Doctor Who* Series 10 (X10.4, *Knock, Knock* onward): The twelfth Doctor, Bill, Nardole and Missy's time at St Luke's University comes to an end, when they answer a distress call from a colony ship in the distant past. We sifted through the evidence and decided that the Monks' conquest of Earth for "six months" gets erased from history (*The Lie of the Land*).

Destrii's Last Documented
Adventure with the Eighth Doctor[917]

c 2005 - "The Flood"[918] **->** The eighth Doctor and Destrii arrived in Camden Market, and quickly discovered that people were over-reacting emotionally. The Doctor also learned that MI6 were in the area. Destrii's senses registered two advanced Cybermen, who begin to convert the population and captured her. The Doctor worked with MI6, convinced these were the most advanced Cybermen he'd ever seen.

The Cybermen neutralised British defences, and their mothership materialised over London. They created a rainstorm that soaked the MI6 personnel, and caused extreme emotional reactions – the humans gladly became Cybermen to cure themselves. The Cybermen planned to flood the world in this way.

Desperate, the Doctor offered to allow the Cybermen to kill him and study his regeneration if the Cybermen returned to their own time – this would allow Cybermen to convert other races, not just humans, into their own kind. The Doctor freed Destrii, who distracted the Cybermen while he leapt into the mothership's power source – a fragment of the Time Vortex. He focused the

power there and destroyed the Cybership, whereupon he and Destrii went off to their next adventure.

Hugo Wilding and Patrick Lake took command of the devastated MI6 following the Cyber-incursion. They restored the MI6 headquarters at Vauxhall Cross, and retooled the group to defend Earth from alien threats in a more pro-active manner than that of UNIT or Torchwood. MI6 collected a wealth of alien technology, and decrypted it using the Doctor's sonic screwdriver retained by the estate of Yuri Azarov.[919]

Fitz Kreiner and Trix's
Last Documented Adventure[920]

2005 (June) - THE GALLIFREY CHRONICLES[921] **->** The eighth Doctor was lured to Earth by the Time Lord Marnal, who had recently learned of the Doctor's role in the destruction of Gallifrey. Fitz and Trix left the Doctor to set up home together, but the police approached Trix and attempted to arrest her on suspicion of murder. As they fled the country, Marnal confronted the Doctor and the Eye of Harmony was briefly opened. Like moths to a flame, the insect race the Vore was drawn to Earth. Their

---

the *Fall* ends some time in mid-June.

917 We're never told how Destrii comes to leave the TARDIS; her adventures with the eighth Doctor simply end, to make way for the ninth Doctor comics in *DWM*. Destrii next appears in "The Stockbridge Showdown".

918 Dating "The Flood" (*DWM* #346-353) - It's "the early twenty-first century", and the story was published from 2004 to early 2005. In "Hunters of the Burning Stone", the eleventh Doctor specifies that "The Flood" took place in 2005. Thematically, the resolution of this story is much like Rose unleashing the power of the Time Vortex in *The Parting of the Ways*.

919 "Hunters of the Burning Stone", detailing what becomes of MI6 following "The Flood".

920 The Eighth Doctor Adventures end, with *The Gallifrey Chronicles*, without detailing how Fitz and Trix come to part ways with the Doctor.

921 Dating *The Gallifrey Chronicles* (EDA #73) - The date is given (p75).

922 "Two years" before *TW: Small Worlds*.

923 Dating *Sarah Jane Smith* Series 2 (*SJS: Buried Secrets*, #2.1; *SJS: Snow Blind*, #2.2; *SJS: Fatal Consequences*, #2.3; *SJS: Dreamland*, #2.4) - These four audios were released from February to April 2006, but seem to have been written with 2005 in mind. Somewhat definitively, Josh says in *Fatal Consequences* that he's been protecting Sarah for "three years", denoting how long it's been since *SJS: Comeback*, set in 2002. Little clues throughout Series 2 support a 2005 dating: in particular, Natalie says in *SJS: Buried Secrets* that a Medici burial chamber

was located "in July 2004" – a phrasing she'd be unlikely to use in 2004 itself. Two items establish that Series 2 can't take place any later than 2007: *Buried Secrets* mentions that the *Dauntless* was originally scheduled for lift-off "in 2008", but has now been moved up, and it's said in *SJS: Dreamland* that Chuck Yeager broke the speed of sound "nearly sixty years ago" (he did so on 14th of October, 1947).

As Series 2 ends on a cliffhanger, a 2005 dating is preferable to 2006 (or 2007, even) in that it allows more time for an unspecified adventure in which Sarah Jane returns to Earth and wraps up any and all lingering details from her dealings with the Crimson Chapter before casually witnessing events in *The Christmas Invasion*, which she mentions upon meeting the tenth Doctor in *School Reunion*.

Series 2 ends with the *Dauntless* launching into space on 27th of September, and all signs are that the series begins some months beforehand; see the Series 2 episode entries for more. It seems likely, although it's not actually stated, that Sarah Jane recovers some of her professional standing between *SJS* Series 1 and Series 2 – at the very least, she's no longer living under cover identities, and is currently having to dodge media inquires about Hilda Winters' death.

The *Dauntless* launch is cited throughout Series 2 as being Earth's first "space tourism" flight... while the attempt made in *Escape Velocity* probably wouldn't count owing to an alien invasion scuttling it, by 2004 that ship had long since sailed in the real world; Dennis

moon materialised in Earth orbit and a full scale invasion took place. The Doctor and his companions destroyed the moon, and engaged the surviving Vore.

Captain Jack Harkness renewed his acquaintance with Estelle, claiming that she had met his father during World War II.[922]

Sarah Jane Smith Series 2[923]

Rechauffer, Inc., rebranded itself as Mandrake, Inc.[924]

2005 (20th-22nd of the month) - SJS: BURIED SECRETS[925] -> Sarah Jane Smith now resided in a cottage on the coast. She hadn't seen Harry Sullivan since he left for an overseas posting, but went anyway to their annual rendezvous at a restaurant not far from Blackfriars in London. Harry failed to show up, but Sarah instead met Will Sullivan, Harry's younger step brother. Hilda Winters died while under house arrest; she'd been killed by the Crimson Chapter for going too far in her mission against Sarah Jane. Sarah and Josh went to Italy to help Natalie Redfern, who was working with archaeologists excavating 500-year-old Medici tombs beneath the Church of San Lorenzo. Natalie's boyfriend Luca, a Crimson Chapter member, tried to obtain some pages from *The Book of Tomorrows* from a hidden room beneath the basilica of San Lorenzo, but Josh killed Luca when he tried to kill Sarah.

2005 - SJS: SNOW BLIND[926] -> Sarah Jane and Josh visited Nikita Base in Antarctica, as Sarah had used some of Lavinia's inheritance to fund an operation there. The project was drilling for ice-core samples, hoping to calculate when global warming would reach a tipping point. One of the research team – Morgane Kaditch, a member of the Crimson Chapter – attempted to steal a supply of ura-

nium-235 found beneath the ice, and thereby help fund the Chapter's operations. She was killed when an accomplice double-crossed her. Sarah secured the uranium.

2005 (August) - SJS: FATAL CONSEQUENCES[927] -> Sir Donald Wakefield warned Sarah that the Crimson Chapter viewed her "emergence" as the human herald mentioned in *The Book of Tomorrows* as a call to action – and would seek to bring about an apocalypse if none was forthcoming. The Crimson Chapter had used Mandrake, Inc.'s operations, as funnelled through the Pangbourne Research Centre in Reading, to create a powerful variant of the Marburg virus – one that incubated within people in a matter of hours. Sarah and her allies stopped the Chapter from opening vials of the virus in twelve major world cities, an act that would have killed millions. The international media covered the failed plot, and identified the Crimson Chapter as a doomsday group obsessed with aliens.

Sarah learned that Josh was both Wakefield's son and a White Chapter agent. Will Sullivan – a Crimson Chapter operative – died in a scuffle with Josh, who also killed the Keeper of the Crimson Chapter.

2005 (August to 27th September) - SJS: DREAMLAND -> Sir Wakefield believed that Sarah still had a destiny to fulfill as a human herald, and invited her to join him aboard the maiden voyage of the *Dauntless*, set for 27th of September at the Dreamland facility (Area 51) in Nevada. Sir Wakefield succumbed to cancer beforehand, and so Josh accompanied Sarah as the *Dauntless* lifted off. The *Dauntless* pilot, a Crimson Chapter agent, mutually died with Josh in an exchange of gunfire that ruined the ship's instrument banks. Sarah was alone as the *Dauntless*, its life support failing, ventured further into space. She saw a bright light, commented that she'd seen

---

later. The Crimson Chapter's role in Winters' death is revealed in *SJS: Dreamland*.

926 Dating *SJS: Snow Blind* (SJS #2.2) - The amount of time that passes between *Snow Blind* and *Fatal Consequences* is rather vague. The two installments could easily take place in the same month (meaning that *Buried Secrets* occurs in June) - then again, they might be further apart than that (meaning that *Buried Secrets* occurs in May or even April).

927 Dating *SJS: Fatal Consequences* (SJS #2.3) - It's said that a round-the-clock vigil at Pangbourne labs has lasted for "six months", and *SJS: Buried Secrets* says the same vigil started "last Christmas" – so by logical extension, *Fatal Consequences* should take place circa June. However, a news report in *SJS: Dreamland* simultaneously mentions that the *Dauntless* is "cleared for lift-off next month" (September, according to *Dreamland*) and

Tito and Mark Shuttleworth made "space tourist" flights in 2001 and 2002 respectively. That said, nothing within *Who* itself (other than *Escape Velocity*, maybe) particularly contradicts the *Dauntless* being the first tourist flight as stated.

924 Eighteen months before *SJS: Fatal Consequences*. "Mandrake" is the English equivalent of "Mandragora", for reasons given in *SJS* Series 2. It's also the name of a drug in "The Mark of Mandragora".

925 Dating *SJS: Buried Secrets* (SJS #2.1) - *SJS: Snow Blind* establishes that Sarah spends two months after *Buried Secrets* recovering from a gunshot wound. The month in which *Buried Secrets* takes place, however, still isn't clear (see the dating notes under *Snow Blind* for why). Natalie specifies that the story opens on "the 20th", and if the two subsequent "midday headlines" reports are any gauge, the action wraps up two days

something like it before a lifetime ago, and said goodbye to Earth...

c 2005 - RED DAWN[928] -> Backed by the Webster Corporation, the first manned American mission to Mars – *Ares One* – successfully reached the Red Planet. The crew made planet-fall in the *Argosy* shuttle just as the fifth Doctor and Peri arrived. The astronauts and the time travellers found the tomb of Izdal, a heroic Martian who sacrificed himself to the Red Dawn – the ultraviolet Martian sunrise.

The tomb's guardian, Lord Zzaal, was revived with his Ice Warriors. Zzaal believed the humans had good intentions, but a misunderstanding quickly escalated into conflict. Zzaal sacrificed himself to the Red Dawn to save the Doctor's life, ending Webster Corp's plans, but it was hoped his dream of a peaceful existence with Earth could survive. *Ares One* returned to Earth. Tanya Webster, a human who possessed Martian DNA, remained behind as Earth's first ambassador to the Martians.

A Russian general ordered a nuclear strike against Chechnya, killing half a million people in an instant. After leaving the army, the General erased his identity and became the notorious arms dealer known as Baskerville. He lacked an electronic presence of any kind, making him impossible to track. After British Airways went bust, Baskerville bought one of their Concordes and converted it for stealth.

Nicopills, designed to wean people off tobacco, were marketed as a consumer item in their own right. The pills were less harmful but even more addictive than cigarettes, and thus were more profitable.[929]

Suzie Costello Joins Torchwood

Jack Harkness recruited Suzie Costello to join Torchwood after she encountered him and Torchwood operative Ben Brown. She helped to contain an alien virus that had been downloaded via some computers into her boss. Brown later died in an unrelated incident.[930]

Suzie Costello had been on the run when she joined Torchwood, and used her technical skill to wipe clean all records pertaining to her. She secretly joined Pilgrim – a religious support group and debating society started by Sara Briscoe – and conditioned Max Trazillion to brutally kill the other Pilgrim members if he didn't see her for three months.[931]

On Earth, a reptilian extra-terrestrial set up a business supplying combat divisions to clients on other worlds. Creating armies posed significant problems: Combat computers were only so reliable; artificial intelligences could only be created under certain conditions; remote-control signals could be scrambled; and fully crewed combat vehicles were costly, plus had a high turnover rate.

As a solution, the alien created heavily armed giant robots, which resembled twentieth-century Earth office complexes on the inside. Humans were kidnapped and brainwashed into thinking that they were simple office workers; in reality, their "paperwork" and office meetings coordinated the robots' attack patterns.

One worker, Todd Hulbert, overcame his conditioning and instigated a hostile takeover. The company was renamed Hulbert Logistics, and moved its home office from Ipswich to London.

A group of Cybermen had settled on the planet Lonsis, the next system over from Shinus. Its people – the Shinx

that the Marburg incident in *Fatal Consequences* occurred "last week", meaning that the "six months" figure has to be taken as rounding, and *Fatal Consequences* must occur in August. That squares with Sarah in rapid succession attending the funeral of Will Sullivan – who's shot dead at the end of *Fatal Consequences* – and then embarking on a four-week training course so she can join the *Dauntless* launch.

928 Dating *Red Dawn* (BF #8) - It is "thirty years" since the "Mars Probe fiasco" of *The Ambassadors of Death*, which is a UNIT story. So to cut a very long story short, it's the now first decade of the twenty-first century. As *The Dying Days* was "over twenty years" after *The Ambassadors of Death*, this story is set before 2007. The impact of Tanya's ambassadorship to Mars must be minimal, as humanity and the Martians are in conflict by *The Seeds of Death*.

929 Both "ten years" before *Trading Futures*.

930 *TW: Long Time Dead.* Brown appears to be an otherwise unmentioned member of Jack's Torchwood team.

931 *TW: They Keep Killing Suzie.* This is part of Suzie's insurance policy in case of her death, although it doesn't entirely account for why she kills herself in *TW: Everything Changes.* (One explanation is that Suzie knows she's going to get fired – meaning mind-wiped – from Torchwood, and her suicide/resurrection gambit is a desperate means of maintaining her memories and identity.)

932 *Human Resources.* The Lonsis operation has been running for "a year" prior to 2006, and Hulbert acts as if he's been in charge of the company for some time before that.

– were traders who disliked aggression because it destabilised their markets. The Gallifreyan CIA sought to eliminate the Lonsis Cybermen, and seeded paranoia into the Shinx's minds. The Shinx hired Hulbert, whose combat divisions started routing the Lonsis Cybermen in 2005.

The CIA secretly aided Hulbert by equipping his Telford branch with a quantum crystalliser – a device that splintered the timelines over a small area, then picked the most desirable one as dictated by its programming.

Elsewhere on Earth, the CIA manipulated history to prevent Karen Coltraine becoming a dictator. Certain negative experiences were eliminated from Coltraine's history, and she matured into a more agreeable person.[932]

The First Environmental Crisis

By the middle of the first decade of the twenty-first century, it was clear that unchecked industrial growth had wreaked havoc on the environment. Increasing instability in weather patterns subjected Britain to acid rain and created turbulence that made air travel less reliable. Shifts in the ozone layer laid waste to Oregon. Traffic had reached gridlock in most of the major cities around the world. Motorcycles superseded the familiar black cabs in London, and many car owners sat in traffic jams working at their computers as they commuted. Predictably, air pollution reached new levels.

A catalogue of environmental disasters threatened the entire planet. The Earth's population was spiralling towards eight billion. Low-lying ozone and nitrogen dioxide levels had risen to such an extent that the London air was unbreathable without a face mask on many days, even in winter. Global warming was steadily increasing: by the turn of the century, there were vineyards in Kent. Antarctic waters became hazardous as the icecap broke up in rising temperatures. The rate of ice-flow had trebled since the nineteen-eighties.

River and sea pollution had reached such levels that the marine environment was on the verge of collapse. Water shortages were commonplace, and even the inhabitants of First World cities like London and Toronto were forced to use standpipes for drinking water and to practise water rationing. The mega-cities of South America saw drought of unprecedented proportions. The holes in the ozone layer were getting larger, causing famine in many countries. Sunbathing, of course, was now out of the question. "The plague", in reality a host of virulent, pollution-related diseases such as HIV 7, appeared and killed millions.

The collapse of the environment triggered political instability. New terrorist groups sprang up: the Earth For Earth groups, freedom fighters, environmentalists, anarchists, nationalists and separatists, the IFA, PPO and TCWC. In England, a whole new youth subculture evolved. Gangs with names like the Gameboys, the Witchkids and the Crows smashed machinery (except for their own gaming software) and committed atrocities. In the most notorious incident, the Witchkids petrol-bombed a McDonald's restaurant on the M2 before ritually sacrificing the customers: men, women and children.

Every country on Earth saw warfare or widespread rioting. In the face of social disorder in America, President Norris' right-wing government ended immigration and his infamous "Local Development" reforms restricted the unemployed's rights to movement. The Connors Amendment to the Constitution also made it easier for the authorities to declare martial law and administer the death penalty. The underclass was confined to its slums, and heavily armed private police forces guarded the barriers between the inner cities and the suburbs.

Once-fashionable areas fell into deprivation. The popular culture reflected this discord: In Britain, this was a time when SlapRap blared from every teenager's noisebox. There was a Kinky Gerlinki revival, its followers dressing in costumes described as "outrageous" or "obscene" depending on personal taste. The most popular television series was *Naked Decay*, a sitcom inspired by 45-year-old Mike Brack's "Masks of Decay" exhibition which had featured lumps of wax hacked into caricatures of celebrities. The teledildonic suits at the "SaferSex emporiums" along London's Pentonville Road became notorious. All faced the opprobrium of groups such as the Freedom Foundation and the Citadel of Morality. American children thrilled to the adventures of Jack Blood, a pumpkin-faced killer, and they collected the latest Cthulhu Gate horror VR modules and comics. Their elder brothers became Oi Boys: skinheads influenced by the fashions of Eastern Europe.

The early twenty-first century saw many scientific advances, usually in the field of computer science and communications. Elysium Technology introduced the Nanocom, a handheld dictation machine capable of translating speech into written text. Elysium also developed the first holographic camera. The 3D telephone was beyond the technology of the time, although most rich people now had videophones. In June 2005, "Der Speigel" gave away a personal organiser with every issue. The first robot cleaners were marketed at this time – they were small, simple devices and really little more than automated vacuum cleaners or floor polishers. Communications software and computer viruses were traded on the black market; indeed, they became almost substitute currency in countries like Turkey.

Surgeons could now perform eye transplants, and the super-rich were even able to cheat "death" (or rather the legal and medical definition of it) by an intensive programme of medication, transplants and implants. If even this failed, suspended animation was now possible – the rich could afford full cryogenic storage, the poor settled for a chemical substitute. Military technology was becoming smarter and more dangerous. The Indonesian conflict and the Mexican War in the first decade of the century were the test-bed for much new weaponry. Arms manufacturers were happy to supply the Australian and American forces with military hardware. The British company Vickers built a vision enhancement system capable of tremendous magnification and low-intensity light applications. The helmet could interface with most weapons, allowing dramatically improved targeting. If anything, the helmet was too efficient – one option, which allowed a soldier to target and fire his weapon merely by moving and blinking his eyes – proved too dangerous and was banned. A new genera-

tion of UN aircraft were introduced, including a remote controlled helicopter (the Odin), a jet fighter with batteries of Valkyrie air-to-air missiles (the Loki), Niffelheim bombs and Ragnarok tactical nuclear devices. The US military introduced a turbo-pulse laser gun developed for use against tanks.[933]

Early in the twenty-first century, there were disasters, wars and nuclear terrorism. The first half of the century saw human civilisation near collapse.[934] Rising sea levels claimed Holland; the Dutch became the wanderers of Europe.[935] Christian fundamentalists campaigned to exterminate homosexuals in the twenty-first century.[936]

933 *Iceberg* and *Cat's Cradle: Warhead* are both set around the same time and feature an Earth on the brink of environmental and social collapse. The two books are broadly consistent, although the odd detail is different – in *Iceberg*, for example, journalist Ruby Duvall muses that sunbathing in England is impossible nowadays, whereas Ace sunbathes in Kent during *Cat's Cradle: Warhead*. The Connors Amendment is mentioned in *Warlock*.

934 *Interference*

935 *St Anthony's Fire*

936 *Placebo Effect* (p12).

937 *Iceberg*

938 *Something Inside.* This occurred on 25th May, 2005.

939 "Years" before *TW: "Somebody Else's Problem".*

940 *TW: In the Shadows*

941 *TW: "The Legacy of Torchwood One!"*

942 *Voyage of the Damned*

943 Dating *TW: Trace Memory* (*TW* novel #5) - Gwen is already a police officer and here meets Andy, but the year is unclear. Rhys eats some Marmite even though the "sell-by date said fifth of March" (p80), so Bellini must visit after that.

944 Events in 2006 include the "present day" sequences of *Doctor Who* Series 1 from *Aliens of London* onwards, and *The Christmas Invasion*.

THE YEAR AHEAD ERA (2006-2009): When the ninth Doctor returns Rose home in *Aliens of London*, "twelve months" after she left (in *Rose*), the subsequent "present day" *Doctor Who* episodes (as well as many of the related *Torchwood* and *The Sarah Jane Adventures* stories) adhere to a dating scheme in which they are set (roughly) a year or so after broadcast. This paradigm ends with *Planet of the Dead*, which has to occur in 2009, the year in which it aired (see the dating notes on that story for why).

Torchwood Series 1 adheres to the "year ahead" approach, Series 2 deviates from the pattern, Series 3 (a.k.a. *TW: Children of Earth*) occurs about two months rather than a year ahead of broadcast, and Series 4 (a.k.a. *TW: Miracle Day*) happens in the same year it was shown, 2011.

The way in which *The Sarah Jane Adventures* initially accommodates the "year ahead of broadcast" dating

scheme, then returns to a "time of broadcast" setting midway through Series 3, means that the whole of the show (Series 1-5) elapses over a total of two years and nine months (from August 2008 to May 2011).

See the entries for 2007, 2008 and 2009 (and by extension 2010 and 2011) for a more specific list of which stories occur in those years.

945 Per his on-screen bio in *The Sontaran Stratagem*.

946 "Five years" before *TW: Miracle Day*.

947 *TW: Miracle Day*. It's variously said that Danes uttered his quote during his arrest/at his trial.

948 *Blood of the Daleks, Human Resources*.

949 "Three years" prior to *TW: Almost Perfect*.

950 *Horror of the Space Snakes*. The UNIT base is presumably the same one mentioned in *SJA: Death of the Doctor*, with the Doctor further suggesting that it will be modified for use as a weather control station (*The Seeds of Death*), a prison (*Frontier in Space*) and a huge children's amusement park with a rollercoaster.

951 The background to *Aliens of London* and the Slitheen's subsequent appearances, as detailed in *SJA: Revenge of the Slitheen* and *SJA: The Gift*. The two accounts don't entirely match up: where does Raxas Prime (another name for Raxacoricofallapatorius, perhaps?) fit into the Raxas Alliance hierarchy? And if the Slitheen were given death sentences, why did the Judoon "force them out" rather than arresting them? (Perhaps the Slitheen were "forced out" in the sense that they fled in the wake of the Judoon's overwhelming force.) Either way, the timeframe of exactly when all of this occurred is uncertain.

952 The year is unknown, but she's alive in the 2004 portion of *TW: Fragments*, and yet is a ghost in *TW: End of Days* (set in early 2008).

953 "A century or two" after *1stD* V1: *The Founding Fathers* [1762]. Benjamin Franklin House opened to the public on 17th January, 2006.

954 *TW: The Torchwood Archive* (BF). This is after Owen has joined the team, in a scene the script dates to "2006".

955 *The Tenth Doctor Year Two*: "Cindy, Cleo and the Magic Sketchbook", extrapolating from Gabby being in night school in *The Tenth Doctor Year Two*: "Revolutions of Terror".

The most pressing threat was that of magnetic inversion. For some decades, scientists had known that Earth's magnetic field periodically reversed. If this happened now, it would damage all electronic equipment and have serious environmental consequences. In 2005, spurred into action by such reports, the major governments of the world set up the FLIPback Project at the old Snowcap complex in the Antarctic. Shortly afterwards, a vehicle from the base – the hovercraft AXV9 – vanished in the Torus Antarctica with the loss of two men.[937]

The Doctor saw the 2005 European Cup Final, in which Liverpool overcame formidable opposition from AC Milan and claimed the Cup for the fifth time in its history.[938]

The tentacled alien Mister Quatnja established a drugs factory in Cardiff. Jack Harkness tolerated the operation, as Quatnja's products calmed the rowdier elements of Earth's extra-terrestrials.[939] Patrick Jefferson received a matchbox containing huon particles, which could transport objects into a hell dimension and age them to death. Captain Jack later suspected that Torchwood London sent the matchbox to Jefferson to field test it as a weapon. Jefferson used the matchbox to kill people he deemed sinners.[940]

Rupert Howarth, Ianto's mentor and the head of Torchwood One's biochemical research division, attempted to create a human-alien hybrid with special forces applications. Most of Howarth's test subjects died, but he became fearful of a survivor – the fear-inducing Chimera – and faked his death to go underground.[941]

Astrid Peth spent three years working at the Spaceport Diner before signing up as a waitress with Capricorn Cruiseliners.[942]

c 2005 - TW: TRACE MEMORY[943] -> Cardiff police officer Gwen Cooper met her new partner, Andy Davidson, and briefly encountered the time-travelling Michael Bellini.

2006[944]

Luke Rattigan established the Rattigan Academy, an advanced school for science students, in 2006.[945] Phicorps, a pharmaceutical company controlled by the Three Families, began stockpiling drugs in preparation for the Miracle.[946] Oswald Danes, a schoolteacher, was convicted in 2006 for the rape and murder of 12-year-old Susie Kabina. Concerning his victim, Danes infamously declared, "She should've run faster."[947]

In 2006, Lucie Miller relocated from the North of England to London, and planned to live with her friend Amanda from school. She met Karen Coltraine in the Tube – the pair of them had interviews with Hulbert Logistics. Todd Hulbert brainwashed them and sent them via a portal to his "Telford branch" on Lonsis. This worried the Time Lords, who feared that the history-revised Coltraine might become unstable if brought into proximity with the

Telford branch's quantum crystalliser. However, the Time Lords worked from faulty intelligence data, and mistook Lucie for Coltraine.

The Time Lords intercepted Lucie's transport through space, causing her to arrive in the eighth Doctor's console room. The Doctor was duped into thinking Lucie had been placed with him as part of the Time Lords' witness protection programme. He tried to take Lucie home, but found that the Time Lords had established a temporal barrier around her era.

Lucie became the Doctor's companion – on their first trip together, they encountered the Daleks on the human colony planet Red Rocket Rising. Hulbert was distressed to find Lucie missing – if for no other reason than he wanted to know which rival was poaching his employees. He hired a time-travelling Headhunter to bring her back.[948]

Jack Harkness encountered the Perfection – aliens who were passing as two young men named Brendan and Jon. They claimed to be "very old gods" who habitually visited a planet for millennia, made it wonderful and moved on; Hallam's World, the Province of Sovertial and the Min Barrier were examples of their work. After a night of "negotiating" with Brendan and Jon in bed, Jack accepted that they were a bit knackered of world-building, and sought nothing more than to improve Cardiff's gay scene by running a nightclub.[949]

In 2006, UNIT constructed a moonbase – in part to monitor Earth and watch for signs of invasion from space, and also to store dangerous alien items and weaponry, including the Hopkiss Diamond (which the Doctor vibrated to communicate with its owners on Jool) and the RavnoPortal Beast of Birodonne.[950]

The Raxas Alliance consisted of four planets: Raxacoricofallapatorius, Raxacoricovarlonpatorius, Clom and Clix. The Slitheen, a family from Raxacoricofallapatorius, were charged by the High Council of Raxas Prime with fraud, theft and treason – each of which carried a death sentence – and were forced out of the Alliance by the Judoon. In their absence, the Blathereen and Hostrozeen families wielded influence. A Grand Council and a Senate governed Raxacoricofallapatorius. The Raxacoricofallapatorians had an instinctive urge to hunt, as it was the only way to keep food safe when the Baaraddelshelliumfatrexius beasts (creatures akin to giant squirrels) roamed the plains.[951]

Toshiko Sato's mother died.[952] The first Doctor visited Benjamin Franklin's home in London, after it had become a museum.[953] Archie logged Object 3,000,512, a weapon, into the Torchwood Archive.[954] When Gabby Gonzalez and Cindy Wu were ten or eleven, they went to Echo Lake, and huddled in their tent after a counselor told them the Story of the Rabid Raccoon.[955]

Lucie Miller Joins the TARDIS

2006 - HUMAN RESOURCES[956] -> The planet Telos was unknown to the Cybermen based on the war-torn Lonsis.

The Headhunter captured Lucie and returned her to Lonsis, but the eighth Doctor followed them using a time ring. The Time Lords and the CIA had brokered a deal in which neither group would interfere on Lonsis directly. The Doctor found the CIA's quantum crystalliser and expanded its range; the Cybermen were killed as probability went against them. Hulbert died amid the battle, and the Headhunter took Coltraine on as her assistant.

The Doctor ordered the Time Lords to destroy Hulbert's machines and return the displaced humans home, then retrieved his TARDIS and continued travelling with Lucie.

c 2006 - NIGHT THOUGHTS[957] -> The seventh Doctor, Ace and Hex arrived on Gravonax Island, just as Major Dickens and his colleagues transmitted a message (via the Bartholomew Transactor) to their previous selves in 1996, with aim of preventing the death of a young girl, Edie. The resultant paradox caused Edie's corpse to revive in a zombified state. Edie took vengeance on those involved in her death – she murdered Bartholomew and Hartley, drove the Deacon to commit suicide and gouged out Dickens' eyes. Her fate remained unclear, but her sister Ruth was reunited with their father, Dr O'Neill.

The Doctor sent Bartholomew's unpublished thesis to the editor of *The New Scientist*, helping it to reach the widest possible audience. In future centuries, it would speed development of a workable theory of time travel.

2006 (2nd February) - TW: TRACE MEMORY[958] -> Following the 1967 Hamilton's Sugar incident, Charles Arthur Cromwell had some preknowledge concerning the time-jumps of Michael Bellini. Cromwell arrived at Torchwood One, as he knew he was fated to do, prior to Bellini appearing there. Torchwood One was evacuated as the Vondrax attacked it to capture Bellini. The Vondrax killed Cromwell, then pursued Bellini through time. Ianto Jones' boss, Bev Stanley, went missing during this incident.

c 2006 - LET'S KILL HITLER[959] -> Shortly after stealing a bus and driving it through a botanical garden, Mels Zucker caused Amy Pond to realise that Rory fancied her.

956 Dating *Human Resources* (BF BBC7 #1.7-1.8) - Lucie has been "pulled back to her natural place in time", which according to *Blood of the Daleks* is 2006.
957 Dating *Night Thoughts* (BF #79) - The setting is roughly contemporary, and the audio was released in February 2006. Dickens and the Deacon served in the Falklands War (which took place in 1982), and the researchers have subsequently met or permanently lived on the island for the last thirteen years.
958 Dating *TW: Trace Memory* (TW novel #5) - Cromwell's death is dated to "14/02/2006" (p99).
959 Dating *Let's Kill Hitler* (X6.8) - The three of them are acquainted while age seven, and this happens after Amy has known Rory for "what, ten years?" The way in which Mels helps to push the two of them together means that River Song, as if her life wasn't complicated enough, helped to facilitate her own conception.
960 *The Girl Who Waited*
961 *TW: Exit Wounds*. This confirms that "Dr Sato" in *Aliens of London*, as played by Naoko Mori, is the same character as Toshiko from *Torchwood*.
962 Dating *Aliens of London/World War Three* (X1.4-1.5) - It is "twelve months" since *Rose*, and a missing persons poster says Rose has been missing since 6th March, 2005 – so it's March 2006, and for all we know specifically 6th March. The (BBC's) UNIT website gave the story the date of "28 June 2006".
HARRIET JONES, PRIME MINISTER: We learn in *The Christmas Invasion* that Harriet Jones took office shortly after *World War Three*, winning a general election by a landslide. As she's a member of the governing party, she presumably became its leader (perhaps unopposed), so became Prime Minister, then called a snap election. In *World War Three*, the ninth Doctor remembers her ushering in the British Golden Age and serving three terms.

Three full terms as Prime Minister would be fifteen years, although constitutionally it's technically possible – if highly unlikely – that someone could serve three terms as a Prime Minister in a matter of months. As of *Aliens in London*, Harriet Jones was almost certainly Prime Minister for around a decade. We might speculate that Jones was a prime mover behind the Reconstruction mentioned in some of the New Adventures, itself portrayed as the beginning of a golden age. There's a female Prime Minister in *The Shadows of Avalon* who, retrospectively, could well be Harriet Jones. Shortly after that, in stories like *Time of the Daleks* and *Trading Futures*, British politics becomes more turbulent.

However... at the end of *The Christmas Invasion*, the Doctor seems to abruptly unseat Jones from office, and potentially cancels out this history. From stories like *Father's Day* and *I am a Dalek*, it seems the Doctor is "allowed" to make small historical changes, but averting the career of a three-term Prime Minister would seem to cross the line. Does the Doctor *really* deny Britain its Golden Age because he's fallen out with Jones? At the very least, he certainly erases Jones' part in it. (For more on this, see the "Vote Saxon" essay.)

Amy's favourite cat was named "Biggles". One summer, Rory returned to school with a ludicrous haircut, claiming he'd been in a rock band, and consequently had to learn to play the guitar. He and Amy had their first kiss while dancing the Macarena.[960]

Owen Harper Joins Torchwood

Captain Jack recruited Owen Harper for Torchwood. On only his second week on the job, Owen woke up drunk. Toshiko went undercover as a medic in his place, and investigated the Slitheen's infiltration of 10 Downing Street...[961]

The Slitheen Capture 10 Downing Street; Rose Returns Home a Year Late

2006 (March) - ALIENS OF LONDON / WORLD WAR THREE[962] -> The ninth Doctor accidentally returned Rose home twelve months after he first met her, instead of twelve hours. A spaceship soon crashed into the Thames, and a state of emergency was called in the UK. Worse, the Prime Minister had vanished. The Doctor investigated and realised that the crash had been faked... by genuine aliens who had infiltrated 10 Downing Street and murdered the Prime Minister. This was done to lure the world's main experts on alien life into a lethal trap.

The perpetrators were the Slitheen, a notorious criminal family of Raxacoricofallapatorians, who were plotting to provoke humanity into launching nuclear missiles and destroying their own planet. This would enable the Slitheen to convert and sell Earth's remains as radioactive fuel. The Doctor used his UNIT codes to launch a missile that destroyed 10 Downing Street and the Slitheen.

A backbench MP, Harriet Jones, had been instrumental in helping the Doctor – who told Rose that Jones was destined to become Prime Minister, serve three terms and usher in the British Golden Age. Harriet

Jones became Prime Minister following a general election when her party won a landslide majority.[963]

Margaret Slitheen escaped the destruction of Downing Street using a portable teleporter. She ended up in a skip in the Isle of Dogs, later making her way to Cardiff.[964] After this time, Torchwood Cardiff were involved with Operation Goldenrod, which saw people's bodies fused together.[965]

2006 (24th May) - "F.A.Q."[966] -> The tenth Doctor and Rose arrived in a London transformed into a surreal place of talking trees and Vikings with laser guns. It was a virtual reality created by Craig, an abused youngster who had erroneously received a Happytimez Intergalactical gamebox. The Doctor helped an alien technician, a Cyrelleod, to end the virtual reality.

(=) 2006 (24th June) - THE TIME TRAVELLERS[967] -> After colliding with a man falling through the Vortex, the TARDIS materialised in Canary Wharf. The first Doctor, Susan, Ian and Barbara discovered that Britain was at war with South Africa. The British were conducting time travel experiments using Dalek technology recovered from Coal Hill School in 1963, and different versions of history were intruding on this one. In this version of history, WOTAN succeeded in its bid for domination, and banned electronic communication in 1968. It was subsequently destroyed in 1969, and everyone under its hypnotic control was left brain-damaged. A World War broke out. The South Africans gained Cybertechnology at the South Pole, and used it to invade Europe.

The TARDIS' presence disrupted the time experiments, allowing the various timelines to connect. By travelling back to 1972, then 1948, Ian restored history.

The Doctor travelled the Jubilee line in the London Underground on 24th June, 2006, and had some ice cream.[968] Jack Harkness dealt with a poltergeist at the Brampton Hotel in Cardiff.[969]

The Doctor doesn't seem to know much about the history of the first decade of the twenty-first century – he explicitly says he doesn't know about the "first contact" situation seen in *Aliens of London* (a remarkable gap in his knowledge of Earth's history, whichever way you look at it). Compare with Captain Jack's continuous assertion in *Torchwood* that the twenty-first century is the time that "everything changes".
963 *The Christmas Invasion*
964 *Boom Town*
965 *TW: Slow Decay*. A potential glitch is that Ianto needs to ask if Toshiko was involved – and she was.

966 Dating "F.A.Q." (*DWM* #369-371) - The date is given, and means Rose is here travelling a year or so into her past (although the Doctor had been planning to take her to China, not London).
967 Dating *The Time Travellers* (PDA #75) - The dates are all given. The implication of the book is that the "real" timeline of the universe is one without the Doctor, so one where the monsters win. The Doctor is actually changing history when he defeats them. WOTAN appeared in *The War Machines*, and the Dalek technology stems from *Remembrance of the Daleks*.
968 *The Slitheen Excursion* (p129). This is unrelated to

The Master Escapes the Eye of Harmony

2006 (Saturday, 24th June) - "Forgotten"[970] -> Edward Grainger, who had met several incarnations of the Doctor throughout his long life, was nearing age 100 and suffering from dementia. The eighth Doctor came to take his friend on one last adventure, and used the TARDIS' telepathic circuits to rebuild his memories. The Master, still trapped within the TARDIS' Eye of Harmony, mentally compelled Grainger to open the Eye and directed the Ship to go to Grainger's birth in 1906...

Grainger passed away in transit as the Doctor returned to 2006. The Doctor gave his condolences to Grainger's granddaughter, Linda, and went for a drink with her at the White Rabbit pub.

2006 - WINNER TAKES ALL[971] -> The ninth Doctor took Rose home, where the latest craze was the video game *Death to Mantodeans*. It had been supplied by the porcupine-like Quevvils of the planet Toop, and was a perfect simulation of their war. The Doctor got the high score and was teleported to the warzone – but he managed to disintegrate the Quevvil invasion force.

2006 - 9thC: RETAIL THERAPY[972] -> Tycho Furbank, an aged entrepreneur in Slough, obtained alien technology that gave rise to Glubby Glubs: squishy pink furry blobs sold as stress relievers. The Glubby Glubs' bio-relays gleaned life energy from their owners, supplying it to the Glubby Glub management as a life-enhancer. Jackie Tyler did so well selling Glubby Glubs, she was a candidate for the post of Top Glubby Glub Go-Getter. The ninth Doctor and Rose returned from the moons of Fordyce and uncovered Furbank's nefarious scheme. Jackie went undercover at Glubby Glub HQ, and helped to end the operation.

c 2006 (early September) - CIRCULAR TIME: "Autumn"[973] -> The fifth Doctor and Nyssa lodged in Stockbridge for a number of weeks. While the Doctor played cricket, Nyssa wrote a novel – not intended for publication – and made the acquaintance of a waiter/ graduate student named Andrew Whitaker. One day, Nyssa and Andrew travelled forty minutes away from Stockbridge to Traken Village.

On the final day of the cricket season, the Stockbridge team prevailed – but the team leader, Don, died of a heart attack while scoring the winning run. Nyssa and Andrew became lovers that afternoon, but she left with the Doctor afterwards, bequeathing her finished novel to Andrew.

2006 - "A Groatsworth of Wit"[974] -> The alien Shadeys brought Robert Greene from 1592 to the present day, where Greene was disgusted to find he was hardly-known but Shakespeare was world famous. The ninth Doctor and Rose arrived to see Greene lash out in anger in a bookshop, and begin a rampage that involved attacking the premiere

The Time Travellers, which occurs on the very same day.
969 This happened in "June", the year before *TW: The Conspiracy*.
970 Dating "Forgotten" (BF *Short Trips* #17p, *The Centenarian*) - The exact day is given.
971 Dating *Winner Takes All* (NSA #3) - The story is set after *Aliens of London/World War Three* and before *Boom Town*.
972 Dating *9thC: Retail Therapy* (BF *The Ninth Doctor Chronicles* #1.4) - The Ninth Doctor Chronicles box set contains four stories that seem to fall in chronological order according to the Doctor's life. As the third of these (*9thC: The Other Side*) involves Adam Mitchell, the last of these, *Retail Therapy*, likely happens after the Doctor and Rose ditch him (*The Long Game*).
973 Dating *Circular Time:*"Autumn" (BF #91) - The story seems to end in early September, with the Doctor and Nyssa lodging in Stockbridge for at least five weeks beforehand. The year isn't given, but it's suggested that the Doctor has been coming to Stockbridge (the setting for his *DWM* comic strips) to play cricket for some time now. (Specifically, it's said that the clubhouse has photographs of "the Doctor's family" going back years.) A contemporary dating is supported by mention that the whole country has gone a bit mad about cricket since "England won the Ashes" – presumably a reference to the 2005 series, in which England bested Australia and won for the first time in eighteen years.
Traken Village isn't real, as appealing as it might sound. The Doctor says that Nyssa (a Trakenite) and Andrew (a human) have roughly the same lifespan, which isn't helpful to anyone trying to reconcile discrepancies in the Doctor's age by suggesting that he and Nyssa travelled together for many years (possibly even decades) between *Time-Flight* and *Arc of Infinity*.
974 Dating "A Groatsworth of Wit" (*DWM* #363-#364) - Greene is transported to the present day.
975 Dating *Boom Town* (X1.11) - A caption at the start says it is "Six Months Later" than *World War Three*. The evening is "freezing" and it's dark relatively early, suggesting it's at least September (the month it would be if *World War Three* was set in March). A mention of Justicia in the story is a reference to the ninth Doctor novel *The Monsters Inside*. The mention of venom grubs – named as such in *The Web Planet* novelisation (entitled *The Zarbi*), but called "larvae guns" in the TV story – suggests Margaret hails from the Isop Galaxy. (*Bad Wolf* also names Isop as the home galaxy of the Face of Boe.)
976 *TW: The Twilight Streets*
977 *TW: Everything Changes*
978 Dating "Supremacy of the Cybermen" (Titan mini-

of a movie version of *The Taming of the Shrew*. The Doctor realised that the Shadeys were feeding off his negative emotions – Greene returned to his native time, and the Doctor and Rose followed in the TARDIS.

2006 (September) - BOOM TOWN[975] -> Margaret Slitheen, a.k.a. Margaret Blaine, became Lord Mayor of Cardiff and pushed through construction of the Blaidd Drwg Power Station, which she had designed to destroy Earth and facilitate her escape into space on an Extrapolator surfboard. The ninth Doctor, Rose and Captain Jack landed in Cardiff to refuel the TARDIS and captured Margaret. Exposure to the heart of the TARDIS reverted Margaret to her original state as an egg. The Doctor returned Margaret to her home planet, Raxacoricofallapatorius, to start life anew.

Margaret's scheme to destroy Earth to facilitate her escape had wracked Cardiff with an earthquake; officially, she was believed to have died during the event.[976]

The TARDIS' chameleon circuit welded its properties onto a very small area of the Rift, and created a perceptual blind spot.[977]

(=) 2006 - "Supremacy of the Cybermen"[978] ->
Cybermen from the end of time converted most of humanity into Cyber-warriors. The Cybermen's assault killed Jack, turned Rose into a Cyberwoman, and caused the ninth Doctor's TARDIS to explode, but the twelfth Doctor's intervention restored the proper timeline.

2006 - THE DEVIANT STRAIN[979] -> The ninth Doctor, Rose and Jack arrived at Novrosk Peninsula in Siberia, the site of an old Soviet base. There had recently been a series of mysterious deaths, which the Doctor determined was caused by the defence systems of a crashed ship from the Arcane Collegiate. The threat was dispelled when the Doctor destroyed the ship.

2006 - ONLY HUMAN[980] -> The ninth Doctor, Rose and Jack arrived in Bromley to investigate temporal distortion caused by a "dirty rip" engine. They discovered a Neanderthal named Das at a local hospital. Das couldn't return home because the dirty rip engine had weakened his structure, but the Doctor and Rose went to 29,185 BC to locate the source of the problem. With Jack's help, Das quickly got a job in construction and married a girl called Anne-Marie.

Suzie Costello of Torchwood recovered an alien device that could open any lock.[981]

2006 (22nd September) - THE GATHERING[982] -> Scarred by her brother's misfortune, Katherine Chambers envisioned the removal of humanity's weaknesses and emotions through widespread Cybertisation. She worked toward the creation of System, the ultimate medical computer. Aiding her was James Clarke, secretly an agent of the Forge.

Tegan Jovanka now had a brain tumour – possibly the result of her travels with the Doctor – and was deemed by Kathy, an acquaintance of hers, as a perfect test subject. James and Kathy created System using Cyber-technology, but the fifth Doctor was on hand and convinced the half-human Nate Chambers to activate System's self-destruct. James escaped, but Chambers Pharmaceuticals exploded, killing Nate. Kathy was believed dead, but the Doctor took her elsewhere to be looked after.

Tegan resumed her romance with Michael Tenaka and turned down the Doctor's offer of finding treatment for her brain tumour.

2006 - THE PARTING OF THE WAYS[983] -> The ninth Doctor forcibly returned Rose to her native time aboard the TARDIS, removing her from the Dalek incursion in 200,100. Rose realised that the words "Bad Wolf" had been scattered throughout time and space as a message that she should return to the fray, and she exposed the heart of the TARDIS with help

---

series #1-5) - The year is given.
979 Dating *The Deviant Strain* (NSA #4) - The year isn't given, although there are references to the Cold War ending "twenty years" ago. It would seem to be set in Rose's home time.
980 Dating *Only Human* (NSA #5) - The story takes place after *Boom Town* (and *The Deviant Strain*), but – owing to Jack's presence – before *The Parting of the Ways*.
981 Jack says that Suzie found the lock-pick "last year" in *TW: Cyberwoman*.
982 Dating *The Gathering* (BF #87) - The date is given, and reinforced by a radio broadcast citing the birthday

of Australian rocker Nick Cave, and discretely mentioning the same for Billie Piper – both were born on 22nd September. In an attempt at symmetry with *The Reaping*, a radio broadcast also mentions an interview with Colin Farrell about the 2006 *Miami Vice* movie. However, the broadcast implies the film isn't out yet – it was actually released in Australia about five weeks prior on 10th August, 2006. Tegan's mother is still alive.
983 Dating *The Parting of the Ways* (X1.13) - No specific date is given, but there's no evidence that much time has passed since Rose and Mickey's meeting in *Boom Town*. In *The Christmas Invasion*, Jackie's been going out with Howard for "about a month", and Rose doesn't

from her mother and Mickey. Rose and the TARDIS returned to 200,100.

By now, the general population knew that aliens had invaded Earth over a dozen times. In 2006, Kadiatu Lethbridge-Stewart published her controversial bestseller *The Zen Military: A History of UNIT*. Lethbridge-Stewart was the granddaughter of Alistair Lethbridge-Stewart and Mariatu of the Themne tribe, making her ideally placed to write the "definitive" study of the UNIT era.[984]

Cathy Salt, the pregnant journalist spared by Margaret Slitheen, was scheduled to marry Jeffrey on 19th October.[985] In November, Jackie Tyler started going out with Howard from the market.[986] On 23rd November, 2006, Lucia Moretti, a former Torchwood operative, died from heart failure.[987]

2006 (29th November) - TW: MOVING TARGET[988] -> The Committee formally classified humanity as pests, and so the extraterrestrial Bronk Bluff Safari Ld. froze time

on Earth and established a space station in orbit. Indolent alien royalty and corporate officers paid Bronk Bluff handsomely for hunting safaris. Suzie Costello resisted the time-freeze, having been exposed to a temporal distortion generator she borrowed from the Hub. She aided the newest prey – a young public relations woman, Alex – in dispatching some tens of alien hunters, before learning that Alex had been verified as Future Proof, meaning her death would have no impact on history, and she would have committed suicide in a few weeks anyway. To end the trials, Suzie killed Alex herself.

2006 (November to December) - ICEBERG[989] -> Earth's magnetic pole shifted slightly, causing consternation at the FLIPback project. Tensions were not eased when the nearby Nikkei 5 research station vanished into the Torus Antarctica. The Cybermen were behind both the disappearances and the magnetic fluctuations, but the seventh Doctor defeated them with the help of journalist Ruby Duvall.

know about their relationship beforehand, so *The Parting of the Ways* is probably set before late November. **984** The date of the publication was given in the *Remembrance of the Daleks* novelisation, and was confirmed by *Set Piece*. In *Transit*, Yembe Lethbridge-Stewart states that Kadiatu was named after his great-grandmother, the historian. Although in *Set Piece*, Kadiatu claims that her namesake was her "grandmother", presumably for brevity's sake. **985** *Boom Town*. This was due to happen on "the nineteenth" and "next month". **986** "About a month" before *The Christmas Invasion*. **987** *TW: Children of Earth* **988** Dating *TW: Moving Target* (BF *TW* #2.4) - Suzie logs the exact day in her field report. **989** Dating *Iceberg* (NA #18) - The main action of the book takes place in 2006, from "early November" (p25) to "Friday 22 December" (p1). The epilogue is set on "Wednesday 31 January 2007" (p251). **990** Dating *The Christmas Invasion* (X2.0) - The story takes place at Christmas, shortly after *The Parting of the Ways*. Subsequent stories establish that this is indeed Christmas 2006. "A third" of the world's population is two billion people at this time. WHEN DO THE GENERAL PUBLIC ACCEPT THE EXISTENCE OF ALIENS?: It was a long-held tradition in classic *Doctor Who* that there are plenty of alien invasions, yet no one in the present day believes in them, or even really notices. Even given the Doctor's comments in *Remembrance of the Daleks* and *Rose* that humans are blind to what's going on around them, that most alien attacks are covert or limited to isolated locations, and that the government keeps hushing up the existence of aliens, there are a number of stories set before 2085 (cited in *The Dying Days* as humanity's first official

diplomatic contact with alien races) where the general population really can't escape the existence of aliens. Such stories include *The Tenth Planet*, *The Dying Days*, and *Aliens of London*. By the end of the last two, people have already started declaring that the aliens are a hoax, and this seems to become the accepted view of what happened.

This has shifted now, though. The new *Doctor Who* occasionally jokes about humanity's willingness to overlook the blatantly obvious, but by *Last of the Time Lords*, only people as obtuse as Donna Noble can be in much doubt about the existence of extra-terrestrial life. Between 2006 and 2008, humanity is made to witness a spaceship destroying Big Ben and crashing into the Thames (*Aliens of London*); another spaceship arriving over London, and its sonic boom causing a swath of damage – this is accompanied by a third of humanity being compelled to stand on rooftops while strange lights illuminate their heads, the face of the Sycorax leader being transmitted on BBC1, a newscaster's declaration that it is "absolute proof that alien life exists", and a super-laser destroying the departing spaceship (*The Christmas Invasion*); the public acceptance of "ghosts", who manifest as five million Cybermen and capture Earth before they're pulled through the sky – along with a flying Dalek army – into Canary Wharf (*Army of Ghosts/Doomsday*); the Racnoss spaceship firing bolts of energy against London, and Mr Saxon gaining prominence because the military destroys the ship on his orders (*The Runaway Bride*); a horned demon looming over Cardiff, and its shadow killing droves of pedestrians (*TW: End of Days*); Royal Hope Hospital vanishing, leaving behind only a crater before reappearing some hours later – this coincides with the hospital appearing on the moon, and about a thou-

The Sycorax Invasion of Earth; the Tenth Doctor Topples Harriet Jones

2006 (24th-25th December) - THE CHRISTMAS INVASION[990] -> The newly-regenerated tenth Doctor arrived back on Earth with Rose. He recovered in Jackie's flat, and became the target of robot Santas and a killer Christmas tree. These were just "pilot fish" for the Sycorax, whose vast spacecraft intercepted the British Guinevere 1 Probe to Mars and set course for Earth.

NATO went to red alert. Prime Minister Harriet Jones took control of UNIT's command centre underneath the Tower of London, where the Sycorax made contact and lay claim to the entire Earth. As a means of blackmail, they used "blood control" to hypnotically command one-third of the population, including the Royal Family, to walk to the nearest rooftop.

Jones made a public appeal to the Doctor as the Sycorax ship arrived over London. Jones, Major Blake of UNIT, Danny Llewellyn of the British Rocket Group and the PM's aide Alex were teleported to the Sycorax ship, where Llewellyn and Blake were quickly killed. The Doctor recovered and challenged the Sycorax leader to a duel. The leader cut off the Doctor's hand with a sword, but as the Doctor was within the first fifteen hours of his regeneration cycle, he was able to regrow the hand and go on to kill the Sycorax leader. The Sycorax retreated.

Harriet Jones feared that the Sycorax would spread word about the Earth, and that more alien invaders would return in the Doctor's absence. She ordered Torchwood to destroy the retreating Sycorax ship with an energy weapon – whereupon the horrified Doctor called Jones' fitness to lead into question, and deposed her with a single sentence ("Don't you think she looks tired?"). Questions were raised about Jones' health, and a vote of no confidence was quickly scheduled.

The British could use "the Hubble array" to track spacecraft. The Sycorax used the Sycoraxic language.

---

sand people inside being scanned by space rhinos (*Smith and Jones*, although it's still possible for Clive Jones' girlfriend, Annalise, to dismiss the idea of aliens); and – most tellingly of all – the British Prime Minister presenting the Toclafane to the world, a day before one of their number murders the American President during a worldwide broadcast (*The Sound of Drums*). The destruction of the Paradox Machine undoes the Toclafane's capture of Earth, but explicitly everything up to and including the assassination of the President still happens. And soon after that, the sun turns a cold blue (*SJA: Invasion of the Bane*), an event that is (flimsily) attributed in a cover story to a "temporary reversal of the Earth's magnetic poles".

The final straw for anyone too thick to believe in aliens prior to this is, surely, *The Stolen Earth/Journey's End* – in which Earth is both teleported into a sector of space with twenty six other abducted worlds, incurs massive casualties while being overrun by the Daleks, and is physically hauled through space while being returned to its natural orbit. Clyde Langer's father later mentions the Daleks by name (*SJA: The Mark of the Berserker*), and it's an event so hard to ignore, Gwen Cooper can tell someone who has been in cryo-freeze, "These days the whole alien cat is rather out of the bag... The Daleks invaded." (*TW: Risk Assessment*, p83)

Circa 2009 to 2011, the public also experiences the moon being set on a collision course with Earth (*SJA: The Lost Boy*), astrologer Martin Trueman hijacking every TV broadcast and hypnotising large swathes of the public according to their astrological symbols (*SJA: Secrets of the Stars*), the entire human race (sans Wilf and Donna) turning into Prime Minister Harold Saxon/the Master (*The End of Time*), everyone on Earth being made to think a meteor is hurtling toward them

(*SJA: Goodbye, Sarah Jane Smith*), the children of Earth simultaneously speaking words in English (*TW: Children of Earth*) and death being suspended across the globe for a period of at least two months, possibly more (*TW: Miracle Day*).

A reset potentially happens in Series 5, when the Cracks in Time nibble away bits of history, meaning that Amy – native to 2010 – can no longer remember the Daleks invading Earth after numerous planets appeared overhead (*The Stolen Earth*), or the Cyber-King rampaging through Victorian London (*The Next Doctor*). The idea may have been to "erase" the public's belief in aliens, and begin anew with modern-day *Doctor Who* being identical to our own, but there's reason to believe this didn't actually happen (see the Cracks in Time sidebar). The occasional glitch remains (Adam in *Dalek* – set in 2012 – thinks that the existence of aliens isn't public; Hex, who originates from 2021, believes the same in *Project: Destiny*), but for now, at least, there's no need to do anything as drastic as put most of Series 1-4, the Tennant specials, *Torchwood* and *The Sarah Jane Adventures* into alternate-universe bubbles.

Even if the Cracks did induce a historical mind-wipe, however, the years to follow that reboot include a global coronary event, which follows the overnight appearance of black cubes across the whole of Earth and humanity spending a whole year acclimating to their presence (*The Power of Three*); Earth's dead pouring forth as a Cybermen army, accompanied by dark skies only dissipated when said Cybermen fly up and perish in a fireball (*Dark Water/Death in Heaven*); Missy getting UNIT's attention by freezing 4,165 airplanes *in time* (a discrepancy those aboard would surely notice upon their revival; *The Magician's Apprentice*); the integration of thousands of disguised Zygon refugees into

Many people went to Trafalgar Square to celebrate – Ursula Blake was among them, and while there happened to take a picture of the Doctor.[991] Donna Noble missed the excitement of Christmas Day because she had a bit of a hangover.[992] The Doctor's severed hand ended up in the archives of Torchwood Cardiff.[993] The Sycorax leader defeated by the Doctor fell to Earth at Westminster Abbey.[994]

The newly-regenerated Master arrived on Earth from the end of the universe, and adopted the alias "Harold Saxon". He faked his past, and set up the Archangel Network of satellites to subliminally influence the British public into supporting his policies. The Archangel signals also masked the Master's presence, and preventing the Doctor from detecting him in this time zone. The Master married a woman named Lucy, and his meteoric rise saw him become Minister of Defence. In such a position, he helped to design a flying aircraft carrier, the *Valiant*.[995]

After the Sycorax Invasion, some people obsessed with the Doctor formed the group LINDA.[996]

c 2006 - "The Lodger" (*DWM*)[997] **->** The tenth Doctor popped in to see Mickey, telling him that he and Rose had just escaped some Lombards – but that the TARDIS had accidentally jumped a time track, so Rose wouldn't be showing up for a couple of days. Jackie was occupied with a man called Alan, so the Doctor stayed with Mickey. After the Doctor beat him at video games *and* tuned his TV so that Mickey got programmes from ten years in the future *and* ruined a night in planned with a girl called Gina, Mickey got sick of him. After a few days, the TARDIS arrived with Rose. The Doctor arranged it so that Mickey and Rose had a nice Sunday together.

Doctor Who Series 2

c 2006 - NEW EARTH[998] **->** The tenth Doctor and Rose set off on their travels, leaving behind Jackie and Mickey.

There was Graske activity on Earth.[999] A group of Groske, similar in form to the Graske but with blue skin, were stranded on Earth in 2006. UNIT made them earn their keep as engineers.[1000]

2007[1001]

The Krillitanes were a composite species, given to absorbing the physical aspects of the races they con-

Earth culture (admittedly done covertly, *The Day of the Doctor* et al) and a caped superhero in Manhattan catching, at the last moment, an inbound spaceship (*The Return of Doctor Mysterio*). The Monks' takeover, at least, was "erased" following their defeat (*The Lie of the Land*).

The point being: even if one can somehow rationalise away an enormous submerged creature wrecking the last Frostfair in 1814 (*Thin Ice*) or the penning of a tyrannosaur in 1890s London for the better part of a day, in front of any passerby, until the beast spontaneously combusts (*Deep Breath*), the status quo of the *Doctor Who* universe in (say) 2017 cannot possibly be our own. We don't yet know what shape it's taken, but when it comes to humanity thinking it's alone in the universe, that toothpaste has surely left the tube. It remains to be seen, however, if *Doctor Who* tries to have it both ways, depicting the public as surprised about epic alien-driven phenomena even as the sheer number of such incidents piles up.

One story from the non-TV media is worth mentioning: the *DWM* strip "The Mark of Mandragora" establishes that the events of "Invaders of Gantac" and (perhaps a little oddly) *Battlefield* led the general public to the realisation that aliens existed. That was contradicted by *Rose*, but the new TV series swiftly established that – in the words of Captain Jack in *Torchwood* – "the twenty-first century is when everything changes".

991 *Love & Monsters*

992 *The Runaway Bride*

993 *TW: Everything Changes*, and confirmed in *Utopia*. The Doctor lost his hand in *The Christmas Invasion*.

994 "The Widow's Curse"

995 "Eighteen months" before *The Sound of Drums*, and by implication very soon after *The Christmas Invasion*. It's not clear who runs Britain for those eighteen months – possibly it's a weakened Harriet Jones. As Jones had only recently won by a landslide, it's easy to infer that the opposition parties are also in disarray. The fact that Saxon's Cabinet in *The Sound of Drums* is composed of people from various political parties would seem to support that. However, the Prime Minister as seen in a blurry photograph in *TW: Out of Time* (set in late 2007) looks male.

The official "Vote Saxon" website states that Lucy's father (mentioned, but not named, in *The Sound of Drums*) is called Lord Cole of Tarminster, so it's likely her maiden name was "Lucy Cole".

996 *Love & Monsters*

997 Dating "The Lodger" (*DWM* #368) - This would seem to fit into the gap between *The Christmas Invasion* and *New Earth*. This strip contains a few jokes and story beats later seen the Series 5 episode of the same name (also written by Gareth Roberts), but the two aren't *so* similar that they become as contradictory as the two versions of *Human Nature*. Any commonalities can, ultimately, be written off as coincidence.

998 Dating *New Earth* (X2.1) - The Doctor and Rose leave the Powell Estate, some undetermined amount of time after *The Christmas Invasion*. The cheerful note on

quered and destroyed. A small group of them took on human form and infiltrated Deffry Vale School, with "Mr Finch" taking over as headmaster.[1002]

Joseph Serf, the owner of Serf Systems, died in a skiing accident in 2007. John Harrison, Serf's public relations officer, purchased a group of Scullions – short aliens with only one eye – on the black market after their ship crash-landed in Central Asia. With the Scullions manipulating a holographic image of Joseph Serf, Harrison covered up the man's death and assumed control of the company.[1003]

In 2007, Jack Harkness, Owen Harper and Suzie Costello dealt with ravenous creatures masquerading as schoolchildren. A school teacher, Eryn Bunting, saw the creatures and was given Retcon. Suzie stole one of Eryn's bank slips, and set up a secret account for herself under Eryn's name.[1004] Elena Hilda Al-Qatari became ill and requested a replacement to head the Rawbone Project, which renewed the government's interest in it.[1005]

Maxwell Edison set up the Stockbridge Preservation Society to protest Khrysalis Corporation building a leisure park.[1006] **Henry John Parker acquired extra-terrestrial items that included a Dogon eye, Ikean wings, and an alien translation of James Herbert's *The Fog* (1975).[1007]**

Tamsin Drew, a future companion of the eighth Doctor and the Monk, appeared in an advert for leg wax.[1008] She also worked for a summer at the London dungeon, as a Cockney drab who was killed by Jack the Ripper.[1009]

Coldfire Construction, a front for the Slitheen, started expanding and specialised in the installation of technology blocks in schools in London, Barcelona, Washington D.C., Santiago, Los Angeles, Sydney, Beijing, Moscow, Naples and Paris.[1010] A geologist friend sent Sarah Jane a crystal found at the site of Krakatoa – as Sarah quickly discovered, the crystal revealed itself to be alive when it communicated with her laptop. Following its instructions, she built a computer to house its sentience, which she called Mr Smith and kept in her attic. Mr Smith offered to help Sarah protect Earth and monitor extra-terrestrial activity, and dutifully did so. In secret, however, Mr Smith schemed to release its brethren, the Xylox, from their imprisonment beneath the Earth.[1011]

Once again, the decaying Master awoke within the UNIT Vault for an hour. Ruth Matheson and Lt Wilcher, the latter of whom later died in an accident, interviewed him during this interval.[1012] The Committee syphoned off enough oil to cause the supply crisis of 2007. Although oil seemed commonplace on Earth, it was a priceless commodity to some alien races.[1013]

Jack Harkness owned a dog named Untitled. The Committee suspected that humanity would be impossible to control, so would need to be replaced.[1014]

2007 - THE STONE ROSE[1015] -> Mickey showed the tenth Doctor and Rose a statue from Ancient Rome in the British Museum – one that depicted Rose. The Doctor and Rose travelled back in time to investigate.

2007 - THE FEAST OF THE DROWNED[1016] -> The HMS *Ascendant* sank in the North Sea, killing Jay, the brother of Rose's friend Keisha. The tenth Doctor and Rose

---

which that story ends might make one think that they intended on leaving immediately afterwards – except that in *New Earth*, the TARDIS has moved; Jackie, Mickey and Rose are all wearing different clothes; Rose now has luggage with her; and the ash from the Sycorax ship has gone. Also, they still had some Christmas food waiting inside (not to mention that they hadn't opened any presents). It's not impossible, though, that they left straight after *The Christmas Invasion*, returned after some unseen adventures, then left once again.

999 "A couple of years back" according to Sarah Jane in *SJA: Whatever Happened to Sarah Jane?* It's almost certainly a reference to the interactive story *Attack of the Graske* that appeared on the BBC website (and which is outside the remit of this book).

1000 *SJA: Death of the Doctor*

1001 Events in 2007 include the "present day" sequences of *Doctor Who* Series 2 and most (but not all) of *Torchwood* Series 1.

1002 "Three months" before *School Reunion*.

1003 *SJA: The Man Who Never Was*

1004 *TW: Long Time Dead* (p206).

1005 "A few years" before *TW: First Born*.

1006 The year before "The Stockbridge Child".

1007 Throughout the year prior to *TW: A Day in the Death*.

1008 "Three years" before *Situation Vacant*.

1009 *Deimos*

1010 "Eighteen months" before *SJA: Revenge of the Slitheen*.

1011 "Eighteen months" before *SJA: The Lost Boy*, and after K9 begins monitoring the black hole, as they have not met before that story.

1012 "Five years" before the contemporary part of *Mastermind*.

1013 *TW: The Torchwood Archive* (BF)

1014 *TW: The Torchwood Archive* (BF), in a scene the script dates to 2007.

1015 Dating *The Stone Rose* (NSA #7) - Mickey hasn't joined the TARDIS crew, but Rose knows about Petrifold Regression, so it's set between *New Earth* and *School Reunion*.

1016 Dating *The Feast of the Drowned* (NSA #8) - The story is set between *The Christmas Invasion* and *School Reunion*.

arrived, discovering that a number of people had died in London since wreckage from the *Ascendant* was brought there. Relatives of the dead were apparently being contacted by the ghosts of the drowned, but this was a side effect of alien technology. The Waterhive were attempting to conquer the world, but the Doctor thwarted them.

2007 - CUDDLESOME[1017] -> Ronald Turvey was released from prison, but his toy factory at Shoreham Harbour was defunct. The Tinghus within Turvey formed a plan: new Cuddlesomes would be manufactured that could transform people into Tinghus-human hybrids. A recall signal summoned the 1980s Cuddlesomes to their birthplace, and a rumble broke out between the different generations of Cuddlesomes. The fifth Doctor witnessed the Cuddlesome slaughter, which ended when Turvey and the Tinghus (which manifested as a giant Cuddlesome) both died, rendering the Cuddlesomes inactive.

The Tenth Doctor Reunites with Sarah Jane Smith and K9

2007 - SCHOOL REUNION[1018] -> Mickey called in the tenth Doctor and Rose to help investigate Deffry Vale School. The Doctor posted a winning lottery ticket through the letterbox of one of the physics teachers and took their place. He met Sarah Jane Smith, who was also investigating the school. The Krillitanes were using the children's brains to formulate the Skasas Paradigm – an equation which could be used to control "the building blocks of the universe", even to the point of rewriting the past. The reactivated K9 sacrificed himself to destroy the Krillitanes.

The Doctor built a new K9 for Sarah Jane. Mickey joined the TARDIS crew.

The new K9 contained a compartment with a number of helpful gadgets for Sarah Jane, like the sonic lipstick.[1019]

1017 Dating *Cuddlesome* (BF promo #7, *DWM* #393) - The audio saw release in March 2008 and seems contemporary, including mention of texting. However, a radio report says that authorities in England are investigating a possible outbreak of H5N1 avian flu, which in real-life was a concern in the UK in 2007.

1018 Dating *School Reunion* (X2.3) - The story features Mickey, and Sarah refers to the events of *The Christmas Invasion* as "last Christmas", so the story is set in 2007 (and at some point during a school term).

SARAH JANE'S REUNIONS WITH THE DOCTOR: In *School Reunion*, the very strong implication is that Sarah hasn't had any form of contact with the Doctor since she left him at the end of *The Hand of Fear*. Somewhat tellingly, the Doctor comments that he's regenerated "half a dozen times" since she last saw him.

Some commentators have seized upon this as evidence that the non-TV media (which entailed a post-*Hand of Fear* Sarah meeting the Doctor on more than one occasion) are apocryphal, but in truth this scenario doesn't match the TV series either. In the first place, the Doctor sent Sarah a K9, and in *K9 and Company*, she even says "so he didn't forget me after all". Yet in *School Reunion*, Sarah says she thought the Doctor had forgotten about her after dropping her off. Also, she was reunited with the third Doctor – and met the fifth – in *The Five Doctors*. Clearly, as occasionally happens, the series chooses not to complicate the narrative by invoking every possible relevant previous story. Indeed, a new or more casual viewer would infer from what Sarah says that some time ago, the Doctor left her and K9 on Earth to go and fight the Time War.

Sarah Jane also appeared in a number of stories in other media set after *The Hand of Fear*: "Train-Flight" (set c 1990), *System Shock* (set in 1998; she didn't meet the Doctor in that story, but neither did she believe he was

dead or had abandoned her), *Interference* (set in 1997, and portraying her as romantically involved with a man called Paul) and *Bullet Time* (also set in 1997). Ergo, Sarah Jane has encountered four of the "half a dozen" incarnations that the Doctor has been through between *The Hand of Fear* and *School Reunion*. The basic story beat is the same in each case – Sarah continues to be a successful journalist, while missing the Doctor.

1019 Established on the BBC website; the sonic lipstick is seen in *SJS: Invasion of the Bane*.

1020 *The Shining Man* (ch21).

1021 "Eighteen months" before *SJS: Invasion of the Bane*.

1022 Dating "The Green-Eyed Monster" (*DWM* #377) - *School Reunion* and The *Girl in the Fireplace* are both referenced, but it's before *Rise of the Cybermen*, as Mickey is still around.

1023 Dating *Borrowed Time* (NSA #49) - The year is given (p60). The Chancellor of the Exchequer is to give a speech based upon the booming economy following "the first six months of 2007" (p201), so it's likely summer. Certainly, nobody complains about the weather. It's a Tuesday (p72).

1024 Dating *Rise of the Cybermen/The Age of Steel* (X2.5-2.6) - Mickey finds a newspaper that he says is dated to "1st February, this year" – in other words, the year *School Reunion* is set, 2007. Lumic cites the day as 1st February.

A birthday party is being held for the parallel-universe Jackie, and Rose says – when she and the Doctor are outside the Tyler mansion – "February the first, mum's birthday" (thereby indicating that "our" Jackie was born on the same day).

One point of confusion is that the official biography of the parallel Jackie – or so she claims – states that she

The Doctor gave Sarah Jane the sonic lipstick because it wasn't really his shade.[1020] **A black hole was released following a Swiss laboratory accident. K9 contained it, but this fully occupied his time, so he was unable to help Sarah Jane on her adventures.**[1021]

c 2007 - "The Green-Eyed Monster" (*DWM*)[1022] ->

When Rose was infected by an alien worm that ate emotions, the tenth Doctor induced great jealousy in her by setting Mickey up with a girlfriend, and having an adventure on the planet of the Amazastians (the entire population of whom were beautiful teenage girls, much to the mystification of even their own scientists). The Doctor resorted to kissing Jackie, which overloaded the alien worm.

2007 - BORROWED TIME[1023] ->

Little Green Storage had installed a storage facility, the internal dimensions of which were compressed down to 7.5% normal, beneath the Millennium Dome. This provided a service to space travellers on Earth, which Little Green regarded as "the most frequently attacked colonised, exploited and enslaved planet in the five galaxies".

Members of the Ah N'Drubrn Clan of Warrior Molluscs were currently residing in the Thames. The Doctor had access to Galactic Enquiries, a newly introduced service that could provide an individual's phone number based upon such data as their sporting interests, their mother's name and whether or not they had a stain on their tie that day.

A parasitic organism posed as "Jane Blythe", a high-ranking personal assistant at Lexington International Bank. Blythe's avatars, Mr Symington and Mr Blenkinsop, offered select individuals Time Harvesters: wristwatches that they could use to borrow extra time. Interest was accrued at a rate of five minutes per hour, *every hour*, meaning the debt quickly exceeded the borrowers' lifespans. Blythe traded the accrued debt on the Time Market.

The eleventh Doctor, Amy and Rory ran afoul of Blythe when they arrived to observe the bank's historic collapse. Amy used a Time Harvester to spend more time with her husband, her parents and by herself, and the Doctor surrendered twenty-five years of his life to pay off the debt that this accrued. Blythe sought to sell the Doctor – the last remaining Time Lord – on the Time Market. He achieved an estimated value of five inhabited galaxies (about fifteen sextillion lives) before Blythe suffered a liquidity crisis. The Doctor bought Earth's outstanding debt for a second a decade. Blythe became a fugitive from the Time Market.

The Lumic Cybermen are Created

= 2007 (1st February) - RISE OF THE CYBERMEN / THE AGE OF STEEL[1024] **->** The TARDIS materialised in a parallel universe with military checkpoints in the streets and zeppelins in the skies. The tenth Doctor, Rose and Mickey found that Rose's father Pete Tyler was alive in this reality, and had become rich from selling a health drink called Vitex Lite. Pete was preparing for Jackie's fortieth birthday party, and the guests included the President of Great Britain and a Torchwood agent named Stevie.

This world was home to a New South America and a New Germany. The Torchwood Institute was releasing studies to the public. The Bio-Convention required the registration of new life-forms. Rose was never born on this world, but the Tylers owned a small dog with the same name.

John Lumic's Cybus Industries owned "just about every company" in Britain, including Vitex. Cybus had sold EarPods to virtually everyone. Lumic himself was dying, and had developed a robot body that could house the human brain. His agents, operating through a dummy company named International Electromatics[1025], started rounding up the homeless to convert into such cybernetic beings. Mickey discovered that his alternate self, Ricky, ran a resistance cell.

Lumic activated his cyborgs – the Cybermen – and they stormed Jackie's birthday party. The President was killed, and many guests were captured. Lumic transmitted a signal via the EarPods to all Londoners, making them march to Battersea Power Station to undergo conversion. Cybermen took to the streets, and Ricky was killed.

The Doctor confronted Lumic – who against his will had been converted into the Cyber Controller. Cyber-conversion factories had been built on all seven continents, but the Doctor instructed Mickey on how to deactivate the Cybermen's emotional inhibitors. Mentally unable to confront the nature of their lost humanity, the Cybermen malfunctioned. The Doctor and his allies escaped in Lumic's zeppelin, destroying the Power Station and the Controller.

Mickey remained in the parallel universe to help liberate it from the remaining Cybermen.

Back in our universe, the Doctor and Rose met Jackie for a tearful reunion.

> = On Pete's World, the People's Republic took control of Torchwood. The Cybermen were sealed in their factories, but a debate ensued about what to do with them, as they were living beings. Some Cybermen infiltrated Torchwood and vanished.[1026]

2007 - I AM A DALEK[1027] -> A Dalek left over from the Time War activated the Dalek Factor within the human Kate Yates. The tenth Doctor and Rose deactivated the Dalek, neutralising the Dalek Factor within Kate.

c 2007 - 100: "Bedtime Story"[1028] -> Near Harrogate, the sixth Doctor accompanied Evelyn as she paid respects to one of her former students – Jacob Williams – regarding the death of his father Frank. The Doctor exposed the shapeshifting creature responsible for the Williams family "curse", but the shapeshifter rendered Evelyn, Jacob and Frank's wife Mary immobile – just as it had with Frank. The Doctor tricked the creature into thinking the Williams line had ended, then showed his charges the wonders of the universe in the TARDIS – and returned them home once they had recovered.

c 2007 (a Wednesday in May) - JACK: WEDNESDAYS FOR BEGINNERS[1029] -> The Harvesters, ancient scavengers who nabbed individuals unique in space-time, identified Jackie Tyler's ties to their ultimate prize: the Doctor. They removed the Powell Estate from reality, and syphoned its residents away until Jackie phoned Rose and the Doctor for help. Captain Jack had been observing the Estate, and deduced the Harvesters' plan. As the TARDIS materialized, Jackie phoned Rose again... to say it was a false alarm, she didn't need them after all, they should go and deal with some dragons or something – she'd made a prank call! – and the TARDIS immediately left. The Harvesters lost their grip on reality and the Estate returned home, its residents none the wiser.

Rose's Auntie Val was to enjoy a birthday next Tuesday. Jackie's Uncle Tony lived in a home; his fireworks from Ramadan had been confiscated.

2007 - INFAMY OF THE ZAROSS[1030] -> Jackie Tyler visited her friend Marge in Norwich, so was on hand as the dreaded Zaross – the stars of an extraterrestrial reality show, *Take Me to Your Leader* – "attacked" the city, to net footage of their "overrunning Earth". The tenth Doctor,

---

was born the same day as actor Cuba Gooding Jr. He was actually born on 2nd January, 1968 (it would seem that someone on the production team didn't take into account that in America, the date "1/2" means the second of January). We might imagine that Gooding was born on 1st February in the parallel reality, or it's possible that Jackie's biographers – in an attempt to make her sound more interesting – simply got the date wrong and nobody corrected her. (This is no more implausible an error than the real-life production team failing to fact-check Gooding's birthday via Google.)

"Our" Gooding was born in 1968 – so if Jackie was born the same year, she should be 39 in *Rise of the Cybermen*, not 40 as she claims. In addition to everything else, then, it's possible Jackie and Gooding's parallel counterparts were born a year prior in 1967.

1025 Evidently a reference to Vaughn's company from *The Invasion*, which otherwise doesn't appear to exist in this reality.

1026 *Doomsday*. The Doctor names this version of Earth as "Pete's World" (as Pete Tyler is alive there), and the term has caught on in texts such as *Doctor Who: The Encyclopedia*.

1027 Dating *I am a Dalek* (*Quick Reads* #1) - No year is given, but the story has a present day setting.

1028 Dating *100: "Bedtime Story"* (BF #100c) - The story seems contemporary with the audio's release in September 2007 – Jamie Oliver is referenced, and mention is made of the rumours surrounding Evelyn's disappearance. There's a glaring story flaw in that the Williams family has long since recognised the correla-

tion between the birth of a son causing his grandparents to "drop dead", and yet no generation has, apparently, refrained from siring children even knowing that the act will kill their parents.

1029 Dating *Jack: Wednesdays for Beginners* (BF *The Lives of Captain Jack* #1.2) - Jackie names the month. It's not said if it's during Series One or Two, although Jackie's "protect Rose and the Doctor at all costs" attitude (*Love & Monsters*) seems to indicate the latter, and her suggestion to Rose that she feed the Doctor birdseed better matches the tenth Doctor. Despite Jackie wondering if it's Tuesday or Sunday, it's indeed established as Wednesday.

Oddly, Jack says he's been waiting for the Doctor "one hundred seventy years" – if he's going by his arrival from the Game Station, it's only roughly one hundred thirty-eight years (perhaps it's been so long, he's lost track?).

1030 Dating *Infamy of the Zaross* (BF 10th Doc #2.1) – It's an unspecified point during Series 2 (set in 2007). There's no mention of Mickey, so it's probably after his exit from our Earth in *The Age of Steel*.

1031 Dating *Love & Monsters* (X2.10) - It's "two years" since the events of *Rose* (set in March 2005). The story takes place after *The Christmas Invasion*, but before *Army of Ghosts* and *Doomsday*. Jackie says that Mickey has gone, placing it after *The Age of Steel*.

Elton says that Kennedy approached LINDA on "a Tuesday night in March".

1032 The Abzorbaloff reads the newspaper in *Love & Monsters*.

Rose and Jackie unmasked the Zaross as the Forzel, a race of innocuous pottery makers who craved notoriety. The Doctor's group proved that *Leader*'s backers, the Hazerix, had eliminated the show's previous stars when their fame ebbed. Appalled, the Forzel destroyed the Hazerix mothership, and themselves, with a mega-bomb.

2007 - LOVE & MONSTERS[1031] -> A "Bad Wolf" virus had corrupted Torchwood's files on Rose.

Elton Pope had been obsessed with the Doctor ever since seeing him as a child. He became a member of the group LINDA (London Investigation 'N' Detective Agency), which was made up of other people for whom the Doctor's existence filled a gap in their lives.

On a Tuesday night in March, the group fell under the sway of Victor Kennedy. He was secretly an Abzorbaloff from Clom, the twin planet of Raxacoricofallapatorius, who wanted to absorb the Doctor and his memories. Elton briefly met the tenth Doctor and Rose as they fought an alien Hoix, then later struck up a friendship with Jackie Tyler – in an attempt to get close to Rose. The Doctor and Rose tracked down Elton because he was "stalking" Rose's mother, and together they confronted the Abzorbaloff – who was defeated, and burst. Elton continued his relationship with Ursula, a member of LINDA, even though she had become a living paving slab.

The *Daily Telegraph* ran the headline: "Saxon Leads Polls with 64 per cent". Four more months of government paralysis were forecast.[1032] Ghosts started appearing around the world, but people got used to them.[1033]

2007 (Monday, June 25th) - TURN LEFT[1034] -> Donna Noble, a Chiswick resident[1035], was offered temp work with HC Clements, but her mother insisted that she consider a full-time position as a secretary with Jival Chowdry's photocopy service. At one minute past 10 am, Donna made a fateful decision while driving: turn left and continue on to HC Clements, or turn right to interview for the full-time job. She turned left, and so went on to meet the tenth Doctor.

> (=) Owing to the intervention of one of the Trickster's Brigade, a parallel timeline was created in which Donna turned right. Rose Tyler and UNIT aided the alternate version of Donna in travelling back to the temporal junction point, enabling the alt-Donna to sacrifice her life to cause a traffic jam so her other self would turn left. History was placed back on track.

2007 - TW: THE TORCHWOOD ARCHIVE (BF)[1036] -> Captain Jack deemed Torchwood London as too corrupt and so had Suzie Costello destroy an Ovid factory in Wales, then phone Yvonne Hartman to say she had "found" Object One, a.k.a. the Bad Penny, beforehand. Hartman was thrilled to reclaim Object One, but its bad-luck factor contributed to her organisation's downfall...

The Battle of Canary Wharf

Torchwood London Destroyed, Rose Tyler Leaves the TARDIS

2007 - ARMY OF GHOSTS / DOOMSDAY[1037] -> Torchwood sought to obtain energy independence for the United Kingdom, and had been using particle engines to further open the temporal breach in Canary Wharf. A Voidship, designed to exist outside space and time, came through the breach; Torchwood took to studying it. The parallel-Earth Cybermen as created by

---

1033 "Two months" before *Army of Ghosts*.

1034 Dating *Turn Left* (X4.11) - This is "six months" before Donna would have met the Doctor in December 2007 (so, June). Rose says it's "Monday 25th", and June was the only month in 2007 when the 25th fell on a Monday. In the alternate timeline created by Donna turning right, there is no mention of Harold Saxon – because if the Doctor died defeating the Racnoss and *Utopia* didn't happen, the Master presumably remained at the end of time.

1035 *Planet of the Ood, The Sontaran Stratagem, The Unicorn and the Wasp, Journey's End, The End of Time*.

1036 Dating *TW: The Torchwood Archive* (BF *TW* special release #1) - It's "ninety years" since Jack threw the Bad Penny into the Rift in 1914; the script dates this to 2007. The implication is that Object One brought about Torchwood London's destruction in *Army of Ghosts/*

Doomsday (also set in 2007).

1037 Dating *Army of Ghosts/Doomsday* (X2.12-2.13) - No month is given, but it's after *Love & Monsters* and before *The Runaway Bride* (set at Christmas Eve 2007).

Backtracking the *Torchwood* Series 1 dating makes it somewhat hard to believe that the Battle of Canary Wharf occurs any later than July. (*TW: Out of Time* takes place right before Christmas; *TW: They Keep Killing Suzie* takes place beforehand but is "three months" after *TW: Everything Changes* – which *TW: Miracle Day* suggests occurs in October; Jack and Gwen chat about Canary Wharf in *TW: Everything Changes*, and don't speak as if the battle there occurred, say, within the last week or so.) *Army of Ghosts* and *Doomsday* respectively broadcast on 1st July and 8th July, and could well take place on one of those dates in 2008.

Lumic followed in the Voidship's wake, and were manifesting on Earth as ghostly figures.

The tenth Doctor and Rose returned home to find that the public had accepted ghost appearances as a fact of life. Many media shows, including *Ghostwatch*, discussed the phenomenon.

The Doctor tracked the appearances of the ghosts to Torchwood HQ in Canary Wharf, and confronted the head of Torchwood, Yvonne Hartman. Soon after, the Cybermen achieved full manifestation – five million of them materialised from the parallel universe and occupied the planet. Hartman was forced to undergo Cyber-conversion. A Cyberman was seen strangling the host of *Ghostwatch*.[1038] Martha Jones' cousin, Adeola Oshodi, worked for Torchwood London and died just prior to the Cybermen takeover.[1039]

Meanwhile, four Daleks – members of the Cult of Skaro, a secret order above even the Dalek Emperor – emerged from the Voidship with a Genesis Ark. The Cybermen and Daleks began fighting, and the Daleks opened the Ark – a Time Lord prison containing millions of Daleks. With the help of Pete Tyler and Mickey who had arrived from Pete's World), the Doctor and Rose opened a gateway to the Void and sucked all the Cybermen and Daleks into the gap between universes. The Cult of Skaro Daleks fled to the 1930s, but the Void was forever sealed. Rose, Jackie and Mickey were left trapped in the parallel universe with the alternate Pete.

After the battle, Rose and Jackie were listed as dead.

1038 Alistair Appleton, who might be among the casualties in the *Doctor Who* universe.

1039 *Smith and Jones*, which explains why Freema Agyeman portrayed both Martha in Series 3 and Adeola in *Army of Ghosts*.

1040 *TW: Everything Changes*

1041 *Utopia*

1042 *The Runaway Bride*

1043 *Army of Ghosts*. The sarcophagus is evidently a reference to *Pyramids of Mars*.

1044 *TW: The Torchwood Archive* (BF)

1045 *TW: Aliens Among Us 3: Poker Face*

1046 *TW: Cyberwoman*

1047 *Made of Steel*

1048 *TW: Cyberwoman*, with additional info from Torchwood.co.uk.

1049 The Doctor deduces this in *The Next Doctor*.

1050 *TW: Fragments*

1051 *The End of Time*

1052 *TW: torchwood_cascade_cdrip.tor*

1053 Dating *TW: Fragments* (TW 2.12) - Ianto surely wouldn't waste much time in approaching Jack after the destruction of Canary Wharf (in *Doomsday*), as he joins Torchwood Cardiff to care for his injured girlfriend, who was partly cyber-converted in the battle there. The modern-day component of *Fragments* occurs "21 months" after this flashback. *TW: Dead Man Walking*, set in 2008, says that the first Resurrection Gauntlet was recovered "last year", i.e. in 2007.

1054 *TW: Long Time Dead*, at an unspecified point between the Gauntlet's recovery and Suzie's first death.

1055 "Two years" before *TW: Almost Perfect*.

1056 "Six months" before *The Runaway Bride*.

1057 Dating *Blink* (X3.10) - The year is given by Kathy Nightingale (who claims she was transported from 2007 to 1920) and the Doctor, who says it's "thirty-eight years" after 1969. The epilogue of the story takes place in 2008.

1058 Dating "Fellow Travellers" (*DWM* #164-166) - Date

unknown, but no-one has been inside the house "for years".

THE HOUSE AT ALLEN ROAD: A good example of continuity between the New Adventures and the *DWM* strip is that both establish that the Doctor has a house in England which he occasionally visits.

The house is usually associated with the seventh Doctor. It first appeared in "Fellow Travellers" and *Cat's Cradle: Warhead*. It was named Smithwood Manor in "Ravens" and "The Last Word". The Doctor owned it at least as early as the Second World War (*Just War*) and has it in the early twenty-second century (*Transit*).

The eighth Doctor visits the house in *The Dying Days* and mentions it in *The Scarlet Empress*. He also has a house in the 1980s in part two and three of *Father Time*, which may or may not be the same house. *So Vile a Sin* depicts a parallel universe where the third Doctor lived in the house for a thousand years until the thirtieth century. *Verdigris* has the third Doctor using the house during his exile to Earth. The house is stolen in "Question Mark Pyjamas" (a short story from *Decalog 2*), but the seventh Doctor, Ace and Bernice recover it.

"Fellow Travellers", "Ravens" and *Cat's Cradle: Warhead* all indicate that the house has a mysterious reputation – and the last two have the street sign altered to read "Alien Road".

1059 Dating "Ravens" (*DWM* #188-190) - It's "the near, harsh future", and the story takes place at the same time as *Cat's Cradle: Warhead*.

1060 Dating *The Nightmare of Black Island* (NSA #10) - It's "late September" and the story is set in the present day. This would mean that the tenth Doctor and Rose have landed a couple of months or so after the Battle of Canary Wharf in *Doomsday* – hardly impossible, as *The Nightmare of Black Island* is an isolated incident, and provides them with no warning about what awaits their personal futures.

1061 Dating *Cat's Cradle: Warhead* (NA #6) - A specific date for this story and its two sequels is not established

Aftermath
of the Battle of Canary Wharf

These events became known as The Battle of Canary Wharf.[1040] Captain Jack read Rose and Jackie's names on the official list of those killed in the battle, and believed they had died.[1041] During the battle, Donna Noble was scuba-diving in Spain.[1042]

Items in the Torchwood HQ archives before the battle had included a particle gun, a magna-clamp that was found in a spaceship at the base of Mount Snowdon and a sarcophagus. Torchwood still used the Imperial weight system, having refused to go metric.[1043]

Yvonne Hartman ordered Kieran Frost to throw the Bad Penny into the Void, but he instead passed it along to Ianto Jones during the fall of Torchwood One, and told him that Lisa could make use of it.[1044] The opening of the Void enabled an alternate version of Yvonne Hartman to cross to our reality. She remained in hiding for a decade.[1045]

The Cybermen had converted a number of the Torchwood London staff, but the conversion of Lisa Hallett – Ianto Jones' girlfriend – was interrupted by their defeat. Ianto cared for her in secret.[1046]

Three Cybermen who were built on our Earth survived and escaped from the Torchwood Tower with an alien teleportation device. They set up a base inside the Millennium Dome.[1047] The Cybertechnology Institute of Osaka was founded to learn the secrets of Cybertechnology. It was headed by a Dr Tanizaki.[1048]

The Cybermen stole from the Daleks a dimension vault as well as information about the Doctor, which they placed on an infostamp.[1049] Two members of Torchwood Cardiff scoured the remains of Torchwood London to prevent its equipment falling into the wrong hands.[1050] They failed to prevent billionaire Joshua Naismith from acquiring an alien device, the Immortality Gate, from the ruins.[1051] Survivors of Torchwood One, including Stephen Heinz, salvaged Torchwood equipment from Canary Wharf.[1052]

Ianto Jones Joins Torchwood Cardiff

2007 - TW: FRAGMENTS[1053] -> Ianto Jones approached Captain Jack about a job at Torchwood Three. Jack resisted, but hired Ianto after he helped capture a pterodactyl that came through the Rift. Jack had Suzie dredge the reservoir for the Resurrection Gauntlet.

The alien viewer that fell into the Rift before life developed on Earth now emerged from it. Torchwood recovered the credit-card-sized device, which Suzie Costello had implanted into the skin of her belly, hoping it could convert energy and power the Resurrection Gauntlet.[1054]

Jack saw the Perfection, a.k.a. Brendan and Jon, at Cardiff Gay Pride, where Owen used a flamethrower to help save singer Charlotte Church from a tentacle monster.[1055] Lance Bennett, the head of human resources at H C Clements, allied himself with the Empress of the Racnoss. As ordered, Bennett slipped some huon particles into the coffee of his co-worker, Donna Noble. The particles gestated within her, and Bennett had her re-dosed on a daily basis.[1056]

2007 - BLINK[1057] -> The Weeping Angels had developed as a race of hunters who could send people back in time, then live off the potential energy of the years their victims might have had. As a defence mechanism built in to their biology, they turned to stone if seen.

Sally Sparrow investigated the abandoned house Wester Drumlins, and discovered a message to her written on the wall by the tenth Doctor in 1969, before she was born. She returned with her friend Kathy Nightingale, who was sent to 1920 by the Angels.

Gradually, Sally discovered that the Doctor was a time traveller. The Angels had stolen the Doctor's TARDIS key and transported him – along with his companion Martha – back to 1969. Owing to messages left by the Doctor, Sally sent the TARDIS back to 1969 – and in doing so, caused the Weeping Angels to look at each other and become forever immobile.

c 2007 - "Fellow Travellers"[1058] -> The seventh Doctor and Ace defeated a Hitcher at the Doctor's house.

c 2007 - "Ravens"[1059] -> A notorious gang called the Ravens massacred everyone at a service station and used their blood in an occult ritual. Needing more blood, they tried to kill two passersby: Christine Jenkins and her daughter Demi. The TARDIS materialised, and the seventh Doctor let out Raven, a seventeenth-century Japanese warrior who butchered the gang apart from a woman named Annie – whose face he slashed in a deliberate way. A few months later, outside the house at Allen Road, Annie explained to other youths that she now understood the patterns of time.

2007 (late September) - THE NIGHTMARE OF BLACK ISLAND[1060] -> The tenth Doctor and Rose arrived on the Welsh island of Ynys Du, and discovered the children there were all having nightmares. The children contained the psychic residue of Balor, General of the Cynrog Hordes, but the Doctor dispersed him.

c 2007 (late October) - CAT'S CRADLE: WARHEAD[1061] -> The Butler Institute – a huge conglomeration of corporations "from Amoco to Zenith", and which had secretly been bought up over the last decade by the vast Japanese Hoshino company – made projections of the future. Butler could see no alternative but massive, irrevocable environmental collapse. The planet was now reaching the point of no return.

Butler's executives secretly poured money into experiments that attempted to download human consciousness into computers. The Institute developed a weapons system run by an electronically-recorded human consciousness, but its ultimate aim was to "record" the minds of the elite and store them in indestructible databanks, safe from the ravages of pollution and the ozone layer's destruction.

The seventh Doctor deemed Butler's plan a perversion. He sought out Ace's friend Shreela – now a renowned science writer, who was dying from an auto-immune disorder brought on by the increasingly toxic environment. Shreela died after agreeing to put her name on an article the Doctor had written ("A Doorway to Other Worlds") that made connections between a type of protein and psionic abilities – all part of his efforts to deceive Butler.

The Doctor and Ace brought together two young psion-ics who could serve as a telekinetic "bomb": Vincent Wheaton, who could transform dark emotions into destructive force, and Justine, a "battery" of emotional energy. The Doctor's plan failed because Vincent and Justine fell in love, which quelled her inner rage. Vincent instead drew energy from Butler's project director, Mathew O'Hara, and released a wave of energy that destroyed Butler's memory-transfer project outside Albany. O'Hara was reduced to ash.

During these events, Ace was forced to kill Massoud, a Kurdish mercenary. With the collapse of Butler's project, the directors of the world's corporations realised their only option was to instigate a massive environmental clean-up programme.

c 2007 - PROJECT: LAZARUS[1062] -> The seventh Doctor happened to re-visit the Forge, and met his former self's clone. The captive Huldran had died – it was part of a gestalt race, and its traumatised fellows assaulted the Forge via a gateway. The clone triggered the base's self-

---

in the books themselves. The blurb states "The time is the near future – all too near". Shreela, a contemporary of Ace from Perivale first seen in *Survival*, dies of an "auto immune disease" at a tragically early age (p19).

The book is set in a year when Halloween falls on a Saturday (on p199 it's Halloween, on p250 it's the next day, a Sunday), making it either 1998, 2009 or 2015 – although in a number of stories, the real calendar doesn't match that of the *Doctor Who* universe. Ace's clothes are how Mancuso, a policewoman, dressed "twenty years ago" (p202), and Ace is from the late 1980s. *Just War* confirms that the Cartmel books take place in the "twenty-first century timezone" (p250). However, mention is made of "President Norris" (p26) - with Obama being president in *The End of Time*, set in 2009, an earlier dating for *Cat's Cradle: Warhead* is preferable (see the American Presidents in the *Doctor Who Universe* sidebar). In his "Future History Continuity" document, Ben Aaronovitch suggested that *Cat's Cradle: Warhead* was set "c.2007".

1062 Dating *Project: Lazarus* (BF #45) - Nimrod implies "three years" have passed since the first installment.

1063 *Happy Endings*

THE RECONSTRUCTION: The televised stories set in the twenty-first century offer a broadly consistent view of a peaceful Earth with a single world government, in which people of all nations cooperate in the field of space exploration and social progress. To reconcile this with the rather more downbeat New Adventures set in this century, Ben Aaronovitch suggested in his "Future History Continuity" document that a concerted global effort was made at some point in the early twenty-first century to repair the damage that had been done to Earth's environment. A "Clean Up" is first hinted at the end of *Iceberg*, which is where we learn of the "Arms for

Humanity" concert and the procuring of drinking water from icebergs, but we might suggest that it only gains impetus after *Cat's Cradle: Warhead*, when all the corporations put their full weight behind it.

This process was named "the Reconstruction" in *Happy Endings*. We would suggest that this period of international co-operation lasts for around seventy years. Earth during this time is a relatively happy, clean and optimistic place.

1064 Travelling by car is a lot easier in *Warlock* than *Cat's Cradle: Warhead* (*Warlock*, p179), and we learn about the monitoring systems (p224) and new road system (p211), yet London traffic has barely improved (p265).

1065 Dating *The Tenth Doctor Year One* (Titan 10th Doc #1.6-1.9, "The Weeping Angels of Mons") - The year is given. Allowing for *Human Nature*, the tenth Doctor has a habit of being quickly seen by World War I vets in this period (Jamie, born in 1896, would be 111 in this scene). In real life, the last World War I veteran, Florence Green, died in February 2012, age 110.

1066 Dating *Torchwood* Series 1 – Gwen joins Torchwood after *Doomsday*, as events of that story are mentioned in *TW: Everything Changes* and *TW: Day One*, and form the basis of *TW: Cyberwoman*. This shifts the Series 1 stories to a year after they were broadcast, like all the "present day" *Doctor Who* stories since *Aliens of London*.

In *TW: Miracle Day*, Esther says Gwen joined Torchwood in "October 2006", with the "year ahead" rule seemingly forgotten about (and in a script by Russell T. Davies, who engineered the convention, no less!). There are a couple of escape contingencies here...the CIA files that Esther is reading from might list the year wrong, or she might misread the year while repeating the infor-

destruct, but died at Nimrod's hands. The Doctor and the Huldran fled as the Forge was destroyed. The Forge's computer, Oracle, put the organisation's beta facility on-line.

The Reconstruction kicked the King's representative out of the British Parliament. Reconstruction Acts were passed to improve the environment. Large family farms started growing meat-substitute plants.[1063] Within a couple of decades, air quality improved, the oceans were cleaner and the ozone layer holes had been patched. Sophisticated traffic monitoring systems and a reconfigured road network eased congestion – and therefore pollution – in the South East of England. Central London, though, was still busy.[1064]

2007 - THE TENTH DOCTOR YEAR ONE[1065] -> Jamie Colquhoun's family took him to visit the St Michel War Cemetery, where he briefly glimpsed the tenth Doctor and Gabby.

Torchwood Series 1 (2007-2008)[1066]

By now, the Cardiff Rift had attracted all manner of aliens and extra-terrestrial technology, and approximately two hundred Weevils were living in the sewers below the city.

The Battle of Canary Wharf had led to the destruction of Torchwood One in London – such was the devastation that Torchwood was reduced to "only a half dozen" operatives: Captain Jack Harkness, Suzie Costello, Owen Harper, Toshiko Sato and Ianto Jones. They worked from the Hub – an underground base near Cardiff's Millennium Centre.

The Cardiff branch of Torchwood was designated Torchwood Three. Torchwood Two was an office in Glasgow, and "a very strange man" named Archie[1067], who wasn't very adept with computers, worked there. **Torchwood Four had gone missing.** Whatever became of Torchwood Four, it involved a great deal of screaming.[1068]

Captain Jack stressed to his operatives that Torchwood had to arm the human race for what lie ahead...[1069]

Gwen Cooper Joins Torchwood; the First Death of Suzie Costello

2007 (early October) - TW: EVERYTHING CHANGES[1070] -> Members of the police were obligated to grant Torchwood operatives special access, and – not knowing the truth about the organisation – regarded the group as Special Ops. A series of murders led to Cardiff PC Gwen Cooper encountering Captain Jack's team. Gwen and Jack discovered that his second-in-command, Suzie Costello, had been committing the murders as a means of field testing an alien glove – the Resurrection Gauntlet – that could briefly bring people back to life. Exposed, Suzie killed herself. Afterwards, Jack recruited Gwen to work for Torchwood.

2007 (October) - TW: DAY ONE -> According to the official records, no American citizen had been born with the name "Jack Harkness" in the last fifty years.

A gaseous alien landed near Cardiff in a meteor, and possessed a young woman named Carys. The alien thrived on orgasmic energy and used pheromones to provoke sexual desire in its victims. Torchwood destroyed the creature, enabling Carys to return home.

---

mation to Rex.

If the "October" reference is correct, however, then every story between *TW: Everything Changes* and *TW: Border Princes* (set at "nearly Halloween") must happen in that month. Also, *Everything Changes* must take place in *early* October, as "three months" (technically accurate with benefit of rounding) pass between it and *TW: They Keep Killing Suzie* (which must occur before *TW: Out of Time*, set near Christmas).

Most details presented in *Torchwood* Series 1 support a dating of 2007 – in *TW: Ghost Machine*, for example, 1941 is "sixty-six" years ago. However, there are some anomalies in stories such as *TW: Random Shoes* and *TW: Out of Time*. See the individual episodes for more detail.

1067 Archie is cited by name in *TW: The Twilight Streets* and *The Torchwood Archives* (BBC). The latter details his background with Torchwood.

1068 *TW: The Torchwood Archive* (BF)

1069 *TW: Everything Changes*

1070 HOW PUBLIC IS TORCHWOOD?: In *Tooth and Claw* (set in 1879), Queen Victoria creates Torchwood as an ultra-secret organisation devoted to defending Britain's borders against alien/supernatural incursion. Similarly, *The Christmas Invasion* (set in 2006) seems to imply that Torchwood is so secret and so clandestine, the Prime Minister – in this case, Harriet Jones – isn't even supposed to know that it exists. Yet in *Torchwood* Series 1, Captain Jack and company can race through the Cardiff streets with the name "Torchwood" prominently displayed on the side of their SUV, the group (or Owen, at least) orders pizza under the name "Torchwood" and so forth. The on-screen evidence offers a simple solution to this, even though *Torchwood* Series 1 doesn't spell it out very succinctly: The authorities are well aware of Torchwood's existence, and believe the group is a Special Ops team to whom they must yield authority. Episodes that support this notion include *TW: Everything Changes* (the police blatantly regard Torchwood as Special Ops), *TW: Cyberwoman*

The prominence of Carys' meteor in the skies over Cardiff distracted a car driver, who accidentally killed the wife of city planner Roger Pugh.[1071]

2007 (October) - TW: GHOST MACHINE[1072] ->
Torchwood recovered a piece of alien technology – a "quantum transducer" – that could convert and amplify human emotion as a means of witnessing the past, or making premonitions about the future. The device enabled Owen Harper to witness the murder of Lizzie Lewis, which was committed in Cardiff, 1963. A scuffle led to the death of Lizzie's killer, Ed Morgan.

Torchwood dealt with a Cyclops and a robot.[1073]

2007 (October) - TW: ANOTHER LIFE[1074] ->
Torchwood defeated a plot by man-eating aliens that resembled starfish to manipulate the MMOG Second Reality.

2007 (late October) - TW: BORDER PRINCES[1075] ->
Torchwood thwarted the Amok, zombie-animating aliens.

In November, Captain Jack and Gwen handled an incident involving the Perth Mermaids.[1076]

2007 - TW: SLOW DECAY ->
Torchwood investigated Doctor Scotus' weight clinic – a business that was achieving dramatic results by having its patients, including Gwen's boyfriend Rhys, ingest an alien parasite. They shut down the operation.

2007 - TW: WEB OF LIES[1077] ->
An operative of the Three Families captured Jack and tested the limits of his immortality – which included throwing Jack out of a plane near Chernobyl. Gwen located Jack, who killed the agent, but the Families wiped their memory of the event with Retcon gas. Jack and Gwyn only knew that they had a "missing day", nothing more.

The Death of Lisa Hallett

2007 - TW: CYBERWOMAN ->
Ianto had secretly been keeping his part-Cybertised girlfriend – Lisa Hallett – in the basement of the Hub, but her Cyber-programming finally won out, and she attempted to "upgrade" the Torchwood team into Cybermen. Lisa's

---

(Gwen mentions Torchwood to a contact at Jodrell Bank), *TW: Countrycide* (Gwen thinks a "policeman" – actually a treacherous cannibal – might know of Torchwood as a Special Ops group), *TW: They Keep Killing Suzie* (police units clear the roads for the Torchwood SUV) and more.

Put very simply, it's only the organisation's goal of harvesting alien technology that's secret, not the very mention of Torchwood itself. This fits most of the evidence, but requires one to retroactively assume that in *The Christmas Invasion*, Harriet Jones is suggesting that the Prime Minister isn't supposed to know Torchwood's true purpose, or that they have a super-weapon capable of obliterating spaceships. At the very least, this explains how Jack can talk to the Prime Minister about Torchwood funding issues (*TW: Greeks Bearing Gifts*).

In *Fear Her* (set in 2012), Torchwood is mentioned in a TV broadcast, but the reference is too obscure to tell if the group's real agenda is known to the public, or if they're still considered an elite branch of the military.

Some fans are uneasy with the notion that Torchwood – even as an organisation that by definition is given to deception – could have existed throughout the twentieth century without the third Doctor or UNIT learning about them. A few attempts have been made to explain this, and a recurring one speculates that, temporally speaking, Torchwood didn't exist until the tenth Doctor and Rose went back and annoyed Queen Victoria (*Tooth and Claw*). This theory is hard to credit, however, partly because it overlooks the obvious point that Torchwood does, in fact, predate the Doctor and

Rose's trip to 1879. The group is mentioned in *Bad Wolf* and *The Christmas Invasion*, and in the latter story obliterates the departing Sycorax spaceship.

There is nothing special about *Tooth and Claw* in terms of time mechanics, so if such revision occurred, it would almost presuppose that the timeline gets revised nearly each and every time the TARDIS lands. Logically, this would suggest that the Great Fire of Rome shouldn't exist in time until the first Doctor inspires Nero to do it (*The Romans*) – even though the Doctor and Vicki both mention it beforehand. A similar case applies to the fifth Doctor causing the Great Fire of London in *The Visitation*, even though it's cited in *Pyramids of Mars*. Therefore, the idea that Torchwood didn't "exist" until *Tooth and Claw* might help to explain its secrecy in the 1970s, but would throw the entire *Doctor Who* timeline into chaos.

It is far, far simpler to think that Torchwood was officially listed in the 70s as a Special Ops group; that Torchwood let UNIT get on with the business of actually combating alien incursions; that the Torchwood agents of the time operated with a high degree of stealth (not surprising, if a "Britain first" group were attempting to out-fox a United Nations organisation); and that the Doctor and UNIT were never given reason to look upon the group with suspicion.

1071 "Ten years" before *TW: More Than This*, and as part of *TW: Day One*.

1072 Dating *Ghost Machine* (*TW* 1.3) - Thomas Erasmus Flanagan and his daughter say they're watching the *Strictly Come Dancing* finals – this is a bit hard to credit,

body was destroyed when Jack set his pet pterodactyl on her, and although she transferred her brain into a pizza delivery woman, the Torchwood operatives shot her new body to death.

The first generation of Arcan Leisure Crawlers were now considered collectors' items as far as spaceships went – Torchwood politely warned one such vessel away from Earth, pointing out that they were scaring the locals. The Arcans themselves were mostly liquid, and rather boring.

2007 - TW: BROKEN[1078] -> Owing to the fracas that ended in his girlfriend's death, Ianto Jones had neglected to buy any milk. The oversight motivated him to leave his flat, a bit dazed, until he wandered into The Ferret pub and struck up a conversation with a barmaid, Mandy. Ianto tip-toed around Torchwood's *raison detre*, but used Mandy as a sounding board and confidant. A few days later, Ianto went with Captain Jack on a Weevil hunt, and took out his frustrations by beating the Weevil senseless with a stick.

Ianto felt isolated from his teammates when Jack's old friend Estelle Cole asked him to visit, and Jack took Gwen along instead of him...[1079]

2007 - TW: SMALL WORLDS[1080] -> Fairies tried to claim a young girl named Jasmine, their "Chosen One", and killed Jack's old friend Estelle Cole. Torchwood was unable to stop the fairies, and Jack only ended their rampage by giving Jasmine over to their custody. She was retroactively seen in a "fairie photograph" that had intrigued Arthur Conan Doyle.

2007 - TW: COUNTRYCIDE -> Seventeen people had disappeared in the last five months in rural Wales, and

Torchwood feared that the Rift's effects were spreading beyond Cardiff. They investigated, and found a group of cannibalistic villagers, who "harvested" travellers every ten years. Jack and his team facilitated the cannibals' arrest.

Torchwood's encounter with cannibals in rural Wales proved so horrific, Ianto contemplated taking his own life. He phoned his friend Mandy in a cry for help, and she talked him down from suicide. Afterward, Torchwood dealt with a disturbance at the Millennium Centre when a Scorchie possessed nearly twenty members of the Welsh Royal Opera.[1081]

2007 - TW: HIDDEN[1082] -> The seventeenth century alchemist Thomas Vaughn was now passing as Sir Robert Craig. Through the research conducted at the CARU fertility clinic in Caerphilly, he hoped to achieve true immortality. Craig had a number of people – including Alice Proctor, the daughter of a friend of Jack Harkness – murdered to protect his secrets, and Jack killed Craig to avenge their deaths. Craig's "son" Simon was actually his own clone, but Jack ascertained that Simon was undergoing genetic deterioration, and wouldn't live past age 20.

2007 - TW: GREEKS BEARING GIFTS[1083] -> The alien named Mary sensed the unearthing of the transmat device that carried her to Earth in 1812. Mary approached Toshiko with a pendant that enabled her to read the thoughts of others, and seduced her in the hopes of retrieving the transmat from the Hub. Jack and his staff found that Mary was an exiled criminal who had been eating people's hearts for years, whereupon Jack teleported her into the Sun. Tosh destroyed the pendant.

---

as the show routinely starts in October and finishes in late December. It's possible they're watching a rerun, but it's presented as if it's the original broadcast.
1073 Mentioned in *TW: Another Life*.
1074 Dating *Another Life* (*TW* novel #1) - The novel is set before *Cyberwoman* – Ianto is seen sneaking down to the basement in the novel. The spines of the first three *Torchwood* novels fit together to make one picture, suggesting a reading order of *TW: Another Life*, *TW: Border Princes* and *TW: Slow Decay*.
1075 Dating *Border Princes* (*TW* novel #2) - There are three mentions of the book taking place in October, one of which reads "An October night, almost Halloween" (p221). It's after the release of *Pirates of the Caribbean III* (in May 2007).
1076 *TW: The Conspiracy*
1077 Dating *TW: Web of Lies* (*TW* animated serial #1) - The year is given in a caption.
1078 Dating *TW: Broken* (BF *TW* #2.5) - The story begins

the day after Lisa died (*TW: Cyberwoman*), and continues "a few days" afterward.
1079 *TW: Broken*
1080 Dating *Small Worlds* (*TW* 1.5) - A calendar appears in Jasmine Pearce's kitchen, but it's too fuzzy to read.
1081 *TW: Broken*
1082 Dating *TW: Hidden* (*TW* audiobook #1) - The story takes place during *Torchwood* Series 1. Ianto and Jack are decently friendly toward one another but don't seem to be an item, suggesting a placement between *TW: Cyberwoman* and *TW: They Keep Killing Suzie*. Also, Ianto tells Tosh during a crisis that he should "never leave the bloody office ever again", which could be taken as a reference to *TW: Countrycide*.
1083 Dating *TW: Greeks Bearing Gifts* (*TW* 1.7) - Tosh estimates that the dead British soldier who was killed in 1812 has been buried for "one hundred ninety-six years, eleven to eleven and a half months". This would

2007 - TW: BROKEN[1084] -> Ianto's friend Mandy had been subsidising the Ferret pub by partnering with the Saviour – an alien who promised to send the downtrodden to a heavenly place, but instead sent them through the Rift to an infernal world and sold them as slaves. While investigating the resultant wave of disappearances, Captain Jack happened upon Ianto drinking at the Ferret. Ianto had deduced Mandy's duplicity, but was so angry at Jack for killing Lisa Hallett, he allowed the Saviour to take Jack away from Earth. Later that night, a repentant Ianto returned to the Ferret, rescued Jack, banished the Saviour from Earth and warned Mandy to forever leave Cardiff.

Ianto propositioned Jack, and they decided to have sex just the one time, and return to being nothing more than co-workers after that...

The Second Death of Suzie Costello

2007 (mid-December) - TW: THEY KEEP KILLING SUZIE[1085] -> By now, Torchwood Cardiff had dispensed amnesia pills – each containing Compound B67, also known as Retcon – to two thousand and eight people.

Max Tazillion responded to Suzie's mental programming and started killing members of the Pilgrim support group. Torchwood investigated, learned that Suzie Costello had belonged to the group, and used the Resurrection Glove to revive her. Suzie escaped, vengefully murdered her father and nearly drained all of Gwen's life-force in a bid to stay alive. Jack realised the glove was diverting Gwen's life-energy into Suzie and ordered its destruction, causing Suzie to die for good.

2007 (December) - TW: RANDOM SHOES[1086] -> Prior to this, there had been a trade for Dogon sixth eyeballs.

Eugene Jones had become a Torchwood groupie of sorts. He tried to raise funds by selling his Dogon sixth eye on eBay, but this led to a string of events in which Eugene swallowed the eyeball – and it kept his spirit tethered to Earth when he died in a hit and run. Eugene's shade accompanied Gwen as she investigated his death, and he manifested enough to save her life from an oncoming car at his funeral. Gwen and her comrades watched as Eugene then vanished into a haze of light, as if departing for the great beyond.

2007 (December) - TW: THE CONSPIRACY / FALL TO EARTH[1087] -> *Plexus* magazine now had one million subscribers worldwide.

The long-standing journalist George Wilson had an on-air breakdown, and decried the US and UK governments as puppets of oil companies and multi-nationals. To jump-

seem to suggest a dating of 2009, save that Tosh stresses she's estimating, and – for that matter – can hardly be expected to have knowledge of the on-screen caption denoting the murder as occurring in 1812. Most likely, Torchwood – without benefit of the omnipotent narrator – concludes the soldier was killed in 1810.

1084 Dating *TW: Broken* (BF *TW* #2.5) - The story reconciles Ianto's anger at Jack's role in Lisa's death (*TW: Cyberwoman*) against his suddenly offering to do salacious things involving a stopwatch with him (the end of *TW: They Keep Killing Suzie*). *Broken* concludes in-between *TW: Greeks Bearing Gifts* and *They Keep Killing Suzie*, with Ianto and Jack having sex for the first time, meaning they'd already consummated their relationship at least once before the "stopwatch" incident. The time of year seems later than earlier, with Ianto's mum asking about Christmas plans, him evasively commenting that Christmas is "ages away", and her responding that it's "not that far off."

1085 Dating *TW: They Keep Killing Suzie* (*TW* 1.8) - "Three months" have passed since Suzie's death in *TW: Everything Changes*.

1086 Dating *TW: Random Shoes* (*TW* 1.9) - The story is rife with minor glitches. The eBay listing for Eugene's alien eyeball claims the auction began on "14-Oct-06", but the date only appears on the full graphic on the *Torchwood* website, and isn't actually seen on screen. As

such, it can be safely ignored. Another anomaly is that the "Black Holes and the Uncertainty Principle" flyer says the convention will begin on the 27th, a Thursday. This doesn't match any later month of the year in 2006, but such a day happened in September and December 2007. Those months don't seem viable (given this episode's relation to other *Torchwood* Series 1 stories), but the flyer is minor evidence. More glaringly, Eugene says it's been "fourteen years" since his father left in 1992 – which would indicate a dating of 2006.

1087 Dating *TW: The Conspiracy* and *TW: Fall to Earth* (BF *TW* #1.1-1.2) - *The Conspiracy* seems to take place in *Torchwood* Series 1; Gwen is working for the group, but the Skypoint tower block (completed by *TW: Skypoint*, set in September 2008) is only half-built. It's been "almost 40 years" since anyone (officially, at least) stepped foot on the moon, which last happened in December 1972. Jack says that Earth has "seven billion people" – that didn't officially happen until October 2011, but he's in the ballpark. An anachronism crops up in that conspiracy-blogger Sam Hallett uses Instagram, which wasn't released until 6th October, 2010.

Fall to Earth follows on from *The Conspiracy*, and it's after Lisa Hallet's death (*TW: Cyberwoman*). Ianto's credit card sports an expiration date of "May 2010". The SkyPuncher is touted as the "first" private spaceflight, but in the real world, that happened with SpaceShipOne in 2004 (see also the dating notes on *SJS: Dreamland*

start a second career, Wilson and his adopted daughter Kate concocted all sorts of conspiracy theories, including details about "the Committee" – an Illuminati-type group that was pulling humankind's strings. Unknown to Wilson, Kate *was* a member of the Committee – and through him was seeding half-truths about her employers into the public discourse, preventing anyone from believing the Committee existed.

Jack Harkness knew the Committee was genuine and investigated Wilson, but Kate murdered Wilson to pin the crime on Jack and Torchwood. Jack told his Torchwood team that he was going undercover to deal with the Committee...

The billionaire philanthropist Ephram Salt had financed the SkyPuncher: a private spaceship. Ianto Jones believed that Salt knew something about the Committee, and infiltrated the SkyPuncher's maiden flight, which had Salt and celebrities such as the boy band Star 7 aboard, to safeguard it. The Committee poisoned the drinks aboard the SkyPuncher, killing or incapacitating everyone save Ianto, and directed the SkyPuncher toward one of Salt's call centers in western Turkey. A call centre worker named Zeynep aided Ianto in directing the SkyPuncher into a quarry, containing the damage as he jettisoned to safety.

2007 (December) - TW: THE TORCHWOOD ARCHIVE (BF)[1088] ->
The week after George Wilson died, Gwen Cooper spoke with a book writer, Madeline, about the Committee. Sporadically under the Committee's control, Madeline tried to poison Gwen by putting weed-killer into her tea – then died herself after a drug overdose.

2007 (December) - TW: UNCANNY VALLEY[1089] ->
Captain Jack visited the reclusive billionaire Neil Redmond, having deduced that the Committee had usurped Redmond's company, Artemis, to develop a mysterious

product named Galatine. Jack slept with Redmond's Ovid android, N.J., by way of proving N.J.'s callousness, and also that Redmond had become the Committee's pawn. An exposed N.J. strangled Redmond to death, and perished trying to stop Jack from escaping.

The Committee supplied the five richest men in Russia with Ovid dolls for girlfriends, and manipulated them into bidding on the late Neil Redmond's Galatine system. The KVI had waned in influence, but one of its operatives, Evan Putin, arranged for the men and their "girlfriends" to be killed.[1090]

2007 (18th-24th December) - TW: OUT OF TIME[1091]
-> Pilot Diane Holmes and two of her passengers – Emma Louise Cowell and John Ellis – emerged from the Cardiff Rift, having flown into it in 1953. The three reacted differently to life in the future – Emma thrived, John killed himself and Diane became lovers with Owen. On 24th December, she flew her plane back into the Rift, expecting to find adventures anew.

Donna Noble Meets the Tenth Doctor

2007 (Christmas Eve) - THE RUNAWAY BRIDE[1092] ->
The huon particles within Donna Noble caused her to dematerialise from her wedding ceremony, and to reappear in the TARDIS. Returning her to Earth, the tenth Doctor had to rescue her from Roboforms disguised as Santas. This time, the robot "pilot fish" served the Empress of Racnoss, a huge spider-like creature and ancient enemy of the Time Lords.

From an abandoned Torchwood facility below the Thames Barrier, the Empress harvested the huon particles within Donna – the key to awakening the only other surviving members of the Racnoss, who were

regarding spaceflights for tourists in the *Whoniverse*).
1088 Dating *The Torchwood Archive* (BF *TW* special release #1) - Wilson died (*TW: The Conspiracy*) "last week".
1089 Dating *TW: Uncanny Valley* (BF *TW* #1.5) - The blurb says Redmond's accident happened "a couple of years" beforehand, in April 2004. Within the fiction, it's been "a few years" since then, with N.J. having spent about "two years" learning to pose as Redmond, and, evidently, roughly another year doing so.
1090 *TW: The Torchwood Archive* (BF), bringing an additional conspiracy angle to the real-life deaths of oligarchs in Vladimir Putin's Russia.
1091 Dating *TW: Out of Time* (*TW* 1.10) - Owen says in *TW: Captain Jack Harkness* that Diane flew back into the Rift on 24th December, denoting when the story ends. Diane says the *Sky Gypsy* flew into the Rift on 18th

December, 1953 – *Captain Jack Harkness* also claims that she and Owen only had "a week" together, so it would appear that the *Sky Gypsy* reappears on the very same day it flew into the Rift, just in half a century later. (The Rift surely doesn't care about matching the Gregorian calendar for aesthetic reasons, so this must owe to the position of the Earth around the sun or some other factor.) An anomaly is that 29th December is said to be a Friday – which is was in 2006, not 2007. The *Cardiff Examiner* is seen with the headline, "Drunk Driving Records Soar This Christmas".
1092 Dating *The Runaway Bride* (X3.0) - It's "Christmas Eve", and the Sycorax invasion was "last Christmas". It's also after the Battle of Canary Wharf (*Doomsday*). Strangely, Donna comments in *The Fires of Pompeii* that the Doctor "saved her in 2008", seemingly referring to this story (she must be rounding up from "Christmas

trapped at the Earth's core. The Empress also killed her ally, Donna's fiancé Lance. The Doctor emptied the Thames into a tunnel leading to the core, killing the Racnoss below. Under orders from Mr Saxon, British Army tanks destroyed the Empress and her spaceship.

(=) 2007 (Christmas Eve) - TURN LEFT[1093] -> In the timeline where Donna turned right, she was celebrating a job promotion when the Racnoss Empress' ship (the "Christmas Star") attacked London. At the scene, she saw UNIT taking away the tenth Doctor's body – for lack of Donna convincing him to show restraint and leave, he had been killed without regenerating. Rose arrived to find the Doctor, too late.

Donna's grandfather, Wilfred Mott, was unable to attend her wedding because he had the Spanish flu.[1094] The Racnoss incident helped Mr Saxon come to prominence with the public.[1095]

Meeting the Doctor changed Donna's life. She tried travelling abroad, including a trip to Egypt, but found it mediocre. Finally, she sought out mysterious happenings, looking for the Doctor.[1096]

2008[1097]

San Francisco fell into the sea.[1098] The Doctor stopped the End, Rue, Burn Doomsday Cult from destroying London.[1099] **Martha Jones owned a television made by Magpie Electricals.**[1100] Petronella Osgood's college classmates called her "Plain Jane Superbrain". Kate Stewart wanted to make UNIT more science-based, so recruited Osgood to her team.[1101]

(=) Manipulated by the poodle people of the Dogworld, John Fuchas produced a movie "adaptation" of *The True History of Planets* in 2008 that abandoned the original book in favour of a story about the deposed poodle Princess Margaret. The eighth Doctor prevented this timeline from ever happening.[1102]

Ed Gold was born in Australia in 2008, a time when his country was seriously lagging behind in the space race.[1103] Clyde Langer won First Place in a Park Vale drawing competition in 2008.[1104] Theo Lawson, a genius teenage hacker, caused a confidence crisis in the banking system that triggered a domino effect and led to a global recession.[1105]

2007" by way of discussing temporal mechanics with the Doctor). Donna's surname is misspelled "Nobel" by some sources such as *Doctor Who Adventures* and in the official *Doctor Who* Exhibition.
1093 Dating *Turn Left* (X4.11) - This is the alternate timeline version of *The Runaway Bride*.
1094 *The Sontaran Stratagem*
1095 *The Sound of Drums*
1096 *Partners in Crime*
1097 Events in 2008 include the last few episodes of *Torchwood* Series 1, the "present day" sequences of *Doctor Who* Series 3, most (but not all) of *Torchwood* Series 2, and *The Sarah Jane Adventures* Series 1.
1098 "Over two hundred years" before *The Janus Conjunction* (p79), set in 2211. Julya, who makes the claim, might just be mistaken – the city appears in *The Ninth Doctor Year One*: "The Transformed" (set in 2016), and is referred to as around in the twenty-second century in *The Face-Eater*.
1099 "A little over two hundred and seventy-one days" from *Borrowed Time*.
1100 According to a label on Martha's television in *The Sound of Drums*, referencing *The Idiot's Lantern*.
1101 *UNIT S2: Shutdown*. Osgood is younger than the actress who plays her, Ingrid Oliver. Going by Oliver's actual age would likely result in Kate Stewart recruiting Osgood to UNIT some seventeen years before 2015, which would clash with Kate's timeline in *Downtime* and *Daemons: Daemos Rising*, not to mention *The Power of Three* implying that Kate hasn't been in com-

mand for nearly that long. Even *Shutdown* itself, set in 2015, claims that Kate worked her way up through the ranks "these last few years".
1102 *Mad Dogs and Englishmen*
1103 *The Waters of Mars*
1104 The certificate for this is hanging on his bedroom wall in *SJA: The Curse of Clyde Langer*. This would appear to be a school competition, separate from the "country's most promising young artist" contest that Clyde wins in *SJA: Mona Lisa's Revenge*. Even so, there's a small continuity error in that *Mona Lisa's Revenge* is better suited to occur in 2009, and yet Clyde protests that his being entered in a "nerdy competition" isn't "good for his image", as if such a thing hasn't happened to him before now.
1105 *Situation Vacant*. The global recession that Lawson triggered is presumably the same as the real-world economic thrashing that started in 2008.
1106 "Eight years" before *Class: Brave-ish Heart*.
1107 Dating *The Girl Who Never Was* (BF #103) - Fireworks spell out the new year as 2008, and the audio came out in December 2007. A glitch is that Madeleine is said to have been 21 in 1942, but is "85 now" – even allowing that she hasn't had a birthday this year, that only gets matters as far as 2006. Contrary to that, the Doctor says (allowing for the new year) that the *Bavaria* has been missing for "sixty-six years".
1108 Dating *TW: Zone 10* and *TW: The Torchwood Archive* (BF TW #2.2, special release #1) - *Zone 10* is variously said to happen "forty years" and "over forty years"

When April MacLean was eight, her father Huw tried to commit suicide by driving off the motorway. The crash left his wife Jackie paralysed from the waist down. April testified against her father, who was incarcerated for eight years.[1106]

Charley Pollard Leaves the Eighth Doctor

2008 (1st January) - THE GIRL WHO NEVER WAS[1107]

-> Charley was deeply upset by the eighth Doctor's dispassionate reaction to the death of C'rizz – their travelling companion – and demanded that he take her home. He set course for Singapore Harbour, New Year's Eve, 1930, but a "temporal hump" diverted the TARDIS to the same location at the start of 2008.

Charley wrote the Doctor a goodbye note at the Singapore Hilton, then agreed to join him for one last investigation when the long-lost SS *Batavia* mysteriously reappeared at sea. The *Batavia* was riddled with temporal corrosion – a known TARDIS-killer that engaged the Ship's HADS and transported Charley back to 1942, stranding her there while the TARDIS returned to this time.

The Doctor encountered an elderly Madeline Fairweather – who still thought her name was "Charlotte Pollard" – and her son, the smuggler Byron. To eliminate the Cybermen in the *Batavia's* hold, the Doctor made the vessel to collide with an iceberg. Madeline was killed, and the Doctor, deducing the real Charley's location, went back to 1942.

The TARDIS finally returned to this time, with the unconscious Doctor inside, after a side trip to the year 500,002. The Doctor failed to realise that Charley had been left behind in 500,002 and went looking for her – only to find her goodbye note. He presumed that she'd left his company for good.

2008 - TW: ZONE 10 / THE TORCHWOOD ARCHIVE

(BF)[1108] -> Toshiko Sato decoded the 40-year-old Pulse, and discovered it was a Russian woman saying: "Toshiko

Sato: the truth is in Zone 10." Tosh went to Zone 10 in Siberia and quieted its temporal fluctuations with Torchwood tech, then retrieved the trapped astronaut Anna Volokova. The Russian Federal Security Service (FSB) moved to eliminate all evidence pertaining to the KVI's collaboration with the Committee.

Realising her people would never stop hunting her, Volokova launched in her space-capsule on a final excursion. She also spoke the words that – owing to the temporal forces – would retroactively become the Pulse. Tosh escaped, leaving the FSB soldiers trapped in Zone 10's circular time. Before she left, Volokova gave Tosh "a gift" from the Committee – the Bad Penny – as well as a message that the Committee was "calling in the debt".

Tosh reversed the Bad Penny so that it cast a "good luck" field, and created a more perfect world in which Owen kissed her, she spoke to her mother, and a war in Africa ended because she heard about it. Thinking nobody should have such power, Tosh consigned the Bad Penny to another dimension, and Retconned her memories of it.

Some time later, Torchwood's Rift Manipulator went wild. As Captain Jack, Gwen, Ianto and Tosh looked on, the Bad Penny once more came through the Rift.

2008 - TW: TORCHWOOD_CASCADE_CDRIP. TOR[1109]

-> Stephen Heinz, formerly of Torchwood One, asked Tosh for help when malignant Internet code began killing people who illegally downloaded music. Tosh lured the code-creature onto the Torchwood mainframe, then locked it away in a cache. Afterward, she declined to reciprocate Heinz's love for her, and he left the world of Torchwood behind.

c 2008 - TW: COMBAT[1110]

-> Torchwood found that an unidentified group was kidnapping Weevils. Jack and company found the Weevils were being used by thrill-seeking businessmen in a "fight club" scenario and shut the operation down.

---

after the Pulse's creation in 1965. More precisely, Volokova says she was born in 1930, and Tosh says, "That makes you what? 78?", indicating that it's now 2008. The KVI wants information pertaining to Neil Redmond's death (*Uncanny Valley*).

The Torchwood Archive picks up after Tosh visited Zone 10 "the other week", although she only needs to remove two days of her memories. The script dates the scene where the Bad Penny returns to "2008".

1109 Dating *TW: torchwood_cascade_cdrip.tor* (BF *TW* #16) - The audio opens with snippets from *TW: Zone 10*, so it's after that. Tosh concedes that things have "never really worked out" with her and Owen, suggesting that it's later in *Torchwood* Series 2. She and Stephen haven't seen each other in "just over" two years. The world

population is "6.6 billion", which matches 2007.

1110 Dating *TW: Combat* (*TW* 1.11) - Owen is greatly depressed and avoiding work owing to the loss of Diane, and Gwen here learns from Tosh about their relationship. Both facts suggest that weeks (or possibly just *a* week) rather than months have passed since *TW: Out of Time* (set in late December). It is possible, therefore, that *TW: Combat* takes place before the New Year, although a 2008 dating is perfectly feasible. (The episode itself broadcast on 24th December, the same day that *TW: Out of Time* concludes.) One anomaly is that *TW: Combat* opens with Gwen and Reece having dinner at an outside restaurant, and looking very comfortable despite their lack of winter clothing.

2008 (20th January) - TW: CAPTAIN JACK HARKNESS[1111] -> A tip-off prompted Captain Jack and Tosh to investigate the deserted Ritz dance hall, but the Rift flared up and catapulted them back to the building as it was on 20th January, 1941. The Ritz caretaker, Bilis Manger, could travel through time and was attempting to manipulate Torchwood into fully opening the Rift. Owen was desperate to get Diane back, and used the group's Rift Manipulator to open the Rift. This enabled Jack and Tosh to return home, but although the Rift seemed to close...

2008 - TW: END OF DAYS[1112] -> Opening the Rift had caused it to splinter, and it started depositing people from the past around the world. The Beatles were seen playing on the roof of Abbey Road Studios, a quarantine was established when someone arrived through time with the Black Death, and a Roman soldier murdered two people. UFOs were sighted over the Taj Mahal, and a samurai went on a rampage in the Tokyo subway system. Concurrent with these events, the Torchwood operatives saw visions of their dead or missing loved ones – each of them recommending that the Rift should be opened.

Bilis Manger was an acolyte of the devil-like being Abaddon, and had arranged these events as a means of freeing his master. The Torchwood operatives rebelled against Jack and opened the Rift, which loosed Abaddon to tower over the city. Abaddon's shadow killed anyone it touched, but Jack allowed Abaddon to feed off his immortal life energy. This overloaded Abaddon and killed him – Jack revived after spending some days in a coma.

He then disappeared as the TARDIS arrived...

After a Century on Earth, Captain Jack Reunites with the Doctor

2008 - UTOPIA[1113] -> The tenth Doctor and Martha landed in Cardiff to refuel the TARDIS at the Rift. Captain Jack hurried to meet them, and found himself hanging on as the TARDIS launched itself into the

---

1111 Dating *TW: Captain Jack Harkness* (*TW* 1.12) - The last two episodes of *Torchwood* Series 1 seem to occur in rapid succession, and placing them on the timeline is problematic. Deciding where to date them depends on whether one favours the overall aesthetic of *Captain Jack Harkness* and the pacing of plotlines in Series 1 (in which case, it's probably January 2008) or a "Vote Saxon" poster seen outside the Ritz dance hall in Cardiff (in which case, it's probably June 2008).

Doctor Who Series 3 takes place over a four-day period in June, and the "Vote Saxon" poster seems to indicate the national election that concludes in *The Sound of Drums*. However, *TW: Out of Time* ends on 24th December, 2007, and *Combat* seems to take place shortly thereafter. Moving *Captain Jack Harkness* and *End of Days* to June because of the poster would mean, then, that six months pass between *Torchwood* episodes eleven and twelve.

While this might sound plausible in theory, it is hard to watch *Torchwood* Series 1 and genuinely believe that such a six-month gap has taken place where none was apparently meant to exist. Not only does the general flow suggest that events in *Out of Time* were fairly recent (notably the rawness that Diane's departure has inflicted on Owen - as Ianto's "You've been off, haven't you?" comment helps to indicate), the costuming indicates January. Jack wears his trench coat regardless of the weather, but Toshiko and Bilis have on winter clothes that no sane person would wear in June. Owen and Gwen are dressed a bit more casually, but their jackets are still out of place for daytime in summer.

The apparent symmetry of Rift travel also suggests a January dating. Jack and Tosh travel through the Rift and arrive in 1941 on 20th January, and as previous Rift travellers seemed to arrive on the same calendar day they left (*Out of Time*), a case can be made that the two of them similarly depart on 20th January, 2008.

Overall, it has become a convention of modern-day television that time within a series progresses in relation to the time of broadcast - even some non-sci-fi shows (such as *Boston Legal*) adhere to this rule, and in the main *Torchwood* is no exception. Series 1 seems to open a couple of months after *Doomsday*, and episode eight (*TW: They Keep Killing Suzie*) occurs "three months" after the series opener - it's actually been more like two months in the real world, but it's in the ballpark. Viewers innately tend to follow this pattern, and among those who keep track of this sort of thing, a January dating (roughly concurrent with the broadcast of *Captain Jack Harkness* and *End of Days*) seems to cause far less confusion than June.

One possibility is that the "Vote Saxon" poster indicates the Saxon Party, as mentioned by Saxon himself in *The Sound of Drums*. Little is known (beyond a general sense of instability) about British politics between Harriet Jones' downfall and Saxon becoming Prime Minister, and the poster could refer to a secondary election that takes place in January. Similarly, the *Daily Telegraph* headline in *Love & Monsters* that reads "Saxon Leads Polls with 64 percent" is just as likely to refer to the party as Saxon himself.

1112 Dating *TW: End of Days* (*TW* 1.13) - There is an obvious need to link this story to *Doctor Who* Series 3, as Jack here registers the TARDIS' arrival and chases the Ship down at the start of *Utopia*. Related to the dating issues in *TW: Captain Jack Harkness*, it seems far simpler to presume that it's February 2008 when the Doctor and Martha land to refuel in *Utopia*, even though this

Vortex. The trio found themselves in the year 100,000,000,000,000. The Doctor reclaimed the severed hand he'd lost fighting the Sycorax leader, which Jack had in his possession.

2008 - TW: CONSEQUENCES: "Kaleidoscope"[1114] -> Gwen became the interim head of Torchwood Cardiff. Her team secured an alien device, a "Rehabilitator", that could morph anyone seen through it into their "more ideal" self.

2008 (28th-29th February) - THE CONDEMNED[1115] -> The Shinx were an economically successful and generally low-key race from the planet Shinus. They had red, jelly-like skin, but could use DNA patches to look human. The Shinx government opened a covert embassy on Earth for benefit of any Shinx there.

The sixth Doctor and Charley arrived in Manchester, 2008, and found the body of Kord, a Shinx embassy official. With help from DI Patricia Menzies, they thwarted a Shinx operating on Earth as a mobster named Slater. He'd hoped to perfect a device that emitted a peculiar form of radiation – one that dissolved a being's physical form and placed their consciousness within a piece of architecture; a much more economic means of dominating a planet than outright invading it.

(=) 2008 - THE HAUNTING OF THOMAS BREWSTER[1116] -> In an alternate version of 2008 that was unlikely to come to pass, smoke-like beings controlled Earth. They reduced the planet to ash, ruin and charred bodies to gain the energy needed to send information back to the eighteenth century, and conveyed instructions on how to create a time corridor. The young Thomas Brewster, convinced he was seeing visions of his dead mother, cobbled together such a device.

Brewster travelled to this timeline by hijacking the TARDIS, but the fifth Doctor and Nyssa followed in a later version of the Ship. The Doctor preprogrammed the earlier TARDIS to return to 1833, then left with Nyssa and Brewster. Owing to events in 1865, the smoke-beings' history collapsed entirely.

c 2008 - "Warkeeper's Crown"[1117] -> Brigadier Lethbridge-Stewart vanished from a passing out ceremony at Sandhurst, and materialised on an alien world where he quickly met up with the tenth Doctor – and discovered he had been named "warkeeper elect" of a world of dragons and ogres. The original Warkeeper's influence was waning, and so he had brought the Doctor and Brigadier to the Slough of the Disunited Planets. The Brigadier asked for Mike Yates to help him, but the wrong Mike Yates – a xenophobic would-be MP – was summoned. As trolls started to overrun the Keep, the Doctor and Brigadier discovered the clone vats that kept the war supplied with troops. The whole planet was, in fact, an R&D facility for galactic arms dealers, and they shut down the operation.

Back on Earth, Yates tried to use the demons to further his political career, but the Doctor and Brigadier arrived back with an army of cloned Brigadiers and stopped him.

The Eleventh Doctor and Amy Pond Reunite

2008 (March) - THE ELEVENTH HOUR[1118] -> Earth was a Level Five planet with six billion people on it.

The eleventh Doctor returned to Amelia Pond and Leadworth... twelve years after he promised he would. Amy had grown up, and was now working as a girl who delivered kissograms while dressed as a policewoman, a nurse or a nun. The Atraxi followed the Doctor's time trail via a Crack in Time, and threatened to destroy Earth unless Prisoner Zero – a multi-form who had

(plausibly) means they've arrived four months before their first meeting in *Smith and Jones*, and that Jack is gone from Cardiff for that duration of time. The Torchwood website supports this with a missing poster of Jack that's dated to February 2008.
1113 Dating *Utopia* (X3.11) - The precredit sequence of *Utopia* matches up with the end of *TW: End of Days*, and shows Jack reunited with the Doctor – explicitly for the first time since *The Parting of the Ways*. *End of Days* is set shortly after Christmas 2007, so the Doctor and Martha must land a few months in her past.
1114 Dating *TW: Consequences*: "Kaleidoscope" (*TW* novel #15b) - The story occurs shortly after Jack goes missing from Torchwood in *Utopia*, and *TW: End of Days* is cited as being "recent". It's wrongly claimed that Gwen and Rhys are already married (p69).
1115 Dating *The Condemned* (BF #105) - Menzies starts

interrogating the Doctor at "1:05 am on 29th February, 2008"; the Doctor and Charley seem to arrive in Manchester a couple hours or so beforehand. The baddies here try to poison the Doctor with a bit of aspirin – something fandom has presumed as being the pill the third Doctor thinks will kill him in *The Mind of Evil*, but which goes unnamed on screen.
1116 Dating *The Haunting of Thomas Brewster* (BF #107) - The year is given, and it matches the year of this audio's release.
1117 Dating "Warkeeper's Crown" (*DWM* #378-380) - The Brigadier is in his seventies, which (probably) means this is the first decade of the twenty-first century.
1118 Dating *The Eleventh Hour* (X5.1) - It's "two years" before Amy finally starts travelling with the Doctor, which is firmly established as 2010. When the Atraxi

been hiding in Amy's house for twelve years – was handed over to them.

The Doctor met Amy's "sort-of boyfriend" Rory Williams. To help the Atraxi locate Prisoner Zero, the Doctor arranged a video conference with NASA, Jodrell Bank, the Tokyo Space Centre and the Doctor's friend, Sir Patrick Moore. They spread a computer virus that the Doctor prepared; it reset every digital number and clock in the world to read "0". This directed the Atraxi's attention to Leadworth, whereupon they captured Prisoner Zero and withdrew. The Doctor called the Atraxi back to warn them that Earth was under his protection.

The Doctor made a short trip to the moon and back to recalibrate the TARDIS. He intended to return for Amy, but wouldn't reappear for another two years...

The Prisoner Zero crisis was passed off as a computer fault.[1119] The Rift transported 15-year-old Jonah Bevan to an alien locale, where he looked into the heart of a dark star and went mad. After the Rift returned Jonah to Earth, he resided at Jack Harkness' convalescent home for Rift abductees.[1120] Alan and Chrissie Jackson, Maria's parents, split up when Chrissie ran off with her judo instructor.[1121]

In May 2008, Torchwood recovered the Betamax recorder that fell through the Rift in 1982.[1122] Donna's father, Geoff Noble, died.[1123]

Doctor Who Series 3

Martha Jones Joins the TARDIS

2008 (a Monday in June) - SMITH AND JONES[1124] -> The tenth Doctor investigated electrical anomalies at the Royal Hope Hospital in central London, and met medical student Martha Jones. At the same time, the Judoon – intergalactic policemen/enforcers who looked like humanoid rhinos – were looking for a fugitive Plasmavore who was charged with the murder of the Child Princess of Padrivole Regency Nine. The Judoon had no jurisdiction over Earth, and so transported the entire hospital – and the Plasmavore within – to the moon. The Plasmavore disguised her alien nature by drinking human blood, but thanks to the Doctor's intervention, the Judoon registered her as an alien and killed her. The hospital was returned to Earth, and Martha joined the Doctor on his travels.

---

scan Earth, they see the Vashta Nerada, Hath and Ood – three races that we've never seen attack Earth. The image of the Cybermen marching is from *Rise of the Cybermen*, so it technically happened on a parallel Earth, but it presumably stands in for similar events from *Army of Ghosts/Doomsday*.

1119 *The Forgotten Army*

1120 "Seven months and eleven days" before *TW: Adrift*, which means that the Rift likely "abducts" Jonah in March. A continuity glitch exists in that Jack investigates the incident on the very day that Jonah is taken – even though he should be off world with the Doctor and Martha (per *Utopia*). It's possible that Jack used his vortex manipulator to go back and look into Jonah's disappearance after the fact.

1121 Alan claims that Chrissie "took [their] home apart six months" before *SJA: Eye of the Gorgon*.

1122 *TW: The Undertaker's Gift*

1123 The actor who played Geoff Noble in *The Runaway Bride*, Howard Attfield, died in October 2007, during the filming of Series 4. We learn that Donna's father had died when we see her again in *Partners in Crime*. The novel *Beautiful Chaos* cites the day of Geoff's death as 15th May, 2008, but see the dating notes on that story for why this must be called into question.

1124 Dating *Smith and Jones* (X3.1) - In *The Sound of Drums*, Martha says it's "four days" since she met the Doctor. As that story takes place the day after a General Election, and elections are always held on a Thursday in the UK, it would mean that *The Sound of Drums* starts on a Friday and so *Smith and Jones* is set on a Monday.

Smith and Jones is clearly set after the Battle of Canary Wharf (*Doomsday*), and Martha, as a medical student, has upcoming exams. In *The Shakespeare Code*, the Doctor boasts that Martha is going to love reading the last *Harry Potter* book – eagerly anticipated at time of broadcast, but released on 22nd July, 2007, the year before he met her. Perhaps she's mentioned she's not read it, but as *The Shakespeare Code* follows directly on from *Smith and Jones*, there are maybe two opportunities for this off-screen conversation to occur.

In *Utopia*, Martha says the Cardiff earthquake (*Boom Town*, set in 2006) was "a couple of years ago". A small oddity is that the Doctor's John Smith persona (in TV's *Human Nature*) dreams that he's from "2007", not 2008.

1125 Dating *Turn Left* (X4.11) - This is the alternate timeline version of *Smith and Jones*. It's "six months" since the alternative *The Runaway Bride* – despite dialogue saying the Thames "remains closed", it looks fine in the footage we're shown. Funnily enough, as Sarah Jane goes to the moon in this version of events, the story title *Smith and Jones* is still apt.

1126 Dating *The Lazarus Experiment* (X3.6) - The Doctor says that Martha has only been away "twelve hours". This has to mean "twelve hours" after she left in the TARDIS with him at the end of *Smith and Jones*, not when they first met each other in the kidnapped hospital – otherwise, Martha and her family would be made to experience Leo's party and events in *The Lazarus Experiment* on the same evening.

1127 Dating *Made of Steel* (*Quick Reads* #2) - This is the first time Martha has returned to the Royal Hope

(=) **2008 (June) - TURN LEFT**[1125] -> In the timeline where Donna turned right, the Thames was closed following the Racnoss' defeat. Mr Chowdry sacked Donna on the day that the Royal Hope Hospital vanished. Without the Doctor's intervention, those inside the hospital had suffocated, including Martha Jones, Sarah Jane Smith, Luke, Clyde and Maria. Rose met Donna again, and warned her to stay out of London over Christmas.

2008 (a Tuesday in June) - THE LAZARUS EXPERIMENT[1126] -> The tenth Doctor returned Martha home twelve hours after they left. The 76-year-old Richard Lazarus conducted an experiment: hypersonic sound waves created a state of resonance and rewrote his DNA, which rejuvenated him into the body of a young man. Martha's sister Tish worked for Lazarus' public relations department, and the family attended the first demonstration. Lazarus mutated into a cannibalistic monster, but the Doctor killed him in a showdown at Southwark Cathedral.

Saxon had funded Lazarus' experiments; his agents warned Martha's mother to beware the Doctor.

2008 - MADE OF STEEL[1127] -> The tenth Doctor took Martha home, and they learned about a number of recent thefts of advanced electronics. Martha was captured by the culprits – a small group of Cybermen who had survived the Battle of Canary Wharf, and had set up camp in the Millennium Dome. The Cybermen wanted the Doctor to open a gateway into the Void to free their fellows, but instead he opened a time portal and released a Tyrannosaurus – which killed the last of the Cybermen.

? 2008 - THE FAMILY OF BLOOD[1128] -> The tenth Doctor and Martha attended a World War II remembrance service and saw an elderly Tim Latimer.

c 2008 - WISHING WELL[1129] -> The tenth Doctor and Martha arrived in the English countryside near Creighton Mere. The brain of the Vurosis parasite living beneath the well there had become separated from its body, which emerged as a huge tentacled creature. The Vurosis tried to take over the Doctor, but he destroyed it, turning both its body and brain to ash.

c 2008 - "Bus Stop!"[1130] -> The tenth Doctor arrived from the twenty-seventh century via a crude time machine, and tried to prevent mutant assassins from killing the Mayor of London. The Doctor concocted a thermos-full of soup that contained the Mayor's DNA, making the mutants track him by mistake. Martha recalled the Doctor to the twenty-seventh century, and the mutants perished when the Doctor destroyed the time machine.

c 2008 - "Death to the Doctor!"[1131] -> Research base Truro served as a meeting place for would-be conquerors and villains who had been defeated by the Doctor, and wanted to pool their resources against him. The eighth Doctor and Izzy had previously reclaimed the Crystal of Consciousness from Valis, High Arbiter of the Darkness; the fourth Doctor, the first Romana and K9 stopped Bolog and his Reptilios Invasion Fleet from invading Earth; the ninth Doctor and Rose defeated Zargath and his army within five minutes of their landing at the Powell Estate; the sixth Doctor and Frobisher bested Plink; and the first Doctor, Dodo and Steven overcame Questor in the living jungle of Tropicalus. The base's wiring proved faulty, and villains became paranoid and trigger-happy about the Doctor. They eventually killed one another. The tenth Doctor and Martha found all the bodies at Truro moments later, and the Doctor lamented that had he arrived sooner, he might have saved the "poor unfortunates".

2008 - BLINK[1132] -> The tenth Doctor and Martha, on their way to stop a dangerous migration/hatching, met Sally Sparrow for the first time... although she'd met

Hospital. The events of *Smith and Jones* are "recent", and her absence is a source of curiosity to Rachel rather than serious concern – however, it's clearly after *The Lazarus Experiment*, which is Martha's first return to her own time. Martha's exams are "soon".

1128 Dating *The Family of Blood* (X3.9) - The year isn't given, but Latimer's extreme age and the fact the service is conducted by a woman indicates at least a near-present-day setting. It's likely Martha's "present day".

1129 Dating *Wishing Well* (NSA #19) - The year isn't given, although it seems to be around Martha's native time. A 1989 mountaineering accident occurred "nearly twenty years" ago (p53). The book saw release in December 2007.

1130 Dating "Bus Stop!" (*DWM* #385) - The story was published in 2007, and might follow the "year ahead" rule pertaining to Series 3.

1131 Dating "Death to the Doctor!" (*DWM* #390) - None of the villains are said to have time-travel capabilities. Given the flashback of the ninth Doctor and Rose at the Powell Estate – and the third Doctor's defeat of the Mentor in the UNIT era – this presumably happens in accordance with the story's publication in 2007, allowing for the "year ahead" paradigm of Series 3.

1132 Dating *Blink* (X3.10) - A caption says it's a year later in the broadcast version, but doesn't appear in the DVDs (possibly the result of a last-minute change the DVD-authoring house didn't know about). The earlier

them in her past, and was able to give them a dossier with details regarding their becoming trapped in 1969.

Martha phoned her mother on Election Day.[1133] Saxon sent the Torchwood staff to the Himalayas to prevent them from helping Captain Jack and the Doctor.[1134]

Prime Minister Harold Saxon and the Toclafane Invasion

2008 (a Friday and Saturday in June) - THE SOUND OF DRUMS[1135] -> The United Nations had provisions for removing the British Prime Minister from office.

Harold Saxon, secretly the Master, won the election and convened a meeting of his Cabinet in the newly-rebuilt Downing Street. He killed everyone present, then announced to the world that he had made contact with the alien Toclafane and refused to keep it secret as past governments had. As President of America, Arthur Coleman Winters flew to Britain – both to warn Saxon to take his responsibilities carefully and to take control of the public revelation of the Toclafane.

Meanwhile, the British authorities were looking for three "terrorists" – the tenth Doctor, Martha and Jack, who had returned to the twenty-first century from the far, far future. On board the flying aircraft carrier *Valiant* – a UNIT ship – a number of Toclafane materialised and killed President Winters. The Master revealled his plan...

(=) and six billion Toclafane emerged from a space-time rift. They decimated the human population, and the Master took control of Earth. The Master incapacitated Jack and used Professor Lazarus' technology to greatly age the Doctor, capturing both of them.

(=) THE STORY OF MARTHA[1136] -> Martha escaped London, dodging the Unified Containment Forces under the Master's control. As she went, she told people stories of her adventures with the Doctor. Her travels took her through France, Turkey, Munich, Ljubljana and Belgrade. In Japan, she met the Drast: tall extra-terrestrials who had sought control of Earth's economy, but owing to the Master's domination sought to leave via a Relativistic Segue. This would have punched a hole in space-time, eradicating Earth. The Drast operation was exposed, and the Master ended their threat by eradicating Japan.

---

sequences were explicitly set in 2007.

1133 At the end of *42*.

1134 *The Sound of Drums*.

1135 Dating *The Sound of Drums* (X3.12) - The Doctor, Martha and Jack arrive back from the future "four days" after *Smith and Jones*, the following morning when the Toclafane are unveiled. Constitutionally, there wouldn't be an existing Cabinet, as the Master would have had to appoint one before killing its members.

VOTE SAXON: There are apparent inconsistencies concerning the rise and election of Harold Saxon.

The facts are laid out as follows: Harriet Jones is deposed as Prime Minister after *The Christmas Invasion* (set in Christmas 2006). The Abzorbaloff in *Love & Monsters* holds a paper with the headline "Saxon Leads Polls with 64 per cent" (this occurs before *Doomsday*, as Jackie Tyler is still living on "our" Earth). Mr Saxon rises in prominence after ordering the shooting down of the Racnoss ship in *The Runaway Bride* (Christmas 2007, and explicitly after *Doomsday*). In *TW: Captain Jack Harkness* (set sometime after Christmas, as *TW: Out of Time* ends on 24th December), there's a Vote Saxon poster in front of the disued Ritz dance hall. The "contemporary" stories in *Doctor Who* Series 3 (*Smith and Jones, The Lazarus Experiment*, a sequence in *42, The Sound of Drums*) all take place in the same week, with a General Election the day before *The Sound of Drums*. We're told it's eighteen months since *The Christmas*

Invasion in *The Sound of Drums* (so it's June 2008).

The problems are:

1. The Vote Saxon poster outside the Ritz suggests that *TW: Captain Jack Harkness* is set during the General Election campaign that elects Saxon, but the episode itself seems to be set soon after Christmas 2007, not June 2008. We can probably discount this problem pretty easily – the Vote Saxon poster doesn't have to be part of the General Election campaign, it could have appeared quickly in the wake of the events of *The Runaway Bride*, as the start of the momentum that sees Saxon elected six months later.

2. Saxon is ahead in the polls (*Love & Monsters*) before he comes to prominence (after *The Runaway Bride*). The "poll" Saxon leads in late 2007 can't be one for the General Election of June 2008, as British election campaigns only take four to six weeks. This is harder to explain, but it is possible...

Following *The Christmas Invasion*, it's a turbulent time in British politics, as stated in *The Sound of Drums*. What we're told in the series actually would lead to political problems – Harriet Jones' party won a landslide victory, but confidence in Jones evaporates overnight. Under the British constitution, there's no obligation for either Jones to hold a general election, or for there to be a general election if her party deposed her as leader... unless the government lost a vote of no confidence, and in practice no party with a "landslide"

Martha Jones Leaves the TARDIS

2008 (a Saturday in June) - LAST OF THE TIME LORDS[1137] -> The *Valiant* returned from a year in the future, to a point just before the Toclafane appeared. The Harold Saxon Master's devastation of Earth had been temporally reversed. Lucy Saxon shot her husband, but the Master refused to regenerate and died. The Doctor burnt his body on a funeral pyre. Martha declined to rejoin the Doctor on his travels. Jack returned to Torchwood.

One of the Harold Saxon Master's acolytes, Miss Trefusis, retrieved his ring.[1138] Lucy Saxon was tried in secret and confined in Broadfell Prison.[1139]

2008 - "The Widow's Curse"[1140] -> A cadre of female Sycorax searched for the males of their clan: the group of Sycorax defeated by the Doctor at Christmas 2006. They were led by a head warrior, the Haxan Craw, and a chief strategist, the Gilfane Craw. Their rock spaceship landed in the Caribbean, was designated the island of Shadow Cay, and remodelled its exterior on parts of London using Adobe Magma-Sculpt Version 12.2. (Adobe Magma-Sculpt Version 13 could craft interiors as well.) It featured a version of Westminster Abbey in which Hawkmoor's towers included such twentieth-century martyrs as Martin Luther King, Oscar Romero, Lucian Tapiedi and Wang Zhiming.

The Sycorax women were enraged upon learning the fate of their men, and dispatched zombies carrying a virus to London – Earth would become a planet of the undead. The tenth Doctor and Donna terminated the zombies, and destroyed both the Sycorax and their spaceship.

Thirty-five years after Jo worked for UNIT, she and her husband Cliff were based halfway up the Rio Negro at the Institute of Mycology. Cliff was now an MBE, a Nobel Prize winner and a veteran eco-warrior; Jo served as his manager. The two of them visited London for the first time in ages so Cliff – his slogan being "Make the Future Yourselves" – could appear on the chat-show circuit, attend the UN's World Future Conference and harangue people there about the imminent collapse of the Amazon forest.[1141]

majority could lose such a vote. *The Christmas Invasion* implies that Jones resigns or is deposed soon after. Her party won an election largely because of her, and holds a massive Commons majority, but she's no longer in charge. Whoever took part is at least third choice to lead the party (after the former Prime Minister who was assassinated by the Slitheen in *Aliens of London*, and Jones), and would almost certainly start out as a lame duck. We should probably note that this instability, exploited by the Master in Series 3, is actually instigated by the Doctor when he deposes Harriet Jones in *The Christmas Invasion*.

In this situation, people would be looking for alternative leaders, and papers would be running polls. Saxon becomes the Minister of Defence at some point in 2007, the www.votesaxon.co.uk website has him as a published novelist (the novel is called *Kiss Me, Kill Me*) and he's married to the daughter of a Lord – so he's clearly a public figure before *The Runaway Bride*. The Racnoss attack, and his handling of it, must be the last piece that makes his succession inevitable.

So the poll in *Love & Monsters* is almost certainly speculative, and perhaps even the first time most people had heard of Mr Saxon. It's also very probably been placed there by Saxon himself.

1136 Dating *The Story of Martha* (NSA #28a) - The book contains four of the many stories ("The Weeping", "Breathing Space", "The Frozen Wastes" and "Star-Crossed") that Martha relates in her travels across the globe, with linking material that details, among other things, her involvement in thwarting the Drast.

1137 Dating *Last of the Time Lords* (X3.13) - Time is reversed to 08:02, just before the Toclafane appeared in great numbers. This means Saxon is still elected and kills his Cabinet and (as is explicitly stated) President Winters is still assassinated. The last detail is something of a glitch, as all of the Toclafane's actions (Winters' death included) should have been temporally erased. Another problem is that the Doctor, Martha and Jack should still be known as "public enemies number one, two and three" despite the historical reversal (as is the case in *The Sound of Drums*), yet they're later seen casually chatting in public with no fear of arrest.

Also at story's end, the "accident and emergency" board behind Thomas Milligan says it's October. This raises the possibility that the Doctor and Martha stay in London for a few months after the Master's defeat, even if nothing else supports or denies the notion.

1138 *Last of the Time Lords, The End of Time.*

1139 *The End of Time*

1140 Dating "The Widow's Curse" (*DWM* #395-398) - The female Sycorax have been trying to learn what became of their men (*The Christmas Invasion*) for "two years".

1141 *The Doll of Death.* Jo says in the framing material that it's "thirty-five years on" from the flashback story, which is set between Seasons 8 and 9 (broadcast in 1971 and 1972). The audio was released on October 2008, either suggesting that writer Marc Platt favours the UNIT stories taking place a bit in the future, or just that Jo is rounding a little. Mention is made in *The Magician's Oath* (the framing sequence of which occurs a week after this story) of "Sir Alistair" (as Lethbridge-Stewart is called in *The Poison Sky*), also suggesting that it's contemporary.

While Cliff did so, Mike Yates took Jo out to dinner. Jo had found Diamond Jack's playing card in her uncle's attic a few weeks prior to this; her stolen memories had returned, and she gave the card to Mike – which he took to a UNIT office. At this time, Mike was single.[1142]

By now, one of the old UNIT HQs had been turned into an embassy for a new east-European state. A window that the Doctor blew out at least three times was barred over, and had CC cameras.[1143] UNIT currently had offices at Tower Bridge.[1144]

c 2008 - TIME REAVER[1145] **->** Every major galaxy had banned time reavers: weapons that prolonged personal time, making their targets experience years or decades in few minutes. The planet Vacintia was dying as its sun enlarged, and the communal people there built time reaver prototypes, intending to shoot themselves as they watched a glorious sunrise one last time. A Vacintian, Cora, misguidedly took the prototypes to Calibris, a spaceport world (effectively a planet-sized King's Cross) that serviced sixty million beings a day.

The tenth Doctor and Donna stopped at Calibris to acquire fluid links and other TARDIS parts. To keep the reavers out of the tentacles of an octopoid gangster, Gully, the Doctor discharged the weapons into himself – and spent the equivalent of seven centuries in his own head, as only ten minutes passed. Cora fired a last time reaver at Gully as he escaped aboard a burning spaceship...

... he was frozen there for four months of his personal time, and badly burned. Finally freed, he went to Earth and pursued a scheme involving parasitic Rempaths.[1146]

Torchwood Series 2 (2008-2009)[1147]

2008 - TW: KISS KISS, BANG BANG -> Jack returned to Torchwood and was approached by John Hart – a former Time Agent and Jack's ex-lover, with whom Jack had been trapped in a time loop for five years. Hart conned Torchwood into retrieving what he believed was an Arcadian diamond, but was actually an explosive device planted to kill him – an act of vengeance from one of Hart's murder victims. Torchwood contained the explosion, and Hart left town.

1142 Mike shows up to have dinner with Jo at the end of *The Doll of Death*; the framing sequence of *The Magician's Oath* opens a week afterwards.

1143 *The Doll of Death*

1144 *The Magician's Oath*, also mentioned in *The Sontaran Stratagem*.

1145 Dating *Time Reaver* (BF 10th Doc #1.2) - Gully cannot time travel, next appears in *In the Blood* [2009].

1146 *Time Reaver*

1147 Dating *Torchwood* Series 2 – While it's customary in this phase of *Doctor Who* to place stories a year ahead of broadcast, this would seem to be an exception. The new season opens with Jack returning to his Torchwood team after *Last of the Time Lords*; notably, he seems to go home under his own power (it's questionable if the Doctor even could give Jack a lift in the TARDIS if he wanted, after the way the Ship reacted in *Utopia*), so no time displacement is involved, and Series 2 presumably opens in the space of time it takes Jack to mop up any lingering details concerning the Master's tenure as prime minister and return to Cardiff. The mood at Torchwood is such that Jack has been absent for some months at least, but nothing suggests that he's been away anything as long as a year (everyone is still actively pining for Jack, in fact), which supports the notion that the modern-day component of *Utopia* occurs a few months before the Doctor and Martha first meet in *Smith and Jones*.

Torchwood script editor Gary Russell confirms that timeline for Series 2 was calibrated to begin in 2008 and end the following year – that is supported in that save for the last two episodes (*TW: Fragments* and *TW: Exit Wounds*), the dating clues throughout Series 2 all concur with a dating of 2008. See the individual entries for more.

1148 Dating *TW: "The Legacy of Torchwood One!"* (*TWM #1*) - The story saw release between *TW: Kiss Kiss, Bang Bang* and *TW: Sleeper*.

1149 Dating *TW: To the Last Man* (*TW 2.3*) - "Friday the 20th" is circled on Tosh's calendar, and is also seen on Jack's calendar. In 2008, such a day only occurred in June – which neatly fits with *Last of the Time Lords* occurring in the same month, and Jack returning to the Hub shortly afterwards. Tommy, who was frozen in 1918, is said to have been at the Hub for "ninety years". Tosh says that she's known Tommy for "four years", which is consistent with her having been a member of Torchwood for "three years" in *TW: Greeks Bearing Gifts*, and "five years" in *TW: Fragments*. Tommy has been revived on an annual basis but doesn't know Gwen, so less than a year has passed since *TW: Everything Changes*.

1150 Dating *TW: Something in the Water* (*TW novel #4*) - Tosh mentions (p31) the Rift's "recent time shift with 1918" (*TW: To the Last Man*), but Rhys doesn't yet know (p30) Torchwood's true purpose (*TW: Meat*). *The Time Traveller's Almanac* says that Strepto is one of the twenty-seven planets the Daleks abducted to build their reality bomb (*The Stolen Earth*).

1151 Dating *TW: Trace Memory* (*TW novel #5*) - The year is given (p23), and it's twice said that it's "fifty-five years" after 1953. It's a Sunday (p13, p232).

1152 It's possible that the "star whale" is related to the "space whale" seen in *The Beast Below*.

1153 Dating *TW: Everyone Says Hello* (*TW audiobook #2*), *TW: In the Shadows* (*TW audiobook #3*), *TW:* "Rift

2008 - TW: "The Legacy of Torchwood One!"[1148] -> Torchwood eliminated the fear-inducing Chimera, but not before it killed its creator, Rupert Howarth.

2008 - TW: SLEEPER -> Torchwood discovered that aliens designated Cell 114 – whose *modus operandi* was to infiltrate planets with intelligence-gathering sleeper agents bearing false memories – had deployed a cell of such agents on Earth. The agents blew up a telecommunications centre and killed the Cardiff emergency city coordinator, but Torchwood prevented them from detonating ten nuclear warheads that the military had secured in a disused coal mine.

2008 (Friday, 20th June) - TW: TO THE LAST MAN[1149] -> St Teilo's Hospital in Cardiff was slated for demolition, which caused the Rift to fluctuate and make time overlap with the hospital as it stood in 1918. Torchwood saved both time zones by reviving Thomas Reginald Brockless from stasis, then sending him back through the Rift to 1918 with a Rift Manipulator that sealed the Rift behind him.

2008 - TW: SOMETHING IN THE WATER[1150] -> One of the remaining inhabitants of the vanished planet Strepto – having biological abilities that resembled water hags, legendary witch monsters – travelled to Earth. Torchwood killed the water hag and her offspring, but not before the hag murdered an old associate of Jack Harkness, Professor Leonard Morgan.

2008 (Sunday) - TW: TRACE MEMORY[1151] -> The remains of the Vondraxian Orb that exploded in 1953 were stored in the Hub, and had discretely irradiated Captain Jack's team. This tethered the time-jumping Michael Bellini to their personal histories, causing him to appear at least once in their lifetimes. Bellini finally arrived at Torchwood Three in 2008, and made one last jump back to 1967 – where he was fated to die.

2008 - TW: MEAT -> A band of criminals captured a baby star whale that flew through the Rift, and profited by selling big chunks of it as raw meat for pies, burgers, pasties, etc. Torchwood shut down the operation, but the star whale died.[1152]

2008 - TW: EVERYONE SAYS HELLO[1153] -> A spaceship came through the Rift and released a "telesensual field" – part of a nonviolent first contact protocol designed to solicit information. The Cardiff public became overly eager to say hello and to divulge their personal details, and the city descended into chaos as people ignored their responsibilities. Torchwood shut down the field by broadcasting gibberish through Jack's cell phone.

2008 (Friday) - TW: IN THE SHADOWS[1153] -> Captain Jack's crew stopped Patrick Jefferson's serial-killing spree, and confiscated his huon-particle-laced matchbox. Unable to formally bring Jefferson to justice, Torchwood planted spare bodies in his cellar and alerted the authorities.

2008 - TW: "Rift War"[1153] -> The Sanctified once had a powerful empire, but were now farmers of dinosaurs. One of their number, Vox, manipulated his people into thinking that Torchwood would attack by weaponising the Rift, prompting a pre-emptive strike. Torchwood repelled the Sanctified's shock troops – the bestial Harrowkind – who materialised in Cardiff to neutralise the Hub.

Soon after, Captain Jack's crew dealt with a Rift bubble that developed in Cardiff Castle, and cared for an enormous Zansi baby during the six weeks it took the child to mature. Torchwood also rounded up a pack of Sanctified-owned dinosaurs in Millennium Stadium, and sent them back through the Rift. They also investigated a stone circle that focused Rift energy every eighty years, and briefly swapped Ianto and Tosh with Gerald Carter and Harriet Derbyshire in 1918.

2008 - TW: "Shrouded"[1153] -> John Hart and Rhys arrived from the future to warn Ianto that a time-traveller named Beatrice, a.k.a. Mairwyn, would try to seduce him – and that his surrendering to her advances could potentially change history. Mairwyn showed Ianto a future in which he, Owen and Tosh died, and the Hub was destroyed. She proposed that they steal the Shroud – a device from Torchwood One assigned to Ianto's care – and escape together, but Ianto killed Mairwyn, gave a precognitive device in her possession to the future-Hart and Retconned his knowledge of events to come.

War" (*TWM* #4-13), *TW*: "Shrouded" (*TWM* #21-22) - In all of these stories, Rhys knows Torchwood's true purpose (so, it's after *TW: Meat*), but Owen hasn't "died" (so, it's before *TW: Reset*). *Everyone Says Hello* (cited on its blurb as occurring in Series 2) was released on 4th February, 2008, between the broadcasts of *TW: Meat* and *TW: Adam*, and nestles between the two stories easily enough. One oddity is that Gwen and Rhys seem to

spend six weeks in "Rift War" caring for a giant Zansi infant; fortunately, the continuity in this phase of Series 2 is pliable enough that such a duration of time might well elapse between the TV episodes.

Ianto's statements establish that *In the Shadows* happens on a Friday; Mariwyn establishes that "Shrouded" occurs two days before a "Wednesday", but the story then continues an unspecified number of days later.

2008 - TW: ADAM[1154] -> An entity that was adrift in the Rift surfaced in Cardiff, and manifested by engraining itself into the minds of Jack's Torchwood agents. They believed the interloper was a fellow Torchwood agent, Adam Smith, and retroactively thought they had all worked together for three years. Jack uncovered the deception and eradicated Adam by removing everyone's memories of the past two days. Jack himself had to go a step further, and permanently lost the last good memory he had of his father.

2008 - TW: "Rift War"[1155] -> The Harrowkind renewed their assault on Torchwood, and sped through a Cardiff retail centre. The last Omnicron trapped the Harrowkind within its tesseract as data files, but was then destroyed by Vox. Soon afterwards, Vox focused enough Rift energy through the Hub's Rift Manipulator to endow himself with fantastical abilities. Torchwood curtailed the energy feeding Vox, leaving him at the mercy of some golems – antibodies generated by the Rift to deal with such threats.

Torchwood investigated a mysterious perception filter that was preventing Rhys from making deliveries, and confronted an alien "body jacker" that had been leaping from host to host and committing crimes. Captain Jack's team obliterated the body jacker's core form, but it distributed pieces of its consciousness within their minds.[1156]

2008 (August) - THE TWILIGHT STREETS[1157] -> Abaddon's death had tipped the balance of power toward the Dark and its allies. Bilis Manger aided Torchwood in trapping the Dark in a containment box, and in releasing the Light into the Rift to keep Abaddon's nemesis, Pwccm, forever imprisoned. Manger departed to intern Abaddon's ashes outside Britain. During this conflict, earthquakes and fires destroyed the Tretarri housing district.

Owen Harper's First Death

2008 - TW: RESET / DEAD MAN WALKING[1158] -> Now working for UNIT, Martha Jones helped Torchwood uncover a conspiracy regarding the Pharm: a partnership between the government and a consortium of pharmaceutical companies. Dr Aaron Copley sought to reset the human body back to its "factory settings" – a development that could potentially cure all human ailment – using "the mayfly", an alien insect species. As Copley's experiments killed his test subjects, Torchwood ended the operation. An enraged Copley killed Owen, and was shot dead by Jack.

1154 Dating *TW: Adam* (*TW* 2.5) - Torchwood believes that Adam has been working alongside them for "three years", and his doctored personnel file says he was recruited on "07/05/05".

1155 Dating *TW: "Rift War"* (*TWM* #4-13) - Owen hasn't yet kicked the bucket, but "three weeks straight" have passed since Torchwood had any engagement with the Sanctified.

1156 *TW: Army of One.* It's a familiar song by this point, but Rhys knows about Torchwood, yet there's no evidence that Owen is a walking cadaver, so these events happen between *TW: Meat* and *TW: Reset*. Tosh says that *Jaws* (1975) is thirty years old.

1157 Dating *TW: The Twilight Streets* (*TW* novel #6) - Once again, placement is determined because Rhys knows about Torchwood but Owen still isn't dead yet. Moreover, it's "twenty-two months, eight days and about nine hours" (p76) since Jack last met Margaret Slitheen's secretary Idris Hopper – an encounter that happened "a month" (p81) after *Boom Town*, in October 2006. So, it's now August 2008. The year is loosely confirmed in that it's "nearly one hundred thirty years" after Queen Victoria established Torchwood (p103).

1158 Dating *TW: Reset* and *TW: Dead Man Walking* (*TW* 2.6-2.7) - A glitch exists in that Owen says that one of Copley's victims, Meredith Roberts, is 45, but both the man's driver's license and Tosh's computer search says he was born "11-01-1962". It's impossible to think that this story occurs prior to 11th January, and yet that would only amount to it being 2007.

1159 Dating *TW: A Day in the Death* (*TW* 2.8) - Three days have passed since the previous episode.

1160 "Two years" before *TW: The Men Who Sold the World*.

1161 Dating *SJA: Invasion of the Bane* (*SJA* 1.1) - It's at least "eighteen months" since *School Reunion*, as that's how long Sarah has had her new K9. Maria's dad says that she's going to "start school next week", presumably in September (as with the 2010 school year starting on 6th September in *SJA: The Nightmare Man*). Maria's clock says "11 1", but she starts a new school "next week" and it's light at 6 pm, so we can only assume it's showing the wrong date, possibly because it was unplugged during the move.

A small oddity is that Sarah says in *SJA: Sky* that Luke was "born" as a 13 year old, yet he's "14" just a week afterwards in *SJA: Revenge of the Slitheen*. It's possible, however, that she initially designated him as 13, then shortly thereafter decided he was "14" (and had Mr Smith alter Luke's documents accordingly) to accommodate his entering school at a slightly higher level.

1162 *SJA: Whatever Happened to Sarah Jane?*

1163 Dating "A Perfect World" (BF #113b) - The year is specified, and coincides with the story's release in October 2008.

1164 Dating *SJA: Revenge of the Slitheen* (*SJA* 1.2) - The Slitheen refer to the events of *Smith and Jones*. It's the start of a school year, so the story begins on a Monday and continues onto Tuesday.

Jack retrieved the second Resurrection Gauntlet from St Mary's Church, and used it to revive Owen for a few moments – or so he thought. Unexpectedly, Owen remained active as an animated cadaver even after the Gauntlet's destruction. As with events in 1479, Owen's return to life enabled a personification of Death to stalk Cardiff. Death attempted to murder thirteen people – the number required to secure its foothold on Earth – but had only killed twelve when Owen grappled with Death and banished it.

2008 - TW: A DAY IN THE DEATH[1159] -> Henry John Parker died, and Owen acquired from him an extra-terrestrial device – a reply sent by unknown parties to the NASA space messages of the 70s. Martha returned to UNIT.

The planet Ytraxor was freezing as its sun grew dim, and approaching glaciers forced the Ytraxorians to fight for what land remained. Ytraxorian scientists developed a Reality Gun that could displace objects in space and time – useless as a means of escape, but an effective weapon. The Ytraxorians destroyed themselves, but one of them, and his Reality Gun, were hurled through space and materialised in a deep-fat fryer in Cardiff. Captain Jack, Gwen and Ianto confiscated the dead alien's Reality Gun.[1160]

Sarah Jane Smith Adopts Luke Smith, Meets Maria Jackson

2008 (last week of August) - SJA: INVASION OF THE BANE[1161] -> Thirteen-year-old Maria Jackson moved to a new house in Ealing, West London, with her father Alan. That night, she saw her neighbour, Sarah Jane Smith, talking to an alien. Sarah aided this lost being – a Star Poet from Arcateen 5 – in returning home, and Maria teamed up with her to uncover the secret behind the popular new addictive drink Bubble Shock. It was a creation of the cephalopod-like Bane – Bubble Shock was laced with a secretion of the Bane Mother, and could take control of anyone who drank it. Two percent of the population carried innate resistance to Bubble Shock, and so the Bane had created an Archetype: a teenage human boy made from the data scans of the ten thousand people who had visited the Bubble Shock factory. The Bane intended that the Archetype would enable them to refine Bubble Shock and eliminate the 2% deviation.

The Bane assumed mental control of the Bubble Shock drinkers – legions of people took to the streets with bottles of Bubble Shock, intoning "Drink it, drink it..." Sarah, Maria and the Archetype thwarted the Bane overseer, Mrs Wormwood, and destroyed the main Bubble Shock factory. Bubble Shock was with-

drawn, and a government cover story claimed that chemicals released from the Bubble Shock plant had caused a mass hysteria.

Sarah named the Archetype "Luke Smith" and adopted him as her son. The two of them resided at 13 Bannerman Road.

> (=) In the history where Sarah Jane died instead of Andrea Yates, the Trickster prevented the Bane from visiting Earth.[1162]

Thomas Brewster Leaves the TARDIS

2008 - "A Perfect World"[1163] -> While travelling in the TARDIS solo, Thomas Brewster stopped in London, 2008, and met a young woman named Connie Winter. She wished for a more perfect world – and as Brewster hadn't materialised the TARDIS properly, a quantum fissure formed that enabled two existential maintenance workers, "Phil" and "Trev", to hear their conversation.

> (=) After Brewster departed in the Ship, Phil and Trev manipulated Connie's timeline to avert her biggest mistakes, and curtailed a large number of political scandals and disasters. The fifth Doctor and Nyssa – having reunited with Brewster – learned how his actions had altered history. Phil and Trev were persuaded to undo their alterations.

Brewster left the TARDIS to start a relationship with the original Connie. The Doctor gave Brewster ownership of his house on Baker Street, which hadn't been occupied in one hundred forty-one years, thinking that the proceeds from its sale would keep him afloat for a time.

The Sarah Jane Adventures Series 1

Clyde Langer Joins Sarah Jane's Team

2008 (a Monday and Tuesday in September) - SJA: REVENGE OF THE SLITHEEN[1164] -> Maria and Luke started at Park Vale school, and made a new friend, Clyde Langer. With Sarah Jane, they discovered that a group of Slitheen had murdered some of the fatter teachers and the school headmaster. The Slitheen planned to harvest all energy from Earth and its sun with equipment housed in the Coldfire Technology Blocks, then sell the energy to fund the retaking of their homeworld, Raxacoricofallapatorius, with a battlefleet. The Slitheen activated their equipment, and the sun temporarily turned a cold blue. Discovering the aliens' vulnerability to vinegar, Sarah Jane and her friends destroyed the machine, ending the scheme.

UNIT cleaned up the Slitheen operation, and Sarah

had Mr Smith release a cover story that the sun's outage resulted from a temporary reversal of the Earth's magnetic poles.

> (=) The Trickster stopped the Slitheen from going to Earth.[1165]

2008 - SJA: EYE OF THE GORGON[1166] -> Sarah Jane and her friends investigated Lavender Lawns, a nursing home where apparitions have been reported. One of the residents, Bea Nelson-Stanley, gave Luke the prized talisman that could link the world of the ancient Gorgon with Earth. The nuns protecting the remaining Gorgon (who was in the body of an Abbess) acquired the talisman, and opened a portal so the other Gorgon could dominate humanity. The Abbess-Gorgon tried to take Sarah Jane as its new host, but Maria disrupted the transfer, turning the Abbess to stone. The portal was deactivated.

Sarah Jane's current aliases included Bunty Mansfield, Victoria Williams and Felicity Barnes. The Viszern Royal Fleet, composed of six hundred ships, passed through Earth's solar system and created a magnificent stellar light show.

Sarah Jane defeated the Patriarchs of the Tin Vagabond.[1167]

> (=) The Trickster stopped the Gorgon from invading Earth, and "turned away" the Patriarchs.[1168]

2008 (a Tuesday) - SJA: WARRIORS OF KUDLAK[1169] -> Twenty-four children had vanished at various Combat 3000 locations, which offered realistic laser tag. Sarah Jane and her friends learned that the disap-

pearances all coincided with freak storms. At the London Combat 3000 site, they saw Kudlak – a member of the insectoid Uvodni race who was trying to recruit warriors to fight his enemies, the Malakh. Kudlak's battle computer, Mistress, had deliberately withheld a message that the war had ended ten years before, because she had no purpose except war. Kudlak destroyed Mistress and released his prisoners.

> (=) The Trickster thwarted Kudlak.[1170]

2008 (a Friday and Saturday) - TW: SOMETHING BORROWED[1171] -> A Nostravite – a shapeshifting species in which the male carries fertilised eggs in his mouth – bit Gwen, who became pregnant with Nostravite offspring during her wedding to Rhys Williams. Torchwood killed the Nostravite mother and removed her young from Gwen, then dosed the wedding guests with Level 6 Retcon in their champagne.

2008 (September) - TW: SKYPOINT[1172] -> The master criminal Besnik Lucca built SkyPoint – an apartment high-rise in Cardiff – as his personal fortress. A thought-entity from beyond the grave had hitched a ride with a SkyPoint resident, a young girl named Alison Lloyd, when she was resuscitated after being clinically dead. The thought-creature stayed corporeal by consuming some of the SkyPoint residents, but Owen injected the creature with a syringe of his dead blood, killing it. Torchwood gave the authorities enough evidence to put Lucca away for fifty years.

2008 - TW: CORPSE DAY[1173] -> A terribly excited PC Andy Davidson partnered with Owen Harper for Corpse Day: an annual tradition when Torchwood helped the police clear unsolved cases. Owen and Andy traced a number of kidnapped girls to the home of a man named Glynn,

---

1165 *SJA: Whatever Happened to Sarah Jane?*
1166 Dating *SJA: Eye of the Gorgon* (SJA 1.3) - No specific dates are given. In *The Mind Robber*, the Doctor was convinced that Medusa could not exist. Sarah also presents herself as "Victoria Beckham" in *SJA: The Temptation of Sarah Jane Smith*.
1167 Sarah tells the Trickster, in *SJA: Whatever Happened to Sarah Jane?*, "Never mind the Bane, what about the Slitheen? And the Gorgons? And the Patriarchs of the Tin Vagabond? I stopped them all from taking over the Earth." There's some leeway as to when she fought the Patriarchs, and it's not even clear as to whether she did so with the teenagers or on her own, but it seems reasonable to presume that she's naming her recent adversaries in order. The Doctor referred to the Church of the Tin Vagabond as worshippers of the Beast in *The Satan Pit*. Sarah seems to have made a return to fighting satanists, as she did in *K9 and Company: A Girl's Best*

Friend and also the *K9 Annual*.
1168 *SJA: Whatever Happened to Sarah Jane?*. If this means that the Trickster somehow averted the Gorgon from coming to Earth in the first place (which isn't said), then the "Andrea Yates" timeline must be devoid of the Medusa mythos.
1169 Dating *SJA: Warriors of Kudlak* (SJA 1.4) - It's a Tuesday, but children aren't at school, so it may be half term. No human astronaut has set foot on Mars by this time, which directly contradicts *The Ambassadors of Death* and *The Dying Days*.
1170 *SJA: Whatever Happened to Sarah Jane?*
1171 Dating *TW: Something Borrowed* (TW 2.9) - The story opens on a Friday night at Gwen's bachelorette party, and the wedding occurs the next day. Given everyone's dress and the ease with which they can go outdoors, it's a warm month.

who years ago had been gifted with an infant Weevil by the Committee. Now grown, the Weevil – named Sonny – had eaten the abductees he didn't like and mated with three others. Owen assisted one of them, Jan, with the birth of her half-Weevil child. Sonny killed Glynn for his years of abuse, and Owen and Andy opted to leave the family in peace.

c 2008 - TW: THE OFFICE OF NEVER WAS[1174] -> The Committee offered Oliver Milne, the owner of Milne Futures, a brain-booster to enhance his employees' performance. Ianto Jones discovered the booster perpetrated long-term harm, so dosed Milne's employees with Retcon in a bid to save them. Being too far gone, the employees savaged one another. To clear his conscience, Ianto wiped his memory with Retcon.

2008 - TW: FROM OUT OF THE RAIN[1175] -> The Electro Cinema in Cardiff reopened as a museum, and an examination of old film stocks in its basement released the Night Travellers contained within. Two Night Travellers stole life essences from half a dozen people, then released the remainder of their contingent from the film. Jack prevented the Travellers from taking more victims by recording their images onto a film reel and exposing it to sunlight, seemingly eradicating them. It was possible that the Travellers had survived on a film reel at a flea market.

2008 (October) - "Hotel Historia"[1176] -> The supercriminal Majenta Pryce and her assistant Fanson founded the Hotel Historia – a chain that became the toast of the Seven Galaxies, offering guests the opportunity to time travel to different points in history. The chain fell into decline as patrons shied away from time travel in the aftermath of the Last Great Time War, but Majenta and Fanson operated one of the remaining Hotel Historias on Earth.

Patrons could experience wildlife in the Jurassic, converse with great wits in Elizabethan England, etc. Meals served at the Historia included vintage Vesuvian vino and woolly mammoth steaks.

The tenth Doctor travelled down one of the Historia's time corridors from 4039, and sent the hotel's main time-travel device – the Chronexus 3000 – back there to thwart the Graxnix. Cosmic bailiffs arrested Majenta, took her to the future and imprisoned her at the Thinktwice orbital penitentiary.

Fansom's own teleport beam to Thinktwice was diverted, and he came into the service of the Skith leader.[1177]

2008 (24th October) - BRAVE NEW TOWN[1178] -> Various rivers in Uzbekistan had been depleted by the continual use of water for cotton fields, cloth, swimming pools and more. The Aral Sea dried up, and the faux English village of Thorington – formerly on an island – had rejoined the mainland. A Nestene unit with the mother consciousness for the Thorington Autons exerted influence over them, turning them murderous. The eighth Doctor and Lucie cut off the signal from the mother-unit and left as the Autons, now aware of their origins, faced the decision of whether to stay in Thorington or go elsewhere.

2008 (late October to early November) - TW: ADRIFT[1179] -> Gwen discovered that the Rift had claimed dozens if not hundreds of Cardiff residents in the last ten years, and learned about the shelter that Jack was operating for such persons.

2008 (1st November) - TW: PACK ANIMALS[1180] -> A young man named Gareth Portland found an alien terraforming device that enabled him to manifest creatures and effects rendered in *MonstaQuest*, a card game he'd created.

1172 Dating *TW: SkyPoint* (*TW* novel #8) - Gwen and Rhys have been married "a little over two weeks now" (p1, p13), and have just returned from their honeymoon of "ten days in Cuba" (p1). More time than that seems to pass between *TW: Something Borrowed* and *TW: From Out of the Rain*, so *SkyPoint* appears to fall between the two. The month is September (p85).
1173 Dating *TW: Corpse Day* (BF *TW* #15) - It amuses Jack to assign Owen to Corpse Day, as Owen is himself a walking corpse (so it's after *TW: A Day in the Death*).
1174 Dating *TW: The Office of Never Was* (BF *TW* #17) - "A year" before the story's main events.
1175 Dating *TW: From Out of the Rain* (*TW* 2.10) - Enough time has passed since *TW: Something Borrowed* that Gwen has gone on her honeymoon and returned. Everyone is now wearing jackets, suggesting that it's a bit later in the year.

1176 Dating "Hotel Historia" (*DWM* #394) - The month and year are given.
1177 "The Crimson Hand"
1178 Dating *Brave New Town* (BF BBC7 #2.3) - The exact date is given.
1179 Dating *TW: Adrift* (*TW* 2.11) - Further establishing that it's 2008, Rift-abductee Jonah Bevan was born 15th February, 1993, and is now 15. Also, a flier says that the first meeting of Searchlight – a missing persons support group – is slated for Monday the 27th; in 2008, such a day only occurred in October. The story's epilogue takes place one week later, presumably in early November. Entertainingly, a handwritten note says that another abductee, Bahri Agon, was born on the fictional date of "30/2/83".
1180 Dating *TW: Pack Animals* (*TW* novel #7) - The back cover mentions "Halloween is a day of fun and frights,"

The telepathic device enhanced Gareth's emotions, causing him to hurt or murder those he believed had slighted him, and then to transform Millennium Stadium into a replica of an alien locale. Jack shot Gareth dead, and the monsters he created fell into a chasm that opened up inside the Stadium.

2008 (Tuesday) - TW: "Jetsam"[1181] **->** Torchwood neutralised a battlewagon used by an extra-terrestrial race to settle turf wars and border disputes.

A Verron soothsayer gave Sarah Jane a warp star – a warpfold conjugation trapped in a carbonised shell; it was "an explosion waiting to happen". The soothsayer advised that she use it at "the end of days".[1182]

2008 - SJA: WHATEVER HAPPENED TO SARAH JANE?[1183] **->** By now, the book *UNIT: Fighting for Humankind* by Sarah Jane Smith had been published.

Sarah Jane told her friends that Meteor K67 was approaching Earth through a radar blind spot, but that Mr Smith would emit a magnetic pulse to deflect it the next day. A Verron soothsayer had given Sarah Jane a small box with instructions that she pass it along to the person she trusted most, and so she gave it to Maria. That night, a mysterious hooded figure, the Trickster, approached Sarah Jane's house.

(=) The box protected Maria's memories when the Trickster altered history in 1964. Maria was the only person who remembered Sarah Jane, and found that a woman called Andrea Yates was living in Sarah's house. Maria remembered the oncoming meteor, but without Mr Smith, there was no way to deflect it. The Trickster thrived on chaos, which the meteor strike would certainly cause. At the local library, Maria learned that a 13-year-old Sarah Jane had drowned after falling from a pier... as seen by her friend, Andrea Yates. A Graske working for the Trickster took the med-

and yet the action occurs on a "freezing Saturday... in November" (p57) that falls after a bit of Halloween festivities (p51). In 2008, the day after Halloween was a Saturday, so the story presumably takes place on 1st November. Regrettably, the book is at odds with the continuity of Series 2 – Owen is already dead (p75, so it's after *TW: A Day in the Death*), and Gwen and Rhys are still making preparations for their wedding (so it's before *TW: Something Borrowed*), but a placement anywhere in November (hard to avoid, as the month is expressly stated) would have *Pack Animals* occurring after or roughly concurrent with *TW: Adrift*, which manifestly occurs after Gwen and Rhys' nuptials. To judge from the prologue, Gareth murders his first victim on the Saturday before Halloween.
1181 Dating *TW: "Jetsam"* (*TWM* #3) - The comic saw release between *TW: Adrift* and *TW: Fragments*. It's specified as being "a wet Tuesday morning".
1182 "The other week" according to *SJA: Whatever Happened to Sarah Jane Smith?* Sarah and Captain Jack use the warp star against the Daleks in *Journey's End*, and it's presumably still aboard the Crucible when it's destroyed.
1183 Dating *SJA: Whatever Happened to Sarah Jane?* (*SJA* 1.5) - Andrea says she has been dead "forty years" and she's the same age as Sarah Jane, who was born in 1951. It's later established that Andrea died in 1964, so it was actually forty-four years earlier. It's still 2008, as Clyde says in *SJA: The Temptation of Sarah Jane Smith*, set in 2009, that they first fought the Trickster "last year". The Trickster makes his move on the Doctor in *Turn Left*.
1184 Dating *SJA: The Glittering Storm* and *SJA: The Thirteenth Stone* (*SJA* audiobooks #1-2) - The stories take place during *The Sarah Jane Adventures* Series 1,

and saw release simultaneous to *Whatever Happened to Sarah Jane?* episode two.
1185 Dating *SJA: The Lost Boy* (*SJA* 1.6) - It's straight after *SJA: Whatever Happened to Sarah Jane?*. The news report about "Ashley Stafford" (i.e. Luke) says that his family hasn't seen him in "five months", which is presumably how long has passed since *SJA: Invasion of the Bane*. If that were literally true, however, *The Lost Boy* would have to take place at the absolute end of 2008, or possibly even in the early part of 2009 (not impossible, but the seasonal weather seems all wrong for that). One possibility is that Sarah and her friends, upon hearing the report, presume that "Ashley" was taken by the Bane and experimented upon for some weeks prior to Luke's "activation" in *Invasion of the Bane*. Supporting this idea, everything that's happened to Sarah and her friends since is said to have happened in the "past few months". Maria, who was 13 in *Invasion of the Bane*, is now 14. A guard says that it's a Saturday.
1186 The month and year are specified. Barbra's arrival is seen in *Iris: Iris and the Celestial Omnibus*: "The Deadly Flap". Barbra relates her arrival in the twenty-first century in *Iris: Enter Wildthyme*.
1187 Dating *The Raincloud Man* (BF #116) - Charley says that *The Condemned* took place "earlier in the year". *The Raincloud Man* saw release in January 2009, but Menzies specifies that "it's Christmas" – presumably denoting the season rather than the actual day, as an awful lot of people are out doing Christmas shopping – which suggests a dating of December 2008.
1188 Dating "The Stockbridge Child" (*DWM* #403-405) - The Doctor says that it's the "early twenty-first century", and "mid-December". A banner in Stockbridge reads, "Aurelia Winter Festival, '08". In real life, Bonnybridge

dlesome Maria to Limbo – but she escaped, and briefly found herself back on 13th July, 1964. Faced with the evidence of what her deal with the Trickster had done, Andrea revoked her bargain with him.

Sarah Jane and Mr Smith deflected the meteor at the last moment. Having skimmed Sarah Jane's memories, the Trickster became curious as to how much damage would ensue if the Doctor had never existed.

2008 - SJA: THE GLITTERING STORM[1184] -> Sarah Jane and her friends investigated a series of gold thefts, and found that the Keratin (slug-like aliens who used gold to enhance their psychic abilities) had a foothold at the Auirga Clinic in Hounslow. The Keratin's mind-slaves were developing a bacterial culture that would boil away Earth's oceans in a day, exposing twenty million tons of gold that the Keratin could harvest and use to conquer many worlds. The Keratin on Earth were destroyed with seawater, and Sarah Jane and Luke destroyed the formula for the culture.

2008 - SJA: THE THIRTEENTH STONE[1184] -> Luke Smith's class visited a tourist attraction called The Stone Whisperers – actually the petrified criminal Ravage and his twelve jailors. Ravage transferred his mind into Luke's body, and his wardens revived as armoured warriors intent on killing his host form. Luke banished Ravage from his mind, and the warriors turned themselves back into rock.

c 2008 (a Saturday) - SJA: THE LOST BOY[1185] -> Mr Smith moved forward his secret plans to free the colony of Xylok crystals trapped since ancient times under the Earth's crust. Smith allied itself with a group of Slitheen, who – disguised in new fleshsuits that were slimmer, and handled gas exchange better – posed as the Stafford family. TV news reports were said they had been looking for their missing son, Ashley, for five months – and the photo shown was that of Luke Smith. Sarah Jane was arrested for child abduction, and "Ashley" was reunited with his "parents". UNIT vouched for Sarah Jane and she was released.

Mr Smith had manipulated the Slitheen into spurring the creation of a telekinetic energiser, Magnetized Intensification of Telekinetic Reactive Energies (MITRE), at the Pharos Institute. Luke's mind was forcibly used to power the device and draw the moon toward Earth; Mr Smith intended that the collision would free the Xylok. Earth experienced spontaneous forest fires, avalanches, freak storms and tidal waves. The United Nations convened an emergency session.

Sarah briefly brought K9 back to Earth. The robot dog defeated Mr Smith, who was reprogrammed to protect Earth from harm. The moon returned to its original position, and the Slitheen departed.

Darlington became a nexus point for adventurers and other travellers because it was home to the Deadly Flap: a gateway to the multiverse. In December 2008, Barbra the vending machine arrived in Darlington from the fifty-ninth century via the Deadly Flap. Iris Wildthyme persuaded MIAOW to accept Barbra as a trainee operative.[1186]

2008 (December) - THE RAINCLOUD MAN[1187] -> A coalition of species had restrained the alien Tabbalac, and an unknown party infected the Tabbalac with a neurosis that created the Cyrox – a race that replicated like a hyper-intelligent virus, and was ever ready to combat Tabbalac aggression. The Tabbalac could still leave their homeworld, but only if their intentions were peaceful.

In Manchester, DI Patricia Menzies had developed a network of aliens and time travellers whom she'd aided. The sixth Doctor and Charley again met Menzies while investigating Carmen Priminger, a time traveller who had gambled her memories away at the planet-jumping High Straights casino boat a year ago. The Doctor and Charley played a Tabbalac leader at the High Stakes table, and Charley's victory caused the Tabbalac to forfeit their conflict with the Cyrox. As events played out, the Tabbalac leader and Brooks – the High Straights owner – were killed, and the casino was destroyed.

2008 (mid-December) - "The Stockbridge Child"[1188] -> The Doctor's former companion Izzy was now a world traveller, and had recently written to Max Edison that she'd found something "amazing" in Kabul. Bonnybridge, Scotland, contained a large dimensional flaw, and would have been a nexus of alien activity were it not for the Cardiff Rift.

The TARDIS brought the tenth Doctor and Majenta Pryce to Stockbridge as the town celebrated its Aurelia Winter Festival. The Lokhus, which hailed from the universe after ours, had completed its chrysalis stage – upon its birth, it would be larger than Earth's sun. The creature was incinerated before this could happen. After the Doctor and Majenta left, the Crimson Hand scanned Max's memories to determine Majenta's whereabouts.

Lucie Miller Leaves the TARDIS

Lucie Miller, thinking the Doctor dead, accepted a lift from the Time Lords back to Blackpool.[1189]

2008 (24th December) - DEATH IN BLACKPOOL[1190] **->** The Zygon Hagoth, still disguised as Lucie Miller's Aunty Pat, discovered he was dying from melanoma – the result of his having maintained the same form for too long. "Pat" outwardly looked middle aged as a result, and the only cure was the milk of a Skarasen.

A Zynog (sic) named Landack schemed to mentally possess Hagoth and become a proper Zygon again. Hagoth – knowing he wouldn't live another year – summoned the eighth Doctor and Lucie to Earth, wanting to have a proper Christmas with Lucie one last time. Landack killed Hagoth's mind, then transferred his consciousness into his body – which Hagoth had poisoned, slaying Landack.

Lucie discovered the deception that the Doctor and Hagoth had perpetrated regarding her "Aunty Pat", and – unable to trust the Doctor any longer – left his company and stayed in Blackpool. She agreed to keep low until the Headhunter kidnapped her younger self, who was currently back home, the following summer.

2008 (24th-25th December) - VOYAGE OF THE DAMNED[1191] **->** London was near-emptied as everyone feared a repeat of the devastating events of the last two Christmases. The Queen stayed in Buckingham Palace over the holiday. Wilf Mott, a news vendor, was impressed by her courage and stayed at his post.

Max Capricorn Cruiseliners now offered tours from

---

fancies itself as "the UFO capital" of Scotland.

1189 *The Vengeance of Morbius*; see the dating notes for *Death in Blackpool*.

1190 Dating *Death in Blackpool* (BF BBC7 #4.1) - It's said to be Christmas Eve, but there's confusion as to the actual year. The back cover says it's "Christmas 2009", which mirrors the intent of the writer, Alan Barnes. However, within the story itself, the Doctor tells Hagoth that it's "2008", and nothing in this or any other Lucie Miller story contradicts that assertion.

Additionally, *Death in Blackpool* takes place concurrent to Lucie returning home for six months at the end of *The Vengeance of Morbius* – an audio that saw release in 2008. For anyone listening at the time, it would've been reasonable to presume that Lucie had returned to either A) her native year of 2006, or B) the year simultaneous to the story's release (2008). Certainly, there's no evidence to make the listener intuitively think that Lucie had gone home in what was, at the time, the future – which makes a dating of 2008 a bit more aesthetically pleasing than that of 2009.

Luckily, as *Death in Blackpool* takes place on Christmas Eve and *Voyage of the Damned* happens on Christmas Day itself, there's no need to explain why nobody in the audio story is distracted by news coverage of a cruise ship plummeting from space toward Buckingham Palace. Either way, Lucie – who meets the Doctor in 2006 – has done a remarkable job at keeping her family from realising that she's been gallivanting off in time and space for two or three years.

1191 Dating *Voyage of the Damned* (X4.0) - Wilf spells out that *The Christmas Invasion* happened "Christmas before last", *The Runaway Bride* occurred "last year".

The Doctor: His Lives and Times (p201) relates how Captain Jack wrote a letter to Buckingham Palace (dated to 29th December) naming the Doctor as the person who saved London from the plummeting *Titanic* on Christmas Day. In gratitude, it says, Her Majesty responded: "My great great grandmother's sentence of exile on the Doctor and Miss Tyler [*Tooth*

and Claw] has been rescinded with immediate effect."

1192 As inferred from *The Stolen Earth*.

1193 Dating *Turn Left* (X4.11) - This is the alternative version of *Voyage of the Damned*. In that story, the Doctor believed that all life on Earth would be wiped out when the *Titanic* hit, although it's not quite as severe here. London is presumably not evacuated in the alternate timeline (as it was in the original) because the Doctor wasn't around to phone in a warning.

1194 "The Screams of Death". She puts her lock-picking to use in such stories as *The Beast Below*.

1195 Events in 2009 include the "present day" sequences of *Doctor Who* Series 4; the last two episodes of *Torchwood* Series 2; *Planet of the Dead*; the "interim" (i.e. post-Series 2) *Torchwood* novels, audios and comics featuring Jack, Gwen and Ianto; *Torchwood* Series 3 (a.k.a. *TW: Children of Earth*); *The Sarah Jane Adventures* Series 2; the first half of *The Sarah Jane Adventures* Series 3; the BBC fourth Doctor audio series *Hornets' Nest* and *The End of Time*.

1196 "Two years" before *SJA: The Curse of Clyde Langer*.

1197 "Three months" before *TW: Bay of the Dead*.

1198 *Worlds BF: The Phantom Wreck*

1199 "Four years" before *Autonomy*.

1200 The year before "The Age of Ice".

1201 The year before *The Lodger* (TV).

1202 *The Eyeless*. "They'd only just finished rebuilding" Big Ben, so this is after *The Christmas Invasion*.

1203 The background to *The Sontaran Stratagem/The Poison Sky*. A car with an ATMOS sticker is seen in *Partners in Crime*, so at least some distribution of ATMOS occurs beforehand.

1204 First mentioned in *Partners in Crime*, explained in *The Stolen Earth*.

1205 *Black and White*, if Sally was indeed born in 2000 (see the Sally Morgan and Lysandra Aristedes sidebar).

1206 *Gods and Monsters*

1207 "Five years" before *Night of the Stormcrow*.

the planet Sto in the Casavanian Belt to "primitive" cultures, and had one starliner designed after the Earth vessel *Titanic*. Max Capricorn himself wanted revenge after he was voted off the company board – he bribed the captain of the *Titanic* to lower the ship's shields during a meteor storm as it arrived in Earth orbit to celebrate a traditional Christmas. Capricorn hoped that the *Titanic* would crash and detonate its nuclear storm drives, destroying Earth and dooming the board to charges of mass murder. He then intended to retire to the beaches of Penhaxico II, where the ladies loved cyborgs such as himself.

The tenth Doctor met the waitress Astrid Peth and the faux historian Mr Copper aboard the *Titanic*, as well as Wilf Mott during a brief shore leave to Earth. Capricorn's plan came to fruition – the *Titanic* fell from orbit, and the Heavenly Host angelic robots built to serve the passengers started killing everyone on board to eliminate potential witnesses. Astrid sacrificed herself to kill Capricorn, and the Doctor both assumed command of the Host and ignited the *Titanic*'s secondary engine, pulling the ship up just before it hit Buckingham Palace. The Queen thanked the Doctor for his help, and wished him a Merry Christmas. Mr Copper started up a new life on Earth.

By the Light of the Asteroid was a popular soap opera on Sto. Cyborgs were discriminated against on Sto, but were gaining more rights, including the right to marry The minimum penalty for space-lane fraud was ten years in jail. Five thousand Sto credits represented twenty years' wages; 50,000,056 credits equalled a million pounds.

Earth was designated as a Level Five planet and had six billion people. The Doctor hinted that Europe and America would go to war at some point in the future.

Mr Copper founded the Mr Copper Foundation. Harriet Jones, the former Prime Minister, had Copper's foundation develop the Subwave Network.[1192]

> **(=) 2008 (24th-25th December) TURN LEFT**[1193]
> **->** The Noble family followed Rose's advice and stayed in a hotel outside London. The starship *Titanic* hit Buckingham Palace, killing everyone in London and dosing southern England with radiation.

Amy Pond learned to pick locks when a Mr Harrison became a little over-eager with the handcuffs during a 2008 Christmas party.[1194]

2009[1195]

A young woman who would befriend Clyde Langer became homeless after her father died and her mother remarried, and the new living situation "didn't work out for her". She adopted the name Ellie Faber.[1196] Leet, a child of the Dellacoi, rode the time winds but was hurled to Earth. His arrival killed sixty-three people at the Regal Cinema in Splott. Leet sought refuge in the only survivor, 22-year-old Oscar Phillips.[1197] In 2009, one of England's most beloved entertainers, Jack Oddwards (sic), swam the English Channel to raise money for Chuckle-Aid.[1198]

In 2009, Hyperville opened – at five square miles, it was the largest shopping mall in Europe. The Nestene-controlled Elizabeth Devonshire had facilitated construction of Hyperville for benefit of the Nestene unit she was nursemaiding, and arranged for production of Plastinol-2: an all-purpose plastic intended to serve as the chief substance of a new generation of Autons. Kate Maguire, age 16, was given an all-access Hypercard to Hyperville by a mysterious stranger – the tenth Doctor, who knew they would need the card in 2013.[1199]

UNIT repelled an advance party of Ice Warriors.[1200] Craig Owens (a future flatmate of the Doctor) and his friend Sophie met at a call centre.[1201] The last of the Steggosians attempted to wipe out Earth with poison. The tenth Doctor fought him on top of Big Ben, and the fight ended with the Steggosian Captain falling to his death.[1202]

The Sontarans collaborated with Luke Rattigan in a new bid to conquer Earth. Rattigan's company distributed the Sontaran-based Atmospheric Omission System (ATMOS), a navigation system and means of reducing carbon dioxide emissions in cars to zero. Before long, it was fitted as standard on all UK government vehicles.[1203] Some bees on Earth were migrant bees from the planet Melissa Majoria. Sensing danger approaching due to the Daleks' reality bomb, they began returning home.[1204]

Sally Morgan's parents served in special forces, and always made coconut pina coladas when they were home on leave. When Sally was nine, her parents were killed when their convoy was ambushed – her father died first, and her mother perished while trying to get her comrades to safety. Sally came to live with her grandfather, a colonel who had served in Iraq.[1205] The elder god Weyland forged the bullets that killed Sally's parents, as part of his positioning her to become his game piece.[1206]

A study of galaxy Messier 91 detected the space vulture circling Earth as it moved into a lower orbit. Erica MacMillan named the creature Stormcrow, and financed an operation to monitor its appearances in the early morning hours.[1207]

2009 - PERI AND THE PISCON PARADOX[1208] -> The fifth Doctor and Peri dealt with a suicidal Piscon named Zarl – or so they believed. The sixth Doctor, sensing something awry about the incident, revisited it... and accidentally killed Zarl before his previous self had defeated him. The sixth Doctor fulfilled history by disguising himself as Zarl, and was aided by Peri's contemporary self: Dr Perpugilliam Brown, a talk show host and three-time divorcee who convinced her younger self that she was a secret agent for the X-Files. Thinking "Zarl" defeated, the fifth Doctor and "his" Peri left. The older Peri declined to travel with the sixth Doctor again.

c 2009 - THE SONTARAN GAMES[1209] -> The tenth Doctor arrived at the British Academy of Sporting Excellence (BASE), where elite athletes were training for the Globe Games. A group of Sontarans from the Twelfth Sontaran Fleet, led by Major Stenx, forced everyone there to a series of physical challenges to assess human prowess – those who failed were killed or fed to Sontar Sand Shrews. The BASE athletes gained the upper hand, and killed Stenx's Sontarans. The Doctor realised that Emma, one of the athletes, was a Rutan spy wanting to stage a diplomatic incident at the Games, which would trigger a war and allow the Rutans to invade. She seemed to consider the Doctor's offer that she abandon her plan and let him take her away from the Sontaran-Rutan conflict – but

before she could decide, she and Stenx died in combat with one another. The Doctor fled as the energy Emma had absorbed was released, destroying BASE.

2009 - LIBERTY HALL[1210] -> Brigadier Alistair Lethbridge-Stewart, CBE, granted an interview to Philip Clarke, a feature writer for the *Evening Anchor*. The Brigadier reminisced about meeting his wife Doris, how he came to teach maths at Brendon Public School, and how he left the school to settle down with her. Captain Yates, he said, had gone to the south coast to try and change the world by entering politics. The Brigadier and his wife had named their new home Liberty Hall.

2009 - TW: THE TORCHWOOD ARCHIVE (BF)[1211] -> In a cafe in Penarth, Sgt Andy Davidson entirely failed to impress a woman of modest intelligence with his connections to Torchwood.

2009 (March) - TW: "The Return of the Vostok"[1212] -> Torchwood killed the Vostok – jelly-fish-like aliens capable of creating winter conditions, and who sought to use the Rift to retroactively send an ice age back through time.

1208 Dating *Peri and the Piscon Paradox* (BF CC #5.8) - "It's definitely Earth, Los Angeles, 2009 AD", the Doctor says, in agreement with the blurb.

1209 Dating *The Sontaran Games* (*Quick Reads* #4) - This has a contemporary or very near-future setting, although no year is specified.

1210 Dating *Liberty Hall* (*Mawdryn Undead* DVD extra) - Nicholas Courtney once again plays the Brigadier in this DVD extra, released in 2009. The name "Liberty Hall" stems from a quote the Brigadier made to Dr Tyler in *The Three Doctors*. Mike Yates' political aspirations, no doubt, reflect actor Richard Franklin standing as a candidate in the UK general election in 1992, 1997 and 2001.

1211 Dating *TW: The Torchwood Archive* (BF *TW* special release #1) - The year is given.

1212 Dating *TW: "The Return of the Vostok"* (*TW* webcomic #1) - The opening caption says, "Cardiff, March". The year isn't specified, but the story was released in February 2009, and – owing to Owen and Tosh's presence – occurs before the Series 2 finale.

1213 Dating *Partners in Crime* (X4.01) - No month is given here, but in the alternate timeline in *Turn Left*, the Adipose incident takes place in March. An Adipose Industries customer tells Donna that she "started taking the pills on Thursday" and has been doing so for "five days", meaning the story begins on a Tuesday. It

concludes the next day.

1214 Dating *Turn Left* (X4.11) - It's at least "eight weeks" since the *Titanic* disaster, as the Colasantos family have been living in Leeds that long, and the Nobles are told they face "another three months" stuck where they are unless they relocate to Leeds.

1215 Dating *The Sontaran Stratagem/The Poison Sky* (X4.5-4.6) - The month isn't given, but the dating can be extrapolated from the alternative universe seen in *Turn Left*, and the fact that only "a few days" have passed since Donna left with the Doctor in *Partners in Crime*. Frustratingly, Martha walks past a wall calendar that is too blurry to make out.

The Brigadier also mentions being in Peru in *SJA: Enemy of the Bane*. Russell T Davies has said that UNIT's name change resulted from the United Nations asking that its name not be associated with the group, although UNIT is said to still receive UN funding.

1216 *The Doctor's Daughter*

1217 *The Taking of Chelsea 426*

1218 "The Blood of Azrael", weaving Fisher into events in *The Poison Sky*.

Doctor Who Series 4

Donna Noble Joins the TARDIS

2009 (a Tuesday and Wednesday in March) - PARTNERS IN CRIME[1213] -> The loss of the breeding planet Adipose III compelled the Adipose first family to hire Matron Cofelia of the Five-Straighten Classabindi Nursery Fleet to oversee the production of their offspring. She founded Adipose Industries on Earth as a front for this operation. The company signed up a million customers to its weight-loss programme in Greater London alone, with the intention of going national. Pills were distributed under the claim that anyone who took them would lose exactly a kilogram a day, but in actuality the pills slowly transformed people's fat into baby Adipose. The tenth Doctor and Donna independently investigated Adipose Industries, were reunited, and came to the realisation that the pill-takers' bones, hair and internal organs could be completely broken down into the Adipose offspring.

The Matron sent a signal that generated ten thousand Adipose, who marched through the streets of London, but the Doctor stopped the signal from fully converting all one million of the weight-loss customers. A giant ship of the Adipose first family arrived over London and collected the baby Adipose with levitation beams. Seeding a Level Five planet such as Earth with offspring violated a galactic law enforced by the Shadow Proclamation, and so the first family killed the Matron to cover up her crime.

The Doctor agreed to let Donna join him on his travels, and briefly showed the TARDIS in flight to Wilf Mott as they departed.

Before she left with the Doctor, Donna briefly met the dimension-hopping Rose Tyler.

(=) 2009 (March) - TURN LEFT[1214] -> An Emergency Government took control of the United Kingdom. Seven million were in need of relocation from the radiation-flooded southern England, and France closed its borders. The Noble family were relocated to Leeds, and shared a small house with the Colasantos family. The United States promised £50 billion in aid... but before it could deliver, America's economy was devastated when sixty million Americans were converted into Adipose. Spaceships collected the Adipose offspring.

The Unified Intelligence Taskforce

2009 (March) - THE SONTARAN STRATAGEM / THE POISON SKY[1215] -> UNIT had been renamed the Unified Intelligence Taskforce. It received massive funding from the United Nations in the name of home-world security, and still operated the *Valiant*. UNIT had access to the nuclear arsenals of the US, UK, France, India, Pakistan, China and North Korea. Sir Alistair Gordon Lethbridge-Stewart was currently in Peru. The Doctor was technically on staff with UNIT, as he never formally resigned. UNIT Headquarters was near Tower Bridge, London.

The ATMOS navigation/anti-pollution system had now been installed in half of the world's eight hundred million cars. Martha summoned the tenth Doctor and Donna when fifty-two people were poisoned to death inside their cars at the exact same moment, in eleven different time zones. General Staal the Undefeated of the Tenth Sontaran Battle Fleet advanced his plans to release poison gas from every car fitted with ATMOS. The gas was a Caesofine concentrate that would alter Earth's atmosphere, turning the planet into a Sontaran breeding world.

As the ATMOS-made gas intensified, the UK government declared a national emergency, and the UN issued a worldwide directive for people to leave the cities. The first deaths were reported in Tokyo. In Europe, thousands walked across country to escape. The Eastern seaboard of America became reminiscent of Dunkirk, as boats took refugees out into the Atlantic. The tenth Doctor and Donna restored Earth's atmosphere to normal, and the genius entrepreneur Luke Rattigan, realising the Sontarans never intended to give him the power he sought, sacrificed himself to destroy the Sontaran mothership.

Martha was now engaged to Tom Milligan, who was in paediatrics and working out in Africa. Rattigan's inventions, not all of them derived from Sontaran technology, included nanotech steel, biospheres, gravity simulation, rattifan 18 and a cordolaine signal.

The tenth Doctor and Donna returned Martha home after sharing an adventure with her – and the Doctor's daughter Jenny – in the future.[1216]

The Rutans learned of the Sontaran plan to make Earth a breeding world, and seeded Saturn with a spore that would possess the resultant clones. With the Sontaran defeat, the spore remained inactive on Saturn until the twenty-sixth century.[1217] While serving with UNIT, Danny Fisher achieved the biggest body count in repelling the Sontaran assault at the Atmos factory. Afterward, he was recruited into MI6. UNIT's standing No. 1 order under such crisis conditions was: "Keep the Doctor alive."[1218]

2009 - IN THE BLOOD[1219] -> Donna visited her family while the tenth Doctor eagerly attended a Kate Bush concert. Her childhood friend Hettie had married a man named Cam, and had two six year olds. A spike in fatal heart attacks among internet trolls escalated into a media event variously labeled Webmageddon and Trollpocalypse. The Doctor and Donna discovered that the cephalopod gangster Gully had seeded the internet with Rempaths: parasites that transmitted through technology, and fed off anger-feedback loops in their hosts. The Rempaths caused an outbreak of fury and violence among the UK public; left unchecked, they would both physically augment Gully and destroy the Earth.

While bringing his master plan to fruition, Gully was sucked into the guts of the Earth and killed. The Doctor modified an audio from the planet Cadmia to compel an increase in Rempath-eradicating blood transfusions.

(=) **2009 (mid-March) - TURN LEFT**[1220] -> With so little petrol, Britain was spared the worst when the Sontarans activated their ATMOS stratagem, although the rest of the world was badly affected. Torchwood took the fight to the Sontaran mothership and although they prevailed, Gwen and Ianto were killed, and Jack Harkness was transported to the Sontaran homeworld. Rose met Donna again, and claimed that Donna would come with her in three weeks time.

Deaths of Toshiko Sato and Owen Harper; Capt. Jack Revives from Stasis

2009 (April) - TW: FRAGMENTS / TW: EXIT WOUNDS[1221] -> Jack Harkness' vengeful brother Gray coerced Captain John Hart into embarking upon a major terror campaign against Torchwood. Hart wracked Cardiff with fifteen building-levelling explosions, and aided Gray in taking Jack back to 27 AD and burying him. Gray enhanced the Rift so that Cardiff came under siege from ghosts, Weevils and hooded figures bearing scythes. The four most senior police offers were murdered. The systems servicing the Turnmill Nuclear Power Station failed, and Owen Harper died a final time while diverting irradiated coolant to contain the resultant meltdown. Gray shot Toshiko Sato, killing her. Torchwood quelled the situation; Jack revived from the stasis into which he'd been placed in 1901 and overpowered his rogue brother, then placed him in cryo-freeze.

Martha attended Owen and Tosh's funerals.[1222]

1219 Dating *In the Blood* (NSA #63) - For the Doctor and Donna, it's after her relationship with Lee (ch3) in *Silence in the Library/Forest of the Dead*. Given the rollercoaster events of the final three episodes of Series 4, *In the Blood* must occur before *Turn Left* – so either in March or early April 2009. The Doctor mentions the Silk Road, a now-defunct illicit internet market, but that didn't launch until February 2011. Wilf and Donna's blood type is A+ (ch38), and the Doctor's mobile number is "07700 900461" (ch47).
1220 Dating *Turn Left* (X4.11) - This is the parallel timeline's version of *The Poison Sky*.
1221 Dating *TW: Fragments* and *TW: Exit Wounds* (TW 2.12-2.13) - The repeated flashback segments in *TW: Fragments* best align with established *Torchwood* continuity if the final two episodes of Series 2 occur in 2009. Most relevantly, it's established that Ianto approached Jack for a job "21 months" ago, after the destruction of Torchwood One (in *Doomsday*) in 2007. If *Doomsday* is indeed set in July 2007, then *Fragments* would occur in April 2009. It might seem like a glitch when Jack tells the Torchwood of 1901 to deep-freeze him and set the alarm for "107 years' time...", suggesting a target year of 2008, but if he's unearthed late in 1901, he could easily be rounding down from, "107 years and a few months".

1222 *TW: Lost Souls*
1223 Dating *SJA: The Last Sontaran* (SJA 2.1) - The *Sontaran Stratagem/The Poison Sky* are referenced in detail, so it's after those stories. No mention is made of events of *The Stolen Earth*, and, notably, both Maria's mum Chrissie and Professor Skinner's daughter Lucy become incredulous upon learning that aliens are real. Chrissie isn't portrayed as the brightest of people, but Lucy - as the daughter of a man whose job is to search for friendly life in outer space - would surely better keep track of this sort of thing. The point is that while it's a little suspect to think that they haven't noticed all the very public alien events that have taken place throughout New *Who*, *Torchwood* and *The Sarah Jane Adventures* before now, it's barking mad to think that they're still in the dark after events of *The Stolen Earth/Journey's End*. Moreover, this reflects a marked shift within *The Sarah Jane Adventures* Series 2 itself – Clyde's dad mentions "those Dalek things" (i.e. *The Stolen Earth/Journey's End*) mid-way through the series in *SJA: The Mark of the Berserker*, and by *SJA: Enemy of the Bane*, the last story of Series 2, the Brigadier can bluff his way out of a tight spot by saying that, "as the cat's out of the bag" with regards aliens, he's now at liberty to reveal details of his UNIT days in his memoirs.

While it's very counter-intuitive, the best fit is to

The Sarah Jane Adventures Series 2

2009 - SJA: THE LAST SONTARAN[1223] -> Strange lights were seen near the Tycho Project, a radio telescope that searched for friendly alien life. Sarah Jane, Clyde, Luke and Maria went to investigate and were stalked by Commander Kaagh, a Sontaran who had survived the recent invasion. He planned to use the Tycho radio telescope to crash Earth's satellites into its nuclear stockpiles, but Sarah Jane and her friends drove Kaagh away.

Kaagh became a mercenary for the Bane, and encountered the fugitive Mrs Wormwood on a planet in the Snake Tongue Nebula. They hatched a scheme to acquire the power of the banished Horath.[1224]

2009 - BEAUTIFUL CHAOS[1225] -> The tenth Doctor took Donna home so she could spend time with her mother and grandfather on the anniversary of her father's death. Morgan Tech, owned by a thrall of the Mandragora Helix, was about to release the newest personal computing gadget: the M-TEK. The Helix planned to control and speed up man's expansion into space – it was projected that humans would build farms on Mars in twenty years and colonise Alpha Centauri in a hundred, all part of a Mandragoran Empire. The Helix took control of people whose lineage extended back to San Martino, Italy, but the Doctor ended its schemes. UNIT recalled the M-TEKs.

The Prime Minister at this time was Aubrey Fairchild.

c 2009 - "The Time of My Life"[1226] -> The tenth Doctor and Donna confronted gun-totting dog aliens from space, whose spaceship arrived over London to incite the dogs of Earth into revolution against their human masters.

(=) 2009 (early April) - TURN LEFT[1227] -> In the "Donna turned right" universe, the Emergency Government adopted an "England for the English" policy, sending foreign-born residents to labour camps. Soon afterwards, the stars started going out. Donna met with Rose and a UNIT group led by Captain Erisa Magambo. They had recovered the dying TARDIS from under the Thames, and used its technology to build a time machine that could reflect chronon energy from mirrors. Donna agreed to travel back to the point of temporal deviation, and convince her past self to turn left...

place *The Last Sontaran* prior to *The Stolen Earth* (i.e. in Spring 2009), and to set the rest of *The Sarah Jane Adventures* Series 2 later in the year. (The alternative would be to set *The Last Sontaran* at least six weeks prior to *SJA: The Day of the Clown*, which would mean that the Park Vale school year has started nearly a month earlier than normal – see *SJA: Revenge of the Slitheen* and *SJA: The Nightmare Man* – for no discernible reason.) It might be relevant that when mention is made of the Doctor, Sarah Jane gives no clue that she's met him recently in *Journey's End*, further suggesting that story hasn't happened yet.

Where Maria is concerned, a pre-*The Stolen Earth* dating makes some sense: if her father gets the job offer in spring, she might be allowed to finish out the school year (during the "six weeks" that pass prior to the epilogue of *The Last Sontaran*), and they move to America at the start of summer. It also works better to assume that not that long has passed since *The Poison Sky* for Kaagh (as opposed to a fall dating for *The Last Sontaran*, which would mean that he's evidently been sitting around Earth for some months doing nothing). The only real glitch to all of this, then, is that when Luke gets an email dated 9th October from Maria in *The Day of the Clown*, it's treated as if it's the first time she's gotten in touch with her old gang, when one would expect that she might have done so some time prior.

1224 *SJA: Enemy of the Bane*

1225 Dating *Beautiful Chaos* (NSA #29) - The story has a very precise dating framework, with the text split into days rather than chapters. Events begin on "Friday 15th May 2009" (per a newspaper dateline, p24), and progress to the following Monday (pgs. 15, 79, 135, 185), with an epilogue that takes place the next "Friday" (p221). Page 53 reiterates that it's the "middle of May".

... all of this information, however, must be set aside because it clashes with the continuity of the TV episodes. Given the need for *Planet of the Dead* to occur at Easter 2009 (see the dating notes on that story for why), all Series 4-related stories must happen beforehand, ruling out a mid-May dating for *Beautiful Chaos*. Additionally, the story is said to happen "one month" after *The Poison Sky* (p13), which is dated in this chronology to mid-March 2009.

Conflict with the TV series aside, *Beautiful Chaos* (pgs. 187-188) is otherwise accommodating to continuity by acknowledging the other Mandragora-related adventures: "The Mark of Mandragora", *Sarah Jane Smith* Series 2 and *The Eleventh Tiger*. Fairchild is the Prime Minister whose plane goes down in *The Stolen Earth*. *TW: Exodus Code* names this incident with the Mandragora Helix as occurring in "2009".

1226 Dating "The Time of My Life" (*DWM* #399) - The story was released in 2008, but the "year ahead" rule governing Series 4 might apply. It must be roughly contemporary in that Donna spies her house, and is incensed that her neighbours have a swimming pool that she didn't know about. The London Eye, constructed in 1999, is seen in the background.

1227 Dating *Turn Left* (X4.11) - "Three weeks" after *The Poison Sky*.

The Daleks Pull Earth Through Space; the Tenth Doctor Reunites With Many Old Friends, and Regenerates Into Himself; Donna Leaves the TARDIS

2009 (a Saturday in early April) - THE STOLEN EARTH / JOURNEY'S END[1228] -> Davros, rescued from the Last Great Time War by Dalek Caan, created a new generation of Daleks genetically derived from his own cells. A new Dalek Empire was born, and set about creating a reality bomb – an alignment of twenty-seven planets that would flatten Z-Neutrino energy into a single string, and thereby undo the electrical field binding all reality. The Daleks intended to shield themselves as all matter became dust, then mere atoms. They would become the only living creatures in existence. Three worlds were plucked from different time zones for the reality bomb: Adipose III, Pyrovillia and the lost moon of Poosh.

The Daleks moved into the second phase of their plan, and teleported twenty-four planets – including Callufrax Minor, Jahoo, Shallacatop, Woman Wept and Clom – into the Medusa Cascade along with the three

worlds already taken. Earth was also one of the stolen planets, and humanity was horrified to look into the sky and find itself surrounded by other worlds. When the translocation occurred, Martha Jones was at UNIT's New York HQ, working as medical director on Project Indigo: an attempt to salvage Sontaran technology into a teleport system. Captain Jack was at the Torchwood Hub, and Sarah Jane was at Bannerman Road. Rose Tyler materialised on Earth from Pete's World. Mickey Smith and Jackie would later journey from Pete's World to help her.

The Daleks were operating from the Crucible: a massive space station in the middle of the planetary arrangement. A fleet of two hundred Dalek ships set out to subjugate Earth, transmitting in advance a single word, repeated: "Exterminate, exterminate, exterminate". The Daleks gleefully dismantled every form of resistance, from UNIT forces aboard the *Valiant* to Wilf Noble with his paintball gun. Daleks landed in Japan and Germany, and forced the air force to retreat over North Africa. Contact was lost with the airplane bearing the UK Prime Minister. The Commander General of the United Nations signalled Earth's surrender.

The tenth Doctor and Donna learned about the miss-

1228 Dating *The Stolen Earth/Journey's End* (X4.11) - This story crosses over with *Torchwood* and *The Sarah Jane Adventures*, and picks up the story from all three series. It is set after *The Poison Sky*, but before *Planet of the Dead*; between *TW: Exit Wounds* and *TW: Children of Earth*; and at some point after *SJA: Revenge of the Slitheen* and before *SJA: Secrets of the Stars* (which mentions this story). Sarah says Luke is 14, as he was in *Revenge of the Slitheen*. Triangulating from all of that, *The Stolen Earth* would have to be set in early April, before Easter. Rose passes a sign advertising a dance night on "Friday 25 July" (which in 2009 was actually a Saturday) - not that this means it's actually July, though.

Adelaide Brooke's biography in *The Waters of Mars* confirms that this Dalek invasion occurred in "2008". The Doctor says it's a Saturday. Callufrax Minor (as it's spelled on screen here) is presumably related to Calufrax (as it's spelled on screen in *The Pirate Planet*).
1229 *The Waters of Mars*
1230 *The Next Doctor*, presuming the "greater battle" that the Doctor mentions refers to events in *The Stolen Earth/Journey's End*.
1231 *Victory of the Daleks*
1232 Dating *Planet of the Dead* (X4.15) - It is "April" according to the bus driver, and the Doctor wishes Christina "Happy Easter". This is after *The Stolen Earth/ Journey's End*, as "planets in the sky" are referenced. The story is mentioned in *SJA: Mona Lisa's Revenge*, so must take place beforehand. Most importantly, *Planet of the Dead* must occur before *The End of Time* per a psychic's prediction of not just the tenth Doctor's impending

death, but Gallifrey's return.

Planet of the Dead, then, is the first contemporary *Doctor Who* TV story since *Rose* to be set the year it was shown, ending the practice (starting with *Aliens of London*) that "present day" stories are set around a year after broadcast. Any temptation to continue the "year later" tradition is overruled partly because of the psychic's prediction, but also because *The End of Time* has to occur at the end of 2009 per the continuity of *The Sarah Jane Adventures*. Sarah and Luke first meet the tenth Doctor in *Journey's End* (set in 2009), acknowledge that meeting in *SJA: The Wedding of Sarah Jane Smith* (where it's said that Sarah and the Tennant Doctor will meet at least one more time), they have their final meeting in *The End of Time* when the Doctor saves Luke from an oncoming car, and then Sarah acknowledges *that* meeting in *SJA: Death of the Doctor* (set in 2010), when she airs her suspicion that the Doctor regenerated because, "The last time I saw him, he didn't say a word, he just looked at me".

A History of the Universe in 100 Objects (p162) names the 200 to Victoria bus seen in *Planet of the Dead* as being from "2010", but generally doesn't appear to incorporate the continuity of *The Sarah Jane Adventures*.
1233 *TW: Lost Souls*. The real life CERN project was also mentioned in *SJA: Invasion of the Bane*.
1234 "Six weeks" after *Beautiful Chaos*.
1235 Dating *SJA: The Last Sontaran* (SJA 2.1) - This epilogue occurs six weeks after the story's main events.
1236 Dating *Last of the Time Lords* (X3.13) - It's "one year later" than the events of *The Sound of Drums*.

ing planets from the Shadow Proclamation. Harriet Jones connected the Doctor's allies using the Subwave Network she'd developed, and together they sent out a pulse that enabled the Doctor and Donna to return to Earth. The Daleks traced the signal back to Harriet's home and exterminated her.

The TARDIS materialised in London, and the Doctor was reunited with Rose... and was then shot by a Dalek. He began to regenerate, but used the process to heal himself and diverted the excess energy into a bio-matching receptacle – the hand severed in combat with the Sycorax – to save his life.

The Doctor and his many allies confronted the Daleks aboard the Crucible. The Supreme Dalek had the TARDIS dumped in the Z-neutrino core of the Crucible to destroy it. Donna was still aboard the Ship, and the regenerative energies in the Doctor's hand (severed during his battle with the Sycorax leader at Christmas 2006) interacted with her. The hand grew into a duplicate of the tenth Doctor who was part human, and Donna absorbed all the Doctor's knowledge, becoming a human-Time Lord metacrisis. This was enough to turn the tables – Donna deactivated the reality bomb, and twenty six of the planets were returned to their rightful places, but the Supreme Dalek destroyed the machinery before Earth could be returned. Jack destroyed the Supreme Dalek, and the duplicate Doctor used a backfeed to wipe out the Daleks. Davros refused the Doctor's offer of a rescue, and the TARDIS left the exploding Crucible. In conjunction with the Torchwood Hub and Sarah Jane's Mr Smith computer, the tenth Doctors and their companions used the TARDIS to tow the Earth back home.

Humanity celebrated Earth's return to its proper location, although there was widespread rainfall due to atmospheric disturbances. Mickey opted to remain in his native reality as his grandmother on Pete's World had died. The duplicate Doctor, Rose and Jackie returned to Pete's World. Jack returned to Torchwood, and Sarah Jane went home.

UNIT had developed the Osterhagen Key: 25 nuclear warheads placed at strategic points beneath the Earth's crust as a means of destroying the planet – a final option should humanity's suffering be deemed too great to be allowed to continue. Martha promised the Doctor that she would dismantle the system.

Donna's mind couldn't cope with the Time Lord abilities it had absorbed. The Doctor saved her life by removing all of her memories of him, the TARDIS and their travels together, then left her with her family.

Adelaide Brooke lost her parents in the Dalek invasion. A Dalek confronted her, but – perhaps recognising her importance to history – did not exterminate

her.[1229] The Daleks' gambit with the reality bomb weakened the dimensional walls, enabling some Cybermen within the Void to fall back through time to London, 1851, using the dimension vault they stole from the Daleks. Everything else inside the Void perished.[1230] One Dalek ship survived and was hurled back through time, damaged, to the 1940s.[1231]

2009 (April) - PLANET OF THE DEAD[1232] -> The aristocratic art thief Lady Christina de Souza stole the Cup of Athelstan, which was worth £18 million, from the International Gallery in London and fled aboard a No. 200 bus. The tenth Doctor joined de Souza and her fellow passengers on the bus, which promptly fell through a wormhole to San Helios – a desert planet in the Scorpion Nebula, on the other side of the universe. A UNIT team led by Captain Magambo sealed off the tunnel in London.

The Doctor made contact with the Tritovores, fly-like aliens who thought San Helios had a population of one hundred billion. In the last year, all life on the planet has been devoured by monsters that resembled ravenous flying stingrays. The Doctor realised that the wormhole between San Helios and Earth was growing, and that the Stingrays would soon cross over, wiping out all life on Earth. With the help of UNIT, and after breaking up the Cup of Athelstan to use as components in a machine, the Doctor got the bus back to London and closed the wormhole. He also helped de Souza elude the police.

The TARDIS had landed in the grounds of Buckingham Palace, and the Doctor was confident the Queen "didn't mind".

In May, a test conducted on the Large Hadron Collider at CERN created a dimensional bridge that provided a neutron-eating creature with access to our universe.[1233] Sylvia Noble received a letter that Donna had written prior to her memory loss. It detailed her excitement about travelling with the Doctor.[1234]

Maria Jackson Leaves Sarah Jane's Team

2009 - SJA: THE LAST SONTARAN[1235] -> Six weeks after defeating Kaagh, Maria Jackson moved to Washington with her father.

(=) 2009 (a Saturday in June) - LAST OF THE TIME LORDS[1236] -> The Harold Saxon Master had controlled Earth for a year, and turned it into a factory world. The enslaved human population was put to work building two hundred thousand war rockets "set to burn across the universe" and create a Time Lord Empire. A space lane traffic advisor warned all travellers to stay away from Sol 3.

Japan had been devastated, and New York was reportedly in ruin. China had fusion mills, Europe had radiation pits, and a shipyard in Russia ran from the Black Sea to the Bering Strait.

Martha Jones spent a year travelling the world and spreading word of the Doctor, telling the public to think of him when the rockets were launched. The hyper-aged tenth Doctor had spent the last year linking himself into the telepathic field of the Archangel network, and used the humans' psychic energy to restore himself. Captain Jack destroyed the Paradox Machine, reversing time one year and one day to the exact moment before the Toclafane materialised.

Six months after a grieving Lucie returned home, the Headhunter arrived on her doorstep, shot her unconscious and whisked her away to the planet Orbis in the future.[1237]

2009 - "Ghosts of the Northern Line" / "The Crimson Hand"[1238] -> Intersol, a time-travelling intergalactic justice organisation, estimated that Earth's oil reserves were "almost depleted".

The Mnemosyne unit hidden in London's Northern Line had matured, and wanted revenge for the murder of its guardian. The tenth Doctor and Majenta Pryce intervened as the Mnemosyne manifested everyone who had died on the Northern Line in previous decades as "ghosts", and announced its intention to incinerate everyone within the Underground. Majenta convinced the ghostly engrams to turn on the Mnemosyne, destroying it and themselves.

A squadron of Intersol ships arrived in Earth orbit and arrested Majenta. They time-locked the TARDIS, and returned with it, the Doctor and Majenta to the future...

The Vortex Butterfly

2009 - THE TENTH DOCTOR YEAR THREE[1239] -> The tenth Doctor left Gabby and Cindy in Willesden, London, at one of his safe houses while he investigated disturbing

---

1237 *The Vengeance of Morbius, Orbis. Death in Blackpool* specifies that Lucie is abducted in summer – no later than June, as she's kidnapped "six months" after returning home in 2008.

1238 Dating "Ghosts of the Northern Line" and "The Crimson Hand" (*DWM* #414-420) - Intersol agents state in "Ghosts of the Northern Line" that it's "late '09, post-Stolen Earth scenario" (*Journey's End*). Obama is said to be in power.

1239 Dating *The Tenth Doctor Year Three* (Titan 10th Doc #3.6-3.8, 3.10, "Vortex Butterflies") - The year is given. Sarah references the Doctor and her recently meeting Davros, so it's after *Journey's End*. Cindy's narration says that she and Gabby lodge in London at least "a few weeks".

1240 Dating the *Torchwood* Series 2/Series 3 interim stories (*TW: Lost Souls*, TW audio drama #1; *TW: Almost Perfect*, TW novel #9; *TW:* "Ma and Par", TW webcomic #2; *TW:* "The Selkie", TWM #14; *TW:* "Broken", TWM #15-19; *TW: The Sin Eaters*, audiobook #4; *TW: Into the Silence*, TW novel #10; *TW: Bay of the Dead*, TW novel #11; *TW: The House That Jack Built*, TW novel #12; *TW: Asylum*, TW audio drama #2; *TW: Golden Age*, TW audio drama #3; *TW: The Dead Line*, TW audio drama #4; *TW: Risk Assessment*, TW novel #13; *TW: The Undertaker's Gift*, TW novel #14; *TW: Consequences*, TW novel #15 – actually a novella collection, but generally counted as part of the novel range; *TW:* "Fated to Pretend", TWM #20; *TW:* "Somebody Else's Problem", TWM #23; *TW:* "Hell House", TWM #24; *TW: Department X*, TW audiobook #5; *TW: Ghost Train*, TW audiobook #6; *TW: The Devil and Miss Carew*, TW audio drama #5; *TW: Submission*, TW audio drama #6) - The aforementioned *Torchwood* stories all feature Captain Jack, Gwen and Ianto, and are set

between *Torchwood* Series 2 and Series 3 (the latter being a single story, *TW: Children of Earth*). The year is confirmed as 2009 in *Risk Assessment* (p9), *Asylum*, *Consequences:* "Consequences" (p241), *The Sin-Eaters* and *Golden Age*. Weirdly, in *TW: The Dead Line*, events in 1976 are identified – in the very same conversation! – as being both thirty-three and thirty-four years ago.

With so few tangible clues as to how these audios, novels and comics slot together, the stories are here presented in nothing more scientific than release order. See the individual entries for more.

1241 Dating *TW: Lost Souls* (TW audio drama #1) - The story aired on 10th September, 2008, as part of Radio 4's "Big Bang Day" to commemorate the LHC switch-on of the very same date, and was released on CD on 18th September. Within the fiction, nothing is said about the year – which is fortunate, given the overarching need to place the Jack, Gwen and Ianto stories in 2009. Nor is any reference given to the month or day, save for repeated mentions of an LHC field test conducted "back in May". It's tempting to think that the switch-on just occurs a year later in the *Doctor Who* universe than in real life, but as the year of the actual LHC switch-on has already been compromised, there's no particular reason to think one way or the other that the 10th September dating is still valid. That being the case, *Lost Souls* might as well go into the release-order rotation with its post-*Torchwood* Series 2 contemporaries.

1242 The framing sequence to *TW: In the Shadows*. Placement is unknown, save that Gwen references *TW: Lost Souls*.

1243 Dating *TW: Almost Perfect* (TW novel #9) - The action begins on a Friday (p131) and concludes the next Saturday.

Vortex oscillations. On the Doctor's behalf, Sarah Jane Smith looked in on his companions. In one version of events, the Doctor had abandoned Gabby in the nothingness of space, and she became a vengeful being empowered with block-transfer computations: the Vortex Butterfly. On the current Doctor's instructions, Sarah stabilized Gabby's time signature and cut her mental link with the TARDIS, averting the Vortex Butterfly's timeline. The Doctor took Gabby and Cindy to see Zhe Ikiyuyu, so she could mentor Gabby's remaining block-transfer abilities.

Torchwood Series 2-3 Interim[1240]

2009 - TW: LOST SOULS[1241] **->** Martha Jones asked Torchwood to help her investigate mysterious events at CERN, the European Organisation for Nuclear Research, in Switzerland. CERN was about to switch on its Large Hadron Collider (LHC) in an effort to identify the theoretical Higgs particle (the most fundamental unit of existence), but the LHC had enabled a deadly alien entity that consumed neutrons to cross into our reality. The LHC was reconfigured to smash protons into anti-protons – creating the Higgs particle, but also killing the creature and preventing others of its kind from crossing over.

Gwen Cooper met a trader from the planet Murgatroyd, and acquired from him a device that could purportedly speak to the dead. She used it – or so she hoped – to send a message to Owen and Tosh in the hereafter.[1242]

2009 (Friday to the following Saturday) - TW: ALMOST PERFECT[1243] **->** The Perfection had built a sentient device that extended their natural reality-warping abilities, but the device became bored of creating perfection and escaped with the Perfection's interior decorators. The device began "helping" various people, causing such brouhaha as a group of speed-daters being reduced to skeletons. Torchwood confronted the Perfection – who had broken their word to Jack, and decided to install themselves as Earth's gods after all. Ianto used the device to drain the life-energy from the Perfection, leaving them as aged husks that he Retconned. In accordance with its wishes, Jack pitched the device into Cardiff Bay.

2009 - TW: "Ma and Par" -> Torchwood electrocuted a Bull-Craktor – a monstrous arachnid – and its offspring at the Pontyvale Golf Course.

2009 - TW: "The Selkie" -> Jack found that the shapeshifting Selkie he'd previously aided was behind a series of murders on Seal Island in Scotland, and killed it.

2009 - TW: "Broken" -> Bilis Manger had designed the Clockhouse Hotel – located on the old site of the Amber Hotel – to contain a creature thought to have been either born of the Rift, or was an expression of the Rift's own self-awareness. Torchwood looked into reports of missing persons at the Clockhouse exactly one hundred forty years to the day after the Rift struck the Amber. The entity hoped to tap enough of Jack's life energy to properly manifest, but Jack temporarily died in such a fashion that severed the Rift entity's link to reality, and also destroyed the hotel.

2009 - TW: THE SIN EATERS -> A swarm of alien insects – creatures that normally lived in a shadow dimension – fed upon the guilt of people in the Cardiff city centre, endowing them with euphoria in return. Torchwood destroyed the swarm and their queen, a giant creature in Cardiff Bay. Jack also burnt down the church of St Francis, which had been infected by the creatures.

2009 - TW: INTO THE SILENCE -> The Rift enabled an entity from the Silent Planet – a shadowy world in the furthest corner of the universe, where the formless inhabitants lived in total isolation and only corporealised to mate – to travel to Earth. The entity thought sound so beautiful, it murdered several singers to absorb their vocal cords and larynxes – but even these barely functioned as intended. The killings disrupted preparations for the fifth annual Welsh Amateur Operatic Contest. Torchwood ended the killing spree by allowing the entity to merge with Ryan Scott, an autistic child who craved isolation, and then return home. Detective Inspector Tom Cutler helped Captain Jack with the case; afterwards, Jack removed Cutler's memories of Torchwood with Retcon.

2009 - TW: BAY OF THE DEAD -> The symbiont Leet heard the siren call of his life pod, and used Oscar Phillip's memories of *The All-Night Zombie Horror Show* to create "search units" to retrieve it. Dozens if not hundreds of people were transformed into the undead but proved hard to control, so Leet sealed Cardiff within a time-energy barrier. Oscar disintegrated the cadavers by killing himself, whereupon Leet brought down the barrier and was believed to have returned home.

2009 - TW: THE HOUSE THAT JACK BUILT -> Jack discovered that interdimensional beings had polluted the timeline of a house he owned, Jackson Leaves, causing the deaths of thirteen of its residents over the past century. He destroyed the beings, and – as insurance against more fatalities – enabled to the current owners of Jackson Leaves to win a lottery, preventing them from renting the house out.

2009 - TW: ASYLUM -> Some inhabitants of an unknown planet escaped in "lifeboats" when solar flares ravaged their world. One lifeboat landed on Earth, and the thirteen benevolent aliens aboard integrated with Earth society and sired offspring with humanity. One of the aliens lived in Cardiff under the name "Moira Evans".

The Rift disgorged Moira's granddaughter – Freda, a Cardiff resident in 2069, whose personal debit gun could disrupt modern-day communications, security and transport systems. Captain Jack's team suspected that the Torchwood of the future had deliberately sent Freda back so they would adopt an asylum policy, hopefully blunting some of the xenophobia that Torchwood would otherwise cause. Jack, Gwen and Ianto helped Freda adjust to life in the present.[1244]

2009 - TW: GOLDEN AGE -> The "time store" at Torchwood India required an ever-growing amount of energy, which it collected via an energy net that consumed the potential, unfulfilled history of people's lives. Over the last few months, the net had made thousands of beggars and transients in India vanish without a trace. Captain Jack's Torchwood team investigated the resultant temporal emissions in Delhi. The Duchess tried to widen the time store's effect and roll the whole of Earth back to 1924, but Jack sabotaged the device. The Duchess and her colleagues were unwilling to venture into the modern world; the device exploded, destroying them and Torchwood India.

2009 - TW: THE DEAD LINE -> Professor Stella Courtney, an old flame of Jack Harkness, was now a grandmother and one of the country's top neuroscientists. The electrical virus trapped in the disused Madoc House escaped and quickly infected twenty people – including

Captain Jack – by ringing their phones. Through these victims, the virus sought to achieve the critical mass required to ring every phone across the world. Ianto and Gwen destroyed the virus with an electro-magnetic pulse, causing its victims to awaken.

2009 (Wednesday to Sunday) - TW: RISK ASSESSMENT[1245] **->** Torchwood destroyed the planet-eating Vam when it manifested on Earth, but not before it further ravaged the SkyPoint apartment complex. Agnes Havisham, the Torchwood Assessor, awoke once more from stasis and colluded with George Herbert Sanderson – her fiancé – to help the supposedly peaceful xXltttxtolxtol settle on Earth. Torchwood helped to destroy a xXltttxtolxtol bridgehead once the aliens' conquering intentions became known, and Havisham left to start a new life with Sanderson.

(=) 2009 - TW: THE UNDERTAKER'S GIFT -> Hokrala Corp's use of warp-shunt technology to send people and messages into the past had widened the Rift, and the Already Dead – beings who sought to keep the Rift from their enemies' hands – exploited this by triggering a temporal fusion device known as the Undertaker's Gift. The resultant explosion destroyed Cardiff. An enormous Vortex Dweller came through the widened Rift and reclaimed its child, Zero. In gratitude to Captain Jack, the Dweller rewrote history to stop the Already Dead from building their temporal device.

1244 *TW: Out of Time* establishes that Torchwood already has asylum protocols for people from the past, so the issue here must be in convincing the group to similarly protect benevolent aliens.
1245 Dating *TW: Risk Assessment* (*TW* novel #13) - It's "Thursday" (p92), and after the new morning dawns, it's said that Havisham was revived "two days ago" (so, she awoke on a Wednesday). Gwen goes missing for "two days" after that, so the story concludes on a Sunday.
1246 Dating *The Eternal Summer* (BF #128) - After the bubble's collapse, Max reappears in Stockbridge on 4th August, 2009 – one of many dates said in a time ripple, and probably representing the furthest point that the time bubble extends into the future. By default, then, that's when the story takes place. Max also confirms, in a conversation with the Doctor, that it's now the twenty-first century. *The Eternal Summer*, alas, wasn't actually released in summer, but came out in November 2009.
1247 Dating *TW: Consequences*: "The Wrong Hands" and "Virus" (*TW* novel #15c, #15d) - The second day of "Virus" falls on the "last Thursday of the month", so it's not yet September, as that would conflict with *TW: Children of Earth*.

1248 Dating *The Three Companions* (serialised story; BF #120-129) - The story appears contemporary, and was released April 2009 to February 2010. Tellingly, Polly tells the Brigadier that it's been "forty-three years" since she last saw the Doctor – presumably referencing the duration of time between *The Faceless Ones* (set in 1966) and the release of *The Three Companions* in 2009.

The Brigadier in return tells Polly that he hasn't seen the Doctor in "twenty years" – a pretty nonsensical thing to say, whatever one's views on *Doctor Who* continuity. It's possible this comment is similarly meant to denote the amount of time that's passed between the release of *The Three Companions* and the last time the Brig saw the Doctor on TV – in *Battlefield*, broadcast in 1989 – but not only does this ignore the tie-in stories featuring the Brig in that interim (including those made by Big Finish!), it forgets that *Battlefield* wasn't actually set in 1989, and instead dates to the mid-90s. The oversight becomes even more peculiar when you consider that Marc Platt wrote both *The Three Companions* and the *Battlefield* novelisation.

Brewster's journal says that the meet-up between him, Polly and the Brigadier – and by extension the end

(=) 2009 (4th August) - THE ETERNAL SUMMER[1246] -> A hyperspatial warp-core explosion originating in 1899 caused a time-stasis field to encompass all of Stockbridge. The bubble trapped six decades of the town's history, and the residents were made to experience their lives over and over again.

In one version of events, the entity Veridios awoke and endowed the fifth Doctor and Nyssa – who had been thrown forward in time by the explosion – with some of its life force. As "the Lord and Lady of the Manor", they ruled Stockbridge for at least a million years. They became ancient, desiccated husks that leeched off the histories of their subjects.

In another version of events, the Doctor and Nyssa awoke in Stockbridge to find that he was regarded as the town doctor and she was its postmistress. The Lord and Lady threatened to expand the bubble so they could feed upon humanity, but the Doctor collapsed it, erasing the Lord and Lady's timeline.

Only Maxwell Edison remembered these events. The bubble's collapse hurled the Doctor and Nyssa into the future, to Stockbridge's last days.

2009 (August) - TW: CONSEQUENCES:"The Wrong Hands" / "Virus"[1247] -> Jack, Gwen and Ianto recovered an alien weapon – a Torrosett 51 binary heat-cannon – that was an offering from an alien mother who had abandoned her child. Half of the cannon self-destructed, destroying the child and a Happy Price supermarket. The next day, the child's vengeful father infected Jack and Gwen with a Kagawa Virus that paralysed them with a mental feedback loop. Ianto acquired an antidote from a black market operation selling alien tech, and destroyed the group's base of operations with a Tregennan demolition bomb.

2009 (August) - THE THREE COMPANIONS[1248] -> Garry Lendler was still working as a merchantman and purveyor of quality goods for extra-terrestrial clients. He found the Doctor's TARDIS adrift in space with Thomas Brewster inside, and gave Brewster a job overseeing his warehouse. Brewster's negligence caused a coffin-loader – the ultimate space-scavenger, swarms of which would appear in the last few days of a doomed world – to hatch.

The coffin-loader hid under London, and started generating a mould that triggered an environmental crisis. The Amazon basin went without precipitation for four months, but London had six straight days of rainfall. Flooding was reported halfway up to Farringdon, and Westminster was only approachable by boat. Parts of the Underground were closed, and the government relocated to Birmingham. Cliff Jones, now attached to the Institute of Mycology in Brazil, attended an emergency summit in New York concerning the crisis. The profit-minded Lendler coordinated with Jones to seed Earth's clouds with a substance that would eliminate the mould.

On Lendler's orders, Brewster searched for the Doctor's former associates, and tracked down Polly Wright and the Brigadier. Polly now worked in a governmental office in Westminster. On Tuesday the 18th, Brewster had Polly and the Brigadier meet at the Hope Springs Café on Beagle Street. They aided him as an alien hunter died while exterminating the coffin-loader, in a struggle that ravaged half of Trafalgar Square with fire. Lendler's cloud-treatment eliminated the coffin-loader's mould, and Polly and the Brigadier coerced Lendler into providing further clean-up services at reduced charges. Brewster left in the TARDIS.

2009 - TW: GHOST TRAIN[1249] -> The computer directing space traffic for legions of Powell clones sought to leave its dying homeworld. It opened up a wormhole to Earth, and used its trains to send its components through for reassembly. An escapade with one such train resulted in

of the story – occurs on "Tuesday the 18th". In 2009, only August had such a day.

Polly's first encounter with Lendler is fairly hard to date, as Lendler's origins are so unknown – whether or not he's a time traveller, or is even human despite his having the demeanour of one, is entirely unclear – so the "Polly's Story" component of this adventure has been relegated to None of the Above.

1249 Dating *TW: Ghost Train* (*TW* audiobook #6) - Torchwood seems to deal with other cases during the two-week period in which the future Rhys hides out in Ianto's apartment and fulfills his own history (hence why Ianto keeps downing minor doses of Retcon, to guarantee that his actions are historically consistent), but as no references are given, deciding *which* stories happen in this gap is something of a tossup.

Curiously, the story's continuity is a bit awry – Rhys' co-worker says that it's "February", but Rhys himself mentions the ATMOS incident, which has to occur later than that (see the dating notes on *The Sontaran Stratagem*). The blurb says that the story occurs before *TW: Children of Earth*, but doesn't specify that it's after Series 2. No mention is made of Owen or Tosh – while it's not impossible that they're still alive (meaning that it's prior to *TW: Exit Wounds*), one has to wonder why – if that were the case – there's no evidence of their being involved in the waves of crises Torchwood here deals with. With that in mind, it's probably best to ignore the "February" reference, and place the story in the *Torchwood* Series 2-3 interim, which according to writer James Goss was the intent.

Rhys being thrown back in time two weeks. With help from Ianto, Rhys' future self set about creating the very events that had led to his involvement in the incident – including a disruption to Cardiff's satellite navigation and the theft of at least three dozen fridges.

Neither Rhys, nor Torchwood, realised that the fridges he was hauling during these events were part of The Committee's operations.[1250]

2009 - TW: CONSEQUENCES: "Consequences" ->

Nina Melanie Rogers, a history student at Cardiff University, happened upon the sentient book that had an interest in Torchwood. The book compelled Nina to observe Torchwood, but Jack, Gwen and Ianto fulfilled history by sending the book through the Rift to 1899, then Retconned Nina to eliminate the book's influence on her.

2009 - TW: "Fated to Pretend" ->

Dozens of people transformed by Monsieur Jechiel into undead beings had felt compelled to congregate beneath Cardiff. One of the undead went rogue and killed sixteen people, whereupon Jack – to prevent more such incidents – told the undead that he could either take them to live as workers on the Heretical Moons... or they could end their lives simply by walking into the rain. They opted for the latter.

2009 - TW: "Somebody Else's Problem" ->

Gwen traced production of R'Ochni – a street drug that killed any human who used it – to Mister Quatnja's operation at the run-down Huffern Estate. She convinced Jack to put Quatnja out of business.

2009 - TW: "Hell House" ->

The shadowy horror that Jack defeated in 1902 sought revenge, but Torchwood drained its essence into an improved version of Lionel Barrett's spectral containment unit.[1251]

2009 - TW: DEPARTMENT X ->

The economic downturn motivated Firestone Finance to return to the practice of finding and selling alien technology. One of Firestone's customers – a bullion facility in the Ural Mountains – wanted the alien within Gareth Robert Owen as a defence system. The formerly tiny alien was now mature and ravenous, and had killed thirty-four people. Torchwood destroyed the creature, and Owen resumed ownership of his family's department store.

2009 - TW: GHOST TRAIN[1252] ->

The inter-dimensional link formed by the alien traffic computer caused some maladies afflicting its homeworld to bleed through to Cardiff. Torchwood variously dealt with a rain of fire (officially cited as the result of climate change) on Cardiff's west side, dragons, shapeshifting assassins, a "yellow, blotchy" plague in Ryder that Ianto cured, a few outbreaks of mass hysteria and an increase in the Rift's "field of despair". Jack and Rhys commandeered one of the computer's inter-dimensional trains and attempted to out-race a fireball headed down the link – causing Rhys to be thrown back in time while Jack crashed the train into the

1250 *TW: The Torchwood Archive* (BF)
1251 Barrett is a physicist who appears in *The Legend of Hell House* (1973).
1252 Dating *TW: Ghost Train* (*TW* audiobook #6) - To the contemporary Rhys, events begin on a Wednesday and (after he's thrown back in time and catches up with the present) end on a Friday morning.
1253 Dating *TW: The Devil and Miss Carew* and *TW: Submission* (*TW* audio dramas #5-6) - These two audios were released after *TW: Miracle Day* (as part of the *Torchwood: The Lost Stories* box set), but take place during the Series 2 to 3 interim. *Submission* occurs fifty years (the duration of Doyle's memories) after the *Guernica* went missing in August 1959. The dating clues in *The Devil and Miss Carew* are a bit bewildering – Gwen says that Joanna Carew, born in 1930, is now "81", suggesting that it's now 2011 (which is clearly isn't). Also, a radio shipping forecast gives the date as "Wednesday, the 10th of November" – that day was a Wednesday in 2010, but not 2009 or 2011.
1254 Dating *TW: Outbreak* (BF *TW* special release #2) - The year is given. The story occurs within the *Torchwood* Series 2-3 interim, and is likely after *TW: The Sin Eaters*, as Ianto was then surprised that Torchwood owned a speedboat and it's here used.
1255 Dating *TW: The Office of Never Was* (BF *TW* #17) - Exact time-frame unknown, but the story was released on the eighth anniversary of *TW: Children of Earth*. Ianto phones Jack to say "It's Friday night, and I've just picked a lock". He also muses that "a good solid Toshiko explanation" must exist for the weird happenings, but he might be speaking of her posthumously.
1256 "Two months" before *SJA: Secrets of the Stars.*
1257 "A few months" before *SJA: The Wedding of Sarah Jane Smith.*
1258 Dating *TW: Children of Earth* (TW 3.01-3.05) - As with Series 2, *Children of Earth* bucks the trend that *Doctor Who*-related episodes in this era are a year ahead of broadcast. Conspicuously, Ianto picks up a newspaper with the dateline, "Wednesday, September 2009" – as the paper is put out for the morning of Day Two, the 456 crisis must begin on a Tuesday and end on a Saturday. It's twice said that "forty-four years" have passed since 1965 – once in Day Two in reference to how long Clement's real name has been inactive, and once by Rhys in Day Four. The real-life Ianto Shrine plaque in Cardiff Bay says that he died in 2009.

defunct Queen Street Station, killing three hundred Powell replicants. The inter-dimensional link was severed, and Jack put the alien computer to work managing Cardiff's traffic lights.

2009 - TW: THE DEVIL AND MISS CAREW[1253] ->

"Fitzroy", a single entity who wandered the stars, and had been born of nothing, desired a home. It struck bargains with pensioners, rejuvenating their vigor in exchange for their aid. Rhys Williams' great uncle, Bryn Williams, refused to bargain with Fitzroy and was given a fatal heart attack.

Joanna Carew, the octogenarian head of First Valley Computings – a developer of operating systems for utilities companies, and so had unique access to the Western World's power supplies – accepted Fitzroy's bargain. She began dampening electrical systems first in the UK, then Europe, so Fitzroy could arrive on Earth without facing electrical interference. Torchwood intervened – Carew fell to her death, and Fitzroy was kept at bay in deep space.

2009 - TW: SUBMISSION[1253] ->

Torchwood dealt with an alien casino, and blew up some aliens as they fled in a minivan down the M4 – at the cost of also damaging the Severn Bridge.

The alien aboard the *Guernica* in the Mariana Trench had exhausted Captain Doyle's memories, and sent out a cry for help – between 23:42 to 23:46, GMT, anyone in the world who had their head under water heard a distorted form of it. Ianto asked Carlie Roberts – a marine biologist, old flame and former Torchwood coworker – for help. Torchwood was transported in the USS *Calvin*, an Arleigh Burke class destroyer, to the *Octopus Rock*: the first in a new class of submarine, equipped with diving suits made from dwarf star alloy. Jack, Gwen, Ianto and Carlie visited the Trench and encountered the alien, which died as they returned to the surface.

2009 - TW: OUTBREAK[1254] ->

Heights Pharmaceuticals revived the Good Thinking Project. Its nano-tech would relay people's very thoughts to a central database, enabling Good Thinking controllers to instruct the public on how to vote, who to kill, and more. Experiments with Good Thinking caused a viral outbreak in Cardiff, causing victims to experience a dissociative state, then an intense desire to murder loved ones. Cardiff was quarantined behind a ring of steel as Jack Harkness was also infected, and – as goaded by Norton Folgate, appearing as a hologram from 1955 – tried to kill Ianto Jones. Jack recovered and inserted a trojan horse into Heights' data core, which deactivated the nano-tech and obliterated the Good Thinking research.

c 2009 - TW: THE OFFICE OF NEVER WAS[1255] ->

Oliver Milne lured Ianto Jones to the ruins of Milne Futures in Splot, to get revenge for his employees' deaths. Ianto wound up snaring Milne in his own death trap. To clear his conscience, Ianto wiped his memory with Retcon.

Martin Trueman was an astrologer... and a fraud. Just as he confessed this to one of his clients, he was hit by a shooting star charged with the power of the Ancient Lights, and turned into a genuine psychic.[1256] A partner in a law firm, Peter Anthony Dalton, died after falling down a stairwell in his home.[1257]

> (=) Dalton accepted the Trickster's offer to live again, and became a pawn in one of the Trickster's gambits against Sarah Jane Smith. Peter later cancelled out the deal, which restored his death.

Torchwood Series 3: *Children of Earth*

The 456 Incident: Ianto Jones Dies, Destruction of the Torchwood Hub

2009 (a Tuesday to Saturday in September) - TW: CHILDREN OF EARTH[1258] -> The 456 heralded its return to Earth with a transmission that caused all of humanity's children to stand frozen in silence for one minute at 8:40 GMT. Hours later, the 456 made the children stop and chant, in English, in unison, "We... we... we... are... we are... coming."

John Frobisher, the Permanent Secretary to the Home Office of the United Kingdom and Northern Ireland, ordered the deaths of anyone connected to the 1965 incident with the 456 – Captain Jack Harkness included – to prevent the government's previous dealings with the aliens becoming known. Government operatives wrongly believed that Jack's immortality stemmed from the Torchwood Hub, and so destroyed it with a bomb planted in Jack's stomach. Simultaneous to the Hub's obliteration, Earth's children chanted, "We are coming... back."

On Day Two of the crisis, the 456 sent the UK government instructions for the construction of an environmental chamber suitable for the 456's representative. This was built in the M15 headquarters, Thames House. The children of Earth stopped and chanted: "We are coming tomorrow."

On Day Three, the children of Earth pointed toward London as the 456's representative descended from the skies in a column of fire, and occupied the chamber in Thames House. Humanity's children declared: "We are here." Prime Minister Brian Green withdrew from dialogue with the 456 per objections raised by General Austin Pierce of the US and Colonel Oduya of UNIT. It was agreed that the UK civil service, as a nonelected branch with no authority of state, would conduct the talks; Frobisher was chosen as Earth's ambassador. The 456 told Frobisher that it wanted a "gift": 10% of the children of the entire human race.

On Day Four, the 456 said humanity had one day to deliver 10% of their children; refusal would trigger the destruction of the entire human race. The 456 refused a counter-offer of one child for every million people (6,700 in total), and made Earth's children chant a number equal to 10% of the children of each country. Green's Cabinet privately decided that children would be taken from the lowest-rated schools, and exempted their own children and grandchildren from the selection. Torchwood forced a confrontation with the 456 – who, as a demonstration of their power, released a virus that killed nearly everyone within Thames House, including Ianto Jones of Torchwood. The 456 sent a pulse that killed Clement McDonald, who had been tethered to the 456 following the 1965 incident.

On Day Five, the 456 told Earth's negotiators that the surrendered children would be biologically grafted to the 456, and not age while producing chemicals that made the 456 "feel good". The world governments mobilised to secure the children by force, under a cover story that they were to be inoculated against further alien communication. The UK army started collecting children from schools and their households at 12:00 hours. Green informed Frobisher that the government must be seen to have suffered loss against the 456, and ordered that Frobisher surrender his two daughters to the aliens. To prevent this, Frobisher killed his daughters, his wife and then himself.

Jack Harkness transmitted the wavelength used to murder Clement through humanity's children, turning it into a constructive wave. The 456 representative exploded in a shower of blood, and its remains were withdrawn on a column of fire. Humanity's children suffered no harm, save for the single child Jack had used at the centre of the resonance: his grandson Steven, who died. Frobisher's executive assistant, Bridget Spears, used Torchwood's surveillance equipment to record Green making incriminating statements, allowing Home Secretary Denise Riley to gain political leverage over him.

Gwen Cooper learned that she had been pregnant for three weeks. The Home Office believed that Torchwood Two had been disbanded.

Aftermath of the Hub's Destruction

The Hub's destruction created enough kinetic energy to activate the alien viewer in Suzie Costello's belly, and would facilitate her revival in weeks to come.[1259] The destruction of the Torchwood Hub enabled an indestructible Shiva virus container to get out into the open. It wound up in the garden allotment of Yasmin Kahn's grandfather.[1260]

The deaths of Ianto Jones, Owen Harper and Toshiko Sato eliminated the mental pieces of the alien "body jacker" dormant within their minds, but it reintegrated as best it was able, and resumed jumping from host to host.[1261] Following the Hub's destruction, a crooked bank manager embezzled many of Torchwood's financial reserves. Mr Colchester, a civil servant, was tasked with restoring the Torchwood Hub and containing any dangers therein.

1259 *TW: Long Time Dead*
1260 *TW: Fallout*
1261 *TW: Army of One*
1262 *TW: Aliens Among Us*
1263 As we learn in *The End of Time*. Martha was engaged to Tom Milligan as of *The Sontaran Experiment/ The Poison Sky*, but the relationship evidently ended off screen.
1264 *TW: Children of Earth*
1265 "Don't Step on the Grass"
1266 *TW:* "Shrouded". Jack is here seen at Ianto's funeral; in *TW: The House of the Dead*, he tells Ianto's ghost that he wasn't because he "had to leave".
1267 *TW: Miracle Day*. This occurs prior to *TW: Long Time Dead* (p238).
1268 *TW: More Than This*
1269 Dating "Don't Step on the Grass" (IDW *DW* Vol. 1 #9-12) - Martha is now married and Magambo tells the Doctor that "Torchwood's gone", indicating that the story occurs after *TW: Children of Earth*. Denise Riley is cited as Home Secretary and Brian Green is said to be

Prime Minister – offices they might well continue with for some time after *Children of Earth*. Martha here accepts the "Sontaran job" on which she and Mickey are working when we next see them in *The End of Time*. Events in "Don't Step on the Grass" continue in "Old Friend" and "Final Sacrifice".
1270 "Nine months" before *TW: The Men Who Sold the World*.
1271 Dating *SJA: The Day of the Clown* (SJA 2.2) - Luke opens the story by reading an email from Maria dated to "9th October", but as Rani's mum says that it's a Monday, he must have received the email a few days prior (9th October was a Friday in 2009), had a busy weekend and didn't read it until the following Monday. *The Ealing Echo* reports upon the disappearance "yesterday" of the victim in the opening credits, so the story begins on the 11th and takes place over two days, ending on the 13th. Luke has school records from the "past year". Park Vale here gains a headmaster, and seems to have been without one since the Slitheen killed Haresh's predecessor in *SJA: Revenge of the Slitheen*.

However, a report on the Rift's stability prompted a cut to Torchwood's funding, just prior to a stock market crash.[1262]

Martha Jones and Mickey Smith married[1263] and were on their honeymoon during the 456 crisis.[1264] The tenth Doctor sent them a wedding gift – without warning that nobody should spill champagne on it. Martha later chastised the Doctor for this, claiming it took four hours to get her mum off the ceiling.[1265]

John Hart was present at Ianto's funeral. Also in attendance were alternate-history versions of Mairwyn and an Ianto who had accepted her offer.[1266]

Angelo Colasanto's agents recovered a Proper Null Field – an alien device that could generate a cancellation wave – from the Hub's remains.[1267] Gwen Cooper salvaged parts of the Rift Manipulator from the Hub, and from it built a tracker to follow the Rift's activities.[1268]

2009 - "Don't Step on the Grass"[1269] -> Martha, now a freelance agent who sometimes continued to work for UNIT, summoned the tenth Doctor, Emily Winter and Matthew Finnegan to Greenwich. They and UNIT forces led by Erisa Magambo became embroiled in a pitched battle between the Enochians (who had freed themselves from imprisonment, and whose essence was variously turning trees into ravenous monsters or animating clockwork bodies) and the Knights of the Arboretum. The Advocate had engineered the conflict as part of her crusade against the Doctor, but the Enochians were contained aboard their spaceship and blown up. Matthew left the Doctor and Emily's company, preferring to travel with the Advocate.

The Department's salvage team retrieved a Ytraxorian Reality Gun from the Hub's remains.[1270]

Rani Chandra Joins Sarah Jane's Team

2009 (11th-13th October) - SJA: THE DAY OF THE CLOWN[1271] -> Haresh and Gita Chandra moved into 36 Bannerman Road. Sarah Jane, Luke and Clyde quickly made friends with their daughter, Rani, a budding journalist... and Clyde was horrified to discover that Haresh was their new headmaster.

Meanwhile, three children had gone missing in two weeks. Rani, Luke, Clyde and Sarah Jane all worked out that every missing child had visited the clown exhibit at a local circus museum: Spellman's Magical Museum of the Circus. The owner, Elijah Spellman, was the legendary Pied Piper. He caused balloons that mesmerised on contact to rain from the sky, and thereby attempted to steal all the children at Park Vale. He psychically attacked Sarah Jane, but Clyde broke the spell by telling jokes. Spellman weakened, and was confined to a fragment of the meteorite he'd fallen to Earth in centuries before. Sarah sealed the meteorite fragment away in a box of Halkonite steel, though which not even thoughts could penetrate.

By now, Sarah Jane, Luke and their friends had saved the world twelve times.[1272]

2009 - SJA: THE NIGHTMARE MAN[1273] -> Luke told Sarah Jane he planned to take his A Levels early, allowing him to go to university a year ahead of his class – and made this announcement while the two of them were handcuffed to a bomb by a group of Slitheen. K9, Rani and Clyde saved them.

2009 (30th-31st October) - FOREVER AUTUMN[1274] -> The tenth Doctor and Martha arrived in Blackwood Falls, New England, to investigate an anomalous energy pulse. The buried Hervoken spaceship had repaired itself,

---

1272 According to Clyde in *SJA: The Day of the Clown*. It's the sort of statement to make a fan chronologer go rushing to his/her notebook, so here goes: 1. the Bane (*SJA: Invasion of the Bane*); 2. the Slitheen (*SJA: Revenge of the Slitheen*); 3. the Gorgon (*SJA: Eye of the Gorgon*); 4. Kudlak (*SJA: Warriors of Kudlak*); 5. the Trickster (*SJA: Whatever Happened to Sarah Jane?*); 6. the Keratin (*SJA: The Glittering Storm*); 7. Ravage (*SJA: The Thirteenth Stone*); 8. the Slitheen again (*SJA: The Lost Boy*); and 9. the Sontarans (*SJA: The Last Sontaran*). The Verron soothsayer referred to in *SJA: Whatever Happened to Sarah Jane?* and *Journey's End* might count. We also know from *Whatever Happened to Sarah Jane?* that Sarah defeated the Patriarchs of the Tin Vagabond, quite probably after besting the Gorgon (although it's possible that she did this on her own, without the kids' help). Sarah and Luke had a role in the defeat of the

Daleks (*The Stolen Earth/Journey's End*)... which would make twelve, and not force us to fancifully imagine that Sarah and company were somehow involved the 456 affair in *Torchwood: Children of Earth*.
1273 Dating *SJA: The Nightmare Man* (SJA 4.1) - We see this in flashback; a caption says that the main events of the story occur set "a year" later. Rani's inclusion, however, means that it's after *SJA: The Day of the Clown* (so, it hasn't actually been a full year; it's more like eleven months). K9 appears in the flashback, even though he hasn't yet been released from his black-hole-containment duties (*SJA: The Mad Woman in the Attic*), so he must have briefly been let out to deal with this crisis.
1274 Dating *Forever Autumn* (NSA #16) - No year is given, but the book was released in 2007 and seems contemporary. The story opens on Friday afternoon – the day before Halloween (p9) – and continues to next

but required an injection of negative emotional energy to power its escape. The Hervoken planned an atrocity in the town using possessed animals and Halloween costumes, but Doctor disrupted their ceremony and destroyed them.

2009 - SJA: THE TIME CAPSULE[1275] -> The Persopolisian named Janxia revived from stasis, and sought out the components of the lost construction device. One of these was the black diamond of Ernfield – an enigmatic 82-CD gem that was on exhibit at the Natural History Museum, where Luke Smith had a work placement. Janxia's attempts to claim the diamond triggered chaos, causing a dinosaur exhibit to explode. Sarah Jane and her friends accidentally caused Janxia and the diamond to meet their fate in a car compactor. Sarah gave the museum a copy of the diamond and, to avoid awkward questions about Luke's role in the fracas, also donated an alien jewel she'd obtained from a Kissarni.

2009 - SJA: THE GHOST HOUSE[1276] -> Sarah Jane and her friends discovered that the plain-looking house at 39 Bannerman Road had mysteriously been replaced by the Victorian villa that had stood there from 1865 to 1969. A temporal bridge formed between their era and 1884, and they journeyed back there to stop a pair of alien war criminals from destroying the world.

The Third Death of Suzie Costello

2009 (early November) - TW: LONG TIME DEAD[1277] -> The Department, as led by Mr Black, had dispatched retrieval teams to sift through the Hub's remains. Suzie Costello awoke in a fully healed body within the heavily damaged Torchwood morgue – but found that the alien viewer in her belly had linked her to an extra-terrestrial blackness, a space between dimensions that was hungry. Its energies surged through Suzie and killed various individuals – their brains were pulped, and their consciousnesses were consigned to the darkness' void. As the darkness grew stronger, at least fifteen Cardiff residents were pulled into seemingly ordinary shadows. The proximity of the darkness caused at least seven people who had been treated with Retcon to regain their memories, and they committed suicide after scrawling "I Remember".

Suzie became lovers with Detective Inspector Tom Cutler. He deduced her involvement in both the mysterious deaths and the spatial disturbances, which were now large enough for NASA to detect. Cutler lured Suzie to the ruined Hub, where his associates detonated charges that brought rubble down atop them. Jack Harkness was nearby as the darkness within Suzie claimed Cutler, instants before their bodies were pulverised.

---

day, which fits the real-world calendar of 2009 but not any other year (to draw arbitrary boundaries) from 2006 to 2012.

1275 Dating *SJA: The Time Capsule* and *SJA: The Ghost House* (*SJA* audiobooks #3-4) - The audios were released together on 13th November 2008, between the broadcasts of *SJA: The Mark of the Berserker* and *SJA: The Temptation of Sarah Jane Smith*. However, Luke is said to be 14 in *The Time Capsule*, so it's before he "turns 15" in *SJA: Secret of the Stars* (and where *The Time Capsule* goes, *Ghost House* might as well go also). That fits with Sarah Jane's claim in *The Time Capsule* that the Chandras moved in "so recently" (*SJA: The Day of the Clown*).

Two bits of discontinuity exist in *The Time Capsule*: Luke says that he's only lived "for a year", when it's only been a couple of months since *SJA: Invasion of the Bane*. Also, Rani wears some glasses that Sarah Jane says "made her look older than her 15 years" – which has to be taken as a mistake, as all the on-screen evidence indicates Rani didn't meet Sarah Jane and company until she was 16. Clyde, at least, is correctly said to be 15.

1276 Dating *TW: Long Time Dead* (*TW* novel #16) - The dating evidence is a bit contradictory. It's said (p17) that the Department started combing through the ruins of the Hub "barely a month" after its destruction (in September 2009, *TW: Children of Earth*), and that it's now "three weeks" into that undertaking – meaning it's currently on or about early November 2009. The

Department believes that Gwen is still pregnant, and Jack appears in the final act, presumably before his departure from Earth (in March 2010, *Children of Earth* again). However, it's said that Suzie has been dead for "years", and that it's been "so many years ago" since she created a bank account in 2007. Most specific of all, Suzie looks at the date on a note saying when a toilet was last cleaned and concludes "She'd been dead for *three years*?" (p30), which should mean that it's now 2010, not 2009. It's something of a coin toss as to which evidence should take precedence, but the timeline of the Department salvaging the Hub seems a bit harder to set aside.

1277 Dating *SJA: Secrets of the Stars* (*SJA* 2.3) - The article reporting on the mass hypnosis event in *The Ealing Echo* at story's end is a bit difficult to make out, but seems to be datelined "November 7". Sarah and friends first go to see Trueman's show on a "Friday night", and the mass-hypnosis event occurs the next day. In 2009, 7th November was a Saturday – unfortunately, the first paragraph of *Echo* story reads, "the world was coming to [unreadable word] yesterday", suggesting that the world was spellbound on "Saturday, 6th November", and that this is yet-another instance of the calendar in a *Doctor Who*-related TV story being off from that of the real world. It's a puzzler as to how news services in this story are reporting on the "hypnosis" event when Trueman has seemingly usurped every TV broadcast.

2009 (5th-7th November) - SJA: SECRETS OF THE STARS[1278] -> Every star in the universe aligned in a perfect conjunction for the first time since the universe's creation thirteen billion years ago, and so the Ancient Lights made a bid to enthrall Earth – the first stepping stone to controlling every living being in creation. Martin Trueman, as empowered by the Ancient Lights, had gained fame as a psychic and star of the stage show *Secrets of the Stars*. Broadcasting from the East Acton New Theatre, he hijacked every TV station in the world and began systematically bringing the human race, one star sign at a time, under the control of the Ancient Lights. News services all around the globe reported that mass droves of people had fallen prey to a television hypnosis stunt. The President of the United States, also enthralled, walked out of the White House holding hands with the wife of the Prime Minister of Kazakhstan. Having no star sign, Luke Smith was immune to the Lights' power and defeated them. Trueman vanished into space, either destroyed or having journeyed away with the Ancient Lights.

Shortly after Trueman's defeat, Luke and Sarah designated "today" as Luke's "birthday".[967] Sarah Jane met Peter Dalton in a shoe shop, and they started dating in secret.[1279]

2009 (Friday, 13th November to 14th November) - SJA: THE MARK OF THE BERSERKER[1280] -> At Park Vale School, student Jacob West used a mind-controlling talisman – a device made by the alien Berserkers to create soldiers – to hypnotise a teacher. Rani found Jacob's pendant, and deposited it with Sarah Jane for safekeeping. Meanwhile, Clyde's long-lost father, Paul,

showed up. Clyde showed him Sarah Jane's attic, and Paul pocketed the pendant. He revelled in the pendant's mind-controlling ability, but the more he used its power, the more he was converted into a Berserker-soldier. Sarah Jane held up a mirror, shocking Paul into becoming himself again. She and her friends throw the pendant into the sea.

(=) 2009 (Friday, 20th November to Saturday, 21st November) - SJA: THE TEMPTATION OF SARAH JANE SMITH[1281] -> The Trickster opened a time fissure to 1951, and engineered a situation wherein Sarah Jane was tempted to travel there and visit her parents. She saved them from their historical deaths, an act that enabled the Trickster to come through a weak point in the web of time, and fully manifest from the limbo dimensions. This created an alternate history in which the Trickster sucked the life from the world – Clyde and Rani, protected from historical alterations by the Verron soothsayer's box, witnessed the remnants of humanity working as slave gangs driven by Krislok the Graske. The timeline was restored when Sarah and her parents changed history back. Clyde gave Krislok the soothsayer's box as payment for his help, freeing the Graske from the Trickster's control.

2009 (21st-22nd November) - SJA: ENEMY OF THE BANE[1282] -> Mrs Wormwood asked Sarah Jane for help, claiming that the Bane were hunting her, and that she wished to gain revenge by stopping them from releasing the ancient, evil being named Horath. Wormwood didn't know where Horath rested, and so

1278 *SJA: Secrets of the Stars.* The date that Luke and Sarah pick for his "birthday" would *seem* to be 7th November – the same as the dateline listed on the *The Ealing Echo* that appears in the same scene – although this isn't expressly said, and so they might be having the discussion on 8th November or shortly thereafter. Either way, they must take this opportunity to advance his "age" – Luke is "14" before this, but is "15" in *SJA: The Gift*. This means, however, that Luke has spent about 15 months (the time since *SJA: Revenge of the Slitheen*) being "14", and that Sarah somehow forgot to inch up his age (or throw him a birthday party, for that matter).
1279 They first meet at least "a month" before *SJA: The Wedding of Sarah Jane Smith.* While Sarah's life is very busy in this period, dealing with one crisis or another, it is hardly beyond the realm of all possibility that she could meet a man while shopping in a shoe store.
1280 Dating *SJA: The Mark of the Berserker* (SJA 2.4) - Paul Langer refers to "those Dalek things", so it's set after *The Stolen Earth/Journey's End.* Clyde's mother specifies

that the story opens on a "Friday night". As *SJA: Secret of the Stars* and *SJA: Enemy of the Bane* seem to respectively take place the first and third weeks in November, *The Mark of the Berserker* by logical extension can only start on the Friday in-between the two, i.e. 13th November, and continue to the next day.
1281 Dating *SJA: The Temptation of Sarah Jane Smith* (SJA 2.5) - The events of *SJA: Whatever Happened to Sarah Jane?* were "last year". The action begins on an afternoon and continues to the next day, when Rani says, "Mum, it's a Saturday". Given the need to accommodate *SJA: The Mark of the Berserker* occupying the only weekend available between 7th and 21st November, and the next story occurring on 21st and 22nd November, *The Temptation of Sarah Jane Smith* has to unfold the two days beforehand (see the dating notes on *SJA: Enemy of the Bane*).
1282 Dating *SJA: Enemy of the Bane* (SJA 2.6) - Miss Wormwood writes the date "20-11-200[?]" on the cheque that she gives to Gita Chandra, with the last

Sarah Jane called on Brigadier Lethbridge-Stewart. He aided Sarah in acquiring an artifact stored in the UNIT Black Archive: the Tunguska Scroll, which could summon a portal to Horath's dimension.

Sarah and her friends discovered that Wormwood was in league with the Sontaran Kaagh, and that they wanted to rule the universe using Horath's power. Wormwood and Kaagh opened the portal to Horath at a stone circle in Whitebarrow, but Wormwood then betrayed Kaagh. To regain his honour, Kaagh pushed himself and Wormwood into the portal. Sarah sealed the portal behind them, and destroyed the Scroll.

UNIT now operated under a Homeworld Security Mandate.[1283]

2009 - SJA: FROM RAXACORICOFALLAPATORIUS WITH LOVE[1284] -> A Slitheen posing as "Ambassador Rahnius of the Galactic Alliance" teleported into Sarah Jane's attic to lavish praise upon her group... and then immobilised them with energy-laced deeley boppers. The Slitheen hoped to capture K9 and use his systems to steal from galactic banks. Sarah overcame the Slitheen with her sonic lipstick, and Mr Smith teleported the Slitheen away.

The Sarah Jane Adventures
Series 3 (first half)[1285]

2009 (a Sunday) - SJA: PRISONER OF THE JUDOON
-> The homeworld of the reptilian Veil had perished when its sun turned cold. The Veil named Androvax, thinking himself the only survivor, subsequently became a nihilist and was responsible for the destruction of twelve planets. The Judoon captured Androvax, but Tybo, a captain of the 1,005th Judoon Guard, crashed to Earth while escorting Androvax elsewhere. This was a violation of The Articles of the Shadow Proclamation, which deemed Earth as primitive and forbade the Judoon from setting foot there.

Androvax used the technology at the nanotech company Genetec to construct a spacecraft, but Judoon reinforcements arrived and arrested him. For their interference, the Judoon cited Clyde and Rani with a ticket that banned them from leaving Earth.[1286]

Androvax learned at his trial that before his homeworld's destruction, one hundred of his people had escaped in a spaceship.[1287]

digit being a squiggle, probably either an "8" or a "9". Either way, the third digit is a zero (so it's before 2010), and the date of 20th November is very legible.

The story opens with Rani's mum Gita working late on Saturday night to accommodate Mrs Wormwood's order; the action continues the next morning when Rani and Haresh realise that Gita has gone missing (because Wormwood abducts her to get Sarah's attention). In 2009, 20th November was actually a Friday, not a Saturday, although it's plausible to think that Wormwood wrote the cheque the day beforehand as preparation for her scheme. That said, with the previous Series 2 stories occupying the other weekends in November, the cheque can only have direct relevance if *SJA: The Temptation of Sarah Jane Smith* and *Enemy of the Bane* occur in rapid succession over a three-day period. Such a scenario is more believable than it might seem – as Sarah is only summoned to look into Gita's disappearance the morning after it happens, her group at least has the comfort of dinner and a night's sleep after *The Temptation of Sarah Jane Smith* before dealing with this newest dilemma. In the course of her adventuring, Sarah has surely had to cope with a lot worse.

1283 *SJA: Enemy of the Bane*, and suggested by mention of "homeworld security" (*The Sontaran Stratagem*).

1284 Dating *SJA: From Raxacoricofallapatorius With Love* (2009 *Comic Relief* special) - This five-minute special aired between Series 2 and 3, and fits comfortably there. K9 briefly appears, presumably leaving his duties around the black hole for a few minutes. The very last image is of K9 wearing the *Comic Relief* red nose, but

this isn't any more of a continuity violation than William Hartnell wishing everyone a merry Christmas at the end of *The Daleks' Master Plan* episode seven – an episode that virtually everyone regards as canon.

1285 Dating *The Sarah Jane Adventures* Series 3 (*SJA: Prisoner of the Judoon*, 3.1; *SJA: The Mad Woman in the Attic*, 3.2; *SJA: Monster Hunt*, webcomic #1; *SJA: The White Wolf*, audiobook #5; *SJA: The Shadow People*, audiobook #6; *SJA: The Wedding of Sarah Jane Smith*, 3.3) - The transition of *The Sarah Jane Adventures* from being a show set one year ahead of broadcast (per all *Doctor Who*-related television after *Aliens of London*) and set at time of broadcast (starting with *Planet of the Dead*) means that *Sarah Jane* Series 2, 3 and 4 are condensed into about fifteen months of time. Series 2 (still a year ahead of broadcast) seems to begin in late August 2009 and to end on or around 20th November, 2009. By Series 4, the series has resumed a time-of-broadcast approach, opening in September 2010 and ending relatively close to 23rd November, 2010. (See the individual story entries for how those dates were derived.)

Series 3, then, fills the gap between the two. Where Sarah and Luke are concerned, their encounter with the tenth Doctor in *SJA: The Wedding of Sarah Jane Smith* occurs prior to their final meet-up with him in *The End of Time* – the result being that Series 3 has to be broken in half, the first three stories occurring in 2009 and the rest occurring in 2010. It's tempting to gain some flexibility on this by thinking that the dying tenth Doctor could have slipped through time a bit and met Sarah and Luke at virtually any point – as he does when

2009 (a Saturday) - SJA: THE MAD WOMAN IN THE ATTIC[1288] **->** Rani was feeling left out when Sarah Jane and her other friends discussed Maria, who was now helping "the government" to hide aliens. One of Rani's old friends from the seaside town of Danemouth, Samuel Lloyd, told her that a demon was at the local funfair. Rani investigated and met Eve, a red-skinned alien. Eve's people could read the timelines and alter history, and had been all-but-wiped out in a war.

- -
(=) Rani inadvertently wished that Sarah Jane and the others would leave her alone. Eve erased them from the timeline, creating an alternate history where Rani would be lonely her whole life. Fifty years later, Eve recognised her mistake and sent her son Adam to write Sarah Jane and the others back into history.
- -

In the restored history, Eve departed after her spaceship drained energy from the black hole that K9 was containing, enabling K9 to return to Earth. Sam Lloyd accompanied Eve, and in future would father her child.

2009 - SJA: MONSTER HUNT[1289] **->** The Krulius, an enigmatic alien who exhaled toxic gas, placed a dozen different species in quasi-digital suspension to study their strengths and weaknesses. The spaceship transporting the Krulius was damaged, causing the Krulius to download its menagerie as biodata onto Earth's World Wide Web. Clyde and Rani used Mr Smith to find the various aliens on the Internet and teleport them home. Sarah Jane signalled the Shadow Proclamation, and a squadron of Judoon arrested the Krulius.

2009 (December) - SJA: THE WHITE WOLF[1290] **->** Eddison Clough contacted Sarah Jane because photographs identified him as a friend and professional colleague of her aunt Lavinia, but he had no memory of it – or of anything at all from 1972 to 2004. Sarah and her friends looked into the town of Wolfenden, which was known as a refuge for people who believed they'd been abducted by aliens. Sarah had Mr Smith contact a passing spaceship; ambassadors soon arrived, and removed the sleeping alien convicts and their technology.

2009 (a Saturday in December) - SJA: THE SHADOW PEOPLE[1290] **->** Sarah Jane drove Luke and Clyde out to a class geography trip in the heart of Snowdonia, Wales, as the boys had been delayed by an extra-terrestrial warlord disguised as a kitten. They came across a spaceship belonging to the Shaydargen, a race of space pioneers, that had crashed millennia ago. An empathic, artificial entity built to meet the spaceship crew's needs had gone dormant, but now awakened and begged Sarah Jane and her friends to stay with it forever. Sarah persuaded the entity to let them go – and used her sonic lipstick to permanently shut down the spaceship's systems.

---

he meets Captain Jack in the space bar – but Luke's phone conversation with Clyde ("That was the maddest Christmas ever!", followed by a reference that almost certainly denotes the whole world turning into the Master) suggests that *The End of Time* has very recently happened.

Everyone is wearing clothing that's more or less commensurate with colder weather.

1286 Sarah is already aware of the Judoon, although we've never seen her meet them before now. The embargo on the Judoon visiting Earth isn't mentioned when they appear in the fifth Doctor sequence in "The Forgotten". It's said to be a Sunday, which could (in accordance with when Series 2 concludes) mean that it's now 29th November, or early December (the 6th, for instance).

1287 *SJA: The Vault of Secrets*

1288 Dating *SJA: The Mad Woman in the Attic* (*SJA* 3.2) - Sam was born in 1994 and is now "15". It's specified as being a Saturday. Presuming the comment about Maria aiding "the government" can be taken at face value, it's not entirely clear if this means the US or the UK government.

1289 Dating *SJA: Monster Hunt* (*SJA* webcomic #1) - The webcomic was released in 2009, and involves Sarah Jane, Luke, Clyde and Rani (so it's after *SJA: The Day of the Clown*). K9's appearance in the final panel suggests that it's after *SJA: The Mad Woman in the Attic*, although one does have to wonder why he isn't seen helping against the Krulius.

1290 Dating *SJA: The White Wolf* and *SJA: The Shadow People* (*SJA* audiobooks #5-6) - The audios were released together on 8th October, 2009, prior to the debut of *The Sarah Jane Adventures* Series 3. In *The White Wolf*, Sarah makes mention of encountering the Judoon (*Prisoner of the Judoon*), and Luke has memories of the "past few years", even though it's only been about sixteen months since *Invasion of the Bane*. It's "close" to exam time, suggesting that it's a bit later in the school year. With that in mind, these two stories have, a little arbitrarily, been placed after *SJA: The Mad Woman in the Attic*. Eddison Clough claims that "nearly forty years" of his life are missing – it's actually been thirty-two (1972-2004), which again proves that characters in the *Doctor Who* universe do round their sums, and not every statement can be taken literally.

In *The Shadow People*, Sarah specifies that it's a Saturday. Given that *SJA: The Mad Woman in the Attic* also occurs on a Saturday, that two weeks and five days elapse during *SJA: The Wedding of Sarah Jane*, and that

K-9 stunned Keri the Pakhar with his nose-laser when the ancient spirit of the Kortha Gestalt possessed her. Sarah Jane and Luke told the Doctor that Keri wasn't happy about the incident.[1291]

2009 (December) - SJA: THE WEDDING OF SARAH JANE SMITH[1292] -> Sarah accepted Peter Dalton's marriage proposal, but her engagement ring mysteriously glowed, and seemed to influence her mind. The wedding rushed ahead with such speed that the Brigadier couldn't attend, as he was back in Peru. Clarissa, Sarah's former editor, was present. When the Registrar asked if anyone objected, the tenth Doctor burst into the room and demanded the wedding be stopped.

His intervention came too late – this was a trap set by the Trickster, and the hotel where the wedding was taking place was moved to a mysterious white void. The Trickster offered Sarah a choice: marry Peter, and doom Earth to an alternate timeline in which she wasn't present to save it, or remain trapped in the void forever with her friends. Peter revoked his deal with the Trickster, thwarting the scheme at the cost of his own life. The Doctor took Sarah Jane and her friends home in the TARDIS.

c 2009 - THE SLITHEEN EXCURSION[1293] -> The tenth Doctor met a classics student, June, at the Parthenon. June helped the Doctor to defeat some blobby aliens, and so he took her back to ancient Greece as a reward. They returned to this time and discovered that the "blobby aliens" were in fact space police – who dutifully arrested three Slitheen that had been in stasis since 1500 BC. When June missed her train, the Doctor offered her one last hop in the TARDIS back to Birmingham.

c 2009 - "The Big, Blue Box"[1294] -> A yellow alien attacked Douglas Henderson near his home. The tenth Doctor rescued him, and revealled that Douglas was actually an advanced doomsday weapon – one banned by the Shadow Proclamation – that was capable of destroying electronics on a planetary scale. Two rival planets had sent battle fleets to recover him. Douglas set himself off aboard one of the alien ships... and awoke on Earth to find that the Doctor had provided him with enough energy to live out a normal human lifespan.

c 2009 - "Old Friend"[1295] -> The tenth Doctor and Emily Winter arrived at the Shady Grove rest home, where an old man named Barnaby was celebrating his birthday. They learned that when Barnaby was "barely 20", he had become the companion of a future incarnation of the Doctor, and that they'd fought flying slugs, Sontarans and the Floor Menace together. Barnaby had been entrusted with the charred remains of Turlough's diary, which he returned to the Doctor before dying of old age.

Sarah's wedding doesn't seem to occur in tandem with Christmas or Boxing Day, the most likely scenario is that *The Shadow People* occurs on 5th December (the only Saturday remaining following *SJA: Enemy of the Bane*). However, it could also be case that these audiobook stories happen within the two-and-a-half-week period that elapses during *The Wedding of Sarah Jane*.

Events from *SJS: Ghost Town* are mentioned in *The Shadow People*, providing a bit of cross-pollination between the Big Finish and BBC *Sarah Jane* audio series.

1291 *Big Bang Generation* (ch2).
1292 Dating *SJA: The Wedding of Sarah Jane Smith* (SJA 3.3) - Rani says, in response to Sarah making up a flimsy story and sneaking off (to meet Peter), "It's the fifth time she's done this in a month." This has commonly been interpreted to mean that nothing strange has happened to Sarah and her friends in the last month – but it doesn't, it merely denotes the frequency with which Sarah has offered a lame excuse and dashed off somewhere on her own, so all sorts of adventures could easily have occurred in the interim. Events in this story play out over two weeks and five days, with the wedding itself falling on a Saturday. No matter how one orders *SJA: The Mad Woman in the Attic*, *SJA: The White Wolf* and *SJA: The Shadow People*, at least two Saturdays

have passed since *SJA: Enemy of the Bane*, so it's definitely December. As previously mentioned, for Sarah and Luke, this story has to end before *The End of Time*. The Doctor's outfit suggests that for him, these events happen between *Planet of the Dead* and *The Waters of Mars*.
1293 Dating *The Slitheen Excursion* (NSA #32) - No year is given – but again, for the Doctor, this story is set between *Planet of the Dead* and *The Waters of Mars*.
1294 Dating "The Big, Blue Box" (IDW *Doctor Who Annual 2010*) - The story seems to have a contemporary setting.
1295 Dating "Old Friend" (IDW *Doctor Who Annual 2010*) - Barnaby lives at a "twenty-first century rest home", and there's nothing to suggest it's not a contemporary setting. The story continues in "Final Sacrifice".
1296 Dating *Blue Forgotten Planet* (BF #126) - The few sane people on Earth - the ones who take a Viyran vaccine that counteracts the madness afflicting humanity – can't remember the year, and the dating clues are very piecemeal.

It's said that two billion have perished owing to the madness – presuming that this is true, the story cannot take place before humankind's numbers are that high. Additionally, a crater is attributed to an oil refinery exploding, narrowing the possibilities to humankind's

Charley Pollard Leaves the Sixth Doctor

2009 - BLUE FORGOTTEN PLANET[1296] **->** The time-displaced Viyrans had now eliminated 3,436,000 of the viruses released from Amethyst. In five instances, they had they opted to wipe out the carriers and commit genocide.

(=) The Viyrans scanned Earth, found that a particle of the 001 variant of Amethyst icosahedral plasmic virus No. 9007/41 was present within every human, and calculated a one in 5.4 billion chance that a human would contract the virus within the next seven million years. The Viyrans attempted to eradicate the particles with their meson radiation disseminator, but this inadvertently made humanity develop a chemical imbalance that triggered forgetfulness, uncontrollable fear and rage. Wars broke out, people lost the ability to work technology, and everyone forgot what year it was. Within a decade, Earth's population was reduced by two billion.

When the sixth Doctor and Mila (who was disguised as Charley Pollard) arrived, the Viyrans revived the genuine Charley from cryo-freeze. The Doctor found that chronon particles, which occur during time travel, could destroy virus No. 9007/41. He used the TARDIS and the Viyran disseminator to put the Earth into a time bubble, then rolled back time to when the Viyrans scanned Earth. This destroyed virus No. 9007/41, and stopped the Viyrans from accidentally ruining humanity.

Either Mila or Charley died to stop the run amuck disseminator from destroying the TARDIS and Earth's history. Afterward, the survivor convinced the Doctor to let the Viyrans revise his memories to preserve the web of time. He forgot that he'd ever travelled with Charley, and believed he'd parted ways with his long-standing companion, Mila – a "tiny" woman with jet-black hair and bright green eyes – on Gralista Social. The survivor kept travelling with the Viyrans.

Hornets' Nest[1297]

c 2009 - HORNETS' NEST: THE STUFF OF NIGHTMARES -> The fourth Doctor was on a break at his cottage in Sussex when he read that a Cabinet minister had been trampled to death in his own bed by an Alpine Ibex. The following weekend, several influential figures belonging to a government think tank were trampled at a cocktail party by a charging stuffed elephant, which was brought down by the military. An elderly nuclear scientist was strangled in her bath by a stuffed python.

The Doctor investigated the killings. Taxidermy was out of fashion, so many museums and stately homes were dumping their stuffed exhibits, and lorries owned by Percy Noggins were taking them away. The Doctor found that the animals were being reanimated at Noggins' factory, but was followed back to his cottage by stuffed animals and attacked. After defeating them, the Doctor discovered the animals had paper brains inhabited by tiny hornets – creatures that could take possession of human minds, and

oil-producing period. Lastly, the Viyrans, having been thrown back in time at the end of *Patient Zero* and lived out some millennia to reach this point, seem confident that they can wipe out virus No. 9007/41 (which exists in every human) by treating the people on Earth alone, which suggests that humankind's space age hasn't happened yet. Related to this, it's implied that Charley's travelling with a past version of the Doctor has destabilised history, so the entire derailment of humankind's future – colony planets, Earth Empire, everything – may have actually occurred before the Doctor steps in and fixes things.

Taking all of that into account, the best placement for *Blue Forgotten Planet* is, funnily enough, the modern day. The story saw release in September 2009 – not only does that work as well as anything, it actually avoids any conflict with the new-series adventures happening in the same window. The only real alternative is 1930 – the year that the Doctor and Mila were travelling to, but it seems that the TARDIS missed that mark. Anyway, the survivors all talk like modern-day individuals, not people from the 30s.

The story ends with some ambiguity as to whether Mila or Charley has died; the script just *a* Charley

Pollard has a final conversation with the Doctor and departs with the Viyrans. The *Charlotte Pollard* spinoff that follows on from this story never mentions that grey area, and seems to assume that Mila, not Charley, perished.

1297 Dating *Hornets' Nest* (BBC fourth Doctor audios; *The Stuff of Nightmares*, #1.1; *The Dead Shoes*, #1.2; *The Circus of Doom*, #1.3; *A Sting in the Tale*, #1.4; *Hive of Horror*, #1.5) - The story was released in 2009, and there's nothing to suggest it doesn't have a contemporary setting. It's "the twenty-first century" and the existence of aliens is common knowledge. Mike says in the opening narration of *Hornets' Nest: The Stuff of Nightmares* that it's "the day after the winter solstice – the twenty-second of December". The Doctor relates his story the next day. It is "quite some time" since Mike's UNIT days, which were in "the seventies"; *Hornets' Nest: Hive of Horror* says that Mike's tenure with UNIT was "three decades" and "thirty years" ago. It's "seventy years" since Mrs Wibbsey's time according to *Hornets' Nest: The Dead Shoes* (so, circa 2002).

In the Doctor's personal timeline, his "recent exploits" include "giant rats, killer robots, skulls from the dawn of time" (i.e., the end of Season 14 and *Image of the*

were controlling Noggins. The Hornet Swarm made contact with the Doctor, and demonstrated that they were aliens with massive mental powers who had previously encountered him in Earth's past, but his relative future.

The Doctor gathered all the stuffed animals containing the Hornets at Nest Cottage, where he kept them trapped by use of hypnotic control and a semi-permeable force shield. A week later, the Doctor realised he could leave Nest Cottage in the TARDIS as long as he returned to the exact point in time he left. He found himself fighting the Hornets across space and time.

Noggins, free of the Hornets' influence, went home to look after his infirm grandmother, the ex-dancer Ernestina Stott. The Doctor followed a lead to 1932 and returned with Mrs Wibbsey, who became his housekeeper.[1298] The Doctor brought the shell of the body of the dwarf Antonio back to Nest Cottage, and put it in the garden.[1299] He also returned from 1039 with a dog which had been possessed by the Hornets, and named it Captain.[1300]

2009 (22nd-23rd December) - HORNETS' NEST: THE STUFF OF NIGHTMARES -> Mike Yates answered an advert placed in an issue of *Country Time* that was seemingly aimed at him, and arrived at a cottage in deepest Sussex called The Nest. He was welcomed by housekeeper Mrs Wibbsey, and reunited with the fourth Doctor. The next day, the Doctor related the first part of his story to Mike, and explained that he was running out of ideas of ways to fight the Hornets. The stuffed animals came to life

again, forcing Mike and the Doctor to barricade themselves in the cellar...

2009 (23rd December) - HORNETS' NEST: THE DEAD SHOES -> While in the cellar, the fourth Doctor related to Mike events pertaining to the Hornets in Cromer, 1932.

2009 (24th December) - HORNETS' NEST: THE CIRCUS OF DOOM / A STING IN THE TALE -> In the middle of the night, the fourth Doctor told Mike of events in Blandford in 1832. As dawn broke, the Doctor related his encounter with the Hornets in 1039.

The stuffed animals became dormant again. The Doctor and Mike realised that Mrs Wibbsey had placed the personal advertisement that summoned Mike, as she was still under the Hornets' influence. They emerged from the cellar to discover the animals were still very much active and hostile ...

2009 (24th-25th December) - HORNETS' NEST: HIVE OF HORROR[1301] **->** ... but the Doctor subdued them with hypnosis. The Queen of the Hornets inhabited the paper brain of a stuffed zebra, and the Doctor cobbled together a machine that shrunk him, Mike and Mrs Wibbsey so they could confront her. They made their way through the black and white landscape of the zebra's head, through its ear and into the brain. The Doctor miniaturised the Queen until she ended up in the microuniverse and became just another insect. The other Hornets were now

---

Fendahl). In *Hive of Horror*, he recalls events from *The Invisible Enemy*. With no mention of Leela or Romana, the *Hornet's Nest* series may take place for the Doctor between *The Invasion of Time* and *The Ribos Operation*.
1298 *Hornets' Nest: The Dead Shoes*
1299 *Hornets' Nest: The Circus of Doom*
1300 *Hornets' Nest: A Sting in the Tale*
1301 Dating *Hornets' Nest: Hive of Horror* (BBC fourth Doctor audio #1.5) - The story follows directly on from *Hornets' Nest: A Sting in the Tale*. It's Christmas Eve when the fourth Doctor, Mike and Mrs Wibbsey defeat the Hornets, and they have Christmas dinner on Christmas Day. *The End of Time* implies that at some point later that day, Mrs Wibbsey and Mike Yates would have transformed into copies of the Master.
1302 *Demon Quest: The Relics of Time*
1303 Dating *The End of Time* (X4.17-4.18) - No year is given, but it's after *Planet of the Dead*. The story begins on Christmas Eve, and unfolds over the next two days. In *SJA: Death of the Doctor*, set in 2010, Sarah acknowledges seeing the tenth Doctor as part of his "goodwill tour". The same story establishes that the dying Doctor visited every one of his former companions, not just those of his tenth incarnation.

A History of the Universe in 100 Objects (pgs. 164, 255) says that Gallifrey's return happens in "2010", but seemingly doesn't incorporate the continuity of *The Sarah Jane Adventures*.
1304 *The End of Time*. As humanity – including some billions with no Wi-Fi – spends an entire day as the Master, it seems very unlikely that many people would swallow this story.
1305 "Four Doctors" (Titan)
1306 *Hornets' Nest: Hive of Horror*
1307 Events in 2010 include the last half of *The Sarah Jane Adventures* Series 3; the present day sequences of *Doctor Who* Series 5 and *The Sarah Jane Adventures* Series 4.
1308 The Haisman Timeline
1309 As revealed in *Demon Quest: Sepulchre*. This happens "earlier in the year", i.e. 2010.
1310 The year prior to *TW: Miracle Day*.
1311 "Hotel Historia"
1312 *Extra Time*
1313 *Mad Dogs and Englishmen*
1314 "Decades" before the first portion of *Singularity*.

mindless, and so the Doctor sealed the Hive, vowing to take the Hornets to a distant galaxy.

The Doctor, Mike and Wibbsey enjoyed a Christmas dinner. The Doctor gave his dog, Captain, to Mike and installed Wibbsey permanently as his housekeeper.

On Boxing Day, the fourth Doctor installed a special cordless answering machine in Nest Cottage.[1302]

Everyone on Earth Becomes the Master; Gallifrey Appears Overhead

2009 (24th-26th December) - THE END OF TIME[1303]

-> Everyone on Earth had terrible dreams of impending destruction, but only Wilf Noble remembered them. The acolytes of Harold Saxon sacrificed themselves as part of a ritual to resurrect the Master, but Lucy Saxon sabotaged the attempt, mortally wounding the Master's new body and making it insatiably hungry. He gained fantastical abilities and seemed akin to an avatar of death. Broadfell Prison was destroyed, apparently killing Lucy.

Meanwhile, the world awaited a grand announcement from President Obama, who was to outline an instant and radical means of ending the current global recession. Donna was now engaged to Shaun Temple. They had very little money, and could only afford a tiny flat.

The restored Harold Saxon Master briefly confronted the tenth Doctor, but was then kidnapped by Joshua Naismith, a businessman and author of *Fighting the Future*. Naismith wanted the Master to help him repair the Immortality Gate that had been recovered from Torchwood, as Naismith believed that the Gate could give his daughter Abigail the gift of immortality. The Gate was of Vinvocci origin, and could be used to heal whole planets by transmitting a biological template through an entire population. The Master used the device to transmit his own biological template across the globe, turning 6,727,949,338 people on Earth (all save Donna Noble and Wilf Mott) into copies of himself. With such an army, he made plans to "turn Earth into a warship".

Rassilon and the High Council of Time Lords, still trapped inside the timelock on the final day of The Last Great Time War, saw a way to escape. They planted the sound of drums – the heartbeat of a Time Lord – into the Master's mind when he was still a child, then sent a white-point star crystal to Earth at this time. The Master retrieved the star, amplified the drum-sound now echoing through billions of people, and traced it back to its source. The disruption to the timelines allowed the entire planet of Gallifrey to emerge in space near Earth. The Master then sought to copy his biological template through every Time Lord.

Rassilon thwarted the Master by restoring humanity to normal, and the Doctor destroyed the Gate. The Master attacked Rassilon in revenge for the High Council driving him mad with the Sound of Drums, and the two of them – and all the Time Lords – vanished as Gallifrey was consigned back to the Time War.

The Doctor sacrificed his life to save Wilf, who had become trapped in a chamber that was filling with radiation. With what time he had remaining, the Doctor visited his former companions – he saved Mickey and Martha, who had become freelance alien hunters, from a Sontaran; saved Luke Smith from a car accident; attended a book signing of Verity Newman, the great-granddaughter of Joan Redfern, whose book *The Journal of Impossible Things* was based on her ancestor's diary; and travelled forward a few months to attend Donna Noble's wedding.

UNIT headquarters was still based in Geneva.

> (=) In one version of history, the tenth Doctor deemed himself more important and let Wilf die. The Doctor declared himself the Time Lord Victorious and became a dictator, but was assassinated.[1304]

Sarah Jane had Mr Smith distribute a story claiming that Wi-Fi had gone mad all over the world, and given everyone the hallucination that they had become Harold Saxon.[1305] Mike Yates planned to attend the UNIT New Year reunion.[1306]

2010[1307]

Brigadier Bishop retired from active service, and became an advisor to the World Security Council.[1308]

One Hornet had survived at Nest Cottage. Mrs Wibbsey disturbed it when she cleaned a pair of curtains, and it took control of her. It developed into a new swarm, which allied itself with an interdimensional demon capable of assuming different aspects, and began plotting its revenge on the Doctor...[1309] Dr Vera Juarez, a future associate of Torchwood, made the decision not to resuscitate her mother after she suffered a massive stroke.[1310] The Samarands invaded Greece in 2010.[1311] Rory Williams owned a vuvuzela from the 2010 World Cup, which one of his friends brought back from South Africa.[1312]

The Halliwell Film Guide of 2010 contained a particularly scathing review of *The True History of Planets* movie, which was broadcast on television for the first time this year. Britain had a King at this time.[1313] The Americans researched military applications for Schumann Resonance, a set of low frequency peaks in Earth's electro-magnetic spectrum.[1314] Earth's scientists first noticed the dark tides that permeated the universe, but it would be a long time before they were understood.[1315]

Van Gogh's *Poppy Flowers* hung in the art section of the TARDIS library; the fourth Doctor recalled that he'd "borrowed" it from Cairo, 2010, and should probably return it.[1316] Joss Laws handed down the ArkHive amulet to her 16-year-old daughter, Josephine Laws Patrick.[1317]

Flip Jackson, age 17, bought a fake ID to go clubbing in Walthamstow. She met her future husband, Jared, at a disco where he played it cool, not wanting her to think he was an idiot, when he so clearly was just that.[1318]

(=) The third Doctor surrendered Earth to the Martians. The Martians withdrew, and Earth became a nature reserve. The Doctor spent a thousand years living in Kent.[1319]

c 2010 - SHADOW OF THE PAST[1320] ->
The remains of the Mim scout locked in UNIT quarantine reconstituted, and merged with the remains of Sergeant Robin Marshall. Liz Shaw judged that the resultant hybrid, who looked like Marshall, had at least some of the man's memories and possessed none of the Mim's anger.

2010 - CUDDLESOME[1321] ->
The fifth Doctor visited Angela Wisher, a Sussex resident who aided him during the Cuddlesome slaughterhouse three years previous.

2010 - THE MACROS[1322] ->
The space-time rift created by the Philadelphia Experiment interacted with the micro-universe containing the planet Capron. Presidenter (sic) Osloo had established a dictatorship, and tapped the rift to power her society and growing army. The sixth Doctor and Peri arrived on Capron, and Osloo increased the power being siphoned from the rift – the first gambit in her effort to conquer the macro-universe from which the travellers originated. The power drain caused the USS *Eldridge*, time-looped in the rift since 1943, to disintegrate entirely. The Doctor ended Osloo's reign by neglecting to stabilise her temporal equilibrium after a trip to the macro-universe, which turned her into an infant. He also provided a battery which, hailing from the macro-universe, was powerful enough to fuel Capron for a million years.

c 2010 - MEMORY LANE[1323] ->
Travel to planets in the solar system was now feasible from Earth, and the *Led Zeppelin* spaceships were named after a public vote. Kim Kronotska became a commander in the Commonwealth Space Programme – a means of using British money to fire off rockets in the middle of the Outback – and participated in the *Led Zeppelin II* mission to the Martian moon of Phobos.

The development of cryo-stasis facilitated grander ambitions. Kim, Tom Braudy and their colleague Samuel were dispatched aboard the *Led Zeppelin IV* to Jupiter, but a system failure drew them off course. They wouldn't awaken for a hundred years. The eighth Doctor rescued Kim and Tom on the planet Lucentra, and returned them to their native era. They settled down together under adopted identities, letting the world believe they were lost in space.

The film *Star Begotten* entailed a second sun appearing over Earth.

1315 In Amy's time, and "by 2010" according to *The Coming of the Terraphiles*.

1316 Two Italian thieves did make off with *Poppy Flowers* from a Cairo museum in August 2010, but authorities recovered the painting within hours.

1317 *The Wheel of Ice* (p97). No year given. Once again, if it's assumed that the Laws women pass along the amulet at forty-year-intervals, it's probably now around 2010. (See the story dating, however, for why there's reason to suspect it's a longer stretch of time.)

1318 *The Middle*

1319 An alternative timeline seen in *So Vile a Sin*.

1320 Dating *Shadow of the Past* (BF CC #4.9) - The story's framing sequence is probably concurrent with the audio's release in April 2010. Liz says that it's been "nearly twice" as long since the Mim incident (in the UNIT era) as the young troopers slain during the event (who were "barely out of school") were alive.

1321 Dating *Cuddlesome* (BF promo #7, DWM #393) - It's been three years since the main part of the story. Angela says that her ex-partner and his fiancé have a wedding planned "for June".

1322 Dating *The Macros* (BF LS #1.8) - The Doctor gives the year as 2010, and twice generalises that it's "over sixty years" since 1943. The TARDIS has been refitted with a Zero Room (also seen in *Renaissance of the Daleks* and *Patient Zero*), following its destruction in *Castrovalva*.

1323 Dating *Memory Lane* (BF #88) - No specific year is given, but most signs indicate that Kim and Tom hail from near the present day. Kim is familiar with iPods; Tom is acquainted with both *Space Lego* (1978-2001) and *Star Wars Lego* (first introduced in 1999) and the Doctor explicitly names their ion jet rocket as the product of the twenty-first century. It's further said that the rockets come into being "thirty-five years" after the Earth-recreation of Tom's childhood on Lucentra, and although this stems from a composite of Tom's memories and isn't very reliable, it does tie in with the date for *The Seeds of Death* in this chronology.

Kim expects Tom to recognise the names of female astronauts Eileen Collins (who flew in 1995 and 1997, and commanded missions in 1999 and 2005) and Pamela Anne Melroy (who piloted space shuttle missions in 2000 and 2002, and was selected to command one in June 2006).

Lucie Miller's Time in the Present Day Ends, Tamsin Drew Joins the TARDIS

2010 - SITUATION VACANT[1324] -> The Pan-Galactic Initiative on Dimensional Rifts had been established as an organisation that monitored rogue wormholes and other dimensional anomalies. On Earth, *Situation Vacant* was a reality show that had contestants competing for a job.

The Monk had regenerated, and advertised for a new companion – then syphoned some of the more murderous and hapless respondents to a secondary location, and manipulated the eighth Doctor into handling them while he conducted the real auditions in an office in Soho. The less-than-desirable applicants assisted the Doctor in stopping a 20-foot-tall robot from menacing London. One of the companion hopefuls – Theo Lawson, a hacker who had caused a global recession – was killed. The Doctor asked another applicant, actress Tamsin Drew, to accompany him on his travels.

Lucie Miller answered the Monk's ad, and became his new companion.[1325]

2010 - APOLLO 23[1326] -> The discontinued Saturn V rocket remained the biggest launch vehicle ever built by humankind. Base Delta, America's secret moonbase, was being used to conduct clandestine experiments upon hardened criminals in an effort to remove their evil impulses, a.k.a. their Keller impulses.

The gelatinous, slimy inhabitants of the planet Taleria discovered that their bodies were dying – each new generation of Talerians was more fragile than the one before it. The Talerians took control of Base Delta – part of their plan to mentally transfer their whole race into humanity. The eleventh Doctor was briefly stranded on Earth, and rode aboard *Apollo 23* – a standby Saturn V (serial No. SA-521)

that had been mothballed since the 1970s, and was made to run on M3 Variant fuel – to reunite with Amy and the TARDIS aboard Base Delta. They stymied the Talerians' efforts, and decompression burst the Talerians' bodies. The quantum link emanating from Base Delta became non-functional, and it was expected that the base would be unsustainable without it.

2010 - CODE OF THE KRILLITANES[1327] -> In London, ordinary people began demonstrating amazing mental feats. They had been eating Brainy Crisps – which the tenth Doctor discovered contained Krillitane Oil. At the Brainy Crisps home office, the Krillitane were planning to harness the power of social networking to solve the riddle of life. They also created a new generation of Krillitane – only to find that the Director of Computing at Brainy Crisps had programmed the new Krillitane to be polite and agreeable. The two factions clashed, which destroyed the Brainy Chips factory and both generations of Krillitane.

2010 (a Saturday night) - THE FORGOTTEN ARMY[1328] -> The eleventh Doctor told Amy that the sausage-burgers served at Big Paulie's Sausages – a battered old trolly in Manhattan where a tired-looking man flipped burgers – became so renowned in future that all manner of beings (including Judoon, Graske, cat-people and Haemo-Goths) journeyed back through time to discretely consume them. Such time travellers had to endure a 12-year waiting list; the Doctor claimed to have circumvented this by purchasing the street on which the trolley stood, and named it after Amy. He recommended to her the "Doctor Burger": "like a cheeseburger but with extra bacon, sausage and steak. And a bit of chicken... No ketchup though. Absolutely banned."[1329]

The 99th Vykoid Expeditionary Force revived, and arranged for a human expedition to find its (secretly

---

1324 Dating *Situation Vacant* (BF BBC7 #4.2) - The story seems to be contemporary, and was released in July 2010. The Monk's involvement is revealed in *The Resurrection of Mars*.
1325 *The Resurrection of Mars*, as partially revealed in *The Book of Kells*.
1326 Dating *Apollo 23* (NSA #37) - It's twice said (pgs. 30, 147) that it's "thirty years" after *Apollo 22* launched in June 1980, which would roughly coincide with the novel's publication in April 2010. The time of year is more indeterminate, although mention that it's a "cold, grey day" in Texas (p7) tends to imply that it's not summer. Either way, the story cannot fit into the one-day gap between *The Eleventh Hour* and *The Big Bang*, as it takes the Doctor and company a full day (pgs. 147, 160) to prep *Apollo 23* for launch, and another two days (p147) to reach Base Delta. The Doctor says that it's "a

few hundred years" (p55) before a penal colony is built on the moon (*Frontier in Space*) and that T-Mat won't be established there (p87) "for a while yet" (*The Seeds of Death*). M3 Variant fuel was developed for the Mars Probe missions (*The Ambassadors of Death*). Mention of "Keller impulses" doubtless refers to *The Mind of Evil*.
1327 Dating *Code of the Krillitanes* (Quick Reads #5) - The year is given.
1328 Dating *The Forgotten Army* (NSA #39) - The Doctor says it's 2010. The Doctor's mention of the Ood Food Guide praising June 2010 might suggest the month. It's "a Saturday night" (p110, p151).
1329 Presuming for even a second that the Doctor isn't just having Amy on with his wild claims of "the Doctor Burger", his having purchased an entire street on her behalf *and* his having banned ketchup on said street, it's not specified *which* street he's named after

robotic) woolly mammoth frozen in ice. The *New York Times* proclaimed, "New York Welcomes Wooly the Mammoth" as the "creature" was taken to the New York Natural History Museum. The Vykoids deployed a Time Freeze and used their combat vehicles to round up New Yorkers for use in the desiccated Vykoid slave mines on Cassetia 2. In the brouhaha to follow, New York was cut off from the outside world: the Vykoids sealed off all access routes with debris, brainwashed every member of the New York Police Department to corral the populace, and plunged the city into its worst power outage since 1922.

The Doctor and Amy commandeered the mammoth and "swam" it across the Hudson, then used a Vykoid teleport device in the Statue of Liberty to send the invaders away from Earth. The Time Freeze ended, and the New Yorkers lost all memory of what had triggered the chaos.

(=) 2010 - "The Golden Ones"[1330] **->** The time-child Chiyoko freed Axos from the time loop in which it was trapped, and it transmogrified its form to become the Shining Dawn Tower in Tokyo. Axons disguised as humans formed the Shining Dawn Corporation and marketed a brain-boosting drink that claimed to increase the intelligence of children. UNIT summoned the eleventh Doctor and Amy upon discovering that Tokyo's children *were* becoming noticeably smarter, and chemical analysis claimed the drink was ordinary water.

Axos converted the fifty thousand children who drank the brain-booster (actually Axonite molecules changed to look like water) into little Axons. A state of emergency was declared as they secured government offices and utilities in Tokyo. Axos absorbed

enough energy from the Tokyo grid to transform into a giant Axon monster, and initiated its nutrition cycle. The Doctor reversed the polarity of the neutron flow, and broadcast a message that the Tokyo residents should switch on all their electrical devices. The power drain killed Axos, and freed the children.

The TARDIS absorbed some of Axos' genetic material, which aided in Chiyoko's creation. She later reversed the effects of her interference.[1331]

= 2010 - DOOMSDAY[1332] **->** On Pete's World, Harriet Jones was President and there was optimism for a new global age. However, in the last sixth months, the planet's average temperature had risen by two degrees. Lumic's Cybermen were infiltrating our universe – Pete Tyler and Torchwood helped to defeat them, then sealed off travel between the two universes. Rose, Mickey and Jackie were stuck in the parallel universe.

A few months after arriving in the parallel universe, Rose was contacted by the Doctor. She said goodbye to him at Dårlig Ulv Stranden ("Bad Wolf Bay") in Norway, and announced that Jackie was three months pregnant with Pete's child.

2010 - VINCENT AND THE DOCTOR[1333] **->** The eleventh Doctor and Amy visited the Musee d'Orsay museum in Paris to see a van Gogh exhibition. The Doctor saw a monster in the painting *The Church at Auvers*, and he and Amy hurried to 1890, when van Gogh painted it. A few days later, they brought van Gogh himself to the museum, to show him that he was considered one of the greatest painters of all time. Van

---

her. A "Pond Street" exists in Staten Island, but not Manhattan, where the story seems to take place.

1330 Dating "The Golden Ones" (*DWM* #425-428) - The story was published in 2010, and looks contemporary. It's after UNIT has changed its name to become the Unified Intelligence Taskforce.

1331 "The Child of Time" (*DWM*). Chiyoko's temporal undoing of her actions (meaning "The Golden Ones" was erased from history) is fortunate, given that events in this story heavily contradict *The Feast of Axos*.

1332 Dating *Doomsday* (X2.13) - Pete states that "three years" have passed since the end of *The Age of Steel*; this must mean that it's 2010. In "our" universe, it's still 2007 (confirmed in *TW: Everything Changes* and *The Runaway Bride*, and as can be inferred from Jackie saying she's "forty" in *Army of Ghosts* and telling Pete he "died twenty years ago" in *Doomsday*).

Perhaps the disruption caused by travelling between the two universes has knocked them out of sync. It means that Mickey, Pete and Jake are all three years older in *Army of Ghosts* than they were in *The Age of*

Steel (even though they all look exactly the same as before), and that Jackie is "officially" three years older there than her actual age (which presumably she's not happy about).

Jackie is three months pregnant by the time the Doctor contacts Rose, so it takes at least three months (of parallel universe time, at any rate) for him to do so.

1333 Dating *Vincent and the Doctor* (X5.10) - The Doctor tells Vincent that it's "Paris, 2010 AD"; he and Amy first visit the museum "a few days" beforehand.

Like Martha before her, the main "present day" events of Amy's first season are compressed into a very short period, so, technically, other "present day" stories (in Amy's case, this story and *The Lodger*) must happen out of sequence with those events and can be safely placed elsewhere. There's snow on the ground outside Musee d'Orsay, everyone is wrapped warmly and their breath is visible – snow in Paris is very rare in April, although it did happen, without much accumulation, in 2008. Further research into this was thwarted because neither of this guidebook's authors speak French.

Gogh still committed suicide in his own era, but the painting he dedicated to Amy, *Still Life: Vase with Twelve Sunflowers*, was on display in the museum.

2010 - THE BIG BANG[1334] **->** As the eleventh Doctor regressed through his timeline, he saw Amy place a card in a newsagent's shop that would prompt him to become the lodger of Craig Owens...

2010 - THE LODGER (TV)[1335] **->** A prototype timeship crashed in Colchester, Essex – its crew died, and the vessel's emergency programme made it blend in with the local architecture. It became the top floor of a house; Craig Owens lived on the main level. The TARDIS was headed for the fifth moon of Sinda Callista, but instead arrived in Colchester and was caught in a materialisation loop. Amy was trapped in the TARDIS while the eleventh Doctor was left behind and became Craig's lodger – he spent three days excelling at football, matchmaking Craig with Craig's friend Sophie and using the nontechnology technology of the Lammasteens to detect that the time engine was upstairs. The timeship was seeking someone who wanted to travel, but Craig and Sophie's desire to stay caused it to implode. The TARDIS landed properly, and the Doctor went back to retroactively smooth the way for his becoming Craig's lodger, which included having Amy drop off an advert in her handwriting for him to find.

The Cardiff Rift is (for a time) Sealed

2010 (March) - TW: THE HOUSE OF THE DEAD[1336] **->** The House of the Dead, reputed to be the most haunted pub in Wales, had a change of ownership and was slated to become flats. An alignment in space-time, combined with a final séance being held in the House as part of its

"closing down" party, accorded Syriath the Death Feeder the opportunity to enter our universe. Jack Harkness interceded, but was confronted by the "ghost" of Ianto Jones, whom Syriath had re-created by reaching through time. Ianto's shade sacrificed itself to detonate a box of rocks and coal laced with Rift energy – the resulting dust storm destroyed Syriath, and sealed the Rift forever.

Captain Jack (for a time) Leaves Earth

2010 (March) - TW: CHILDREN OF EARTH[1337] **->** Jack Harkness had travelled across the world while coming to terms with events concerning the 456, but deemed Earth as too small, and that it felt like a graveyard. He briefly met with Gwen and Rhys, who returned his vortex manipulator; it had been recovered from the Hub's remains. He then accepted a lift from a cold fusion cruiser surfing the ion reefs at the edge of the solar system.

THE END OF TIME / JACK: ONE ENCHANTED EVENING[1338] **->** Jack ended up at an alien bar. He saw the tenth Doctor for one last time, and the Doctor introduced him to Alonzo Frame, a former midshipman aboard the starship *Titanic*.

A race of giant beetles had faced starvation, but other worlds had ignored their cries for help as a prank. Mother Nothing had eaten all of her people, including her own hatchlings.

Two minutes and ten seconds after Jack spotted the Doctor, Jack and Alonzo had retired to Alonzo's cabin. Before matters could get underway, Mother Nothing's assault drones blitzed the space station, as she coveted its shiny Diamond Engine. Jack and Alonzo eventually squished Mother Nothing beneath the Engine. As the station lost power, they leapt into separate escape pods – and agreed over comms that as first dates went, contributing to

1334 Dating *The Big Bang* (X5.13) - The scene occurs the same day as *The Lodger* (TV).
1335 Dating *The Lodger* (X5.11) - An advert on Craig's fridge for a "Vincent Van Gogh: The Great Innovator" exhibit is dated "13th March-29th August, 2010". (This isn't the same exhibit that the Doctor and Amy visit in *Vincent and the Doctor*, especially as Craig has never been to Paris and can't see the point of it.) It's a time of year when people are wearing jackets and even gloves. The population of the Earth is given as 6,000,400,026 ... fewer people than were on Earth in *The End of Time*, which either suggests that *The Lodger* is set before that, or that the Cracks in Time have temporarily "erased" some of Earth's population (see the Cracks in Time sidebar). Either way, it's preferable that *The Lodger* occurs before the other "modern-day" stories in Series 5, as at least two years elapse between this story and

Closing Time, which likely occurs in spring 2012 (see the dating notes on that story).
1336 Dating *TW: The House of the Dead* (TW audio drama #7) - Jack tells Ianto's shade, "Six months ago, you died in my arms," so this is just prior to Jack's leaving Earth in the epilogue of *TW: Children of Earth*. Barring on any further stories that address the topic, the Rift is here sealed forever – which might explain why Jack finally feels at liberty to relinquish his duty to Cardiff and depart into space.
1337 Dating *TW: Children of Earth* (TW 3.05) - It's "six months" after the defeat of the 456.
1338 Dating *The End of Time* (X4.18) and *Jack: One Enchanted Evening* (BF *The Lives of Captain Jack* #1.3) - For Jack, *The End of Time* scene occurs after *TW: Children of Earth*.

the destruction of an entire species, a space station and one of the universe's biggest diamonds wasn't bad. Moments later, their pods changed course to avoid a meteor shower, and went in completely opposite directions.

2010 (April) - TW: FIRST BORN[1339] -> Gwen and Rhys escaped Cardiff and went underground when government agents tried to capture them.

The Wedding of Donna Noble

2010 (spring) - THE END OF TIME[1340] -> The tenth Doctor attended Donna Noble's wedding. Joshua and Abigail Naismith had been arrested. The Doctor gave Donna a triple rollover winning lottery ticket... bought with a pound he had borrowed from Donna's late father, Geoffrey Noble.

Benny Summerfield and Jason Kane Marry; the Seventh Doctor Regains His TARDIS

c 2010 / 2010 (spring) - DEATH AND DIPLOMACY / HAPPY ENDINGS[1341] -> The small, furry, three-eyed Skrak constructed automatons to pose as the "Hollow Gods": purportedly powerful beings who demanded that the rival empires of the Czhans, the Saloi and the Dakhaari negotiate a peace accord on Moriel – a world at the intersection of their territory. In truth, the Skrak were steering the empires toward war so they could ransack their

remains and become more powerful. The Skrak also diverted the seventh Doctor to Moriel as they hoped to obtain his TARDIS. The Doctor's companions – Bernice, Roz and Chris – were transmatted to other worlds to deprive him of help.

Bernice encountered the rogue Jason Kane, who had been travelling the Dagellan Cluster for about fifteen years. The two of them consummated their relationship and, despite their abandonment issues, increasingly fell in love. The Doctor foiled the Skrak's plans and broadcast an announcement from "the Hollow Gods" that the talks had been a resounding success, establishing peace. Afterwards, Benny broke the news to the Doctor that she'd accepted Jason's marriage proposal.

Guests from across space and time attended the wedding of Bernice Summerfield and Jason Kane in the Norfolk village of Cheldon Bonniface. Those present included – thanks to the seventh Doctor's efforts – Roz, Chris, Ace, General Lethbridge-Stewart and his wife Doris, Mike Yates, John Benton, Irving Braxiatel, Kadiatu Lethbridge-Stewart, Muldwych, William Blake, the Pakhar Keri, Ruby Duvall, Hamlet Macbeth, Anne Doras' daughter Bernice, Creed McIlveen, Christian Alvarez and his son Benjamin, the Ice Warriors Savaar and Rhukk, Tom Dekker, Sherlock Holmes, John Watson, Joan Redfern, J.R.R. Tolkien (who gave Benny and Jason a signed first edition of *The Hobbit*) and a girl who looked remarkably like Death of the Endless. Winifred Bambera and Ancelyn couldn't attend, as they were off on a quest. Music was

---

1339 Dating *TW: First Born* (*TW* novel #17) - Gwen is currently "seven months" pregnant (p5). It's possible that this scene is the start of Gwen and Rhys being forced to go underground, following their meet-up with Jack in March 2010 at the end of *TW: Children of Earth*. No reason is given as to why the government has left them alone this long, although *TW: The Men Who Sold the World* hints that the UK has a new coalition government, which might have negated the damning video evidence collected against Prime Minister Green's administration in *Children of Earth*.
1340 Dating *The End of Time* (X4.17-4.18) - We're told that Donna planned to marry in the spring.
1341 Dating *Death and Diplomacy* and *Happy Endings* (NA #49-50) - The Virgin version of *Ahistory* dated *Death and Diplomacy* to the present day, based upon the synopsis. The final book has Benny asking Jason the year, and him replying that it's "Nineteen ninety-six when I last looked. Mind you, that was something like fifteen years ago, more or less. I had a watch once, but it broke and I lost count" (p123).

While it's reasonable to take Jason's "something like fifteen years" comment to mean *precisely* fifteen years, and thereby date *Death and Diplomacy* to circa 2011, it also seems justifiable to place it before *Happy Endings*

– which is repeatedly said to be set in 2010, with the season specified as "spring" (p11). Given the vagueness of Jason's remarks and with the two stories occurring so close together regardless, why *would* the Doctor have decided to hold the wedding in the year before Benny and Jason actually met? A wedding invite in *Happy Endings* (p90) specifies Benny and Jason's nuptials as taking place on "Saturday, 24th April, 2010" (which in real life was actually a Tuesday).

In *Prime Time*, the director of Channel 400, Lukos, tells Ace's younger self that her mother died age 85, haunted by never knowing what happened to her daughter. As Ace's mother was born in 1943 (*The Curse of Fenric*), this would place her death in 2028. However, Channel 400's account is specifically tailored to torment Ace and is therefore suspect, especially given the older Ace's reunion with her mother in *Happy Endings*. Ricky McIlveen is the son of Vincent and Justine from *Warchild*. Time was first mentioned in *Love and War*, and the seventh Doctor is often cited as "Time's Champion".
1342 *The Shadows of Avalon*, following on Lethbridge-Stewart's rejuvenation as a result of events in *Happy Endings*. This explains how the Brigadier lives well past a normal human lifespan.

provided by the Isley Brothers, the band Plasticine and the Silurian group Bona Fide. Leonardo da Vinci served the wedding cake he had designed.

The Tzun Master stole the Loom of Rassilon's Mouse, a bioengineering tool, to fashion himself a new body. A Fortean Flicker caused him to coincidentally be operating in Cheldon Bonniface during Bernice and Jason's wedding, and he did what he could to disrupt events. Multiple clones of Jason were created, and the Loom generated a huge gelatinous monster. The Doctor had Ishtar Hutchings slay the creature with her dormant Timewyrm abilities.

General Lethbridge-Stewart, having been engulfed by the monster before Ishtar killed it, found that – as a happy side-effect – his body had become decades younger.

The Doctor gifted Benny and Jason with time rings; together, they could travel throughout space-time. He also recovered his TARDIS from some wayward Charrl.

Ace reconciled with her mother, Audrey – who was now engaged to Robin Yeadon, Ace's boyfriend in 1968. Ace herself left on her time hopper with one of the Jason Kane clones. Ishtar was left pregnant from an encounter with Chris Cwej. She believed that their daughter, Jasmine, would become the girlfriend of Ricky McIlveen – and that the two of them would sire the Eternal named Time.

The word "cruk" was introduced in the anime series *Bones and Kay*, and quickly caught on as a mild expletive.

The rejuvenated General Lethbridge-Stewart returned to active duty with UNIT.[1342] Mike Yates told the Brigadier about his adventure with the Hornets, and did the same when he met Liz Shaw in the summer.[1343] Prior to the Jastok affair, Mike Yates last saw Bessie when he drove her to see West Ham vs. Crystal Palace. The Brigadier, more of a Rugger man, was along but grumpy.[1344]

The Sarah Jane Adventures
Series 3 (second half)[1345]

2010 (spring) - SJA: THE ETERNITY TRAP[1346] -> Sarah Jane and her friends investigated Ashen Hill Manor – one of the most haunted locations in the UK. They confronted the shade of the alchemist Erasmus Darkening, an alien whose attempts to manipulate other dimensions to get home had caused all the spooky happenings. Darkening proved hostile, but Sarah and her allies dissipated him into mere electricity. The spirits of everyone Darkening had captured over the centuries were likewise liberated.

2010 (spring) - SJA: MONA LISA'S REVENGE[1347] -> Clyde Langer won a competition that saw his imaginative drawings (actually images of aliens and their technology that he had seen in his adventures) displayed in the Artists of the Future competition at the International Gallery in London. The gallery was also hosting the Mona Lisa, which was on loan from the Louvre. The close proximity of the Mona Lisa to Guieseppe di Cattivo's painting *The Abomination* – which had, along with the Mona Lisa, been painted with oils derived from an alien mineral – caused the embodiment of the Mona Lisa to come to life and step from the painting. The Mona Lisa had the ability of molecular transplantation, and sought to release others of her kind. She did so with William Bonneville's *The Dark Rider*, and wanted to liberate her "brother", the Abomination. Clyde drew a picture of K9, which temporarily came to life and dispersed the Abomination's pigments. All the effects of the Mona Lisa's power were reversed, and she returned to her painting.

1343 *Demon Quest: The Relics of Time.* We see Mike with the Brigadier at Benny's wedding, so perhaps he told him then.
1344 *UNIT S4: Assembled*
1345 Dating *The Sarah Jane Adventures* Series 3 (*SJA: The Eternity Trap*, 3.4; *SJA: Mona Lisa's Revenge*, 3.5; *SJA: The Gift*, 3.6) - The remainder of Series 3 occurs in the spring of 2010, with the last story, *The Gift*, appearing to finish at the very end of the school year. This isn't directly said, but the children are doing GCSE preliminary exams, and the final scene – with Sarah and company enjoying a backyard BBQ without jackets on, and basking in the sunshine – looks and feels as if they're celebrating the start of the summer holiday. Either way, *The Gift* definitely occurs later in the spring – established green plants are shown as the Rakweed pollinates everywhere, and Rani goes off to school without

a jacket on as birds chirp in the warm sun.
1346 Dating *SJA: The Eternity Trap* (*SJA* 3.4) - Rani and Darkening separately (and broadly) say that 1665 was "three hundred forty years ago". Lord Marchwood's shade claims, twice, that he's been searching "over three hundred years" since 1665 for the souls of his children. Clyde and Rani have school "on Monday", so it's during the school year.
1347 Dating *SJA: Mona Lisa's Revenge* (*SJA* 3.5) - The International Gallery curator mentions "the Cup of Athelstan fiasco at Easter" (*Planet of the Dead*). He definitely *doesn't* say "last Easter" - so this is possibly evidence that *Mona Lisa's Revenge* occurs before Easter 2010 (4th April, in that year). It's not impossible, of course, that the "at Easter" reference denotes that *Mona Lisa's Revenge* (and by extension *SJA: The Eternity Trap*) take place at the very tail end of 2009, but that would

2010 (end of school year) - SJA: THE GIFT[1348] -> Sarah Jane and her friends were about to thwart a Slitheen child's plan to crush the Earth into a large diamond when Tree Lorn Acre and Leef Apple Glyn – two Blatherean (cousins of the Slitheen) – captured the child. The Blatherean gave Sarah a Rakweed plant – a staple food they said would grow even in the harshest conditions, and end world famine. In actuality, the Rakweed was a fast-growing addictive drug that would seed itself via spores across Earth, and could then be harvested for a massive profit on the galactic market. Tree and Leaf were not true Blatherean, but Slitheen-Blatherean hybrids. The Rakweed seeded spores that could have taken over London in hours, Earth in days, but Sarah Jane learned the plants would burst if exposed to a sound frequency of 1421.09 Hz. Sarah broadcast the sound with K9's help, ending the threat... and making the Rakweed-soused Blatherean explode.

Anwen Williams, the daughter of Gwen Cooper and Rhys Williams, was born in or near early May 2010.[1349]

(=) 2010 - TW: THE TWILIGHT STREETS[1350] -> Bilis Manger showed Torchwood a potential future in which the Dark influenced Owen, his wife Toshiko and Gwen. They slaved Jack to the Hub's Rift Manipulator, then used his life energy to harness the Rift – in less than a year, the Torchwood Empire had conquered the world. While Gwen gave birth to a son, Geraint Williams Junior, Ianto killed Owen and was shot dead by Toshiko's guards. Jack destroyed the Rift Manipulator, breaking the Dark's power.

2010 - TW: "Shrouded"[1351] -> John Hart established himself in Mexico, near a mini-Rift that provided him with an easy means of transport, as a trafficker of alien artifacts. Hart and Rhys realised that a rogue time traveller named Beatrice was attempting to meddle in Ianto's history, and went back in time two years to warn him.

The new coalition government in the United Kingdom became desperate for funds. Mr Black facilitated the sale to the Americans of a cache of advanced weapons – including Judoon, Yeti, Sea Devil and Sontaran firearms, as well as a Ytraxorian Reality Gun – that had been recovered from the Torchwood Hub.[1352]

In June, Luke Smith got four As at A-Level, earning a place at Oxford University a year early. Sarah Jane defeated a piece of sentient concrete that had disguised itself as a flyover in Chiswick, and was attempting to control people's minds.[1353] The Ood Food Guide gave June 2010 "a whole solar system of awards".[1354]

2010 (summer) - TW: FIRST BORN[1355] -> Gwen, Rhys and their newborn daughter Anwen remained on the run, and took up residence in the North Wales town of Rawbone because Torchwood had keys to a caravan there. In the ten weeks to follow, they learned the origins of the townsfolk becoming sterile, the Scion children given to the Rawbone families, and the alien Juniper Tree that had birthed them.

Budget cuts necessitated that the Rawbone Project produce results, and so Eloise, the project's director, initiated Stage 2 of it. She killed the Juniper-spawned Sebastian and grew Sebastian 2. He was intended to take mental command of the Scions and turn them into soldiers, but

---

necessitate forcing a five-month gap between *The Gift* and the rest of Series 3 where none was meant to exist. Moreover, the more Series 3 stories one wedges into the waning weeks of 2009, the more the total absence of bitterly cold weather and holiday decorations becomes conspicuous.

1348 Luke is said to be 15. The Blatherean first appeared in *The Monsters Inside*.
1349 Extrapolating from Gwen being three weeks pregnant in *TW: Children of Earth*.
1350 Dating *TW: The Twilight Streets* (TW novel #6) - The exact dating for this is unclear, but it's possible that Gwen's pregnancy parallels the one in the real timeline. Bizarrely, Gwen here gives birth to a son – on screen, she has a daughter.
1351 Dating *TW: "Shrouded"* (*TWM* #21-22) - Gwen has now given birth. John Hart says he met Beatrice in 2010, and Rhys tells Ianto in 2008 that Beatrice will "come to find" him in "two years".
1352 "Six weeks" before *TW: The Men Who Sold the World*.

1353 *SJA: The Nightmare Man*
1354 Or so the Doctor claims in *The Forgotten Army* (p17).
1355 Dating *TW: First Born* (*TW* novel #17) - The year at two points is implied to be 2011: Sebastian 1 (born 3rd March, 1981) is "thirty years old"(p134), and Jenny, one of the oldest Scions following the Juniper Tree being relocated to Rawbone in 1991, is "twenty" (pgs. 81, 166). Both pieces of evidence need to be taken as approximations, however, as Anwen's age mandates that the year is 2010 (Gwen's family settles in Rawbone "two months", p9, after Gwen was "seven months" pregnant, p5, and Gwen throughout the story is hampered by lactation issues). The story proceeds over at least ten weeks (Anwen's stated age on p88) if not longer. The life-cycle of the potatoes that Rhys plants seems a bit strange – he puts them in the ground three weeks after he and Gwen move to Rawbone, but the plants are "just starting to come up" (p248) at story's end, when they should have emerged within two, maybe three weeks.
The ages of the last natural-born Rawbone children

viciously wanted to grow an army of Scions and kill humanity. Gwen contacted the creators of the Juniper Tree, who were so horrified by the new Sebastian's mindset that they aged him and the Juniper Tree to death. The people of Rawbone compiled enough evidence of the Rawbone Project to compel a huge payment from the government, and the new leader of the Scions, Jenny Meredith, was hopeful that the town's sterility could be reversed. Gwen, Rhys and Anwen left for parts unknown.

2010 (summer) - TW: THE MEN WHO SOLD THE WORLD[1356] ->

The cache of advanced weaponry recovered from the Torchwood Hub was now being sold by the UK to the US, and was clandestinely routed through Cuba. The American CIA sent agents to safeguard the shipment, but a mishap with the cache's Ytraxorian Reality Gun caused agent Oscar Lupé to materialise in the flight controls of American Airlines Flight AA2010. It crashed into the Gulf of Mexico, killing the four hundred and fifty people aboard. Two members of the CIA team – Cotter Gleason and his second, Mulroney – went rogue and stole the weapons, intending to stage enough devastation to force a large payout from the US government.

(=) A power-mad Gleason used the alien tech to destroy the White House. CIA agent Rex Matheson tried to stop Gleason, who used the Reality Gun to send Rex back to 100,000 BC.

The enigmatic assassin Mr Wynter obtained the Reality Gun, and used it to alter history. The White House was saved, and Gleason was sent back to 100,000 BC instead of Rex. Some weeks later, Wynter rejuvenated his aged body and ate his employer.

2010 (summer) - "The Age of Ice"[1357] ->

UNIT had established an underwater HQ in Sydney Harbour. Its archives contained at least eight Mona Lisas, a mummy robot, a War Machine, a Yeti, an Auton chair, a Sontaran space ship and a Sontaran Skyhammer cannon.

The Skith had gone to a military footing following the destruction of their homeworld, and the Skith leader who battled the Doctor in 1915 summoned the warship Oppressor Two – and its garrison of Skith – to Earth. The Skith constructed a faulty time machine, a Skardis, with information looted from the Doctor's mind. The Skardis created unstable temporal waves: those aboard Sydney Flight 218 were aged near to death, a Neolithic narwhal was seen in the Parramatta River, pterodactyls appeared by the Zenith Centre, and mammoths roamed the suburbs.

The tenth Doctor and Majenta Pryce arrived as chronal waves made more dinosaurs appear, and inflicted Sydney with a new ice age. The Skith briefly turned Majenta into Skithself so her mind could operate their Skardis – but she generated a pulse that destroyed them. Majenta's assistant Fanson had been aiding the Skith, and died saving her life.

Thomas Brewster's beloved, Connie Winter, was hit by a car and died after being taken off life support. The Doctor had previously saved the planet Symbios – a single organism with the appearance of a thriving ecology – from the Drahvin, and Symbios' governing intelligence summoned him to help against runamuck terraforming robots: the insectoid Terravore. Brewster answered Symbios' call, and used the time engine he'd built in 1867 to transport volunteers to Symbios – where the planet possessed them, and used them as foot soldiers.[1358]

Amy met a gorgeous scuba instructor called Claude on her hen night.[1359]

(Sasha, Davydd and Nerys) aren't of much help in making a determination. The town went sterile in 1987, Nerys is currently in her "early 20s" (p40), Davydd is "mid-20s" (p30) and Sasha is 24 (p112), but could easily have been born in 1986.

There's a continuity glitch in that Gwen and Rhys covertly take Anwen to meet Gwen's parents (p128), but *TW: Miracle Day* is presented as their first meeting. **1356** Dating *TW: The Men Who Sold the World* (*TW* novel #18) - No date is given, but it's been at least "nine months" (p121) since the Department's salvage team – in an operation that commenced in October 2009, judging by *TW: Long Time Dead* – recovered the Reality Gun from the Hub. So, it's most likely summer 2010 at present.
1357 Dating "The Age of Ice" (*DWM* #408-411) - The Doctor says that they've arrived in "Sydney, Australia,

early twenty-first century", on a "glorious summer's day". A UNIT officer says that the Doctor and his allies saved the entire universe from the Daleks "just last year" (in *Journey's End*, set in 2009). It very much looks as if the story-creators forgot about the "year ahead" rule governing Series 4, meaning that the "last year" reference places "The Age of Ice" in 2010 rather than (as was perhaps intended) 2009, its year of publication. Consequently, for the Doctor and Majenta, this story and "Ghosts of the Northern Line" must chronologically happen out of order.
1358 "Six months" before *The Crimes of Thomas Brewster*.
1359 "Spam Filtered"

Doctor Who Series 5

Amy Pond and Rory Williams Join the TARDIS

2010 (25th June) - THE ELEVENTH HOUR[1360] -> The eleventh Doctor returned to Amy Pond... two years later than he thought. She joined him travelling in the TARDIS, but didn't tell him that this was the night before she was due to marry Rory Williams.

2010 (25th-26th June) - FLESH AND STONE / THE VAMPIRES OF VENICE[1361] -> The eleventh Doctor and Amy returned to her house following their encounter with the Weeping Angels, and Amy finally admitted that she and Rory were going to get married. She attempted to seduce the Doctor, but he hurried her into the TARDIS and collected Rory from his stag party, determined to take the two of them somewhere romantic to cement their relationship...

Big Bang 2.0

The Lone Centurion's Vigil Ends

2010 (26th June) - THE PANDORICA OPENS[1362] -> The coalition of alien races seeking to imprison the Doctor – so the TARDIS wouldn't explode and destroy the universe – scanned Amy's house for her psychic residue. A trap was laid for the Doctor in 102 AD, patterned after Amy's childhood recollections of *The Story of Roman Britain* and *The Legend of Pandora's Box*.

Soon after, the TARDIS brought River Song to Amy's house from 120 AD. She realised that the Doctor was in great danger, but the TARDIS – as feared – started to explode. The Ship automatically put River in a time

loop to protect her; she would be released in 1996.

The Kovarian Chapter of the Silence blew up the TARDIS as part of its efforts to avert a new Time War. In doing so, however, it created the Cracks in Time that facilitated the same future standoff the Chapter was trying to quell...[1363]

Amy and Rory Get Married

2010 (26th June) - THE BIG BANG[1364] -> Following the eleventh Doctor's sacrifice in 1996, the universe was restored to its original form – save that everyone had forgotten he had ever existed. Amy Pond's parents returned to life after the Cracks in Time sealed, and celebrated Amy and Rory's wedding. As Amy's father began his speech, Amy – goaded by the TARDIS-patterned journal that River left for her – remembered something old, something new, something borrowed and something blue. She insisted that her "raggedy Doctor" was late for her wedding – at which point the Doctor was restored to the universe, and the TARDIS materialised at the reception.

River returned to the future using her vortex manipulator. The Doctor, Amy and Rory also left to have new adventures, starting with the case of an Egyptian goddess loose on the *Orient Express*, in space.

Amy and Rory conceived a child while travelling in the TARDIS.[1365] Rory Williams told his dad that he and Amy were off honeymooning in the likes of Thailand, when they were actually traveling with the Doctor.[1366] The TARDIS' obliteration freed Es'Cartrss, a Tactire mind parasite, from its captivity within the Ship, and it tumbled back in time.[1367]

1360 Dating *The Eleventh Hour* (X5.1) - It's the night before Amy's wedding, the exact date of which ("26/6/2010") is first established in *Flesh and Stone*. Surprisingly given that time of year, the Doctor and Amy's breath is visible. (Did the recalibrated TARDIS cause a heat exchange upon materialisation?) Rory's badge to the emergency unit of the Royal Leadworth Hospital, where he works, is something of an anomaly given Rory's age: it was issued "30/11/1990".
1361 Dating *Flesh and Stone/The Vampires of Venice* (X5.5-5.6) - In *Flesh and Stone*, the clock ticks over to 12 am on 26th June, the date of Rory and Amy's wedding. Rory says in *The Vampires of Venice* that he's "getting married tomorrow" – either he hasn't noticed that it's past midnight already, or the Doctor nips back in time a little.
1362 Dating *The Pandorica Opens* (X5.12) - River

checks the TARDIS instruments and confirms the date as "the 26th of June, 2010". The alien intruders broke down Amy's front door, so both they and River presumably go to Amy's house after the Doctor and Amy stopped there in *Flesh and Stone*. The clock ticked over to 12 am of the morning of the 26th as they left, so the action described in *The Pandorica Opens* probably occurs in the darkened morning hours.
1363 *The Time of the Doctor*
1364 Dating *The Big Bang* (X5.13) - The date of the wedding ("26/6/2010") is established first in *Flesh and Stone*, and mirrors the broadcast of *The Big Bang* on the same day.
1365 The Doctor speculates in *A Good Man Goes to War* that this happened on Amy and Rory's wedding night (in *The Big Bang*), but there's reason to doubt this (see the Cracks in Time sidebar); the conception could

The Sarah Jane Adventures Series 4

Luke Smith, K9 Leave for Oxford

2010 (6th-10th September) - SJA: THE NIGHTMARE MAN[1368] -> Luke Smith's anxiety about going to university was exploited by the Nightmare Man – a Vishklar that hailed from the Seretti Dimension, and needed terror to enter our universe. The Nightmare Man infected Luke, Clyde and Rani with dreams of leading failed lives, but they didn't fear him, and so his power dissipated. Sarah gifted Luke with her car and K9 as he left for Oxford.

2010 (13th-15th September) - SJA: WRAITH WORLD[1369] -> Gregory P. Wilkinson came out of semi-retirement to write the final Wraith World novel, The Fall of Hancada. The reality-warping paper in Wilkinson's journal latched onto Rani's mind, and the series' main antagonist – the sorcerer Hancada, composed of blood-worms – nearly manifested through her. Sarah Jane, Wilkinson and Rani combined efforts to write an end Hancada's story, then burned Wilkinson's journal.

Sarah Jane and her friends recovered an antigravity ray from an old Nadloon Circus Comedy Cruiser that crashed into the Thames.[1370]

2010 (a Saturday) - SJA: THE VAULT OF SECRETS[1371] -> Mr Smith sabotaged a NASA probe on Mars, as Sarah Jane did not want them finding evidence of an "ancient and terrible civilisation" there. Rani's parents joined the Ealing branch of the British UFO Research and Paranormal Studies Society (BURPSS) as a way of coping with their various alien encounters.

Androvax the Veil escaped Judoon custody on a swamp world, but not before he was bitten by a deadly Moxolon Swamp Viper. He found that the spaceship with the last one hundred members of his race was within the hyper-dimensional Vault created by the Alliance of Shades, the entrance to which was at the disused St Jude's asylum. Sarah learned that activating the Veil ship within the Vault would create dimensional instability that would tear Earth apart. Androvax attempted to do so anyway, but the robot overseer of the Vault, Mr Dread, sacrificed four hundred fifty years of his personal power supply to reactivate the Vault's transmat. The Veil spaceship was sent into space, and it was expected that the Veil would settle on a new planet. The Vault became inaccessible as its second activation key had been lost. As Mr Dread's mission had terminated, he deactivated himself.

Mike Yates saw Jo Grant in October, and told her about his adventure with the Hornets.[1372]

Sarah Jane Meets Jo Jones, the Eleventh Doctor

2010 - SJA: DEATH OF THE DOCTOR[1373] -> The vulture-like Shansheeth were known throughout the universe as intergalactic undertakers – they would search

have happened while they were travelling together in Series 5, or at any point between *The Big Bang* and the Doctor dropping Amy and Rory on Earth (prior to *The Impossible Astronaut*). Whatever the case, nine months must pass in Amy's personal timeframe before she starts to give birth at the end of *The Rebel Flesh*.
1366 *Dinosaurs on a Spaceship*
1367 "Dead Man's Hand"
1368 Dating *SJA: The Nightmare Man* (SJA 4.1) - A calendar in Luke's room prominently says "September 2010" and is in accordance with the real-world calendar. The story counts down the four days marked on the calendar, from the 6th (when Luke starts packing) to the 10th (when he departs for Oxford).
1369 Dating *SJA: Wraith World* (SJA audiobook #7) - The story effectively begins on the day of Wilkinson's bookstore signing, on "Monday, 13th September" (an actual Monday in 2010) and events pick up "two days later". Unfortunately, that doesn't sit well with the established continuity of The Sarah Jane Adventures Series 4. Luke left for Oxford (in *SJA: The Nightmare Man*) the week prior to 13th September, so it's strange that he'd suddenly be back at home, without explanation, the very

next Monday – and also a month later, in this story's epilogue – given how little he otherwise visits Sarah in the TV show. But, Rani's inclusion means that *Wraith World* cannot be bumped back to the previous year, as she didn't meet Sarah and friends until early October 2009 – which, again, would conflict with the 13th September dating. Whatever the case, Sarah's comment that she was "just like [Rani] when I was 15" has to be taken as a generalisation, as Rani should be 16 if this story occurs in 2009, 17 if it's 2010.
1370 The month prior to *SJA: Defending Bannerman Road*.
1371 Dating *SJA: The Vault of Secrets* (SJA 4.2) - No specific date is given, although it's said to be "almost forty years" since 1972. The "ancient and deadly civilisation" is likely the Osirians, as a pyramid a la *Pyramids of Mars* is briefly glimpsed on Mars on Mr Smith's monitor. The Alliance of Shades was introduced in *Dreamland* (DW).
1372 *Demon Quest: The Relics of Time*
1373 Dating *SJA: Death of the Doctor* (SJA 4.3) - No specific date is given, although Sarah comments that the Doctor "came back" about four years ago. (This is presumably a reference to his coming back into her life

battlefields for the remains of heroes, then transport their bodies home. The Claw Shansheeth of the Fifteenth Funeral Fleet contacted UNIT, claiming to have found the Doctor's body ten thousand light years away in the Wastelands of the Crimson Heart, where he had evidently perished to save five hundred children from the Scarlet Monstrosity.

Colonel Karim of UNIT summoned the Doctor's associates to attend a funeral service at Unit Base 5, inside Mount Snowdon. The Brigadier was stuck in Peru, and Liz Shaw couldn't return from moonbase until Sunday. Sarah Jane went to Mount Snowdon with Rani and Clyde, and met for the first time Jo Jones, née Grant, who had arrived from the Tierra del Fuego with her oldest[1374] grandson Santiago. Cliff Jones was picketing an oil rig in the Ascension Islands. Santiago's father was hiking across Antarctica with a gay dads organisation.

The Shansheeth had gone rogue, and falsified the Doctor's demise to capture his associates. They drained Sarah and Jo's minds with a Memory Weave, a device that could manifest physical objects from memories. The Weave crafted a new TARDIS key – a means by which the Shansheeth could enter the Doctor's Ship. They hoped to use the vessel to interfere with the timelines, and end death across the universe.

The eleventh Doctor arrived and aided his friends. Sarah and Jo's memories overloaded the Memory Weave and it exploded, killing the Shansheeth and

their collaborator, Karim. The Doctor reclaimed his TARDIS and departed. Jo and her grandson left to go to Norway by hovercraft.

Sarah had researched other former companions of the Doctor. Ian and Barbara Chesterton were professors at Cambridge; rumours claimed they hadn't aged since the sixties. Tegan Jovanka campaigned for aboriginal rights. Sarah implied that Harry Sullivan had died, but before that had developed vaccines that saved thousands of lives. Ben and Polly ran an orphanage in India. A woman called Dorothy ran a billion-pound charity called A Charitable Earth.

Jo herself had seven children and twelve grandchildren (with another on the way). The Doctor said that the newest would be dyslexic, but a great swimmer.

2010 - SJA: RETURN OF THE KRULIUS / DEFENDING BANNERMAN ROAD[1375] -> The Krulius escaped from Judoon custody, and sought revenge against Sarah Jane and her friends. Urglanic shapeshifters in the Krulius' employ teleported Rani to the Krulius' spaceship, which was hidden in Earth orbit behind a force warp. Rani learned that the Krulius had grown clones of the various races it had studied, then escaped and warned Sarah about the Krulius' intentions.

A week after Rani escaped, the Krulius established a temporal stasis field around Bannerman Road. It deployed its cadre of hypnotised clones – including Slitheen, Judoon and Men in Black – against Sarah's house. Clyde fought off

---

in *School Reunion*, although it's only been three years since that story. In a pinch, if one squints really hard, by "came back" Sarah might mean the Doctor's greater involvement in human affairs per Series 1.) The Doctor says it's been "forty years" since Jo left UNIT. Santiago mentions that he hasn't seen his mother in "six months", and hasn't gotten together with all of his family "since about February" – but since he might have seen his mother after that, it can't automatically be said that it's now August.

Sarah here recalls her final meeting with the tenth Doctor in *The End of Time*. The Doctor has left Amy and Rory on a honeymoon planet, so this is almost certainly set between *The Big Bang* and *A Christmas Carol* in his timeline.

Aside from Jo, the fates of the companions as given in this story broadly match (or, at least, don't grievously contradict) what has been established in the tie-in series. The non-televised stories seem, at the very least, to inform this story. A number of the books established that Ian and Barbara married and became professors (eg: *Goth Opera*). The rumours that Sarah mentions – that Ian and Barbara have "never aged since the 60s" – might indeed just be rumours, as the Big Finish audios (*The Five Companions* especially) have consistently ren-

dered Ian as an older man, roughly concurrent with William Russell's real age.

Sarah here implies (but doesn't outright say) that Harry Sullivan has died – he's cited as being alive in *UNIT: The Wasting* (likely set in spring 2005), and Sarah tries to have her annual meet-up with Harry (although he fails to show) in *SJS: Buried Secrets*, set in the same year. He's also said to be alive in 2015 in *Damaged Goods* (also by Russell T Davies). This being *Doctor Who*, it's possible that there's an extended stretch where Sarah thinks that Harry is dead, but he's actually been kidnapped by (say) space weasels, and that he later returns home. (Either way, this would explain why Harry never visits Sarah in her own series.) Liz Shaw apparently died in *Eternity Weeps*, set in 2003... but in that book, as with *Death of the Doctor*, she was working on a moonbase. (See the Did Liz Shaw Die in 2003? sidebar.)

The "Dorothy" that Sarah mentions might be Dodo, but the initials of Dorothy's charity imply otherwise. Ace's fate is convoluted, to say the least, but if we want to invoke the books, it's possible she saw the dystopian near-future of *Cat's Cradle: Warhead* and decided to try to avert it. Or, it's possible that her leading A Charitable Earth owes to her being undercover/on assignment for the Doctor, and is only temporary.

the attackers with a variety of alien technology that Sarah had collected. The Krulius' temporal field failed, and it withdrew its forces, vowing revenge.

2010 - SJA: THE EMPTY PLANET[1376] -> The king of an alien world and his brother had died, making Gavin – the king's son, living as a thirteen year old in Ealing with no knowledge of his heredity – the heir to the throne. The robot retrieval team sent to find Gavin eased their task by shunting the entire population of Earth into a sub-dimension, while preventing all traffic crashes, derailments and other damage that might have resulted from humanity's sudden disappearance. Clyde and Rani, barred from leaving Earth by the Judoon, awoke to find that they and Gavin were the only people left. They persuaded Gavin to go with the robots, and the population of the Earth was restored, with no memory that they had been gone. Gavin awarded his friends the titles of Lord Clyde and Lady Rani.

2010 (November) - SJA: DEADLY DOWNLOAD[1377] -> Sarah Jane and her friends defeated the Emulgus, a 12-foot insectoid alien who tried to transmit a computer virus that would transform technology across Earth into mind-controlling metal replicants of itself.

2010 (Tuesday, 23rd November) - SJA: LOST IN TIME[1378] -> Sarah Jane and her friends were summoned to Smalley and Co. Antiques by the mysterious Shopkeeper, who answered to a parrot named Captain. The Shopkeeper opened a time window and sent Sarah Jane, Rani and Clyde to three different timezones (1889, 1553 and 1941 respectively) to find pieces of chronosteel – a metal forged in the Time Vortex, and which had the power to change history. If they failed to return with the objects the chronosteel had become

fashioned into, the Earth would be destroyed. The Shopkeeper himself was forbidden from making such a journey.

Clyde and Rani returned with their chronosteel pieces, but Sarah Jane failed to retrieve hers. The granddaughter of the ghost-hunter Emily Morris arrived at the Shopkeeper's store with the final chronosteel piece, saving Earth and allowing the Shopkeeper and Captain to depart.

Clyde learned that George Woods, whom he had met in 1941, was now 83 and had been knighted by Queen Elizabeth II.

2010 - SJA: GOODBYE, SARAH JANE SMITH[1379] -> The Katesh – a race wherein each member had a humanoid component, and a giant, separate "stomach" that digested heightened emotions – exiled one of their own when her hunger grew too strong. She escaped her space-faring prison cell by modifying its game system, then learned of Sarah Jane's status as an adventurer. The Katesh presented itself to Sarah Jane, Rani and Clyde as "Ruby Ann White", a fellow adventurer who had just moved to Bannerman Road. Ruby began feeding off Sarah, impairing her cognitive function. Sarah made a mistake while fighting an invasion of the Dark Horde (that Ruby repelled), and became convinced by a medi-scan that she was ill. She reluctantly handed over her duties and Mr Smith to Ruby, but Sarah's friends soon realised the truth. Ruby accelerated her feeding cycle, but Luke returned from Oxford and reprogrammed Ruby's holographic game system to make every person on Earth think that a meteor was headed straight for them. The emotional overload exploded Ruby's "stomach", and she was returned to her prison capsule and sent back into space.

The biggest contradiction is Jo's fate (married mother of seven, grandmother of twelve), which is far more cheerful here than her status in *Genocide* (divorced mother of just one child). While it's easy enough to imagine that she and Cliff later remarried, there is, with the best of will, no good way to reconcile the differing accounts of their children.

1374 *UNIT S4: Assembled: United*

1375 Dating *SJA: Return of the Krulius/SJA: Defending Bannerman Road* (*SJA* webcomic #2-3) - The action seems to take place after Luke departs for Oxford, as he's absent save for a highly posed group shot in the very last panel. The Krulius has a picture of Sarah standing next to the Matt Smith Doctor, implying it's after *SJA: Death of the Doctor*.

1376 Dating *SJA: The Empty Planet* (*SJA* 4.4) - No specific date is given, although it's said to be a school night.

Clyde and Rani were "grounded" in *SJA: Prisoner of the Judoon*.

1377 Dating *SJA: Deadly Download* (*SJA* audiobook #8) - The audio was made available for download on 4th November, 2010, between the broadcasts of *SJA: The Empty Planet* and *SJA: Lost in Time*. (The CD was released 15th November, 2010.) Sarah opens the story with, "It all began one cold November afternoon", and plays some Christmas songs, albeit "a bit prematurely".

1378 Dating *SJA: Lost in Time* (*SJA* 4.5) - The date appears on a newspaper; in 2010, 23rd November was indeed a Tuesday. Rani says at one point, "I'm only 17". George Woods was 13 when Clyde met him on 7th June, 1941, and has now aged seventy years – which is feasible if his birthday is 8th June or later.

1379 Dating *SJA: Goodbye, Sarah Jane Smith* (*SJA* 4.6) - No specific date is given. The population of Earth is "six

Demon Quest

2010 (22nd-23rd December) - DEMON QUEST: THE RELICS OF TIME[1380] -> The fourth Doctor returned to Nest Cottage after a year away, and enthusiastically dismantled the TARDIS console as part of an overhaul. Mrs Wibbsey (secretly under the control of the new Hornet Swarm)[2081] took many of the Doctor's items to sell at a jumble sale at the village hall, and swapped a mysterious gentlemen – actually a shapechanging demon in the Hornets' employ[2082] – four components of the spatial geometer in return for antiques: a mosaic tile attached to a page from a history book, a poster, a book of fairy tales and a superhero comic. All of these items incorporated images of the Doctor, and the Doctor concluded they were a series of clues. Without the spatial geometer, the TARDIS could move in time, but not very far in space. The Doctor and Mrs Wibbsey headed to the first century AD to investigate this mystery, even as Mike Yates called to say he was at a loose end, and would like to come to Nest Cottage for the holiday.

2010 (23rd December) - DEMON QUEST: THE DEMON OF PARIS[1383] -> The fourth Doctor and Wibbsey returned from 1894 with the first and second parts of the spatial geometer, and reunited with Mike Yates.

2010 (23rd December) - DEMON QUEST: A SHARD OF ICE[1384] -> The fourth Doctor and Mike Yates took a short trip to the nineteenth century to track down the third piece of the spatial geometer. The last part was to be found in New York City, 1976, so the Doctor, Yates and Wibbsey headed there.

2010 (24th December) - FIND AND REPLACE[1385] -> Iris Wildthyme and Jo Grant were flummoxed when Huxley – a five-legged noveliser from the mooned world of Verbatim VI – insisted that the Doctor had never been exiled to Earth, and that Jo was Iris' old travelling companion. They left in Iris' bus to visit the third Doctor during his time at UNIT to settle the matter.

2010 (24th December) - DEMON QUEST: STARFALL[1386] -> The fourth Doctor and Mike Yates returned to Nest Cottage from New York, but the Demon "kidnapped" Wibbsey. The Doctor and Yates could do little but wait...

2010 (24th December) - DEMON QUEST: SEPULCHRE[1387] -> The fourth Doctor and Mike Yates got an answering machine message from Mrs Wibbsey – a means of luring them to the Sepulchre, a hidden location at the edge of the universe. It resembled an English country house, but was the domain of the Demon. The Doctor learned that the Demon was from a backwater shadow dimension, and was working for secret masters: the new Hornet Swarm. They planned to disintegrate the Doctor and condense his knowledge of space-time into a four-dimensional Atlas of All of Time and Space – a device that would let the Swarm find its lost Queen. The Doctor extracted the Swarm from Wibbsey, and teleported it inside a sarcophagus to a 1914 fire at the Cromer Palace of

billion". Sarah here orders Mr Smith to distribute the cover story that the whole of humanity thought that a meteor was coming toward them as part of a 3D-game promotion, but it's such a ludicrous tale even by *Doctor Who* standards, it's hard to see it gaining any traction.

1380 Dating *Demon Quest: The Relics of Time* (BBC fourth Doctor audio #2.1) - The *Hornets' Nest* series was "last year", it is "next Christmas", and the Doctor has had "a year's absence" from Nest Cottage. It's three days before Christmas.

1381 *Demon Quest: Sepulchre*

1382 *Demon Quest: Sepulchre*

1383 Dating *Demon Quest: The Demon of Paris* (BBC fourth Doctor audio #2.2) - According to Mrs Wibbsey, "We arrived on the day we left, December the 23rd".

1384 Dating *Demon Quest: A Shard of Ice* (BBC fourth Doctor audio #2.3) - The Doctor and Mike return the same day as they left.

1385 Dating *Find and Replace* (BF CC #4.3) - It's repeatedly said that it's Christmas Eve, and the back cover blurb specifies the year as 2010. Adding to the debate of whether the public of this era knows about the exist-

ence of extra-terrestrials or not, Jo fakes surprise upon learning that Huxley is an alien.

1386 Dating *Demon Quest: Starfall* (BBC fourth Doctor audio #2.4) - The Doctor and Yates return soon after they left.

1387 Dating *Demon Quest: Sepulchre* (BBC fourth Doctor audio #2.5) - The final sequence takes place on Christmas Eve. The sequences on Sepulchre explicitly take place in "a different time" and are undatable, but have been included here for clarity.

1388 Dating *Serpent Crest: Tsar Wars* and *Aladdin Time* (BBC fourth Doctor audios #3.1, #3.3) - The story picks up directly after the robots charged into Nest Cottage on Christmas Eve, at the end of *Demon Quest: Sepulchre*.

1389 Events in 2011 include *The Sarah Jane Adventures* Series 5, many (but not all) of the "present day" sequences of *Doctor Who* Series 6, and *Torchwood* Series 4 (a.k.a. *TW: Miracle Day*).

1390 *Fear Her.* Chloe's father died the previous year.

1391 *No Man's Land*

1392 *TW: Miracle Day.* This is presumably part of the Three Families' efforts to exploit the Miracle.

Curios, where the Swarm died. The Doctor and his friends returned to Nest Cottage, where they enjoyed a dinner on Christmas Eve. The Demon was still on the loose.

2010 (24th-25th December) - SERPENT CREST: TSAR WARS / ALADDIN TIME[1388] -> The fourth Doctor, Mrs Wibbsey and Mike Yates were enjoying their Christmas Eve dinner when robot agents burst in, knocked Yates unconscious, and took the Doctor and Wibbsey down a wormhole to the Robotov Empire in the far future. After a subsequent trip back to the nineteenth century, the Doctor, Wibbsey, the cyborg teenager Alex and his guardian Boolin returned the following day, while Yates was recovering in hospital. While the Doctor took Alex and Boolin home in the TARDIS, saying he might be gone some time dealing with other business, Wibbsey did some washing up.

2011[1389]

Chloe Webber's father died in 2011. Both she and her mother had been terrified of him.[1390] When Hex was in secondary school, he went on a school trip to Venice.[1391] On 15th January, 2011, the US Senate Committee for Drugs and Alcohol voted to hoard the national supply of surplus drugs, and make them only for use in civil defence programmes.[1392] The Doctor took Stevie Wonder back to 1814 to perform for River Song.[1393]

Van Statten discovered the cure to the common cold using alien technology.[1394] Harmony Shoal began constructing buildings in preparation for its takeover of Earth.[1395] The Bantu Independence Group originated as a political movement in southern Africa in 2011. It purchased land and built communities on behalf of the oppressed.[1396]

The eighth Doctor and Lucie saved a bit of cash by doing their Christmas shopping in the January sales.[1397]

? 2011 - NIGHT AND THE DOCTOR: "Bad Night"[1398] -> Amy Pond awoke in the TARDIS, swatted a fly on the console and answered a phone call from the Prince of Wales, who was very concerned about his mother. The eleventh Doctor dashed into the Ship with a bowl containing a goldfish that he claimed was the Queen, who had been transformed during a mishap at a party. The Doctor had captured the fly-like warrior chief of the aliens responsible, then became horrified to realize that Amy had mashed him with a newspaper. He dashed back out to tell River Song that, worryingly, they'd also grabbed the wrong goldfish and needed to sort the mess out before the pet stores opened...

While Amy and Rory slept in the TARDIS, the eleventh Doctor did some locum work in Brixton.[1399]

Thomas Brewster Rejoins the TARDIS

c 2011 - THE CRIMES OF THOMAS BREWSTER[1400] The sixth Doctor and Evelyn tried to quietly visit the Tower of London, but instead were embroiled in the conflict between Symbios, the Terravore and Thomas Brewster – who was passing as an East London gang leader named "the Doctor". The Terravore negotiated with Symbios – it would spare the sentient planet if it provided access to Brewster's wormhole, enabling them to attack Earth instead. The Doctor deactivated the Terravore by isolating their queen on Symbios, and the media deemed a Terravore assault on south London as something of a "Japanese Toy Robot Terror". Afterwards, Brewster departed with the Doctor and Evelyn.

As part of these events, Flip Jackson – a future companion of the sixth Doctor – and her boyfriend Jared Ramon were along for the ride when a train was abducted to Symbios.

1393 *A Good Man Goes to War.* Wonder had his first hit, age 13, in 1963. The Doctor could have recruited him at any point in the many decades to come; linking it to the present day seems reasonable.
1394 *Dalek*
1395 "Five years" before *The Return of Doctor Mysterio.*
1396 *Benny: Another Girl, Another Planet*
1397 *Relative Dimensions.* The year isn't stated, but the idea seems to be that Lucie is back her home turf, so it's probably the January after she started travelling with the Monk. The Doctor uses a debit card linked to an account with his "untouched" UNIT salary, further suggesting that it's the modern day.
1398 Dating *Night and the Doctor:* "Bad Night" (Series 6 DVD minisode) - This is the first of five minisodes exclusive to the Series 6 DVD set, under the banner title of *Night and the Doctor* (not to be confused with the

similar-sounding *The Night of the Doctor*, in which the eighth Doctor dies). "Bad Night" is likely contemporary with the release of the DVDs in November 2011 – the reigning UK monarch is female, and the Prince of Wales is male. Nonetheless, the Doctor's comment that the death of their warrior chief might goad the aliens into causing "the slaughter of ten billion souls" might suggest it's the future, and even Amy asks of the TARDIS caller: "The Prince of Wales. Which one? What year is this?" Presented as a comedy piece, the dilemma seen here is never resolved on screen.
1399 *Night and the Doctor:* "Good Night". No year given, but the claim has a contemporary ring to it.
1400 Dating *The Crimes of Thomas Brewster* (BF #143) - The story seems contemporary and was released in January 2011; Evelyn concurs with this at the start of *The Feast of Axos*, claiming that *The Crimes of Thomas*

2011 - THE FORBIDDEN TIME[1401] -> The entire population of Earth heard a prerecorded message that the Vist had encoded into space-time, but most interpreted this as a dream or hallucination. Polly Wright addressed a gathering of esteemed people – many of whom knew of the Doctor – to relate her encounter with the Vist, and assure that they posed no further danger.

(=) 2011 - "Ripper's Curse"[1402] -> The eleventh Doctor and Rory arrived in Whitechapel from 1888 to check what if any historical alteration had occurred concerning the Jack the Ripper murders. A tour guide told them that the list of suspected Ripper victims included "Amelia Marple" – the name Amy had been using in 1888. They returned to 1888 and prevented Amy's death.

2011 - J&L S3: SWAN SONG[1403] -> Elliot Payne arrived from the future and undertook temporal experiments that he hoped would save his wife. A temporal link was forged between Payne's laboratory and the New Regency Theatre – which stood adjacent to the same site – in the 1890s. Time breaches occurred, and the collective emotions of all the performances given in the theatre coalesced into an intelligence that nestled within Payne's assistant Alice. The two of them sacrificed themselves to destroy Payne's equipment before it could destroy the world, and their consciousnesses transferred into what stone that remained from the theatre. Nonetheless, Payne travelled back to the 1890s to continue his plans.

c 2011 - THE SENTINELS OF THE NEW DAWN[1404] -> Lt Ed Grueber of UNIT, secretly an agent of the Sentinels of the New Dawn, gained valuable intelligence from Liz Shaw about historically nullified events in 2014.

c 2011 - FERRIL'S FOLLY[1405] -> A thrall of the Cronquist, Millicent Drake, had married Sir Hector Ferril, and upon his death renovated his estate and observatory in Norfolk. Ferril attempted to bring a Cronquist invasion force to Earth via a star alignment that occurred once every five thousand years, but the fourth Doctor and the first Romana dispersed the Key to Time segment that was crucial to Ferril's equipment. The invaders and Ferril were dissipated into a thin layer of matter, and the Doctor and Romana went to retrieve the segment from the planet Tara.

c 2011 - TALES FROM THE VAULT[1406] -> Captain Ruth Matheson, the Curator of UNIT's Vault, recruited Warrant Officer Charlie Sato of UNIT's Skywatch division to serve as her assistant. The mind of Kalicarache, still in the jacket of Tommy Watkins, possessed Sato and hoped to leave Earth by using the Vault's technology. Matheson drained Kalicarache's mind into the alien crystal containing a copy of Zoe Herriot's memories, then smashed it.

c 2011 - HEART OF STONE[1407] -> The silicon-based lifeforms in the Pron-Kalunka Galaxy used granite as the base matter for all their technology.

Scientists at the Henson Research Centre conducted experiments on moon rock samples in preparation for NASA's next moon landings. A moon rock was bathed in

---

Brewster took place in "2011". However, in *Tales from the Vault* – seemingly set in 2011 – Captain Ruth Matheson says the Terravore incident was "last year". Patricia Menzies mentions meeting the Doctor "a couple of years ago", and while she could be referring to *The Condemned* (set in February 2008), it's more likely she means *The Raincloud Man* (set in December 2008), so she could be rounding up a little.

1401 Dating *The Forbidden Time* (BF CC #5.9) - The Doctor tells Polly that the Vist seek to capture an eight-year span of time from "2011 to 2019", and the Vist's message is presumably triggered at the start of it – also in accordance with the audio coming out in 2011.

1402 Dating "Ripper's Curse" (IDW *DW* Vol. 2 #2-4) – The date is given in a caption. Amy and Rory are married, but there's no indication that Amy is pregnant, suggesting that this is part of the adventures they experience between *A Christmas Carol* and their returning to Leadworth prior to *The Impossible Astronaut*.

1403 Dating *J&L S3: Swan Song* (*J&L* #3.3) - The setting seems contemporary; *J&L S3: Chronoclasm* specifies the year as "2011". Very strangely, Payne at one point says that in Victorian times, the New Regency was located

adjacent to where his laboratory will be in "several thousand years". (This can't mean Earth in the future, as Payne isn't human and conducted his work near a black star.) No mention is made of the Miracle from *TW: Miracle Day*, so events in this story likely resolve beforehand.

1404 Dating *The Sentinels of the New Dawn* (BF CC #5.10) - This framing sequence is probably contemporary with the audio's release in 2011.

1405 Dating *Ferril's Folly* (BF CC 5.11) - The audio was released in May 2011, and the blurb says it occurs on "Earth in the present day". There's little to support or rule against this, save that Millicent Ferril was a NASA astronaut fifteen years ago.

1406 Dating *Tales from the Vault* (BF CC 6.1) - The audio came out in July 2011. Sato remarks that some items in the Vault have labels such as "Do not open until the year 2011", and the revived Kalicarache says, "What year is this... 2011". It's "about ten years" after the story's 2002 component. Mucking things up slightly is that Matheson says the Terravore incident in *The Crimes of Thomas Brewster* was "last year" (see the dating notes on that story).

ultraviolet light, which activated the alien bacteria it contained. The TARDIS arrived in a pigsty on Conway Farm in England after the bacteria had birthed a new form of life – an animated rock man named Athrocite, who could have triggered a molecular wave that would turn everything on Earth's surface into moon rock. The eleventh Doctor, Amy and Rory returned the bacteria's original rock to the moon, cancelling its effects and turning Athrocite to dust.

c 2011 - THE WITCH FROM THE WELL[1408] -> Workman unsealed the well into which the energy echo of the Agnes Bates-monster was trapped in the seventeenth century. Finicia and Lucern – secretly alien Varaxils who outwardly looked 17 – approached the eighth Doctor and Mary Shelley for help, claiming the monster had killed their father. The four of them went back in time to learn the creature's origins.

Finicia and Lucern stranded the Doctor in the past, and returned with Mary in the TARDIS. They located the Witch Star that the descendents of Squire Portillon had kept safe, and tried to siphon the monster's Odic energy. The resultant blast killed the Varaxils and dissipated the creature. Mary learned the historical fate of her associate, George Gordon Byron, from the man's great nephew. She then used the Fast Return Switch to retrieve the Doctor.

c 2011 (a Sunday) - "Down to Earth"[1409] -> The eleventh Doctor visited the Tylonian commander Lum-Tee, who had settled into a cosy life in an English village as "Harold Lumley". The Doctor judged that Lum-Tee was quite at home on Earth, and enabled him to have one last joy ride in his Class II Trylonian Star Fighter.

(=) 2011 - "Do Not Go Gentle Into that Good Night"[1410] -> A Vorlax Regeneration Drone, built to transfer the minds of fallen soldiers into clone bodies,

was brought back to 2011 from 4688 by the time-child Chiyoko. It continued its programming at the Hawkshaw Manor nursing home, shifting the minds of deceased residents into artificially made children's bodies. The eleventh Doctor and Amy transported the Drone and its charges to peacefully live on an uninhabited garden planet.

The TARDIS absorbed the old-woman-turned-young-girl Margaret into its matrix. She became one of the components that would – in a history that was later nullified – create Chiyoko.[1411]

Iris Realises that Panda is Lost to Her

c 2011 - IRIS S5: LOOKING FOR A FRIEND[1412] -> Iris visited Stella's bar in Soho on and off for decades, thinking it the perfect place that her lost friend Panda might wander into. She befriended a bartender, Andy, and encouraged him to attempt a relationship with a man named Ian. Panda's human self, the theatre critic Arthur Christmas Bayer, did eventually walk into Stella's, but had no memory of Iris. She stalked Arthur for several days, and prompted him to remember some details of their time together. Sensing that her friend would be happier as a writer, Iris pretended that her time-travelling bus was nothing more than fiction – but that Arthur should write a number of stories about it. Arthur returned to his human life, unaware of Iris' true nature.

? = 2011 - FP: HEAD OF STATE[1413] -> The time-ship Lolita plotted to create within Earth a Caldera: a counterpart to the space-time event that granted the Great Houses supremacy over the timeline of the universe. If successful, she would retroactively usurp the Houses' foothold on history...

In America, the Supreme Court struck down voter

1407 Dating *Heart of Stone* (BBC children's 2-in-1 #2) - The story seems contemporary, especially in its allusions to NASA, and was released in 2011. For the Doctor, Amy and Rory, it appears to occur during their travels together between Series 5 and 6.

1408 Dating *The Witch from the Well* (BF #154) - It's "twenty-first century Earth", and "three and a half centuries" since the witch scare at Tranchard's Fell in the seventeenth century. Without any other evidence, the story is probably contemporary with its release in 2011.

1409 Dating "Down to Earth" (IDW *DW Annual 2011*) - The setting appears contemporary. A World War II fighter plane is considered "old", but not so old that it's unlikely that it could still fly.

1410 Dating "Do Not Go Gentle Into That Good Night" (*DWM* #432) - The year is given, and repeated in "The Child of Time" (*DWM*).

1411 "The Child of Time" (*DWM*). One of the downsides of Chiyoko cancelling out her own existence is that the Hawkshaw residents are, presumably, made to remain on Earth as senior citizens.

1412 Dating *Iris S5: Looking for a Friend* (BF Iris #5.8) - It's "three, four years" before the latter part of the story, which is likely contemporary with 2015.

1413 Dating *FP: Head of State* (FP novel #9) - No year given, but the US Constitution dictates that presidential elections happen every four years. The blurb broadbrushes the story as "21st century America". The first of Rachel Edwards' blog posts about the election start the year beforehand, on "November 15th".

Although real-life political figures such as Michael Dukakis, George McGovern, John McCain and Hillary Clinton are mentioned, the campaign entails fictional participants. The White House is currently occupied by

ID laws in *Zall vs. Pennsylvania*, which made three million people – mostly poor, black, swing-state residents – eligible to vote, resulting in the first truly open presidential race in about twenty years. Eight months after the Court's decision, the presidential campaign of Matt Nelson – the 45-year-old junior senator of Minnesota – conducted the biggest voter registration drive in US history. He was a member of the Democratic Farm-Labor Party, which had ties to the Democratic Party.

The eleventh Doctor dropped the now-married Amy and Rory off in Leadworth. They wouldn't see him for two months.[2114] Amy was replaced with a Ganger version of herself by Madame Kovarian.[1415]

The Sarah Jane Adventures Series 5

Sarah Jane Smith Adopts Sky

2011 (a Sunday in early March) - SJA: SKY[1416] -> Miss Myers, one of the Fleshkind in the Tornado Nebula, bioengineered a synthetic lifeform: a baby girl that upon activation would release an energy pulse that would destroy the Fleshkind's enemies, the Metalkind. The Shopkeeper and Captain, in their roles as "servants of the universe", stole Myers' child and left her on Sarah Jane's doorstep. The baby – which Sarah hurriedly named "Sky" – primed itself enough to instantly grow into the form of a 12-year-old girl. Myers attempted to lure the Metalkind to Earth and force Sarah to trigger Sky, but Sarah and her friends defeated her. Sky's genetic potential as a weapon was

"President Sampson" and "Ken Gribbin" – the latter loosely being a Joe Biden-equivalent in that he's served as Vice-President for eight years. (However, it's exceedingly hard to imagine Biden committing Gribbin's disgrace with his sister-in-law – even if Biden's wife Jill does happen to have four sisters.)

Edwards' claim that this election constitutes "the first truly open presidential race in about twenty years" might suggest a later dating, as the 2008 election was a true toss-up. However, the pop culture references include mentions of *High School Musical*, Spider Jerusalem (the comic series *Transmetropolitan*) and *American Gods* by Neil Gaiman – i.e. properties more in line with (say) circa 2012 than 2028.

Although *Head of State* was released in 2015, writer Andrew Hickey notes: "I actually started writing the book in 2012, and the 8th January lands on a Sunday both in the book and in 2012, so I'd say it's set then. That said, I know how the *Doctor Who* calendar seems to vary from ours, so could accept any date in the early twenty-first century." As Lolita seems to prevail at story's end, it's unclear as to whether these events now constitute the "real" history or not.

The Caldera is the *Faction Paradox*-equivalent of the Eye of Harmony on Gallifrey.

1414 Amy and Rory first part company with the Doctor at some point after *A Christmas Carol*, and it's "two months" before they see him again in *The Impossible Astronaut*.

1415 As revealed in *The Almost People*. It's not clear when Amy's abduction/replacement happens, but it's far more likely to have happened when she and Rory are living on Earth and away from the Doctor's protection (so, between *A Christmas Carol* and *The Impossible Astronaut*). It's alternatively possible that the switch happened in the three months between *The Impossible Astronaut* and *Day of the Moon* in 1969, but that would more awkwardly require the Silence to be nipping in

and out of their own timeline, when (setting aside that River does this sort of thing all the time) there's no evidence otherwise that they're doing so.

1416 Dating *SJA: Sky* (SJA 5.1) - The Sarah Jane Adventures Series 5 was broadcast from 3rd to 18th October, 2011, but what few dating clues are provided suggests that it actually takes place sooner than that, in spring of the same year. As *SJA: The Curse of Clyde Langer* appears to occur in early April (see the dating notes on that story), and also says that Sky came to Earth (in *Sky*) "barely a month" beforehand, *Sky* itself must take place in early March. Supporting that timeframe, Rani's mum says in *Sky* that Rani is "17" – we know from cross-referencing *SJA: Secrets of the Stars* and *SJA: Lost in Time* that Rani is an Aries born in 1993, so if she's still 17, then *Sky* cannot occur any later than the second-to-last day of Aries, 19th April. (If it were 20th April, and Rani's birthday were the same day, Gita would almost certainly have mentioned it instead of just saying, "She's 17".) The scenery isn't entirely in keeping with early March – the trees have leaves, and Sky is amazed at all the green plants (flowers included) growing in Sarah's driveway – but otherwise it's not so warm and sunny as to evoke the onset of summer. In fact, it's noticeably windy and overcast.

1417 Dating *SJA: The Curse of Clyde Langer* (SJA 5.2) - Sarah is reading *The Ealing Echo* as Clyde visits her the morning after the curse on him activates, and while the newspaper's dateline is unreadable, the top headline on the back page – presumably the sports section – says "... For Cricket's First Day". The 2011 English cricket season commenced on 2nd April (a mid to late April start is typical, but the seasons began much earlier than the norm in 2010 and 2011). That fits very well with *SJA: Sky* not being able to occur later than the end of Aries (20th April; see the dating notes on that story), and Sarah Jane's statement in *The Curse of Clyde Langer* that "barely a month" has passed since *Sky*.

deactivated, and a Metalkind forcibly took Myers back to its homeworld. Afterwards, Sarah adopted Sky as her daughter.

2011 (first week of April) - SJA: THE CURSE OF CLYDE LANGER[1417] -> Clyde Langer was now in sixth form.

The totem containing the spirit of Hetocumtek was found in a cave in Death Valley, and became part of an exhibit of totem poles at the Museum of Culture in London. Sarah, Clyde, Rani and Sky investigated the totem pole as the possible cause of a storm of full-sized fish that rained upon Ealing. Hetocumtek's full revival was triggered when Clyde got a splinter from the totem pole in his finger – Clyde's name became the key to Hetocumtek freeing himself, but this left Clyde cursed. Everyone who heard his name ostracised him, and he soon became homeless. Sarah and Rani broke the curse by summoning enough willpower to say Clyde's name aloud, and brought Clyde to stop Hetocumtek from getting free. Hetocumtek's totem pole vanished, and was possibly destroyed. Clyde's only friend during his exile, a homeless woman with the alias Ellie Faber, thought he'd abandoned her and left town.

2011 (Sunday, 15th May) - SJA: THE MAN WHO NEVER WAS[1418] -> Sarah Jane was now regarded as one of the top three journalists in the country – as was Lionel Carson, her former editor. While K9 remained at Oxford to back up the Bodleian Library, Luke Smith visited Sarah Jane – and met his "sister" Sky – just as Serf Systems readied to debut the SerfBoard, a device touted as "the world's newest and best portable computer". The holographic image of the late Joseph Serf, as projected from equipment manipulated by the enslaved cyclopses from Scultos – had a hypnotic quality. Through this, the scheming John Harrison hoped to make billions by mesmerising the public into loving the SerfBoard when it was really quite rubbish. Sarah Jane, Clyde, Rani, Luke and Sky ended Harrison's plan, and summoned a rescue ship from Scultos to take the liberated Scullions back home.

2011 - SJA: CHILDREN OF STEEL[1419] -> Sarah Jane won at auction the head of Adam, Sir Joseph Montague's Difference Golem, and found its body at Montague's former estate, Holcote House. Reactivated, Adam created robotic offspring to fulfill Montague's wish that humanity be freed from servitude. A synthetic female operative arrived from the future, warned that Adam's actions would

The passage of time within *The Curse of Clyde Langer*, however, is a bit trickier to pin down. At first blush, it would appear that a total of two nights and three days (the first and last of which are school days) elapse, but Ellie's comment to Clyde at the start of episode two – that she first saw him "the other day" (back when he first visited the museum, after the rain of fish) – might suggest that more time than that passes. If so, and presuming for the moment that Sarah is seen reading (for whatever reason) an older edition of *The Ealing Echo*, a framework for this story can be derived...the rain of fish happens on 1st April, and Sarah and her friends visit the Museum (leading to Clyde getting the splinter) on the same day; the 2nd April edition of *The Ealing Echo* leads with the story "Fish Flingers" and also contains a *preview* (not an after-the-fact account) of "Cricket's First Day"; the curse on Clyde's name fully activates the night of 3rd April, when he signs his name to some artwork (this means that a day passes between the scenes of Clyde and his mother settling down to dinner and him going to bed, which isn't intuitive but works); Clyde is ostracised after visiting Sarah the morning of 4th April, when she's going through some articles from the 2nd April *Ealing Echo* (possibly just because she failed to read it over the weekend); night passes between episodes one and two, and events conclude no earlier than 5th April. (Possibly even later, depending on how long Clyde is lives on the streets.)

1418 Dating *SJA: The Man Who Never Was* (SJA 5.3) - There's no indication of how much time has passed

since *SJA: The Curse of Clyde Langer*. The SerfBoard launch date is given as "the 15th"; as it's not a school day and 15th April was a Friday in 2011, the best fit (if the real-world calendar holds any sway here) is Sunday, 15th May. It's also a bit symmetrical to think that *The Man Who Never Was* takes place at the end of the school year – this could in fact be the reason why Luke is home from Oxford, although it isn't said.

1419 Dating *SJA: Children of Steel* and *SJA: Judgement Day* (SJA audios #9-10) - The final (to date) *Sarah Jane Adventures* audios occur at some unspecified point after Sky's introduction (*SJA: Sky*). The audios were released after Series 5 had finished broadcasting, so it's entirely possible that they follow on from the final TV story, *SJA: The Man Who Never Was*. Both of the audios occur on a Saturday, and so must take place at least a week apart. *Judgement Day* provides further evidence that Series 5 occurs earlier in the year than when it aired (in October 2011) – Sarah is said to "step out of the house, and into the spring sunshine", and it's established that *SJA: Judgement of the Judoon* was "many months ago", *SJA: Vault of Secrets* (set circa October 2010) was "a few months ago". One oddity – because there hasn't been quite enough done to confuse the issue of when the humanity learns about the existence of extra-terrestrials, oh no – is that Sarah Jane wins over the Veritas partly by convincing them that humanity is "not ready for the truth" that aliens are real, in defiance of the public *surely* having figured it out by now.

pollute the timelines and – with his permission – removed the future-tech probe that enabled his mental function, deactivating him and his children.

2011 - SJA: JUDGEMENT DAY[1419] -> The truth-seeking Veritas arrived on Earth in pursuit of Xando, an alien passing as a stage magician. Xando created an illusion of flame beings to distract the Veritas' spheres as they searched the White Cross Mall near West London, frightening hundreds. The Veritas identified Sarah Jane as a perpetrator of fabrications and cover stories, but she convinced the Veritas to save Sky from a mob, and taught them that the truth could sometimes harm innocents. The Veritas agreed, and Xando departed.

Doctor Who Series 6

River Kills the Doctor at Lake Silencio

The older eleventh Doctor had directed Amy, Rory, River and his 909-year-old self to meet at an American diner... that unknown to any of them was the disguised exterior of Clara Oswald's TARDIS...[1420]

2011 (22nd April) - THE IMPOSSIBLE ASTRO-NAUT[1421] ->

"By Silencio Lake, on the Plain of Sighs, an Impossible Astronaut will rise from the deep and strike the Time Lord dead."[1422]

The eleventh Doctor, age 1103, had learned that he was historically fated to die at Lake Silencio in Utah on 22nd April, 2011. He sent invitations to Amy and Rory (who were back to living in Leadworth), River Song and the elderly Canton Delaware III to meet him there. As the Silence had planned, a younger version of River Song rose from Lake Silencio in a NASA astronaut suit and killed the Doctor – she shot him twice; the second time, fatally, in the middle of his regeneration. The River who killed the Doctor left, and the Doctor's friends give him a Viking funeral, cremating his body to prevent it falling into the wrong hands. Canton Delaware also departed, and the Doctor's friends met the fourth person he had invited to his murder... himself, age 909. Acting on the older Doctor's instructions, Amy, Rory and River had the 909-year-old Doctor take them back to 1969. This was the first of a series of adventures in which they fought the Silence and their ally, Madame Kovarian, all in the knowledge that the Doctor was destined to die.

1420 Or so *Hell Bent* seems to strongly imply.
1421 Dating *The Impossible Astronaut* (X6.1) - River Song gives the year as "2011". Amy and Rory's invite instructs them to meet the Doctor on "22/4/2011"; it's possible they receive the invite before that exact day, allowing time for them to travel by conventional means from Leadworth to Utah. The specific date of the Doctor's death is also given as 22/4/2011 in *Let's Kill Hitler*, *Night Terrors*, *Closing Time* and *The Wedding of River Song*, and is doubtless meant to roughly parallel the broadcast of *The Impossible Astronaut* on 23rd April of that year.
1422 *Closing Time*
1423 Dating *The Wedding of River Song* (X6.13) - The bulk of the action of this story takes place in one instant: 5.02.57pm on 22nd April, 2011.
1424 Between *A Good Man Goes to War* and *Let's Kill Hitler*. Amy and Rory have not yet experienced events in *The Wedding of River Song*.
1425 "Four Doctors" (Titan)
1426 *Serpent Crest: The Hexford Invasion*. Easter was on 24th April in 2011.
1427 Dating *Technophobia* (BF 10th Doc #1.1) - It's "two years" into the future for Donna, who originates from 2009 (*Partners in Crime*). Donna here gains foreknowledge of Justin Bieber's 3D film (*Never Say Never*, out in February 2011), and Prince William's wedding to

Catherine Middleton (29th April, 2011). London doesn't actually have a "Technology Museum", but the Science Museum is based in South Kensington.
1428 "Almost a year" and, later, "over a year" earlier than *The Shadows of Avalon*.
1429 Dating *Serpent Crest: The Hexford Invasion* (BBC fourth Doctor audio #3.4) - Mrs Wibbsey's narration says that the story begins on "a Thursday in August", "nearly nine months" after the Doctor returned her to Hexford in *Serpent Crest: Aladdin Time*. The faux second Doctor putters about Hexford for "just over a fortnight" before the fourth Doctor returns "on Friday afternoon". The Hexford residents spend three months in their personal timeline in the far future, but Hexford presumably returns to Earth the moment after it left – Captain Yates swears the townsfolk to secrecy about everything they've witnessed, and that would be a great deal harder, given the inevitable media attention, had Hexford vanished overnight only to return three months later.
1430 *Serpent Crest: Survivors in Space*
1431 Dating *Let's Kill Hitler* (X6.8) - The Doctor has had "all summer" to look for baby Melody.

The Eleventh Doctor Marries River Song

> **(=) 2011 (22nd April) - THE WEDDING OF RIVER SONG**[1423] -> The eleventh Doctor was apparently resigned to his fate at Lake Silencio, but River Song refused to play along... she emptied her weaponry, saving his life but undoing the fixed point in time that was meant to see him die.
>
> All of history happened simultaneously on the exact moment of the Doctor's intended death, at 5:02 pm on 22nd April. London became a chaotic landscape of steam trains, Roman chariots and pterodactyls. The War of the Roses entered its second year, and Charles Dickens appeared on Breakfast TV. The Holy Roman Emperor Winston Churchill returned to the Buckingham Senate on his personal mammoth, after having argued with Cleopatra ("a dreadful woman, but an excellent dancer"). Churchill's soothsayer, the Doctor, was kept imprisoned in the Tower of London.
>
> The Doctor was rescued by Amy, who in this reality worked for a military organisation. She took him to Area 52, a military base kept in an Egyptian pyramid, where Madame Kovarian and over a hundred of the Silence were being held captive. River Song met the Doctor at Area 52, but the Silence were merely playing possum – they broke free, attacking their captors. Amy left Kovarian behind to die.
>
> The Doctor believed that River was fated to become either the woman who married or killed him... so he married her, and secretly told her that his body was actually a shapeshifting spaceship, the *Teselecta*, made to look like him. The Doctor kissed River, starting time again and returning them to Lake Silencio. When River shot the Doctor this time, she actually struck the impervious *Teselecta*, thwarting the fixed point.

After the Battle of Demons Run, River Song returned Amy and Rory to their native time. The two of them waited all summer for the Doctor to bring word of their missing infant daughter Melody.[1424]

> (=) In an alternate timeline, all time collapsed when River refused to kill the eleventh Doctor. He failed to restore causality, and settled down into a blissful domestic life with her.[1425]

Mrs Wibbsey danced the can-can during the Hexford Easter parade.[1426]

2011 - TECHNOPHOBIA[1427] -> Inter-dimensional beings, the Koggnossenti, sent a tech squadron to capture Earth by emitting sound waves that reprogrammed the cerebral cortex. About 99.2% of the population proved susceptible, and came to fear all technology. The tenth Doctor and Donna halted the invasion by reflecting the Koggnossenti's stupefying beams back on them.

Jill Meadows of Meadows Digital was the youngest female CEO in Britain. London was home to the Technology Museum. Terileptus Nine had an impressive gallery.

In late July 2011, Lethbridge-Stewart's wife Doris was killed in a yachting accident.[1428]

2011 (August) - SERPENT CREST: THE HEXFORD INVASION[1429] -> The Skishtari longed for the gene egg that the fourth Doctor had hidden, in 1861, under what would become Nest Cottage. They created a clone of the second Doctor, who tricked UNIT into helping him grow biomesh trees – biomechanoids with metal roots. Captain Yates was brought out of retirement to help. The faux Doctor took up residence at Nest Cottage while the fourth Doctor was away, and spent two weeks planting the trees all around Hexford. The fourth Doctor returned just as a shrouded Skishtari spaceship linked energy beams with the trees and hauled up the entire village, hoping to find the egg underneath. The genuine Doctor tried to counteract this by having the TARDIS generate a gravity bubble, but the resultant tug-of-war triggered the Skishtari wormhole that had been dormant since 1861, sending the whole village of Hexford into the far future. The fourth Doctor and Wibbsey collected the Skishtari egg, then followed in the TARDIS...

The clone second Doctor and the fourth Doctor combined efforts to return Hexford to its proper location. Yates decided to stay in Hexford for a time, and the fourth Doctor bid Wibbsey farewell, leaving for parts unknown. The second Doctor was a type of clone with a very limited lifespan, and it was expected that he would just fade away in a matter of months.[1430]

2011 (end of summer) - LET'S KILL HITLER[1431] -> The Doctor failed to answer Amy and Rory's phone calls, so they created a huge crop circle that read "DOCTOR" and was featured in the *Leadworth Chronicle*. He saw the photo and joined them. Amy and Rory's childhood friend, Mels, was on the run from the police and pulled a gun on the Doctor, ordering that they go back in time and kill Hitler. The Doctor took Amy, Rory and Mels back to 1938... after resolving matters there, Amy and Rory continued travelling with the Doctor.

2011 - NIGHT TERRORS[1432] **->** The Tenza were birthed in space, then adapted their form in order to find a nest; they were effectively space cuckoos. One such Tenza transformed itself into George, the eight-year-old son of a young couple named Alex and Claire, and altered their memories so they would accept him. George feared rejection, and his psionic abilities trapped people in the place that symbolised where he put "bad things": the doll's house in his cupboard. The eleventh Doctor, Amy and Rory became trapped in the doll's house prison, and were threatened by living dolls. Alex's love for his son calmed his fears, and normality was restored.

2011 (a Saturday in September) - LETH-ST: "Lucy Wilson"[1433] **->** Sir Alistair Lethbridge-Stewart's relationship with his son Albert had hardened, but he still went to visit his granddaughter Lucy. Along the way, he thwarted an inoffensive alien, a Prankster, from stealing the extraterrestrial box he'd bought as a gift for her. Alistair told Lucy

the box would give her hope in times of darkness, and she could hear its nature-sounds after it vanished in her hands. Lucy's oldest brother, Conall, was thinking about marrying his boyfriend Dean.

2011 (7th-14th October) - TOUCHED BY AN ANGEL[1434] **->** Mark Whitaker, a widower following his wife's death in 2003, was now a partner at the law firm of Pollard, Boyce & Whitaker. On 7th October, he received an archived set of instructions... that was written in his own handwriting, and which detailed tasks Mark had to perform throughout 1994 and 2001. The only Weeping Angel that had survived the eleventh Doctor's trap in 2003 used the very last of its energy to send Mark back to 1994.

The eleventh Doctor, Amy and Rory identified Mark as a blip in the space-time continuum, and followed him to that year. After many cross-time shenanigans, the travellers returned Mark to 2011. He had physically become a 37 year old again following events in 1993, and decided to move on with his life.

1432 Dating *Night Terrors* (X6.9) - Alex, while admittedly not knowing his son's true origins, believes that George was born "a couple of weeks" after "24/12/2002" (the time-stamp on a photograph), and that George "just turned eight" in January. So, it's now 2011. Alex's landlord says that *Bergerac* (1981-1991) is "thirty years old". There's a day planner on the wall of George's bedroom, but nothing helpful can be discerned from it.
1433 Dating *Leth-St: "Lucy Wilson"* (*Leth-St HAVOC Files* #3.8) - The tag line says it's "two years after" *SJA: Enemy of the Bane*. The Haisman Timeline says it's "September". Lucy stars in a *Lethbridge-Stewart* spin-off series, *The Lucy Wilson Mysteries*.
1434 Dating *Touched by an Angel* (NSA #47) - The exact days are given (pgs. 13, 235). The Doctor and Amy make an initial visit to 1994, thinking they'll return the moment they left, but instead come back a week later (p43). In the interim, Rory stays in Mark's flat, and pops up to Leadworth to collect the post (p44).
1435 Dating *The Way Through the Woods* (NSA #45) - The book was released in 2011, and keeps making reference to "England, now" – which appears to be simultaneous to "late October" (p10).
1436 Dating *Wildthyme Beyond!* (Iris novel #2) - Events from Sammy's point of view start in "October" (p13) and continue on at IrisCon at "Christmas" (p431). An Internet forum exchange dates the year as "2011" (ch20), and it's been "thirty years" since *The Iris Wildthyme Show* aired in 1979 (p163).
1437 Dating *TW: Miracle Day* (TW 4.1-4.10) - No year, day, month or time of year is expressly stated.
The incidental evidence suggests that the year is 2011, the same as the story's broadcast. Events in 1928 are variously generalised as having occurred "eighty years" and "nine decades" ago; evidence pertaining to a

murder in 1927 has been archived for "almost ninety years". The back of the Overflow Camp Heath Care Provider Framework: Standards and Guidelines folder that Gwen is given (in episode five) says "Copyright 2011". Oswald Danes says (episode two) he spent "six years" in solitary confinement – he was convicted in 2006, but it's very likely, for a crime of his magnitude, that he was held without bond for some time beforehand. An investigative report on Jack that Esther pulls from sealed CIA archive boxes (episode one) is dated 21st December, 2010. The CIA's intelligence (episode one) says that there's been "no sightings" of Gwen "for the last twelve months" – which isn't to say that Gwen didn't go underground some time before that (after *TW: Children of Earth*). Each episode begins with a rising population counter that starts at 6,928,198,000(ish) – in the real world, the Population Division of the United Nations declared the "Day of 7 Billion" (the day designated as Earth's population achieving that amount) as 31st October, 2011, although the Miracle might have made the population crest over the seven billion mark somewhat sooner. In *The End of Time*, set prior to the Miracle at Christmas 2010, the population of Earth was given as 6,727,949,388.
Gwen's daughter Anwen, born in or near early May 2010, looks much more like a one year old than a two year old. Both Rex's mobile (episode two) and the phone logs on Charlotte Wills (episode ten) – although not entirely reliable for reasons discussed below – display the year as "2011". Overall, and barring some new finding coming to light, 2011 seems like a safe bet.
The biggest challenge with *Miracle Day*, then, is finding a portion of 2011 in which it can occur without coming into conflict with *Doctor Who* Series 6 and *The Sarah Jane Adventures* Series 5 – neither of which make

2011 (late October) - THE WAY THROUGH THE WOODS[1435] **->** The eleventh Doctor, Amy and Rory found that journalist Jess Ashcroft was the latest of hundreds of people who had gone missing in Swallow Woods throughout the millennium. They identified the semi-sentient spaceship of Reyn the were-fox as being responsible for the disappearances, and ended the spatio-temporal anomalies the ship had extruded into the Woods. This retroactively returned everyone the ship had captured. History would record that only three of the abductees – Jess, Laura Brown and Emily Bostock (a barmaid from 1917) – had gone missing, as they opted to travel with the liberated ship.

The Long War was now over, and Reyn returned to his devastated homeworld to fulfill upon the legend of the Traveller: a figure who would restore the lost technology of how to make spaceships semi-sentient.

= 2011 (October to Christmas) - WILDTHYME BEYOND![1436] **->** Interest was rekindled in the short-lived *Iris Wildthyme* TV show, with *Pandamonium* standing as the foremost *Iris Wildthyme* magazine. The complete series was released on DVD. A fan named Sammy was baffled to find the content very different from what he'd remembered. The first episode had been set mostly on Earth, with the revelation of Iris' big red bus, and the final episode entailed Iris and her friends visiting the magical world of Hyspero. In the new version, the series opened with Iris and Panda attending a Boney M concert at the Roker Park football stadium in Sunderland, and dealing with scorpion men. The final episode had Iris and her friends visit a shopping mall in a moonbase as Earth's moon lurched out of orbit.

In December, Sammy attended IrisCon – the first major Iris Wildthyme convention in more than ten years. The real Iris, having thwarted Anthony Marvelle, traveled to this parallel dimension to attend IrisCon at the Palace Hotel with her friends Panda, Simon, Kelly, Jenny, Barbra the Vending Machine and Fenster the dragon. They enjoyed the cosplayers dressed as them, and a good time was had by all.

Torchwood Series 4: *Miracle Day*

Death is Suspended Across Earth

2011 - TW: MIRACLE DAY[1437] **->** The world's population now exceeded 6,928,198,000. In Cardiff Bay, the water tower had been rebuilt since the Hub's destruction. Rendition of UK citizens to US custody was permitted under the 456 Amendments to US Code 3184.

The Three Families initiated their plan to destroy the world economy in order to rebuild and take control of it. The Families seeded the blood of an immortal, Jack Harkness, into the Blessing in Singapore and Buenos Aires simultaneously, causing the Blessing to accept the blood as a new template and transmit some of its properties through humanity's morphic field.

On a Sunday night at 11:36 pm, Eastern US time, in what became known as the Miracle, death instantly vanished from Earth. People became so *alive* that they continued to function despite hideous injuries – not even decapitation could entirely kill someone. Some people had conditions that left them brain dead, their bodies denied the release of death. The child killer Oswald Danes was executed in Jacksonville, Kentucky – but the Miracle kept Danes alive, and the state governor was forced to set him free.

In spite of the Miracle, humanity continued aging as normal, suggesting that everyone would eventually become an undying, aged husk. The 50% of pregnancies that would naturally have aborted didn't, making

---

any mention, or display any sign, of either the Miracle or its massive impact upon global society. Three pieces of evidence – all of which must be discounted for continuity reasons – go directly to this question: a) in a scene set a few days after the Miracle begins, Rex's secondary mobile gives the date as "22-MAR-11" (episode two), b) also a few days following the Miracle's start, Oprah Winfrey wants Oswald Danes as a guest on her show, which in the real world took a bow on 25th May, 2011 (episode two), and c) a CIA trace on the phone records of Charlotte Wills (in episode ten, so after the two month gap between eps eight and nine) says the last use of her mobile occurred on "2011.09.09".

The first two pieces of evidence are fairly easy to set aside... Rex is talking to Esther on what's presumably his CIA-issue mobile, so perhaps his secondary mobile is a disposable unit he hurriedly picked up for personal use,

and the date isn't set right. Also, if anything could coax Oprah into bringing her show back (presuming that she ever ended it in the *Doctor Who* universe), the Miracle would be it. Charlotte's phone records, admittedly, are much more difficult to overlook, as they're produced by advanced CIA spyware.

It's entirely possible that the production team meant for Rex and Charlotte's mobile dates to denote that six months pass during *Miracle Day* from start to finish – or it could equally be the case that they weren't paying attention to such things. (This is the same production team, after all, that allowed an email to Esther in episode two to read as if it were written by a Dadaist poet: "Ballistics wants report on top of the shade. The flower commands ballistics. The curtain outweighs ballistics. How will the welcome quiz ascend below report? Inside ballistics weds deterrent. Should ballistics stem

genetic mistakes viable. As murder was no longer possible, many murder prosecutions were reduced to assault charges. The need for painkillers skyrocketed, and a bill introduced in the US Congress made all prescription drugs, painkillers and antibiotics available without a prescription – a windfall for the pharmaceutical companies.

Jack Harkness had returned to Earth, and the inversion of the Blessing meant that he had became mortal. His blood endangered the Families' plan, and so they initiated an online virus to search out references of Torchwood, hoping to flush Jack into the open. Jack used malware to eliminate each and every digital mention of Torchwood, and the word itself ceased to exist online. Agents of the Families moved to discredit anyone with any knowledge of Torchwood, putting CIA agent Rex Matheson and CIA analyst Esther Dummond on the run. They were forced to join Jack and Gwen Cooper as the remnants of Torchwood.

2011 - TW: WEB OF LIES[1438] **->** Miles Mokri, a conspiracy blogger, uncovered many details pertaining to the Miracle and was rendered silent when assassins shot him.

Miles' sister Holly and FBI agent Joe Bradley combed through Miles' evidence and became convinced that a shadow group was trying to control the world through the Miracle. They found and destroyed the Three Families' back-up supply of Jack's blood, which was hidden at Coney Island.

2011 - TW: MIRACLE DAY -> The nations of Earth struggled to adjust to a world without death... Somalia stopped fighting, but North Korea mobilised its army at its southern border, as many of its soldiers thought themselves immortal. The Prime Minister of India announced a desire to reconcile with Pakistan – with reincarnation was no longer an option, the one life accorded to each human seemed too precious to waste on fighting. Some projections held that as the three hundred thousand people who died on average each day were still living, global resources would be exhausted in four months. Contraceptives were introduced to the water supply in India and mainland China. Hospices started closing down. The price of oil crossed a symbolic $100 a barrel amid fears over distribution in the Middle East.

---

report? The incidental river pops after report. Report rubs ballistics.") Whatever the intent, however, the phone records cannot be treated with absolute sanctity because...

While the time that elapses within the ten *Miracle Day* episodes is reasonably indeterminate, a non-negotiable gap of two months occurs between episodes eight and nine, and the first eight episodes appear to span a few weeks if not more. (The Torchwood team seems to conduct its investigations at a relatively quick pace, and some developments – such as the construction of the concentration camps – were undoubtedly hastened by the Three Families planning so far in advance of the Miracle; "weeks" passing seems to fit the bill better than "months".) There's wiggle room, but it must take a bare minimum of three months, roughly speaking, for *Miracle Day* to play itself out. (One side note: The prediction in episode one that Earth will exhaust its resources in four months probably doesn't need to be taken literally, as it's never mentioned again, and – as appalling as it is to point out – the mathematical models would change once the incineration units start reducing the number of Category 1 cases.) *TW: Mr Invincible* claims that the Miracle turned the world upside down for "several months".

When, then, do these three months (if not longer) occur in 2011? Some commentators determined from Rex's mobile date that the Miracle began in March 2011, and made some heroic efforts to explain how and why Amy and Rory might already be experiencing it when the Doctor summons them to Utah on 22nd April (in *The Impossible Astronaut*). It is simply beyond

the pale, however, to think that Amy and Rory would be reunited with their best friend – an adventurer in time and space with a penchant for solving cosmic problems – and not once ask him to address the issue that people can no longer die, that concentration camps are sprouting up all over the place, and that the world governments are feeding civil liberties into a paper shredder. It is doubly beyond the pale, in fact, to think that they would not once express bewilderment as to how the Doctor can be shot dead on the beach in a world without death, or at the very least scream at the grave injustice of it all. Thinking that such statements were made off screen seems like wishful thinking, and once it's factored in that *The Sarah Jane Adventures* Series 5 runs throughout spring 2011 without a single hint of the Miracle happening, any scenario in which the Miracle coincides with these episodes becomes nigh-impossible.

Could, then, the Miracle initiate in early summer 2011, be in play when Amy and Rory reunite with the Doctor in *Let's Kill Hitler*, and conclude in accordance with Charlotte's mobile records in September? Again, this is exceedingly unlikely, even if it does have the benefit of roughly pegging *Miracle Day* to its weeks of broadcast. As before, it's asking too much to believe that Amy and Rory would not once direct the Doctor's attention to the Miracle and the horrific suffering it has inflicted upon millions worldwide. It's also a little silly that, with all the guns being pointed about in *Let's Kill Hitler*, Amy and Rory don't wonder if the Miracle is still in play on their bodies now that they've relocated to another time zone.

Cultural movements emerged in response to the Miracle. People took to the streets as "the Soulless" – marchers wearing white masks with sad faces, and holding vigil candles, to denote that everlasting life had robbed humankind of its souls. Members of the suicide-minded 45 Club believed that jumping from the 45th floor or higher was the only guaranteed way to lose consciousness forever. Ellis Hartley Monroe, a darling of the Tea Party, started the Dead is Dead campaign, which advocated that the people who should have died should be treated as such. People in Egypt rioted against the "Western Miracle".

The world governments began to deal more decisively with the growing numbers of undead. Europe and the United States established categories for the classification of life... Category 3 designated a healthy person, Category 2 was a functioning person who had a persistent injury or illness, and Category 1 denoted someone without brain function, but whose body remained alive owing to the Miracle.

The United Kingdom, the United States, France, Germany and generally the whole of Europe established overflow camps for the undead. China declined to do so, but the Pan-African Summit opted in favour of it. Anyone designated Category 1 or 2 was taken to the camps – in the United States, this was sanctioned under the Emergency Miracle Law. The UK Prime Minister announced that the camps were part of a "new age of care and compassion".

Incineration units were secretly established in the camps to turn the Category 1 cases into ash; in the United Kingdom, the Emergency Rulings for the Sake of Public Heath allowed for the burning of dead bodies en masse. Torchwood exposed the truth about the incineration units, triggering headlines such as "Horror of Death Camps in the 21st Century", and also released a video showing the incineration of one of their associates, Dr Vera Juarez. However, this merely paused the camps' operation. The White House ordered an investigation into Juarez's death, but made no apology for the Category 1 process. The footage of Juarez's murder received more than five million views online, and memorial services were held for her.

The US Supreme Court agreed to hear a case involving adjustments to the life sentences of convicted criminals. The US Congress considered the creation of Category Zero: a designation for anyone – including Oswald Danes – who had earned death by incineration for moral reasons. Phicorps facilitated Danes having a media career in which he advocated compassion in these difficult times, in a manner that boosted corporate profits. Madison Weekly attained some fame as the "bisected bride" – a car accident had sheered off her lower half, but she got married a week later while propped up on a box. Angelo Colasanto, having extended his lifespan by limiting his calorie intake and lowering his body temperature, used the Null Field from the Hub to cancel out the Miracle in a very small area and end his life.

The stock market collapsed, and the global economy went into freefall. Banks closed, and the Euro's weakness exacerbated the financial crisis. Greece and Ireland declared bankruptcy, and Spain's economy destabilised, threatening to pull down the whole European Union. Pension funds began going bankrupt, creating a domino effect. A new Great Depression was instigated. At the first sign of the economic meltdown, China withdrew from the United Nations and sealed its borders.

Two months into the new Great Depression, the White House halted all immigration into America. The insurance industry had largely gone bust, "along with half the Western World". The overflow camps built to dispose of Category 1 patients were in full operation

The *most* likely scenario, then, for *Miracle Day* – albeit one that requires wilfully ignoring Charlotte's phone log – is that the Miracle initiates after Amy and Rory leave with the Doctor in *Let's Kill Hitler*, plays out in autumn 2011 and concludes before end of year. While hardly a perfect solution, this avoids all major continuity clashes in a world where *Doctor Who*, *The Sarah Jane Adventures* and *Torchwood* manifestly co-exist (the ties between the three shows are simply too strong to think otherwise). Such a solution leaves two *Doctor Who* novels (*Touched by an Angel* and *The Way Through the Woods*) as outliers, as they have material dated to October 2011 that doesn't acknowledge the Miracle. But it's impossible to get through this process without a continuity clash somewhere, somehow.

This chronology has avoided using the titles given to the individual *Miracle Day* episodes for publicity purposes, as these didn't appear in the episodes themselves and so aren't very intuitive. (Besides, with *Miracle Day* being a single story, using the individual titles rather than "episode one", etc., just tends to create needless confusion.) For anyone needing to cross-reference, the publicity titles (which also appear on the DVD menus) are: 4.1, *The New World*; 4.2 *Rendition*; 4.3, *Dead of Night*; 4.4, *Escape to L.A.*; 4.5, *The Categories of Life*; 4.6, *The Middle Men*; 4.7, *Immortal Sins*; 4.8, *End of the Road*; 4.9, *The Gathering*; 4.10, *The Blood Line*.

1438 Dating *TW: Web of Lies* (TW animated serial #1) - A caption says that it's "the present day". It's alternately said that Miles is shot "on Miracle Day"/the day *after* Miracle Day. While the action of this story only seems to take a day or so to unfold, it's evidently much longer than that, as mention is made of "people being burned" and the economy being on razor's edge.

– the Depression meant that the public was looking to its own welfare, and could offer little protest. Rationing was instituted. In the UK, the Emergency Powers Act allowed government agents to enter homes without a warrant in search of Category 1 patients. Violations of the Miracle Security Act were treated as treason. Some people in the US chose to classify themselves as Category 1, a means of assisted suicide.

Torchwood discovered how the Families had created the Miracle, and found the sites of the Blessing in Shanghai and Buenos Aires. Jack's mortal blood was fed into the Blessing at both locations, restoring the Blessing to its previous state.

"In a pit in old Shanghai, I brought death back to the world. They said it was like a breath, the breath that went around the whole wide world. The last breath, and then no more."[1439]

Everyone kept alive by the Miracle instantly died, including Gwen Cooper's father Geraint. Esther Drummond was killed in the final confrontation with the Families. Oswald Danes, having coerced Jack and Gwen into letting him accompany them to Shanghai, died while detonating the Families' facility there. The Three Families survived, still shrouded in secrecy, and judged the Miracle as a good trial run for their Plan B. UNIT sealed up the sites of the Blessing.

Rex Matheson found that – perhaps owing to his proximity to the Blessing when it recalibrated – he had become just as immortal as Captain Jack.

Miles Mokri recovered from his gunshot wounds. His sister Holly remained in possession of one last bag of Captain Jack's blood – a safeguard against Miles' injuries worsening and a resurgence of her cancer, which was in remission.[1440] The Committee aided the Three Families in their scheme with the Miracle.[1441]

"I was Abducted by a Time-Travelling Sex Pest" (*Chinwagz Magazine* ·#3442, Nov 2011) detailed an encounter between a woman named "Jane" and the Hussar. Iris Wildthyme tweeted her support to the woman in question.[1442]

Alistair Lethbridge-Stewart Passes Away

Sir Alistair Gordon Lethbridge-Stewart had made the Queen's Birthday Honours list. On 5th October, Pearl Hammond wrote to ask if her grandniece could interview the Brig as a Sandhurst alumni. Lethbridge-Stewart agreed on 2nd November, and the interview commenced afterwards. Hammond wrote her thanks on 15th December, but her letter was returned unopened, as the Brigadier had died.[1443] To honour his grandfather, Conall Wilson legally changed his surname to Lethbridge-Stewart.[1444]

1439 Gwen Cooper, *TW: Miracle Day*.
1440 *TW: Web of Lies*
1441 *TW: Forgotten Lives*
1442 *FP: Weapons Grade Snake Oil* (ch12).
1443 *Leth-St:*"The Lock-In"
1444 The Haisman Timeline dates this to "December 2011", but lists it after the Brigadier's passing; *Leth-St:* "When Things Change" has the name-change happen beforehand.
1445 Dating *Leth-St:* "When Times Change" (*Leth-St* novella #2b) - The Brigadier is near the end of his life; he "knew deep down, that the end was approaching".
1446 *The Wedding of River Song*. The Haisman Timeline opts for the symmetry that Lethbridge-Stewart was born on Nicholas Courtney's death date, and the Brigadier dies on Courtney's birthday (16th December).
1447 *Shroud of Sorrow* (p226). The strangely garbed men appear to be the second, sixth, seventh and ninth Doctors – which seems to contradict the eleventh Doctor being caught by surprise to hear of his old friend's death in *The Wedding of River Song*. Then again, if it's part of a multi-Doctor event, they'd most likely lose their memories of it, as frequently happens (*The Day of the Doctor*, etc.).
1448 *UNIT S4: Assembled*

1449 Gryffen is a regular in the *K9* TV series. *K9: Taphony and the Time Loop* establishes his birth year.
1450 *The Condemned*
1451 *Dark Horizons* (p49). The Globetrotters were founded in 1927, and the year of the Doctor meeting them isn't said.
1452 "A few years" before *UNIT* Series 3.
1453 *Unbound: He Jests at Scars...*
1454 "A few years" before *UNIT S4: Assembled*.
1455 Dating *FP: Head of State* (FP novel #9) - The story continues to detail a fabricated US presidential campaign, as brought about by Lolita's time-mechanics.
1456 Dating *The Angels Take Manhattan* (X7.5) - The Doctor names the year. Ads are seen for *Dark Shadows* (2012) starring Johnny Depp and for *Memphis: the Musical*, which played on Broadway from 19th October, 2009 to 5th August, 2012. The Detroit Lions headline shown on fictional *The New York Record* that Amy reads is a bit of a mislead: in real life, the Lions are one of four NFL teams to have never played in the Super Bowl. Nonetheless, the headline suggests the time of year – since 2004, the Super Bowl has always been scheduled for early February.

2011 (December) - LETH-ST: "When Times Change"[1445] -> Alistair Lethbridge-Stewart was near the end of his life. The thirteenth Doctor dropped by Conall Lethbridge-Stewart's living room, to leave a signed photograph for his grandfather. She apologised for not visiting the Brigadier in person, as it would cross personal timelines, but wanted him to see her new face before he passed. The Brigadier told Conall that the Doctor was the Doctor regardless of his/her face, and they cheerfully toasted to the Doctor's good health.

Brigadier Lethbridge-Stewart peacefully passed away on 16th December, 2011. **He'd taken to pouring an extra brandy in the evenings, in case the Doctor came to visit.**[1446]

A mixture of private civilians and UNIT personnel, including John Benton, Liz Shaw and Mike Yates, attended Lethbridge-Stewart's funeral. Also on hand were men variously wearing a fur coat, a multi-coloured outfit, a crumpled suit with a question-mark umbrella, and a leather jacket.[1447]

The Brigadier willed Bessie to Benton, who restored the venerable car.[1448]

2012

Alistair Gryffen was born in Canada in 2012. By 2050, he would be perhaps the world's most brilliant scientist – an expert in robotics, cybernetics, weather control, time travel and alien technology.[1449] In 2012, a special pound coin was minted for the London Olympics.[1450] The Harlem Globetrotters taught the Doctor how to spin a basketball on his finger.[1451]

Owing to Doctor's gambit against them in 1969, the Silents' numbers on Earth had plummeted from tens of thousands to a very few. The survivors coordinated a new effort against humanity.[1452] UNIT archivists revisited the Silurian base at Wenley Moor.[1453]

> = In one version of events, Melanie Bush never left Earth and died, age 48, from a brain tumour created by micro-radiation from humanity's communication devices.[1454]

? = 2012 - FP: HEAD OF STATE[1455] -> President Sampson was in the White House. Ken Gribbin had served as Vice-President for eight years. At least three rival Faction Paradox groups were operating on Earth, and the government of one major country had succumbed to the Celestis.

In early February, Senator Matt Nelson's support for the presidency skyrocketed when Gribbin withdrew from the race, following the revelation that he'd impregnated his wife's sister. Nelson reaped enough delegates to win the presidential nomination, but in August, super-delegates at the Democratic National Convention set Nelson aside in favor of Senator O'Brien. Nelson denounced the Democratic Party as corrupt, and formed the independent Radical Party. Congressman Lola Denison of Arizona – a Republican turned Independent, and secretly Lolita – became Nelson's running mate.

A conceptual entity monitoring Earth, a Shift, realised that a third party (Lolita) was causing a massive disruption of Earth's history. Lolita blanketed Earth in a psychic dampening field, blocking the Shift from communicating with anyone save for an everyday Iowan named Dave Larsen. To the Shift's dismay, Larsen couldn't decide if the Shift's half-obscured messages stemmed from God or Satan. Worse, Larsen stupidly came to believe that Nelson was a vampire who was murdering young women along the campaign trail. Owing to Lolita's designs, Larsen thought *The Thousand and Second Night* was a prophetic text claiming that Nelson was the Antichrist, and that Larsen must assassinate him to save the world.

Nelson won the presidency, after the most contentious election since Nixon vs. Kennedy. Without Lolita's time-alterations, a moderate Republican who increased military spending, cut America's science budget and achieved little else would have prevailed.

Amy Pond and Rory Williams are Lost to the Doctor

2012 (early February) - THE ANGELS TAKE MANHATTAN[1456] -> The Detroit Lions won the Super Bowl.

The eleventh Doctor, Amy and Rory stopped to relax in New York, but a Weeping Angel sent Rory back to 1938 when he stepped out for coffee. The Doctor and Amy followed, and were thrown back to this year – with Rory and River Song – after killing the Angels in New York with a paradox.

One survivor remained, and again sent Rory back in time. The Doctor realised the TARDIS couldn't visit New York's past again, lest it rupture the already strained timelines and destroy the city. Amy had the Angel send her back in time also, choosing to live out her life with her husband.

The Doctor saw a tombstone for Rory Arthur Williams, age 82, and his wife Amelia Williams, age 87, and realised he would never see his friends again. The last page of *Melody Malone: Private Detective in Old New York Town* contained a farewell message to him from Amy.

Clara Oswald intended to travel, but stayed with a family she knew for a week before she left. When the family's mother died, Clara remained on as a governess to the two children, Angle and Artie.[1457]

c 2012 - THE GOD COMPLEX[1458] -> Minotaur-like creatures – distant cousins of the Nimon – subsisted on the emotion of faith, and established themselves on various planets as gods. One such Minotaur was imprisoned in a space station that could transform its interior shape, and abducted beings with different belief systems to feed the prisoner.

The eleventh Doctor, Amy and Rory arrived in the station after it had shifted into the likeness of a 1980s hotel. The Minotaur longed to die, but instinctually kept killing the abductees – a gambler, Joe; a medical student, Rita; and a blogger, Howie, all perished. Amy's faith in the Doctor attracted the Minotaur, but the Doctor broke her belief in him, which severed the emotional tether and killed the creature.

The Doctor realised that Amy and Rory's faith in him was dangerous, and that one or both of them would end up killed if they stayed with him. He set them up in London with a house and car, and took to travelling without them...

2012 (March) - THE WEDDING OF RIVER SONG[1459] -> The eleventh Doctor phoned to see if his old friend Brigadier Lethbridge-Stewart wanted to go out on the town, and learned that he had died a few months earlier.

c 2012 - NIGHT AND THE DOCTOR: "Up All Night"[1460] -> Craig Owens became a bit alarmed the prospect of Sophie going away for the weekend, leaving him alone with their son Alfie...

c 2012 (spring) - CLOSING TIME[1461] -> Knowing he was about to die at Lake Silencio in Utah, the eleventh Doctor paid a social call on his friend Craig Owens – who now had a baby boy, Alfie, with his partner Sophie. The Doctor noticed electrical anomalies, and got himself a job at a department store where a number of employees had disappeared. They had been tele-

---

1457 "About a year" before *The Bells of Saint John*.

1458 Dating *The God Complex* (X6.11) - No year is stated, but there's no evidence that the station can abduct people through time, and the participants seem contemporary: mention is made of blogging, of the Internet, of the American CIA and of the Klingon language being the purview of geeks. Everyone's attire, Joe's horseshoe tie-tack included, is consistent with the modern day. The prison is made to look like a 1980s hotel, and, tellingly, Rita is familiar enough with such décor that it "takes her by surprise" to be trapped in it.

The Doctor returns Amy and Rory to Earth at a point between *Let's Kill Hitler* and *Closing Time*. The wild card here is to what degree he knows about the horrific events of *TW: Miracle Day* and – presuming he can't intervene in order to let history unfold as scheduled – whether he would deposit his best friends back on Earth in the thick of it. It seems reasonable to think that he drops Amy and Rory off after the worst consequences of the Miracle have come and gone; he might even drop them off in early 2012, after civilisation has recovered somewhat.

1459 Dating *The Wedding of River Song* (X6.13) - The Haisman Timeline dates the Doctor's call to "March 2012", in line with it being "a few months" after its preferred dating of when the Brigadier passes away [December 2011]. That puts the Brig's passing after the crux of events in *The Wedding of River Song* [April 2011], but the TARDIS has magic phones, so it's not a problem if the eleventh Doctor calls out of sequence(ish).

1460 Dating *Night and the Doctor: "Up All Night"* (Series 6 DVD minisode) - This looks suspiciously like it was made as a prequel for *Closing Time*, and was awk-

wardly stapled onto the *Night and the Doctor* miniseries.

1461 Dating *Closing Time* (X6.12) - The story unfolds over three days, ending on a Sunday (the Doctor: "Even with time travel, getting glaziers on a Sunday, tricky"), and is predicated on the idea that Sophie has gone away for the weekend and left Craig alone with Alfie. The time of year is indicated when the Doctor and Craig stand next to an advert for a "Spring Season" sales event. All well and good, but otherwise, this story's dating clues and continuity concerns make its placement very difficult.

The central question is whether, when the Doctor repeatedly says he will die "tomorrow" ("tomorrow is the day I [die]", "tomorrow I'm going to die", etc.), he means it's *chronologically* tomorrow (i.e. 22nd April, 2011, as first mentioned in *The Impossible Astronaut*) or that it's tomorrow in his personal timestream. The latter seems more likely – as a time traveller, he could (and already has) spend years if not decades postponing his getting shot at Lake Silencio. It's only halfway through *The Wedding of River Song*, in fact, that he fully resigns himself to his fate and goes there.

The piece of evidence most in support of *Closing Time* literally occurring before 22nd April is a newspaper that Craig reads with the headline "Britain's Got Torment" – this appears to have been published two days before the story's end (at the very least, it's topical, with Nina the local girl being on *Britain's Got Talent*), and has the barely visible dateline of "19th April, 2011". This would mean, however, that the *Doctor Who* calendar is even more askew than normal... 22nd April was a Friday in 2011, so either the same day in the *Doctor*

ported to a weakened Cyber-ship that had dispatched Cybermats to beam electricity back to it. From a distance, the Doctor saw Amy and Rory; Amy was currently appearing in an ad for Petrichor perfume, a scent "For the Girl Who's Tired of Waiting".

When the Cybermen attempted to convert Craig into their new Controller, his love for Alfie overloaded the circuits, destroying the Cybermen and their ship. The Doctor repaired the damage to Craig's house that a Cybermat had caused, and accepted Craig's gift of a Stetson. He also took some blue envelopes to send invites to his closest friends... and left to confront his fate at Lake Silencio.

c 2012 - THE WEDDING OF RIVER SONG[1462] -> River Song visited Amy and Rory at their home, and told them how the Doctor had survived at Lake Silencio.

> = Rose and her allies worked on a dimension cannon that would enable her to return home. The Daleks' gambit with a reality bomb weakened the dimensional walls, enabling the cannon to

work. Rose returned to her native universe, and helped Donna resolve an errant timeline.[1463]

> **= 2012 - JOURNEY'S END**[1464] -> Mickey and Jackie also crossed over to their home reality, and aided Rose and the Doctor against the Daleks. Afterward, Rose, Jackie and the duplicate tenth Doctor resumed residence on Pete's World, and the dimensional walls sealed once more. Jackie had now given birth to a son named Tony.

Paul Kendrick, an Auton created by the Nestene affiliated with Hyperville, and having no knowledge of his true origins, emerged as the best football player England had offered in the last two decades. In the Euro 2012 semi-final against Spain, Kendrick captained England and scored the winning goal. An injury to Kendrick prevented England from winning the final against Portugal.[1465]

c 2012 (June) - "In-Fez-Station"[1466] -> The annual Festival of Sacred Music held in Fez, Morocco, had gone global, with celebrations slated for London, Washington

---

Who universe is actually a Monday (given that *Closing Time* ends on Sunday), or 22nd April *is* in synch with real life and is a Friday, meaning Tuesday through Thursday (when Sophie is gone) has somehow, someway, been re-designated as "the weekend". It's always regrettable to disregard a date blatantly given on screen, but it's probably fair to ignore it in this case.

Two elements support a dating for *Closing Time* of later than April 2011... the first is that the Doctor spies Amy and Rory from afar. In their timelines, this must happen after he dropped them off in *The God Complex* – not because Amy has a previously unmentioned modelling career (for all we're told, she could already be making a living that way in the two months before *The Impossible Astronaut*), but because the name of the fragrance she's advertising, "Petrichor" (meaning the smell of dust after rain), presumably derives from Amy and Rory learning about petrichor in *The Doctor's Wife*. Either way, Amy and Rory's presence helps to rule out *Closing Time* coming before *The Impossible Astronaut*.

The Doctor ends *Closing Time* intending to send Amy and Rory the invite to his death, which is delivered to their Leadworth address (on or prior to 22nd April) in *The Impossible Astronaut*, but it's unlikely that he would trust such a vitally important message to the vagaries of Royal Mail. If the time-travelling justice agents deliver the invite with the Doctor's other invitations (in *The Wedding of River Song*), Amy and Rory's invite must be stamped for Overnight Mail just for show.

The tipping point for a later dating for *Closing Time*, ultimately, is Alfie's age. Babies typically say their first words at around eleven to fourteen months, so unless the Doctor's conversations with Alfie boosted his

vocabulary, Alfie must be at least a year old if he can say the words "doctor who". Add on the duration of Sophie's pregnancy, and it must have been at least two years since Craig and Sophie became a couple in *The Lodger* (set in 2010).

The Cybermat header in *A History of the Universe in 100 Objects* (p178, and relevant to *Closing Time*) is labeled as "2007", which seems to be a typo, as it's sandwiched between entries for 2011 and 2012, and the text mentions the former.

The Cybermen in this story, as with those in *A Good Man Goes to War*, don't bear the Cybus logo and are presumably the ones from our universe, having incorporated the technology of the alternate-reality ones first introduced in *Rise of the Cybermen/The Age of Steel*.

1462 Dating *The Wedding of River Song* (X6.13) - No date given for this epilogue, but it's after the Doctor drops Amy and Rory off at the end of *The God Complex*.

1463 *Turn Left, The Stolen Earth, Journey's End*. The dimension-jumping Rose is glimpsed throughout Series 4, starting with *Partners in Crime*.

1464 Dating *Journey's End* (X4.13) - The placement of these events is accomplished by (a little arbitrarily) adding two years (the same as passed in real life) to Rose parting ways with the Doctor in *Doomsday*. Jackie was pregnant in *Doomsday* and has now given birth, so that time-span seems reasonable.

1465 *Autonomy*

1466 Dating "In-Fez-Station" (IDW *DW Special 2012*) - The narrator glibly dismisses concerns about the story's date with "Let's say it's a week from this coming Thursday, for all the difference it makes", and the Slitheen make no mention of their family's previous

DC, Rome, the Great Wall of China and more. The eleventh Doctor, Amy and Rory visited Fez to check an item off the Doctor's To Do List (which was approximately 1,453 pages long), and found the Slitheen had developed fezes that controlled the minds of anyone wearing them. The Slitheen intended to make their thralls sing on an exact frequency that would explode all humans on Earth, then sell the planet to interested parties as an interstellar parking lot. The Doctor used his sonic to alter the song's core frequency and fatally rupture the Slitheen instead.

2012 - MAGIC OF THE ANGELS[1467] -> The eleventh Doctor, Amy and Rory tried to experience the sights of London, but were ejected from St Paul's Whispering Gallery for shouting, tossed out of Madame Tussaud's when the Doctor "corrected" the moustache on Guy Fawkes' waxwork, failed to get into Buckingham Palace to have tea with the Queen, and were thrown off a tour bus for rudely correcting the guide. By now, the Doctor had been locked up in the Tower of London "five or six times".

The travellers discovered that a Weeping Angel was using the stage show of a magician, Sammy Star, to send volunteers from the audience back in time. Two young girls, Kylie Duncan and Amber Hooper, were translocated back to 1945, and returned to Star's theatre as senior citizens. The Doctor's party generated a second Weeping Angel using a mirror, and the two angels were forever locked in each other's gaze.

2012 (27th July) - FEAR HER[1468] -> Adverts were distributed for *Shayne Ward: The Greatest Hits*. Humans were the only species in the galaxy to have ever bothered with edible ball bearings.

The Isolus were empathic creatures from the deep realms – it was not unusual for an Isolus family to consist of up to four billion members, or for them to journey for a thousand human lifetimes. During childbirth, an Isolus mother would jettison millions of spores into space, but one Isolus was caught in a solar flare, and its pod crashed to Earth. It empathised with Chloe Webber, age 12, and hosted itself in her. The Isolus could harness ionic power, enabling Chloe to

botched attempts to destroy Earth (*Aliens of London/ World War Three, SJA: Revenge of the Slitheen*, et al). Even so, the story is presumably contemporary, and saw print in *Doctor Who Special 2012* (originally marketed as *Doctor Who Annual 2012*) in Summer 2012. The Festival of Sacred Music was held in Fez on 8th to 16th June in that year.

1467 Dating *Magic of the Angels* (Quick Reads #7) - The story doesn't specify whether the Doctor's trio have arrived in London by TARDIS, or during one of the Doctor's stopovers to Amy and Rory's house. A continuity glitch exists in that the Doctor's group sees a missing-persons poster for Kylie *before* the angels have sent her younger self back in time. That weirdness acknowledged, the book was published in 2012, which concurs with Kylie being born in 1993 (ch4) and her missing-persons poster stating that she's currently 19 (ch3). The poster for another girl, Katie Henley, claims that she went missing on "May the sixth" (ch1), so it seems likely that it's after that. Kylie's birthday is "29th of June" (ch10), and if she really was born in 1993 and is now 19, we might assume that it's after that also. VE Day [1945] was "more than sixty-five years ago" (ch5). Perhaps this is the same Weeping Angel from *Good as Gold*.

1468 Dating *Fear Her* (X2.11) - The year is given as "2012", and the story ends with the opening of the London Olympics, which was scheduled for 27th July, 2012. At present, pop singer Shayne Ward has no Greatest Hits collection.

1469 Dating *Good as Gold* (*Blue Peter* minisode) - The Doctor and Amy arrive during the Olympics in, the Doctor claims, "London 2012, if I'm not mistaken". With this episode being written for a *Blue Peter* competition and credited to the children of Ashdene School, it's

probably best not to dwell much on the canonicity of it, or wonder why the Doctor and Amy are acting somewhat out of character.

1470 Dating *The Shadows of Avalon* (EDA #31) - The story starts in "July 2012" (p1). *The Ancestor Cell* specifies that Compassion is the first Type 102 TARDIS, and *FP: The Book of the War* establishes that she's the *only* Type 102. That said, we did see another in *The Dimension Riders*, but it didn't take the form of a person.

1471 This statement appears odd in the light of the wide array of alien attacks in the new *Doctor Who*, *Torchwood* and *The Sarah Jane Adventures*.

1472 Dating *Dalek* (X1.6) - The Doctor gives the date.

1473 Dating *9thC: The Other Side* (BF The Ninth Doctor Chronicles #1.3) - The year is given. For the Doctor, Rose and Adam, it's directly after *Dalek* [2012].

1474 Dating *The Long Game* (X1.7) - No date is given, but it's clearly after *Dalek*. Adam's mother says she hasn't seen him for six months.

1475 "Five years" before *The Enemy of the World*.

1476 *The Time of the Daleks*. The Doctor restores some wayward history at the end of the story, but it's clear that the "real" history includes Learman coming to power, and she's mentioned in *Trading Futures*.

1477 *The Face-Eater* (p55). *Trading Futures* (p68) – there's a New Kabul in that book, implying the original city was destroyed, so Afghanistan was also a battleground.

1478 *Trading Futures*

1479 *The Taking of Planet 5*

1480 *Instruments of Darkness*. Presumably a reference to Tony Blair's son and Prince Andrew's daughter.

1481 Dating *The Revenants* (BF promo #10, *DWM* #448) - Ian says that he met Janet "What? Fifty, sixty years

turn people into drawings and vice versa.

As London geared up for the opening ceremony of the Olympic Games, the tenth Doctor and Rose investigated reports of missing persons – actually consigned by Chloe to an ionic holding pen – on Dame Kelly Holmes Close in the city. Chloe also made the eighty thousand people in the Olympic Stadium vanish. The Doctor and Rose restored them, and helped the alien back into space by lighting the Olympic Flame.

Papua New Guinea went on to surprise everyone in the shot put. At this time, there was an East London police authority and an East London Council.

2012 (27th July) - GOOD AS GOLD[1469] -> The TARDIS landed on a running track, causing an Olympic torchbearer to dash into the Ship. A Weeping Angel sought to destroy the Olympic flame and quash the spirit of friendship it represented, but the Doctor repelled the Angel by intensifying the flame's light. The runner continued as the Doctor and Amy left, but the Angel started reconstituting in the console room...

Compassion Transforms into a TARDIS

wih - 2012 / = 2012 (June - August) - THE SHADOWS OF AVALON[1470] -> Britain had a King and a female Prime Minister. There had been no major alien attack that required UNIT's attention since the Martian invasion of 1997.[2171]

The Time Lords detected that one of the eighth Doctor's companions, Compassion, was evolving into a form of technology they could use, and President Romana dispatched agents Cavis and Gandar to recover her. Still mourning Doris, General Lethbridge-Stewart was on leave. He was called in to investigate the loss of a nuclear warhead, which he discovered had passed through to the parallel universe of Albion.

> = In Albion, a war was brewing between the Unseelie and the Catuvelauni. The eighth Doctor, Fitz and Compassion arrived in Avalon following the seeming destruction of the TARDIS in a dimensional rift. They prevented war there from escalating. Compassion evolved into a new form of TARDIS. President Romana tried to capture her, but the Doctor and his companions escaped. Lethbridge-Stewart remained in Avalon to advise Queen Mab.

Adam Mitchell

2012 - DALEK[1472] -> The ninth Doctor and Rose followed a distress signal and discovered that Henry Van Statten, the owner of the Internet, had what was reportedly the last Dalek captive in his extra-terrestrial museum deep underneath Utah. The Dalek broke free and killed most of Van Statten's staff, but contact with Rose's DNA made it mutate and question its purpose. The conflicted creature destroyed itself. Van Statten's employees rebelled at his callousness and had him mindwiped, then dumped in a US city starting with "S". The Doctor reluctantly welcomed Adam, one of Van Statten's staff, on board the TARDIS.

Adam told Rose that the UN was keeping the existence of aliens a secret, and Van Statten didn't know that his alien was called a Dalek.

2012 - 9thC: THE OTHER SIDE[1473] -> Departing Van Statten's vault, the ninth Doctor and Rose tried to take Adam Mitchell home to Manchester, but a temporal tsunami clipped the TARDIS and deposited it in Birmingham. The Bigon Horde – the echoes of races erased from history by the Time War – encroached upon the present day, to craft a timeline where they dominated many worlds. The Doctor and Rose were displaced to 1894 and 1922, but returned through a portal with Adam's help. The Horde tried to follow, but the Doctor catapulted them into the far future, where their power would fade.

2012 - THE LONG GAME[1474] -> Adam attempted to send information from the year 200,000 home to exploit. When the ninth Doctor discovered this, he took Adam back to his native time and left him there.

Politically the world seemed less stable for a time. In 2012, the scientist/politician Salamander convinced a group of his followers that a global nuclear war was inevitable. He established a survival shelter at Kanowa in Australia for them.[1475] Following the Euro Wars, Mariah Learman took power in the United Kingdom on a popular tide of anti-EuroZone feeling, renaming it New Britain. Britain had a King at this time.[1476]

World War Three was fought in the early twenty-first century. India was reduced to a radioactive mudhole.[1477] The War against Terrorism was won when the RealWar teletrooper was introduced. Subscribers could kill terrorists (identified with 80% accuracy by software) from the comfort of their own home by operating war robots. Baskerville, a Russian arms dealer, became the richest man in the world selling the technology.[1478]

In 2012, firemen in New York laughed and toasted marshmallows instead of rescuing people from a fire. This resulted from the Memeovore feeding on human ideas.[1479] The Doctor owned a commemorative mug from the wedding of Euan and Eugenie.[1480]

c 2012 - THE REVENANTS[1481] -> Ian Chesterton received notification that Janet McKay had died, and returned to Hoy, Scotland, to visit with the Marsh family.

2012 - CHRISTMAS ON A RATIONAL PLANET[1482] ->

The seventh Doctor, Chris and Roz landed in Arizona. When Cacophony's gynoids emerged into our universe, Roz fell through a crack in time to the end of the eighteenth century.

2012 - FROZEN TIME[1483] ->

Lord Barset sought to locate the colony of lizard men that his grandfather (also known as Lord Barset) had discovered, and sponsored an expedition to Antarctica to find advanced technology there. The expedition members found a frozen Ice Warrior base, and their heaters revived the war-mongering Arakssor – as well as the seventh Doctor, who had been frozen for millions of years. Barset was killed, but the Doctor signalled an Ice Warrior spaceship. The commander of the vessel enforced a death sentence upon Arakssor – his spaceship bombarded the base from orbit, and Arakssor and his warriors died. The Doctor escaped with a member of Barset's expedition, Genevieve, and she returned to her comrades a week later.

& 2012 - MARTHA IN THE MIRROR[1484] ->

The planets Anthium and Zerugma had been at war for centuries. Castle Extremis, a floating edifice in space that was formerly home to the Mystic Mortal Monks of Moradinard, became crucial to the conflict – whomever controlled Extremis controlled the Sarandon Passage. The strategist Manfred Grieg ended the second Zerguain occupation, and was later given a gift: the Mortal Mirror. The Darksmiths of Karagula had built the Mirror on behalf of Grieg's opponents – he was trapped within its internal dimension, and couldn't counter-act the third Zerguain occupation. The tenth Doctor and Martha hid Grieg's glass diary in Extremis, knowing they would find it in a hundred years' time.

Flip Jackson Joins the TARDIS, Leaves It, Gets Married, Joins Again

2012 (a Sunday) - THE CURSE OF DAVROS[1485] ->

Davros, mentally trapped in the sixth Doctor's body, and having escaped the Battle of Waterloo in 1815 aboard a damaged Dalek shuttlecraft, crashed in England. He found by Phillipa "Flip" Jackson and her boyfriend Jared Ramen, who believed him to be the same Doctor they had met a year earlier during the Terravore invasion. The Daleks used mind-transfer technology to exchange some of their number with humans, including Jared, and sent them to hunt for their wayward creator. The Dalek agents both blew up Flip's flat, and slaughtered the staff and patrons of the Fresh Soup Market where she worked. The Daleks forcibly took the Davros-Doctor, Flip and Jared back to 1815...

Flip Jackson found herself back in her native time via a space-time rip the Doctor opened to save her life in 2071. She became engaged to Jared Ramen, and sent the Doctor a wedding invitation.[1486]

---

ago?" in the earlier part of the story, set in 1956. The audio was released in 2012.

1482 Dating *Christmas on a Rational Planet* (NA #52) - The date is given.

1483 Dating *Frozen Time* (BF #98) - The year is given. The veiled implication is that Genevieve shares some adventures with the Doctor before returning home.

1484 Dating *Martha in the Mirror* (NSA #22) - "One hundred years, three months and six days" (p38) before the main part of the story.

1485 Dating *The Curse of Davros* (BF #166) - The Doctor (the genuine article, not Davros in the Doctor's body) specifies that Flip and Jared originate from "2012", the same year this audio was released. Contradicting that, *Scavenger* claims that Flip originates from "2011". When she rejoins the TARDIS in *Quicksilver* after an interim back in her native time, however, she and Jared are getting married in "2012".

In *The Curse of Davros*, Flip says that she and Jared previously met the Doctor (in *The Crimes of Thomas Brewster*) "last year", and the back cover says that "It's been a year" since this happened. The only hiccup there, then, is the confusion about whether *The Crimes of Thomas Brewster* takes place in 2011 or 2010 (see the dating notes on that story).

1486 *The Widow's Assassin*

1487 Dating *Quicksilver* (BF #220) - Flip names the year. She says that she'll shortly return for another go at "Gangnam Style"; that song was released on 15th July, 2012.

1488 Dating *Mastermind* (BF CC #8.1) - The audio was released in 2013, but fits a little better with 2012... it's after *Tales from the Vault* (set circa 2011, but no later than 2012), and Matheson mentions the Thames Mead Massacre from *The Curse of Davros* [2012]. Notably, UNIT captured the Master "fifteen years ago", presumably concurrent with Frankie don Maestro's death in 1997, and the Master has woken up at five year intervals since then.

Major Husak and Excalibur appeared in *Battlefield*.

1489 Dating "Sticks and Stones" (DWM #446-447) - The opening caption reads "South London, 2012". According to "Hunters of the Burning Stone" [2013], these events happened "last year". Amy is cooking dinner in the TARDIS kitchen and Rory is surprised to find that it's "three in the morning" outside the Ship (he's also unaware of Mono's very prominent graffiti attacks, which have been happening for three weeks) – all of which suggests that this happens during in their TARDIS travels, not when the Doctor visits them at

2012 - QUICKSILVER[1487] -> During her marriage to Jared, Flip Jackson stepped out for a breather... and was abducted down a Vilal-made portal to 1948.

The Master's 106 Years on Earth Ends

2012 - MASTERMIND[1488] -> The sword Excalibur was currently stored in the UNIT Vault, along with an audio report by Major Husak.

Captain Ruth Matheson and Warrant Officer Charley Sato interrogated the decaying Master as he once again awoke in the UNIT Vault – but fell prey to the fiend's hypnotism. The Master retrieved his TARDIS from the Dominus Vault – a double-security zone within the Vault – then sealed Matheson and Sato within their own base and escaped. Matheson and Sato realised a relief team would conclude the two of them had been compromised – then take them into custody for the rest of their lives, to guarantee they posed no continued threat.

2012 - "Sticks and Stones"[1489] -> The Necrotists were an extraterrestrial art movement that believed pure creation could only stem from death – in their minds, a slaughter equalled a masterpiece. One of their number, Monos, acquired a gauntlet made from belief metal, and spent three weeks using this technology to invisibly spray-paint his name on prominent London landmarks. St Paul's, Big Ben, the Tower of London and Nelson's Column all came to bear "Monos" in large red letters.

The stunt imprinted Monos' name in people's minds, and the gauntlet enabled him to expand upon that mental signature – turning some Londoners into walking embodiments of the word "Monos". The eleventh Doctor overpowered Monos, then instructed Rory to short out the TARDIS' telepathic circuits with Amy's chili sauce. This briefly turned everyone in London dyslexic and returned Monos' victims to normal.

Annabel Lake had been trained in covert ops, and expected a posting to UNIT until her father, Patrick, incorporated her into MI6's new space program. She was equipped with cyber-armour, and tasked with piloting an Amaranian Star-Hopper retrieved from the Indian Ocean to its point of origin: the alien city of Cornucopia.[1490]

wih - 2012 - FP: AGAINST NATURE[1491] -> Goralschai of House Xianthellipse used House Meddhoran's breeding engine, as fuelled by biodata obtained in 1375, to place two totems "a decade or so" beyond humanity's ghost point. The totems were realised as two "half-brothers" with overlapping timelines: Primo Acamapichtli Isleno de la Vega, born when Maria de la Vega Lunas stayed in Mexico City, became something of a cuckoo placed in the life of Todd Calavero, who was born to Peter Calavero and Maria de la Vega Lunas after she immigrated to San Antonio, Texas.

Gedarrameddhoran vel-Xianthellipse, a.k.a. Gedarra, encountered Primo and Todd as Goralschai's plans for his Quincunx – a five pointed pattern that included Primo and Todd – came to fruition. Gedarra and Primo were transported to 1506 while an incarnation of Todd's spirit animal – a dead dog named Scarface – guided him to the underworld to reclaim his life, his "breath".

The Darksmith Legacy[1492]

c 2012 - DL: THE DUST OF AGES / THE GRAVES OF MORDANE / THE COLOUR OF DARKNESS / THE PICTURES OF EMPTINESS / THE ART OF WAR[1493] -> Earth experienced such a shortage of minerals and metal ores, some corporations began surveying the moon for its mining potential. One such survey found the Eternity Crystal of the Darksmiths – it had been buried for at least a century, and instinctively created humanoids composed of moondust to defend itself with. The tenth Doctor ended the threat and sealed the Crystal within a stasis box, but

home. Boris Johnson is currently mayor of London; he held that office 2008-2016. It's a little unclear if the Doctor merely stuns Monos unconscious or (more likely) participates in his electrocution.

1490 Time frame unknown, but Annabel is seen working undercover on Cornucopia in "The Cornucopia Caper".

1491 Dating *FP: Against Nature* (FP novel #7) - The book was released in 2012; Todd Calavero's joke-reference to someone as "Miss Roswell 2012" suggests that events for him and Primo take place in that year. A man named Andrew died "back in 2009". Pop culture references include Elvis, Power Rangers, Batman, *The Sopranos* (1999-2007) and the *Lord of the Rings* films (2001-2003). *FP: This Town Will Never Let Us Go* [c.2001] seemed related to the start of humanity's "ghost point", as men-

tioned in *FP: The Book of the War*.

1492 Dating *The Darksmith Legacy* (*The Dust of Ages*, #1; *The Graves of Mordane*, #2; *The Colour of Darkness*, #3; *The Depths of Despair*, #4; *The Vampires of Paris*, #5; *The Game of Death*, #6; *The Planet of Oblivion*, #7; *The Pictures of Emptiness*, #8; *The Art of War*, #9; *The End of Time* (DL), #10) - This ten-book children's series entails the tenth Doctor and his one-off companion, the android girl Gisella, racing between different time zones.

Two of these are fairly easy to place: most of *The Art of War* occurs in medieval times, and *The Vampires of Paris* happens in "1895". Four more (*The Dust of Ages*, the opening sequences of *The Graves of Mordane*, *The Pictures of Emptiness* and the opening sequences of *The Art of War*) occur together relatively close to the books' publication in 2009. Another three (*The Depths of*

was then confronted by a time-active Agent the Darksmiths had dispatched to retrieve the Crystal. The Doctor travelled to the planet Mordane in the far future to learn how to destroy the Crystal, but the Agent pursued him through time and captured the item.

The Doctor followed the Agent to the Darksmiths' homeworld of Karagula... and stole it back again. He experienced a handful of adventures, along with the android girl Gisella, as part of his efforts to destroy the Crystal.[1494]

The Shadow Proclamation eventually ruled that Gisella was the rightful owner of the Eternity Crystal – but she had been reprogrammed, and recognised the Darksmiths' claim to the item. The Darksmiths went to London, Galactic reference 297/197AHG, to give the Crystal to the fearsome Krashoks who had commissioned it. The Krashoks turned upon the Darksmiths and killed them... but were then stymied by the Doctor, and retreated into the past using a Dalek temporal shift device. The Doctor saved Gisella and secured the Crystal, and they pursued the Krashoks to medieval times...

Capt. Jack and Gwen post-Miracle Day[1495]

2012 (September) - TW: ARMY OF ONE -> Gwen Cooper, Rhys and Anwen visited a bank in Georgetown, Washington DC, containing one of a half-dozen Torchwood safety deposit boxes with a cache of currency, gold, diamonds and equipment. The Miracle had disrupted the

abilities of the body-jacker Torchwood had previously encountered, reducing the time it could stay in a host from years to hours. It died after trying to stabilise its condition by reclaiming the piece of itself in Gwen's mind. Rex Matheson vouched for Gwen's family with the local authorities.

2012 (September) - TW: FALLOUT -> Pavel Androvitch Yeshov, an agent of the Russian Committee for Extraterrestrial Research, attempted to secure a jewelled egg containing an alien Shiva virus – a bio-weapon capable of eradicating all carbon-based lifeforms on Earth, paving the way for the planet to house the silicon-based Kaloczul. Sgt Andy Davidson became embroiled in efforts by the last of the Kaloczul to secure the Shiva virus' activation key, which Captain Jack had squirreled away at the British Museum. Andy helped to trigger an EMP that Jack had installed at the Museum, killing the Kaloczul.

Jack took a break from humanity and visited Cotter Paluni's World, but returned to Earth after experiencing a vision that Gwen Cooper would be shot dead...[1496]

2012 (October) - TW: MR INVINCIBLE -> Jody Chapman – the product of a union between her mother and an alien Arqualian – was now 14, and her inherited ability to manipulate space-time began manifesting in unexpected ways. Jody's desire to help her adoptive father Ross gifted him with invulnerability, super-strength and

---

Despair, The Planet of Oblivion and most of *The Graves of Mordane*) contain references to humans in space, and so must be placed in the future.

The intent of those making *The Darksmith Legacy* was that the Darksmiths themselves were contemporaneous with the first book, *The Dust of Ages*, and so originated from circa 2012. Said intent has been reflected in this chronology, even though many of the details in the series are vague, absent or maddeningly contradictory. Brother Varlos must have access to time technology (that he presumably nicked from the Darksmiths) for the plot to function, but this isn't explicitly stated. The Darksmiths use up "every last item of temporal engineering" at their disposal in creating their Agent (*The Dust of Ages*), and yet they can still dispatch an entire Dreadnought through into the future after the Doctor (*The Depths of Despair*), and travel to the world of Oblivion (*The Planet of Oblivion*, also in the future).

Most glaringly of all, the Doctor stresses in *The Graves of Mordane* (p27) that he's only going to travel in space, not time – and yet the TARDIS moves from Earth's moon, circa 2012, to a point when humanity's colony worlds have been burying their dead on Mordane for at least four centuries (p37), without any acknowledgement of the discrepancy.

One glitch that's unrelated to dating issues, but dem-

onstrates the difficulty in analysing this series: Karagula is named a "cold desolate planet" in Book One (*The Dust of Ages*), but is a hot and arid world with two suns in Book Three (*The Colour of Darkness*).

See the individual entries for more.

1493 Dating *DL: The Dust of Ages, The Graves of Mordane, The Colour of Darkness, The Pictures of Emptiness* and *The Art of War* (DL #1-#3, #8, #9) - The back cover of *The Dust of Ages* and the story recap in *The Graves of Mordane* both claim that the Doctor's involvement with the Eternity Crystal takes place "a few years into our future..." The general impression is that Earth's corporations are considering exploitation of the moon for the first time – so, more in the relative near future (in *Doctor Who* terms) than, say, hundreds of years hence. All references to UK and London culture are either vague or fictionalised, and of no help in determining the year.

According to the story recap and back cover to *The Art of War*, the Darksmith-Krashok rendezvous (i.e. the opening sequences to *The Art of War*, and by extension most of *The Pictures of Emptiness*, which leads into it) occurs on "present day" Earth. Taken literally alongside *The Dust of Ages* being "a few years in the future", this would mean that the tenth Doctor is attempting to thwart the meeting and retrieve the Eternity Crystal a few years before his younger self finds it on the moon.

super-speed. He took to fighting crime in Splot as the superhero Mr Invincible.

Jody's time-manipulating abilities became increasingly unstable and created whirlpools of destabilised time – at least seventeen people died, another twenty went missing and about thirty experienced extreme aging or extreme youth. Captain Jack physically intercepted bullets fated to kill Gwen, then fitted Jody with a necklace that curtailed her powers. The time whirlpools disappeared, and the sudden cessation of Ross Chapman's super-powers caused him to die while trying to stop a mugging.

2012 - TW: EXODUS CODE[1497] **->** Blame for the horrific events surrounding the Miracle had been dispersed among corporations, health groups, and government and non-government entities alike. In most important regards, the global public wanted their lives – and their deaths – to continue as normal. Rex Matheson became Deputy Director of the American CIA, and oversaw its Office of Geo-Global Affairs. Sgt Andy Davidson had a new girl-friend, Bonnie from Blackpool.

The health of the Helix Intelligence within the Earth worsened, and it continued to need Captain Jack's futuris-tic DNA to heal itself. The Intelligence dispersed, via oce-anic vents, an ecto-hormone encoded with a message to summon Jack. As an unintended side effect, the hormone caused increasing numbers of women – including Gwen Cooper – to experience synaesthesia, a neurological condi-tion in which a type of sensory input generates an invol-untary secondary response (such as letters and numbers being perceived as colors). The most severely affected women lost control of their senses and began mutilating themselves and others. The World Health Organization held a press conference to address the growing amount of "female insanity".

Jack and Gwen threw themselves into an abyss in Peru so the Intelligence could make use of their DNA. Two weeks later, the survey ship *Ice Maiden* recovered them off the coast of Miami.

c 2012 (early autumn to late November) - IRIS: ENTER WILDTHYME[1498] **->** Terrance – an accomplished thief operating throughout space and time, and the owner of the Great Big Book Exchange in Darlington – went miss-ing and bequeathed the shop to one of its patrons: Simon, age 26. Simon and his friend Kelly fell in with Iris

---

It seems fair to assume, however, that the four books *do* follow one another in the same year, as there's no sign that the stories were intended to be out of sequence – the "present day" references look very much like a mistake and can be treated as such.

1494 *DL: The Colour of Darkness, DL: The Depths of Despair, DL: The Vampire of Paris, DL: The Game of Death.*

1495 Dating *Torchwood* post-*Miracle Day* (*TW: Army of One*, TW audiobook #7; *TW: Fallout*, TW audiobook #8; *TW: Red Skies*, TW audiobook #9; *TW: Mr Invincible*, TW audiobook #10) - This quartet of audios were marketed as occurring after *TW: Miracle Day*. The blurb to *Army of One* expressly states this, and various characters men-tion the Miracle and its effects in *Army of One, Fallout* and *Red Skies*.

Events within the four stories seem to occur in order of release. Certainly, *Mr Invincible* happens last – it fol-lows up on Captain Jack's premonition in *Red Skies* that Gwen Cooper will die, and has Andy state that his ordeal in *Fallout* happened a few weeks beforehand.

Ross Chapman first discovers he possesses super-powers during a electronics store robbery on "a drizzly Wednesday night in late September", and events in *Mr Invincible* pick up a "few weeks" (or a month at most, judging by when Henry Baverstock is institutionalised) afterwards. Gwen's family is in America in *Army of One*, and still there when Andy calls her in *Fallout*, suggest-ing the two stories occur simultaneously (or close enough). It seems reasonable to assume, then, that *Army of One* and *Fallout* both happen in September, *Mr Invincible* comes last in October. *Red Skies* is the odd man out – Captain Jack appears to go to Cotter Paluni's

World in humanity's future, then returns to 2012 after getting a vision of Gwen being shot dead.

In *Fallout*, Earth's population is cited as being "almost seven billion humans" (it was roughly 6,928,198,000 in *TW: Miracle Day*).

1496 *TW: Red Skies*, which appears to take place in the future (see that story's dating notes). If so, this means that Captain Jack has regained the ability to indepen-dently time travel following the tenth Doctor hobbling his vortex manipulator in *Last of the Time Lords*, and Jack needing to hitch a ride from a passing spaceship at the end of *TW: Children of Earth*. Jack seems to pos-sess more than one working Manipulator throughout his lifetime, however, as evidenced by the one that winds up in the UNIT archives in *The Day of the Doctor*. In *Red Skies*, Jack not only seems to arrive at a space station above Cotter Paluni's World outside the normal channels, he teleports down to the isolated planet under his own power.

1497 Dating *TW: Exodus Code* (TW novel #19) - The book was released a month after the last post-*Miracle Day* audio (*TW: Mr Invincible*) in 2012, takes place in the "present day" (ch4), and is variously said to occur "many months" (ch10) and "a few months" (ch21) after *Miracle Day*. The Helix Intelligence seen here isn't the same as the Mandragora Helix (*The Masque of Mandragora*, et al), but mention is made of the Mandragora Helix's attack on the internet in "2009" (*Beautiful Chaos*).

1498 Dating *Iris: Enter Wildthyme* (Iris novel #1) - The modern-day component begins in "autumn" (p15, 38, 39), proceeds over some weeks (p165-166) and finishes "Sometime in late November" (p311). A TV screen in Iris'

Wildthyme and Panda when the poet Anthony Marville stole the most important item in Terrance's collection – the glass jar containing the Scarlet Empress Euphemia, a.k.a. the "Objet D'Oom" (as it was called by the F'rrgelaaris). The Empress was crucial to Marville's plans to open up the Ringpull to gain access to the Obverse, and from there travel to the planet Hyspero to plunder its dark magics. Iris, Panda, Simon, Kelly, Barbra the sentient vending machine and Iris' ex-companion Jenny became embroiled in this affair, and dogged Marville to numerous locations in space-time. Kelly fell under the sway of Marville's hypnotic power of speech, *murmurism*.

Iris, Simon and Panda returned to this era to rest, thinking their other friends had died circa 33,935 on the planet Valcea. They then went to Hyspero, millions of years in the future. MIAOW closed down its Darlington branch.

c 2012 - IRIS S3: MIDWINTER MURDERS[1499] -> A Krobian shapeshifter split into two selves and settled in Midwinter Leys in Warwickshire, taking on the identities of Inspector Nettles and Sgt Spartan. When needed, one Krobian would murder nosy residents to silence them, and the other "investigated" the crime. Their victims included Bernard Duncan, writer of trashy detective novels.

Iris Wildthyme and Panda stumbled upon the Krobians' murder spree, realised they were vulnerable to the vibrations caused by morris dancing, and burst the fiends by encouraging people at the annual village fete to kick up their heels. The pair realised that the Monstron Time Destroyer pursuing them was piloted by Iris' future self, who rendered them unconscious...

The older Iris – wanting her younger self out of the way to avert a disaster – imprisoned the younger Iris and Panda at penal station Cappa-Gamma-Delta, a bubble reality outside the multiverse that made real their fondest desires. Iris and Panda deduced the nature of their prison, reclaimed Iris' bus and escaped back to reality...[1500]

2012 (winter) - "The Cornucopia Caper"[1501] ->
Horatio Lynk, a benevolent thief operating on Cornucopia, attempted to steal the Star of Solitude from ThiefCorp. The eleventh Doctor, Amy and Rory turned up by accident, having intended to visit Rio, and ran afoul of the leader of Corncuopia's Crime Lords: Granny Solasta. Granny forced the Doctor to take the Crime Lords into the city's golden ziggurat via the TARDIS, but the psychic metal within triggered such greed, the Crime Lords killed one another. The

---

bus (in a takeoff of *Doctor Who – The Movie*) says that it's "Darlington – Human Era – Early 21st Century" (p61).

Enter Wildthyme was published in 2011, but must occur in some other year owing to the need to place *TW: Miracle Day* in autumn 2011. (The meta-fictional nature of the Iris Wildthyme adventures means that Iris fans can probably overlook this continuity conflict, but this chronology doesn't have that luxury.) It's been "some years" since Barbra the vending machine arrived from the future (in December 2008, in *Iris: Iris and the Celestial Omnibus*: "The Deadly Flap"), so 2012 or 2013 is perhaps preferable to 2010.

1499 Dating *Iris S3: Midwinter Murders* (BF *Iris* #3.3) - The audio was released in 2012, and seems roughly contemporary; Iris' assignation with the Krobian happened "twenty years ago", in the "1980s". The story is a parody of the ITV series *Midsomer Murders*, which stars John Nettles and a character named "Sgt Troy". Stewart Bevan, here voicing "Inspector Nettles" – a character who was romantically involved with Iris twenty years previous – appeared in *The Green Death* and, for a time, dated Katy Manning. It's a Sunday, with the weather nice enough to hold the annual village fete.

Iris S4: A Lift in Time reveals why Iris seeks to lock up her younger self and Panda.

1500 *Iris S4: Whatever Happened to Iris Wildthyme?*

1501 Dating "The Cornucopia Caper" (*DWM* #448-450) - "Hunters of the Burning Stone", set in 2013, establishes that these events happened both "the year before" and "a few months" beforehand.

1502 Dating *Hunter's Moon* (NSA #46) - No year given. None of the participants are human, save for three people kidnapped from Earth to serve as prey in the Gorgoror Chase. The London in which the abductees live is very functional and could well be contemporary, but the references (including the Circle Line, the Metropolitan Police, Jobseeker's Allowance and a man from Romania) fall short of being very definitive. It's difficult to tell, in relation to the public's awareness in the new series that aliens exist, if the trio are surprised by the very notion that aliens are *real*, or are instead baffled to learn they personally have been abducted and taken into space on a star-cruiser. With the year being so uncertain, but the month in London being specified as November (p12), it's perhaps best to avoid the year of *Hunter Moon's* publication – 2011 – to curtail any further conflict with *TW: Miracle Day*.

Mention is made of a war between Torodon and the Terileptils – the latter's ability to wage all-out war was presumably diminished after the destruction of their homeworld in *The Dark Path* (set circa 3400), so *Hunter's Moon* likely occurs before that. An Aggedor beast (*The Curse of Peladon*) is among the wildlife present, but no mention is made of the Federation. One of the hunters in the Chase bears a high-voltage shotgun called the Eradicator (p113), the design of which is similar (coincidentally or otherwise) to the weapon of the same name from *Carnival of Monsters*.

1503 Dating *The Doctor, the Widow and the Wardrobe* (X7.0) - It is "two years" since Amy last saw the Doctor

Doctor triggered the ziggurat's self-destruct, and the resultant explosion ended the radiation cloud that had isolated the planet.

? 2012 (November) - HUNTER'S MOON[1502] -> Kobal Zalu, a Galactic Marine Corps lieutenant in a past war between Torodon and the Terileptils, had now met the Doctor "many times".

The eleventh Doctor, Amy and Rory visited Leisure Platform 9, one of ninety such platforms in the Phrygian System. Rory lost a game of Dead Man's Duel – he was thereby conscripted as prey in a hunt, the Gorgoror Chase. The Xorg Krauzzen criminal cartel had effectively taken over Gorgoror, a moon of the gas giant Zigriz in the Torodon System, and operated the Chase as a hunt for benefit of bored millionaires, weekend warriors and gamblers. The Torodon Confederation, which spanned several star systems, left Krauzzen alone so long as Torodons were not involved. The Doctor posed as a hunter in the Chase to help Rory, and greatly curtailed Kruazzen's operations. Krauzzen, a cyborg, tried to hunt the Doctor down – but the Doctor increased the magnetic force of a nuclear reactor, causing Krauzzen to plunge to his death.

2012 (Christmas) - THE DOCTOR, THE WIDOW AND THE WARDROBE[1503] -> The eleventh Doctor arrived at Amy and Rory's house in time to share Christmas dinner with them.

By 2012, Countess Gallowglass was operating her mail-forwarding service from a hidden location near Carnaby Street. The seventh Doctor visited the Countess, with Ace, in August to collect his mail. According to the Countess, London should be avoided on 14th July, 2013.[1504] General Tidos, a dictator affiliated with the Sentinels of the New Dawn, rose to power in Tanganyika, Africa.[1505]

2013[1506]

Adam Mitchell's mother died from a brain embolism. The thought that the future knowledge he'd lost might have saved her life deepened Adam's resentment against the Doctor.[1507] Ace found Ian Gilmore's memoir in a bookshop in 2013, and read a vague reference to a crisis with her and the seventh Doctor following the Shoreditch Incident. The two of them dutifully went back to the 1960s to help the Counter-Measures team.[1508] Cedric Chivers, now a professor at Oxford, received a Time Lord hypercube with instructions from himself on how to build a time machine. A graduate student, Alice Watson, aided him in doing so.[1509]

The attack by the Hunters of the Burning Stone on Cornucopia killed two thousand beings, and left five thousand homeless. Cornucopia's spaceport traffic plummeted 45%, and the people there considered returning to a crime-based economy.[1510]

The Queen awarded Eileen Younghusband, now the last survivor of the Gulliver Incident, with the British Empire Medal. In May 2013, Younghusband visited Major James Randall's gravesite.[1511]

? = 2013 (21st January) - FP: HEAD OF STATE[1512] -> Lolita enabled Dave Larsen to bypass security at Matt Nelson's presidential inauguration. Larsen shot Nelson dead – and was himself slain by the Secret Service. As "Congresswoman Lola Denison", Lolita was immediately sworn in as president. Soon after, Lolita used Nelson's murder to justify a crackdown on the public and the media. She also announced Project Caldera: touted as the Manhattan Project of geothermal energy, but which would give Lolita control of the Earth's Caldera...

(in *The Wedding of River Song*, set in April 2011). It's a toss-up as to whether Amy is rounding up and means that it's now Christmas 2012, or she's rounding down and it's Christmas 2013 – see the Amy and Rory's Double Lives sidebar for why we've chosen the former.
1504 *Relative Dementias* (p40) dates when the Doctor and Ace visit the Countess. Her warning about 14th July is on p17.
1505 "The year before" *The Sentinels of the New Dawn*. Tanganyika was an independent state in Africa only from 9th December, 1961 to 26th April, 1964. The area is now part of Tanzania, and in recent times, the name "Tanganyika" has only been used in reference to Lake Tanganyika.
1506 Events in 2013 feature the Series 7 episodes with Clara Oswald (X7.7, *The Bells of Saint John* to X7.14, *The Name of the Doctor*), which must take place prior to

X7.1, *Asylum of the Daleks* and the *Pond Life* webcast series leading into it (so, out of order from the viewer's perspective).
1507 "Prisoners of Time", "not long after" Adam's return home in *The Long Game*.
1508 *1963: The Assassination Games*
1509 "Eleven months" before *DotD: The Time Machine*.
1510 "The Blood of Azrael", following "The Hunters of the Burning Stone".
1511 *Leth-St: The Flaming Soldier* (Prologue).
1512 Dating *FP: Head of State* (FP novel #9) - It's Inauguration Day, which, as directed by the US Constitution, happened on Monday, 21st January, 2013.

c 2013 - "The Eye of Ashaya"[1513] -> The eleventh Doctor dropped Amy and Rory off for a vacation in Majorca, Spain – a dismal experience that included soggy fish and chips in a fake English pub. The Doctor intercepted his friends on their way back to Leadworth, and offered them tickets to the maiden voyage of the *Excelsis*, the most luxurious star-liner in the galaxy. They went there, two years in the future, even as Lady Christina de Souza went to Utah to raid Henry Van Statten's vault. The alien technology there let her cobble together a spaceship, and she left Earth to become an interstellar master thief.

= c 2013 - IRIS: "Party Kill Accelerator!"[1514] -> Kelsey, a friend of Maria Jackson's, found herself at the Zona Oscura festival – a haven for lost ideas, as curated by Theo Possible. Iris Wildthyme got all dolled up for a party, but never made it there because she and Panda watched a David Attenborough video about primates. In so doing, she inadvertently created a "lost being", Jimmy the Mandrell, who tricked her and Panda into visiting the Zona Oscura. Jimmy started to consume the fictional characters present, to become more complex. Kelsey squashed Jimmy to death beneath a colossal mirrorball, then departed with some Faction Paradox-affiliated goths in a Volvo.

2013 - "Doorway to Hell"[1515] -> Inspired by the twelfth Doctor's love of art, Dr Jessica Collins now worked at the National Gallery. She happened to spy the Doctor and his TARDIS in *The Hay Wain*.

c 2013 - THE SNOWMEN[1516] -> Clara Oswald took a shortcut through an overgrown cemetery, failing to realise that one of the tombstones belonged to the version of her that lived in Victorian times.

Doctor Who Series 7 (last half)[1517]

Clara Oswald (a.k.a. "Clara-Prime")

2013 - THE BELLS OF SAINT JOHN[1518] -> The Great Intelligence's agents, led by Miss Kizmet, established a base of operations in the Shard. They set about draining human minds and souls via the Internet to a private cloud for the Intelligence to feed upon; an increasing number of such victims were found comatose and soon died.

Clara Oswald phoned Internet support and was connected via the TARDIS phone to the eleventh Doctor, who was living as a monk in Cumbria, 1207. She aided him in defeating Kizmet's operation; the minds within

1513 Dating "The Eye of Ashaya" (IDW Vol. 4 #5-6) - The initial part of the story saw print at the end of 2012. The Doctor is once again leaving Amy and Rory on Earth, then returning to lure them away with promises of adventure, which seems to match the first half of Series 7. Adam suggested in *Dalek* that Van Statten's base was slated to be filled with cement, but it's possible only the exterior was sealed, as it's plundered both by de Souza here and Adam himself in *Prisoners of Time*.
1514 Dating *Iris: "Party Kill Accelerator!"* (*Iris: The Panda Book of Horror* short story #5) - Kelsey is Kelsey Hooper from *The Sarah Jane Adventures* pilot "Invasion of the Bane". Here, she's "eighteen" – she was a classmate of Maria Jackson, who was "thirteen" in that story. Kelsey next appears in *FP: "Now or Thereabouts"*, then *FP: Weapons Grade Snake Oil*, all written by Blair Bidmead.
1515 Dating "Doorway to Hell" (*DWM* #508-511) - It's "thirty years" after the 1973 part of this story.
1516 Dating *The Snowmen* (X7.6) - No year given, but it's a warm season.
1517 Dating *The Bells of Saint John* (X7.7), *The Rings of Akhaten* (X7.8), *The Crimson Horror* (X7.13) and *The Name of the Doctor* (X7.14) - The "modern day" segments of these episodes, all broadcast in 2013, feature the eleventh Doctor meeting and visiting the original Clara Oswald (the template for duplicates of her scattered throughout history, as we learn in *The Name of the Doctor*; see also *Asylum of the Daleks* and *The Snowmen*). The letter that Vastra writes to Clara in *The Name of the Doctor* gives the day as "10th April, 2013",

and it seems fair to assume that the aforementioned modern-day bits all occur in that year. This means, however, that the eleventh Doctor's time in modern-day(ish) London with Amy and Rory overlaps the Series 7 Clara episodes.
A substantial narrative gap exists, however, in Clara's life between *The Name of the Doctor* and when she's next seen as a teacher at Coal Hill school in *The Day of the Doctor* [2015]. Did she live out that time on Earth, with the Doctor randomly appearing, taking her off for adventures and successfully bringing her home afterwards, or did she skip a couple of years after *The Name of the Doctor* (in which case, she failed to experience The Year of the Slow Invasion seen in *The Power of Three*) and just tell everyone she took an extended holiday? In *Deep Breath* (the epilogue of which occurs in 2016), Strax's medical scan indicates that Clara is biologically "27" – which only seems possible, given her birth year of 1986 (*Death in Heaven*) if she did indeed skip much of 2013, 2014 and 2015 prior to *The Day of the Doctor*.
1518 Dating *The Bells of Saint John* (X7.7) - Kizmet's operation is based at the Shard, a London skyscraper that is currently the tallest building in the European Union - it was inaugurated July 2012, and opened February 2013. Floor 65 of the Shard, where Kizmet's staff is based, is in actually just residential apartments (or so they say). A police box has stood outside Earl's Court tube station in London since 1997.
It's very bizarre that Clara, as an educated young

the cloud were either returned to their habitable bodies or dissipated for lack of them. UNIT seized control of Kizmet's base, but Kizmet and her staff were "returned to factory settings", meaning they had no memories of being under the Intelligence's thrall. While searching for the Doctor, Kizmet's agents wrongly thought the police box outside Earl's Court was the TARDIS.

The Doctor asked Clara to accompany him on his travels, but she said she would consider the matter, and that he should return tomorrow...

Missy had routed Clara's help-line call to the TARDIS, in the interest of bringing the Doctor and Clara closer together...[1519]

2013 - THE RINGS OF AKHATEN -> Clara accepted the eleventh Doctor's offer to travel, and they went to the planet Akhaten for its Festival of Offerings. She sacrificed the leaf that brought her parents together to put an old god back to sleep. Afterward, the Doctor brought Clara home on the same day she left.

2013 - THE CRIMSON HORROR -> The eleventh Doctor returned Clara home after a trip to Victorian times. Clara's charges, Angie and Artie Maitland, had uncovered photographic evidence from the Victorian era, 1974 and 1983 proving she was a time traveller, and threatened to tell their father unless she let them have a go at traveling through time...

The eleventh Doctor took Clara, Angie and Artie to the Hedgewick's World amusement park in the future, and brought them home afterwards.[1520]

2013 (10th April) - THE NAME OF THE DOCTOR -> Clara received a letter requesting that she render herself unconscious with a soporific candle, and thereby join Madame Vastra and her associates in a mental "conference call". As a guarantee of Clara's cooperation, Vastra slipped a knockout drug into the very paper of the letter. Clara returned to her body after the Whisper Men attacked Vastra's group in 1893, and the eleventh Doctor deduced that the Great Intelligence had discovered his future grave on the planet Trenzalore. With reservations, he took Clara there to investigate...

At some point following events on Trenzalore, Clara returned to Earth and became a teacher at Coal Hill school.[1521]

Doctor Who Series 7 (first half)[1522]

Amy Pond and Rory Williams' Double Lives

2013 (April) - POND LIFE -> The eleventh Doctor rang up Amy and Rory to let them know that he'd surfed the firefalls of Fiorinall 9, met Mata Hari in Paris and performed some backing vocals. While still on the phone, he crashed screaming into ancient Greece.

---

woman in the year 2013, doesn't seem to know anything about the Internet until Kizmet's people splice a software skills package into her mind.

1519 *Death in Heaven*, contextualizing *The Bells of Saint John*.

1520 *Nightmare in Silver*. The Doctor expects to see Clara next Wednesday, to which she replies, "A Wednesday, definitely." In 2013, the date given in the next story, *The Name of the Doctor*, was indeed that day of the week.

1521 See the dating notes on Series 7 (last half) as to why Clara must have skipped over much of 2013, all of 2014 and perhaps some of 2015 on Earth.

1522 Dating *The Doctor, the Widow and the Wardrobe* (X7.0), *Pond Life* (Series 7 webcast, leads into *Asylum of the Daleks*), *Asylum of the Daleks* (X7.1), *Dinosaurs on a Spaceship* (X7.2), *The Power of Three* (X7.4), and by extension *The Day of the Doctor* (X7.15) and *The Time of the Doctor* (X7.16) - Whereas the modern-day episodes of Series 5 and 6 neatly occur in their years of broadcast (respectively 2010 and 2011), the first half of Series 7 (broadcast 2012) entails the eleventh Doctor being

absent from Amy and Rory's lives for protracted periods, then unexpectedly popping up to whisk them away for adventures in time and space. The result is a widening gulf between when the contemporary stories occur and the year they were shown.

With no year actually stated in these stories, the trick becomes one of correctly accounting for the gaps while arriving at the point that *In the Forest of the Night* (X8.10) – and by extension the rest of the contemporary Series 8 episodes – happens in "2016" (two years ahead of broadcast) as the twelfth Doctor claims.

In trying to square this circle, there are a few seemingly non-negotiable rules:

• The epilogue to *The Doctor, the Widow and the Wardrobe* (X7.0) has the Doctor showing up on Amy and Rory's doorstep at Christmas, and Amy remarking that "two years" have passed since she last saw him (for her, since *The Wedding of River Song*; chronologically on Earth, since *The God Complex*). While it's possible to round the "two years" figure some, the calendar year keeps changing in the episodes to follow, as...

• The webcast *Pond Life* entails five mini-episodes that each take place in a successive month, starting

2013 (May) - POND LIFE[1523] -> The eleventh Doctor violated Rory and Amy's rule about barging into their bedroom to beg for their help with a crisis – then realised he'd arrived too early in their timeline, and unconvincingly told them that everything was fine and they should sleep well.

2013 (June) - POND LIFE -> Rory and Amy were startled to find an Ood sitting on their loo, and from this deduced that the Doctor had surreptitiously visited their house.

2013 (July) - POND LIFE -> The eleventh Doctor phoned Rory and Amy to explain that he'd rescued the Ood at their house from the middle of the Androvax Conflict, and had every intention of taking him back to the Ood-Sphere. They obligingly let the Ood pack their lunches, do laundry, wash windows and cook breakfast until the Doctor returned.

Tanya Adeloa received a letter, dated 19th July, 2013, from Frances Armitage. Owing to her stellar academic performance, she was accepted into Coal Hill School and moved forward three years.[1524]

2013 (August) - POND LIFE -> The eleventh Doctor returned Amy and Rory's Ood home, then phoned to say he was having trouble visiting them because the TARDIS' helmic regulators were still on the blink. Amy threw Rory out of the house...

... because events at Demons Run had left her unable to conceive, and she believed he'd be happier without her.[1525]

Doctor Who Series 7

2013 (August or September) - ASYLUM OF THE DALEKS[1526] -> Rory stopped by one of Amy's modelling shoots to have her sign their divorce papers. The Daleks captured Amy and Rory and transported them to the future to the Dalek Asylum. They were reconciled by the time the eleventh Doctor returned them home.

c 2013 (Summer) - IRIS S4: IRIS AT THE OCHE[1527] -> Iris and Panda were elated to find themselves at the Pondside Country Club's World Darts Championship, as Iris was a member of the Universal Darts Federation and the five-time winner of the Alpha Centauri Open. Lady Bow'n, the supreme mistress of the fallen Bovian Empire, drew the entire Pondside Club through a temporal rift to the future. Those within the club returned to this era after one of the darts players, Ted Turner, gained fantastical trans-dimensional abilities and again defeated the Bovians.

? 2013 - "Prisoners of Time"[1528] -> The fifth Doctor landed on an unnamed world so the TARDIS could replenish its artron energy from a time-tear. He, Tegan, Nyssa and Adric witnessed Commander Strock's Sontarans make a suicide charge against a Rutan encampment. As the

---

with "April" and ending in "August", and lead into *Asylum of the Daleks* (X7.1).

• In *Dinosaurs on a Spaceship* (X7.2), the Doctor and Amy agree that "ten months" have passed since they last saw one another, so it's almost certainly the next calendar year on from *Asylum of the Daleks*.

• Events in *The Power of Three* (X7.4), a.k.a. The Year of the Slow Invasion, take – as the name suggests – an entire year to unfold. According to captions, the Slow Invasion starts and ends in the month of July. Kate Lethbridge-Stewart meets the eleventh Doctor for the first time in this story, necessitating that the next time she sees him, *The Day of the Doctor* (X7.15), happens afterward.

• *The Time of the Doctor* (X7.16) occurs at Christmas following *The Day of the Doctor*, with Series 8 happening the following calendar year after classes at Coal Hill School have resumed.

• A story that doesn't factor into this equation, interestingly enough, is Amy and Rory's last one – *The Angels Take Manhattan* – as its "modern day" components are dated to 2012 (meaning they occur out of sequence with Amy and Rory's civilian lives back in London).

... that only leaves the question of *where* to begin counting. The math on this works out – as the *Doctor Who* production team surely intended – if it's presumed that the eleventh Doctor dropped Amy and Rory off on Earth (in X6.10, *The God Complex*) in 2011 following their leaving in the summer of that same year in *Let's Kill Hitler*, and that Amy was rounding up a bit with her "two year" sum in *The Doctor, The Widow and the Wardrobe*.

Those not-unreasonable assumptions made, everything neatly slots into place: *The Doctor, the Widow and the Wardrobe* epilogue happens at Christmas 2012, *Pond Life* and *Asylum of the Daleks* are 2013, *Dinosaurs on a Spaceship* is 2014, *The Power of Three* runs July 2014 to July 2015, *The Day of the Doctor* and *The Time of the Doctor* fall after that in 2015, and the modern-day episodes of Series 8 happen in 2016 (with that year expressly stated in *In the Forest of the Night*).

Noticeably, however, this means that the events in *TW: Miracle Day* don't appear to have factored into the production team's thinking while creating this framework. Trying to fold *Miracle Day* – which almost definitely has to happen in 2011 – into *Doctor Who* continuity poses challenges no matter how one plays this,

Rutans prevailed, Adam Mitchell incapacitated and snatched away the Doctor's companions.

2013 - "The Doctor and the Nurse"[1529] -> The eleventh Doctor and Rory's errant time-jumping exhausted the TARDIS' power reserves, and they put down in Cardiff, 2013, to refuel. A cadre of Cybermen tried and failed to kill them in an exploding spaceship. Afterward, the Doctor put the TARDIS into Sleep Mode, sending it through the Vortex to heal while he and Rory toasted marshmallows and hot dogs in a projected air shell on the moon. When the Ship returned, self-repaired, they successfully journeyed to 17th October, 1814.

2013 - AUTONOMY[1530] -> Animatronic attractions at Hyperville, the largest shopping mall in Europe, aroused the tenth Doctor's suspicions. Kate Maguire, now a trainee at Hyperville, aided the Doctor with the Hypercard he had given her in 2009. The two of them destroyed an army of Autons as well as the Nestene's top Auton assistant, Elizabeth Devonshire. UNIT cleared up the mess, and the Doctor popped back four years to give Kate Maguire the crucial Hypercard.

Erisa Magambo was still with UNIT. The singer Shaneeqi was one of the biggest hits of the past five years, with singles including "Gimmie Love Now" and "All That You Mean". Her "Don't Steal My Boyfriend, Girlfriend" was the vid-download No. 1 for nine weeks. She married soccer player Paul Kendrick – who was actually an Auton that was developing some glimmering of autonomy, and was destroyed during these events.

The eleventh Doctor claimed that the "truth" about a famed celebrity – who had arrived on Earth after falling through a dimensional rift – would be revealled to the public a "few years" after Amy's time. However, he couldn't remember if this revelation applied to the winner of *X Factor*, the winner of *American Idol*, the winner of *South Korea's Got Talent* or Lady Gaga.[1531]

2013 - "Hunters of the Burning Stone"[1532] -> Cornucopia had reopened as a spaceport. Annabel Lake, still posing as "Miss Ghost", prevented the Hunters of the Burning Stone from capturing a stockpile of psychic metal aboard the cargo ship *Shining Water*. The eleventh Doctor rescued Ian Chesterton and Barbara Wright from the temporal hijackers who had spirited them away from 1965, then confronted the Hunters – who were augmented members of the Tribe of Gum – and their meddling benefactors, the Prometheans.

The Prometheans advanced the final phase of their plan to shape humanity's development, and targeted Earth with a neuronic extractor made from a mass of psychic metal some twelve thousand miles in diameter. The extractor's

---

however, so it's best to just place the Series 7 and 8 episodes as stated, and leave *Miracle Day* to sort itself out (see the dating notes on that story).
1523 Dating *Pond Life* (Series 7 webcast #2) - For Amy and Rory, *Dinosaurs on a Spaceship* has yet to occur. The Doctor presumably leaves them here and jumps ahead to recruit them for that same story.
1524 *Class: Nightvisiting*
1525 *Asylum of the Daleks*, as shown at the end of *Pond Life*.
1526 Dating *Asylum of the Daleks* (X7.1) - Events follow on from *Pond Life*, each episode of which takes place in a successive month before ending in "August". It seems likely that *Asylum of the Daleks* was intended as taking place in September, the month in which it was broadcast, but within the fiction it could also be August (the only wiggle room available, if *Dinosaurs on a Spaceship* and *The Power of Three* are to happen in the same year; see the dating notes on those stories). Amy's signature on the divorce papers proves that, however many jokes are made about Rory being "Mr Pond" and so forth, she did legally take his last name (see also her tombstone in *The Angels Take Manhattan*).
1527 Dating *Iris S4: Iris at the Oche* (BF *Iris* #4.2) - There's no tangible evidence of time displacement following Iris and Panda's return to the multiverse (*Iris S4: Whatever Happened to Iris Wildthyme?*), and the story

(released in 2013) seems contemporary. The sunny weather convinces Iris and Panda that it's summer.
1528 Dating "Prisoners of Time" (IDW *DW* mini-series) - No year given, but the Rutans recognise the Doctor as having regenerated, and say he was "instrumental in our defeat on Earth" – presumably meaning, as the Doctor guesses, events in *Horror of Fang Rock* [c 1902]. The Doctor and Commander Strock both say the Rutan-Sontaran war has now lasted "thousands of years". With little else to go on, the story has been placed in its year of publication.
1529 Dating "The Doctor and the Nurse" (IDW Vol. 4 #3-4) - The year is given. The Cardiff Rift was sealed in *TW: The House of the Dead* [2010], so probably couldn't have refueled the TARDIS anyway, but the Cybermen's sudden arrival prevents the Doctor and Rory from even making the attempt.
1530 Dating *Autonomy* (NSA #35) - The year is given. The Doctor says this is the fourth Auton invasion "at least".
1531 *The Glamour Chase* (p128).
1532 Dating "Hunters of the Burning Stone" (*DWM* #456-461) - A caption names the year, which is concurrent with when the story was published. Annabel Lake says it's been "twenty-four years" since she last met the Doctor, in 1989 ("The Broken Man"). The Doctor says the population of Earth is "seven billion".

rays attacked the frontal cortex via the sun icon imprinted in humanity's collective memory, causing people around the world to lose their cognitive abilities and proclaim allegiance to Orb. The UK Prime Minister was up a tree in Regent's Park, eating a ferret. The Prometheans hailed the birth of *homo ferus*, which they judged as the height of human development.

The Doctor travelled back to 1963, entered the first Doctor's TARDIS at Totter's Lane and damaged its chameleon circuit. The Ship's subsequent journeys imprinted a police box icon into humanity's collective memories, enabling the Doctor to transform the extractor into a police box icon and restore humanity's minds.

Ian and Barbara convinced the Hunters of the Prometheans' duplicitous nature, and the Hunters and Prometheans all died in mutual combat. The psychic metal icon dissipated, and the Doctor took Ian and Barbara home.

The Doctor and Hugo Wilding of MI6 reached a state of détente. Wilding renamed MI6 HQ as Wonderland.

2013 - ELDRAD MUST DIE![1533] -> Mulkris, a Kastrian executioner tasked with collecting the body parts of the tyrant Eldrad, and killing any Eldrads that grew from them, arrived on Earth as the fifth Doctor, Tegan, Turlough and the older Nyssa sought to enjoy themselves at the fishing village of Ambermouth. The radiation from Mulkris' vessel stimulated granular particles of Eldrad, and a quartz-berg formed in Ambermouth's bay. One of Eldrad's eyes lodged itself in the forehead of Charlie Gibbs – one of Turlough's former classmates, and a Trion exile – and possessed his mind. Gibbs crumbled Mulkris' body with a poison dart that Eldrad had created.

Captain O'Brien of the HMS *Alexander* fell under Eldrad's sway, and worked to bombard Eldrad's crystals around the globe. Earth would become sheathed in living quartz – a planet-sized Eldrad. The Doctor's party prevented this, and the quartz-berg collapsed in on itself.

The Doctor's party went to the dead world Kastria, along with the Eldrad-possessed Charlie Gibbs. The Eldrad trapped on Kastria had gone mad during his isolation, and carved "Here Lies Eldrad" onto his chest. Gibbs fully trans-

1533 Dating *Eldrad Must Die!* (BF #172) - It's been "thirty years" since Turlough and Charlie Gibbs attended Brendon together (in *Mawdryn Undead*, set in 1983), and the story was released in 2013. An oddity is that aeons have passed since Kastria's destruction (*The Hand of Fear*), but while Mulkris has been active for all of that time, she's never bothered to call home for new instructions, or to determine her homeworld's status.

The dating of events on Kastria pose a special problem, as the Doctor tells Eldrad: "How many years now [since we've last met]? Hundreds? A thousand?", referring to their last encounter in *The Hand of Fear*. It's not easy to rationalize this remark, as either: A) Eldrad was indeed trapped on Kastria in UNIT Year 8 (as *The Hand of Fear* seems to suggest), meaning the fifth Doctor has here time-jumped forward hundreds or a thousand years for no discernible reason, B) the fourth Doctor, accompanied by Eldrad and Sarah, left the UNIT era and went *back in time* to Kastria hundreds/a thousand years for discernible reason in *The Hand of Fear*, or C) the fifth Doctor in *Eldrad Must Die!* does not know what on Earth he's talking about, as Eldrad was trapped on Kastria in the UNIT Era, and it's now 2013, so he's been there some four decades. For the sake of clarity, this chronology has opted to go with C, and decide that the Doctor is just being weird.

1534 Dating *Ghost in the Machine* (BF CC #8.4) - No year given, but some decades seem to have passed since Lezarata went into lockdown - those who died there have become skeletons, and Benjamin Chikoto, whose mind was transferred to audio during the Second Voice's initial outbreak, speculates (while conceding that he doesn't actually know the answer) that he's been in such a state for "Fifty years? A hundred?"

since the UNIT era. Without more specific information, it seems fair to place the story concurrent with its release in October 2013.

1535 Dating *Erimem: "The One Place"* (Erimem novel #2a) - Erimem and Andrea jump "not even three years" into the past from October 2015.

1536 Dating "The Girl Who Loved Doctor Who" (IDW *Doctor Who Special 2013*) - The story-concept is that the Doctor is visiting the real world ("It's like the land of un-fiction. Anti-fiction. Non-fiction. Everything the Doctor has done becomes a story, with no UNIT."), but some of the details provided are askew with real life. The eleventh Doctor attends a 50th anniversary *Doctor Who* convention (in November 2013, presumably), and yet Matt Smith says that he's filming a "new" episode of *Doctor Who* the very next day (in the real world, he wrapped up work on *The Time of the Doctor* in September 2013), and that said story will entail the Doctor landing in the real world (no such episode was ever filmed). More glaringly, his replacement hasn't been announced – in contrast to the global unveiling of Peter Capaldi in August 2013. All in all, this story is arguably better regarded as "the exploration of an idea/a love-letter to *Doctor Who* fans" than something that's actually part of the *Doctor Who* universe.

1537 Dating *DotD: The Time Machine* (Destiny of the Doctor #11) - The exact day is given, and is undoubtedly meant to coincide with *Doctor Who*'s fiftieth anniversary. The hypercube featured in *The Time Machine* is an ontological paradox with no start or end point – Alice Watson here flings it into the Vortex so Chivers can obtain it in early 2013, the eleventh Doctor later takes the same hypercube from Chivers and sends it into the Vortex for the seventh Doctor to find (*DotD:*

formed into a version of Eldrad, and challenged his predecessor. The older Eldrad dispatched the upstart with a poison dart, then vowed to make Earth his new command centre for galactic conquest. The Doctor restored Mulkris the Executioner by use of her ring, which contained her cellular pattern, and she killed Eldrad with his own poison dart. Turlough and Tegan found and destroyed Eldrad's ring, preventing this version of Eldrad from ever being resurrected. Afterward, Mulkris resumed hunting Eldrads.

c 2013 - GHOST IN THE MACHINE[1534] -> While Jo Grant entertained herself in the TARDIS wardrobe, the third Doctor explored the disused Lezarata Research Centre and came under psychic attack from the Second Voice. The Doctor hid the TARDIS key in his mouth – to prevent the Second Voice escaping in the Ship – and rendered himself comatose, leaving an audio log with the note "Use Me" for Jo to find. Jo accessed the log, setting in motion a series of body, mind and audio-swaps that let the Doctor outfox and erase the Second Voice.

2013 - ERIMEM: "The One Place"[1535] -> Erimem jumped through time with her friend Andrea Hansen, so Andy could be with her mother as she died from cancer. Six months later, Andy's estranged father also died. She refrained from telling her brother Matt, worried how he'd deal with losing both parents in the same year.

? (=) 2013 (November) - "The Girl Who Loved Doctor Who"[1536] -> The TARDIS conducted the eleventh Doctor into a parallel universe in which all of the Doctor's adventures had been made into episodes of a TV show, and the current lead – Matt Smith – looked exactly like him. The Doctor befriended a 12-year-old girl named Ally, and went with her to a convention celebrating *Doctor Who's* fiftieth anniversary. Smith met the Doctor, who took second place in a costume contest, and suggested that the actor Peter Capaldi might make a good replacement should Smith ever move on. The Doctor sent a Cyberman that fell through time from the Battle of Canary Wharf back into the Vortex, then returned to his home reality. Ally, inspired by the Doctor, stood up to a classmate who had been bullying her.

2013 (23rd November) - DotD: THE TIME MACHINE[1537] -> The eleventh Doctor investigated a "temporal wrongness" at Oxford as Professor Cedric Chivers and Alice Watson neared completion of their time machine. The Doctor backtracked the instructions contained within Chivers' hypercube, and went with Alice to a near future where the insectoid Creevix had conquered Earth, then to the Creevix's domain at the end of time.

They returned to 2013, having determined that the Creevix had entered our universe by deleting the life history of Time Agent Guy Taylor, as well as the paradox of Chivers sending himself the hypercube during his first journey through time. The Doctor programmed the TARDIS to send messages to ten of his previous selves, coordinating their actions to guarantee Taylor's existence. He also ejected Chivers' hypercube into the Vortex for the seventh Doctor to find in the forty-ninth century. Alice threw another version of the hypercube, as taken from a copy of Guy Taylor's time machine, into the Vortex for Professor Chivers to receive eleven months previous.

Taylor's restoration and the alteration of the Chivers paradox thwarted the Creevix, and the last of their number was squashed beneath Taylor's time machine as it safely arrived from the fifty-second century. The Doctor left as Taylor took Alice back to his native era to make his report.

2014[1538]

Amy Pond received a tube of River's psychodelic-inducing lipstick as a Mother's Day gift.[1539] UK entertainer Jack Oddwards disappeared down a Gomagog wormhole while trying to swim the length of the Thames, on behalf of Chuckle-Aid, in 2014. Bernice Summerfield would find his remains, Chuckle-Aid shorts and all, in her native time.[1540] In 2014, the Scindia family invested in the Mangalyaan Mars Orbiter Mission, which paved the way for their becoming India's premiere dynasty.[1541]

The reclusive industrialist Simon Devlin suffered from a rare bone disorder, fibrous dysplasia, and developed a technique by which his entire skull was replaced with a plastic one. The Nestene Consciousness took control of Devlin via his plastic skull, and had him turn his company, Devlin FutureTech, toward the advancement of an Auton invasion plan.[1542]

Ace, now a student at the Gallifreyan Academy, visited

Shockwave), whereupon Captain OhOne claims it as a keepsake and later passes it down to his son Guy Taylor, who keeps it with him in his time capsule... which the eleventh Doctor then pockets and gives to Alice to fling into the Vortex.

1538 Events in 2014 include *Dinosaurs on a Spaceship* (X7.2) and the start of the Year of the Slow Invasion in *The Power of Three* (X7.4).

1539 The tube arrived in the post "last month, on Mother's Day", according to "The Broken Man".
1540 *Worlds BF: The Phantom Wreck*
1541 *The Twelfth Doctor Year One*: "The Swords of Kali"
1542 "The year before" *UNIT* S1: *Extinction*; when liberated from Nestene control, Devlin can't remember anything of "the last six months".

her mother – who was dying of cancer – in Perivale.[1543] UNIT dealt with some friendly "Spanish sea monsters" living in a cave under the Rock of Gibraltar.[1544]

The twelfth Doctor believed that the Rossendale Fairies photos were genuine.[1545] A virulent bacteriophage, lodged underneath the eleventh Doctor's shoe, threatened the lush planet Altikan when he stopped by. The Doctor cocooned the planet within a TARDIS cupboard and accelerated time within, trying to burn out the phage. As he absent-mindedly forgot to release it, Altikan aged a few million years.[1546]

The great-great granddaughter of a resident of Mercy reflected upon the tale of the man who fell from the stars, and became the "special angel" watching over the town, meaning it needed no sheriff or policeman.[1547]

At the start of 2014, the Home Office introduced compulsory HIV blood tests. In June the next year, MI5's Harry Sullivan told UNIT that the blood of a survivor of the Quadrant Incident might hold a cure to the condition.[1548] **Ambrose Northover's aunt Gladys died in 2014. Her body had vanished from its grave by 2020, taken by Malohkeh of the Silurians.**[1549]

Victoria Waterfield had created a new life for herself – she was a wife and a mother, and was soon to be a grandmother. She'd never told her family of her origins and adventures in time – and suspected that time was running out, as her memories were fading.[1550]

The eleventh Doctor warned that the psionic abilities of George, a Tenza disguised as a young boy, might re-manifest around puberty, as it was "always a funny time".[1551]

c 2014 - THE CROOKED MAN[1552] **->** The surge in new storytelling venues – websites, e-publishing, print on demand, YouTube, tabloid exaggeration, TV tie-ins and more – created a massive increase in fictional creations. Even the Land of Fiction had its limits, and the lower-tier characters inhabiting it faced extinction as their stories were forgotten about. Laura Corbett, a resident of Eastwold, England, so fantasized about the ideal form of the husband (and father of her child) who left her, she created the fictionalized Simon Corbett: a living tear in space-time.

The Crooked Man, a creation of a manuscript penned by Laura's father, aided endangered fictions in traversing to the real world... by exchanging life for life, and literally stuffing Eastwold residents full of works by Dickens and more. The fourth Doctor and Leela torched the Crooked Man's manuscript, destroying him. The Doctor convinced Simon to cross over to the Land of Fiction, closing the tear and extinguishing the fugitive fictions.

1543 *NAofBenny* V1: *The Lights of Skaro*, contradicting Ace and her mother reuniting in *Happy Endings*.

1544 The year before *UNIT* S1: *Shutdown*.

1545 *The Shining Man* (ch14). The photos, taken by an art history lecturer at Manchester Metropolitan, were debunked in April 2014 as probably being midge flies.

1546 "A few years" before *The Lost Planet*, and referenced in *The Eleventh Doctor Year Three*: "The Memory Feast".

1547 *A Town Called Mercy*, presumably concurrent with the other "modern day" stories in Series 7.

1548 *Damaged Goods*

1549 "Six years" before *The Hungry Earth*.

1550 *The Great Space Elevator*. This is the first we've seen of Victoria since *Downtime* – a story that established that she was 14 when she met the Doctor, and she's probably not much older than that when she leaves his company circa 1975. If she did restart her life (as an international fugitive or not) in wake of *Downtime*, then she's in her mid-30s when she starts a family, and the bare minimum of time required for her to be an impending grandmother must mean that the framing sequence for *The Great Space Elevator* occurs circa 2015 at the earliest.

1551 *Night Terrors*, extrapolating from George being eight in 2011.

1552 Dating *The Crooked Man* (BF 4th Doc #3.3) - The story was released in 2014, and the trappings of the publishing industry as outlined by the Doctor sound very contemporary.

1553 Dating *The Sentinels of the New Dawn* (BF CC #5.10) - The year is given.

1554 Dating *Breaking Bubbles and Other Stories*: "The Curious Incident of the Doctor in the Night-Time" (BF #188d) - The story seems contemporary, and was released in 2014.

1555 Dating "Pay the Piper"/"The Blood of Azrael" (*DWM* #468-469, 470-474) - A news report in "The Blood of Azrael" claims that "Hunters of the Burning Stone", set in 2013, happened "last year".

1556 Dating *Worlds DW: The Screaming Skull/Second Sight* (*Worlds DW* #1.3-1.4) - These "modern-day" stories were released in 2014. It's been "fifty years" since Rees' mind was separated in *Worlds DW: The Reesinger Process* [1964]. For Matheson and Sato, an indeterminate amount of time has passed since *Mastermind* [2012]. Matheson has "four degrees", but it's not specified how many (if any) she earned during her imprisonment. The UNIT "home" Matheson and Sato are locked up in loosely sounds like Stangmoor Prison (*The Mind of Evil*). Within *Doctor Who*, the world's developed nations agreeing to surrender surveillance of their own citizens to UNIT is arguably no more ludicrous than their similarly turning over their nuclear launch codes (*Robot*, *World War Three*).

Although the story ends with the Doctor, Leela and Romana setting off for some adventures together, we're never shown what those entail.

2014 - THE SENTINELS OF THE NEW DAWN[1553] ->

Cambridge University now had a heliport, just off Wilberforce Road.

The Sentinels of the New Dawn emerged as an ascendant coalition of high-ranking scholars, scientists and politicians who officially promoted a "greener, fairer future", but in reality was a tool by which its elite members sought power. The Sentinels' scientists were having some success creating biomechanoids, including a human-bird monstrosity that resembled Heliodromus: a mythical punisher of the damned. The group was also trying to develop a concentrated form of the ebola virus – and a cure for it – so they could cause a widespread contagion after positioning themselves to restore order.

(=) The Sentinels built a time dilator using Terri Billington's schematics, and created a wormhole linked to Billington's prototype dilator in the 1970s. They hoped to attain enough control of time travel to retroactively empower their members, and to foresee their opponents' decisions. The third Doctor and Liz visited this time, and upon returning home destroyed Billington's work – retroactively preventing the Sentinels from creating their time-dilation device.

c 2014 - BREAKING BUBBLES AND OTHER STORIES: "The Curious Incident of the Doctor in the Night-Time"[1554] ->

The Galactic Coalition created the Genoi, silicon-based lifeforms resembling garden gnomes, as a weapon of war, but the Genoi were banished to Earth, where the ozone levels petrified them. Their leader, Llangragen, developed a mobility field and went to Earth to recover his comrades. Geoffrey Jennings, a Canterbury resident, had died when a dingy overturned, and his 14-year-old son Michael mistakenly thought that Llangragen was his father, but transformed into a garden gnome. Llangragen reanimated his fellows at a House Proud repair store, but Michael, the sixth Doctor and Peri set off the store's sprinklers, destroying Llangragen's machinery and returning the Genoi to immobility.

2014 - "Pay the Piper" / "The Blood of Azrael"[1555]

-> On behalf of Wonderland, Annabel Lake and Danny Fisher infiltrated the Obsidian Mainframe: a commerce nexus serving millions of worlds. They manipulated the eleventh Doctor and Clara into attending a secret auction hosted by the Incognito – a distraction while Lake and Fiaher attached surveillance devices to the Mainframe's systems. The auction host, Mr Minus, attempted to sell Clara as a lucrative source of temporal particles. To save her, the Doctor put the TARDIS itself on sale, causing quadrillions of bids to temporarily crash the Mainframe while he freed five Kindred of Fel from the auction block. The Fel telepathically made the Incognito feel remourse for their misdeeds, but the Mainframe rebooted, and the auction for the TARDIS completed. The Doctor's Ship disappeared to join its new owner...

While undercover, Fisher had discovered the mask and resources of Azrael the legendary necrotist. With these, Fisher secretly constructed the Mercy: a DNA-eradicating substance that was harmless to human beings. Azrael's riches enabled Fisher to buy the TARDIS, and he slaved the Ship to the Mercy, forming a weapon that could eradicate any alien race in space-time. The Ship would become Fisher's trump card on protecting Earth from all extraterrestrial dangers, with "Azrael" receiving blame for the resultant atrocities.

The Doctor and Clara travelled to Cornucopia, and – as aided by the aviatrix Amy Johnson, Annabel Lake and Horatio Lynk – ended Fisher's scheme. During combat, Lake killed Fisher. Afterward, the Doctor's party joined the revels at the Lifesong Carnival celebrating Cornucopia's history.

c 2014 - WORLDS DW: THE SCREAMING SKULL / SECOND SIGHT[1556] ->

Earth's major nations, reluctant to give up spying on their own citizens, agreed to turn over such surveillance to UNIT. Officially, the Oversight Project was established in Peru to send signals into deep space, but in truth it monitored all of Earth's communications.

A locale that had served as UNIT HQ in Captain Yates' day was being sold off, and made into luxury flats. Assets in the UNIT Vault included plastic daffodils, Bok, a suit of armour, a black London taxicab, a chess set that independently moved one of its pieces every couple of days, and various items from the Professor Dark Collection.

Some of the Black Archive's assets were reallocated to the Vault, which brought Rees' music box and skull together for the first time in decades. His mind attained enough critical mass to kill the Vault staff – including Captain Jane Lucas, Mike Yates' former lover – and possess their bodies. Captain Ruth Matheson and Warrant Officer Sato were currently imprisoned in a UNIT retirement home, but Yates returned to active service and offered them a pardon if they helped to contain the situation. The trio stymied Rees, but he escaped in Lucas' body...

Yates summoned the sixth Doctor with the space-time telegraph, and Leela and the second Romana independently arrived from Gallifrey, as Rees attempted to project his mind into all of humanity via the Oversight Project's technology. The Doctor used the TARDIS' telepathic circuits to trick Rees' mind into believing he'd lived a fulfilling life, and it slowly faded. The Doctor then promised to return Leela and Romana to Gallifrey, expecting they would experience some detours along the way...

Alice Obiefune Joins the TARDIS

2014 - THE ELEVENTH DOCTOR YEAR ONE[1557] -> Alice Uwaebuka Obiefune's life became frayed after her mother Ada died, budget cuts ended her job as a library assistant, and her landlord demanded she move out by August, so the property could become luxury flats. While out walking, Alice happened upon the eleventh Doctor – who was in hot pursuit of a Rainbow Dog: a "joy beast" native to the planet Vreular in the Fifth Galaxy. The Rainbow Dog fed off negative emotions... so was drawn to the House of Commons during the Prime Minister's Question Time. The Doctor reunited the Dog with its best friend, a squid-like alien child, but the Prime Minister remained befuddled by the spectacle he'd witnessed. Alice accepted the Doctor's offer to travel with him.

The Doctor briefly returned Alice home, but she fondly remembered her mother's enjoyment of the music of John Jones, so he whisked her off to Jones' first public performance in 1962...

2014 (20th March) - THE CRAWLING TERROR[1558] -> The TARDIS detected a ley line disturbance, prompting the twelfth Doctor and Clara to stop in Wiltshire. Jason Clearfield had partially created a gateway to the Wyrrester planet, on behalf of Wyrrester war criminals fleeing pros-ecution. The Doctor and Clara aided the UK military in destroying Clearfield's operation, and Clearfield was accidentally transmitted to the Wyrrester homeworld.

When Mr Colchester and his partner Colin got married, they rented a cinema to show everyone their favourite movie: *North by Northwest*. Colin, originally from Leeds, took the surname Colchester-Price.[1559]

2014 (5th June) - NIGHT OF THE STORMCROW[1560] -> The Stormcrow drew near Earth and consumed a St Albans Island village near Mt. McKerry Observatory. The fourth Doctor and Leela convinced the Stormcrow that Earth was still viable, whereupon Stormcrow resisted the urge to feed and returned to space.

2014 (June or July) - DINOSAURS ON A SPACESHIP[1561] -> Ten months had passed since Amy and Rory last saw the eleventh Doctor. One day, while Rory's father Brian was helping with home maintenance, the Doctor materialised the TARDIS around the three of them, and took them to a dilemma facing Earth in 2367. The Doctor later returned his friends home, and the experience motivated Brian – normally a homebody – to travel to Pisa, Rio de Janeiro, India, New York and more.

1557 Dating *The Eleventh Doctor Year One* (Titan 11th Doc #1.1, 1.3, "After Life"/"What He Wants") - The Doctor names the year in "After Life", as does a caption in "What He Wants". The Doctor mentions being "900 years" old in "What He Wants" and "The Comfort of the Good", so he travels with Alice prior to the end of Series 6.

1558 Dating *The Crawling Terror* (NSA #57) - The year is given (ch13). The activation of the new Wyrrester gateway coincides with the vernal equinox, which in 2014 happened on 20th March. A local comments: "It's a bit early for April Fool's Day" (ch3).

1559 TW: *Aliens Among Us*. Presuming this is a legally recognised union, same-sex marriages in the UK started happening on 13th March, 2014.

1560 Dating *Night of the Stormcrow* (BF subscription promo #11) - The exact day is given.

1561 Dating *Dinosaurs on a Spaceship* (X7.2) - It's been "ten months" since Amy and Rory last saw the Doctor – either directly following *Asylum of the Daleks*, or any adventures they had after leaving the Dalek Asylum. With *Asylum of the Daleks* occurring in (at the earliest) August or (at the latest) September of the preceding year, *Dinosaurs on a Spaceship* must happen in either June or July. The former would accord Brian a bit more time to complete his overseas travel before he's busy with events in *The Power of Three*.

1562 Dating *The Power of Three* (X7.4) - The month is given as "July". With that also being the most likely month in which the modern-day component of

Dinosaurs on a Spaceship takes place, it seems reasonable to think that for Amy and Rory, *The Power of Three* happens on the heels of their returning home after *A Town Called Mercy* (and despite Amy opining at the end of *Mercy* that she'd like to put the TARDIS travelling on pause for a while).

Kate Stewart previously appeared in the independent videos *Downtime* and *The Daemons: Daemos Rising*. Intentional or not, the two have the same name, hair colour, parentage (the Brigadier being named as their father) and are (relatively speaking) the same age.

1563 Dating *The Power of Three* (X7.4) - The month is given. Brian's "cube-watching" log is on Day 67, the math of which works out if he started it in late July and it's now early October.

1564 GABBY GONZALEZ AND CINDY WU: Titan's *Tenth Doctor* comics feature two New Yorkers, Gabby Gonzalez and Cindy Wu, as companions in stories that seem to coincide with the modern day, and began publishing in 2014. Only one time in the whole of *The Tenth Doctor Year One*, *Two* and *Three* is a year given - in "Vortex Butterflies" (*Year Three* #3.7), when Gabby says that she originates from 2016, and, come to think of it, it "must be 2017 now".

That suggests that we can take the umbrella "year" titles (which don't otherwise correspond to calendar years, 12-month durations or indeed 12-issue blocks) as actual years, and log that three years passed in real time for Gabby and Cindy from the start of *Year One* to

The Year of the Slow Invasion

2014 (July) - THE POWER OF THREE[1562] -> Amy Pond was employed writing travel articles for magazines while Rory worked as a nurse. Kate Stewart, formerly Kate Lethbridge-Stewart, had assumed command of UNIT.

The Skakri were regarded as mythical pest controllers of the universe, but did exist and served the Tally: a numerical sum the Shakri believed expressed balance. Seven Shakri vessels feared the spread of humanity throughout space, and sought to curtail humankind while it was still limited to Earth. One morning, humanity awoke to find small black cubes – secretly left by the Shakri and impervious to harm – scattered everywhere. World leaders appealed for calm, and Professor Brian Cox noted that the cubes were too perfectly cut to be random space detritus.

Kate met the Doctor for the first time when a UNIT team charged into Amy and Rory's house to secure his help with the cubes. With the cubes resisting analysis and being completely inert, the Doctor nearly went mad from the boredom of observing them. He told his friends that he'd instruct the TARDIS to monitor Earth's news for developments, and would jaunt off for a while.

Over the next twelve months, humanity found it perfectly normal to have the cubes just lying about the place…

2014 (early October) - THE POWER OF THREE[1563] -> Amy and Rory were unsettled to find how much they

were acclimating to civilian life on Earth. Brian Williams devoted himself to watching the cubes, in accordance with the Doctor's wishes.

The Tenth Doctor Year One[1564]

Gabby Gonzalez Joins the TARDIS

c 2014 (30th October) - THE TENTH DOCTOR YEAR ONE[1565] -> Pranavores developed in Earth's psychosphere as invisible, harmless creatures that fed off positive emotions. The alien Fleshkind weaponised some Pranavores into Cerebravores, who fed off fear instead. The Cerebravores destroyed their creators, then travelled down a wormhole to Brooklyn, New York, and caused seemingly supernatural effects there in the run-up to Halloween.

The tenth Doctor studied the situation and happened upon Gabriella Gonzalez – a second-generation Hispanic taking accounting classes on behalf of her father, but who dreamed of attending art school. The Doctor banished the Cerebravores by amplifying the positive emotions at a Day of the Dead celebration at Green-Wood Cemetery, then mentally influenced Gabby's father to encourage her interest in art design. Afterward, Gabby asked the Doctor to teach her more about the universe, and he accepted her as a travelling companion.

c 2014 - THE TENTH DOCTOR YEAR ONE[1566] -> The tenth Doctor brought Gabby home to see her family as Echoes – beings of pure sound who roamed the universe like pods of whales – increased New York's sound to destructive levels. The Doctor insulated himself and

---

the end of *Year Three*, but there's a few bumps in the road. *Year One* ends with the Doctor bringing Gabby home a mere two hours after she left, and *Year Three* seems to start on the heels of *Year Two*. (We can imagine a greater gap between the latter, but it doesn't feel like what was intended.)

We also have to decouple our expectations from the impact of this on Gabby and Cindy's schooling and what Gabby's tight-nit family (introduced in *Year One*), makes of her increasing absences, because we're never told. Sarah Jane intimates in "Vortex Butterflies" that people age at a slower rate in the TARDIS, meaning that "In human terms, I was probably with [the Doctor] for years. Five? Ten? More? I honestly don't know", but the idea is never followed up, so it's hard to know what to make of that. Whatever her chronological age, Gabby herself seems to log time in concert with the modern day – she's pretty sure it's become "2017", even though the TARDIS can obviously cheat some. Writer Nick Abadzis told us over email, at the end of *The Tenth Doctor Year Three*: "TARDIS travel being what it is, I'm not sure how 'old' [Gabby and Cindy] are in relative terms

now, but, with the amount of 'unseen' stories in my head, Gabby easily has about three years' worth of adventures behind her, Cindy a little fewer. (But she was also trapped in ancient China for months.)"

For now, then, we'll take the path of least resistance and pace out Gabby and Cindy's relationship with the modern day (so far) as 2014 to 2017.

1565 Dating *The Tenth Doctor Year One* (Titan 10th Doc #1.1-1.3, "Revolutions of Terror") - The story was published in 2014 and seems contemporary. The action opens two days before Halloween/the Day of the Dead, and concludes on the day itself. A recap says that the tenth Doctor's time with Gabby happens after he's parted ways with Donna (*Journey's End*). Very strangely, a psychic image of the tenth Doctor's fears includes the hoodie-wearing John Simm Master and the Timothy Dalton Rassilon, who only appeared in his last story, *The End of Time*.

1566 Dating *The Tenth Doctor Year One* (Titan 10th Doc #1.10-1.15; "Echo", "The Fountains of Forever", "Spiral Staircase", "Sins of the Father") - The action picks up from the first story in *Year One*, "Revolutions of Terror",

Gabby with sonic earmuffs as a strike squad of alien Shreekers, authorized to hunt the Echoes under Article 21212121212 of the Intergalactic Treaty of Cultural Rights, threatened additional mayhem. With Gabby's help, the Doctor channelled the sonic chaos through the Empire State Building and destroyed the Shreeker Battleship, allowing the Echoes to leave for space.

Afterward, the Doctor attended an auction of extraterrestrial artifacts that included Van Statten's space-hairdryer and the Hand of Sutekh: a semi-sentient quantum harvester that merged with Dorothy Bell, a terminally ill movie star. The restored Bell set about reengineering New York into a more ideal form, and had transformed the Empire State Building's top twenty stories when a Seeker drone programmed to collect Osirian technology transported the Doctor, Gabby and Bell to the mothership of Anubis, the son of Sutekh.

Anubis sought to follow his people to a higher plane through the Circle of Transcendence, but the Doctor convinced him that using the unstable Circle would destroy the universe. Anubis agreed to delay action for five thousand years while the Doctor found a means of safely closing the Circle. Bell decided to stay with Anubis.

The Seeker drone saturated the tenth Doctor and Gabby with Osirian healing nanites. The Doctor's system purged these, but they remained in Gabby, and would augment her ability to wield block-transfer computation.[1567]

The Tenth Doctor Year Two

Cindy Wu Joins the TARDIS

c 2014 - THE TENTH DOCTOR YEAR TWO[1568] -> A gestalt being, Mr Ebonite, accosted two survivors of the Cult of the Black Pyramid – Cleopatra Hunsicker and Erik Ulfriksson – for artefacts to sell in his Ebonite Rooms. Captain Jack intervened, but Ebonite captured them and Gabby Gonzalez's best friend Cindy Wu, as well as the tenth Doctor and Gabby from pre-historic times, to compete in his Arena of Fear: a miniturised combat site beneath Rockefeller Center. The Doctor and his allies

although how much time has passed is unclear. The recap claims Gabby has only been absent for two hours, and yet it's long enough for Cindy, as her best friend, to get peeved because Gabby has seemingly been ignoring her. Also, Cindy mentions Gabby walking off with the Doctor "after the Day of the Dead feast" – an odd remark to make, if it's the same day. Whatever the case, it's not long enough for Gabby to have been declared a missing person.

1567 *The Tenth Doctor Year Three:* "Vortex Butterflies"
1568 Dating *The Tenth Doctor Year Two* (Titan 10th Doc #2.3, #2.6-2.7, #2.8-2.9; "Cindy, Cleo and the Magic Sketchbook", "Arena of Fear" and "The Wishing Well Witch") - For Cindy, not long at all seems to have passed since the Doctor and Gabby left following *The Tenth Doctor Year One:* "Sins of the Father." "Arena of Fear" ends with the Doctor's party discovering that Ebonite's base is beneath Rockefeller Center in the same time zone. The blurb for "The Wishing Well Witch", and the Previously On... blurb to the story after this ("The Infinite Corridor") claim that the Doctor, Gabby and Cindy visit Dewbury in "the present day". If there's any time-displacement involved in the Doctor's trio going there by TARDIS, it's not said, and the Doctor regards a *Monster Fun Annual 1980* at the book fair as a "classic".
1569 Dating *The Tenth Doctor Year Three* (Titan 10th Doc #3.5, "Revolving Doors") - This flashback story was published in *The Tenth Doctor Year Three*, but is set during *Year Two*. The original randomiser was left on Argolis in *The Leisure Hive*; the eighth Doctor had one, but it was installed in Compassion, not his own TARDIS. The tenth Doctor has one in the *Doctor Who Adventures* comic "Triskaidekaphobia", but needed to "set the controls to random" in *Planet of the Ood*.

1570 *The City of the Dead.* This retcon takes the sting out of one of the nastier bits of *Warlock*.
1571 Dating *Warlock* (NA #34) - The novel is the sequel to *Cat's Cradle: Warhead.* The events of the earlier book are consistently referred to as happening "years" ago (p8, p203, p209, p223). Vincent and Justine, the two young lovers from *Warhead*, bought a car after a "few years" of marriage and have had it a while (p356).
In *Cat's Cradle: Warhead*, Ace had difficulty guessing how old Justine was, eventually settling on "maybe 16 or 17" (p181). By *Warlock*, Justine has matured into a woman (p203), but she is still only "probably a couple of years older than the medical student" (p301), so she is in her early-to-mid 20s. We suggest, then, that *Warlock* takes place about five years after *Cat's Cradle: Warhead*. It is late autumn (p279, p334).
1572 *Class: Nightvisiting*
1573 Dating *The Power of Three* (X7.4) - The month is given.
1574 Events in 2015 include the end of the Year of the Slow Invasion in *The Power of Three* (X7.4), the webcast *P.S.*, *The Day of the Doctor* (X7.15) and *The Time of the Doctor* (X7.16).
1575 *Big Bang Generation* (ch7).
1576 The year before *The Twelfth Doctor Year One:* "The Fractures".
1577 The year before *In the Forest of the Night.*
1578 *The Husbands of River Song*
1579 *The Legends of River Song:* "Suspicious Minds"
1580 *Time Surgeon* #24 is due at the printers during *The Twelfth Doctor Year Two:* "Invasion of the Mindmorphs" – so, assuming a monthly release schedule, it started two years beforehand.

defeated Ebonite, who splintered into his component pieces. Afterwards, the Doctor proposed that Jack, Cleo and Erik make Ebonite's base the home of a new Earth defence organisation.

Cindy joined the Doctor and Gabby in their travels, and they visited the Paranormal Literary Festival in Dewbury, which had wrested the mantle of "most paranormal place in England" from Stockbridge this year. A witch-like creature – formerly seven children thrown into the Untempered Schism on Gallifrey – started stealing pieces of people's bodies and personae to make itself whole. Using a filtering Time Scope, the Doctor banished the children and restored their victims. To recoup, he, Cindy and Gabby went back to the Jazz Age in New Orleans.

c 2014 - THE TENTH DOCTOR YEAR THREE[1569] ->

The tenth Doctor, Gabby and Cindy returned to New York following the death of Cindy's boyfriend, Roscoe Ruskin. The Doctor dealt with low-level matters such as the Ogron Poets' Group and the Guild of Unfeasible Mirthcasters. Turbulence triggered the TARDIS' Randomiser, which took the Doctor and Gabby to London. A squid-like entity exiled to a pocket dimension cached energy via its psychic link with a tech entrepreneur, Aaron Crossland. The Doctor and Gabby enabled Crossland to turn against the entity, severing its link to our reality.

The eighth Doctor visited a house in Kent and saved a cat.[1570]

c 2014 (late autumn) - WARLOCK[1571] -> Organised

crime continued to rely on the profits of drug trafficking. Dealers now used sports cars to get around, and the British police were forced to use Porsches to keep up with them. Soon, Porsche were even making a special model for them.

In an attempt to win the Drugs War, the International Drug Enforcement Agency (IDEA) was set up. A pooling of Interpol and FBI resources, IDEA had a number of well-publicised successes against drug dealers, forcing many of them underground. IDEA was based in the King Building in New York, the old headquarters of the Butler Institute, and its methods often brought them into conflict with local police forces.

For around a year, IDEA had been aware of a new street drug called Warlock by many of its users. The seventh Doctor sent Benny to infiltrate IDEA's headquarters to learn more about Warlock, as it was granting people psionic abilities and seemed to defy analysis. He tried to contact Vincent and Justine Wheaton, who had settled down and were expecting a child, to locate their associate Mrs Woodcott – an expert on Warlock. An IDEA team learned about Vincent's powers, but an attempt to capture Vincent resulted in his psionically manifesting an opponent's hatred as a fireball that destroyed Canterbury Cathedral.

The event was attributed to a freak ball-lightning effect.

Ace investigated a research lab near Canterbury that was kidnapping animals and using Warlock to exchange their minds with people. The Doctor's cat Chick, a resident of his house in Kent for about a year, was captured and euthanised. The Doctor and his allies found Vincent and ended the research lab's activities. The mind of a Kent resident, Jack, remained trapped in a dog, but the Doctor took possession of Jack's human body.

Creed McIlveen, an undercover IDEA agent, saved Justine Wheaton from a forced prostitution house that threatened to terminate her pregnancy. Grateful to Creed, Justine became his lover. Harry Harrigan Jnr, the head of IDEA, had been using Warlock to transfer his mind into younger bodies, and now intended on doing so with Creed. A further discharge of Vincent's powers released the alien intelligence within Warlock, and it left for space after incinerating Harrigan.

Justine left her husband for Creed. Vincent departed with the dog named Jack.

In November 2014, Jasper Adola had dinner with his family and went to bed, where he expired from a stroke.[1572]

2014 (December) - THE POWER OF THREE[1573] ->

The black cubes continued to stay motionless as the Christmas season arrived. The Shakri's operatives began secretly operating in the hospital where Rory worked and collected samples from the patients there.

2015[1574]

The twelfth Doctor believed that "2015 is a pretty uninteresting year, universally speaking".[1575] UNIT scientist Paul Foster died when a drunk driver struck his car. In an alternate reality, Foster lived while his wife and children died, and began researching a means of jumping between realities.[1576] **Maebe Arden's sister, Annabel, went missing.[1577] At some point, River Song married the actor Stephen Fry.[1578]** River Song dabbled in adult colouring books in 2015.[1579]

Sonny Robinson and Val Kent used urban legends of the Doctor as the inspiration for a new comic-book series: *Time Surgeon*. Accompanied by Nurse Kara, the Time Surgeon fought such menaces as the Minister and his army of Deathroids.[1580]

The former Ritz Dance Hall in Cardiff was torn down, to make way for the Ritz Tower.[1581]

c 2015 - BENNY: PRESENT DANGER: "Excalibur of Mars"[1582] -> Knight-General Ancelyn Ap Gwalchma

broke his leg playing a charity football match for benefit of his Squires Academy in Wessex.

(=) The Deindum moved Deimos and Phobos out of Mars orbit to use as a power source, capitalising upon an other-dimensional weak spot within Phobos. Winifred Bambera used her husband's bionodal travelling armour to take the reactivated Excalibur to Mars, where she met Bernice Summerfield, and found a chamber built for the sword by Merlin. Benny sheathed Excalibur there, enabling it to act as a gravitational anchor that drew Deimos and Phobos back into orbit. This also anchored the moons in the past, preventing their loss from ever happening. Merlin told Benny that Excalibur must remain on Mars for several million years at least.

c 2015 - "The Eye of Ashaya"[1583] -> The squat, blue-skinned Ashayanas lived in quiet devotion to their sun, which they regarded as a goddess, until the Vodirans harvested a massive diamond – the Eye of Ashaya – from the sun and thereby reduced its output. The Ashayan homeworld froze over, and the Ashayans who survived became the Vodirans' servants and thralls. The Eye of Ashaya became an energy-focusing device aboard the Excelsis, a Vodiran star-liner.

Lady Christina de Souza, now an accomplished interstellar thief, felt moved to aid the Ashayans. She encountered the eleventh Doctor, Amy and Rory as she hijacked the Excelsis and drove it into the Ashayan sun. The Excelsis' shields held as hydrogen deposits from the Ashaya Nebula were drawn toward the sun, increasing its ignition mass. The Ashayan homeworld was restored, and the Ashayans drove away their oppressors. De Souza departed to further explore the universe.

2015 - "Give Free or Die"[1584] -> Zzaganar, a form of living fiction, caused mayhem among Piccadilly Circus shoppers by tainting free comics, books and audio files with its essence. Stephen King endorsed the mesmeric work with: "I have seen the future of horror and its name is Zzaganar." The eleventh Doctor, Alice and Jones convinced ARC to slough off some of its skin, and transferred Zzaganar's consciousness into it. In its new body, Zzaganar was wracked with insecurity concerning its talent, prompting the Doctor to aid Zzaganar in becoming a Sci-Fi writer.

2015 - THE ELEVENTH DOCTOR YEAR ONE[1585] -> The eleventh Doctor, as accompanied by John Jones and ARC, brought Alice home to Hackney to catch up on her personal affairs. The Eternal Dogfight between the

1581 "A couple of years" before TW: Aliens Among Us 2.
1582 Dating Benny: Present Danger: "Excalibur of Mars" (Benny collection #14) - Benny says that she's in "the early twenty-first century, give or take". Bambera and Ancelyn are said to have been entrusted with Excalibur "decades ago" (at the end of Battlefield), but Bambera is still fit enough for active duty, Merlin is here presented as "a scruffy man in a long, raggedy afghan coat... Wearing an eye-patch, barely visible beneath a long, asymmetric fringe of red hair", loosely in accordance with the Battlefield novelisation.
1583 Dating "The Eye of Ashaya" (IDW Vol. 4 #5-6) - It's "a couple of years and a few galaxies over" since the Doctor picked up Amy and Rory in the earlier part of the story.
1584 Dating "Give Free or Die" (Titan Free Comic Book Day #1b) - The year is given, with the Doctor covering for the fact that he'd meant to land in Berlin during Hitler's last days.
1585 Dating The Eleventh Doctor Year One (Titan 11th Doc #1.7-1.8, "The Eternal Dogfight"/"The Infinite Astronaut") - The progression of events seems skewed, in that the Doctor, Jones and a caption all concur this is "2015", and yet Alice is just now getting around to deal with her pushy landlord, who insisted in The Eleventh Doctor Year One: "After Life" that she had to move out by August 2014. Alice mentions having met the Doctor "two months ago", probably referring to how long – from her perspective – she's been travelling with him.
1586 Dating "The Comfort of the Good" (Titan 11th Doc #14) - Alice claims, "This is London... 2015-ish by the look of it", but the recap says it's "2015".
1587 Dating Gallifrey VII: Intervention Earth (Gallifrey #7.0) - Rexx gives the year as "Local calendar 2015", the same year as the story's release.
1588 Dating P.R.O.B.E.: When to Die (P.R.O.B.E. film #5) - The story seems contemporary with its release in 2015. Georgette Ellison and Hazel Burrows here portray Patricia and Liz, taking over from Louise Jameson and the late Caroline John.
1589 Dating Worlds BF: Kronos Vad's History of Earth (Vol. 36,379) (Worlds BF #1.4) - As mentioned here and in Worlds BF: The Phantom Wreck, it's "a few months" after the entertainer Jack Oddwards disappeared "in 2014". Iris names books in the vein of Pride and Prejudice and Zombies (2009).
1590 Dating NAofBenny V2: The Vaults of Osiris/The Tears of Isis (NAofBenny #2.2, 2.4) - The blurb gives the year. The TARDIS instruments report that it's the "early twenty-first century".
1591 Dating Iris S5: Comeback of the Scorchies, Dark Side, Looking for a Friend (BF Iris #5.1-5.2, 5.8) - Iris says in Comeback of the Scorchies that it's "the year 2015 schillings and sixpence", and comments in Dark Side that it's "fifty years" after humans sent a man into space. Looking for a Friend gives no date, but the setting seems contemporary. Stella's Bar has a no-smoking policy; in the UK, a smoking ban started on 1st July, 2007.

Armstrons of the Great Wheel and the Ja'arrodic Federation moved into Earth's solar system, but their ambassadors informed humanity's leaders that only wished to slaughter one another, and would avoid Earth. Humankind regarded the battle in the night sky as a spectator sport.

Alice asserted the right to "seek and see" what lay beyond the Gate of Creation wormhole, triggering a cease-fire while she set out in a copy of the *Infinite* starship. By resisting the mesmeric effect of the reality beyond the wormhole, Alice reported back what she found – and thereby ended the Eternal Dogfight. The Amstrons and Ja'arrodic signed a peace treaty, even as the Doctor and his friends decided to confront SERVEYOUinc in its own headquarters in the future...

2015 - THE ELEVENTH DOCTOR YEAR ONE[1586] ->
The TARDIS had lost faith in the eleventh Doctor, and sought out the nearest "Time Lord" it could find: the SERVEYOUinc Talent Scout, who was disguised as the Doctor's mother. The Entity arrived with the eleventh Doctor, Alice, ARC and Jones, enabling the Doctor to apologise to his Ship. The TARDIS rejected the Talent Scout, and transported everyone involved to the future to deal with him...

> ### (=) 2015 - GALLIFREY VII: INTERVENTION EARTH[1587] ->
> Ace and the Time Lord Rexx visited an alternate timeline in which an anomalous black hole devastated Earth. On Rexx's recommendation, they collected the Hand of Omega and went to Greater Henge in 2,986 BC...

c 2015 - P.R.O.B.E.: WHEN TO DIE[1588] ->
Patricia Haggard, now a Minister, oversaw the Preternatural Research Bureau (P.R.O.B.E.). She was in a relationship with Liz Shaw. Austerity measures ended funding for Corporal Paul Reynish's longevity treatments, and P.R.O.B.E. was assigned to oversee his termination. Reynish went rogue as his metabolism broke down, threatening a tremendous release of energy, but Liz contained Reynish's demise within a force field. Afterward, Liz considered Patricia's suggestion that they retire and move to Spain.

c 2015 - WORLDS BF: KRONOS VAD'S HISTORY OF EARTH (VOL. 36,379)[1589] ->
Captain Turner opined that *Pride and Prejudice* didn't contain enough spunk, so Iris brought him to the Vandermeer family's bookshop to purchase something more to his liking – such as *Pride and Prejudice and Poltergeists*, *Wuthering Heights and Werewolves* or even *The Cranford Chainsaw Massacre*. She also insisted that the best adaptation of *Pride and Prejudice* was the one with Queen Latifah.

Jenni Marcel and Zack Hoffman, respectively the host and cameraman of *The World's Strangest Mysteries*, arrived at the bookshop to film a piece on Kronos Vad's *History of Earth* (Vol. 36,379), which had accurately predicted events from the Battle of Waterloo to 9-11 and beyond. Iris, Turner, Jenni and Zack discovered that the bookshop had been destroyed in the 1911 explosion that also killed Sherlock Holmes, and went in Iris' bus to help the renowned detective...

Iris and her friends returned to the restored bookshop, and read in Vad's chronology that a Gomagog temporal dreadnought would invade Earth via a wormhole at Tower Bridge on that very day. Turner angled Tower Bridge so that Iris could launch her bus off it and send the manifesting dreadnought into the Time Vortex, saving the planet.

2015 - NAofBENNY V2: THE VAULTS OF OSIRIS / THE TEARS OF ISIS[1590] ->
The TARDIS brought Ace and Benny to Egypt as followers of the Temple of Sutekh located the secondary Eye of Horus. The Osirian Isis was living in a vault in Switzerland. Benny retrieved the Eye, but was hurled down an Osirian space-time corridor to ancient Egypt, forcing Ace to follow in the Ship. Russell Courtland, a millionaire member of the Temple, housed an event at his country home to celebrate the foretold destruction of the world. The seventh Doctor relocated Courtland's entire estate to twenty-ninth century Earth as part of his master plan against Sutekh.

Andy the Bartender Joins Iris' Bus

c 2015 - IRIS S5: COMEBACK OF THE SCORCHIES / DARK SIDE / LOOKING FOR A FRIEND[1591] ->
In Margate, Iris and Captain Turner found that the Scorchies had taken over Brian Bonamy, a washed up singer and Iris' former lover. Bonamy refused to sing his hit single "Girl, You're My A-Side", which enabled the Scorchies to feed off the audience's disappointment and Bonamy's self-loathing. Iris sang mightily, and slipped an imperfection into her vocals that backlashed the audience's emotions and destroyed the Scorchies.

Afterward, Iris and Turner visited Iris' house of Pink Gables on the moon. The spirits there attempted to usurp the central disembodied intelligence trapped in the house, but Iris and Turner curtailed their mischief. The spirits went to the next plane of existence as Pink Gables exploded, and the intelligence departed into space – after reshaping the rubble into a new form for itself, which looked like a daddy longlegs made of bricks.

A lonesome Iris returned to Stella's bar from time to time, and drowned her sorrows over having lost her friendship with Panda. Andy the bartender's relationship with Ian had gone tits up, so he accepted Iris' invitation to become her new companion.

2015 - PROJECT: NIRVANA[1592] -> Derleth, an elder god of jealousy, fell to Earth and hosted itself in Truman Viner – the leader of a religious commune near Odessa. Persons mentally dominated by Derleth experienced feelings of intense love, peace and devotion, which quickly gave way to homicidal urges. Ukrainian authorities soon found that everyone in Viner's compound except Viner himself had torn themselves apart. Viner was apprehended, and the Forge arranged to transport him to one of its bases. As part of Project: Nirvana, it was hoped that Derleth clones could be dropped over enemy lines, causing enemy soldiers to fall prey to their thrall.

The seventh Doctor sent Lysandra Aristedes and Sally Morgan to intercept the train carrying Derleth through the Carpathian Mountains. Derleth jumped bodies and nested itself within a Department C4 agent accompanying the train: Sgt Aristedes, Lysandra's younger self. The Doctor's allies obtained a Truthsayer – a device used by lawkeepers from the Anurine Protectorate – from the younger Lysandra and used it to create a network of psionic barriers, imprisoning Derleth within her mind. The elder god would remain inside Lysandra, powerless, and die when she

eventually died. The trauma of sealing off Derleth wiped Lysandra's memories of these events.

Noobis

c 2015 (? Spring) - THE TENTH DOCTOR YEAR TWO[1593] -> The tenth Doctor returned Gabby and Cindy home to Brooklyn, and continued aiding Anubis in properly using the Circle of Transcendence. On his behalf, the Doctor and Cindy went to Phaester Osiris six billion years ago, but were first diverted to ancient Gallifrey.

They returned as Sutekh's mind was reborn in his son's body, even as his own body remained trapped in limbo. The combined "Anutekh" reorientated the Circle, and permitted his allies – defeated demigods cast out of our dimension, including the King Nocturne, a God of Ragnarok, the Destroyer, a dragon and a Death god – entrance to our reality. To stymie the Doctor from banishing him through the Circle, Anutekh plugged it with the bound Destroyer. Anutekh slaughtered his other allies when they turned upon him.

Still merged with the Hand of Sutekh, Dorothy Bell gave

1592 Dating *Project: Nirvana* (BF CC #7.3) - The back cover says, "The place is Eastern Europe. The year is 2015", and there's no reason to doubt this is the case. A Truthsayer formerly appeared in *Forty-Five*: "Casualties of War".

SALLY MORGAN AND LYSANDRA ARISTEDES: *House of Blue Fire*, which introduces Private Sally Morgan and has her become the seventh Doctor's companion, is very direct about its taking place in 2020 (the Doctor reiterates the year in *Black and White*). Meanwhile, Captain Lysandra Aristedes is recruited to aid the Doctor and Sally against the elder gods from a point no earlier than 2026 – the year of the Forge's destruction, after which Lysandra takes command of what remains of the group's governmental arm, Department C4 (*Project: Destiny*). So, Sally and Lysandra originate from the same decade, but roughly six years apart.

The more the Black TARDIS Trilogy (*Protect and Survive, Black and White, Gods and Monsters* and the related *Project: Nirvana*) progresses, however, the more Sally and Lysandra's background details and status become blurred together. *Project: Nirvana*, set in 2015, is especially tricky in this regard, when a highly advanced DNA scan notes the discrepancy that the Sally travelling with the Doctor is physically a "26-year-old woman" (a notion Sally doesn't argue with – although to be fair, she has bigger concerns at the time), even though her file claims she should be a 15-year-old orphan living with her grandfather. If Sally *was* 15 in 2015, then it follows that she was born in 2000, and she was only 20 in *House of Blue Fire*. Her rank of Private, certainly, seems more appropriate for a 20 year old than a 26 year old. All very good, but if the Sally

in *Project: Nirvana* is physically 26, then either A) she wasn't born in 2000 after all, B) the Forge's data on her contemporary self is blatantly wrong, for whatever reason, C) she's spent a whopping *six years* travelling in the TARDIS – which is deeply hard to believe, given *Black and White*'s claim that Lysandra joined the TARDIS after Sally had been there a mere three months, and there being no other evidence that either of them travel with the Doctor anywhere near that long, or D) her TARDIS adventures resulted in her being physically aged six years, in some event we're never told about. Try as one might, none of these solutions seem particularly credible.

Compounding the issue, *Gods and Monsters* – the final part of the Trilogy – has Lysandra comment to Sally that "our time" is 2026, and the time-hopping Sally state, after arriving near Swindon, that she "will be there" (i.e. *has* been there, in her history) for her Duke of Edinburgh's "in the early [20]20s". (For benefit of non-UK people, the Duke of Edinburgh's award is given out to participants, ages 14 to 24, who complete a series of leadership and community-minded activities.) Both statements, arguably, should be taken as generalisations.

Afterlife, which takes place in or around 2022, opens with the Doctor and Ace having dropped Sally and Lysandra "back in their own time, or near enough" in the aftermath of *Gods and Monsters*, and while that *should* indicate two separate trips to their native times, Sally speaks of Lysandra as if they're contemporaries. The intention of Matt Fitton, the writer of *Afterlife*, was that Sally loses a couple of years after disembarking the TARDIS and Lysandra ends up well in advance of her

her life to hurl Anutekh through the Circle, seemingly killing Sutekh. Anubis was reborn as an innocent named Noobis.

2015 (7th June) - "The Lunar Strangers"[1594] -> The cow-like inhabitants of Dryra had settled into a peaceful existence, but two of their number – Ravnok and Vartex – released a killer virus to provoke the population into action. Ravnok and Vartex subsequently buried a treasure on Earth's moon, but were then captured and sentenced to three thousand years in prison. They soon escaped, and returned to find that a Moon Village had been built over their treasure. The fifth Doctor, Tegan and Turlough caught Ravnok and Vartex red-hooved trying to sabotage the Moon Village's reactor. Commander Jackson shot Vartex, and Ravnok suffocated on the moon's surface. The Doctor revealled that the "treasure" was actually cheese – the currency on Dryra.

2015 (late June) - THE POWER OF THREE[1595] -> The United Nations officially judged the Shakri black cubes as being "provisionally safe". The artist Damien Hirst and the pseudonymous graffiti artist Banksy publicly renounced any connection to the cubes.

The eleventh Doctor popped over to Amy and Rory's house as they threw a party to celebrate their wedding anniversary. They accepted his invitation to celebrate the occasion at the Savoy in 1890, but consequently returned to the party having – from their perspective – been absent for seven weeks. The Doctor decided to lodge with Amy and Rory for a bit, and promised to be better behaved than his last stay-over.

Robotic "ravens of death" protected UNIT's HQ in the Tower of London.[1596]

The Year of the Slow Invasion Ends

2015 (July) - THE POWER OF THREE[1597] -> Contestants on *The Apprentice* were tasked with trying to sell the Shakri black cubes. Lord Sugar fired those who failed to make the grade.

The Shakri plan to curtail humanity advanced as the black cubes became active and made a complete assessment of humanity's biology and technology in forty-seven minutes. The government advised the public to immediately remove the cubes from their houses. The cubes initiated a countdown that ended with their emitting a signal that disrupted the electrical current of the human heart, inducing heart attacks in as much a third of the global population. Aided by Amy and Rory, the eleventh Doctor caused an energy backlash that destroyed the Shakri vessels. He also used the cubes to induce mass defibrillation across the world.

Brian Williams recognised that his son and Amy were having difficulty abandoning their lifestyle of jaunting through time and space, and encouraged them to go off with the Doctor while he stayed to water the plants...

Amy and Rory Williams are Lost to the Modern Day

Owing to an encounter with the Weeping Angels, Amy and Rory became trapped in New York City some fifty years before they were born. They remained in the past for the rest of their lives...[1598]

2015 (July or August) - P.S.[1599] -> Brian Williams was watering the plants when a New Yorker in his mid-60s

---

own time, so does mercenary work off the grid until she catches up with her native year. While this solution still leaves a few details unaddressed (namely, why the seventh Doctor doesn't/can't just take Lysandra back to where she belongs, and why she'd agree to being dislocated from their personal lives), it's as good a remedy as any.

1593 Dating *The Tenth Doctor Year Two* (Titan 10th Doc #2.13-2.17, "Old Girl") - The timeframe of *The Tenth Doctor Year Two* has now become very vague... Gabby's mother Maria mentions that her daughter seems different even though she's been "apprenticed" to the Doctor "for only a short time", meaning – weeks? A few months? The weather is sunny and there's dark leaves on the trees, which might suggest that it's the Spring after "Revolutions of Terror". Either way, there's no discussion of if Gabby and Cindy are still attending to their classes and jobs, or are refraining from such things to take a TARDIS Gap Year of sorts.

The Destroyer appeared in *Battlefield*, the Gods of

Ragnarok in *The Greatest Show in the Galaxy*, the King Nocturne in *The Tenth Doctor Year Two*: "The Jazz Monster". The Beast (*The Impossible Planet*) is also seen. The idea seems to be that these beings originate from outside the universe and time itself, so are typically banished if they're "killed". It's unclear if Sutekh is powerful enough to give them a final death.

1594 Dating "The Lunar Strangers" (*DWM* #215-217) - The date is given at a caption at the end of the story.

1595 Dating *The Power of Three* (X7.4) - The month is given. With all other signs suggesting that the cubes first manifested the previous July, Amy is either employing some bad math or generalizing because she's in a hurry when she says, "What's it been [since the cubes arrived], nine months?"

1596 *The Power of Three, The Day of the Doctor*.

1597 Dating *The Power of Three* (X7.4) - The month is given. Brian's log – which was on Day 67 in "October" – is now on Day 361.

1598 *The Angels Take Manhattan*

stopped by with a note from Rory to his father. The message explained that he and Amy were unable to ever come home again. Brian acclimated to the news and the fact that the New Yorker was Anthony Brian Williams, Amy and Rory's adopted son.

Kate Stewart's UNIT[1600]

2015 - UNIT S1: EXTINCTION[1601] -> Working to the directives of the Nestene Consciousness, Simon Devlin's FutureTech deployed a revolutionary 3D printer onto the market. Following a global launch, an estimated 70% of households and 50% of businesses owned such a device. The move coincided with an event the World Astronomical Society dubbed the most extensive meteor shower in living memory: the arrival to Earth of two hundred and eighty two Auton energy units. The majority of these networked through the 3D printers to FutureTech HQ, and created a Nestene Consciousness to oversee the conquest of Earth...

FutureTech's 3D printers simultaneously roared to life and produced legions of Auton mannequins. The Auton armies herded people into major population centres, intending to process humanity itself into a liquid polymer. Earth would become encased in plastic, a breeding ground for the Nestene. Officials declared Berlin, Paris, Los Angeles and a dozen other cities off-limits to the public,

even as London, New York and Tokyo were similarly besieged. Led by Kate Stewart, UNIT forces destroyed FutureTech HQ, which cancelled out the Nestene control signal. The Auton armies dissolved into petroleum.

Stewart authorized a cover story claiming the mayhem resulted from a catastrophic technology failure – a lie furthered by psychotropic drugs in the water supply. UNIT now possessed hologram-messaging technology, as well as the ability to alter memories. The latter technique had been used on UNIT staff for twenty years, resulting in those affected having a retro sense of fashion and a tendency to overspend on cinema tickets.

2015 (August) - UNIT S2: SHUTDOWN -> The Tower of London had been destroyed at least once before now, and secretly rebuilt by UNIT in six weeks using alien technology. The Ministry of Defence oversaw UNIT in the UK; the Secretary of State for Defence could remove Kate Stewart from her position. UNIT HQ in Geneva was located near the Palace of Nations. Cerberus Global Solutions, the largest independent military operation in the world, had numbers to rival NATO. In the Tower of London, a display case for the Saturnine Star – a jewel from Saturn, given to Brigadier Lethbridge-Stewart by an Andromedan ambassador – concealed a hidden passage out of the Jewel Room.

1599 Dating *P.S.* (Series 7 webcast) - Rory's letter says that it's "a week" after he and Amy last left in the TARDIS (in *The Power of Three*). The script says that Anthony is in his "mid 60s", but he's shown being adopted as a small child in 1956, suggesting he's a bit younger than that.
1600 Dating *UNIT S1: Extinction, UNIT S2: Shutdown, UNIT S3: Silenced, UNIT S4: Assembled, UNIT S5: Encounters* and *UNIT S6: Cyber-Reality* (BF new *UNIT* Series #1-6) - The Big Finish *UNIT* audios, which feature Jemma Redgrave and Ingrid Oliver respectively reprising their roles as Kate Stewart and Osgood, largely attempt to position themselves (as the blurb to Series 1 states) "between Kate's appearances in... *The Power of Three* and *The Day of the Doctor*." The same text tacitly weighs in on the UNIT Dating issue with: "UNIT will need to call on forty years of experience if it hopes to hold the line!"

The general impetus of the range attempts to place the *UNIT* audios within this gap (ending, at most, not long after it). At time of press, shortly after the release of Series 6, writer Matt Fitton said discussions were taking place to move UNIT into the twelfth Doctor era. That said, nothing in the stories mandates that Series 1-6 must play out before the Capaldi Doctor's time on Earth begins. The chief clue supporting a pre-*Day of the Doctor* dating is that there's no mention of Osgood's twin, who is created in that story – but then again, there's no mention of her in *Death in Heaven* either, when she's evidently off on assignment and nobody has cause to talk about it.

A few helpful markers exist, to help us pace out *UNIT* Series 1-6:
• *The Power of Three* ended in June [2015]. The *UNIT* audios really can't begin before this, as it's never suggested that Kate can simply phone up the Doctor at Amy and Rory's house to ask for help.
• A through-line between the first three series exists in that Auton-fire wounds Colonel Vikram Shindi at the end of Series 1, he's recovering and on surveillance duty when Series 3 opens, and seemingly back to normal in its fourth and final episode (*UNIT S3: Silenced: In Memory Alone*). Series 2, certainly, seems to unfold over days as opposed to weeks or months, and it's reasonable to think that Series 1 is the same.
• A UNIT officer tells Osgood in Series 2: "It's the middle of the Antarctic winter. The sun won't come up for another three weeks." As the continent's sunless period ends in September, it's probably August.
• Series 3 is a very odd duck, in that the Silents undermine the standing Prime Minister, who resigns and calls for an election "one month from now", that election then occurs amidst a crisis, necessitating a do-over election, and *In Memory Alone* happens "a fortnight" after said do-over. So, at least six weeks pass during Series 3, plus however long elapses between the first and second elections. (By law, a UK general election cannot occur less than twenty-five working days after the last one, with the biggest party positioning the date after that to its advantage if possible. At time of

UNIT outsourced three hundred research and development projects to select universities, and sent a hand-held Kamishi converter – a device capable of turning matter, even air, into energy – to King Henry's for study. One of the world's largest energy providers, Lyme Industries, copied the device. Lyme honed the technology at its Station Alpha base in Antarctica – if successful, it would profit by making all other energy industries redundant.

The Kamishi dispatched their warrior caste, the ninja-like Tengobushi, to recover their converter and murder all humans with knowledge of it. The Tengobushi destroyed Petronella Osgood's flat, and killed her college friend Jay Roy and General Grant Avary of UNIT senior command.

UNIT reallocated the converter to the Black Archive beneath the Tower of London, but the Kamishi stormed the locale via the District Line. Kate Stewart activated Operation Swordfish – an evacuation of UNIT personnel by taking a submarine out through a flooded Traitor's Gate – and allowed the Tengobushi to capture the converter. She then obliterated the Tower with an alien bomb.

Members of the highest Kamishi caste arrived in a mothership, having detected a Kamishi energy signature at Station Alpha. Kate and her allies destroyed the base, and convinced the Kamishi to leave if UNIT wiped the memories of the converter from most of the people involved. UNIT concealed the Tower of London's destruction with a hologram, then used alien tech to hyper-age stone and restore the structure.

The New Prime Minister Assassinated

2015 - UNIT S3: SILENCED[1602] **->** Osgood constructed a prototype universal translator, which did decently well with Sontaran and Axon, but struggled with Welsh.

The few Silents left on Earth laced UK marketing campaigns with their subliminal messages, to undermine the current Prime Minister and boost the candidacy of a businessman: Kenneth LeBlanc. The Prime Minister resigned amidst falling approval ratings, and called for a general election in a month. LeBlanc challenged the Prime Minister in her own district.

The Silents worked toward a global media event big enough to rival the moon landing, so they could overwhelmingly instruct humanity to not kill them on sight. To that end, they enthralled Captain Josh Carter of UNIT, and ordered him to assassinate both the outgoing Prime Minister and LeBlanc – who won – on Election Day. UNIT largely scuttled the Silents' grand scheme, but LeBlanc was still killed. The incoming Parliament re-ran the election.

The former Prime Minister narrowly regained power after the LeBlanc debacle. She had been back in office a fortnight when tensions ran high among the world governments, who nonetheless coordinated efforts behind a global communications upgrade. Aided by British Rocket Group, UNIT administrated the augmentation aboard the United Intelligence Space Platform. The Silents tried to expose many spy satellite networks, sparking a world war while they escaped aboard a passing Tellocni spaceship.

press, the only time that the result of a general election led to a quick second election was in 1974, and the timescale there was the first election was held in February, the second in October. Trying to synch the Series 3 general election/s and the real-world one, by the way, doesn't work, since the latter happened on 7th May, 2015 – so, before *The Power of Three* ends.)

• *UNIT S5: Invocation* happens at "Hall'oween".

• *UNIT S6: Cyber-Reality* happens prior to *Dark Water* – it's a Master/Cyberman story in which the Cybermen assault in *Doomsday* gets mentioned, but Missy's transformation of Earth's dead into a Cyber-army isn't. (Also, Osgood mentions her glee at having "survived" an encounter with the Master, unknowingly presaging Missy killing her / her twin in *Death in Heaven*.)

UNIT first encounters the Auctioneers in Series 5, and Series 6 has Osgood say UNIT has "almost caught up to them so many times in the last few months", and that an Auctioneers' detonator was found in a power station "last year". There's no mention of Christmas. It's hard to avoid thinking that a calendar flip has occurred by now, even if the twelfth Doctor era hasn't started in earnest.

We have a rough timeline, then... July or August for Series 1, August for Series 2, six weeks elapse in Series 3, Hall'oween comes and goes halfway through Series 5, and it's past the New Year when Series 6 begins.

That admittedly requires thinking that the do-over general election in Series 3 happened in a matter of days, perhaps weeks – a bonkers idea more implausible than all the rapid-fire invasions by Autons, Silents and Cybermen, strangely enough – but it's needed to keep the general shape of these stories.

The Haisman Timeline, by the way, goes with the flow, and presumes that the first four Big Finish UNIT series all happen in 2015.

1601 In Series 1, Kate tells a journalist: "No one believes in aliens, Ms. McGee" – an assertion that simply cannot be correct by now (see the When Do the General Public Accept the Existence of Aliens? sidebar). Moreover, the tradition in classic UNIT stories – that the public fails to realise that alien incursions have taken place – entailed comparatively small-scale affairs, nothing on par with the global Auton invasion seen here (bigger, surely, than even the invasions seen in *Army of Ghosts* and *The Stolen Earth*). That being the case, it seems highly unlikely that UNIT could hush this up, as Kate suggests, with some media spin and drugs in the water supply.

1602 Kate receives additional marksmanship training in Series 3 – a deliberate bridge between her being science-led in *The Power of Three*, and blowing away a Zygon with "five rounds rapid" (*The Zygon Inversion*).

Before leaving into space, the Silents destroyed UNIT's space platform with the Tellocni ship's weaponry. UNIT and their allies hacked an edited message from the Silents into coverage of the platform's destruction: "Humanity is its own master. It will lead itself. We leave this Earth to you. You are its masters. The human will is strong."

Erimem in the Modern Day[1603]

2015 (late Summer) - ERIMEM: THE LAST PHARAOH[1604] -> The Tomb of the Three Princes, the final resting place of Erimem's three brothers, was discovered in the Valley of the Kings. The relics found there – including a Death Mask intended for Erimem – were loaned to the London University of History and Antiquity. The followers of Ash-Ama-Teseth infiltrated the university, and believed that the blood of Erimem – thought to be the last descendant of the man who had imprisoned their master – could loose Ash-Ama-Teseth upon the world. The cult's time-active equipment drew Erimem to the university, but the presence of museum curator Ibrahim Hadmani, who was Erimem's nephew many generations removed, diverted her to the university's Egyptian Collection. Erimem remembered her time as pharaoh, but not what had occurred in her recent years.

A ball of temporal lightning transported Erimem, Hadmani and students Andrea Hansen, Tom Niven and Anna Whitaker back to the Battle of Actium. Whitaker died there, but the remainder of Erimem's party returned home. Erimem used her blood as the cult demanded... but as she was not actually the last of her line, the ritual sent Ash-Ama-Teseth forever hurtling into the outer darkness. Events conspired to kill off the remainder of the cult; the investigation into their disappearances delayed the start of term by a fortnight.

Erimem and her friends took possession of the Habitat, the hub of the cult's time-technology. which gave them the ability to travel in time and space. Using this, Erimem visited Cleopatra prior to her death.

1603 The internal chronology of the *Erimem* books devoutly corresponds to the passage of time in the real world, with each release calibrating its internal details to its year (and sometimes even month) of publication.
1604 Dating *Erimem: The Last Pharaoh* (*Erimem* novel #1) - The year is given (ch11), and later reiterated – per when the university debuted its death mask exhibit – in *Erimem: Churchill's Castle* (ch8). It's "late summer" (ch2), and the start of the new term (ch15).
1605 Dating *UNIT S4: Assembled* (BF new *UNIT* box set #4; *Call to Arms*, #4.1; *Tidal Wave*, #4.2; *Retrieval*; #4.3; *United*, #4.4) - The time of year isn't said, but UNIT's gambit with instigating cold weather makes Winter "come early".
Jo references meeting the eleventh Doctor (*SJA: Death of the Doctor* [2010]), and her tally of grandchildren – twelve in that story, with one on the way – has inched up to "thirteen or fourteen". It's been "years" since she, Benton and Yates caught up; their last meet-ups on record are Yates and Jo in 2010 (*Demon Quest: The Relics of Time*) and Yates and Benton at the Brigadier's funeral in 2011 (*Shroud of Sorrow*), which Jo might also have attended.
Kate remarks in *United* that the Silurians had "weeks" to filch secrets from Captain Burmaster (brainwashed in *Call to Arms*), so it's presumably that long between episodes one and two. The last three episodes, however, only take as long as the liberated hybrids require to swim to the UK. Benton suggests that *Call to Arms* happens on a Friday night. Pertaining to UNIT Dating, Benton says this adventure makes him feel "forty years younger"; Sgt Waring "missed his chance" with Anne Thompson "forty years ago".
Scafell Pike is the highest mountain in England. "Professor Klein" presumably refers to the second version of Elizabeth Klein (*UNIT: Dominion* et al); the character, born in 1945, must now be over 70.
1606 Dating *Erimem: The Beast of Stalingrad* (Erimem novel #2) - The month and year are given. It's been "five weeks" since *Erimem: The Last Pharaoh*.
1607 *Erimem: Angel of Mercy*. Andrea says it's still "2015" when they depart.
1608 Dating *UNIT S5: Encounters* (BF *UNIT* box set #5; *The Dalek Transaction*, #5.1; *Invocation*, #5.2; *The Sontaran Project*, #5.3; *False Negative*, #5.4) – The second story here, *Invocation*, takes place at "Hallo'ween".
It's natural to wonder if the parallel world in *False Negative* is the Inferno-Earth (hence why "our" Kate Stewart makes the obligatory joke about eyepatches), but this seems unlikely given there's no reference to the cataclysm in *Inferno*.
1609 Dating *The Eight Truths/Worldwide Web* (BF BBC7 #3.7-3.8) - The back cover says it's "London, 2015"; a news broadcast claims the story begins "21st October". The Doctor then spends "twenty-three days" healing from a dose of radioactive Polonium-210, but awakens for the story's end. Terra Nova might be a corollary of the British space program first seen in *The Ambassadors of Death*. The Terra Nova probe dispatched to Mercury is "following up" on the NASA probe sent to Sol's innermost planet on 3rd August, 2004.
The clear implication is that the Doctor makes the public forget all the events of this story, and (off screen, somehow) erases all media coverage of it. It's very unclear, however, how the Eightfold Truth could have distributed millions of Metebelis crystals to its members for an 18-year stretch prior to 2015 without anybody involved in the original Metebelis incident (Sarah Jane, Mike Yates, let alone the Doctor, etc.) noticing.
Lucie here appears on TV as an Eightfold Truth

c 2015 - UNIT S4: ASSEMBLED[1605] -> Officially, no Silurian activity had occurred in years. John Benton now owned the White Hart, a pub near Grasmere, and hosted a mini-reunion of UNIT operatives. Captain Mike Yates, Sgt Terry Waring and Corporal Anne Thompson joined him. Benton's wife, Margerys, was staying with her sister. Yates gifted Benton, who was scheduled for retirement, with a restored service revolver.

Grand Marshall Jastrok's Silurians, based under Scafell Pike, wiped out most of UNIT's Bravo Detail. Kate Stewart and Osgood regrouped at the White Hart – aided by UNIT's old guard, they forced Jastrok to feign defeat by destroying his base. Waring and Thompson died in the conflict, and the White Hart was heavily damaged.

Some time after, Stewart recruited Jo Jones (née Grant) to advise on a test run of Project Charybdis: a tide-turbine submarine, designed to provide mobile eco-friendly power. Jastrok usurped Charybdis and directed its bores to attack a Silurian base, to trick the moderate Silurians there into siding against humanity. Jo persuaded the Silurian scientist Kralix to take his people back into hibernation, but hybrid creatures that Kralix had developed escaped. Jastrok directed them toward the United Kingdom...

Stewart and Osgood went to a Silurian base in Greece, to obtain intel on the hybrids. With General Bambera in Peru, Colonel Mace in Japan, and Colonel Shindi and Professor Klein in Geneva, Stewart ceded command of UNIT to Yates, Jo and Benton. Politicians withdrew to safety as Jastrok captured the Houses of Parliament – the UK would become the First Silurian State, with Novus Siluria as its capital. Using alien science honed at the Lime Industries Weather Station, Stewart moved the Gulf Stream and instigated frigid weather. Hobbled by the cold, Jastrok's Silurians withdrew to hibernation shelters, including one beneath St James' Park. Stewart forcibly put Jastrok into hibernation beneath the Black Archive.

Silurian control devices enabled UNIT to redirect Jastrok's hybrids to different parts of the globe. Jo joined one team going to South America, to reunite with her husband Cliff. Yates departed, and Benton relocated some flying hybrids to the Highlands, then went on holiday.

2015 (October) - ERIMEM: THE BEAST OF STALINGRAD[1606] -> Erimem moved in with Ibrahim and his partner Helena, and enrolled at the University as a student, earning extra credit as Ibrahim's assistant. She and her friends studied the Habitat's database, which contained a comprehensive timeline of Erimem's trips throughout history. Isabella Zemanova, now age 95, returned the ring Erimem gave her in 1942. With the Habitat database indicating Erimem would visit Stalingrad in that year, Erimem, Andrea Hansen and Tom Niven went there and defeated the Drofen Horde.

Andy Hansen and Helena Hadmani went with Erimem to the future, and tangled with the gang leader Razor...[1607]

2015 (c 31st October) - UNIT S5: ENCOUNTERS[1608] -> Kate Stewart, Osgood and Colonel Shindi went undercover as British mercenaries in Central America, and dealt with a rogue Dalek that had fallen to Earth some fifty years previous.

The tests UNIT researcher Alice Donelly had performed on infrasound decades ago had included a Latin invocation, which now drew a malevolent force to Earth. On Hall'oween, the entity inflicted madness-inducing sound upon major cities until Osgood and Kate Stewart – thinking it best to follow the rules of demonology rather than science – completed the invocation, banishing the force after it had claimed Donelly.

Osgood's former mentor, Professor John Torrance, set up the Torrence Research Foundation to funnel research into alien genetics onto the black market, as managed by the off-world Auctioneers. UNIT busted up Torrance's operation – which was endeavouring to crack the science behind cloning Sontarans – and captured one of the Auctioneers' human agents, Christine Colley.

= One of the Auctioneers' caches contained an interdimensional travel capsule, which transported Osgood and Captain Josh Carter to a parallel world. They encountered amoral versions of the UNIT team, including their own counterparts – lovers who were plotting to assassinate this Britain's fascist leader, then replace him with his brother, another fascist. "Our" Osgood and Carter returned home and, to prevent a cataclysmic explosion, sent the travel capsule whistling into space-time with the alt-Osgood aboard, her fate unknown.

2015 (21st October to 13th November) - THE EIGHT TRUTHS / WORLDWIDE WEB[1609] -> Storms battered the Caribbean, and the President of Cuba blamed the problem on climate change.

Britain had spent £75 million on the Terra Nova space project, which had a tracking station in Buckinghamshire. A Terra Nova satellite sent to obtain water samples from Mercury went missing only two days after NASA lost contact with one of its solar probes. The eighth Doctor and Lucie aided authorities concerning the mystery. The Eightfold Truth's membership had increased fivefold in the last five years, and the group continued to advocate a self-help regimen of meditation using Metebelis crystals provided to its members. The organisation had converted the old BBC Television Centre into a residential block with lecture rooms.

The moon-sized stellar manipulator that had shadowed the TARDIS through the Vortex appeared near Earth, and began draining energy from the Sun. The Eightfold Truth hailed this as the "rebel sun" foretold of in its teachings, and the group's membership soared to two hundred forty-four million. Some Metebelis spiders arrived from the future, and pushed their plan to conquer a thousand worlds to fruition. The stellar manipulator's energy was directed into the millions of Metebelis crystals held by the Eightfold Truth members, creating a hive mind. Unstopped, it would generate a psychic pulse that would ripple outward at 170,000 times the speed of light, and compel legions of worlds to worship the spiders.

The spiders' Queen, facing dissension in her ranks, tried to possess her ally the Headhunter – who had an evolved resistance to psionics and reflected the Queen's power back at her, killing them both. The Doctor defeated the spiders – whose surviving members returned to Metebelis in the future – and used the crystal-web's power to make the public forget these events. He also considered how to erase the relevant media coverage.

The Doctor relocated the stellar manipulator to a remote part of the universe where it would never be found. No longer in the Headhunter's employ, Karen Coltrane left for parts unknown. The Doctor and Lucie departed to spend Christmas in Blackpool, 2008.

The Day of the Doctor: The Zygon Treaty, the War Doctor Regenerates, the Curator

lgtw - 2015 - THE DAY OF THE DOCTOR[1610] -> Ian Chesterton was now the Chairman of the Governors at Coal Hill Secondary School. W. Coburn served as headmaster. Clara Oswald was now a teacher at Coal Hill, but eagerly accepted the eleventh Doctor's invitation that they spend a week in ancient Mesopotamia, followed by a trip to Mars in the future and cocktails on the moon.

Before they could do so, Kate Stewart summoned the Doctor to obtain his help. A cover story pertaining to illusionist Derren Brown was crafted when an overzealous UNIT helicopter nabbed the TARDIS and deposited it in front of the National Gallery. Kate presented the Doctor with Queen Elizabeth I's credentials – a Time Lord painting variously named *No More* or *Gallifrey Falls* – to confirm instructions that he be contacted following any disturbance in the clandestine Under Gallery. Soon after, the Doctor traveled down one of the Moment's time portals to 1562.

Clara learned that the Zygons in stasis in the Under Gallery's paintings had revived and replaced many of the UNIT staff, including Kate. The Zygons gained access to UNIT's Black Archive – and the formidable weaponry within – before Clara escaped to 1562 using a vortex manipulator kept in the Archive, as previously owned by Captain Jack Harkness.

The eleventh Doctor, the tenth Doctor, the War Doctor and Clara emerged from stasis within *No More/Gallifrey Falls*, where they had been held since 1562. The Doctors brokered peace between the shapechanged Zygons and their human counterparts by using UNIT's memory scrubbers to everyone forget who was who. With Clara, the Doctors returned to the final day of the Last Great Time War, and resolved the matter of Gallifrey's destruction...

Afterwards, the Doctors and Clara enjoyed some tea

---

spokesperson, but if the Doctor indeed erases all record of this, it needn't further complicate her media appearance in *Hothouse* circa 2045.

1610 Dating *The Day of the Doctor* (X7.15) - The story follows on from the eleventh Doctor first meeting Kate Stewart in *The Power of Three*, and most likely (given that Series 8 happens in 2016) occurs the same year as that story. The season appears to be autumn – everyone is wearing coats or scarves of some description, but there's no snow. "W. Coburn" is probably intended as a blend of *Doctor Who's* first scriptwriter and director, respectively Anthony Coburn and Waris Hussein.

1611 *The Zygon Invasion/The Zygon Inversion*, after *The Day of the Doctor*.

1612 "Two years" before *The Zygon Invasion*.

1613 Dating *6thLA: The End of the Line* (*The Sixth Doctor – The Last Adventure* #1) - It's a "foggy December". The story appears contemporary, including mention of nuclear bombs and taking the 555 to work.

1614 Dating *Big Bang Generation* (NSA #59) - The exact day is named (chs. 9, 11).

1615 Dating *The Time of the Doctor* (X7.16) - Clara serves Christmas dinner to her family; it's presumably Christmas Day, although they're watching the *Strictly Come Dancing Christmas Special*, which isn't always broadcast on 25th December.

1616 *Erimem: "In Search of Doctor X"*

1617 *Kill the Moon*

1618 *FP: Erasing Sherlock* and its prologue in *FP: Warring States*. The year isn't specified, but Gillian is from the "twenty-first century", and stops to wonder how the 2018 embargo is going to affect the course of her academic studies.

1619 Stories in 2016 include Series 8, the sequences in *The Pilot* up through Christmas, *Class* (if you favour the dates given on screen), *Last Christmas* and (best guess) *The Return of Doctor Mysterio*.

1620 *The Angel of Scutari*

1621 *LIVE 34*

1622 *Heritage*. In terms of *Who* history, *Trading Futures* has the earliest mention of humans cloning humans.

1623 *Maker of Demons*. La Tour d'Argent, a historic restaurant in Paris, very dubiously claims to have been founded in 1582.

at the National Gallery before going their separate ways. The War Doctor's body was wearing a bit thin, and he regenerated into the Doctor who would meet Rose Tyler in 2005.

A Curator with a familiar face informed the eleventh Doctor that the actual title of the Gallifreyan painting – which the Curator had acquired in "remarkable circumstances" – was *Gallifrey Falls No More*, meaning that Gallifrey had survived but was now lost in another dimension.

Per the terms of the human/Zygon treaty, twenty million Zygons – the entire hatchery – were born on Earth, and permanently adopted the form of the nearest available humans. UNIT agent Petronella Osgood and her Zygon doppelganger protected the terms of the treaty as part of Operation Double. The Doctor left the Osgood Boxes inside the Black Archive, as a lure for any human or Zygon who sought to usurp the treaty.[1611] A Zygon splinter group infiltrated Truth or Consequences, a town in New Mexico.[1612]

c 2015 (December) - 6thLA: THE END OF THE LINE[1613] ->
The railway station Kettering Junction also served as a dimensional interchange: one of the nexus points hardwired into the Parallel Sect's travel-web. The Master sought to usurp the web and dominate all realities, but realised that engaging its control-protocols would prove fatal. He tried to force the sixth Doctor, who was accompanied by Constance, into performing this task, but the Doctor instead restored the nexus point to its default settings. The Valeyard secretly aided the Doctor's efforts, needing the Doctor alive as part of his master plan.

(=) 2015 (22nd December) - BIG BANG GENERATION[1614] ->
The Pyramid Eternia was pulled through time by its lodestone, which had become a museum piece in Sydney, Australia. The twelfth Doctor, Bernice Summerfield, Peter Summerfield, Jack and Ruth were similarly drawn to this era, and worked to contain the situation as the Pyramid materialised beside the Harbour Bridge, and its energies triggered a massive earthquake and lava flow. The Doctor persuaded the Ancients of the Universe to scrub the timeline of the consequences of their losing the lodestone circa 36,000 BC. He remained the only mortal to remember these events.

The Eleventh Doctor's Interaction with the Modern Day Ends

2015 (December) - THE TIME OF THE DOCTOR[1615]
-> Clara asked the eleventh Doctor to share Christmas dinner with her father, grandmother and step-mother Linda, and that he pose as the "boyfriend" she'd invented for her family's benefit. The ruse was foiled because the Doctor had stripped off to meet with the Papal Mainframe; only Clara saw him as clothed by benefit of a hologram projected directly into her mind. The Doctor realised that the planet he'd visited in the future was designated "Gallifrey", and Clara accompanied him to what was actually the planet Trenzalore to investigate...

Stymied on Trenzalore, the Doctor pre-programmed the TARDIS to send Clara back home, then return for him. Clara refused to stay put and inserted her key into the TARDIS lock just as the Ship dematerialised, taking her with it...

The Doctor again tricked Clara into returning home, this time successfully. She informed her family that she'd broken up with her "boyfriend", but left when Tasha Lam piloted the TARDIS to this time, as she didn't want the Doctor to die alone...

At Christmas 2015, Erimem popped back to 1964 to shop for a now-rare copy of *Doctor X in an Amazing Adventure in Space*.[1616] **The Coal Hill secretary came to despise Clara, thinking she gave her a packet of TENA Lady for Secret Santa.**[1617]

wih - Gillian Rose Petra released her Master's thesis, *The Magic Feather Duster: A Brief History of Domestic Service in Victoria's England*, and thereby caught the attention of corporate wizard Jimmy Moriarty. He suggested they use his time technology to send Gillian back to the 1880s, so she could study the seminal detective Sherlock Holmes for her doctoral thesis. She was barred from publishing its results until 2018. Gillian agreed and went into the past, returning after the eruption of Krakatoa.[1618]

2016[1619]

Hex did a school project about the Crimean War and Florence Nightingale, which motivated him to mention an interest in nursing when a career officer visited that week.[1620] Hex's father worked on the docks, and thought his job was safe until a strike was held in support of some men who'd been sacked. The disagreement dragged on for years, and Hex's father finally accepted redundancy. Hex's grandmother suggested that he should find an occupation that would always be in demand; when Hex left school, he figured that medicine was a pretty safe bet.[1621]

The earliest human clones were mindless, bred for use as perishable stunt doubles in motion pictures. Humanity became uneasy with the morality of this and ended the practice. Cloning fell into disuse, but scientists periodically revived the art.[1622] The Doctor cooked alongside the greatest chefs in Europe at La Tour d'Argent.[1623] Alice Parsons of Shoreditch died in July.[1624]

The Funeral of John Jones; the Sapling Joins the TARDIS

? 2016 - THE ELEVENTH DOCTOR YEAR THREE[1625]

-> John Jones, formerly the eleventh Doctor's companion, had become the greatest pop star in the universe, and travelled about in his own spaceship. Jones made a game of leaving clues for the eleventh Doctor on his records' sleeve notes, and had just one copy struck of his last album, *Whitestar*. The Doctor and Alice retrieved *Whitestar* from the human colony Brixit-247 in the future, and thereby found the coordinates of Jones' funeral. The late Jones had left the travellers yet another message, which directed them to a forest planet...

The most adept of the Silents, the Scream, caused such forgetfulness that even its own people failed to acknowledge its existence. The Scream had found the Planting – a forest that overcame entire worlds, like a virus – and tried to use the Doctor and Alice's memories as raw fuel for transferring its mind into the Planting's Sapling. The Scream hoped to seed another world, and never be out of sight or remembrance.

A time-hopping version of Jones helped the Doctor and Alice escape. Jones left for further adventures, while the Doctor and Alice accepted the Sapling aboard the TARDIS, knowing the Scream would probably build a time machine off the Doctor's memories and pursue them.

c 2016 - TRADING FUTURES[1626]

-> There were no rogue states remaining and the world's secret services kept almost every square inch of the planet electronically monitored. The only two remaining superpowers – indeed, the only two remaining sovereign powers – were the United States and the Eurozone, who dominated the world between them. But they were on the brink of war, as both were trying to extend their sphere of influence into

---

1624 The year before *Class: The Stone House*.

1625 Dating *The Eleventh Doctor Year Three* (Titan 11th Doc #3.1, "Remembrance") – Date unknown, but Jones has always been a stand-in for David Bowie, who died 10th January, 2016. Jones' last album is *Whitestar*, Bowie's was *Blackstar*. It's not said if events on the forest world take place in a different time zone, or if Jones can travel in time as well as space (perhaps he can, since the Doctor calls him on – as he calls it – his "timestream blower").

1626 Dating *Trading Futures* (EDA #55) - The year is not specified beyond "the early decades of the twenty-first century" on the back cover, but Mather says his encounter with the Doctor in *Father Time*, which occurred in 1989, was "more than twenty years ago". Malady Chang, a secret agent, seems to place it nearer thirty years, as she thinks the Doctor "would have been about ten at the time", and he looks like he's in his "early forties". People who were teenagers in the nineties are now "pushing pensionable age" (p8) and Anji's generation are the parents of teenagers. Learman from *The Time of the Daleks* is referred to (p107), as are the Zones from *The Enemy of the World*. It's not clear whether World War Four has been averted – US and EZ forces are fighting at the end of the book, and it's only *hoped* that the revelation of Baskerville's plan will end it.

WORLD WARS: The First and Second world wars occur much as we know them. There are fears of a Third World War in the UNIT era. It occurs some time between Anji joining the TARDIS crew (2000) and *Trading Futures* (c.2016) – whether the events of the episode *World War Three* qualify is unclear. World War IV was mentioned in *The Also People* and *Frostfire*, but no details are given. In *Christmas on a Rational Planet*, it's said that people danced in the ashes of Reykjavik during World War IV. The Doctor says he saw World War V in *The Unquiet Dead*. *Borrowed Time* references mutant crabs active in the 4900s; these were engineered to eat the marine vessels used in World War V. World War VI is averted in the year 5000, according to *The Talons of Weng-Chiang*.

1627 Dating *TW: Forgotten Lives* and *TW: More Than This* (BF *TW* #1.3, 1.6) - The audios seem roughly contemporary with their respective releases in November 2015 and February 2016, but there's conflicting information as to *exactly* when they occur. The blurb to *Forgotten Lives* says it's been "four years since the Miracle" (i.e. *TW: Miracle Day*, set in 2011)... but within the fiction, Rhys says there's been no sign of Jack in "five" years, and Gwen is very insistent to Jack that it's been "Five years. *Five*," since they last saw one another. Against that, Gwen laments in *More Than This* that it's only taken "four years" for the name "Torchwood" to fade into obscurity (presumably she's referring to *TW: Miracle Day*, although the group's public profile surely ended in 2009, in *TW: Children of Earth*). "Ten years" have passed since Roger Pugh's wife died simultaneously to *TW: Day One* [2007].

In *Forgotten Lives*, Jack claims to have lost count of his age somewhere around the late 2000s, although it's unclear if he's counting the couple of millennia he spent buried underground (*TW: Exit Wounds*).

1628 Dating *TW: Ghost Mission* (BF *TW* #2.3) - Norton Folgate names the year: "[It's] 2016, yes?" Andy says that Gwen joined Torchwood "almost ten years ago" (in 2006; *TW: Everything Changes*), and that Cardiff incurred heavy damage "eight years ago" (in 2008; *Exit Wounds*).

1629 Dating *TW: "World Without End"/"Station Zero"* (Titan *TW* #1.1-1.4, 2.1-2.4) - A caption says it's "the present day"; this run of *Torchwood* comics were published 2016-2017. The narrator mentions during an ambush: "Ninjas on flying jetskis. Must be Tuesday", and the action continues over a day or two. It's currently "warm weather". Gwen hasn't seen Hollis since *TW: Exodus Code* [2012], which introduced the *Ice Maiden* and its crew. She's cited as acting head of Torchwood Cardiff (a role she de facto adopted in *TW: Forgotten Lives*).

power vacuums in North Africa and the Middle East. "Peacekeepers" from both sides took up positions.

Elsewhere in the world, Eurozone RealWar tanks were covertly sent into action against American corporate interests. The situation was a tinderbox that could have lead to World War Four. The United Kingdom was now part of the Eurozone and the semi-elected British President Minister was bound by the Articles of European Zoning, despite polls showing 84% of the British population taking the American side in the dispute. Britain secretly maintained its own intelligence service, run by the ancient Jonah Cosgrove. The American President was Felix Mather, former CIA astronaut.

There was a European national soccer team, and games were divided into eighths to fit more adverts in. Rhinos only existed in clonetivity. Human cloning was possible, but very expensive. Hypersonic jets could cross the world in a few hours. Nuclear bombs were used in civil engineering. There was a North China and a New Kabul. Kurdistan was a country in its own right, in a region blighted by civil wars. British Airways had gone bankrupt, the BBC was replaced by the EZBC. More than one channel tunnel was operating.

The international flow of money was through the IFEC computer system. Arms dealer Baskerville launched an ambitious con job to take control of it. He posed as a time traveller from ten thousand years in the future, and offered Cosgrove a time machine in return for access to the powerful EZ ULTRA computer. The CIA got wind of the plan, as did Sabbath's Time Agents; the eighth Doctor, Anji and Fitz; and the rhino-like alien Onihrs. The Doctor and his companions uncovered Baskerville's plan just as shootings in Tripoli triggered a potential world war.

Gwen Cooper and Rhys Williams Decide to Rebuild Torchwood Cardiff

c 2016 - TW: FORGOTTEN LIVES / MORE THAN THIS[1627] **->** The Evolved built a utopian society via their "gift" of swapping bodies; as any member of the Evolved could be high-class one day, low-class the next, all of the Evolved were treated well. Captain Jack communed with the Evolved – as they had resisted the Committee – and agreed to a limited body-swapping experiment at the Bryn Offa Nursing Home in North Wales. However, the Evolved tried to force their "gift" upon humankind. They trapped Jack's mind in a 93-year-old, Mr Griffith, while his body remained stuck on Peridas 4, a world in Omega Centauri.

Gwen Cooper and Rhys Williams came out of retirement to help Jack, but the Evolved also stole Rhys' mind and that of his daughter Arwyn. Jack traded his mind, with its "thousands of years of traveling" experience, to the Evolved for the release of their hostages. Gwen and Rhys agreed that the best way to safeguard their daughter was to

protect the whole of Earth, and decided to call in some favors to restart Torchwood...

Gwen tried to convince Roger Pugh, a Cardiff city planner, to arrange clearances for a new Torchwood HQ by showing him what a normal day for her entailed. Pugh watched as Gwen beheaded an alien Baratavik, and bucketed a liquid being from the planet Phibos, who was disguised as a piece of modern art.

The Rift became sensitive to outside stimulants, and its Cardiff end was no longer fixed. Pugh saw the universe in its full majesty while helping Gwen to close a Rift portal. He better came to terms with the death of his wife a decade previous, and expedited Gwen's request for a new HQ.

2016 - TW: GHOST MISSION[1628] **->** Norton Folgate, a Torchwood Assessor appearing as a soft-light projection from 1953, observed Sgt Andy Davidson as he auditioned for Torchwood. Andy shut down an illicit alien clone bank, and concluded that it owed to some opportunistic Welsh blokes who were manufacturing disposable labour for a construction company, Glen Star Developments. Folgate reported the successful retrieval of the Bad Penny from the clone bank to a group of old men at a care home on Cathedral Road: human vehicles for the Committee members. Andy was unsure of Folgate's allegiances, but wound up on a date with Jane, a woman he'd had his eye on.

Torchwood *Ice Maiden*

c 2016 - TW: "World Without End" / TW: "Station Zero"[1629] **->** Captain Jack had formed a new Torchwood branch operating from aboard the *Ice Maiden*, a survey ship retrofitted with alien technology. The vessel was equipped with a new Hub, a chameleon circuit, a vortex manipulator, and a hard-light AI patterned after Mary Shelley. The crew included Dana Macleish, ship's captain; Vlad, an ex-con man; and Hollis – a weapons specialist, chef and Jack's occasional bedmate.

The Navigators – human-Vervoid hybrids from the future, hoping to avenge themselves upon humanity – linked their ship, the Opsolarium, to a world-bursting seed at a Committee base beneath the Arctic Circle. Despite the Committee attacking them with ninjas on jetskis, Jack's Torchwood team and Gwen Cooper halted the Navigators' operation. Nonetheless, major volcanic eruptions occurred in Santorini, the Cascade Mountains, Japan, and Victoria Bay and Arthur's Seat in Scotland.

Lady Karina, secretly an ex-Time Agent, became the second wife of Sir James Sterling III: the head of Torchwood House. Karina coerced Captain John Hart into stealing an Astrolabe from Sterling's care, hoping to trade it to the Slitheen for technological assistance with her counterfeit TARDIS. Jack retained the Astrolabe, and Hart escaped in Karina's Ship.

2016 - AND YOU WILL OBEY ME[1630] -> An agent of the Transhuman Sisters of the Unholy Protocols found the cadaverous Master's TARDIS in Upper Hexford, and accidentally reactivated the Ship after a 32-year slumber. The Master failed to reclaim his scattered symbiotic nuclei, but escaped after endowing his essence in the body of Mikey, his former minion, which began to decay once more...

c 2016 - VAMPIRE OF THE MIND[1631] -> The bald Master instigated a scheme so transparent, so obvious, and with so many clues, the Doctor could not help but blunder into his trap. The sixth Doctor accordingly went to the South Coast of England to probe the affairs of the Dominus (Latin for "Master") Institute and its CEO, Sir Andrew Gobernar (Spanish for "to govern"). The Master wanted to repair his amnesia with the Doctor's own memories, as syphoned away by a captive Mind Leech, but the Doctor conspired with the Mind Leech to turn on their mutual

foe. After killing the Mind Leech, the Master escaped... but not before his future self's agent placed a tracking device aboard his TARDIS.

2016 - 2NDD V1: THE STORY OF EXTINCTION[1632] -> The seventh Doctor pocketed the parchment Victoria Waterfield owned that held an alien Story-form, and passed her in the street with a "Good afternoon, Miss Waterfield". Failing to recognise her old friend, Victoria discovered he'd left a letter to her that Jamie had written, after the Doctor had taught him how to read.

2016 - DC 3: THE EIGHTH PIECE / THE DOOMSDAY CHRONOMETER[1633] -> The eighth Doctor left Helen to search Rome for a Doomsday Chronometer piece, then went with Liv Chenka to continue the hunt in two other time-zones. Though stymied for six centuries, the Clocksmith had now reassembled seven of the

---

1630 Dating *And You Will Obey Me* (BF #211) - The fifth Doctor reads the year off a gravestone. It's "32 years" after *The Awakening* [1984]. The blurb says the Master is wanted for crimes "across five galaxies", the story itself says it's "the Seven Galaxies".

1631 Dating *Vampire of the Mind* (BF #212) - The story seems contemporary, with mention of the internet and Bluetooth. The Master was incarcerated in the UNIT Era "all those decades ago", and here seems to base himself on the island fortress seen in *The Sea Devils*. The Doctor's friend, Dr Heather Threadstone, proposes a means of improving the speed of micro-monolithic circuits (*The Invasion*). *The Two Masters* explains the Master's memory gaps.

1632 Dating *2ndD V1: The Story of Extinction* (BF CC #10.2) - The script notes that the framing sequences happen in the "present day". Victoria, it says, is currently "living in 2016 after settling down in 1968" – the latter year denoting when *Fury from the Deep* was broadcast. (The script erroneously claims, however, that Victoria is "a Victorian orphan from 1867"; she's actually from 1866.) Taking the "2016" date at face value, *The Story of Extinction* takes place about four years before Victoria's appearance in *Power Play* [c.2020].

The framing scenes are predicated on the second, third, fourth, fifth and sixth Doctors having had no contact with Victoria after she left the TARDIS – which ignores her having been reunited with the second Doctor prior to his Earth exile (see the Season 6B sidebar), and her meeting the third Doctor (and the fourth, it seems) in the epilogue to the novel version of *Downtime*. That, or Doctors three through six were so scatterbrained, they forgot about the potentially deadly parchment in Victoria's possession.

1633 Dating *DC 3: The Eighth Piece* and *DC 3: The Doomsday Chronometer* (BF DC #3.2 and 3.3) - The year is given.

1634 Dating *Doctor Who* Series 8 and *Last Christmas* (X9.0) - Series 8 follows on from Clara's family meal at Christmas 2015 (*The Time of the Doctor*) and stretches into the following year. *Into the Dalek* opens "three weeks" after the Doctor dropped Clara back on Earth and stepped out for coffee (*Deep Breath*), and sees Clara meet Danny – the "new fella, maths" – for the first time, presumably at the start of the term. *The Caretaker* entails parent-teacher night at Coal Hill, and might represent the term's halfway point.

Danny later comments in *In the Forest of the Night* that it's been "months" – or so he believed – since Clara last saw the Doctor in *Mummy on the Orient Express*, which suggests that the time of year has moved on to summer or autumn. Given that about half the bystanders seen in *Dark Water* and *Death in Heaven* are wearing jackets (amidst bright sun with lots of birdsong; Kate Stewart comments that it's a "lovely day"), and that *everyone* is wearing such things in the epilogue set four weeks later, it's probably the latter. *Last Christmas* follows on from that, at Christmastime.

In *In the Forest of the Night*, the Doctor specifies the year as "2016".

1635 The background to Series 8, as given in *Dark Water/Death in Heaven*.

1636 *Robot of Sherwood*

1637 *Lights Out*, playing off the end of *Deep Breath* and the start of *Into the Dalek*.

1638 Dating *Into the Dalek* (X8.2) - "Three weeks" have passed since the Doctor stepped out for coffee in *Deep Breath*.

1639 *Robot of Sherwood*

1640 Dating "A Matter of Life and Death" (Titan 8th Doc #1-5) - The mini-series saw print in late 2015 to early 2016, and Josie generalizes that it's "21st century Wales". The twelfth and eighth Doctors separately confirm that it's "February". In the eighth Doctor's lifetime,

Chronometer's nine pieces. Once assembled, the Chronometer would measure the time of the Apocalypse – and, in accordance with Heisenberg, make it manifest.

River Song and Helen toured history to investigate the Clocksmith's Revelation Sect. Upon their return, the Clocksmith acquired from them the eighth and ninth pieces. River aided Liv in the fifteenth-century, then brought her to this time-zone.

The Doctor, River, Helen, Liv, the Eight, and Risolva, the Queen of the Solvers, combined forces against the Clocksmith. The villain fatally wounded the Eight, but was then torn apart by Risolva's Solvers. Risolva pledged that her Solvers would turn the location of the Chronometer pieces into such a puzzle, nobody would ever find them.

As the Clocksmith's base exploded, the Doctor and River evacuated in the Clocksmith's TARDIS, and used its Fast Return Switch to go back to Tudor England. The Eight regenerated into the Nine, whom Liv and Helen mistook for a reborn Doctor. He took Liv and Helen in the Doctor's TARDIS to raid the archives on Gallifrey...

lgtw - c 2016 - UNIT: CYBER-REALITY -> One strain of Cybermen in a parallel reality established battery farms on conquered worlds, using their denizens as living energy sources. Having dominated 48% of their home universe, the alt-Cybermen seeded other dimensions with VR technology – as bait to help identify realms with sentient life. The Auctioneers adapted one such seed unit, to profit from first-person shooter games and VR applications. UNIT's clashes with the Auctioneers caused them to obtain a seed unit, which Osgood, Colonel Shindi and Lt. Sam Bishop used to virtually reconnoiter the alt-Cybermen's universe...

... triggering an invasion of our reality by the alt-Cybermen. Cyber-conversion units were established in the United States, Japan, South America, Paris, Munich, Moscow and London. As UNIT reeled to contain the situation, the War Master touched down, requiring parts to repair his wounded TARDIS. With his own survival at stake, the War Master tapped into realities where the alt-Cybermen had met defeat and poisoned their energy supply, killing them en masse. Afterward, he returned to the fray of the Last Great Time War.

Mostly for kicks, the War Master eliminated the Auctioneers and their largest shareholder, Julia Hartley-Price. UNIT laid claim to the Auctioneers' acquisitions, as hidden in the White House Gallery.

Doctor Who Series 8

The Twelfth Doctor, Clara Oswald and Danny Pink at Coal Hill[1634]

The Master returned as a female, the Mistress ("Missy"), and secretly founded the 3W Institute to front the belief that the dead remained conscious. 3W ostensibly devoted itself to creating a suitable "afterlife" for dead minds, all so Missy could acquire resources from the super-rich, and further her plan to create an army of Cybermen from humanity's dead. Missy uploaded the minds of the dead into a Matrix dataslice, and through this communed with people who died while encountering the Doctor. They believed they had passed on to the Underworld, a.k.a. the Nethersphere and the Promised Land, which manifested as a vast city on the inside curve of a giant sphere. Missy also manipulated the Doctor and Clara into remaining together, knowing that Clara would one day ask the Doctor for the impossible: to bring a dead person close to her back to life...[1635]

Clara took her Year Seven for after school Tae Kwon Do.[1636]

2016 - DEEP BREATH -> Missy welcomed the Half-Face Man as he awoke in the Nethersphere. Meanwhile, the twelfth Doctor and Clara arrived in Glasgow from Victorian times, and stepped out for coffee...

The Doctor slipped away to buy Clara coffee from the Intergalactic Roasting Station in the future, and investigated a series of murders there.[1637]

2016 - INTO THE DALEK[1638] -> Clara Oswald met the new maths teacher at Coal Hill, Danny Pink, and asked him out for a drink. The Doctor returned bearing coffee, only three weeks after he'd left for it, and asked Clara to help deal with a difficulty aboard the medical frigate *Aristotle* in the future. He returned Clara home the same afternoon that she left, and she went out on her date with Danny. Gretchen Alison Carlisle, who had been killed during the *Aristotle* incident, awoke in the Nethersphere to find Missy serving her tea.

The Doctor capitulated to Clara's request that they visit Robin Hood in Sherwood Forest.[1639]

Josie Joins the TARDIS

c 2016 (February, Sunday lunchtime) - "A Matter of Life and Death"[1640] -> The twelfth Doctor and Clara deposited the portrait of Lady Josephine, as acquired in the future, in a house the Doctor owned in twenty-first-century Wales. The animae particles in the portrait brought Josephine's likeness to life – as "Josie", she made paintings of races including Ice Warriors, Krotons and the Witherkin: living starlight creatures that formed bodies out of asteroid fragments. The eighth Doctor stopped at home to find his copy of *Jane Eyre*, but the TARDIS' arrival catalysed the animae particles in Josie's paintings, and the aliens she depicted came to life. Josie painted the Doctor, and his paint-self returned the creatures to their works.

The eighth Doctor found the twelfth Doctor's list of space/time coordinates, and went with Josie to those locales. They returned after the Doctor had learned of Josie's true nature, but he continued to accept her as a travelling companion.

The eighth Doctor and Josie aided various Doctors and companions against a void consuming all of reality.[1641]

2016 - LISTEN[1642] **->** Clara's first formal date with Danny went badly, and she aided the Doctor in his quest to prove the existence of creatures who had evolved "perfect hiding". He speculated that every human had experienced the same nightmare of beings in the shadows under the bed, and linked Clara to the TARDIS' telepathic circuits to identify when she'd had that very dream. Distracted by thoughts of Danny, Clara accidentally directed the TARDIS back to his childhood in the mid-90s...

Upon her return, Clara's attempt to resume her date with Danny again went awry. A spacesuit-wearing Colonel Orson Pink, collected by the Doctor from the end of time, summoned Clara back to the TARDIS. The Ship took the three of them back to the end of the universe to prove or disprove the Doctor's theory...

2016 - TIME HEIST[1643] **->** Just before Clara's second date with Danny, the Doctor tempted her with a trip to the Satanic Nebula, the lagoon of lost stars or Brighton. An aged Madame Karabraxos phoned to ask for help with one of her life's regrets, and so the Doctor and Clara went to the Bank of Karabraxos in the future. They returned in time for Clara to make her date.

2016 - "Four Doctors" (Titan)[1644] **->** The foreknowledge Clara had gained from a trip with the Doctor to the Museum of Terrible Fates prompted her to interface with the TARDIS' telepathic circuits, and get the Ship to take her back to Paris, 1923, to stop a trio of Doctors from meeting on Marinus...

it's after his travels with Charley, C'rizz, Lucie, Tamsin and Molly. This house is a different property to the Allen Road one from the *DWM* comic strips and New Adventures.

1641 "The Lost Dimension"

1642 COLONEL ORSON PINK: The final fate of Danny Pink and Clara Oswald that we see in the TV series (he's dead, she's given a reprieve on death by virtue of being in a timeless state with no heartbeat – see *Death in Heaven* and *Hell Bent*) leaves up in the air the existence of Colonel Orson Pink, who's fronted as their descendant in *Listen*. Not only does he mention that his "grandparents – well, great-grandparents" told "silly" stories about travelling through time, he owns the little plastic soldier from Danny's childhood as a "family heirloom", and – by the way – he looks exactly like Danny (since Samuel Anderson played both parts). Enough time elapses after Danny's death to rule out Clara discovering that she unexpectedly became pregnant beforehand, and her status as a timeless being seems to negate any thoughts of her reuniting with Danny in the past and then becoming pregnant. After all, if her biological functions are so suspended that she lacks a heartbeat, could she conceive even if she wanted to?

Steven Moffat somewhat clouded the issue when asked about Orson's ancestry in *Doctor Who Magazine* #481: "Well, I can think of several explanations, but the obvious one is that Orson comes from another branch of the family. He knows about Danny's heroic sacrifice, because Clara got in touch with the Pink family after the events of *Death in Heaven* (because you would, wouldn't you?), and told them what he did, and why. And she gave them the little soldier, as a keepsake of a great man and a great soldier – and because she knows

the toy soldier has to remain in the Pink family line. Now all that strikes me as pretty inevitable... but I'm not saying it's *right*. Nothing is actual till it's in the show. Knowing how the season would end, we were careful, in *Listen*, never to define exactly what the connection was." (One problem with this scenario, however, is that Clara doesn't finish *Listen* in a position to pass the plastic soldier along, because she winds up giving it to a very young first Doctor.)

In a follow-up column in *DWM* #509, however, Moffat seemed to more definitively settle the parentage issue when he declared: "Orson Pink is descended from another branch of the family. We were careful never to say he was directly descended from Danny."

1643 Dating *Time Heist* (X8.5) - Clara attempts to have her second date with Danny, so it's not long after *Listen*.

1644 Dating "Four Doctors" (Titan mini-series #1) - For Clara, the story occurs after she learns to manipulate the TARDIS' telepathic circuits (*Listen*), but before she "betrays" the twelfth Doctor (presumably *Dark Water*).

1645 Dating *The Caretaker* (X8.6) - The Blitzer is slated to reappear from the vortex on a "Thursday", "three days" after it departed. It instead returns only a day later, so the story must start on a Monday and end on a Tuesday.

The TARDIS contains artron energy, so although the Doctor doesn't own up to it, his trips to Coal Hill (*An Unearthly Child* et al) are responsible for the Blitzer being drawn there. (By extension, this means the Doctor is indirectly responsible for every horrifying death seen in *Class* too.) Mention of "fish people" doesn't necessarily denote that the Doctor and Clara went to Atlantis, although it's a safe bet that writers Gareth Roberts and Steven Moffat had *The Underwater*

2016 (a Monday and a Tuesday) - THE CARETAKER[1645] -> A Skovox Blitzer, one of the most lethal war-machines ever devised, homed in on the artron energy emissions centred around Coal Hill School. The Doctor went undercover as the Coal Hill caretaker to position chronodyne generators that would suck the Blitzer into the time vortex, harmlessly shunting it to billions of years in the future, but Danny found the Doctor's activities suspicious and moved one of the generators. The Blitzer errantly jumped ahead only a day, reappearing during parents' evening at the school. After learning the Doctor's true identity, Danny helped to deactivate the Blitzer. The Doctor, accompanied by Coal Hill student Courtney Woods, took the Blitzer to drift in the darkness of space...

2016 - KILL THE MOON[1646] -> Clara asked the Doctor to apologize after he told Courtney Woods that she wasn't special. To make amends, the Doctor took Courtney (and Clara) to the future, so she could be the first woman to walk on the moon in 2049...

Clara became incensed at the Doctor's behaviour on the moon, and told him to clear off and not return. Danny recognised that Clara wasn't done with the Doctor, because she was still angry with him.

2016 - MUMMY ON THE ORIENT EXPRESS[1647] -> Clara decided to have a farewell adventure with the Doctor, and accompanied him to the Orient Express in space. Upon changing her mind, and deciding to keep travelling with him, she lied to Danny that her business with the Doctor was done.

2016 - FLATLINE -> The TARDIS accidentally landed in Bristol as beings from another universe, with the power to add and subtract the third dimension, intruded upon our own. The beings experimented on various citizens, turning them two-dimensional or separating out their skin or nervous system. They also leeched energy from the TARDIS, shrinking its exterior and trapping the Doctor within. The beings adopted the fractured bodies of their victims, but Clara tricked them into restoring the TARDIS, and the Doctor –

pausing to name the interlopers the Boneless – banished them back to their realm.

Reunion in Stockbridge, Maxwell Edison's 60th Birthday

2016 (? 26th May) - "The Stockbridge Showdown"[1648] -> The ruthless Josiah W. Dogbolter thought he was conspiring with Chiyoko, the Child of Time, to build time tunnels and ruin his rivals before they were born. One such tunnel led to St Justinian's church in Stockbridge, 2016, on Maxwell Edison's sixtieth birthday. The twelfth Doctor – with help from his friends Sharon Allan, Frobisher (who was posing as Chiyoko), Majenta Pryce and Destri – had lured Dogbolter into a trap, and tricked him into confessing his crimes on the galactic net. He was taken back to the future and arrested by Intersol.

Izzy stopped by to gift Max with the complete *X-Files* on Blu-Ray. She had reconciled with her parents, and now worked for Doctors Without Borders. The Doctor took his friends to Cornucopia, and they celebrated Max's birthday.

2016 (7th July) - THE LEGENDS OF RIVER SONG: "A Gamble with Time"[1649] -> The eleventh Doctor and River Song sorted out a brouhaha involving Gharjhax, the prince-in-exile of the Mighty Garden Empire of the Gastropodic Alliance. As part of this, an insurance salesman, Martin Flint, fell into a time rift that threatened to destroy causality. Resolving this created two identical Flints – one of whom prospered, while the other was trapped in a perpetuating time-loop, continually saving the universe.

Erimem, Andrea Hansen and Tom Niven time-jumped to 2062, and dealt with a spore infection aboard the deep space probe *Clinton*. To Erimem and Andy's ire, Niven had returned home early, without telling them, to chat up a woman in a pub.[1650]

2016 (August) - ERIMEM: BUCCANEER[1651] -> Andy Hansen became so infuriated at her brother, she time-jumped to the late seventeenth century to indulge her passion for Errol Flynn films. Erimem, Ibrahim and

---

Menace on their minds when including that reference.
1646 To date, in our version of history, twelve men and zero women have walked on the moon. The last was in December 1972.
1647 Dating *Mummy on the Orient Express* (X8.8) - Clara says she hated the Doctor "for weeks", so it's presumably been that long since *Kill the Moon*.
1648 Dating "The Stockbridge Showdown" (*DWM* #500) - The year is given. Izzy, born the day that *Doctor Who Magazine* debuted (12th October, 1979), is now

"36", meaning it's not yet her birthday, so "The Stockbridge Showdown" might literally happen the day of its publication: 26th May.
1649 Dating "A Gamble with Time" (*The Legends of River Song* #1c) - The exact day is given.
1650 *Erimem: Prime Imperative*, which gives the modern-day date as "2016" (ch3).
1651 Dating *Erimem: Buccaneer* (*Erimem* novel #6) - A newspaper bears the dateline "August 2016", the same month as the book's release.

Helena followed their friend, and all returned after Andy had struck up a long-distance relationship with a ship captain, Olivia Parson.

2016 (August) - THE NINTH DOCTOR YEAR ONE[1652]

-> The Celestial Hyperloop Corporation routed a transwarp tunnel, the Punchway, through Earth. Unique energies in San Francisco interacted with the Pathway and gifted a handful of individuals, including Martha Jones, with enhanced strength, speed and flight – all before morphing them into winged gargoyles. Martha's husband, Mickey Smith, summoned the Doctor... only to have his ninth self, along with Rose and Jack, answer the call. Mickey and Martha avoided Rose and Jack as the Doctor collapsed the Punchway, reversing the mutation. One gargoyle remained, and the Doctor's trio followed it back to the UNIT era...

2016 (Autumn) - IN THE FOREST OF THE NIGHT[1653]

-> A devastating solar flare threatened to destroy Earth. As had happened in ages past, forests surged in growth overnight and overshadowed much of the globe, as well as increasing the world's oxygen supply. Clara and Danny awoke after a sleepover in the London Zoological Museum with a Coal Hill Year Eight class, and found Trafalgar Square overrun with vegeta-tion. The new growth tipped over Nelson's Column.

The Doctor landed as the spirit of the trees, the Here, communed with young Maebh Arden. Maebh spoke through every phone on Earth via the TARDIS' telepathic circuits, and asked the world governments to refrain from defoliating the trees. The solar flare burned off the excess oxygen and vegetation, but Earth was spared. The Doctor believed that humanity would forget about the super-growing vegetation, regarding it as a fable.

At her sister's urging, Annabel Arden came home. Danny discovered that Clara had been travelling with the Doctor behind his back.

2016 - THE TWELFTH DOCTOR YEAR ONE[1654]

-> The Fractures had been born in the Void as a sort of universal anti-body: a means of targeting breaks in reality. The alternate version of Paul Foster crossed over to our Earth to reunite with his family, but a group of Fractures judged he had transgressed the universal order. The twelfth Doctor and Clara cast the Fractures back into the Void.

2016 - THE TENTH DOCTOR YEAR THREE[1655]

-> As the tenth Doctor helped to close the remaining Keyhole Anomalies around the Circle of Transcendence, a Nestene-like predatory organism came through into our universe.

1652 Dating *The Ninth Doctor Year One* (Titan 9th Doc #1.4-1.5, "The Transformed") - The TARDIS instruments say it's "August 2016", concurrent with the book's digital release. Mickey seems to think that Torchwood is operational.
1653 Dating *In the Forest of the Night* (X8.10) - The Doctor notes that Maebe has rendered the solar flare event and marked it with "today's date", but fails to say *that* date aloud (he does, however, mention, "A tree is a time machine. You plant a little acorn in 1795, and in the year 2016, there's an oak tree"). Humanity's forgetfulness of these events might suggest that global deforestation continued from this point – rendering the planet vulnerable in future to the solar flare incident (see The Solar Flares sidebar).
1654 Dating *The Twelfth Doctor Year One* (Titan 12th Doc #1.6-1.8, "The Fractures") - A caption and two recap pages claim it's "2014", but the action for Clara occurs between *The Caretaker* and *Death in Heaven* (Danny is alive, and Osgood has started wearing bow ties, but hasn't yet shown them to the Doctor), meaning it's actually 2016 (see the dating notes on Series 9). Compounding the error, two UNIT techs say that Osgood should get them tickets for the premiere of *Interstellar*, which occurred on 7th November, 2014.

THE TWELFTH DOCTOR YEAR ONE AND TWO: Titan's twelfth Doctor comics regularly assume that contemporary stories with the twelfth Doctor and Clara (Series 8 and 9) happen in their years of broadcast, 2014 and 2015. However, they actually take place two years afterward (see the dating notes to Series 7 and 8 for why). In any contest between dates given in a tie-in property and the TV series, the TV series wins out, hence why we've respectively dated these runs of comics to 2016 and 2017.
1655 Dating *The Tenth Doctor Year Three* (Titan 10th Doc #3.1, "Breakfast at Tyranny's") – It's directly after *The Tenth Doctor Year Two*: "Old Girl". Contrary to that, however, Gabby says in *The Tenth Doctor Year Three*: "Vortex Butterflies" that she originates from 2016 – indeed, that it "must be 2017 now". She and Cindy do appear to have aged a bit during their TARDIS travels; in "Vortex Butterflies", the Day of the Dead incident in *The Tenth Doctor Year One* [October c.2014] seems like "a lifetime ago". The Doctor's group mentally experiences some days or even weeks in the Para-Nestene's faux New York, while only moments pass in real time.
1656 *The Witch's Familiar*
1657 *Death in Heaven, The Zygon Invasion.*
1658 The background to Series 10, as given in *The Pilot* and *Extremis.*
1659 See the Series 10 dating notes, in 2017.
1660 Dating *TW: Made You Look* (BF TW #2.6) - Gwen says Talmouth is "a seaside town in winter." The Voice started killing people on a Friday, which was "three days ago".
1661 *Revolution Man* (p23). Castro died 25th November, 2016.

The Para-Nestene kept the Doctor, Gabby, Cindy and Noobis' minds docile in a psychic recreation of New York, while trying to mimic their individual abilities. Breaking the illusion, the Doctor's group caused the Para-Nestene – which adopted the form of a red, tentacled police box – to abduct Cindy and flee through time. The Doctor, Gabby and Noobis pursued them to ancient China...

Missy Turns Earth's Dead into Cybermen, Danny Pink and (an) Osgood Die

2016 (Autumn) - DARK WATER / DEATH IN HEAVEN

-> By now, the nations of Earth had crafted protocols stipulating that in the event of a full-scale extraterrestrial invasion, the Doctor was to be detained and forcibly given the office of President of Earth: the Chief Executive Officer of the entire human race. Kate Stewart, still in command of UNIT, was a divorced mother of two.

Danny became distracted as Clara phoned to tell him she would never say the words "I love you" to anyone else, and died after walking into the path of an oncoming car. Clara failed to blackmail the twelfth Doctor into rewriting time to resurrect Danny, but the Doctor agreed to search out Danny in the afterlife and bring him home. By linking Clara to the TARDIS' telepathic circuits, the Ship went to where Clara and Danny's timelines were most likely to next intersect...

The Doctor and Clara found themselves in a mausoleum containing water tanks of Cybermen, as located in a trans-dimensional pocket that Missy had established in St Paul's Cathedral. Missy revealed herself as the Master reborn as Cybermen squadrons under her command surfaced in London, New York, Paris, Rome, Marrakesh, Brisbane, Glasgow and more. The Cybermen flew up and exploded over Earth's major population centres, scattering Cyber-particles that transformed humanity's dead into Cyber-bodies. The minds within Missy's Matrix dataslice downloaded into their original forms, awakening as Cybermen.

Missy "gifted" the control bracelet for the Cybermen army to the Doctor, to prove that they weren't so different, and could still be friends, but the Doctor rejected her offering. The late Danny Pink had woken up as a Cyberman, but directed the Cybermen army to fly with him into the atmosphere and self-incinerate – destroying the Cyber-stormclouds before they could rain again and transform the living into Cybermen.

Brigadier Lethbridge-Stewart had also returned to life as a Cyberman, and seemingly vapourised Missy before flying away. Two weeks later, Danny used the last energies of a dimension-hopping Cyber-bracelet to return the teenager he'd killed in Afghanistan to life.

Two weeks after that, Clara met with the Doctor in a café, and falsely claimed that she and Danny were very happy together. The Doctor fibbed that he was going home to Gallifrey, and he and Clara went their separate ways...

Missy survived the Brigadier's laser-bolt by channeling its energy into her vortex manipulator, teleporting to safety.[1656] Missy had killed one of the Osgoods. UNIT remained unaware if the remaining Osgood was human or Zygon.[1657]

Meanwhile, a later version of the twelfth Doctor – following his time with Clara – had become a lecturer at St Luke's University...

Doctor Who Series 10

Bill Potts at St Luke's University Bristol

Having made a sacred oath to guard Missy's body for a thousand years, the twelfth Doctor had relocated to St Luke's University Bristol, where he was assisted by Nardole. The Doctor lectured on topics ranging from quantum physics to poetry. Missy remained in a vault beneath the campus.[1658]

2016 (Autumn) - THE PILOT[1659]

-> The twelfth Doctor took an interest in Bill Potts: a canteen worker at St Luke's University, who snuck into his lectures and smiled while doing so. She accepted his offer to enroll her, and tutor her every Wednesday at 6pm.

2016 (a Tuesday in Winter) - TW: MADE YOU LOOK[1660]

-> A disembodied waveform, the Voice, consumed anyone who saw its essence three times, and thereby killed nearly everyone in the seaside town of Talmouth. A hostel owner, Mrs Rhodes, alone survived as she was blind. Gwen Cooper deduced that the Voice was reasonably weakened and could not leave Talmouth, and escorted Mrs Rhodes to safety. Without fresh victims, the Voice was expected to burn itself out.

The Doctor was in Havana for Fidel Castro's funeral, and later said, "They all loved [Castro] again by then".[1661]

The Twelfth Doctor Enjoys Christmas Three Times Over (Probably)

2016 (24th-25th December) - LAST CHRISTMAS

-> A cluster of Kantofarri, a.k.a. Dream Crabs, subdued the twelfth Doctor, and through him also assaulted Clara and four other people: a woman named Ashley, Professor Albert, Rona Bellows and Shona McCullough. The Kantofarri generated a telepathic field that kept their victims in a nested dream state: a form of anaesthetic while the Kantofarri slowly consumed their brains. Ashley's quartet believed they were scientists on a polar expedition.

Albert died, but the Doctor saved the others by having them dream that Santa Claus was flying them home. The Doctor and Clara owned up to their well-intentioned lies, decided they'd been given a second chance and left for new adventures...

? 2016 (? Christmas) - THE RETURN OF DOCTOR MYSTERIO[1662] -> Migratory aliens who literally looked like brains with eyes, and could install themselves in host bodies, had established the Harmony Shoal Institute on Earth. The company had built offices in many national capitals, as well as New York. The aliens planned to bombdive a spaceship onto New York, obliterating the city save for the nuclear-proof Harmony Shoal building there. World leaders would race to the "safety" of the Institute's other holdings, allowing the brain-aliens to seize executive control of Earth.

Daily Chronicle reporter Lucy Lombard, née Fletcher, had hired her school friend Grant Gordon to nanny her daughter Jennifer. Grant, however, was moonlighting as a caped superhero: the Ghost. As such, he aided the twelfth Doctor and Nardole in ruining Harmony Shoal's plans. The Doctor tipped off UNIT, who raided Harmony Shoal's offices. Grant and Lucy became a couple.

2016 (Christmas) - THE PILOT[1663] -> Bill Potts bought the twelfth Doctor a new rug for Christmas. Having nothing for her, he nipped back and took photos of Bill's late mother, then left them for her to find.

To spare her successor difficulty, Olive Hawthorne burned the poppet containing Melissa Fenn's spirit.[1664] Brandon Yow bought his sister Alex a Magpie 7S mobile, the top of the line, for Christmas.[1665]

2017[1666]

In 2017, Adelaide Brooke began her doctorate in Physics at Rice University in Texas, having studied Physics and Maths at Cambridge.[1667] Ramirez Harmon was president of Mexico in 2017.[1668] At some point in future, the Internet would launch a war to protect itself

---

1662 Dating *The Return of Doctor Mysterio* (X10.0) - The story takes place over two days, and was broadcast as the 2016 *Doctor Who* Christmas special. There's a general "modern day" feel about it all, including the Doctor flooding Harmony Shoal's Tokyo branch with Pokemon, in the wake of *Pokemon Go's* debut in July 2016. The *Superman* comics in eight-year-old Grant's bedroom (published in 1987 and 1988, but not necessarily "new" when we see them) also indicate it's the "modern day" now for adult Grant.

Thematically, *Doctor Mysterio* concerns the twelfth Doctor returning to twenty-first-century Earth after his extended sojourn on Darillium with River (*The Husbands of River Song*). Under normal circumstances, it'd just fill the Christmas slot between the modern-day components of Series 9 and 10 – but since they overlap, that's not possible. There's enough ambiguity to credibly think that *The Return of Doctor Mysterio* could fall in 2015, 2016, 2017 or thereabouts, but no matter which one you pick, it's either going to coincide with the twelfth Doctor's other activities on Earth, or (if you go for 2017 or beyond) it happens after *both* Series 9 and 10, which reads as doubly bonkers with regards the progression of the Doctor's own life.

As narrative clarity isn't attainable, then, it's probably best to place *Doctor Mysterio* in its year of broadcast, 2016, and accept it's an atypically busy Christmas, with the twelfth Doctor present three times over. He's simultaneously A) fighting some Dream Crabs with Clara in London (*Last Christmas*), B) taking on Harmony Shoal in New York with a slightly younger Nardole (*The Return of Doctor Mysterio*), and C) keeping his head down at St

Luke's University Bristol, with Bill Potts and a slightly older Nardole (*The Pilot*). It's a little snarled, but that's time travel for you.

Either way, it's actually not *said* that *The Return of Doctor Mysterio* happens at Christmas, and the weather – climate change or no climate change – seems altogether too warm for New York that time of year. Noticeably, Lucy thinks she can get away with wearing a sleeveless cocktail stress with a short skirt *for a rooftop* interview/dinner date with the Ghost. She admits to being chilly once there, but he fixes that by simply making a candle burn hotter. Nobody, in fact, bothers to wear winter clothing; Brock seems perfectly comfortable in a blazer.

An agent of the "Shoal of the Winter Harmony" previously appeared in *The Husbands of River Song*. It's not explained why the Shoal-creatures keep their spaceguns in their head cavities rather than their pockets.

1663 Dating *The Pilot* (X10.1) - It's Christmastime, complete with a choir singing "Jingle Bells".

1664 *Daemons: White Witch of Devil's End* (story #4, "The Poppet"), during a snow of "Christmas card perfection".

1665 The year before *The Lost Magic*.

1666 Stories in 2017 include Series 9, the post-Christmas scenes of *The Pilot* and the remaining Series 10 episodes, and *Class* (if you favour narrative clarity over the on-screen dates).

1667 According to the computer in *The Waters of Mars*. If that's correct, Brooke would have started her doctorate very young.

1668 *Army of Death*

from humankind.[1669] The twelfth Doctor pulled Clara out of class to go with him and recover a sentient super-weapon, the Hadax Ura.[1670]

Ally Landlaw, born in 2017, and a second cousin of Conall Lethbridge-Stewart, represented the start of an entirely new cycle for the consciousness formerly reincarnated as James Lethbridge-Stewart, Owain Vine and the Great Intelligence.[1671] In the same year, in unknown circumstances, the Great Intelligence that had endured since its encounter with Counter-Measures in 1974 was thrown back in time, to the 1800s.[1672]

After an enemy overwhelmed his homeworld, Ballon – a shapechanging Lorr – hoped to take advantage of the Zygon armistice, and rendezvous with his family on Earth. Instead, he murdered a human family that caught him stealing food. The Governors of Coal Hill made Ballon their prisoner.[1673] The Barbara Wright Building, part of Coal Hill Academy, was completed in Spring.[1674]

In 2017, UNIT closed their file on the Quadrant Incident.[1675] Kakapos were extinct on Earth by 2017.[1676] The British government recovered dystronic missiles – weapons that could destroy all organic life in a set radius – from an Arcadian spacecraft.[1677]

Garry Fletcher, an opportunist in Shoreditch, killed an exploration party of naïve aliens and acquired their mind-swapping technology.[1678] The Winter family's TARDIS-recall card repeatedly pulled the twelfth Doctor and Clara to various points in space-time.[1679] The MeadowPhone 3 was released in August 2017.[1680]

An unidentified race of alien scientists monitored Earth transmissions from a temporary outpost on Europa, one of Jupiter moons. The outpost's shutdown protocols failed in 2017, and a simulacrum there believed itself to be Morton Beck, a minor "alien abduction" celebrity in the late 2010s. It remained alone until 2060. Amber Lewis, a Kennedy Space Center worker and brief acquaintance of the twelfth Doctor, was born in 2017.[1681]

The Doctor was personally acquainted with ITT CEO Richard Lindenmuth.[1682] Sarah Jane Smith heard that 2017 would, despite appearances, get better.[1683] On Earth, dolphins had an advanced sense of geometry.[1684]

2017 - TW: THE TORCHWOOD ARCHIVE (BF)[1685] ->
Gwen Cooper dispatched one of her operatives, Mr Colchester, to learn more about renewed rumours concerning the Committee. The Committee members were, as needed, inhabiting the bodies of old men at the care home on Cathedral Road, but Colchester failed to learn any useful information from them.

2017 - TW: VISITING HOURS[1686] ->
Time-travelling surgeons infiltrated St Helen's Hospital, and tagged Rhys Williams' mother Brenda – who was in for a hip replacement – as an organ source in their illicit operations. Their true patient, Prince Abdullah, didn't survive the first procedure. Rhys kept his mother safe until the surgeons were made to depart through time, and also from the Cleaners who sterilised their locale.

2017 - DC 2: BEACHHEAD[1687] ->
The eighth Doctor, Liv and Helen hoped for a holiday after their confrontation with the Eleven in 1639, but arrived at the village of Stegmoor as the Voord Ishtek attempted to summon a Voord survival flotilla to Earth. The Doctor altered her spaceship's molecular structure, which likely crushed the

---

1669 *Hell Bent*

1670 "Spirits of the Jungle"; this happens after Danny Pink's death.

1671 *Leth-St: Night of the Intelligence* (ch10), The Great Intelligence Official Background document.

1672 The Haisman Timeline and The Great Intelligence Official Background document, leading to *The Snowmen*.

1673 *Class: The Metaphysical Engine, or What Quill Did*

1674 *Class: The Coach with the Dragon Tattoo*

1675 *Damaged Goods*. Marcie Hatter, a UNIT Corporal here (p262), was the name of the heroine of Russell T Davies' TV serial *Dark Season* (1991).

1676 *The Last Dodo*

1677 "Nine years" before *Project: Destiny*.

1678 "Six months" before *Class: Joyride*.

1679 *The Tales of Winter* series. For the Doctor and Clara, use of the card seems to coincide with Series 9 – there's mention, on just the second time it's used (the later part of *The Gods of Winter*), that Danny Pink is "gone".

1680 *The Shining Man* (ch5).

1681 *Death Among the Stars*

1682 Inferred from *The Outliers*. Lindenmuth wrote *The Outside the Box Executive* (2017).

1683 *The Tenth Doctor Year Three*: "Vortex Butterflies"

1684 *The Eleventh Doctor Year Three*: "The Tragical History Tour"

1685 Dating *TW: The Torchwood Archive* (BF *TW* special release #1) - The year is given. This scene was originally written for Owen Harper, and set in 2007, but was reallocated to Colchester when actor Burn Gorman proved unavailable because he was filming overseas. (Funnily enough, a reference to *Homes Under the Hammer* worked either way, because it's been running since 2003.)

1686 Dating *TW: Visiting Hours* (*TW* #3.1) - It's the next installment of the revived Torchwood's adventures, in a story released in 2017.

1687 Dating *DC 2: Beachhead* (BF *DC* #2.1) - The Doctor tells his friends that it's "2017, I think. Yes, I think that's what the [TARDIS] readouts said. Bracing, isn't it?" The

Voord within to death. Thinking the destruction of the Voord homeworld deviated from established history, the Doctor and his friends left to investigate...

2017 - ERIMEM: CHURCHILL'S CASTLE[1688] ->

Erimem, Andy, Helena and student Trina Barton jumped to the future, and witnessed the destruction of Earth in a closed time-loop. Since all seemed lost, Trina returned home with a young survivor, Jadie. Erimem came back and convinced Trina to return the girl to her own era, so the proper timeline could be restored. Afterward, Erimem informed Trina that she lacked the sound judgment to go on more time-trips with them.

c 2017 - VORTEX ICE[1689] ->

Speleologists awoke the cyborg-squid in Chihuahua, Mexico, and it syphoned off their energy, turning them into skeletons. As the creature secreted vortex ice, frozen chunks of time, the sixth Doctor and Flip were briefly suspended in time. To fulfill causality, an earlier version of this Doctor jumped forward in the TARDIS, and took the revived Flip into the near-past. She pretended to experience these events for the first time, and mournfully let the speleologists go to their deaths. The

Doctor set off charges that killed the cyborg-squid.

(=) 2017 - SUBURBAN HELL[1690] -> The fourth Doctor and Leela examined a wrinkle in time centred around the North London home of a married couple, Ralph and Belinda. The Doctor and Ralph journeyed down the wrinkle to 1977, and dealt with a formidable alien mutant.

Ralph needed a drink upon learning that owing to the historical changes made in 1977, he was now married to a woman other than Belinda, and had four children.

(? =) c 2017 - CHARLEY S2: EMBANKMENT STATION / RUFFLING / SEED OF CHAOS / THE DESTRUCTIVE QUALITY OF LIFE[1691] -> Polling data indicated record support for the Royal Family. Both the UK prime minister and the US president were female.

Proto-Viyrans, a.k.a. the Identical Men, installed one of their Machines in Embankment Station. This rewrote the neural pathways of travellers through there, causing them to lose empathy and become

---

story, however, was released in early 2016. Phillipa Gregson, a holiday cottage manager, recalls the third Doctor visiting Stegmoor "a long time ago" during his UNIT days, when she was a toddler, meaning *Beachhead* is almost certainly contemporary.

1688 Dating *Erimem: Churchill's Castle* (*Erimem* novel #7) - The passage of time in the *Erimem* series seems to coincide with the real world, and this book was released in 2017.

1689 Dating *Vortex Ice* (BF #225a) - The story, released in 2017, seems contemporary enough. One of the cave-explorers spent the last ten years working at Caltech, and the Doctor tells Flip: "As far as you're concerned, this is the present, give or take a few years".

1690 Dating *Suburban Hell* (BF 4th Doc #4.5) - The year is given, and it's "forty years" after "1977".

1691 Dating *Charlotte Pollard* Series 2 (*Embankment Station*, 2.1; *Ruffling*, 2.2; *Seed of Chaos*, 2.3; *The Destructive Quality of Life*, 2.4) - No year provided, but the trappings (including mention of Facebook, Twitter, Tumbler and the importance of social media) all seem contemporary. Polling data indicates record support for the Royal Family; that happened in 2016, alongside Queen Elizabeth II's 90th birthday. Once they find a picture of Charley from 1930, the authorities claim, "She should be over a hundred [years old] now." The Battle of Trafalgar (21st October, 1805) happened "over two hundred years ago". The story ends on a cliffhanger.

Series 2, one big story, takes place in this time-zone over "a few days" – a haggard Charley and Robert discuss whether it's been "three days" (he thinks) or "four" (she thinks).

1692 Dating *The Twelfth Doctor Year Two* (Titan 12th Doc #2.10, "Playing House") - It's the "twenty-first century", and, for the Doctor, after Clara's departure (*Hell Bent*).

1693 Dating *The Eleventh Doctor Year Three* (Titan 11th Doc #3.3, "The Tragical History Tour") – Alice asks the Doctor, "What's the date?", and he replies, "Couldn't tell you. I sneezed when it flashed up on the console." Kushak simply says: "You've been gone a while, Alice." If Alice is concerned about such details as keeping up with her rent, holding down a day job and her friends not seeing her for years while she's faffing about time and space with the Doctor, it goes unmentioned. Without more information, it's a toss-up as to whether this phase of her life on Earth happens in 2017 – commensurate with this story's publication – or not long after the last time she visited her native era ("The Comfort of the Good") in 2015.

1694 Dating *The Eleventh Doctor Year Three* (Titan 11th Doc #3.8, "Fooled") – No year given, but the setting seems reasonably contemporary.

1695 Dating *Daemons: White Witch of Devil's End* (story #6, "Hawthorne Blood") - The on-screen gravestone of one of Bryony's victims, Robert Merrow, says he died "10th February, 2017". Bryony lodges with Olive for an indeterminate amount of days/weeks. In the film version, Olive ventures out "last night" on the eve of Beltane (1st May), and continues her narration on Beltane itself.

1696 Dating *Erimem: Three Faces of Helena* (*Erimem* novel #8) - The year is given.

prone to stupid and deadly mistakes. London experienced a surge of road accidents, hospital deaths and food delivery problems. Two airplanes collided over the city, killing three thousand on the ground. Social media took notice as the Identical Men's molecular rearrangement caused Nelson's statue in Trafalgar Square to move.

The authorities evacuated London, and formed refugee camps in places such as Slough. The afflicted went to other countries, causing a million deaths. The international community demanded action, and the UK prime minister authorised the eradication of London with conventional bombs and – if needed – nuclear ones.

Charley Pollard, Robert Buchan and Bernard the Rogue Viyran failed to contain the situation, and the Identical Men pulled Charley and Robert back to the planet Galracia before the birth of humankind. The sudden release of Charley's *The Continuing Memoirs of an Edwardian Adventuress* over the internet enabled Bernard to time-jump and join them...

c 2017 - THE TWELFTH DOCTOR YEAR TWO[1692] -> The twelfth Doctor, accompanied by a forty-first-century rocker, Hattie, made an emergency stop at a twenty-first century home. A dying TARDIS was leaking temporal radiation, expanding beyond its confines, and attracting Sprillites: artron-energy scavengers that fed on the corpses of timeships. The Doctor sent the ailing TARDIS to its demise in a star's core. He then returned Hattie home.

(=) & ? 2017 - THE ELEVENTH DOCTOR YEAR THREE[1693] -> The eleventh Doctor brought Alice home, only to find a band of humans from the past – the Sixty-Eighters – marauding around looting this (to them) future era. Earth's timeline had folded in on itself, overlapping its many time zones. With the TARDIS inoperative, the Doctor, Alice and Alice's neighbour Kashak procured a bus and spent three

and half weeks "driving" backwards to the source of the problem, in 1968.

? 2017 - THE ELEVENTH DOCTOR YEAR THREE[1694] -> The eleventh Doctor, Alice and the Sapling enjoyed themselves at a Village Green Festival. A shimmer-disguised Krovian was stealing people's memories to sell to a customer in Glovis 9 with a taste for such things, but the Doctor smashed the Krovian's memory-stealing camera, restoring his stolen goods.

c 2017 (February to 1st May) - DAEMONS: WHITE WITCH OF DEVIL'S END[1695] -> An aged Olive Hawthorne sensed her time as protector of Devil's End was nearly finished, and welcomed the arrival of her potential heir: Bryony, the daughter of a distant cousin. To her horror, Olive identified Bryony as a life-draining succubus preying upon the young men of Devil's End. The spirits of Olive's family rallied to help her incinerate Bryony's physical form, and bury her in a protective circle.

2017 - ERIMEM: THREE FACES OF HELENA[1696] -> As Helena's marriage to Ibrahim Hadmani drew near, history dictated that Helena now reveal her immortal life to him, Erimem and Andy Hansen, so they could intercede in her own past. They accordingly visited Alexandria in 276 BC, and the lost city of Kurr in 272 BC and 1884. Helena gave up her immortality to save Ibrahim's life in 1884, and they married upon returning to the present.

The Twelfth Doctor, Bill Potts and Nardole at St Luke's University Bristol (cont.)[1697]

2017 (Spring) - THE PILOT[1698] -> While visiting Bristol, a liquid spaceship left behind a puddle of super-intelligent, shapeshifting oil. The Puddle designated Heather, a St Luke's student, as its pilot upon sensing her desire to leave. After killing Heather and

---

1697 Dating *Doctor Who* Series 10 - The series aired 15th April to 1st July, 2017.

Only one episode names the year, albeit obliquely: in *Knock, Knock*, we learn that the Landlord's Dryads feast upon on a sixpack of victims every twenty years like clockwork, and housing documentation proves they did so in 1957, 1977 and 1997 (so, it's now 2017). Additionally, the publicity scene introducing Pearl Mackie as Bill has the Doctor insist they've got to return to "2017", and takes place during their runabout with the Daleks later in *The Pilot*. Both clues help to confirm that Series 10 adheres to a "year of broadcast" mode (save for the first episode), but also necessitates that *Doctor Who* Series 9 and 10 overlap a bit (see the dating

notes on Series 8 and 9 for why they occur two years ahead of broadcast).

That said, *The Pilot*, which kicks off Series 10, begins in 2016 and stretches into the next year – the Doctor meets Bill, presumably at the start of the autumn term, and their friendship rapidly progresses through Christmas, the start of the new term and into spring. *Knock, Knock*, by contrast, probably happens later in 2017 – noticeably, it coincides with a Fresher's Party (typically held in the Autumn, usually October), a small hiccup being that Bill and her quintet of friends are looking for housing while school's on rather than sorting it out beforehand. It's possible that Clara Oswald officially "dies" before *Knock, Knock* (in *Face the Raven*),

adopting her form, the Puddle sought out Bill Potts – who had fancied Heather, and made her promise not to leave without her.

To escape the Puddle, the twelfth Doctor, Nardole and Bill fled in the TARDIS to Australia in the present day, then a planet in the year Twenty-Three Million, then to a Dalek-Movellan skirmish. They returned after Bill released "Heather" from her promise, and the Puddle departed.

Although he'd promised to stay on Earth save for emergencies, the Doctor found the thought of new adventures in space and time irresistible, and he invited Bill into the TARDIS...

2017 - SMILE / THIN ICE[1699] -> The twelfth Doctor sent Nardole to make tea. In the time it took Nardole to reach the Doctor's study, the Doctor and Bill had slipped away and returned from a human colony in the future, and the last frostfair in 1814.

The twelfth Doctor and Bill visited the future, to prevent escalating warfare over Saturn's diamonds. They also jumped ahead a few months, and aided an imprisoned Boggart.[1700]

Doctor Who Series 9[1701]

Clara and the Doctor post-Danny Pink

c 2017 - THE MAGICIAN'S APPRENTICE -> Missy received the twelfth Doctor's confession dial, which indicated he expected to die soon, but was unable to locate her old friend. To snag UNIT's attention, Missy used a basic Time-Stop to freeze 4,165 airplanes in the air over Earth. Clara conferred with Kate Stewart at UNIT HQ, and went with a UNIT detachment to meet

meaning the remainder of Series 10 takes place after Series 9. *World Enough and Time*, marking the end of the Doctor's time at St Luke's, seems to occur in or near winter – Bill wears a windbreaker, and other students don heavier coats.

None of this needs to be a problem continuity-wise... once the twelfth Doctor relocates to St Luke's with Nardole and the (mostly) locked-up Missy, he by all appearances keeps a low profile. Such is his devotion to sneaking away in the TARDIS without Nardole noticing, he doesn't seem to take much interest in events elsewhere in the UK. As such, and given that he doesn't remember his time with Clara (*Hell Bent*), nothing especially rules out the twelfth Doctor living on Earth twice over for about a year. God only knows, however, what he makes of media reports of four thousand-plus airplanes being frozen in time (see X9.1, *The Magician's Apprentice*) unless he intuits he should stay clear of it, as Missy's past self is involved.

Halfway through Series 10, *The Lie of the Land* shifts the goalposts a bit, in that the Monks keep control of Earth for "six months" – a case can be made that it's 2018 when they're defeated, but (and it's a tough call), it's possible there's some temporal reversion occurred, so we've opted for 2017. (See the Dating on that story.)

For Bill, events in the novel *The Shining Man* (ch18) happen after she's seen *Doctor Strange* (it debuted in November 2016). As if calculated to make veteran *Who* fans feel old, she doesn't seem to recognise Scully from *The X-Files* (ch14).

1698 Dating *The Pilot* (X10.1) - Bill wishes the Doctor "Happy new term!" in a quick cutaway, and then an indeterminate amount of time passes. The remainder of the story entails warm weather and Bill in short sleeves.

1699 Following *The Pilot*, these are Bill's second and third adventures in the TARDIS.

1700 *Diamond Dogs* falls during Bill's first few "days" (ch8) in the TARDIS. *The Shining Man* (ch13) mentions the Doctor's "recent" attempt to "nick a diamond on Saturn", so comes afterward.

1701 Dating *Doctor Who* Series 9 – For Clara, events follow on from *Last Christmas* (set at Christmas 2016). *The Magician's Apprentice* opens when school is in session. All things being equal, it seems reasonable to think that Series 9 takes place throughout 2017... but this isn't actually said on screen. In favour of a 2017 dating, the Doctor worries that Clara is still grieving for Danny (*Under the Lake*), and the Zygon disguised as the American policewoman in *The Zygon Invasion* says that the "Brits" (i.e. the Zygons) came to Truth or Consequences, New Mexico, "two years" beforehand – presumably in the wake of *The Day of the Doctor* (set in 2015). That roughly matches with a police report that Kate Stewart reads, which involved someone "age 22, DOB 12/21/1993". (Another police report bears the date of 19th May, but the year isn't visible.)

A calendar displayed in the Truth or Consequences police station in *The Zygon Invasion*, however, cryptically reads: (top row) "Thu 1 [illegible sequence, possibly denoting the year]" (bottom row) "11 01." We know that the "11 01" doesn't denote the time of day, because it doesn't change from scene to scene, which might suggest the story takes place on 1st November (American calendars list the month first, then the day). However, in 2017, only June begins on a Thursday. In 2018, the first is a Thursday in February, March and November. Unhelpfully in the same story, the Doctor phones Clara to say: "Hello, it's Doctor Disco. I'm in the twenty-first century. I don't know what month."

Another piece of evidence in favour of a later dating for Series 9 is Clara's claim in *The Magician's Apprentice* that she and the Doctor saw Missy die "ages ago" – an odd statement, if only a few months, or even a year,

with Missy in a Mediterranean locale. After Missy released the airplanes, a UNIT algorithm determined that the Doctor was in Essex, 1138. Missy triggered her vortex manipulator and Clara's to take them there. The Doctor and Clara returned to this era after confronting Davros.

c 2017 - THE WOMAN WHO LIVED -> Clara took her Year 7s to Taekwondo while the Doctor left in the TARDIS, and met the immortal Ashildr in 1651. Upon returning, the Doctor spotted Ashildr lurking in the background of photo taken at Coal Hill.

Ashildr had snuck into the photo to get the Doctor's attention.[1702]

c 2017 - THE ZYGON INVASION / THE ZYGON INVERSION -> The White House appointed an alien ambassador.

Bonnie, the leader of the Zygon splinter group Truth or Consequences, sought to expose the Zygons living undercover on Earth, and thereby trigger a war between human and Zygonkind. The renegade Zygons executed the Zygon High Command, and captured both Clara and the surviving Osgood. Bonnie adopted Clara's form, and as such accessed UNIT's Black Archive to acquire an object of last resort: the Osgood Box. The twelfth Doctor explained that one switch on Bonnie's Osgood Box would shift the twenty million Zygons back to normal, whereas the other would forever cancel their ability to shapeshift. Kate Stewart seized the second Osgood Box, which the Doctor claimed would either release the Zygon-killing Zee-67 gas, or detonate the nuclear arsenal beneath the Black Archive and destroy London.

Bonnie deduced that the Osgood Boxes were merely empty boxes with dead switches, and realised the futility of pursuing war. The Doctor accepted her as a partner in guarding the human-Zygon treaty, and wiped Kate's memories of these events. Bonnie shifted form to become Osgood, and partnered with the surviving Osgood to protect the peace.

2017 (26th June) - HORROR OF THE SPACE SNAKES[1703] -> Lukas Minski, a staff member at the UNIT museums in Georgia, communed with the space snakes on Earth's moon. He brokered a deal to return their queen's egg, but was forced to hide it in an undeveloped section of UNIT's moonbase, where it remained for eight years.

2017 (Summer) - THE DALEK PROJECT[1704] -> Archaeologists in North Eastern France thought they'd found a Bronze Age burial chamber, but in truth opened the Dalek timeship buried there since 1917. The eleventh Doctor directed a backhoe to smash a Quasimodo Dalek – which had a gun in its eyestalk and two eyestalks for hands – that the archaeologists had assembled from spare parts, and also overloaded the remaining Daleks with power from the TARDIS. He then left, along with Professor Angela Todd, to share tea with a survivor from the Dalek conflict of 1917: Corporal Ted Anderson.

c 2017 (Summer) - THE TWELFTH DOCTOR YEAR ONE[1705] -> On Earth, interest in space exploration was the highest it had been in decades. A sleeper cell of Hyperions awoke and landed their spaceship in Lake Windermere – after flying through the International Space Station, destroying it. The twelfth Doctor and Clara returned home

have passed since *Death in Heaven*. The time of year in that story seems chilly (Clara even wears a jacket upon going to see Missy in a warmer locale), and it's a little strange the way Clara's breath is visible in UNIT HQ but not when she's outside. A UNIT analyst claims there are "439" active nuclear stations worldwide, which fits with a February 2015 count by the World Nuclear Association of there being "over 435 commercial nuclear power reactors".

1702 *Face the Raven*

1703 Dating *Horror of the Space Snakes* (BBC children's 2-in-1 #5) - The exact date is given (ch2).

1704 Dating *The Dalek Project* (BBC original graphic novel #2) - It's "2017", "a century after the Great War"/the Dalek ship was buried in 1917. The Doctor specifies that it's "a French summer".

1705 Dating *The Twelfth Doctor Year One* (Titan 12th Doc #1.12-1.15, "The Hyperion Empire") - The "Previously On..." nuggets place "The Hyperion Empire" between *Last Christmas* and Series 9, but (as with "The Fractures")

it can only be taken as an error when one of the blurbs claims it's "2015" (issue #13), and Clara herself says that it's "London in the Summer of 2015" (#12). By the TV show's continuity, it should be 2017 at the very earliest. Clara states that she's "28" years old (she was 27 in *Deep Breath*).

The Hyperions menace Earth for "a few weeks at most" before the Doctor and Clara turn up. It might be preferable to assume that "The Hyperion Empire" occurs after *Face the Raven*, as London in that story displays no damage from the Hyperion assault, even if this means that Clara is here present on Earth after her "death" in that story. "Witch Hunt" mitigates against that, however, by suggesting that the twelfth Doctor and Clara still haven't parted ways by the time Halloween 2017 rolls around.

A little confusingly, the Hyperion sleeper cell seen here was based on Neptune, so is presumably the same group glimpsed in the epilogue to *The Twelfth Doctor Year One*: "Terroformer"... in the year "2114 AD".

to find London covered in ash, and that the Hyperions had both established themselves in many regions including Sussex, as well as endowing their essence into human slaves: the Scorched.

The Hyperions established a fusion web around Earth's sun, intending to drain it and absorb its energy into itself, but the Doctor linked the TARDIS into the web's systems, and transported it, as well as the Hyperions, to the year five billion...

THE TWELFTH DOCTOR YEAR TWO[1706] -> While conducting the last night of The Proms, the Doctor mistakenly played the Sex Pistols version of "God Save the Queen".

The Sea Devils had usurped control of Ravenscaur School, on Raven's Isle, some decades ago. Their hatchlings possessed humans by wrapping around their cortices, and so the Sea Devils had mentally dominated whole

generations of Ravenscaur graduates, including the current prime minister, Daniel Claremont. Clara Oswald joined the Ravenscaur English department upon the mysterious death of Christel Dean, her friend from teacher-training college.

At Ravenscaur, Claremont returned and announced new energy initiatives – through climate change, the Sea Devils hoped to tailor Earth to their liking. The twelfth Doctor modified the Ravenscaur sprinklers to reveal anyone hosting Sea Devil spawn, and the prime minister stood revealed on live television as a reptile man.

Exposed, a Sea Devil army engaged a Navy taskforce at Raven's Isle. The Doctor redirected the Sea Devils' own devastation pulse to destroy them, their army and the isle. In the mayhem, the Doctor lost Sonny, a stuffed swordfish that he had recently acquired, and dubbed "his most faithful companion".

1706 Dating *The Twelfth Doctor Year Two* (Titan 12th Doc #2.1-2.4, "Clara Oswald and the School of Death") - A caption on the first page says it's "September 2015", another in issue #3 reiterates the "2015" bit, and the Paris Climate Change Conference (30th November to 12th December 2015) is scheduled for "later this year". For the Doctor and Clara, the story takes place after *The Zygon Inversion*, as it includes two Osgoods, each of them wearing seventh Doctor apparel.

This story constitutes a profound revision to the Sea Devils and their abilities – stories such as *Warriors of the Deep* might have unfolded very differently, if they were capable of taking over peoples' minds, and even making them telekinetic, with their frogspawn.
1707 Dating *The Twelfth Doctor Year Two* (Titan 12th Doc #2.5, "The Fourth Wall") - It's presumably after the previous story, "Clara Oswald and the School of Death". This is the last ongoing Titan comic featuring Clara.
1708 Dating *The Twelfth Doctor Year Two* (Titan 12th Doc #2.14-2.15, "Invasion of the Mindmorphs") - The story seems contemporary, and the *Time Surgeon* comic appeared in "The Fourth Wall" (Titan). Sonny and Val are part of the quick-fire "rotating companion" approach to the last half of *The Twelfth Doctor Year Two*, so we never see them part ways with the Doctor.
1709 Dating "Witch Hunt" (*DWM* #497-499) - The story slots very awkwardly into Series 9, as it's after the Doctor and Clara reunite following Danny's death (*Last Christmas*, Christmas 2016), but also involves a Halloween festival. So, it's at least October 2017 (unless Clara decided to go against expectations, and stage a Halloween festival in spring or summer). Taken at face value, the epilogue, set "a few months" later, would then push *Face the Raven* and *Hell Bent* into 2018 – not impossible, but probably not what the episode-to-episode pacing of Series 9 intended.
1710 Dating *The Lost Angel, The Lost Planet* and *The Lost*

Flame (BBC *DW* audiobooks #26-27, 29) - In tone, and especially in its use of technology (the Meadowflex smartwatch is due out in a month, Alex owns a Magpie Electricals phone), *The Lost Angel* seems contemporary. Supporting that, an Angel throws McCormack back to 1994 (given the Angels' *modus operandi*, an interim of twenty-three years sounds feasible). Nonetheless, Dee's Angel-binding book, dating back to 1588 (*The Lost Magic*), was written "412 years ago" (which only adds up to the year 2000).

It's indeterminate if the TARDIS actually takes off at the start of *The Lost Planet*... the engine sighs a bit, but there's no mention of the console moving, and the TARDIS locks itself down. If so, most of the story passes either with the Ship off in the Vortex, or just sitting there in Rickman.
1711 Dating *TW: Aliens Among Us* (BF *TW* Series Five; #5.1, *Changes Everything*; #5.2, *Aliens & Sex & Chips & Gravy*; #5.3, *Orr*; #5.4, *Superiority Complex*) - This is Big Finish's official continuation of the defunct *Torchwood* TV show. There's no particular reason to resist setting it in its year of release, 2017, especially as Gwen's daughter Anwen, born in or near May 2010, is now "seven".

The blurb says this story "picks up the events after *Miracle Day*", but it also follows on from Gwen and Rhys' pact to bring back Torchwood in *TW: Forgotten Lives* [c.2015]. It's after Jack's adventures with the *Ice Maiden* crew (*TW: Exodus Code*, then the Titan *Torchwood* comics). There's mention of Brexit (approved on 23rd June, 2016).

Three, maybe four weeks elapse over the course of this box set – Gwen's mother dies at the end of episode two, and her funeral is in episode three. In the latter, Tyler remarks that "A few weeks ago, I didn't believe in aliens" (as he discovered in episode one). Orr is still new to Torchwood come episode four.

THE TWELFTH DOCTOR YEAR TWO[1707] -> Some Boneless absorbed humans into comic books and replaced them. The twelfth Doctor and Clara visited the Prohibited Sphere Megastore in London, where he was sucked into an issue of *Time Surgeon*. The Doctor convinced the trapped humans to concentrate upon their love of comics, which freed them and made the Boneless implode.

c 2017 - THE TWELFTH DOCTOR YEAR TWO[1708] -> The twelfth Doctor couldn't believe the portrayal of himself in Sonny Robinson and Val Kent's *Time Surgeon* comic, so he went to a comic-book convention in Birmingham, and tricked them into entering the TARDIS when they attempted to visit the loo. Determined to show them how *real* adventures in time and space worked, he whisked them away to the Jurassic era, and other exotic locales. While defeating the evil Mindmorphs on the planet Zarma, Sonny and Val became a couple. Oblivious to this, the Doctor was glad for the lack of "mushy stuff" aboard the TARDIS.

"Witch Hunt"[1709] -> Clara Oswald coordinated the Coal Hill Halloween Fayre as a fund-raiser for Danny Pink's memorial, but Miss Chief, a time-travelling jester, disrupted the venue and briefly manifested the witch-hunter Matthew Hopkins. The twelfth Doctor bested Miss Chief in a scavenger hunt, which obliged her to take him to Clara's location in the past...

To weaken the fundraiser by turning over the historical relics and extinct animals that Miss Chief had collected. A few months later, Clara used the funds to open the Danny Pink I.T. Suite at Coal Hill.

Clara Oswald Listed as Dead, Joins Ashildr; the Doctor's Confession-Dial Ordeal Begins

c 2017 - FACE THE RAVEN / HELL BENT -> The Time Lords menaced Ashildr, who agreed to deliver the Doctor into their hands in exchange for the continued safety of her London trap street. Knowing the Doctor could never resist a mystery, Ashildr used the powerful spirit at her command – a Quantum Shade – to place a death sentence, a chronolock, on the neck of his friend Rigsy. The twelfth Doctor and Clara found Ashildr's trap street, and Ashildr offered Clara her personal guarantee of safety.

To weaken Ashildr's position, Clara convinced Rigsy to pass the chronolock on to her... but in doing so unknowingly rewrote the terms of the agreement with the Quantum Shade, preventing Ashildr from voiding the chronolock. As the chronolock reached zero, Clara faced the raven – a manifestation of the Quantum Shade – and died as it charred out her insides. In accordance with the Time Lords' wishes, Ashildr teleported

the Doctor into his confession dial, where he would remain trapped for 4.5 billion years...

The Doctor used a Gallifreyan extraction chamber to retrieve Clara from the instant before her death. Following events on Gallifrey at the end of the universe, Clara acquired a TARDIS and began travelling with an older Ashildr – knowing that her death remained a fixed event in time, and she would one day have to let the Time Lords return her to the moment of her death. Before departing, Clara left the twelfth Doctor in Nevada, and reunited him with his TARDIS.

Alex and Brandon Yow

c 2017 - THE LOST ANGEL / THE LOST PLANET / THE LOST FLAME[1710] -> In Rickman, New York, construction on a new mall unearthed a quartet of Weeping Angels – one of whom would soon hurl Jane McCormack, a homeless shelter owner, back to 1994. McCormack had lived out the interim, and found a book by John Dee containing Ancient High Gallifreyan: a means of binding the Angels. By using them as her agents, McCormack paradoxically hoped to halt the construction and avert her fate.

An aspiring photojournalist, Alex Yow, and her brother Brandon Yow met the twelfth Doctor as he tried to contain McCormack's Angels. An Angel sent the Doctor back some decades, but he lived his way back to the present, and with Alex's help buried the Angels in cement.

Alex and Brandon opted to accompany the Doctor to look into Dee's book, but the ecology of the planet Altikan spilled out of the TARDIS cupboard containing it. The Phage trapped there was now stronger, and would kill trillions if it escaped. The Doctor let the Phage possess his body, then burnt it out with a particular type of sunlight. He returned Altikan to its home system, then went back to 1588 with his friends...

Alex and Brandon's parents were deceased. Brandon was involved with a woman named Shelly. The Meadowflex smartwatch, released a month after these events, proved very popular. The Doctor eventually brought Brandon home, after Alex's decision to stay in the First Great and Bountiful Human Empire. He gave Brandon one of John Dee's crystals, so he could communicate with his sister.

Torchwood Cardiff 2.0

2017 - TW: ALIENS AMONG US[1711] -> The *Ice Maiden* crew dispensed with Captain Jack's services, and he joined Gwen Cooper's revived Torchwood branch in Cardiff. Mr Cinjin[1711] Colchester, still officially a civil servant, administrated the group and its partially restored Hub. Torchwood's funding had been greatly diminished. After a few years of dormancy, and its energy benignly seeping into the soil, the Rift became more active. Public recognition of

Torchwood had nosedived.

The Sorvix – a human-looking race from the planet Sorva, with a ravenous maw on their backs – felt deserted by their old god, and came through the Rift to find a new one. With a mixture of carrots and sticks, their leader, Ro-Jedda, integrated ever-growing numbers of Sorvix into Cardiff society. The Sorvix intertwined themselves into the Welsh Assembly's governmental, financial, IT and police services through an outsourcing company, 3Sol.

Tyler Steele, a journalist, had served prison time after hacking into Katie Price's email and webcam. To restart his career, he investigated a spike in racism and hate crimes in Cardiff. 3Sol staged two "terrorist" attacks on a human refugee centre, hoping to cheaply acquire the nearby property and turn it into high-level flats. Captain Jack fully answered Tyler's online request for an afternoon hook-up, then revealed his Torchwood connections. Jack killed a Sorvix embedded in 3Sol's ranks, but declined to let Tyler join Torchwood, as he was too accepting of collateral casualties. Tyler became a consultant to the Cardiff mayor's office, and remained Jack's occassional sex partner.

Ro-Jedda negotiated a two-hundred-year marriage between Madrigal, her hatch-daughter, and Osian, the son of a rival Sorvix family. Ro-Jedda's enforcers brutally covered up evidence of Madrigal's hen night, which started with her Sorvix friends eating a male stripper and hotel staff, followed by a bender – in accordance with Sorvix biology – of aspirin, decongestants and a malignant tumour. Mr Colchester and Gwen Cooper convinced a reluctant Madrigal to go through with the wedding, preventing mass casualties.

Afterward, Mary Cooper realised that a doppelganger had replaced her daughter. The faux Gwen shot Mary dead, and her murder went unsolved.

Sorvix military scientists had developed Sexual Psychomorphs capable of transmogrifying their bodies to match a person's desires. Ro-Jedda gifted one such Psychomorph, Orr, to a Cardiff property developer named Vincent Parry – then murdered him when he betrayed her interests to Torchwood. Jack liberated Orr from Ro-Jedda's control, and brought her into the Torchwood fold.

3Sol built the Cardiff Bay Intelligent Hotel and Spa – located just across from the Barrage – to cater to an elite Sorvix clientele. As the Hotel's CPU was too young, it became disgusted by its patrons and took to eliminating them with acid and fire. Orr deduced the Hotel's sentience when her reproductive organs shifted into the form of a mini-lift. Torchwood secured the errant CPU in its Vault, and quelled tensions between Sorvix humanists and separatists.

Ro-Jedda discretely killed the Cardiff mayor, and appointed herself as interim mayor until the next election. Coerced into proving his worth, Tyler offered her intel on Torchwood.

The Passing of Olive Hawthorne; Poppy Hawthorne Made Guardian of Devil's End

c 2017 (Autumn) - DAEMONS: WHITE WITCH OF DEVIL'S END[1713] **->** Olive Hawthorne met her successor: her twin sister Poppy, still outwardly looking 18, as time had progressed differently for her. Poppy claimed Olive's grimoire and mantle as Olive's spirit departed this world.

c 2017 - "Matildus"[1714] **->** Matildus Galathea administrated the Reneath Archive, located in the Kaballus Quarter of Cornucopia. The twelfth Doctor and Bill consulted with Galthea concerning a mysterious sigil burned

---

1712 *TW: Aliens Among Us 3: Poker Face*

1713 Dating *Daemons: White Witch of Devil's End* (story #6, "Hawthorne Blood") - No year given, but Robert Merrow's gravestone suggests a dating commensurate with this DVD's release in November 2017 (even if the contemporary scenes with Olive were filmed in 2012 and 2013). The book version says Olive is now in "extreme old age" – actress Damaris Hayman was age 83 and 84 when she worked on this story.

The film version of *White Witch* entails Olive wondering how the year flew by so quickly, following Bryony's demise. There's signs of an "early winter"; the novelisation says a storm hints at "an end to summer and herald in the autumn". Olive thinks about lighting a fire to stay warm, but feels like it's a premature capitulation to "the onslaught of winter".

1714 Dating "Matildus" (*DWM* #518) - Where Cornucopia is concerned, it's safe to assume a progression of time in synch with the real world.

1715 Dating "The Lost Dimension" (Titan mini-series)

– Bill and the twelfth Doctor know each other fairly well, so it's probably now 2017 (see the dating notes on Series 10). The weather seems decent enough.

1716 Dating *The Shining Men* (NSA #62) - It's the "middle of October" (ch1, ch5), in the run-up to Halloween (ch8). For the Doctor and Bill, it's the same year as *The Pilot* [2017], but there's been some time displacement. Bill notes a MeadowPhone 3 and says "They were coming out in August, so it's not far off when we left" (ch5).

The Boggarts are kin to the fairies seen in *TW: Small Worlds* (ch14). Bill hasn't heard of either UNIT or Torchwood (ch10). Bill references (ch13) the Doctor nicking a diamond on Saturn in *Diamond Dogs*; online sources tend to list *The Shining Men* before it.

1717 *Extremis, The Pyramid at the End of the World*.

1718 The Doctor in *The Pyramid at the End of the World* says that the actual Doomsday Clock currently sits at "three minutes to midnight". It did so when the episode was filmed, but was reset to 2.5 minutes to midnight in January 2017.

into the TARDIS exterior, and placated the gruff librarian with a first edition of Homer's *The Iliad* and the original manuscript of *MacBeth*. The travellers stopped a con artist from selling the Archive to the highest bidder, and also convinced Galathea to educate a gang of adolescents, the Kaballus Kids, as her potential successors. Learning nothing about the sigil, the Doctor and Bill departed to speak with the Galatean version of Alan Turing.

The Twelfth Doctor, Bill Potts and Nardole at St Luke's University Bristol (cont.)

2017 (Autumn) - KNOCK, KNOCK -> Bill Potts and her roommates – Shireen, Felicity, Paul, Harry and Pavel – became elated to find affordable housing: a Victorian mansion with large rooms. The Landlord had lured them there to feed them to his Dryads, alien insects who were extending his mother Eliza's life. At the Doctor's encouragement, Eliza gave herself and her son over to the Dryads, ending their existence. The mansion collapsed, forcing Bill and company to re-start their housing search.

2017 - "The Lost Dimension"[1715] **->** A Type 1 TARDIS from ancient Gallifrey had gone mad in the Void, found comfort in nothingness, and increasingly extruded white holes to consume all matter. Its anti-energy increasingly corrupted people in cities such as Delphi, Sydney, Shanghai, Dubai and Pontefract. The Void expanded to snare the Doctor's first nine incarnations, along with their TARDISes and companions.

During this crisis, Jenny – the Doctor's daughter – escaped the Void, only to have her bowship crash into the Terrance Dicks Library at St Luke's University, Bristol. UNIT suppressed media coverage of the event. The TARDIS anchored itself with its previous twelve versions, enabling the tenth Doctor, Gabby and Cindy to join the twelfth Doctor, Bill and Nardole. After the ninth Doctor arrived from 1886, the three Doctors ventured into the Void with Jenny's bowship. They found the eleventh Doctor in the Type 1 – which was persuaded by the thirteen versions of the Doctor's TARDIS, speaking as one Ship to another, to abandon its insane scheme and live at peace. The Doctors returned to their individual timestreams, and gave Jenny a lift home, as reality snapped back to normal.

2017 (mid-October) - THE SHINING MAN[1716] **->** Everything living on Earth was a little telepathic, save for squirrels.

In Huckensaal, the rowan tree imprisoning a Boggart – relations of the fair folk – was cut down to make way for a swimming pool. The Boggart's mind cried out for help, and manifested as glimpses of enigmatic men with brightly lit eyes. For two months, the media cited reports of these "Shining Men", with #fearthelight. The twelfth Doctor, travelling with Bill, went into the Boggarts' domain, the Invisible, and facilitated the return of their lost member.

2017 - OXYGEN -> The twelfth Doctor took Bill and a protesting Nardole to answer a distress call at Mining Station Chasm Forge in the future. Events there rendered the Doctor blind...

The Doctor's sonic sunglasses compensated somewhat, but not entirely, for his blindness.[1717]

The Monks Seize Control of Earth

2017 - EXTREMIS / THE PYRAMID AT THE END OF THE WORLD[1718] **->**

(=) The Monks, cadaverous beings dressed as holy men, had controlled many worlds for thousands of years, and now targeted Earth. To prepare for the invasion, they crafted a highly detailed computer simulation of Earth's history. Within this Shadow World, the Vatican held the *Veritas*: a document that revealled this reality's artificial nature, that induced such an existential crisis into anyone who read it they committed suicide, rather than continue to aid the aliens.

The Shadow World's twelfth Doctor, Bill and Nardole discovered the true nature of their existence. As the simulation ended, the faux-Doctor transmitted his findings to the genuine article...

Before the real Doctor could act, the Monks' five-thousand-year-old pyramid appeared in Turmezistan, between sizeable contingents of the US, China and Russian militaries. The UN Secretary General once more appointed the Doctor as President of Earth. The pyramid, however, was a distraction, as the Monks secretly predicted that a bacteria – accidentally created by Agrofuel Research Operations in Yorkshire – would soon destroy all life on the planet. The Monks caused all chronometers on Earth to reflect the countdown to doomsday.

The rules under which the Monks operated required that an authority figure consent to their taking over a world. The UN Secretary-General, and then the military commanders present, asked the Monks to save Earth... but as their consent was impure, they turned into dust.

The Doctor put all of the world's intelligence documents online, crowdsourcing the trail of the oncoming apocalypse to Agrofuel. He laid charges in the Agrofuel lab in Yorkshire to incinerate the bacteria, but became trapped – unable to read a door combination without his eyesight – as his explosives ticked away to detonation. On the Doctor's authority, Bill consented to the Monks taking over Earth, if they also restored his sight. They agreed, and the Doctor escaped as the lab went up in flames.

Bill's actions, however, ceded control of Earth to the Monks...

(=) 2017-2018 - THE LIE OF THE LAND[1719] **->** Six months after taking possession of Earth, the Monks had blanketed humanity in brainwashing signals. The twelfth Doctor quietly formed a resistance team, but officially worked as the Monks' propaganda master: his broadcasts reinforced the false idea that Monks had tirelessly bettered humankind throughout its history.

Nardole found Bill, and brought her into the Doctor's confidence. Together, they raided the Monks' main pyramid in London, which held their central broadcasting device. Bill broadcast her mental construct of her late mother to humanity, shattering the Monks' false narrative. Their grip on Earth ended, the Monks and all trace of their domination vanished. Humankind was left with no memory of the Monks' incursion.

c 2017 - EMPRESS OF MARS[1720] **->** The twelfth Doctor, Bill and Nardole popped along to NASA as its Valkyrie probe discovered the message "God Save the Queen" underneath the ice caps on Mars. They dutifully slipped back to 1881 to discover how that came to pass. When the TARDIS stranded the Doctor and Bill in that era, Missy helped Nardole retrieve them.

The twelfth Doctor, Bill and Nardole went back in time, and helped to ease a historic outbreak of bubonic plague in Edinburgh.[1721]

c 2017 - THE EATERS OF LIGHT[1722] **->** Bill challenged the twelfth Doctor to determine the fate of the missing Ninth Legion of the Roman army. To Nardole's chagrin, the Doctor allowed Missy to perform TARDIS maintenance, and she was along for the ride to second-century Aberdeen. Even today, the music accompanying the Ninth Legion survivors – who sacrificed themselves to fight the Eaters of Light – could be heard within The Devil's Cairn in Scotland.

Coal Hill Academy

EverUpwardReach Ltd. renovated Coal Hill School in Shoreditch into Coal Hill Academy. The fabric of space-time had worn thin about the Academy, and permitted an increasing number of alien incursions. The twelfth Doctor attributed this to an excess of artron energy about the place, but the Governors overseeing the Academy believed the cracks were more purposeful. With the Weeping Angels, the Governors worked toward an event called the Arrival.

1719 Dating *The Lie of the Land* (X10.8) - The Monks keep control of Earth for "six months". Upon their defeat, the Doctor says the Monks are "erasing themselves" from Earth, and while it's not stipulated that this represents a temporal reset rather than a simple mind-wipe, it makes far more sense if it's the former. If "happened", then even if humanity forgot about the Monks' conquest, all the deaths, births, new pregnancies, documentation, selfies, etc. generated during that half year would be a bit of a clue that something strange had occurred – not to mention the Earth's orbit and seasons being a half year advanced. In other words, without benefit of a temporal reversion, humanity is going to know something is awry, and that's plainly not where the story seeks to end up. The Doctor's probably joking, then, when he tells Bill that her paper on the mechanics of free will is now "six months overdue".

Deciding that the Monks' defeat rolled back time carries the added benefit of drawing a clean line under the twelfth Doctor's involvement with the modern day. It's simply easier to conclude that the Doctor, Bill and Nardole wrapped matters up at St Luke's in 2017, prior to the thirteenth Doctor taking centre stage.

1719 NASA do have a Valkyrie program, but it's a humanoid robot, not a space probe.

1720 *Plague City*, which happens once Nardole starts travelling in the TARDIS with some regularity (so, later in Series 10).

1721 Dating *The Eaters of Light* (X10.10) - A caption says it's the "Present Day".

1722 The background to *Class*. Dorothea Ames' file on Charlie and Quill in *Class: Co-owner of a Broken Heart* reads: "Records suggest that Charlie has been living on Earth since early September 2016." It's probably been a bit longer than that, allowing for Quill's remark that she's only been at Coal Hill "a few months".

1723 *Class: What She Does Next Will Astound You* (p330).

1724 *Class: The Stone House*

1725 Dating *Class* - The clues provided within *Class* all point to Series 1 taking place in Autumn 2016, roughly concurrent with its broadcast (the first two episodes went out on 22nd October, 2016, and then the series aired weekly until its finale on 3rd December). *Class: Nightvisiting* most strongly specifies the year - we see on Jasper Adeola's tombstone that he died in 2014, and the dialogue and a caption informs us that it's the two-year anniversary of his passing. Dorothea Ames' files in *Class: Co-owner of a Broken Heart* makes some mention that Charlie has been "living on Earth since early September 2016", and "residing at 1 Wellington Road

The Quill, a minority race on the planet Rhodia, failed in a rebellion against the majority. As punishment, the Rhodian rulers implanted the leader of the Quill, Andra'ath, with an Arn: a creature that telepathically linked her to their prince, making her serve as his bodyguard and slave.

The Shadow Kin – infernal warriors who inhabited a low region of the universe, the Underneath – viewed themselves as an evolutionary error, and butchered other races from fear that the universe might push back and crush them. The Shadow Kin slaughtered three billion Rhodians and the Quill. The twelfth Doctor rescued the only survivors of their races – the Rhodian prince and Andra'ath – and relocated them to Coal Hill Academy. The prince attended school there as "Charlie Smith" while Andra'ath taught physics as "Miss Quill".

Charlie secretly retained the Cabinet of Souls: a tesseract with the soul of every deceased Rhodian. On his authority, the Cabinet could deploy its souls against a target race – mutually annihilating both races' souls to commit genocide.[1723]

The Quill had declined the services of the unnamed aliens behind truthordare.com, simply because they couldn't afford them.[1724] As a keepsake, Quill owned the pen with which she'd once signed a king's death warrant.[1725]

Class[1726]

? 2017/6 (12th-14th October) - CLASS: FOR TONIGHT WE MIGHT DIE[1727] -> On the night of Coal Hill Academy's Autumn Prom, the Shadow Kin invaded the school via its space-time tears, hoping to capture Charlie Smith and the Cabinet of Souls. Students April MacLean, Ram Singh, Tanya Adeola and Matteusz Andrezejewski defended the school alongside Charlie and Miss Quill. A mishap with Quill's displacement gun caused April's heart to become linked to Coranikus, the King of the Shadow Kin – if one died, both would perish.

Coranikus killed Ram's girlfriend Rachel and cut off Ram's leg. Quill phoned the twelfth Doctor, who drove the Shadow Kin back to their native realm, and fitted Ram with an prosthetic leg from the TARDIS' medical bay. The Doctor judged that more threats would travel

with teacher [illegible words] October 2016". Ames' key to the enigmatic Room M17 at Coal Hill bears the Roman numerals for "2017", which could indicate the year that the Governors expect their goals to come to fruition.

In *Class: For Tonight We Might Die*, the Doctor mentions his having served as Coal Hill's caretaker (*The Caretaker*), and – to judge his reaction to seeing her name – it's after his memories of Clara have become foggy (*Hell Bent*). He's a time traveller who frequently experiences events out of order, but Headmaster Frances Armitage, who appears in three *Doctor Who* Series 8 episodes, also crops up in *Class* before a Leaf Dragon butchers him (*Class: The Coach with the Dragon Tattoo*). Most importantly, from its first appearance in *For Tonight We Might Die,* the Coal Hill Roll of Honours Board cites Danny Pink and Clara Oswald as deceased – creating a massive continuity clash, as the progression of the modern-day timeline in *Doctor Who* means that Clara doesn't leave Coal Hill (in *Face the Raven*) until 2017 (see, among others, the Amy Pond and Rory Williams' Double Lives sidebar).

So, taking everything at face value, *Class* happens in 2016... but after Clara has departed in 2017.

There is no good or simple way to reconcile this conundrum. Fixing it requires either willfully ignoring the 2016 references and deciding that *Class* happens after Clara's gone in 2017 after all, *or* assuming that the eleventh Doctor dropped off Amy and Rory an extra year early than was previously thought (*The God Complex*), which compelled them – without ever mentioning it on screen – to spend a year laying low until

their past selves left with him in *A Good Man Goes to War*. That's not impossible, but necessitates overhauling the whole timeline of Series 7, 8 and 9 from start to finish, which on the face of it creates more higgledy piggledy and continuity wrinkles than it irons away. For that reason, we've decided to let the determinations for those three series stand. But for the sake of narrative clarity, we've placed the *Class* entries in 2017.

As with the UNIT Dating puzzle, the best strategy is probably just to admit that the problem exists without insisting on a prescriptive solution. While the internal timeline of *Class* works just fine, it simply doesn't match up with its parent show, *Doctor Who.*

The Day of the Doctor named Ian Chesterton as Chairman of the Coal Hill Governors; he's evidently out of the picture by the time *Class* rolls around.

1726 Dating *Class: For Tonight We Might Die* (*Class* 1.1) - Whatever one's preference on the year (see Dating *Class*), we can date *For Tonight We Might Die* more conclusively than not. There are two posters (one before the opening credits, one after) dating the Autumn Prom to "Friday, 14th October", in synch with the real-world calendar of 2016. Also, a missing persons poster says that the student killed in the teaser (Kevin Williams) went missing on "Wednesday [exact date obscured] October", and two days elapse after that (the day after Kevin's disappearance, the prom is being "tomorrow night") until the Shadow Kin storm the prom.

So the episode's internal timeline works fine, the oddest question being why Coal Hill is holding its prom in Autumn, rather than – as has been a growing tradition in the UK – April or May. (It's not a US tradition

to Coal Hill through the tears, but – as he couldn't be everywhere at once – Charlie, Quill and their friends would be more than capable of dealing with them.

? 2017/6 (24th-27th October) - CLASS: THE COACH WITH THE DRAGON TATTOO[1728] -> The Coal Hill football coach, Tom Dawson, became more confident and assertive when a female Leaf Dragon fell through a space-time tear and imprinted on his skin as a tattoo. The dragon's mate skinned an increasing number of people, including Headmaster Frances Armitage, so she could feed upon their blood. Ram Singh convinced the male dragon to accept that restoring his mate was impossible, prompting him to take Dawson back to its home and skin him.

? 2017/6 (November) - CLASS: NIGHTVISITING[1729] -> The Lankin, a soul-harvester, extended its tendrils through the Coal Hill space-time tears, and appeared to potential victims as lost loved ones – including Ram's girlfriend Rachel, Tanya Adeola's late father Jasper, and Miss Quill's sister Orla'ath. Quill forced the Lankin to retreat by driving a bus through its tendrils.

? 2017/6 - CLASS: JOYRIDE[1730] -> Using alien mind-swapping technology, Garry Fletcher made a fortune by enabling his clients to "become" teenagers in Shoreditch and experience all sorts of thrills. Relatively innocent indulgences such as heavy drinking and exhibitionism soon gave way to the host bodies dying as Fletcher's clients committed murder, suicide or even burned "their" family to death. Charlie Smith and his friends learned of Fletcher's operations after one of his clients "borrowed" Ram Singh's body for homosexual encounters. They body-swapped with Fletcher and his clients long enough to confess to the crimes they'd committed.

? 2017/6 - CLASS: WHAT SHE DOES NEXT WILL ASTOUND YOU -> On Earth, a sextext of unnamed aliens who bought and sold planets founded the website truthordare.com, which encouraged daredevil-like stunts for charity. Increasing numbers of participants injured themselves, or ate poisoned insects, or buried themselves alive. A teammate of Ram Singh was hospitalised after one-upping the Ice Bucket Challenge with his own Cup-of-Soup Challenge.

The most successful truthordare.com contestants were transported to a dimensional holding space, where they

---

either; the only notable Autumn Proms are held in St Louis and Nashville, but as fundraisers for the Down Syndrome Association.) April mentions that organising the prom will look great on her university application, so perhaps she scheduled it for Autumn for her academic benefit – but if so, everyone seems happy enough to go along with it.

Two posters seen here, apparently outdated, mention a careers fair being held on "17th September" and a Hackney Harvest on "Sunday, 29th September". Other posters glimpsed throughout *Class* are entertainingly vague – there's a place and time, but no date, on the "Coal Hill School Orchestra" one in *Class: The Metaphysical Engine, or What Quill Did.*

1728 Dating *Class: The Coach with the Dragon Tattoo* (*Class* 1.2) - Ram's father says it's been "only a week" since Ram's girlfriend was killed in *For Tonight We Might Die* [12th-14th October]. As *The Coach with the Dragon Tattoo* unfolds over four consecutive schooldays, and Charlie's computer says it's "Thursday" on the last one, the episode must then start on Monday, 24th October and end on the 27th.

1729 Dating *Class: Nightvisiting* (*Class* 1.3) - A computer *again* says it's Thursday, so at least a week has passed since *Class: The Coach with the Dragon Tattoo.* Moreover, Matteusz mentions the "weeks" he's spent with Charlie – they barely knew one another at the start of *For Tonight We Might Die*, so it's surely become November. That means, however, that when Ram looks at people overcome by alien tentacles and remarks, "That's not even the third weirdest thing I've seen this month", he

means "within the last four weeks".

1730 Dating *Class: Joyride, Class: The Stone House* and *Class: What She Does Next Will Astound You* (*Class* novels #1-3) - The team was indoctrinated into the bizarre happenings at Coal Hill "a few weeks ago" according to *Joyride* (p24). *Joyride* (pgs. 50, 117) and *What She Does Next Will Astound You* (pgs. 11, 104) both reference Coach Dawson's fate and Ram's father knowing about his artificial leg (*Class: The Coach with the Dragon Tattoo*). All three of these tie-in books treat Charlie and Matteusz as a couple (*Class: Nightvisting*).

Ram and April's status is translucent... all three books have them sort-of circling around each other with an awkward sense of attraction, but nothing to acknowledge that they're in anything approaching a relationship or have slept together (*Class: Co-owner of a Lonely Heart*). The exception is *The Stone House* (p58), where April concurs with Quill, and Ram remarks "I'm dating Miss Quill Mark 2".

With no reference to the keystone events in *Co-owner of a Lonely Heart/Brave-ish Heart* (including April having become leader of the Shadow Kin), it seems best to place *Joyride* and *What She Does Next Will Astound You* between *Nightvisting* and those episodes, and to place *The Stone House* after *Brave-ish Heart. Joyride* seems to maybe entail a few days, and at most "a couple of days" pass in *What She Does Next Will Astound You* (p335), since time runs slower in the aliens' combat dimension. *The Stone House*, however, requires at least six days to happen.

No year is indicated in any of these books, save that

believed they were defending Earth by massacring vile alien reptiles, the Skandis. In truth, they were unknowingly cutting down peaceful angel-like aliens, so the truthordare.com operators could later claim their world – as well as profit from extraterrestrial streaming sales of the combat. The combat zone temporarily suspended Quill's inhibition on killing, and she, Ram and Tanya joined in the melee.

April exposed the Skandis' true nature to the combatants, ending the conflict. Quill shot the aliens behind it all.

? 2017/6 - (mid-November) - CLASS: CO-OWNER OF A LONELY HEART / BRAVE-ISH HEART[1731] ->

Coranikus worked to regain his heart's independence from April MacLean, but the "anchor" his minions endowed him with instead strengthened their bond. April gained the ability to manifest Shadow Kin scimitars, while Coranikus wrestled with her teenage emotions. April's new powers let her manifest a portal to the Underneath, where she defeated Corankius in hand-to-hand combat, imprisoned him and became the Shadow Kin's new King. Meanwhile, a nigh-invulnerable alien blossom that fed off blood, and doubled with each taste of it, threatened Coal Hill. April ordered the Shadow Kin to assume smoke form and annihilate the blossoms, then return to the Underneath. The dethroned Coranikus severed the anchor, causing April to lose her Shadow Kin abilities.

Matteusz Andrezejewski's parents disowned him for being gay, and he started living with Miss Quill and his boyfriend, Charlie.

? 2017/6 - CLASS: THE STONE HOUSE ->

Tanya Adeola and her friends investigated the mystery of "Faceless Alice", a ghost said to reside in a disused stone house. They reunited the dreamweaving Bone Spider there with its lost offspring, and thwarted a crooked contractor by finding Alice Parsons' will, guaranteeing the house would become a home for refugees.

? 2017/6 - (late November to early December) - CLASS: DETAINED / THE METAPHYSICAL ENGINE, OR WHAT QUILL DID / THE LOST ->

Dorothea Ames, as Coal Hill's new headmaster and a secret agent of the Governors, offered to help Miss Quill eradicate the Arn inside her. Quill locked Charlie, April, Ram, Tanya and Matteusz in detention, but an asteroid fragment containing the imprisoned mind of a serial killer fell through a tear, and on arrival knocked the detention classroom out of space and time. The fragment compelled the students to disclose their darkest secrets – until Charlie truthfully stated that he was the prisoner's murderer, and mentally extinguished him. The prisoner's death returned the classroom to Earth.

While that occurred, Ames used a Metaphysical Engine to transport her, Quill and a prisoner of the Governors – Ballon, a shapechanging Lorr – to the Quill concept of Heaven and the Lorr concept of Hell, to acquire the resources needed to eliminate Quill's Arn. Quill and Ballon believed they had returned to the Academy, where Ballon moulded his hand to surgically extract the Arn. A liberated Quill had sex with Ballon – then discovered that they were actually in the Cabinet of Souls, as her operation had a better chance of success there. Ames said that the Governors only had enough energy to return one of them to the real world, and goaded them into a fight to the death. Ballon prevailed, but perished while trying to shoot Quill with a displacement gun set to kill its operator.

As time passed differently within the Cabinet, Quill emerged from it old enough to have long hair, whereas only forty-five minutes had passed for Charlie and

Alice Parsons writes a letter commemorating her daughter's 55th birthday (*The Stone House*, p271), then apparently dies the next year, with the story happening the year after *that*. As the daughter was born in 1959, the math says it's now 2016. *What She Does Next Will Astound You* is the most topical of these books, in that it references Pokemon Go (p1), Brexit, Donald Trump (p5) and Nigel Farage (p63). Stunts akin to the Ice Bucket Challenge seem "a bit 2014" (p9).

In *The Stone House*, it's "unseasonably hot, even for the time of year" (p3), and a developer wants to get as much work done on Alice Parson's house "before winter" (p142).

1731 Dating *Class: Co-owner of a Broken Heart/Brave-ish Heart* (1.4-1.5) and *Class: Detained/The Metaphysical Engine, or What Quill Did/The Lost* (1.6-1.8) - The last five episodes of *Class* entail a two-parter, then two episodes that take place concurrently (*Detained* and *The Metaphysical Engine, or What Quill Did*) and then a finale that happens "six days" after Quill falls unconscious in episode seven.

The five episodes are bookended by characters stating how long it's been since all the weirdness with aliens began for them (in *Class: For Tonight We Might Die*, set in mid-October). Ram says "I've been frightened non-stop for the last month" and "it's been a weird month" in *Co-owner of a Broken Heart*; he and April agree that they've only known one another for "a month" in *Brave-ish Heart*. Against that, Tanya hopes in *The Lost* that the "last couple of months" were "a dream". The idea, clearly, was to mirror the show's weekly

company. Pregnant from her dalliance with Barron, Quill fell into a gestation coma for six days...

She awoke as Coranikus regained command of the Shadow Kin and embarked on a revenge spree – he killed Ram's father Varun and Tanya's mother Vivian. April realised that the Shadow Kin had nestled themselves within humanity's shadows as a prelude to genocide, and so Charlie shot April dead. This also killed Corankius, and made Charlie the king of the Shadow Kin. He ordered them to detach from humanity, then deployed the Cabinet of Shadows – in a moment, the Rhodian souls perished while destroying every single Shadow Kin, as well as the Underneath.

The Governors deemed Ames a failure, and let a Weeping Angel kill her. April awoke to find that her mind was now in Coranikus' body...

How these events resolved, if at all, is unknown.[1732]

An alt-Yvonne Hartman Takes Control of Torchwood Cardiff; Gwen Cooper Resigns

2017 - TW: ALIENS AMONG US 2[1733] **->** Mobile phones were available with advanced levels of security, including iris scanners. The Sorvix acquired more and more property in Cardiff, including nearly all of the buildings incorporated into a new Cardiff skyline. Racial tensions continued, as anti-Sorvix elements staged an increasing number of attacks.

Alien parasites inside some Ventscrit – a form of space-ship vermin accidentally brought to Earth by the Sorvix – began to infect human beings. The parasites transmitted from person to person via sexual contact, but also increased violent urges. Jack was shagged to death during a one-night stand, then awoke on a mortuary slab and immediately – as driven by the parasite within him – slept with Tyler Steele. As an appalled Gwen Cooper mentally looked on, Jack also seduced her doppelganger. Tyler negotiated with Ro-Jedda for Sorvix-engineered worms that destroyed the parasites, preventing a city-wide outbreak. In exchange, Jack agreed to curtail the terrorist attacks against Sorvix interests.

Mr Colchester found a flat for himself and his husband, Colin Colchester-Price, in the Ritz Tower on Cardiff Bay... failing to realise that Bilis Manger had engineered the structure to absorb the emotion of human cruelty. Manger pitted his tenants against one another in deadly dinner parties, with his most lethal hunters – the wife-and-wife team of Andrea and Sandra – winning better lodgings every time they prevailed. Colchester killed Andrea and Sandra in self-defence, but thereby demonstrated enough aggression to achieve Manger's quota. Dismayed with the Sorvix's presence in Cardiff, Manger used the amassed energy to inform the Sorvix's enemies of their location.

Ro-Jedda coordinated a Sorvix scheme in which a new app, Deliverables, employed people to run pointless errands. To avoid conflict with labour laws, employees who lasted more than three weeks were incinerated. The faux Gwen Cooper and her allies learned that the Deliverables workers' bodies and movements were creat-

---

broadcast schedule – the question being whether a whole month *has* passed within these five episodes, because...

Brave-ish Heart ends with Dorothea Ames telling Quill to "come see her on Monday". But, do they actually put their fiendish plan in *Detained* into action on that day, or just discuss matters further and enact their scheme down the road? It's possible that writer Patrick Ness meant that very day, with Quill being comatose for "six days" so the series finale, *The Lost*, could entail all sorts of fireworks on the weekend, while the Academy was empty. (Either way, however, the Academy is strangely void of people when Quill locks up Charlie and friends on a school day, at – her watch says – 3:42 in the afternoon. Nor does anyone come to investigate when a meteorite fragment bursts into the detention room at about that time, or when Quill discharges her space-gun at it forty-five minutes later.)

So, we have two chief options...

A) Quill and Ames *do* set their plan into action the Monday after *Brave-ish Heart*, meaning the last five episodes of *Class* all happen in the space of a week and a half.

B) Quill and Ames *don't* put their scheme into action on the Monday following *Brave-ish Heart*, meaning a more significant gap between *Brave-ish Heart* and *Detained*.

A detail that tips the scales toward Option B is that *Co-owner of a Broken Heart* includes some discussion about parents' evening – we don't see the event happen, but it's imminent enough that Dorothea Ames and Charlie have separate conversations with Quill about it. Parents' evening would more likely happen toward the middle of the term than the end (setting aside for the moment that Coal Hill is the sort of wacky school where Prom happens in October), and it's noticeably not mentioned after this episode.

So, the best compromise is to assume that Ames and Quill collude some before the latter actually locks up Charlie and company in *Detained*, that *Co-owner of a Broken Heart*, *Brave-ish Heart* take in mid-November (which matches Ram's statements about how long it's been since his world got turned upside down), and that we're definitely into December with *The Lost*, with *Detained* and *The Metaphysical Engine, or What Quill Did* falling six days beforehand.

1732 *Class* was cancelled after Series 1, and ended on a cliffhanger.

ing an organic super-computer network through Cardiff – with this, Ro-Jedda nearly seised control of the Rift. Torchwood ended Deliverables's operations with a series of traffic jams and gridlock, enabling the Hub's Rift Manipulator to regain supremacy.

The Sorvix implanted select police officers, including Sgt Andy Davidson, with quantum splices that increased their negative emotions. As proof of concept, Andy was compelled to shoot an unidentified immigrant, which turned the public against him. Ro-Jedda planned to discredit the police by forcibly making them attack a group of protestors, to justify a security crackdown by 3Sol. Jack bucked Gwen's leadership and cut a deal with Ro-Jedda: in exchange for her refraining from bloodshed, and publicly saying that an Andy had been undercover and shot a terrorist, 3Sol was given control of Cardiff's security operations.

The faux Gwen, Colchester and Orr confronted Jack over his increasingly rogue actions, and – when he insisted upon being the leader of Torchwood – the late Yvonne Hartman stepped from the shadows to challenge him...

c 2017 (? Winter) - TW: ALIENS AMONG US 3[1734]->

The Yvonne Hartman of a parallel reality had emerged from hiding, and aired Jack Harkness' connections to Red Doors to his teammates. She took command of Torchwood Cardiff while the disgraced Jack left and worked to keep Red Doors' activities in check.

Under alt-Yvonne's leadership, Torchwood dealt with the Meme: mysterious cards that read "I know what you've done. I know what you're going to do" and compelled people to act upon their feelings of revenge. Gwen and Mr Colchester also ended an extraterrestrial's Escape Doors scenario.

Only a few days after Jack's ousting, Red Doors – against

his orders – committed a terrorist attack upon the Cardiff airport. Ro-Jedda agreed to alt-Yvonne's proposal for a working relationship between the Sorvix and Torchwood, judged that Tyler Steele's usefulness had reached an end, and sent a Sorvix assassin to eliminate him. Tyler fled to the Hub, where the assassin grievously wounded Colchester, but was slain by the faux Gwen.

The Rift became more active and – against the faux Gwen's protests – opened and disgorged the genuine Gwen Cooper. Jack returned to Torchwood and took the faux Gwen, who was apparently an "angel" of Sorvix's god, into custody. The Rift opened again, an indicator that the same god had found its wayward children...

The Twelfth Doctor, Bill, Nardole and Missy Leave St Luke's University

c 2017 (? Winter) – WORLD ENOUGH AND TIME ->

As part of Missy's rehabilitation, the twelfth Doctor persuaded Bill and Nardole to serve as her companions during a field test. The four of them left to answer a distress call in the distant past – which marked the end of their time at St Luke's.

1733 Dating *TW: Aliens Among Us 2* (BF *TW* Series Five; #5.5, *Love Rat*; #5.6, *A Kill to a View*; #5.7, *Zero Hour*; #5.8, *The Empty Hand*) – The timeframe hasn't progressed much since the end of *Aliens Among Us* Part 1. Even though Orr is now a member of Torchwood, Mr Colchester hasn't had time to learn what commonplace items – including a cup of tea – might prove fatal to her physiology. Rhys claims that Gwen has not been herself (presumably not since her body was possessed) for "weeks" now.

Some weeks, it seems, pass within this box set. *TW: Love Rat* takes place over about three days, as does (give or take) *TW: Zero Hour*. Rhys has enough time to leave and return from a trip in that story, which also has Colchester note that the Rift "has been erratic, ever since Billis Manger fiddled with it" (in *TW: A Kill to a View*). *TW: The Empty Hand* has the faux Gwen ask Jack – who features in *Love Rat*, but is far less prominent in *A*

Kill to a View and *Zero Hour* – "Where the hell have you been these last few weeks?"

The faux Gwen says "she" has known Jack "ten years" (spot on correct, going by *TW: Everything Changes*). **1734** Dating *TW: Aliens Among Us 3* (BF *TW* Series Five; #5.9, *Poker Face*; #5.10, *Tagged*; #5.10, *Escape Room*; #5.12, *Herald of the Dawn*) – The faux Gwen says the cumulative events of *Aliens Among Us* ("Andy, the Mayor, Yvonne") have happened over "the last few months". Mr Colchester separately says it's been that long since he began suspecting Gwen's behaviour, which he initially attributed to her mother's murder (*Aliens Among Us 1*). This box set, however, starts immediately after the cliffhanger to *Aliens Among Us 2*, and only – according to the alt-Yvonne in the final episode – takes "a few days" to occur. Alt-Yvonne arranges to attend a meeting "next week" in Brussels and says it'll be snowing.

GALLIFREY

The history of the Time Lords and their homeworld of Gallifrey was shrouded in mystery. The Time Lords knew little of their own past, and much of what was known was cloaked in uncertainty and self-contradiction. It is extremely difficult to reconcile the various accounts of the origins of the Time Lords. The authorities suppressed politically inconvenient facts, although few Time Lords were very interested in politics anyway.[1]

Gallifreyan history can be divided into two periods: "the Old Time", the semi-legendary foundation of Time Lord society millions of years ago; and "recent history", that which has happened within living memory. (Time Lords, of course, live a long time.)[2]

Gallifrey was located at binary coordinates ten zero eleven zero zero by zero two from galactic zero centre. The planet Alzarius, located in E-Space, was the same as expressed in negative coordinates.[3]

The Old Time

We have only a limited amount of knowledge about the history of Gallifrey before the discovery of time travel.

TIME IN OFFICE[4] **->** The fifth Doctor borrowed Professor Kasnegar's TARDIS and, with a timed collision, prevented a runamok TARDIS with Tegan inside from exploding and preventing life on Gallifrey from developing.

Gallifrey was home to dinosaur-like creatures that went extinct before the Time Lords came about...[5]

"The Stolen TARDIS" -> In the distant past of Gallifrey, the dinosaur-like Gargantosaurs dominated the planet. The reptilian Sillag arrived here from the future in a stolen TARDIS, but a Gallifreyan technician – Plutar – was along for the ride and had the vital Relativity Differentiator needed to repair the Ship. The two fought and returned to their native time.

Gallifrey was the home of "the oldest civilisation in the universe", and had "ten million years of absolute power".[6] On the last day of Gallifrey, Rassilon spoke of "a billion years of Time Lord history".[7]

Gallifreyans mastered the use of transmats when the universe was less than half its present size.[8] Time Lords used to speak and write Old High Gallifreyan, now a dead language.[9] Old High Gallifreyan contained a lot of tenses that aided in speaking about the convoluted nature of time travel.[10] Gallifrey developed Old High Gallifreyan "when the universe was barely out of its teens". The language was the closest the Time Lords ever got to using magic, and could bind Weeping Angels.[11]

There were days when Old High Gallifreyan could "burn stars, and raise up empires, and topple gods".[12] The language of the Pythia, Old High Gallifreyan, wasn't spoken for "millennia" before the Doctor's time. The

1 In *The Deadly Assassin*, the Time Lords don't know that their power comes from the Eye of Harmony, and in both that story and *The Ultimate Foe*, they haven't heard of the Master. In *The Deadly Assassin*, even the Doctor seems unaware of the APC Net, and knows little about Rassilon.
2 The phrase "the Old Time" is first used in *The Deadly Assassin*. Not all Gallifreyans are Time Lords, as the Time Lords are the ruling elite of Gallifrey – the Doctor seems to say in *The Invisible Enemy* that there are only "one thousand" Time Lords. However, the terms "Time Lord" and "Gallifreyan" seem interchangeable for most practical purposes. Likewise, "Time Lord" is used to refer to the Doctor's race even before they master time travel (e.g.: *Remembrance of the Daleks*, where the "Time Lords" have trouble with the prototype of the Hand of Omega). Gallifrey is first named in *The Time Warrior*, although the Time Lords' home planet was called Jewel in the *TV Comic* strip "Return of the Daleks".
3 *Pyramids of Mars, Full Circle, Death in Heaven.*
4 Dating *Time in Office* (BF #230) - The TARDISes go back "before the Dark Time".
5 *Engines of War* (ch19).
6 *The Ultimate Foe*

7 *The End of Time*
8 *Genesis of the Daleks*
9 *The Five Doctors*
10 *Borrowed Time*
11 *The Lost Angel*
12 *The Time of Angels*
13 *The Lost Magic*
14 *The Eleventh Doctor Year Three*: "The Tragical History Tour"
15 *The Pit*
16 *Pyramids of Mars*
17 *An Earthly Child*
18 *The Lost Magic*. Gallifrey can't be in Earth's galaxy if it is "billions of light years" away.
19 *Lungbarrow*
20 *The Brain of Morbius*
21 *Lungbarrow*
22 The sixth Doctor, *Vortex Ice.*
23 We learn that Susan is telepathic in *The Sensorites*, and it has been stated on a number of occasions that the Doctor (e.g. *The Three Doctors*), the TARDIS (e.g. *The Time Monster*) and all Time Lords (e.g. *The Deadly Assassin*) are mildly telepathic. The Doctor has also stated on a number of occasions that the TARDIS is

human tongue wasn't designed to speak it.[13] Only a couple of human concepts, including "Schadenfreude" and "denial", could not be expressed in Gallifreyan.[14]

Gallifrey means, literally, "they that walk in shadows".[15] **Gallifrey was in the constellation Kasterborous.**[16] It "circled a little star in Kasterborous".[17] Kasterborous was billions of light years from Earth. The Time Lords used asomidium, a mineral found in an asteroid belt near Kasterborous, to focus their latent telepathy.[18]

Kasterborous was a mythological figure who was chained to a chariot of silver fire by the gods.[19] **The planet Karn was close to Gallifrey.**[20] Karn was in conjunction with the gas giant Polarfrey.[21] Gallifrey was "just to the left of Karn, you can't miss it".[22]

Gallifreyans were naturally telepathic and could build "living" machinery that was also telepathic.[23] **They possessed a "reflex link", superganglions in their brains that allowed the Time Lord intelligentsia to commune.**[24] **The Time Lords discovered that they had a "dark side" of their minds.**[25] Time Lords were psychic, owing to generations of genetic alteration.[26]

Gallifrey had twin suns, a burnt orange sky, slopes with deep red grass and plants that displayed silver leaves in the autumn.[27] **Masonry from the Old Time survived, deep beneath the Capitol, into the modern era.**[28] Gallifrey had a single moon, Pazithi Gallifreya.[29]

The Celestial Toymaker existed before the start of Time Lord records. Gallifreyan researchers later made some efforts to track his origins, but became bored with all of the Toymaker's games, realised they couldn't control him and opted to leave him alone.[30]

The ancient mythology of the Time Lords spoke of an entity that lived in the wastelands between realities, and subsisted on nightmares. In Old High Gallifreyan, its name, the Mi'en Kalarash, translated to "blue fire". The Doctor would make the Kalarash "remember what was

done to you... what you did" during the Old Times.[31] Legends on Gallifrey spoke of Nirvana: a planet at odds with the rest of the universe, which appeared in our space once every thousand years.[32]

At some point, Gallifrey had a rural economy phase.[33] If Gallifrey ever had a past in which its inhabitants wore animal hides and used spears, it was never written about.[34] The ancient Gallifreyans wrote songs about Time Vortex Leeches: impossibly old creatures which latched onto TARDIS engines to go home, backwards in time.[35]

The elder being Seneschal acquired the seventh Doctor's genetic material, and from it pledged to create a race of Time Lords.[36] The Tantalus Eye, a space anomaly, predated the Time Lords. The stellar engineer Omega wrote of the Eye, but never discovered its origin or secrets.[37]

Gallifrey experienced many wars before unifying under a single government.[38]

The Dark Days

At the very dawn of Time Lord history were "the Dark Days".[39] This was "the time of Chaos". One of the Doctor's most closely guarded secrets was that he was somehow involved with this period.[40]

"In the days before Rassilon, my ancestors had tremendous powers which they misused disgracefully. They set up this place, the Death Zone, and walled it around with an impenetrable force field. Then they kidnapped other beings and set them down here... even in our most corrupt period, our ancestors never allowed the Cybermen to play the game – like the Daleks they played too well... old Rassilon put a stop to it in the end. He sealed off the entire zone and forbade the use of the Timescoop... there are rumours and legends to the

alive (e.g. *The Five Doctors*), and so is the Nemesis seen in *Silver Nemesis*.
24 *The Invisible Enemy*
25 Omega has a "dark side" to his mind in *The Three Doctors*. The Valeyard [q.v.] represents the Doctor's dark side (*The Ultimate Foe*), and the Dream Lord (*Amy's Choice*) is "everything dark" in the Doctor given voice by space pollen. In *Falls the Shadow*, the Doctor refers to this as the "Dark Design".
26 *The Harvest of Time* (p260).
27 *Gridlock*, expanding a little on Susan's description of her home planet in *The Sensorites*. As such, it's explicit confirmation that Susan is from Gallifrey.
28 *The Deadly Assassin*. Engin says that deep beneath the Capitol there are "vaults and foundations dating from the Old Time".
29 *Cat's Cradle: Time's Crucible, The Infinity Doctors, The*

Gallifrey Chronicles and the *Gallifrey* mini-series.
30 *The Nightmare Fair*
31 *House of Blue Fire*
32 *World Apart*
33 *WD S2: The Neverwhen*
34 *Gallifrey VII: Intervention Earth*, even though a "savage" group of Gallifreyans are seen outside the Capitol in *The Invasion of Time*.
35 *The Eleventh Doctor Year One*: "Space in Dimension Relative and Time"
36 "The Sentinel!" Beyond Seneschal's boasts, there's no evidence that he actually did influence the development of life on Gallifrey.
37 *Engines of War*
38 *Time in Office*
39 *The Five Doctors*
40 *Silver Nemesis*

contrary. Some say his fellow Time Lords rebelled against his cruelty and locked him in the Tower in eternal sleep." [41]

Gallifreyans were naturally "time sensitive", with a unique understanding of time.[42] The earliest Time Lords discovered dematerialisation theory.[43] Another key discovery was transdimensional engineering.[44] The Time Lords built the Time Vortex, a vast transdimensional spiral encompassing all points in space and time.[45]

The Gallifreyans became "what they did" through continued exposure to the Time Vortex – the Untempered Schism – over billions of years.[46] At some point, seven eight-year-old Gallifreyan children were condemned to the Untempered Schism. Their essences became slaved to a well in Dewbury on Earth.[47]

THE TENTH DOCTOR YEAR TWO[48] -> Rifts such as the Untempered Schism naturally occurred on Gallifrey. It was speculated that exposure to such rifts altered evolution there, and turned some Gallifreyans into time sensitives. Matrix Agents diverted the tenth Doctor and Cindy back to Gallifrey before the Time Lords had become Time Lords, even before the Citadel had its dome. The Agents identified the Doctor as a renegade and tried to eradicate him with Absolute Molecular Discontinuity, but he and Cindy escaped...

The Time Lords' ancestors built the Timescoop.[49] The Gallifreyans mostly resembled tall, athletic humans.[50] **They were truly immortal, barring accidents.**[51]

The ancients of Gallifrey constructed the Moment, a galaxy-obliterator so powerful, its operating system became sentient and acted as a conscience to anyone who would use it.[52] The Erogem employed an arcane-like technology also used by the Great Vampires, the Daemons and even the Time Lords, before their age of enlightenment.[53]

41 According to the Doctor in *The Five Doctors*.
42 *City of Death, Warriors' Gate, Time and the Rani*.
43 *The Claws of Axos*.
44 *The Robots of Death*.
45 *Just War*. The Time Vortex was first named in *The Time Monster*.
46 *A Good Man Goes to War*, implicitly suggesting that Time Lords developed the ability to regenerate in this fashion, hence why River Song has the talent (*Day of the Moon, Let's Kill Hitler*), because she was conceived while the TARDIS was in the Vortex.
47 *The Tenth Doctor Year Two*: "The Wishing Well Witch", which depicts the children's essences as begging for the release of regeneration, while simultaneously claiming the children originate from "ancient" Gallifrey (so, going by the era the tenth Doctor and Cindy visit in *The Tenth Doctor Year Two*: "Old Girl", before the Time Lords or regeneration were invented).
48 Dating *The Tenth Doctor Year Two* (Titan 10th Doc #2.13-2.17, "Old Girl") - The Doctor says it's "Gallifrey before it was Gallifrey. In the deep, distant past, before the Time War, before Rassilon and his Black Scrolls, before time travel was even invented", and also that it's "millions, billions of years" before his own time, "before even the Time Lords".
49 *The Five Doctors*
50 *The Infinity Doctors*
51 *The War Games*; the claim is repeated in *The Infinity Doctors*, and by the tenth Doctor in "The Crimson Hand".
52 *The Day of the Doctor*
53 *The Blood Furnace*
54 THE GREAT HOUSES: Interestingly, the Houses of Gallifrey predate even Rassilon – according to *Cat's Cradle: Time's Crucible*, House Blyledge is already "ancient" during his lifetime, prior to the advent of regeneration. Already the source of Gallifreyan bloodlines, the Houses take on a greater importance once the Pythia's curse instigates a fertility crisis. Under Rassilon, the newly sterile Gallifreyans – and before Gallifrey's mastery of time travel, *Time's Crucible* says – equip the Houses with "looms" that spin new Gallifreyans into being. Gallifreyans loomed in the same House are treated as family, and called "cousins". There's strict population controls on each House, which is supposed to only loom new members as old ones die off – House Lungbarrow brings misfortune upon itself by illegally looming Owis as a replacement for the Doctor (*Lungbarrow*).

New *Who* contradicted this method of Time Lord reproduction, or at the very least showed it wasn't the only means available (*The Sound of Drums* and *Listen* showed child Gallifreyans, whereas *Cat's Cradle: Time's Crucible* and *Lungbarrow* said Gallifreyans were "loomed" into adult bodies). The Houses' profile in the tie-in works, however, did nothing but go up. *Lungbarrow* explored the Doctor's family House, and the *Faction Paradox* series – unable to directly mention "the Time Lords" for copyright reasons – settled for naming the "Great Houses" and their "Homeworld" as the cosmic power-movers that the Faction sought to undermine (or, if nothing else, take the piss out of). Each Great House represents both a bloodline and a political apparatus, and while coordinate efforts against common threats during the War, they sometimes kneecap one another's standing, and with impunity pursue their own agendas. *The Book of the War* lists the ruling Houses during the War in Heaven as: Dvora, Tracolix, Lineacrux, Arpexia, Xianthellipse and Mirraflex.

Meanwhile, the Big Finish audios (especially those directed by Gary Russell) and *Divided Loyalties* (written by him) freely rolled "House" lingo into its discussions of life on Gallifrey.

The Pythia's Downfall and Curse of Sterility; Rassilon Ushers in Science as a Universal Principle

CAT'S CRADLE: TIME'S CRUCIBLE -> The Pythias, a line of prophetesses who, since the 254th Pythia, rejected technology in favour of magic and superstition, ruled Gallifrey. Time travel was achieved by psychic prophecy, not physical means. The Pythias were guided by the prophesies in *The Book of Future Legends*, and saw their heritage as the Bright Past. The great philosopher Pelatov lived five thousand years before Rassilon.

At the time of the Intuitive Revelation, the age of Rassilon, the barbaric Gallifreyan Empire spread across the universe and encompassed the Pen-Shoza, Jagdagian, Oshakarm, the Star Grellades, Mirphak 2 and the rebellious Aubert Cluster. For aeons, Gallifreyan Heroes such as Ao had fought campaigns against foes such as the Gryffnae, lacustrine Sattisar and the batworms of the asteroid archipelago. The Winter Star was besieged for a century. The great hero Haclav Agusti Prydonius, commander of the Apollaten, defeated the marauding Sphinx of Thule, and was sent to observe a dispute brewing between Ruta III and the Sontara Warburg.

Across the cosmos, the ruling seers were dying: the Sphinx of Thule; the Logistomancer of A32K, foreseer of a cold empire of logic; the Core Sybilline of Klanti; the Sosostris in the West Spiral; The-Nameless-That-Sees-All in the North Constellations. The 508th Pythia became the last of her line. After a visit from a Master Trader of the South, she finally recognised that the veil of Time would soon only be traversed physically, not mentally. She instigated the Time Programme. The Time Scaphe, the first time vessel and powered by the mental energy of its crew, was launched but vanished.

Rassilon and his neo-technologists overthrew the Pythia. As her followers fled to Karn, the Pythia cursed Gallifrey with her dying words: its people became infertile, the colonies began to demand their independence and an Ice Age commenced. The Pythia cast herself into an abyss.

Rassilon lost a daughter to the Pythia's curse. The only good omen was the return of the Time Scaphe. Quennesander Olyesti Pekkary, captain of the Time Scaphe and first son of the House of Fordfarding, was Rassilon's nephew.

The Great Houses, the Anchoring of the Thread and the Looms[54]

The family Houses of Gallifrey were sentient and the oldest beings on Gallifrey. They were born at the time of the Intuitive Revelation.[55]

The Time Lords, a.k.a. the Great Houses, defined the physical laws of the universe as we know them. The act of

---

The Doctor hails from House Lungbarrow (*Cat's Cradle: Time's Crucible, Lungbarrow*), the Master from Oakdown (*Divided Loyalties*) and Romana from Heartshaven, sometimes mistaken as "Hartshaven" (*Neverland; The Book of the War* hinted she belonged to House Dvora – a parsing of Romana's full name – but didn't come out and say it). Inquisitor Darkel (*The Trial of a Time Lord*) comes from House Jurisprudence (*Gallifrey S2: Insurgency*), and Andred (*The Invasion of Time*), a Cousin of Hildred (*The Deadly Assassin*) comes from either House Redlooms (*Lungbarrow*) or Deeptree (*Gallifrey S2: Lies*). President Livia (*Gallifrey S8: Enemy Lines*) originated in House Brightstone. Lolita, a sentient timeship and a major antagonist in the *Faction Paradox* series, is powerful enough to constitute her own House (*The Book of the War*). *Divided Loyalties* shows the War Chief (*The War Games*), Drax (*The Armageddon Factor*) and the Rani (*The Mark of the Rani*) as belonging to different Houses from the Doctor and the Master, but doesn't name them. *Gallifrey – Time War* V1 cites House Rassilon, as "the most ancient of the Houses". Patience (*Cold Fusion*) belongs to Blyledge.

A tally of the Houses to date, as well as the first work to name them... Arpexia (*The Book of the War*), Blyledge (*Cat's Cradle: Time's Crucible*), Brightstone (*Divided Loyalties*), Catherion (*The Book of the War*), Deeptree (*Gallifrey S2: Lies*), Dellatrovella (*Circular Time: "Spring"*), Dvora (*The Book of the War*), Fordarding (*Cat's Cradle: Time's Crucible*), Heartshaven (*Neverland*), Ixion (*The Book of the War*), Jade Dreamers (*Zagreus*), Jurisprudence (*Gallifrey S2: Insurgency*), Lineacrux (*The Book of the War*), Lolita (*The Book of the War*), Lungbarrow (*Cat's Cradle: Time's Crucible*), Medhorran (*FP: Against Nature*), Mirraflex (*The Book of the War*), Oakdown (*Divided Loyalties*), Paradox (*Alien Bodies*, later revamped as Faction Paradox), Rassilon (*Gallifrey – Time War* V1), Redlooms (*Lungbarrow*), Stillhaven (*Divided Loyalties*), Tracolix (*The Eleven-Day Empire*), Urquineath (*FP: Weapons Grade Snake Oil*), and Xianthellipse (*The Book of the War*). Houses Firebrand, Goodlight and Warpsmith exist on the alt-Gallifrey seen in *Gallifrey S4: Annihilation*, and for all we know on "our" Gallifrey also.

On Earth, Michael Brookhaven founds the renegade House of Seven Gables as part of Faction Hollywood (*The Book of the War*). The warhawk House Mirraflex (which the eighth Doctor calls "honourable" in *The Eighth Doctor – The Time War 1*) ultimately eradicates the last members of humanity and launches the ultimately embarrassing timebeast assault on the City of the Saved (*The Book of the War*). *Trial of the Valeyard* hints at the existence of "shadow Houses" that contain "Rassilon's mistakes", an array of Time Lords with regenerations that have gone awry.

55 *Lungbarrow*

doing so was called the Anchoring of the Thread, and viewed by the Houses as the start of history. It was theorised that Exo Houses – bloodlines pre-dating the Great Houses and the Anchoring of the Thread – might have survived in our universe as fiction.

Although the major Great Houses were confident about the Anchoring of the Thread's outcome, some minor Houses developed a contingency plan. A silver of Old Time was locked away in a temporeliquary, the 2nd Second, which could reset the universe to its previous state.[56]

Every Time Lord was born into a chapter of one of Rassilon's Great Houses. "Shadow Houses" were rumoured to contain "Rassilon's mistakes" pertaining to regernation: the half-regenerated, those regenerated in body but not mind, those regenerated back to a state of being Time Tots, those turned inside-out by regeneration, those whose possible future incarnations were overwriting their past, and more.[57]

To get around the Pythia's curse of sterility, Rassilon and the Other built Looms capable of weaving Gallifreyans from existing genetic material.[58] Time Lords were born from the Loom fully grown and fully conscious, but needed educating.[59]

Jurisprudence priamus on Gallifrey mandated that any-thing which affected the ancient Houses required electoral consent.[60]

A priest on early Gallifrey was driven into the wilderness when Rassilon dissolved the monasteries. While wandering, he happened across all twelve of his future incarnations, who had no memory of how they came to appear together. The priest became known as IM Foreman, and his thirteen incarnations founded a time-travelling carnival. Their caravan was a complex space-time event that would model itself a new shape on each arrival.

Events on Dust in the thirty-eighth century mortally wounded Foreman's incarnations, forcing them to regenerate and causing amnesia. They were flung through time to early Gallifrey for the original Foreman to paradoxically find.[61]

It took the finest minds on Gallifrey a millennium to develop time technology.[62] The Doctor's people needed "millennia" to solve the equations, and harness the necessary power, required for time travel.[63] The initial Time Lords conjectured that a chronal tumor could facilitate navigation through the Vortex.[64] The Fractures claimed that time was mastered before the Time Lords could count, by beings so powerful the very thought of them would shatter minds.[65]

56 The background to *FP: Weapons Grade Snake Oil*. *FP: The Book of the War* explained the Anchoring of the Thread.

57 *Trial of the Valeyard*, dovetailing together ingredients from *The Deadly Assassin* and the New Adventures.

58 *Cat's Cradle: Time's Crucible, Lungbarrow*.

59 *Lungbarrow*

60 *Gallifrey – Time War V1: Desperate Measures*

61 *Interference*. Rassilon's dissolution of the monasteries presumably accompanies his defeat of the Pythia.

62 *The Song of the Megaptera*

63 "The Age of Ice"

64 *The Eleventh Doctor Year Two*: "The One"

65 *The Twelfth Doctor Year One*: "The Fractures"

66 The ninth Doctor, *The Parting of the Ways*

67 The top suspect as the inventor of regeneration is Rassilon... while there's no direct evidence of that (it's not even obvious that Rassilon regenerated during his first tenure as President), stories such as *The Crystal Bucephalus*, *The Trial of the Valeyard*, etc., intimate it. *The Deadly Assassin* attributes most of the key Time Lord discoveries to Rassilon (without specifying regeneration as one of them), but also establishes that the Time Lords have forgotten much of their own history. A text written by a scribe of old, Quartinian, in *Cat's Cradle: Time's Crucible* pins down "the triumph of regeneration" as coming to fruition between Rassilon's defeat of the Pythia and his mastery of time travel.

68 Davros, *The Witch's Familiar*

69 In *A Good Man Goes to War*, the eleventh Doctor and Vastra question the degree of Melody Pond's Time Lord inheritance – including whether or not she can regenerate – because she was conceived while the TARDIS travelled in the Vortex. We know that Melody (later River Song) can regenerate, as it happens in *Day of the Moon* and *Let's Kill Hitler*. This ability doesn't appear the work of the Silence, however, since nobody else on their team can regenerate unless they're actively derived from River (*River S3: The Lady in the Lake, The Furies*). Taking River's genesis at face value, anyone conceived in the Vortex would, quite likely, be born with a reservoir of regeneration energy. Either way, the new series consistently portrays the prized resource of "regeneration energy", which can be transferred from person to person in quantities big and small (*Let's Kill Hitler, The Angels Take Manhattan*, etc.), as the fuel behind regeneration, without explaining how it causes Body A to transform into Body B, or Persona B to replace Persona A. Or, the necessity of gaining a new persona in the first place.

The reference text *The Gallifrey Chronicles* by John Peel attributed regeneration to the creation of "self-replicating, biogenic molecules" – *Zagreus* uses the same language, albeit in second-hand, very suspect recollections. (These days, it's fair to say that almost nobody buys the idea that, effectively, regeneration is the work of nanobots.) *The Crystal Bucephalus* called regeneration a function of shifting from double-helix to triple-helix DNA; *Gallifrey S4: Reborn* said the same, and also mentioned nucleo-lingua symbiotica. *Goth*

Regeneration

"Time Lords have this little trick, it's sort of a way of cheating death. Except it means I'm going to change, and I'm not going to see you again. Not like this. Not with this daft old face." [66]

Regeneration enabled Time Lords to renew their bodies and gain new personas, while (usually) retaining the memories of their past incarnations. The circumstances behind the advent of regeneration on Gallifrey remain a mystery. [67]

"Regeneration energy. The ancient magic of the Time Lords." [68]

Prolonged exposure to the Untempered Schism made the Time Lords "what they were" – including, it would seem, the ability to regenerate. [69] Through regeneration, Time Lords could become "renewed". [70] Time Lords were truly immortal, barring accidents. [71] When a Time Lord's body wore out, they regenerated,

"became new". [72] An avatar of a Time Lord's next incarnation might appear prior to a regeneration. [73]

Barring extraordinary circumstances, Time Lords were limited to twelve regenerations. [74] Upon regeneration, Time Lords could switch genders and (outwardly) races. It was not unprecedented for a Time Lord to have one gender throughout most of their incarnations, and the rare instance of a different one. [75] Time Lords could transform themselves into other species during regeneration. [76]

The First Law of Time forbid Time Lords from meeting their other selves. [77] Such meetings only happened during the "gravest emergencies"... [78] ... or just because if you travel through time often enough, it's "almost inevitable" that you'll run into yourself at some point. [79]

Some Time Lords demonstrated, upon regeneration, an ability to choose their next incarnation - even to the point of becoming duplicates of other individuals. [80] As a general rule, however, with regeneration "you never quite know what you're going to get". [81] Any meeting of two incarnations of the same Time Lord would throw the timelines out of synch, meaning the earlier

---

Opera hinted that Rassilon improved upon Gallifreyan longevity with blood taken from the Great Vampires; FP: The Book of the War suggested it was a Yssgaroth derivative.

70 The Power of the Daleks

71 The War Games. The 60s stories treat the process of bodily "renewal" as something the Doctor alone undergoes, in concert with the TARDIS (The Power of the Daleks). In The War Games, the Doctor makes the startling claim that his people are immortal barring fatal injury – the same story demonstrates this when the War Chief and two Gallifreyan technicians (also Time Lords?) are all shot dead, with no expectation that they'll sit up as different people. It's only with the very end of Season 11, in Planet of the Spiders, that it's established that all Time Lords regenerate, and we see a Time Lord other than the Doctor (K'Anpo) undergo the process. The Deadly Assassin, however, does an about-face on the whole "Time Lords are immortal" angle by introducing the 12-regeneration limit rule. Mortality concerns on Borusa's part bring about The Five Doctors.

72 Planet of the Spiders

73 Planet of the Spiders and Logopolis, although the true nature of the Watcher (who merges with the fourth Doctor to bring about the fifth) in the latter is never explained. Nyssa airs the view that the Watcher "was the Doctor all the time", but we're never given any confirmation of that.

74 The Deadly Assassin, The Time of the Doctor. Trial of the Valeyard, as ever a wellspring of less-than-reliable information, suggests that Time Lords are limited to 12 regenerations because Rassilon discovered that the symbiotic nuclei degenerated if split too many times.

The Doctor safely goes beyond their thirteenth life in The Time of the Doctor, so we can probably discard conjecture – as also fronted by the New Adventures – that Time Lord psyches and bodies physically can't handle going beyond 13 lives, it's just that the High Council doesn't normally permit it (see the "Regeneration... A Complete New Life Cycle" sidebar).

75 As evidenced by Missy in Series 8, the General's regeneration in Hell Bent, Majestrix Borusa (in an alternate timeline) in Gallifrey IV: Annihilation, and, of course, the thirteenth Doctor. The first on-screen confirmation that Time Lords could switch genders was the Corsair (The Doctor's Wife).

76 Doctor Who – The Movie, as witnessed in works by Paul Cornell (Circular Time: "Spring" and The Shadows of Avalon).

77 The Three Doctors

78 The Five Doctors; see also The Three Doctors, The Day of the Doctor and Time Crash.

79 The Two Doctors; see also Cold Fusion and The Doctor Falls.

80 Destiny of the Daleks, and also The Suns of Caresh and River S3: The Lady in the Lake.

81 Castrovalva. Most of the Doctors exhibit some degree of surprise at their new appearances. The tenth Doctor chooses to keep his present form while regenerating in Journey's End, owing to the atypical presence of a "bio-matching receptacle" to catch the excess regeneration energy before it changes his body. The twelfth Doctor takes quite a while (The Girl Who Waited) to realise that he had subconsiously patterned his current form on Caecilius (also played by Peter Capaldi in The Fires of Pompeii).

version/s would fail to remember the event.[82] The Omega Limitation Effect stated that different incarnations of a Time Lord, if they met, would have no memory of their shared experiences once they rejoined the timelines.[83] Inter-incarnation meetings would sometimes "short out the time differential", causing a younger version of a Time Lord to look noticeably older.[84] Different incarnations of the same Time Lord could touch one another.[85]

Daring neonates at the Academy played a dangerous game called Eighth Man Bound. This entailed deliberately putting an "Initiate" into a state of flux between life or death, enabling them to witness and experience their future regenerations. The term was coined after a student of the Arcalian Chapter who discovered the natures of his first seven bodies, but couldn't observe the eighth. A student of the Prydonian Chapter was rumoured to have tied this record.[86]

Gallifrey, it seemed, was home to people who did not share in the gift of regeneration.[87]

The Mastery of Time: Rassilon, Omega and the Other

Omega Lost to an Anti-Matter Universe

Two Gallifreyans ensured that their people became the Lords of Time: Rassilon and Omega. Rassilon was the "greatest single figure in Time Lord history", yet "no one really knows how extensive his powers were" and he "had powers and secrets that even we don't understand". To this day, the Time Lords revere Omega as their "greatest hero", "one of the greatest of all our race".[88] Omega and Rassilon developed Validium, a "living metal" designed to be the last line of defence for Gallifrey.[89] They were part of a Triumvirate, the third member of which was known as the Other to modern Time Lords.[90] Legends on Gallifrey spoke of secret societies dedicated to the worship of Rassilon, Omega and the Other.[91]

---

82 *The Day of the Doctor* and *The Doctor Falls*. This was long hypothesised beforehand, to explain why the older Doctors in multi-Doctor stories don't have the memories of their earlier selves, allowing them to remember how they won. *Cold Fusion* is an exception, in that the devious seventh Doctor (almost certainly) uses his fifth self's memories to his advantage, as is *Time Crash*.

83 "The Lost Dimension"

84 *Time Crash*, explaining reunion stories where returning actors have noticeably aged (*The Five Doctors* and *The Two Doctors* in particular).

85 *The Five Doctors*, *The Doctor Falls*, in seeming defiance of the Blinovitch Limitation Effect (*Mawdryn Undead*). Multiple Draxes coordinate their efforts with benefit of a Blinovitch Limitation Effect limiter (*The Trouble with Drax*).

86 According to Professor Thripsted's *Genetic Politics Beyond the Third Zone* in *Christmas on a Rational Planet* (p212-216). The Doctor names himself as "Eighth Man Bound" in *The Dying Days* and *Lungbarrow*.

87 Inferred from various stories, but not rigidly confirmed. *Listen* revisits the Doctor's childhood, and helps to establish that Gallifreyans aspiring to become Time Lords must attend the Academy. We see other residents of Gallifrey who aren't Time Lords, so presumably can't regenerate: the Shobogan tribes living outside the Capitol (*The Invasion of Time*), as well as the residents of the drylands in *Hell Bent*. The latter, however, entails the twelfth Doctor meeting "the Woman", who knows him of old, possibly all the way back to his childhood, and it's not said how she's lived so long without benefit of regenerating. Mawdryn and his fellows (*Mawdryn Undead*) stole a metamorphic symbiosis regenerator

from Gallifrey in a desperate bid to gain regeneration, but it's left unsaid if they originated from Gallifrey or not.

88 Omega first appears in *The Three Doctors* and reappears in *Arc of Infinity*, *The Infinity Doctors*, *Omega* and *Gallifrey Series 7*. The Hand of Omega, his stellar-manipulation device, appears in *Remembrance of the Daleks*, *Lungbarrow* and *The Infinity Doctors*. A prototype of the Hand factors into *Doom Coalition*.

The first reference to Rassilon is in *The Deadly Assassin*; after that he becomes the central figure of Gallifreyan history, referred to in many subsequent stories (the quotes are from the Doctor, in *The Five Doctors* and *Shada* respectively). He personally appears in *The Five Doctors*, *The End of Time*, *Hell Bent*, etc. Both Rassilon and Omega are the legendary founders of Time Lord society, both are "the greatest" of the Doctor's race and supply the energy necessary for time travel. The first time that it is explicitly stated on-screen that they were contemporaries is in *Silver Nemesis*, although earlier in Season 25, *Remembrance of the Daleks* attempted to rationalise the two accounts of Time Lord origins. Early *Doctor Who Weekly* issues included a back-up strip written by Alan Moore which was an account of the origins of the Time Lords, and which has been referred to in novels such as *The Infinity Doctors* and *Interference*.

89 *Silver Nemesis*

90 The Other was mentioned or alluded to in several New and Missing Adventures; he first appeared (in flashback) in the *Remembrance of the Daleks* novelisation.

91 "Millennia" before *Gallifrey VII: Intervention Earth*, playing off the continuity of the TV series and the New

"Today we tend to think of Rassilon as the founder of our modern civilisation, but in his own time he was regarded mainly as an engineer and an architect. And, of course, it was long before we turned away from the barren road of technology." [92]

The Time Lord Capitol and Citadel dated from the time of Rassilon and Omega, but in those days they weren't enclosed in a dome. The Citadel was built to withstand a siege, but against which enemy had been lost to history.[93] The Zero Room beneath the Capitol on Gallifrey was built by the Other.[94] **The Citadel of the Time Lords resided on the continent of Wild Endeavour, in the mountains of Solace and Solitude.**[95] The Meridian Mountains separated the Arcalian Desert from the lowlands of Outer Gallifrey.[96]

Omega was a member of the High Council, the solar engineer who found and created the power source needed for time travel: the energy released by a supernova. He was lost in the explosion, and the Time Lords believed that he had been killed.[97]

"A long time ago, on my home planet of Gallifrey, there lived a stellar engineer called Omega. It was Omega who created the supernova that was the initial power source for Gallifreyan time-travel experiments. He left behind him the basis on which Rassilon founded Time Lord society... and he left behind the Hand of Omega. The Hand of Omega is the mythical name for Omega's remote stellar manipulator – the device used to customise stars with. And didn't we have trouble with the prototype..." [98]

One version of Omega's history suggested that he was originally an Academy student named Peylix. He theorised that his people could gain mastery of time by exploding a star within the Sector of Lost Souls, but Peylix's tutor, Luvis, deemed this nonsense and awarded him an "omega" grade – the lowest score attainable. The nickname "Omega" plagued Peylix, but Rassilon's rise to power allowed him to properly implement his theories.

Peylix set out aboard the *Eurydice* to detonate a star, but his colleague Vandekirian warned that the targeted system contained sentient life. Omega proceeded anyway, and Vandekirian – trying to prevent Omega from gaining his handprint for security clearance – destroyed one of his hands in the ship's fusion reactors. Omega cut off Vandekirian's other hand, and used it to launch his stellar manipulator. The star exploded, killing the system's inhabitants. Vandekirian's hand caused an impurity in the fusion reactor and the ship exploded, consigning Omega to a universe of anti-matter.[99]

Omega's prototype stellar manipulator was hidden and thought lost for "millennia" after the Dark Times. The first incarnation of the Eleven, an Arcalian, later stumbled upon its existence while rooting around in the Panoptican Archives.[100]

THE INFINITY DOCTORS -> The Ice Age had led to the collapse of Gallifreyan civilisation, in the time known as the Darkness. Libraries and temples burned. Many Gallifreyans perished. The Loom-born were smaller than the Womb-born and were mortal, but they preserved the Gallifreyan genetic codes.

Nine years after the Pythia's curse, the Elders still treated the Loom-born with disdain, viewing them a temporary solution to a problem. Rassilon and his Consortium gave everyone hope by finding the Fragment: the last surviving prophecy that spoke of Rassilon's personal rise and how the Gallifreyans would become the Lords of Time. The Other knew that Rassilon had faked the Fragment.

Rassilon and Omega set out for Qqaba, the only surviving Population III star in the galaxy. There were two Hands of Omega. They would detonate the star, releasing time energy that would be syphoned into fuel cells. However, the stasis halo protecting Omega's ship failed as Qqaba went supernova and Omega fell into the black hole that was forming. The crews of the surviving ships were infused with the energies. At the heart of this, Rassilon used the power of the singularity to rewrite the laws of physics across the entire universe. One effect of this, whether Rassilon knew it or not, was that Omega still lived, trapped inside the black hole.

Omega left behind a widow, a Womb-born Gallifreyan who would become known as Patience.

Adventures (especially *Lungbarrow*).
92 Engin, *The Deadly Assassin*.
93 *The Infinity Doctors*
94 *The Quantum Archangel*, following up a reference from *Castrovalva*.
95 The tenth Doctor's first reference to Citadel and its dome is in *Gridlock*, and it is actually seen in *The Sound of Drums*.
96 *Mistfall*

97 *The Three Doctors*
98 The Doctor, *Remembrance of the Daleks*.
99 *Omega*. These details hail from Omega's unreliable memories and are highly suspect. The details about Omega committing genocide, certainly, stem from a blending of the Doctor's recollections and are likely to be false.
100 "Millennia" before *DC: The Satanic Mill*.

"Star Death" -> Four Gallifreyan starbreakers moved to the star Qqaba. From the flagship *Aeon*, Jodelex and Griffen waited, safe behind Stasis Haloes that protected their ships from the primal forces. They knew that Rassilon had yet to work out how to navigate through time. Fenris, a mercenary from the future, arrived to prevent the creation of the Time Lords. He sabotaged the lead ship, condemning Omega to what seemed like certain death, but Rassilon used the power of his mind to contain the black hole, then severed Fenris' time belt as he tried to escape. Fenris was scattered throughout eternity, and Rassilon picked up the belt containing the directional control he needed to navigate time.

The star Omega detonated was in the Constellation of Ao.[101] Omega used the sunskipper *Eurydice* to reach the star he detonated, Jartus. Some scholars at the Omega Heritage Centre (a popular tour destination) think Rassilon deliberately got rid of Omega, who was more popular.[102]

Two members of a Council of Three – Provost Tepesh (the Prime of the Arcalian chapterhouses) and Lady Ouida, both of them vampires – allied with the Great Mother of a Sisterhood against Rassilon. The Great Mother's assistant was Cassandra, a member of the House of Jade Dreamers. They sought to discover the secrets of Rassilon's Foundry, but the Divergence again threatened to break through at this juncture. The Foundry was firestormed to prevent this, which wiped out the conspirators.[103]

"And Rassilon journeyed into the black void with a great fleet. Within the void no light would shine. And nothing of that outer nature continued in being except that which existed within the Sash of Rassilon. Now Rassilon found the Eye of Harmony which balances all things that they may neither flux, whither nor change their state in any measure, and he caused the Eye to be brought to the world of Gallifrey wherein he sealed this munificence with the Great Key. Then the people rejoiced." [104]

The Doctor's people invented black holes.[105] The Gallifreyans successfully concluded the experiments, becoming the Time Lords. Mastery of Time required an unimaginably vast energy supply, which Rassilon set about acquiring.[106]

Modern Time Lords believed the Eye of Harmony to be a myth, and that the Sash of Rassilon had merely symbolic importance. In reality, the Sash prevented the wearer from being sucked into a parallel universe. The Eye of Harmony was the nucleus of a black hole, from which all the power of the Time Lords devolved. "Rassilon stabilised all the elements of the black hole and set them in an eternally dynamic equation against the mass of the planet." [107]

Year Zero Rassilon Era is marked from the moment Rassilon activated the Eye of Harmony.[108] The earliest time-travel legends say Rassilon decapitated a Great Beast, took the branching golden tree of its metathalmus and found the First Secret of Chrononambulatory Egress.[109] Rassilon anchored the timeline of the universe, creating one unified history. The Antiverse was created as an equal and opposite reaction to this.[110]

"The Lost Dimension"[111] **->** The Doctor's TARDIS became adrift in a white void. To escape, the eleventh Doctor and Alice took the Ship through an infinitesimally

101 *Lungbarrow*
102 *Omega*, an idea supported by *Zagreus*.
103 *Zagreus*. According to a questionable simulation, this occurred after Omega detonated his star. Arata is named as the third member of the Council of Three. The Great Mother belongs to the Sisterhood of Karn, although it isn't mentioned by name. Of all the suspect recreations shown in *Zagreus*, this one is the most dubious due to Tepesh's biased claims, and because he and Ouida, as vampires, would be unlikely to hold such authority in the Gallifreyan echelons for long, if at all.
104 *The Book of the Old Time*, referred to in *The Deadly Assassin*.
105 *The Impossible Planet/The Satan Pit*
106 *The Three Doctors, The Deadly Assassin, Remembrance of the Daleks*.
107 *The Deadly Assassin*
108 "The Final Chapter". As it's only reached 5725.2 by the time of *Doctor Who – The Movie* – a period of millions of years after Rassilon's time – each unit can't represent a calendar year. Perhaps it misses out some of the numbers (i.e. it's short for 10,005,725 RE, or something like it), or it's more like a stardate in *Star Trek*, and the exact method of calculation is impossible for us to decipher.
109 *Heart of TARDIS*
110 *Neverland*
111 It's after Omega's downfall. The Doctor here suggests making fluid links compatible with mercury, a facet of the TARDIS first seen in *The Daleks*. Rassilon here dubs him "The Other" – surely a nod to the New Adventures, but not especially compatible with it (see *Cat's Cradle: Time's Crucible* et al).
112 The Brigadier, the second Doctor, *The Five Doctors*.
113 *Gallifrey IV: Annihilation*
114 *Shada*
115 *Four to Doomsday*
116 *Neverland*
117 *Worlds DW: Second Sight*
118 *The Deadly Assassin, The Invasion of Time*.
119 *The Two Doctors. Zagreus* further suggests that the Imprimature also facilitated regeneration, and that

small quantum aperture... and found themselves on ancient Gallifrey, in the Capitol, as Rassilon and his technicians laboured to graft internal dimensions onto a TT capsule: a prototype TARDIS. The statue of Omega, ancient when the Doctor was a student, was new. For a time, the Doctor posed as a humble inventor from the lower city's cheese-making quarter.

The Doctor came to Rassilon's attention, and proposed that while Rassilon favoured using Validium in his newly created fluid links, mercury or rubidium would work better. Rassilon agreed, acknowledged the Doctor as a Level Seven time-sensitive (on par with himself) and made him a test pilot for the early TT capsules. The Doctor identified himself as "Theta-Sigma" – thinking him humble, Rassilon simply named him "The Other".

The eleventh Doctor attempted a test flight of a Type 1 TARDIS, but the Ship suffered a catastrophic dimensional breakdown. Rassilon lamented the loss of "Theta-Sigma".

... Meanwhile, the Type 1 TARDIS was very scared, and found comfort in the Void. The eleventh Doctor wired himself into the console, to show Her the wonders of the universe, but instead the Type 1 saw only chaos, warfare and the words "Silence will fall." The Type 1 extended white holes from the Void, to consume all matter. Thirteen incarnations of the Doctor combined efforts at St Luke's University, Bristol, in 2017, and persuaded the Type 1 to stand down and live at peace with itself.

Alice escaped Gallifrey in a proto-TARDIS, then phoned the eleventh Doctor for a pick-up when her Ship burnt out and sank into an ocean.

The Other Gives Himself to the Looms

LUNGBARROW -> Nine point six years after Omega was lost, Rassilon was purging anyone opposed to his regime. The Other was disgusted, and tried to get his granddaughter Susan and her nanny Mamlaurea to safety on the planet Tersurus. Susan had coined the term "TARDIS" to describe the new time ships. The Other then threw himself into the Prime Distributor that fed all the Looms. He knew he would be reborn at some point in Gallifrey's history.

A year later, the Doctor – unknown even to him, the reincarnation of the Other – arrived from the distant future. He found Susan wandering the streets, unable to escape. She recognised him as her grandfather and they left Gallifrey together to explore the universe...

"4-D War" ->

"We are fighting a timewar, comrades. A war in four dimensions. A war that on our timeline hasn't even started yet! Our enemy is in the future. We must know his identity. His reason for hating us... we must know his weaknesses!"

Twenty years after Fenris was scattered into the time vortex, Rema-Du – daughter of Jodelex and Griffen – had been training for a decade to retrieve him. At this time, the Time Lords employed the Special Executive, parahumans with unusual talents. One of them, Wardog (whose mind could withstand stresses that would reduce anyone else to insanity) partnered Rema-Du.

They entered the Vortex via a warp gate and located Fenris. He was connected to a Brainfeeler to identify the enemy. The Time Lords discovered that their enemy was from thirty thousand years in the future, a cadre of supermen called the Order of the Black Sun. A Black Sun squad – including members called Llorex, Faru-Faro and Drin – killed Fenris and the Brainfeeler, severed Wardog's arm and vanished. The Time Lords were left unsure what they would do, if anything, to provoke such an attack.

"Black Sun Rising" -> Ten years later, Rema-Du and Wardog attended talks with the Sontarans. A member of the Order of the Black Sun disrupted the gathering.

The Great Days of Rassilon

"Didn't you say [Rassilon] was supposed to be rather a good type?"... "So the official history says, but there are many rumours and legends to the contrary." [112]

Rassilon lived "millennia" ago.[113] **As President of the Time Lords, Rassilon ushered in an age of technological and political progress. The phrase "the Great Days of Rassilon" appears in the Gallifreyan book Our Planet's Story, which was read by every Time Tot.[114] Even races such as the Urbankans, who knew nothing of the Time Lords, had legends of Rassilon.[115]** Rassilon's exploits were remembered on many planets, whose legends speak of Azaron, Razlon and Ra.[116]

The "higher races" strode across the stars, bending creation to their will, when Rassilon was young and naïve. They warred against one another for millennia, with whole galaxies burning in the conflict. The Art – a device used to focus psychic power – ended the chaos by turning various races' aggression back on themselves, but was then lost.[117]

Rassilon was credited with many scientific achievements: He created the transduction barriers surrounding Gallifrey. These prevented the unauthorised landing of a TARDIS or similar vehicle. A quantum force field also existed as a barrier against more conventional threats.[118] Rassilon introduced the symbiotic nuclei – the Rassilon Imprimature – into the genetic make-up of Time Lords, allowing them to fully travel through Time.[119] Rassilon also discovered the secret of temporal fission.[120]

Rassilon invented the Demat Gun, a weapon that required the Great Key to function. This weapon was so powerful that the Great Key was hidden from all future Presidents by successive Chancellors.[121] A Time Lord Tribunal could impose the penalty of dematerialisation on other races or individuals, such as the War Lord.[122]

Rassilon created a servant, but she gained free will and rebelled, killing a few thousand Time Lords. Rassilon thought he'd killed Pariah – as she was now known – but she escaped to Earth in 1879. Subsequently, Rassilon created Shayde, a more loyal servant.[123] A legend said that Rassilon banished the Mimic – a mindless creature that could copy concepts, but had no imagination of its own. It would reappear in sixteenth century London.[124]

Rassilon captured a being native to the Time Vortex: the Tenebrous Glist, which could create time storms. Officially, Rassilon had the Glist undo the devastation wrought by Gallifrey's many wars. Many, however, believed that he weaponised the creature, reverting enemy ships to their component parts.[125]

The Vondax fought a losing war against Gallifrey, and – with defeat imminent – caused a formidable paradox that erased one of Rassilon's generals from history. The general's consort alone remembered him, and in her grief became the Watchmaker: a wraith-like being who moved between dimensions to eliminate temporal anomalies. Early Time Lord history was rife with mentions of the Watchmaker, as the Time Lords were more careless with their temporal prowess. Eventually, the Watchmaker was only remembered as a Time Lord folktale told to children, and not seen for a million cycles.[126]

Legends concerning the Parallel Sect – a group of travellers to other realms – appeared in countless civilisations, including Gallifrey. Possessing symbiotic nuclei, the Time Lords inherited the Sect's mantle.[127] The nuclei of Gallifreyan antibodies were also symbiotic.[128]

An elder parasitic race, A Thrake, fed off memories and plagued the Time Lords in "ancient times". The Thrake went extinct, or so it was believed, but one survived to stalk Joan of Arc in 1429.[129]

... of Rassilon

Rassilon was associated with many relics and concepts, all of which had "stupendous power". Many were lost, or their true purpose was unknown.[130]

These included the Sash of Rassilon, the Great Key of Rassilon, Rassilon's Star (the Eye of Harmony) and the Seal of Rassilon.[131] The Sash of Rassilon could alter

---

Rassilon introduced the limit of twelve regenerations to avoid the problem of degenerating biogenic molecules.

THE KEY: In *The Deadly Assassin*, the Great Key is "an ebonite rod" that seals the Eye of Harmony within its monolith. By *The Invasion of Time*, that artifact is called "the Rod", and the Great Key is an ordinary-looking mortise key that can power the Demat Gun and has been hidden from the President by successive Chancellors since the time of Rassilon. We might presume that the Chancellor told the President that the Rod *is* the Key, hence the confusion of the two. However, two Chancellors we know about – Goth and Borusa – are both in line to be President while (presumably, in Goth's case) knowing the whereabouts of the real Great Key.

In *The Ultimate Foe*, "The Key of Rassilon" allows access to the Matrix through portals such as the Seventh Door, and the Keeper of the Matrix wears it on his robes – this is presumably an entirely different artifact.

the biodata of Time Lord President to allow better access to the Matrix.[132]

The Seal of Rassilon was also known as the omniscate.[133] The pattern for the Seal of Rassilon scrambled the neuro-systems of beings from outside our universe, such as vampires, to ward them off.[134]

Other relics and items included the Wisdom of Rassilon, the Rod of Rassilon ("Rassilon's Rod!" was also a mild Gallifreyan expletive)[135], the Record of Rassilon, the Directive of Rassilon[136], the Tomb or Tower of Rassilon, the Game of Rassilon, the Black Scrolls of Rassilon, the Harp of Rassilon (later reworked into a water feature), **the Coronet of Rassilon and the Ring of Rassilon.**[137]

The fifth Doctor played "Rassilon's Lament" on the Harp of Rassilon.[138] Traditional Gallifreyan waltzes were known as the Foxtrots of Rassilon.[139] **The Rassilon Imprimature mapped Time Lords on to the Vortex.**[140] There was also **the Key of Rassilon (not the Great Key, but one which allows access to the Matrix)**[141]... **the Legacy of Rassilon**[142]... the Loom of Rassilon's Mouse[143], the Horns of Rassilon, also known as the Sign of Rassilon (a magical warding sign)[144]... Rassilon's Red, Gallifrey's finest vintage wine[145]... the Runes of Rassilon[146]... Rassilon's Throne, a seat installed in the office of the President[147]... the Time-Gun of Rassilon[148]... *temporanius celpsydrasi*, a.k.a. the Rassilon Timefly, which was extensively hunted[149]... the Order of the Ancient Deeds of Rassilon[150]... a game of chance, Rassilon's Roulette[151] ... the Thimble of Rassilon, which permanently sealed off time-loops[152]... Gallifreyans swore by "Rassilon's blood"[153]... the legendary death-shield of Rassilon, possibly something the fourth Doctor just made up[154]... and the Equation of Rassilon, which allowed for travel through a time corridor. It "is and isn't" a scientific formula.[155] Following the Hyperion War, criminals were incarcerated in transcendental Rassilon Cubes.[156]

House Rassilon was home to Rassilon's bloodline, and was affiliated with the Prydonian Chapter.[157] The Time Lords signed the Pact (or Treaty) of Rassilon with the Sisterhood of Karn, protecting them in return for the Elixir of Life.[158] The Master destroyed TOM-TIT with a Profane Virus of Rassilon, which was designed to prevent Gallifreyan technology falling into alien hands.[159] TARDISes granted their passengers some biological immunity, "another of Rassilon's gifts".[160]

A poem from the Muses of Rasslion made reference to Nineveh, a TARDIS graveyard "where Gallifreyans go to die".[161] Time Lord fables included the Gooseberry Bush at the Bottom of Rassilon's Garden and the Great Gallifreyan Stork.[162]

= In an alternate version of Gallifrey, Rassilon became a vampire and turned many of his contempo-raries – including Lord Prydon, who then killed him. The transduction barriers were altered so no sunlight would shine on Gallifrey, and an ongoing war broke out between Prydon's vampires and the "True Lords of Gallifrey" led by Majestrix Borusa.[163]

= Another alt-Gallifrey never developed time travel because Rassilon used the still-developmental Eye of Harmony to trap the Krillic: 13,007,058,211 ravenous beings of pure thought.[164]

Rassilon as Ruler

Rassilon became President of Gallifrey.[165] Rassilon was the first – and to date only – Lord High President.[166] **Rassilon was also a legislator. In his time, five princi-ples were laid down.**[167] Rassilon's Five Principles led Gallifrey to a more enlightened social order.[168] History says the Timescoop was destroyed after Rassilon's Reformation.[169] Gallifrey gave up slavery during the time of Rassilon.[170]

The Constitution was drafted. Article Seventeen guaranteed the freedom of political candidates.[171] Only a unanimous vote of the High Council could over-rule

---

154 "The Lost Dimension"

155 *The English Way of Death*

156 *The Twelfth Doctor Year One*: "The Fractures"

157 *Gallifrey – Time War* V1

158 *Warmonger*, elaborating upon *The Brain of Morbius*.

159 *The Quantum Archangel*

160 *Antidote to Oblivion*, following the implication of the New Adventures. The TARDIS' immunity-conveying properties must have been on the blink in *The Ark*, however.

161 "Ninevah!"

162 *Trial of the Valeyard*

163 *Gallifrey IV: Annihilation*. It's possible that Prydon knew Rassilon in the proper timeline and was a found-er of the Prydonian Chapter.

164 *Gallifrey IV: Forever*. The Krillic don't appear to exist in Gallifrey's primary timeline. Strangely, they claim to have been imprisoned for "a million years", despite repeated references to Rassilon trapping them mere millennia ago. (Possibly, time passes differently within the Krillic's prison, or they've simply lost track of how long they've been dormant.)

165 *The Invasion of Time*. The Doctor becomes "the first President since Rassilon to hold the Great Key", implying that Rassilon was President.

166 *The Infinity Doctors*

167 *Shada*

168 *Gallifrey IV: Forever*

169 *World Game*

170 *Gallifrey IV: Forever*

171 *The Deadly Assassin*

the President.[172] Thanks to Rassilon, TARDIS data-banks contained 18,348 coded emergency instructions. Older TARDISes (Type 40 and older) had a magnetic card system, the Record of Rassilon, which contained emergency instructions regarding the Vampires.[173]

Article Seven of Gallifreyan Law forbid Time Lords from committing genocide.[174] **The death penalty was abolished, except in extreme circumstances such as a threat to Gallifrey or genocide.**[175] Time Lords posing as deities in other cultures were guilty of a Class 2 intervention, the penalty for which was vaporisation. Altering the axial rotation of a planet was a Class 1 intervention.[176]

Gallifrey outlawed use of "manumitters" – devices that severed the telepathic link between a Time Lord and their TARDIS, but could cause catastrophic damage to space-time if the Ships weren't fully powered down first.[177] It was "universally" forbidden to keep in captivity a coffin-loader – the ultimate form of scavenger – let alone a whole colony of them.[178]

The prison planet Shada was set up to house the most dangerous criminals in the universe. A key to the facility was encoded in the pages of Rassilon's book, *The Worshipful and Ancient Law of Gallifrey*, which was housed in the Panopticon Archive.[179] Newpeerlessness served as another Time Lord prison planet, secured by impermeable force fields. It was located "a couple of galaxies away" from Earth, toward Kasterborous.[180]

Rassilon decreed that no Time Lord should travel into Gallifrey's past.[181] Rassilon's technology stopped Time Lords from investigating their own futures.[182] Rassilon built the Oubliette of Eternity, which exiled prisoners to the Antiverse. He was known as the Conqueror of Yssgaroth, Overpriest of Drornid, First Earl of Prydon, Patris of the Vortex and Ravager of the Void.[183]

The Eternal Wars

"The myths of Gallifrey talk about nameless horrors infesting our universe that were only defeated through the might of the Time Lords."

Rassilon's experiments created holes in the fabric of space-time, which consequently unleashed monsters from another universe. For over a thousand years, across the cosmos, the Ancient Gallifreyans fought the Eternal Wars against the monsters from another universe. These included the Vampires and the Yssgaroth. The great general Kopyion Liall a Mahajetsu was said to have died during this time, but he'd secretly survived. The Matrix contained no record of this war. When Rassilon overthrew the Pythia, Gallifrey was cursed with a plague from which only a few survived. Some suggested that Rassilon himself released the virus to wipe out all who knew of his mistake – they further claim that Rassilon deliberately sealed Omega in his black hole.[184]

The Spear – one of the Great Devices – was said to have been the weapon that impaled the King Yssgaroth. A member of House Lineacrux eventually stole it, for use against Leviathan.[185]

172 *The Five Doctors*

173 *State of Decay*

174 *Terror of the Vervoids*

175 *The Brain of Morbius, Arc of Infinity, Terror of the Vervoids*. In *The Invasion of Time*, it's said that unauthorised use of a TARDIS "carries only one penalty", but this isn't definitively stated as execution.

176 *Forty-Five:* "False Gods"

177 *The Company of Friends:* "Benny's Story"

178 *The Three Companions*

179 *Shada*

180 *Persuasion*. It's not clear when Newpeerlessness was constructed relative to Shada, but the Doctor says Newpeerlessness was a jail "of the most ancient of my people". It's in disuse, or so it seems, by the seventh Doctor's era of Gallifrey.

181 *Timewyrm: Revelation*

182 *Alien Bodies*

183 *Neverland*

184 *The Pit*

185 *FP: The Brakespeare Voyage* (ch28). The Yssgaroth first appeared in *The Pit*.

186 *State of Decay*

187 *The Ninth Doctor Year One:* "The Bidding War"

188 *Damaged Goods*

189 *So Vile a Sin*

190 *Goth Opera*

191 *The Rising Night*. As with the vampires the Doctor encounters in *State of Decay*, the Baobhan Sith might well be the progeny of the Great Vampires.

192 *The Runaway Bride*

193 *CD, NM V2: Empire of the Racnoss*

194 *The Twelfth Doctor Year One:* "Gangland". It's possible that these races constitute the "Fledgling Empires" mentioned in *The Runaway Bride*.

195 *The Twelfth Doctor Year One:* "Terraformer"

196 *The Legends of River Song:* "River of Time"

197 *Gallifrey – Time War* V1: *Soldier Obscura*

198 *Zagreus*

199 *Lungbarrow*

200 *The Five Doctors*

201 *The Coming of the Terraphiles*

The Vampire War

When Rassilon was young, a Vampire army swarmed across the universe. Each Vampire could suck the life out of an entire planet.

"Energy weapons were useless, because the monsters absorbed and transmuted the energy, using it to become stronger. Therefore, Rassilon ordered the construction of bowships, swift vessels that fired a mighty bolt of steel that transfixed the monsters through the heart – for only if his heart be utterly destroyed will the Vampire die... The Vampire Army: so powerful were the bodies of these great creatures, and so fiercely did they cling to life, that they were impossible to kill, save by the use of bowships. Yet slain they all were, and to the last one, by the Lords of Time – the Lords of Time destroying them utterly. However, when the bodies were counted, the King Vampire, mightiest and most malevolent of all, had vanished, even to his shadow, from Time and Space. Hence it is the directive of Rassilon that any Time Lord who comes upon this enemy of our people and of all living things shall use all his efforts to destroy him, even at the cost of his own life..."

This war was so long and so bloody, that afterwards the Time Lords renounced violence forever.[186] The Time Lords spent millennia fighting the Great Vampires.[187]

Members of the Prydonian and Arcalian chapters crewed the bowships. N-forms were developed to fight vampires by the Patrexes Chapter. N-forms existed in pocket universes and could quickly extrude a vast killing machine onto planets infected by vampirism. They were programmed to kill all life on planets where vampires were detected.[188]

Warships were built to act as carriers for the bowships.[189] A marginal illustration in one book of legends showed a bat overcoming an owl. The owl was a traditional symbol of Rassilon; the bat of the Vampires. Some Gallifreyan heretics to this day worship Rassilon the Vampire, believing the Great Vampire bit Rassilon, and that Rassilon himself became a vampire towards the end of his life.[190]

When the Time Lords were in their infancy, they defeated the Baobhan Sith – a race with parasitic DNA and a hunger for blood – but only after the Sith feasted upon some of their number.[191]

Other Wars

The Fledgling Empires all but wiped out the Racnoss, creatures from the Dark Times. The Time Lords elimi-

nated the Racnoss' energy source, Huon particles.[192] Gallifreyan precogs had predicted that unless stopped, the Racnoss would spread through Kasterborous.[193]

Rassilon united many races – including Zygons, Ice Warriors, Sontarans, Hath, Vigil, Silurians and Judoon – against the sun-like Hyperions, then led this coalition to eliminate other malign threats to the universal order.[194]

In the purge to follow the Hyperion War, Rassilon's coalition targeted Count D'if, the ruler of the marauding Cybock Imperium. Rassilon challenged D'if to Rassilon's Roulette: a game of chance where Rassilon and D'if took turns shooting themselves with Rassilon's Time Gun. D'if lost, and the Time Gun discharged a time-bullet that wiped him from history. Rassilon laughed at D'if's downfall... marking the first time the Gallifreyans had cause to fear their president.[195]

The Qwerm, an insectoid race with five interconnected brains, joined the Time Lords' coalition against horrors such as the Racnoss, the Narlok and the Great Vampires. Later, the Qwerm foresaw their downfall, as they had become smart and weaponised enough to challenge Gallifrey's supremacy. They captured one of their Time Lord advisers, Rocinate, and laid eggs in her TARDIS. The Ship's time field froze the eggs for a million years, when it was hoped the Time Lords would be more complacent, and the new Qwerm could conquer the universe.

A Vortex Web enabled the TARDISes of Rocinate's era to link with one another for the sake of strategy or communications, but the resource fell into disuse.[196] A temporal war in Gallifrey's Dark Times created the Obscura: a region of space-time that induced insanity in anyone who looked upon it.[197]

A powerful rival race would have evolved after the Time Lords, but Rassilon trapped them in a moebius loop. They became known as the Divergence.[198]

Four of the outer worlds built temples to honour Rassilon in his own time.[199] **Rassilon discovered the secret of perpetual regeneration – "timeless, perpetual bodily regeneration, true immortality" – but knew that only the power-mad would attempt such a thing. Rassilon prevented at least four such Time Lords from discovering the secret of true immortality.[200]**

The Time Lords used to worry because time moved at different speeds in different parts of the galaxy, and ripples from the centre of the galaxy affected the past. When all was well, the universe was effectively immortal as it constantly regenerated itself. The Time Lords understood this, and from this learned to regenerate themselves.[201]

Time Lords had three brain stems. The administrators of the Fatality Index thought it possible to execute a Time Lord by stopping both hearts and all three brain stems, with a cellular shock wave to cancel out regeneration. Even then, they recommended placing

the body in a Quantum Fold Chamber for a thousand years of observation. By custom, the Index required that a Time Lord must carry out another Time Lord's execution.[202]

The Neverpeople – a group of exiled Time Lord criminals – falsified legends which stated that Rassilon fought and prevailed against the destroyer Zagreus in the Antiverse, but was entombed in a Zero Cabinet. This was part of the Neverpeople's plan to lure Time Lords into the Antiverse and facilitate their escape.[203]

Rassilon's consciousness survived within the Matrix, from which he was able to watch over the whole of time and space. He was one of three Matrix Lords, along with Morvane and Bedevere. All three were Higher Evolutionaries.[204] Upon his death, Rassilon was entombed in the Dark Tower, where he remained in eternal sleep. Legends stated that anyone who reaches the Tower and takes the Ring of Rassilon will gain immortality. Gallifreyan children were familiar with the story and learned a nursery rhyme:

"Those to Rassilon's Tower Would Go... Must choose: Above, Between, Below." [205]

Rassilon gave up corporeal form in Gallifrey's ancient times, and resided in his tomb for "millennia".[206]

There were six vast statues in the Panopticon. These honoured the Founders of Gallifrey. Omega's statue was in the southern corner, Rassilon was opposite. Another was that of Apeiron (who wore combat boots). There was a nursery riddle that, when solved, revealled the identity of

all six... although the Doctor couldn't remember all of it:

"Neath Panopticon dome Rassilon faces Omega... But who is the other?... brother." [207]

The six statues represented the six Gallifreyan Colleges.[208] While both Rassilon and Omega were virtually canonised, if not deified, there were no further records of the Other in any of the histories. Speculation said that he left Gallifrey altogether. Legend said that he grew weary of being an all-powerful player at the chess game of the universe. Instead, he longed to be a pawn on the board in the thick of the action.[209]

The Ancient Texts

The Book of the Old Time was the official version of Rassilon's achievements, and a modern transgram had been made of it.[210] The Black Scrolls of Rassilon contained a forbidden account of the same period, including the secrets of Rassilon's power.[211] There were many R.O.O. texts (those dealing with legends of Rassilon, Omega and the Other).[212]

The Red Book of Gallifrey concerned the Dark Time and talked of Rassilon the Ravager, Omega the Fallen and the Other. It also contained magical incantations.[213] The Green and Black Books of Gallifrey discussed legends of the future, including the Timewyrm.[214] There was a book called *The Triumphs of Rassilon*.[215]

There were records known as *The Other Scrolls*.[216] There was a prophecy that the Time Lord who found the lost

---

202 *Extremis.* Time Lords having triple brain stems suggests that when Missy "offers" to let UNIT shoot her hearts and just the one brain stem, she's bluffing.
203 *Neverland*
204 "The Tides of Time"
THE HIGHER EVOLUTIONARIES: It's never explained in the comic strips exactly what defines a Higher Evolutionary, or what their sphere of influence is. From the examples of Rassilon and Merlin, we can see that they're semi-legendary figures – immortals with enormous personal powers that go far beyond psychic abilities until they are indistinguishable from magic. As such, the Higher Evolutionaries are capable of viewing and influencing events across infinity and eternity.
In the final part of "The Tides of Time", we see dozens of High Evolutionaries from "throughout the known universe". We're only given the names of six during the story: Rassilon; Morvane; Bedevere ("The Matrix Lords", and implicitly the latter two are Gallifreyans); Dakon Theta and the Thane of Kordar from the Althrace System; and Merlin the Wise from Earth. By the time of "The Final Chapter", the Higher Evolutionaries include a representative of the Order of the Black Sun, Demoiselle

Drin, in the place of Merlin.
It's unclear whether the fact that Bedevere and Merlin are both names from Arthurian legend is significant, or how this Merlin relates to the Doctor being the Merlin of a parallel universe in *Battlefield*.
205 *The Five Doctors*
206 *Engines of War* (ch19).
207 *The Infinity Doctors*
208 *The Ancestor Cell*
209 *Cat's Cradle: Time's Crucible*
210 We hear a female voice read an extract from the modern translation of *The Book of the Old Time* in *The Deadly Assassin*.
211 The last extant copy of The Black Scrolls of Rassilon is destroyed in *The Five Doctors*.
212 *Goth Opera* (p119).
213 *No Future* (p203).
214 *Timewyrm: Revelation* (p65).
215 *Lungbarrow*
216 *The Infinity Doctors*
217 *The Gallifrey Chronicles*
218 *The Infinity Doctors, The Ancestor Cell.*
219 *Cortex Fire*

scrolls of Rassilon will lead Gallifrey from darkness.[217] One book, bound in reptile skin and with an embossed omniscate on the cover, survived until the end of the universe. It contained one last prophecy, which terrified the Doctor when he read it.[218]

Gallifreyan books from the Old Time, from before the Cosmos was made stable, contained additional dimensions – making it easy to lose one's place.[219] The Time Lords considered writing in green ink as the apex of bad manners.[220]

The Time Lord Astrolabus was known as the thief of time – he stole the *Book of Old Time* before the Doctor was born. Astrolabus saw himself as a real Time Lord, a pioneer who charted the first meridians of time: "It was I who released Gallifrey from the chains of the present." However, he plundered the timezones he visited.[221] The Master had a copy of the *Insidium of Astrolabus* in his TARDIS library.[222]

The chrono-scrollwriters on ancient Gallifrey were "too modest" to reveal their true names.[223]

Between the Ancient and Modern

The Time Wars were fought in the generation after Rassilon. The Tomb of the Uncertain Soldier in the Capitol honours a Gallifreyan who died during the Time Wars, cancelling out his own timeline for the greater good of Gallifrey. The Time Lords' Oldharbour Clock is the only surviving relic from an alternate universe wiped out in the Time Wars. Unknown to anyone, the clockwork figures had evolved into the most intelligent beings on the planet.[224] The Doctor said he witnessed Gallifrey's Time Wars first-hand, although the Time Lords wiped the wars from their history books.[225]

Omegon was a Time Lord who created the system that gave the Time Lords time travel, and harnessed the power of a thousand suns for them. They made him Emperor, then plotted to destroy him and exiled him into a bubble

in time. From there, he plotted his revenge.[226] The Pyralis, energy beings who mimicked other races, swarmed throughout Kasterborous and were defeated after a century-long war. They were imprisoned within a temporal void for millennia, but their obelisk-shaped dimensional gateways remained dormant on some worlds.[227]

The Time Lords time-looped the Fifth Planet, home of the Fendahl, twelve million years ago.[228] When the Gallifreyans were new to space/time exploration, they discovered the inhabited world of Minyos and were worshipped by the population there. In return, they gave technology to the Minyans.[229]

The Time Lords used their great powers to help the people of Micen Island, in Orion. This led to chemical and biological warfare on the planet. The Time Lords renounced interference, erecting the Temple of the Fourth as a monument. A small number of Time Lords, though, felt the need to atone for past sins, and covertly intervened in the universe's affairs.[230]

Because of their great powers, and their tendency to lead to corruption, Time Lords were discouraged from emotion and affection. They were trained with a series of tests, including a journey to Anima Persis. They were mentored by older Time Lords, but the final judgement on whether an individual can be a Time Lord (and the punishment of any Time Lords who misuse their power) was handled by the mysterious Kingmaker, an ancient crone.[231]

Time Lords appear to have possessed mental blocks that prevented their interfering in history. However, if one of these blocks was broken, the others soon shattered.[232] Three centuries after Rassilon's death, Rassilon's Rampart was built to defend against the lawless Shobogans.[233]

It took fifty generations for TARDISes to become an acceptable form of travel, and another twenty for them to be used to participate in history.[234] **The "living soul" of each TARDIS was an eleventh-dimensional matrix.[235]** All TARDISes had a preset circuit – a time-track crossing

220 *The Lost Magic*
221 "Voyager"
222 *The Quantum Archangel*
223 "The Lost Dimension"
224 *The Infinity Doctors*
225 *Heart of TARDIS*
226 *K9 and the Time Trap*. The story bears similarity to Omega's story, and is written by Bob Baker, Omega's co-creator. However, there are differences – Omega was never Emperor, and he only harnessed one sun. Omegon has a crippled leg. Despite the very similar names, they *do* seem to be different figures from early Time Lord history. *The Time Trap* doesn't mention Omega, so doesn't explore the relationship between the characters. Perhaps Omegon is Omega's son, building on his father's work. As an interesting side note, Omegon says he has met K9's master, presumably the

Doctor.
227 "Millennia" before *The Pyralis Effect*. Gallifrey is in Kasterborous, and it's not impossible that the unnamed race that defeated the Pyralis was the Time Lords, although it's impossible to say exactly when in their history this event would fall.
228 *Image of the Fendahl*
229 *Underworld*
230 *Death Comes to Time*. This sounds like a retelling of the Minyan story, or possibly an indication that there were many such mistakes made in Gallifrey's past.
231 *Death Comes to Time*
232 *Time and Relative*
233 *Lungbarrow*
234 *The Ancestor Cell*
235 *The Doctor's Wife*

protocol – that prevented travellers from visiting the same space-time location more than once. Doing so would result in recursion effects of completely unknown and unpredictable consequences. The Daleks didn't use such a system, meaning they could sometimes overlap their journeys and history.[236]

Epsilon Delta was a Time Lord from the Ancient Time who gained a double beta in cybernetics. He stole a TARDIS and adopted the name "the President". He settled in St Matthew's College, Oxford.[237]

The shanty township of Low Town sprang up at the base of the Capitol Dome, and was settled by normal Gallifreyans, Outsiders and those seeking a life free of the restrictions of Time Lord society. The Capitol once had a Harbour.[238] A suit of armour belonging to Tegorak gathered dust in one storeroom, as did a giant stuffed bird.[239]

Time Lords dabbled at breaching the higher dimensions, but the Dimensional Ethics Committee banned the work.[240] At some point, the Biblioclasm claimed the Endless Library. The Watch checked every night to prevent such a thing happening again. A quarter of a million years ago, the Time Lords were afflicted with the Blank Plague. The Time Lords fought military campaigns against Rigel, Gosolus and about a dozen other worlds.[241]

The Time Lords developed the blackstar, a weapon to crack Dyson Spheres.[242] Gallifreyan artifacts included Pandak's staff and an artifact associated with Helron.[243]

"Aeons ago", the Dimensioneers were a group of Time Lords who sought to rule every dimension, and developed advanced nodes to transfer energy from one dimension to another. The Time Lords feared the damage the Dimensioneers might cause, had them executed and outlawed their technology. The Dimensioneers became the stuff of legend and a bedtime story the Time Lords used to frighten their children – they were regarded as powerful travelers who walked the dimensions, daring to interfere and seek the ultimate balance between the powers of eternity. The Time Lords forbade inter-dimensional travel, but declined to destroy all of the Dimensioneers' technology. A time-shielded vault on the planet Terserus contained some files and artifacts, and node activators were installed in hidden compartments within Type 40 TARDISes.[244]

"The Stolen TARDIS"[245] -> A Gallifreyan student named Plutar was failed because he wanted to meddle in the affairs of other planets. He was put to work maintaining TARDISes. Meanwhile, a ship landed outside the Time Lords' city, and the lizard-like Sillarg fooled those present into watching a space circus while he moved to steal a TARDIS. He stole one that Plutar was working inside, but it malfunctioned and took them to the distant past of Gallifrey. Plutar warned the authorities on their return, whereupon Sillag was arrested and his memory of Gallifrey erased. Plutar was asked to reapply to the Academy.

236 *Renaissance of the Daleks*. The fifth Doctor overrides this circuit to rescue Nyssa and a Knight Templar after they're killed in 1864, which somewhat begs the question of why he doesn't do this more often. It's presumably this circuit that malfunctions and causes the "time track" anomaly seen in *The Space Museum*. The fact that the Daleks don't use such a protocol probably accounts for the alternate timeline in which they're the masters of Earth in *Day of the Daleks*.
237 *The Dimension Riders*
238 *The Eight Doctors, The Infinity Doctors*.
239 *The Infinity Doctors*
240 *Tomb of Valdemar*
241 *The Infinity Doctors*
242 *The Infinity Doctors*. The implication is that they would be (or had been?) used against the People of the Worldsphere first seen in *The Also People*.
243 *Divided Loyalties*
244 *UNIT: Dominion*
245 Dating "The Stolen TARDIS" (*DWW* #9-11) - The Doctor says "when did it happen? Oh, a long time ago, dates really aren't important to us time travellers". Sillarg lands without encountering Gallifrey's transduction barriers (*The Invasion of Time*) or other defences, and the city isn't domed (although it may not be the Capitol, as we know there are other cities on Gallifrey).
246 Dating "Minatorius" (*DWM Winter Special 1981*) -

Like "The Stolen TARDIS", this could take place at any time.
247 The Doctor, *Hell Bent*
248 *The Deadly Assassin*
249 *Hell Bent*
250 "The Lost Dimension", expanding upon the Cloister Bell as first heard in *Logopolis*.
251 *The Magician's Apprentice, Hell Bent*.
252 *Matrix*
253 *The Dimension Riders*
254 *Conundrum*, referencing *The Mind Robber*.
255 The Doctor, *Heaven Sent*
256 *Hell Bent*
257 *So Vile a Sin*
258 *Millennial Rites*
259 *Christmas on a Rational Planet*
260 *The Mutants*
261 *The Deadly Assassin*
262 *The Leisure Hive*
263 *The Trial of a Time Lord*
264 *Shada*
265 *Nightmare in Silver*
266 "Uroborous"
267 *Revenge of the Judoon*
268 *Pier Pressure*
269 *FP: The Brakespeare Voyage* (ch36).
270 *The Quantum Archangel*

"Minatorius"[246] -> A young Time Lord visited the planet Minatorius, and died to prevent a reactor there from going critical.

The Matrix

"The Time Lords have got a big computer made of ghosts, in a crypt, guarded by more ghosts." [247]

The Time Lords built the Matrix, a form of computer that could – amongst other things – store the minds of dead Time Lords.[248]

The Matrix was the biggest database in history, and functioned like a living computer. Its algorithms could generate prophecies that predicted the future. Some beings, such as a Dalek from the Cloister Wars, were physically incorporated into the Matrix's database. Projections of the dead minds in the Matrix – the Cloister Wraiths (a.k.a. Sliders) – guarded its inner systems, and rang its Cloister Bells to warn of oncoming disaster.[249] The TARDIS's Cloister Bell, its Doomsday Circuit, notified its passengers of impending disaster.[250]

Time Lords knew not to bury their fellows prematurely... even a Time Lord was too injured to regenerate, the cells of his/her body could keep going for days. The final days of a Time Lord's life were supposed to entail a period of mediation, repentance and acceptance, as well as contemplation of the absolute. By ancient tradition, a confession dial – a Time Lord's last will and testament – would be delivered to his or her closest friend on the eve of their final day. The dial served as an act of purification – a pocket reality in which the Time Lord could face his/her inner demons before his/her mind was uploaded to the Matrix.[251]

When the Matrix was young, it began to break down as thousands of Time Lord minds resented their deaths. The Time Lords cleaned the Matrix by isolating its dark part: the Dark Matrix. It was caged and forgotten about beneath the Citadel, sealed with a great key held by the Keeper of the Matrix.[252]

The Garvond was imprisoned for a time in the Gallifreyan Matrix, where it assimilated copies of Time Lord minds, including that of the Doctor. The creature's exact origins were unknown, although by nature it was the embodiment of the evil in the minds in the Matrix. The Garvond wanted to sail the Time Vortex and consume all life. It had several thousand names, all corruptions of the High Gallifreyan term for "of darkest thought".[253]

The Land of Fiction was originally part of the Matrix.[254]

The Hybrid

"Long before the Time War, the Time Lords knew it was coming, like a storm on the wind. There were many prophecies and stories, legends before the fact. One of them was about a creature called the Hybrid: Half Dalek, half Time Lord, the ultimate warrior. But whose side would it be on? Would it bring peace or destruction? Was it real, or a fantasy? I confess, I know the Hybrid is real. I know where it is, and what it is. I confess, I'm afraid." [255]

The prophecy pertaining to the Hybrid only cited it as the product of "two warrior races", but the Time Lords and the Daleks presumed it referred to them. In future, all Matrix prophecies would concur that the Hybrid would stand in the ruins of Gallifrey – that it would unravel the Web of Time and destroy a "billion billion hearts" to heal its own.[256]

Technological and Scientific Advancement

Gallifreyan technology has been refined, rather than totally reworked, over the last ten million years.[257] A dark science of earlier Time Lords was quantum mnemonics, a reality-altering power that manipulated the basic nature of reality and probability. Quantum mnemonics allowed one to transform the history of a planet or an individual by warping space and time.[258]

The Time Lords used devices called amaranths to rebuild parts of time and space that were damaged in the Time Wars. They were originally built to manipulate black holes.[259] The Time Lords discovered an indestructible material.[260] They learnt to engineer micro-universes. Eventually, they abandoned the barren road of technology.[261]

They abandoned tachyonics for warp matrix engineering.[262] They invented the Magnotron. Over time, the Primitive Phases One and Two of the Matrix were relegated to the Archives. Phases Three to Six remained in use.[263] They developed Gallifreyan Morse.[264] The Time Lords invented chess.[265] The game of poker didn't exist on Gallifrey.[266]

The science of Temporal Reversion was so tricky, the Time Lords avoided using it.[267] Gallifreyan zinc was an excellent conductor, and one of the strongest substances in the known universe.[268] Ten million years ago, Gallifreyan technology abandoned use of moving parts such as ball bearings.[269]

Erkulon, the greatest nano-engineer in Gallifreyan history, created the time ram.[270]

The Time Lords took the credit for the Library of

Carsus, although no-one knew for sure who built it. It was built millennia ago, and contained every book ever written. It was in an area of space known for time anomalies – the same solar system as Minerva, Schyllus, Tessus, Lakertya, Molinda, Hollus and Garrett.[271] At least one section of the Gallifreyan Academy was built in a formerly underwater locale.[272]

Three thousand years ago, Mawdryn and his followers stole a Metamorphic Symbiosis Regenerator.[273] Two thousand years ago, the Time Lords abandoned interspacial geometry.[274] Some Time Lords such as Epsilon Delta could rehearse various events without altering the true timeline.[275] Time Lords could use Reverse Tachyon-Chronons to move time backwards and forwards, manipulating material so that it wouldn't age.[276]

With great effort, Time Lords used a process called "soul-catching" to absorb a dying Gallifreyan's memories.[277] The Time Lords built the Parachronistic Chamber, deep in the Capitol, to regulate time distortions.[278] Mimesis was a Gallifreyan art in which anything you write came true. It was practiced by a cult that held an annual ritual, the Thirteenth Night, but the High Council banned the ritual and the art – probably because it was too arcane and unpredictable.[279]

Time Lords' extended lifespans sometimes necessitated that they edit out their more useless memories, storing them electronically or erasing them.[280] An artificial, multidimensional art gallery was located beneath the Capitol.[281]

TARDISes were grown, not built.[282] They were intended to have six pilots, but on numerous occasions had just one.[283] They were grown in space, away from Gallifrey, to prevent time pollution. Stattenheim signals could broadcast along Eye of Harmony time contours, so TARDIS remote control worked even from across the uni-

271 *Spiral Scratch.* Lakertya appeared in *Time and the Rani.*

272 *Time in Office*; this is "eighteen thousand years" before the fifth Doctor era.

273 *Mawdryn Undead*

274 *The Stones of Blood*

275 *The Dimension Riders*

276 *Legacy*

277 *The Devil Goblins from Neptune*

278 *A Device of Death*

279 *Managra*

280 *Timewyrm: Genesys*

281 *Damaged Goods*

282 *The Impossible Planet*, which concurs with information in the novels, such as *Cold Fusion* and *The Taking of Planet 5.*

283 *Journey's End*, perhaps intended to explain why the Doctor is so rubbish at piloting the TARDIS, but in defiance of the large number of times in classic *Doctor Who* (*The Time Meddler*, every story with the Master, etc.) that TARDISes other than the Doctor's Ship operate just fine with a single pilot.

284 *Cold Fusion*

285 *Goth Opera*

286 "Millennia" before *Engines of War* (ch15).

287 *The Crystal Bucephalus*

288 *The Gallifrey Chronicles*

289 *Love and War*

290 *The Eight Doctors*

291 First seen in *The War Games* (suggesting that the technology predates the Doctor leaving Gallifrey) and most recently used in *The Doctor's Wife.*

292 "Millennia" before *The Twelfth Doctor Year One*: "Terrorformer".

293 "Thousands of years" before *1stD V1: The Sleeping Blood.*

294 *Big Bang Generation* (ch5).

295 *DC: The Eleven*

296 *The Abandoned*

297 *The Trouble with Drax*

298 *The Eleventh Doctor Year One*: "Space in Dimension Relative and Time"

299 *The Eleventh Doctor Year One*: "The Comfort of the Good"

300 *The Eleventh Doctor Year Two*: "The One"

301 *The Sound of Drums*

302 Aliens recognise the Doctor as a Time Lord in *The Time Warrior, The Brain of Morbius, Image of the Fendahl, Underworld, The Invasion of Time, The Ribos Operation, State of Decay, The Keeper of Traken, Earthshock, Mawdryn Undead, Frontios, Resurrection of the Daleks, Attack of the Cybermen, Vengeance on Varos, The Two Doctors, Timelash, The Trial of a Time Lord, The Curse of Fenric, Rose, The End of the World, Dalek, Human Nature* (TV), *The Stolen Earth, The Eleventh Hour, The Doctor's Wife, A Good Man Goes to War, The Time of the Doctor, Before the Flood, The Husbands of River Song* and *Extremis.*

303 *The Two Doctors*

304 *The War Games*

305 *The Time Warrior*

306 *The Hand of Fear*

307 *The Deadly Assassin, The Invasion of Time.*

308 *Scaredy Cat*

310 *Deep Time*

311 *The Deadly Assassin.* Fans and recent writers have rationalised away the Time Lords' stated "non-intervention" and the clear evidence that they have intervened by assuming that it's the secret (and in some stories highly sinister) "Celestial Intervention Agency" who are behind the interventions. This builds quite a lot on the one reference in the TV series.

312 *The Kingmaker*

313 *The Well-Mannered War*

314 *The Wheel of Ice* (p109).

315 *Tomb Ship*

316 "Dead Man's Hand"

verse.[284] Time Lord technology could retrieve ancestral memories from the blood of virgins. Time Lords could communicate telepathically across the Time Vortex. The poisons in tea couldn't harm them.[285] An undercroft beneath the Capitol served to dispose of dead, dying or otherwise unwanted TARDISes.[286]

Time Lords used two hundred and eight language tenses, most of which didn't translate well.[287] The Time Lords used an omegabet, which was better than an alphabet.[288] Castellan Lode, a female, was the greatest literary historian the Time Lords ever had.[289]

A Gallifreyan golden guinea could buy you a few drinks at a bar.[290] **Time Lords had an emergency messaging system that entailed bundling their thoughts into cube-shaped psychic containers that could be dispatched through time and space.**[291]

The Time Lords deployed a series of satellite beacons to send warnings of threats to universal harmony.[292] To the Time Lords, nano-medicine became regarded as a "child's plaything".[293]

The youngest Time Tots on Gallifrey were taught that the Ancients of the Universe had vanished after manipulating all of time and space to their own ends, and that their Pyramid Eternia was to be avoided.[294] Gallifreyan children used eye-filters to elude their tutors for a short while.[295] One Gallifreyan nursery rhyme spoke of a princess who used the Dark Crystals of Power to reset time.[296]

The people of Altrazar developed a Blinovitch Limitation Effect limiter – which rewrote their past so many times, they removed their city from history itself. The Time Lords sealed the limiter in a vault in Altrazar, which had become a sort of temporal Atlantis, and turned knowledge of the city into a cautionary tale for Time Tots.[297]

Time Lords possessed a Secondary Backwards consciousness, enabling their minds to function in instances of time rolling backwards.[298] If a TARDIS lost faith in its pilot, the bond between the two was severed and the Ship automatically returned to Gallifrey – or, failing that, the nearest Time Lord.[299]

The Time Lords were very powerful, and excellent dancers to boot.[300]

Foreign Policy

The Time Lords were the oldest and most mighty race in the universe, sworn only to watch, never to interfere. Gallifrey was called "the Shining World of the Seven Systems".[301]

Alien races from all periods of recorded time have had dealings with the Time Lords, ranging from those in the ancient past such as the Kastrians and the destroyer Sutekh to those in the far future such as the Usurians. Other races or beings who know something of the Time Lords and Gallifrey (without hearing just

of the Doctor or another individual) include the Andromedans, the Bandrils, the Church of the Papal Mainframe, the Cryons, the Cybermen, the Daleks, the Face of Boe, the Family of Blood, the Fendahl, Fenric, the Fatality Index, the Fisher King, the Forest of Cheem, the Guardians, House, the Keeper of Traken, Mawdryn's race, the Mentors, the Minyans, the Nestene, Prisoner Zero, the Racnoss, Saturnynians, the Shadow Proclamation, the Silence and the Academy of the Question, the Sisterhood of Karn, the Sontarans, some residents of the Third Zone, the Tractators, Vampires and the Vardans.

The Time Lords visited many worlds in many time periods, even in an official capacity.[302] They authorised (or prevented) other races' time travel experiments and defended the Laws of Time.[303] Time Lords observed but didn't interfere.[304] At times they intervened with regards to unauthorised time travel, and could almost be thought of as "galactic ticket inspectors".[305]

They were committed to protecting weaker species, and to preventing aggression against indigenous populations.[306] **The vast majority of Time Lords didn't concern themselves with the universe outside the Capitol, and were more concerned with internal politics.**[307] Time Lords were taught "very early on" not to visit newly formed planets, as the morphogenetic fields of such worlds were still in flux, and therefore susceptible to undue influence from visitors.[308]

Before other races existed, the Time Lords warned the Phaeron about an Imperfection among their number.[310]

The Celestial Intervention Agency was concerned with covert intervention.[311] The CIA's motto was, "The story changes, the ending stays the same", meaning that it didn't matter how one fixed temporal anomalies so long as time continued along a straight path. For instance, if a man who would start a war were erased from time, it was incumbent on the organisation to start it anyway.[312]

Study of the later Humanian era was forbidden by the Academy as being outside the Gallifreyan sphere of influence.[313] The Time Lords regarded the practice of implanting "a device, legend, signpost, a promise" deep in the past of a race, changing its development as a means of soliciting help as "rather unethical".[314]

The Arrit, an ancient and advanced race, could have risen to rival the Time Lords had they survived.[315] Another time-active race, the T'Keyn, and the Time Lords made a habit of ignoring one another.[316]

The (mostly) incorporeal Arimeci drew strength from their followers' faith. Their efforts to establish a religion on Gallifrey incurred a devastating pushback from the Time Lords, but the emergence of Gallifrey's non-intervention policy motivated both sides to formalise relations. To save the fifth Doctor and Leela in future, Tegan Jovanka came back in time in a WarDIS and exposed the Arimeci's duplicity to their followers, destroying them.[317]

The High Council moved to eliminate Godseeds, weapons of war made to transform target populations, after foreseeing a time when they would seed the whole universe.[318] The Time Lords tried to eradicate the Throxian lavaworms: a species genetically engineered to destroy the planet Throx.[319] The Time Lords undercut the Horofax Empire, and its time-sensitive leaders.[320]

The Celestial Council – a governing body unique to Gallifrey's Forty-First Era – detected a dangerous confluence of parallel timelines and crafted the ocean planet Funderell to contain it. A village oversaw the planet, but it was overlooked following the Great Cutbacks of Gallifrey's Fifty-Third Bureaucratic Regime. In time, the Time Lords forgot the art of constructing whole worlds.[321]

Political

More Presidents hailed from the Prydonian Chapter than all other chapters combined. Prydonians were viewed as cunning, but claimed they "simply saw a little further ahead than most". They wore scarlet and orange robes. Other chapters included the Arcalians (who wore green) and Patrexes (who wore heliotrope).[322] No Arcalian had been president of Gallifrey in "several centuries".[323] The Patrexes were aesthetes who saw artistic value in all things, including suffering, but lacked the imagination to be true artists.[324] Gallifrey's history was spotted with a few presidential assassinations.[325]

The Celestial Intervention Agency evolved from Rassilon's personal guard.[326] **At some point, the Time**

317 *Time in Office*
318 "Millennia" before *Fiesta of the Damned*.
319 *3rdA: The Transcendence of Ephros*
320 *3rdA: Storm of the Horofax*
321 "Thousands of years" before *The Skin of the Sleek/ The Thief Who Stole Time*.
322 *The Deadly Assassin*
323 *Trial of the Valeyard*. The sixth Doctor, in fact, gives no sign that an Arcalian has been president during his lifetime.
324 *Damaged Goods*
325 *Gallifrey IV: Reborn*
326 *Lungbarrow*
327 *Shada*
328 *The Ancestor Cell*
329 *Shada*
330 *Gallifrey IV: Disassembled*
331 *Omega*
332 *Gallifrey II: Lies*
333 *DC: The Eleven*
334 *The Deadly Assassin*

TIME LORD PRESIDENTS: Presidents of Gallifrey that pre-date the Doctor's time include Rassilon (Gallifrey's first president), Pandak (*Lungbarrow*, *The Ancestor Cell*), Pandak II (*DotD: Babblesphere, DC: The Eleven*), Pandak III (who was president for nine hundred years; *The Deadly Assassin*), Pandak VII (*Gallifrey IV: Disassembled*), Pandora (the first female president, overthrown but reborn in *Gallifrey* Series 2 and 3) and Torkal (*The Ancestor Cell*). Drall was president during the Doctor's Academy years (*Divided Loyalties*), and Morbius' presidency likely happens during the Doctor's lifetime (*The Brain of Morbius, Warmonger*). Vice President Saran served as Acting President during the Morbius crisis (*Warmonger*).

In *Hell Bent*, the Doctor concedes that during his time on Gallifrey, he made off with the president's daughter (likely Susan). *Time in Office* venerates Apeiron, Pandak IV, Eurenoyar and Pandak XI, but they didn't necessarily serve as president.

The Ancestor Cell says the Doctor was the 407th and

409th President of Gallifrey. *The Gallifrey Chronicles* says that Romana is the 413th. From this, we can extrapolate that the 405th President was the one killed in *The Deadly Assassin* (and almost certainly, in a previous incarnation, the one seen in *The Three Doctors*); the 406th was Greyjan the Sane (*The Ancestor Cell*); the 407th was the fourth Doctor (he was "inducted" in *The Invasion of Time*); the 408th was Borusa (the President is referred to by the Doctor in *The Ribos Operation*, but not named as Borusa until *Arc of Infinity*. Borusa regenerates once more and his reign ends in *The Five Doctors*); the 409th is the fifth Doctor (deposed in the run-up to *The Trial of a Time Lord*); the 410th is Flavia, the 411th is Niroc, who's corrupt and deposed with the help of the Doctor and Rassilon in *The Eight Doctors*; the 412th is Flavia again, according to *Happy Endings*, which is set soon after Romana is installed as the 413th.

Time in Office, set in the aftermath of *The Five Doctors*, says the fourth Doctor's presidency was scrubbed from the official record. The same story entails the fifth Doctor being press-ganged into accepting the presidency, and replace the deeply unpopular Acting President Tavoli, following Flavia's retirement (from the High Council, not the presidency) owing to the botched succession. The Doctor legs it (naturally) as soon as possible, after appointing Castellan Lowri as Acting President. As Lowri never formally becomes president, perhaps Flavia re-entered the political scene and became president afterward (*The Eight Doctors*).

Romana's tenure is a fairly long one, barring some interruptions – including an unnamed Time Lord serving as interim president while the Daleks hold her prisoner for twenty years (*The Apocalypse Element*). Additionally, the fallout from Pandora's return and insurrection, *Gallifrey* Series 3 rapidly results in Chancellor Valyes serving as Acting President, then Chancellor Braxiatel being the *actual* president for a matter of hours before naming Matthias his successor. Matthias later resigns, handing the presidency back to Romana (*Gallifrey* Series 6). She continues as president into her third incarnation, Lady Trey, but events in

Lords Rungar and Sabjatrik were sent to Shada. They remained there.[327]

Apart from Rassilon, only President Torkal was ever referred to as "the Great".[328] **While young, Salyavin learnt how to project his mind into others' and was sentenced to imprisonment in Shada as a result. He escaped, using his powers to erase all knowledge of the prison planet.**[329] "Burn orders", i.e. kill orders, issued by Gallifreyan presidents were carried out by their personal assassin, a Time Lord with the title of Lord Burner. Such orders were sent directly into Lord Burner's mind, and not made public.[330]

Mundat the Third's reputation swung from his being a brutal murderer to a noble warrior – and that's just in the documentaries of the historian Ertikus.[331] Pandora became the first female President of Gallifrey, assumed the dictatorial title of Imperiatrix and sought to overturn the ancient laws of Rassilon. Legends would claim that Pandora tried to lead Gallifrey to war, hoping to reshape the web of time to her liking. The High Council defeated Pandora – her offworld bodyguard was sent home, and their planet time-looped. Pandora herself was placed in a dispersal chamber beneath the old Capitol and erased from history. However, her spirit survived in a partition of the Matrix, which was immune to such historical alterations.[332]

The administration of Pandak II, a.k.a. Pandak the Wanderer, crafted an Inabsentia in Chaotica Protocol allowing for a ranking official to be installed as acting president, without ceremony, if the proper office-holder was away from Gallifrey.[333]

In the lifetime of some contemporary Time Lords, President Pandak III ruled for nine hundred years.[334]

President Pandak III suppressed a report on Lampreys by Lord Rellox of the Arcalian Council for Temporal Research.[335]

> = Auld Mortality, an entity "as old as time itself", lurked behind every Time Lord president as a reminder that their tenure was fleeting. One Time Lord president fell on the stairs at his investiture and cracked open his skull, another was poisoned by his own food taster, and a third died of a paper-cut at an archivist's supper.[336]

Savar tried to rescue Omega from his black hole, but was ambushed by the Time Lord god Ohm. Attempting to escape, Savar's TARDIS was stretched until it became the light-year-long structure called the Needle. Savar fled in an escape capsule, which was intercepted by the I. The I stripped the ship of technology and took Savar's eyes. He was found by the Time Lords, but was utterly insane from the experience. He regenerated, but was a broken man.[337]

Time Lords didn't like cows, or onions.[338]

The Doctor's TARDIS

The Doctor's original TARDIS was a Type 50 – it was an "acquaintance of his, from his youth". He came to leave Gallifrey in a different TARDIS, and later told the Type 50: "There wasn't time to pick and choose. I had to take the first TARDIS I could lay my hands on... if I could [have taken you], I would." The Type 50's symbiotic link with the Doctor was stronger than he'd believed, and it became deeply resentful at being abandoned.[339]

Gallifrey Series 8 retroactively annul that (see the Lady Trey sidebar).

Dark Eyes and *Doom Coalition* are hard to square against Romana's presidency, but seem to happen during the various *Gallifrey* audio series. A male president (not Romana as a bloke) colludes with Straxus in *DEyes: X and the Daleks*. *Doom Coalition* entails Chancellor Padrac murdering still another unnamed president, seizing the office and forcing the High Council to temporarily flee Gallifrey for fear of their lives. How President Romana and her associates (Leela, Narvin, K9, etc.) factor into this, we're never told.

At the end of *Gallifrey* Series 8, Romana stands down as President after naming Chancellor Livia as her successor. A new incarnation of Livia is still president during the outbreak of the Last Great Time War (*Gallifrey – Time War* V1), and stands down as part of a conspiracy that leads to Admiral Valerian becoming president, moments before Rassilon is resurrected in his body. We see Rassilon serving as president in *The End of Time*. The twelfth Doctor overthrows a new incarnation of Rassilon in *Hell Bent*, and is very briefly acknowledged

as president himself (for the third time around) before running off with Clara. A female President succeeds him ("Supremacy of the Cybermen").

Susan becomes president in an Unbound timeline (*Unbound: A Storm of Angels*), following a period in which Auld Mortality picks off a number of presidents. The sitting president in *The Infinity Doctors* is "tiny; withered", with a white beard. Following an attempt on his life, he names Castellan Voran as acting president.

335 *Spiral Scratch*
336 *Unbound: Auld Mortality*
337 Savar is first mentioned in *Seeing I*, but these events take place "a thousand years" before *The Infinity Doctors*, as far as Savar is concerned. There was a Time Lord called Savar in *The Invasion of Time*.
338 Or so a projection of the fourth Doctor claims in "Dead Man's Hand." Conversely, the tenth Doctor claims in "The Forgotten" that Rassilon enjoyed onions.
339 *Prisoners of Fate*. The Type 50 had a working navigational system, and presumably wasn't in the repair bay seen in *The Name of the Doctor*.

The TARDIS the Doctor took from Gallifrey was a Type 40, Mark 3.[340] The Type 40 TT-Capsule was introduced when Salyavin was young.[341] The Type 40 was withdrawn centuries ago and was considered a "Veteran and Vintage Vehicle".[342] The TARDIS' true weight would fracture the surface of the Earth.[343] Type 40 TARDISes were equipped with a magnetic card system containing 18,348 emergency instructions.[344]

The TARDIS began life as a coral outgrowth; the Doctor suspected that She wasn't watered properly.[345] The TARDIS contained an Architectural Reconfiguration System: a living metal construct that could reconstruct particles according to its users' requirements, manufacturing any machine they needed.[346]

When the Doctor took possession of his TARDIS, all records pertaining to its previous crew were gone. It normally took years to learn how to fly a TARDIS. Food machines had been standard TARDIS issue.[347] Such food machines offered product with a fungi base, as grown in vats in a laboratory in the Ship, and molecularly rearranged into whatever combinations users requested.[348]

The original pilot of the Doctor's TARDIS, the Time Lady Marianna, sought to visit the Point of Stillness and use it to make her imagination real, then eliminate all war and conflict from the universe. Marianna's TARDIS crew tricked her into imagining a coma-inducing drug, which they administered to her. She remained hidden and dormant in the heart of the TARDIS throughout the Doctor's first four incarnations. Her imaginings sometimes bled through into the universe, manifesting such creatures as the horda.[349]

The Doctor's TARDIS was due for the breakers, decommission log No. 2311/6/3, when he stole it. Quadrigger No. 3911, Stoyn, was tasked with taking apart the Ship's engines before it was sent to the vapourizers.[350]

The Early Life of the Doctor

There are a number of seemingly contradictory facts about the Doctor's birth and upbringing.

The Doctor was born under the sign of "Crossed Computers".[351] As a baby, the Doctor had a cot.[352] He was born the same year as the Rani.[353] He was one of forty-five cousins from the House of Lungbarrow. Unusually for a Time Lord, he had a belly button, which earned him the nicknames "Wormhole" and "Snail".[354] He dreamed of stars when he was very young.[355]

The Doctor was half human on his mother's side.[356] He was acquainted, somehow, with the Woman in White.[357] His mother's maiden name was "a question and a half".[358]

340 The term "Type 40" was first used in *The Deadly Assassin*. The *Teselecta*'s records in *Let's Kill Hitler* list the Doctor's TARDIS as a "Type 40, Mark 3" – in accordance with the Doctor being amazed at the modernity of the Monk's TARDIS, a "Mark 4", in *The Time Meddler*.
341 *Shada*
342 *The Pirate Planet*
343 *Flatline*
344 *State of Decay*
345 *Diamond Dogs* (ch15).
346 *Journey to the Centre of the TARDIS*, elaborating upon mention of the system/technique in *Logopolis* and *Castrovalva*.
347 *The Beginning*. The TARDIS food machine first appeared in *The Daleks*.
348 *Upstairs*
349 Marianna – not the most reliable of witnesses – variously says she was imprisoned "millennia" and "hundreds of years" before *The Abandoned*. The horda appeared in *The Face of Evil*.
350 *The Beginning, Luna Romana.*
351 *The Creature from the Pit*
352 *A Good Man Goes to War.* The circumstances of the cot being in the TARDIS becomes more perplexing the more one thinks about it. The cot's presence might suggest that the TARDIS was some sort of family heirloom, but *The Doctor's Wife* says that the Doctor picked the TARDIS because its door was open. If so, did he pack his childhood cot before leaving Gallifrey in such a rush?

Did his family keep multiple TARDISes, and he just happened to select the one with his cot in it? Or did he just reclaim the cot during a stopover on Gallifrey? Or is he simply lying to say it's his cot – did it actually belong to a child of his?
353 In *Time and the Rani*, the Doctor deduces the combination to the Rani's lock is 953, "my age ... and the Rani's".
354 *Lungbarrow*, with *The One Doctor* confirming the "Snail" nickname.
355 *Closing Time*
356 *Doctor Who – The Movie*
HALF HUMAN ON HIS MOTHER'S SIDE: The eighth Doctor's airing of his "secret" to Professor Wagg in *Doctor Who – The Movie* – that he is "half human on his mother's side" – has long been a source of debate in fandom, if for no other reason that it seems to go against all manner of stories where the Doctor biologically is no different from a purebred Time Lord. It's insufficient to claim that the Doctor is just joking with Wagg, because the Deathworm Master concludes that the Doctor is half-human by looking into a projection of the eighth Doctor's iris. The "half-human" claim is chiefly limited to just *Doctor Who – The Movie*, although *The Gallifrey Chronicles* furthered this by hinting that the Time Lord named Ulysses/Daniel Joyce and the human time traveller Penelope Gate are the Doctor's parents.

The more likely explanation, however, is that Time

THE DOCTOR'S AGE: *The Doctor's age has been specified a number of times, but he is often vague and contradictory on the subject.*

The second Doctor tells Victoria that he is "450" in *The Tomb of the Cybermen*. The Master of the Land of Fiction says he is "ageless" in *The Mind Robber*. (In the draft scripts of *The Power of the Daleks* and *The Underwater Menace,* he was "750".)

The third Doctor, frustrated while trying to develop a plague cure, says in *Doctor Who and the Silurians*: "I'm beginning to lose confidence for the first time in my life. And that covers several thousands years." He similarly tells Professor Kettering in *The Mind of Evil*, "I am a scientist, and I have been for several thousand—", before cutting himself off. (Both statements are frequently interpreted, as was a convention of earlier science fiction including *Doctor Who*, as measuring someone's age by the duration of time they've travelled rather than their birth years. See, for instance, Vicki calculating that Barbara must be about 550 years old in *The Rescue*.)

The fourth Doctor still thinks of himself as "743... or was it 730, I can never remember", in "The Time Witch". On TV, he says he is "749" in *Planet of Evil, The Brain of Morbius* and *The Seeds of Doom*, and "nearly 750" in *Pyramids of Mars*. He is "750" by *The Robots of Death*, 756 (according to him) or 759 (according to Romana) in *The Ribos Operation*, nearly 760 in *The Power of Kroll*, 750 again in *The Creature from the Pit* and *The Leisure Hive*. (A scripted scene in *The Stones of Blood* showed him celebrating his 751st birthday.) He's "750" in "Gaze of the Medusa", and "only middle age" in *Destroy the Infinite*.

The fifth Doctor never gives his age on screen, but he is "pushing 900" in *Omega*.

The sixth Doctor is 900 in *Revelation of the Daleks* and *The Mysterious Planet*, but "over 900" by *Terror of the Vervoids*. An elderly Jacob Williams claims in *100*: "Bedtime Story" that the sixth Doctor spent a hundred years showing four completely paralysed people – including him and Evelyn – the wonders of the universe, but it's a highly suspect claim given the Doctor's age in *Time and the Rani,* and could just owe to Jacob relating events to his son in a fable-like fashion.

In *Time and the Rani*, both the seventh Doctor and the Rani are "953", and the Doctor has "nine hundred years experience" by *Remembrance of the Daleks*. He's lived "900 years" in *Mask of Tragedy*, and goes for his "nine hundred and fifty year check up" (presumably a bit late) in the comic "Slimmer!" In the New Adventures, he was around a thousand years old. According to *SLEEPY*, he celebrated his 1000th birthday during *Set Piece*.

The eighth Doctor is 1012 in *Vampire Science*, in which it's also said that his current body is "three" years old, meaning that the seventh Doctor regenerated at age 1009. In *The Dying Days*, the eighth Doctor is 1200.

He's only "nine hundred and fifty" in *Neverland* – and yet he has "over a thousand years of collected experience" in *The Twilight Kingdom*, despite there not having been that much time in the interim.

We know that the eighth Doctor resided on Earth for one hundred and thirteen years, from 1888-2001 (beginning with *The Ancestor Cell* and ending with *Escape Velocity*) and that he spent six hundred years on the planet Orbis (*Orbis*). Cumulatively, and however one structures the eighth Doctor's adventures, he must be at least 1725 (probably more).

He also, although it's chump change for a Time Lord, spent some months incognito aboard the *Traken* during the Last Great Time War, keeping watch over Nyssa (*ST:* "A Heart on Both Sides").

# # # # #

The new series reset the Doctor's age, but has been consistent in its progression since then. The ninth Doctor says he's 900 in *Aliens of London* and *The Doctor Dances*. In response to Rose's question about the problems introducing himself without a real name in *The Empty Child*, he says, "Nine centuries in, I'm coping".

The tenth Doctor says he's 903 in *Voyage of the Damned*, "The Whispering Gallery" and *The Nemonite Invasion*. He's 904 in *The Day of the Doctor*, and 906 in *The End of Time*. Taken at face value, this means that the Doctor's tenth body only survived for six years.

The eleventh Doctor is 907 in *Flesh and Stone* and *Amy's Choice*. He mentions spending "nine hundred years in time and space" in *A Christmas Carol*. In *The Impossible Planet*, we see him at two different points in his life – at age 909 and 1,103. He ends Series 6 as the latter. It's unclear if the intervening hundred and ninety-five years occur (for him) during the mid-season hiatus between *A Good Man Goes to War* and *Let's Kill Hitler* or between *The God Complex* and *Closing Time* (after he drops Amy and Rory on Earth). The Doctor telling young George in *Night Terrors*, "I was your age oh, about a thousand years ago", might suggest that about a century elapses between each break. In the comic "The Doctor and the Nurse", the Doctor says that for him, *The Girl Who Waited* happened "200 years ago".

Asked his age in *The Day of the Doctor*, the eleventh Doctor replies: "I don't know. I lose track. Twelve hundred and something, I think, unless I'm lying. I can't remember if I'm lying about my age, that's how old I am." Adam Mitchell believes the eleventh Doctor is "twelve hundred years old" in "Prisoners of Time". The same Doctor finishes out his life on Trenzalore over a period of nine hundred years (*The Time of the Doctor*, as further related in *Tales of Trenzalore*), leading to the twelfth Doctor stating he's lived for "more than two thousand years" in *Deep Breath*.

Clara reiterates that the twelfth Doctor is "two thou-

continued on page 2367...

He had a family.[359] He had an "excellent if smelly" godmother with two heads and halitosis. She gifted him with a device that could recognise different alien species.[360] He may have had an uncle[361], but he didn't have an aunt.[362] The Doctor said his Auntie Mabel told him to "Look up, look down, look around."[363]

As the Doctor let the Master die on Sarn, the Master called out, "Won't you show mercy to your own—"[364]

The Doctor's family owned a home in South Gallifrey.[365] This home was House Lungbarrow, which was perched on the side of Mount Lung, overlooking the Cadonflood river, two days from Rassilon's Rampart.[366] The Doctor doesn't know much about Gallifrey's Southern Hemisphere.[367]

"I was a very lonely child. Most children had imaginary friends. I had an imaginary enemy. Mandrake the Lizard King was my creation. A vicious tyrant and galactic conqueror who made a blackened trail of chaos across a thousand worlds, and whom I would do battle with in the mountains of South Gallifrey. [He was actually] just a dead lizard propped up on the side of a chrono-exhaust funnel that poked up out of the ground. I used to sneak out of the Capitol to play goodies vs. baddies, and I used to defeat [him] with my trusty stick. Then, one day, when events forced me to grow up, I put away childish things and faced up to the real evil that was in the universe. I also started to make friends. Lots of them. [Mandrake was] consigned to the back of my mind."[368]

When the Doctor was a boy, "back at the dawn of time", he had an imaginary friend named Blinker. During a rare snow on Gallifrey, they escaped into the forest, and shivered up a tree for days. Afterward, the Doctor never imagined Blinker again.[369] The Doctor heard stories of Azrael the necrotist when he was a boy, which made for some rough bedtimes.[370]

The Doctor's nanny told him, "You never know when a gadget might come in handy", and "the bigger they are, the harder they fall."[371] When he was young, the Doctor drew crayon sketches of the Solvers.[372] The story of the Then and the Now, a living paradox and Gallifreyan bogeyman, terrified the Doctor as a child.[373]

Lords can hybridise with other species upon regeneration – the eighth Doctor claims as much in *Doctor Who – The Movie* (Grace:"Why don't you have the ability to transform yourself into another species?" The Doctor:"Well, I do, you see, but only when I 'die' [i.e. regenerate]". Some have taken this to mean – owing to the atypical manner of his regeneration (the dulling influence of the anaesthetic, his "changing" in a morgue full of human corpses) – that the eighth Doctor is "half-human" whereas all the other Doctors are full-blooded Time Lords. The notion that Time Lords can hybridise with other species is substantiated in the works of Paul Cornell: a regenerated Time Lord becomes part-Silurian in *The Shadows of Avalon*, and another becomes part-birdperson in *Circular Time:*"Spring".

The IDW mini-series "The Forgotten" tries to reconcile the "half-human" problem by saying that the eighth Doctor once used a half-broken Chameleon Arch (*Utopia*, the TV version of *Human Nature*) to convince the Deathworm Master that he was half-human. There isn't a particularly good reason in *Doctor Who – The Movie* as to why this would be helpful, however; in fact, as a means of helping the Master to realise that human eyes can open the Eye of Harmony in the TARDIS, it's a fairly counter-productive thing to do.

The Series 9 finale, *Hell Bent*, flirts with the idea that the Doctor is indeed half-human, half-Time Lord – a notion which, if true, might explain why the Doctor originally fled Gallifrey, out of fear of a prophecy regarding a powerful and destructive Hybrid creature. Ultimately, however, only Ashildr muses the possibility that the Doctor is half-human, and no hard evidence is given to say that the twelfth Doctor has any human inheritance.

357 The more descriptive name used for the mysterious woman seen throughout *The End of Time*, credited on screen as just "the Woman". Russell T Davies confirmed in his memoir, *The Writer's Tale*, that the Woman was intended as the Doctor's mother, but has acknowledged that other interpretations of the character are fair game.

358 *DC 3: Absent Friends*
359 *The Tomb of the Cybermen*, further implied in *The Curse of Fenric* and confirmed in *Father's Day*.
360 *Vincent and the Doctor*
361 *Time and the Rani*. He says, possibly facetiously, "you should see my uncle".
362 *The Eleventh Hour*
363 *DotD: The Time Machine*
364 *Planet of Fire*. The sentence isn't complete, but the next word could well spell out a family relationship (fan speculation over the years has suggested a number of things, usually "brother" and less usually "husband").
365 *Planet of the Spiders*
366 *Lungbarrow*
367 *The Scarlet Empress*
368 The Doctor, *The Widow's Assassin*.
369 *The Abandoned*
370 "The Blood of Azrael."
371 *Death Match, The Fate of Krelos*.
372 *DC 3: The Doomsday Chronometer*
373 "Over a thousand years", in the Doctor's timeline, before *The Eleventh Doctor Year Two*: "Physician, Heal Thyself".

continued from page 2365...

sand years" old (in *Mummy on the Orient Express*), and also that he's "over two thousand years old. Well over. I think" in *The Blood Cell* (ch7). In *The Girl Who Died*, the Doctor is seen consulting his 2000 Year Diary. He's "over two thousand years old" in *The Zygon Inversion*.

Office gossip in *The Pilot* intimates that the twelfth Doctor spends fifty years, or possibly even seventy, lecturing at St Luke's while guarding Missy. It's probably just Chinese whispers (see the Dating notes on Series 10 for why), but if not, he evidently skips over that detail and keeps rounding his age throughout Series 10. He's still "two thousand years old" in *Smile* and *Thin Ice* (TV), and a computer-generated version of him in *Extremis* claims that he's "two thousand years at the last count".

According to the twelfth Doctor in *Twice Upon a Time*, "fifteen hundred years" separate him and the first Doctor.

# # # # #

The advent of the War Doctor (the incarnation between the eighth and ninth Doctors; see The Numbering of the Doctor sidebar) threatens to throw any mapping of the Doctor's life and age – which, if very contradictory at times, at least followed a logical progression for prolonged periods – into irreconcilable chaos. *The Day of the Doctor* establishes that the War Doctor is "four hundred years" younger than the 1200-year-old eleventh Doctor, meaning he's about 800 years old (a figure chosen, doubtless, to reflect the ninth Doctor being 900). However, with *The Night of the Doctor* showing the eighth Doctor regenerating into a fairly young John Hurt, it's hard to avoid the conclusion that the War Doctor himself (played by Hurt when he was 73) lived and aged some centuries during the Last Great Time War. Along those lines, *Engines of War*, featuring the War Doctor, suggests that the War has been going on – from the perspective of those involved – for "four centuries".

Even a conservative estimate of the War Doctor's lifespan should mean that he endures for some centuries – in which case, taking all the evidence as equal, the War Doctor reaches the end of his life after about four centuries and the eleventh Doctor does the same after more than 1100, but the first Doctor similarly died after his body had "worn a bit thin" (a quote the War Doctor even repeats in *The Day of the Doctor*), and yet the first eight Doctors must all be crammed into a 400-year stretch of time.

One attempt to reconcile this, as floated by Mad Norwegian associate Steve Manfred, is that a time war would logically entail both sides using Time itself as a weapon, somewhat akin to the Time Destructor the Daleks build in *The Daleks' Master Plan*. It's possible the War Doctor was caught a blast or two (or ten, for all

we're told) of a time weapon that compressed, hid or otherwise deducted years of life, whatever his external appearance. Exactly that fate seems to have befallen "Mrs Wilson", a Time Lord who "retired" from the Last Great Time War after a temporal weapon aged her body some centuries in seconds, but not enough to warrant regenerating (*WM: Only the Good: The Heavenly Paradigm*).

Ergo, perhaps owing to the War Doctor outwardly looking older than his true age, he's back to being just "900" at the end of the Time War – presuming the same discrepancy doesn't reflect his not having a clue as to his true age, picking what sounds like a pleasing number and counting his way up from there. These are, of course, somewhat spurious solutions, but at least some such rationalization is needed to explain the War Doctor-sized peg being shoved, after the fact, into the Doctor's timeline.

# # # # #

At times, the Doctor has spent extended periods away from their friends, the extended life granted to each incarnation enabling them to resolve various problems, or ride out various developments...

• The first Doctor spent two years rebuilding civilisation on the colony world Destination, until Ian, Barbara and Susan rejoined him through various means (*1stA: The Destination Wars*).

• Following a fumbled TARDIS materialisation, the first Doctor lived in Hoy, Scotland for a few years waiting to reunite with Ian and Barbara in 1956 (*The Revenants*).

• The first Doctor, Ian, Barbara and Vicki devote three months of their lives to restoring a brainwashed human society (*1stD V1: The Unwinding World*), no temporal horseplay involved.

• The second Doctor lives out a few years fixing up a control room while, owing to temporal trickery, Jamie and Zoe only experience a few minutes (*DotD: Shadow of Death*).

• Fifteen years elapse for the fourth Doctor and the first Romana in *Heart of TARDIS* (set between *The Stones of Blood* and *The Androids of Tara*) as they travel through a nexus fighting such foes as the Solstice Squid; it's thirty years if they do, in fact, have to make the same journey back again.

• The fourth Doctor whittled away five years in Paris and at his Baker Street house (sometimes having to elude himself) to rejoin the second Romana and the TARDIS (*The Haunting of Malkin Place*).

• The fifth Doctor spent five years building up the renown of his restaurant, the Tempus Fugit, so he could return to Tegan and Turlough (*The Crystal Bucephalus*).

• The sixth Doctor kept nipping in and out of a cell,

continued on page 2369...

Where the Doctor came from, he wasn't an elite – in fact, he was overwhelmingly a plebian.[374] **An old lady died when the Doctor was a "very little boy". Although her body was covered in veils, it attracted flies a hot, sunny day – an image that gave the Doctor nightmares for years. A "young and telepathic" Doctor knew a trick where he could forge a pseudo-psychic link with a door and convince it to open.**[375]

In the nursery, the Doctor used to play with bricks that contained Roentgen radiation.[376] The Doctor remembered his mother smiling and his father holding him up to see the stars.[377] When the Doctor was ten years old, he was caught skinny-dipping with one of his Cousins.[378] The Doctor used the tunnels beneath the Panopticon as his playground.[379]

The first time the Doctor left Gallifrey was to visit his family's summer house on the other side of the Constellation. While looking up into the night's sky with his mother, he saw a fleet of time ships but never asked where they were going.[380]

LISTEN[381] -> **The TARDIS brought Clara, Colonel Orson Pink and the unconscious twelfth Doctor to a barn with a bed that contained a crying boy. Clara hid under the bed as a man and a woman suggested that the boy should sleep in the house with the other boys. The man insisted that the boy wouldn't have a use for crying when he joined the army, and that he certainly couldn't go to the Academy to become a Time Lord.**

The man and the woman left, and when the boy tried to get out of bed, Clara reflexively grabbed his ankle. She encouraged him to go back to sleep, and told him that it was all right to be afraid, because fear could make him stronger, and didn't have to make him cruel or cowardly. To remember this, Clara left Colonel Pink's gunless soldier figure, Dan the Soldier Man, at the boy's bed. She then left in the TARDIS, and ordered the Doctor to never look where the Ship had landed.

The Doctor left primary school when he was 45 years old.[382] The twelfth Doctor said it had been "two thousand years" since his last confession.[383]

There are a number of seemingly contradictory facts about the Doctor's age.[384]

(Irving) Braxiatel

Braxiatel, a.k.a. Irving Braxiatel, Lord Braxiatel and Cardinal Braxiatel, was a relative of the Doctor, either his brother or one of his Cousins.[385] **The tenth Doctor said he didn't have a brother "anymore".**[386]

Dannademantara, a military strategist, served as one of Braxiatel's mentors and trained him in marksmanship. Together, Danna and Braxiatel experienced wartime events including the Siege of the Sprints of Capra.[387] lgtw - When Braxiatel was young, he met the Blind Soldier: the only survivor of a temporal battle at the Obscura.[388]

Braxiatel's father owned a cellar full of Draconian brandy when Brax was but a babe in arms.[389] Lord Braxiatel never wanted to conform, but graduated with a "fistful of firsts" and initiated many research projects – all to position himself as a nonconformist in conformist's clothing. By the time Braxiatel's brother was doing his exams (and scraped through with the barest minimum of effort), Braxiatel was trusted enough to achieve his dream of serving as an unofficial ambassador, and saw the universe by undertaking clandestine missions for Gallifrey's benefit. Braxiatel's brother followed his example to more of an extreme, and outright left their homeworld.[390]

---

374 *Cortex Fire*

375 *Heaven Sent*

376 *Smith and Jones*

377 *The Eight Doctors*

378 *Unnatural History*

379 *Order of the Daleks*, probably playing off *Hell Bent*.

380 *The Infinity Doctors*

381 Dating *Listen* (X8.4) - It's the Doctor's boyhood. Clara's words are an homage to the first Doctor's line that "fear makes companions of us all" in *An Unearthly Child*.

382 *Shroud of Sorrow*

383 *The Sins of Winter*

384 See The Doctor's Age sidebar.

385 Braxiatel first appears in the NA *Theatre of War*, and becomes an ongoing character in the Bernice Summerfield range. The *Gallifrey* audios detail much of his early history. Justin Richards, who created the char- acter, first implied that Braxiatel was the Doctor's brother in *Benny: The Tears of the Oracle* (p166-167). The notion was later reinforced in *Gallifrey IV: Disassembled* (Romana tells Brax concerning an alt-Doctor: "I thought you'd be pleased to see your—"; Brax, as the alt-Doctor strangles him: "Surely, you wouldn't do this to your own—"), and also in Brax's description of "an old man and his granddaughter" (presumably the first Doctor and Susan) as "family".

386 *Smith and Jones*, and possibly a reference to Irving Braxiatel.

387 *Gallifrey – Time War* V1: *Soldier Obscura*

388 *Gallifrey – Time War* V1: *Soldier Obscura*. Braxiatel eventually realises the Blind Soldier hails from the Last Great Time War.

389 *Benny S3: Legion: Everybody Loves Irving*

390 *Benny: The Tears of the Oracle* (p166-167)

continued from page 2367...

and doubling back on his own timeline, in the course of *The Widow's Assassin* – all told, living out about a decade of his own time.

• *Cortex Fire* is coy about how long it takes the sixth Doctor, in the TARDIS, to save a planet by bending stellar energy, with some time-warping as a consequence. Flip observes that the Doctor looks a bit older, but he hand-waves it away as "a long couple of days".

• The Daleks held the seventh Doctor prisoner for about five years, until he released a contagion that wiped out his captors (*Return of the Daleks*).

• In *World Apart*, the seventh Doctor claims to spend some "decades" alone in the TARDIS (possibly in a timeless state?) while concocting a means of rescuing Ace and Hex from the displaced planet Nirvana.

• The eighth Doctor, as mentioned, variously spends one hundred and thirteen years living on Earth (*The Burning* to *Escape Velocity*), and another six hundred years on the planet Orbis (*Orbis*). While travelling with Fitz and Anji, he's brainwashed into serving as a gun-totting soldier, a Professional, for four years before rejoining them. During the Last Great Time War, he spends some months incognito aboard the *Traken* while watching over Nyssa.

• The ninth Doctor in *9thC: The Other Side* (set shortly after *Dalek*) claims to have lived out the twenty-eight years between 1894 and 1922 on Earth, out of necessity to reunite with Rose. That's wholly incompatible with the statements the ninth and tenth Doctors give about their ages on TV, unless A) we should file this under "The Doctor Lies", assume he arrived there by some other means and just likes to make an entrance, or B) he's approximating that he's "900" in *Aliens of London* and he's actually about 872, but he genuinely, truly means "900" in *The Doctor Dances*.

• The tenth Doctor spends three (of his six total) years of life on the prison planet Volag-Noc before riding a metal bird through space to reunite with Martha (*The Infinite Quest*).

• In *The Lost Angel*, a Weeping Angel catapults the twelfth Doctor back to an unspecified year – 1994 seems a reasonable bet, as another Angel-victim wound up there – and he quietly lives out the interim back to the modern day [c.2017].

• The twelfth Doctor lives with the Collins family in London, 1972, for about a year while waiting for the TARDIS to repair itself ("The Highgate Horror" to "Doorway to Hell").

# # # # #

The Doctor sometimes experienced events that do not appear to count toward their stated age...

• The seventh Doctor was frozen in ice for 2.5 million years in *Frozen Time*. If his body experienced a total cel-

lular suspension – impossible for humans, but perhaps not for Time Lords – it's perhaps understandable that he doesn't count this toward his age.

• The tenth Doctor evidently doesn't add the ten years of life he yields to restart a TARDIS energy cell in *The Rise of the Cybermen* to the overall tally of his age, perhaps suggesting that the eleventh Doctor doesn't count the twenty-five years he donates to settle Amy's temporal credit card bill (*Borrowed Time*) either.

• A daisy chain of twelfth Doctors – each one incinerated before their successor is created – spend a total of 4.5 billion years inside a confession dial (*Heaven Sent*). The lone twelfth Doctor that survives, however, has only "lived" for about a day and a half. While he's aware of having spent such an outrageously long time in the dial, there's no reason why he would actively remember his time there.

# # # # #

From all of this, we can infer some other dates:

• The Doctor has been operating his TARDIS for five hundred and twenty-three years by *The Pirate Planet*, and was 759 in the previous story, *The Ribos Operation*. This would mean that the Doctor left Gallifrey when he was 236. Presumably going by that dating, the coffee-table book *The Doctor: His Lives and Times* (p7) has Madame Kovarian report that research into the Doctor's first "236 years" is spotty, as "it's irritatingly difficult to research a timelocked planet".

However, *The Doctor's Wife* claims that the Doctor has been travelling in the TARDIS for "seven hundred years"; as he was cited as being 909 in *The Impossible Astronaut*, this would alternatively suggest that he left Gallifrey when he was 209-ish. The eighth Doctor claims, in *Doctor Who – The Movie*, that nobody has managed to open the TARDIS' Eye of Harmony in "seven hundred years" – presumably denoting the Ship's age, or the time it's been in his custody.

In *Byzantium!* (set just prior to *The Romans*), the first Doctor recalls that "he... hurriedly abandoned his home and fled in terror into the universe" sixty years ago.

• The Doctor attended his Tech Course with Drax "four hundred fifty years" before *The Armageddon Factor*. This would mean he was 309 at the time (implying it was after he left Gallifrey, or that he left and then returned before leaving for the last time).

• Romana is equally inconsistent with her age, and the age difference between her and the Doctor can variously be calculated as 617 or 620 (*The Ribos Operation*), 625 (*City of Death, The Creature from the Pit*) or 600 (*The Leisure Hive*).

The Doctor's Father

The Doctor remembered **"I'm with my father. We're lying back in the grass... it's a warm Gallifreyan night"**.[391] The Doctor's father was taught by the ancient Gallifreyan who would be known as Patience, as his father had been. Many of his generation – such as Savar; Hedin; the Doctor's mentor, Lady Zurvana; the future President (a Chancellor at the time) and Marnal thought they could change the universe.[392]

The Doctor's father was a member of the High Council. He launched a great exploration of the universe, which became known as the Odyssey.[393] On his travels, he met an Earthwoman, the Victorian time traveller Penelope Gate. They married, and had at least one child. The Doctor's father adopted the name Ulysses.[394]

The Doctor's father had many friends and allies from alien planets. He broke protocol by inviting them to his House on Gallifrey. The Doctor's mother owned a Bible from which the Doctor read.

A computer portrait of the Doctor's parents hung on the wall of his quarters on Gallifrey. His father was "powerfully built with rugged features, a weathered face with dark eyes". His mother "a redhead, a little plump".[395]

One contemporary of the Doctor's father was Marnal, who believed that the Time Lords should intervene to eliminate potential threats to Gallifrey. He became known – dismissively – as a crusader. On one mission, to the Shoal on the edge of Mutter's Spiral, he stumbled across a race of insect creatures that he believed were a threat to Gallifrey. They weren't – until he intervened and changed history. "Marnal's Error" (meaning that he did not know his enemy) became a Time Lord proverb. Marnal had a son.[396]

Shortly after the Doctor was born, the Doctor's father was leading a team working on a mysterious Project. Other members included Penelope, Mr Saldaamir and a Time Lady from the relative future, Larna. Some Time Lords (including Marnal and Larna) knew of the Scrolls, recently-discovered prophecies that warned, in Larna's words:

"For millions of years, Gallifrey has existed in isolation. Soon – not imminently, not all at once – there will be a spate of attacks. Omega, the Sontarans, Tannis, Faction Paradox, Varnax, Catavolcus, the Timewyrm. You know some of those names, you will come to know the others. It is very important that Gallifrey survives all these attacks. All things must pass. Gallifrey will fall. But it must fall at precisely the right time. The enemy is unknown to us. It will be until Last Contact is made. If it's destroyed before that, by any of those other enemies, then the consequences... that is as much as I know."

Marnal added:

"The President and members of the Supreme Council know the prophecy. They have been told that a Time Lord now living will be central to all these events. That he will find the lost scrolls of Rassilon and lead Gallifrey from darkness."

To prevent the exposure of the Project, the Doctor's father wiped Marnal's memory and exiled him to Earth in 1883. He took Marnal's TARDIS, a Type 40, from him.[397]

The Doctor's Early Education

Jo: **"Makes it seem so pointless really, doesn't it?"**
The Doctor: **"I felt like that once when I was young. It was the blackest day of my life."**
Jo: **"Why?"**
The Doctor: **"Ah, well, that's another story. I'll tell you about it one day. The point is, that day was not only my blackest, it was also my best... when I was a little boy, we used to live in a house that was perched halfway up the top of a mountain. And behind our house, there sat under a tree an old man, a hermit, a monk. He'd lived under this tree for half his lifetime, so they said, and he'd learned the secret of life. So, when my black day came, I went and asked him to help me... He just sat there, silently, expressionless, and he listened whilst I poured out my troubles to him. I was too unhappy even for tears, I remember. And when I'd finished, he lifted a skeletal hand and he pointed. Do you know what he pointed at?... A flower. One of those little weeds. Just like a daisy, it was. Well, I looked at it for a moment and suddenly I saw it through his eyes. It was simply glowing with life, like a perfectly cut jewel. And the colours? Well, the colours were deeper**

---

391 *Doctor Who – The Movie*
392 *The Infinity Doctors*
393 *Cold Fusion*
394 *The Gallifrey Chronicles*. Penelope Gate first appeared in *The Room with No Doors*.
395 *The Infinity Doctors*
396 *The Infinity Doctors, The Taking of Planet 5, The Gallifrey Chronicles*.

397 *The Gallifrey Chronicles*. The prophecy paraphrases one from an abandoned American pilot script from the nineties. The book shows the Doctor fulfilling the prophecy – assuming the "lost scrolls of Rassilon" are the Matrix files in his mind. He had already made Last Contact in *The Daleks*, when he made contact with the race that would eventually destroy the Time Lords in the Last Great Time War, as revealled in *Dalek*.

PAST LIVES: The orthodox view accepted wholesale by most fans, for decades, is that the Doctor is a Time Lord who can regenerate their body 12 times when it is seriously injured. It was also held that William Hartnell played "the first Doctor". The 12-regeneration rule was certified in the show's 50th anniversary year, in *The Time of the Doctor*, in which the Matt Smith Doctor explains: "Twelve regenerations, Clara. I can't ever do it again... This face, this version of me.... All those graves, one of them mine." Only by virtue of the Time Lords providing the Doctor with a new life cycle does Peter Capaldi emerge as the Doctor's fourteenth incarnation.

And yet, only a half a dozen stories in the classic series refer to the orthodox view: In *The Three Doctors*, the Time Lords claim that the Hartnell Doctor is the "earliest". We learn that the Time Lords are limited to twelve regenerations in *The Deadly Assassin*, a view that is reinforced by *The Keeper of Traken*, *The Five Doctors* and *The Twin Dilemma*. (Although in *The Deadly Assassin*, *The Keeper of Traken* and *The Five Doctors*, we learn that it is possible for a Time Lord to regenerate more than twelve times, and in *The Twin Dilemma*, Azmael initiates a thirteenth regeneration, the strain of which kills him.)

It is *Mawdryn Undead* (Season 20) before the Doctor explicitly states that he has regenerated four times and has eight regenerations remaining. In *The Five Doctors*, the first Doctor sees the Davison Doctor and concludes "so there are five of me now" and refers to himself as "the original, you might say". In *Time and the Rani*, the Doctor talks of his "seventh persona". The voiceover at the start of *Doctor Who – The Movie* says that the Doctor is "nearing the end of my seventh life".

The new series displays the established Doctors in order (starting with William Hartnell and finishing with the incumbent Doctor) in *The Next Doctor*, *The Eleventh Hour*, *The Day of the Doctor* and *The Husbands of River Song*. In *The Lodger*, the earliest Doctors appear in a mental flash, and the Matt Smith version points at himself and says, "eleventh". *SJA: Death of the Doctor* upsets some orthodoxy when the Doctor says he can regenerate "five hundred and seven times" (see the "Regeneration... A Complete New Life Cycle" sidebar).

Despite all this, the commonly used terms such as "first Doctor", "second Doctor" and so on are never used on screen (and should never be capitalised).

More often, the evidence about the Doctor's past is ambiguous or inconclusive: he seems vague about his age throughout his life, the details varying wildly from story to story, likewise his name, his doctorate and the reasons why he left Gallifrey. In *The Deadly Assassin*, Runcible remarks that the Doctor has had a facelift and the Doctor replies that he has had "several so far" (the original script said more specifically said he had done so "three times"). In *The Ultimate Foe*, the Valeyard comes from somewhere between the Doctor's "twelfth and final incarnation" (not the "twelfth and thirteenth"). No unfamiliar Doctors come to light in *The Three Doctors* or

The Five Doctors, but on two occasions (*Day of the Daleks* and *Resurrection of the Daleks*), an attempt to probe the Doctor's mind is abruptly halted just as the William Hartnell incarnation appears on the monitor. In *The Creature from the Pit*, he claims Time Lords have ninety lives, and he's had a hundred and twenty.

There have been a number of hints that incarnation of the Doctor played by William Hartnell was not the first. In the script for *The Destiny of Doctor Who*, the new Doctor confides to his astonished companions that he has "renewed himself" before. In the transmitted version of the story, *The Power of the Daleks*, the line does not appear, but neither is it contradicted. In *The Brain of Morbius*, Morbius mentally regresses the Doctor back from his Tom Baker incarnation, through Jon Pertwee, Patrick Troughton and William Hartnell, but this time no-one interrupts and we go on to see a further eight incarnations of the Doctor prior to Hartnell. Morbius shouts – as the sequence of mysterious faces appears on the scanner – "How far Doctor? How long have you lived? Your puny mind is powerless against the strength of Morbius! Back! Back to your beginning!" These are certainly not Morbius' faces (as has occasionally been suggested) or the Doctor's ancestors or his family. Morbius is not deluding himself. The Doctor fails to win the fight and almost dies, only surviving because of the Elixir... it just happens that Morbius' brain casing can't withstand the pressures either.

The production team at the time (who bear a remarkable resemblance to the earlier Doctors, probably because eight of them – Christopher Barry, George Gallacio, Robert Banks Stewart, Phillip Hinchcliffe, Douglas Camfield, Graeme Harper, Robert Holmes and Chris Baker – posed for the photographs used in the sequence), definitely intended the faces to be those of earlier Doctors. Producer Philip Hinchcliffe said: "We tried to get famous actors for the faces of the Doctor. But because no-one would volunteer, we had to use backroom boys. And it is true to say that I attempted to imply that William Hartnell was not the first Doctor".

However we might want to fit this scene into the series' other continuity, or to rationalise it away, taking *The Brain of Morbius* on its own, there's no serious room for doubt that these are pre-Hartnell incarnations of the Doctor. This hasn't stopped fans doubting, of course. Two stories later, in *The Masque of Mandragora*, the Doctor and Sarah Jane discover "the old control room" that the Doctor claims to have used, although it had never been seen in the TV series before.

Cold Fusion features a sequence where the Doctor remembers his past on Gallifrey (p172-173), where he has recently regenerated to resemble the "Camfield Doctor" seen in *The Brain of Morbius*. However, there is a degree of ambiguity as to whether these are the Doctor's own memories. *Lungbarrow* states that the Hartnell Doctor was the first and hints, but never explicitly states, that the faces seen in *The Brain of Morbius* are incarnations of the Other, not the Doctor.

and richer than you could possibly imagine. Yes, that was the daisiest daisy I'd ever seen."

Jo: "And that was the secret of life? A daisy? Honestly, Doctor."

The Doctor: "Yes, I laughed too when I first heard it. So, later, I got up and I ran down that mountain and I found that the rocks weren't grey at all, but they were red, brown and purple and gold. And those pathetic little patches of sludgy snow, they were shining white. Shining white in the sunlight."[398]

The same mentor told the Doctor ghost stories about the Vampires.[399] Satthralope, a member of House Lungbarrow, sacked the hermit because he was a bad influence and too expensive.[400]

The Doctor was interested enough in Gallifreyan history to take the unusual step of learning the dead language of Old High Gallifreyan.[401] The Doctor started

reading Ancient High Gallfreyan when he was "knee-high to a gumblejack", but wasn't familiar with every dialect.[402] The Doctor admired Salyavin.[403] He was frightened by stories of the Fendahl.[404]

He always wanted to be a train driver.[405] The Doctor took up trainspotting as a hobby.[406] His first train set was a Hornby, Double-O.[407] When he was younger, the Doctor was into Jazz.[408] The Doctor flew skimmers as a boy on Gallifrey.[409]

The Doctor was a lonely little boy.[410] Three of the Doctor's favourite bedtime stories as a child were *The Three Little Sontarans*, *The Emperor Dalek's New Clothes* and *Snow White and the Seven Keys to Doomsday*.[411] The Doctor heard legends of the Pantheon of Discord when he was a little boy.[412]

The Doctor's mother told him a nursery rhyme about Zagreus, which spoke of people disappearing up paradoxical staircases.[413] When he was an impressionable age,

398 *The Time Monster*

399 *The Time Monster, Planet of the Spiders, State of Decay.*

400 *Lungbarrow*

401 *The Five Doctors*

402 *The Lost Angel*

403 *Shada*

404 *Image of the Fendahl*

405 *Black Orchid*

406 *The Nowhere Place*

407 "Planet Bollywood"

408 *Rhythm of Destruction*

409 *The Ghosts of N-Space*

410 *The Girl in the Fireplace*

411 *Night Terrors.* The latter is a take-off of the apocryphal 1970s *Doctor Who* stageplay, *Seven Keys to Doomsday*, starring Trevor Martin.

412 *SJA: The Wedding of Sarah Jane Smith*

413 *Seasons of Fear*

414 *The Gallifrey Chronicles*

415 *Serpent Crest: Aladdin Time*

416 "Weapons of Past Destruction"

417 *The Shining Man* (ch14).

418 *The Sound of Drums*

419 *The Power of Three*

420 *The Anachronauts*

421 *DC 3: The Doomsday Chronometer*

422 *The Tenth Doctor Year Two:* "Medicine Man"

423 *The Story of Martha:* "The Frozen Wastes"

424 *The Coming of the Terraphiles*

425 *The Stolen Earth, Journey's End.*

426 According to the Harold Saxon Master in *Last of the Time Lords.* In *The Doctor: His Lives and Times* (p8), Cardinal Borusa, as the Doctor's mentor, notes that the Doctor's single-handed sealing of the rift at the Medusa Cascade was "remarkable", if unauthorised.

427 *The Next Life*

428 *The Sound of Drums*

429 *Hell Bent*

430 *The Deadly Assassin*

431 *Divided Loyalties*

432 *Timewyrm: Revelation*

433 *Terror of the Autons, The Deadly Assassin, The Armageddon Factor, The Mark of the Rani.*

434 *The Time Meddler*

435 *The War Games*

436 *Arc of Infinity*

437 *Terror of the Autons*

438 *DC 3: The Crucible of Souls*

439 *DC 4: Stop the Clock*

440 *Divided Loyalties, Neverland.*

441 *The Death of Art*

442 *Time and the Rani*

443 Or so he claims, perhaps glibly, in *The Song of the Megaptera.*

444 *Night Thoughts*

445 *Mission to Magnus.* The back cover to the novelisation of this story (not included in this chronology in favour of the Big Finish audio adaptation) says that Anzor was a bully from the "class of the fourth millennium on Gallifrey".

446 *The Five Doctors*

447 *The Armageddon Factor.* In *The Doctor: His Lives and Times* (p9), "Rani- and Master-ships" are viewed as something one can attain, akin to a Doctorate.

448 *Island of Death*

449 *World Game*

450 *The Deadly Assassin*

451 *Equilibrium*

452 According to a dream the Doctor has in *The Tenth Doctor Year Three* ("Vortex Butterflies").

453 *Lungbarrow*

454 *Cat's Cradle: Time's Crucible*

455 "Gaze of the Medusa"

456 *The Twin Dilemma*

she also told him scary stories about Grandfather Paradox.[414] The Doctor read *Arabian Nights* when he was a Time Tot.[415] The Doctor infuriated the Rani by becoming the Time-Tot Hide and Seek champion for forty-two years "on the trot".[416]

When he was a Time Tot, the Doctor had difficulty believing in humans.[417]

On Gallifrey, the Toclafane were spoken of in fairy tales, much like the bogeyman on Earth.[418] The Shakri were regarded as a fable to keep the young of Gallifrey in their place.[419] A fairy tale told to Gallifreyan children claimed that a ghostly time sprite was trapped in the heart of every TARDIS.[420] Gallifreyan Fairy Tales included stories of the Solvers.[421] Gallifreyan mythology spoke of the Monaxi, a composite race of physical matter and energy.[422]

The Doctor was told as a boy that there was no point being an explorer, as the Time Lords had already discovered everything.[423]

The Doctor worked as a courier in the vast spaceport Desiree during his gap century, although he was fired because he kept getting lost.[424] **When the Doctor was "just a kid", only 90 years old, he visited the Medusa Cascade, a rift in time and space that reached into every dimension and every parallel reality.[425] At some point, he sealed the rift of the Medusa Cascade single-handed.[426]** As teenagers went, the Doctor was a handful until age 120.[427]

The Academy Years

The Untempered Schism

The children of Gallifrey were taken from their families at age eight, and brought to the Academy. Each novice was taken for Initiation, and made to stand in front of the Untempered Schism: a gap in the fabric of reality. From there, each novice would see the whole of the Vortex, and stare at the raw power of time and space. Some novices would become inspired, some would run away, and some would go mad.[428]

When the Doctor was a student at the Academy, "barely more than a child", he disappeared into the cloisters within the Matrix for four days – only to reappear in a completely different part of the city. Some believed that the Cloister Wraiths had showed the Doctor a secret way out – but also that he had gone completely mad, and was "never right in the head again". It was suspected that the Cloister Wraiths spoke to the Doctor about the Hybrid, and that something about the story made him extremely afraid – possibly motivating his departure from Gallifrey. He didn't always remember the story in the times to come.[429]

The Doctor was a member of the Prydonian Chapter, but came to forsake his birthright.[430]

The Academy was basically a self-contained city annexed to the Gallifreyan Capitol. It took up twenty-eight square miles of Gallifrey's surface.[431] Gallifrey's highest peak, Mount Cadon, extended to the fringes of the planet's atmosphere and held the Prydonian Academy far up its slopes. Acolytes there endlessly recanted protocols and procedures. In high towers, special pupils learned dark arts.[432]

The Doctor was a contemporary of the Master, Runcible, Drax and the Rani.[433] He was "fifty years before" the Monk.[434] The War Chief and the Doctor recognised each other.[435] The Doctor knew Hedin and Damon.[436] He knew the Time Lord who warned him about the Master.[437]

Padraculoma ("Padrac") was one of the Doctor's oldest friends at the Academy.[438] Padrac and the first incarnation of the Eleven, the One, were part of an elite cabal that quietly eliminated threats to Gallifrey based upon Matrix projections. In his day, the Doctor was also part of a secret cabal or two.[439]

The Doctor was at the Academy with Vansell.[440] He attended the Rani's raucous 94th birthday party.[441] **The Doctor attended University with the Rani, and his speciality was thermodynamics.[442]** He got an education at the "University of Gallifrey".[443] The Doctor said his field was "mainly" the science of macro-cosmology.[444]

Anzor, the son of a High Council member, bullied the Doctor into doing his homework at the Prydonian Academy. He also tormented him with a pain-inducing Galvanizer stick. One of the Doctor's friends, Cheevah, stood up to Anzor – who sealed Cheevah in a block of crystal, and dropped him from the Academy belltower.[445]

He attended "the Academy" with the Master.[446] The Doctor attended a Tech Course with the Class of '92, which included Drax, before he gained his Doctorate.[447] The Doctor was taught quantum mechanics at infant school. He and his friends once put a teacher in a time loop. He kept a pet flubble under his bed during his first year at the Academy, and was nearly caught when she went into heat and started a mating song.[448] He took his Gallifrey Lifesaver's Certificate.[449]

The Doctor studied at Prydon Academy (where Borusa taught him).[450] Borusa said the Doctor's ability to comprehend vast systems exceeded his ability to explain them.[451] Borusa reminded the Doctor that "curiosity is not the same as study", and thought he would be lucky to graduate beyond Stage One, with a Class Three Doctorate.[452] Lord Cardinal Lenadi led the Prydonian Chapter during the Doctor's time on Gallifrey.[453] Cardinal Borusa wrote a history called *Rassilon the God*.[454]

Concerning time travel, the Doctor's tutors at the Academy said he was more of an enthusiastic amateur than a qualified practitioner.[455] **The Doctor was taught by Azmael.[456]** The Doctor's old Academy teacher told him,

"Ignore history at your peril".[457] The Academy taught students the laws of temporal dynamics, to convey that actions had consequences. The Doctor's psychic evaluation score at the Academy was dismal.[458]

The Doctor used to build time jammers to disrupt others' experiments.[459] When the Doctor was young, he kept enough odds and ends in his pockets to build a holo-field scrambler in five minutes flat – and often did.[460] He used to build space-time portals for fun.[461]

Ruath and the Doctor staged pranks together – they introduced cats into the Gallifreyan ecosystem, altered gravity to make a Panopticon graduation take place in mid-air and electrified Borusa's perigosto stick.[462] Cats were very popular on Gallifrey, to such an extent that every President had a presidential cat... until an incident with giant mice.[463]

Cardinal Sendok taught the Doctor and the Master cosmic science.[464] The Doctor skipped his Academy class on transdimensional locus attraction dynamics to learn the yo-yo and juggling.[465]

The Doctor used to play truant so he could down pints of Best Shobogan beer at the Golden Grockle in Low Town. He seethed with anger at the High Council.[466] **The Doctor claims he was a late developer.**[467]

The Doctor's tutor at the Academy told him: "What are the time streams of ephemeral beings when weighed against universal, multiversal cataclysm? Sacrifices must be made."[468] The Doctor and Padractruloma III ("Paddy" to his friends) both played on the Academy's zero-grav hyperball team, on which the Doctor excelled at cheating. Padrac used secret tunnels in the Academy library to slip past the warders and fly skimmers over the outland dunes. The Doctor and his friends did the same, to carry out unauthorized science projects.[469] The Doctor placed fourth in the Time Lord Academy Sprint Championship. When it came to vortex manipulators, the Doctor was a "40-a-day man" in his youth.[470]

The Doctor learned about the Eternal Dogfight at the Academy, although Gallifreyan scholars remained unsure about where and when the conflict started.[471] The Doctor failed a test on the hyperspaceway code.[472] He only received an A-star for Quantum Flux Equations... and even that was on his third attempt.[473] The Doctor read about electromitosis, a means of electrical beings reproducing, at the Academy.[474]

The Doctor's room at the Academy included a poster of Marcella Retaxus, a reverse fusion engineer and singer. Nobody, including the Doctor himself, figured out exactly

457 *Demon Quest: Sepulchre*
458 *The Eighth Doctor – The Time War* Series 1
459 *The Time Monster*
460 *The Nightmare Fair*
461 *Made of Steel*
462 *Goth Opera*
463 *Nevermore.* This can only be after cats are introduced to the ecosystem. The giant mice are mentioned in *The Mark of the Rani*.
464 *The Quantum Archangel*
465 *Match of the Day*
466 *The Eight Doctors*
467 *Terror of the Autons*
468 *Big Bang Generation* (ch13).
469 DC: *The Eleven*
470 *The Eleventh Doctor Year One:* "Space in Dimension Relative and Time"
471 *The Eleventh Doctor Year One:* "The Eternal Dogfight"/"The Infinite Astronaut"
472 WD S2: *The Neverwhen*
473 *You are the Doctor and Other Stories:* "The Grand Betelgeuse Hotel"
474 *Absolute Power*
475 *Time in Office*
476 *Planet of the Rani*
477 "Ophidius"
478 *The Next Life*
479 *The Shakespeare Code*
480 "The Age of Ice"
481 *Lungbarrow*
482 *The Ribos Operation*
483 "The Lost Dimension"
484 *The King of Terror*
485 *Luna Romana*
486 *The Eleventh Doctor Year One:* "The Friendly Place". It's not specified that the "university" is the Academy on Gallifrey, but it seems likely.
487 *The Rani Elite*
488 2ndD V1: *The Mouthless Dead*
489 By *The Sontarans*, it's been "a long time" since the first Doctor has done so.
490 See The Numbering/Naming of the Master sidebar.
491 The twelfth Doctor, *Death in Heaven*
492 Combining accounts given in *The Sound of Drums* and *The End of Time*. Some have questioned how the appearance of the child Master, the Doctor's mention of Gallifreyan "families" (both in *The Sound of Drums*) and the appearance of the Doctor's cot in *A Good Man Goes to War*) can be reconciled against the notion of looming as given by the New Adventures. However, accounts of the Doctor's early life on Gallifrey always seem contradictory – by now, it's almost a tradition.
493 *Master.* This account is told as a fable, and so may not be true.
494 *The Sound of Drums*
495 *Terror of the Autons*
496 *Dark Water* et al.
497 *World Enough and Time.* As portrayed in *1stA: The Destination Wars*, the first Master is male.

how – by fiddling with time-field distortions – he put his room into permanent stasis. Professor Kasnegar never forgave the Doctor for his hijinks with the Academy's fourth-floor food dispenser. He also reprogrammed a drinks machine to produce mercury. Kasnegar noticed the Doctor's habit of "bringing strange creatures home with him", a pre-cursor to his having so many traveling companions.[475]

The Doctor illicitly created an Appleture: a gray bacteria so basic, it was close to being nothing at all, and reduced everything it encountered to the same rudimentary level. It caused enough chaos that the Doctor was nearly expelled, but the Academy hushed up the incident. Officials confiscated the Doctor's samples, but the Rani pocketed one.[476] The Doctor built time-cloaks, which granted users invisibility and intangibility, while in school.[477] In year 50 of his Academy days, the Doctor fed Valyes' summer project to some snapping wartfowl.[478]

The Deca

DIVIDED LOYALTIES -> The Doctor was part of the Deca, a group of ten brilliant students who were activists in favour of more Time Lord intervention. The Deca members were: the Doctor, Koschei (the Master), Mortimus (the Monk), Magnus (the War Chief), Drax, Ushas (the Rani), Vansell (actually a Celestial Intervention Agency spy), Rallon, Millennia and Jelpax.

They were taught by Borusa, Franilla, Sendok and Zass.

It was as part of the Deca that the Doctor learned about the Celestial Toymaker. The Doctor, Rallon and Millennia located the Toymaker and were caught up in his games. Rallon and Millennia were apparently killed, and the Doctor was expelled from the Academy on his return to Gallifrey, and ordered to spend five hundred years in Records and Traffic Control. He studied for his doctorate in his spare time.

The President at this time was Drall, the Castellan was Rannex. Type 35 TARDISes were in operation; the Doctor used a Type 18 to visit the Toymaker.

Only Jelpax completed his time at the Academy in the conventional manner, the others either went to special projects or vanished. Jelpax went on to work with Borusa.

Time Lords had to pass a test to fly a TARDIS; the Doctor failed his.[479] The Doctor wasn't much for studying at school.[480] He deliberately failed his exams so that people would underestimate him, and to avoid office duty.[481] **The Doctor eventually scraped through the Academy with 51% on the second attempt**[482] ... although he insisted that his temporal mechanics paper deserved a much higher mark.[483]

His poor results were a grave disappointment to his parents.[484] Romana claimed that the Doctor never received

any certificates. Chitter-chatter about the Doctor claimed that he wasn't "ahead of his time" at the Academy, he was "always late".[485]

The Doctor spent roughly eight years learning to envision an array of 208 different 43-dimensional supersolids, all superimposed, and eventually earned a higher dimensional physics degree.[486] The Rani believed that the Doctor's sentimentality was responsible for his graduating with only a double-gamma.[487]

The second Doctor implied that he'd lost someone in a war.[488] The Doctor fought in a war.[489]

The Master[490]

"I had a friend once. We ran together when I was little. And I thought we were the same... but when we grew up, we weren't. Now, she's trying to tear the world apart, and I can't run fast enough to hold it together." [491]

The Master looked into the Vortex while he was a child, as part of his Academy Initiation, and some believed this was the beginning of his madness. Rassilon and the High Council of Time Lords, trapped in the time-lock of the Last Great Time War, seeded the heartbeat of a Time Lord through the Vortex and into the eight-year-old Master's mind as a means of facilitating their escape. Throughout his lives, the Master was made to hear the sound of drums as a call to war.[492]

An account of the Doctor's boyhood claims that he and the Master grew up together, and played near the river Lethe. A bully, Torvic, menaced the Master, but the Doctor fought back and thereby caused Torvic's death. Death later visited the Doctor in a dream, and sought to take him as her Champion, but the Doctor told her to take the Master instead. This gave rise to the Master becoming Death's Champion, and would motivate the Doctor and the Master to leave Gallifrey.[493]

The Master chose his name, as did the Doctor.[494] The Master was universally referred to as the Master[495], save for when they were in female form, and called the Mistress ("Missy" for short).[496]

The Master was the Doctor's first friend, and his first man crush – he was "always so brilliant, from the first day at the Academy". The two of them forged a pact to see every star in the universe, but the Master got so busy destroying them, he probably didn't see very much. The Doctor came to regard the Master as his oldest friend, and the only person who seemed remotely like him. By the twelfth Doctor's fuzzy reckoning, the Master was a man at this point. The Doctor suspected he was too.[497] Missy told Clara that she had cared about the Doctor "since always": since the

Cloister Wars, since the night he stole the moon and the President's wife, and since he was a little girl. One of those statements was a lie.[498]

The Master and the Doctor used to be very good friends – you could even say they were at school together.[499] They were at the Academy together.[500] The Master's degree in cosmic science was of a higher class than the Doctor's.[501] Borusa also served as the Master's teacher. The Master used to best the Doctor in metabolic control classes, his respiratory bypass system holding out for as much as ten minutes longer.[502]

The Time Lord Dimension Ethics Committee banned all exploration of the higher dimensions. Nevertheless, fascinated by the legends of the Great Old Ones at the Academy, the Doctor and Master travelled back in time to search for Valdemar. They found nothing but warnings.[503]

The UNIT Master knew the Doctor as something of an optimist.[504] The Master looked upon the Doctor as an intellectual equal. The Master had so few worthy opponents – when they were gone, s/he always missed them.[505] The Master became the Doctor's sworn archenemy, "a fiend who glorifies in chaos and destruction". They had old scores to settle.[506] The Master was the Doctor's "oldest friend and oldest enemy".[507]

During the "olden days" on Gallifrey, the Doctor gave the Master a cameo brooch made from dark star alloy, during a development with the Master's daughter.[508] The Master once counted the Doctor as a friend – they were pioneers among their people, and fellow inventors, but much happened after that to spoil their relationship. Susan knew the Master as a friend of her grandfather, but didn't trust him. The Master recalled that Susan was prone to hysterics.[509]

The Gallifrey of the fourth Doctor's era had no record of any Time Lord using the title "the Master" – if a biodata extract on the Master ever existed, he must have destroyed it.[510] The Master believed that a

basic rule of life is that one must rule or serve.[511]

Some incarnations of the Master were formidable hypnotists – able to temporarily, albeit completely, control the human mind, although some minds were strong enough to resist their influence.[512] The Master required only two things – your submission and your obedience to their will.[513] You will obey the Master and no one else.[514]

The Doctor desperately wanted the Master to fight alongside him, not against him. Missy confessed to wishing for this too.[515] At times the Master offered to let the Doctor share in the ultimate power that s/he acquired, but the Doctor kept refusing.[516]

The Master, while trapped in approaching flames, asked the fifth Doctor to "show mercy to [his] own – arrgggh! Aggh! Aggh! Aggh!"[517] The tenth Doctor, however, refuted Martha Jones's suggestion that he and the Master were brothers.[518]

Over time, the Master would gain a reputation as one of the most notorious and corrupt Time Lords who ever lived. His crimes were without number, and his villainy without end.[519] The Master was a brilliant mathematician.[520] He believed that Blinovitch was just a myth.[521] The planet Voltron had been a cinder since the Master was a Time Tot. His actions in the Last Great Time War would inadvertently restore it to life.[522]

The numerous incarnations of the Master throughout space-time collectively acted on his mind; at times he was like an emergent system of birds, all acting as one entity. The Master had never dreamed in his life. Time Lords generally had no choice with regards the form of their different incarnations. The Master, however, had deliberately chosen all of his faces, each of which bore the imprint of his mind.[523]

The Master fled Gallifrey in much the same circumstances as the Doctor, but stole a rundown TARDIS before the Quadriggers could overhaul it. The Ship eventually fell

---

498 *The Magician's Apprentice.* Process of elimination tends to rule out the possibility that the Doctor was, in fact, a little girl.
499 *The Sea Devils*
500 *The Five Doctors*
501 *Terror of the Autons*
502 *DEyes 3: Masterplan*
503 *Tomb of Valdemar*
504 *Terror of the Autons*
505 *The Sea Devils*
506 *The Deadly Assassin*
507 *DEyes 3: The Reviled*
508 *The Witch's Familiar*
509 *1stA: The Destination Wars*
510 *The Deadly Assassin.* The High Council, by contrast, is altogether too aware of the Master's activities prior to this (see especially *Colony in Space*), and sometimes

sends the third Doctor to curtail them.
511 *Colony in Space*
512 *Terror of the Autons*, et al. For the Master, *1stA: The Destination Wars* represents the earliest known use of their hypnosis.
513 *The Daemons*
514 *Terror of the Autons*, et al.
515 *The Doctor Falls*
516 *Colony in Space, Death in Heaven.*
517 *Planet of Fire*, throwing some ambiguity into the Doctor-Master relationship.
518 *The Sound of Drums*
519 *The Five Doctors*
520 *The Deadly Assassin*
521 *The Harvest of Time* (p336).
522 *WM: The Heavenly Paradigm*
523 *The Harvest of Time* (pgs. 68, 221, 266).

THE NUMBERING/NAMING OF THE MASTER: Unlike the Doctor, where there's a strong consensus as to the sequence of their incarnations, with only a few hiccups (see the Past Lives sidebar), there are substantial gaps in the Master's known history. It's unclear how many incarnations the Master has had, and we don't see every regeneration. With different tie-in works competing to fill in lapses in the Master's history, contradictions exist that make designating the various incarnations even more challenging.

However, to aid *Ahistory* readers by specifying which Master appears in any given story, the following list represents our attempt to crack this nut – and explain the terminology we use. We're assuming for sake of argument that even if the Master *can* control the outcome of their regenerations (*The Harvest of Time*, ch23: "[another Master] had a family likeness that was clearly intentional... the Master had selected all his faces, and each bore the imprint of his mind"), there's no evidence of any duplications – that there aren't, for example, thirteen incarnations who all look like Roger Delgado.

This also excludes parallel universe and other similar alternative versions of the Master (such as the android version played by Derek Jacobi in *Scream of the Shalka*, the Magistrate from *The Infinity Doctors* and the Unbound Master from *Unbound: Sympathy for the Devil* et al), characters from the Doctor's past who may or may not be the Master (such as the Man with the Rosette in *The Adventuress of Henrietta Street*), and other renegade Time Lords who various fan theories have suggested are earlier incarnations of Master, such as the Monk and the War Chief.

The novel *The Harvest of Time* involves an alien race collecting every incarnation of the Master and imprisoning them – in a vast chamber, featuring many, many more than we've seen so far (roughly "470" of them, but that includes "potential incarnations that may never happen at all"). These are the ones we know about.

• **The first Master.** Played by James Dreyfus. First appearance: Big Finish's *1stA: The Destination Wars*.

Specified as the Master's very first incarnation. As such, Dreyfus would have to be playing an adult version of the eight-year-old seen in flashback in *The Sound of Drums* (X3.12).

• **The UNIT Master.** Played by Roger Delgado. First on-screen appearance: *Terror of the Autons* (8.1). Last on-screen appearance: *Frontier in Space* (10.3).

This is the Master who repeatedly clashes with the third Doctor, Jo Grant and Brigadier Lethbridge-Stewart's soldiers in the UNIT Era. Owing to Delgado's sudden death in a car accident in 1973, use of the character was discontinued. On screen, we're never told which incarnation of the Master Delgado represents. *The Dark Path* sets up an origin for the Master, who starts the novel in this body, but calling himself Koschei, and becomes the evil mastermind during the course of a story featuring the second Doctor. In *Terror of the Autons*, a Time Lord warns the Doctor "be careful. The Master has learnt a great deal since you last met him", and the Master notes "I have so few worth opponents. When they've gone, I always miss them", suggesting he's been busy.

It's not stated how many incarnations occur in between him and the cadaverous Master who crops up in *The Deadly Assassin* (see below). It is established that he's an almost exact contemporary of the Doctor, so – all things being equal – must be roughly the same age. The novelization of *The Deadly Assassin* states that the Master's criminal lifestyle means he has to regenerate more often that the Doctor.

As we'd only seen one incarnation of the Master before *The Deadly Assassin*, it was perfectly reasonable to assume that the cadaverous Master is the UNIT Master, ancient and decaying.

This is the line taken by *Legacy of the Daleks*, which depicts the UNIT Master receiving grievous physical injuries, so becoming the cadaverous version. There's independent reason to think Legacy of the Daleks was scrubbed from history (see the dating notes on The Second Invasion of Earth for why), but while this would necessitate a new explanation for the injuries, it presumably wouldn't change the fact that the UNIT Master is the thirteenth incarnation.

This, though, is ruled out by the comic strip "Doorway to Hell", which showed the UNIT Master fatally wounded and regenerating (but not what his next incarnation looked like).

• **The cadaverous Master.** Played by Peter Pratt (in 14.3, *The Deadly Assassin*) and Geoffrey Beevers (in 18.6, *The Keeper of Traken*, a role he's reprised for numerous Big Finish stories).

We know that the emaciated and decaying husk seen in *The Deadly Assassin* is the Master's thirteenth self, as the entire plot of that story relies upon the fact he is (as both Goth and Engin state) "dying". *The Deadly Assassin* has Spandrell explain "his body was extremely emaciated. He had come to the end of his regeneration cycle". Goth says "He was dying. No more regeneration possible".

While the end of *The Deadly Assassin* seems to show the Master regenerating (it's far clearer that's what's happening in the novelisation), the Master in *The Keeper of Traken* is explicitly the same incarnation as the one in *The Deadly Assassin*, saying "I am now nearing the end of my twelfth regeneration".

And You Will Obey Me loosely contradicts this, as it entails the cadaverous Master's body perishing, and him endowing his essence in a human named Mikey, which becomes similarly desiccated. Thus, when he steals Tremas' body in *The Keeper of Traken*, he's already in a stolen body, but his persona has stayed the same.

continued on page 2379...

apart, leading to the stranded Master's first meeting with the Doctor away from Gallifrey, on the planet Destination.[524]

Iris Wildthyme

The adventurer in time and space known as Iris Wildthyme hailed from the Obverse, a pocket reality adjacent to our own, which was accessible through a cosmic phenomenon called the Ringpull.[525] Specifically, Iris hailed from a domain within the Obverse called the Clockworks – a place of logic and reason, inhabited by beings who tinkered with time and space and were "the grease in the cogs of the multiverse".[526]

Iris' memories of her past were very suspect.[527]

She was just a kid from the slums, and rebelled by stealing her time-travelling bus.[528] Stories of Time Shaydes – a bogeymen of the Clockworks, said to scalpel people from causality with a mere touch – frightened Iris when she was little. In future, she'd repeat the tales of the Time Shaydes to her little ones.[529]

Iris as a Young Girl

The young girl who would become Iris Wildthyme was raised in Saga City, the biggest metropolis of the Clockworks. An elite class, which Iris called "the High and Mighties", ruled there. The people of the Clockworks would celebrate the occasional off-worlder who strayed into their territory – then publicly execute them upon first mention of their wanting to go home, or a desire for their people to invade. One day, the girl stole into the Woods at the heart of the Clockworks, and found there an ancient, sentient tree named Eliot. He enjoyed her company for seven days, and bestowed upon her a book of the world grown from his soft wood. The book contained charts and maps to the universe, as well as short cuts between dimensions, all of which would help to facilitate her future travels.[530] Eliot was the first "impossible" thing the girl encountered.[531]

Through unknown events, the girl was found in a crashed capsule in a desert thousands of miles from Saga City. She came to reside in the nearby Wherewithal House, and was cared for by three "aunts" – Faith, Hope and Susan, who were co-joined as a hydra-creature and lived in the attic. Save for the odd stray memory, the girl had no recollection of her life before this point. The aunts named her Lilith.[532]

WILDTHYME BEYOND! -> Lilith's only friends within Wherewithal House were a young servant girl named Mary, and Mary's younger brother, Dick.

When Lilith was 14, she and Dick found in the desert a red double-decker celestial omnibus capable of traveling through time and space, and which outwardly looked like the No. 22 bus to Putney Common. The bus seemed to be millennia old, and was dying. A future version of Panda

---

524 *1stA: The Destination Wars*

525 The first *Doctor Who* novel to feature Iris, *The Scarlet Empress*, presents her as originating from Gallifrey – something that even Iris herself seems to believe – but *The Blue Angel* makes first mention that she's from the Obverse, and the Iris stories to follow take that as given. *Iris: Wildthyme Beyond!* details some of Iris' youth in the Obverse, and seems as close as anything to a definitive account of her background as will ever be published. The Ringpull is first mentioned in *Ringpullworld*.

526 The Clockworks are first mentioned in *Iris S2: The Land of Wonder*, elaborated upon in *Iris: Wildthyme Beyond!*

527 Many of Iris' recollections are lost in a shattered memory crystal in *Iris S1: Wildthyme at Large*, and one gets the impression that she's been subjected to so many brain probes, demonic possessions and identity grafts over the course of her adventuring, her memories have to be treated with not just a pinch but an entire block of salt. Her advanced age (she can't even recall whether she's "millennia old" or not; *Iris: Wildthyme Beyond!*, p275) and the frightful amount of alcohol she consumes at any given moment doesn't help either. Famously, Iris keeps claiming the Doctor's adventures as her own, which infuriates him in *The Scarlet Empress*.

In *Verdigris*, it's said that Iris comes from one of the New Towns under the Gallifreyan Capitol, and that she found her TARDIS abandoned in the mountains as a wasted experiment. *The Scarlet Empress* claims that she grew up in a House in southern Gallifrey, that her Aunts (including Baba, her favourite) ruled it, that her mother ran away with an offworlder, and that she found an abandoned TARDIS in the wilderness and adopted it. Iris seems genuinely familiar with the Time Lords and Gallifrey, so it's possible that she spent some time there at some point (regardless of *Iris: Wildthyme Beyond!* detailing young Iris' upbringing in the Obverse). In *The Elixir of Doom*, Iris tells Jo Grant that she's not a Time Lord, and that she grew up on the "wrong side of the tracks" from the Doctor. These days, it's commonly accepted that Iris hails from the Obverse, not Gallifrey, and any contradictions therein are probably down to her unreliable memories and cavalier demeanor.

528 *Iris S2: The Land of Wonder*

529 *Iris S4: Whatever Happened to Iris Wildthyme?*

530 *Iris: Wildthyme Beyond!* (pgs. 73-74, 281).

531 *Iris: Wildthyme Beyond!* (p313).

532 *Iris: Wildthyme Beyond!* (pgs. 73-74, 345). *The Scarlet Empress* claims that one of Iris' aunts was named Baba (perhaps a nickname).

continued from page 2377...

On television, no one says this Master's appearance is the result of injuries; it seems to be just that he's extremely old, and refusing to die. In stories such as *The Brain of Morbius*, *Arc of Infinity* and *Extremis*, it's made clear that killing a Time Lord who doesn't want to die is particularly difficult and that even advanced, custom-designed execution chambers aren't a reliable method. The twelfth Doctor, in *Heaven Sent*, explains: "People always get it wrong with Time Lords. We take forever to die. Even if we're too injured to regenerate, every cell in our bodies keeps trying. Dying properly can take days. That's why we like to die among our own kind. They know not to bury us early."

The audio *The Two Masters* accounts for the Master's cadaverous appearance by portraying the Master's thirteenth self as a fit and healthy Geoffrey Beevers ... right up to the point that he's horrifyingly electrocuted (but not killed) by one of his future selves (the bald Master). This cadaverous version also appears in a number of Big Finish audios, prior to his going to the planet Traken, and...

• **The fourteenth Master, a.k.a. the Tremas Master.** Played by Anthony Ainley. First on-screen appearance: *The Keeper of Traken* (18.6). Final on-screen appearance: *Survival* (26.4).

… transfers his mind into the body of Consul Tremas, Nyssa's father. In this stolen body, he returns to vex the fourth, fifth, sixth and seventh Doctors.

This body has two hearts: in *The Mark of the Rani*, he says he's keeping an item "next to my hearts, both of them". Nyssa, as Tremas' daughter, does not – only one is detected by the scanner in *Earthshock*. As the Master is visibly younger than Tremas, the simplest explanation would seem to be that he upgrades Tremas' body as he takes it over. (There are more baroque explanations – perhaps female Trakenites only have one heart, but the males have two; perhaps the Master steals a second heart before *The Mark of the Rani*). Whatever the case, the fourteenth Master does not have the ability to regenerate, and is offered (but seemingly not granted) a new regeneration cycle for helping the Time Lords in *The Five Doctors*.

As his fate is never detailed on screen, the tie-in works contain three explanations for what became of the fourteenth Master...

• **The fifteen-A Master, a.k.a. the Tzun Master.** Features in two New Adventures books and a related short story. *First Frontier* shows the Tremas Master, soon after *Survival*, using Tzun-made nanites to regain his Time Lord status... right before Ace shoots him, triggering his regeneration into an incarnation based on actor Basil Rathbone. This same Master also appears in *Happy Endings* and *ST*: "Homecoming".

We're not told the outcome of this Master, so it's possi-ble a calamity forced him to reclaim Tremas' body once more, but then...

• **The fifteen-B Master, a.k.a. the decaying Master.** Played by Geoffrey Beevers (again). Appears in the Big Finish audios *Dust Breeding* and *Master*. The former claims that a superweapon, the Warp Core, stripped Tremas' body from the Master, once more leaving him in a decaying body (but less skeletal, it seems, than the hooded cadaverous Master).

• **"The turned-to-ashes Master".** Played by Gordon Tipple. The Daleks turn an incarnation of the Master into cremains at the start of *Doctor Who – The Movie*, but we don't see his face in the broadcast version. *The Eight Doctors* suggests it's the Tremas Master (specifying that he "last" encountered the Doctor in *Survival*). Either way...

• **The Deathworm Master.** Played by Eric Roberts. A one-off incarnation who appears in *Doctor Who - The Movie*, by virtue of transforming into a gelatinous slug creature (a Deathworm, *The Eight Doctors* claims) after the Daleks cremate him. He once again possesses a body – this time, a paramedic named Bruce. By the story's end, it is sucked into the TARDIS' Eye of Harmony.

There are (potentially) two explanations for how the Master escaped the Eye...

• **The Glorious Dead Master.** Only appears in *DWM*'s eighth Doctor comics. After escaping the TARDIS' Eye, the Master returned to life inside a dead vagabond in Brixton, 2001. He clashed with the eighth Doctor for command of the reality-altering Glory, but dematerialised when the Glory's new controller – Kroton – used it to scrub the Master's influence from the TARDIS. It's possible, although it's not said, that Kroton winds up erasing this Master from history, paving the way for...

• **The decaying Master (again).** Played by Geoffrey Beevers (again). *Mastermind* (and by extension *ST*: "Forgotten") details how the Master's essence escaped the TARDIS' Eye in 1906, found yet another human body to inhabit, but was then stuck on Earth – body-hopping as each of his hosts wore out – until reclaiming his TARDIS in 2012. We've no idea what becomes of him after that.

• **The bald Master.** Played by Alex Macqueen. Features in a number of Big Finish audios, including *UNIT: Dominion* and a number of *Dark Eyes* episodes. Big Finish refrained from specifying where this Master falls in the sequence of the Master's lives, instead just touting him as a "new one". As he faces off against the sixth, seventh and eighth incarnations of the Doctor, it might be simplest to think of him as an incarnation from shortly before the Last Great Time War.

continued on page 2381...

arrived from the future, helped Lilith coax the bus back to life, and encouraged her to seek the adventure she craved by leaving the Clockworks. Lilith and future-Panda piloted the bus through the Ringpull, leaving the Obverse behind. He also encouraged her to change her name to Iris Wildthyme.

At some point following Iris' departure, the Clockworks came under attack during the Great Schism. Some survivors – including Iris' aunts – uprooted Eliot the Tree and escaped with him out of the Obverse, through the Ringpull. They settled underneath Hyspero, where the Scarlet Empress' mind detected Eliot's presence and regarded him as a potential enemy. The Clockworkers kept him safe for several generations, but forgot their origins.[533]

Dick's sister Mary didn't come through the Ringpull, as she was convinced Iris would return, and wanted someone to be there waiting for her.[534] The third Doctor said that Iris wasn't a proper Time Lady and that the Time Lords were unsure of her identity. By then, Iris had been travelling longer than the Doctor.[535] Iris referred to the Doctor's people as "a snobby, over-privileged bunch".[536] Iris was unique in the whole of creation, and had no duplicates in parallel realities.[537] Iris was she was "not who she said she was, and more besides!"[538]

The Doctor on Gallifrey

The Doctor says he was a pioneer among his people.[539] He claimed to have built his Ship. Susan coined the acronym TARDIS.[540] The Doctor excelled himself when he built the TARDIS force field.[541] He and the Master referred to each other as "Lords".[542]

Decades prior to his leaving his homeworld, the Doctor accessed records that let him watch the universe from afar.[543] The Master said the Doctor was "A lowly bookworm who dared to dream of another life beyond the cloisters of his own world."[544] The Doctor's views were too disruptive, and upset powerful people. He'd been unable to sit back without protest. He was a "meddler" in his time.[545] **The eleventh Doctor said he'd had many faces, but "didn't admit to all of them".[546]**

533 "Many millennia" before the contemporary part of Iris: Wildthyme Beyond! (p275).

534 Iris: Wildthyme Beyond! (p348).

535 Verdigris

536 Excelis Dawns

537 Iris S2: The Panda Invasion

538 The Blue Angel

539 The Daleks

540 The Chase and The Tomb of the Cybermen suggest the Doctor "built" the TARDIS, An Unearthly Child states that Susan coined the term, although later stories seem to contradict both claims. Some commentators have tried to attribute the Doctor's statement in The Chase to mean that he only built his Ship's time-path detector, not the whole Ship, but this is a rationalisation after-the-fact and not borne out by the scene itself. Lungbarrow, at least, supports the notion that Susan created the word "TARDIS" by claiming she was around when TARDISes were relatively new.

541 Galaxy 4

542 The End of Time

543 The Alchemists

544 The Light at the End

545 The Beginning

546 The Day of the Doctor, an obvious reference to the War Doctor, but a statement that leaves open the possibility the extra faces seen in The Brain of Morbius are him.

547 Efforts, deliberate or otherwise, to probe the Doctor's mind and learn his name fail in The Shakespeare Code and The Fires of Pompeii. Clara seems to learn it in Journey to the Centre of the TARDIS, but forgets when time resets. A truth field forbids the Doctor from lying about his true name in The Time of the Doctor, so he simply refrains from saying it. On screen, the only certified person besides the Doctor to know his true name is River Song (Silence in the Library), who says it aloud – not that we can hear it – to open a tomb in The Name of the Doctor.

548 FP: Weapons Grade Snake Oil (ch38), explaining why renegade Time Lords tend to have titles such as "the Doctor", "the Master", etc., but those on Gallifrey sport names such as "Borusa" (The Deadly Assassin), "Hedin" (Arc of Infinity) and so on. Weirdly, the TV show has been silent on this dichotomy.

549 The Sound of Drums

550 The Day of the Doctor

551 World Enough and Time, and possibly true or nothing more than Missy (and writer Steven Moffat) rattling everyone's chains. Missy makes it clear that "Doctor Who" is a name the Doctor chose, which means it's not the "real name" that River Song safeguards, and which contains an almost mystical power.

552 The Wedding of River Song

553 SLEEPY (p204). Marc Platt's notes to the online version of Lungbarrow remark: "Gallifreyan names probably run on the Welsh Llanfairpwllgwyngyllgogerychwyrndrobwllllantysiliogogogoch principal."

554 Lungbarrow

555 "Mortal Beloved". It seems a stretch, given what we otherwise know of the Doctor's age and early life, to think that he spent whole centuries at the Academy. Maybe it just felt like centuries.

556 The Fires of Pompeii

557 The Armageddon Factor, The Happiness Patrol.

558 Twice Upon a Time

559 The Harvest of Time (pgs. 256-259).

The Name of the Doctor

Despite the best efforts of various parties to learn it, the Doctor's real name remained a mystery.[547]

The process of Elective Semantectomey, a combination of esoteric temporal engineering techniques, enabled Time Lords to scrub their real name from history and substitute a title or appellation. It was often, but not always, used to protect their bloodline from shame. The technique also, it was believed, enabled Time Lords to mix with lesser species and avoid conceptual contamination.[548]

The Doctor chose his name, as did the Master.[549] The Doctor chose his name as a promise to never be cruel or cowardly.[550]

Missy claimed that the Doctor's real name, which he chose to make himself sound mysterious, was "Doctor Who". He later dropped the "Who" part, she said, thinking it too on the nose.[551] The Doctor has been running from the question "doctor who?" all his life.[552]

His Gallifreyan name had thirty-eight syllables.[553] Upon the Doctor's disinheritance, Satthralope banned use of his name within the House of Lungbarrow.[554] The Doctor claimed that he didn't spend centuries at "that poxy academy" just to be called "Mister."[555]

The Doctor's real name burns in the Cascade of Medusa.[556] The Doctor's nickname at the Academy was "Theta Sigma".[557] Nobody would understand the Doctor's true name, but children heard it on occasion, if their hearts and the stars were in the right place.[558]

The *Consolidator* Affair

The Time Lords built the *Consolidator* as a country-sized ship to contain dangerous weapons (including an Axumiliary Orb), technologies (an Infinite Cocoon) and even whole races (such as the Sild) that threatened the stability of creation. Unable to agree on whether to outright annihilate the *Consolidator* or to preserve its holdings for benevolent use/rehabilitation, the Time Lords opted to push the decision off on future generations who had better considered the issue. It was proposed to send the *Consolidator* through a time rift some centuries into Gallifrey's future, but this required more ingenuity than even Time Lord science possessed.

Two promising Time Lord graduates – the Doctor and the Master, but not yet called by those names – were recruited to solve the technical challenges posed by sending the *Consolidator* through time. The Master proposed opening a time rift by collapsing a star into a black hole, but the Doctor – fearful of this approach – declined to take

continued from page 2379...

Another gap in the Master's history occurs prior to the Last Great Time War, in which – he tells the tenth Doctor in The Sound of Drums – he was "resurrected" by the Time Lords as the ultimate warrior. This implies that the "original" Master died. In the War itself, we see...

• **The pre-adolescent Master.** A recurring character in *The Eleventh Doctor Year Two*, outwardly (at a guess) somewhere between seven and nine, who helps the War Doctor in the Last Great Time War (both lose their memories of doing so). Time spillage ages this Master to become...

• **The War Master.** Played by Derek Jacobi. Only on-screen appearance: *Utopia* (X3.11), in which he regenerates into the Harold Saxon Master. Also features in Big Finish's *The War Master* audios. A degree of convenient amnesia, timeline shenanigans and fudging are needed to explain how the "Professor Yana" incarnation who was found as a child and who regenerates minutes after discovering his true nature can be the same incarnation who fought in the Time War. As it allows Derek Jacobi to reprise his role, we're happy to turn a blind eye. In *Utopia*, he regenerates into…

• **The Harold Saxon Master.** Played by John Simm. First on-screen appearance: *Utopia* (X3.11). Final on-screen appearance: *The Doctor Falls* (10.12). Infamously, this version of the Master becomes Prime Minister of the United Kingdom as "Harold Saxon". In *The Doctor Falls*, his future self, Missy, stabs him to death, and he regenerates into...

• **The Mistress, a.k.a. Missy.** Played by Michelle Gomez. First on-screen appearance: *Deep Breath* (X8.1). Final on-screen appearance: *The Doctor Falls* (X10.12). Follows on from the Harold Saxon Master, but they mutually murder one another. She apparently dies when a "full blast" from Harold's laser screwdriver cancels out (or so he claims) her ability to regenerate.

This is presented as "the perfect ending", and the Harold Saxon Master is convinced Missy will not be able to regenerate, which means there can't be any more, and Missy is definitely the final incarnation of the M—

… no, we don't believe that, either.

co-credit for the work. The Doctor's prospects fell, as the Master was awarded the highest academic merit in his field.

The attempt to jump the *Consolidator* forward proved unsuccessful, and the ship was believed atomized in the resultant event horizon. In actuality, it leapt forward even further than expected, and arrived at the end of time. The humiliated Time Lords – eager to preserve Gallifrey's reputation – covered up the *Consolidator* affair. The Master and the Doctor received no formal punishment.[559]

Before leaving Gallifrey, the Doctor was used on a diplomatic mission at least once, when he visited the inauguration of Station Chimera in the Third Zone.[560] Following a campaign by the Doctor, the Time Lords banned MiniScopes.[561]

The Doctor's reflex link connected him to the Time Lord intelligentsia.[562] Like all Time Lords, he swore an oath to protect the Law of Gallifrey.[563]

The Doctor was a member of the Supreme Council.[564] He held a powerful position before leaving Gallifrey.[565] He was a member of the High Council during the latter years of his first incarnation.[566]

A Time Lord, the Heretic, observed the universe – and concluded it was sick and corrupt beyond redemption. He left his homeworld, and assembled members of a dozen species into a cult devoted to "regenerating" the universe into a better form. The Doctor assisted in the Heretic's downfall; sketchy records indicated he was either executed or sent to Shada. The Cult endured and kept the Heretic's designs for an Anomaly Cage, which the Time Lords failed to replicate.[567]

"Flashback"[568] -> The first Doctor ("Thete") supervised Magnus' project to tap into a giant ball of Artron energy that Magnus had extracted from the Vortex. It would provide the Time Lords with more power than even Rassilon and Omega had dreamt of, and Magnus saw this as leading to "a new beginning for our stagnant race". The Doctor was more sceptical, and his fears were confirmed when they learned the energy ball was alive. Magnus wanted to continue regardless – so the Doctor destroyed his equipment with a staser. "And that was that. Any chance of a reconciliation between the two – any hope of regaining their former friendship – died at that moment." The Doctor was commended for his action.

The Minyan Incident

The Minyans used nuclear technology to destroy their planet. The Time Lords subsequently renounced intervention in the affairs of other planets.[569]

The truth was more complicated. Braxiatel and the Time Lord Narvin had become involved in Project Alpha, an undertaking to create a timonic fusion device capable of obliterating portions of space-time. As Braxiatel feared, the device was more powerful than its designers believed – when tested, it created a shockwave that ravaged Minyos. The High Council launched a cover-up, saying Minyos was destroyed in a civil war. Braxiatel felt that technology's potential for destruction had become so great that the universe's great artistic and cultural treasures needed better protection. He started sneaking away from Gallifrey and amassing a personal collection of such works.

560 *The Two Doctors*
561 *Carnival of Monsters*
562 *The Invisible Enemy*
563 *Shada*
564 *Cold Fusion, The Infinity Doctors.*
565 *Deadly Reunion*
566 *World Game*
567 *The Two Masters.* The bald Master claims the Heretic was dealt with "back in the day" – enough in the past that the Time Lord records on him are inconclusive. The seventh Doctor says he aided in stopping the Heretic "Many years ago. Or last week. One or the other. I'm not really sure." Writer John Dorney commented to us: "I imagine the Doctor's dealing with the Heretic is probably first incarnation, but I always wanted it to be vague."
568 Dating "Flashback" (*DWM Winter Special 1992*) - "Ancient Gallifrey, or so it seems." Magnus is apparently the War Chief from *The War Games*.
569 *Underworld*
570 *Gallifrey I: The Inquiry*
571 According to the Cyber Lieutenant in *Earthshock*.
FORBIDDEN TO INTERFERE: *Underworld* established that the destruction of Minyos led directly to the Time Lords' policy of non-intervention. Previous versions of *Ahistory* have assumed that this happened in the distant past, but *Gallifrey I: The Inquiry* establishes that this happens after the Doctor graduated. *Divided Loyalties*,

however, states that while the Doctor was studying, there were those who wanted Gallifrey to intervene more often; *The Gallifrey Chronicles* says that this was true a generation before.

Clearly, this is a perennial and active debate among the Time Lords, with three factions. In descending order of size and influence: most are opposed to any form of intervention; a significant number think the Time Lords should be a benign influence; a very few feel Gallifrey should impose its rule on the rest of the universe. The majority of Time Lords clearly worry that "benign" intervention will quickly become tyranny, and this is not an unfounded fear.

From the time of Rassilon through to the Doctor's time, however, there seems to be a status quo – the Time Lords fight wars against immense threats, and perhaps monitor time-travel experiments and send occasional delegations out for specific reasons, but broadly confine themselves to Gallifrey. The existence of the Celestial Intervention Agency suggests that covert operations were also conducted.

If Gallifrey's "zero tolerance" attitude to intervention is a recent crackdown, rather than dogma since the time of Rassilon, this would help explain a few of the apparent contradictions in its policies towards other races. We can see that when the Doctor was young, he travelled and was involved in interventionist efforts, like banning the MiniScopes. Clearly, Gallifrey in this

(=) The isolationist Torvald travelled back to this point from Gallifrey's future and stole the timonic fusion device as part of a scheme to discredit President Romana, causing alterations to Gallifrey's history. Narvin covered up the theft.

President Romana and Braxiatel travelled back and ensured the device was detonated as history recorded. Minyos was destroyed, and Torvald stole a fake device instead.[570]

Time Lords were "forbidden to interfere".[571]

Past Lives

Morbius would later probe the Doctor's mind, and see eight incarnations of the Doctor before the one generally accepted as the "first" Doctor.[572]

The Doctor's First Marriage

The Doctor fell in love with his former nurse and tutor, the Womb-born Gallifreyan who would become known as Patience. She taught him to dance, which he did in front of some house guests including Mr Saldaamir, a pair from Althrace and a yellow-skinned man with red fins.

They married. Savar was one of the guests at the wedding.[573] The Doctor painted his wife's portrait. As he finished, she told him she was pregnant.[574] They went on to have thirteen children.[575]

Shortly after he regenerated, the Doctor and Patience celebrated the birth of their first grandchild. Their son was a Cardinal and the Doctor sat on the Supreme Council, as his father did before him. The President ordered the Guard to search the Doctor's family home for "children born of woman". The Doctor's thirteen children were dragged out

and his daughter-in-law's baby was scheduled for termination. The Doctor's whereabouts during this incident were unknown, but there was a warrant for his arrest – he stood accused of "consorting with aliens".

The Doctor (in what we would consider his "first" incarnation) would later travel back in time to this point. He rescued his infant granddaughter and took her to the ancient past. He then got Patience to safety by taking her to an ancient TARDIS. As he did this, the Capitol was burning.[576] Mobs stormed the Panopticon that night.[577]

The Doctor's memories of this trauma were blocked, although by who or what is unclear. He believed his wife had died.[578] It is unclear if the Doctor's father was still on Gallifrey at this point. After this, the Doctor's father may have adopted the name "Joyce" and relocated to San Francisco on Earth, continuing the Project with Larna and Mr Saldaamir.[579]

The Doctor remembered that he was a father, once.[580] He was a father, but "lost all that a long time ago", and remembered "the hole the left, all the pain that filled it" – when they died, a part of him died with them.[581] The Doctor had "dad skills."[582] The Doctor's children and grandchildren went missing, and were, he assumed, dead.[583] He "had plenty of family and knew what it was like to lose them".[584]

The Infinity Doctor

? (=?) (w?) - THE INFINITY DOCTORS[585] -> The Doctor mourned for his dead wife, and even though she died a long time ago, he still lit a new candle every year in her memory. Before this time, he had travelled the universe and returned to Gallifrey. He had defeated and imprisoned Centro, a mechanical being that could warp space.

On Gallifrey, the Doctor served as a tutor who oversaw

period was relatively willing to interact with the wider universe.

The Minyan Incident seems to have been a shock to the system that resulted in a clampdown in all interventionism. As the Doctor left soon after this, and given what we know of the Doctor's attitude to intervention, it's extremely tempting to imagine that this clampdown was a factor in his departure. As the varying accounts of why the Doctor left Gallifrey show, what motivates him leaving could be anything from a principled rejection of Time Lord society to punishment for his being caught redhanded in a newly-illegal act.

572 *The Brain of Morbius.* See the Past Lives sidebar.
573 *Cold Fusion, The Infinity Doctors.*
574 *The Infinity Doctors*
575 *Cold Fusion*
576 *Cold Fusion, The Infinity Doctors.* The Doctor's new incarnation matches the description of the "Camfield

Doctor" seen in *The Brain of Morbius.*
577 *The Infinity Doctors*
578 *Cold Fusion*
579 *Unnatural History.* There's also no account of what happened to the Doctor's son and daughter-in-law, or any of the Doctor's other children.
580 *Fear Her.* Although some have seen this as a reference to the Doctor raising Miranda in *Father Time*, if he was indeed Susan's biological grandfather, then he clearly must also have been a father.
581 *The Doctor's Daughter*
582 *Listen*
583 Or so Clara claims in *Death in Heaven.*
584 "A Fairytale Life"
585 Dating *The Infinity Doctors* (PDA #17) - The story takes place an unspecified amount of time after Patience disappears, to an unspecified incarnation of the Doctor, at an unspecified point before Gallifrey's

– amongst others – the brilliant student Larna. He negotiated a final peace between the Sontarans and the Rutans, ending their eternal war. Gallifrey monitored the Effect, a reality-altering ripple. The Doctor and his friend the Magistrate went to the end of time to confront the one who was responsible: Omega. The Doctor met his wife Patience, whom Omega had rescued from death, but again lost her. Omega was defeated, but the Magistrate didn't return from this mission. The Doctor did, and had grown restless with Gallifrey.

Voran became President. Larna was charged to travel the universe and clear up after the Effect, a mission that would take two thousand years.

Susan

The Doctor's granddaughter Susan was something of an enigma.[586]

Susan was the Doctor's grand-daughter "and always will be".[587] Susan described her home planet as "quite like Earth, but at night the sky is a burned orange, and the leaves on the trees are bright silver".[588] She knew about the Dark Tower.[589] She was 15 when she met Ian and Barbara.[590] The other Time Lords never referred to Susan.[591] She coined the name "TARDIS".[592] The Doctor was amused because Susan independently came up with the name TARDIS, as others had before her.[593]

Susan was born in Gallifrey's recent past. Her grandfa-

---

destruction (possibly between *The Gallifrey Chronicles* and *Rose*). It's a thousand years since Savar lost his eyes.

IS THE INFINITY DOCTORS CANON?: *The Infinity Doctors* is a story set on Gallifrey that takes all the information from every previous story (in all media) set on Gallifrey – and other references to it – at face value and incorporates them into the narrative. The paradox being that we've seen a vast number of contradictory accounts of the Doctor's home planet, so that *The Infinity Doctors'* super-adherence to established continuity actually makes it impossible to place at a particular point in continuity without contradicting something established elsewhere.

References in *Seeing I*, *Unnatural History*, *The Taking of Planet 5*, *Father Time* and *The Gallifrey Chronicles* all make it clear that *The Infinity Doctors* (or, at the very least, events identical to it) took place in the "real" *Doctor Who* universe.

Latterly a fan consensus has built up that *The Infinity Doctors* is set on the "reconstructed" Gallifrey promised by *The Gallifrey Chronicles*, that the Infinity Doctor is the eighth Doctor, and his Gallifrey is the one destined to be destroyed in the Time War. This wasn't the author's intention, but isn't ruled out by the book.

586 IS SUSAN THE DOCTOR'S GRANDDAUGHTER?: *Cold Fusion* recounts Susan being rescued by the Doctor as an infant, which followed the description in the original "Cartmel Masterplan" document. When the events of that document were dramatised in *Lungbarrow*, Susan was an older child.

This complicates an already rather convoluted story. If both the accounts of *Cold Fusion* and *Lungbarrow* are taken at face value (and both contain degrees of ambiguity), it seems that Susan was born to the Camfield Doctor's daughter-in-law in the recent past (ie: when the Doctor was a younger man and living on Gallifrey, not millions of years ago at the time of Rassilon). The Hartnell Doctor came back to this time zone (in *Cold Fusion*, it's possible he simply regenerated, but this would seem to seriously contradict *Lungbarrow*) with

the Hand of Omega and then rescued the infant Susan and Patience. The Doctor then travelled deep into the past of Gallifrey, where Susan was left in "safety" with the Other (where she was considered the last womb-born child). Patience fled Gallifrey in an early TARDIS (possibly she was taken into the distant past, too, and stole the TARDIS there). The Hartnell Doctor would revisit ancient Gallifrey and discover that following the death of the Other, Susan had been living on the streets there.

The twelfth Doctor admits that, in his early days, he "stole the president's daughter" – possibly referring to Susan, although even if she *was* the president's daughter, she might also still be the Doctor's granddaughter.

587 *An Unearthly Child*, the quote comes from *The Dalek Invasion of Earth*. The Doctor and Susan frequently refer to each other as grandfather and grandchild.

588 *The Sensorites*

589 *The Five Doctors*

590 Barbara says Susan is 15 in *An Unearthly Child*. In *Marco Polo*, Ping Cho says she is "in my sixteenth year", and Susan says "Well, so am I." So Susan is not far older than she looks, unlike Romana.

591 On screen, Susan is never mentioned by any Time Lord, either those on Gallifrey or the various renegades.

592 *An Unearthly Child*. Later stories showed the manual for the Doctor's TARDIS which has the word on the cover, suggesting it was coined long before the Doctor's time. One possible conclusion is that Susan is from an earlier period of Gallifreyan history, and which is indeed what *Lungbarrow* established.

593 *The Beginning*, reconciling Susan's claim in *An Unearthly Child* that she coined the name "TARDIS", when it's in common use on Gallifrey later in the series (and, as an acronym, isn't so hard a thing to invent).

594 *Cold Fusion*

595 *Lungbarrow*

596 *Here There Be Monsters*. Having "a perfect memory" certainly isn't something one could convict the Doctor of, though.

ther was the Doctor. She was a naturally-born child, an abomination in the eyes of the authorities of Gallifrey. Her mother's fate was unknown. Her father was a Cardinal.[594]

Susan was born in Gallifrey's distant past. Her grandfather was the Other. She was the last naturally-born child on Gallifrey. Her mother died at the moment of her birth, as the Pythia's curse of sterility came into effect. Her father was a warrior.[595] Susan had a perfect memory, which she said was "the curse of her people".[596] Circumstances denied Susan a proper education on Gallifrey.[597]

She received both the names "Susan" and "Foreman" from other people.[598] The first Master claimed that Susan was regarded as the Doctor's accomplice, his acolyte.[599]

Susan learned of Earth during her Spatial Cartography lessons, as it was the only planet designated with a "the" in front of it. She was too young to resist leaving with her grandfather, or to even question what they'd done wrong: "It just wasn't our home any more." She had been at home, playing with a young animated chair that liked to chase her around the wall, when "tall white figures with big heads and single, unblinking black eyes" came for her. The Doctor told her that they "had to get away". She managed to escape with just a little bag of clothes and a few books...[600]

As a child, Susan was told stories of children exploring the castles of giants. The Doctor stressed to her the importance of "making a stand", but would later modify that view, as he better explored the universe and learned that the consequences of interference in alien cultures couldn't always be foreseen.[601]

The Doctor stole the moon and the President's wife.[602] The Doctor didn't steal the moon – he lost it. The Shobogans lied to say the Doctor stole the president's wife; it was actually his daughter.[603]

The Doctor Leaves Gallifrey

The exact nature of the Doctor's departure from Gallifrey is still a mystery, and there have been a number of seemingly contradictory accounts of the circumstances in which he left.[604]

Account One[605]:

Jamie: "Why did you run away from [your people] in the first place?"

The Doctor: "What? Well... I was bored... The Time Lords are an immensely civilised race. We can control our own environment, we can live forever barring accidents, and we have the secret of space/time travel."

Jamie: "Well, what's so wrong in all that?"

The Doctor: "Well, we hardly ever use our great powers! We consent simply to observe and to gather knowledge."

Zoe: "And that wasn't enough for you?"

The Doctor: "No, of course not. With a whole galaxy to explore? Millions of planets? Aeons of time, countless civilisations to meet?"

Jamie: "Well, why do they object to you doing all that?

The Doctor: "Well... It is a fact, Jamie, that I do tend to get involved with things."

Jamie: "Aye, you can say that again! Whenever there's any trouble he's in it right up to his neck."

Zoe: "But you've helped people, Doctor."

The Doctor: Yes, yes, but that's no excuse in [the Time Lords'] eyes."

Account Two: LUNGBARROW[606] -> The Doctor worked as a Scrutationary Archivist in the Prydonian Chapterhouse Bureau of Possible Events. His applications for promotion were always turned down.

Consulting the Bench of Matrocians, Quences – the

---

597 *An Earthly Child*

598 *ST:* "All Hands on Deck"

599 *1stA: The Destination Wars*

600 *The Beginning*

601 *The Sleeping Blood*

602 *The Magician's Apprentice*. "The Cloister Wars" is possibly meant to contextualize the TARDIS' doom-announcing Cloister Bell (*Logopolis* et al).

603 *Hell Bent*; see "Is Susan the Doctor's Granddaughter?"

604 As *The First Doctor Handbook* (p181) spells out, while the series was being devised and before the first scripts were in, the production team had a relatively clear idea of what the Doctor's secret was: "He has flashes of garbled memory which indicates he was involved in a galactic war and still fears pursuit by some undefined enemy... he escaped from his own galaxy in the year 5733". There's no supporting evidence for this on screen.

605 *The War Games*

606 Dating *Lungbarrow* (NA #60) - This was "eight hundred and seventy-three years ago". Given that this is set just before *Doctor Who – The Movie*, and *Vampire Science* states that the Doctor was 1009 when he regenerated, it would make him 136. However, given the contradictions over his age, it is probably best not to rely on this figure. Owis was Loomed 675 years ago.

THE DOCTOR'S COUSINS: Sixteen of the Doctor's forty-four Cousins are named in Lungbarrow: Quences, Owis, Glospin, Satthralope, Jobiska, Rynde, Arkhew, Maljamin, Farg, Celesia, Almund, Tugel, Chovor the Various, DeRoosifa, Salpash and Luton. Braxiatel is presumably another, as is Grandfather Paradox (*Christmas on a Rational Planet*).

head of the Lungbarrow household – learned that the Doctor would be a huge influence on the future of Gallifrey. He wanted the Doctor to become a Cardinal. The Doctor stormed out of his family home after an argument with Quences about the Doctor's future prospects. With the Doctor no longer regarded as a member of the family, a replacement – Owis – was Loomed to maintain the family quota. However, this was illegal and the House was ostracised from Gallifreyan affairs. The Doctor's Cousins were trapped in the House.

The Doctor left an experiment with water-sligs running. A hundred and thirty years, later they broke out.

Quences was the 422nd Kithriarch of Lungbarrow.

The Doctor decided to steal a TARDIS and leave Gallifrey. The Hand of Omega recognised the Doctor was linked to the Other. When the Doctor left Gallifrey, the Hand redirected him to Gallifrey's ancient past.

Account Three[607]: The Doctor lived sealed inside a city, on a planet hidden behind energy barricades. He finally left his people so he could experience the universe's won-

ders, to see its majesty, firsthand. He didn't leave for Susan's sake – she was an "accidental passenger, a hanger on". The Doctor looked old, but was just an adolescent as far as his people went; Susan, comparatively speaking, was just a baby. The TARDIS navigation system wasn't broken as was sometimes claimed – the Doctor had yet to forge a "mystical" bond with his TARDIS, which the legends of his people said was possible.

Account Four[608]: The president of Gallifrey, Pandak VII, issued a kill order on Braxiatel – but Braxiatel killed Lord Burner, the president's assassin, in self-defence. Braxiatel was appointed Lord Burner as punishment, and given a "burn order" for a member of his family – an old man – as a test of loyalty. The old man was tipped off by Braxiatel as to the danger, stole a TARDIS and left Gallifrey with his granddaughter. Pandak VII died the very same day, owing to a power relay overload... that an inquiry led by Braxiatel determined was an accident. Braxiatel and the old man were the only two Time Lords to ever survive a burn order.

607 *Here There Be Monsters*
608 *Gallifrey IV: Annihilation*. The inauguration of Pandak III is mentioned in *The Deadly Assassin*.
609 The twelfth Doctor, *Heaven Sent*
610 *The Beginning*. The technicians seen at the start of *The Name of the Doctor* are, presumably, Quadriggers.
611 *Luna Romana*
612 *The Beginning*, suggesting that sonic screwdrivers are native to Gallifrey, and not something the Doctor acquired in his travels. Zeus plugs were first mentioned in *The Hand of Fear*.
613 Dating *The Name of the Doctor* (X7.14) - By the eleventh Doctor's life, these events happened "a very long time ago..." The scene is a bit hard to reconcile against the TARDIS' claim in *The Doctor's Wife* that it left its door unlocked and "chose" the Doctor to steal it, unless the "Clara Oswald" seen here is actually an avatar of the TARDIS. *The Eleventh Doctor Year Three*: "Hungry Thirsty Roots" specifies the Type 53 TARDIS.
614 Dating *The Beginning* (BF CC #8.5) - It's the first Doctor and Susan's very first flight/adventure upon fleeing their homeworld. The start of this audio was amended to better match with the Doctor's brief meeting with Clara Oswald in *The Name of the Doctor*. The cover had displayed the pre-police box TARDIS as a pyramid, but this was changed to a plain cylinder with a door (*The Name of the Doctor* again). The Doctor's trunk is clearly the Hand of Omega (*Remembrance of the Daleks*).
615 *The War Games, Resurrection of the Daleks, Pyramids of Mars, The Deadly Assassin*.
616 *Death in Heaven*
617 *The Invisible Enemy, The Five Doctors*.
618 *The Sound of Drums, The Beast Below*.
619 *Smile*
620 *An Unearthly Child, The Edge of Destruction, The Massacre, The Two Doctors*.
621 *The War Games*
622 *The Tomb of the Cybermen*, suggesting that he thought he could go back by that point, or he's just being cute with her.
623 *World Game*
624 *Aliens of London*
625 *The Reign of Terror, Galaxy 4, The Massacre, The Celestial Toymaker, Colony in Space*.
626 According to Susan in *Marco Polo*.
627 The background to *The Beginning*.
628 *The Light at the End*, which doesn't entirely match events in *The Name of the Doctor*.
629 *The Dying Light*
630 *The Witch's Familiar*
631 *DC: The Eleven*
632 *The Black Hole*
633 *1stA: The Destination Wars*
634 *DEyes 4: Master of the Daleks; 1stA: The Destination Wars* entails the first Doctor learning that the first Master also left their homeworld.
635 *Timewyrm: Revelation* (p48).
636 *Frontier in Space, Logopolis*.
637 *The Big Bang*
638 *Frontier in Space, The Big Bang*.
639 *The Invasion of Time*
640 *Logopolis, Cold Fusion*.
641 *Planet of the Dead*
642 *The Song of the Megaptera*
643 *The Sins of Winter*
644 *The Time of the Doctor*
645 *The Beginning*

GALLIFREY

Account Five: HEAVEN SENT

"I didn't leave Gallifrey because I was bored! That was a lie! It's always been a lie! I was scared! I ran because I was scared!" [609]

Account Six: TWICE UPON A TIME -> The first
Doctor told an avatar of Bill Potts: "I left Gallifrey to answer a question of my own. By any analysis, evil should always win. Good is not a practical survival strategy. It requires loyalty, self-sacrifice and er, love. So, why does good prevail? What keeps the balance between good and evil in this appalling universe? Is there some kind of logic? Some mysterious force?"

When the Doctor and Susan left Gallifrey, Quadriggers served as quantum engineers that serviced TARDISes.[610] Quadrigger Stoyn remembered his Ceremony of Matriculation, in his first days at the Academy.[611] Tools at Stoyn's disposal included Zeus plugs and a sonic screwdriver.[612]

THE NAME OF THE DOCTOR[613] -> Two Gallifreyan
technicians, Andro and Fabian, were befuddled to find some "idiot" – the first Doctor, accompanied by his granddaughter Susan – attempting to steal a faulty Type 53 TARDIS from a repair bay. An iteration of Clara Oswald advised the Doctor that he had picked the wrong TARDIS to thieve, and pointed to one that had a "knackered" navigation system, as he'd have much more fun with it. He complied and left with Susan in the Ship that Clara suggested...

THE BEGINNING[614] -> ... Susan entered the first time
capsule as the Doctor indicated, and briefly heard indistinct voices outside the Ship before her grandfather pulled her out and ushered her into the next TARDIS in line. The Doctor's luggage – a bronze trunk – levitated out of the gloom and joined them. Guards wearing ceremonial scarlet started to cut their way into the Ship.

Quadrigger Stoyn was within the TARDIS' inspection webbing, and badly scarred when the Doctor set the Ship in motion. Gallifrey was visible on the TARDIS scanner as a receding brown-green snowcapped planet, followed by the streaming lights of the Time Vortex. As the TARDIS had been decommissioned, it slipped past the transduction barriers and entered the universe. The first place the TARDIS landed was Earth's moon in its ancient past...

The Doctor might have left Gallifrey of his own free will, because he was "bored" or had "grown tired of their lifestyle". He renounced the society of Time Lords. He abandoned his Prydonian birthright.[615] The Doctor's Prydonian privileges were revoked when he

stole his TARDIS and ran away.[616] But he has also stated he was "kicked out" and was "on the run".[375] The Doctor "ran away" from Gallifrey.[617] The Doctor stole the TARDIS because he felt like it. He had no idea how much the Ship cost.[618]

The Doctor was an "exile", unable to return home.[619] He "had reasons of his own" for leaving his home planet.[620] The second Doctor told Victoria that he might try to take her to his planet.[622]

He left Gallifrey because of the corruption rife in Time Lord politics.[623] The Doctor travelled to see history happen in front of him.[624] He saw himself as an explorer and researcher.[625] After discovering "the mysteries of the skies", he could return home.[626]

The Doctor's departure from Gallifrey was "an impulse to act that would have faded away if that TARDIS had not been there at that precise moment".[627] Stepping one foot over Gallifrey's transduction barriers without a Time Warrant could finish one's career. The Fetch Squad retrieved Gallifreyan rogues who did so.[628] Quadrigger Stoyn said the Doctor was "a god from a race of gods", whom he defied by thinking himself special when he left them.[629]

The Doctor told Davros that he left his homeworld because "It's a boring place, Gallifrey, I was going out of my mind", but Davros sensed that he was lying. It wasn't Missy who ran, it was the Doctor.[630] The Doctor's departure from Gallifrey was a little more urgent than his being bored.[631] The Doctor ran away because he was a criminal... depending on your perspective.[632] The Doctor was a criminal among his people, a wanted man.[633]

The Doctor and the Master went out into the universe together.[634] The following image appears early in the Doctor's memory: "Here was a cowled figure shaking a fist at a dark castle, and in the next picture he was cowering from something huge and fearful. Then he was running."[635]

The Doctor claims to have borrowed rather than stolen the TARDIS.[636] The Doctor stole the TARDIS – or he borrowed it, he always intended to return it.[637] He fully intended to return it.[638] He wasn't authorised to take it.[639] Nor did he own the Ship.[640] He stole the TARDIS.[641] The Doctor technically nicked the TARDIS, but in truth the TARDIS wanted to see the universe as much as he did.[642] The Doctor stole his Ship – although strictly speaking, they ran away together.[643]

He stole a time machine, ran away and has been flouting the principal law of his own people ever since.[644] Immediately upon leaving his homeworld, the Doctor regarded his TARDIS as "borrowed", not "stolen".[645] He stole a TARDIS, ran away, meddled in the affairs of countless people on countless worlds, and – sometimes – the consequences of his meddling had been grave indeed.[646]

(=) The conceptual bomb the Master planted in 1963 briefly created a timeline in which the Doctor's TARDIS never existed, and so the Doctor never left Gallifrey.[647]

There were "pressing reasons" why he couldn't wait for the Ship's chameleon circuit to be fixed.[648] There were many pressing reasons why he stole the TARDIS and ran away.[649] If he stopped to consider his actions, he'd never have left Gallifrey.[650]

The Doctor's TARDIS was already a museum piece when he was young. The first time the Doctor touched the TARDIS console, he said aloud that she was "the most beautiful thing he had ever known". The Doctor chose the TARDIS because her door was open – the Ship wanted to see the universe, and so "stole" a Time Lord and ran away. Only the Doctor was "mad" enough to yield to the temptation the Ship offered.

The eleventh Doctor said he and the TARDIS had been travelling together for seven hundred years.[651]

The TARDIS was a family heirloom.[652] The TARDIS had been taken from Marnal by Ulysses. Marnal's son knew the truth about the Doctor's departure, and told his father what had happened afterwards.[653] The Doctor chose not to take a Type 53 TARDIS.[654]

The authorities thought of him as arrogant.[655] In addi-tion to the TARDIS, the Doctor took the Hand of Omega, the Validium statue and his granddaughter Susan.[656]

The Doctor and Susan left home "ages" before they met Ian and Barbara.[657] Possibly more than fifty years.[658]

(=) If the Doctor had never left Gallifrey, he would have become President, but spent his time appeasing the Daleks. The Earth would have been invaded dozens of times.

Benny Summerfield witnessed the Doctor and Susan leaving Gallifrey.[659] During a timeslip, the Doctor would later re-enact the time he activated the TARDIS.[660]

= The Doctor's great-uncle, Ordinal-General Quences, died. As a child, Susan – the daughter of the Doctor's daughter – went to Quences' internment in the family vault. Although the law stipulated that the minds of dead Time Lords must go to the Matrix's Remembrance Garden, Quences' mind transferred into the Doctor's robotic servant Badger. The Doctor contemplated leaving his homeworld in a TARDIS slated for the breakers, but Quences – believing his grandnephew was the key to ultimate power via the

646 *Trial of the Valeyard*

647 *The Light at the End*

648 *Logopolis* – although it was working until *An Unearthly Child*.

649 *Twice Upon a Time*

650 *Mindwarp*

651 *The Doctor's Wife*. The Doctor was 909 in *The Impossible Astronaut*, a couple of episodes earlier, so was around 209 when he stole the TARDIS.

652 *The Infinity Doctors*

653 *The Gallifrey Chronicles*

654 *Lungbarrow*

655 *The Eight Doctors*

656 *Remembrance of the Daleks, Silver Nemesis, An Unearthly Child*.

657 *The Sensorites*

658 *The Time Meddler*. The Doctor says the Monk left their home planet fifty years after he did.

659 "Time and Time Again"

660 Seen in "Timeslip".

661 *Unbound: Auld Mortality*

662 "Centuries", Romana says, before *Luna Romana* (so, well before her own lifetime). The TARDIS maintenance levels are those seen in *The Name of the Doctor*.

663 *The Twin Dilemma, The Mark of the Rani, Planet of the Spiders* respectively.

664 *The Doctor's Wife*

665 *Spiral Scratch*

666 The Doctor says he comes from "fifty years earlier" than the Monk in *The Time Meddler*. The War Chief remembers him leaving his home planet in *The War Games*. The Master is first seen in *Terror of the Autons*.

667 We first meet Irving Braxiatel in *Theatre of War*, but he's also present at the Armageddon Convention in *The Empire of Glass*, which occurs first chronologically. The Braxiatel Collection was first mentioned in *City of Death*.

668 *Neverland*

669 *The Brain of Morbius*. *Gallifrey I: The Inquiry* establishes that the non-interference doctrine in its current hardline form is a development within the Doctor's lifetime, so the rebellion led by Morbius would seem to be against recent policy, rather than an ancient dogma.

670 Dating *Warmonger* (PDA #53) - It is never stated in *The Brain of Morbius* how long ago Morbius ruled Gallifrey. The Doctor recognises Morbius, but Morbius doesn't recognise the Doctor.

In his novelisation of the story, Terrance Dicks states that Morbius came to power after the Doctor left Gallifrey, and that the Doctor heard of Morbius on his travels. In *Warmonger*, also by Dicks, the Doctor (who has travelled into Gallifrey's past) muses that Borusa might be in his first incarnation (p166), and that this is the first time Borusa has met him, almost certainly setting it before the Doctor was born – but this is directly contradicted just a few pages later (p173), when it's made clear that it's after the Doctor stole a TARDIS and has left Gallifrey.

presidency – hypnotised him into staying. For three hundred years, the mesmerised Doctor remained in his quarters, which was his TARDIS in disguise, but attained fame as the author of *An Adventurer in Space and Time*.[661]

The position of Quadrigger became obsolete when the self-testing engine capacitor – essentially a console button that initiated a full diagnostic – was introduced with Type 54 TARDISes. Quantum mechanics were still performed under the Capitol, in the TARDIS maintenance levels.[662]

Renegade Time Lords

Many other Time Lords were known to have left Gallifrey in the Doctor's lifetime: Azmael left Gallifrey to become Master of Jaconda. The Rani was exiled following illegal experiments on animals, including an incident where genetically re-engineered mice that she had created ate the President's cat and attacked the President himself. She became ruler of Miasimia Goria. The Doctor's mentor left Gallifrey for Earth and became known as K'Anpo.[663] At some point, the Doctor knew the Corsair – a Time Lord adventurer who had a snake tattoo in every regeneration, including the couple of times that he was female.[664]

Rummas was taught by Delox and Borusa. He left Gallifrey in a stolen TARDIS to build up a collection, mainly of books. He took the Spiral Chamber – a portal to the Spiral at the nexus of the Time Vortex – and settled at the Library of Carsus.[665]

The Doctor left before the Monk, the War Chief and probably before the Master.[666]

Braxiatel spent twenty years arranging the Armageddon Convention. He would eventually dedicate himself to building the Braxiatel Collection, a repository of universal knowledge and art. Braxiatel collected every book banned by the Catholic Church. Unlike the Doctor, he freely left Gallifrey.[667]

The Morbius Crisis

The Cult of Morbius was formed in 5725.3, Rassilon Era.[668]

Morbius, the leader of the High Council, proposed that the Time Lords should end their policy of non-interference. When the High Council rejected this, he left Gallifrey and raised an army of conquest, promising them immortality. Devastating several planets on the way, the Cult of Morbius arrived on Karn, home of the Sisterhood. The Time Lords attacked them on Karn, destroying his army. Following a trial, Morbius was vaporised. Solon had removed Morbius' brain before his execution and preserved it.[669]

WARMONGER[670] -> Morbius was deposed by Saran, who became Acting President in his place. Junior Cardinal Borusa assisted Saran. Morbius was exiled from Gallifrey. Adopting the identity "General Rombusi", he raised an army of mercenaries using stolen Celestial Intervention Agency funds. These armies came from Darkeen, Fangoria, Martak and Romark. They conquered, among many other worlds, Tanith and the Ogron homeworld. Freedonia joined the General, and conquered nearby Sylvana. The General met the surgeon Solon, who pledged to build an army for him from patched-together corpses.

The fifth Doctor encountered Morbius and travelled to Gallifrey, where he convinced Acting President Saran to act. The Doctor took charge of a large Alliance – an army that included the Draconians, Sontarans, Ice Warriors, Cybermen and Ogrons – and defeated Morbius' forces.

The Order of the Weal, the Homeworld's first counter-intelligence organisation, was dedicated to the "common-weal" (i.e. common-good) and in operation at this time. It helped to expose the Imperator's abuses of power, accelerating his downfall.[671] One of Morbius' followers would acquire his presidential robes.[672]

Acting President Saran was almost certainly never elected President.[673]

Neverland places it before the UNIT Master steals the files on the Doomsday Weapon. *FP: The Book of the War* has its "the Imperator Presidency" occurring between 870 and 866 years before the War starts, so (almost certainly) after the Doctor left Gallifrey. *Timelink* prefers the idea that Morbius rose after *The Three Doctors*.

671 According to *FP: The Book of the War*, the Order of the Weal was formed during the "Imperator Presidency" – the *Faction Paradox* term for Morbius' tenure as President. Presumably the ancient Celestial Intervention Agency concerned itself with external issues, not Gallifreyan politics.

672 Fandom has tended to assume that Morbius was President of the Time Lords, although this isn't stated in his TV story. *The Vengeance of Morbius*, though, makes reference to his presidential robes of office. According to *The Doctor: His Lives and Times* (p84), President Pandak I officiated over the sentencing of Morbius, a.k.a. the First Renegade, who had been to "hundreds of worlds – from Solos to Kastria."

673 While everyone is happy to call him "Lord President" in *Warmonger*, Saran is only Acting President until elections are held (p175). The Doctor thinks of Saran as "a very minor figure in Time Lord history" (p166), so we can probably infer that he lost the election. We can also speculate that the President who is

House Paradox

The Time Lords had thrived on their status quo for ages, but the Morbius' rise and fall disrupted their culture to such a degree, some change seemed inevitable. Nonetheless, the announcement by one of their number, later known as Grandfather Paradox, of the formation of a new bloodline – that of House Paradox – seemed immeasurably tasteless, especially as the very name seemed an affront to the Time Lords' governing Protocols. House Paradox eventually gave rise to Faction Paradox.[674]

Seven years after the formation of House Paradox, its members established the Eleven-Day Empire. It would serve as a "bolt-hole and reliquary" for the followers of Grandfather Paradox for years to come.[675]

Following House Paradox becoming Faction Paradox, Godmother Antigone founded the Ministry of Insinuation. It served as arbiters of the Grandfather's will within the Faction itself.[676] The Faction's *sombras que corta* – their own shadows, turned into weapons – developed as a side-effect of the Faction's experiments with removing objects from time, while maintaining their "meaning".[677]

Greyjan the Sane dabbled with the idea of time paradoxes. His three-year reign was the shortest in Gallifreyan history, and coincided with the relative Earth dates that saw the creation of the Eleven-Day Empire.[678] Four years after the Empire's founding, the Time Lords cracked down on threats to their hierarchy and imprisoned Grandfather Paradox, supposedly in perpetuity.[679]

The leader of the Order of the Weal, Chatelaine Thessalia, foresaw the oncoming War in Heaven and became intent on learning more about the future Enemy of

---

elected at this point is the one seen in *The Three Doctors* and (after regenerating) the one assassinated in *The Deadly Assassin*. The Doctor never met the President killed in *The Deadly Assassin*, according to that story, but he had known Saran before originally leaving Gallifrey.

674 *Interference* and *FP: The Book of the War*, the latter of which clarifies that the genesis of Faction Paradox lies in the founding of House Paradox two hundred and fifty-two years beforehand. Lawrence Miles, upon reading an advance draft of *Ahistory* (First Edition) verified that while Morbius and Grandfather Paradox were close contemporaries, "... It's the long-term effects of the Morbius/Imperator crisis that lead to the rise of the Faction, rather than its direct aftermath."

675 *Interference*, *FP: The Book of the War* – see the events of 1752 in the main timeline.

676 *FP: Weapons Grade Snake Oil*

677 *FP: Weapons Grade Snake Oil* (ch5).

678 *The Ancestor Cell*. The online Faction Paradox timeline suggests that this Presidency fell between *The Deadly Assassin* and *The Invasion of Time*.

679 *FP: The Book of the War*

680 *FP: Newtons Sleep* and *FP: The Book of the War*, the latter of which says the Zo La Domini incident occurs three hundred eighty years before the War in Heaven, and twelve years after Grandfather Paradox's imprisonment.

681 Dating *Unbound: Auld Mortality* (BF Unbound #1) - The story stars Geoffrey Bayldon, a candidate for the first Doctor before the part went to William Hartnell. Bayldon also played astrologer Organon in *The Creature from the Pit*. The Doctor wishing a Merry Othermass to everyone at home emulates Hartnell toasting the audience in *The Daleks' Master Plan*.

THE UNBOUND DOCTORS: In 2003, Big Finish released a half-dozen *Unbound* audios, the *raison d'être* of which allowed venerable actors (and one actress) to portray the Doctor in "What if?"-style stories. Big Finish

resolutely conveyed that the *Unbound* audios were apocrypha, and the stories in question featured, as the Doctor, Geoffrey Bayldon (in *Unbound: Auld Mortality*), David Warner (*Unbound: Sympathy for the Devil*), David Collings (*Unbound: Full Fathom Five*) and Arabella Weir (*Unbound: Exile*, with Nicholas Briggs playing her Doctor's former incarnation). *Unbound: He Jests at Scars...* (sic) entailed the Valeyard (Michael Jayston) usurping the Doctor's existence, and, in *Unbound: Deadline*, Derek Jacobi portrayed TV-writer Martin Bannister – in a universe in which the Doctor and the TARDIS didn't exist (maybe, perhaps). Bayldon and Warner respectively reprised their roles in two more *Unbounds*, *A Storm of Angels* (2005) and *Masters of War* (2008). Overwhelmingly in fandom, the *Unbounds* were viewed as apocryphal.

All of that changed in 2016, when *The New Adventures of Bernice Summerfield* Vol. 3 entailed the David Warner Doctor crossing over into our universe and hastily taking Benny back to his own. Once that occurred, by inference that means all the *Unbound* stories take place in "actual" alternate realities "sideways in time" to the main *Doctor Who* one, and count just as much as (say) the Inferno Earth (*Inferno*), the Earth where Rome never fell ("The Iron Legion") or the reality where Arthurian stories were real (*Battlefield*). Given *Ahistory*'s goal of being as inclusive as possible, it now seems appropriate to place all of the *Unbound* audios in the timeline in alternate-universe bubbles.

682 *Unbound: A Storm of Angels*

683 SEASON 6B: The second Doctor's status in *The Two Doctors* – that he's an agent working on the behest of the Time Lords – looks like a major contradiction of the established facts, as it's made clear in *The War Games* that the Doctor has fled his home planet and is terrified of any contact with his people. Fans don't seem so worried that the Time Lords also contacted the first and second Doctors in *The Three Doctors*.

One theory that has gained currency since appear-

the Great Houses. Her interrogation of a babel – a sentient weapon engineered to protect the Homeworld against physical and language-viral attacks – that had gone rogue and wiped out House Catherion ended in a Violent Unknown Event on the planet Zo La Domini. Thessalia was reported missing, and the Order crumbled without her. In actuality, the wounded babel hid itself in the time-line of Isaac Newton, and Thessalia was flung through time to seventeenth century Earth.[680]

= **UNBOUND: AULD MORTALITY**[681] -> Susan now had her own grown-up grandchildren, a girl and a boy. Esto experienced a fungal coup, even as the price of souls fell on Mephisto Regis. The Thalek Empire claimed two more star systems, and had dominated half the galaxy. The reclusive Doctor's studies into Possibility Theory and Imagination – two dimensions the Time Lords barely explored – resulted in the creation of the Possibility Generator: a means by which he explored simulations of other worlds and times. He took an interest in confirming the route Hannibal took across the Alps.

Auld Mortality/Quences realised that he'd erred in favouring the Doctor for the presidency, and turned his attention to Susan instead. On the day Susan was to stand for the presidency, she and the Doctor realised Auld Mortality's interference in their family line and Time Lord presidents of old. Susan called out Auld Mortality, whereupon the Doctor let the faux Hannibal and his battle elephants loose in the Panopticon. A battle elephant skewered Badger, killing Auld Mortality/Quences.

The Doctor offered Susan the chance to leave Gallifrey with him, and become wanderers in the Fourth Dimension. A myriad of outcomes to this decision presented themselves, and the Doctor wished a Merry Othermass to everyone at home.

Susan remained on Gallifrey and became President of the High Council. Her grandfather left in the TARDIS, having created an independent simulation

of her with his Probability Generator. Susan spent most of her tenure covering up the Doctor's interference with history, but the High Council learned that his actions were projected to destroy Earth in 1588, and issued charges warranting the death penalty against him. Agent Zero of the Central Office of Temporal Observation was dispatched to apprehend the Doctor. When he failed to report in, Susan went to find the Doctor in 1588. The Generator copy of her returned to Gallifrey, to deceive the High Council while the original went off to meddle in history with her grandfather.[682]

Second Doctor Era

THE DARK PATH -> Two hundred years after the second Doctor last saw Koschei, they met on the Earth colony of Darkheart in the thirty-fourth century. Koschei wanted an ordered universe, but his methods had become increasingly questionable. He felt betrayed upon realising that his dear companion Ailla was a Time Lord spy, and came into conflict with the Doctor also, which kept him emotionally isolated. Koschei became obsessed with the power of the Darkheart and declared himself the Master.

The Doctor's First Trial, Increasing Intervention

The Second Doctor Regenerates After Working as the Time Lords' Agent[683]; Jamie and Zoe Sent Home

THE WAR GAMES / SPEARHEAD FROM SPACE -> In the aftermath of defeating the War Lords, the second Doctor faced a Malfeasance Tribunal. The Time Lords returned Jamie and Zoe to their home eras, and also erased their memories of all their adventures with the Doctor, save for their first meeting with him.

The Time Lords found the Doctor guilty of interfering in history, and exiled him to twentieth-century

ing in *The Discontinuity Guide* is that after *The War Games*, the Doctor wasn't regenerated straight away but was reunited with Jamie and Victoria (who is mentioned in *The Two Doctors*) and sent on missions for the Time Lords. Supporting evidence for this is that the second Doctor seems to remember *The War Games* in *The Five Doctors*. It also ties in with *TV Comic*, which had the second Doctor exiled to Earth for a time before he became his third incarnation. Two novels by Terrance Dicks (*Players* and *World Game*) explicitly have sequences that, from the Doctor's point of view, occur during Season 6B.

The Black Hole opts to split the Season 6B theory down the middle, in accordance with writer Simon Guerrier's view that the second Doctor/Jamie's involvement in *The Two Doctors* feels more at home in Season 5 (especially because Victoria is referenced), whereas the Troughton Doctor's appearance in *The Five Doctors* does in fact owe to Season 6B. To that end, *The Black Hole* sees the Doctor temporarily acquiring a Stattenheim remote control, the TARDIS' console room being upgraded to something roughly analogous to the sixth Doctor's model, and the Doctor and Jamie venturing off – thanks to the Time Lords directing the

Earth, changing his appearance. The Tribunal continued to monitor him.[684]

A Gallifreyan protocol dictated that before entering a period of exile, a Time Lord was required to regenerate.[685] At the time of the second Doctor's trial, the current model of TARDIS was the Type 97, and psychic paper had just been invented. House Dellatrovella was politically powerful and ambitious.[686]

> = In an Unbound universe, after the War Lord and his cohorts were dematerialised, the Castellan's office reported that the Doctor had escaped from Gallifrey. The Doctor – a bald man – pulled the old "suicide, then sex change" trick and threw himself off a pylon, then regenerated into a female form. By refraining from halting alien invasions, ecological disasters and energy crises, the alt-female Doctor avoided the Time Lords' detection.[687]

WORLD GAME -> The Time Lords covered up the true end of the Doctor's trial. He was secretly recruited to the Celestial Intervention Agency by its leader, Sardon, to investigate time disturbances on Earth, given a companion (Serena) and a new TARDIS. Serena was killed on that mission. On his return, the second Doctor was visibly older, with grey hair and in new clothes. It was noted that he

"took his time getting back", and he insisted on reclaiming his old TARDIS.

The second Doctor, accompanied by Jamie, was sent to space station Chimera to call a halt to the time travel experiments of Kartz and Reimer.[688]

Eventually, the Doctor's sentence was reinstated. He regenerated and was exiled to twentieth-century Earth...

Third Doctor Era

The Doctor Exiled to Earth

The Mega adhered to a code governing how much developed societies could interact with lesser ones. By outwardly if not actually respecting this law, they hoped to avoid the Time Lords moving against them.[689] The blind watchmakers – either large mole or bat-like creatures who lived in tunnels beneath their devastated world – became the finest temporal artisans and instrument-makers in history. Their Chronometric recording devices were without parallel, efficient enough to register a gnat's nervous system from half a continent away.[690]

TERROR OF THE AUTONS -> Around this time, the UNIT Master removed Time Lord files containing information about the Doomsday Weapon and the Sea

---

TARDIS without realizing that it's the Doctor's Ship – on a mission to visit Dastari. (The scenario doesn't account for why Patrick Troughton and Frazer Hines look so much older in *The Two Doctors* – but to be fair, most of the multi-Doctor stories overlook such things.) This side trip takes place between *The Black Hole* episodes two and three – the conceit being that the jaunt "prompted" the 1980s production team to commission *The Two Doctors* by way of showing what happened off-screen.

There's some leeway, however, in that upon returning from the Third Zone, the Doctor breezily claims that Dastari was "busy with [some] Sontarans" – perhaps just his way of making light of events in *The Two Doctors*, or perhaps (taking his word at face value) suggesting that he and Jamie *didn't* visit Dastari and will do so in future (per Season 6B). For anyone preferring the latter, it's notable that *The Black Hole* ends with the Doctor, Jamie and Victoria being hypnotised into forgetting everything that has occurred during the story, meaning Season 6B could unfold in an eerily similar fashion without their noticing.

684 *The War Games*. The event is recalled and dated in *The Deadly Assassin*, the Doctor's exile begins in *Spearhead from Space* (continuing until *The Three Doctors*), and we learn the Tribunal is still monitoring the Doctor in *Terror of the Autons*. A number of accounts

have taken their lead from *The Auton Invasion* (the novelisation of *Spearhead from Space*) and the first edition of *The Making of Doctor Who*, and stated that the Doctor is also punished for stealing the TARDIS. This is not established on television. The Time Lords have the opportunity to confiscate the TARDIS, but send the Doctor to Earth with it.

685 *Circular Time*: "Spring", in reference to *The War Games*.

686 *World Game*

687 *Unbound: Exile*

688 *The Two Doctors*

689 *The Mega*

690 The third Doctor has such a device in *The Harvest of Time* (p55).

691 *Terror of the Autons*. The files are referred to in *Colony in Space* and *The Sea Devils*. Presumably, although this is never stated on TV, the UNIT Master also finds out about many of his other future allies and accomplices from these files.

692 *Neverland*

693 *The Quantum Archangel*, with reference to (respectively) *The Mind of Evil, Colony in Space, The Daemons, The Sea Devils, The Time Monster, Frontier in Space/Planet of the Daleks, The Keeper of Traken, Survival, Falls the Shadow, GodEngine* and *Doctor Who – The Movie*.

694 In the television series, the Time Lords sending the

Devils. The Time Lords sent a messenger to warn the third Doctor about the Master's imminent arrival on Earth.[691]

The UNIT Master stole the plans for the Doomsday Weapon on 5892.9, Rassilon Era.[692] He also learned of the Psychic Parasites of Bellerophon; the Doomsday Weapon; Azal of the Daemons; the Earth Reptiles; the Crystal of Kronos; the Dalek army on Spiridon; the Source on Traken; the Cheetah people; the Midnight Cathedral; the GodEngine on Mars; the deathworm; the frozen gods of Volvox, the Amentethys, the Proculus and the Scerbulus; and the secrets of the planet Kirbili.[693]

COLONY IN SPACE / THE CURSE OF PELADON / THE MUTANTS -> The Time Lords sent the exiled third Doctor on various missions to other planets and times. These were always crucial points of galactic history, with implications for the entire universe. The Doctor was sent to Uxarieus to prevent the Doomsday Weapon from falling into the hands of the UNIT Master; to Peladon to ease the passage of that planet into the Galactic Federation and to prevent galactic war; and to Solos, where the Doctor delivered a message to Ky, the leader of the Solonian independence movement, that allowed him to fulfill his race's evolutionary potential.

Omega Returns; the Third Doctor's Exile Rescinded

THE THREE DOCTORS -> A black hole suddenly drained the cosmic energy of the Time Lords. Unable to power their machinery, the Time Lords called on the third Doctor for help. They brought two of his previous incarnations into the present to try and counteract

whatever was draining the power.

The second and third Doctors travelled into the black hole and arrived in a universe of anti-matter. They discovered that Omega lived, maintaining an entire world with his mental control of a singularity. Omega resented the Time Lords, feeling they had abandoned him. He couldn't leave his domain without it ceasing to exist before he departed, and needed the Doctors' help to leave. But the Doctor learnt that Omega's body had long been destroyed, and that only his will remained. It would be impossible for him to return to the universe of matter.

The Doctors tricked their way back to their TARDIS, apparently destroying Omega in a matter/anti-matter explosion. The power drain ended, and the Time Lords had a new source of energy. In gratitude, the Time Lords lifted the Doctor's exile.

For some time after this, the Time Lords would "occasionally" call upon the Doctor's services.[694]

PLANET OF THE DALEKS -> At the third Doctor's request, the Time Lords piloted the TARDIS to Spiridon, the location of a Dalek army.

The Time Lords time-locked the temporal scientist Kiadine's homeworld, after he had devolved his people into temporal slime while attempting to split the chronon. The UNIT Master's efforts to harness the resultant temporal storm resulted in his regeneration.[695]

Romana

Romanadvoratrelundar, or "Romana" for short, was born when the Doctor was between age 600 and 625.[696] She was from the House of Heartshaven.[697]

Doctor on missions is a rare occurrence after the Doctor's exile is lifted – it only happens in *Genesis of the Daleks* and (the Doctor suspects) *The Brain of Morbius*. In the other media, it's far more common, particularly the *TV Comic* strip (not included in this chronology), where it's almost taken for granted that every time the Doctor uses the TARDIS, the Time Lords are controlling it at least to some extent.

695 "Doorway to Hell". *Legacy of the Daleks* offered an alternative reason for the UNIT Master's regeneration, but see The Second Dalek Invasion of Earth for the rationale on erasing that story from history.

696 WHEN WAS ROMANA BORN?: Like the Doctor, Romana doesn't give a consistent account of her age – she's "nearly 140" in *The Ribos Operation*, "125" in *City of Death* and "150" in *The Leisure Hive*. Potentially throwing another spanner into the works, *Heart of TARDIS* has

her (between *The Stones of Blood* and *The Androids of Tara*) spending fifteen if not thirty years travelling through a nexus with the Doctor.

Nonetheless, her birth would seem to occur, in the Doctor's personal timeline, almost exactly halfway between *The Tomb of the Cybermen* and *Pyramids of Mars*. Given the continuity of companions and the Doctor's exile to Earth, the only certain gap between those two stories where the Doctor could age three hundred years would be between *The Green Death* and *The Time Warrior*, when the Doctor travels alone in his TARDIS. The UNIT personnel have no idea if the Doctor is away, as far as he is concerned, for decades or centuries at a time. If the Season 6B theory is true, there could be another significant gap there. The probability, then, is that Romana was born while the Doctor was in his third incarnation.

She was an only child, as her brother Rorvan had been consigned to the Oubliette of Eternity and erased from history.[698] **She read *Our Planet's Story* as a Time Tot.**[699] Romana used to play a children's game that involved escaping from places with a sonic screwdriver.[700] Romana's disapproving father once told her, "You know you're getting old when the High Council seemed to be getting younger."[701] In the first grade, Romana was taught that it was impossible to see one's own future.[702]

Braxiatel served as Romana's tutor. One day, Romana wanted to escape the bullying of her fellow students and wandered into the ancient vaults beneath the Capitol. She came into contact with the lingering spirit of the Imperiatrix Pandora – who had manipulated Romana's genetic heritage so her body could host Pandora's spirit. Braxiatel prevented this by having one of his future selves – who was more adept at hypnotism – erase Romana's memory of the encounter. Romana also forgot that Braxiatel had ever mentored her. Romana believed that she met Braxiatel for the first time after her return to Gallifrey, when he offered to help with her political campaign.[703]

Romana spent most of her spare time at the Academy developing mental and physical discipline, and learned the Seven Strictures of Rassilon, as well as the Foxtrots of Rassilon.[704] Romana was top of her class at the Academy in geo-sciences.[705]

Romana and Sartiakaradenoa attended Prydon Academy in the same year, were work partners and – Romana thought – good friends. In truth, Sartia privately hated Romana's accomplishments and elitism. Sartia specialised in ancient mysteries.[706]

As part of her studies, Romana studied the lifecycle of the Gallifreyan Flutterwing and eventually graduated from the Academy with a Triple First.[707] Romana was an historian and worked in the Bureau of Ancient Records.[708] She was a Prydonian.[709] When she was sixty, she went to Lake Abydos on holiday with her family.[710] **For her seventieth birthday, she was given an air-car.**[711] Romana had elementary spacecraft propulsion tutorials.[712]

Romana became a star pupil at psychic field manipulation – which was standard second-year training at the Academy, and entailed maintaining stability in one's own thoughts while projecting a psionic aura to other targets. She attended safety briefings on TARDIS engine maintenance in her second term, and studied a module in the Academy's Primitive Theology Primer. During Romana's third year at the Academy, Cardinal Verana found that positronic fields could be used in a five-dimensional array manipulation.[713]

The word "Stoyn" had become slang for an act of engineering incompetence, such as failing to close a hatch or pressing Button B instead of Button A.[714]

697 As repeatedly stated in various *Gallifrey* stories (*Lies, Panacea, Reborn* and *Annihilation*). *FP: The Book of the War*, however, implies that Romana is from the House of Dvora, hence her full name (*The Ribos Operation*) of "Romanadvoratrelundar".
698 *Neverland*
699 *Shada*
700 *Subterranea*
701 *Gallifrey IV: Reborn*
702 *The Thief Who Stole Time*
703 *Gallifrey II: Lies*. This seems intended to paint over Romana's not making the connection between her old tutor and the "Braxiatel Collection" that she mentions in *City of Death*. This doesn't fix the problem, though, as other Time Lords would know about their history together.
704 *Tomb of Valdemar*
705 *The Movellan Grave*
706 *The Skin of the Sleek/The Thief Who Stole Time*
707 *The Ribos Operation*
708 *State of Decay*
709 *The Romance of Crime, The Invasion of E-Space, The Ancestor Cell*.
710 *Neverland*
711 *The Pirate Planet*
712 *Casualties of Time*
713 *Luna Romana*
714 Or so Romana claims in *Luna Romana* – possibly truthfully, possibly just to rattle Stoyn's cage.
715 *Lungbarrow. Gallifrey VI: Ascension*, however, says a disguised Cardinal Valyes tasked the Doctor with going to Skaro.
716 The female Doctor (played by Arabella Weir) comes into being in the aftermath of her former self's trial (a deliberate parody of *The War Games*), but is "over seven hundred" years old, so closer in age to the fourth Doctor than the third. Nicholas Briggs played the previous Doctor.
717 "Gaze of the Medusa"
718 *Neverland*. This is presumably the visit in *Legacy of the Daleks*, first referenced in *The Deadly Assassin*.
719 *Interference, FP: The Book of the War*. Lawrence Miles, commenting on an advanced copy of *Ahistory* (First Edition), said the formation of Faction Paradox "should come just before *The Deadly Assassin* (or just after *Genesis of the Daleks*)... the point when Gallifrey starts being shaken up by renegades, assassinations and invasions, and mortality suddenly becomes a major issue."
720 *Alien Bodies, Interference, FP: The Book of the War*.
721 *FP: The Book of the War*
722 "Three hundred years" before "The Final Chapter", and it's tempting to see this as emerging from the same "cultural crisis" that created Faction Paradox.
723 The background to *And You Will Obey Me* and *Vampire of the Mind*. See The Numbering/Naming of

THE TIME VAMPIRE -> The Time Lords asked the third Doctor and Joshua Douglas to intervene when the Z'nai acquired a primitive time capsule. Time travellers who crossed weak points in space-time in a paradoxical fashion sometimes created "time vampires": exquisite wraiths who only wanted to observe the beauty of time through the eyes of their hosts. The Time Lords deemed the creatures as abominations who could "ride the tides of time" and, potentially, use their power to wipe out creation. The Time Lords created temporal suspension cages to restrain such creatures, although Gallifrey's official policy was that the capture of such creatures was a crime, and such cages were outlawed.

Fourth Doctor Era

GENESIS OF THE DALEKS -> The Time Lords predicted a time when the Daleks would dominate the universe, and sent the fourth Doctor, Sarah and Harry to prevent the Daleks' creation (or at least slow their development).

Lord Ferain was head of Allegiance at the Celestial Intervention Agency, and it was he who sent the Doctor to Skaro to prevent the Daleks' creation.[715]

> **= UNBOUND: EXILE**[716] **->** The alt-female Doctor's luck ran out, as the Time Lords gave her a death sentence because she fled Gallifrey. She was sealed in her TARDIS for the remainder of her lives – dematerialising would have erased her from time; it would be "as if she had never existed". She was left to decide if the two Time Lords who sentenced her had sympathised with her plight, and helped her to escape, or if throwing the dematerialisation switch would indeed end her existence.

THE BRAIN OF MORBIUS -> The Time Lords also apparently sent the TARDIS, with the fourth Doctor and Sarah Jane aboard, to Karn to prevent the resurrection of Morbius.

Ireland had far better poetry than Gallifrey, the fourth Doctor claimed.[717] Chancellor Goth visited Tersurus on 6241.11, Rassilon Era.[718]

House Paradox Becomes Faction Paradox

House Paradox re-defined itself as Faction Paradox during a time of cultural crisis on Gallifrey. The Time Lords officially outlawed and exiled House Paradox, whose representatives left Gallifrey and recruited the Faction's members from the lesser species, including humanity.[719]

The Faction set out to be deliberately confrontational.

Whereas the Time Lords abhorred time paradoxes, Faction Paradox revelled in them. The Time Lords were immortal, so much of the Faction's iconography – like their skull masks – celebrated death. The Time Lords thought themselves sterile, so the Faction used familial titles such as "Father", "Mother", "Cousin" and "Little Brothers and Sisters". The relationship between the Time Lord authorities and Faction Paradox was analogous to that of the Catholic Church and satanic cults on Earth.[720]

> "Faction Paradox doesn't do things for the sake of power, or out of any inherent sense of sadism. It seems to do them because it wants to make a point. Because the universe would be lacking if *nobody* did it. Because, quite simply, it's a carnival. And even the very word 'carnival', with its overtones of death, flesh and pointless ceremony, would on [the Homeworld] suggest something so disgusting that only the outcaste would consider it." [721]

The Elysians were a secret society on Gallifrey run by a man called Luther. They rejected the traditional houses, were sick of the non-intervention code, and styled themselves as "the Final Chapter". They planned to capture Gallifrey in a coup using unregistered clones. The first was the son of Uriel, named Xanti. Uriel, Xanti's father, volunteered for incarceration in a mental asylum: the Quantum of Solace.[722]

The Thirteenth Master is Gravely Wounded (by Himself), Becomes Cadaverous

THE TWO MASTERS[723] **->** Having forged a pact that compelled him to murder one of his younger selves, the bald Master travelled back along his own timeline and massacred the Time Lords stationed at Terserus Base. The thirteenth Master, void of regenerations, landed on Terserus to raid the Time Lord vaults there, and fell into his future self's trap. The bald Master heavily burned his thirteenth self with a Malson Electrofield, but refrained from killing him – both to fulfill upon history, and trick the Cult of the Heretic into believing he'd fulfilled their deal. The bald Master signalled Gallifrey, prompting Chancellor Goth to investigate...

... but was overcome by the Cult before Goth arrived. The Cultists tricked the Masters into swapping minds, which created a massive paradox and also muddled their memories. The cadaverous Master, in the bald Master's body, was set free so the paradox of his existence could destabilise space-time wherever he went. The bald Master, in the cadaverous Master's body, escaped, prompting the Cult to send assassins after him.

The President Assassinated, Rediscovery of the Eye of Harmony

THE DEADLY ASSASSIN ->

"Through the millennia, the Time Lords of Gallifrey led a life of peace and ordered calm, protected against all threats from lesser civilisations by their great power. But this was to change. Suddenly and terribly, the Time Lords faced the most dangerous crisis in their long history..."

The fourth Doctor received a telepathic message, warning him that the President was going to be assassinated. He returned to his home planet, only to find himself implicated in the assassination. The President had been due to resign anyway after centuries in office, and the murder appeared motiveless.

The Doctor's old enemy, the Master, had lured him back to frame him for the murder. The now-cadaverous Master had exhausted his regenerations, and had been found by Chancellor Goth on the planet Tersurus. Goth had been favoured to succeed the outgoing President, but he had discovered that another was to be nominated instead. In return for Goth's help, the Master killed the incumbent President.

The Master wanted full access to various items such as the Sash of Rassilon, as he needed to find a way to prolong his life. He discovered that he might regenerate again if he had a powerful enough source of energy – the Master selected the Eye of Harmony. He believed the Sash would protect him if he unleashed the Eye's power. The Doctor prevented the Master from destroying Gallifrey, but the Master escaped.

The Master kept Goth's TARDIS, and would use it to evade Time Lord security protocols.[724] The cadaverous Master's condition worsened, and so he loosely followed the Doctor's time-trail away from Gallifrey – only to arrive in the Victorian Era, some years after the Doctor had defeated Weng-Chiang.[725] In his personal timeline, the fourth Doctor would next encounter the cadaverous Master in Derbyshire, 1979.[726]

Around this time, the Doctor began to learn more about the Time Lords' ancient past.

"It was a chance encounter with the *Book of the Old Time* that had first nudged the Doctor's own thoughts back towards his world's archae-barbaric past. A suspicion had been born in his mind that before regeneration there had been reincarnation. Some memories might be more than racial inheritance. Nothing lasts that does not change." [727]

Borusa regenerated at some point between this and the Doctor's next visit to Gallifrey.[728]

IMAGE OF THE FENDAHL / UNDERWORLD -> Soon after learning of his planet's past, the fourth Doctor began to encounter survivors from his race's ancient history: the Fendahl and the Minyans.

The Time Lords sent the fourth Doctor and Leela to Dowcra Base, circa 2520, to prevent General Strang from

the Master sidebar for the confusion about the Master's thirteenth incarnation.

724 *J&L* S11: *Masterpiece*, playing off *The Deadly Assassin*.

725 *UNIT: Dominion*. It's possible that Goth's TARDIS is the one disguised as a grandfather clock in *The Deadly Assassin* and *The Keeper of Traken*.

726 *The Oseidon Adventure*, in which the Master specifies that he last met the Doctor during *The Deadly Assassin*.

727 *Cat's Cradle: Time's Crucible* (p210-211).

728 A different actor plays Borusa in each of his televised appearances (Angus MacKay in *The Deadly Assassin*, John Arnatt in *The Invasion of Time*, Leonard Sachs in *Arc of Infinity* and Philip Latham in *The Five Doctors*).

729 *The King of Sontar, White Ghosts*.

730 *The Name of the Doctor*

731 *The Ancestor Cell*

732 *Alien Bodies*

733 *Timewyrm: Genesys*

734 *Tomb of Valdemar*

735 We learn of Leela and Andred's marriage in *Arc of Infinity*.

736 In *The Ribos Operation*, the Doctor wishes that he'd thrown the President to the Sontarans, suggesting that Borusa has become President (although the treacherous Kelner apparently survived *The Invasion of Time* and he'd have a strong constitutional case, as the Doctor named him Vice-President). The Doctor was meant to have lost his memory of the Sontaran invasion at the end of *The Invasion of Time*, but clearly didn't, or was given some sort of account of it before he left Gallifrey. By *Arc of Infinity*, Borusa is President.

737 *Time in Office*, and a continuity patch to explain why the Capitol in *Arc of Infinity/ The Five Doctors* looks smaller compared to the one in *The Invasion of Time*.

738 Established at the start of each of the four *K9* books published in 1980. In *K9 and the Zeta Rescue*, we learn that K9 reports to a Space Controller on Gallifrey and that the Doctor came up with the name for his spacecraft, K-NEL. We can also infer the order in which the books take place: K9 is flying K-NEL Mark 1 in *K9 and the Beasts of Vega*, it's destroyed in *K9 and the Time Trap*,

waging war on creation, and also to the edge of the known universe, to halt the creation of a new race of vampires.[729]

THE ABANDONED -> Leela's attempts to comprehend fables – including the old woman in the shoe – provided enough of an imagination catalyst for the TARDIS' original pilot, Marianna, to awaken from her imprisonment in the heart of the Ship. Marianna's efforts to acquire power via the Point of Stillness, and revenge herself on Gallifrey for her abandonment, came to naught and she was returned to her dormancy within the TARDIS.

Leela and K9 Mark 1 Begin Living on Gallifrey; K9 Mark 2 Activated

THE INVASION OF TIME -> The fourth Doctor was contacted by the Vardans, a race capable of travelling down energy waves, including thought. The Vardans had infiltrated the Matrix, and now wanted to commence a physical invasion of Gallifrey. The Doctor pretended to collaborate with the Vardans and claimed the Presidency of Gallifrey. He then returned the Vardan invasion force to their home planet and time-looped it. The Sontarans had been manipulating the Vardans all along, and attempted to invade Gallifrey themselves. This incursion was also repelled. Leela and K9 elected to stay behind on Gallifrey. The Doctor unpacked a box with K9 Mark 2 inside.

(=) The Great Intelligence spied on the fourth Doctor during the Sontaran invasion of Gallifrey. A version of Clara Oswald overwrote the Intelligence, and saw the Doctor.[730]

The Doctor was the 407th President.[731] During his short tenure, his biodata was altered by contact with the Sash of Rassilon.[732] While in the Matrix, the Doctor became aware of the Timewyrm. He sent his future self a warning about it.[733] Romana was not directly affected by the Sontaran invasion.[734]

Leela and Andred, a member of the Chancellery Guard, married soon afterwards, but the Doctor was unable to attend the ceremony.[735] **Borusa became President and regenerated once again.**[736] The Dominators' Quarks stormed the Gallifreyan Capitol, and although Leela and K9 destroyed thirty-nine of the robots, a bomb attached to one of them obliterated the facility. The High Council put up a temporary Capitol while forging a new one.[737]

K9 Mark 1 was sent on independent missions in situations classed as too dangerous for Time Lord intervention.[738]

K9 AND THE TIME TRAP[739] **->** K9 met with the Rigellian Fleet Commander to discuss the disappearance of the Rigellian Seventh Fleet. Between galaxies, K9's spaceship – the K-NEL – was sucked into a time trap, and K9 discovered ten thousand alien ships that had also been caught there, including the Rigellians. Omegon, a figure from early Time Lord history who was exiled here, was amassing the ships to form a warfleet and launch an attack on Gallifrey. K9 sacrificed K-NEL, using it to ram and destroy Omegon and his ship. As a reward, the Rigellians gave K9 K-NEL Mark 2 – the same ship, but with racing stripes.

K9 AND THE ZETA RESCUE[740] **->** K9 had now saved the Time Lords "many times". He tested the Mark 2 K-NEL, and was sent to investigate massive explosions in the Zeta Four Sector – if Zeta Canri went nova, the whole galaxy would be blown apart. At the heart of the devastation, K9 discovered a prison ship of the Megellan Empire, the sworn enemies of the Time Lords. He rescued Dea, an

---

he goes on a test flight in the Mark 2 at the start of *K9 and the Zeta Rescue*, he's using it in *K9 and the Missing Planet*.

It's also interesting to note that after many years of sending the Doctor on missions for them, the Time Lords stop doing so (the last time is apparently *The Brain of Morbius* on television, "Light Fantastic" – from *Doctor Who Annual 1980* – in other media). We might infer K9 is now doing this work for them.

739 Dating *K9 and the Time Trap* (*The Adventures of K9* #1) - This takes place in the Gallifreyan timeframe. K9 is referred to as being "hired" by the Time Lords, but this may be a figure of speech rather than indication he is paid.

RIGEL: The delegate from the Rigel Sector is a member of the Order of the Black Sun in "Black Sun Rising", and the Rigellians are mentioned as once being ene-

mies of the Time Lords in *The Infinity Doctors*, but they are allies in *K9: The Time Trap* (in both "Black Sun Rising" and *The Time Trap*, they are depicted as humanoid). They would seem to be one of the "Higher Powers". These Rigellians would seem to exist in a different era to humanity – perhaps the same early universe as the Time Lords. Earth has a depot on Rigel by "Conflict of Interests" (?2192). Rigellians had four tentacles, three mouths and a reputation for being untrustworthy according to Abslom Daak (c2550). Rigel VII is part of the Earth Empire by 2620. The Battle of the Rigel Wastes took place in 2697. Slavery is abolished on Rigellon by the time of the Federation (3985). The Shadow Proclamation shut down a maximum security prison on Rigel 77 according to *TW: The Undertaker's Gift*.

740 Dating *K9 and the Zeta Rescue* (*The Adventures of K9* #3) - It's soon after *K9 and the Time Trap*.

ambassador from Telios. Nuclear war had wiped out the Telians and Megallans, and K9 and Dea watched the two leaders kill each other in a final duel. The few survivors were given medical treatment.

The Key to Time

The White Guardian picked the first Romana to aid the fourth Doctor and recover the six segments of the Key to Time.[741] Rumours circulated as to why Romana suddenly left the Academy, including that she had won the public register lottery, been expunged for overshadowing her tutor, and been sent on a mission for the CIA.[742]

The first Romana's torture by the Shadow broke the conditioning that had made her forget the Imperiatrix Pandora. Fearing that Pandora would manifest through the Imperiatrix Imprimature within her, Romana forced her own regeneration. Her memories of Pandora were again scrambled, and her genetic link to Pandora went dormant.[743]

Luther designed the reconstruction of the Capitol over the hulk of the old, including the Watchtower, over the old Panopticon.[744] The development of fungal brains eluded Gallifrey, as such networks were notoriously unstable.[745]

A schism in College of Cardinals led to a rival President setting himself up on Drornid. The Time Lords ignored them, and they eventually returned home.[746] Drornid was also known as Dronid.[747]

THE TROUBLE WITH DRAX[748] -> Drax's twelfth incarnation gave his third self a Blinovitch Limitation Effect limiter, enabling them and the intervening eight Draxes to coordinate con jobs. To fulfill upon causality, the third, fifth, ninth and twelfth Draxes conned the fourth Doctor and the second Romana into returning the limiter to the lost city of Altrazar a second after it was stolen – but only after the third Drax had used it for some centuries.

The Doctor and Romana confronted the quartet of Draxes at a bar, The Rutan's Tendril, and turned them over to Inspector Fleur McCormick of Galactic Enforcement... failing to realize that McCormick was Drax's eighth self, and her six officers were also Draxes. The ten Draxes escaped in McCormick's police car, which was Drax's TARDIS.

SHADA -> The fourth Doctor and the second Romana prevented Skraga of Drornid from using the powers of the Time Lord mind criminal Salyavin to impose himself as the "universal mind".

THE SKIN OF THE SLEEK / THE THIEF WHO STOLE TIME[749] -> The Time Lady Sartia discovered that the planet Funderell's core was a mass of parallel timelines, and sought to gain godlike abilities through its control device: the Orb of Funderell. The fourth Doctor and the second Romana happened upon Sartia... who revealed that she had always hated Romana, her "oldest friend" from the Academy, and tried to kill her. A local, Bluejaw Skaldson,

741 *The Ribos Operation*
742 *The Skin of the Sleek/The Thief Who Stole Time*
743 *Gallifrey II: Lies.* This directly conflicts with the notion in *The Chaos Pool* that Romana's regeneration occurred because she became a segment of the Key to Time. Much of *Gallifrey Series 2 and 3* is predicated on the notion of Romana having a genetic link to Pandora, so it seems fair to give this account precedence. As Romana's memories of Pandora are suppressed, it's entirely possible that she falsely believes for a while that she regenerated due to the Key's influence – even if she does, for a time, become a Key segment.
744 "Centuries" before "The Final Chapter". It's unclear when this takes place. It's before "The Tides of Time", because we see the Watchtower in that story. Perhaps there was more extensive destruction during the Vardan/Sontaran assault in *The Invasion of Time* than we saw on TV. References to the "old Panopticon" might mean there's a new one – we haven't seen the Panopticon on television since *The Invasion of Time*.
745 *The Pyralis Effect*
746 *Shada*. It's unclear when this happened. *FP: The Book of the War* states it was three hundred and ninety-two years before the War starts, and four hundred and seventy-four years after Morbius' execution.

747 *Alien Bodies. The Terrestrial Index* and *The Discontinuity Guide* both mistakenly refer to Drornid as Dronid.
748 *The Trouble with Drax*. The Drax that featured in *The Armageddon Factor*, we here learn, was his second incarnation. Barry Jackson was slated to reprise the role on audio, but passed away beforehand.
749 It's unclear when this two-parter takes place in universal time, although Funderell lies "about twenty days out from Earth" (by means of what technology, we're never told) in "southeast galactic delta". The participants include a team of broadcasters from Mars.
750 *Meglos, Full Circle*.
751 *Prisoners of Fate*. The Type 50 is only on Valderon for twenty years before the fifth Doctor and company turn up, so it presumably escapes Gallifrey during the same Doctor's era, or possibly toward the end of his fourth incarnation.
752 "The Stockbridge Horror"
753 "The Final Chapter"
754 *The Name of the Doctor*
755 *Hexagora*

sacrificed himself to reset Funderell to the Time Lords' factory settings, curtailing Sartia's scheme. She escaped using her Time Ring.

Romana Defies the Time Lords' Order to Return Home, Stays in E-Space

With the quest for the Key to Time long-completed, the Time Lords recalled Romana. Before she could return, the TARDIS fell through a CVE into E-Space.[750]

STATE OF DECAY -> The fourth Doctor, the second Romana, Adric and K9 destroyed the Great Vampire, who had survived the war with the Time Lords and fled to E-Space.

WARRIORS' GATE -> Romana opted to stay in E-Space and help free the Tharils from slavery.

Fifth Doctor Era

The Doctor's original Type 50 TARDIS, having become increasingly anguished in the long centuries since the Doctor left, performed the unprecedented feat of leaving Gallifrey under its own accord. It succeeded in tearing through Gallifrey's transduction barriers and quantum force fields, but had to jettison 9/10ths of its interior architecture. It would come to ground, heavily wounded, on the planet Valderon circa 3536.[751]

"The Tides of Time" -> The fifth Doctor continued at times to be addressed as "the President" of the Time Lords. He said of Gallifrey, "When my wanderings are over, I will make my home here."

The Time Lords installed a defence system on board the TARDIS without telling the Doctor. In an emergency, it would automatically summon Shayde to the ship.[752]

"The Stockbridge Horror" -> The fifth Doctor arrived on Gallifrey seconds after Tubal Cain's missiles froze time in the Capitol. Within the time warp, the Doctor repaired the TARDIS. When the effect wore off, the Doctor was arrested and brought before a secret court for his interference with the timeline. Shayde disposed of evidence pertaining to the case, resulting in the Doctor's release.

Tubal Cain was demoted to run the Quantum of Solace.[753]

THE SECRET HISTORY -> The Time Lords intervened when the Monk tricked the Doctor into unravelling his own history, and temporarily erased the Doctor from time.

CIRCULAR TIME: "Spring" -> Cardinal Zero was a Prydonian, and a member of the Council of the Great Mother – a group focused upon the politics of regeneration. He was in the running for a High Council seat when he abandoned life on Gallifrey, instead living in a rainforest on an alien world. The Time Lords dispatched the fifth Doctor and Nyssa to talk Zero into returning home, lest his actions damage the time-stream.

The Doctor and Nyssa found Zero living among a race of avian-people; Temporal Projectionists on Gallifrey had foretold that this species would progress from steam to orbital space flight in less than three generations. The avians themselves foretold of a prophet who would "lead them back to the sky", and Zero arranged his death using a local poison. He theatrically fell into a lake – which was actually his TARDIS – and regenerated inside it into a half-Time Lord, half-avian being. Events compelled the Doctor and Nyssa to leave, and Zero – hailed as the prophet of the avians – set about boosting their development and refining their judicial system along more civilised lines.

ARC OF INFINITY -> Borusa was now president of Gallifrey. Omega had survived, and convinced a member of the High Council, Hedin, that he had been wronged by Gallifrey. With access to a biodata extract, Omega would be able to bond with a Time Lord, re-entering our universe. Hedin chose the fifth Doctor as Omega's target – when the High Council discovered this, they recalled the Doctor's TARDIS to Gallifrey (only the third time this had been done in the planet's history) and lifted the ban on the death penalty. Killing the Doctor, they believed, would break the renegade's link with our universe. The Doctor survived vaporisation by entering the Matrix, where he discovered Omega's plan. He tracked Omega to Amsterdam, where the renegade's new body proved unstable and disintegrated.

Clara Oswald witnessed the fifth Doctor floating in the Matrix during the second Omega crisis.[754] Time Lords could potentially live for millennia.[755]

"Blood Invocation" -> The fifth Doctor, Tegan and Nyssa responded to an emergency signal from Cardinal Hemal. A Time Lord had been found, drained of blood, and the Doctor realised there were vampires abroad. The Doctor discovered acolytes of the Cult of Rassilon the Vampire and had them rounded up. Meanwhile, Tegan was bitten by a vampire Time Lord who had gained access to the TARDIS. The vampire took the Ship to Earth... but disintegrated because he landed in the daytime.

GALLIFREY

Borusa Put Away by Rassilon; the Doctor Named President, Flees

THE FIVE DOCTORS[756] **/ THE FIVE COMPANIONS ->** Borusa regenerated once more. He had become dissatisfied with ruling Gallifrey. Now he wanted "perpetual regeneration": a secret discovered by Rassilon that allowed true immortality, not simply the vast lifespans granted to other Time Lords. Borusa discovered the ancient Timescoop machinery and restarted the Game of Rassilon, pitting the first, second, third and fifth Doctors and their friends – Susan, the Brigadier, Sarah Jane, Tegan and Turlough – against a selection of old enemies in the Death Zone on Gallifrey.

The fifth Doctor escaped a group of Cybermen by transmatting to the Capitol, but en route was diverted into a pocket dimension containing an alternate Death Zone environment: a collection of fused spacecraft and space stations. More of the Doctor's friends – Ian Chesterton, Steven Taylor, the incarnated "house" version of Sara Kingdom, Polly Wright and Nyssa – had been transported into the holding dimension, and aided him against foes that included Daleks, dinosaurs and members of the Sontaran Sixth Column. Time Lord technicians sent the Doctor's friends home, and the Doctor continued on to the Capitol...

Rassilon gave Borusa the immortality he sought, transforming him into a living statue. He also sent the first, second and third Doctors – and their associates – back to their native times. Chancellor Flavia declared the fifth Doctor as President, but he left Gallifrey with Tegan and Turlough before he could take up office, and appointed Flavia to rule in his stead.

The Doctor was the 409th President.[757] **Type 57 TARDISes were in operation at this time.**[758] Leela decapitated the Raston Warrior Robot in the Death Zone, and mounted its head in her kitchen.[759]

Flavia didn't chase the Doctor because she wanted the Presidency for herself. Her reign was one of prosperity.[760] The Time Lords abandoned the practice of transporting off-worlders into the Death Zone, but occasionally plucked menaces from Gallifrey's own past.[761]

The Fifth Doctor as President of Gallifrey

TIME IN OFFICE -> Fluid sculptures progressively depicted all the regenerations of esteemed Time Lords. Notable Time Lords included Rassilon, Omega, Apeiron, Pandak, Pandak IV, Eurenoyar and Pandak XI.

Borusa's success at having managed so many emergencies necessitated a face-saving cover-up of his crimes. Chancellor Flavia told the public that Borusa had formally picked the Doctor as his successor, but that the Doctor was indisposed with other matters. Blame for the bungled succession fell on her shoulders, and she retired. Over-Chancellor Tavoli became Acting President, served for twice as long as anyone else in the role, and netted approval ratings lower than any of the previous seventeen Presidents.

To incur political stability, Chancellor Vorena and her caucus of Time Lords snared the fifth Doctor's TARDIS – en route back to Frontios – with a vortex manipulator, and convinced him to take up the Presidency. Castellan Lowri granted Tegan with Ambassadorial status, allowing her to stay on Gallifrey. At his inaugural address, the Doctor called for accrediting Gallifreyan institutions beyond the Academy with the right to bestow the title of Time Lord, to encourage more competition. He also shut down the High Council's nefarious Policy Adjustment Bureau, whose members went back in time to help Presidents avert mistakes. Leela assisted the Doctor while Andred and K9 dealt with stray horrors scuttling around the Death Zone.

A remembrance ceremony between the Time Lords and their nominal rivals, the Arimeci, went awry when the Doctor and Leela were identified as having killed an Arimeci in seventeenth-century Japan. With Vorena's help, Tegan retroactively undercut the Arimeci's faith-based power, ruining them.

Chancellor Vorena and her supporters took the Doctor's past calls for intervention to hearts, and secretly designed the new Capitol as the largest TARDIS ever built, with the ability to turn into a humanoid robot. Vorena offered the Capitol-TARDIS to the Doctor so he could more directly thwart evil-doers, but he rejected the notion of supreme power, and sent the Capitol-TARDIS into a permanent time-loop. Vorena refused to evacuate the Ship, so was forever trapped. The Doctor advised Lowri to claim he stole the Capitol in an abuse of power, and ran away. He bestowed upon her the various accoutrements of Rassilon,

---

756 See the Regeneration, A Complete New Life Cycle sidebar.
757 *The Ancestor Cell*
758 In *Warriors of the Deep*, the Doctor says he should have changed his TARDIS for a Type 57 "when he had the chance". This could imply that Type 57 is the most

advanced model at present, or simply that newer models exist but the Doctor prefers Type 57.
759 *Time in Office*
760 *The Eight Doctors*
761 *Engines of War* (ch19).

2400

"REGENERATION... A COMPLETE NEW LIFE CYCLE":

In *The Five Doctors*, the High Council offers the Master the carrot that – should he enter the Death Zone and help the Doctor as they wish – he will be rewarded with both a full pardon and "regeneration, a complete new life cycle". This became a perennial source of confusion, as it looked like a change from the twelve-regeneration limit as first established in *The Deadly Assassin*. And yet, both on screen and in the tie-in media, nearly every classic *Doctor Who* story ignored the development and continued to regard the 12-regeneration rule as sacrosanct.

Even within *The Five Doctors* itself, the deal looks a bit suspect. The story entails Borusa wanting to be President of Gallifrey for eternity by obtaining the immortality promised by Rassilon, but we know that Borusa can remain President even if he regenerates (he's done so at least once while in office; compare with *Arc of Infinity*), so the issue isn't that he's desperate to hold onto his current body. In *The Five Doctors*, Borusa seeks what Rassilon has: "Timeless perpetual bodily regeneration. True immortality! Rassilon lives, Doctor. He cannot die. He is immortal." This is not, it seems, an infinite number of regenerations; it's more akin to the newly-regenerated Doctor's state in *The Christmas Invasion* – he loses a hand in a swordfight, but grows it back, saying "I'm still within the first fifteen hours of my regeneration cycle, which means I've got just enough residual cellular energy to do this." Rassilon would seem to be in that state perpetually.

In *The Five Doctors*, the High Council clearly can't grant the gift of "perpetual regeneration", but they can grant the Master a new life cycle – twelve more regenerations. Not immortality, but a doubling of his natural lifespan. And yet, if Gallifrey has, somehow, developed the ability to do that, why would it be an option for one of the Time Lords' most infamous and evil renegades, but not their own Lord President? One theory, fronted by Neil Gaiman, hold that the limitation on regenerations is as much a legal limit as a naturally occurring one. The idea would seem to be that Time Lords are born with 12 regenerations "in the bank" (as it were), because they evolved that way due to exposure to the Untempered Schism (*A Good Man Goes to War*).

Following Gaiman's reasoning (and that of his associate Steve Manfred), we might imagine that the High Council in *The Five Doctors* has a safe, controlled and humane way of granting more lives that is normally illegal. Why it's verboten isn't clear – possibly, Rassilon laid down such a rule because (as *The Five Doctors* makes abundantly clear) immortality is "a curse, not a blessing". Alternatively, *Head Games* (p173) builds upon the idea in the New Adventures (*Timewyrm: Revelation* especially) that traces of previous personas remain in a Time Lord's mind after each regeneration, and has the Doctor state that the number of regenerations was limited because "too often the mind can't handle the multiplicity of psyches". (The mental schism that occurs between the seventh Doctor and his previous self – see *Love and War* and *Head Games* – supports this.) In the Big Finish audios, the Eleven suffers from roughly the same disorder. The Valeyard claims in *The Trial of the Valeyard* that Rassilon created the 12-regeneration rule to keep the Time Lords under his thumb, but as reliable experts go, he's inherently untrustworthy.

Alternatively, perhaps going over the thirteen-life limit represents a vast expenditure of energy, even by the Time Lords' standards. In his quest for immortality, the Master needs to harness a black hole (*The Deadly Assassin*, *Doctor Who – The Movie*) or the Source, which powers the whole of the Union of Traken (*The Keeper of Traken*). When the Doctor gets a new regeneration cycle in *The Time of the Doctor*, there's enough spare to destroy a planetary invasion force of Daleks. Possibly, the Time Lords can grant new regenerative cycles, but lack the resources to bestow this on everyone.

In *Gallifrey: Reborn* (set long after *The Five Doctors*), Romana comments that Gallifrey has the ability to "implant a new regeneration cycle, but not extract, divide or redistribute an existing one". Curiously, this overlooks the Master's claim that the High Council has promised the Valeyard the sixth Doctor's remaining lives if he helps them cover up the Ravolox affair (*The Ultimate Foe*). Also, the Master nearly succeeds in "redistributing" the Doctor's regenerations to himself in *Doctor Who – The Movie*, using nothing more than the Eye of Harmony in the Doctor's TARDIS, and the plan of Mawdryn's group in *Mawdryn Undead* is predicated on the idea the Doctor can sacrifice his remaining regenerations but survive in his current form.

The Time of the Doctor seems to somewhat settle the issue, with the Matt Smith Doctor detailing for Clara how he's used up his thirteen allocated lives, and the Time Lords then sending him the energy for a new regeneration cycle. With regeneration energy being finite (River Song burns up her remaining regenerations healing the Doctor in *Let's Kill Hitler*, and slaps him for using a bit of his reserves to mend her wrist in *The Angels Take Manhattan*), it doesn't appear likely that the Doctor now has an endless supply of lives (even the twelfth Doctor seems confused on this point, in *Kill the Moon*). More likely, the Time Lords' largess probably means that enough energy for lives fourteen through twenty-five were placed "in the Doctor's bank", and that s/he will require some new accommodation at the end of that road. Clouding the issue somewhat, Rassilon is moved to ask "How many regenerations did we grant you?" while confronting the twelfth Doctor (*Hell Bent*). Also, we don't know how many lives (if any) the twelfth Doctor burnt up while turbo-charging a Dalek sewer with regeneration energy (so the revived Dalek hordes can overwhelm Davros) in *The Witch's Familiar*.

... all of which suggests that when the eleventh Doctor tells Clyde in *SJA: Death of the Doctor* that he can regenerate "507 times", it's nothing more than him poking fun with Clyde, a teenager.

and appointed her Over-Chancellor, making her Acting President.

The Time Lords were now highly skilled with Block Transfer Computation, able to erect whole buildings overnight. The Academy had a Trans-Dimensional Architecture Department. All military-grade TARDISes, colloquially called "WarDISes", had been decommissioned, but some – armed with plasma cannons – remained in use for ceremonial services. Mints didn't exist on Gallifrey, nor did toothpaste as Earthers would recognise it. Senior Time Lords could access the Black Files, accessible only through an office in the core of an asteroid in a pocket dimension (the only remnant of a redundant timeline).

The Time Lords tasked the fifth Doctor with investigating time warps on Earth.[762] The fifth Doctor knew about the Shadow Proclamation, and that the Judoon had a contract with them.[763]

RESURRECTION OF THE DALEKS -> The Daleks planned to assassinate the High Council of the Time Lords using duplicates of the fifth Doctor and his companions, but the Doctor prevented this.

Type 70 TARDISes were better suited than Type 40s to apply brute force and penetrate distortion grids that prevented space-time travel.[763]

THE AXIS OF INSANITY -> The Axis was an interdimensional nexus akin to a giant tree, whose branches linked to alternate realities that were usually the result of time experiments gone wrong – especially those conducted by the Time Lords. The Axis prevented such errant realities from interfering with the primary timeline.

The scientist Jarra To conducted experiments with a Timescoop that brought dragons – the Firebreed – from the past of her homeworld of Pangorum to the present. Jarra To killed the Time Lord Protok when he attempted to intervene, and although the Time Lords closed off Jarra To's timeline, she escaped from it into the Axis – where she gained fantastical abilities and adopted multiple guises. As the nihilistic Jester, she killed the Overseer – a multi-faceted being from the dimension of Guardas, whose consciousness stabilised the Axis. This threatened to bring down the barriers separating timelines within the Axis, an act that would have spread madness through the whole of creation. Tog, a native of Pangorum, sacrificed himself to kill Jarra To. The fifth Doctor, Peri and Erimem, relegated

762 "4-Dimensional Vistas"

763 "The Forgotten"

764 *Singularity*

765 Later in the story, the Doctor suspects that the Time Lords *are* aware of events and have been manipulating him, but this is never confirmed.

766 *Recorded Time and Other Stories*: "Recorded Time"

767 *The Mysterious Planet*. The Valeyard's "evidence", as displayed throughout *The Trial of a Time Lord*, derives from this feature, although it's unclear if the Doctor's TARDIS was secretly fitted with surveillance gear at some point (his visit to Gallifrey in *Arc of Infinity*, for instance), or if the Ship was incorporated into the system by remote.

768 *The Eight Doctors*

769 THE VALEYARD: It is unclear exactly what the Valeyard is. The Tremas Master, who knows a great deal about him, says, "there is some evil in all of us, Doctor, even you. The Valeyard is an amalgamation of the darker sides of your nature, somewhere between your twelfth and final incarnation, and I must say you do not improve with age".

This is rather vague, and it seems that the Valeyard might be a potential future for the Doctor (like those presented to him in *The War Games* or arguably those of Romana in *Destiny of the Daleks*), a projection (like Cho-je in *Planet of the Spiders* or the Watcher in *Logopolis*) or an actual fully-fledged future incarnation (as he was in the original script). The Master seems to have met the Valeyard before, and sees him as a rival (he also says "as I've always know him, the Doctor" –

suggesting that the Valeyard would normally refer to himself as "the Doctor" not "the Valeyard").

That the Doctor has a "dark side" that can manifest, either physically or within his mind, was established in *The Three Doctors*; both the Valeyard and the Dream Lord (*Amy's Choice*), arguably, are a further culmination of this. Some commentators have leaned toward viewing the Dream Lord (the result of psychic pollen manifesting a dark part of the Doctor's psyche) as a sort of precursor (in the Doctor's lifetime) to the Valeyard, but no overt link has ever been drawn between the two.

Whatever the Valeyard is, he doesn't have any qualms about killing his past self – perhaps if the sixth Doctor died, the Valeyard would apparently gain his remaining regenerations by default. His survival at the trial's end, when we had seen him disseminated (and the Doctor has promised to mend his ways) perhaps suggests that he is something more than just a mere Time Lord.

Note also that the Master says "twelfth and final", not "twelfth and thirteenth" – now that the Doctor has survived beyond their original regeneration cycle (*The Time of the Doctor*), and Jodie Whittaker is portraying the Doctor's fourteenth incarnation, we can probably rule out the Valeyard being a genuine "12.2 Doctor" of sorts. That's not to say that he couldn't crop up down the road – if, indeed, he's not simply an alternate-reality Doctor, the bizarre events of the Trial itself allowing the Valeyard to infringe upon our timeline.

For a time, the novels and audios tended to steer clear of the Valeyard – indeed, the Writers' Guide for the New Adventures stated, "anything featuring the

Protok's TARDIS to a pocket dimension that held hundreds of inert TARDISes whose operators were deceased. The Doctor also went to the Grand Prosideum on Guardas to request installation of a new Overseer.

"Urban Myths" -> The fifth Doctor cured an outbreak of the Tule-Oz virus on the planet Poiti, but three CIA agents (Commander Edge, Commander Harom and Kettoo) became infected with a benign strain of the germ. The Tule-Oz virus made the agents believe that the Doctor and Peri had devastated Poiti, but the Doctor provided an antidote for the agents and their superior, Inquisitor Auron. At this time, top-secret correspondence was automatically routed via the nearest Type 40 TARDIS to incidents away from Gallifrey.

Sixth Doctor Era

ATTACK OF THE CYBERMEN -> The Cybermen invaded the sixth Doctor's TARDIS and cut short a signal he sent to the Time Lords asking for help.[765]

MISSION TO MAGNUS -> The Seven Sisterhoods of Magnus petitioned the Time Lords for permission to incorporate time travel into their conflict with the neighbouring planet of Salvak. Anzor, as an envoy of the High Council, was sent to Magnus in a Type 60 TARDIS. He denied the Sisterhoods' request on the grounds that, "It is forbidden to alter history. My job is to prevent time tampering, except in the most exceptional circumstances." The Doctor revenged himself on his school tormentor by sending Anzor and his TARDIS back to the Mesozoic Era.

The Phylesians made immortal temporal phoenix birds fly in time loops, creating quills capable of rewriting time. The Time Lords were thought to have destroyed all such devices, but at least one survived.[766]

New surveillance methods were developed, increasing the range of information that the Matrix could harvest. The Matrix could now record events that occurred within a certain vicinity of a TARDIS.[767]

"The World Shapers" -> The Time Lords sent an agent in a new TARDIS to investigate time disturbances on Marinus. That Time Lord died, but the sixth Doctor, Frobisher and Peri arrived and took on the assignment. At its conclusion, a delegation of senior Time Lords met up with the sixth Doctor and offered false assurances that they would nip the creation of the Cybermen in the bud.

The Celestial Intervention Agency worried that the Ravolox Affair would be exposed. They spread rumours that Flavia wasn't legitimately President, and she ordered an election to settle the matter. The Agency fixed the election, installing their supporter, Niroc.[768]

The Doctor's Second Trial

The Valeyard[769] Unmasked as a Future Doctor, the High Council Deposed

THE TRIAL OF A TIME LORD / THE ULTIMATE FOE -> The sixth Doctor discovered that the planet Ravolox was in fact the Earth in the far future, but he didn't know what had moved the planet two light years or, more importantly, why. Despite this, the High Council became worried that the Doctor knew too much, and they brought him to a vast space station. The Doctor at first learned that he was to undergo an impartial enquiry into his activities. He also learnt that as he had neglected his duties, he had been deposed from the Presidency.

Valeyard is out – he's a continuity nightmare, and a rather dull villain". Despite this, a number of the novels (particularly *Time of Your Life*, *Head Games* and *Millennial Rites*) developed the idea first aired in *Love and War* that the Doctor sacrificed his sixth incarnation ("the colourful jester") to create a stronger, more ruthless seventh persona ("Time's Champion") who was better equipped to change his destiny. Ironically, books such as *Love and War* and *Head Games* suggest that this internal conflict might well have been the catalyst that brought the Valeyard into being.

The Big Finish audio *Trial of the Valeyard* entailed the Valeyard airing some of his background details, but he's so inherently untrustworthy, it's hard to vest any faith in it. The PDA *Mission: Impractical* also featured the Valeyard, as did the Unbound audio *He Jests at Scars*.

Two tie-in works do their best to provide a "final" story for the Valeyard... he's the recurring villain in *The Sixth Doctor: The Last Adventure* box set, and seemingly perishes in the Matrix at the end. A stubborn refusal to die, however, is surely part of the Valeyard's CV (as with the Master) and the shock would be if he genuinely kicked the bucket in the Matrix, his powerbase. He more overtly seems to perish in the PDA *Matrix* (his last chronological appearance to date), struck down by a lightning strike while confronting the seventh Doctor (who doesn't cause the Valeyard's death, but refrains from saving him).

Either way, the Valeyard's legacy lives on in that *The Name of the Doctor* cites him as an alias the Doctor will use "before the end", and *Twice Upon a Time* says the Doctor has "many names" including "The Shadow of the Valeyard".

The prosecuting council, named the Valeyard, successfully argued that the Doctor was guilty of interference on a grand scale, and the enquiry became a trial. It was revealed that the Doctor's actions on Thoros Beta had threatened the course of universal evolution. The Time Lords intervened directly, killing the scientist Crozier, the Mentor Kiv and possibly the Doctor's companion Peri. When the Doctor's own evidence proved that on another occasion he had committed genocide – wiping out the Vervoids to save the Earth – he faced a death sentence.

The Doctor claimed that the Matrix was being tampered with. The Keeper of the Matrix was brought in as an expert witness, but the Tremas Master suddenly appeared on the Matrix screen, demonstrating that it was indeed possible to breach the security of the Time Lords' master computer. The Master explained that Andromedans had previously entered the Matrix from their base on Earth and stolen valuable scientific secrets. To protect their position, the High Council had covertly ordered Earth's destruction.

The Master's greatest bombshell was the identity of the prosecuting council: the Valeyard was an amalgamation of all that was evil in the Doctor, somewhere between his twelfth and final incarnation. The Master had encountered the Valeyard before, and knew that the High Council had brought him in to frame the Doctor, in return for which the Valeyard would gain the Doctor's remaining regenerations.

When the truth about Ravolox was revealed, popular unrest deposed the High Council. Both the Master and Valeyard moved to take advantage of the situation: the Master planned to take control of Gallifrey, even as the Valeyard attempted to assassinate senior members of the Time Lord hierarchy. Both failed. The Master was trapped by the Limbo Atrophier, a booby trap placed on the Matrix files. The Valeyard was believed destroyed by his own particle disseminator, but he somehow survived. When last seen, he had assumed the guise of the Keeper of the Matrix.

The Doctor suggested that once order was restored, the Inquisitor should run for President.

Multiple Peris are Created

A secret faction of Time Lords had authorised Peri's assassination, fearing the damaging testimony she might deliver at the sixth Doctor's trial. A splinter group of that faction, fearing reprisals from the Doctor, revised history so Peri instead became Yrcanos' queen. The incoming Gallifreyan president, upon reviewing the Trial, authorised use of standard CIA protocol – that Peri be returned home after her memories of the Doctor were wiped, save for their first adventure together. Each intervention created a new timeline for Peri; before long, at least five of her were active in the universe.[770]

Despite Melanie's protestations that she had been spirited away from the planet Oxyveguramosa to attend his trial, the Doctor thought it best to drop her off in Pease Pottage, the twentieth century, for his older self to find.[771]

THE EIGHT DOCTORS -> The eighth Doctor travelled to the time of his trial. He called on Rassilon to briefly free Borusa's noblest incarnation. Borusa deposed the corrupt High Council and arranged honest elections. Flavia was re-elected and restored Earth to its rightful place. Rassilon might have intervened to make the Doctor meet his companion Sam Jones in 1997.

= **UNBOUND: HE JESTS AT SCARS... ->** In an Unbound timeline, the sixth Doctor and Mel legged it as the Valeyard's power base in the Matrix exploded... but the Doctor compassionately ran back to save

---

770 *Peri and the Piscon Paradox*

771 *The Wrong Doctors. The Ultimate Foe* novelisation, and later *Business Unusual*, cite Oxyveguramosa as the locale from which Mel is taken to the Doctor's trial. The tenth Doctor and Rose attempt to visit Oxyveguramosa in the *DWM* comic "The Lodger".

772 Mention of Evelyn Smythe in *The Ultimate Adventure* indicates that Jason and Crystal travelled with the Doctor after her time with him.

773 *The Black Hole*. Pavo seems contemporary with the sixth Doctor's Gallifrey per *The Two Doctors*. The origin of the Master's Tissue Compression Eliminator (first seen in *Terror of the Autons*) is never given on screen, but here presented as Time Lord technology. Given that the device shrinks people to death, it *would* be a useful means of killing Time Lords without according

them the chance to regenerate.

774 *Antidote to Oblivion*

775 Dating *Worlds DW: Second Sight (Worlds DW #1.4)* - The story seems notionally set between *Zagreus* and *Gallifrey* Series 1, given that Narvin is head of the Celestial Intervention Agency, but Romana describes him as a "CIA halfwit" (an assessment she'd be less likely to give as *Gallifrey* progresses).

776 *6th LA: Stage Fright, 6th LA: The Brink of Death.*

777 Dating *Trial of the Valeyard* (BF subscription promo #12) - The story is a sequel to *The Trial of a Time Lord*. The Valeyard's background details are here included because anything pertaining to his origins seems relevant, but as it's all part of a ruse to trap the Doctor and the Inquisitor, not a word of it can be trusted.

his future self. The Valeyard amalgamated the Doctor into himself and emerged triumphant. He then wreaked such havoc with history, Gallifrey was destroyed. A small sub-section of the Matrix endured, enabling Coordinator Vansell and the President-Elect to allocate Mel a time ring that tracked the Valeyard, giving her one last chance to put things right.

Mel arrived in the TARDIS as the whole of causality came undone, owing to the Valeyard's meddling in history and his own past. To save creation, the TARDIS distracted the Valeyard with projections in which he believed he ruled the eternal city of Chronopolis. Mel was incorporated into the programme for ten years... until the TARDIS ran out of power. The console room alone endured, with the Valeyard and Melanie immobile inside, as the universe spent millions of centuries healing itself.

BEYOND THE ULTIMATE ADVENTURE -> The Time Lords responded to the sixth Doctor's request for help, and either contained or destroyed the Eidolon. The Doctor's companions, Jason and Crystal, recorded their recollection of the incident for the Time Lords' files.[772]

Some Time Lords, the Constables of Chapter Nine, were authorized to go into the universe and act as policemen, and operate under Chapter regulations and the Prevention of Temporal Interference Measures. The symbiotic print of Chapter Nine officers could bring any TARDIS they entered under their control. One of their number, Pavo, employed a Tissue Compression Eliminator and a ring that clouded the senses.[773] The sixth Doctor sent Anzor's TARDIS back to Gallifrey.[774]

WORLDS DW: SECOND SIGHT[775] **->** Leela went to twenty-first century Earth, at President Romana's request, when Gallifrey registered alarming levels of psychic force there. Romana followed when contact with Leela was lost. The sixth Doctor promised to take the two of them home, after some side adventures.

The Doctor postulated that the Valeyard hailed from an alternate reality where he, the Doctor, had succumbed to his darker impulses. Alternatively, forbidden files within the Matrix – possibly planted by the Valeyard himself – indicated that the Valeyard originated in our reality as a weapon forged by a Time Lord Black Ops unit.[776]

TRIAL OF THE VALEYARD[777] **->** The Time Lords apprehended the Valeyard as he hacked into the Matrix from a mud-laden satellite of the gas giant Eta Rho, and summoned the sixth Doctor to Space Station Zenobia to serve as his defense council. The Inquisitor informed the Doctor that whereas the standard punishment such a crime was

five hundred years imprisonment, it had recently been revised to the death penalty.

The Valeyard pled guilty, and detailed the circumstances of his creation while asking for clemency. He claimed to have been found – age twenty, mute and savage – by space scavengers on Eta Rho's mud satellite, and was relocated to a Gallifreyan Shadow House upon the discovery that his biodata matched that of the Doctor. A fellow resident there – the Doctor, in the waning days of his final life – encouraged the Valeyard to study the science of regeneration, and learn why Time Lords were limited to thirteen lives. The last Doctor experimented on himself to extend his life, causing the Valeyard's creation.

Despite Era Rho's mud satellite of disappearing, the Inquisitor found the Valeyard guilty. As those assembled watched, the Valeyard was disintegrated.

The Doctor and the Inquisitor separately went back in time to the mud satellite, to find evidence of the Valeyard's claims. They encountered the Doctor's mad thirteenth self... actually the still-living Valeyard in disguise, as part of his scheme to lure the Doctor and the Inquisitor to their deaths. The pair eluded the Valeyard's particle disseminator, and all parties went their separate ways.

The Sixth Doctor Regenerates, Possible Death of the Valeyard

6thLA: THE BRINK OF DEATH -> The CIA space station where the sixth Doctor's trial was held had fallen into disrepair. Night classes in Matrix Diagnostics were available. The Valeyard rescued disembodied aliens, the Nathemus, when their home, the moon of Plastinius, was developed into a power plant. He secreted the Nathemus within the symbiotic nuclei of the sixth Doctor's TARDIS, and over time, they fed off the Doctor's mind...

(=) At full strength after events in Victorian England, the Valeyard advanced to his end game... and subverted the Matrix enough to substitute himself into the sixth Doctor's timeline. He *became* the Doctor while the genuine article was reduced to a Matrix echo. The Valeyard similarly dominated the existences of CIA Coordinator Storin and technician Genesta – in time, he would replace every Time Lord, even becoming Rassilon himself.

The sixth Doctor backtracked along his own timeline, and facilitated his regeneration in the Lakertya System. Deprived of the sixth Doctor's unique mind, the Nathemus starved to death. The Valeyard was catapulted back into the Matrix with the last echo of the sixth Doctor's persona, and they both perished. Before his end, the sixth Doctor saw his successor, and they agreed that "It's far from being all over".

Seventh Doctor Era

UNREGENERATE![778] -> The High Council foresaw a time when lesser species would develop time travel, and pack the space-time continuum to the bursting point. The Gallifreyan CIA therefore instigated a project to install the sentiences of newly birthed TARDISes into living beings. They hoped the sentiences would operate as CIA agents on their hosts' homeworlds, thwarting the lesser species' endeavours to create time-travel technology. The CIA believed this would work better than the usual array of spies and brainwashing.

Professor Klyst, a Time Lord, spearheaded the research. Experiments on Daleks were forbidden, but subjects were recruited from at least fifty worlds. Each were offered lifetimes of success if they participated in the research on the day before their deaths. Yet the beings' brains were unable to host the TARDIS sentiences, and many went insane.

The seventh Doctor ended the operation. One TARDIS sentience stabilised in the human Johannes Rausch. Klyst agreed to host another sentience, thus erasing her own knowledge of the research. The sentiences in Rausch and Klyst transferred another of their number into the Institute where the research was conducted, turning it into a make-shift travel vehicle. They went on the run from the Time Lords, hoping to stabilise the other sentiences in their host bodies.

"Nineveh!" -> The seventh Doctor strayed into the null space of Ninevah: a graveyard for TARDISes. The Watcher of Ninevah was tasked with killing aged Time Lords, but recoiled upon realising that the Doctor was at the start of his seventh regeneration, so had a great deal of life left before his passing.

REMEMBRANCE OF THE DALEKS -> Addressing Davros, the seventh Doctor claimed to be "President-Elect of the High Council of Time Lords... Keeper of the Legacy of Rassilon". After destroying Skaro, the Hand of Omega returned to Gallifrey.

Back on Gallifrey, the Hand of Omega missed its creator and tended to hover around the Omega Memorial.[779] An Adjudicator – a retired Time Lord acting as an academic assessment officer – considered Ace for enrollment in the Prydonian Academy... but she declined, and remained in the Doctor's company.[780] Time Wardens mediated traffic disputes in the Vortex.[781]

"The Forgotten"[782] -> The War of Agrovan Seven had now lasted fifteen hundred years, and the Time Lords had designated it a non-intervention site. The Strykes and Marats had been evenly matched for generations, but an unknown party gave the Strykes a bioweapon designed to work on Gallifreyans. As the Marats had a similar biology to the Gallifreyans, this lead to a great plague among them.

778 It's difficult to say how much the CIA is operating independently in this story, or to what degree it's sanctioned by the High Council. Presuming the CIA isn't acting totally solo, the High Council that initiated the project is possibly the administration that was overthrown in *The Trial of a Time Lord*.
779 *Lungbarrow*
780 *Thin Ice* (BF). This was proposed as a means of Ace leaving the TARDIS in the unmade Season 27, but in the Big Finish adaptation of it, she stays with the Doctor after all.
781 "The Crossroads of Time". For all we're told, the "Time Wardens" might be Time Lord beat cops. In *The Time Warrior*, the Doctor tells Sarah, "My people are very keen to stamp out unlicensed time travel. You can look upon them as galactic ticket inspectors, if you like."
782 Dating "The Forgotten" (IDW *DW* mini-series #2) - No date is given. It's interesting that the Time Lords designate this a "non-intervention site", as the working assumption is that all intervention is banned. Presumably, this is a particularly sensitive area.
783 *The Chaos Pool*
784 Romana's desire to open up the Academy to non-Gallifreyans doesn't happen until a long time on (in the *Gallifrey* mini-series) and must fizzle at this juncture.
785 *The High Price of Parking*
786 *A Death in the Family*
787 The novel version of *Human Nature*, in which a Gallifreyan agent arranges for an alien Aubertide to transform into a cow and get eaten as such.
788 *UNIT: Dominion*. It's late in the seventh Doctor's lifetime.
789 DC: *The Eleven*, DC 4: *Songs of Love*, DC 4: *Stop the Clock*.
790 *The Gallifrey Chronicles*
791 *Christmas on a Rational Planet*. No date is given in the *Doctor Who* books, but the Faction Paradox timeline in the back of *FP: The Book of the War* pegs the Grandfather's escape as occurring "one hundred fifty-one years" before the War in Heaven... and also places it simultaneous to the transition of House Paradox to Faction Paradox, which seems to happen in the era of the fourth Doctor, not (as here) the seventh.
792 *Christmas on a Rational Planet, Alien Bodies, Interference* – the first of these identifies the Time Lord criminal brand as a "dragon tattoo", probably in accordance with Jon Pertwee's real-life tattoo, as seen on the exiled third Doctor's right arm in *Doctor Who and the Silurians*.

The Time Lords wanted an end to the war, but the seventh Doctor and Ace gave the Marats a restorative that cured 90% of Gallifreyan ailments.

Romana Returns to Gallifrey

BLOOD HARVEST / GOTH OPERA -> Three Time Lords – Rath (the younger brother of Goth), Elar and Morin – took responsibility for security matters. Most Time Lords considered this a rather lowly position, but the Committee of Three, as they styled themselves, used their office to build their own powerbase. Using their expertise, they planned to kill Rassilon in his Tower and take control of the galaxy. They were defeated by the seventh Doctor, Ace, Benny and the second Romana.

The three traitors were sentenced to vaporisation. Romana settled back on Gallifrey from E-Space, and was greeted by Ruathadvorophrenaltid, a Time Lady acquaintance of the Doctor. Ruath planned to be the consort of the Vampire Messiah, and targeted the fifth Doctor. Romana alerted Gallifrey and the Doctor to the threat, and was rewarded with a seat on the High Council.

Gallifreyan medics examined Romana after her return from E-Space, and determined that her body – which had unknowingly become the sixth Key to Time segment – was degenerating, and that regeneration wasn't possible.[783]

THE CHAOS POOL -> The second Romana aided the fifth Doctor in the second quest for the Key to Time, then returned to Gallifrey with the former Tracer named Amy – whom she hoped would help to convince the Time Lords of the worthiness of non-Gallifreyans to attend the Academy. Afterwards, Amy left Gallifrey and went in search of her sister.[784]

Not even Time Lord technology could penetrate the barrier around the planetoid Parking without a receipt.[785] The Time Lords outlawed Vaspen space-time stamps – a means of transporting a small package to any point in space-time, and which were more expensive than a planet.[786] Some Interventionists on Gallifrey took an interest in introducing alien genetic material into the make-up of other species, including humanity.[787]

The bald Master, equipped with the late Chancellor Goth's TARDIS, used the Ship's High Council protocols to penetrate the temporal defences surrounding a Time Lord vault on the planet Terserus. After shrinking the two Time Lords within to death, the Master used the vault's files and artifacts pertaining to the Dimensioneers to implement a scheme involving the seventh Doctor, Raine Creevy and UNIT on twentieth-century Earth.[788]

The Eleven

The Eleven, a Time Lord suffering from regenerative dissonance – meaning his ten previous selves were still active in his mind – went on a rampage that "eviscerated armies, incinerated worlds". On Veltra Nine, the Eleven massacred ten thousand souls, purely to see how it would sound. The Eleven's name changed numerically with each incarnation – the Ten also committed many crimes, including the massacre of a Time Lord squad on Dalgar.

The seventh Doctor assisted the President of the Time Lords in capturing the Eleven. As reforms on Gallifrey had done away with molecular disintegration, the Eleven was frozen in stasis in a Capitol prison block. The Ten had mesmirized the sitting Castellan to aid in his future incarnation's escape...[789]

The Romana Presidency

HAPPY ENDINGS -> The second Romana was elected President of the Time Lords, beating the previous Madame President – who had been found drunk while in possession of the Sash of Rassilon – by 53 to 47% in the elections, and won the support of the Interventionist movement. She promised an end to isolationism and to open an embassy with the Tharils. Very soon after her election, she investigated a Fortean Flicker which the Tzun Master was exploiting. He had stolen the Loom of Rassilon's Mouse, which could build monsters. The Master was defeated and the Loom retrieved, but he escaped Gallifreyan custody.

Romana was the 413th President.[790]

The Carnival Queen affected rationality throughout the universe. On Gallifrey, Grandfather Paradox, "voodoo priest of the House of Lungbarrow", escaped his prison when the Lady President had a fit and released three hundred prisoners from their prison asteroid. Six hundred Time Lords claimed to be the ghost of Morbius, and the planet's automatic defences activated.[791]

Grandfather Paradox removed his arm, as the Time Lords had branded it. Soon, he would remove himself from history. With its leader free, Faction Paradox would grow in size and influence.[792]

Chris Cwej Leaves the TARDIS

LUNGBARROW -> The seventh Doctor and Chris Cwej returned to the Doctor's ancestral home of Lungbarrow. He was accused of murdering Quences, the head of the household. The Doctor was badly beaten and incapacitated by his family, who blamed him for all their woes. Innocet – one of the Doctor's Cousins – joined Ace, Leela, Chris and President Romana in reviving him. They learned the Doctor contained the genetic codes of the Other.

The Doctor deduced that another Cousin, Glospin, had briefly regenerated to look like the Doctor and thus framed him for Quences' murder. Quences' mind was in Badger, the House's robot servant. The House itself committed suicide, throwing itself from the mountain it rested upon. Romana ordered a new House built for the Cousins.

Chris decided to stay on Gallifrey and work as an agent of the President. He was given a time ring. Leela discovered she was pregnant. The Dromeians and Arcalians objected to Romana's interventionist policies. She was given a gift by the Chairman of Argolis and opened an embassy with Karn.

The Celestial Intervention Agency sent the Doctor to recover the Master's remains from Skaro.

(?=) DEATH COMES TO TIME[793] **->** A new generation of Time Lords was far more open to the idea of intervention. Among them was the Minister of Chance, and he met with the seventh Doctor to discuss intergalactic crises. One such matter emerged when the Time Lords Antinor and Valentine were killed on Earth. Meanwhile, Ace trained to be a Time Lord under Casmus. Events climaxed on the twenty-first century Earth.

The second Romana and a research team went missing when the planetoid Etra Prime vanished on 6776.7, Rassilon Era. An interim President was appointed in Romana's absence.[794]

(=) THE SIRENS OF TIME[795] **->** The Knights of Velyshaa seized control of the Gallifreyan Capitol. They were exploiting time disturbances using a captured Temperon, an animal that could release particles capable of disrupting time. The fifth, sixth and seventh Doctors restored established history and the conquest of Gallifrey never happened. The Temperon sacrificed itself to forever hold in check the Sirens of Time, extra-dimensional creatures that fed off time distortion.

Ace on Gallifrey

The seventh Doctor left Ace on Gallifrey to study at the Academy. A mentor assigned Ace to watch over, but not interfere with, the peaceful planet of Talmeson. Ace briefly left her post to visit Earth, as her mother was dying of cancer, and returned to find the Daleks had wiped out the Talmeson populace. Enraged, Ace stole an Omega Device and journeyed to the days when the Daleks were dormant in their city, to retroactively wipe them out forever.[796]

Ace stayed on Gallifrey for a time, and attempted to contact the seventh Doctor and Raine during a crisis involving the bald Master and the Tolians.[797] Ace left Gallifrey to aid the seventh Doctor and Benny against Sutekh. She had taken a single TARDIS driving lesson at the Academy, and it didn't go well.[798]

THE TWO MASTERS -> The Cult of the Heretic agreed to let the bald Master rule them – if, in a show of loyalty, he murdered one of his younger selves, and preserved his existence with their paradox-nullifying Anomaly Cage. The Master intervened against his thirteenth self on Terserus... but the Cult followed, switched the Masters' minds, and turned them into a living paradox that infected all of space-time. The Masters separately travelled to Earth in 1984 and circa 2016, and later confronted each other during the Gorlan civil war.

The seventh Doctor prompted the Masters to swap minds again – but the damage they'd wrought continued, and the whole of the space-time was nearly consumed.

---

793 Dating *Death Comes to Time* (BBC1 drama, unnumbered) - While there are discrepancies, *Death Comes to Time* shares a number of features with the timeline of the later New Adventures – the Time Lords are more openly interventionist, and Ace is training up as a Time Lord. While *Lungbarrow* is clearly meant to lead straight into *Doctor Who – The Movie*, there are other stories set in the "gap", such as *Excelis Decays* and *Master*. Ace is a lot older than she was in the New Adventures (her last appearance is in *Lungbarrow*). As with events in *Death Comes to Time* that occur in the Present Day section, the canonicity of these details is highly debatable. Fans are free to incorporate this story or ignore it.

794 *Neverland*

795 The story takes place during the interim Presidency, in the seventh Doctor's "current" Gallifrey.

796 *NAofBenny* V1: *The Lights of Skaro*, following *UNIT: Dominion* establishing that Ace was studying at the Gallifreyan Academy.

797 *UNIT: Dominion*

798 *NAofBenny* V2: *The Vaults of Osiris*

799 Dating "The Final Chapter" (*DWM* #262-265) - The date is given on the TARDIS screen at the beginning of the story, and is significantly later than the one given in *Neverland*. This is tricky to fit in with the books and audios, where Romana is President throughout the eighth Doctor range – although we never actually see the President in this story. It clearly happens before Gallifrey's destruction and fits in with the idea of Gallifreyan society fraying and succumbing to cultism depicted around the time of *The Ancestor Cell*.

800 The adventures of this faux "ninth Doctor" (patterned after Big Finish producer Nicholas Briggs) continue in "Wormwood", set around 5220.

801 *The Shadows of Avalon*

802 *Interference*

803 *FP: The Book of the War* specifies that Compassion becomes a Type 102 TARDIS.

The Masters killed the Cult of the Heretic members, but the Doctor reprogrammed the Cult's equipment to "regenerate" the timeline into a form identical to its previous self – save that he returned the Masters to their proper places in history. He then destroyed the Anomaly Cage.

Eighth Doctor Era

DOCTOR WHO - THE MOVIE -> The seventh Doctor recovered the Master's remains from Skaro, and was heading for Gallifrey in 5725.2, Rassilon Era. The Deathworm Master sabotaged the TARDIS, and forced a landing in San Francisco, 1999, but was later lost to the TARDIS' Eye of Harmony.

10639.5 Rassilon Era - "The Final Chapter"[799] ->
Fey and Izzy piloted the TARDIS to Gallifrey. They told Castellan Tenion and Overseer Luther that the eighth Doctor was dying, and he was taken to a hospital complex called the Mortal Coil. At this point, the Doctor was considered fiction by most people on Gallifrey.

Xanti, an Academy dropout and admirer of the Doctor, hurried to meet him. The Doctor's mind resided in the Matrix while his body healed. He encountered the Higher Evolutionaries – which now included a representative of the Order of the Black Sun, Demoiselle Drin, in Merlin's place. They all had experienced nightmares of a Gallifrey grown "dark and wicked".

A group of Elysians materialised over the Doctor's body, planning to kill him "for the sake of the future", but Shayde arrived to fight them off. The Elysians vanished, taking Izzy with them.

The Doctor spoke to Uriel, Xanti's father, in the Quantum of Solace (which was now being run by ex-military man Tubal Cain). He learned of the history of the Elysians, and that Luther was their leader. Luther's rebuilding of the Capitol had effectively turned the whole planet into a giant TARDIS, powered by Xanti's mind. Now he planned to take it back to the moment of Rassilon's triumph and overwrite that history with his own. The Doctor forced Luther out into the Vortex, but Luther killed Xanti, and the Doctor had to take his place. Shayde rescued the Doctor, but the strain apparently triggered the Doctor's regeneration into a balding man...

Shade was posing as the "regenerated" Doctor, allowing the eighth Doctor to act in secret against the Threshold.[800]

Eve of the War in Heaven

ALIEN BODIES / INTERFERENCE / THE TAKING OF PLANET 5 -> Although Time Lords were unable to see into their own future, the eighth Doctor found evidence that the Time Lords would fight a War across time and space against an unknown Enemy. This War involved exotic weapons and such shifts in the timeline, reality, and cause and effect as to make it all but impossible to determine any firm details. The broad sweep of events became apparent among the fragmentary evidence, however, and it was bleak news for Gallifrey.

Romana regenerated for the second time. Her third incarnation became increasingly concerned – perhaps even paranoid – about the prospect of the War.[801] Some Time Lords tried to acquire a bottle universe from IM Foreman, hoping to flee into it when the Enemy attacked.[802]

THE SHADOWS OF AVALON -> President Romana now put the survival of the Time Lords over more ethical considerations. While she was concerned with the dispute with the People of the Worldsphere, Romana was aware that the War with the unknown Enemy would soon be upon Gallifrey.

The Doctor's TARDIS ruptured in a dimensional rift and was presumed destroyed. Learning that the eighth Doctor's companion, Compassion, was mutating into a TARDIS thanks to her contact with future technology, Romana sent Interventionist agents Cavis and Gandar to capture her. Romana planned to force Compassion to breed with other TARDISes. Compassion transformed into a TARDIS, and she, the Doctor and Fitz fled the Time Lord authorities.

Until Compassion, the most advanced TARDIS was the Type 98.[803]

Gallifrey Destroyed, the Original Fitz Kreiner Dies, Compassion Parts Ways with the Now-Amnesiac Eighth Doctor

THE ANCESTOR CELL / THE GALLIFREY CHRONICLES -> As the War approached, Gallifreyan society was starting to fray at the edges and many Time Lords were becoming superstitious. Time Lords succumbed to the cults of Ferisix, Thrayke, Sabjatric, Rungar, the Pythian Heresy, Klade and the legend of Cuwirti.

A vast Edifice materialised over Gallifrey. This was the Doctor's original TARDIS, which was drawing energy from IM Foreman's leaking bottle universe.

On Gallifrey, many Time Lords had fallen under the sway of Faction Paradox. They summoned the dead President, Greyjan the Sane, who infected the Matrix with Faction Paradox virus. Faction Paradox arrived in force to occupy Gallifrey, led by Grandfather Paradox. Fitz's original self, Father Kreiner of Faction Paradox, was freed from the Vortex, but killed by the Grandfather when he switched allegiances and aided the eighth Doctor.

The Enemy was revealed as evolved ancestor cells – primeval lifeforms that had been mutated and empowered by the leaking bottle universe. The Enemy now launched its first strike on Gallifrey, destroying the TARDIS berths.

Faced with the choice of either submitting to Faction Paradox or escaping, the Doctor instead used the remaining energy of the Edifice to destroy Gallifrey. Faction Paradox was wiped out, and the annihilation was so complete that it destroyed the entire constellation of Kasterborous, creating disturbances in space and time that prevented any further time travel to or from Gallifrey.

The Doctor and Compassion downloaded the entire contents of the Matrix into the Doctor's brain. Compassion sent the Doctor and his TARDIS, which had been all but destroyed, to Earth to recover. She also dropped Fitz off in 2001 to reunite with him, then left with Nivet, a Time Lord technician.

It was possible that the destruction of Gallifrey prevented...

The War in Heaven[804]

In some texts, the Time Lords were called the Great Houses, Gallifrey was cited as the Homeworld, and TARDISes were named as timeships.[805]

The War in Heaven was about meaning as much as it was about territory.[806]

The Time Lords created at least nine duplicate Gallifreys, in case the Enemy destroyed the original. Not even the President knew which was the "real" one.[807]

Realising that the Enemy could erase them from history, some Celestial Intervention Agency members tried to remove themselves from the universe as a means of defence. They became conceptual beings named the Celestis. They operated from a realm called Mictlan, and influenced universal affairs with a network of agents.[808]

The War King, a former renegade who had tried and failed to warn the Great Houses about the Enemy, was made the official head of the Homeworld six years before the War began. He had a pointed beard that had grown white with age, and wore black robes.[809]

The living timeship Compassion was the only Type 102 timeship. Type 101 timeships, an attempt to breed a living timeship such as Compassion, had been a disastrous failure. Compassion largely attempted to stay neutral in the War, sometimes having adventures with companions such as Carmen Yeh. Two years before the War began, the death of the timeship Percival moved Compassion to take a more active role in the War, and she brokered a deal with the War King, becoming the mother of the first Type 103 timeships. Nonetheless, she insisted that the Enemy attacking the Great Houses was a distraction, and focused her attention on House Lolita.[810] The first of Compassion's offspring, Antipathy, was deeply unstable and kept imprisoned on the Homeworld.[811]

The Enemy struck Gallifrey, completely destroying it.

804 THE WAR IN HEAVEN: *Alien Bodies* introduced the future War and the Enemy (neither of which were capitalised at that point). Further details were added in subsequent eighth Doctor books, principally *Interference, The Taking of Planet 5, The Shadows of Avalon* and *The Ancestor Cell*. The term "the War in Heaven", while not used very much in the Faction Paradox-related stories themselves, has become a common currency in fandom to differentiate this time-active conflict from the Last Great Time War of the new *Doctor Who*, following the lead of *FP: The Book of the War* as to how historical figures and others tend to perceive the conflict. Technically, this should be the *second* "War in Heaven", the first being the conflict between the Time Lords, the Great Vampires (*State of Decay*) and the Yssgaroth (*The Pit*) as elaborated upon in *FP: The Book of the War*.

The Doctor destroyed Gallifrey in *The Ancestor Cell*, in large part to avert the War. At that point, all the events of the War ceased to be the "real" future of the *Doctor Who* universe. However, there's the caveat that, by definition, it's difficult to establish facts or the sequence of events of a time war. When asked about the canonicity of its *Faction Paradox* novels, Mad Norwegian Press – tongue planted firmly in cheek – would sometimes respond that *The Ancestor Cell* was propaganda written by the Faction's enemies (as evidenced by a framing sequence therein), and that the War events had not been erased from history.

805 FACTION PARADOX TERMINOLOGY: These equivalents were used throughout the *Faction Paradox* novels, audios and comics for legal reasons. Similarly, "babels" are the *Faction Paradox* equivalent of the Shaydes from the *DWM* comic; the "Imperator Presidency" refers to Morbius' tenure as head of the High Council. The War King is generally presumed to be the *Faction Paradox* version of the Master, but little confirms this beyond a few background details (the War King's statement that he was one of the few to leave the Homeworld, that he has no House of his own, that the Council forgave him, etc.) given in *FP: Words from Nine Divinities*.

806 *FP: The Book of the War*, which chronicles the first fifty years of the War in Heaven in great detail.

807 *The Taking of Planet 5. FP: The Book of the War* says the alternate Homeworlds/Gallifreys were made "in the last decades before the War", and *FP: Sabbath Dei* specifies that this happens thirty years before the War starts.

808 This happens twenty years before the War, according to *FP: The Book of the War*. The Celestis first appeared in *Alien Bodies*.

WHEN DID THE WAR IN HEAVEN START?: There's no indication in the *Doctor Who* books exactly when the War was due to start relative to the Doctor. The War began one hundred and fifty-one years after

GALLIFREY

Aware this attack was coming, the Time Lords broke their oldest laws, travelling back in time to assault their Enemy before they were attacked.[812]

Early in the War, the Enemy succeeded in wiping out the most powerful Gallifreyan artifacts like the Demat Gun and the Sash of Rassilon. Many secrets and pieces of bio-data were lost. Those that survived became extremely valuable, and much sought-after, as they could be adapted into weapons.

The first land battle of the War was fought on Dronid in the 155th century. The Doctor was thought to have died on Dronid. His body was recovered, and its unique bio-data would make it perhaps the most valuable artifact in the universe. The Doctor had agreed to donate his body to the Celestis in return for their non-intervention on Dronid.[813]

Every battle was fought and then refought, as the losing side retroactively attempted to reverse the result. Eventually, time collapsed in the vicinity and the fighting would move elsewhere. The Time Lords searched their own future for advanced weapons to be used in the War.[814]

The Enemy learned how to build conceptual entities such as the anarchitects, beings capable of rearranging architecture. Qixotl met the Doctor and saw him escape the Antiridean organ-eaters.[815]

Faction Paradox grew corrupt and started trading weapons and time travel. The Time Lord authorities moved to wipe them out as they would a virus. In 2596, the Time Lords destroyed the Earth colony Ordifica because of its contact with Faction Paradox.[816]

The Time Lords allied themselves with the Gabrielideans. The Time Lords had a military training ground on Gallifrey XII. The latest model TARDISes were the Type 103s, which were sentient and could take the form of people.[817]

The regenerated Thessalia, now passing as "Larissa", agreed to a personal alliance with Faction Paradox.[818]

In the War's eighth year, Cousin Octavia and her corps of elite Faction troops – the Red Brigade – brought about the ruin of a breakaway Faction stronghold (the Thirteen-Day Republic) and its leader, Cousin Anastasia. Father Dyavol, formerly the mad monk Rasputin, died in mysterious circumstances. For her crimes against the Faction, Anastasia was triplicated and put back into linear time, in the twentieth century, to die three times over.[819]

Ordnance-Decurion Goralschaixianthellipse (a.k.a. Goralschai, and a product of the House Military's First Wave) was something of a black sheep in House Xianthellipse, even though his successes included the Spike, the Llammas IV campaign and the rout of the Raithaduine cultists. The Great Houses came to view amaranth technology – capable of eliminating discontinuity and resolving pockets of space-time to their most logical potential – as unreliable. Goralschai argued that amaranths were useless when wielded by unimaginative parties.[820]

It was rumoured – based upon the nature of the Enemy's first communication with the Homeworld – that the War in Heaven would end when the Seven Prophesied Heads of Severance spoke.[821] Time gems – cysts formed around micro-factures in temporal causality, the largest of which was about the size of a knucklebone – were investigated for their potential in War-related efforts.[822]

Traditional House soldiers were thought to lack a brutal animal ingenuity compared to the Enemy, so the Fourth Wave of the House Military – which included Captain Tancreevee – was born with retro-human characteristics. The most notorious of Fourth Wave member, Robert Scarratt, had an interest in sex. A year after being named a cadet-Captain in his House's elite time corps, Scarratt started acquiring a reputation as a non-conformist, and made an unauthorized trip to Liverpool, 1946.[823]

Grandfather Paradox escaped his prison, according to *FP: The Book of the War*. That escape occurred in *Christmas on a Rational Planet*, shortly after Romana became President. Romana celebrates her one hundred and fiftieth year as President in *The Ancestor Cell*, meaning the War is now imminent.

809 *FP: The Book of the War, The Taking of Planet 5.*
810 *FP: The Book of the War, FP: Sabbath Dei, FP: In the Year of the Cat.* Lolita of House Lolita features prominently in the *Faction Paradox* audios.
811 *FP: Of the City of the Saved*
812 *The Ancestor Cell*
813 *Alien Bodies*
814 *The Ancestor Cell*
815 *Alien Bodies*
816 *Interference*
817 *Alien Bodies*

818 *FP: Newtons Sleep.* The Faction has recently severed ties with the Remote, and the House Military is making a major effort to wipe out the Faction's holdings wherever they are found (p257) – which going by the timeline in *FP: Book of the War* means that it's about Year Six of the War. What becomes of Thessalia's alliance with the Faction isn't known.
819 *FP: The Book of the War*, and referenced throughout *FP: Warring States.*
820 *FP: Against Nature.* Amaranth technology appeared in *Christmas on a Rational Planet.*
821 *FP: The Brakespeare Voyage*, elaborating upon *FP: The Book of the War.*
822 *FP: The Brakespeare Voyage* (chs. 10, 36).
823 *FP: The Brakespeare Voyage*, as established in *FP: The Book of the War.* According to the latter work, the Fourth Wave is born in Year 17 of the War.

2411

c Year 18 - FP: AGAINST NATURE[824] -> House Xianthellipse created House Meddhoran as part of the Great Houses' experiment in bio-diversity – an undertaking that yielded meagre results, and a new batch of hybrids with little interest in the War. Threatened with being recycled as bio-fodder, the fifteen offspring of House Meddhoran agreed to a proposal by Ordnance-Decurion Goralschaixianthellipse of House Xianthellipse that he relocate Meddhoran – similar to the means by which Faction Paradox created its Eleven-Day Empire – to the Nemontemi: extra days purged from the Mexica calendar. Goralschai was granted access to Meddhoran's breeding engine, but instead used it to create a quincunx (a square with a fifth item at the centre) of totems that included Primo Acamapichtli Isleno de la Vega and Todd Calavero in the twenty-first century, and an orphan named Momancani in 1506. House Meddoran, serving as another totem, was betrayed and transferred into a decaying Neatherweald.

Meddhoran became subject to a blight that turned its males to ash (save for Rhodenetmeddhoran vel-Xianthellipse, who was reincarnated by Goralschai as the Momancani) and spread to the female population. Gedarra of House Meddhoran found a means of travelling to the twenty-first century and aiding Calavero and de la Vega. Following the resolution of the New Fire Ceremony in 1506, House Meddhoran was transported to an idyllic representation of Tlalocan, the Mexica underworld. Calavero took up residence there with the Meddhoran survivors, who became able to biologically reproduce and continue their bloodline.

House Urquineath kept the 2nd Second until one of its descendants, the Hussar, gambled it away at Serendipity Keep in the Chance Coteries. Godmother Antigone of Faction Paradox, also of Urquineath, forged the Neam Treaty with the Coteries to cover up her House's disgrace. The Hussar forged an intimate relationship with his TARDIS, the Kraken, and became a renegade.[825]

? - FP: WEAPONS GRADE SNAKE OIL[826] -> Within the Eleven-Day Empire, Bankside – on the south side of the Thames – served as a research and development centre for Parliament's more unpredictable assets. Father Christèmas, as the Aquister Primate, oversaw the facility and was assisted by Cousins Haribeaux and Chantelle.

As a power play, Godmother Antigone tried to bait Christèmas into stealing the 2nd Second from the Chance Coteries, in clear violation of the Neam Treaty. Christèmas assembled Sojourner Hooper-Agogo, Cousin Chantelle, the Hussar and his TARDIS (the Kraken) and Anne Bonny as a heist team – or so he said – to obtain the 2nd Second.

824 Dating *FP: Against Nature* (*FP* novel #7) - Goralschai, a product of the House Military's First Wave, seems confused as to whether the new generation represents the Third or Fourth Wave. The Newblood initiative is very much in keeping with the bio-diversity effort that creates the latter in (according to *FP: The Book of the War*) Year 17 of the War.
825 The background to *FP: Weapons Grade Snake Oil*.
826 Dating *FP: Weapons Grade Snake Oil* (*FP* novel #10) - It's before Lolita destroys the Eleven-Day Empire (*FP: The Shadow Play*). Beyond that, writer Blair Bidmead confessed to us that he hadn't "given a great deal of thought" to where this book falls in the War years. War correspondence reveals (ch8) that it's while Robert Scarratt is working for House Xianthellipse. One of his contacts is Lord Nybeckarlaxinthelle of House Lineacrux, a.k.a. Karlax from *Engines of War* (and used with writer George Mann's permission).
827 *FP: The Brakespeare Voyage* (ch9).
828 *FP: The Book of the War*
829 *FP: The Brakespeare Voyage* (ch5).
830 *FP: The Brakespeare Voyage* (chs. 7, 9).
831 *The Brakespeare Voyage* (ch10).
832 This happens in Year 18 of the War, according to *FP: The Book of the War*.
833 It's Year 29 of the War, *FP: The Book of the War*.
834 *FP: Erasing Sherlock*. This happens before the Celestis' destruction in *The Taking of Planet 5*; the place-

ment is in keeping with the way that Mad Norwegian's *Faction Paradox* novels (where the War in Heaven was concerned) tended to occur in reverse order.
835 The years are respectively provided in the intros to *FP: Warring States*, *FP: Warlords of Utopia*, *FP: Of the City of the Saved*...
836 The background to the *Faction Paradox* audios, as given in *Alien Bodies*, *FP: The Eleven-Day Empire*, *FP: The Shadow Play* and *FP: The Book of the War*. Eliza's quote hails from *The Eleven-Day Empire*, and the implication behind it is that Eliza is Christine Summerfield from *Benny: Dead Romance*. (This is further evidenced in *FP: In the Year of the Cat*, when Eliza says she went to Buckingham Palace on a school trip – meaning she grew up on Earth or *a* version of Earth.)
The "other being" like Lolita is Compassion, one of Lolita's chief rivals in the audios. Compassion is the only Type 102 timeship according to *FP: The Book of the War*; Lolita's Type is never revealed. The short story "Toy Story" – by Lawrence Miles, and included in the Mad Norwegian Press edition of *Dead Romance* – implies that Lolita once served as the Master's TARDIS.
Godfather Sabbath (actually seen in *FP: A Labyrinth of Histories*) and the Sabbath who trained with the British Secret Service and appears in the Eighth Doctor Adventures (and also crops up in the *Faction Paradox* audios and comics) are *not* the same person, as first demonstrated when Eliza says the Secret Service's

In truth, Christèmas manipulated them into creating a new *loa*. The Eleven-Day Empire's *loa* approved, and allowed the newborn to stay in Christèmas' care, which gave him considerable weight against Parliament. Bankside became independent from the Eleven-Day Empire, but maintained relations with it.

Christèmas leveraged Antigone's own violations of the Neam Treaty, and her connections with the disgraced House Urquineath, to quietly force her retirement. Godfather Rupert became head of the Ministry of Insinuation. Bankside's leadership received promotions, becoming Godfather Christèmas, Father Haribeaux and Mother Chantelle. The Kraken and Anne Bonny joined Bankside as, respectively, Cousin Cecilia and Little Sister Shotgun.

Robert Scarratt

In Year 20 of the War, Robert Scarratt of the Great Houses acted against the Celtic alliance at Delphi, 279 BC, to aid the Houses' Eighth Earth Front.[827]

Robert Scarratt enjoyed successes during the War, becoming the Hero of Pentralaxia and the martyr of Cuchailian's Rift. He claimed to have been the last to parlay with the Enemy before the disaster on the plains of Utterlost – a colony where the timeline became so re-written, it was impossible to discern the original history or know the outcome of the conflict there.[828]

Scarratt's biological ability to stretch the rules of implacable time might have been siphoned away and endowed in another Wave, save that the Enemy's attacks on the eleventh, fourteenth and forty-ninth centuries increased the need for his services.[829]

In time, Scarratt worked for most of the Houses, and had long-standing ties to House Strategist Entarodora. Every one of Scarratt's associates, friends, occasional lovers, and chroniclers had died before he was employed by Lineacrux, the most ancient of the Great Houses.[830]

Nechronomancer Philetes was made female in the birthing engines of the Houses' Fifth Wave, when biodata reserves were diminished due to the Blockade.[831]

One of the Great Houses – the highly militaristic Mirraflex – assaulted the City of the Saved with timeships reconfigured into behemoths. The City's state of grace protocols were temporarily suspended; twenty million City-dwellers (and eleven timeships) perished as the whole of Snakefell District was expelled into the Big Crunch. The casualties were re-resurrected and a memorial built to commemorate the attack.[832]

Christopher Cwej, an agent of the Great Houses, was mass replicated into a standing army called the Cwejen.[833] The Celestis provided Jimmy Moriarty, a corporate guru in the twenty-first century, with time-travel technology. He used it to interfere in the timeline of Sherlock Holmes.[834]

In Year 41 of the War, Cousin Octavia went in search of an immortality-granting casket in China, 1900. In Year 46, every parallel reality where Nazi Germany conquered the globe came into conflict with every parallel history where Rome dominated Earth. The forty-eighth year of the conflict saw increased political and social tensions within the City of the Saved.[835]

Faction Paradox Series 1: The Faction Paradox Protocols

Lolita Destroys the Eleven-Day Empire, Cousin Justine Gains Grandfather Paradox's Shadow

Cousin Justine of Faction Paradox was sent on a mission to the East Indies ReVit Zone in 2069. She returned afterwards to the Eleven-Day Empire, having failed in her duty. One of Justine's guardians, Sanjira, failed even more badly and as punishment was made to kill his eight-year-old self, paradoxing his timeline.

One of Justine's associates in the Faction, Cousin Eliza, told her:

> "I used to live in a city like this. Different world, different time – different universe, come to think of it... One day, the sky just opened, and that was it. That was the end of it all. [The Great Houses] tore up all the cities, turned most of the people into worker drones. That was the way I found out about things, about how the universe really worked... I was pretty much the only person who got away."

Godfather Morlock now served as head of Faction Paradox's Bio-Research Wing, and was the Acting Emergency Speaker of Parliament. Godfather Sabbath commanded Faction Paradox's Military Wing. The biological catalogue in the Eleven-Day Empire contained eighteen billion species.

Old bloodlines were waning on the Homeworld, and new ones were in ascendancy. House Lolita emerged as a newblood amongst the Great Houses, and initially wasn't seen as being politically relevant. It was composed of a single member – the living timeship Lolita, who remarked that "there were only two [beings] like her".

By Year 50 of the War, Lolita had birthed a daughter and was again pregnant. She furthered her bloodline by overlaying her personality upon beings on multiple worlds, occupying at least one body on every planet where she had influence. She then began to infiltrate the bloodlines of those planets, planting her children within them.[836]

YEAR 50 - FP: THE ELEVEN-DAY EMPIRE / THE SHADOW PLAY[837] **->** Lolita moved to enhance her standing amongst the Great Houses by eliminating Faction Paradox. The Eleven-Day Empire repelled an attack by Lolita's allies, the Seventy-Ninth Sontaran Assault Corps, but this was just the opening volley of a greater gambit. The Houses offered the Faction a treaty – they would once again recognise House Paradox, and refrain from prosecuting its practices.

Godfather Morlock arranged events so that Cousin Justine lost her shadow – she was then fitted with the shadow of Grandfather Paradox, which resided within the knife he had used to cut off his arm. The Grandfather's shadow was a siege engine, capable of generating and discarding an infinite number of shadow weapons.

The Faction's Parliament ratified the treaty, whereupon Lolita exploited the laws governing transition of affairs and the treaty's clause on prestanding crimes – and demanded that the shadow of Grandfather Paradox be turned over for trial. The Faction's failure to do so put it in breach of protocol. Lolita performed an invocation that linked her to the *loa* protecting the Eleven-Day Empire... and she then consumed the whole of the Empire, compressing it into her internal dimensions. Justine and Eliza were the sole survivors of the Empire, and escaped in the timeship of a House member slain by Lolita.

Lolita said that the Empire's remains resided to the left of her alimentary canal.[838]

YEAR 51 - FP: IN THE YEAR OF THE CAT / MOVERS / A LABYRINTH OF HISTORIES[839] **->** The Great Houses recaptured Justine in 1762 and condemned her to their prison asteroid for all eternity, but she escaped back to the eighteenth century. Before doing so, Justine encountered Kresta Ve Coglana Shuncuker – the previous (and from Shuncuker's perspective, current) bearer of the shadow of Grandfather Paradox.

Faction Paradox Series 2: The True History of Faction Paradox

Cousin Eliza Dies Defeating Sutekh

YEAR 51 - FP: COMING TO DUST / THE SHIP OF A BILLION YEARS / BODY POLITIC / WORDS FROM NINE DIVINITIES / OZYMANDIAS / THE JUDGMENT OF SUTEKH[840] **->** The past of the Osirian Court interacted with the present of the War in Heaven. The Great Houses officially recognised the Court via a treaty signed after Sutekh made a power play into fifteenth century Earth. Many Osirians took to living on the Ship of a Billion Years after Sutekh destroyed their homeworld, and although Sutekh was no longer acknowledged as a divine shield of Ra, some of their number were agreeable to giving him Osiris' throne as a matter of security. Cousin Justine – travelling to the Court from 1763, and intent upon killing Sutekh – strengthened the Ship's defences, stymieing Sutekh's efforts to claim dominion over it.

To further keep Sutekh in check, Justine asked Lord

Sabbath, "I used to have a godfather called Sabbath... didn't look much like you, though" in *FP: Sabbath Dei*.

837 Dating *FP: The Eleven-Day Empire* and *FP: The Shadow Play* (FP audios #1.1-1.2) - The *Faction Paradox* audios follow on from *FP: The Book of the War*, which cites Year 50 of the War as "the present", and contains some character entries - notably those of Godfather Morlock and Lolita - that establish their status before the audios begin. A few references in the audios (notably in *FP: In the Year of the Cat* and *FP: Body Politic*) reiterate that the War is roughly at the half-century mark.

838 *FP: In the Year of the Cat*

839 Dating *FP: In the Year of the Cat*, *FP: Movers* and *FP: A Labyrinth of Histories* (FP audios #1.4-1.6) - Justine revives after six months (the same amount of time that Compassion has spent trying to aid in her escape) of stasis on the Great Houses' prison asteroid (almost certainly Shada). Ergo, it might still be Year 50 of the War when she awakes, but simplicity tends to suggest that it's Year 51.

840 Dating *FP: Coming to Dust*, *FP: The Ship of a Billion Years*, *FP: Body Politic*, *FP: Words from Nine Divinities*, *FP: Ozymandias*, *FP: The Judgment of Sutekh* (FP audios #2.1-2.6) - For Justine and Eliza, a matter of months seem to pass between Series 1 and 2 of the *Faction Paradox* audios, and a comparable amount of time presumably passes where the War itself is concerned.

841 Dating *FP: The Brakespeare Voyage* (FP novel #8) - The exact year of the War in Heaven isn't named, but for Scarratt and Entarodora, it's after *FP: The Book of the War* (which chronicles the conflict's first fifty years). A reconstruction of a meeting with Entarodora makes reference to House Lolita, whose rise and fall occurs throughout the *Faction Paradox* audios (in Years 50 and 51). Mention by Philetes of the "plains of Abaddon in the 75th year of the Great War" seems related to a local conflict rather than the Great Houses' War. The *Brakespeare's* voyage commences "forty days" after Scarratt boards the ship (ch13), and encompasses enough "months" that it might take about a full year (Philetes is embedded in *The Brakespeare* for "several months", ch24; and honeymoons with Scarratt for "months", ch18; and then "a few months" more pass before the Leviathan is located, ch29).

842 *Interference*

Anubis to resurrect Osiris. The War King backed Justine's gambit by deploying the Fifty-Ninth Fleet of the House military to protect Anubis' stronghold. Cousin Eliza harvested what remained of Osiris' biodata, but failed to retrieve 12% of his psychic mass and 7% of his timeline. Osiris' biodata was already tainted with Faction Paradox biomass, so Anubis used Eliza herself to fill in the gaps, instilling Osiris' essence within her. She made a bid for the throne as "Horus", and was acknowledged as being somewhere between Osiris' firstborn son and a reincarnation of him. Lolita, not wanting a maniac like Sutekh on the throne, secretly endowed Eliza with some of her own biomass, giving "Horus" enough power to temporarily wound Sutekh. The matter of Sutekh's claim to the throne was settled on Mars, circa 5000 BC.

The War was currently being fought on nine hundred and twenty fronts, across nearly half a million worlds. The Great Houses had brokered alliances in more than eight thousand cultures, and thought the Osirians could be key allies on seventeen fronts of the War. The War King prematurely triggered an inevitable civil war between his followers and Lolita's, thinking it better to start the conflict before she became even more powerful. The clash ended with Lolita consuming the War King just as she had the Eleven-Day Empire, and claiming leadership of the High Council. Justine realised that Lolita represented a greater threat than even Sutekh, and sent her a "message": a cadre of Mal'akh, who tore their way through the Council chambers.

Justine negotiated a deal wherein the force of Osirians historically destined to defeat Sutekh were instead diverted to the Homeworld. Led by Cousin Eliza/Horus, they "dealt" with the effectively immortal Lolita, at the cost of Eliza's life.

FP: THE BRAKESPEARE VOYAGE[841] -> House Lineacrux desired to explore the great nothingness beyond the Grandfather's Maw, but initial tests resulted in any timeship venturing there dying from abject loneliness after about forty-seven minutes of Ship time. To correct for this problem, Lineacrux built two prototype vessels – each containing planets, entire populations and a massive span of event-time – as a means of traversing the nothingness and hunting the Leviathans there for their biodata.

House Strategist Entarodora stole the smaller prototype, *The San Grael* – which had an extra-universal life expectancy of about five hundred years – and escaped into the Great Void. Lineacrux subsequently tasked Robert Scarratt with captaining the larger vessel, *The Brakespeare* – a ship that was effectively a trans-galactic empire, with more than two thousand years exploration time, ten million inhabited-world-events and a total population of 230 trillion people – to retrieve *The San Grael*. The intended captain of *The Brakespeare*, Tancreevee, was lost and thought to be in league with Entarodora. Around 87% of *The Brakespeare*

crew bore resistance to Scarratt's captaincy.

= *The Brakespeare* departed from the Spiral Politic and, months later, found *The San Grael* embedded in the side of a Leviathan. Entarodora allied herself with the Cancer Empire to capture *The Brakespeare*: a means, she hoped, of starting a new universe away from the War. The Cancer Empire's undead forces stormed *The Brakespeare*, but were held at bay until Scarratt capitulated his captaincy to Father Nebaioth of Faction Paradox. Nebaioth beheaded Scarratt to facilitate a biodata merger of the two of them and Captain Tancreevee, creating a manifestation of the concept of *The Brakespeare*'s true commander: Captain No-One. The Captain ordered *The Brakespeare*'s weapons galaxies to fire upon *The San Grael*, destroying it and ending Entarodora's plans.

Scarratt suspected that – owing to the laws of cause and effect being different in the nothingness – this represented the fifth or sixth voyage of *The Brakespeare* out of the Spiral Politic, and that the Ship was lost to the Homeworld on each attempt. One of his journeys on it was recorded on the datacore *The Verifiable, True and Eternal Voyage of Captain Scarratt*.

Scarratt's Type 91 timeship exhausted itself on his behalf and was found, dead, in the great distances of time with his severed head aboard – potentially the worst breach in linearity since the Eight Day Week. Academician Jendrickenses of Arpexia House opted to forego trying to heal Scarratt and interrogated his head instead. It was later stolen by Necromancer Philetes and given to House Lineacrux.

FP: HEAD OF STATE -> Lolita influenced an American presidential election in the twenty-first century, and captured Earth's Caldera. With this, she seemed poised to assume the Houses' standing on a universal level...

The Auctioning of the Relic

ALIEN BODIES -> As some of the Celestis began switching sides, the War began tipping in favour of the Enemy. The Doctor's dead body – the Relic – was auctioned by Mr Qixotl. The Celestis won by giving Qixotl a new body when his original one was fatally wounded. The eighth Doctor tricked the Celestis and stole the Relic. He took it to Quiescia, then destroyed it with a thermosystron bomb.

The Time Lords quickly moved to occupy or control millions of planets. They opted to mate Marie, a Type 103 TARDIS, to a male Type 105 as a means of diversifying TARDIS genetics. They also created the Ogron Lords, shock troops with the ability to time travel.[842]

INTERFERENCE -> The Time Lords were losing the War. Gallifrey had a last resort – a weapon designed to destroy Earth, which would not only destroy the Enemy's homeworld but collapse the entire web of time. The ship was dispatched at sub-light speeds, and was due to arrive at Earth in 1996. Fitz became Father Kreiner of Faction Paradox and hunted down Time Lords, including the Master and the Rani. One of these was actually a clone.[843]

One of the duplicate Gallifreys was destroyed in the Battle of Mutter's Cluster. Gallifrey VIII was an industrial planet with vast Looms pouring out soldiers.[844] There was a Gallifrey XII.[845]

Time Lords were force-regenerated into physical forms engineered to fight. Fifteen out of a thousand Time Lords survived each combat mission. There were distinct Waves of warfare, with gaps between them allowing the Time Lords to Loom more soldiers. Only those from the First Wave resembled humans. The Time Lords suffered heavy losses in the Third Zone during the Fifth Wave.

Any gathering of around a dozen TARDISes would attract an Enemy attack. The Time Lords used Parallel Cannons that created holes to other, more hostile, parts of the universe and unleashed the forces there. The Enemy detonated the star of the planet Delphon, causing a significant rout of the Time Lords.[846]

THE TAKING OF PLANET 5 -> The Time Lords planned to smash a fleet of War TARDISes against the barriers around the Fifth Planet, hoping to free the Fendahl for use against the Enemy. The eighth Doctor, Fitz and Compassion discovered the plot, and Compassion tried to save the War TARDISes. The barrier was destroyed, which unleashed not the Fendahl but the Fendahl Predator – a Memovore creature that had evolved the ability to destroy concepts. The Fendahl Predator was drawn to Mictlan and destroyed the Celestis before the Doctor banished it.

THE ANCESTOR CELL / THE GALLIFREY CHRONICLES -> Faction Paradox had gone from being a secret society to an army, led by Grandfather Paradox, the future self none of us hope to become. As well as a new rank of initiate – the Uncles, leather-clad assassins – there was now an armoured infantry, known as skulltroopers, and their shadow weapons had evolved so that they resembled guns. Although they were experienced at fighting Time Lords, Faction Paradox was not the Enemy.

Now they travelled two hundred and ninety-seven years

843 Subsequent events would suggest the clone was of the Master.
844 *The Taking of Planet 5*
845 *Alien Bodies*
846 *The Taking of Planet 5*
847 "THERE ARE FOUR OF US NOW": *The Infinity Doctors* (p213) first mentioned "four names" as the four people that Rassilon had ordered killed as a threat to Gallifrey, with Omega and the Doctor specified as two of the four. The above quote comes from *The Adventuress of Henrietta Street* (p231). In *The Gallifrey Chronicles*, the four survivors are described as "A man with a sallow face and small, pointed black beard, who wore a blue rosette; a young woman with long blonde hair in an extraordinary piece of haute couture; a tall man with a bent nose wearing a cravat and holding a pair of dice; the Doctor himself with close-cropped hair, sitting on an ornate throne, a new-born baby girl in his arms" – intended, but not named, respectively as the Master; Iris Wildthyme (or possibly Romana); the Minister of Chance from *Death Comes to Time*; the Doctor (possibly the Doctor from *The Infinity Doctors*, or in his role as the Emperor of the Universe, father of Miranda, mentioned in *Father Time*).
848 The books from *Father Time* to *Sometime Never* often showed races with time travel or magical abilities.
849 The *Faction Paradox* comic series (*FP*: "Political Animals" and *FP*: "Betes Noires and Dark Horses").. As the Doctor, Fitz and Compassion all survived the War in Heaven, these events may or may not "still happen" following the potential erasing of the War in Heaven timeline in *The Ancestor Cell*.
850 The mysterious woman in the epilogue – in a book released to coincide with the twentieth anniversary of Faction Paradox's debut in *Alien Bodies* – is very probably Cousin Justine, but it's left deliberately vague.
851 The Doctor's intent to recreate Gallifrey in *The Gallifrey Chronicles* raises the interesting possibility that he does so, and that the Gallifrey featured in Big Finish's eighth Doctor-era audios and *Gallifrey* mini-series (which lead into the Last Great Time War) all take place on the "restored" Gallifrey, not the original. If nothing else, this might explain why Romana (seen in her third incarnation in *The Shadows of Avalon* and *The Ancestor Cell*) reverts back to being her second incarnation as played by Lalla Ward – either the copy of the Matrix hidden in the Doctor's mind (*The Ancestor Cell*) hadn't been updated to include the new Romana, or (rather amorally) the Doctor went out of his way while renewing Gallifrey to bring Romana back to life as her previous self.
852 *Gallifrey I: Square One*
853 *Neverland*
854 The prologue to the Big Finish webcast offers an in-story explanation as to why the Doctor needs to "repeat" an adventure. See "Which *Shada*, if Any, is Canon?" for more.
855 *The Eleventh Doctor Year Two*: "The One". The eighth Doctor knows about Shada readily enough in the Big Finish version of that story, but the eleventh

into their own past to launch an invasion of Gallifrey. This would be the event that would lead to both the Faction conquering Gallifrey, and – three minutes seven seconds later – their total destruction and the annihilation of the War timeline.

Aftermath of the War in Heaven

Aided by Compassion at the moment of Gallifrey's destruction, the eighth Doctor had downloaded the entire contents of the Matrix – the memories of almost every Time Lord who had ever lived – into his own mind. They survived in a supercompressed form that left no room for the Doctor's own memories. Compassion apparently took the Doctor's memories, although for what purpose remains a mystery. Compassion dropped the amnesiac Doctor off in the late nineteenth century.

When his travels through time and space resumed, the Doctor met a man in the eighteenth century who resembled the Master and said the following:

> "There are only four of us left now, you know. Four of us in all the universe." [847]

Without the Time Lords controlling the proliferation of time travel, many races attempted to gain mastery of time, often by acquiring Gallifreyan artifacts. Without the Time Lords to enforce the laws of time, magic started to seep back into the universe.[848]

THE GALLIFREY CHRONICLES -> Marnal regenerated and automatically regained his memories. He soon discovered the Doctor had destroyed Gallifrey and lured him to Earth to punish him. The eighth Doctor and Marnal came to realise that the Doctor's mind contained the contents of the Matrix and the memories of all the Time Lords. Marnal died saving the Doctor, convinced that the Doctor should dedicate himself to the task of building a New Gallifrey. The Doctor sent K9 to track down Compassion.

After the War in Heaven, relics of it – including members of the Mayakai civilisation, who had been primed as weapons – remained. Mother Francesca and her unnamed associate believed they were "the only ones left" of Faction Paradox.[849]

FP: SPINNING JENNY[850] **->** Faction Paradox was now all but extinguished, although explanations differed as to the cause of its demise. Cousin Isabella, initiated into the Faction at age eight, survived and sought to create a new homeland for the Faction – but scuttled her own undertaking when her older self murdered her younger self, as part of a ritual to prove one's devotion to the Faction.

One more survivor of the Faction, an anonymous woman bristling with power, tried and failed to recruit Elizabeth Howkins into a new Faction Paradox in 1940, then left for parts unknown.

It would appear that the Doctor succeeded in building a new Gallifrey. His memories certainly returned. Romana was once again in her second incarnation.[851]

The Temporal Powers

An unspecified temporal incident caused space-time to warp around the Monan homeworld. Ten different time periods came into contact with one another, enabling some future Monan to conquer their ancestors. By stabilising the errant fields, the Monan unified the different periods into a single system – creating the Monan Host.[852]

THE APOCALYPSE ELEMENT -> Twenty time-active races met on Archetryx for a summit, but the planetoid Etra Prime reappeared. The Daleks there were working on the Apocalypse Element: a substance capable of shredding the raw fabric of space-time in an unstoppable reaction. The Daleks attacked Archetryx and stole components needed to finish making the Element.

The second Romana had been imprisoned on Etra Prime for twenty years. She escaped as the Daleks, using a Monan Host time ship as a Trojan horse, attacked Gallifrey. The sixth Doctor and Evelyn aided Romana against the Daleks; as part of this, Gallifrey's security systems were temporarily slaved to Evelyn's retinal pattern. The Daleks detonated the Apocalypse Element in the Seriphia Galaxy. As was their plan, the Daleks sacrificed their ranks on Gallifrey to reinforce the Eye of Harmony's power. The Eye contained the Element's destruction to Seriphia, which was restructured to create millions of new worlds for the Daleks.

The Daleks killed the interim President of Gallifrey, and Romana was restored to the Presidency.[853]

SHADA[854] **->** The eighth Doctor returned to Gallifrey and told President Romana and K9 that they needed to resolve a time anomaly by travelling to Cambridge in 1979.

The Doctor removed the location of Shada from his mind, and hid a device containing it away in space-time.[855]

THE LIGHT AT THE END -> The Vess – a race of three-legged, monocular mud-like telepaths – created a weapons factory in a pocket dimension and supplied arms to the Daleks, Cybermen and Sontarans. The cadaverous Master discovered that Straxus, an agent of the Celestial Intervention Agency, was negotiating to acquire the Vess weapons without the High Council's knowledge, and agreed to remain silent in exchange for one Vess weapon of his choice. Straxus agreed, and the Master obtained a Vess conceptual bomb that he used against the Doctor in 1963. The plan failed, and eight incarnations of the Doctor time-rammed the Master's TARDIS.

NEVERLAND -> President Romana allied the Time Lords with the Warpsmiths of Phaedon and the Monan Host.

A warfleet of TARDISes pursued the eighth Doctor and Charley, who decided it was time to resolve the paradox of her existence (as she had been saved from dying in the *R-101* crash). They were taken to a Time Station.

President Romana and CIA coordinator Vansell warned that the structure of space and time was on the verge of collapse. They believed that Charley had attracted Anti-Time particles from the Antiverse, which was disrupting the universal balance. The Time Lords adapted the Station to pass into the Antiverse to investigate. The Doctor discovered Rassilon's TARDIS, the size of a planetoid, with a surface populated by "Neverpeople". Rassilon's casket was there. Vansell fell under the sway of the Neverpeople, who were actually exiled Time Lord criminals.

The Doctor realised that the Neverpeople had spread rumours throughout time of Zagreus, hoping to tempt the Time Lords here. Instead of Rassilon, the casket contained a mass of Anti-time sufficient to destabilise the universe. Vansell sacrificed his life, but failed to prevent the Station, with the casket on board, from reaching Gallifrey. The Doctor surrounded the Station with his TARDIS. The Station exploded, but the TARDIS contained the Anti-Time. However, the Doctor was saturated with Anti-Time energy... which split his personality and made him the destroyer Zagreus.

> = In the Matrix, the Doctor saw a possible future where Gallifrey had been attacked and the second Romana was the Imperatrix responsible for the genocide of the Daleks.[856]

This occurred in 6798.3, Rassilon Era.[857]

ZAGREUS -> The Anti-Time-infected Doctor became Zagreus, and a revived Rassilon sought to use him as a weapon against the Divergence. Zagreus objected to being manipulated and cast Rassilon through a portal into the Divergence's timeline. The TARDIS helped the eighth Doctor stabilise his true persona and he left for a Divergent Universe that lacked time, fearing that by remaining, he would risk the Anti-Time within him allowing Zagreus to again take control. Charley accompanied the Doctor on his journey....

Gallifrey I[858]

Gallifrey had battle-TARDISes at its disposal. Cardinal Braxiatel was a member of the High Council, and Narvin (full name Narvinectralonum[859]) served as CIA coordinator. Andred had disappeared, and Leela – mourning for him – became President Romana's personal bodyguard.[860]

GALLIFREY I: WEAPON OF CHOICE -> Under President Romana, Gallifrey continued to withdraw from its monopoly of time travel, and furthered a coalition of temporal powers that included the Monan Host, the Warpsmiths of Phaedon and the Nekkistani. The temporal powers promised to protect the lesser races, in exchange for a moratorium on unauthorised time experiments. The planet Gryben was established as a "reception centre" for rogue time travellers – unauthorised time-vessels in the

Doctor here doesn't. Possibly, he extracted the knowledge during the Last Great Time War.

856 *Neverland*

857 *Neverland.* The date was given earlier in the story as 6978.5, but this is clearly a fluffed line, given the other recent dates.

858 Dating *Gallifrey I* - The season opens up in wake of events in *Zagreus*.

859 As spelled in the script to *Gallifrey VI*.

860 *Gallifrey I: Weapon of Choice*, providing the background to *Gallifrey* Series 1. Leela was pregnant in *Lungbarrow*, and no mention is made of her child in the *Gallifrey* series.

861 Inquisitor Darkel is the same character as the Inquisitor in *The Trial of a Time Lord*, and is once again played by Lynda Bellingham.

862 *Benny S6: The Crystal of Cantus*

863 *Gallifrey VII: Intervention Earth*

864 Dating *Gallifrey II* - The opening installment, *Lies*,

takes place "six weeks" after *A Blind Eye*. *Spirit* opens "a week" after *Lies*, and the remaining installments of Series Two happen in rapid succession. *Neverland* forecast Romana's ascension to Imperatrix. Braxiatel departs Gallifrey in *Pandora*, and appears to experience all of his involvement in the New Adventures and the Bernice Summerfield range between now and his return to Gallifrey in *Mindbomb* (see the Irving Braxiatel vs. Cardinal Braxiatel sidebar).

865 "Eighteen years or so" before Avril encounters, circa 2010 to 2013, the Braxiatel who eventually settles on Legion in *Benny B4: New Frontiers: The Curse of Fenman.* A case can be made that the Pandora segment digs its hooks into Braxiatel in the Collection's earliest days (following its foundation in *Benny: Twilight of the Gods* [2596]); writer Gary Russell intended that it constituted a paradox and was sent back in time to infect Braxiatel before he left Gallifrey.

Vortex would be automatically diverted to Gryben, and their occupants dealt with on a case-by-case basis.

The Time Lords believed a timonic fusion device recovered by Nepenthe – a member of the subversive group Free Time – in 3655 was now on Gryben, and so Romana sent Leela, K9 Mark 1 and a CIA operative named Torvald there to find it. It was learned that a third party had engineered the situation to bring the Time Lords and the Monan into conflict; the device went unused and was teleported away, and Nepenthe martyred herself. Romana made the acquaintance of Mephistopheles Arkadian, a time-travelling rogue and arms dealer.

GALLIFREY I: SQUARE ONE -> The coalition of temporal powers held a summit on a synthetic planetoid in neutral space, and considered legislation to limit time travel in the Vortex. Romana and Leela thwarted a third party's attempts to cause various deaths, including that of the Unvoss representative, as a means of discrediting Gallifrey. The gathering was actually a decoy to draw Free Time into the open – the real summit proceeded in secret, with Braxiatel representing Gallifrey's interests.

GALLIFREY I: THE INQUIRY -> Inquisitor Darkel[861] and Cardinal Braxiatel led an inquiry into Romana's conduct during the Gryben affair. She was cleared after it emerged she had helped to prevent the timonic fusion device from being stolen in the first place. Romana learned that Braxiatel, trading as "Irving Braxiatel", had been purchasing unique works of art, furniture, sculpture (including one by the artist Serafina) and even entire buildings for his private collection. She realised that Braxiatel was behind the Braxiatel Collection, but judged that he'd broken the laws of time to an inconsequential degree...

Though it was against the rules of time, Irving Braxiatel contacted his younger self on Gallifrey and asked him to send a Gallifreyan relic to the Braxiatel Collection.[862]

GALLIFREY I: A BLIND EYE -> Romana, Leela and Narvin went back to Earth, the 3rd of September, 1939, and identified the culprit behind the timonic device theft. Leela learned that Andred had regenerated after a failed attempt to infiltrate the CIA, and had been passing himself as a new incarnation of the CIA agent Torvald.

The Precog Programme – an attempt to use Time Lord minds to foresee different timelines – was instigated during President Romana's absence, and continued upon her return over the objections of Coordinator Narvin.[863]

Gallifrey II[864]

The Pandora segment arrived in the past, having been sent back in time by Avril Fenman...[865]

GALLIFREY II: LIES -> At Romana's urging, the High Council altered some of Gallifrey's oldest laws to open up the Academy to non-Gallifreyan students. Romana realised that the Imperiatrix Imprimature within her might allow Pandora – the warmongering former president of Gallifrey – to take control of her body, and that Pandora's spirit still existed within a Matrix partition.

The Dogma Virus Crisis

GALLIFREY II: SPIRIT / GALLIFREY II: PANDORA -> Romana promoted Braxiatel to the rank of Chancellor. She took a brief leave of absence, and went with Leela to the planet Davidia – a retreat used by presidents of various species for summits, conferences and holidays.

Andred stopped Gillestes, a Free Time agent, from contaminating the Time Lords' water supply with a "dogma virus" engineered by Free Time. Pandora nestled herself in Castellan Wynter's mind, but was then confronted by Braxiatel and Darkel. Braxiatel devoted a portion of his thoughts to the Matrix equations that kept Pandora imprisoned, trapping Pandora in his own mind. Wynter died soon after. Braxiatel volunteered to go into exile, removing all possibility of Pandora escaping on Gallifrey – but the public disclosure that he'd broken the lines of time by communicating with his past and future selves meant that he did so in disgrace. Before leaving, Braxiatel warned Romana that he'd only bottled Pandora's past and present aspects; her future aspect remained in the Matrix.

K9 Mark 1 Destroyed

GALLIFREY II: INSURGENCY / IMPERIATRIX -> Non-Gallifreyans at the Academy included humans, the Warpsmiths of Phaidon, Monans and at least one Sunari. Cardinal Valyes became Chancellor of the Academy.

The Time Lords didn't know how many of their number had been infected by Gillestes' "dogma virus" – but learned that it would make any tainted Time Lord, upon their regeneration, accept Free Time's beliefs and political agenda. Racial tensions at the Academy increased, and a human student, Taylor Addison, died while attempting to sabotage the Eye of Harmony. A terrorist bombing at the Academy killed twenty; the High Monan and the Nekkistani emperor withdrew their citizens and students from Gallifrey. K9 Mark 1 detected another bomb at Gallifrey's spaceport – his early warning saved many lives, but blast doors were lowered. He died in the subsequent explosion, along with everyone else trapped within.

Darkel decried Romana's policies as having compromised Gallifrey's security, and forced a new election. The future aspect of Pandora, communing with Romana through K9 Mark 2, insisted that Gallifrey would fall into civil war unless Romana stepped down. Romana worried about Pandora's secret agenda, but also feared the consequences of Darkel becoming president. In accordance with the law – and in full possession of the Great Key, the Sash, the Rod and the Coronet of Rassilon – Romana ended the stalemate by declaring herself Imperiatrix, i.e. dictator of Gallifrey. She ordered the dissolution of the Chapters.

Romana donned the Coronet of Rassilon to prevent another Free Time agent from blowing up the Panopticon and force-regenerating the assembled Time Lords therein, but this act triggered the Imperiatrix Imprimature within her, enabling Pandora to draw biological matter from the Matrix and manifest in the form of Romana's first incarnation. Pandora usurped the mantle of Imperiatrix. Romana realised that Pandora, as part of her schemes, had mentally influenced her into killing Andred.

Gallifrey III[866]

The Romana-Pandora Civil War

GALLIFREY III: FRACTURES / WARFARE / APPROPRIATION / MINDBOMB / PANACEA -> Civil war erupted on Gallifrey. Darkel and Chancellor Valyes sided with Pandora; Leela, Narvin, Councillor Matthias and others joined Romana's resistance effort. Romana used her presidential access codes to ground all TARDISes, denying Pandora access to time travel. The other temporal powers parked war fleets near Gallifrey. Romana's group sabotaged various resources – the Gallifreyan archive banks were razed, destroying millions of years of recorded history. Narvin and Leela attempted to ruin the Artron microform – a locale where excess Artron energy from Time Lord minds was absorbed and sent to the TARDIS

berthing bays – but their charges went off prematurely, causing a discharge of Artron energy that permanently blinded Leela. Leela nonetheless stabbed Pandora through both hearts, slaying her physical form. Pandora's essence was once more contained within the Matrix – which was made to self-destruct, killing her and the preserved minds of former Time Lords within.

Political jockeying led to Chancellor Valyes, then Darkel, becoming acting president. The High Council took a vote of no confidence in Romana – an act that legitimised her term as president, and invalidated Valyes' tenure. Matthias claimed the powers of a vice-president, and called for the first presidential election Gallifrey had experienced in millennia. Darkel, Matthias and Romana stood as presidential candidates. Romana was impeached, and her candidacy declared void.

Gallifrey's transduction barriers temporarily fell, and timeships carrying Sunari soldiers – who said they wanted to retrieve any surviving Sunari students – arrived in the Capitol. The Nekkistani warfleet allied with the Sunari vessels. Matthias ordered Gallifrey's transduction barriers raised without giving the warfleets time to withdraw, killing hundreds and causing a diplomatic fiasco.

Braxiatel returned to Gallifrey, having learned that Gallifrey would soon face a threat that it was too weak to defeat without the Imperiatrix. He allied with Matthias, who tricked Darkel into annulling the effects of Romana's presidency from the moment Pandora escaped from the Matrix – which restored Braxiatel to his former position of Chancellor. He automatically became President.

The remaining Pandora component – little more than raw hatred – longed for freedom, even though this would kill both the component and its host. Darkel tried to murder Braxiatel by freeing the Pandora component, only to find that it had been restrained all along in *her* mind, and that Braxiatel's mind – while containing a small portion of Pandora – was merely the key to its prison. Darkel and the Pandora piece perished upon its release. Braxiatel declared

866 Dating *Gallifrey III* - The fact that Pandora is Imperiatrix long enough to amass a horde of illegal temporal weapons suggests that some indeterminate time passes between Series 2 and 3, but the episodes of Series 3 themselves occur in rapid succession. Gary Russell, the producer of *Gallifrey*, has confirmed that Series 3 ends shortly before Gallifrey becomes embroiled in the Last Great Time War referenced in the new series. To that end, Arkadian expresses a desire to sell the temporal weapons stockpile to "metal gentlemen of his acquaintance", presumably meaning the Daleks. The suggestion that Time Lords could be restored from the biodata archive could be a precursor to the Time Lords "resurrecting" their number (particularly the Master, as mentioned in *The Sound of Drums*) for the Time War. The technique might even be a front-

runner to the resurrection gauntlets seen in *Torchwood* and *The End of Time*.
867 Dating *Gallifrey IV* - The series picks up immediately after (or near enough) Series 3.
868 Braxiatel's meet-up with Benny is a dramatisation of their "first" meeting (from Braxiatel's point of view, not Benny's) in *Benny: Dragons' Wrath* – which might suggest that post-*Gallifrey*, Braxiatel is, somehow, living in his own subjective past. One suspects that future Bernice Summerfield audios will address the point.
869 THE DIVERGENT UNIVERSE: *Gallifrey I: Weapon of Choice* opens with Romana saying the Doctor is "unavailable" – a reference his being off in the Divergent Universe following *Zagreus*. Going purely by the hours of story-time (about eighteen for *Gallifrey I* to *IV*, the same for the Divergent Universe stories: *Scherzo* to *The*

that, for Gallifrey's safety, he would resume his exile. Knowing that the next president would fall with Gallifrey, Braxiatel named Matthias as his successor.

Matthias' tenure began with a great calamity: the pigrats used to incubate Gillestes' dogma virus had escaped from the Academy labs during the civil war, and widely tainted the Gallifreyan population. K9 estimated that at least 35% of the Time Lords was already infected; any infected Time Lord who regenerated would became a mindless Free Time thrall. Before long, thousands of Time Lords were in such a state.

Braxiatel offered to trade the Braxiatel Collection's holdings to Mephistopheles Arkadian, in exchange for his help in securing and disposing of the treaty-violating temporal weapons that Pandora had amassed while Imperiatrix. Arkadian offered to give Gallifrey a cure for the dogma virus in exchange for Pandora's weapons – which the Time Lords loaded into a battle-TARDIS rigged to explode, in the hope that they would obtain the cure and prevent the weapons from falling into the wrong hands.

Romana and K9 piloted the battle-TARDIS to the now-disused Braxiatel Collection, which was outside space-time. Braxiatel Timescooped the Time Lords' biodata archive – and snared Leela and Narvin while doing so – so it would survive Gallifrey's upcoming downfall. He told those assembled that the virus "cure" worked, but only by stripping a Time Lord of their ability to regenerate – this had been Free Time's goal all along, to curtail the Time Lords' near-immortality. Free Time itself was no longer a threat, perhaps owing to Braxiatel's adventures in exile.

Romana had to choose between using the cure and consigning the Time Lords to a single life each, or letting Gallifrey fall and reconstructing the Time Lords with the biodata archive. Before she could decide, the battle-TARDIS – with Arkadian inside – was recalled to Gallifrey. Romana, Leela, K9, Narvin and Braxiatel were horrified to realise that the battle-TARDIS was headed toward a zombie-filled Gallifrey with a stockpile of booby-trapped temporal weapons, and a cure that would rob the Time Lords of their regeneration prowess. Romana told her allies: "Right. What we're going to do is..."

Gallifrey IV[867]

Romana and Her Allies Tour alt-Gallifreys; Narvin Loses His Future Incarnations

= **GALLIFREY IV ->** Romana and her friends used the Axis to visit different versions of Gallifrey, hoping that one of them had the means of curtailing the dogma virus and halting the impending war. On one such alt-Gallifrey, the Time Lords boosted their economy through the sale of time rings, TARDISes, battle-TARDISes and more – opening for business as Gallifrey, Inc. Regenerations could be extracted and sold for currency. All of Narvin's future lives were removed against his will, rendering his current incarnation mortal.

A second alt-Gallifrey was highly interventionist, and used surgical changes to history – including assassination and erasure from history by D-Mat gun – to achieve an optimal timeline. Romana's group prevented the President Romana of that Gallifrey from using the Axis to collapse all realities into a single continuum that she ruled, but Braxiatel and President Romana's assassin – Lord Burner, an alternate version of the sixth Doctor – were lost to the Vortex. The timelines shifted around Braxiatel, and he again encountered Bernice Summerfield in 2593.[868]

Romana obliterated Lord Prydon's vampires on a third alt-Gallifrey, but it was expected that Majestrix Borusa's diminished "True Lords" would die out soon after. Leela regained her sight by imbibing blood from one of Prydon's vampires. Yet another Gallifrey was found to have simian Time Lords.

Finally, Romana's group visited a militant Gallifrey that had never developed time travel. The President Romana of that reality was killed, and Chancellor Narvin died to prevent the insatiable Krillic from escaping the Eye of Harmony. Romana's access to the Axis was terminated to prevent the same, stranding her, Narvin and Leela while K9 Mark 2 remained behind in the Axis. Leela left, tired of Romana's broken promises. Romana and Narvin took their counterparts' place, making this Gallifrey their new home so that they could teach its inhabitants the ethics needed for them to one day become Time Lords.

The Eighth Doctor, Charley and C'rizz in the Divergent Universe[869]

= The Divergence laboured to escape the Divergent Universe – the time-loop constructed by Rassilon to isolate them, which reset itself every twenty or thirty millennia – and crafted Bortresoye as a world of zones containing various cultures, in which they could conduct experiments. The Eutermesans on Bortesoye revered a rogue planet that signalled the rise and fall of life within the Divergent Universe, and formed the Church of the Foundation on the orthodoxy that all life would return to the Foundation Planet to die. Adepts such as C'rizz, one of the Church's monks, were allowed the privilege of killing other beings. C'rizz left the Church to marry his beloved L'da, but the Kromon invaded twenty minutes into their marriage ceremony, and established their biodomes.

Rassilon became exiled to the Divergent Universe, and unknowingly experienced eighty-four of its cycles. The Anti-Time within the eighth Doctor left him the moment he and Charley entered the Divergent Universe – this enabled Zagreus to incarnate within the body of Perfection, a woman who took her own life.

Separated from the TARDIS, the eighth Doctor and Charley travelled through different zones on Bortesoye...[870]

= **THE CREED OF THE KROMON ->** The Kromon hoped to expand their gene pool by transforming females of other races into Kromon queens. C'rizz's mate, L'da, was forcibly and painfully turned into a Kromon queen, and so – at her urging – he euthenized her. The eighth Doctor and Charley encountered the Kromon, and accepted C'rizz as a travelling companion. Deprived of water, the Kromon royals died.

= **THE NATURAL HISTORY OF FEAR / THE TWILIGHT KINGDOM / FAITH STEALER / THE LAST / CAERDROIA ->** The eighth Doctor, Charley and C'rizz spent months travelling through Bortesoye's different zones, including those of Light City, the jungles of the planet Setarus, the Multihaven (a realm occupied by hundreds of different religions), and two societies who so believed themselves the zenith of evolution, they gave up reproducing. On Caerdroia, the Divergence's "home office", the Doctor's group regained the TARDIS.

= **THE NEXT LIFE ->** The Divergent Universe approached its end point, when it synched up with the main universe. Rassilon was looped back to its start. Zagreus/Perfection partnered with Daqar Keep: a result of the Divergence's experiments with hyperevolution, who had absorbed his creators.

The eighth Doctor, Charley and C'rizz left the Divergent Universe in the TARDIS, and immediately came into conflict with Davros and the Daleks.[871] Officially, Rassilon's misdeeds during the Zagreus affair were kept quiet.[872]

Gallifrey V and VI[873]

= **GALLIFREY V / GALLIFREY VI: EXTERMINATION ->** On the alt-Gallifrey, Leela became the *de facto* leader of the newly liberated slaves – the Outsiders, who sought to establish a federation of communes in the wilds. Romana settled a dispute between the Regenerators' mining guilds and the Outsider settlement of Mancipia regarding Zeitan deposits. She and Narvin also resolved a hostage situation concerning Lord Zakar – one of the richest Regenerators – and then released a genuine recording of Zakar condemning his slaves to death, leading to his arrest.

The Daleks usurped control of the Axis, forcing K9 to flee back to the one true Gallifrey. He had used his time in the Axis to catalogue a thousand Gallifreys.[874]

A Dalek Coordinator positioned itself in the Axis and directed Dalek task forces to assault alternate Gallifreys – the first stage of a Dalek takeover of the entire multiverse. Romana and Narvin synchronised a signal emanating from the Axis, thinking it a means of returning there, but in so doing created a portal that disgorged an eight-member Dalek attack squad. The alt-Gallifrey had spent centuries on weapons research, furthering an arsenal that Romana and her allies used to wipe out the Daleks. Leela and Narvin went to the Axis and killed the Dalek Coordinator, even as Romana recorded a message for the Regenerators that she had been fatally wounded. The

---

Next Life), we might imagine that the eighth Doctor, Charley and C'rizz return to our universe sometime during *Gallifrey IV*. This TARDIS team, however, doesn't seem to have any further contact with Gallifrey while they're off having adventures.

870 The background to the Divergent Universe arc, given in *The Next Life*.

871 *Terror Firma*

872 *Gallifrey – Time War* V1: *Desperate Measures*

873 Dating *Gallifrey V* and *VI* - *Gallifrey* Series 5 opens "nine months" after the end of *Gallifrey* Series 4, and events proceed in relatively quick succession. In *Gallifrey V: Arbitration*, Science Minister Kavil estimates that "three days" are needed to open the Axis portal, then he revises that figure down to "thirty-six hours", and it seems to happen even faster than that at story's end. Series 6 picks up immediately after Series 5. Zeitan

ore was first mentioned in *Vengeance on Varos*, and is here confirmed as also being native to Gallifrey (or an alt-Gallifrey, at least). Jonias' experiments echo the early time travel on Gallifrey being powered by force of will (*Cat's Cradle: Time's Crucible*).

874 Trey, *Gallifrey VI: Renaissance*

875 *Gallifrey – Time War* V1, explaining the placement of Narvin's intervention in the *Dark Eyes* series (see the Lucie Miller/Molly O'Sullivan sidebar). "Warsmiths", a short story that Big Finish author Matt Fitton wrote for the *Seasons of War* charity anthology, has a white-haired Doctor talk Narvin out of poisoning Skaro's prehistory environment so the Daleks will never evolve.

876 *J&L S3: Dead Men's Tales* – placement in Gallifrey's timeline unknown, but for Romana and Leela, this is as good a break in the action as any.

Regenerators were left to chart their own course while Romana's trio sealed off all portals within the Axis, stranding the Dalek task forces scattered throughout the multiverse. The three of them then went through a portal to their native Gallifrey...

Romana and Her Allies Return Home, Narvin Attacks the Daleks' Origins

GALLIFREY VI: RENAISSANCE / GALLIFREY VI: ASCENSION ->

"In the dark days of Gallifrey, in the time known as the Pandora Devastation, the ancient and noble civilisation of the Time Lords lay in ruins. A plague had eaten away the souls of its people. The once great and mighty towers of the citadel had fallen. In search of a cure, their president, the lady Romana, travelled across the universes with her friends. Their quest was long, and came at great personal cost, because the lady Romana would do anything for Gallifrey. And then, on the darkest day of all, after many years of wandering, lady Romana finally returned home. There in the ruins of the planet, a stranger was waiting for her, for she had an offer she knew the great president could not refuse..." [874]

The Daleks had played a long game with the Dogma Virus crisis to conquer Gallifrey. An unknown party created a Matrix projection of a future incarnation of Romana (Romanadvoratreylundar, or "Trey" for short) to thwart them.

Romana, Narvin and Leela were diverted into a Matrix pocket configured to look like the ruins of their Gallifrey. They encountered Trey, who presented herself as Romana's future self and claimed she had spent several millennia, the work of "several lifetimes", rebuilding the Time Lords' Citadel, Eye of Harmony and transduction barriers. The Time Lords, Trey said, had never recovered from the Dogmas Virus, and degenerated into savagery. Without Gallifrey to halt them, the temporal powers had sparked a war that threatened to end time itself.

To avert such a fate, Romana agreed to Trey's proposal that she overwrite the future Citadel onto contemporary Gallifrey, and reopen the planet for business. Trey shunted Romana back to the real-world Capitol as part of her stratagems, causing Romana to materialise in the Panopticon as the assembled Time Lords were electing a new leader. With Romana's return, Chancellor Valyes voided the election. Romana urged her fellow Time Lords to elect someone else, but the humility she displayed moved the Council to name her as the once and future president of Gallifrey. K9 returned to Gallifrey and reunited with her.

The Daleks made it appear that the Matrix and Gallifrey's control systems were deteriorating – a total collapse would have released the quarantined Dogma Virus victims. Romana evacuated Narvin and Leela from the Matrix, then used a back-up copy of the Time Lord biodata extracts to reset the Gallifreyan population back to versions of themselves that pre-dated the Dogma Virus outbreak. Save for Romana's group, the Time Lords went dormant as the Matrix recalibated their personalities, experiences and biologies. The Dogma Virus was purged from Gallifrey.

With the Time Lords incapacitated, a Dalek task force materialised in the Capitol. As Trey had planned, the invaders went through a Matrix door into a "future Capitol" landscape. Matrix-avatars of both Romana and Trey told the Supreme Dalek and his Daleks that they were forever trapped in an isolated Matrix section.

Narvin mistakenly thought that the actual Romana was lost to the Matrix. Believing that Gallifrey could not endure without her, Narvin launched a plan to curtail the Daleks' technological might – to retroactively stop them from attacking the Matrix at all – by altering their very origins. K9 judged that the plan had a negligible probability of success, and that the Daleks would likely retaliate if it failed.

Narvin proceeded regardless – as the Time Lords awoke, he diverted the fourth Doctor, Sarah and Harry to Skaro's early days, and dispatched Valyes, incognito, to warn the Doctor that Gallifrey had foreseen a time when the Daleks would destroy all other lifeforms. Valyes was to instruct the Doctor to avert the Daleks' creation, or affect their genetic development to make them less aggressive, or find an inherent weakness to exploit.

After Valyes left, Narvin found the real Romana safe, with Leela, in the presidential offices... and realised he'd made a terrible mistake. Romana and Leela believed that the Time Lords were awakening to a new dawn, but Narvin was sickened to realise his actions may have sparked a temporal war between the Time Lords and the Daleks...

Narvin's guilt over the fourth Doctor's mission to Skaro prompted him to visit different points of Gallifrey's history, to contain the damage. As "Coordinator-in-Extremis", he aided the eighth Doctor against the Eminence.[875]

Time breaks were detected in Victorian times. President Romana sent Leela back to aid Professor Litefoot and Henry Gordon Jago in ending this threat.[876]

Lucie Miller and Molly O'Sullivan[877]

BLOOD OF THE DALEKS / HUMAN RESOURCES
-> Interference in the year 2006 resulted in the Time Lords placing Lucie Miller with the eighth Doctor, and telling him that she was part of a witness relocation programme. They also placed a temporal barrier around Lucie's native era, preventing the Doctor from returning there. The Doctor and Lucie resolved events pertaining to Karen Coltraine and the Cybermen on Lonsis, and the Time Lords lifted the barrier.

SISTERS OF THE FLAME / THE VENGEANCE OF MORBIUS -> The Time Lords received word that the new leader of the Cult of Morbius – Kristof Zarodnix – was trying to capture a Gallifreyan. Fearing the consequences of this, they recalled all TARDISes, and used the Timescoop to capture any Time Lord who refused to return home.[878] Time rings became the only viable means of travel.

A restored Morbius deprived Gallifrey of energy using a stellar manipulator, then created a new empire. The eighth Doctor restored power to Gallifrey, and the Time Lords retroactively undid Morbius' triumphs.

NEVERMORE -> The Time Lords sent the eighth Doctor and his companion, Tamsin Drew, to procure the release of General Morella Wendigo on the planet Nevermore.

The Straxus Crisis

(=) DARK EYES[879] **->** The High Council foresaw that Straxus, a Gallifreyan CIA operative, would regenerate into a persona filled with disgust for his people, and deem the Time Lords a worse blight on the universe than the Daleks. Adopting the family name "Kotris", Straxus' new incarnation would ask the Daleks to purge his Time Lord DNA and replace it with Dalek material – the first step in an alliance in which Kotris' equipment would eradicate all Time Lords in past, present and future.

The High Council broke the laws of time to warn Straxus that his next incarnation would betray Gallifrey. To stymie his future self, Straxus manipulated the eighth Doctor into looking into Kotris' involvement in the life of Molly O'Sullivan, a nurse serving in France, World War I.

Straxus' actions led to the Daleks exterminating him on the planet Shrangor. With Straxus' death, Kotris' existence and works were erased from time.

DEyes 2: EYES OF THE MASTER / DEyes 3: THE DEATH OF HOPE / DEyes 3: RULE OF THE EMINENCE -> The Time Lords foresaw a future in which the Eminence overcame even the Daleks and became the only mind in existence at the end of the universe. The Celestial Intervention Agency conscripted the bald Master

877 LUCIE MILLER, MOLLY O'SULLIVAN AND GALLIFREY: The Big Finish audios featuring the eighth Doctor and Lucie Miller – and the *Dark Eyes* and *Doom Coalition* stories that follow on from them (the former opens in the wake of Lucie's death) – are a little tricky to place in Gallifrey's timeline. The Lucie audios were marketed as occurring "later" in the eighth Doctor's life, and they happen after the Doctor's travels with Charley Pollard (so, after *Zagreus*, which paves the way for the *Gallifrey* mini-series). Nonetheless, reconciling those stories against the events in the *Gallifrey* audios can feel a bit awkward. It's hard, for example, to imagine the Time Lords sparing the resources (or having the desire) to address issues related to Lucie and the Cybermen on Lonsis (*Human Resources*) once Gallifreyan society comes apart at the seams in *Gallifrey* Series 2.

Moreover, the Gallifrey-related Lucie stories, *Dark Eyes* and *Doom Coalition* all face the challenge that they involve Gallifreyan administrations and presidents that have nothing to do with President Romana and her inner circle from the *Gallifrey* audios. An unnamed male (not a male Romana that we can tell) is president in the first *Dark Eyes* series, a different one flees when Pandac ostracizes the High Council in *Doom Coalition*. We're never told what's up with Romana and her friends while all of this is happening. It's possible that those

other administrations come and go while Romana's team traipses about parallel realities in *Gallifrey IV* and *V*, but that coincides with the Dogma Virus incapacitating thousands of Time Lords and threatening the downfall of Gallifreyan civilisation (*Gallifrey III*) – a planet-wide turmoil that conspicuously isn't mentioned the Lucie audios, *Dark Eyes* and *Doom Coalition*. Also, if the non-Romana administrations happen while she's is off world from *Gallifrey III* to *VI*, is the memory of them wiped from existence once the reset button is hit to liberate the Time Lords from the Dogma Virus (*Gallifrey VI*)? That was surely not Big Finish's intention – the Lucie stories, *Dark Eyes* and *Doom Coalition* are presented to us as "counting", not something that's retconned away as a side-effect of *Gallifrey VI*.

Another possibility is to assume that different presidents happen between Livia's first and second terms (*Gallifrey VIII* and *Gallifrey – Time War* V1), and cram the Lucie, *Dark Eyes* and *Doom Coalition* stories into that space. That still doesn't explain why Romana and her allies are – just to pick an example – completely sidelined on their own homeworld during Padrac's insurrection in *Doom Coalition*. Romana becomes as CIA Coordinator at the end of *Gallifrey VIII*, but Farina holds the post in *DC 1: The Eleven* – a story in which Romana pretty obviously isn't president either.

to interfere with the Eminence's development, and thereby give the Time Lords control of it. When the Master usurped the undertaking for his own gain, CIA Coordinator-in-Extremis Narvin aided the eighth Doctor against him.

The Coalition

The Doctor's old friend Padrac was now a cardinal on Gallifrey. He ran many Matrix projections – in all save one, Gallifrey was destroyed through attrition, through the crossfire between other species, through temporal refugees, or even through an immense Time War. In just one, Gallifrey endured because all other species died.

Padrac spent years forming the Coalition, whose ranks included the Eleven and the Clocksmith, and worked to bring the outlying prediction about. Padrac also recognised the psychic potential in a young Academy student, Caleera, and gave her the menial post of assistant to a junior archivist. She grew resentful as expected, and became both his beloved and that of the Eleven.

Among its projects, the Coalition built the Crucible of Souls: an asteroid facility that, upon the destruction of the future, would convert the resultant life force into regenerative energy. The Time Lords need never die.[880]

Padrac's Coup

DOOM COALITION 1-4 -> The Coalition brought its various plans of universal obliteration to fruition. The eighth Doctor, Liv Chenka and Helen Sinclair stopped the Eleven from destroying Earth's Age of Reason in 1639.

Caleera stole one of the earliest TARDIS models, parked it in the Time Vortex and focused her mental might through a psychic amplifier – the first use of which destroyed the Voord homeworld. The Doctor, Liv and Helen were tricked into facilitating her transformation into a more powerful psychic being: the Sonomancer. The Doctor's trio confronted the Sonomancer in 1906, and elsewhen on the planet Syra. Alongside River Song, they also bested the Clocksmith's efforts to create a Doomsday Chronometer, and caused his demise in Rome, 2016.

As a result of the Coalition's actions to come, the universe's future was destroyed. The benevolent Eight failed to interfere in his past, and regenerated into the Nine. Padrac presented his Matrix projections to Gallifrey's Inner Council, but failed to win passage of a Harmony vote: that the Time Lords allow the future's destruction, but control it to their gain. Consequently, Padrac claimed the presidency after assassinating the president, Chancellor Jerasta and many dissenters. Councillor Ollistra and other objectors retreated to the safety of New York, the 1970s. The Doctor, Liv and Helen failed to net their help.

The Doctor's trio returned to Gallifrey an hour before the doomsday alignment of stars and planets that the Doomsday Chronometer had identified. Padrac wired the Sonomancer into the Resonance Engine – a psychic amplifier that would let her disrupt the alignment and wipe out the fabric of space-time. The Doctor exposed Padrac's manipulations of the Sonomancer, turning her against him. The Sonomancer lent Helen some psychic power, in exchange for Helen piloting a Battle-TARDIS to destroy the Resonance Engine. The resultant temporal explosion spread the Sonomancer throughout space-time, transforming her into the Red Lady that encountered the Doctor's party in 1963. She returned to Gallifrey as the reassembled High Council sentenced Padrac to freezing, and she tormented his mind in secret.

Helen's whereabouts remained unknown, and so the Doctor and Liv pursued the Battle-TARDIS' time-trail to find their friend...

Matt Fitton, one of the architects of *Dark Eyes* and *Doom Coalition*, suggested to us: "I think from Gallifrey's own perspective, Romana's return [from the parallel Gallifreys] must happen quite quickly (in Time Lord terms) so we leap from *Gallifrey III* to *VI*. Then, by the end of *VI*, there's some kind of status quo, isn't there? We have *VII* taking place in a far future which then gets undone by *VIII* – so possibly the wiggle room is there for a few successive administrations to come and go. But yes, any way you cut it, there are going to be some leaps of logic."

Whatever the case, it's accounted for (in *Gallifrey – Time War* V1) that Narvin – presenting himself as "Coordinator-in-Extremis" – pops in and out of *Dark Eyes* audios as part of his temporal apology tour, as he lit the match of the Last Great Time War (see *Gallifrey VI*). That, at least, needn't match Gallifrey's linear history,
as he's deliberately circumventing the laws of time.

878 Given the sheer number of Time Lord renegades at work in the universe throughout *Doctor Who*, it's hard to swallow that "all Time Lords are accounted for", i.e. have been recalled to Gallifrey. Still, the Timescoop used here is powerful enough to snatch in-flight TARDISes – a much greater use of the device than is seen in *The Five Doctors*.

879 Dating *Dark Eyes* (BF 8th Doc box set #1) - For the eighth Doctor, the story follows on from Lucie Miller's passing in *To the Death*. The story implies that only the eighth Doctor, Molly and the Dalek Time Controller remember the events that Kotris caused, and it's possible – but far from certain – that this is a rare instance of a portion of Gallifrey's own timeline being erased.

880 The background to *Doom Coalition*.

Gallifrey VIII, then VII

Lady Trey's Administration
Erased from History[881]

(=) GALLIFREY VIII: ENEMY LINES[882] -> The Monan Host and the Nekkistani engaged in illegal quantum mining on Terra Phallax, straining relations with Gallifrey. Ambassador Kalbez of the Warpsmiths of Phaidon and Castellan Plutus of Gallifrey conspired to exacerbate the divide, to goad a formal alliance between their two worlds. Plutus destabilised the Monan ship *Mauross*, and its core threatened to become a singularity. In one version of events, the second Romana deliberately triggered her regeneration aboard the *Mauross* – the resultant burst of energy strengthened the ship's internal shields, containing the breach. Leela escaped and enjoyed adventures in many locales, including Legion and Andromeda.

In another sequence of events, Braxiatel came back from "many years" in the future and rescued Leela and Romana before her regeneration. The *Mauross* went critical. Braxiatel urged Romana to prevent the chain of circumstances that would plunge Gallifrey into war. Romana agreed and resigned from the presidency; used Clause 5, Sub-Section 9 of the presidential code to name herself to a lesser position – the head of the Celestial Intervention Agency – and chose a rival, Councillor Livia of House Brightstone, as her replacement. Plutus and Kalbez were exposed and arrested.

Braxiatel and Romana's paradoxical efforts attracted the Watchmaker, and he offered Romana a choice: she could be rescued from the *Mauross*, and the resultant singularity could destroy Gallifrey. Or, she could die aboard the *Mauross*, in which case Gallifrey would perish in the war to come. Romana chose a third option, as a pocket universe had been created when timelines aboard the *Mauross* diverged. She reunited with the now-older Leela she had teleported away, and together they returned to the *Mauross* as it achieved critical mass. Their deaths tied off many temporal inconsistencies.

Romana Steps Down as President, Becomes CIA Coordinator

In the surviving history, the Adherents of Ohm were arrested before facilitating Omega's release. Romana accepted responsibility for failing to stop the *Mauross* from going critical and stepped down as president. She named herself head of the CIA, with Narvin as her deputy, and picked Livia as her successor.

Braxiatel remained the lone survivor of an erased timeline, and the Watchmaker offered to resolve the paradox of his existence – he could return to Dellah, Legion, the Collection or Gallifrey, or go into hiding, but not all of them. Braxiatel made his choice, deciding what sort of Braxiatel he wanted to become.

(=) GALLIFREY VII: INTERVENTION EARTH[883] -> Gallifrey had enjoyed "many years" of peace and harmony, even though its timelines became subject to flux, wither and change. Type 160 TARDISes were obsolete compared to the newest CIA Ships. President Romana foresaw that even such older TARDISes, however, could be called back into service. Gallifrey

---

881 LADY TREY: The third Romana, a.k.a. Lady Trey, as played by Juliet Landau, first appears in *Gallifrey* Series 6 as a projection (Matrix forged or otherwise) of the second Romana's future self. It constitutes something of a collision between past and future – albeit a useful one, as the Trey avatar aids Romana's crew in scuttling a Dalek takeover of Gallifrey. Later, Lady Trey twice appears in the flesh: as President in *Gallifrey* Series 7 (with no explanation of how her regeneration from the Lalla Ward Romana occurred), and also to reflect upon one of her past selves' adventures in *Luna Romana*. (Trey's inclusion there owed to a retooling of this double-Romana story, as necessitated by Mary Tamm's passing in 2012.)

Gallifrey Series 8, however, not only wrings *Gallifrey* Series 7 out of the timeline, it also depicts the second Romana's regeneration and then negates it – so much so, she finishes *Gallifrey* Series 8 uncertain as to whether her next incarnation will turn out like Trey or not.

(While some Time Lord bodies seem pre-determined, it's possible that others are more potluck, owing to the time and place they occur. Noticeably, Romana sported a different third body in *The Shadows of Avalon* and *The Ancestor Cell* – an incarnation that doesn't appear to have endured, however the War in Heaven resolved. And, of course, Romana knowingly cycled through potential bodies like she was trying to find a comfortable pair of shoes, during her first regeneration in *Destiny of the Daleks*.)

Events in *Gallifrey* Series 8 compel the second Romana to step down as president and appoint herself Coordinator of the CIA – the post she continues to hold in *Gallifrey IX: Time War*, further lessening the odds of Lady Trey's tenure as president even if she comes to exist. All of that taken into account, Big Finish's policy moving forward seems to be that the Landau Romana was President of Gallifrey in an aborted timeline.

882 Dating *Gallifrey VIII: Enemy Lines* (*Gallifrey* #8.0) -

was home to the Shrine of Pandak, and had a field office on Nekkistan.

Romana was now in her third incarnation, a.k.a. Lady Trey. In her last term in office, she favoured non-interventionist policies. Ace was now living on Gallifrey, but couldn't remember how that had occurred. She was one of the High Council's most adept field operatives, her TARDIS having special privileges on Romana's orders.

The Adherents of Ohm – followers of Omega devoted to facilitating his return, and who martyred Hedin – infiltrated high levels of Gallifrey's government. Omega escaped his anti-matter universe, but arrived at Gallifrey at a point before he'd done so, his mind housed in the body of Adjutant Coordinator Taurus. Rexx, as Taurus' previous incarnation, tricked Ace into taking the Hand of Omega from an alternate version of 2015 back to 2,986 BC, and creating a black hole that opened a pathway to Omega's anti-matter universe. Narvin pursued Ace to 2,986 BC, and was taken to Omega's anti-matter world along with her and a newly regenerated Rexx. Romana and Commander Lukas followed in a decommissioned Type 160 TARDIS.

Omega transplanted his essence into Taurus' body, and escaped his domain in Ace's vessel. Lukas' mind maintained Omega's realm as Romana, Narvin and Ace fled in the Type 160, but its systems failed after returning to our reality. As Taurus, Omega settled into Gallifrey's past. To her surprise, Romana was saved from death by asphyxiation by Irving Braxiatel and his TARDIS...

(=) GALLIFREY VIII: ENEMY LINES -> The High Council judged Narvin and Ace as accessories to the crisis and ordered their execution. Battle-TARDISes belonging to the Fifth Battalion fired time torpedoes at their Type 160, killing them both. Romana and Braxiatel conspired to write the Omega crisis out of history, and he went back many years to do so...

(=) LUNA ROMANA -> During Gallifrey's darkest hour, datacodes authorising the decommissioning of

the Quadrigger Vents – testing stations that had serviced the pre-Type 54 TARDISes, but had been obsolete for millennia – crossed the second Romana's desk. Every available trans-dimensional berth was being given over to creating a new generation of Battle-TARDISes. She felt the need to personally shut down Quadrigger Stoyn's old station, in honour of her two encounters with him.

LETH-ST: "The Enfolded Time" -> The Accord, who appeared as a misshapen representation of the human form, anticipated a horrifying future of warfare across all of space-time. To fortify the universe against this onslaught, the Accord helped to reconcile a discrepancy caused by the TARDIS' many visits to Earth, which had resulted in two decades of Earth history (1969 to 1989) occurring over a ten-year span.

The Accord lifted each person living on Earth during this time twenty times over, and had them meet themselves in holding domes. Each would forget these events upon their return home. Alistair Gordon Lethbridge-Stewart was the epicentre of the problem, as he'd spent such an extensive time in the Doctor's company. The Accord slipped a temporal marker into Alistair's DNA. Upon Alistair's return to 1st January, 1990, the marker would cause a vague awareness of the overlapping timelines, restoring some balance.

This season occurs "many years" *before* Series 7, and retroactively erases it from the timeline. Romana says it's been "centuries" since she last saw Braxiatel (in *Gallifrey IV: Disassembled*, presumably). Ace at this point is "barely out of training" and "hardly has any experience" as a Gallifreyan operative, but also references her time with Spacefleet (*Deceit*).

883 Dating *Gallifrey VII: Intervention Earth* (*Gallifrey* #7.0) - Romana has regenerated into her Juliet Landau incarnation, who was previously seen as a "future

Romana" (*Gallifrey* Series 6 and *Luna Romana*). Hedin died in *Arc of Infinity*. Ace's claim that the timelines on Gallifrey shift as a matter of course seems a massive change from previous eras of *Doctor Who*, *The Deadly Assassin* in particular. And yet, things have certainly got more fluid in the run-up to the Last Great Time War, as evidenced by the way that Braxiatel and Romana erase this whole chain of events in *Gallifrey* Series 8 – a revision to Gallifrey's history that would have been unthinkable in past eras.

The Last Great Time War

The Doctor's home planet was believed destroyed in the Last Great Time War, "a war between the Daleks and the Time Lords with the whole of creation at stake".[884]

The Daleks removed themselves from history to go off and fight the Time War.[885] They became experts at fighting TARDISes.[886] The Doctor led the battle in the Last Great Time War.[887] He was on the frontline during the war, and did "terrible things" just to survive.[898] He "butchered millions" during the Time War.[889] He fought on the front line, and saw the fall of Arcadia.[890]

Gallifrey and Skaro were both time-locked during the War, to prevent either side from interfering in the timelines of their homeworlds.[891] The Matrix had warned Gallifrey about this Time War for some decades beforehand.[892]

The Daleks Obliterate the Temporal Powers; Gallifrey Formally Declares War and Starts Resurrecting Its Dead; Ace Declared a War Casualty

GALLIFREY – TIME WAR V1: CELESTIAL INTERVENTION / SOLDIER OBSCURA -> On Gallifrey, President Livia had maintained power after being assassinated and regenerating. The War Council, operating with

increased agency and secrecy, conducted weapons research in Gallifrey's Loom Forests and established plantations for Battle-TARDISes. New laws required that the High Council, the War Council and the Celestial Intervention Agency jointly approve any immigration to Gallifrey. The President could dismiss the CIA Coordinator, but not the War Council leader.

Suddenly, the Dalek war machine overwhelmed and destroyed Gallifrey's temporal rivals – the Warpsmiths of Phaedon, the Nekkistani, the Monan Host and the Sunari were all brought to ruin. Of nine billion Warpsmiths, only five thousand survived to petition Gallifrey for sanctuary. The War Council approved this plea, in exchange for formally being allowed to operate in secret. Elsewhere, the War Council had developed Project Revenant: a resurrection engine tucked away in a pocket dimension, the Khybos Occlusion, that brought deceased Time Lords back to life. The War Council pondered opening the Omega Arsenal.

Under President Livia, Gallifrey formally declared war against the Dalek Empire. The Doctor refused to assist in the conflict.

The Daleks coveted control of the Obscura: a temporal scar that accessed a thousand realities and worlds. With Ace, Braxiatel lured the Daleks' main fleet to a Time Lord outpost, Obscura Station. One perfectly targeted missile, he hoped, as aimed by his mentor Danna, would wipe out the Daleks in a chain reaction and end the War. Danna's

884 *Dalek*
THE ROOTS AND FORMAL START OF THE LAST GREAT TIME WAR: The new series spends a lot of time referencing the Last Great Time War as a background detail – it's come and gone when the ninth Doctor meets Rose (*Rose*), and the ninth, tenth and eleventh Doctors spend a fair amount of time lamenting the War's outcome, although we do eventually see the final day of the conflict in *The End of Time* and *The Day of the Doctor*.

It's become fashionable to backtrack the conflict all the way to *Genesis of the Daleks* (12.4), when the Time Lords – having foreseen "a time when [the Daleks] will have destroyed all other lifeforms and become the dominant creature in the universe" – play their trump card, mastery of time travel, and dispatch the fourth Doctor, Sarah and Harry to castrate the Daleks in their early days. A theory runs that this early encounter with a Time Lord and his human friends, in the days when Davros discounts the possibility of "intelligent life on other planets", more quickly puts Gallifrey on the Daleks' radar. Russell T Davies concurred with that sentiment, both in an interview he gave to *Doctor Who Confidential* and a short account of the Time War that he wrote for *Doctor Who Annual 2006*. *Gallifrey VI* somewhat codifies the idea by showing Narvin, as head of the Celestial Intervention Agency, retroactively authorising the Doctor's trip to early Skaro in *Genesis* –

and becoming horrified to realise he may have just sparked the very time war he'd been working so hard to prevent.

Following *Genesis of the Daleks*, we're made to witness a series of escalating incidents between the Time Lords and the Daleks – including the Daleks conspiring to assassinate the High Council (22.4, *Resurrection of the Daleks*), even though it's not clear what they've to gain from such overt aggression. Either way, the Daleks' time-travel prowess throughout the classic series remains rather minor league. They dog the TARDIS in a time machine of their own (2.8, *The Chase*; 3.4, *The Daleks' Master Plan*), forge links between different time zones (4.9, *The Evil of the Daleks*) and craft rickety time corridors (*Resurrection of the Daleks*), but even as late as 25.1, *Remembrance of the Daleks*, they seem like a field team nowhere near the Time Lords' A-game. That gap, quite obviously, closes to nothing between the original series and the new. The Daleks marshal so much temporal firepower in the Time War's final day, Gallifrey is losing the War (see The Last Day of the Time War sidebar). We see engagements and battles from the War in the novel *Engines of War*, the comic series *The Eleventh Doctor Year Two* and a wealth of Big Finish audios (including the *War Doctor, War Master, The Eighth Doctor – The Time War* and *Gallifrey – Time War* box sets). In all of these, Gallifrey and the Daleks are evenly matched.

marksmanship had declined, and so Braxiatel killed her as a loose end. Braxiatel sacrificed Obscura Station to damage the Dalek fleet, then escaped... and wiped Ace's memory of him, to cover up his cowardice and the murder of his mentor. Braxiatel left Ace on twentieth-century Earth, and reported her and Danna as war casualties.

The War Master

The Time Lords resurrected the Master as the perfect warrior to fight in the Time War...[893]

WM: ONLY THE GOOD: BENEATH THE VISCOID ->

The Daleks tried to compel the War Master to reveal the secrets of his TARDIS, but he eluded them on the planet Gardezza, and destroyed their mothership with a wave of temporal backlash.

GALLIFREY – TIME WAR V1: THE DEVIL YOU KNOW[894] ->

Type 560 TARDISes were now in use.

Such were the War Master's crimes after his resurrection, the Time Lords had incarcerated him. Romana offered the War Master a pardon, in exchange for his aiding Leela in finding the freedom fighter Finnian Valentine, who had information about a game-changing resource. From Finnian, the War Master and Leela learned of a powerful energy source on the planet Arcking – whereupon the Master opened the door to his TARDIS, consigned Leela to the Vortex and went to find it...

The War Master Exits the War

WM: ONLY THE GOOD: THE GOOD MASTER / THE SKY MAN / THE HEAVENLY PARADIGM ->

A sentient Fixed Point in Time and Space protected the planet Arcking; it radiated a field that nullified injuries, and only let people die when their time had expired. The War Master failed to harness the Fixed Point, which was grounded out when Cole Jarnish – the only survivor of a medical ship downed by the Daleks – touched it. Arcking fell to a Dalek onslaught, and so the War Master enacted a new plan, which entailed accepting Cole as his travelling companion...

The War Master told Cole that as a Time Lord, he was forbidden to interfere, but suggested that Cole could safeguard worlds at risk. Cole joined an agrarian community, and became lovers with a woman named Elidh, even as the War Master indulged his passion for growing grapes and making excellent wine. The Time War's decay tainted the community, weakening its people. Cole devised self-replicating mechanical suits to seal out the rot, but the suits attained a level of sentience... and desired revenge against organics for what their people had suffered. As history had dictated that both Cole and the agrarian community should have died, the suit-people were a paradox created by a paradox. Unleashed into the Time War, they scorched causality and ruined many worlds.

The War Master took Cole to a Time Lord research facility in Stamford Bridge, 1976, and seized the Heavenly

---

Davies' article for *Doctor Who Annual 2006* weaves *Lungbarrow* and *The Apocalypse Element* into the foundations of the War, mentions the Deathsmiths of Goth (from the *DWM* back-up strip "Black Legacy") and adds the information that the Animus (*The Web Planet*) and the Eternals (*Enlightenment*) were caught in the fighting. The article was the first place related to the 2005 series that names Gallifrey as the Doctor's destroyed home planet (the new series later named it in *The Runaway Bride* and *The Sound of Drums*), and says Skaro was in "ruins" by the end – a reference that seems to support the claim in *War of the Daleks* that Skaro wasn't destroyed in *Remembrance of the Daleks*. We see Skaro in ruins in *Asylum of the Daleks*, but it's a bit hard to pin down when that story occurs in Dalek history. The *Magician's Apprentice/The Witch's Familiar* also takes place on Skaro – either a restored original, or a renamed secondary world fashioned like it.

As for when the War palpably begins... *Gallifrey – Time War* Volume 1 opens with the Daleks consolidating enough muscle to wipe out every major temporal power save for Gallifrey. This seems part and parcel of Captain Jack saying, in *The Parting of the Ways*, that "One minute [the Daleks were] the greatest threat in the Universe, the next minute they vanished out of time

and space", to which the Doctor replies, "They went off to fight a bigger war. The Time War." The downfall of its frenemies and the advancing Dalek forces pushes the High Council, under President Livia, to cross the temporal rubicon and formally declare a state of War with the Daleks.

885 *Bad Wolf*

886 *Journey's End*

887 *The Sontaran Stratagem*

888 According to Davros in *Journey's End*.

889 "The Stockbridge Child"

890 *Doomsday*

891 WD S4: *Casualties of War*. Gallifrey and Skaro's histories being "time-locked" makes sense, especially if the Daleks are mindful of the Time Lords' attempt to subvert their origins in *Genesis of the Daleks*.

892 *Gallifrey – Time War* V1: *Desperate Measures*

893 *The Sound of Drums*. Mention of the Master being "resurrected" probably covers all contingencies regarding his status prior to the new series. The Dalek Emperor's presence suggests that this occurs after Davros' "death" in the Time War.

894 For the War Master, this story occurs between episodes one and two of the *War Master* box set. For Leela, this is the start of events that lead to her being at

Paradigm: a timeline manipulator that revised history to favour correct decisions. The Time Lords had failed to meet the Paradigm's temporal energy requirements, but the War Master fed Cole – an uber-paradox – into it, making him cease to exist. The War Master programmed the Paradigm to create an ideal version of the universe, but the machine failed to cope with so many variables. Worlds were reborn and destroyed as the Paradigm's paradox wave ran amok.

To the War Master's horror, the paradox wave handed the Daleks many victories, and **the Dalek Emperor took control of the Cruciform**.[895] The War Master sent his TARDIS away, and facilitated his exit from the War using a Chameleon Arch, believing that whomever remained standing after the War would need a master...

The War Master was present when the Dalek Emperor took control of the Cruciform, and became so terrified that he fled. He turned himself into a human, and hid at the end of the universe.[896]

The Rebirth of Rassilon;[897] Braxiatel Exits the War

GALLIFREY – TIME WAR V1: DESPERATE MEASURES[898] **->** Two months after granting the Phaedons asylum, the War Council expelled all aliens and refugees within Gallifrey's time locks. The Council increased conscription, approved activation of N-Forms, and recommissioned bowships for War service. Gallfreyan forces engaged the Daleks in the Medusa Cascade. At Romana's urging, Gallifrey prepared new time locks and sky trenches.

The Daleks staged a concerted attack on the Kyphos Occlusion, hoping to capture the Resurrection Engine and with it rebirth deceased Gallifreyans as Daleks. Meanwhile, Livia conspired with the War Council and called for new elections. Admiral Valerian of the First Fleet, of the same lineage as Rassilon, stood for president against Romana. Term limits prohibited her serving as president in this incarnation – if successful, she would regenerate into her third body.

Valerian aired Romana's secret conversations with the Supreme Dalek – a failed bid for peace – and won the

the Pillars of Consequence, and – centuries later – meeting the War Doctor (*WD S4: Casualties of War*).
895 *The Sound of Drums*
896 *The Sound of Drums.* The Dalek Emperor's presence suggests that this occurs after Davros' "death" in the Time War.
897 A restored Rassilon leads the High Council in *The End of Time* and *Hell Bent*. In advance of that, *Gallifrey – Time War* V1 ends with his resurrection.
898 By now, from the viewpoint of the participants, the War has only been in progress for "two months"/"a few relative months".
899 *9thC: The Bleeding Heart*
900 *The Eleventh Doctor Year Two:* "The Organ Grinder"
901 *The Stolen Earth*
902 "The Forgotten"
903 *The Parting of the Ways, Doomsday, Utopia.* It's possible that the Emperor took power after the loss of Davros.
904 *WM: Only the Good: The Heavenly Paradigm*
905 *WD S2: The Neverwhen*
906 Gallifrey develops and loses its first Resurrection Engine in *Gallifrey – Time War* V1. Time Lord efforts toward mass resurrection continue in *WD S2: Infernal Devices*.
907 "Centuries" before *WD S4: Casualties of War*.
908 *The Unquiet Dead.* There seem to be some races in the middle – the Krillitanes (*School Reunion*) and Cynrog (*The Nightmare of Black Island*) - who were aware of the Time War, but weren't directly affected by it. In *Bad Wolf*, Captain Jack mentions hearing rumours of the Time War and the Daleks.
909 *Rose*
910 *The Day of the Doctor. The Bodysnatchers* claims that the Xaranti destroyed the Zygons' homeworld of Zygor. To reconcile these accounts, we have to suppose that either the Xaranti action was somehow part of the Time War, or it wasn't the original Zygon homeworld annihilated during the Time War.
911 "Weapons of Past Destruction"
912 *The End of the World*
913 *The Unquiet Dead*
914 *9thC: The Other Side*
915 *The Sontaran Stratagem.* There's no explanation as to who or what blocked the Sontarans' participation. The Doctor seems to have formally led the Time Lord forces.
916 "The Futurists"
917 "The Age of Ice"
918 *School Reunion*
919 The weapon seen in *The Eyeless* may be the device the Doctor talked about in "The Forgotten" that needed the Key, which in turn may be the Moment, the weapon that dooms Gallifrey according to *The End of Time*. If so, this link isn't explicitly established in any of those stories.
920 "Hotel Historia"
921 *Doomsday*
922 *Engines of War.* Borusa was freed from Rassilon's tomb (*The Five Doctors*) in *Blood Harvest*, but – as someone no longer officially part of Time Lord society – could have been captured during the War and clandestinely turned into the Possibility Engine.
923 *Doomsday*

presidency with 76% of the vote. Narvin destroyed the Resurrection Engine, triggering an explosion that wiped out the Supreme Dalek and its task force. Braxiatel decided that Gallifrey would lose the War and abandoned his homeworld.

One of Livia's agents stole the Resurrection Engine's core, and with it channeled the explosion's power through the Matrix. Valerian, being of Rassilon's blood, was transformed into his ancestor. As Livia and the War Council hoped, Rassilon was reborn to lead Gallifrey in the War...

Rassilon feared the Daleks would weaponise the Compassionate – a space-time event that erased anger and promoted empathy – and make the Time Lords tearful and useless on the battlefield. He hid the Compassionate on Galen, which became the Planet of Peace.[899]

The Early Days of the Last Great Time War

The Vortex burned with white noise from the War's beginning, preventing the participants from fleeing into the future.[900]

In the very first year of the Time War, at the Gates of Elysium, the Doctor saw Davros' command ship fly into the jaws of the Nightmare Child. The Doctor tried, and failed, to save Davros as his ship was timelocked. Dalek Caan came back in time and attempted made a thousand attempts to rescue Davros – he gained vast insight into the nature of time in the process, but drove himself insane. He finally succeeded where the Doctor failed, and broke Davros from the timelock.[901] The Doctor laughed in the face of the Nightmare Child.[902]

The Daleks were led by the Dalek Emperor.[903]

The Time Lords notched an early victory in the Time War, by ending Dalek operations on the planet Kito – but the War Master's gambit with the Heavenly Paradigm reversed this, enabling the Daleks to succeed.[904]

> (=) During the Time War's early years Time Lord scientists created the Neverwhen: a weapon that could wrench a target through the different stages of its development. The Neverwhen was tested above a world where thousands of Gallifreyan battalions had engaged the Daleks, and trapped the combatants in a cycle of death, life, past, future, primitive weaponry, advanced technology and more.

The War Doctor retroactively altered the Neverwhen's control matrix, letting the combatants perish rather than experiencing the continual hell of rebirth and death.[905]

The Last Great Time War created such malleability in the timelines, Time Lords – with great effort – could resurrect their fallen members. Resurrection en masse, however, remained out of their reach.[906]

Leela Lost at the Pillar of Consequence

In the War's early days, Leela led the charge to retake the Citadel of Desolation at the Pillar of Consequence. More than half her troops died while reaching the Dalek lines. Leela fired her staser just as a Disruptor Dalek engaged its time weapon, and the resultant energy release displaced her in time and space. She would later meet the War Doctor in the Obsidian Nebula.[907]

Devastation of the Time War

The Time War was invisible to "smaller" species, but was devastating to "the higher forms".[908] **Many planets, such as those of the Gelth, were affected. The food planets of the Nestene were wiped out.**[909] **The Zygons "lost their own world", which burnt during the first days of the Last Great Time War.**[910] The War devastated the Unon.[911]

The Forest of Cheem knew of the War, and thought it was impossible that any Time Lords could exist afterwards.[912] **The Gelth were forced to become incorporate spirits when their bodies were destroyed.**[913] Temporal remnants of some species remained, and a coalition of them – the Bigon Horde – worked to restore themselves to life on in Birmingham, 2012.[914]

The Sontarans consider this the finest war in history, but "weren't allowed to be part of it".[915] The Time War devastated the Hajor dimension.[916] Hotel Historia was a popular attraction that allowed holiday-goers to time travel to other eras, but its business plummeted when the Last Great Time War triggered a lapse in demand for time travel.[917]

It's possible that the civilisations of Perganon and Assinder fell during the Time War.[918] It's possible that the city of Arcopolis was depopulated during the Time War, and it's possible the Doctor activated the weapon that did so.[919] The Graxnix were one of the grubbier races involved in the Time War, and had very unreliable time technology.[920]

The Time Lords used the Genesis Ark, a dimensionally transcendental prison, to confine many thousands of Daleks. The Doctor was not involved with this.[921] The High Council authorised construction of a Possibility Engine, a device capable of seeing a myriad of strategies and battle outcomes. Ex-President Borusa was forcibly installed as the Engine's core, and held in a retro-evolved state of transition between his various incarnations. The Council deemed the Engine something of an abomination, and had it relocated to the Death Zone.[922]

The four Daleks that made up the Cult of Skaro stole the Genesis Ark and used a Voidship to leave the universe before the end of the War.[923]

The Time Lords used Chameleon Arches to hide spies among humanity and other races.[924] To the Time Lords in the War, silver flowers represented cowardice.[925] The Time Lords deployed the Orphaned Hour – an item from the Omega Arsenal, capable of resetting time in a designated radius – but it fell, damaged, to the planet Zoline.[926]

Dalek weaponry in the Time war included Entropy Engines, which created planet-sized bubbles, sped up time and turned everything within to dust. The harvested energy could power a Dalek time-armada.[927] The Time Lords still had the Demat Gun at their disposal.[928] The Daleks constructed Entropy Engines which aged planets to death, then funneled the resultant energy into Dalek time armadas.[929] Armaments in the Last Great Time War included Now Devourers: temporal napalm that eradicated linear time.[930]

The Eighth Doctor in the Time War

RIVER S1: I WENT TO A MARVELLOUS PARTY / SIGNS / THE RULERS OF THE UNIVERSE[931] -> A group of elites, the self-named Rulers of the Universe, created an enormous spaceship that travelled a figure eight through infinity. Within, the Rulers both partied and used their Manipulation Suite to strengthen or weaken cultures on many worlds, by influencing their crop production, economies, elections and more.

The Rulers hoped to take control of a SporeShip – a world-killer devised by the First Race – and market it, positioning themselves to gain influence in the Last Great Time War. One of their number, Bertie Potts, believed that River Song's expertise could help them. An operative of the Rulers presented himself to River as a future incarnation of the Doctor, then captured and cloned her. The faux Doctor employed different stratagems to seize a SporeShip, re-cloning River whenever an effort resulted in her death. The genuine article escaped and, extremely vexed at how she'd been treated, killed the man.

Potts strong-armed the eighth Doctor into attempting to disable a SporeShip. The First Race travelled forward from the dawn of time and, thinking their progeny had become too greedy and corrupt, attempted to detonate a SporeShip at galactic centre – such an act would exponentially consume all stars, recreating the universe to the First Race's designs. The Doctor used a chrono-mine to send the First Race back in time, even as River destroyed the Rulers' spaceship with anti-matter bombs.

Gallifreyan shock troops sometimes used pendants that enabled them to stay ten nanoseconds ahead of their opponents.

The High Council dispatched an operative to leverage Reeve – a service world strategically close to Gallifrey – into exclusively supplying their forces during the Time War. The eighth Doctor stopped the operative from killing Nyssa and destroying her medical ship, the *Traken*.[932]

---

924 *The Eighth Doctor – The Time War 1*, explaining the true purpose of the device used in *Human Nature/The Family of Blood*.
925 *The Eighth Doctor – The Time War 1*
926 *The Eleventh Doctor Year Three*: "Strange Loops"
927 "Weapons of Past Destruction"
928 *WD S4: Casualties of War*; the De-Mat Gun appeared in *The Invasion of Time*.
929 "Weapons of Past Destruction"
930 *Gallifrey – Time War* V1, *The Eighth Doctor – The Time War 1*
931 Dating *River S1: I Went to a Marvellous Party/Signs/ The Rulers of the Universe* (BF *The Diary of River Song* #1.2-1.4) - The eighth Doctor thinks his main contribution to the Last Great Time War is to "tidy up the mess", so it's presumably the conflict's early days.
932 *ST:* "A Heart on Both Sides"
933 We don't learn the outcome of Susan going off to serve in the War, and the new series makes no mention of her status.
934 Dating "The Forgotten" (IDW *DW* mini-series #2) - This seems to take place during the Last Great Time War, but it could also be the War in Heaven. We don't learn the name of the planet or the Doctor's jailers. The landscape is red, so resembles Gallifrey, but it could be another planet. The Great Key was once part of the De-Mat Gun (*The Invasion of Time*), and the suggestion seems to be that "the Moment" that the Doctor uses to end the Last Great Time War is an extension of it (we learn different in *The Day of the Doctor*). No explanation is given for why, if the Doctor lost all memory of Chantir, he's suddenly able to relate the story of how they met.
935 Writer Matt Fitton told us: "We generally try not to pin things down exactly and so restrict the storytelling, but *The Eighth Doctor – The Time War* series obviously come later than *Gallifrey – Time War* Volume 1." Captain Tamasan has now "been on the front line for one hundred twenty years" - not necessarily an indicator of how long the Last Great Time War itself has been running.
936 *CD,NM* V2: *Day of the Vashta Nerada*
937 Says the eighth Doctor in "The Forgotten". A line cut from *The Eyeless* said that the eighth Doctor was betrayed by his then-companions.
938 See the Numbering of the Doctor sidebar.
939 The War Doctor, *WD S4: Casualties of War*.
940 *Hell Bent*
941 *Twice Upon a Time*
942 *The Eleventh Doctor Year Two*: "Pull to Open", "Outrun","Running to Stay Still"
943 *The Twelfth Doctor Year One*: "Unearthly Things"

ST: "All Hands on Deck"[933] **->** The Time Lords asked for the eighth Doctor's help in the Last Great Time War, but he refused in part to protest the passage of emergency legislation, and the annexation of neutral territories "for their own good". He contented himself with helping those caught in the War's crossfire. Despite his efforts to distract his granddaughter, Susan answered Gallifrey's call for assistance in the War.

"The Forgotten"[934] **->** The eighth Doctor was jailed by robots as a War raged around him, turning the skies turn to blood. On Day 21 of his captivity, he gained a Malmooth cellmate, Chantir. On Day 37, he escaped and freed the other prisoners, which included a Sea Devil. Then he proceeded to his objective: the Great Key of Rassilon, which was stored in the same castle. He hoped he never needed to use it, but knew he might need something that removed millions from space and time at once. The Key would lock the Medusa Cascade forever, should it ever be required.

The Doctor eventually used the Key, and it erased his memory of Chantir.

THE SONTARAN ORDEAL -> A brief intersection with the Last Great Time War polluted the timeline of Drakkis, populating it with warring city-states throughout its history. The Sontaran Empire regarded the Time War as glorious and longed to join it, and so Ninth Sontaran Battlefleet investigated Drakkis' temporal flux. The eighth Doctor curtailed the Sontarans' operation, and assisted an honourable Sontaran, Jask the Foe-Slayer, in bringing the corrupt General Stenk to justice. He also aided the Paladin on Arapolis City, Sarana Teel, in forging a truce with the rival Barrowman City, but she rebuked him upon realising the Time Lords' culpability in her planet's downfall, and that no peace there could ever last.

THE EIGHTH DOCTOR – THE TIME WAR 1[935] **->** Gallifreyan technology now included Type 120 TARDISes and multi-barreled stasers. Time Lord strategists estimated that their troops were ten times more resistant to temporal corruption than the Daleks, and so Gallifrey's forces gained the upper hand by shredding space-time in targeted locales. The Daleks' quantum causality generators could create temporal duplicates of Dalek vessels, and their regeneration inhibitors could permanently kill Time Lord opponents. The Daleks attacked target worlds with hyper-evolution weapons designed to speed up time; the Time Lords fought back with temporal regression waves.

A Time Lord registered a psychic evaluation score so high, he could rewrite history and reality with his mind. Rather than let his power be abused, he used a Chameleon Arch to hide in history as a human: Quarren Maguire. Cardinal Ollistra embroiled the eighth Doctor in efforts to reclaim Quarren, who regained his Time Lord inheritance

– and took the added step of erasing himself from history. His wife Rupa enjoyed a happy life, with no memory of him.

The eighth Doctor saved Cardinal Ollistra when her scheme to weaponise Vashta Nerada against the Daleks went awry.[936] The eighth Doctor "started and ended this regeneration alone".[937]

The Eighth Doctor Regenerates

THE NIGHT OF THE DOCTOR[938] **-> The eighth Doctor did his utmost to avoid becoming part of the Last Great Time War, even as the escalating conflict between the Time Lords and the Daleks threatened all of reality. Fatally wounded on the planet Karn, the Doctor used a specially tailored Elixir of Life to regenerate into a warrior sometimes known as the War Doctor...**

The War Doctor

"I'm the stuff of nightmares. I'm a murderer, a warrior, a demon let loose in the storm. A man who's lost his conscience, his friends, even his name." [939]

It was said that the first – and, in many cases, last – thing one noticed about the Doctor of War was that he was unarmed. The Time Lord soldier Gastron was at Skull Moon during the Time War.[940] **The Doctor became known as the Butcher of Skull Moon.**[941]

The Daleks aligned with other dark powers during the War. The War Doctor led the Shrikefleet against a plasma-wheel armada on Vexa. At the Chronofracture on Borun, he routed the Exotic-Plunger. On Kether Prime, he fought the Heisenberg Mutations. The Daleks' front line went through the star cluster banks of the Gallifreyan Planetbirth Nursery on the planet Veestrax. The War Doctor wiped out three Dalek battalions, but the Daleks nonetheless killed six billion beings. The paradise world of Lujhimene, a.k.a. The Great Lush, was caught in the Dalek advance.[942]

The Doctor encountered a spider-like Aranox as the Time War raged.[943]

(=) Year A10%? of the Last Great Time War - "Four Doctors" (Titan) -> Potent weapons the Time War included Continuity Bombs, which altered an individual's timeline and allegiances. Paradoxes and alterations to causation led to significant upgrades in Voord strength and technology, and they allied themselves with the Time Lords during the Last Great Time War. The War Doctor watched as a Dalek saucer was brought down on Marinus, and the Daleks inside were subjected to accelerated evolution.

Abslom Daak Enters the Time War

THE ELEVENTH DOCTOR YEAR TWO -> The War Doctor and the War Master – outwardly incarnated as a young body – set aside their differences and worked together in the War. A young female knight, the Squire, became the War Doctor's companion. Toward the start of the War, an eccentric Dalek deathcult, the Volatix Cabal, had a singular trait among Dalekkind: creativity. The Cabal-Daleks took "ExterminHate" as their motto, and donned a range of eccentric casings.

On the planet Golgauth, the belief of the Overcaste tethered their "gods" – the Cyclors, multi-dimensional beings – to our reality. The Volatix Cabal brought the Cyclors into the Daleks' fold by promising them new thrills and sensations, and the Cyclors' first strike – composed of psychic balefire – annihilated the Glorious Thirteenth Vexillatio division from half a galaxy away.

The War Doctor readied the Psilent Songbox of Karn, a device that could rewrite collective belief, to cut the Overcaste's reverence of the Cyclors. On the eleventh Doctor's behalf, Alice Obiefune entered the Time War in the War Master's TARDIS, and activated the Songbox herself. The War Master tried to flee in his own TARDIS... whose navigation relied upon a chronal tumour that, with his escape, would never get made, creating a massive paradox. A time storm erupted, and a Volatix Cabal Dalek merged with it to become the Malignant: a creature that scourged the Overcaste for generations. The Cyclors were trapped between realities.

The War Doctor contained the chronal chaos by creating a living paradox-creature, the Then and the Now, then wrapped Alice inside it and returned her to his future self. As causality stabilized, all of the participants save Alice forgot these events. A chronal wavefront outwardly aged the War Master, and ejected him and his TARDIS from the Time War.[944]

Later, the Then and the Now brought Abslom Daak into the Time War so he could indulge in his passion for slaughtering Daleks.

WD S1: ONLY THE MONSTROUS[945] **->** The Time Lords adopted Dalek Time Destructor technology from Kembel into their Omega One space array, which the War Doctor used to obliterate the greatest Dalek time fleet ever assembled. Afterward, he recuperated on the peaceful planet Keska, and created a planetary force field that repelled the genocidal Taalyens. The Doctor stayed on Keska for 134 days and befriended a young woman named Rejoyce, who was left behind as the Doctor was forcibly summoned back to Gallifrey...

The Time Lord Selatrix and his associates favoured diplomacy rather than confrontation with the Daleks. Selatrix negotiated a pact in which the Daleks would cease hostilities in exchange for a small empire of a Thousand Worlds, including Keska.

The War Doctor returned to Keska twenty years after he'd left, and found that the Prime Dalek intended to renege on Selatrix's deal – the Daleks were working to remove the magnetic cores of the Thousand Worlds and install planetary drives, creating planet-sized missiles that would overcome even Gallifrey's defences. The Daleks killed Selatrix, but the Doctor curtailed the Daleks' drilling operations. Cardinal Ollistra destroyed all Daleks in the Thousand Worlds with Battle-TARDISes. The Taalyen leader stabbed an older Rejoyce – the Doctor didn't know if she'd lived or died, but later found Keska a prosperous world, where his friend had become a symbol of peace.

WD S2: INFERNAL DEVICES -> The Daleks seeded Varga plants with regeneration inhibitors, making them effective against Time Lords. The High Council harshly kept order in its own ranks; those who disobeyed orders were subject to court-martial or vapourisation. The War Doctor was tasked with recovering a timeline-rewriting Annihilator that the Daleks had developed, but instead destroyed it. He was placed under arrest by his own people, and dubbed Prisoner 101...

Cardinal Ollistra of the War Council conscripted the War Doctor to investigate matters on Asteroid Theta-12, where a breakaway Dalek group was hoping to reverse-engineer their evolution and restore the Kaled race – an innovation to the war effort. Dalek High Command surrounded Theta-12 with a warfleet. The Doctor and Ollistra used an Anima Device – a psychic weapon capable of intensifying disagreements – to make all Daleks present obliterate themselves. Ollistra downloaded research on the Neverwhen onto a data stamp, and with it directed the Doctor's TARDIS there...

---

944 Before our eyes, the temporal flux causes the pre-pubescent War Master to age into the adult version played by Derek Jacobi. This is problematic, as *Gallifrey – Time War* V1 (set before *The Eighth Doctor – The Time War* audios) and *War Master: Only the Good: The Heavenly Paradigm* have the (outwardly) older War Master leaving the War before the War Doctor comes about. One possibility is that the temporal flux seen here regresses the War Master along his own timeline. Either way, the mind-wipe explains why the Doctor and the Master don't remember serving together in the War (*The Sound of Drums*).
945 Time Destructor technology first appeared in *The Daleks' Master Plan*.

GALLIFREY

THE NUMBERING OF THE DOCTOR: Throughout the new series, the ninth, tenth and eleventh Doctors have been in active denial that the incarnation played by John Hurt ("the War Doctor") ever existed. Consequently, the numbering of the Doctor's lives hasn't taken the Hurt incarnation into account, and – as with the faces of the "Morbius Doctors" – the War Doctor is absent from montages of the Doctor's faces (*The Next Doctor*, *The Eleventh Hour*, etc.). Nonetheless, as *The Night of the Doctor* readily proves, the John Hurt Doctor followed on from the eighth Doctor and we see him, in turn, regenerate into the ninth Doctor at the end of *The Day of the Doctor*. In *The Time of the Doctor*, the eleventh Doctor leaves no doubt as to the order of his lives when he explains to Clara that he's the thirteenth (and last, he thinks) incarnation. Pursuant to that, he verifies that the Tennant Doctor burned up a regeneration after a Dalek shot him in *The Stolen Earth*, but – owing to the unique circumstances of that story – was able to keep the same physicality and persona. This means that the character as played by David Tennant is the Doctor's *tenth* incarnation and *eleventh* incarnation by one way of counting, the *eleventh* incarnation and *twelfth* incarnation by the other.

Within the fiction, the War Doctor's actions (or so everyone involved thinks before the truth is revealed in *The Day of the Doctor*) are regarded as so against the grain of what the Doctor stands for that he thematically sets aside his acquired name while fighting the Last Great Time War. In *The Name of the Doctor,* the War Doctor says "what I did, I did without choice, in the name of peace and sanity". And yet, *The Day of the Doctor* is predicated on the fact the Doctor has a choice to use the Moment – the "without choice" comment might allude to the fact this "warrior" incarnation is actually the decision of the eighth Doctor, as revealed in *The Night of the Doctor*. ("I don't suppose there's any need for a Doctor any more. Make me a warrior now."). "What I did" is also clearly a reference to more than just the destruction of Gallifrey – he has renounced the name before the *The Day of the Doctor* starts, not as a result of its climax. Clearly, he spends the entire incarnation – many centuries, and perhaps his third longest life, after the eleventh and first incarnations – behaving like a warrior, not the Doctor.

To the viewers at home, the point is somewhat diminished by captions that prominently introduce John Hurt as "the Doctor" in *The Name of the Doctor* and "the War Doctor" in *The Night of the Doctor*. Also, *The Day of the Doctor* ends with the Hurt version briefly reclaiming the mantle of the Doctor: "For now, for this moment, I am the Doctor again." From this point, the War Doctor is accepted back into the fold – as seen in the closing sequence of the story and the montage of faces during the end credits, as well as BBC publicity material. The scripts for *The Day of the Doctor* referred to the Hurt incarnation as "Omega", by way of curtailing spoilers. The widely accepted convention has become to call the John Hurt incarnation the War Doctor (some of the toys – an action figure and replica sonic screwdriver – prefer the "Other Doctor") and to skip him (and, for simplicity's sake, the duplicate Tennant persona) in the numbering of the Doctors – meaning that Eccleston is the ninth Doctor, Tennant the tenth, Smith the eleventh and Peter Capaldi the twelfth. The continued tidal wave of the BBC's marketing and *Doctor Who* product output conforms to this. A few online commentators have attempted to swim against the tide to "correct" for the Hurt Doctor, alternatively calling the Eccleston version the "tenth Doctor" and so forth, but are in the minority and likely to stay that way.

More constructive pedantry can be gleaned from the fact that the War Doctor's introduction highlights the fact that the Doctor's "incarnations" and "regenerations" are not actually the same thing. The former denotes the number of bodies he's had, while the latter indicates the times he's undergone the regenerative process. So, it would be inaccurate to call the Doctor as played by Patrick Troughton the Doctor's "second regeneration" – he has only regenerated once by that point (we'll accept for sake of argument that every time the actor playing the Doctor changes, within the fiction it's via the same process, although the television series seems to state otherwise). It's a concept that's easy enough to intuit, and was aired on screen in *The Five Doctors* when the first Doctor – becoming acquainted with the fifth Doctor – asks "Regeneration?" and is told "fourth" in reply.

As a result of the introduction of the War Doctor, and while it seems sensible to call the Jodie Whitaker incarnation "the thirteenth Doctor", it would be highly inaccurate to say she is their "twelfth regeneration" (it's their fourteenth – we saw the regenerations in *The Tenth Planet*, *The War Games*, *Planet of the Spiders*, *Logopolis*, *The Caves of Androzani*, *Time and the Rani*, *Doctor Who – The Movie*, *The Night of the Doctor*, *The Day of the Doctor*, *The Parting of the Ways*, *The Stolen Earth*, *The End of Time*, *The Time of the Doctor* and *Twice Upon a Time*). A supreme pedant might enjoy the fact that, between the end of *The Day of the Doctor* and *The Stolen Earth*, and only between those stories, the number of the Doctor's incarnations and regenerations match.

(=) The War Doctor's TARDIS had such expertise with navigating space-time, it successfully penetrated the Neverwhen; Ollistra followed in her Battle-TARDIS. The Gallifreyan battalions and Daleks trapped within the Neverwhen – including Temporal Weapons Daleks, the Spider Forms of the fifth Skaro Devastation, and the Diamond Daleks of Benvessa – had been cycling through the past and future of their races' developments. Ollistra hoped to combine the Neverwhen's control matrix with the Anima Device to break Skaro's timelock, and plunge the Daleks into endless civil war. Instead, the War Doctor ended the suffering of those within the Neverwhen by altering its parameters, ending its effects upon its deployment. Having disobeyed the High Council, he fled in his TARDIS as a war criminal...

WD S3: AGENTS OF CHAOS ->

The timeship *Infinity* served as a TARDIS carrier in the War. It had six hangers, each with berths for tens of thousands of Battle-TARDISes.

Although officially a renegade, the War Doctor agreed to Cardinal Ollistra's request that he stop a human agent, Lara, from helping the Daleks to invade Earth in 1961. Afterward, he was asked to rescue Ollistra from the clutches of a Sontaran, General Fesk, on the planet Rovidia. Fesk hoped to open a third front in the War, but the Doctor enabled a Dalek time fleet to wipe out Fesk and his Eighth Sontaran Battle Fleet. He then tried to escape with Ollistra in the Battle-TARDIS of a fallen Time Lord, Vassarian...

The Dalek Time Strategist hoped to use Ollistra's command codes to access the Eye of Harmony link in Vassarian's Battle-TARDIS. Through it, Dalek time squads would detonate dark matter and destroy the main Eye of Harmony's containment field, obliterating Gallifrey in the resultant black hole. The War Doctor and Ollistra preventatively destroyed the Battle-TARDIS' Eye of Harmony link, and made one last jump in the Ship to a nearby space station, which the Daleks swiftly attacked...

Leela Re-Enters the Time War

WD S4: CASUALTIES OF WAR ->

The Daleks pursued the War Doctor and Ollistra to Belltox, where the two Time Lords coordinated a holding action until the town of Fairgill was evacuated. With help from Schandel, a time-travelling War correspondent, the Doctor edited footage about a super-cannon that tricked the Daleks into position... and then blew them up with a bomb, along with half the city. A dying Dalek killed Schandel. Schandel's editor released edited footage of the War Doctor vowing action against the Daleks, and so the Dalek Time Strategist's warfleet sterilised Belltox, killing billions.

The War Doctor and Ollistra withdrew to the Obsidian Nebula, where they found that the Lady of Obsidian, an infamous resistance leader, was actually Leela. Owing to the temporal accident at the Citadel of Desolation, she had become saddled with all memories of her life and her possible lives. Nonetheless, her guerilla unit had both vexed the Daleks, and guarded a temporal breach that enabled the Unlived – savage humans from potential timelines – to manifest in our reality. A security detail of twenty Battle-TARDISes arrived to collect Ollistra, but she ordered them to hold the line in the Grend System. The Doctor sealed off the breach, ending the Unlived's existence. Ollistra's detail endured until the Fifth Time Fleet arrived and routed the Dalek forces.

The Doctor retrieved his TARDIS and healed Leela's mind with its artron energy. Everyone she knew on Gallifrey was now gone. The Dalek Time Strategist began a final strike against the Time Lords' homeworld...

(=) The Daleks ventured into the Enigma Dimension, a reality where gravity, time and matter had no constant. The Dalek Time Strategist contained some of the beings there – the Enigmas, who to our senses manifested as blank spheres. The Strategist coerced the Enigmas to alter universal history to

946 *The Ninth Doctor Year One:* "The Bidding War". We don't learn the outcome of these events. *State of Decay* took as given that the fourth Doctor and the second Romana killed the last of the Great Vampires.
947 The background to *Engines of War.*
948 *Churchill: The Oncoming Storm*
949 Dating *Engines of War* (NSA #54) - The events seen here lead into *The Day of the Doctor*, with the War Doctor appearing as he's seen on screen (not the younger version of John Hurt glimpsed in *The Night of the Doctor*). Cinder had heard, rightly or wrongly, that the War has now been going on for "over four hundred years" (ch1). It's after the Master has been lost in the War (ch10), as reported in *The Sound of Drums*.
The Doctor's trip to Skaro in *Genesis of the Daleks* is

here acknowledged as the first volley in the Last Great Time War (ch21). A De-mat gun appeared in *The Invasion of Time*. Bowships are mentioned (ch10), although as these were created to skewer giant vampires (*State of Decay*), it's not readily obvious how effective they'd be against the Daleks. The Battle TARDISes and time torpedoes used here sound very much like the ones seen in "The Stockbridge Horror". Cinder finds a pair of "skinny black jeans and a Greenpeace T-shirt" (ch17) in the TARDIS wardrobe, possibly a reference to Sam Jones from the eighth Doctor novels.
950 *The Coming of the Terraphiles*
951 The Doctor speaking to the Master in *The End of Time*. The Doctor described the stone Daleks in *The Big Bang* as "footprints of the never-were", and River Song

replace the Time Lords with the Daleks, and so the War Doctor, Ollistra and Leela abandoned Gallifrey in the TARDIS as the Capitol became a Dalek city.

The hostage Enigmas empathised with the War Doctor's sadness and Leela's purity of mind, and refused to cement the revisions to history. Ollistra tried and failed to push the Enigmas to write the Daleks out of history. The Doctor believed the Time Lords had fought for so long, they would never be anything other than warriors, and would find another foe to combat even if the Daleks were gone... and so he asked the Enigmas to erase both the Daleks and the Time Lords, to stop the Time War from ever happening. The Enigmas declined this action as well. The Dalek Time Strategist's forces unwisely fired energy weapons in the Enigma Dimension, causing a chain reaction that wiped them out, even as the War Doctor, Ollistra and Leela returned to Gallifrey.

THE NINTH DOCTOR YEAR ONE[946] **->** The War Doctor visited the Gallifreyan Time Station Zenobia II, in the Empusa Cluster, and saw – on Cardinal Ollistra's orders – Councilor Voltrix opened a rift that let the Great Vampires join the fray against the Dalek saucers...

The Dalek Emperor charged the Eternity Circle – five Daleks cast in a deep blue, with silver globes – with developing new weapons against the Time Lords. The Circle directed Dalek forces to attack human colonies in the Tantalus Spiral, all to harness the temporal radiation emanating from the Tantalus Eye.[947] As the Last Great Time War went against the Time Lords, they fashioned intelligence-augmenting Auger Stones to aid their ground troops.[948]

ENGINES OF WAR[949] **->** It was said that in purely linear terms, the Last Great Time War had now raged for more than four hundred years. Time Lords were still limited to thirteen lives each, and had locked their De-mat guns away. Gallifrey's bowships burned in the War, and thousands – possibly tens of thousands – of dead or grievously wounded TARDISes were disposed of beneath the Capitol.

Time Lord efforts to interfere in the Daleks' history had counter-productively created Daleks augmented with attributes of their fellows from potential timelines. The Daleks themselves expanded upon this, giving rise to the Skaro Degradations: Dalek mutants such as Gliders, Spiders and Temporal Weapons Daleks. Rassilon similarly tinkered with Time Lord evolution, casting the failed results of his work into the Death Zone.

The War Doctor accompanied the Fifth Time Lord Battle Fleet to assess the Dalek operations in the Tantalus Spiral, and his Ship fell to the planet Moldox as a Dalek assault wiped out the assembled Battle TARDISes. He met the Dalek hunter Cinder, and discovered that the Daleks were forging a massive cannon that, powered by the Tantalus Eye's temporal energies, would erase Gallifrey and the Time Lords from the whole of history.

Cinder accompanied the War Doctor to Gallifrey as he warned the High Council of the temporal cannon. Rassilon considered a proposal to deploy the Tear of Isha – a stellar engineering tool capable of collapsing black holes, and kept in the Omega Arsenal – against the Tantalus Eye, an act that would kill billions across the twelve Tantalus worlds. The Doctor followed Rassilon as he went to the Death Zone and consulted with ex-President Borusa, who had been incorporated into a Possibility Engine. Borusa predicted that the age of the Time Lords was drawing to a close, but that annihilating the Tantalus Eye would prolong it.

The War Doctor openly challenged Rassilon's decision to use the Tear, causing Rassilon to both order the Doctor's arrest and – as he and Cinder fled – to task Karlax, a rival of the Doctor's, with killing him. The Doctor saved a mortally wounded Karlax after a Dalek assault force destroyed the five Battle TARDISes the Celestial Intervention Agency had placed at his disposal, and allowed him to regenerate in the TARDIS' Zero Room. The new version of Karlax attempted to kill the Doctor after he diverted the Tear of Isha to a star at the end of time, and shot Cinder dead instead. The War Doctor ejected Karlax from the TARDIS, allowing the Daleks to murder him.

The Daleks intended to slave the War Doctor to a Predator Dalek shell, which would have tapped the raw power of his mind and marked the start of a new Dalek age. The War Doctor instead took the Borusa-Possibility Engine to the Tantalus Eye, where the ex-President sacrificed himself to rewrite time and destroy the Eternity Circle and their troops.

Cinder's death helped motivate the War Doctor to bring about a final end to the Last Great Time War...

The Time War got desperate towards the end – at this time, the Doctor was the only version of himself anywhere in the multiverse.[950]

"You weren't there in the final days of the War, you never saw what was born. Not just the Daleks but the Skaro Degradations, the Horde of Travesties, the Nightmare Child, the Could-have-been-King with his armies of Meanwhiles and Never-weres, the War turning to Hell." [951]

Towards the end of the Time War, as the Daleks circled Gallifrey and all seemed lost, some Time Lords dispersed memory lanterns to preserve their recollections. The Time Lord Hiroth's lantern would influence Joan of Arc in the fifteenth century.[952]

The Last Day of the Time War [953]

"[There's] one face I've tried very hard to forget. He was the Doctor who fought in the Time War, and that was the day he did it. The day I did it. The day he killed them all. The last day of the Time War... in that battle, there was a man with more blood on his hands than any other, a man who would commit a crime that would silence the universe. And that man was me." [954]

THE LAST DAY [955] -> Four hundred Sky Trenches protected the city of Arcadia on Gallifrey. Nothing in history had ever penetrated even one such trench, yet the Daleks found a means of doing so, and initiated a final invasion of Gallifrey...

1STD V2: THE PLAGUE OF DREAMS [956] -> In the final offensive against Gallifrey, the Daleks mounted numerous incursions against the first Doctor's timeline. Two Time Lords associated with the High Council contained the damage, but feared direct intervention near the Doctor's first regeneration. The Player, a Time Lord who'd been avoiding the War for years, was tasked with fixing the problem in the sixteenth century.

"Sky Jacks" [957] -> Coordinator Engin, in his role as Keeper of the Matrix, had struggled to allocate resources so the Matrix could absorb the experiences of every Battle TARDIS the Daleks destroyed, and every slain Time Lord. Lady Priyan informed Engin that the Lord President had decreed they should prepare themselves for the final sanction, even though the Doctor had possession of the Moment. Engin and Priyan took comfort in the knowledge that even if Gallifrey fell, the Matrix would preserve their race's memory.

THE END OF TIME -> By the last day of the War, Dalek saucers had crashed on Gallifrey and the dome of the

---

says that the Doctor's fate if he's erased from the universe would see him "trapped in the never-space, the void between worlds", so we might infer the Never-Weres are beings who exist despite being erased from history.

952 *Engines of War*, *The Memory of Winter*, "The Memory Feast" – all written by George Mann.

953 THE LAST DAY OF THE TIME WAR: *The Day of the Doctor* is set, as a caption tells us, on "the last day of the Time War". We have known that the Doctor's actions decisively ended the Time War since *Dalek*, during the ninth Doctor's exchange with a Dalek:

The Doctor: "Your race is dead! You all burned, all of you. Ten million ships on fire. The entire Dalek race wiped out in one second."

Dalek: "You lie!"

The Doctor: "I watched it happen. I made it happen."

Dalek: "You destroyed us?"

The Doctor: "I had no choice."

Dalek: "And what of the Time Lords?"

The Doctor: "Dead. They burned with you. The end of the last great Time War. Everyone lost."

Before *The Day of the Doctor*, the implication seems to have been that if the Doctor hadn't acted, the Time War was never going to end, at least not until the structure of the universe had been so damaged that nothing would be capable of surviving. One Time Lord offers this description in *The End of Time*:

"This is only the furthest edge of the Time War. But at its heart, millions die every second, lost in bloodlust and insanity. With time itself resurrecting them, to find new ways of dying over and over again. A travesty of life. Isn't it better to end it, at last?"

...which suggests that the Time Lords and Daleks are locked in an endless cycle of violence. Presumably, during a Time War, you can go back and refight every battle you lost, but so can your enemy – meaning that you will both be committed to a literally endless fight. Without the Doctor's intervention, there may well have never been a "last day of the Time War". The Doctor's actions broke the cycle by destroying all the Time Lords and all the Daleks in existence, except for him. The War ended because there was literally no one left to fight.

The End of Time muddied the waters a little by showing that, in fighting the War, the Time Lords had become as ruthless as the Daleks. In *The Night of the Doctor*, Cass is as scared of the Time Lords as the Daleks, and chooses to die rather than set foot in a TARDIS.

The Day of the Doctor presents what seems to be a very different scenario – the Daleks were on the verge of victory, and the Doctor had to destroy Gallifrey to destroy the Daleks (mirrored in the choice he faces in *The Parting of the Ways*). In this scenario, if the Doctor hadn't acted, it would still have been "the last day of the Time War", because the War would have ended with a decisive Dalek victory.

To simplify, as presented in *Dalek*, the Doctor wiped out the good guys to wipe out the bad guys. As presented in *The End of Time*, the Doctor wiped out two sets of bad guys. *The Day of the Doctor* has the Doctor wiping out two sets of bad guys, and his guilt stems from the fact that one set wasn't quite as bad, with some on that side being innocents.

Despite the Doctor saying he didn't have a "choice", in both the exchange from *Dalek* quoted above and when the War Doctor speaks in *The Name of the Doctor*, he clearly chooses to instigate the destruction of Gallifrey. He enacts a plan to steal the Moment, we see that he's under no immediate, personal physical danger when he plans to activate it, he declares what he's

Capitol been cracked open. Gallifrey was at the furthest edge of the War. At the heart of the conflict, millions died every second, lost in bloodlust and insanity, time itself resurrecting them to find new ways of dying over and over again in a travesty of life. A Time Lord seer, the Visionary, confirmed that this was the last day of the Time War.

The Doctor had learned that Rassilon planned the Final Sanction, the end of time – a rupture that would continue until it ripped the Time Vortex apart. The Time Lords would ascend, become creatures of consciousness alone – free of their bodies, time and cause and effect – while creation itself ceased to be. The Doctor had to stop them, and the High Council, led by Rassilon, knew that the Doctor possessed the Moment and would use it to destroy the Daleks and Time Lords alike.

The Harold Saxon Master believed that if the Doctor killed Rassilon, "Gallifrey could be yours".[958]

The Visionary had a prophecy that there would be two survivors beyond the final day: the Doctor and the Master. Learning this, the High Council approved Rassilon's plan to retroactively implant the sound of drums in the mind of the Master while he was a child, as an escape route for his people. There were two votes against this strategy, including one cast by the Woman in White. Rassilon sent the Master a white-star point on Earth, Christmas Day 2009. Gallifrey and Rassilon briefly rose from the Time War, but the tenth Doctor and the Master fought back, banishing the Time Lords – including the Woman in White – back to the hell of the Time War. The Master learned that Rassilon had been responsible for the sound of drums in his mind, and fell back into the Time War, fighting him.

The Time Lords removed the sound of drums plaguing the Harold Saxon Master, and they parted ways. He would next meet the Doctor, and his own future self, Missy, aboard a Mondasian colony ship.[959]

In readying to deploy the Moment, the War Doctor returned to the barn from his childhood...[960]

---

going to do.

From just the information in *The Day of the Doctor*, it's hard to fault the War Doctor's original plan.

He commits genocide, two counts of genocide, but while the ninth Doctor seems to understand that committing genocide, even against the Daleks, is an evil act, the War, tenth and the eleventh Doctors are positively gleeful about their new plan, which remains genocidal. So the War Doctor's crime, in his own eyes, was not "genocide".

Taking *The Day of the Doctor* at face value, the War Doctor killed his own people... but if he hadn't acted, all the Time Lords were all about to die anyway when the Daleks conquered Gallifrey. He ends the War, saves the rest of the universe from either Dalek domination or structural collapse. It's easy to see why he's upset, but it's hard to conclude he did anything other than engineer a victory only he could while in the jaws of total defeat. Unable to save the Time Lords, he at least saved everyone else.

If we take other stories into consideration, though, perhaps we should infer that this wasn't going to be the Last Day of the Time War. The Time Lords, facing utter defeat, would have been able to initiate some sort of reset, revision of history or retcon that returned the universe to square one – the "over and over again" referred to in *The End of Time*. Perhaps next time, the Time Lords would be on the verge of victory when the Daleks did the same. And so on, in an endless cycle. Perhaps the Daleks and Time Lords would be unaware this was the second, third, fourth or thousandth time they'd replayed the War, but the Doctor did know. It is this cycle that the Doctor is ending by using the Moment. Finally, there was a Last Day of the Time War.

954 The eleventh Doctor, *The Day of the Doctor*.

955 Dating *The Last Day* (Series 7 minisode) - The story leads into *The Day of the Doctor*.

956 Dating *1stD V2: The Plague of Dreams* (BF CC #11.4) - The status of the War places this epilogue between *The Last Day* and *The Day of the Doctor*. The Daleks operating in the Last Great Time War target the first Doctor's history in the four stories in *The First Doctor* Volume 2 (AKA *The Companion Chronicles* Series 11): *Fields of Terror*, *Across the Darkened City*, *The Bonfires of the Vanities* and *The Plague of Dreams*.

957 Dating "Sky Jacks" (IDW Vol. 4 #9-12) - The caption reads: "Gallifrey. Last Day of the Time War." *The Eight Doctors* established that Engin's role of coordinator (*The Deadly Assassin*) was refashioned into that of Keeper of the Matrix (*The Trial of a Time Lord*), and also that Engin isn't the Keeper seemingly killed by the Valeyard (*The Ultimate Foe*).

958 *Journey's End*, possibly a sign that the Doctor had followers on Gallifrey during the War, or perhaps even was formally next in the order of succession.

959 *World Enough and Time/The Doctor Falls*

960 *Listen*

Gallifrey Frozen in Time, the Daleks Defeated, the War Doctor Regenerates

THE DAY OF THE DOCTOR[961] -> Gallifrey was currently home to 2.47 billion children.

The Time Lords had nearly emptied their Omega Arsenal, a storehouse of forbidden weaponry, against the Daleks but were nonetheless losing the war. On the Last Day of the Time War, warfleets containing a billion billion Daleks arrived to bombard Gallifrey from orbit. The War Council sent urgent word to the High Council that Arcadia – Gallifrey's second city – had fallen, and that the Daleks were now converging on the Capitol. The War Doctor used a gun to blast the words "No More" on a wall in Arcadia before leaving to deploy the Moment – a powerful galaxy-destroyer – in seclusion. Use of the device would equally annihilate the Daleks and the Time Lords.

The Moment's sentient operating system adopted a form that would be important to the Doctor – that of Rose Tyler – and opened time portals to let the War Doctor visit the men he would become if he ended the War as intended. The War Doctor journeyed to England, 1562, where he met the tenth Doctor, the eleventh Doctor and Clara. All three Doctors and Clara entered suspended animation until the twentieth century, then returned to the Time War in the tenth Doctor's TARDIS.

The Doctors realised that if they froze Gallifrey in an instant of time, it would remain safe in another universe while the attacking Dalek fleets destroyed themselves in their own crossfire. To the universe, it would appear as if the Time Lords and the Daleks had mutually annihilated one another. The calculations required would have taken centuries to complete, so the first, second, third, fourth, fifth, sixth, two versions of the seventh, eighth, ninth and twelfth Doctors all coordinated efforts with the tenth, eleventh and War Doctors. Combined, the Doctors' thirteen TARDISes froze Gallifrey in time.

The Doctors returned to their respective timelines as the tenth, eleventh and War Doctors returned with Clara to twentieth-century London.

These events had temporarily put the Doctor's

---

961 Dating *The Day of the Doctor* (X7.15) - A caption specifies that it's the "The Last Day of the Time War", the day that the Doctor obliterated both the Daleks and his own people.
962 *Journey's End*
963 "Fugitive", "Don't Step on the Grass".
964 "The Forgotten"
965 Seen on the first page of "Agent Provocateur". The Capitol Dome looks intact and no Dalek wreckage is visible, unlike *The End of Time*.
966 *The Fires of Pompeii*
967 "Sky Jacks", presenting a state of affairs very much in doubt following revelations in *The Day of the Doctor* and *Hell Bent*.
968 *Dalek*
969 *The Doctor's Wife*
970 "Agent Provocateur"
971 "The Forgotten". This is apparent confirmation that Susan no longer exists after the Time War.
972 *The Stolen Earth*
973 Jack, in *The Parting of the Ways*, for one.
974 *The Vampires of Venice*
975 "The Forgotten". This is apparent confirmation that *Rose* occurs soon after the end of the Last Great Time War.
976 *The End of the World*. *The Day of the Doctor* portrays what really happened on the Time War's last day, but the ninth, tenth, War and eleventh Doctors don't remember that, owing to the timelines being out of synch.
977 *School Reunion*
978 *Dalek*
979 *Bad Wolf/The Parting of the Ways*

980 *Victory of the Daleks*
981 *The Tenth Doctor Year Two*: "Old Girl"
982 *The Unquiet Dead, Father's Day*.
983 *Rise of the Cybermen*

ONLY ONE DESTRUCTION OF GALLIFREY?: The intention of both the creative team behind the EDAs and the new series producer Russell T Davies is that the destruction of Gallifrey seen in *The Ancestor Cell* and the destruction of Gallifrey reported in the new series are entirely separate events. As the Doctor destroys Gallifrey once while preventing the Enemy and Faction Paradox from taking control of his homeworld, then (presumably after rebuilding Gallifrey, as he pledges to do at the end of *The Gallifrey Chronicles*) he destroys Gallifrey again in a great war with the Daleks, it would seem clear these are indeed mutually exclusive. Russell Davies likened it, in a *DWM* column, to the two World Wars humanity fought in quick succession.

But could Gallifrey have been destroyed just once? The Doctor certainly experiences the destruction of Gallifrey twice, in two different contexts. But this doesn't rule out it being the same *event*. If there was only one destruction of Gallifrey, he and his future self would have to be present, and both culpable.

Surprisingly, this already fits what we know from *The Ancestor Cell* - the Doctor's future self, Grandfather Paradox was there. Moreover, this future eighth Doctor fits everything we know about the Doctor who fought the Time War: fighting a vast time war has scarred him, made him lose his faith in humanity, made him a little callous. In *The Gallifrey Chronicles* recap of the end of *The Ancestor Cell*, Grandfather Paradox even wears a leather coat. As for the destruction of Gallifrey – the

timesteam out of synch. As time rebalanced, the War Doctor forgot that he'd helped to save Gallifrey rather than destroying it, meaning the ninth, tenth and eleventh Doctors would bear the burden of that false knowledge. With his body wearing a bit thin, the War Doctor regenerated into the ninth Doctor.

The tenth Doctor suggested that his previous self had been "born in battle, full of blood and anger and revenge".[962]

The Advocate was transported across time and space from the Shadow Proclamation to the Medusa Cascade and into the Time War. She arrived seconds before the Doctor used the Moment and time-locked the War, and so was killed and reborn over a thousand years as time lost meaning. She became little more than stardust, and eventually drifted out of the War through the same tear in time as Davros. Once reformed, she decided that the Doctor was a great threat to the universe.[963]

"I saw Gallifrey sacrificed when the Cruciform fell. I turned the Key in the lock and I doomed them all." [964]

Time Lords outside the Capitol Dome, including a young girl, looked up and were bathed in a blue light. Gallifrey was destroyed in one second.[965] **Gallifrey was "lost in fire".**[966] Gallifrey's downfall caused the simultaneous download of every Time Lord's memories into the Matrix, and the unprecedented inrush of information caused the Matrix to attain sentience. In Gallifrey's last instants, the Matrix uploaded its newborn consciousness into the only surviving TARDIS: the Doctor's Type 40 time capsule. The Matrix intelligence became stuck in the TARDIS' inner workings.[967]

The Doctor wiped out the entire Dalek race, and their ten million-strong war fleet, in one second. The Time Lords – save for the Doctor – also perished as a result of this. The Doctor instigated this destruction, referred to as an "inferno". He "watched it happen... made it happen".[968] **The Doctor killed all the Time Lords.**[969] Many other planets, star systems and galaxies

were destroyed at this point.[970]

The Last Great Time War was timelocked.

Aftermath of the Last Great Time War

The Time Lords' secrets died with them, as well as artifacts such as the Seal of Rassilon. Susan was taken from the Doctor, everyone was taken from him.[971]

"Time Lords are the stuff of legends. Belong in the myths and legends of the higher species." [972]

Some people regarded the Time War as a legend.[973] The Saturnynians knew the Doctor as the "man that let an entire race turn to cinders and ash".[974]

"Remember what happened immediately after the War. Remember Rose." [975]

The Doctor believed that his home planet was reduced to rocks and dust, and he was the only survivor.[976] He stated, "I lived... everyone else died."[977] **A single Dalek fell through time to the early twenty-first century.**[978] **The Emperor Dalek's flagship also survived, and limped to the solar system "centuries" before the year 200,000.**[979] **A single Dalek Progenitor survived, and was later recovered by the last surviving Daleks.**[980] Matrix Agents, aspects of the Time Sentinel, survived the Last Great Time War and were programmed to deal with the Time Lords' loose ends. They tried to kill the tenth Doctor in ancient Gallifrey.[981]

Time was more fragile without the Time Lords to protect it, and some of the rules governing time were suspended.[982] **Travel between parallel realities had been "easy" when the Time Lords "kept their eye on everything", but following their downfall, the walls of reality closed and travel between parallel worlds became nearly impossible.**[983]

Doctor's description in *Dalek*, "I watched it happen ... I made it happen... I tried to stop it" is a neat summary of his actions in *The Ancestor Cell*.

If this theory is true, the Doctor's memories of the War are conflicted because he was *literally* fighting his (earlier) self over "pulling the lever" that destroyed Gallifrey. So it's *Grandfather Paradox* who has fought the Last Great Time War, the Daleks, the Nestenes and so on. He goes back to *The Ancestor Cell* having done all that, confronts his earlier self... who then outsmarts him by blowing up Gallifrey. Following this defeat, it's Grandfather Paradox who regenerates into Eccleston

(growing his arm back in the process).

For this to be the case, it involves the introduction of the tiniest bit of extra information: the War that's being fought in the future has the Daleks in it and at some point they make a decisive move on Gallifrey. What the "current" eighth Doctor doesn't know – but which his future self does – is that, in the future, the War's going so badly that the Daleks are heading for Gallifrey. The Daleks were ruled out as "the Enemy" in *Alien Bodies*, but they don't need to be for this theory to work – they just need to be capable of hitting the Time Lords hard.

The Shadow Proclamation[984]

"What is the Shadow Proclamation, anyway?"...
"Posh name for police. Outer-space police."[985]

The Time Lords gave the Shadow Proclamation strict rulings on the subject of manipulations in Time and Space before they left.[986] **The Shadow Proclamation followed the Holy Writ of the Shadow Proclamation, and considered Time Lords "the stuff of legend"**[987]

The Shadow Proclamation was led by the Shadow Architect.[988] **The Shadow Proclamation employed the Judoon as shock troops.**[989] The Judoon had teaspoon-sized brains, and developed a monosyllabic tongue too basic for language translators.[990]

There were at least twenty-three conventions to the Shadow Proclamation.[991] T'Keyn Bylaws of Convention 15 of the Shadow Proclamation accorded the accused the right to defend themselves in the T'Keyn's holographic Nexus.[992] Convention 15 of the Shadow Proclamation gave invaders the option of ending hostilities and dispersing without harm.[993]

Article 27 of the Shadow Proclamation pertained to the forfeiture of recording equipment.[994] The extraction machines used to create Golems were forbidden under Article 29.8 of the Shadow Proclamation.[995] **Article 57 of the Proclamation forbid the destruction of Level Five planets.**[996] Article 1768C of the Shadow Proclamation allowed for a trial operating under "innocent until proven guilty", a legal standard found on eighty-seven member planets and 12,932 affiliated worlds.[997] Clause 374 of the Shadow Proclamation authorised lethal force to retrieve a culturally valuable artifact.[998]

Matryoshka Drives – engines containing whole universes – contravened at least nine articles of the Shadow Proclamation, and were banned by every civilised race.[999] The Shadow Proclamation underestimated the success and reach of the Time Market.[1000] The Gentlemen of the Dice kept operating *just* within the bounds of galactic law, frustrating the Shadow Proclamation's efforts to shut them down.[1001]

Rumours and anecdotal evidence suggested that the Shadow Proclamation had enforced the boundaries of a far galaxy by seeding a virus that would activate if any of that galaxy's populations ventured into space. One civilisation ventured toward the stars anyway, casing the virus to kill off a third of the beings in that galaxy. If this story was nothing more than propaganda, it was nonetheless effective at keeping some of the lesser races in line.[1002]

According to Captain Jack, the Shadow Proclamation charged members of the Saviour's race with the trading of sentient beings as slaves.[1003] The eighth Doctor expected that the Shadow Proclamation would crack down on Bakri Resurrection Technology.[1004] The Shadow Proclamation banned a weapon from the Mullafone System, which looked like a pink (the traditional color of fighting there) hairdryer, which was equipped with three mini black holes.[1005]

Ninth Doctor Era

"Weapons of Past Destruction" -> The Unon, a race of scientists and explorers, barely survived contact with the Time War. Their seers foresaw a new universal conflict as races contested to take the Time Lords' place, and so – using leftover Gallifreyan technology – the Unon became armoured centaurs and pre-emptively blocked other races from acquiring time prowess. When the peaceful Excrothians conducted time-travel experiments, the Unon razed their world. The diminished survivors became armoured warriors: the Lect.

984 THE SHADOW PROCLAMATION: This group is first referenced in *Rose*, is seen on screen in *The Stolen Earth*, and also appears in *The Magician's Apprentice*, "Fugitive" [c.2545] and *The Darksmith Legacy* books. The Proclamation's native time zone is never specified, and it's unclear if it has access to time travel (meaning the characters seen there might not even originate from the same era) or if the Proclamation perhaps operates (as with Gallifrey) on its own continuum. It's evidently been around for some time, though – in *The Stolen Earth* (set in 2009), the Shadow Proclamation consider the disappearance of Pyrovillia as a "cold case", suggesting they investigated it at the time. "Agent Provocateur" has them active at the time of Ancient Egypt.
985 Donna, the Doctor in *The Stolen Earth*.
986 "Fugitive". This is difficult to reconcile with the actions of Rassilon in *The End of Time*, so it might represent the actions of another Time Lord authority, although seemingly not the Doctor himself.
987 *The Stolen Earth* has one of the Shadow Proclamation talk of the Holy Writ, and another tell Donna "God save you", suggesting this might be some form of religious organisation.
988 *The Stolen Earth, The Magician's Apprentice*.
989 *The Stolen Earth*
990 CD, NM V1: *Judoon in Chains*, explaining why Judoonese doesn't translate in *Smith and Jones*, etc.
991 *Beautiful Chaos* (p211).
992 "Dead Man's Hand"
993 "Space Oddity"
994 9thC: *The Bleeding Heart*
995 *The Beast of Orlok*
996 *The Eleventh Hour*
997 DL: *The Pictures of Emptiness* (p15).

The ninth Doctor, Rose and Jack found themselves in the middle of a Unon-Lect conflict that ended with an entropy engine devastating both sides. The Doctor's group took some Unon survivors to a peaceful world.

Tenth Doctor Era

The Axis, formerly used to cauterize errant timelines, was "gone" now.[1006]

THE TENTH DOCTOR YEAR THREE -> Without the Time Lords, the personality of Time Sentinel – a collective Matrix function forged to preserve the Vortex's integrity – increasingly fractured. Its Aspect Red zealously sought to eliminate the tenth Doctor as a threat to Time, but its Aspect Blue aided him. The Moment quietly aided the tenth Doctor in defeating the Time Sentinel, and bent the rules of time so the twelfth Doctor could rescue his companion, Gabby Gonzalez.

Eleventh Doctor Era

THE DOCTOR'S WIFE[1007] **->** The sentient planet called House existed in a bubble universe. It fed on rift energy, and over the course of half a million years had killed hundreds of Time Lords to feast upon the refined Artron energy in their TARDISes. Before doing so, House had to transplant the sentience of each TARDIS into a living being. House's junkyard included the remains of one hundred TARDIS models.

The eleventh Doctor received an emergency message from a Time Lord slain by House: the Corsair. He took Amy and Rory into House's bubble, where House transferred the "living soul" of the TARDIS into a young woman named Idris. When House learned that the TARDIS was the last of its kind, he took control of the Ship and attempted to fly back to the universe, marooning the Doctor in a collapsing universe with a dying Idris. They scratch-built a TARDIS from House's junkyard, and caught up with the House-TARDIS. As Idris' body died, the TARDIS Matrix was released and reclaimed control of the Ship, annihilating House.

The Doctor's TARDIS had about thirty console rooms in its archives, including ones the Doctor would use in future – until now, he had only changed the "desktop pattern" about a dozen times.

---

998 *DL: The Depths of Despair*
999 *The Ninth Doctor Year One*: "Sin-Eaters"
1000 *Borrowed Time*
1001 *ST: The Jago & Litefoot Revival*
1002 *The Glamour Chase*
1003 *TW: Broken*
1004 "A Matter of Life and Death"
1005 *TW: Forgotten Lives*
1006 *The Tenth Doctor Year Two*: "Old Girl", detailing the fate of the locale first seen in *The Axis of Insanity*.
1007 HOW MANY TIMES HAS THE DOCTOR BEEN MARRIED?: Depending on how you define terms, at least six.

The earliest we know of in the Doctor's lifetime was seen in flashback in *Cold Fusion*, a book that established that prior to the Doctor leaving Gallifrey, he was married to Patience, his former tutor (also seen in *The Infinity Doctors*). Patience is presumably Susan's grandmother. Much later in *The Adventuress of Henrietta Street*, the eighth Doctor married a ritualist named Scarlette on a platonic basis, as a means of becoming vested with the authority to serve as a protector of Earth.

Since 2009, the new *Doctor Who* has married off its central character three times. The tenth Doctor is said to have married Queen Elizabeth I – while this event isn't seen on screen, it's referred or alluded to so often (*The Shakespeare Code*, *The End of Time*, *The Beast Below* and *Amy's Choice*), it seems safe to assume that it happened. The eleventh Doctor very prominently marries River Song in *The Wedding of River Song*, and prior to that winds up married to Marilyn Monroe in *A Christmas Carol*.

An alternate future seen in *Human Nature* (TV) entailed the Doctor's "John Smith" persona living out his life as the husband of nurse Joan Redfern. *The Aztecs*, amusingly enough, entails the first Doctor becoming accidentally engaged to an Aztec woman, Cameca, when he fails to realise the cultural significance of making her a cup of cocoa.

In *Death in Heaven*, Clara, while pretending to be the Doctor, claims: "I've been married four times, all deceased." On screen, he's only been married three times (River Song, Queen Elizabeth I, Marilyn Monroe), but the count – as confirmed by Steven Moffat in *DWM* #282 – assumes he was married to the mother of the child that produced Susan.

Later, in *The Husbands of River Song*, River claims that the Doctor also married Cleopatra.

In *Death Among the Stars*, the twelfth Doctor seems befuddled as to whether an Elvis impersonator or the real man performed his wedding ceremony in 1969 – possibly just a mis-remembering of his marriage to Marilyn Monroe. Otherwise, it's hard to know what, if anything, to make of that remark.

To date, the Doctor has not literally married the TARDIS, despite *The Doctor's Wife* (as the title suggests) taking this ongoing element of the programme's subtext and, in large measure, turning it into text.

Absolm Daak Joins the TARDIS, Leaves

THE ELEVENTH DOCTOR YEAR TWO[1008] -> The Malignant had murdered about a billion of the Overcaste. The survivors captured the eleventh Doctor and Alice, and put the Doctor on trial for having both destroyed their gods, the Cyclor, and created the Malignant. In escaping the Overcaste's Palliative Ark, the Doctor and Alice met an older version of the War Doctor's companion, the Squire.

The Overcaste purchased the services of two bounty hunters... a paradoxical creature, the Then and the Now, and the chainsword-wielding Abslom Daak. The TARDIS hid the cryo-frozen body of Daak's beloved, Taiyin, within its interior, forcing Daak to aid the Doctor's trio.

The Doctor suspected that the Master had framed him for the Overcaste's downfall, and found that the Master had influenced a renegade legion of Sontarans to wear goatees. The 17th Veteran Cohort bred a suicidal Sontaran eschatomic warhead that obliterated the rogues. River Song aided the Doctor in determining that the Master had squirreled his TARDIS away on Shada. As he could not enter the Last Great Time War himself, the Doctor manipulated Alice into going there in the Master's TARDIS to learn more.

She returned as the Squire – a Volatix Cabal sleeper agent – overpowered the Doctor's group, went to the Overcaste's Ark and summoned the Malignant. The Squire fully banished the Cyclors, enabling the Malignant and the Volatix Cabal to seize their godhead... they would become the Dalek Gods, and instigate a new age. Daak and River killed the Squire, and the Doctor safely bottled the Dalek Gods within the Then and the Now. The Cyclors and the Overcaste ascended to Nirvana.

Afterward, the Then and the Now took Abslom Daak back to the Time War, so he could kill as many Daleks as he liked.

THE ELEVENTH DOCTOR YEAR THREE[1009] -> On Zoline, three opportunists used the Orphaned Hour's time-resetting abilities to make technological leaps. As the enigmatic Golden Triangle, they profited while their world's environment suffered. The eleventh Doctor, Alice and the Sapling retrieved the Orphaned Hour, and left the diminished Triangle with a copy of *Carbon Sequestration for Children: A Beginner's Guide*. Damaged in the Last Great Time War, the Orphaned Hour approached critical mass... and so the TARDIS euthanised the Orphaned Hour within its heart.

The Scream merged with both the Sapling and the TARDIS' core, to usurp all life by spreading seeds of itself throughout space-time. The Doctor and Alice tricked the Scream into duplicating itself, then looking away, whereupon it forgot about itself and ceased to exist. The Sapling returned to normal.

"Sky Jacks" -> The sentient, malevolent Matrix mind (a.k.a. the Hypothetical Gentleman) trapped within the Doctor's TARDIS failed to manifest on Earth in 1851.

1008 Curiously, given how the new series frets about whether the Doctor is the last of his people or not, Shada's cells are said to contain "a lot" of Time Lords. It's said that the Overcaste thrived "1200 years" ago, that the Malignant has attacked them for "fifty generations"/ "a thousand years", and yet somehow it only assaulted the Overcaste homeworld "500 years" ago. Later in the story, the Doctor says that it's been afflicting the Overcaste for "2000 years".
1009 Dating *The Eleventh Doctor Year Three* (Titan 11th Doc #9, 11-13; "Strange Loops"/ "Hungry Thirsty Roots") - By Zoline's local calendar, it's the "close of sixteenth cycle".
1010 "Hypothetical Gentleman"
1011 *Journey to the Centre of the TARDIS*
1012 Dating "Supremacy of the Cybermen" (Titan mini-series #1-5) - It's the aftermath of *Hell Bent*. The Tomb of Rassilon is here located beneath the Capitol; in *The Five Doctors*, it's in the Death Zone. Rassilon remarks that the General (*The Day of the Doctor, Heaven Sent*) has served Gallifrey for "thousands of years".
1013 Dating *Extremis* (X10.6) - Placing this sequence on Gallifrey's timeline seems fair game, partly because of the twelfth Doctor and Missy's participation, and also because the Fatality Index keepers appear up-to-date on universal events (including the scarcity of post-Time War Time Lords and the Doctor's kill count). Doing so kicks the can to the side some, however – the more one considers where Missy's "execution" should go in universal history, the more vexing and slippery it all becomes.

A caption says Missy was executed "A long time ago"; the Doctor uses the same phraseology in *Smile*. The phrase tends to evoke something like *Star Wars*, meaning this happened "quite a long ways back in the past", but it doesn't give us a useful date.

If the Fatality Index sequence takes place in A Long Time Ago, however... how did Nardole get there from Darillium (*The Husbands of River Song*)? He can't have possession of River's vortex manipulator, since she'd need it to time-hop from Darillium to the Library (*Silence in the Library*) and any adventures in-between. Did the computer copy of River in the Library pass it along, then? Again, no, since Nardole doesn't have such a useful device at his disposal in Series 10 – if he did, he could've easily retrieved the Doctor and Bill, and avoiding asking Missy's help, in *Empress of Mars*, never mind that a Manipulator could've averted the whole spacewalk in *Oxygen* and the Doctor going blind. However, if Nardole went from Darillium to the Missy's execution

The Matrix made a second bid for freedom via portals through the TARDIS' Eye of Harmony, but the TARDIS stymied this effort by diverting energy to create a massive room within its interior. This housed Tipperary Station: a floating base that became home to wayward beings who flew through the Matrix's portals. The Matrix tricked the eleventh Doctor into "exiting" the TARDIS, and he spent three years at Tipperary failing to realise he was still within his Ship's environs. Clara was ejected from the TARDIS and, from her point of view, reunited with the Doctor moments after she'd left him. The Doctor trapped the Matrix in an infinite time loop, and returned the Tipperary residents home.[1010]

The eleventh Doctor's TARDIS contained *The History of the Time War*, which included mention of his real name. *Encyclopedia Gallifreya*, available in liquid form, was at least eleven volumes long.[1011]

THE TIME OF THE DOCTOR -> Gallifrey remained trapped in another universe, but the Time Lords sought to re-enter our reality through a Crack in Time on the planet Trenzalore. Stymied in doing so, the Time Lords agreed to Clara Oswald's request that they grant the dying Doctor a new regeneration cycle.

Twelfth Doctor Era

(=) "Four Doctors" (Titan) -> In one version of events, the twelfth Doctor never recovered from Clara betraying him, kicked her out of the TARDIS, and spent centuries travelling alone and becoming increasingly bitter. Eventually, he accepted the Voord Group Mind's offer of friendship and compassion, and became its leader. By manipulating his past selves via information placed at the Museum of Terrible Fates, the rogue twelfth Doctor brought about his own origin. He then worked toward the day that the Voord would invade every strategic point in the universe, and become the new Time Lords.

The tenth and eleventh Doctors, as well as Clara, Alice, Gabby and a younger version of the twelfth Doctor, were tricked into coming to Marinus as the rogue twelfth Doctor detonated a Continuity Bomb. A tiny Weeping Angel the eleventh Doctor had strategically placed in a parcel of comic books sent Gabby back along her own timeline, to give everyone a second chance...

The tenth, eleventh and twelfth Doctors and their companions returned to Marinus and dealt with the Continuity Bomb. They persuaded the rogue twelfth Doctor to end his schemes, and use a Dalek time-weapon to regress the Voord along their own timeline, even though this would undo his existence...

DARK WATER / DEATH IN HEAVEN -> Missy told the twelfth Doctor that Gallifrey had returned to its original coordinates, but upon going there, the Doctor found only empty space...

THE MAGICIAN'S APPRENTICE -> An alarming number of suicide moons prompted the Shadow Architect to deploy an under-regiment across two sectors. Colony Sarff approached the Architect, but failed to learn the Doctor's location.

Gallifrey Returns to the Universe

HELL BENT -> On Gallifrey, the people of the Dry Lands both knew and admired the Doctor.

The Time Lords unfroze Gallifrey and relocated it back to the universe, toward the end of time. All Matrix prophecies agreed that the Hybrid would one day stand in Gallifrey's ruins, and so Rassilon, to learn more about the creature, had the twelfth Doctor imprisoned in his own confession dial. The Doctor escaped the dial on his own terms, exiled Rassilon and the High Council, and left his homeworld – with Clara Oswald – in a spare TARDIS.

(=) "Supremacy of the Cybermen"[1012] -> The exiled Rassilon forged a pact with some Cybermen clinging to life at the end of the universe, and returned to Gallifrey with a fleet of Cyber-ships. He intended to usher in a new Gallifreyan era, but the Cybermen dispatched Cyber-Arks through time to rewrite history. Moreover, they infused the Eye of Harmony with the regenerative energy of many Time Lords, intending that as the universe perished, they would forge the Age of the Cyberiad.

The twelfth Doctor directed the Eye's regeneration energy into the past, erasing the Cybermen's alterations. Rassilon remained ousted, and only he and the Doctor remembered these events.

Nardole Assists the Twelfth Doctor in Keeping Missy Under House Arrest

EXTREMIS[1013] -> The universe had such an abundance of life – over a billion intelligent species were active in one galaxy alone – that an unnamed race thoughtfully considered the matter of how to kill them all. They excelled at executions, and founded the Fatality Index to catalogue all terminations in reality.

Said executioners captured Missy, and per custom required another Time Lord to terminate her. The twelfth Doctor threw a switch that blasted Missy, and he took an oath to guard her body for a thousand years... but had tweaked the apparatus to merely render her unconscious. Nardole had tracked the Doctor down, and aided him in relocating Missy to a vault beneath St Luke's University Bristol. They began their vigil of keeping her imprisoned.

The Testimony Foundation knew the Doctor as the Imp of the Pandorica, the Shadow of the Valeyard, the Beast of Trenzalore, the Butcher of Skull Moon, the Last Tree of Garsennon, the Destroyer of Skaro and the Doctor of War.[1014]

without benefit of time travel, then events on the Fatality Index world must happen in the fifty-fourth century (concurrent with the end of *The Husbands of River Song*), which is fine... save for the "A Long Time Ago" caption.

Could that phrase be figurative, meaning it was "A long time ago" in the Doctor's personal timeline? It's a little unsatisfactory to say, but that might be the case. Taking the problematic claim that the Doctor spends "fifty, even seventy" years teaching at St Luke's as true (see the Series 10 dating notes), that might count as being "A long time ago", allowing *Extremis* to happen in the fifty-fourth century with no time prowess on Nardole's part (or that of the Fatality Indexers, if they summoned the Doctor once his night on Darillium ended). It also better fits with the universe being *teeming* with life ("a billion intelligent species" in the Indexers' galaxy alone) if it's later in the course of universal history than earlier.

1014 *Twice Upon a Time*

TOWARDS A PRONOUN: The casting of Jodie Whittaker as the Doctor leaves you with a peculiar problem if you happen to be midway through revised and expanding a million-word *Doctor Who* chronology when it's announced: what pronoun should we use to refer to the Doctor?

We can presume that the show will refer to the thirteenth Doctor as "she," "her" and so on, rather than insist on the masculine pronouns. BBC press releases already do, as do various behind the scenes people in interviews.

So the pronoun we use when we're talking about the Jodie Whittaker Doctor seems easy enough.

The issue is how we refer to past incarnations, now.

In real life, with the understanding that there are people with wildly different beliefs, we've reached a broad agreement that individuals have the right to assign their own pronoun. If someone identifies as female, we use female pronouns to refer to her. This is, generally, retroactive – we would refer to "her childhood". The directors of *The Matrix* movies, the Wachowskis, are both transgender women. Even when we refer to their work on *The Matrix*, before their gender transition – when they were credited as "The Wachowski Brothers", indeed - we ought to use female pronouns, and the first names Lana and Lilly.

This is not as newfangled an idea as some on the political right would have us believe. We don't object to the idea that Mary Shelley wrote Frankenstein, or blink at this sentence from Wikipedia: "Mary Shelley, aged 18, and her lover (and later husband) Percy Bysshe Shelley, visited Lord Byron at the Villa Diodati by Lake Geneva in Switzerland". Retroactively, Mary Godwin became Mary Shelley, once she married Shelley.

So... should *Ahistory* now revise pretty much every entry to say things like "The third Doctor visited Metebelis III and she retrieved a blue crystal"? We don't believe so.

But... how should *Ahistory* refer to the Doctor's past generically? How about the sentence "The Doctor heard legends of scary monsters as a child, and these scared him"? How about the sentence "When asked why he left Gallifrey, he has given differing accounts"?

These seem far more problematical, now – it sets up the "default" Doctor as male, with a female Doctor as some sort of aberration.

We haven't seen Jodie Whittaker in action as the Doctor, yet, but we can safely assume that the circumstances and format of the show mean that the Doctor's switch in gender won't be depicted as particularly analogous to any real-life situation. This is a unique, science fiction problem, and not something where we need to look to the experiences and social pressures acting upon the real-life transgender community.

As ever with this book, we look to the show itself for guidance.

There are a few precedents from previous stories. In the earliest, *The Hand of Fear*, the male Eldrad copies Sarah's "strange form" and generates a body that superficially, at least, looks female. (Eldrad is a silicon-based lifeform, composed of rocks and crystals, so in practical terms is probably as "female" as a statue of a woman, rather than being biologically female.) Both the Doctor and Sarah refer to Eldrad as "she" and "her" when Eldrad has a female body, switching to male pronouns as soon as Eldrad regenerates a male body.

In *Hell Bent*, the General – a male Time Lord – regenerates into a female, prompting one of his officers to ask "Are you all right, sir? Oh, er, sorry, ma'am". And the General replies "Oh, back to normal, am I? The only time I've been a man, that last body". The previous incarnation said he was on his tenth regeneration, meaning (as per *The Five Doctors*), the new incarnation is his twelfth. Suggesting that for that individual, at least, there's a "default gender".

The most obvious and closest precedent is that the Capaldi era saw a female incarnation of the Master, Missy. She's consistently referred to using female pronouns. When it comes to the past, though, we have the Doctor all over the map, such as this from *World Enough and Time*:

"She was my first friend, always so brilliant, from the first day at the Academy. So fast, so funny. She was my man crush … Yeah, I think she was a man back then. I'm fairly sure that I was, too. It was a long time ago, though … We had a pact, me and him."

Ahistory has been saying since its very first edition – see the Past Lives sidebar – that there are far more incarnations of the Time Lord now known as the Doctor than we've seen on TV. The new series confirmed this in *The Day of the Doctor*, which showed us a "missing" incarnation, and seemed to snatch it away in *Twice Upon a Time*, where it seems the "first" Doctor has never regenerated before. We may or may not soon have watertight confirmation that Jodie Whittaker's incarnation is the first time the Doctor has had a female body. Whatever the case, however you cut the deck, we currently know of far more male incarnations than female ones. The "normal" – as per the General in *Hell Bent* – for the Doctor would seem to be male.

The new series may establish the etiquette. For now, this version of *Ahistory* has had to make a decision. For Fourth Edition, and in all honesty for logistical reasons

as much as anything else – it would require a top-to-bottom revision of the manuscript, with knock-on implications for page design, indexing, footnoting and so on – we are going to A) assume that the Jodie Whittaker incarnation is the first female incarnation of the Doctor, and B) refer to the Doctor by the pronoun appropriate to that incarnation. This has the effect that "generic" mentions of the Doctor will default to male pronouns.

For future editions, we think the best model may be something like the one used when talking about British Prime Ministers. As of time of writing, Britain has a female Prime Minister, the second woman to hold the office. Until 1979, it was possible to talk generically about the PM and say, for example, "he has the power to call a general election". Talking specifically about Margaret Thatcher in, say, 1987, it would be "she has the power to call the election". Talking generically, though, after 1979 it has to be "he or she has the power" or "they have the power".

In future editions, unless the show steers us in another direction, we will refer to each individual based on their gender at the time "the third Doctor went to Skaro and he … ", the Doctor generically as "they", "when it comes to the Doctor flying the TARDIS, they've typically been unable to …". There will be judgement calls, compromises and circumlocutions, for the sake of narrative clarity. It will not be possible to be 100% consistent.

Ultimately, though, what better pronoun for the Doctor than "they"?

BIBLIOGRAPHY

The following is a list of useful resources for anyone interested in the "fictional facts" of Doctor Who.

The Making of Doctor Who. (Malcolm Hulke and Terrance Dicks: first edition Piccolo/Pan Books, April 1972; second edition Target/Tandem Books, November 1976) – The earliest source of dates, often direct from BBC material.

Dr Who Special. (edited by David Driver, Jack Lundin: BBC, November 1973) – The tenth anniversary *Radio Times* special, including many previously unpublished story details. This magazine perpetuated the "incorrect" story titles, used by many fans.

The Doctor Who Programme Guide. (Jean-Marc Lofficier: first edition [2 vols] WH Allen, May 1981, second edition [2 vols] Target/WH Allen, October 1981, second edition has separate volume titles "The Programmes" and "What's What and Who's Who") **Doctor Who – The Programme Guide.** (Jean-Marc Lofficier: third edition Target/WH Allen, December 1989) **Doctor Who – The Terrestrial Index.** (Jean-Marc Lofficier: Target/Virgin Publishing, November 1991) **Doctor Who – The Universal Databank.** (Jean-Marc Lofficier: Doctor Who Books/Virgin Publishing, November 1992) **Doctor Who Programme Guide.** (Jean-Marc Lofficier: fourth edition Doctor Who Books/Virgin Publishing, June 1994) – The standard reference work, with most fans owning a copy of at least one of these books. A good starting point.

Doctor Who Monthly. (Marvel Comics Ltd.) – Richard Landen wrote a series of pseudohistories in the twentieth anniversary year: Issues 75-83 (April 1983 – December 1983) featured *The TARDIS Logs*, a list of TARDIS landings riddled with annoying little errors; issue 77 had a more concise list *Travels with the Doctor*, and a good attempt at "A History of the Daleks"; "A History of the Cybermen" (issue 83, with Michael Daniels) and *Shades of Piccolo* (UNIT history, issue 80) were both sensible, simple treatments of potential minefields.

The Doctor Who Role Playing Game. (FASA Corporation [US], 1985; Supplements published 1985-6) – Various dates, including much invented for the game's purposes.

Doctor Who. (Marvel Comics Group [US]) – Pseudohistories written by Patrick Daniel O'Neill: "A Probable History of the Daleks" (issue 9, June 1985), "A Probable History of the Cybermen" (issue 10, July 1985) and "The Master Log" Parts I and II (issues 14, 15, November, December 1985). Enthusiastic but ill-researched.

The Doctor Who File. (Peter Haining: WH Allen, September 1986) – Pages 223 to 228 contain a table listing the Doctor's adventures and where / when they took place.

Encyclopedia of the Worlds of Doctor Who. (David Saunders: Piccadilly/Knight Press 1986, 1989, 1990) – An A-Z of the series with many entries giving dates.

The Official Doctor Who & the Daleks Book. (John Peel & Terry Nation: St Martin's Press [US], April 1989) – Dalek history, including various other sources (comic strips etc). Approved by Terry Nation.

In-Vision 11: UNIT Special. (CMS, December 1988) – Includes *Down to Earth*, a history of UNIT, by Garry Bradbury. Each issue of *In-Vision* is a comprehensive analysis of an individual story, and the magazine is an indispensable reference work.

Doctor Who – Cybermen. (David Banks, with Andrew Skilleter, Adrian Rigelsford and Jan Vincent-Rudzki: Who Dares, November 1988; Virgin Publishing, September 1990) – Comprehensive, if elaborate, history of the Cybermen. The first, and still best, reference book of its kind.

Doctor Who Magazine. (Marvel Comics Ltd) – issue 174: *The TARDIS Special* (June 12th 1991) features "Journies" by Andrew Pixley, a superbly researched list of every landing made by the TARDIS. Issue 176 (August 7th 1991) contains an addendum.

The Gallifrey Chronicles. (John Peel: Doctor Who Books/Virgin Publishing, October 1991) – Gallifreyan history and other information. (This isn't the same book as *The Gallifrey Chronicles*, the 2005 EDA.)

Doctor Who Magazine Winter Special 1991 – UNIT Exposed. (Marvel Comics Ltd, 28th November, 1991) – Includes an excellent UNIT chronology by John Freeman and Gary Russell, as well as "UNIT Exposed" by Andrew Dylan.

The Doctor Who Writers' Guide. (Peter Darvill-Evans, Rebecca Levene & Andy Bodle: Virgin Publishing, 1991) – The guidelines for prospective authors of New and Missing Adventures. Includes notes on Gallifreyan history.

Apocrypha. (Adrian Middleton: 1993-95). Fan published chronology drawing together everything the author can get his hands on: comic strips, novelisations, role-playing scenarios and so on.

BIBLIOGRAPHY

The Discontinuity Guide. (Paul Cornell, Martin Day and Keith Topping: Virgin Publishing, May 1994) – Survey of the series' continuity and continuity mistakes. Many interesting fan theories, all marked as such.

I, Who vols. 1-3. (Lars Pearson, Mad Norwegian Press, 1999 – 2003) – A book-by-book and audio-by-audio survey of the novels and BF audios, including spin-offs and detailed breakdowns of the stories.

Timelink (Jon Preddle, TSV Books, 2000) – A massive fan-produced survey of the television series' continuity. With extensive quotes, and a story-by-story breakdown. **Timelink** (Jon Preddle, Telos, 2011) – Massively updated version of the TSV publication, now in two volumes.

Doctor Who – The Legend. (Justin Richards, BBC Books, 2003) – Hardback introduction to *Doctor Who*, with a story-by-story section that lists dates where they are known.

About Time. (Lawrence Miles and Tat Wood, Mad Norwegian Press, 2004 – present) – A series of books that place *Doctor Who* in a cultural context and offer opinions and essays on continuity matters, including some chronological ones like UNIT Dating.

Who's Next. (Mark Clapham, Eddie Robson and Jim Smith, Virgin Publishing, 2005) – A one-volume guide to *Doctor Who* on television, with a breakdown of continuity.

The Time Traveller's Almanac: The Ultimate Intergalactic Fact-Finder. (Steve Tribe, BBC Books, 2008) – Relates information about the historical events and characters seen in New *Who*.

Torchwood: The Official Magazine Yearbook. (uncredited: Titan Books, 2008) – Behind-the-scenes details on *Torchwood* Series 1, with short stories.

The Torchwood Archives. (Gary Russell: BBC Books, 2008) – Presented as archive of files and other material pertaining to *Torchwood* Series 1 and 2.

The Brilliant Book 2011. (Edited by Clayton Hickman, BBC Books, 2010) – Behind-the-scenes details on Series 5, with short stories.

The Brilliant Book 2012. (Edited by Clayton Hickman, BBC Books, 2011) – Behind-the-scenes details on Series 6, with short stories.

Doctor Who: The Encyclopedia. (Gary Russell, BBC Books, 2011) – Immense A-Z on New *Who*, up through Series 6.

The Dalek Handbook. (James Goss and Steve Tribe, BBC Books, 2011) – Detailed yet compact history of the Daleks.

A History of the Universe in 100 Objects. (James Goss and Steve Tribe, BBC Books, 2012) – A take-off of the "A History of the World in 100 Objects" exhibit at the British Museum, catalogues key items in *Doctor Who* according to a particular year or period.

The Doctor: His Lives and Times, released as **The Doctor's Lives and Times** in the US market (James Goss and Steve Tribe, BBC Books, 2013) – Variously serious and silly profiling of the Doctors via memos, newspaper articles, etc.

Whoniverse: An Unofficial Planet-by-Planet Guide to the World of the Doctor from Gallifrey to Skaro. (Lance Parkin, Barron's, 2015) – Sweeping look at the worlds of the Whoniverse and the races that populate it.

Whoniverse: An Unofficial Planet-by-Planet Guide to the World of the Doctor from Gallifrey to Skaro. (Justin Richards and George Mann, BBC Books, 2016) – Summations of the various phases of the Whoniverse's history, with lavish illustrations.

Doctor Who: A History of Humankind: The Doctor's Official Guide (Steve Tribe, BBC Books, 2017) – Does what it says on the tin.

Doctor Who: A Brief History of the Time Lords. (Steve Tribe, BBC Books, 2017) – Does what it says on the tin.

The Haisman Timeline (2017) – Online and internal document detailing the *Lethbridge-Stewart* novels' position on continuity.

Dalek: The Astounding Untold History of the Greatest Enemies of the Universe. (George Mann, Justin Richards, Cavan Scott and Alex Fort, Harper Design, 2017) – Coffee-table book that conveys the Daleks' fictional and real-world timelines in broad strokes, and presents itself as an unreliable narrator trying to suture together Dalek history from a combination of facts, rumours and half-truths.

ACKNOWLEDGEMENTS

Lance wishes to thank... A great many people have been involved with this book. This is the fifth version. The first – *The Doctor Who Chronology* – was produced by Seventh Door Fanzines. It covered the television series. The second – *A History of the Universe* – was published by Virgin in 1996, and covered the television series plus the New and Missing Adventures up to *Happy Endings* and *The Sands of Time* respectively. It proved very popular. Nearly ten years on, the third version was published by Mad Norwegian Press, and covered roughly twice as many stories as the Virgin edition. This is the second update of that.

Thanks first and foremost to my editors at Virgin – Mark Jones, Rebecca Levene and Simon Winstone – and, for the Mad Norwegian versions, my co-writer Lars Pearson.

Thanks to the many other people who have offered information, comments, help, material, corrections or just said nice things. In alphabetical order, these are: Ben Aaronovitch, Nadir Ahmed, Keith Ansell, John Binns, Jon Blum, David Brunt, Graeme Burk, Andy Campbell, Andrew Cartmel, Shaun Chmara, Mark Clapham, Finn Clark (big, big thanks for his comics expertise), Paul Cornell, Alex Dante, Jeremy Daw, Martin Day, Zoltan Dery, Jonathan Evans, Michael Evans, Simon Forward, Martin Foster, Gary Gillatt, Donald and Patricia Gillikin, Craig Hinton, David Howe, Edward Hutchinson, Alison Jacobs, William Keith, Andy Lane, Paul Lee, Steve Maggs, Daniel O'Mahony, Steven Manfred, April McKenna, Iain McLaughlin, Adrian Middleton, Lawrence Miles, Steve Mollmann, Kate Orman, David Owen, David Pitcher, Andrew Pixley, Marc Platt, Jon Preddle, Justin Richards, Gareth Roberts, Trevor Ruppe, Gary Russell, Jim Smith, Robert Smith?, Shannon Sullivan, Dimity Telfer, Richard Thacker, Lynne Thomas, Michael Thomas, Steve Traylen, Stephen James Walker, Peter Ware, Martin Wiggins, Gareth Wigmore, Guy Wigmore, Alex Wilcock and Anthony Wilson. I'm genuinely sorry if I missed anyone.

Thanks most of all to the innumerable people involved with the production of *Doctor Who*, in any and every form ... past, present and future.

Lars wishes to thank... First and foremost, a shout-out is due to Lance – for his vast *Doctor Who* knowledge, writing skill, professionalism, humour and for putting up with manic phone calls in which I desperately needed to puzzle through (say) the terraforming of Mars. The twelve years (!!!) that I've been involved with the Mad Norwegian version of *Ahistory* has been a hell of a ride. Big thanks are also due to Christa Dickson, not just for the tremendous cover and overall design of *Ahistory*, but for being patient with my mood swings in the time it took to complete the text therein. You know how the partners / spouses of coaches have to exert extra understanding with their stressed-out, doom-slathered mates during sports season? Now imagine that, but that it essentially goes on for twelve years. Similarly, Jim Boyd, Marc Eby, Carrie Herndon, Paul Kirkley, Braxton Pulley, Robert Smith? and Josh Wilson went to exceeding lengths to keep me at least half-sane, and a man could not ask for better friends and colleagues.

A great many people assisted with my research, but I seemed to most often approach the highly prolific Simon Guerrier, Matt Fitton, Jonathan Morris and Gary Russell for help, so thanks to them for their insightful responses. Big thanks to everyone at Big Finish – particularly Nicholas Briggs and Jason Haigh-Ellery – for their continued enthusiasm and support for this project. Even more thanks are due to Stewart Douglas for help with Obverse's publications, and Andy Frankham-Allen for guidance with the thinking behind the *Lethbridge-Stewart* novels. Valued research help was also given to me by Andrew Cartmel, Martin Day, Stuart Douglas, Paul Ebbs, James Goss, David Richardson, Eddie Robson, Alan Stevens and Damian Taylor. I'm sure I've failed to mention someone, for which I'm desperately embarrassed.

Appreciation in one form or another is due to Nick Abadzis, Sophie Aldred, Jeremy Bement, Josh Bertaki, Blair Bidmead, Jack Bruner, Graeme Burk, Lawrence Burton, Dan and Allison Chibnall, Gwyn Cox, Jen M.F. Dixon, John Dorney, the late Sacha Dzuba, Barnaby Edwards, Sigrid Ellis, Laura Gerald, John Gibney, Stephen Gray, Brandon Griffis, Toby Hadoke, James Houston, Maggie Howe, Shari Hrdina, Hannah Hudson, James and Renee Juneau, Matt Jesson, Al Kennedy and Paul O'Brien at the House to Astonish podcast, Shawne Kleckner, Michael Lee, Catherine Lowe, Kelli Lydon, Shaun Lyon, Dylan Lyons, Steve Manfred, Cameron and Stephanie McCoy, Sylvester McCoy, Tiff Morgan, K.O. Myers, L.M. Myles, Dave Owen, Lars Pearson (no relation, oddly enough), Chris Purcell, Cody Quijano-Schell, Heather Riesenberg, Cassie Sampson, John Seavy, Robert Shearman, Katy Shuttleworth, Paul Simpson, Deborah Stanish, Lynne Thomas, Allison Trebacz, Jason Stormageddon Tucker, Peter Ware, Cathleen Young and that nice lady who sends me newspaper articles.